D0907156

THE
CAMBRIDGE
MEDIEVAL HISTORY

VOLUME IV

THE MACMILLAN COMPANY
NEW YORK · BOSTON · CHICAGO · DALLAS
ATLANTA · SAN FRANCISCO

THE MACMILLAN CO. OF CANADA, LTD.
TORONTO

THE CAMBRIDGE MEDIEVAL HISTORY

PLANNED BY

J. B. BURY, M.A., F.B.A.

REGIUS PROFESSOR OF MODERN HISTORY

EDITED BY

J. R. TANNER, Litt.D.
C. W. PREVITÉ-ORTON, M.A.
Z. N. BROOKE, M.A.

VOLUME IV

THE EASTERN ROMAN EMPIRE (717—1453)

NEW YORK
THE MACMILLAN COMPANY
1923

PRINTED IN GREAT BRITAIN

PREFACE.

IT will be seen from the title-page that the *Cambridge Medieval History* has again suffered the loss of one of its Editors by the resignation of Professor Whitney, to whom the first three volumes owed so much. Volume IV, however, a good part of which was in type before the War, stands indebted to him nearly as much as its predecessors have done, and much of the revision in proof has benefited by his co-operation. Mr Z. N. Brooke has been appointed by the Syndics of the University Press to succeed him.

Our chief thanks are also due to Professor Bury, without whose aid our task in a volume treating of Byzantine history could hardly have been accomplished. He has read most of the chapters in proof, and has made a number of invaluable suggestions upon them. Besides contributing a summary to Chapter V, he has written for us the Introduction to the volume, in which he explains its general plan and defines the place of Byzantium in universal history.

A volume dealing with subjects which lie apart from the more frequented paths of medieval studies has laid the Editors under many obligations to specialists. Professor A. A. Bevan has given the kindest help in the transliteration of Arabic, and Professor E. G. Browne in that of Turkish names, while Dr E. H. Minns has revised the forms of names in Slavonic languages; we owe much to their criticism and advice.

The long delays which the War imposed on Volume III have reacted also on Volume IV, and we regret that Sir Edwin Pears did not live to see his chapter in proof, nor M. Ferdinand Chalandon more than the first proofs of his chapters; but we have been fortunate in the second revision of M. Chalandon's proofs by Madame Chalandon.

The scope and proportion of the volume have occasionally necessitated the abbreviation of a chapter; and here we owe a special debt to Professor Macler, who has allowed us to reshape his exhaustive contribution on Armenia in accordance with the limitations on our space, and to Mrs E. A. Benians, who undertook the task of compression, enabling us to give to a chapter abbreviated from the French the characteristics of an original composition in English.

Our thanks are also due to Mr E. W. Brooks for the Bibliography of

Chapter V (B), since it has not been possible to communicate with the author, Professor A. A. Vasil'ev; to Dr Paul Wittek for the revision of the oriental portion of the Bibliography of Chapter XXI; to Mrs Goulding Brown for her care and accuracy in compiling the Index; to Miss A. Greenwood for time and labour devoted to the difficult task of preparing the maps; and to Mr C. C. Scott, Sub-Librarian of St John's College, for invaluable help in the peculiarly exacting task of preparing for the press Bibliographies which include works in some twenty languages. To the officials of the University Press we also owe many thanks, and especially to the late Mr J. B. Peace, who with his expert knowledge helped us in the technical problems of map-making.

A word must once more be said in conclusion on the vexed and thorny question of the forms of proper names. Byzantine names as a rule have been represented by their Latinised forms, saving in the first place such as are distinctly sobriquets, and in the second place the little-known names of medieval Greece, which are given in their original Greek spelling. These last in Chapters XV to XVIII, by request of the author Dr Miller, have been provided with their Greek accents as an aid to pronunciation. Arabic, Persian, and Slavonic names, unless a form has become familiar in English literature, have been transcribed in accordance with the systems approved by the British Academy.

J. R. T.
C. W. P.-O.
Z. N. B.

July, 1923.

INTRODUCTION.

THE present volume carries on the fortunes of a portion of Europe to the end of the Middle Ages. This exception to the general chronological plan of the work seemed both convenient and desirable. The orbit of Byzantium, the history of the peoples and states which moved within that orbit and always looked to it as the central body, giver of light and heat, did indeed at some points touch or traverse the orbits of western European states, but the development of these on the whole was not deeply affected or sensibly perturbed by what happened east of Italy or south of the Danube, and it was only in the time of the Crusades that some of their rulers came into close contact with the Eastern Empire or that it counted to any considerable extent in their policies. England, the remotest state of the West, was a legendary country to the people of Constantinople, and that imperial capital was no more than a dream-name of wealth and splendour to Englishmen, except to the few adventurers who travelled thither to make their fortunes in the Varangian guards. It is thus possible to follow the history of the Eastern Roman Empire from the eighth century to its fall, along with those of its neighbours and clients, independently of the rest of Europe, and this is obviously more satisfactory than to interpolate in the main history of Western Europe chapters having no connexion with those which precede and follow.

Besides being convenient, this plan is desirable. For it enables us to emphasise the capital fact that throughout the Middle Ages the same Empire which was founded by Augustus continued to exist and function and occupy even in its final weakness a unique position in Europe—a fact which would otherwise be dissipated, as it were, and obscured amid the records of another system of states with which it was not in close or constant contact. It was one of Gibbon's services to history that the title of his book asserted clearly and unambiguously this continuity.

We have, however, tampered with the correct name, which is simply *Roman Empire*, by adding *Eastern*, a qualification which although it has no official basis is justifiable as a convenient mark of distinction from the Empire which Charlemagne founded and which lasted till the beginning of the nineteenth century. This Western Empire had no good claim to the name of Roman. Charlemagne and those who followed him were not legitimate successors of Augustus, Constantine, Justinian, and the Isaurians, and this was tacitly acknowledged in their endeavours to obtain recognition of the imperial title they assumed from the sovrans of Constantinople whose legitimacy was unquestionable.

Much as the Empire changed after the age of Justinian, as its population became more and more predominantly Greek in speech, its descent from Rome was always unmistakably preserved in the designation of its subjects as Romans (Ῥωμαῖοι). Its eastern neighbours knew it as Rūm. Till the very end the names of most of the titles of its ministers, officials, and institutions were either Latin or the Greek translations of Latin terms that had become current in the earliest days of the Empire[1]. Words of Latin derivation form a large class in medieval Greek. The modern Greek language was commonly called *Romaic* till the middle of the nineteenth century. It is only quite recently that *Roumelia* has been falling out of use to designate territories in the Balkan peninsula. Contrast with the persistence of the Roman name in the East the fact that the subjects of the Western Empire were never called Romans and indeed had no common name as a whole; the only "Romans" among them were the inhabitants of the city of Rome. There is indeed one district in Italy whose name still commemorates the Roman Empire—*Romagna*; but this exception only reinforces the contrast. For the district corresponds to the Exarchate of Ravenna, and was called Romania by its Lombard neighbours because it belonged to the Roman Emperor of Constantinople. It was at the New Rome, not at the Old, that the political tradition of the Empire was preserved. It is worth remembering too that the greatest public buildings of Constantinople were originally built, however they may have been afterwards changed or extended—the Hippodrome, the Great Palace, the Senatehouses, the churches of St Sophia and the Holy Apostles—by Emperors of Latin speech, Severus, Constantine, Justinian.

On the other hand, the civilisation of the later Roman Empire was the continuation of that of ancient Greece. Hellenism entered upon its second phase when Alexander of Macedon expanded the Greek world into the east, and on its third with the foundation of Constantine by the waters where Asia and Europe meet. Christianity, with its dogmatic theology and its monasticism, gave to this third phase its distinctive character and flavour, and *Byzantine* civilisation, as we have learned to

[1] Examples: (1) *ἀσηκρῆτις* (*a secretis*), *δούξ*, *κόμης*, *μάγιστρος*, *πατρίκιος*, *δομέστικος*, *πραιπόσιτος*, *πραίτωρ*, *κουαίστωρ*, *κουράτωρ*; *ἰδίκτον*, *πάκτον*; *κάστρον*, *φοσσάτον*, *παλάτιον*, *βῆλον* (*velum*); *ἀπληκεύειν* =(*castra*) *applicare*, *πραιδεύειν*, *δηριγεύειν*; *μοῦλτος* =(*tu*)*multus*; (2) (ancient equivalents of Latin terms) *βασιλεύς*, *αὐτοκράτωρ* (*imperator*), *σύγκλητος* (*senatus*), *ὕπατος* (*consul*), *ἀνθύπατος* (*proconsul*), *ὕπαρχος* (*praefectus*), *δρόμος* (*cursus publicus*).

call it, is an appropriate and happy name. Its features are very fully delineated in this volume by Professor Diehl (chapter XXIV). The continuity which links the fifteenth century A.D. with the fifth B.C. is notably expressed in the long series of Greek historians, who maintained, it may be said, a continuous tradition of historiography. From Critobulus, the imitator of Thucydides, and Chalcocondyles, who told the story of the last days of the Empire, we can go back, in a line broken only by a dark interval in the seventh and eighth centuries, to the first great masters, Thucydides and Herodotus.

The development of "Byzantinism" really began in the fourth century. The historian Finlay put the question in a rather awkward way by asking, When did the Roman Empire change into the Byzantine? The answer is that it did not change into any other Empire than itself, but that some of the characteristic features of Byzantinism began to appear immediately after Constantinople was founded. There is, however, a real truth in Finlay's own answer to his question. He drew the dividing line at the accession of Leo the Isaurian, at the beginning of the eighth century. And, in fact, Leo's reign marked the consummation of a rapid change which had been going on during the past hundred years. Rapid: for I believe anyone who has studied the history of those centuries will agree that in the age of the Isaurians we feel much further away from the age of Justinian than we feel in the age of Justinian from the age of Theodosius the Great. Finlay's date has been taken as the starting point of this volume; it marks, so far as a date can, the transition to a new era.

The chief function which *as a political power* the Eastern Empire performed throughout the Middle Ages was to act as a bulwark for Europe, and for that civilisation which Greece had created and Rome had inherited and diffused, against Asiatic aggression. Since the rise of the Sasanid power in the third century, Asia had been attempting, with varying success, to resume the rôle which it had played under the Achaemenids. The arms of Alexander had delivered for hundreds of years the Eastern coasts and waters of the Mediterranean from all danger from an Asiatic power. The Sasanids finally succeeded in reaching the Mediterranean shores and the Bosphorus. The rôles of Europe and Asia were again reversed, and it was now for Byzantium to play on a larger stage the part formerly played by Athens and Sparta in a struggle for life and death. Heraclius proved himself not only a Themistocles but in some measure an Alexander. He not only checked the victorious advance of the enemy; he completely destroyed the power of the Great King and made him his vassal. But within ten years the rôles were reversed once more in that amazing transformation scene in which an obscure Asiatic people which had always seemed destined to play a minor part became suddenly one of the strongest powers in the world. Constantinople had again to fight for her life, and the danger was imminent and the strain unrelaxed for eighty years. Though the Empire did not succeed in barring the road to Spain and Sicily, its rulers held the gates of Europe at the Propontis and made it impossible for them to sweep over Europe as they had swept over Syria and Egypt. Centuries passed, and the Comnenians guarded Europe from the Seljūqs. The Ottomans were the latest bearers of the Asiatic menace. If the Eastern Empire had not been mortally wounded and reduced to the dimensions of a petty state by the greed and brutality of the Western brigands who called themselves Crusaders, it is possible that the Turks might never have gained a footing in Europe. Even as it was, the impetus of their first victorious advance was broken by the tenacity of the Palaeologi—assisted it is true by the arms of Tīmūr. They had reached the Danube sixty years before Constantinople fell. When this at length happened, the first force and fury of their attack had been spent, and it is perhaps due to this delay that the Danube and the Carpathians were to mark the limit of Asiatic rule in Europe and that St Peter's was not to suffer the fate of St Sophia. Even in the last hours of its life, the Empire was still true to its traditional rôle of bulwark of Europe.

As a civilised state, we may say that the Eastern Empire performed three principal functions. As in its early years the Roman Empire laid the foundations of civilisation in the West and educated Celtic and German peoples, so in its later period it educated the Slavs of eastern Europe. Russia, Bulgaria, and Serbia owed it everything and bore its stamp. Secondly, it exercised a silent but constant and considerable influence on western Europe by sending its own manufactures and the products of the East to Italy, France, and Germany. Many examples of its embroidered textile fabrics and its jewellery have been preserved in the West. In the third place, it guarded safely the heritage of classical Greek literature which has had on the modern world a penetrating influence difficult to estimate. That we owe our possession of the masterpieces of Hellenic thought and imagination to the Byzantines everyone knows, but everyone does not remember that those books would not have travelled to Italy in the fourteenth and fifteenth centuries, because they would not have existed, if the Greek classics had not been read habitually by the educated subjects of the Eastern Empire and therefore continued to be copied.

Here we touch on a most fundamental contrast between the Eastern Empire and the western European states of the Middle Ages. The well-to-do classes in the West were as a rule illiterate, with the exception of ecclesiastics; among the well-to-do classes in the Byzantine world education was the rule, and education meant not merely reading, writing, and arithmetic, but the study of ancient Greek grammar and the reading of classical authors. The old traditions of Greek education had never died out. In court circles at Constantinople everyone who was not an utter parvenu would recognise and understand a quotation from Homer. In consequence of this difference, the intellectual standards in the West where book-learning was reserved for a particular class, and in the East where every boy and girl whose parents could afford to pay was educated, were entirely different. The advantages of science and training and system were understood in Byzantine society.

The appreciation of method and system which the Byzantines inherited both from the Greeks and from the Romans is conspicuously shewn in their military establishment and their conduct of war. Here their intellectuality stands out in vivid contrast with the rude dullness displayed in the modes of warfare practised in the West. Tactics were carefully studied, and the treatises on war which the officers used were kept up to date. The tacticians apprehended that it was stupid to employ uniform methods in campaigns against different foes. They observed carefully the military habits of the various peoples with whom they had to fight—Saracens, Lombards, Franks, Slavs, Hungarians—and thought out different rules for dealing with each. The soldiers were most carefully and efficiently drilled. They understood organisation and the importance of not leaving details to chance, of not neglecting small points in equipment. Their armies were accompanied by ambulances and surgeons. Contrast the feudal armies of the West, ill-disciplined, with no organisation, under leaders who had not the most rudimentary idea of tactics, who put their faith in sheer strength and courage, and attacked all antagonists in exactly the same way. More formidable the Western knights might be than Slavs or Magyars, but in the eyes of a Byzantine officer they were equally rude barbarians who had not yet learned that war is an art which requires intelligence as well as valour. In the period in which the Empire was strong, before it lost the provinces which provided its best recruits, its army was beyond comparison the best fighting machine in Europe. When a Byzantine army was defeated, it was always the incompetence of the general or some indiscretion on his part, never inefficiency or cowardice of the troops, that was to blame. The great disaster of Manzikert (1071), from which perhaps the decline of the Eastern Empire may be dated, was caused by the imbecility of the brave Emperor who was in command. A distinguished student of the art of war has observed that Gibbon's dictum, "the vices of Byzantine armies were inherent, their victories accidental," is precisely the reverse of the truth. He is perfectly right.

Military science enabled the Roman Empire to hold its own for many centuries against the foes around it, east and west and north. Internally, its permanence and stability depended above all on the rule of Roman law. Its subjects had always "the advantage of possessing a systematic administration of justice enforced by fixed legal procedure"; they were not at the mercy of caprice. They could contrast their courts in which justice was administered with a systematic observance of rules, with those in which Mohammedan lawyers dispensed justice. The feeling that they were much better off under the government of Constantinople than their Eastern neighbours engendered a loyal attachment to the Empire, notwithstanding what they might suffer under an oppressive fiscal system[1].

The influence of lawyers on the administration was always great, and may have been one of the facts which account for the proverbial conservatism of Byzantine civilisation. But that conservatism has generally been exaggerated, and even in the domain of law there was a development, though the foundations and principles remained those which were embodied in the legislation of Justinian.

The old Roman law, as expounded by the classical jurists, was in the East considerably modified in practice here and there by Greek and oriental custom, and there are traces of this influence in the laws of Justinian. But Justinianean law shews very few marks of ecclesiastical influence which in the seventh and following centuries led to various changes, particularly in laws relating to marriage. The law-book of the Isaurian Emperor, Leo III, was in some respects revolutionary, and although at the end of the ninth century the Macedonian Emperors, eager to renounce all the works of the heretical Isaurians, professed to return to the pure principles of Justinian, they retained many of the innovations and compromised with others. The principal reforms of Leo were too much in accordance with public opinion to be undone. The legal status of concubinate for instance was definitely abolished. Only marriages between Christians were recognised as valid. Marriages between first and second cousins were forbidden. Fourth marriages were declared illegal and even third were discountenanced. It is remarkable however that in the matter of divorce, where the differences between the views of State and Church had been sharpest and where the Isaurians had given effect to the un-Roman ecclesiastical doctrine that marriage is indissoluble, the Macedonians returned to the common-sense view of Justinian and Roman lawyers that marriage like other contracts between human beings may be dissolved. We can see new tendencies too in the history of the *patria potestas*. The Iconoclasts substituted for it a parental *potestas*,

[1] Compare Finlay, *History of Greece*, II. 22–4; I. 411–2.

assigning to the mother rights similar to those of the father. Other changes are mentioned below in Chapter XXII, pp. 709–10[1].

In criminal law there was a marked change in tendency. From Augustus to Justinian penalties were ever becoming severer and new crimes being invented. After Justinian the movement was in the direction of mildness. In the eighth century only two or three crimes were punishable by death. One of these was murder and in this case the extreme penalty might be avoided if the murderer sought refuge in a church. On the other hand penalties of mutilation were extended and systematised. This kind of punishment had been inflicted in much earlier times and authorised in one or two cases by Justinian. In the eighth century we find amputations of the tongue, hand, and nose part of the criminal system, and particularly applied in dealing with sexual offences. If such punishments strike us to-day as barbaric (though in England, for instance, mutilation was inflicted little more than two centuries ago), they were then considered as a humane substitute for death, and the Church approved them because a tongue-less or nose-less sinner had time to repent. In the same way, it was a common practice to blind, instead of killing, rebels or unsuccessful candidates for the throne. The tendency to avoid capital punishment is illustrated by the credible record that during the reign of John Comnenus there were no executions.

The fact that in domestic policy the Eastern Empire was far from being obstinately conservative is also illustrated by the reform of legal education in the eleventh century, when it was realised that a system which had been in practice for a long time did not work well and another was substituted (as is explained in Chapter XXII, p. 719). That conception of the later Empire which has made the word Byzantine almost equivalent to Chinese was based on ignorance, and is now discredited. It is obvious that no State could have lasted so long in a changing world, if it had not had the capacity of adapting itself to new conditions. Its administrative machinery was being constantly modified by capable and hardworking rulers of whom there were many; the details of the system at the end of the tenth century differed at ever so many points from those of the eighth. As for art and literature, there were ups and downs, declines and renascences, throughout the whole duration of the Empire. It is only in quite recent years that Byzantine literature and Byzantine art have been methodically studied; in these wide fields of research Krumbacher's

[1] It has been commonly held that the codes known as the Rhodian (Maritime) Law, the Farmer's (Rural) Law, and the Military Law were the work of the Isaurian Emperors, and this view is taken below in Chapter I (pp. 4–5) and Chapter XXII (pp. 708, 710). In the opinion of the present writer the investigations of Mr Ashburner have rendered it quite untenable, at least in regard to the two first.

Byzantine Literature and Strzygowski's *Orient oder Rom* were pioneer works marking a new age. Now that we are getting to know the facts better and the darkness is gradually lifting, we have come to see that the history of the Empire is far from being a monotonous chronicle of palace revolutions, circus riots, theological disputes, tedious ceremonies in a servile court, and to realise that, as in any other political society, conditions were continually changing and in each succeeding age new political and social problems presented themselves for which some solution had to be found. If the chief interest in history lies in observing such changes, watching new problems shape themselves and the attempts of rulers or peoples to solve them, and seeing how the characters of individuals and the accidents which befall them determine the course of events, the story of the Eastern Empire is at least as interesting as that of any medieval State, or perhaps more interesting because its people were more civilised and intellectual than other Europeans and had a longer political experience behind them. On the ecclesiastical side it offers the longest and most considerable experiment of a State-Church that Christendom has ever seen.

The Crusades were, for the Eastern Empire, simply a series of barbarian invasions of a particularly embarrassing kind, and in the present volume they are treated merely from this point of view and their general significance in universal history is not considered. The full treatment of their causes and psychology and the consecutive story of the movement are reserved for Vol. V.

But the earlier history of Venice has been included in this volume. The character of Venice and her career were decided by the circumstance that she was subject to the Eastern Emperors before she became independent. She was extra-Italian throughout the Middle Ages; she never belonged to the Carolingian Kingdom of Italy. And after she had slipped into independence almost without knowing it—there was never a violent breaking away from her allegiance to the sovrans of Constantinople—she moved still in the orbit of the Empire; and it was on the ruins of the Empire, dismembered by the criminal enterprise of her Duke Dandolo, that she reached the summit of her power as mistress in the Aegean and in Greece. She was the meeting-place of two civilisations, but it was eastern not western Europe that controlled her history and lured her ambitions. Her citizens spoke a Latin tongue and in spiritual matters acknowledged the supremacy of the elder Rome, but the influence from new Rome had penetrated deep, and their great Byzantine basilica is a visible reminder of their long political connexion with the Eastern Empire.

CORRIGENDA.

Vol. I.

p. xvi. *For* The Visigoths to the death of Euric *read* The Visigoths to the death of Alaric II.

Index.

p. 731. *Under* Marcellinus, Roman general, *delete* cited, 399, 431.
p. 731. *Insert entry* Marcellinus, count, his chronicle cited, 399, 431.

Vol. II.

Index.

p. 839. *Under* Columbanus (Columba), St, *delete* 510; in Scotland 512 sq., 526, *and* 527.
p. 839. *Insert entry* Columba, St, apostle of Scotland, 510, 512 sq., 526 sq.

Vol. III.

p. xxi, l. 13. *For* Taube *read* Tauber.
p. 150, l. 6 from end. *For* Moslem *read* Muslim.
p. 157, l. 19. *For* Anscari's *read* Anscar's.
p. 177, l. 18. *For* on the Tiber *read* near the Tiber.
p. 178, l. 5. *For* 1006 *read* 1005.
p. 301, l. 14 from end. *For* Archbishop *read* Bishop.
p. 404, l. 20. *For* Fores *read* Forest.
p. 460, l. 4. *For* Ardre *read* Ardres.
p. 460, l. 11. *For* Terouanne *read* Térouanne.
p. 467, l. 8 from end. *For* flay *read* flog.
p. 560, l. 20. *For* St Germigny *read* Germigny.
p. 561, l. 16. „ „ „ „ „
p. 567, l. 7. „ „ „ „ „

Index.

p. 669. *Insert entry* Germigny, church at, 560 sq., 567.
p. 691. *Delete entry* St Germigny.
p. 692. *Under* Severus *for* Archbishop *read* Bishop.

Maps.

No. 29. *For* Maconais *read* Mâconnais.

TABLE OF CONTENTS.

INTRODUCTION.

PAGE

By Professor J. B. Bury, F.B.A. vii

CHAPTER I.

LEO III AND THE ISAURIAN DYNASTY (717—802).

By Charles Diehl, Member of the Institute of France, late Professor of Byzantine History at the University of Paris.

Character of the Period 1
Leo III the Isaurian 2
Repulse of the Arabs from Constantinople . . . . . *ib.*
Domestic administration: the themes 3
the finances 4
the Codes and the *Ecloga* 5
Religion: the cult of images 6
Edict against images (726) 9
Opposition in East and West 10
Constantine V Copronymus 11
The revolt of Artavasdus 12
Successes at home and abroad 13
Reopening of the iconoclastic struggle 14
Persecution of image-worshippers 15
Defeat of the monks 16
Alienation of Italy and the Papacy 17
Italy lost to the Empire 18
Leo IV the Chazar 19
Regency of Irene 20
Restoration of images 21
Irene and Constantine VI 22
Constantine VI sole ruler: intrigues of Irene 23
Irene reigns as Emperor 24
Deposition of Irene 25
The achievements of the Isaurian Emperors 26

CHAPTER II.

FROM NICEPHORUS I TO THE FALL OF THE PHRYGIAN DYNASTY.

By Professor Charles Diehl.

Nicephorus I 27
Opposition of the monks 28
Michael I Rangabé 29
Leo V the Armenian 30
Theodore of Studion and the freedom of the Church 31

PAGE
Murder of Leo V: accession of Michael the Amorian 32
Michael's tolerant policy 33
Theophilus: revival of persecution 34
Civil wars (802—823) 35
Recognition of the Western Empire (812) 36
Losses to the Arabs and Bulgarians 37
Struggle with the Caliphs 38
Internal government of Theophilus 39
Regency of Theodora 40
Final restoration of image worship (843) 41
Persecution of the Paulicians 42
Michael III and the Caesar Bardas 43
Intellectual revival under Bardas 44
Conversion of Bulgaria to Orthodoxy 45
External dangers 46
The Photian schism with Rome 47
Murder of Bardas and of Michael III 48

CHAPTER III.

THE MACEDONIAN DYNASTY FROM 867 TO 976 A.D.

By the Rev. the Abbé Albert Vogt, late Extraordinary Professor of History at the University of Fribourg.

Basil I (867—886) 49
His early life 50
The finances 51
Revival in legislation and the arts 52
Religious questions 53
Close of Basil I's reign 54
Leo VI (886—912) . . . . *ib.*
End of the Photian schism 56
Leo's four marriages 57
Administration and legislation 58
Constantine VII Porphyrogenitus (912—959) 59
Alexander: the Council of Regency 60
Romanus I Lecapenus (919—944) 61
His policy 62
End of the house of Lecapenus 63
Constantine VII and his entourage 64
Religious affairs 65
Administration 66
Intellectual movement 67
Romanus II (959—963). . . . . *ib.*
Foreign affairs 69
Early career of Nicephorus Phocas . . . . . . *ib.*
The regency of Theophano 70
Usurpation of Nicephorus Phocas (963—969) 72
His marriage with Theophano 73
His hostility to the monks 74
Ecclesiastical and military legislation 75

	PAGE
General discontent	76
Murder of Nicephorus	77
John Tzimisces (969—976)	78
First measures as Emperor	79
Ecclesiastical affairs	80
Secular affairs	81
Death of John Tzimisces	82

CHAPTER IV.

THE MACEDONIAN DYNASTY FROM 976 TO 1057 A.D.

By the Rev. the Abbé ALBERT VOGT.

Basil and Constantine	83
First years of Basil II	84
Revolt of Bardas Sclerus	85
Defeat of Sclerus: fall of the eunuch Basil	86
Conspiracy of Phocas and Sclerus	87
Collapse of rebellion	88
Ecclesiastical affairs	89
Conversion of Russia	90
Religious controversies with the Latins	91
Attempt at a compromise	92
Legislation against the "powerful"	93
Secular relations with the West	94
Recurrence of revolt	95
Death of Basil II	96
Constantine VIII	*ib.*
Accession of Zoë	98
Character and government of Romanus III	99
Foreign affairs and conspiracies	100
Michael IV succeeds Romanus	101
Character of Michael IV	102
Government of John the Orphanotrophos	103
Death of Michael IV	104
Michael V: fall of the Orphanotrophos	105
Exile of Zoë: popular rising	106
Fall of Michael V	107
Zoë and Theodora	108
Constantine IX associated in the Empire	109
Revolt of Maniaces	110
Revolt of Tornicius	111
Annexation of Armenia: Michael Cerularius	112
Schism of the Eastern and Western Churches	113
Literary renaissance	114
Deaths of Zoë and Constantine IX	115
Death of Theodora. Michael VI Stratioticus	116
Discontent of the army: revolt under Isaac Comnenus	117
Fall of Michael VI	118

CHAPTER V.

(A)

THE STRUGGLE WITH THE SARACENS (717—867).

By E. W. Brooks, M.A., King's College, Cambridge.

	PAGE
The last Arab attempt upon Constantinople	119
Character of the wars	120
Battle of Acroïnon	121
Campaigns of Constantine V	122
Expedition of the Caliph Mahdī	123
Expedition of Rashīd	124
Campaigns of Constantine VI	125
Nicephorus and Rashīd	126
Recovery of Camacha	127
Campaigns of the Caliph Ma'mūn	128
Sack of Sozopetra	129
Fall of Amorium	130
Disintegration of the Caliphate	131
Expeditions to Damietta	132
Battle of Chonarium	133
Battle of Poson	134
Muslim invasion of Sicily	135
Fall of Palermo	136
Fall of Enna	137
Expeditions of Khafāja	138

(B)

THE STRUGGLE WITH THE SARACENS (867—1057).

By A. A. Vasil'ev, late Professor of History at the University of Dorpat.

Favourable position of Basil I	139
Loss of Syracuse	140
Disasters under Leo VI	142
Constantine VII: the decline of the Caliphate	143
War on the Euphrates	144
Advance under Nicephorus Phocas	145
Capture of Antioch and Aleppo	146
John Tzimisces in Syria	147
Basil II	148
War with the Fāṭimites	149
The successors of Basil II	150

(C)

SUMMARY 151

By Professor J. B. Bury, F.B.A.

CHAPTER VI.

ARMENIA.

By Frédéric Macler, Professor of Armenian at the École nationale des Langues orientales vivantes, Paris.

PAGE

Position of Armenia 153
Periods of Armenian history 154
Persians and Greeks in Armenia 155
The Arab Conquest 156
Armenian Principalities 157
The Bagratuni Dynasty 158
The Katholikos: Ashot I: Smbat I 159
Armenia and Azarbā'ījān 160
Friendship between Armenia and the Arabs 161
The civilisation of Greater Armenia 162
Civil war between John-Smbat and his brother 163
Armenia threatened by Greeks and Turks 164
Constantine Monomachus betrays Gagik II 165
Greater Armenia conquered by the Seljūqs 166
Character of the Armeno-Cilician kingdom 167
The foundation of Armeno-Cilicia 168
Armeno-Cilicia attacked by Greeks and Turks 169
Thoros II successful against the Greeks 170
The Greeks driven from Cilicia 171
European connexions of Leo the Great 172
Leo's achievements in peace and war 173
Succession problems after Leo's death 174
Armenian alliance with the Mongols 175
War with the Mamlūks and Seljūqs 176
Unstable government of Hethum II 177
Loss of the Mongol alliance 178
Overtures to the West. Nationalist reaction 179
The Mamlūks conquer Armenia. The Lusignans 180
Failure and exile of Leo VI 181
Armenia under Muslim rule 182

CHAPTER VII.

(A)

THE EMPIRE AND ITS NORTHERN NEIGHBOURS.

By Dr Charles Kadlec, Professor of Slavonic Law at the Charles University of Prague.

Scythians and Sarmatians 183
Alans, Goths, and Huns 184
Bulgars, Avars, and Turks 185
The Avars in Europe 186
Chazars and Turks 187

	PAGE
Growing power of the Chazars	188
Relations with the Empire	189
Chazar institutions	190
Religious tolerance	191
The Burdas	192
The White Bulgars	193
The Magyars	194
Admixture of races	196
Magyar customs	197
Patzinaks and Magyars	198
The Magyars migrate to Hungary	199
Russia. The "Varangian" theory	200
The Eastern Slavs	201
Trade Routes	202
The *vólosti*	203
Settlement of the Varangians	204
Oleg and Igor of Kiev	205
Trade and tribute	206
Beginnings of Christianity in Kiev	207
Reign of Svyatoslav	208
Vladímir the Great	209
Russia accepts Christianity	210
The Magyars in Hungary	211
The Magyar raids	212
The Magyars become a settled people	213
Christianisation of Hungary	214
St Stephen	215

(B)

CONVERSION OF THE SLAVS.

By Dr V. Jagić, Member of the Jugoslav Academy of Science and Art at Agram, Emeritus Professor of Slavonic Philology at the University of Vienna.

Cyril (Constantine) and Methodius	215
Sources for their history	216
Constantine's youth at Constantinople	217
His disputations	218
Relations with Photius: mission to the Chazars	219
Discovery of the relics of St Clement	220
The invitation to Moravia	221
The invention of the Slavonic alphabet	222
Constantine and Methodius in Moravia	223
Their journey to Rome	224
Cyril's death: his literary achievements	225
Methodius in Pannonia	226
His imprisonment and return to Moravia	227
His victory at Rome	228
Opposition of Svatopluk: death of Methodius	229

CHAPTER VIII.

THE RISE AND FALL OF THE FIRST BULGARIAN EMPIRE (679—1018).

By WILLIAM MILLER, M.A., Hertford College, Oxford, Hon. LL.D. of the National University of Greece.

PAGE

Bulgarian settlement in Europe 230
Early Greco-Bulgarian Wars 231
Krum 232
Omurtag 234
First Serbo-Bulgarian War 235
Conversion of the Bulgarians 236
Simeon's love of learning 237
A Bulgarian Tsar and Patriarch 238
The Bogomile heresy 239
Fall of Eastern Bulgaria 240
Samuel and Basil II 241
Fall of Western Bulgaria 242
Bulgaria a Byzantine province 243
Bulgarian rising of 1040 244
Further risings 245

CHAPTER IX.

THE GREEK CHURCH: ITS RELATIONS WITH THE WEST UP TO 1054.

By LOUIS BRÉHIER, Professor of History at the University of Clermont-Ferrand.

The Greek Church and Rome 246
Ignatius and Photius 248
Conflict between Photius and Nicholas I 249
The schism of Photius 250
Deposition of Photius 251
Ecumenical Council (869—870) 252
Re-instatement of Photius 253
His disgrace and death 254
Contemporary judgments on him 255
Restoration of communion with Rome (898) 256
Leo VI and Nicholas Mysticus 257
Concord of the two Churches 258
Lessened prestige of Rome 259
Independence of the Greek Church 260
Strained relations with Rome 261
Eustathius and the *autocephalia* 262
The party of reform in the West 263

PAGE
The two Churches up to 1054 264
Michael Cerularius 265
The Eastern Empire, Leo IX, and the Normans 266
Michael Cerularius and Rome 267
Correspondence between the Pope and the Patriarch . . . 268
The Roman legates at Constantinople (1054) 269
Excommunication of Michael Cerularius 270
The Synodal Edict of 1054 271
Definitive rupture (20 July 1054) 272
The results of the Schism 273

CHAPTER X.

(A)

MUSLIM CIVILISATION DURING THE ABBASID PERIOD.

By Sir THOMAS W. ARNOLD, C.I.E., Litt.D., Hon. Fellow of Magdalene College, Cambridge, Professor of Arabic at the University of London.

The Abbasid Empire 274
Character of the Abbasid dynasty 275
Decline of the Abbasid Caliphate 276
Ascendancy of the Buwaihids 277
The Seljūq Empire 278
The Mongol conquests 279
Muslim political theory 280
Theory of the Caliphate 281
Organisation of administrative machinery 282
The postal system 283
Censorship of morals: judiciary: army 284
The Turkish guard 285
Slavery: commerce 286
Toleration 287
Religious persecution 288
Position of Christians 289
Literature under the Abbasids 290
Exegesis: law 291
Dogmatic systems 292
Mysticism. Historical literature 293
Belles lettres 294
The encyclopaedists and geographers 295
Philosophy 296
Medicine 297
Mathematics and Astronomy 298

(B)

THE SELJŪQS.

By Herbert M. J. Loewe, M.A., Queens' College, Cambridge.

	PAGE
Importance of the Seljūqs	299
Decay of the Caliphate	300
The Shīʿites	301
Islām saved by the Seljūqs	302
The dynasty of Seljūq	303
Ṭughril Beg	304
The Vizier Niẓām-al-Mulk	305
Alp Arslān	306
Malik Shāh	307
Intrigues of the Turkān Khātūn	308
Barkiyāruq: civil wars	309
Muḥammad	310
Sanjar, the last Great Seljūq	311
Revolts of Atsiz of Khwārazm	312
The Ghuzz: death of Sanjar	313
The Atābegs and local Seljūq dynasties	314
The Seljūqs of Rūm	315
Coming of the Crusaders	316
End of the Seljūq power	317

CHAPTER XI.

THE EARLIER COMNENI.

By the late Ferdinand Chalandon, Archiviste Paléographe.

First appearance of the Comneni	318
End of the Macedonian dynasty	319
Revolt of Isaac Comnenus	320
Fall of Michael VI	321
The reign of Isaac Comnenus	322
Michael Cerularius	323
Constantine Ducas	324
Situation of the Empire	325
Anna Dalassena	326
Accession of Alexius Comnenus	327
Alexius and the Ducas family	328
War with the Normans of Italy	329
The Patzinaks and Cumans	330
The Empire and the Turks in Asia Minor	331
Unpopularity of Alexius	332
The First Crusade	333
Alexius Comnenus and the crusaders	*ib.*
The first crusaders at Constantinople	336
Hugh of Vermandois. Godfrey of Bouillon	337
Bohemond and Alexius Comnenus	338
Siege of Antioch	339

	PAGE
Alexius and the crusaders of 1101	340
Bohemond Prince of Antioch	341
Bohemond's expedition against the Byzantine Empire	342
Peace with Bohemond	343
Alexius and the Turks	344
Alexius and the Papacy	345
Intrigues of Anna Comnena	346
The Byzantine army and navy	347
Financial administration	348
Alexius and the Church	349
Estimate of Alexius	350

CHAPTER XII.

THE LATER COMNENI.

By the late Ferdinand Chalandon.

John Comnenus	351
Expedition against the Turks	353
The Venetians	354
The Hungarians	355
The Serbs	356
John Comnenus in Asia Minor	357
Italian affairs	358
John in Syria and Cilicia	359
John and the Western Empire	360
John and the Principality of Antioch	361
Accession of Manuel Comnenus	362
His character	363
His administration	364
Turkish attacks	365
The Second Crusade	366
Conrad III and Louis VII	367
Manuel and Roger II	368
The Greeks in Italy	369
Manuel and Alexander III	370
Manuel, Venice, and Barbarossa	371
Manuel and Hungary	372
Manuel and Serbia	373
The Latin East	374
Manuel's marriage with Mary of Antioch	375
Amaury of Jerusalem	376
Wars with the Turks	377
Battle of Myriocephalum	378
Death of Manuel	379
Alexius II	380
Andronicus I	381
His *coup d'état*	382
His administration	383
His death	384
The Angeli	*ib.*

CHAPTER XIII.

VENICE.

By Horatio F. Brown, Hon. LL.D., New College, Oxford.

PAGE

Earlier history of Venice 385
Lombard invasion. The *Tribuni* 386
Growth of the community 387
The first Doge 388
Relations with the Lombards 389
Relations with Byzantium 390
The Franks 391
Olivolo. Charles the Great 392
Fortunatus of Grado 393
Pepin of Italy's attack 394
Rialto, the City of Venice 395
Commerce 396
Constitution. Dynastic tendencies 397
The *pactum* of Pavia 398
Secular *versus* ecclesiastical power 399
Pacta and *praecepta* 400
The Candiani 401
The Emperor Otto I 402
Peter Orseolo I 403
Peter Orseolo II 404
Relations with East and West 405
Dux Dalmatiae 406
New Venice 407
The Normans 408
The First Crusade 409
The Levant 411
The Emperor Manuel 412
The Constitution 413
The Peace of Venice 414

CHAPTER XIV.

THE FOURTH CRUSADE AND THE LATIN EMPIRE.

By Professor Charles Diehl.

The beginning of the Crusade 415
The Crusaders and Venice 416
The diversion of the Crusade to Constantinople . . . 417
Arrival at Constantinople 418
Breach with the Byzantine Government 419
Sack of Constantinople 420
Partition of the Empire 421
Assises of Romania 422
Weakness of the Latin Empire 423
Defeat and death of the Emperor Baldwin I 424
Accession of Henry of Flanders: his early successes . . . 425

PAGE
His internal government 426
Decline of the Empire after Henry's death 427
Wars with Greeks and Bulgarians 428
Reign of Baldwin II 429
Gradual advance of the Greeks 430
End of the Latin Empire 431

CHAPTER XV.

GREECE AND THE AEGEAN UNDER FRANK AND VENETIAN DOMINATION (1204—1571).

By WILLIAM MILLER, M.A.

Partition of the Greek lands in Europe 432
Conquest of Athens and the Morea 433
Corfù and Crete 434
Euboea and the Archipelago 435
The Despotat of Epirus 436
Organisation of Achaia 437
The Latin Church 438
Prosperity of Achaia 439
Guy I of Athens 440
Battle of Karýdi 441
Battle of Pelagonía 442
The Ladies' Parliament 443
The Angevins and Greece 444
Career of Licario 445
Nicholas II de St Omer 446
The Theban Court 447
Philip of Taranto 448
Walter of Brienne. The Catalans 449
Battle of the Cephisus 450
Catalan organisation of Athens 451
The Infant Ferdinand of Majorca 452
The Duchy of Neopatras 453
Rise of the Acciajuoli 454
The Serbians in Northern Greece 455
The Navarrese Company 456
Florentine capture of Athens 457
Nerio Acciajuoli 458
Condition of Athens 459
Greek revival in the Morea 460
Turkish capture of Joánnina 461
Constantine Palaeologus in Greece 462
Mahomet II in the Morea 463
Turkish capture of Athens 464
The Gattilusi of Lesbos 465
The dynasty of Tocco 466
The Duchy of the Archipelago 467
Turkish capture of Naxos and Chios 468
History of Cyprus 469

PAGE
The Genoese in Cyprus 470
Cyprus becomes a Venetian colony 471
Loss of the last Venetian colonies 472
Frankish society 473
Frankish culture 474
Tables of Rulers . . . . *ib.*

CHAPTER XVI.

THE EMPIRE OF NICAEA AND THE RECOVERY OF CONSTANTINOPLE.

By WILLIAM MILLER, M.A.

Theodore Lascaris 478
Description of Nicaea 479
Partition of Asia Minor 480
The Franks in Asia Minor 481
Theodore I proclaimed Emperor 482
Second Frankish Invasion 483
Defeat and death of Kai-Khusrū I 484
Third Frankish Invasion 485
Theodore's death. His character 486
John III Vatatzes succeeds 487
Conspiracies against him 488
Greco-Bulgarian alliance 489
Triple League against Vatatzes 490
First attack on Salonica 491
Reconquest of Macedonia from the Bulgarians . . . 492
Annexation of Salonica 493
Recovery of Rhodes. Defeat of Michael II . . . 494
Second marriage of Vatatzes 495
Career of Constance of Hohenstaufen 496
Futile attempts at Union with Rome 497
Ecclesiastical policy. Material prosperity . . . 498
Literature 499
Death and canonisation of Vatatzes 500
Theodore II Lascaris: his education and writings . 501
His Bulgarian campaigns 502
Early career of Michael Palaeologus 503
War in Epirus 504
The Union of the Churches. Domestic policy . . . 505
Illness and death of Theodore 506
Regency and murder of Muzalon 507
Michael VIII Palaeologus crowned Emperor . . . 508
First attack on Constantinople 509
Diplomatic manœuvres of Palaeologus 510
Treaty of Nymphaeum 511
Capture of Constantinople 512
Nicaea merges in Byzantium 513
History of Trebizond 514
Vitality of Hellenism 516
Table of Rulers . . . . *ib.*

CHAPTER XVII.

THE BALKAN STATES.

I. THE ZENITH OF BULGARIA AND SERBIA (1186—1355).

By WILLIAM MILLER, M.A.

PAGE

The foundation of the Serbian monarchy 517
The Bogomile heresy 518
Second Bulgarian Empire 519
Kalojan's success 520
Stephen the "First-crowned" 521
Zenith of Bulgaria 522
John Asên II 523
Decline of Bulgaria 524
Constantine Asên 525
History of Bosnia 526
Stephen Uroš I 527
Ivailo the Swineherd 528
The Dowager-Empress Maria 529
The Tartars in Bulgaria 530
Peaceful development of Serbia 531
Stephen Uroš II 532
His Greek marriage 533
Serbia and the Papacy 534
Policy of Stephen Uroš II 535
Stephen Dečanski and his court 536
Condition of Serbia 537
Battle of Velbužd, 1330 538
Accession of Stephen Dušan 539
Foundation of Wallachia and Moldavia 540
Dušan and Cantacuzene 541
Dušan crowned Emperor, 1346 542
Serbo-Greek treaty of 1350 543
First Turkish settlement in Europe 544
Dušan invades Bosnia 545
His death, 1355 546
Dušan's Code 547
His ecclesiastical policy 548
Contemporary Slav culture 549
Character of Dušan's Empire 550
Its lack of unity 551

CHAPTER XVIII.

THE BALKAN STATES.

II. THE TURKISH CONQUEST (1355—1483).

By WILLIAM MILLER, M.A.

Break-up of the Serbian Empire 552
Vukašin's usurpation 554
Battle on the Maritza, 1371 555
Hegemony of Bosnia 556
The Turkish advance 557

PAGE

Battle of Kossovo, 1389 558
Zenith of Tvrtko I 559
End of the Bulgarian Empire 560
Battle of Nicopolis, 1396 561
Battle of Angora, 1402 562
Reign of Stephen Lazarević 563
Venice in Albania 564
The Bosnian King-maker 565
Civil war in Bosnia 566
Mirčea "the Great" of Wallachia 567
Condition of Moldavia and Serbia 568
Branković at Semendria 569
The loss of the last Serbian ports 570
John Hunyadi 571
Battle of Varna, 1444 572
Third Battle of Kossovo, 1448 573
The "Duchy of St Sava" 574
Policy of Mahomet II 575
Siege of Belgrade, 1456 576
Death of George Branković, 1456 577
End of medieval Serbia 578
Coronation of Stephen Tomašević 579
Turkish conquest of Bosnia, 1463 580
Hungarian *banats* of Jajce and Srebrenik 581
Turkish conquest of the Herzegovina 582
Venice in Albania 583
Career of Skanderbeg 584
Turkish conquest of Albania 585
History of Montenegro 586
End of the "Black Princes" 587
The Danubian Principalities 588
Jealousies of the Powers 589
Tables of Rulers 590

CHAPTER XIX.

ATTEMPTS AT REUNION OF THE GREEK AND LATIN CHURCHES.

By Professor Louis Bréhier.

Hindrances to the Union 594
The different points of view 596
Last attempts at alliance against the Normans 597
Union and the danger from the Turks 598
Union and the First Crusade 599
The Papacy and the Germanic Empire 600
Manuel Comnenus and the Union 601
Failure of Manuel's policy 602
Rupture between Byzantium and the West 603
The Fourth Crusade 604
The compulsory Union 605
Innocent III and the Greek Church 606

PAGE
Fall of the Latin Empire 607
John Vatatzes and attempts at union 608
Policy of Michael Palaeologus 609
Schemes of Charles of Anjou 610
Gregory X and Michael Palaeologus 611
Union at the Council of Lyons 612
Breach of the Union 613
Policy of Andronicus II 614
Clement VI and the Union 615
John VI Cantacuzene 616
John V Palaeologus 617
Manuel Palaeologus in the West 618
The Battle of Angora, 1402 619
The Greeks and the Council of Basle 620
The Council at Ferrara, 1438 621
The Council at Florence, 1439 622
The Union of Florence 623
Byzantine opposition to the Union 624
Fall of Constantinople 625
Conclusion 626

CHAPTER XX.

THE MONGOLS.

By Herbert M. J. Loewe, M.A.

Character of Mongol history 627
Extent of the Mongol invasions 628
Unification of Asia 629
Mongol and Tartar 630
Other tribes in the Mongol Confederation 631
Jenghiz Khan 632
Conquest of Turkestan and Khwārazm 633
Empire of Jenghiz Khan 634
Conquest of Northern China 635
Advance westward 636
Invasion of Europe 637
The recall of Bātu saves Europe 638
The Papacy and the Mongols 639
Ogdai and Kuyuk 640
Downfall of the Assassins 641
The fall of the Caliphate of Baghdad 642
Defeat of the Mongols by the Mamlūks, 1260 643
Hūlāgū and the Īl-khāns 644
Mangu 645
The reign of Kublai 646
Change in the Mongols 648
Fall of the Mongols in China 649
The western Mongols: Tīmūr 650
Conquest of India: defeat of the Ottomans 651
The Golden Horde 652

CHAPTER XXI.

THE OTTOMAN TURKS TO THE FALL OF CONSTANTINOPLE.

By the late Sir Edwin Pears, LL.B. London, President of the European Bar at Constantinople.

PAGE
Infiltration of Turkish nomads into Asia Minor 653
Ertughril 655
Accession of Osmān 656
The Catalan Grand Company 657
First entry of Turks into Europe, 1308 658
Progress of Osmān 659
Capture of Brūsa 660
Capture of Nicaea 661
Capture of Nicomedia 662
Orkhān styled Sultan 663
The Janissaries . . . . ib.
Organisation of the army 664
Orkhān in alliance with Cantacuzene 665
Venetian *versus* Genoese influence 666
The Ottomans in Europe 667
Murād I 668
European policy of the Ottomans 669
Defeat of the Serbs on the Maritza, 1371 670
Subservience of the Empire to Murād 671
Battle of Kossovo, 1389 672
Causes of Murād's success 673
Bāyazīd the Thunderbolt 674
Western crusade against the Turks 675
Victory of Bāyazīd at Nicopolis, 1396 676
Boucicaut at Constantinople 677
The appearance of Tīmūr 679
His capture of Aleppo and Baghdad 680
Battle of Angora, 1402 682
Tīmūr's conquests in Asia Minor 683
Deaths of Tīmūr and Bāyazīd 684
Civil war among the Ottomans 685
Mahomet I 687
Character of his reign 688
Murād II . . . . ib.
Increasing numbers of the Ottomans 689
European conquests of Murād 690
Crusade of Vladislav and Hunyadi 691
Murād's victories at Varna and Kossovo 692
Accession of Mahomet II 693
Preparations for the siege of Constantinople 694
Western assistance for the Emperor 695
The besieging force 696
The defences of Constantinople 697
The dispositions of the besieged 698
Defeat of Mahomet's fleet 699
The Turkish fleet in the Golden Horn 700

PAGE
Preparations for a general assault 701
Commencement of the assault, 29 May 1453 702
The Janissaries force the stockade 703
Capture of Constantinople 704
Character of Mahomet II 705

CHAPTER XXII.

BYZANTINE LEGISLATION FROM THE DEATH OF JUSTINIAN (565) TO 1453.

By Paul Collinet, Professor of Roman Law at the University of Paris.

Periods of legislation 706
Commentaries on Justinian's work 707
Novels of Justin II, Tiberius, and Heraclius 708
The *Ecloga* 709
The Military, Maritime, and Rural Codes 710
Canon law of the sixth century 711
Legislation of Basil I 712
Legislation of Leo VI: the Basilics 713
The Novels of Leo VI 714
Novels from 911 to 1045 715
Legal education under Leo VI 716
Legal treatises based on the *Ecloga* and *Basilics* . . . 717
The Πεῖρα 718
Canonical collections . . . . *ib.*
The law school of Constantinople (1045) 719
Novels from 1045 to 1453 720
Monographs of the eleventh century 721
Later legal works 722
Later canonical collections 723
The *Syntagma* of Matthew Blastares 724
The diffusion of Byzantine legislation 725

CHAPTER XXIII.

THE GOVERNMENT AND ADMINISTRATION OF THE BYZANTINE EMPIRE.

By Professor Charles Diehl.

The Basileus 726
Limitations of imperial authority 729
The twofold hierarchy of rank and office 730
The ministers 731
Institution of the themes 732
The themes in the tenth century 733
Officials of the themes 734
Importance of the bureaucracy 735
Hellenisation of the Empire 736
Assistance of the Church 737
The army 738
The fleet 741

CHAPTER XXIV.

BYZANTINE CIVILISATION.

By Professor CHARLES DIEHL.

	PAGE
Splendour of Constantinople	745
Twofold aspect of Byzantine civilisation	746
Constantinople's extent and walls	747
Its plan in the tenth century	748
The population of Constantinople	750
Religion	751
St Sophia	752
The power of Monasticism	753
The Sacred Palace	754
Imperial ceremonial	755
Court life: intrigues	756
Part played by women	757
Luxury of society	758
The Hippodrome and the factions	759
The populace	760
Bazaars and gilds	761
Commerce	762
Culture	763
The University of Constantinople	764
History	765
Theology	766
Poetry	767
Art	*ib.*
The provinces	770
The towns	*ib.*
The countryside	771
Power of the great nobles	772
The Byzantine character	773
Oriental, Greek, and Christian influences	774
Virtues and defects of the Byzantines	775
The inheritance of Europe from Byzantium	776
Byzantium and the Renaissance	777

LIST OF BIBLIOGRAPHIES.

CHAPS.		PAGES
	Abbreviations	779—781
	General Bibliography for Volume IV . .	782—794
I.	Leo III and the Isaurian Dynasty . . .	795—797
II.	From Nicephorus I to the Fall of the Phrygian Dynasty	798—800
III and IV.	The Macedonian Dynasty	801—804
V (A).	The Struggle with the Saracens (717—867) .	805—809
V (B).	The Struggle with the Saracens (867—1057) .	809—813
VI.	Armenia	814—818
VII (A).	The Empire and its Northern Neighbours .	819—821
VII (B).	Conversion of the Slavs	822—825
VIII.	The Rise and Fall of the First Bulgarian Empire	826—827
IX.	The Greek Church: its relations with the West up to 1054	828—830
X (A).	Muslim Civilisation during the Abbasid Period	831—835
X (B).	The Seljūqs	836
XI.	The Earlier Comneni	837—840
XII.	The Later Comneni	841—845
XIII.	Venice	846—849
XIV.	The Fourth Crusade and the Latin Empire .	850—851
XV.	Greece and the Aegean under Frank and Venetian domination	852—866
XVI.	The Empire of Nicaea and the recovery of Constantinople	867—870
XVII and XVIII.	The Balkan States	871—876
XIX.	Attempts at Reunion of the Greek and Latin Churches	877—879
XX.	The Mongols	880—882
XXI.	The Ottoman Turks to the fall of Constantinople	883—889
XXII.	Byzantine Legislation	890—893
XXIII.	The Government and Administration of the Byzantine Empire	894—895
XXIV.	Byzantine Civilisation	896—898

Chronological Table of Leading Events	899—907
Index	909—993

LIST OF MAPS.

VOLUME IV.

(See separate portfolio.)

38. The Break-up of the Caliphate.
39. Asia Minor, shewing the Themes of the Tenth Century, and Armenia.
40. Northern neighbours of the Empire in the Tenth Century.
41. Bulgaria and the Balkans in the Tenth Century.
42. The Empire of the Comneni about 1130.
43. The Latin States in the East in 1214.
44. The Empires of the Palaeologi and Stephen Dušan.
45. The Turkish Sultanate in 1481.
46. The Mongol Empire about 1250.
47 (a). The City of Constantinople.
47 (b). The environs of Constantinople.

CHAPTER I.

LEO III AND THE ISAURIAN DYNASTY (717–802).

The history of the Byzantine Empire under the rule of the Isaurian dynasty is one of the periods in the prolonged evolution of the monarchy least easy of comprehension. The work of the sovereigns usually called the Iconoclast Emperors has been, in fact, recorded for us practically only by opponents or victims, and their impassioned reports have obviously no claim to be considered strictly impartial. On the other hand, the writings defending and justifying the policy of the Emperors have nearly all disappeared in the fierce reaction which followed the defeat of the Iconoclasts, and we are thus but imperfectly acquainted with the real objects which the Isaurian Emperors set before themselves. Further, the true aspect of their rule has been completely obscured and distorted by the hatred and prejudice excited against them. The nature of their religious policy has been, and still is, frequently misconceived. In truth, the controversy as to images was only a part of the great work of political, social, and economic reconstruction undertaken by Leo III and Constantine V on the emergence of the Empire from the serious dangers which it had passed through in the seventh century. It would thus be a misunderstanding of the meaning and scope of this religious strife to consider it apart from the vast aggregate of which it merely forms a portion, just as it would be a wrong estimate of the Isaurian Emperors to find in them mere sectaries and heretics. The striking testimony rendered them by their very detractors at the Council of 787 should not be forgotten by any who undertake to relate their history. While severely condemning the religious policy of a Leo III or a Constantine V, the bishops assembled at Nicaea recall "their great deeds, the victories gained over enemies, the subjugation of barbarous nations," and further, "the solicitude they showed for their subjects, the wise measures they took, the constitutions they promulgated, their civil institutions, and the improvements effected by them in the cities." "Such," the Fathers in Council add, "is the true title of the dead Emperors to fame, that which secures to them the gratitude of all their subjects."[1]

[1] Mansi, *Concilia*, XIII, 355.

I.

When on 25 March 717 Leo III was crowned by the Patriarch Germanus, the exterior circumstances of the monarchy were notably difficult. For ten years, thanks to the anarchy laying waste the Empire, the Arabs had been persistently advancing in Asia Minor; in 716 they laid siege to Amorium, in 717 they took Pergamus; and Maslamah, the most distinguished of their generals, who had pushed his way nearly into the Opsician theme, was, with his lieutenant Sulaimān, making ready for a great attack upon Constantinople itself. But the new Emperor was equal to defending the Empire. Of Asiatic origin, an Isaurian, according to Theophanes, but more probably descended from a family of Germanicea in Commagene, he had, since the time of Justinian II, displayed remarkable qualities in the shaping of his career. On a mission to the Caucasus he had shewn himself a wary diplomatist, and had given proofs also of energy, courage, presence of mind, and the power of disentangling himself from the most embarrassing situations. As strategus of the Anatolics since 713, he had held the Arabs in check with some success in Asia Minor, proving himself at once a good general and a skilful diplomatist; he was well acquainted with the Musulman world and perhaps even spoke Arabic. In short, eager as he was to vindicate the high ambitions he cherished, he appreciated order and was desirous of restoring strength and security to the Empire; a good organiser, a man of resolute will and autocratic temper, he had all the best qualities of a statesman. In the course of his reign of twenty-three years (717–740) he was to shew himself the renowned artificer of the re-organisation of the Empire.

Barely a few months from his accession the Arabs appeared before Constantinople, attacking it by land and sea (15 August 717). During the whole year which the siege lasted (August 717 to August 718) Leo III dealt firmly with every difficulty. He was as successful in stimulating the defection of a portion of the crews composed of Egyptian Christians serving in the Arab fleet as he was in prevailing on the Bulgars to intervene on behalf of the Byzantines. He shewed himself as well able to destroy the Musulman ships with Greek fire as to defeat the Caliph's armies on land and secure the re-victualling of the besieged city. When at last Maslamah decided upon retreat, he had lost, it is said, nearly 150,000 men, while from a storm which burst upon his fleet only ten vessels escaped. For Leo III this was a glorious opening to his reign, for Islām it was a disaster without precedent. The great onrush of Arab conquest was for many years broken off short in the East as it was to be in the West by the victory of Charles Martel at Poitiers (732). The founder of the Isaurian dynasty stood out as the saviour of the Empire, and pious Byzantines declared in the words of Theophanes "that God and the most blessed Virgin Theotokos ever protect the city of the Christian Empire, and that God does not forsake such as call upon Him faithfully."

In spite of this great success, which contributed powerfully to establish the new dynasty, the Arabs remained formidable. After some years respite, they again took the offensive in Asia Minor (726), and the struggle with them lasted until the end of the reign. However, the victory of Leo III and his son Constantine at Acroïnon was a stern lesson to the Musulmans. The successes of the reign of Constantine V, facilitated by the internal quarrels which at that time disturbed the Empire of the Caliphs, were to crown these happy achievements, and to avert for many years the Arab danger which in the seventh century had so seriously threatened Constantinople[1].

The domestic administration of Leo III was no less fortunate in its consequences to the Empire.

After twenty years of anarchy and revolution the monarchy was left in a very distracted state. In 718, while the Arabs were besieging Constantinople, the strategus of Sicily, Sergius, proclaimed an Emperor in the West. In 720 the ex-Emperor Anastasius II, who was interned at Thessalonica, attempted, with the support of the Bulgars and the complicity of several high officials, to regain the throne. Both these movements were firmly suppressed. Meanwhile, Leo III was planning how he might give permanence to his dynasty. At the time of his accession, having no sons of his own, he had married his daughter Anne to Artavasdus, strategus of the Armeniac theme, and formerly his chief supporter in his revolt against Theodosius III, conferring on him the high rank of *curopalates*. When in December 718 a son, Constantine, was born to him, an even better prospect of length of days was opened to his house. By 25 March 720 Leo had secured the throne to the child, having him solemnly crowned by the Patriarch. Thus master of the situation, he was able to give himself up wholly to the great task, so urgently necessary, of reconstituting the State.

Above all things it was imperative to provide for the defence of the frontiers. Leo III set about this by completing and extending the system of *themes*. He cut off the Western part of the immense government of the Anatolics to form the Thracesian theme. He likewise divided the Maritime theme, in order to constitute the two governments of the Cibyrrhaeots and the Dodecanese. The military reasons, which dictated the creation of provinces less extensive and more easily defended, were reinforced by political considerations. Leo III knew by his own experience how dangerous it was to leave too large stretches of territory in the hands of all-powerful strategi, and what temptations were thus offered them to revolt and lay claim to the Empire. For the same reasons Constantine V pursued his father's policy, reducing the area of the Opsician theme, and forming out of it the Bucellarian theme, and, perhaps, the Optimatian. Thus under the Isaurian Emperors was com-

[1] For the details of the Arab War, see *infra*, Chapter V (A), pp. 119–21.

pleted the administrative organisation sketched out in the seventh century. Leo III and his son made a point of nominating to be governors of these provinces men of worth, good generals and capable administrators, and, above all, devoted to the person and the policy of their master. The *Military Code* (νόμος στρατιωτικός), which probably dates from the reign of Leo III, was designed to provide these rulers with well-disciplined troops, and to secure the formation of an army with no care or interest apart from its work, and strictly forbidden to concern itself with agriculture or commerce. Out of this force Constantine V, by throwing into one body contingents drawn from every theme in the Empire, was to set himself to create a truly national army, ever more and more removed from the influence of local leaders and provincial patriotism.

If the administration and the army were to be re-organised, it was of the first necessity to restore order to the finances. At all costs, money must be found. To secure this, Leo III hit upon a highly ingenious expedient, known as doubling the indiction. The fiscal year from 1 September 726 to 1 September 727 was the tenth in the period of fifteen years called the indiction. The Emperor ordered that the following year, reckoning from 1 September 727 to 1 September 728, instead of being the eleventh year of the indiction, should be the twelfth, and consequently in one year he levied the taxes which should have been paid in two years[1]. The Exchequer officials received orders to get in all contributions with rigorous exactness; and the Popes complained bitterly of the tyranny of the fiscal authority (725). In spite of this, new taxes were devised. In 732 Leo III increased the capitation tax, at least in the provinces of Sicily, Calabria, and Crete, and seized the revenues of the pontifical patrimonies in the south of Italy for the benefit of the treasury. Finally in 739, after the destructive earthquake in Constantinople, in order to rebuild the walls of the capital, he raised existing imposts by one twelfth (*i.e.* two *keratia* upon the *nomisma*, or golden *solidus*, which was worth twenty-four *keratia*, whence the name *Dikeraton* given to the new tax). Thus it was that the chroniclers of the eighth century accused Leo III of an unrestrained passion for money and a degrading appetite for gain. As a fact, his careful, often harsh, administration of the finances supplied the treasury with fresh resources.

Leo was at no less pains to restore economic prosperity to the Empire. The *Rural Code* (νόμος γεωργικός), which appears to date from this period, was an endeavour to restrain the disquieting extension of large estates, to put a stop to the disappearance of small free holdings, and to make the lot of the peasant more satisfactory. The immigration of numerous Slav tribes into the Balkan peninsula since the end of the sixth century had brought about important changes in the methods of land cultivation. The colonate, if it had not completely disappeared, at

[1] For the confusion caused by this in the chronology of part of the eighth century, see the note by Professor Bury, *History of the Later Roman Empire*, II, 425.

any rate had ceased to be the almost universal condition. Instead were to be found peasants (the μορτίται) much less closely bound to the soil they cultivated than the former *adscriptitii*, and paying a fixed rent (μορτή) to the owner, or else communities of free peasants holding the land in collective ownership, and at liberty to divide it up among the members of the community in order to farm it profitably. The *Rural Code* gave legal sanction to existing conditions which had been slowly evolved: it witnesses to a genuine effort to revive agriculture and to restore security and prosperity to the husbandman; apparently this effort was by no means wasted, and the moral and material condition of the agricultural population was greatly improved. The *Maritime Code* (νόμος ναυτικός), on the other hand, encouraged the development of the mercantile marine by imposing part of the liability for unavoidable losses on the passengers, thus diminishing the risk of freight-owner and captain.

Finally, an important legislative reform brought the old laws of Justinian up to date in relation to civil causes; namely, the publication of the code promulgated in 739 and known as the *Ecloga*. In the preface to the *Ecloga* Leo III has plainly pointed out the object aimed at in his reform; he intended at once to give more precision and clearness to the law, and to secure that justice should be better administered, but, above all, he had at heart the introduction of a new spirit into the law, more humane—the very title expressly mentions this development (εἰς τὸ φιλανθρωπότερον)—and more in harmony with Christian conceptions. These tendencies are very clearly marked in the provisions, much more liberal than those in Justinian's code, of the laws dealing with the family and with questions of marriage and inheritance. In this code we are sensible that there is at once a desire to raise the intellectual and moral standard of the people, and also a spirit of equal justice, shewn by the fact that henceforth the law, alike for all, takes no account of social categories[1]. And there is no better proof than the *Ecloga* of the vastness of the projects of reform contemplated by the Iconoclast Emperors and of the high conception they had formed of their duty as rulers.

Leo III's work of administrative re-organisation was crowned by a bold attempt at religious and social reform. Thence was to arise the serious conflict known as the *Iconoclastic struggle*, which for more than a century and a half was profoundly to disturb the interior peace of the Empire, and abroad was to involve the breach with Rome and the loss of Italy.

The long struggle of the seventh century had brought about far-reaching changes in the ideas and morals of Byzantine society. The influence of religion, all-powerful in this community, had produced results

[1] Cf. on the laws established by the *Ecloga*, *infra*, Chapter XXII, pp. 708–10.

formidable from the moral point of view. Superstition had made alarming progress. Everybody believed in the supernatural and the marvellous. Cities looked for their safety much less to men's exertions than to the miraculous intervention of the patron saint who watched over them, to St Demetrius at Thessalonica, St Andrew at Patras, or the Mother of God at Constantinople. Individuals put faith in the prophecies of wizards, and Leo III himself, like Leontius or Philippicus, had been met in the way by one who had said to him: "Thou shalt be King." Miracle seemed so natural a thing that even the Councils used the possibility of it as an argument. But, above all, the *cultus* offered to images, and the belief in their miraculous virtues, had come to occupy a surprisingly and scandalously large place in the minds of the Byzantines. Among the populace, largely Greek by race, and in many cases only superficially Christianised, it seemed as though a positive return to pagan customs were in process.

From early times, Christianity in decorating its churches had made great use of pictures, looking upon them as a means of teaching, and as matter of edification for the faithful. And early too, with the encouragement of the Church, the faithful had bestowed on pictures, especially on those believed to have been "not made by human hands" (ἀχειροποίητοι), veneration and worship. In the eighth century this devotion was more general than ever. Everywhere, not merely in the churches and monasteries, but in houses and in shops, on furniture, on clothes, and on trinkets were placed the images of Christ, the Blessed Virgin, and the Saints. On these cherished icons the marks of respect and adoration were lavished: the people prostrated themselves before them, they lighted lamps and candles in front of them, they adorned them with ribbons and garlands, burned incense, and kissed them devoutly. Oaths were taken upon images, and hymns were sung in their honour; miracles, prodigies, and marvellous cures were implored and expected of them; and so absolute was the trust in their protection that they were sometimes chosen as sponsors for children. It is true that, in justification of these aberrations, theologians were accustomed to explain that the saint was mystically present in his material image, and that the respect shewn to the image penetrated to the original which it represented. The populace no longer drew this distinction. To them the images seemed real persons, and Byzantine history is full of pious legends, in which images speak, act, and move about like divine and supernatural beings. Everybody was convinced that by a mystic virtue the all-powerful images brought healing to the soul as well as to the body, that they stilled tempests, put evil spirits to flight, and warded off diseases, and that to pay them the honour due to them was a sure means of obtaining all blessings in this life and eternal glory in the next.

Many devout minds, however, were hurt and scandalised by the excesses practised in the cult of images. As early as the fifth and sixth centuries, Fathers of the Church and Bishops had seen with indignation the Divine Persons thus represented, and had not hesitated to urge the destruction of these Christian idols. This iconoclastic tendency had grown still more powerful towards the end of the seventh century, especially in the Asiatic provinces of the Empire. The Paulicians, whose heresy had spread rapidly in Asia Minor during the second half of the seventh century, proscribed images, and were opposed to the adoration of the Cross, to the cult of the Virgin and the Saints, and to everything which was not "worship in spirit and in truth." The Messalians of Armenia also rejected image-worship, and the clergy of that province had succeeded in gradually purifying popular religion there. It must by no means be forgotten that the Jews, who were very numerous in Christendom, and at this time shewed great zeal in proselytising, were naturally hostile to images, and that the Musulmans condemned them no less rigorously, seeing in the devotion paid to them an actual revival of polytheism. Leo III himself, Asiatic in origin and subjected from childhood to the influence of an iconoclastic atmosphere, would as a matter of course sympathise with this opposition to images. Like many Asiatics, and like a section even of the superior clergy of the orthodox party, he seems to have been alarmed by the increase of idolatry among the people, and to have resolved on a serious effort to restore to Christianity its primitive loftiness and purity.

Mistakes have often been made about the character of the religious policy of the Isaurian Emperors, and its end and scope have been somewhat imperfectly understood. If faith is to be reposed in contemporaries, very hostile, be it said, to Leo III, the Emperor was actuated by strangely petty motives. If Theophanes is to be trusted, he was desirous of pleasing the Musulmans with whom he was in close intellectual agreement (σαρακηνόφρων), and the Jews, to whom he had, as was related, promised satisfaction on this head if ever the predictions which bade him expect the throne should be realised. These are mere legends; it would be difficult to believe that a prince who had just won so resounding a victory over Islām should have been so anxious to spare the feelings of his adversaries, and that a ruler who in 722 promulgated an edict of persecution against the Jews should have been so much affected by their views.

The historians of our day have credited the iconoclasts with other intentions, and have attributed a much wider scope to their policy. They have seen in them the champions of the lay power, the opponents of the interference of the Church with the affairs of the State. They have represented them as rationalists who, many centuries before Luther, attempted the reformation of the Church, as freethinkers, aspiring to found a new society on "the immortal principles" destined to triumph in the French Revolution. These are strange errors. Leo III and his son were men of their time, sincerely pious, convinced believers, even theologians, very anxious, in accordance with the ideas of the age, to cast out everything which might bring down the Divine anger upon the Empire, very eager, in sympathy with the feelings of a section of their people and their clergy, to purify religion from what seemed to them idolatry.

But they were also statesmen, deeply concerned for the greatness and the safety of the Empire. Now the continuous growth of monasticism in Byzantine society had already produced grave results for the State. The immunity from taxation enjoyed by Church lands, which every day became more extensive, cut down the receipts of the Treasury; the ever-increasing numbers who entered the cloister withdrew soldiers from the army, officials from the public services, and husbandmen from agriculture, while it deprived the nation of its vital forces. The monks were a formidable element of unrest owing to the influence they exercised over souls, which often found its opportunities in image-worship, many convents depending for subsistence on the miraculous icons they possessed. Unquestionably, one of the objects which the Iconoclast Emperors set before themselves was to struggle against this disquieting state of things, to diminish the influence which the monks exercised in virtue of their control of the nation's education and their moral guidance of souls. In proscribing images they aimed also at the monks, and in this way the religious reform is intimately connected with the great task of social rebuilding which the Isaurian Emperors undertook.

It is true that by entering on the struggle which they thus inaugurated the iconoclast sovereigns ushered in a long period of unrest for the monarchy; that out of this conflict very serious political consequences arose. It would, nevertheless, be unjust to see in the resolution to which they came no more than a caprice of reckless and fanatical despots. Behind Leo III and his son, and ready to uphold them, stood a whole powerful party of iconoclasts. Its real strength was in the Asiatic population and the army, which was largely made up of Asiatic elements, notably of Armenians. Even among the higher clergy, secretly jealous of the power of the monks, many bishops, Constantine of Nacolea, Thomas of Claudiopolis, Theodosius of Ephesus, and, later on, Constantine of Nicomedia and Sisinnius of Perge, resolutely espoused the imperial policy, and among the Court circle and the officials high in the administration many, less perhaps from conviction than from fear or from self-interest, did likewise, although among these classes several are to be found laying down their lives for their attachment to images. And even among the people of Constantinople a violent hostility to monks shewed itself at times. But in the opposite camp the Isaurian Emperors found that they had to reckon with formidable forces, nearly the whole of the European part of the Empire: the monks, who depended upon images and were interested in maintaining the reverence paid them; the Popes, the traditional and passionate champions of orthodoxy; the women, bolder and more fervent than any in the battle for the holy icons, whose vigorous efforts and powerful influence cannot be too strongly emphasised; and, finally, the masses, the crowd, instinctively faithful to time-honoured religious forms, and instinctively opposed to the upper classes and ready to resist all change. These elements of resistance formed the majority in the Empire, and upon their tenacious opposition, heightened by unwearying polemics, the attempted reforms were finally to be wrecked.

Leo III was too capable a statesman and too well aware of the serious consequences, which, in the Byzantine Empire, any innovation in religion would involve, not to have hesitated long before entering upon the conflict. His course was decided by an incident which shews how thoroughly he was a man of his time. In 726 a dangerous volcanic eruption took place between Thera and Therasia, in which phenomenon the Emperor discerned a token of the wrath of God falling heavily upon the monarchy. He concluded that the only means of propitiation would be to cleanse religion finally from practices which dishonoured it. He resolved upon the promulgation of the edict against images (726).

It has sometimes been thought, on the strength of a misunderstood passage in the life of St Stephen the Younger, that the Emperor ordered, not that the pictures should be destroyed, but that they should be hung higher up, in order to withdraw them from the adoration of the faithful. But facts make it certain that the measures taken were very much more rigorous. Thus keen excitement was aroused in the capital and throughout the Empire. At Constantinople, when the people saw an officer, in the execution of the imperial order, proceed to destroy the image of Christ placed above the entrance to the Sacred Palace, they broke out into a riot, in which several were killed and injured, and severe sentences necessarily followed. When the news spread into the provinces worse things happened. Greece and the Cyclades rose and proclaimed a rival Emperor, who, with the support of Agallianus, turmarch of the Helladics, marched upon Constantinople, but the rebel fleet was easily destroyed by the imperial squadrons. In the West results were more important. Pope Gregory II was already, owing to his opposition to the fiscal policy of Leo III, on very bad terms with the Government. When the edict against images arrived in Italy, there was a universal rising in the peninsula in favour of the Pope, who had boldly countered the imperial order by excommunicating the exarch and denouncing the heresy (727). Venice, Ravenna, the Pentapolis, Rome, and the Campagna rose in revolt, massacred or drove out the imperial officers, and proclaimed new dukes; indeed, matters went so far that the help of the Lombards was invoked, and a plan was mooted of choosing a new Emperor to be installed at Constantinople in the place of Leo III. The Emperor took energetic measures against the insurgents. The new exarch Eutychius, who received orders to put down the resistance at all costs, marched upon Rome (729) but did not succeed in taking it.

And it may be that imperial rule in Italy would now have come to an end had not Gregory II, like the prudent politician that he was, discerned the danger likely to arise from the intervention of the Lombards in Italian affairs and used his influence to bring back the revolted provinces to their allegiance. Thus peace was restored and Italy conciliated, her action being limited to a respectful request that the honour due to images should again be paid to them[1].

Meanwhile opposition was growing in the East. The clergy, with Germanus, Patriarch of Constantinople, at their head, had naturally condemned the imperial policy openly. Leo III determined on breaking down resistance by force. The Church schools were closed, and a later legend even relates that the Emperor burned the most famous of them, along with its library and its professors. In January 730 he caused the deposition of the Patriarch Germanus, who refused to condemn images, and in his place he had the Syncellus Anastasius elected, a man wholly devoted to the iconoclast doctrine. This caused fresh disturbances in the West. Gregory II refused to recognise the heretical Patriarch. Gregory III, who succeeded in 731, relying on the Lombards, assumed an even bolder and more independent attitude. The Roman Synod of 731 solemnly excluded from the Church those who opposed images. This was to go too far. The Emperor, who now saw in Gregory merely a rebel, sent an expedition to Italy with the task of reducing him to obedience; the Byzantine fleet, however, was destroyed by a tempest in the Adriatic (732). Leo III was obliged to content himself with seizing the Petrine patrimonies within the limits of the Empire, with detaching from the Roman obedience and placing under the authority of the Patriarch of Constantinople the dioceses of Calabria, Sicily, Crete, and Illyricum, and with imposing fresh taxes on the Italian population. The breach between the Empire and Italy seemed to be complete; in 738 Gregory III was to make a definite appeal to Charles Martel.

Even outside the Empire orthodox resistance to the iconoclast policy was becoming apparent. St John Damascene, a monk of the Laura of St Sabas in Palestine, wrote between 726 and 737 three treatises against "those who depreciate the holy images," in which he stated dogmatically the principles underlying the cult of icons, and did not hesitate to declare that "to legislate in ecclesiastical matters did not pertain to the Emperor" (*οὐ βασιλέων ἐστὶ νομοθετεῖν τῇ ἐκκλησίᾳ*). Legend relates that Leo III, to avenge himself on John, had him accused of treason to the Caliph, his master, who caused his right hand to be cut off, and it adds that the next night, by the intercession of the Blessed Virgin, the hand was miraculously restored to the mutilated arm, that it might continue its glorious labours in defence of orthodoxy.

In reality, despite certain harsh acts, dictated for the most part by political necessity, it seems plain that the edict of 726 was enforced with

[1] Cf. Vol. II, Chapter VIII A.

great moderation. Most of the churches and the Patriarch's palace were still, at the end of the reign, in undisturbed possession of the frescoes and mosaics which adorned them. Against persons there was no systematic persecution. Even the chronicler Theophanes, who cannot sufficiently reprobate "the impious Leo," acknowledges that the deposed Patriarch, Germanus, withdrew to his hereditary property of Platonion and there peacefully ended his days. If his writings were burnt by the Emperor's orders, he himself was never, as legend claims, subjected to measures of violence. The rising in Greece was suppressed with great mildness, only the two leaders being condemned to death. Finally, the *Ecloga*, promulgated in 740, inflicted no punishment on iconodules. Nevertheless, when Leo died in 740, a serious struggle had been entered on, which was to become fatally embittered as much by the very heat of the combat and the desperate resistance of the monks as by the formidable problems which it was soon to raise. In the quarrel over images the real collision was between the authority of the Emperor in religious matters and the desire of the Church to free herself from the tutelage of the State. This became unmistakable when Constantine V succeeded his father.

II.

Constantine V (740–775) has been fiercely attacked by the iconodule party. They surnamed him "the Stable-boy" (καβάλλινος) and "Copronymus" (named from dung), on account of an unlucky accident which, they said, had occurred at his christening. They accused him of nameless debaucheries, of vices against nature, and attributed to him every kind of infamy. "On the death of Leo," says the deacon Stephen, "Satan raised up in his stead a still more abandoned being, even as to Ahab succeeded Ahaziah, and to Archelaus Herod, more wicked than he." In the eyes of Nicephorus he outdid in cruelty those tyrants who have most tormented the human race. For Theophanes he is "a monster athirst for blood," "a ferocious beast," an "unclean and bloodstained magician taking pleasure in evoking demons," in a word "a man given up from childhood to all that is soul-destroying," an amalgam of all the vices, "a precursor of Antichrist."

It would be childish to take these senseless calumnies literally. In fact, if we consider the events of his reign, Constantine V appears as an able and energetic ruler, a great warrior and a great administrator, who left behind him a glorious and lasting reputation. He was the idol of the army, which long remembered him and many years after his death was still the determined champion of his life-work. He was, in the eyes of the people, "the victorious and prophetic Emperor," to whose tomb in 813 they crowded, in order to implore the dead Caesar to save the city which was threatened by the Bulgars. And all believed themselves to have seen the prince come forth from his tomb, mounted on his war-horse and ready once more to lead out his legions against the enemy. These are not facts to be lightly passed over. Most certainly Constantine V was, even more than his father, autocratic, violent, passionate, harsh, and often terrifying. But his reign, however disturbed by the quarrel concerning images, appears, none the less, a great reign, in which religious policy, as under Leo III, merely formed part of a much more important achievement.

It must be added that the early occurrences of the reign were by no means such as to incline the new prince to deal gently with his opponents. In 741 the insurrection of his brother-in-law Artavasdus united the whole orthodox party against Constantine V. The Emperor had just left Constantinople to open a campaign against the Arabs; while the usurper was making an unlooked-for attack on him in Asia, treason in his rear was handing over the capital to his rival, the Patriarch Anastasius himself declaring against him as suspected of heretical opinions. A year and a half was needed to crush the rebel. Supported by Asia, which, with the exception of the Opsician theme where Artavasdus had been strategus, ranged itself unanimously on the side of Constantine, the rightful Emperor defeated his competitor at Sardis (May 742) and at Modrina (August 742) and drove him back upon Constantinople, to which city he laid siege. On 2 November 742 it was taken by storm. Artavasdus and his sons were blinded; the Patriarch Anastasius was ignominiously paraded round the Hippodrome, mounted on an ass and exposed to the mockery of the crowd; Constantine, however, maintained him in the patriarchal dignity. But we may well conceive that the Emperor felt considerable rancour against his opponents, and continually distrusted them after events which so plainly shewed the hatred borne him by the supporters of images.

Yet Constantine shewed no haste to enter upon his religious reforms. More pressing matters demanded his attention. As with Leo III, the security of the Empire formed his chief preoccupation. Profiting by the dissensions which shook the Arab Empire, he assumed the offensive in Syria (745), reconquered Cyprus (746), and made himself master of Theodosiopolis and Melitene (751). Such was his military reputation that in 757 the Arabs retreated at the bare rumour of his approach. To the end of the reign the infidels were bridled without the necessity for any further personal intervention of Constantine.

The Bulgars presented a more formidable danger to the Empire. In 755 Constantine began a war against them which ended only with his life. In nine successive campaigns he inflicted such disastrous defeats on these barbarians, at Marcellae (759) and at Anchialus (762), that by 764 they were terror-stricken, made no attempt at resistance, and accepted peace for a term of seven years (765). When in 772 the struggle was renewed, its results proved not less favourable; the Emperor, having won the victory of Lithosoria, re-entered Constantinople in triumph. To the last day of his life, Constantine wrestled with the Bulgars, and if he did not succeed in destroying their kingdom, at least he restored the prestige of Byzantine arms in the Balkan Peninsula[1]. Elsewhere he repressed the risings of the Slavs of Thrace and Macedonia (758), and, after the example of Justinian II, he deported part of their tribes into Asia, to the Opsician theme (762).

At home also, Constantine gloriously carried on the work of his father. We have already seen how he continued and completed the administrative and military organisation set on foot by Leo III; he bestowed equal care on restoring the finances of the Empire, and his adversaries accuse him of having been a terrible and merciless exactor, a hateful oppressor of the peasants, rigorously compelling the payment of constantly increasing taxes. In any case, at this cost was secured the excellent condition in which he certainly left the imperial finances (Theophanes speaks of the vast accumulations which his son, on his death, found in the treasury). Also, despite the havoc caused by the great pestilence of 747, the Empire was prosperous. The brilliancy of the Court, the splendour of buildings—for Constantine V, while battling against images, encouraged the production of secular works of art intended to replace them—are a proof of this prosperity. And the Emperor, who from as early as 750 had shared the throne with his son Leo, and who in 768, in order to increase the stability of his house, had associated his four other sons in the imperial power with the titles of Caesar and Nobilissimus, might flatter himself that he had secured the Isaurian dynasty unshakably in the imperial purple, and restored to the Empire security, cohesion, and strength.

Constantine V had no hesitation, in order to complete his work, in re-opening the religious struggle.

The Emperor had received the education of a Byzantine prince; he was therefore a theologian. He had composed sermons which he ordered to be read in churches; an important theological work, which the Patriarch Nicephorus made it his business to refute, had been published under his name, and he had his own doctrine and his personal opinion on the grave problems which had been raised since 726. Not only was he, like Leo III, the enemy of images, but he condemned the *cultus* of the Blessed Virgin and the Saints, he considered prayers addressed to them useless, and punished those who begged for their intercession. All the writers tell us of the want of respect which the Emperor shewed to the Theotokos; all the authorities represent him as charging the upholders of images with idolatry, and the Fathers of the Council of 753 congratulate him

[1] For details of the Arab and Bulgar wars, see *infra*, Chapters v (A), pp. 121–3, and viii, pp. 231–2.

on having saved the world by ridding it of idols. Further, he was deeply sensible of the perils of monasticism. He reproached the monks with inculcating a spirit of detachment and of contempt of the world, with encouraging men to forsake their families and withdraw from the court and from official life to fling themselves into the cloisters. Thus, as with Leo III, political considerations added weight to religious ones in Constantine V's mind. But, more passionate and fanatical than his father, he was to carry on the struggle by different methods, with greater eagerness in propaganda, and with a more unyielding and systematic bitterness in the work of repression.

Yet up to 753 the Emperor confined himself to enforcing Leo III's edicts in no very harsh spirit. At the most, it may be thought that he was preparing the ground for his future action when in 745 or 751 he removed to Thrace a number of Syrians and Armenians hostile to images, and when in 747, after the pestilence, he practically re-peopled Constantinople with men not less devoted to his opinions. But he waited until his power had been consolidated by eleven years of glory and prosperity before resolving on any decisive step. Towards the end of 752 Constantine had made sure of the devotion of the army, and of the sympathy, or at least the acquiescence, of a large proportion of the secular clergy. The people of the capital had become very hostile to the monks. Finally, the patriarchal chair was vacant since the death of Anastasius (752). The Emperor convoked a Council to decide the question of image-worship; on 10 February 753 three hundred and thirty-eight bishops met in the palace of Hieria on the Bosphorus.

The Council intended to deal seriously with the task entrusted to it. Its labours were long and onerous, lasting without interruption from 10 February to the end of August 753. It does not at all appear that the prelates in their deliberations were subjected to any pressure from the imperial authority. They in no wise accepted all the opinions professed by Constantine V; they resolutely maintained the orthodox doctrine concerning the intercession of the Blessed Virgin and the Saints, and anathematised all who should deny to Mary the title of Theotokos. But they solemnly condemned the worship of images "as a thing hateful and abominable," and declared that whoever persisted in adoring them, whether layman or monk, "should be punished by the imperial laws as a rebel against the commandments of God, and an enemy of the dogma of the Fathers." And after having excommunicated the most illustrious champions of the icons, and acclaimed in the persons of the Emperors "the saviours of the world and the luminaries of orthodoxy," and hailed in Constantine V "a thirteenth apostle," they separated.

The decrees of the Council involved one serious consequence. Heretofore the iconodules had only been proceeded against as contravening the imperial ordinances. They were, for the future, to be treated as heretics and rebels against the authority of the Church. By entrusting to the imperial power the task of carrying the canons into effect, the bishops were putting a terrible weapon into Constantine's hands, and one specially fitted to strike at the priests and monks. Any spiritual person refusing to support the dogma promulgated by the Council might, in fact, be condemned with pitiless rigour.

Yet the Emperor, it would seem, was in no haste to make use of the means put at his disposal. During the years that followed the Council, two executions at most are mentioned (in 761). The sovereign appears to have been bent rather on negotiating with his opponents in order to obtain their submission by gentle methods. Also, at this moment the Bulgarian war was absorbing his whole attention. It was not until peace had been signed in 765, and he realised the futility of his controversy with the most famous of the monks, that Constantine decided on crushing resistance by force. The era of martyrs then set in.

"In that year" (September 764—September 765), writes Theophanes, "the Emperor raged madly against all that feared God." The oath to renounce images was imposed upon all subjects, and at the ambo of St Sophia the Patriarch Constantine was forced to be the first to swear to abandon the worship of the forbidden "idols." Thereupon persecution was let loose throughout the Empire. At Constantinople all the still numerous images left in the churches were destroyed; the frescoes were blotted out, the mosaics broken, and the panels, on which figures of the Saints were painted, scraped bare. "All beauty," says a contemporary, "disappeared from the churches." All writings in support of images were ordered to be destroyed. Certain sacred buildings, from which the relics were removed, were even secularised; the church of St Euphemia became an arsenal. And everywhere a scheme of decoration secular in spirit took the place of the banished pictures.

Measures no less harsh were taken against persons. The great officials, and even the bishops, eagerly hunted down everyone guilty of concealing an image or of preserving a relic or amulet. The monks especially were proceeded against with extreme violence. Constantine V seems to have had a peculiar hatred of them; "he called their habit," says one authority, "the raiment of darkness, and those who wore it he called *ἀμνημόνευτοι* (those who are no more to be spoken of)." "He set himself," says another witness, "to destroy the monastic order entirely." The Fathers of the later Council of 787 recall with indignation "the tortures inflicted on pious men," the arrests, imprisonments, blows, exile, tearing out of eyes, branding of faces with red-hot irons, cutting off of noses and tongues. The Emperor forbade his subjects to receive communion from a monk; he strove to compel the religious to lay aside their habit and go back to civil life. The property of convents was confiscated, the monasteries secularised and bestowed as fiefs on the prince's favourites; some of them were converted into barracks. The Emperor, to effect the suppression of the monastic orders, scrupled at no expedient. There were terror-striking executions, such as that of St Stephen the Younger, Abbot of Mount St Auxentius, whom Constantine, after vainly attempting to bring him over to his side, allowed to be done to death by the crowd in the streets of Constantinople (20 November 764). Scandalous and ridiculous exhibitions took place in the Hippodrome, where, amidst the hootings of the crowd, monks were forced to file past, each holding a woman by the hand. In the provinces the governors employed the same measures with equal zeal. Michael Lachanodraco, strategus of the Thracesians, assembled all the monks and nuns of his province in a square at Ephesus, giving them the choice between marriage and death. And the Emperor, writing to congratulate him, says: "I have found a man after my own heart: you have carried out my wishes."

The monks stubbornly resisted the persecution. If, acting on the advice of their leaders, many left Constantinople to seek a refuge in the provinces, the leaders themselves, with courageous insolence, defied the Emperor to his face, and, in spite of the edicts, carried on their propaganda even among those nearest to his person. This was conduct which Constantine V would not tolerate. On 25 August 765, nineteen great dignitaries were paraded in the Circus as guilty of high treason, and in particular, says Theophanes, of having kept up intercourse with St Stephen and glorified his martyrdom. Several of them were executed, others were blinded and exiled. Some days later the Patriarch Constantine was, in his turn, arrested as having shared in the plot, exiled to the Princes Islands, and superseded in the patriarchal chair. In the following year he was brought back to Constantinople, and, after long and ignominious tortures, was finally beheaded (15 August 767). During the five or six years from 765 to 771 persecution raged furiously, so much so, that, as was said by a contemporary, no doubt with some exaggeration, "Byzantium seemed emptied of the monastic order" and "no trace of the accursed breed of monks was to be found there."

Without accepting literally all that chroniclers and hagiographers have related, it is certain that the struggle gave occasion for deeds of indescribable violence and nameless acts of harshness and cruelty; but it is certain also that several of the party of resistance, by the provocations they offered, drew down upon themselves the severity of those in power and let loose the brutal hostility of the populace. It must also be remarked that, if there were some sensational condemnations, the capital executions were, taken altogether, somewhat rare. The harsh treatment and the punishments usual under Byzantine justice undoubtedly struck down numerous victims. The government was even more bent on making the monks ridiculous than on punishing them, and frequently tried to rid itself of them by banishing them or allowing them to flee. Many of them crossed over to Italy, and the Emperor was well pleased to see them go to strengthen Byzantine influence in the West. Many also gave way. "Won over by flattery or promises or dignities," writes the Patriarch Nicephorus, "they forswore their faith, adopted lay dress, allowed their hair to grow, and began to frequent the society of women." "Many," says another authority, "preferred the praise of men to the praise of God, or even allowed themselves to be entangled by the pleasures of the flesh." On the other hand, in the provinces many communities had resigned themselves to accept the decrees of the Council, and although in Constantinople itself many monks still lived in hiding, Constantine V might on the whole flatter himself that he had overcome the opponents upon whom he had declared war.

In Italy this victory had cost the Empire dear. We have seen that from the beginning of the eighth century the people of the peninsula were becoming more and more alienated from Constantinople. At Rome, and in the duchy of which it was the capital, the real sovereign was in fact the Pope rather than the Emperor[1]. Yet since in 740 Gregory III had been succeeded by a Pope of Greek origin, Zacharias, relations between the Empire and its Western provinces had been less strained. Zacharias, at the time of the revolt of Artavasdus, had remained loyal to the cause of the legitimate sovereign, and during the subsequent years he had put his services at the disposal of the Empire, to be used, with some success, in checking the progress of the Lombards (743 and 749). But when in 751 Aistulf obtained possession of Ravenna and the Exarchate, Zacharias' successor, Stephen II, was soon induced to take up a different attitude. He saw the Lombards at the gates of Rome, and, confronted with this imminent danger, he found that the Emperor, to whom he made desperate appeals for help, only replied by charging him with a diplomatic mission to the Lombard king (who proved obdurate) and perhaps also to the King of the Franks, Pepin, whose military intervention in Italy, for the advantage of the Emperor, was hoped for at Constantinople. Did Stephen II, realising that no support was to be expected from the East, consider it wiser and more practical to recur to the policy of Gregory III, and did he take the initiative in petitioning for other help? Or else, though the Emperor's mandatory in France, did he forget the mission entrusted to him, and, perhaps influenced by accounts received from Constantinople (the Council of Hieria was at that very moment condemning images), allow himself to be tempted by Pepin's offers, and, treacherously abandoning the Byzantine cause, play for his own hand? The question is a delicate one, and not easy of solution. A first convention agreed to with Pepin at Ponthion (January 754) was, at the Assembly of Quierzy (Easter 754), followed up by more precise engagements. The Frankish king recognised the right of the Pope to govern in his own name the territories of Rome and Ravenna, whereas, up to then, he had administered Rome in the name of the Emperor,

[1] See Vol. II, pp. 231–232 and 576–580.

and when Pepin had reconquered them from the Lombards, he did in fact solemnly hand them over to Stephen II (754)[1].

It was not till 756 that the real meaning of the Frankish king's intervention was understood at Constantinople, when, on the occasion of his second expedition to Italy, Pepin declared to the ambassadors of Constantine V that he had undertaken the campaign in no wise to serve the imperial interest, but on the invitation of the Pope. The Frankish king's language swept away the last illusions of the Greeks. They understood that Italy was lost to them, and that the breach between Rome and Constantinople was final.

The Emperor had no other thought henceforth than to punish one in whom he could only see a disloyal and treacherous subject, unlawfully usurping dominion over lands which belonged to his master. On the one hand, from 756 to 774 he did his utmost to break off the alliance between Pepin and the Papacy, and to induce the Frankish king to forsake his protégé; but in this he met with no success. On the other hand, he sought by every means to create difficulties for the Roman Pontiffs in the peninsula. His emissaries set themselves to rouse resistance to the Pope, at Ravenna and elsewhere, among all who were still loyal to the imperial authority. In 759 Constantine V joined forces with Desiderius, King of the Lombards, for the re-conquest of Italy and a joint attempt to recover Otranto. And, in fact, in 760 a fleet of three hundred sail left Constantinople to reinforce the Greek squadron from Sicily, and to make preparations for a landing. All these attempts were to prove useless. When in 774 Charlemagne, making a fresh intervention in Italy, annexed the Lombard kingdom, he solemnly at St Peter's confirmed, perhaps even increased, the donation of Pepin[2]. The Byzantines had lost Italy, retaining nothing but Venice and a few places in the south of the peninsula. Again, too, the Synod of the Lateran (769), by anathematizing the opponents of images, had completed the religious separation between Rome and the East. When in 781 Pope Hadrian ceased to date his official acts by the regnal year of the Emperor, the last link disappeared which, on the political side, still seemed to bind Italy to the Empire.

The Greeks of the eighth century appear to have been little concerned, and the Emperor himself seems to have regarded with some indifference, the loss of a province which had been gradually becoming more detached from the Empire. His attention was now bestowed rather on the Eastern regions of the Empire which constituted its strength, and whose safety, unity, and prosperity he made every effort to secure. Perhaps also the intrinsic importance which he had come to attach to his religious policy made him too forgetful of perils coming

[1] See, for details of these events, Vol. II, pp. 582–589.

[2] See Vol. II, pp. 590–592 and 597–600.

from without. When on 14 September 775 the old Emperor died, he left the Empire profoundly disturbed by internal disputes; under Constantine V's successors the disadvantages of this state of discontent and agitation, and of his over-concentration on religious questions, were soon to become evident.

III.

Constantine V before his death had drawn from his son and successor a promise to carry on his policy. Leo IV, surnamed the Chazar, during his short reign (775–780) exerted himself to this end. Abroad he resumed, not ingloriously, the struggle with the Arabs; in 778 an army of 100,000 men invaded Northern Syria, besieged Germanicea, and won a brilliant victory over the Musulmans. The Emperor gave no less attention to the affairs of Italy; he welcomed to Constantinople Adelchis, son of Desiderius, the Lombard king dethroned by Charlemagne, and in concert with him and with the Duke of Benevento, Arichis, he meditated an intervention in the peninsula. At home, however, in spite of his attachment to the iconoclast doctrines, he judged it prudent at first to shew himself less hostile to images and to the monks. He dreaded, not without reason, the intrigues of the Caesars, his brothers, one of whom he was in the end forced to banish to Cherson; he was anxious, feeling himself in bad health, to give stability to the throne of his young son Constantine, whom at the Easter festival of 776 he had solemnly admitted to a share in the imperial dignity; and, finally, he was much under the influence of his wife Irene, an Athenian by origin, who was secretly devoted to the party of the monks. Leo IV, however, ended by becoming tired of his policy of tolerance. Towards the end of his reign (April 780) persecution set in afresh: executions took place even in the circle round the Emperor; certain churches, besides, were despoiled of their treasures, and this relapse of the sovereign into "his hidden malignity," as Theophanes expresses it, might have led to consequences of some gravity, but for the death of the Emperor on 8 September 780, leaving the throne to a child of ten, his son Constantine, and the regency to his widow the Empress Irene.

Irene was born in a province zealously attached to the worship of images, and she was devout. There was thus no question where her sympathies lay. She had indeed towards the end of the preceding reign somewhat compromised herself by her iconodule opinions; once at the head of affairs her first thought would be to put an end to a struggle which had lasted for more than half a century and of which many within the Empire were weary. But Irene was ambitious also, and keenly desirous of ruling; her whole life long she was led by one dominating idea, a lust for power amounting to an obsession. In pursuit of this end she allowed no obstacle to stay her and no scruple to turn her aside. Proud and passionate, she easily persuaded herself that she was the instrument to work out the Divine purposes, and, consequently, from the day that she assumed the regency in her son's name, she worked with skill and with tenacious resolution at the great task whence she expected the realisation of her vision.

In carrying out the projects suggested by her devotion and in fulfilling the dreams of her ambition, Irene, however, found herself faced by many difficulties. The Arabs renewed their incursions in 781; next year Michael Lachanodraco was defeated at Dazimon, and the Musulmans pushed on to Chrysopolis, opposite the capital. An insurrection broke out in Sicily (781), and in Macedonia and Greece the Slavs rose. But above all, many rival ambitions were growing round the young Empress, and much opposition was shewing itself. The Caesars, her brothers-in-law, were secretly hostile to her, and the memory of their father Constantine V drew many partisans to their side. The great offices of the government were all held by zealous iconoclasts. The army was still devoted to the policy of the late reign. Finally the Church, which was controlled by the Patriarch Paul, was full of the opponents of images, and the canons of the Council of Hieria formed part of the law of the land.

Irene contrived very skilfully to prepare her way. Some of her adversaries she overthrew, and others she thrust on one side. A plot formed to raise her brothers-in-law to the throne was used by her to compel them to enter the priesthood (Christmas 780). She dismissed the old servants of Constantine V from favour, and entrusted the government to men at her devotion, especially to eunuchs of her household. One of them even became her chief minister: Stauracius, raised by Irene's good graces to the dignity of Patrician and the functions of Logothete of the Dromos, became the undisputed master of the Palace; for twenty years he was to follow the fortunes of his benefactress with unshaken loyalty.

Meanwhile, in order to have her hands free, Irene made peace with the Arabs (783); in the West she was drawing nearer to the Papacy, and made request to Charlemagne for the hand of his daughter Rotrude for the young Constantine VI. Sicily was pacified. Stauracius subdued the Slav revolt. The Empress could give herself up completely to her religious policy.

From the very outset of her regency she had introduced a system of toleration such as had been long unknown. Monks re-appeared in the capital, resuming their preaching and their religious propaganda; amends were made for the sacrilegious acts of the preceding years; and the devout party, filled with hope, thanked God for the unlooked-for miracle, and hailed the approaching day when "by the hand of a widowed woman and an orphan child, impiety should be overthrown, and the Church set free from her long enslavement."

A subtle intrigue before long placed the Patriarchate itself at the Empress' disposal. In 784 the Patriarch Paul abruptly resigned his office. In his place Irene procured the appointment of a man of her own, a layman, the imperial secretary Tarasius. The latter, on accepting, declared that it was time to put an end to the strife which disturbed the Church, and to the schism which separated her from Rome; and while repudiating the decisions of the synod of 753 as tainted with illegality, he skilfully put forward the project of an Ecumenical Council which should restore peace and unity to the Christian world. The Empress wrote to this effect to Pope Hadrian, who entered into her views, and with the support of these two valuable allies she summoned the prelates of Christendom to Constantinople for the spring of 786.

But Irene had been too precipitate. She had not reckoned with the hostility of the army and even of some of the Eastern bishops. On the opening of the Council (17 August 786) in the church of the Holy Apostles, the soldiers of the guard disturbed the gathering by a noisy demonstration and dispersed the orthodox. Irene herself, who was present at the ceremony, escaped with some difficulty from the infuriated zealots. The whole of her work had to be begun over again. Some of the provincial troops were dexterously won over; then a pretext was found for removing from the capital and disbanding such regiments of the guard as were ill-disposed. Finally, the Council was convoked at Nicaea in Bithynia; it was opened in the presence of the papal legates on 24 September 787. This was the seventh Ecumenical Council.

Three hundred and fifty bishops were present, surrounded by a fervent crowd of monks and igumens. The assembly found a month sufficient for the decision of all the questions before it. The worship of images was restored, with the single restriction that adoration (*λατρεία*) should not be claimed for them, but only veneration (*προσκύνησις*); the doctrine concerning images was established on dogmatic foundations; finally, under the influence of Plato, Abbot of Sakkudion, ecclesiastical discipline and Christian ethics were restored in all their strictness, and a strong breeze of asceticism pervaded the whole Byzantine world. The victorious monks had even higher aims in view; from this time Plato and his nephew, the famous Theodore of Studion, dreamed of claiming for the Church absolute independence of the State, and denied to the Emperor the right to intermeddle with anything involving dogma or religion. This was before long to produce fresh conflicts graver and of higher importance than that which had arisen out of the question of images.

In November 787 the Fathers of the Church betook themselves to Constantinople, and in a solemn sitting held in the Magnaura palace the Empress signed with her own hand the canons restoring the beliefs which she loved. And the devout party, proud of such a sovereign, hailed her magniloquently as the "Christ-supporting Empress whose government, like her name, is a symbol of peace" (*χριστοφόρος Εἰρήνη, ἡ φερωνύμως βασιλεύουσα*).

Irene's ambition was very soon to disturb the peace which was still insecure. Constantine VI was growing up; he was in his eighteenth year. Between a son who wished to govern and a mother with a passion for supreme power a struggle was inevitable. To safeguard her work, not less than to retain her authority, Irene was to shrink from nothing, not even from crime.

Formerly, at the outset of the reign, she had, as a matter of policy, negotiated a marriage for her son with Charlemagne's daughter. She now from policy broke it off, no doubt considering the Frankish alliance less necessary to her after the Council of Nicaea, but, above all, dreading lest the mighty King Charles should prove a support to his son-in-law against her. She forced another marriage upon Constantine (788) with a young Paphlagonian, named Maria, from whom she knew she had nothing to fear. Besides this, acting in concert with her minister Stauracius, the Empress kept her son altogether in the background. But Constantine VI in the end grew tired of this state of pupilage and conspired against the all-powerful eunuch (January 790). Things fell out ill with him. The conspirators were arrested, tortured, and banished; the young Emperor himself was flogged like an unruly boy and put under arrest in his apartments. And Irene, counting herself sure of victory, and intoxicated, besides, with the flatteries of her dependents, required of the army an oath that, so long as she lived, her son should never be recognised as Emperor, while in official proclamations she caused her name to be placed before that of Constantine.

She was running great risks. The army, still devoted to the memory of Constantine V, was further in very ill humour at the checks which it had met with through Irene's foreign policy. The Arab war, renewed by the Caliph Hārūn ar-Rashīd (September 786), had been disastrous both by land and sea. In Europe the imperial troops had been beaten by the Bulgars (788). In Italy the breach with the Franks had led to a disaster. A strong force, sent to the peninsula to restore the Lombard prince, Adelchis, had been completely defeated, and its commander slain (788). The troops attributed these failures to the weakness of a woman's government. The regiments in Asia, therefore, mutinied (790), demanding the recognition of Constantine VI, and from the troops in Armenia the insurrection spread to the other themes. Irene took the alarm and abdicated (December 790). Stauracius and her other favourites fell with her, and Constantine VI, summoning round him the faithful counsellors of his grandfather and his father, took power into his own hands.

The young Emperor seems to have had some really valuable qualities. He was of an energetic temper and martial instincts; he boldly resumed the offensive against the Arabs (791–795) and against the Bulgars (791). Though the latter in 792 inflicted a serious defeat on him, he succeeded in 796 during a fresh campaign in restoring the reputation of his troops. All this recommended him to the soldiers and the people. Unfortunately his character was unstable: he was devoid of lasting suspicion or resentment. Barely a year after the fall of Irene, yielding to her pressing requests, he restored to her the title of Empress and associated her in the supreme power. At the same time he took back Stauracius as his chief minister. Irene came back thirsting for vengeance and more eager than ever in pursuit of her ambitious designs. She spent five patient years working up her triumph, and with diabolical art bred successive quarrels between her son and all who were attached to him, lowering him in the eyes of the army, undermining him in the favour of the people, and finally ruining him with the Church.

At the very beginning she used her newly regained influence to rouse Constantine's suspicions against Alexius Muselé, the general who had engineered the *pronunciamento* of 790, succeeding so well that the Emperor disgraced him and had him blinded. On learning this usage of their leader the legions in Armenia mutinied, and the Emperor was obliged to go in person to crush the revolt (793). This he did with great harshness, thus alienating the hearts of the soldiers who were his best support. At the same time, just as on the morrow of the Bulgar defeat (792), the Caesars, his uncles, again bestirred themselves. Irene persuaded her son to put out the eyes of the eldest and to cut out the tongues of the four others, an act of cruelty which availed little, and made the prince extremely unpopular with the iconoclasts. Then, to excite public opinion against him, she devised a last expedient.

Constantine VI had become enamoured of one of the Empress-mother's maids of honour, named Theodote, and Irene had lent herself complaisantly to this passion. She even counselled her son to put away his wife in order to marry the girl—as she was well aware of the scandal which would follow. The Emperor lent a ready ear to this advice. In spite of the opposition of the Patriarch Tarasius, who courageously refused a demand to facilitate the divorce, he dismissed Maria to a convent and married Theodote (September 795). There was a general outburst of indignation throughout the religious party at this adulterous connexion. The monks, especially those of the Sakkudion with Plato and Theodore at their head, abounded in invective against the bigamous Emperor, the "new Herod," and condemned the weakness of the Patriarch in tolerating this abomination. Irene surreptitiously encouraged their resistance. In vain did Constantine VI flatter himself that, by courtesy and calmness, he could allay the excitement of his opponents, even going so far as to pay a visit in person to the monks of the Sakkudion (796) and coolly replying to their insults "that he did not intend to make martyrs." At last, however, in the face of their uncompromising mood, he lost patience. He caused the monks of the Sakkudion to be arrested, beaten, imprisoned, and exiled. These severities only exasperated public opinion, which Irene turned to her own advantage. While the court was at the baths of Prusa, she worked up the plot which was to restore her to power. It burst forth

17 July 797. The Emperor was arrested and imprisoned at the Palace, in the Porphyry Chamber where he had been born, and by his mother's orders his eyes were put out. He was allowed, with his wife Theodote, to end his days in peaceful obscurity. Irene was Empress.

The devout party were determined to see in this odious crime of a mother against her son nothing but the just punishment of an adulterous and persecuting Emperor, and traced the hand of Providence in an event which brought back to power the most pious Irene, the restorer of orthodoxy. She, quite unmoved, boldly seized upon the government, and, as though intoxicated with her omnipotence and with the delight of having realised her dreams, did not hesitate—such a thing had never been seen and never was to be seen again in Constantinople—to assume, woman as she was, the title of Emperor. Skilfully, too, she secured her authority and maintained her popularity. She banished to Athens the Caesars, her brothers-in-law, who were again conspiring (797), and a little later she had the four younger blinded (799). To her friends the monks she gave tokens of favour, building new monasteries and richly endowing the famous convents of the Sakkudion in Bithynia and the Studion in Constantinople. In order to win over the people, she granted large remissions of taxation, lowering the customs duties and the taxes on provisions. The delighted capital greeted its benefactress with acclamations.

Meanwhile, secret intrigues were being woven around the Empress, now aged and in bad health. Irene's favourites, Stauracius and Aëtius, had dreams of securing the throne for one of their relatives, there being now no legitimate heir. And for more than a year there raged round the irritated and suspicious Irene a heated and merciless struggle. Stauracius was the first to die, in the middle of 800. While the Byzantine court wore itself out in these barren disputes, the Arabs, under the rule of Hārūn ar-Rashīd, again took the offensive and forced the Empire to pay them tribute (798). In the West, peace was signed with the Franks, Benevento and Istria being ceded to them (798). Soon an event of graver importance took place. On 25 December 800, in St Peter's at Rome, Charlemagne restored the Empire of the West, a deep humiliation for the Byzantine monarchy which claimed to be the legitimate heir of the Roman Caesars.

It is said that a sensational project was conceived in the brains both of Charlemagne and Irene—that of a marriage which should join their two monarchies under one sceptre, and restore, more fully than in the time of Augustus, Constantine, or Justinian, the ancient unity of the *orbis Romanus*. In spite of the distinct testimony of Theophanes, the story lacks verisimilitude. Intrigues were, indeed, going on round the old Empress more eagerly than ever. Delivered from his rival Stauracius, Aëtius was pushing his advantage hotly. Other great lords were opposing him, and the Logothete-General, Nicephorus, was utilising the common dissatisfaction for his own ends. The iconoclasts also were secretly planning their revenge. On 31 October 802 the revolution broke out. The palace was carried without difficulty, and Nicephorus proclaimed Emperor. Irene, who was absent at the Eleutherian Palace, was arrested there and brought back to the capital; she did nothing in her own defence. The people, who were attached to her, openly shewed themselves hostile to the conspirators, and the coronation, at which the Patriarch Tarasius had no scruple in officiating, was somewhat stormy. Irene, "like a wise woman, beloved of God," as a contemporary says, submitted to accomplished facts. She was exiled, first to the Princes Islands, and then, as she still seemed too near, to Lesbos. She died there soon afterwards (August 803).

Her contemporaries forgave everything, even her crimes, to the pious and orthodox sovereign, the restorer of image-worship. Theophanes, as well as Theodore of Studion, overwhelm with praise and flattery the blessed Irene, the new Helena, whose actions "shine like the stars." In truth, this famous sovereign was essentially a woman-politician, ambitious and devout, carried away by her passion for empire even into crime, one who did more injury than service to the interests of the monarchy. By her too exclusive absorption in the work of restoring images, she weakened the Empire without and left it shrunken territorially and shaken morally. By the exaggerated deference which she shewed to the Church, by the position which, thanks to her, that Church, with strength renewed by the struggle, assumed in the Byzantine community, by the power which the devout and monastic party under such leaders as Theodore of Studion acquired as against the State, the imperial authority found itself seriously prejudiced. The deep divisions left by the controversy over images produced a dangerous state of discontent and unrest; the defeated iconoclasts waited impatiently, looking for their revenge. Finally, by her intrigues and her crime, Irene had made a perilous return to the period of palace revolutions, which her glorious predecessors, the Isaurian Emperors, had brought to a close for nearly a century.

And yet at the dawn of the ninth century the Byzantine Empire still held a great place in the world. In the course of the eighth century, through the loss of Italy and the restoration of the Empire of the West, and also through the preponderance in the Byzantine Empire of its Asiatic provinces, that Empire became an essentially Oriental monarchy. And this development in a direction in which it had for a long time been tending, finally determined its destiny and the part it was to play. One of the greatest services rendered by the Isaurian Emperors had been to put a period to the advance of Islām; the Empire was to be thenceforward the champion of Europe against the infidel. In the same way, as against barbarism, it was to remain throughout the East of Europe the disseminator of the Christian Faith and the guardian of civilisation.

Despite the bitterness of the quarrel over images, the Byzantine State came forth from the ordeal with youth renewed, full of fervour and vigour. The Church, not only stronger but also purer for the conflict, had felt the need of a moral reformation which should give her fresh life. Between 797 and 806, in the Studion monastery, the Abbot Theodore had drawn up for his monks that famous rule which, with admirable feeling for practical administration, combines manual work, prayer, and regard for intellectual development. In lay society, taught and led by the preaching of the monks, we find a like stress laid on piety, chastity, and renunciation. No doubt among these devoted and enthusiastic spirits a strange hardness may sometimes be noticed, and the heat of the struggle occasionally generated in them a singular perversion of the moral sense and a forgetfulness of the most elementary ideas of justice, to say nothing of a tendency to superstition. But these pious souls and these holy women, of whom the eighth century offers so many examples, lent an unparalleled lustre to the Byzantine Church; and since for some years it was they who were the leaders of opinion, that Church drew from them and kept throughout the following century a force and a greatness never equalled.

The opponents of images, on their side, have contributed no less to this splendour of Byzantine civilisation. Though making war upon icons, the Isaurian Emperors were anything but Puritans. In place of the religious pictures which they destroyed they caused secular and even still-life subjects to be portrayed in churches and palaces alike—scenes of the kind formerly affected by Alexandrine art, horse-races, hippodrome games, landscapes with trees and birds, and also historical scenes depicting the great military events of the time. In the style of this Iconoclastic art, especially in its taste for the decorative, there is a genuine return to antique traditions of the picturesque, mingled with influences derived from the Arab East. This was by no means all to be lost. The renascence of the tenth century owed more than is generally thought to these new tendencies of the Iconoclastic period.

The same character is traceable in the thoroughly secular and oriental splendour with which the Byzantine court surrounded itself, in the lustre of its fêtes, which were still almost pagan, such as the Brumalia, in which traditions of antiquity were revived, in the taste for luxury shewn by private individuals and even by churchmen. With this taste for elegance and art there was a corresponding and very powerful intellectual advance. It will suffice to recall the names of George Syncellus and Theophanes, of John Damascene and Theodore of Studion, of the Patriarchs Tarasius and Nicephorus, to notice the wide development given to education, and the breadth of mind and tolerance to be met with among certain men of the day, in order to realise that here also the Iconoclastic period had been far from barren. Certainly the Empire in the ninth century had still many years to go through of disaster and anarchy. Yet from the government of the Isaurian Emperors a new principle of life had sprung, which was to enrich the world for ever.

CHAPTER II.

FROM NICEPHORUS I TO THE FALL OF THE PHRYGIAN DYNASTY.

I.

THE religious policy of the Empress Irene, the concentrated and impassioned devotion which she brought to the task of restoring the cult of images, had produced, in the external affairs of the Empire no less than in its internal condition, results which were largely injurious. Her financial policy, and the considerable remissions of taxation which she had agreed to in the hope of assuring her popularity and of recommending herself to the Church, had had no better success. An onerous task was thus laid upon her successor. He had to remedy the penury of the exchequer, to restore order to a thoroughly disturbed State, by prudent administration to extinguish the memories of a bitter and lengthy quarrel, and thus to quiet its last convulsive heavings.

Such was the end aimed at, it would seem, from the opening of his reign by the new Emperor Nicephorus I (802–811). From his opponents he has met with hardly better treatment than the great iconoclast sovereigns of the eighth century. Theophanes declares "that on all occasions he acted not after God but to be seen of men," and that in all his actions "he shamelessly violated the law," and he severely blames his "unmeasured love of money," comparing him to "a new Ahaz, more covetous than Phalaris and Midas." In reality, Nicephorus seems to have been a talented ruler, anxious to fulfil his duties as Emperor, a man of moderate temper and comparatively tolerant. He renounced the violent courses adopted by the Iconoclast Emperors, but he was determined to maintain the great work of reform which they had carried out. A good financier—before his accession he had filled the high office of Logothete-General—he desired to restore to the treasury the supplies of which it stood in need, and in the very first year of his reign he reimposed the greater part of the taxes imprudently abolished by Irene, until in 810 he had thought out a comprehensive scheme of financial reorganisation, of which the most essential feature was the abrogation of the numerous fiscal exemptions enjoyed by Church property. A man very jealous of his authority—he bitterly reproaches his predecessors with having had no idea of the true methods of government—he would never tolerate the idea of any person being more powerful than himself, and claimed to impose his will upon the Church as well as the State. His adversaries the monks forgave nothing of all this, and have depicted him as a tyrant, oppressive, cruel, hypocritical, and debauched, while it is also plain that, owing to the harshness of his financial measures, he was highly unpopular. "Everybody," as one of his courtiers said to him, "exclaims against us, and if any misfortune happens to us, there will be general rejoicing at our fall." Yet it would appear that Nicephorus, in difficult times, possessed some of the qualities which go to make a good Emperor.

But passions were still so much heated that everything offered matter for strife. The monks were outraged at the idea of ecclesiastical property being liable to taxation and Church tenants subject to a poll-tax. They vehemently denied the right of the Emperor to interfere in religious matters. They even resisted the authority of the Patriarch Nicephorus, who in 806 had succeeded Tarasius. Yet Nicephorus brought to his high office a fervent zeal for the reform of the monasteries and the destruction of heresy, and thus would have seemed likely to be acceptable to the monks of the Studion and their fiery Abbot Theodore. But, before attaining to the patriarchate, Nicephorus had been a layman, and it was necessary to confer all the grades of holy orders on him at the same time. Consequently the Studite monks violently protested against his election. But above all the new Patriarch was, like the Emperor, a statesman of opportunist tendencies desirous of pacifying men's minds and of obliterating the traces of recent struggles. At the request of the Basileus, he summoned a Synod to restore to his sacerdotal functions the priest Joseph, who had formerly been excommunicated for having solemnised the marriage of the Emperor Constantine VI and Theodote. The assembly, despite the protests of Theodore of Studion, complied with the Patriarch's wish, and even restored Joseph to the dignity of Grand Oeconomus (807). This was the origin of the long quarrel called the "Moechian controversy" (from μοιχός, adulterer, whence the name *Moechiani* given to the supporters of Joseph's rehabilitation).

The monks of the Studion resolutely withdrew from communion with the Patriarch. "We shall endure everything," Theodore declared, "death itself, rather than resume communion with the Oeconomus and his accomplices. As to the Patriarch, he makes us no answer, he refuses to hear us, he is, in everything, at the Emperor's orders. For my part, I will not betray the truth despite the threat of exile, despite the gleaming sword, despite the kindled faggots." And indeed the Emperor quickly became impatient of an opposition which disturbed the peace of the Church afresh, and which irritated him the more keenly in that it claimed to subject the conduct and marriage of an Emperor to canonical rules. Another Synod, held in 809, reiterated therefore the lawfulness of Constantine VI's espousals, declared that the Emperors were above the law of the Church, and pronounced sentence of excommunication upon all gainsayers. The old Abbot Plato, Theodore of Studion, and his brother

Joseph, Archbishop of Thessalonica, were banished to the Princes Islands; the seven hundred monks of the Studion, who vehemently refused to go over to the side of the temporal power, were scattered, imprisoned, maltreated, driven into exile. For two whole years persecution raged. The fact was, as Theodore of Studion truly wrote, "it was no longer a mere question of ecclesiastical discipline that was at stake. A breach has been made in faith and morals and in the Gospel itself." And in opposition to the Emperor's claim to set himself above the laws of the Church and to make his will prevail, Theodore boldly appealed to Rome, and to secure the liberty of the Eastern Church he invoked the judgment of the Pope, "the first of pastors," as he wrote, "and our apostolic head."

Thus, despite the good intentions of the Emperor and his Patriarch, passions flared up afresh; and such was the fanaticism of the devout party that they ignored the grave dangers threatening the Empire, and even looked upon the death of the Emperor, who fell fighting against the Bulgars on the disastrous day of 25 July 811, as a just punishment from God upon their cruel foe.

Michael I Rangabé (811–813) succeeded his father-in-law Nicephorus, after the short reign of Stauracius, the son of the late Emperor. He was a prince after the Church's heart, "pious and most orthodox," writes Theophanes; his chief anxiety was to repair all the injustices of the preceding reign, "on account of which," adds Theophanes, "Nicephorus had miserably perished." He recalled the Studites from exile, caused the Oeconomus Joseph to be condemned anew, and at this cost succeeded in reconciling the monks with the Patriarch. He shewed himself a supporter of images, anxious to come to an understanding with Rome, and firmly opposed to the iconoclasts. Such a policy, at a time when the Bulgarian war was raging and the terrible Khan Krum threatening Constantinople, was grossly imprudent. The iconoclasts, indeed, were still strong in the capital, where Constantine V had settled numerous colonists from the East, and where the Paulicians, in particular, occupied an important place; besides which almost the whole army had remained faithful to the memory of the illustrious Emperors who had formerly led it to victory. Thus Constantinople was in a state of tense excitement; plots were brewing against Michael; noisy demonstrations took place at the tomb of Constantine V. When in June 813 Michael I was defeated by the Bulgars at Versinicia, near Hadrianople, the iconoclasts considered the opportunity favourable for dethroning the Emperor. The army proclaimed one of its generals, Leo the Armenian, Strategus of the Anatolics, begging him "to watch over the safety of the State, and to defend the Christian Empire." On 11 July the usurper entered Constantinople. His accession was to be the signal for a supreme effort to impose iconoclast ideas upon the Empire.

The new Emperor, who was of Eastern origin, was, although secretly, an iconoclast at heart. But so great was the peril from outside—the Bulgars were besieging Constantinople—that he was at first obliged to cloak his tendencies, and to sign a confession of faith by which he pledged himself to defend the orthodox religion and the veneration of the sacred icons. But when he had inflicted a severe defeat on the barbarians at Mesembria (813), and when the death (14 April 814) of the terrible Khan Krum had led to the conclusion of a truce for thirty years with his successor Omurtag, Leo no longer hesitated to make his real feelings known. Drawing his inspiration from the same ideas as those on which the resolutions of Leo III had been based, he declared that if the Christians were always beaten by the pagans, "it is because they prostrate themselves before images. The Emperors who adored them," he proceeded, "have died in exile or in battle. Only those who destroyed them have died on the throne and been buried in the Church of the Holy Apostles. It is their example that I shall follow." He therefore ordered the learned John Hylilas, surnamed the Grammarian, to collect the authorities favouring the condemnation of images, and in particular to draw from the archives of the churches the acts of the Council of 753. On the other hand, he attempted to win over the Patriarch Nicephorus to his views, and, with the hope of shaking the resistance of the party opposed to him, he summoned a conference at the imperial palace, where under his presidency orthodox and iconoclasts might hold a debate. The speech with which he opened the assembly was answered by courageous remonstrances from Theodore of Studion. "Church matters," he boldly declared, "are the province of priests and doctors; the administration of secular things belongs to the Emperor. This is what the Apostle said: 'God has instituted in His Church in the first place the apostles, then prophets, then evangelists,' but nowhere does he make mention of Emperors. It is to the former that it appertains to decide matters of dogma and faith. As for you, your duty is to obey them and not to usurp their place." Leo, exasperated, suddenly brought the assembly to a close, and next day a decree appeared forbidding thenceforward the discussion of religious questions. The resistance of the opposition party only gathered strength. "For my part," declared Theodore of Studion, "I had rather have my tongue cut out, than fail to bear testimony to our Faith and defend it with all my might by my power of speech. What! are you to have full liberty to maintain error, and are we to keep silence concerning the truth! That we will never do. We will not give our tongue into captivity, no, not for an hour, and we will not deprive the faithful of the support of our words." Did the Emperor dread the influence of the Studites? At all events, he pretended to yield, and at the Christmas festival 814 he solemnly did reverence to the icons at St Sophia. But before long he took his resolve.

In the month of March 815 the Patriarch Nicephorus was banished, and in his place was set up an official of the palace, Theodotus Cassiteras, wholly devoted to the Emperor's policy. It was in vain that the monks of the Studion arranged solemn demonstrations in honour of the holy images, and that on Palm Sunday 815 more than a thousand religious walked in procession round the monastery, each bearing an icon in his hands and singing the canticle, "We venerate your sacred images, O blessed Saints." The Emperor retorted by convoking a Council at St Sophia (815), which confirmed the canons of the Synod of 753, proscribed images after its example, declaring that they were mere "idols," and recommended "worship in spirit and in truth." Nor did the assembly resist the temptation to cast parenthetic reproach on the memory of Irene, recalling the happy state of the Church "up to the day when the imperial sceptre had fallen from the hands of men into those of a woman, and when, through the folly of that woman, the Church of God was ruined." It was the controversy over images breaking out afresh. But while the earlier iconoclast movement had lasted more than half a century, the second was to endure barely twenty-five years (815–842). This time the enemies of icons were to find confronting them, particularly in the monks of the Studion, a resistance better organised, more vigorous, and more dangerous also. In its defence of images the Byzantine Church now really aspired to something beyond. She openly aimed at casting off the authority of the State and winning her freedom, and in order to secure her independence she did not hesitate to appeal to the Pope against the Emperor and, despite her former repugnance, to recognise the primacy of the Roman Church. This is the characteristic feature distinguishing the second phase of the great controversy. Between Church and State, then, there was waged at Constantinople much the same conflict which, in the West, took later on the form of the struggle over Investitures.

However, Leo V at first tried moderate methods. But the Studites were immovable, and the opportunists, fearful of seeing the struggle reopened, lent their support to the uncompromising monks. Theodore of Studion was banished (815) and his monks scattered, while against images as well as their defenders persecution was let loose. "The altars have been overthrown," writes Theodore of Studion, "and the temples of the Lord laid waste; a lamentable sight it is to see the churches of God despoiled of their glory and disfigured. Among my brethren, some have had trial of cruel mockings and scourgings, others of chains and prison on a little bread and water, some have been condemned to exile, others reduced to live in the deserts and mountains and in dens and caves of the earth, others after receiving many stripes have gone hence to the Lord as martyrs. Some there are who have been fastened in sacks and thrown by night into the sea." Again, he says, "The holy vessels are melted down, the sacred vestments cast to the flames, with the pictures and the books which contain anything concerning images. Inquisition is made, and questions put from house to house, with threats and terrorism, so that no single picture may escape the heretics. He who most signalises himself by his rage against Christ is judged worthy of the most honour. But for those who resist—scourges, chains, prison, the tortures of famine, exile, death. They have only one thought—to compel everyone to yield. The persecution we endure is beyond any persecution by the barbarians."

From his distant exile, Theodore, without truce or intermission, valiantly encouraged the resistance. "Are we to yield," he wrote, "are we to keep silence, and out of fear give obedience to men and not to God? No, never. Until a door is opened unto us by the Lord, we shall not cease to fulfil our duty as much as in us lies." He renewed and repeated, therefore, the letters and exhortations which he addressed to Pope Paschal, appealing for justice and help: "Listen to us, O Apostolic Head, charged by God with the guidance of Christ's sheep, porter of the heavenly kingdom, rock of the Faith on which is built the Catholic Church, for you are Peter, you are the successor of Peter, whose throne you honourably fill." The Pope, with no great success, attempted to intervene, and the struggle went on, becoming ever more embittered. In the face of the Emperor's severities many ended by giving way. "Nearly all spirits quail," writes Theodore of Studion himself, "and give attestations of heresy to the impious. Among the bishops, those of Smyrna and Cherson have fallen; among abbots, those of Chrysopolis, of Dios, and of Chora, with nearly all those of the capital." Leo the Armenian seemed to have won the day.

But his fall was at hand. Even in his own circle plots were hatching against him, and one of his old companions in arms, Michael the Stammerer, Count of the Excubitors, was at the head of the conspirators. Leo V had him arrested, and to save him his friends hazarded a bold stroke. On 25 December 820, while the Emperor was attending the morning office of the Nativity, mingling, as was his custom, his voice with those of the choristers, the plotters, who had contrived to slip in among the congregation, struck him down at the foot of the altar. Michael, instantly set at liberty, was proclaimed, and, while his feet were still loaded with fetters, was seated on the imperial throne. With him began the Phrygian dynasty (Michael was a native of Amorium), which for three generations, from 820 to 867, was to rule the Empire.

The new sovereign (820—829) was, it would appear, somewhat indifferent in religious matters. "I have not come," he said to the former Patriarch Nicephorus, "to introduce innovations in matters of faith and dogma, nor to question or overthrow what is fixed by tradition and has gained acceptance. Let every man, then, do as seems him good and right; he shall have no vexation to undergo, and no penalty to fear." He began, therefore, by recalling the exiles; he set at liberty the victims of the preceding reign, and flattered himself that by assembling a conference, in which the orthodox and the iconoclasts should deliberate together over the question of images, he could bring them to an agreement and restore peace. Theodore of Studion, who had returned to Constantinople, flatly refused to enter into any relations with the heretics, and, faithful to the doctrine which he had always maintained, he declared to the prince: "There is no question here of human and temporal things in which kings have power to judge; but of divine and heavenly dogmas, which have been entrusted to those only to whom God has said: 'Whatsoever thou shalt bind on earth shall be bound also in heaven, and whatsoever thou shalt loose on earth shall be loosed also in heaven.' Who are they who have received this power? The Apostles and their successors. As to emperors and sovereigns, their part is to lend their support and approbation to what has been decreed. No power has been granted them by God over the divine dogmas, and if they exercise such, it will not be lasting."

The Emperor was ill-inclined to accept these admonitions. He signified his pleasure by setting on the patriarchal throne, at the death of Theodotus Cassiteras (821), not the former Patriarch Nicephorus, whose restoration the Studites demanded, but an avowed enemy of images, Anthony, Bishop of Syllaeum. Much displeased also at the negotiations which his opponents were carrying on with Rome, he gave a very ill reception to the monk Methodius who brought him letters from Paschal I; he caused him to be scourged, and imprisoned him for more than eight years in a little island in the Gulf of Nicomedia. It is true that, when in 822 the formidable insurrection of Thomas broke out in Asia Minor, Michael thought it prudent to recall to Constantinople the monks, whom he had again banished from it; "it was by no means," says the biographer of Theodore of Studion, "from any tenderness towards them, but in dread lest some should espouse the cause of Thomas, who passed for a supporter of image-worship." But on the ending of the civil war by the defeat of the rebel (823), Michael thought himself in a position to act more vigorously. Convinced that it was above all the support of Rome which encouraged the uncompromising temper of his adversaries, he began a correspondence with the Emperor of the West, Louis the Pious, and, in a curious letter of 824, denounced to him the abuses of image worship, and requested his intervention at Rome, in order to induce the Papacy to put an end to them. Under these conditions it became difficult for the defenders of icons to remain at Constantinople. Theodore of Studion withdrew to a convent in Bithynia and died there in 826. The iconoclast policy was triumphant; but, faithful to the promises of toleration made on the morrow of his accession, Michael refrained from all violence against his opponents; while personally constant to his resolve to render no worship to images, he left those who thought otherwise freedom to cling to what seemed to them the orthodox faith.

Theophilus, his son and successor (829–842), shewed more zeal in combating icons. Sincerely pious, and delighting, like the true Byzantine prince he was, in theological discussions, of a systematic turn of mind, and obstinate to boot, it was not long before he came to consider Michael II's politic tolerance inadequate, and, under the influence of his former tutor, John Hylilas, whom he raised to the patriarchal throne in 832, he resolved to battle vigorously with the iconodule party. Severe measures were ordered to prevent its propaganda and to strike at its leaders; to banish, especially from Constantinople, the proscribed pictures, and to punish any painter who dared to produce them. Once again terror reigned: convents were closed, the prisons were filled with victims, and some of the punishments inflicted were of extraordinary cruelty. The two Palestinian monks, Theodore and Theophanes, who stand out, after the death of Theodore of Studion, as the foremost champions of the icons, were first banished, then recalled to Constantinople, where the Emperor caused to be branded on their foreheads with red-hot irons certain insulting verses which he had composed for the purpose. Hence the name of *Graptoi*, bestowed on them in hagiographical writings. Lazarus, the painter of icons, was also imprisoned and barbarously tortured; Theophilus ordered, it is said, that his hands should be burned with red-hot irons. Other supporters of pictures were exiled. But the work of the iconoclast Emperor was ephemeral. Even in the palace, the sympathies of the prince's own circle were secretly with the forbidden images: the Empress Theodora and her mother Theoctiste hardly concealed their feelings, and the Basileus was not unaware of it. He also realised that the whole Empire besides was weary of an interminable struggle leading to no result. It was vain for him to exact on his death-bed from his wife Theodora, whom he left Regent, and from the ministers who were to assist her, a solemn oath to make no change in his policy, and not to disturb in his office the Patriarch John, who had been its chief inspirer (842). Rarely has a last injunction been made more utterly in vain.

II.

While the second phase of the quarrel of the images was thus developing, events of grave importance were taking place within the Empire as well as without.

Irene's crime against her son, by diverting the succession from the Isaurian dynasty, had re-opened the chapter of revolutions. The old Empress had been overthrown by a plot; other conspiracies were constantly to disturb the reigns of her successors.

First in time (803) came the rising of Bardanes Turcus, who, originally strategus of the Anatolics, had been placed by Nicephorus in supreme command of all the troops in cantonments in Asia Minor. Intoxicated by this great position and by his popularity among the soldiers, Bardanes proclaimed himself Emperor. But the insurrection was short-lived. The rebel leader, betrayed by his chief partisans and unable to take Constantinople, threw up the game and entered the cloister. In 808 another plot was set on foot to place on the throne the Patrician Arsaber, who held the high office of quaestor; in 810 there was an attempt to assassinate the Emperor. Things were much worse after the death of Nicephorus. During the few months that his son Stauracius reigned (after escaping wounded from the defeat inflicted by the Bulgars on the Byzantines) unending intrigues went on with the object of raising his brother-in-law, Michael Rangabé, to power, and the Patriarch Nicephorus himself took part with the Emperor's ministers in fomenting the revolution which dethroned him (October 811). Less than two years afterwards, the disasters of the Bulgarian war, the discontent of the army after the defeat of Versinicia, and the great danger threatening the Empire, caused the fall of Michael; the soldiers proclaimed their general, Leo the Armenian, Emperor. Entering Constantinople he seized upon supreme power (July 813). It has already been seen that, thus raised to the throne by an insurrection, Leo fell a victim to plotters who assassinated him on Christmas morning 820.

Under Michael II, there was, for two years, little or no improvement in the state of things; the Empire was convulsed by a terrible civil war let loose by the insurrection of Thomas the Slavonian, an old brother-officer of the Emperor. Professing to be Constantine VI, the dethroned son of Irene, Thomas had won over the whole iconodule party, proclaiming himself its defender; he appealed to the lower classes, whose social claims he supported, and, in this almost revolutionary movement, he gathered round him all who were discontented. Finally, he had secured the support of the Arabs: the Caliph Ma'mūn had recognised him as Emperor, and authorised the Patriarch of Antioch to crown him with all solemnity. Master of nearly the whole of Asia Minor, leader of an army of more than eighty thousand men, Thomas had now only to get possession of Constantinople. He succeeded in leading his soldiers into Europe, and the fleet of the themes of the Aegean and of the Cibyrrhaeots being at his disposal, he attacked the capital by land and sea. A first attempt failed (December 821–February 822), but in the spring of 822 Thomas returned to the charge, and reinforced by contingents supplied to him from the European provinces which were warmly in favour of images, he pushed on the siege throughout the year 822 with so much vigour that the fall of Michael II seemed merely a question of days. Only the intervention of the Bulgars saved the Emperor. In the spring of 823 the Khan Omurtag made a descent upon Thrace. Thomas had to bring himself to abandon Constantinople to go to meet this new enemy, by whom he was completely beaten. Some weeks later, having been defeated by the imperialist troops, he was compelled to throw himself into Arcadiopolis, where he held out until the middle of October 823. In Asia Minor also, where the troops of the Armeniac and Opsician themes had remained unshakably loyal to the Emperor, the last attempts at resistance were crushed. But the alarm had been great, and if the defeat of Thomas' rising had made the Phrygian dynasty safe for long years to come, on the other hand it is certain that the continual outbreaks, coming one after another from 802, had notably impaired the strength and exhausted the resources of the Empire.

This was plainly to be seen in the disasters both in the East and in the West encountered by the foreign policy of the State.

From the early days of his reign Nicephorus had made efforts to come to a settlement of the Italian question with Charlemagne, and the treaty of 803, which left to the Eastern Empire Venice, the Dalmatian coast, Naples, Calabria, and Sicily, abandoned, *per contra*, Istria, the interior of Dalmatia, the Exarchate of Ravenna, the Pentapolis, and Rome to the Franks. But, as Constantinople refused to recognise the Emperor of the West, it was not long before hostilities broke out afresh, and Frankish intrigues in the Venetian lagoons decided Nicephorus on taking energetic steps. A Greek fleet appeared at the head of the Adriatic (807) without, however, enabling the Byzantines to hinder Pepin, the young Frankish King of Italy, from taking, after a long siege, the islands of the lagoon (810). Negotiations were therefore reopened with Aix-la-Chapelle, and the treaty of 812, while restoring Venice to the Eastern Empire and in other respects renewing the convention of 803, provided for the recognition by Constantinople, although reluctant, of Charlemagne's imperial title. Thus the Greeks accepted the events of 754 and renounced their historic rights to Italy; thus, as Charlemagne wrote, the Western Roman Empire officially took its place side by side with the Eastern Empire; thus, as Einhard expressed it, every occasion of stumbling was definitively removed between them. But for Constantinople it was a deep humiliation to have been forced to recognise even momentarily, even with the secret intention of withdrawing the concession, the event which, on Christmas Day 800, had taken place in St Peter's at Rome.

Still heavier blows fell upon the Empire in the East. The resolution arrived at by Nicephorus, immediately upon his accession, to refuse the tribute which Irene had been forced to pay to the Arabs, had renewed the war between the Empire and the powerful Caliphs of the Abbasid dynasty. It proved disastrous to the Byzantines, at least for the first ten years; from 814 to 829, however, internal disturbances in the Mohammedan world restored to the Greeks some degree of tranquillity in Asia. But elsewhere the Musulmans gained alarming advantages. In 826 some Arabs, who had been driven from Spain, seized upon Crete, and founded the stronghold of Chandax. All the efforts of the Byzantines in the reign of Michael II to re-conquer the island proved useless, and the Musulman corsairs, masters of so excellent a strategic position, were to become, for a century and a half, the terror of the Eastern Mediterranean. About the same time, the rising of Euphemius in Sicily had consequences no less serious for Constantinople. In 827 the rebel called the Musulmans of Africa to his help, and the Aghlabid Emir, Ziyādatallāh, landed in the island. The Arabs were not to evacuate it before the end of the eleventh century. It is true that they failed at first before Syracuse, but then the troops despatched from Constantinople were completely defeated at Mineo (830), and soon after that the great town of Palermo fell into the hands of the infidels (831). And if more than a quarter of a century, up to 859, was still needed to complete the conquest of Sicily, yet the Arabs, from this time onward, held in Western waters a position analogous to that which the possession of Crete gave them in the East, and were soon from thence to menace Southern Italy[1].

The war which had been waged against the Empire, during the early years of the ninth century, by Krum, the Khan of Bulgaria, ran an even more terrible course. Let loose by the imprudent offensive of Nicephorus, it was marked by sanguinary disaster. In 809 Sardica fell into the hands of the Bulgars, and its garrison was massacred. In 811 the great expedition which Nicephorus led into Bulgaria came to an end in the Balkan passes with a severe defeat, in which the Byzantine army, surrounded on all sides, was cut to pieces, and the Emperor himself slain. Thereupon Krum committed frightful ravages in Thrace and Macedonia, and Michael I, attempting to check him, was completely defeated at Versinicia near Hadrianople (June 813). Even Constantinople was threatened. Krum appeared under the walls of the capital, which was saved by the energy of Leo V, though the surrounding districts were fearfully wasted by the exasperated Bulgarian prince. Hadrianople fell into his hands; but Leo's victory at Mesembria (Autumn 813) restored the fortunes of the Empire, and the death of Krum (April 814) just as he was preparing a fresh onslaught upon Constantinople, sufficed to reassure the Byzantines. Shortly afterwards a peace for thirty years was concluded between the Empire and the new ruler of Bulgaria, Omurtag: the frontier of Thrace, dividing the two states, was now marked by a line of fortifications running from Develtus to Makrolivada, between Hadrianople and Philippopolis. The fact was that the Bulgars had, at that moment, more pressing anxieties on their western frontier; the Frankish threat was sufficiently engrossing to make them ready to live on good terms with the Byzantine Empire[2].

One last incident had disturbed the reign of Nicephorus. In 807 the Slavs of the Peloponnesus had risen and laid siege to Patras. Legend relates that the town was miraculously saved by its patron, St Andrew the Apostle. At any rate, it seems that, after this outbreak, the Slav tribes were compelled to adopt more regular habits of life, less dangerous to the security of the country.

[1] For details of these events see *infra*, Chapter v, pp. 126–8, 134–6.
[2] For details of these events see *infra*, Chapter viii, pp. 232–4.

In face of the difficulties which they had had to overcome, the early Emperors of the ninth century had not been devoid of real merit. Nicephorus was an energetic and courageous prince and a capable administrator. Leo V was a skilful general, solicitous for the military defence of the Empire and for the sound organisation of justice, whose great qualities his very enemies acknowledged. The Patriarch Nicephorus said of him on the morrow of his assassination: "The Empire has lost an impious prince, but a great defender of the public interest." The second sovereign of the Phrygian dynasty was no less remarkable, and his reign (829–842) was marked by decided improvement in the situation at home as well as abroad.

In the East, the Caliphate had for several years been greatly disturbed and weakened by the insurrection of Bābak and the communistic sect of the Khurramites of which he was the leader. Theophilus, from the moment of his accession, turned these conditions to good account. He entered into negotiations with the rebels, and gave a hearty welcome to those of them who, under the command of Theophobus, a Persian officer, came (it is said, to the number of thirty thousand) to ask leave to serve in the imperial army (830). The war with the Arabs immediately broke out again. As long as the Caliph Ma'mūn lived, it was marked by varying success, and the Emperor was more than once obliged to bring himself to make overtures for peace. But after Ma'mūn's death (833) he assumed the offensive more boldly. The campaign of 837 on the Euphrates proved fortunate. Zapetra and Samosata were taken, and Theophilus celebrated his victory by a triumphal entry into his capital. The following year, however, the Byzantines met with a serious defeat at Dazimon, now Tokat, and Amorium, the cradle of the royal house, was taken by the Musulmans and sacked. The Emperor had to submit to negotiate and a truce was signed (841). Fortunately the death of the Caliph Mu'taṣim, who was already meditating an attack on Constantinople (842), and a disaster suffered by the Arab fleet attempting the enterprise, caused a temporary cessation of the struggle[1].

About the same time the Byzantine Empire, through its diplomatic relations, was extending its influence and increasing its reputation. In 833, at the request of the Khan of the Chazars, a Byzantine officer built at the mouth of the Don the fortress of Sarkel. It was intended to protect the district against the attacks of the Patzinaks, and especially of the Russians, who were beginning to threaten the shores of the Black Sea, and who for the first time sent ambassadors to Constantinople in 838. The Byzantine court was, besides, on good terms with the Western Emperors; in 839 Theophilus applied to Louis the Pious for his support in an attack on Syria or Egypt. Similar negotiations took place with the Umayyad Emirs of Cordova, at all times the enemies of the Abbasid

[1] For details see *infra*, Chapter v, pp. 128–31.

Caliphs. Thus from the shores of the Crimea to the limits of the West, Byzantine diplomacy, after a long time of isolation, resumed its earlier activity.

But it is especially on account of his home government that Theophilus is still remembered. The chroniclers picture this prince much as the Arab tales represent Hārūn ar-Rashīd, as a ruler ever anxious to render absolute justice to all his subjects, accessible to every comer, willingly taking part in the life of the people in order to gain more accurate information, severe towards the guilty, and eager to redress all injustices. A good administrator, he applied himself to bringing the finances into order, and at his death left a large reserve; the financial prosperity enjoyed by the Empire is proved most clearly by the fact that the gold coins (*solidi*, bezants) of Byzantium were current throughout the world[1].

Theophilus set himself with no less energy to secure the defensive organisation of the Empire. In Asia, besides the ancient "five themes" there were the new themes of Paphlagonia and Chaldia, without reckoning the small military governments, or *clisurae*, of Seleucia, of Charsianum, of Cappadocia, and of Colonea. On the Black Sea, the free town of Cherson was also made into a theme, in order to strengthen the defence against the Patzinaks and the Russians. Finally, in the European territories where, from 813, the Peloponnesus had been constituted a separate theme, Theophilus created the themes of Thessalonica, of Cephalonia, and of Dyrrhachium, in order to ward off the Bulgarian threat to Macedonia and the Arab danger in the Adriatic. Thus the military defence of the Empire was completed and perfected.

Lastly, Theophilus was a great builder. He loved pomp and splendour and all that might enhance the prestige of his throne. On two occasions, in 831 and 837, he dazzled Constantinople by the magnificence of his triumphs. He added to the beauty of the imperial palace by wonderful buildings, in which he plainly sought to rival the glories of Baghdad. Around the new throne-room, the Triconchus, to which the Sigma terrace led, he raised numerous and sumptuous pavilions, glorious with many-coloured marbles, and glittering with golden mosaics.

Still further to emphasise the beauty of his palace, he adorned it with admirable specimens of the goldsmith's art. In the great hall of the Magnaura was a plane-tree made of gold, shading the imperial throne, on the branches of which golden birds were perched; at the foot of the throne were lions couchant of gold, and on either hand golden griffins stood sentinel; opposite was set up a golden organ, adorned with enamels and precious stones. These masterpieces of splendour and luxury were at the same time marvels of mechanical skill. On audience-days, when foreign

[1] On the finances of the Empire at this period cf. Bury's *Eastern Roman Empire* (802–867), Chapter VII, pp. 210 sqq.

ambassadors entered the hall, the birds in the plane-tree fluttered and sang, the griffins sat up on their pedestals, the lions arose, lashed the air with their tails, and gave forth metallic roars. Elsewhere, a great coffer of gold, the Pentapyrgion, served to hold the imperial insignia and the crown jewels. Again, Theophilus had renewed the imperial wardrobe with unheard-of splendour, the gala robes worn on days of ceremony by the Basileus and the Augusta, the cloth of gold or gold-embroidered garments which adorned the great dignitaries of the court when they walked in solemn procession. He also, at great cost, restored the ramparts of Constantinople. All this conveys a strong impression of wealth (it is estimated that Theophilus spent more than a million a year on his building operations), of magnificence, and of beauty. Certainly Theophilus was lacking in several of the outstanding qualities of a statesman; his religious policy was ill-judged, and his wars not always successful. Nevertheless, his reign is conspicuous as a time of unusual brilliancy, a proof of the moral and material revival of the Byzantine Empire towards the middle of the ninth century.

III.

Theophilus at his death left the throne to a child of tender age, his son Michael III, who was not more than three or four years old. The Empress Theodora, therefore, assumed the regency during the minority of the young sovereign, her counsellors being her uncle the Magister Manuel, and the Logothete Theoctistus. They were religious men, secretly attached, as was the Basilissa herself, to iconodule principles, men of good sense also, who regarded with natural anxiety the long continuance of the religious strife and the serious consequences that it might have for the dynasty. The execution of the iconodule Theophobus, the successful general, the Emperor's own brother-in-law, which Theophilus had ordered from his death-bed, looks like a recognition of the threatening appearance of the situation, the champions of images waiting only for a leader to attempt a revolution. The Regent's ministers, especially her brother Bardas, who had great influence with her, strongly urged her to hasten the restoration of orthodoxy. The Basilissa, however, hesitated. She had been deeply attached to her husband and put great faith in the correctness of his political views, she was unwilling to consign his last instructions to oblivion, and, finally, she was much concerned at the prospect of the anathema likely to be pronounced against the late Emperor if iconoclasm were condemned. Nearly a year was needed to overcome the Regent's scruples. At last, however, fearing for the throne of her son, she came to a decision.

It was of the first importance, if the restoration of images was to be successfully carried out, to get rid of the Patriarch John, a clever and formidable man, whose enemies had created for him a sinister reputation as a magician, and who was nicknamed Lekanomantis. The prelate was therefore invited to sit on the council which had just been convoked in order to restore images to honour. John refused, and was consequently, not without some slight maltreatment, deposed and relegated to a monastery. In his seat was installed the monk Methodius, in former days so harshly persecuted by Michael II, but whom Theophilus, by a singular caprice, had admitted to intimacy on account of his scientific attainments. Highly favoured by Theodora, the new Patriarch assumed full control of the council which met in February 843. To please the Empress, the bishops hastened to except Theophilus from the condemnation directed against heretics, admitting without discussion the pious fraud which represented the Emperor as having, in his last moments, repented of his errors. Thanks to this compromise, the restoration of orthodoxy was accomplished without opposition. The pictures were solemnly reinstated in honour; the exiles and the proscribed were recalled and welcomed in triumph; the prisoners were set at liberty; the remains of the martyrs who had died in the struggle were brought back in state to Constantinople; and anathemas fell upon the most famous of the iconoclasts. Then, the work of the council having been accomplished, on the first Sunday in Lent (19 February 843) a triumphal procession, headed by the Empress herself, marched through the streets of the capital, from the church of the Virgin in Blachernae to St Sophia, where the enthusiastic people returned thanks to the Most High. In the evening, at the Sacred Palace, Theodora gave a great banquet, at which were assembled the prelates and confessors and those who had suffered for the cause. It was the festival of Orthodoxy, which from that time the Greek Church has solemnly celebrated on the first Sunday in Lent every year, in commemoration of the reinstatement of images and of the blessed Theodora.

Thus, after more than a century of strife, peace was at last restored to the Empire. But if, from the dogmatic standpoint, the victory of the iconodule party was complete, the Church, on the other hand, was forced to give up the tendency towards independence which some of her most illustrious champions had shewn. One of the essential objects to which the policy of the Iconoclast Emperors had been directed was the reduction of the Church to entire dependence on the State. In spite of the protests of their opponents, who, from Gregory II and John Damascene down to the Fathers of the Council of 787 and Theodore of Studion, had with one voice refused to the Emperor the right περὶ πίστεως λόγον ποιεῖσθαι, it was this imperial policy which now proved victorious. "In the struggle," writes Harnack, "which for a century the Byzantine Church maintained against the State, not her religious constitution alone, but her liberty was at stake. On the first point, she was the victor; in the struggle for liberty, she yielded." Thus, in spite of the re-establishment of orthodoxy, the Studite party and the freedom for which they had fought were defeated, and the work of the Iconoclast Emperors proved not to have been in vain.

Theodora's government, however, which lasted up to 856, assumed, as might have been expected, somewhat of a religious complexion. The Empress, priding herself highly on having restored orthodoxy, held it no less important to wage war upon heresy. From the end of the seventh century, the Paulicians, so called from the great respect which they professed for the Apostle Paul, had been spreading their doctrines through Asia Minor, from Phrygia to Armenia. Their progress had been furthered by the patronage of the Iconoclast Emperors, and the Orthodox Church saw with great anxiety the growth of the influence and the spread of the propaganda of sectaries whom she characterised as Manichaeans. Theophilus, it is not exactly known why, had allowed himself to be persuaded into persecuting them, and part of the heretical community had from that time sought refuge in Arab territory. Theodora was only too happy to be able in this point to continue her husband's policy. By her orders, the Paulicians were called upon to choose between conversion and death, and, as they refused to yield, the imperial government set itself to break down their resistance. Blood was shed in torrents in the parts of Asia Minor where they were settled; it is said that one hundred thousand persons suffered death. The survivors, led by Carbeas, one of their chiefs, went to ask shelter from the Emir of Melitene, and settling around Tephrice, which became their main citadel, they soon made it clear to the Byzantines how ill-advised they had been in thrusting into the arms of the Musulmans men who, up till then, had valiantly defended the frontiers of the Empire. It has been said with justice that the persecution of the Paulicians was "one of the greatest political disasters of the ninth century."[1]

The pious zeal which inspired the Regent suggested to her more fortunate projects elsewhere. She initiated the great missionary enterprise through which, some years later, the Gospel was to be brought to the Chazars, the Moravians, and the Bulgars. In order to subdue the ever restless Slav tribes of the Peloponnesus, she despatched thither the Strategus Theoctistus Bryennius (849) who, except in the Taygetus region where the Milengi and the Ezerites kept their autonomy, succeeded in establishing the imperial authority on a firm basis throughout the province, and in preparing the way for the conversion of the Slavs. Finally, Theodora, by her sound financial administration, did no small service to the state. Unfortunately, as is often the case under feminine government, the imperial palace was a hive of intrigue. The Logothete Theoctistus, the Regent's chief minister, had her entire favour, and against him her brother Bardas sought support from the young Emperor Michael, his nephew, who, as he grew up, shewed deplorable tendencies. Bardas used his influence to embitter the resentment of the young prince against the Logothete, and in 856 a plot was concocted which ended in the

[1] Bury, *History of the Eastern Roman Empire*, p. 276.

murder of Theoctistus. This was a blow aimed full at Theodora, and thus she understood it. For two years more she lived in the palace, until in 858 she was requested to withdraw into a convent. But her political career was already over. From the day after the assassination of Theoctistus, Michael III had taken power into his own hands; Bardas, appointed Magister and Domestic of the Scholae, and at last in 862 almost admitted to a share in the Empire under the title of Caesar, was for ten years (856–866) to exercise supreme power in the name of his nephew.

In spite of the sedulous care which his mother had bestowed on his education, Michael III, who was now about seventeen or eighteen years old, was a prince of the worst type. Without taking too literally all that has been related of him by chroniclers too much bent on excusing the murder which gave the throne to Basil the Macedonian, and therefore disposed to blacken the character of his victim, it is certain that the behaviour of the miserable Emperor was calculated to scandalise both the court and the capital. He cared for nothing but pleasure, hunting, riding, racing, wrestling of athletes; he delighted in driving a chariot on the palace race-course and in shewing himself off before his intimates. He frequented the lowest society, was ever surrounded by charioteers, musicians, buffoons, and players; he spent part of his nights drinking (history has bestowed on him the surname of Michael the Drunkard); he amused himself and his unworthy favourites with coarse and indecent jests, turning religion into ridicule, parodying the sacred rites, and in his low and tasteless jests sparing neither the Patriarch nor the Empress-Mother. He wasted the money amassed by his parents in ridiculous extravagances; public business was to him an unwelcome infliction, a mere hindrance to his amusements, an interruption to his course of folly; in fine, he was the natural prey of favourites for ever contending for his good graces, and his court, where he ostentatiously displayed his mistress, Eudocia Ingerina, was the home of ceaseless intrigue.

Bardas, who governed the Empire in the name of Michael III, was a man of another stamp. Keenly ambitious, greedy of power and wealth, little troubled with scruples or morals, he was, despite his vices, a man of unquestionable capacity. Even his enemies have been unable to deny his great qualities. A good administrator, he prided himself on his love of strict justice and on his incorruptibility as a minister, and in this way he made himself highly popular. A man of great talents, he loved letters and was interested in scientific studies. Theophilus had already appreciated the importance of restoring Constantinople to its intellectual pre-eminence in the Eastern world; he had been the patron of learned men, and had heaped favours on the Patriarch John and on the great mathematician, Leo of Thessalonica. Bardas did more. To him is due the honour of having founded the famous school of the Magnaura, where he gathered the most illustrious teachers of the day. Its direction was put into the hands of Leo of Thessalonica, one of the greatest minds of the ninth century, whose universal learning—he was equally versed in mathematics, medicine, and philosophy—had gained for him among his contemporaries the reputation of a wizard and magician. Around him were others teaching geometry, astronomy, and philology, and to encourage the zeal of the professors and the eagerness of their pupils, Bardas used to pay frequent and diligent visits to the school. He counted other learned men among his intimates: Constantine, some years afterwards to become the apostle of the Slavs, and then teaching philosophy at the University; Photius, the most distinguished and brilliant intellect of the time as well as the man of most learning, who was shortly, by the favour of the all-powerful minister, to attain the patriarchal throne of Constantinople. Under the influence of Bardas, a great wave of intellectual revival was already passing over the capital, presaging the renaissance of the tenth century, and already, by its secular and classical character, arousing the anxiety of the Church. It has been justly remarked that henceforward there was to be no more interruption, no further period of darkness breaking into the literary activities of the Byzantines, until the fall of Constantinople, and that one of the most valid claims to glory of the Amorian dynasty in the history of civilisation is undoubtedly the interest which the court then shewed in education and learning[1].

Bardas had still another honour, that of successfully accomplishing, with the help of the Patriarch Photius, the great work of the conversion of the Slavs[2]. Two men were the renowned instruments in the work, Constantine, better known under his name in religion, Cyril, and his brother Methodius, "the Apostles of the Slavs," as history still calls them to-day. Constantine, the younger of the two, after having been at first a professor at the University of Constantinople, had, about 860, successfully carried out a mission to Christianise the Chazars; he was thus marked out for the work when, towards 863, Rostislav, Prince of Great Moravia, requested of the Byzantine court that his people might be instructed in the Christian Faith. In 864 Cyril and Methodius set out, and they carried with them the means of assuring the success of their undertaking. Natives of Thessalonica, and thus quite familiar with the language and customs of the Slavs, who on all sides dwelt around that great Greek city, the two missionaries well understood the necessity of speaking to those whom they desired to convert in their own tongue. For their benefit, therefore, they translated the Gospel into a dialect akin to that spoken by the Moravians, and, in order to transcribe it, they invented an alphabet from the Greek minuscule, the Glagolitic script. At the same time, Cyril and Methodius introduced into Moravia a Slav liturgy, they preached in the language, and did their utmost to train a Slav clergy. Thus it was that their success was achieved, and after their

[1] Bury, *op. cit.* p. 435. [2] See *infra,* Chapter VII B.

first stay in Moravia, Rome herself expressed her approbation of the methods they had employed in their undertaking (868). It is true that later on, owing to the opposition and intrigues of the German clergy, the work so magnificently begun was quickly ruined. But nevertheless, the glory remained to Constantinople of having, at the same time that she brought the orthodox faith to the Slavs, created the alphabet and the liturgical language in use amongst them to-day.

The conversion of Bulgaria was another triumph for Constantinople. From the first thirty years of the ninth century, Christianity had begun to make its way among the Bulgars, and imperial policy watched its progress with interest, seeing in it a means of strengthening Byzantine influence in this barbarian kingdom. On his side, Tsar Boris, placed as he was between the Greek Empire and that great Moravia which, at this very time, was accepting Christianity, realised that he could no longer remain pagan. But he hesitated between the orthodoxy of Constantinople and the Roman faith offered him by Germany, whose ally he had become. Constantinople could not allow Bulgaria to come within the Western sphere of influence. A military expedition recalled the prince to discretion (863), and as his conversion, besides, was to be rewarded by an increase of territory, he made his decision. He asked to be baptised into the Orthodox Church, receiving the christian name of Michael (864); and the Patriarch Photius, realising to the full the importance of the event, delightedly hailed the neophyte as "the fairest jewel of his efforts." Despite the resistance of the Bulgarian aristocracy, the Tsar compelled his people to adopt Christianity with him. But he was soon made uneasy by the apparent intention of Constantinople to keep him in too strict a dependence, and so turned towards Rome, requesting the Pope, Nicholas I, to set up the Latin rite in his kingdom. The Pope welcomed these advances, and Roman priests, under the direction of Formosus, began to labour in Bulgaria (866–867). This did not suit Byzantine calculations; the imperial government had no intention of loosing its hold upon Bulgaria. In the council of 869 Rome was obliged to yield to the protests of the Greeks; the Orthodox clergy were reinstated in Bulgarian territory, and the Tsar had to reconcile himself to re-entering the sphere of action of the Greek Empire.

IV.

The government of Bardas had thus to a remarkable degree increased the prestige of the Empire. Beyond the frontier, however, Arab successes provided the shadows in the picture. The piracies of the Musulmans of Crete brought desolation to the Aegean, and the great expedition which the Logothete Theoctistus led against them in person (843) had produced no better results than did the enterprise attempted against Egypt, despite the temporary success achieved by the capture of Damietta (853). In

Sicily the infidels were proceeding successfully with the conquest of the island; Messina fell into their hands in 843, and Leontini in 847; Castrogiovanni, the great Byzantine fortress in the middle of Sicily, yielded in 859, and the Greek expedition sent to re-conquer the province (860) was completely foiled. In Asia, where the defection of the Paulicians had been a heavy blow to the Empire, affairs prospered no better. It is true that, in 856, Petronas, brother of the Empress Theodora, made his way into the country of Samosata and Amida, and attacked Tephrice. But in 859 the Byzantine army, commanded by the Emperor himself, was beaten before Samosata, and not long afterwards (860) at Chonarium, near Dazimon. In 863 Omar, the Emir of Melitene, took Amisus. This time the Greeks braced themselves for a great effort, and the brilliant victory won by Petronas at Poson, near the Halys (863), restored for the moment the reputation of the imperial arms[1].

Whilst these events were taking place, a serious and unforeseen danger had menaced Constantinople. While the Emperor was in Asia and the imperial fleet busied in Sicily, some Russian pirates had unexpectedly crossed the Bosphorus and attacked the capital (860). In this emergency, the Patriarch Photius nobly sustained the spirit of the people, and it was rather to his energy than to the supposed intervention of the Blessed Virgin, that the capital owed its safety. Further, the approach of the army from Asia Minor, returning by forced marches, determined the barbarians upon a retreat which proved disastrous to them. And the treaty not long afterwards concluded with the Russians, lately settled at Kiev, opened up, towards the north, vast future prospects to the Empire.

One last event, pregnant with future consequences, marked the administration of Bardas. This was the breach with Rome. For some considerable time the chief minister had been on bad terms with the Patriarch Ignatius, that son of the Emperor Michael Rangabé who, having been tonsured on the death of his father, had in 847 been raised to the patriarchate. On the feast of the Epiphany (January 858) the prelate had thought it his duty to refuse communion to Bardas, and this the latter never forgave. He therefore set to work to implicate Ignatius in an alleged treasonable plot. The Patriarch was arrested and deported to the Princes Islands, while in his place the minister procured the election of Photius, a layman, who within six days received all the ecclesiastical orders, and on 25 December 858 celebrated a Solemn High Mass at St Sophia. The accession to the patriarchate of this man of mark, who was, however, of consummate ambition, prodigious arrogance, and unsurpassed political skill, was to bring about a formidable crisis in the Church. Ignatius, in fact, though evil-intreated and dragged from one place of exile to another, resolutely declined to abdicate, and his supporters, above all the monks of the Studion, violently resisted the

[1] For details of these events see *infra*, Chapter v, pp. 131–4, 136–8.

usurpation of Photius. The latter, in order to compel their submission, attempted to obtain recognition from Rome, and, by means of a most diplomatic letter, entered into communication with Nicholas I. The Pope eagerly seized the opportunity to interfere in the dispute. But the legates whom he sent to Constantinople allowed themselves to be led astray by Photius, and the council which met in their presence at the church of the Holy Apostles (861) summoned Ignatius before it, deposed him, and confirmed the election of Photius. Nicholas I was not the man to see his wishes thus ignored. Ignatius, besides, appealed to Rome against his condemnation. At the Lateran synod (April 863) Photius and his partisans were excommunicated, and were called upon to resign their usurped functions immediately; Ignatius, on the other hand, was declared restored to the patriarchal throne.

It was the wonderful astuteness of Photius which turned a purely personal question into an affair of national importance. Most skilfully he turned to account the ancient grudges of the Greek Church against the West, the suspicion and dread always aroused in it by the claims of Rome to the primacy. He made even greater play with the ambitious and imprudent designs of Nicholas I upon the young Bulgarian Church; and he won over the whole of public opinion to his side by posing as the champion of the national cause against the Papal usurpers. The encyclical, which in 867 Photius addressed to the other patriarchs of the East, summed up eloquently the grievances of the Byzantines against Rome. The council, which was held soon after at Constantinople under the presidency of the Emperor, made the rupture complete (867). It replied to the condemnations pronounced by Nicholas I by anathematising and deposing the Pope, and condemning the heretical doctrines and customs of the Western Church. The breach between Rome and Constantinople was complete, the schism was consummated, and Photius, to all appearance, triumphant. But his triumph was to be short-lived. The murder of Michael III, by raising Basil the Macedonian to the throne, was suddenly to overthrow the Patriarch's fortunes.

While these events, portending such serious consequences, were taking place, Michael III continued in his course of pleasure, folly, and debauchery. By degrees, however, he became weary of the all-powerful influence wielded by Bardas. From the year 858 or 859 the Emperor had a favourite. This was an adventurer, the son of a poor Armenian family which circumstances had transplanted to Macedonia, a certain Basil, whose bodily strength and skill in breaking horses had endeared him to Michael III. This man became chief equerry, and in 862 grand chamberlain and patrician. His obliging conduct in marrying the Emperor's mistress, Eudocia Ingerina, put the finishing touch to the favour he enjoyed. His rapid advance could not fail to disquiet Bardas, all the more because Basil was unquestionably clever, and obviously extremely ambitious. Thus it was not long before the two men were engaged in a bitter struggle.

It ended in 866 by the murder of Bardas, who, during a campaign in Asia, was slaughtered by his enemies under the very eyes of the Emperor. Thus Basil was victorious. Some weeks later the Emperor adopted him and raised him to the dignity of Magister; soon after, he associated him in the Empire (May 866). But with a prince such as Michael III favour, however apparently secure, was still always uncertain, and Basil was well aware of it. The Emperor, more addicted than ever to wine, was now surpassing himself in wild follies and cruelties. Basil, knowing that many were jealous of him and attempting to undermine him with the Emperor, must have been perpetually in fear for his power and even for his life. An incident which revealed the precariousness of his situation decided him on taking action. On 23 September 867, with the help of some faithful followers, Basil, in the palace of St Mamas, murdered the wretched Emperor who had made him great, and, next morning, having gained possession of the Sacred Palace, seized upon power. It seems plain that the Empire joyfully acquiesced in the disappearance of the capricious and cruel tyrant that Michael III had become. But Basil was more than a skilful and lucky aspirant, he was a great statesman; by setting a new dynasty on the throne, he was destined, through his vigorous government, to usher in for the Empire two centuries of glory and renown.

CHAPTER III.

THE MACEDONIAN DYNASTY FROM 867 TO 976 A.D.

THE race of Leo the Isaurian, which in no inglorious fashion had filled the whole of the eighth and ninth centuries with its iconoclastic struggles, social reforms, and palace intrigues, nominally died out in 867 in the person of a debauched and incapable young Emperor, Michael III, known as the Drunkard. The man who in consequence ascended the throne by means of a crime, and founded the Macedonian dynasty, was Basil I. To study the personal character and home policy of the sovereigns directly or indirectly descended from him down to 1057, is, in effect, to depict the leading aspects of the period, save for the ever-present struggle for existence against external foes.

BASIL I (867–886).

The founder of the Macedonian dynasty was born about 812[1] in the neighbourhood of Hadrianople, of a humble Macedonian family engaged in agriculture and probably of Armenian extraction. As always happens in such cases, no sooner had Basil ascended the throne than the genealogists provided him with illustrious ancestors. His obscure family history was made the subject of legendary embellishments, as were his infancy and early years. The Arsacides, Philip of Macedon, Alexander, and Constantine, were attributed to him as his remote progenitors. It was related that marvels and prodigies had attended his birth, foreshadowing a glorious future for him. As a matter of fact, Basil's father and mother were poor peasants. "While still in swaddling clothes" he was, with his family, carried captive into Bulgaria by the troops of Krum, and there he remained until he was about twenty years old. On his return to Macedonia, finding himself rich in nothing but brothers and sisters, he set out for Constantinople and took service in the first instance with the

[1] In an article in the *Byzantinische Zeitschrift* (Vol. xx, pp. 486–491) Mr Brooks contests this date, and, consequently, the whole chronology of Basil I. Here he puts the future Emperor's birth between 830 and 835. In spite of the arguments which he brings forward, the writer of this chapter has thought it necessary to adhere to the date already adopted by him in *Basile Ier*, as the reasons alleged by Mr Brooks appear by no means conclusive.

Strategus of the Peloponnesus, Theophylitzes. Here he rose to fortune, having on a voyage to Patras had the good luck to make acquaintance with a rich widow named Danielis, who showered favours upon him. A very handsome man and of herculean strength, he attracted notice at Constantinople, and in 856 the Emperor Michael took him into his service as chief groom.

In this way Basil was brought into intimate association with the sovereign, whose confidant he soon became. While the government was left to Bardas, Michael amused himself and Basil became the self-appointed minister of the imperial pleasures. Amidst the corruptions of the court the shrewd peasant contrived to make a place of his own and gradually to render himself indispensable. He rose in favour, obtained ancient dignities for himself, and, in order that he might have no rival to fear, in April 866 he assassinated the Caesar Bardas, Michael's uncle. This was a preliminary crime. Having thus got rid of the real ruler of the state, Basil prevailed upon the Emperor, on 26 May following, to declare him associated in the imperial authority. Thus the path to the crown was thrown open to him. It was quickly traversed. Having lost the affection of the Emperor, who had taken a fancy to a boatman named Basiliscianus and wished to have him crowned, Basil, no longer feeling himself secure, formed a plot with several of his relations and friends, and on the night of 23 September 867 procured the assassination of Michael in the St Mamas palace. This done, he instantly returned to Constantinople, took possession of the imperial palace, and had himself proclaimed sole Emperor. The Macedonian Dynasty was founded. It was to last for nearly two centuries.

According to the chroniclers, the revolution of September 867 was welcomed by the population as a whole. The Senate, the nobles, the the army, and the people made no difficulty about acclaiming the man of the moment, for it was generally understood that the Empire was passing through a serious crisis, and that it was of the first importance to have the throne filled by one who was a good soldier, a wise administrator, and a valiant leader. Now there was no doubt that Basil possessed these qualifications.

Having reached the age of fifty-six when he mounted the throne, the new Emperor did not arrive at power unaccompanied. He brought his family with him, a strange family, to tell the truth, and one which laboured under the disadvantage of doubtful legitimacy. While still young, Basil had married a Macedonian girl named Maria, from whom he procured a divorce in 865 when his fortunes shewed signs of soaring. The Emperor Michael immediately married him to his own mistress, Eudocia Ingerina, who nevertheless continued to live with her imperial lover. On Basil's accession, she mounted the throne with him as Empress, dying in 882. Ostensibly Basil had two sons, Constantine and Leo. Who were these children? The elder, Constantine, was his father's favourite. He was probably born about 859. In 870 Basil associated him in his government, and took him on the campaign which he made in 877 against Germanicea. Unfortunately he died in 879, to the despair of his father, whose mind became affected. The mother of this son was unquestionably Maria, and he would have been the natural heir. There were probably also four daughters of the same marriage, who were sent to a convent and ignored on all hands. One of them, however, must have married, for Basil had a son-in-law, a celebrated general, Christopher. As to Leo, he was almost certainly born at the palace of St Mamas on 1 December 866. Whatever Constantine VII says in his life of his grandfather, Leo was not Basil's son but the offspring of Michael and Eudocia Ingerina. He was consequently illegitimate. The evident antipathy with which Basil regarded him is thus easily understood. He was nevertheless Basil's successor. After becoming Emperor, Basil had two more sons by Eudocia, Alexander, who reigned jointly with Leo VI and died in 912, and Stephen, who became Patriarch of Constantinople. Basil had, besides, brothers and sisters, but none of them played a part of any importance. One of his sisters, Thecla, made herself notorious by her misconduct, and his brothers took an active and prominent share in the murder of Michael.

On the morrow of Michael's assassination, Basil, already co-regent, was proclaimed sole Emperor by Marianus, Prefect of the City, in the Forum. Then, having at St Sophia solemnly returned thanks to God, he set himself to the task of government. The first matter which seems to have engaged his attention was the exchequer. The finances were in a truly deplorable state. Michael III had wasted all his resources, and in order to raise money had sold, broken up, or melted down a large number of works of art. When Basil came to examine the treasury, nothing was left in it. But a statement of accounts was found in possession of one of the officials, proving that serious malversations had been committed. The thieves were forced to restore half of the sums abstracted, and in this way a certain amount was brought into the treasury. Other sums of importance reached it in due time, helping to restore the finances to solvency.

But this, in itself, was little. The first urgent reform was the reorganisation of the financial machinery of the State. Social questions at this juncture had become acute. The feudal class, which was all-powerful, was striving to accentuate more and more the formidable distinction between the rich and the poor, the *δυνατοί* and the *πένητες*, and crying abuses were springing up in every direction. Basil tried to protect the small men against the great, by shewing favour to the lesser landholders; he appointed honest and trustworthy officials over the finances, and exerted himself to maintain the peasant in possession of his plot, and to secure him from being ruined by fines or taxes out of all proportion to his wealth. Then, taking a step further, he endeavoured to reform the method of collecting the taxes by revising the register of lands, and compelling the officials to set down in clear, legible, comprehensible figures the fixed quota on which depended the amount of tax payable. Finally, he took a direct and personal share in financial administration, verifying the accounts, receiving the complaints which reached Constantinople, and acting as judge of final resort. It is probable that exertions such as these brought about a temporary improvement in the state of the poor and labouring classes. Nevertheless, as we shall see, Basil's successors were in their turn to find the social and financial tension more acute than ever.

While thus attending to the finances, Basil also applied himself to the task of legislative and judicial re-organisation. Here, as elsewhere, he made a point in the first place of choosing officials of integrity, and also just and learned judges. He cared little from what stratum of society his judges were drawn, provided that they discharged their duties faithfully. Basil required that they should be numerous and easily accessible, and that their pay should be sufficient to make them independent. Justice was to be administered daily at the Chalce Palace, at the Hippodrome, and at the Magnaura, and more than once Basil himself was seen to enter the court, listen to the trial, and take part in the deliberations.

But it is plain that the chief legislative work of Basil was the revision of the Justinianean Code and the issue of new law-books. In 878 or 879, without waiting for the completion of the work of re-modelling which he had planned, he promulgated the *Prochiron*, a handbook or abridgment which determined the laws and unwritten customs in force, and abrogated those no longer in use. The *Prochiron* was, above all, concerned with civil law. It maintained its authority up to 1453. A second and fuller edition was prepared by Basil about 886. This was the *Epanagoge*, which besides formed an introduction and a summary, intended for a more important collection in forty books, the *Anacatharsis*. The last-named work is no longer in existence. No doubt its substance, as well as that of the *Epanagoge*, was included in the *Basilics*. But apparently neither of these earlier works was ever officially published. In any case, they did not remain in force for long[1].

During the most glorious period of his reign, Basil gave a new impulse to the fine arts which was destined to outlast his life. Under his direction, large numbers of churches were re-built, repaired, and beautified. In architecture we get the type of cupola intermediary between the large and dangerous dome of St Sophia and the elegant lantern-towers of a later age, while buildings on the basilica model become rarer, and architects are chiefly eager to construct splendid churches with gilded roofs, glittering mosaics, and marbles of varied hues. It was to Basil that his contemporaries owed, among other buildings, the magnificent church

[1] Cf. *infra*, Chapter XXII, pp. 711–12.

begun in 876 and consecrated in 880, called, in contradistinction to St Sophia, the New Church, with its scheme of decoration in many colours, and its unequalled mosaics forming a great assemblage of religious pictures, a church worthy to stand beside that which Justinian had built. We know it fairly well through the descriptions of Photius and Constantine VII.

Basil's artistic enterprise also found free scope in the erection of secular buildings which he raised for his own use, such as the palace of the Caenurgium, with its famous historical decorations and its ornamented pavements. The lesser arts also entered on a period of revival, and among works which have come down to us one in particular is famous, the celebrated manuscript of St Gregory (Parisinus 510) with its full-page illuminations and its varied ornamentation. It is of the highest interest for the reign of Basil, as it leaves us some trace of the portraits, unfortunately in a very imperfect condition, of Basil, Eudocia, Leo, and Alexander.

The religious question was the chief concern of Basil's reign. At his accession, the dispute with Rome which had arisen over Photius had reached an acute stage, and the Eastern Church was deeply divided. Photius had been chosen Patriarch in very irregular fashion on 25 December 858, a month after the banishment of the rightful Patriarch, Ignatius. Bardas had been the cause of the whole trouble, and, as early as 860, Rome had intervened. In spite of the Roman legates who, in 861, had allowed themselves to be intimidated into recognising Photius, Nicholas I had deposed and anathematised him and his adherents. The result was anarchy. Basil, therefore, who disliked "the knavery of this sage" and was also desirous of conciliating the Roman See and restoring religious peace to the Empire, hastened to recall Ignatius on 23 November 867, and to demand a council to put an end to the schism. This Council met in St Sophia on 5 October 869 and sat until 28 February 870. Basil, though in an indirect and covert way, took a leading part in it, and brought about the triumph of his own policy. On 5 November Photius was anathematised, declared to be deposed, and exiled to the monastery of Skepes.

The Emperor had, in part at least, gained his end. The solemn sitting of a council had, in the eyes of the public, set a seal upon his usurpation, and the Church found itself in the position of having implicitly recognised his title. And, what was more, the arrival of ambassadors from Bulgaria, who came at this juncture to inquire of the Council to which of the two Churches, Rome or Constantinople, their own belonged, was a further advantage for Basil. Thanks to the support given him by the Patriarch Ignatius, against the will of Rome and its legates, the Emperor obtained a decision that Bulgaria came under the jurisdiction of the Patriarchate, and Ignatius consecrated a bishop for that country. The result of all these religious transactions was clear. Basil's authority at home and abroad was strengthened, but at the same time he had broken with the Pope, Hadrian II[1].

The settlement, however, brought some measure of peace to the Church. In 875 or 876 Photius even returned to Constantinople as tutor of the imperial children, entered again into communication with Pope John VIII, and waited for the death of the aged Ignatius, which occurred on 23 October 877. Three days later, Photius again took possession of the patriarchal throne, and the Pope, upon certain conditions which were never carried out, confirmed his title. A temporary end was thus put to the schism, and the two authorities were again in harmony. A Council was held at Constantinople in 879–880 to decide the religious question. But by that time Basil's reign was virtually ended. Having lost his son Constantine he allowed things to take their own course, and Photius profited by his apathy to weave the conspiracy which proved his ruin.

Basil's reign ended gloomily. The nineteen years during which he had governed the Empire had not been free from complications. More than once he had had to foil a conspiracy aimed against his life; serious difficulties had arisen with his successor Leo; his armies had not been uniformly successful. It was, however, Constantine's death in 879 which really killed Basil. From this time onwards his reason was clouded; he became cruel and left to others all care for the administration. He himself spent his time in hunting, and it was while thus employed that he was overtaken by death at Apamea as the result of an accident perhaps arranged by his enemies. He was brought back seriously injured to Constantinople, where he died on 29 August 886, leaving the Empire to Leo VI under the guardianship of Stylianus Zaützes, an Armenian, who later became father-in-law of the Emperor.

Leo VI (886–912).

The revolution of 867 which had raised Basil to the throne was now undone, so far as its dynastic significance went, since with Leo VI the crown returned to the family of Michael III. Although the offspring of an adulterous connexion, the new sovereign was none the less of the imperial blood, and his accession really meant that the murderer's victim in the person of his son thrust aside the impostor in order to take his proper place. Officially, however, Basil's successor was regarded as his legitimate heir, and many no doubt believed that he was in fact his son and

[1] As we are here considering only the internal government of the sovereigns of the Macedonian house, no mention is made of the religious enterprises of Basil and his successors in the mission field, a subject which appears to belong too exclusively to Basil's foreign policy. To the Emperors, missions were a method of conquest as much as or more than a purely apostolic work. See *infra*, Chapter vii b.

Eudocia's. It is this false situation which explains the estrangement between Basil and Leo, the conduct of the latter, and doubtless also the existence of a party at court which remained permanently hostile to Basil and constant to Michael's dynasty in the person of Leo VI.

Leo, when he ascended the throne at Constantinople (886), was twenty years old. Up to that time his life had been a painful one. It is true that Basil had given him an excellent education, and that his care had not been thrown away. We know that Leo VI was surnamed the Wise, or the Philosopher, probably on account of his writings, his eloquence, and his learning. But this was certainly the sole advantage which the new ruler owed to his nominal father. While he was still quite young Basil had him tonsured; then, as he had an heir in the person of Constantine and as public opinion looked upon him as the father of the second child also, he associated him in the Empire with Constantine, and soon afterwards with Alexander. As long as Constantine lived, the relations between Basil and Leo were in no way unusual, but on the death of the eldest son the situation was changed. Leo now became the heir, the second place only falling to Alexander. It will easily be understood that this was a grief to Basil. At all costs he desired to set Leo aside in favour of Alexander. In the winter of 880–881 the Emperor married his adopted son to a young girl for whom he had no affection and who might be supposed unlikely to bear him children. This was Theophano, a relation of Eudocia Ingerina, afterwards St Theophano. A daughter was, nevertheless, born of this marriage, named Eudocia, but she died in 892. Her birth no doubt caused an increase of hatred on both sides. Leo roused himself, the party which he led took shape, and in 885 a revolt broke out under John Curcuas, Domestic of the Hicanati, supported by sixty-six fellow-plotters, all great dignitaries of the court. The conspirators were discovered and severely punished. Leo, who had been concerned in the affair, was betrayed by a monk named Theodore Santabarenus, and thrown into prison with his wife and little daughter. The Emperor threatened to have his eyes put out, but was dissuaded from this course by Photius himself, and some of the courtiers. Leo was restored to his dignities, but the Emperor gave him neither his confidence nor his affection. Before long, Basil died, as a result of a hunting-accident which may well have been a murder.

A light was at once shed upon the doubtful paternity of Leo by his conduct on the death of Basil I. Without bestowing much attention on the remains of his supposed father, he reserved all his care for those of his real parent, Michael III. Immediately on his accession he ordered that the body of the murdered Emperor should be solemnly removed from Chrysopolis, where it had been hastily interred in 867, and brought to Constantinople, where a magnificent funeral service was held over it in the church of the Holy Apostles. It thus appeared that he wished to emphasise the renewal, in his own person, of a dynastic tradition which had been momentarily interrupted. He then applied himself to the task of government, in theory jointly with Alexander but practically as sole ruler. The reign of Leo VI is in one sense the completion and crowning of that of Basil. All the reforms adumbrated during the late reign were achieved and codified under Leo, and the majority of the questions then left unsolved were now dealt with. To pronounce the reign a poor and feeble one is grossly unfair. It is true that, as far as foreign affairs are concerned, there is little to record and that little not of a fortunate kind. Leo VI evidently was not built on the scale of Basil. Far more at home in court and cabinet than his predecessor, he had none of the qualities of a general. This did not, however, prevent his doing useful work as a ruler.

The first religious question which confronted the new government was that of Photius. Leo was certain to be a foe to the Patriarch, who, with the help of his friend Santabarenus, had done his utmost to exacerbate Basil against his heir. He had hoped to profit by the late Emperor's weakened condition and by the youth of his successor to thrust one of his own relatives into the chief authority. In any case, it was he who, through the agency of Santabarenus, had procured the imprisonment of Leo and his family. Thus, when after his three months' disgrace Leo's dignities had been restored to him by Basil, Santabarenus had been driven to his see of Euchaita near Trebizond, there to hide himself in oblivion. But unfortunately for both parties Leo did not forget. By the new Emperor's orders, immediately upon the death of Basil, Photius was removed from his office, and a tribunal met to try his case as well as that of his accomplice. Their guilt could not in point of fact be proved, but this did not affect the result of their trial. The Patriarch was sent into exile, dying at Bordi or Gordi in Armenia in 891; Santabarenus was scourged and banished to Athens, where his eyes were put out. Then Leo's young brother Stephen, aged sixteen, was raised to the Patriarchal See at Christmas 886. His tenure of it was but brief, for he died on 17 May 893. Finally, in 900, after letters and legates had passed between Rome and Constantinople, the act uniting the two Churches was solemnly signed, Anthony Cauleas being Patriarch. By these various means the schism was brought to an end, and some measure of peace was restored to the Church.

This repose was not, indeed, of long duration, for during Leo's reign an obscure religious question arose to rekindle popular excitement and theological passion, namely, the successive marriages of the Emperor. On 10 November 893 Theophano died, and Leo was at last free to think of re-marrying. Now for a long time, to the great displeasure of Basil, Leo had maintained a mistress named Zoë, a woman, it would appear, of the worst possible reputation. Her father was Stylianus Zaützes, Leo's guardian, who had probably encouraged his sovereign's passion, for immediately upon his accession Leo loaded him with favours, put the direction of public business into his hands, and before long, having already raised him to the rank of *magister*, created for him the sounding title of *Basileopator* (894). He then married Zoë as his second wife, but a few months after her marriage she also died, during the summer of 896, without having borne a male heir to the Emperor. Contrary to all rule and custom, Leo determined on a third marriage, and in the spring of 899 he took as his wife a young Phrygian girl named Eudocia, by whose death he was again left a widower on 20 April 900. Not long after he was attracted by the daughter of a noble and saintly family, Zoë, who in allusion to her black eyes was surnamed Carbonupsina. The Emperor at first could not venture to marry her. He several times manifested his intention of doing so, but met with such general reprobation that he felt forced to refrain, until the day when Zoë gave birth to a son, afterwards Constantine VII. This was in the autumn of 905. In January 906 the child was solemnly baptised by the Patriarch, but only upon condition that Leo should dismiss Zoë. This stipulation was in accordance not only with the canons of the Byzantine Church but also with the civil laws enacted by Leo himself. Both alike forbade a fourth marriage.

It will be readily understood that this austere provision commended itself neither to Leo nor to Zoë. The Emperor wished to legitimate his sole heir and successor; Zoë hoped to become Empress and to reign. Now the Patriarch had already refused to concur in the marriage with Eudocia, and had suspended the priest who blessed the union. And, moreover, that Patriarch was Anthony Cauleas, and the question was merely of a third marriage. What was likely to be the attitude of the new Patriarch, Nicholas, towards a fourth union? Leo, however, persisted. Three days after Constantine's baptism, he married Zoë and created her Augusta. Nicholas, though he had been a friend of the Emperor from childhood and had been named Patriarch by him, did not temporise. Having in vain endeavoured to influence his master, he refused to recognise the marriage, and at the end of 906 forbade the guilty Emperor to enter St Sophia. The Patriarch had on his side the Church, the court, and the city. It was, however, agreed that Rome should be consulted on the subject. Both Nicholas and Leo wrote to the Pope, who despatched legates, and in the end granted a dispensation for the marriage. The Eastern Patriarchates also sanctioned this relaxation of the established law, and immediately Nicholas was driven into exile and resigned his office. He was succeeded by Euthymius, a saintly man, in January 907. But the conflict of course was not to be so easily extinguished. In June 911 the debates on the Emperor's fourth marriage were still going on. They lasted, indeed, up to the death of Leo (11 May 912) and even beyond it.

Leo's legislative activity shewed itself in the ecclesiastical domain as well as in the civil. Between 901 and 907, in conjunction with his friend the Patriarch Nicholas, he published a list of the Churches in dependence upon Constantinople and the order of their precedence. He thus carried through a genuine reorganisation of the outer framework of the Byzantine Church, including Illyricum in its jurisdiction, despite the repeated protests of the See of Rome. These Νέα Τακτικά which form the sequel to the Παλαιὰ Τακτικά of the preceding period shew us, in fact, the ecclesiastical provinces of the Balkan peninsula grouped around Constantinople.

Independently of this new set of regulations, and before it was issued, Leo, as soon as he succeeded to power, had addressed to his brother Stephen a series of Novels dealing with ecclesiastical affairs, the interior organisation of the Church, and religious discipline, just as the Patriarch himself might have done. It was he also who created certain new ecclesiastical honours, or gave greater importance to others already existing, such as the office of syncellus held by his brother before he became Patriarch. These measures formed part of a general scheme of reform already initiated by Basil, which Leo desired to follow up to a successful issue.

To whatever branch of the civil administration we turn, traces appear of the handiwork of Leo VI. His energy seems to have been enormous. The book of "Ceremonies," a collection published by Constantine VII, dealing with the organisation and working of the court and the different civil and religious ceremonies, contains material compiled under Leo VI. At any rate, to it was appended the Κλητορολόγιον, or ceremonial treatise of precedence at court, composed in 899 by the *atriclines* (*dapifer*) Philotheus[1]. It is plain that a re-organisation of the court was in process during Leo's reign.

With regard to the policing of the city and the regulation of commerce, we have a valuable document, the Book of the Prefect[2], containing ordinances or regulations applicable to the numerous gilds dwelling and working at Constantinople. This edict is addressed to the Prefect of the City.

For the army and navy we possess a "Tactics," *τῶν ἐν πολέμοις τακτικῶν παράδοσις*. Attempts have been made to transfer its authorship from Leo VI to Leo the Isaurian. It seems certain, however, that this work also belongs to the reign with which we are now dealing. But the great legislative achievement of Leo VI, besides his Novels dealing with civil affairs addressed to Stylianus between 887 and 893, was the publication of the important work on law initiated by Basil, which bears the name of *τὰ βασιλικά*, the *Basilics*[2]. This vast collection of the writings of Justinian and the Novels of his successors extends to sixty books. The jurists who drew up this work made a point of preserving

[1] See Bury, *The Imperial Administrative System in the Ninth Century*, which also contains a revised text of Philotheus.

[2] See *infra*, Chapter XXII, pp. 713–14.

all the writings of Justinian that had not fallen into disuse. To this they added the customs which had grown up in the course of centuries and had acquired the force of law, and also the provisions set down and promulgated by Basil in the *Prochiron* and the *Epanagoge*. To these were added a certain number of the decrees of the Iconoclast Emperors, in spite of the avowed unwillingness of the legists to make use of this heretical legislation. The work saw the light between 887 and 893.

For the sake of completeness, and in order to give a general idea of the activities of Leo VI, it is important to mention the direct share taken by the Emperor in developing the civilisation of his day. He is known as an orator. On all great public occasions, and especially at religious festivals, he was fond of delivering orations and homilies. The greater part of these have not yet been edited. Religious literature seems, indeed, to have been attractive to Leo, for besides his homilies he published liturgical works and odes, and even a letter on dogma addressed to the Caliph Omar. We have, besides, from his pen "Oracles" on the destiny of the Empire, and some secular poems.

With regard to the fine arts, Leo, like his father, restored and constructed a large number of religious buildings. The best known of these are the churches which he erected in honour of his first two wives, Theophano and Zoë, and the convent of Nossiae. Finally, the museums of Europe still preserve many specimens of artistic work, ivories and jewellery, of Leo's period.

Constantine VII Porphyrogenitus (912–959).

In some respects the character of Constantine VII bears a striking resemblance to that of his father Leo. But the father's defects, as reproduced in the son, outweigh his good qualities. Like Leo VI the Porphyrogenitus was a savant, an artist, and a scholar. Unfortunately he was not endowed with an organising mind and the same indefatigable energy. His reign, moreover, was a prolonged minority. His uncle Alexander, the Council of Regency, and Romanus Lecapenus in turn directed the government. Constantine VII himself never governed officially until 944.

Alexander (912–913).

In spite of the family hatred which divided Leo from Alexander, and in spite of the fruitless efforts of the latter to rid himself of his brother by a conspiracy formed in 900, Leo VI at his death entrusted the guardianship of his seven-year-old son to Alexander as the only genuine representative of Basil. The reign of this prince had never been more than nominal. During his brother's lifetime he had been excluded from the administration; indeed, he had excluded himself, having made himself impossible by his disgraceful behaviour. Now, jointly with his nephew and under cover of his name, he was about to attempt to govern. His attempt was short-lived, and fortunately so, for his administration brought nothing but disturbances and violent reaction in the Empire.

To the blundering policy of Alexander was due the re-appearance of schism at Constantinople, a schism on the one hand religious and on the other national. The first act of the protector, as early as May 912, was to recall the Patriarch Nicholas from exile, and to drive Euthymius with insult and violence from his see. This was a wanton outrage to the memory of Leo VI; it was also the way to confirm the people in the opinion that Zoë had never been a wife and that Constantine was not legitimate. The Church was divided as to the two Patriarchs; each had his supporters. The nation was divided on the far graver question of the legitimacy of Constantine. All the ministers of the last reign were disgraced, and Zoë was driven from the palace. In his hatred Alexander even thought of proceeding to the mutilation of his nephew. Time failed him, and he died at the most opportune moment on 6 June 913.

The Council of Regency (913–919).

According to the wish expressed by Alexander on his death-bed, a Council of Regency was appointed to govern the Empire. At the head of it was the Patriarch Nicholas, with one man of great weight, but only one, to second or counter his efforts, John Eladas. Returning as he did in triumph, the Patriarch, naturally enough, had only one idea, to maintain his own judgment as to the unlawfulness of Leo's fourth marriage. He consented, however, to wait for the death of Euthymius, which occurred on 5 April 917, before publishing his *Tomus Unionis*. Meanwhile, other events took place. His first care was to drive out Zoë, who on Alexander's death had returned to the palace, and his next was to open negotiations with all those ambitious men who were already in fancy assuming the crown, such as Constantine Ducas, Lecapenus, and Leo Phocas. The threatening aspect of foreign affairs gave these aspirants an opportunity of thrusting their services upon the State. One of them, Constantine Ducas, had narrowly failed of success. But he died just as he was about to assault the palace. The domestic situation was thus very serious, and anarchy reigned. Happily John Eladas was there to supply a remedy. Taking advantage of the unpopularity incurred by the Regents, especially through the bloody revenge which they exacted for the abortive attempt of Ducas, he skilfully contrived, with the help of one of the members of the council, to exclude the Patriarch and to recall Zoë (October 913). All the partisans of Alexander were now in their turn disgraced and banished. Nicholas received orders to confine himself henceforward to his ecclesiastical administration.

The Empire was, in fact, divided into two camps. Two hostile parties confronted each other in the army, the court, and the city. Both were military, and each was struggling to put its own leader at the head of affairs; one was for Phocas and the other for Romanus Lecapenus. Zoë had embraced the interests of Phocas, but among her entourage a certain Theodore, the influential tutor of Constantine, was negotiating with Romanus Lecapenus. It was the latter who prevailed. Thanks to the favour and skilful exertions of Theodore, Romanus obtained a footing in the palace, married his daughter Helena to Constantine, filled all the offices with his partisans, and himself assumed the title of *Basileopator*. Leo Phocas, indeed, tried the chances of a revolt. It was in vain. Being promptly abandoned by his fellow-conspirators, he was taken prisoner and suffered mutilation.

Romanus I Lecapenus (919–944).

In this manner Romanus on 25 March 919 made himself sole Regent of the Empire. He was merely a poor soldier of the Armeniac theme, a plebeian[1], as Basil had been. Leo VI had become attached to him and had thrown open the path to honours to his favourite. When the Emperor died Lecapenus was Drungarius of the fleet. He did not allow himself to be hampered by gratitude. As soon as he was left master of the situation by the exile of his opponent Phocas, he shewed himself as he really was, a hardy upstart and insatiably ambitious but a capital administrator.

He promptly seized upon the supreme power and shewed every intention of keeping it. Zoë found herself relegated to her convent, Theodore was exiled, and Constantine VII abandoned. Romanus' friend, the Patriarch Nicholas, regained his influence and governed under the name of the Regent. As early as September 919 Lecapenus had himself crowned Caesar, then on 17 December Emperor. Thenceforward his position seemed to him secure. He had, indeed, made himself master of the throne and was soon to become master of the Church.

It was with this object and in the hope of founding a new dynasty to his own advantage, that in 921, imitating the course taken by Basil, he had his wife Theodora crowned Empress and his eldest son Christopher Emperor. Feeling his power daily increasing despite the conspiracies incessantly woven around him, in 923 he set the imperial crown on the head of his daughter-in-law, and in 924 crowned his other two sons, Stephen and Constantine. From 922, besides, the coinage and official documents shew that he already took precedence of the rightful sovereign.

In political matters Romanus was unquestioned master, and it

[1] "The Lord Emperor Romanus was a man without breeding or education, who had not been brought up in the Palace, was ignorant of Roman law and custom, was not of noble and imperial birth, and was all the more rash and audacious in his actions." He is thus described by Constantine VII.

must be acknowledged that his government was not wanting in greatness. Shrewd and clever, he received in magnificent fashion in 923 Ashot II, King of Armenia, Adernesih, the Curopalates of Iberia (at this time a vassal of the Empire), and the princes of the family of Taron. We find him (as well as the Patriarch Nicholas) keeping up continuous relations with most of the rulers of these distant lands, receiving them hospitably, giving them help against the Arabs, and above all making treaties with them through his diplomatists, greatly to the advantage of Byzantium, which thus acquired considerable influence in their countries. On another frontier of the Empire, the Bulgarians, during the Tsar Simeon's reign, had caused him much anxiety and serious injury. All his diplomatic skill had been useless before the arms of the Tsar. But on Simeon's death more amicable relations were resumed with his son Peter, and Romanus, imitating earlier Emperors, bestowed his granddaughter Mary in marriage upon the young king on 8 September 927, and signed a peace with Bulgaria. In this manner he very adroitly detached the Bulgarian Church from the Papacy and bound it to Constantinople, which, both in ecclesiastical and political matters, was obtaining an evident preponderance.

In home politics, Romanus' attention, like that of his predecessors, was drawn to social problems. The provincial aristocracy were nothing short of a scourge. By their wealth and their grinding of the poor the "powerful" ruined the peasantry and the government with them. Again it became imperative to retrace the steps that had been taken. This was the object of the numerous Novels which the government of Lecapenus put forth. In 922 and 934 two laws were enacted forbidding the rich to acquire land belonging to the poor or to the military class. Those who were injured in this way received a preferential right of repurchase for their protection. Two other Novels allowed the seller a right of re-entry, on repayment, in case of a sale forced by famine, and pronounced a sale null and void if effected to the prejudice of the right of re-purchase. All these Novels had as their object the protection of the small holdings, the basis of general prosperity. No doubt the occasion that called them forth was the suffering caused by the terrible winter of 933, when famine brought about the ruin and death of large numbers of the population.

In the domain of religion, the influence of the Patriarch Nicholas Mysticus remained predominant up to his death on 15 May 925. His correspondence shews him busying himself with political and foreign affairs. He is in touch with Simeon, Tsar of Bulgaria, and with the Pope at Rome. Nor is it strange that he should have sought to impose his opinion on the vexed question of fourth marriages. In June 920 a Council met at Constantinople to deal with the subject, and it was on this occasion that he published the Τόμος τῆς ἑνώσεως, the decree of union which condemned fourth and cast blame on third marriages.

Nevertheless, something had been gained. The Council had restored harmony among all Byzantines.

The authority of Romanus, so long as Nicholas lived, was exercised mainly upon political matters. Religious concerns were felt to be in safe hands. But, on the death of the Patriarch, the Emperor, carrying on the system of Basil I, wished to put the government of the Church in the hands of his youngest son, Theophylact. Unfortunately, though already syncellus (patriarchal secretary), Theophylact was only a child of eight or ten years old. It was necessary to wait. Two Patriarchs appointed *ad interim*, Stephen and Tryphon, filled the post until 931. In 933, after a vacancy of eighteen months, Theophylact was at last elected and John XI ratified the choice. The new Patriarch, to the great scandal of Constantinople, was to remain in office up to his death on 27 February 956. It was during this wretched patriarchate, in 942, that the famous "Image of Edessa" was brought to Constantinople. It was a linen cloth on which, it was said, our Lord had left the trace of His features, and which He had sent to Abgar as a token of friendship. Curcuas, the general, had acquired it in exchange for a prisoner and had sent it to Constantinople, where it was received with great solemnity.

This acquisition of a famous relic was the last triumph of Lecapenus. In spite of the charity which he shewed towards the inhabitants of his capital during the famine of 927 and the severe winter of 933, in spite of the substantial sums which he distributed to the poor, the hospitals which he erected, and the public works of all kinds which he undertook, Romanus was not in the least beloved at Constantinople. Constantine VII still had supporters and friends. He was both pitied and respected. "He who should have been first found himself made fifth," and this excited great displeasure. Deprived of everything, of power and of the appearance of power, it was said that he was even obliged to work as an artist in order to maintain himself. On the other hand, Romanus Lecapenus had implacable enemies, even in his own sons, who were jealous of his authority and eager to seize upon it for themselves. Perhaps these domestic broils were fomented by the influence of Constantine's friends; possibly it was these faithful servants of the real Emperor who counselled the "Lecapenides" to rebel. No one knows. Only one thing is certain, that, after the death of Christopher, the sons of Romanus on 16 December 944 carried off their father, banished him to a convent in the Island of Proti, and forced him to take the monastic habit. They counted upon succeeding to his place. But they only met with the just punishment of their guilt. At the very hour when they were to have dethroned Constantine, the Emperor had them seized and despatched them to join their father on 27 January 945. Romanus Lecapenus died, a few years after his fall, in 948.

Constantine's Personal Government (944–959).

The family of Romanus Lecapenus before long survived only in the female line. Stephen was deported to Rhodes and Lesbos, where he was poisoned in 963; Constantine was relegated to Samothrace and assassinated by his guard; while of the other Lecapenides whose fate is known, Romanus, Michael, and Basil only suffered mutilation, and thus survived to reappear later in political life. Alone of his family, the despised Theophylact remained at Constantinople.

The first steps taken by Constantine naturally began a reaction. He dismissed the relations, friends, and partisans of Romanus Lecapenus, and surrounded himself with members of the rival faction of Phocas, which, thanks to Constantine's patronage, we shall soon find in possession of the imperial throne. This violent reaction did not fail of the usual result, in the shape of numerous conspiracies. Both in 945 and in 947 the supporters of Romanus made a move. But it was in vain, and cruel punishments and mutilations followed. Constantine, who thus at the age of thirty-nine took the reins of government into his own hands, was much more of a student than a man of action. Though usually of a mild and even timid disposition, he was subject to terrible fits of anger, when he became violent and even cruel. For the rest, although an accomplished judge of wine and cookery, he was evidently not the man destined to restore the Empire's former glories. The government at once fell into the hands of his wife Helena, and a favourite, Basil, known as the Bird (πετεινός). Apparently neither of them accomplished anything of importance, and they confined themselves to selling public offices to the highest bidders. Scandals took place which the Emperor, buried as he was in his books, had not the resolution to punish and put down. Such, for example, was the conduct of that Prefect of the City who was "a notorious robber" but nevertheless administered the police of Constantinople, loaded with favours conferred by the Emperor.

It must, however, be acknowledged that Constantine's family circle was a singular one. His wife, the Empress Helena, was by no means above reproach, but she compares favourably with others of his connexions. In 939 a son had been born to him, Romanus II, who from his early days gave promise of utter worthlessness, in spite of the affection which his father shewed for him and the care which he bestowed on his education. In the reign of Lecapenus, in 944, the Regent had arranged a marriage for him with Bertha, the illegitimate daughter of Hugh of Provence and Pezola. This unequal connexion was an insult to the Macedonian House, but worse was in store. The poor Provençale lived only five years at Constantinople, and is said to have died a virgin. But after her death not merely disparity but shame and crime entered the palace in the person of Romanus' second wife, a courtesan, the daughter of a tavern-keeper, whom he married at the end of 956. She had been known as Anastaso at the Hippodrome; as Empress she took the name of Theophano. According to the majority of the chroniclers, she was the Brinvilliers of her age. Before practising as a poisoner herself, she induced her husband to poison Constantine VII, and with partial success, for the Emperor died, if not immediately, still in the end from the effects of the drug administered to him. This was but her first step in the path of crime, as was tragically shewn in the succeeding reigns. As to the rest of the court dignitaries whose names have come down to us, they were little more to be respected. The only sound portion of the governing body was to be found in the army.

The Church, as represented by the Patriarch Theophylact, kept pace with the court. Doubtless among the occupants of monasteries and bishoprics it would not be difficult to find shining examples of holy living. But the patriarchate was given up to disorder, license, and impiety. So great was the scandal caused by Theophylact's conduct that the Emperor, who tolerated it, was involved in the discredit. Consequently, when the Patriarch was killed by a fall from his horse in February 956, Constantine was compelled, in order to repair the mischief that had been done, to seek out an austere monk of Proti whose fame was widespread, named Polyeuctes. The new Patriarch was a reformer, and fully resolved to impose on all alike a discipline which had become a necessity. In his solitary life he had acquired great spiritual exaltation and a resolute will; he was, in the full sense of the word, a man of faith. At first he was joyfully received on all hands. The Emperor fully expected that this poor monk, bred at a distance from worldly intrigues, could be held in the hollow of his hand; pious folk looked forward to the reforms which the Patriarch desired to carry out; and the court bishops promised themselves that they could always bring about Polyeuctes' resignation should he prove disposed to interfere too much with their habits. This seemed all the more feasible, inasmuch as Polyeuctes' consecration had not been performed according to the customary rules. He was, in fact, consecrated on 3 April 956 by Basil, Metropolitan of Caesarea. This was quite contrary to precedent, for according to law the right belonged to Nicephorus, Bishop of Heraclea; but as the latter was in bad odour at court, his services were refused by Constantine, who deliberately set him aside. Nothing more was needed, it was supposed, to quash the appointment of Polyeuctes and send him back to his convent. And in fact, from the very outset of his patriarchate, cabals were formed against him, of which Theodore, Bishop of Cyzicus, was the moving spirit. His rigour was at once made a reproach to him, as also was his narrowness of view and his action in restoring the name of the Patriarch Euthymius, formerly struck out of the diptychs by Nicholas. Efforts were made to ruin him. But Polyeuctes was not the man to yield. Far from cringing before his adversaries, he attacked the Emperor himself, and on one occasion openly demanded that he should make good all the injuries inflicted on the Church by his family and by the preceding patriarchate. To put forward such a claim was to make a public declaration of his independence. Constantine so well understood this that he was preparing to have the election of Polyeuctes quashed when he died.

From the administrative and political point of view the personal government of Constantine Porphyrogenitus is undeniably of small importance. Some of the chroniclers even represent the Emperor as an idler and a do-nothing. But this is a grotesque exaggeration. On the other hand, we cannot place entire confidence in the flatterers who depict Constantine as an administrator ever on the alert to lessen the evils afflicting his people, to give orders to his provincial governors, to keep himself well informed of all that was happening, to give brilliant receptions to ambassadors, and to keep in touch with the rulers of East and West. It is nevertheless certain that Constantine endeavoured on the one hand to do the work of an administrator, and on the other shewed himself throughout his life by his intellectual activity and his numerous writings not to be the indolent trifler of the chronicler Cedrenus. In the first place, we have nine Novels of his to prove that he too paid attention to the juridical and social questions which had caused such constant anxiety to his predecessors. Like them, he forbids the wealthy nobles to acquire lands belonging to the poor or the military class; like them, he legislates on certain points of civil law, such as wills, inheritance, the salaries payable to notaries, the right of sanctuary, and so forth. But he did more than this. Towards the end of his reign he issued an alphabetical abridgment of the *Basilics* intended to be of service to lawyers. Finally, during the time of his personal government he granted a chrysobull in favour of the monastery of St John the Baptist at Thessalonica, and another to the convent of the Iberians on Mount Athos.

Apart from these beneficent laws, Constantine, who piqued himself on his knowledge of the rules of etiquette, and was fond of holding himself up as an example to the splendid and stately court which surrounded him, seems to have taken special pleasure in the reception and despatch of great numbers of ambassadors. In 945 and 949 we find him sending diplomatic missions to Otto I in Germany; in May and in August 946 he received the ambassadors of the Caliph and the Emir of Amida with great magnificence; in October it was the turn of the ambassadors from Spain; in 948 that of Liudprand, Berengar's envoy; and finally in 957 he gave a brilliant welcome to the Russian Princess Olga and the splendid cortège which accompanied her, including both men and women. All the indications point to this visit to Constantinople as the time when the baptism of Olga took place[1].

But the true glory of Constantine VII is the share which he had in the intellectual movement of his day. Like Bardas under Michael III, he

[1] See, however, *infra*, Chapter VII (A), p. 207, for another view.

made great efforts to revive education, which, outside Constantinople, was hardly to be obtained; he appointed to the university chairs savants of reputation, historians, writers, philosophers, men of science, jurisconsults; like Basil I he gave a new impetus to all the arts, architecture, painting, sculpture, and music; while, more than any of his predecessors, he interested himself in students, receiving them, helping them, and when their studies were finished promoting them to great civil and ecclesiastical posts. He himself helped forward this general literary renaissance by working at painting, music, and the industrial arts, as also by publishing, especially for his son's use, several works, some of which are lost, though others have come down to us. About 934 or 935 he wrote the *Book of the Themes* or provinces of the Empire; in 952 or 953 he published the *Book of the Administration of the Empire*, and composed the first eighty-three chapters of the *Book of Court Ceremonies* which bears his name; finally in 958 or 959 he gave to the public the *Life of Basil.* Thus it is not strange that under his government literary and artistic production should have been abundant. Thanks to him, numberless religious and secular buildings were erected, restored, and embellished; such works as the *Continuation of Theophanes*, the *Discourse upon the Image of Edessa*, and other compositions of literary and religious importance were begun and finished, so that it is in fact almost solely to the learned labours of an Emperor, so often decried, that we owe such knowledge as we possess of the period in which he lived and reigned.

Either in the summer or in the autumn of 959, Constantine, feeling himself near to death, went, in search of some measure of physical and mental repose, to the slopes of Mount Olympus in Bithynia, then celebrated for the medicinal waters of Sotiriopolis, and for its monasteries and hermits. He was to find there nothing but gloomy presages of his speedy end. He returned to Constantinople only to die, expiring on 9 November 959 at the age of fifty-four.

Romanus II (959–963).

The new ruler, Romanus II, was twenty years old when his father died, probably as the result of the poison which he and his wife administered to him. Despite his youth and his bodily and mental advantages, despite his excellent education, Romanus II was to make but a transitory appearance as Emperor, and to leave a most unworthy reputation behind him. At his accession he was surrounded by his mother Helena, his wife Theophano, his five sisters, and his son Basil II. He had been crowned and had received a share of the imperial power, in accordance with the Basilian tradition, in 945, and he now at once took possession of the government, or rather handed it over to his wife Theophano. We have already seen who this wife was. The daughter of Craterus, a poor tavern-keeper of Laconian origin, she owed the unhoped-for honour of ascending the throne solely to her beauty and her vices. While her husband eagerly pursued, surrounded by unworthy companions, the life of debauchery and dissipation which was destined to lead him to an early grave, she for her part took upon herself the task of government with the help of a noble eunuch, Joseph Bringas, whom Constantine on his death-bed had recommended to Romanus.

This reign would be utterly insignificant were it not lighted up by the eventful military triumphs of Nicephorus Phocas and his brother. Indeed, within the imperial circle things immediately began to take a mischievous turn: Helena and her daughters, by order of Theophano and with the consent of Romanus II, were forced to quit the palace for a convent. Helena, it is true, obtained leave to remain in the palace, where she died on 19 September 961, but her daughters, Zoë, Theodora, Theophano, Anne, and Agatha were sent first to the convent of Canicleum, and soon after to separate houses. It was probably the harsh treatment dealt out to Constantine's family which, in March 961, brought about the conspiracy, formed, with the help of other lords, by that Basil the Bird who had been the favourite, perhaps the lover, of Helena in the preceding reign. Knowing that Romanus was about to visit the Hippodrome, Basil resolved on his assassination, but being informed against by a converted Saracen named Johannicius, he was seized, tortured, and finally died insane in Proconnesus.

Though dying young, Romanus was to leave a large family to the Empire. In addition to Basil II, he had a second son by Theophano in 961, the future Constantine VIII whom the Patriarch Polyeuctes crowned in April the same year. He had, besides, two daughters, of whom one, Theophano, born perhaps as early as 956, became the wife of Otto II of Germany, and the other, Anne, was married to Vladímir of Russia. The two sons of Romanus II were to reign in Constantinople between Tzimisces and the daughters of Constantine VII.

Historians and chroniclers record no event of importance in the internal administration of the Empire during the years from 959 to 963. The government under Romanus gave its whole attention to events beyond the frontiers. And in this field it unquestionably acted with judgment and ability. Immediately upon the death of Constantine, Theophano and Bringas shewed themselves desirous of maintaining or creating advantageous relations with the rulers of the East and the West. They sent ambassadors to every court. Then on 22 April 960 they had the little Basil II crowned. But it was above all by planning the campaign of Nicephorus against the Saracens that they gave proof of political discernment. They felt the need of making an end once for all with these enemies, who were ever increasing in aggressiveness, and in Nicephorus Phocas they had a man great enough to engage these perennial foes at an advantage. In spite of unending court intrigues, the government in July

960 laid upon this general, though he was suspected by many, the task of attacking the Arabs of Crete, supported him energetically, supplied him with reinforcements, and thus prepared the way for the great victory which Nicephorus won on 7 March 961 resulting in the conquest of Chandax (now Candia) in Crete. Accordingly when the general returned to Constantinople he received in the Circus the honour of a pedestrian ovation, a foretaste of the triumphs which later were to be his. Both concentration on foreign affairs and skilful diplomacy were displayed by Theophano's government on the morrow of Nicephorus' victory. He returned covered with glory and accompanied by the defeated emir, 'Abd-al-'Azīz. This chief was well treated and splendidly lodged, and Constantinople had no reason to regret her generosity, for his son, having become a Christian, won renown in 972 in the Byzantine army.

It appears that, during the short time that he remained at the head of affairs, Bringas also paid attention to the material interests of the population. In October 961 there was a great dearth, and corn was at an extravagant price. He brought into the capital ship-loads of corn and barley, which, despite his reputation for avarice, he sold at half-price.

Then came a check. The Byzantine armies were winning brilliant successes in Asia, due entirely to the two Phocas brothers, when Nicephorus suddenly learned that Romanus had died at the palace on 15 March 963. Though the end was sudden it was not unforeseen, for the Emperor's health had been declining all the winter. Theophano was nevertheless accused of having rid herself of her husband by poison in order to marry Nicephorus. The crime was never proved, but the sequel was just what had been prophesied. With Romanus II the glory of the Macedonian House and the intellectual renaissance which it had initiated departed for a time. Government by women and successful soldiers was about to begin.

Nicephorus Phocas (963–969).

At the moment when Romanus II was gathered to his fathers in the church of the Holy Apostles, leaving the Empire in the hands of Theophano, Bringas, and two crowned children, the already illustrious name of Phocas had, in the course of four years from 960 to 963, reached the highest pitch of glory. This was owing to the achievements of Leo and even more of Nicephorus, who was at that time the chief personage of the Empire. The Phocas family, which originated in Cappadocia, was indeed well known to fame. It was, with the families of Curcuas and Tzimisces, among the noblest in Asia Minor. In the days of Basil I, a Nicephorus Phocas, grandfather of the future Emperor, had won renown by his warlike exploits in Italy and Sicily, and since then all of the family, from father to son, had been soldiers, and successful soldiers. The uncle and father of Nicephorus had been specially distinguished by their valour—the former, Leo, by his share in the war with the Bulgarians, and the latter, Bardas, by his victories in Asia Minor. The man who now, by his marriage with Theophano, was about to ascend the throne of Constantinople had, with his brother Leo, followed the glorious path marked out for him. Magister, and generalissimo of the armies of the East, under Constantine VII, he had long warred successfully in Asia Minor, and had since covered himself with glory by the siege of Chandax. He was born probably about 913, and was thus nearly fifty when the death of Romanus II took place. At this period, monk and soldier were united in him. Having lost his wife and his only son a little before 963, he had often thought of going to join his friend St Athanasius, the founder of the Great Laura, on Mount Athos. It was through his interest and his gifts that the first convent on the "Holy Mountain" had been built, and a cell there had long awaited him. A man of iron temper, mystical to the highest degree, and yet none the less a man of passions, he had devoted himself to his army and his men, and at the same time to prayer and the severest mortifications. He was reported to be unbendingly stern, uncompromisingly just, and rigidly pious, but he was also considered miserly. In spite of his failings, his shining qualities won for him general love and deep respect, above all in the camp. On the other hand he was dreaded by many, and especially by Bringas, on account of his military fame and the brilliant campaign with which his name was inseparably joined. After the conquest of Crete, he had, however, returned to Asia Minor and to his brother, conquering Cilicia between 961 and 963. He had then flung himself upon Syria, and had just taken Aleppo when the news of the death of Romanus forced him to pause.

Theophano (16 *March*–14 *August* 963).

At Constantinople the death of Romanus had created a most difficult situation. Theophano, at twenty years of age, naturally desired to retain power and to act as Regent, as she was authorised to do by her husband's last dispositions. But Bringas had to be reckoned with, and his projects, it would appear, tended in quite another direction. He, with his partisans, counted upon seizing sole power at the first favourable moment and governing the Empire. Thus, though he had supported Nicephorus at the time of the Cretan expedition, yet out of dread of his popularity and perhaps also from other motives he had made haste to send him back to Asia Minor. This, however, had not prevented Nicephorus, doubtless without Bringas' knowledge, from being kept informed by the Empress herself of all that went on. It was, indeed, of importance to Theophano, if she was to make herself safe in all contingencies, to be able to make use of Nicephorus, before whom she had held out the hope of supreme power and even of something more. As the general was on his way through Constantinople she had, with great skill, contrived to plant in the austere soldier's heart the germs of a passion which she intended to turn to account, and which was to drive from his mind any pious aspirations after the monastic life and permanently to deflect the current of his existence. It was this, probably, which had so greatly excited the alarm of Bringas.

Nevertheless, for the moment, the expressed wishes of Romanus were respected. The Patriarch Polyeuctes proclaimed Theophano Regent, with Bringas as her minister. Immediately afterwards, however, Theophano secretly called back Nicephorus, who reached Constantinople as early as April. Officially he came to receive the reward of his conquests, a military triumph and the confirmation of his authority. In reality he came to measure himself against the head of the government. So well did Bringas understand this that he at once attempted to rid himself of his formidable adversary. He proposed that he should be forbidden to enter Constantinople, that a triumph should be refused him, and even that his eyes should be put out. All these attempts failed before the universal popularity of Nicephorus, probably helped by the intrigues of Theophano. The people welcomed Nicephorus with all possible honour and magnificence. But on the morrow of this ceremonial reception, which so greatly increased his prestige, being alone and without his army, he felt himself in danger and took refuge in St Sophia. There he obtained from the Patriarch and his clergy the protection of which he stood in need. Thanks to his reputation for piety, his valuable connexion with the monks, his services, and the animosities which divided the three most powerful forces in Constantinople—Theophano, Bringas, and Polyeuctes—Nicephorus found a steadfast supporter in the Patriarch. In spite of Bringas, and thanks to Polyeuctes, the Senate fully confirmed the authority of Nicephorus, and promised that nothing should be done without his being consulted. Nicephorus, in return, swore to engage in no design injurious to the rights of the young princes. The Patriarch's eloquence had saved Nicephorus, who, as soon as Easter was over, lost no time in returning to Asia Minor at the head of his army. Bringas had been outwitted. The Patriarch had no suspicion of what his own future would be under Nicephorus.

The chief minister, however, did not acknowledge himself defeated. At any cost, whether Nicephorus were present or absent, he sought his life. For this he manoeuvred, but clumsily enough. Through a confidential agent he made splendid offers to two of Nicephorus' generals, Curcuas and Tzimisces, if they would betray their chief to him. They, however, far from lending an ear to such proposals, revealed the intrigue to Nicephorus, and in order to cut matters short, prevailed on him without difficulty to hasten the realisation of his plans, to assume the crown, and to march upon Constantinople. Accordingly on 3 July 963 the army, instigated by the two generals, proclaimed Nicephorus Emperor at Caesarea. The next day, the troops set out to accompany him to St

Sophia and there to have him crowned. As soon as the news was known at Constantinople the mutterings of revolt began. Bringas tried to make head against it, and to organise the defence. His partisans were numerous, even among the troops in the capital, and he had valuable hostages in his hands in the persons of the father and brother of Nicephorus. The new sovereign reached Chrysopolis on 9 August and there awaited events. After three days of furious revolution had dyed the streets of Constantinople with blood, the supporters of Bringas were defeated. Nicephorus' father was saved by Polyeuctes, and on 14 August 963, under the aegis of Basil, the illegitimate son of Romanus Lecapenus and a bitter enemy of Bringas, Nicephorus entered Constantinople. On 16 August he was crowned in St Sophia, declaring himself the guardian of the imperial children.

Government of Nicephorus.

The revolution to which Nicephorus had just put the finishing touch was the culmination of hypocrisy, for everyone knew, by the recent example of Romanus Lecapenus, the real meaning of the title of guardian, or joint sovereign, in connexion with Emperors who were still minors. Whatever fictions might adorn official documents, it was Nicephorus who became Emperor, and sole Emperor. The monks, his former friends, were scandalised. St Athanasius, quite in vain, reminded the Emperor of his former vocation for the religious life. And it soon appeared that still more ruthless disillusionments were in store. Apart from this, the action of Nicephorus was, politically speaking, of great gravity. Once again he severed the dynastic chain. And this time the breach in the succession was made not merely in his own name and for his personal benefit, or out of family ambition, but in the name and with the support of the army, which was now to re-learn the lesson of thrusting its weighty sword into the scale in which the internal destinies of the Empire were balanced. It is true that for all this Nicephorus paid a heavy penalty, and it is no less true that the course he took was to have the most disastrous influence on the fortunes of Constantinople.

At the very outset, as soon as he was master of the palace and the city, Nicephorus hastened to deal out titles and rewards to those who had aided him. His father was declared Caesar, his brother Leo magister and curopalates, while in the East John Tzimisces succeeded to the post, rank, and honours which Nicephorus had held. Basil received the title and appointment of *Proedros* or President of the Senate. As to Bringas, he was of course dismissed, and was detained at a distance from Constantinople in a monastery, where he died in 971. These arrangements made, Nicephorus turned his thoughts towards a marriage with Theophano, both from personal and from political considerations. The matter, however, was not quite so simple as at first it looked. Both the Church and lay society might have something to say on the subject. It was probably in order to gain time to reconcile the public mind to the idea, as well as to observe the proprieties, that Nicephorus, acting in accord with the Empress, sent her away to the palace of Petrion on the Golden Horn until the day fixed for the wedding. It took place on 20 September, six months almost to a day after the death of Romanus. As might have been expected, it aroused great displeasure among the clergy. St Athanasius was much incensed against his old friend, and Polyeuctes, finding himself tricked, steadily refused communion to Nicephorus for a whole year. For, on the one hand, there was to the monks, of whom the Patriarch was one, something distinctly scandalous in the spectacle of this man of fifty marrying a woman in the twenties; this austere general, ascetic almost to a fault, who had vowed to end his days as a celibate in a monastery, now, having by the help of the Church attained to supreme power, suddenly uniting himself to Theophano, one of the most ill-famed and vicious of women, utterly repulsive in the eyes of the religious world. On the other hand, the newly-wedded couple, having both been widowed, could not, without doing penance, enter upon a second marriage. The determined refusal of Polyeuctes was, however, very offensive both to Nicephorus and Theophano. We are told that Nicephorus never forgave the Patriarch. This Polyeuctes was soon to learn, and not only he but the whole body of the clergy was to suffer in consequence.

The ecclesiastical struggle, thus inauspiciously begun on the marriage-day of Nicephorus, ended only with his death. If the chroniclers are to be trusted, it was further envenomed by the rumours set afloat by a court chaplain named Stylianus. He claimed, indeed, that the Emperor's marriage with Theophano was unlawful and void, because Nicephorus had stood godfather to one, if not two, of the Empress' children. The canons were absolutely conclusive against such unions, which were forbidden by "spiritual affinity." It is not very easy to determine how much foundation there was for the statement. It is certainly strange if Polyeuctes were ignorant of a circumstance so serious and notorious, and if Nicephorus and Theophano on their side took no notice of this ecclesiastical impediment. Was the allegation of Stylianus made before or after the marriage ceremony? Even on this point the chroniclers give us no answer. However this may be, one thing is plain, that Polyeuctes was roused, and he demanded of Nicephorus under the heaviest canonical penalties the repudiation of Theophano. Naturally the Emperor refused, and at once gathered together an assembly, half ecclesiastical and half lay, to discuss the question. This miniature council, composed of court bishops and officials devoted to the royal family, made no difficulty about coming to the decision which Nicephorus would be likely to desire. The regulation on which Polyeuctes relied was, it was decided, invalid, although its meaning was unmistakable, because it had been put forth in the name of a heretical Emperor, Constantine

Copronymus. Further, to bolster up this rather pitiful decision, Stylianus came forward to declare solemnly that Nicephorus had never been godfather to any one of the imperial children, and that he himself had never spoken the incriminating words. It is not known whether Polyeuctes was convinced, but it is probable, for, averse from compromise as he was, he yet admitted the Emperor to the Holy Communion. But what after all do these stories amount to? Nothing can be positively known. It is plain that they fit in badly with what knowledge we have of the manners of the age and the characters of its chief personages. It would appear that, if the struggle had been as heated and as much founded in reason on the part of the Patriarch as is represented, the latter would not then have hesitated to maintain his condemnation and Nicephorus would probably have deposed him. If both consented to an apparent reconciliation, we must believe that the chroniclers either exaggerated, or what is more likely, misunderstood the nature of the dispute. It is not impossible that at bottom the whole affair was merely a quarrel got up by the monks, who were indignant at the conduct of Nicephorus and at his marriage.

This explanation of these events is supported by the fact that at once, in 964, Nicephorus, as though to take his revenge, published a Novel as strange as it was revolutionary against the monks. He, who had once so greatly loved the religious, turned suddenly to scoffing at and sitting in judgment on his old friends. "The monks," he says, "possess none of the evangelical virtues; they think only of acquiring worldly goods, of building, and of enriching themselves. Their life differs in nothing from that of the thorough worldling." They were ordered to leave the cities and go forth into the wilderness, abandoning all their lands and goods. It was no doubt to help them along this path that he forbade (though he had himself given large sums to St Athanasius when he founded his convent on Mount Athos) that new monasteries should be established or others enriched by new donations, or that lands, fields, or villas should be left by will to convents, hospitals, or clergy.

This celebrated Novel had, it would seem, a double object. It gave Nicephorus the means of avenging himself upon the monks for the humiliations they had lately inflicted on him, and it enabled him also to find the necessary supplies which he wanted to carry on the war. "The revenues were intended indeed," he said, "to be distributed to the poor, but in reality they profited none but the clergy, and this while the soldiers, who were going forth to fight and die for God and the Emperor, lacked even necessaries." The fact was that Nicephorus wished as Emperor to prosecute the expeditions which he had begun as a private subject. From 964 to 966 the Empire resounded with the clash of arms. While his generals were fighting the African Arabs in Sicily and Cyprus, Nicephorus himself twice went forth to encounter the Asiatic Saracens in Cilicia, Mesopotamia, and Syria. For these distant wars he needed large sums of money, and it was the property of the clergy, which as long as he lived he never spared, that supplied him with funds.

This doubled-edged policy was made clear and obvious during the winter of 966–967, immediately upon the Emperor's return to Constantinople. Thanks to the court bishops, in residence at the capital and thus in the Emperor's power, he embodied in an edict a measure in the highest degree injurious to the Church. For the future it was declared unlawful to nominate any subject to a bishopric without the Emperor's consent. In this way Nicephorus made sure of having bishops entirely at his devotion, and at the same time he could seize upon the Church revenues, whether during the vacancy of a see or after an appointment had been made. There are many examples to prove this. It is not known what attitude the clergy took up on this matter. In no quarter do we hear of revolts or of coercive measures, but doubtless such a policy must have powerfully furthered the rise of the popular movement which thrust Nicephorus from power. In any case, the first demand of Polyeuctes on the accession of Tzimisces was to be for the abrogation of these anti-clerical measures.

The last fact which the chroniclers record in connexion with ecclesiastical matters in this reign, is the strange idea conceived by the Emperor of constraining the Church to venerate as martyrs those who had fallen in the warfare against the infidel. Naturally, nobody was found willing to comply with this eccentric demand, and Nicephorus was compelled to abandon a project opposed by Polyeuctes and the whole of the clergy.

Putting aside this perennial quarrel with the churchmen, which itself had a military aim, Nicephorus seems during his short reign to have had little attention to spare for anything but his soldiers and the army. It was this, indeed, which before long predisposed the populace towards that movement of revolt which was to bring about his speedy ruin. Quite early in the reign, after the example of his predecessors, Nicephorus revived the laws favouring the small military holdings and protecting them against the vexatious and extortionate purchase of them by the great. He granted his soldiers the widest facilities for regaining possession of their lands when they had been sold or stolen, and this evidently with a view to retaining their services in the army. Then, legislating in accordance with his own experience, he issued a Novel dealing with the Armenian *fundi*, that is, the fiefs belonging to those Armenian soldiers, mercenaries in the service of the Empire, who had obtained military lands in return for their services but did not always fulfil the obligations which their tenure imposed upon them. In 967 and at another date not exactly known, Nicephorus issued two more Novels touching landed property, and especially the property of the rich. The Emperor required that each man should keep what he possessed, or at least should acquire lands only from those set apart for his caste. A noble might only possess noble fiefs; a commoner only commoners' fiefs;

a soldier only military allotments. This was plainly to protect and strengthen the very framework of Byzantine society. Unfortunately these laws, the character of which was further emphasised by countless instances, were too exclusively military in their scope. The exaggerated importance attached to the army was shewn in every possible way, and ended by irritating and exciting the public mind. About 966 and 967 the mutterings of revolt began to be heard on every side.

If the many excesses of the army, and the marks of exclusive favour which Nicephorus lavished on it, were the chief causes of the Byzantine revolution which swept away the Emperor, they were not the only ones. The anti-clerical policy of Nicephorus had already alienated numbers of his subjects. His military policy fostered the spread of this disaffection. But, above all, his fiscal measures provoked general discontent. In consequence of the wars of the Empire, more and more money was constantly being required by the government. Taxes increased at a prodigious rate, while in other directions retrenchments were made in habitual expenditure, which estranged all classes, nobles and commoners. As if all this had been insufficient, exceptional measures were now taken. Not only did the tax-gatherers receive strict orders to exact the taxes, but, more serious still, the Emperor himself trafficked in corn, wine, and oil, of which commodities the government had a monopoly, thus causing such a rise in the cost of living that riots began to break out in almost every direction. On Ascension Day (9 May 967), as Nicephorus was returning from his devotions, he was stopped by crowds of people and insulted in the heart of Constantinople, stones and tiles being thrown at him. He would certainly have perished, but that his faithful bodyguard covered his hasty retreat to the palace. This insurrection had no other effect than to make Nicephorus aware of his danger. It did not avail to change his line of policy. For his own defence, without reckoning with his recent fresh expenditure, he had a strong high wall built to surround the Great Palace completely, and within its circuit, close to the sea, he erected the fortress of Bucoleon where he was to meet his death.

Like the earlier years of Nicephorus, his last two were entirely given up to war on all sides. There were wars in Bulgaria and Italy, and in Syria, where Antioch and Aleppo were taken. Among home events, two only are worth recording. One was the arrival at Constantinople in 967 of the Bulgarian ambassadors, claiming the tribute which the Empire had been accustomed to pay to the Tsar. Nicephorus, who was on the watch for a pretext to declare war against his neighbour, received the ambassadors roughly, insulted them before the whole court, and drove them ignominiously away. Soon afterwards, he set out at the head of his troops for Bulgaria. The other event, which was of the same character, was the embassy of Liudprand, Bishop of Cremona, now sent for the second time to Constantinople by the Emperor Otto. Liudprand arrived in the East on 4 June 968. His master, after his usurpations in southern Italy and his assumption of the title of Emperor, had made him the bearer of a pacific message and a proposal of marriage. The German sovereign hoped to bring the struggle in Italy to an advantageous conclusion, and to secure quiet possession of the provinces which he had conquered, by means of a marriage between his son and Theophano, daughter of Romanus II. The embassy met with wretched success. Liudprand, detained as a half-prisoner and publicly insulted by Nicephorus and his court, spent four months at Constantinople, and was obliged to leave without having obtained any concession. For the time the marriage fell into abeyance; the idea was only resumed later, and the union did not take place until 972.

Immediately after Liudprand's embassy, about the end of July 968, Nicephorus set out for a campaign in Asia Minor, and did not return to Constantinople until the beginning of 969. Notwithstanding the fresh laurels which he had reaped in Syria, only death awaited him. Disaffection to his rule was daily growing and plots were openly discussed. On the other hand, Theophano had found a new lover, and John Tzimisces had become the Emperor's successful rival in love as he had already been in war. As Schlumberger has pointed out, the whole clue to the palace drama, in which these two were the chief actors, escapes our grasp. How and why did Theophano and Tzimisces decide upon ridding themselves of Nicephorus? We do not know, nor do contemporaries seem to have known. All the conjectures put forward by chroniclers, Byzantine, Arab, and Western, are possible, but of none is there a shadow of proof. Two things only are certain, first, the passion of Theophano for Tzimisces, secondly, the plot to kill the Emperor, which they jointly concocted with the help of several other conspirators. The murder took place in the night of 10–11 December 969. By Theophano's means the palace was opened to Tzimisces and his confederates, and they, without difficulty, made their way into Nicephorus' chamber. They found the Emperor asleep, lying on a tiger-skin. Arousing him with kicks, they then struck at his face with a sword, inflicting a great wound. In this state, the conspirators, after tying his legs together, dragged him before Tzimisces, who loaded him with insults, spurning him with his foot and plucking out his beard. Finally he completed his work by shattering the Emperor's skull with a sword, while another assassin ran him through the body. This done, in order to check the revolt which was beginning, Tzimisces immediately had himself crowned, and ordered that the head of Nicephorus should be exhibited at a window. Next day, in great secrecy, the murdered Emperor was buried in the church of the Holy Apostles, and thus came to a bloody end one of the most glorious reigns, if it be looked at solely from the military point of view, in the whole of Byzantine history.

John Tzimisces (969–976).

John Tzimisces, whose true surname was Chemshkik, or Chemishgig, which the Byzantines made into Tzimisces, belonged to an ancient and noble Armenian family. Through his father he was related to the illustrious house of Curcuas, and through his mother to that of Phocas. He was born at Hierapolis in Armenia (now Chemishgadzak, *i.e.* birth-place of Tzimisces) about 924 and, like Nicephorus and all his other relatives, was a soldier from his boyhood. He early attached himself to his cousin, and made the great campaigns of Cilicia and Syria in his company. At this time a close friendship united them, and we know that it was Tzimisces who prevailed upon Nicephorus to ascend the throne. His military renown and his exploits in battle almost equalled those of the Emperor, and his popularity was great in the army, on account of his bravery, his liberality, and also his personal beauty, although he was short of stature. On the accession of Nicephorus, he received the post vacated by the Emperor, that of Domestic of the Scholae of Anatolia, became magister, and was entrusted with the task of prosecuting the conquests of Nicephorus, work which he accomplished with signal success chequered by occasional reverses. Was it these successes which alienated the Emperor from Tzimisces? It may be so, but the truth is not known. One thing, however, is certain, that in 969 Tzimisces fell from favour. It is possible, it is even probable, that there were other causes for this disgrace. Tzimisces was not long in discovering that his former brother-officer, though under obligations to him, did not shew him proper consideration, treated him just like the other generals, and was ungrateful towards him. Moreover, what may very well have determined him to throw in his lot with the discontented, and to weave the conspiracy which put an end to the reign of Nicephorus, was the influence of Theophano herself, who had at this time a strong passion for him. In any case, it was she who helped him in his revolt and urged him on to assassinate Nicephorus. Finally, Leo Phocas was an inveterate foe of Tzimisces and constantly accused him to his brother, doing all in his power to embitter the relations between them. All these causes combined to bring about first a complete breach and finally a violent hatred between these two old friends and kinsmen. In 969 Tzimisces had been deprived of his military rank, had been driven from court, and had received orders to live in exile on the Asiatic coast on his estates in Chalcedon, whence he was forbidden to depart. It was, however, from thence that he set out on the night of 9–10 December to perpetrate the murder which seated him on the throne. On attaining supreme power Tzimisces was forty-five years old. He was the widower of a certain Maria, a sister of Bardas Sclerus, was the lover of Theophano, and was childless. In order to succeed to the throne after the murder of Nicephorus, he was ready to accept any conditions which might be laid upon him.

Immediately after his coronation, Tzimisces, as Nicephorus had done, declared that he would look upon himself merely as the guardian and protector of the legitimate sovereigns, Basil and Constantine, and as Regent therefore of the Empire. After this, he set to work to organise his government. He took as his chief minister the famous Basil, illegitimate son of Romanus Lecapenus and favourite of Constantine VII, who has already appeared as the zealous supporter of Nicephorus at the time of his accession, who became his Parakoimomenos, or chief Chamberlain, and received the post, created for him, of President of the Senate. Basil, for the same reasons no doubt as Tzimisces, had abandoned the Emperor, and when the conspiracy of 969 was formed made common cause with the plotters. Thus, as soon as Tzimisces was seated on the throne, Basil became the real head of the government, and by him the first measures taken were inspired. By his orders the new sovereign was proclaimed in every quarter of the city, and public gatherings, disorder, and pillage were forbidden, under pain of beheading. It was not desired that the revolutionary scenes which had marked the accession of Nicephorus should be re-enacted in Constantinople. The next step was to dismiss all functionaries who were in favour of the former Emperor, and to replace them by new men. Leo Phocas and his sons, with the exception of Peter, a eunuch, were banished to Methymna and Amasia. In this way the position of Tzimisces was secured.

The Patriarch Polyeuctes, who had reached a great age, was near his end when the events of 10 December 969 took place. What was his attitude on first hearing of the revolution we do not know, but on the other hand we know how, despite the burden of his years, he received Tzimisces, when the new Emperor, a week after his crime, presented himself at St Sophia in order to be crowned. The Patriarch firmly refused to take part in any religious ceremony until Tzimisces should have done penance, exculpated himself from the murder of Nicephorus, and denounced the criminals. Polyeuctes went further. On this solemn occasion he took the revenge of his lifetime, issuing to John this ultimatum: "Drive first of all from the Sacred Palace the adulterous and guilty wife, who planned and directed everything and who has certainly been the chief mover in the crime." Finally, feeling perhaps the moral strength of his own position as against this suppliant murderer, the Patriarch took another step in advance and exacted, as a striking reparation, the repeal of the whole of the religious legislation of the late Emperor, the recall to their sees of all the exiled bishops, and the distribution of the usurper's private fortune to the poor and the hospitals. John agreed to everything. The Novels were immediately abrogated, the bishops recalled, Theophano exiled to Proti and later to Armenia, while John himself made no scruple of swearing that he had not lifted his hand against Nicephorus, and denounced on oath several of his late accomplices as guilty of the crime. Then, as much from necessity as policy, he gave great largess to the poor, the peasants, and even the aristocracy. This done, Polyeuctes crowned John at Christmas 969. Before his death the Patriarch had a last gratification, that of seeing Tzimisces faithfully fulfil his promises as to his religious policy. The Church of Antioch having lost its Patriarch, Christopher, Tzimisces caused Polyeuctes to appoint in his place a holy hermit, Theodore of Colonea, who had long been known to him. The Patriarch was spared long enough to perform the consecration on 8 January 970. His death followed on 28 January.

The successor to Polyeuctes was proposed by Tzimisces to a synod which he assembled when the vacancy occurred. Basil, like Theodore of Colonea, was a poor monk of the Olympus, famous for his saintliness and his prophecies. He was a friend of the Emperor, and when his consecration took place on 13 February John might certainly flatter himself that he had made a wise and fortunate choice both for the Church and for himself. Yet this did not prove to be altogether the case, for, in fact, in 974 a conflict broke out between the two authorities; Basil, who had less discernment doubtless than Polyeuctes, would have liked to turn the Church into one vast convent, and to enforce reforms which were distasteful to the bishops. Perhaps, indeed, he went further, and, if we are to believe Leo the Deacon, unwisely began to supervise the conduct of his subordinates rather too closely. With all his merits, we are told, "he was of a curious and investigating turn of mind." What is certain is that complaints were laid against him on this account, and he was also reproached with maladministration of the Church. In short, the Emperor was obliged to interfere. He called upon the Patriarch to appear before his court and clear himself. Basil refused to take any such step, alleging that he came under no jurisdiction but that of an Ecumenical Council, which would necessarily bring in the West. This led to his fall. While Polyeuctes, strong in his right, had maintained himself in the see of Constantinople against all comers, Basil for his part, being very possibly guilty of the errors laid to his charge, was deposed and sent into exile at his monastery on the Scamander. His syncellus, Anthony of the Studion, succeeded him. Perhaps this deposition of Basil may have some vague connexion with affairs in Italy, and with the presence at Constantinople of the exiled anti-Pope Boniface. But it seems rather unlikely, and in any case our authorities do not make the statement. All that has been said by historians on the subject is mere conjecture.

The death of its patron Nicephorus did not hinder the building and extension of the Great Laura (monastery) of St Athanasius, founded in 961. In 970 the community there was numerous enough to allow of the saint's imposing upon them a rule, a *typikon* determining the laws which should govern the monks of the Holy Mountain. Unfortunately the *typikon* was ill-received and ill-observed, so much so that a revolt broke out against the Abbot. The mutineers considered St Athanasius and his rules too severe, and appealed to the Emperor. This was the reason that Tzimisces, after holding an inquiry, granted to the Laura the chrysobull of 972 confirming the *typikon* of St Athanasius and the privileges granted by Nicephorus. The monastery was declared "autocephalous" under the sole authority of the Abbot (Igumen). The Golden Bull laid down rules for the administration of the convent, and its provisions are still in force to-day.

The reign of the soldier John Tzimisces, like that of Nicephorus Phocas, was military in character, and events of note in home politics (with the exception of religious events) are few in number. One of the most important was certainly the revolt of Bardas Phocas in 971. Son of Leo and nephew of Nicephorus, Bardas had been banished to Pontus on the death of the Emperor. Thanks to the good offices of his father and other members of his family, of some of the strategi who had remained loyal to Nicephorus, and even of some among the clergy, he succeeded in breaking prison and in surrounding himself with partisans. Then, taking advantage of the Russian war, which Tzimisces was just beginning, Bardas had himself proclaimed Emperor at Caesarea, amidst large numbers of adherents. Fortunately, civil war had not time to break out. The Emperor's brother-in-law, Bardas Sclerus, was immediately sent against the usurper, who, before he had struck a blow, found himself deserted by his friends and forced to surrender. He was relegated with his family to a monastery in the island of Chios. Next year, while Tzimisces was at the siege of Durostolus (Silistria), Leo Phocas attempted to regain power, but unsuccessfully. Being taken prisoner at Constantinople he was blinded and in this state re-consigned to his monastery.

While the ineffectual revolt of Bardas Phocas was just about to break out, and the preparations for the war with Russia were being pushed feverishly on, Tzimisces took advantage of the situation to form a fresh union. Being debarred from marrying Theophano, he fell back upon Theodora, a princess of mature age, daughter of Constantine VII and aunt of Romanus II. This prudent marriage gave great satisfaction at Constantinople, for it confirmed the legitimate descendants of Basil I upon the throne.

Before setting out for the brief and victorious Russian war, in the spring of 972, Tzimisces found time to receive another German embassy, which sought Constantinople in order to renew the negotiations, broken off under Nicephorus, respecting the marriage of Theophano, daughter of Romanus II, with the youthful Otto II. The embassy headed by Gero, Archbishop of Cologne, reached Constantinople about the end of 971. The girl, in spite of certain doubts which have been raised, certainly appears to have been a genuine princess, born in the purple, and sister of Basil II; she was betrothed, and set out for Italy. The marriage took place at Rome on 14 April 972.

So far as we can judge from the scanty documents which have come down to us, Tzimisces seems not to have given much of his personal attention to the work of internal administration. His wars occupied him sufficiently. Only one Novel issued in his name has been preserved; it concerns the slaves taken in war. Basil the Parakoimomenos remained chief minister up to the death of Tzimisces, and used his position to enrich himself to a scandalous extent. This meant that the social difficulty remained unsolved, and became even graver. All the efforts of his predecessors had thus been fruitless. And yet the Emperor behaved liberally to all classes of society. He made large distributions from his private resources. But the only genuinely useful legislative measure which he carried out was the abolition of the highly unpopular tax called the *Kapnikon*, or poll tax, which was paid only by plebeians.

The reign of John Tzimisces was being made illustrious by his victories, when suddenly, on his return from a second campaign in Asia, he died in Constantinople on 10 January 976. Many discussions have arisen as to this unexpected death. Did the Emperor fall a victim to poison or to sickness? It cannot be certainly known, but according to Schlumberger it is most probable that he succumbed to typhus. However this may be, John Tzimisces left the Empire devoid of all apparent support and likely soon to be given up to all the fury of revolution. No one, it is plain, foresaw what manner of man Basil II would prove himself to be.

With Tzimisces the tale of great soldiers raised to the throne breaks off for the time. Henceforward, power was to return to the Macedonian House until the rise of the Comneni. The Emperors who were to reign from 1028 to 1057 might be foreigners or men of no account. For in fact, in contrast to what followed on the death of Romanus II, the reins of power were now to be held by the female members of the reigning house.

CHAPTER IV.

THE MACEDONIAN DYNASTY FROM 976 TO 1057 A.D.

THE death of John Tzimisces not only closed for a time the period of great if usurping generals, but also, except for the reign of Basil II, put an end to the great military successes of the Empire. Thenceforward, from the death of Basil II in 1025 down to the day when a new dynasty, that of the Comneni, came to take up the sceptre of Constantinople, the imperial sovereignty, while its condition became ever more and more critical, remained in the hands of the descendants of Basil I. It was held first by men and afterwards by women, and was discredited and degraded by most extraordinary palace intrigues which are barely conceivable to the Western mind.

John Tzimisces left no heir capable of succeeding him. Besides, as we have seen, he, like Nicephorus Phocas, had always strictly reserved the rights of the two imperial children, Basil and Constantine, the sons of Romanus II and Theophano, of whom he had declared himself the guardian. It was to them, consequently, that the imperial crown, according to the hereditary principle, now fell. Basil II was the elder of the two. He was probably born some time in the year 958, and was crowned on 22 April 960. His brother Constantine was two years younger, having been born in 960 or 961. He, in his turn, was crowned Emperor on 7 April 961. They both spent their early years under the guardianship of their mother and of the two generals who successively raised themselves to the throne, probably without suffering much, unless morally and intellectually, from the political events which took place. Few men can have differed more from each other than these two brothers, whose actual reigns in Constantinople covered a period of 52 years. Basil II, above all a warrior and a ruler, had no taste for luxury, art, or learning. He was a rough and arbitrary man, never able to throw off the soldier, a sort of Nicephorus Phocas with a better title. Constantine, on the other hand, reminds us of his father, and especially of his great-great-uncle, Alexander. Like the latter, he always chose a soft and easy life, preferring the appearance of power to its reality[1] and pleasures of every kind to the discipline of work. Thus Constantine while his brother lived no more governed than did Alexander. Admitted

[1] Though Psellus tells us that it was Basil who refused to share power with his brother.

to a purely honorary share in the sovereignty, he enjoyed its dignities while knowing nothing of its burdens. Yet, in contrast to Alexander, Constantine appears on certain occasions to have shewn himself a brave soldier, and at all events he never at any time manifested the evil and mischievous characteristics of Leo VI's brother. He was a weakling, who thought himself lucky to have someone more capable than himself at his side to undertake the direction of affairs. Of the two brothers only Constantine seems to have married. At some unstated time he took to wife Helena, the daughter of the patrician Alypius, who was the mother of his three daughters, Eudocia, Zoë, and Theodora, two of whom were to be rulers of Constantinople after his death up to 1056. When by the death of Tzimisces the two young men succeeded to power, their mother was in a convent, and there was no influential member of their family with whom their responsibilities might have been shared. They had no one to depend upon except their great-uncle, the famous eunuch and parakoimomenos Basil[1], who had been chief minister under four Emperors, and Bardas Sclerus the general, brother-in-law of the late Emperor John Tzimisces, who had promised him the succession.

The first years of Basil II (976–989).

As might be expected, Basil and Bardas detested one another, and both aspired to the chief power. The former, however, was actually in Constantinople, and easily seized upon the helm in Basil II's name and perhaps with his consent, while the other, who was with the army, could only lay his plans for the future. The eunuch Basil thus, at the outset of the new reign, remained what he had heretofore been, the real and all-powerful minister of the Empire.

The first action of the new government was to recall Theophano from her convent; then immediately afterwards, in order to strengthen his own position, Basil deprived his rival of the title of Stratelates of the armies of the East, and gave him the office of Duke of the frontier theme of Mesopotamia. Other great officers, friends of Sclerus, were dealt with in the same way: for instance, Michael Burtzes, who was sent to Antioch with the titles of Duke and magister. The patrician Peter Phocas succeeded Sclerus as commander of the armies of Anatolia.

At this juncture, Bardas Sclerus appeared in Constantinople, no doubt to be invested with his new command. The diminished importance of his position had exasperated him, and he made so little secret of it in his conversation that Basil ordered him to leave Constantinople at once and rejoin his troops. This was the signal for revolt. As soon as he reached Mesopotamia, he stirred up his army to revolt against the eunuch, having first taken care to recall his son Romanus to his side.

[1] Basil, it will be remembered, was brother of Romanus II's mother.

Like other revolts, this one, which was destined to last four years, began with the proclamation of Bardas as Emperor, some time during the summer of 976. The troops made no difficulty about acclaiming their commander, and Bardas soon drew fresh and substantial contingents from Armenia and even from several emirs with whom he negotiated. By his orders the military funds were seized upon and the rich landowners taxed, and in this way he obtained the money that he needed. Then immediately opening the campaign, he made himself master of several fortresses such as Kharput and Malaṭīyah, and set out for Constantinople. Peter Phocas was at once despatched against him to Caesarea in Cappadocia. Meanwhile the Bishop of Nicomedia received orders to approach him with a view to an accommodation. It was labour lost. Sclerus was bent on empire or war.

The rebel army was for long successful. After a preliminary affair between vanguards which resulted to the advantage of his troops, Bardas won a great victory over Peter Phocas at Lepara-Lycandus in the autumn of 976 which threw Asia Minor open to him. The revolt spread from place to place. Whole provinces, with their soldiers, sailors, officials, and rich landowners, quickly ranged themselves on the side of the victor. Civil war was everywhere, and, in consequence, Bardas and his army penetrated by way of Caesarea to Cotyaeum. Constantinople was panic-stricken, but Basil's energy did not fail him. At the opening of 977 he sent off the protovestiary Leo with discretionary powers, to lead the imperial army and to buy off the mutineers. He was no more fortunate than Peter Phocas had been. If, at the very outset, thanks to his skilful tactics, he gained an appreciable advantage at Oxylithus over a detachment of the rebels, he incurred a defeat at Rhegeas, where Peter Phocas fell, towards the end of 977. Through this victory, Asia Minor with its fleet and troops fell into the hands of Sclerus. It was with this great accession of strength that in the spring of 978 he again set out for Constantinople and laid siege to Nicaea, which was defended by Manuel Comnenus, surnamed Eroticus. But Manuel, after a blockade of several weeks, was forced to surrender, and Sclerus entered Nicaea, his last halting-place before Constantinople. It was also the scene of his last triumph.

While Sclerus was gaining this brilliant success, his fleet under the Admiral Curticius was being defeated and annihilated by the imperial admiral, Theodore Carantenus. Nevertheless, the imperial pretender advanced upon Constantinople, which was in a state of terror. The situation was rendered graver by a revolt of the Bulgarians and a scarcity of soldiers. But once again the aged Basil saved the Empire, this time by making an appeal to one of his former enemies, Bardas Phocas, himself once a leader of revolt, who had been reduced to impotence by the very Bardas Sclerus whom he was now about to meet and overthrow. Bardas Phocas, having received full powers, did not spend time over the defence of Constantinople. He threw himself into Caesarea, where the broken remains of the imperial army lay under the command of Maleinus, in order to take the army of Sclerus in the rear, and oblige him to retrace his way into Asia Minor. This, in fact, was what happened. Sclerus was forced to retreat from before Constantinople in order to meet the danger from Phocas, whom he encountered not far from Amorium in the plain of Pancalia. Here Phocas was defeated on 19 June 978, but was able to retire in good order to Charsianum, where he was again beaten by Sclerus. Nevertheless, the game was not lost for the imperialists. During the winter of 978–979 they obtained help from the Curopalates of Iberia, and in the spring of 979, on 24 March, a fresh battle was fought at Pancalia, ending, after a single combat between the two namesakes, in the complete triumph of Phocas, the final defeat of the rebel army, and the flight of the defeated pretender to Saracen soil. Constantinople was thus saved.

Bardas Sclerus took refuge at Amida, and soon afterwards in the summer of 979 was imprisoned at Baghdad with his family by the order of the Caliph. At Constantinople it was desired that the rebel should be handed over, and to obtain this object the parakoimomenos sent an embassy to Baghdad headed by Nicephorus Uranus. It was unsuccessful. The Caliph would not relax his hold on the prisoner, and Sclerus remained in durance up to December 986. As to his followers, they were granted an amnesty as early as 979 or 980.

But now it was the turn of the eunuch Basil. Hardly had the Empire been momentarily saved from the revolt of Bardas Sclerus, when the military conspirators within its borders, unmindful of the very serious position of affairs in Italy, Bulgaria, and Syria, began plotting anew as they had done under preceding Emperors. The parakoimomenos Basil, on the one hand, to whose energy the defeat of Sclerus was due, felt himself, in spite of his immense services, more and more deserted by Basil II, who was becoming eager to govern in person; while on the other hand, the great military leaders, Bardas Phocas and Leo Melissenus, were dreaming of a military dictatorship and looking back to their illustrious predecessors such as Nicephorus and Tzimisces. They wanted a part to play, and thought the rôle assigned them by the Emperor altogether inadequate. For these reasons, and many others of which we are ignorant, the whole body of great officers resolved to join hands in order to rid themselves of Basil II. The conspiracy was hatched at Constantinople, and appears to have had its ramifications in Syria and Bulgaria. Unluckily for the plotters, the Emperor received timely warning, and the latent antagonism between him and his old minister burst forth with startling suddenness and violence (985). Roughly and without warning, Basil snatched power from the hands of the parakoimomenos, drove him from the palace, confined him to his house, and then banished him to Bosphorus. The rest of the conspirators were now reduced to impotence, but the Emperor was not yet strong enough to punish all his enemies. Melissenus and Phocas were spared. As to the parakoimomenos, his immense fortune was confiscated, and he died soon after his fall, stripped of everything and in a mental state bordering upon madness. Once again plotting had ended in a fiasco. It had served no other end than to make the Emperor sure of himself, and to transform him wholly and completely. "Basil," says Zonaras, "became haughty, reserved, suspicious, implacable in his anger. He finally abandoned his former life of pleasure."

Basil II had not seen the last of ill-fortune with the fall of his minister. Hardly was he set free from the arbitrary domination of the eunuch Basil, when he was called upon to face fresh dangers. In the autumn of 986 he had just returned to Constantinople, after having been defeated by the Bulgarians on 17 August owing to lack of zeal on the part of his lieutenants. Suddenly, while the Byzantine generals, Bardas Phocas at their head, were plotting against their sovereign, the news came that Sclerus had escaped from Baghdad, and for the second time had put forward his pretensions at Malaṭīyah. It was the beginning of the year 987. Whether he would or no, in order to win over Bardas Phocas, Basil was forced to restore him in April to his dignity of Domestic of the Anatolian Scholae, from which he had been dismissed after the plot of 985, and to despatch him against Sclerus. Unfortunately, Phocas was devoid of scruples. Instead of doing the duty imposed on him, he betrayed his master and entered into negotiations with Sclerus. This shews us in what peril Basil stood. His position was further made worse by the fact that Phocas also on 15 August 987 had himself proclaimed Emperor for the second time with great pomp at Chresianus, nearly all the military officers rallying round him[1]. Again civil war divided the Empire, while on the frontiers the Bulgarians were making ready to invade its territory. Basil II could not have escaped ruin had the two pretenders acted loyally towards one another. Like professional thieves, they had agreed to march together upon Constantinople and there to divide the Empire. Phocas was to have the capital and the European provinces, Sclerus Asia Minor. But the following incident intervened. More discerning than his father, young Romanus Sclerus, divining Phocas' bad faith, refused to agree to the proposed treaty, and going straight to Constantinople opened the Emperor's eyes to the true state of affairs. And in truth he was right in his suspicions, for during an interview between the two pretenders on

[1] This shews what strange revulsions of fortune might be seen within a few years at Constantinople. In 971 Bardas Phocas had himself proclaimed Emperor in opposition to Tzimisces. Sclerus opposed and defeated him, and he retired into a convent as a monk. In 976–977 it was Sclerus who broke out into revolt, while Phocas was despatched against him. Ten years passed, and the two hostile leaders were again on the scene, but this time they were acting in concert, both pretending to the throne and both declared Emperors.

14 September 987, Phocas had Sclerus seized and deprived of his imperial dignity, after which he was sent under a strong guard into confinement at the castle of Tyropaeum in custody of Phocas' wife.

Phocas, now left to be the only pretender, at once hastened to advance upon Constantinople, nearly all Asia Minor being in his favour. He arrived under the city walls probably in the early days of 988. Part of his army encamped at Chrysopolis, the other half going to besiege Abydos in order to seize at once upon the Straits, the fleet, and the convoys which secured the food-supply of Constantinople. Basil II faced ill-fortune with splendid energy. He had recourse to Russia, and signed a treaty at Kiev which brought him the help of 6000 Varangians. The famous *druzhina* arrived during the spring of 988, probably in April, and a few months later, in the summer, crossing over to the coast of Asia Minor under Basil II, it met the enemy's forces in the terrible battle of Chrysopolis, where victory remained with Basil. Meanwhile, in the direction of Trebizond, a member of the princely Armenian family of Taron was causing disquiet to the eastern wing of Phocas' army, and forced the pretender to despatch his Iberian contingents to the defence of their homes, while he himself hurried to the help of his lieutenant, Leo Melissenus, at Abydos. It was around this town that the final act in the drama took place. Constantine, Basil's brother, was the first to set out for Abydos. He was soon followed by Basil with the Russians, and in the spring of 989 the two armies met. The decisive action took place on 13 April. By some accident which has never been explained, Phocas suddenly hurled himself in person against Basil, and narrowly missing him fell dead without ever having been wounded. The battle was now won. The rebel troops dispersed, and were cut in pieces by the imperialists. Many prisoners were taken, and the leaders of the revolt, with the exception of Melissenus, were executed. Basil II had definitely triumphed over all rivals. Bardas Sclerus, it is true, was set at liberty by Phocas' wife as soon as she learned the fate of her husband, but his release profited him little. The new rebellion, begun in the summer of 989, was quickly ended by a reconciliation between Basil II and Sclerus. The latter secured his pardon, and the title of Curopalates. All his adherents were also pardoned. The pacification was sealed by an interview between Basil II and Sclerus in October 989. Sclerus, however, did not long survive his fall. He died blind and in semi-captivity at Didymotichus on 6 March 991.

During the thirteen years from 976 to 989 contemporary records, which by the way are extremely meagre, speak of little beyond the civil strife which dyed the Empire with blood. It is probable indeed that all other administrative concerns were thrust into the background by the ever fresh perils which menaced the Empire, for the few events that are mentioned during the period all have a close connexion with the civil war. One of the most important was unquestionably the resignation of the Patriarch, Anthony of Studion, in 980. We do not know what caused his retirement from the Patriarchate, nor have we any explanation of the fact that his successor, Nicholas Chrysoberges, was not elected until 984. It seems, however, that the reason must be sought in the revolt of Sclerus. Numerous small coincidences, indeed, lead us to conjecture that Sclerus, who was brother-in-law of Tzimisces and was chosen by him on his death-bed to be his successor, was always the favourite candidate of the clergy, as Bardas Phocas was of the army. Now as we know that it was on the occasion of the first defeat of Sclerus in 980 that Anthony was obliged to abdicate, we may conjecture the cause of this event to have been the zeal displayed by the Patriarch and his clergy in the cause of the pretender. For the rest, Anthony died soon after his abdication in 980. But it was not until 984 that he was succeeded by Nicholas Chrysoberges, who governed until 996, and of whom we know nothing except that it was under his pontificate that the baptism of Vladímir and his Russian subjects took place.

Another bishop, Agapius of Aleppo, distinguished himself at this time by his share in the Sclerian revolt. On 28 May 986 Theodore of Colonea, Patriarch of Antioch, died at Tarsus, as he was journeying by sea to Constantinople. His city had fallen into the hands of Sclerus, and the government desired above all things to regain possession of so important a place. Agapius, Bishop of Aleppo, promised that if he were appointed Patriarch he would bring about the return of the town to its allegiance. He was consequently nominated and made his entry into Antioch on 23 November 977. Thanks to his connivance and that of the governor, ʻUbaid-Allāh, a Saracen who had become Christian, the town did in fact come again into the Emperor's possession. This state of affairs continued up to the time of the revolt of Bardas Phocas, who succeeded in seizing upon Antioch. It is probable that the Patriarch received the new pretender amicably, for after the victory of Abydos he sought to approach the Emperor with explanations of his conduct. At all events, in consequence of his machinations, he was exiled by order of Phocas in March 980, and, on the other hand, was unable to regain favour with the Emperor. Summoned to Constantinople at the end of 989 or the beginning of 990, he was imprisoned in a monastery, and in September 996, in exchange for a large pension, he signed his abdication. He died a little later, in September 997.

We have only one law belonging to this part of the reign of Basil. It is dated 4 April 988, and deals with religious matters, being the famous Novel which abrogated the anti-clerical legislation of Nicephorus Phocas. It is more than likely, as the preamble states, that Basil put forth this Novel, menaced as he was by imminent danger, with the idea that he was performing an act of piety, and thinking to assuage the Divine anger by restoring to the monks the right of acquiring and erecting new monasteries; but it also appears highly probable that the

Novel had besides a political bearing. In publishing it at the moment when he was preparing to attack Bardas Phocas at Abydos, Basil judged it well to recall to the minds of the clergy what Nicephorus had been to them, and to convince them that the rightful Emperor had no intention of maintaining or imitating the religious policy of his earliest guardian. Finally, it is worth noting as a curious circumstance that it was just at the time when the Empire was convulsed by civil war and when misery was rife on every side, that the most vigorous renascence of the monastic life took place. It was from Mount Athos, whither they had retired, that John and Tornicius, hearing the news of the civil war, came forth to intervene in arms on behalf of the Emperor. Tornicius (or Tornig) and John fought valiantly at Pancalia in 979, and with the booty that he won Tornicius built the famous convent of Iviron, which Basil II by his golden bull of 980 considerably enriched. Already in 978 the Emperor had made royal gifts to the Laura of St Athanasius, and about 972 had authorised the founding of Vatopedi. Thus it is not surprising, after this, that apart from any other considerations he should have meditated the abrogation of laws which he had not scrupled to be the first to contravene.

The great transaction, half political and half religious, which marks this period of Basil II's reign was unquestionably his treaty of alliance with Vladímir of Russia, and the baptism of the Russians to which it led. The negotiations arose over the visit to Constantinople of an embassy from the great Russian Prince of Kiev, sent to collect information touching the Orthodox religion. The Emperor at the moment was in the thick of the civil struggle, in want of both men and money. He used the opportunity to attempt to bring about with the Russians, heretofore his enemies, an understanding which should supply him with the help of which he stood in need. It was accordingly arranged that the Prince of Kiev should send six thousand Varangians to Constantinople, and in exchange should receive in marriage the princess Anne, Basil's sister (born March 961), the bridegroom becoming a Christian. This was carried out. The Varangians arrived, and were instrumental in saving the Empire, but Basil showed less promptness in handing over his sister. It needed an attack upon the Crimea by the Russians in the summer of 989 to bring him to the point. It was about the end of that year, indeed, that Anne set out for Kiev and that Vladímir received baptism, thus bringing Russia permanently within the circle of the political and religious influence of Constantinople.

Rule of Basil II (989–1025).

In the reign of Basil II, the year 989 stands for the complete end of civil strife, and the unquestioned victory of the imperial authority as well as of the legitimist principle. For the future, his only task was to consolidate his power and to make head against the two great enemies of his empire, the Bulgarians and the Saracens. This implies that the reign of the "Bulgaroctonus" was primarily a military one. Nevertheless, in the course of home affairs, there are several events of the first importance to be noted.

On the death of Nicholas Chrysoberges the court named as his successor Sisinnius. His consecration took place on 12 April 996. This Sisinnius was a layman of the high rank of magister. He was also a physician, and was besides deeply versed in letters and endowed with many virtues. Yet he did not seem to be marked out for so distinguished an office, and it is probable that the Emperor was actuated by political motives. However this may be, one thing seems certain, that during his very brief pontificate Sisinnius came to a more or less complete breach with Rome. The grounds of this fresh quarrel were doubtless quite unconnected with theology. They were, in fact, purely personal. The Pope, Gregory V, was a nominee of Otto III of Germany, while Basil's candidate for the Papacy, a Greek named Philagathus, had been defeated in spite of having had the support of Crescentius the Patrician of Rome. In enmity to Gregory, Crescentius set up the Greek as anti-Pope, and in due course, at the beginning of 998, Gregory excommunicated his rival. Hence came the rupture. The pontificate of Sisinnius was, however, signalised by other measures. Reverting to the ever-irritating question of second marriages, he issued a regulation concerning unlawful unions between persons related in various degrees, and another which condemned even second marriages. This was at the same time a direct attack upon Rome, which had sanctioned the fourth marriage of Leo VI. Sisinnius had not time to go further. He died about the month of August 998. One encyclical letter of his has come down to us, addressed to the bishops of Asia Minor and treating of the Procession of the Holy Ghost.

His short pontificate ended, a successor to Sisinnius was sought, according to the traditional practice, in the ranks of the clergy. The Emperor's choice, in fact, fell upon an aged monk of distinguished birth named Sergius, Igumen of the Manuel Monastery. Hardly anything is known of his pontificate or of the events which took place within it, but dissensions broke out between Constantinople and Rome about 1009, which were caused in all probability by the Emperor's policy in Italy, and which ended in schism[1]. We feel, indeed, that we are approaching the days of Michael Cerularius, for, monk as he was, Sergius certainly appears to have carried on the struggle initiated by Sisinnius. Several of our authorities, questionable it is true, tell us that the Patriarch assembled a synod in 1009 at Constantinople, and that he resumed the policy formerly inaugurated by Photius, procured the confirmation of his pronouncements against Latin innovations, and struck out the Pope's

[1] But cf. *infra*, Chapter IX, pp. 261–62.

name from the diptychs. In fact, at this time separation and schism were put on an official footing. Apart from this event, which does not appear to have had any immediate consequences, we find that Sergius very courageously attempted to induce the Emperor to abolish the tax which he had just re-imposed, the *allelengyon*, but without success. Basil refused his consent. It was also during this pontificate that a certain number of liturgical and canonical books were translated from the Greek into Russian for the use of the recently-founded Church, and that the monastery of St Anne was founded on Mount Athos. Finally we have an ordinance of Sergius dated in May 1016 authorising devout persons to give donations to churches and monasteries.

The successor of Sergius was a eunuch named Eustathius, almoner of the imperial chapel, elected on 12 April 1020. The appointment was dictated solely by political reasons. Relations between Rome and Constantinople were much strained, if not wholly broken off. In Italy things were not going prosperously for the Empire; German influence was preponderant there, and Benedict VIII had not hesitated to employ the Normans against the Byzantines. It will readily be understood that, in these circumstances, Basil's whole idea would be to countermine papal influence at Constantinople. But a Western chronicler tells us that in 1024, immediately on the death of Benedict VIII, Eustathius asked for the title of Ecumenical Patriarch from John XIX, and in this way resumed spiritual relations with Rome. John XIX was about to concede the privilege, which would have been tantamount to granting autonomy to the Church of Constantinople, when the protests of Western Europe compelled him to draw back. Matters had reached this stage when Eustathius and Basil II died, within a few days of each other, in December 1025. The successor to the dead Patriarch was at once chosen. He was Alexius, Igumen of the Studion.

The reign of Basil II is notable for a certain number of laws of importance. Some are concerned merely with gifts made to the great monasteries; others have a more general significance. It was in January 996 that Basil issued his famous Novel against the continual encroachments of the great territorial proprietors. If this question had been, as we have seen, a constant preoccupation of the Emperors of the preceding century, it had become for Basil II a matter of life and death. For it was the great landholders who had raised the standard of revolt, and they it was who, with their money and their men, had maintained the cause of the rebel pretenders. It was of the utmost importance, then, for Basil to carry out the advice which had been given him (it is said, by Bardas Sclerus after his defeat), to break down this formidable power, and dry up the source that fed it, territorial wealth. This he did by means of the Novel of January 996, "condemning those who enriched themselves at the expense of the poor." This provision in fact merely confirms and gives precision to that of Romanus Lecapenus, and extends its scope. Prescription, even for forty years, was now to avail nothing against the right of redemption; the power to reclaim property was declared inalienable by any lapse of time. Any estate acquired by its owner before the date of the Novel of Lecapenus was to remain in the hands of its actual proprietor, provided that he could furnish authentic documentary proof that his rights dated from a time anterior to the ordinance. The title to any estate illegally acquired since the publication of the Lecapenian Novels was declared null, and the peasants might at once reclaim their original property, which would be restored to them without the payment of any compensation. Estates unjustly come by, even if their possession had been sanctioned by a golden bull from the Emperor, were subject to the same provision, any such bulls being declared null.

Special provisions gave precision also to the Novel of 4 April 988 concerning ecclesiastical property, and finally very severe penalties were decreed against high officials who used their position to enrich themselves outrageously at the expense of the crown lands. The principle underlying all this formidable legislation was that any estate, whether noble, ecclesiastical, or burgher, should remain permanently what it was, and that thus commoners' lands were never to pass to either of the other two classes.

This Draconian law was, in truth, only justice, for the "powerful" had in the end agreed that they were rightful possessors of land taken from the poor only if, by any means or methods whatsoever, they had debarred their victims for a period of forty years from lodging a complaint in due legal form. The injustice of the practice is clear, and so is the social danger to which it led. It was by such means that the fortunes of the great feudal houses had been founded, such as those of Phocas, Maleinus, Tzimisces, Sclerus, and of the parakoimomenos Basil; it was by such means too that the exchequer was depleted, for all these great nobles, like convents, were privileged with regard to taxation.

The new laws appear to have met with no great success. The penalties were irregularly applied, even if we take it that they were capable of being enforced. In 1002 the Emperor, having paid him a visit, did indeed disgrace Eustathius Maleinus, whom he carried prisoner to Constantinople, awaiting the opportunity of his death to confiscate his estates to the profit of the crown. But this was an isolated instance, which goes to shew how difficult, slow, and inefficacious was the application of the Novel of 996. It was moreover in these circumstances that Basil II, in order to provide for the enormous cost of the war with Bulgaria, as well, probably, as to pursue his controversy with the great feudal lords, re-imposed the famous tax called the *allelengyon*, by which the rich and the poor were declared jointly and separately liable with respect to all obligations, whether financial or military, and the rich were required, in default of the poor, to discharge for them both their taxes and their service in the field. This mutual warranty was an old legacy from the Roman law as to the *curiales*, which had no other result than to ruin the mass of the great landholders and to stir up the bitterest of social hatreds. Thus Basil's work had no element of permanence. If for a time the Emperor found some profit in exacting the tax, his successors were before long forced to repeal it.

If Constantinople was on far from amicable terms with Rome, and if Italian affairs were frequently the cause of disputes with the Saxon Emperors, yet from 983 onwards, the date at which Theophano took power into her own hands, the relations between the two imperial courts were excellent. Otto III had been educated by his mother in great reverence for Constantinople and according to Greek ideas, and, as soon as he was old enough, he hastened in May 996 to send an embassy to Basil II asking for the hand of one of his imperial cousins, no doubt Zoë or Theodora. We know nothing of the results of this first embassy, but apparently it was warmly received, for in 1001 a fresh mission left Italy, headed by Arnulf, Archbishop of Milan, charged on this occasion to bring back the promised princess. This second embassy was received by Basil II with honours such as in themselves shew how cordial were the relations between the two courts. Unfortunately neither had laid its account with death. When the wedding cortège reached Bari, the news came that Otto III had died in January 1002, and all dreams, diplomatic and matrimonial, vanished like smoke. The Byzantine princess who had been about to assume the imperial crown of the West must needs return to Constantinople, and before long be a witness of the ruin of the Byzantine power in Italy, which her marriage would perhaps have hindered or at any rate delayed.

At Venice, in contrast to the Italian mainland, the Doge Peter Orseolo II (elected 991) made every effort to maintain a thoroughly good understanding with Basil. In 991 or 992 he sent ambassadors to Constantinople, who were very well received, and by a chrysobull of March 992 secured valuable commercial privileges. Later on, relations became even more intimate. In 998 the Doge's son John spent some time at Constantinople, and some few years afterwards, in 1004, Basil gave him as his wife a young Greek of illustrious race, Maria Argyrus, sister of Romanus Argyrus, the future Emperor of Constantinople. Unfortunately both husband and wife died of the plague in 1007.

One of the most important of Basil's diplomatic achievements was the political and religious organisation which he imposed upon Bulgaria after his final victory in 1018. We are to some extent acquainted with this work of his through three Novels addressed by the Emperor to John, Archbishop of Ochrida, which have been discovered in a golden bull of Michael Palaeologus dated 1272. By these Novels Basil set up an autonomous Church in Bulgaria, having as its sphere the ancient Bulgarian Patriarchate as it existed from 927–968, with the addition of a whole series of bishoprics taken from various metropolitan sees of Macedonia,

Epirus, Thessaly, Serbia, etc. It is probable that in this he was influenced by political motives, but on this point we have very little information[1].

The reign of Basil II, full of importance from the domestic point of view, was even more so in a military sense. An Emperor who strove so energetically and successfully to enable Byzantium to triumph over her foreign enemies, after having bravely contended for his own rights against his personal foes, was naturally, during the greater part of his reign, often absent from Constantinople. While going forth on his military expeditions and while returning to his capital he had, what was very rare for an Emperor, an opportunity of visiting every part of his vast dominions, and his sojourn at Athens in 1018 has always been famous. His military triumphs, celebrated at Constantinople after his great victories, were also magnificent, as beseemed the reward which his warlike achievements had deservedly earned.

Yet before his death Basil, about 1022, was called upon once again to experience the anxieties of his younger days, through the revolt of two of his generals, Nicephorus Xiphias and Nicephorus Phocas, son of Bardas. The Emperor was at Trebizond, about to set forth on an expedition to Iberia, when he learned in rapid succession that in his rear the two generals had broken out into revolt, that a conspiracy had been formed to dethrone him, that the traitors had probably an understanding with one of his worst enemies, the King of the Abasgians, and that an army was gathering together against him in Cappadocia. The situation was likely to become even more threatening, for Phocas was proclaimed Emperor. But, as before, Basil profited by the rivalry which soon declared itself between the two rebels. Xiphias, jealous of Phocas, drew the crowned pretender into an ambush on 15 August 1022, and had him assassinated. It was now all over with the revolt, and also with the family of Phocas, which with this Nicephorus disappears from the pages of history. As to Xiphias, he was made prisoner, tonsured, and sent into exile on one of the Princes Islands, his property being confiscated. The Emperor, thus delivered, was able to continue his march to Iberia.

A reign so essentially military as Basil's was unfavourable to letters and the arts, which indeed the Emperor always looked upon with indifference or contempt. Nevertheless, whatever the period to which the work of Simeon Metaphrastes should be assigned, hagiographical compilation was actively carried on, as we see from the famous *Menologium of Basil* dedicated to that sovereign, a marvellous illuminated manuscript now preserved in the Vatican Library. Basil's name is also associated with another great work, this time an architectural one. In the night of the 25–26 October 989 Constantinople was visited by a fearful earthquake. The destruction was enormous. The cupola of St Sophia and the eastern apse gave way. It was necessary that they should be at once repaired,

[1] See also, *infra*, Chapter VIII, p. 243.

and also that the ramparts and the aqueduct of Valens which had been partially destroyed should be reconstructed. An Armenian architect, Tiridates, was entrusted with the work at St Sophia, fine mosaics being executed for the adornment of the western arch. The same was the case with the Baths of Blachernae, which Basil caused to be re-built and re-decorated in sumptuous fashion. Commerce, especially, seems to have prospered during this reign, and the great silk manufactories seem to have been always at work. The industrial museum at Düsseldorf preserves a superb silk stuff, dating from the reign of Basil and the year 1000, into which are woven figures of lions facing one another.

From the time of Basil's return from his campaign in Iberia nothing is recorded of him until his death. We only know that as the conqueror of Musulmans, Russians, and Bulgarians he had extended his empire as far as the Caucasus, when at the age of sixty-eight he desired, in spite of the glories which already made his reign illustrious, to accomplish still more and to go in person to carry the war into Sicily. He was prevented only by death, which cut him off on 15 December 1025 after a reign of forty-nine years and eleven months. As he left no direct heirs, he named his brother Constantine to succeed him, and to take up the splendid inheritance which his own energy and valour had enabled him to leave behind. Never, indeed, had the Empire been stronger, wider, or more prosperous than in this year 1025, the high-water mark in the history of the Macedonian House and, in fact, of the Byzantine Empire. With Basil II's death a period of miserable decadence was to set in.

Constantine VIII (1025–1028).

The new Emperor, to whom Basil in dying had committed the imperial crown, was already an old man, sixty-four or sixty-five years of age, having first seen the light in 960 or 961. Unlike his brother, he had spent his life almost wholly within the palace precincts, amidst all the refinements of luxury and lowest excesses of debauchery. As we have seen, he was crowned on 7 April 961, and associated in the Empire as the honorary colleague of Basil in 976. When he succeeded to the throne he had a wife, Helena, and three daughters, Eudocia, Zoë, and Theodora. The eldest daughter makes no figure in history. Disfigured from her early days by small-pox, she entered a convent and died before 1042. The other two were to have their names in all men's mouths and to represent the Macedonian dynasty up to 1056.

The Emperor Constantine VIII bore the worst possible reputation at Constantinople, and unfortunately with only too much reason. Psellus has left us an unflattering portrait of him, which, however, seems to be fairly accurate. Inheriting, as he did, the blood of Michael III and Alexander, during his reign of three years his one object seemed to be to empty the treasury, and, as Scylitzes says, "to do a vast amount of mischief in a very short time, to pursue his merely voluptuous way of life as the absolute slave of gluttony and lust, and to indulge without reflection in the amusements of the Hippodrome, the table, the chase, and games of hazard." His first measures were taken solely with a view to getting rid of the whole of the late Emperor's staff, and to dealing out offices and honours to the habitual companions of his debauches, men of base origin, several of whom were pagans and barbarians. The government was handed over to six eunuchs, and in order, no doubt, to found his authority on terror, the new Emperor disgraced a certain number of men of mark such as Constantine Burtzes and Nicephorus Comnenus, Bardas Phocas and the Metropolitan of Naupactus, all of whom he caused to be blinded. Then, notwithstanding the enormous sums left in the imperial treasury by Basil, Constantine VIII demanded with covetous insistence not only the strict and yearly exaction of the taxes in full, but also the arrears of two years, which Basil had not exacted. This was a grievous burden for the whole Empire and spelt ruin to many families. But such considerations were powerless to disturb the equanimity of Constantine VIII.

Except for these few incidents, the reign of three years was marked by no event of importance, unless it be the marriage of Zoë. However, the military and political conditions which Constantine, quite apart from any will of his own, inherited of necessity from his brother in Armenia, Iberia, and Italy, brought embassies to Constantinople of which an account has been preserved. In 1026 the Katholikos of Iberia came to appeal for the protection of the Emperor for his Church. At the beginning of 1028 came the embassy sent by Conrad II with the ostensible object of proposing a marriage of ridiculous disparity between his son, aged ten, and one of the two princesses born in the purple, but in reality to attempt to conclude an alliance between East and West which might have restored the ancient unity of the Roman Empire, as the Macedonian House had now no male heirs. Werner, Bishop of Strasbourg, and Count Manegold were received with great splendour at Constantinople, but the negotiations led to no practical result, and that for several reasons: in the first place, because they aimed at the impossible, and in the second, because on 28 October 1028 Werner died, as did a fortnight later the Emperor himself. Nevertheless, some good effect seems to have come of the mission, for from this time onwards the relations between Germans and Greeks were, temporarily at least, marked by a genuine cordiality.

We have a somewhat curious new departure dating from the reign of Constantine VIII and the year 1027, described by the Arab writer, Maqrīzī. It was actually agreed upon by treaty between the Emperor and the Fāṭimite Caliph Ẓāhir that for the future the Egyptian ruler's name should be mentioned in all the prayers offered in mosques situated in the imperial territory, and that the mosque in Constantinople should be restored and a muezzin established there. On his part, the Caliph agreed to the rebuilding of the church of the Holy Sepulchre at Jerusalem, which had been destroyed in 1009, and to the return to the orthodox faith of those Christians who through force or fear had become Mohammedans. There is besides in existence a Novel of Constantine VIII dated June 1026 anathematizing seditions.

When on 9 November 1028 Constantine fell dangerously ill, he bethought himself of settling the succession. He had near him only his two younger daughters, neither of whom was married. A solution of the question had to be found without delay. It was resolved that Zöe should be married on the spot, and the Emperor made choice of Constantine Dalassenus, but at the last moment palace jealousies caused him to be set aside, and the final choice fell on Romanus Argyrus. But he was married. By the order of the Emperor and by threats of the most horrible punishments, Romanus was brought to consent to a divorce, and his wife to retire from the world into a convent. There she died in 1032. Romanus was at once proclaimed Caesar and heir to the Empire. In spite of the existence of his real wife and the nearness of relationship between the two[1], the Patriarch made no objection to solemnising this remarkable union, on account, it would seem, of the State interests involved, and in order to avert a political crisis. At all events, nobody seems to have raised any protest against the morals displayed, and Constantine tranquilly expired on 11 November 1028, aged seventy.

Zoë and Romanus III Argyrus (1028–1034).

Zoë, when in right of her birth she ascended the Byzantine throne, was forty-eight years old, having been born in 980. "Of a haughty temper and great personal beauty, with a brilliant mind," says Psellus, she had languished into old age in the women's apartments of the palace, imperial policy having been neither able nor willing to find her a husband. Her marriage with Romanus Argyrus meant to her emancipation and liberty, and she was to make use of her position to recall into being, nay, to unite in her own person and display to the world, all that had brought shame upon her race, and to give herself up to the worst excesses. There is something in Zoë of Theodora, something of Romanus II, and again something of Constantine VIII. Her accession began the hopeless decline of her dynasty.

The husband whom accident had given her was in himself a worthy man. Up to the day of his unwelcome marriage, he had lived at Constantinople as a great noble, deeply attached to his affectionate wife,

[1] Constantine VII, grandfather of Constantine VIII, and Romanus Argyropulus, great-grandfather of Romanus Argyrus, had married sisters, Helen and Agatha, daughters of Romanus Lecapenus. It was probably for this reason that Romanus was chosen for Zoë's husband and for future Emperor.

much given to works of piety, and to study as understood by a man of the world, that is to say, of a rather superficial description. He was a man of ability, but unfortunately not a little vain, and as Emperor during his six years' reign he strove to govern well, and dreamed (a strange dream, considering the age which both he and Zoë had reached) of establishing an Argyrus dynasty at Constantinople. Unluckily his intelligence did not keep pace with his good intentions, and owing to his self-deception as to his own military qualifications and to his too eager appetite for glory, he ended by bringing the worst calamities upon Constantinople, and upon himself the most bitter disillusionment.

On his accession, the first measures taken were fortunate, and shew the importance which Romanus always attached to being on good terms with the clergy. The first Novel which he issued on his accession increased the contribution made by the imperial exchequer to relieve the strain on the very limited resources of St Sophia. He then abolished the famous tax known as the *allelengyon* which Basil II had re-imposed, and bestowed lavish alms on all who had been ruined by the late reign. Going further, he flung open the prison doors and set free those who were detained for debt, himself paying a great part of what was due to private creditors and remitting what was claimed by the State. He restored to liberty numberless victims of the late reign, replacing them in their old positions, and, when feasible, bestowing great offices on them.

These first steps, however, unfortunately led nowhere. Hardly had the edicts gone forth, when a series of calamities fell upon the Empire which changed not only the aspect which Romanus had given to his government but the very character of the sovereign himself. The account of the disasters experienced by the Emperor and his army in Syria must be omitted here. They did not come alone. Soon money began to fail, and Romanus was forced to concentrate all his energy upon the financial side of the administration, and from having been liberal and munificent, he became, except where the clergy and his buildings were concerned, severe, harsh, and even, it was said, avaricious, to a degree which brought him many enemies. He was compelled to raise the money needed by fresh taxes, and it happened further that under his government the Empire passed through a time of fearful crisis. In the winter of 1031–1032 there was an awful famine in Asia Minor accompanied by prodigious mortality; with the spring came the plague, then an army of locusts which made havoc of the crops, and then, as though all this had not been enough, on 13 August Constantinople was shaken by a terrific earthquake which destroyed numberless houses, hospitals, and aqueducts. Romanus III was forced to come to the relief of all the unfortunate sufferers with money. He did it on a generous scale, but the finances felt the effects grievously.

In spite of the emptiness of the treasury, of which, indeed, his propensities were partly the cause, Romanus III was a great builder. Like

Justinian and Basil I, he desired to erect at Constantinople a new architectural marvel, a worthy rival of St Sophia and the New Church. This was the church of St Mary Peribleptos, and he added to it a large laura for men. He endowed both church and monastery richly, alienating lands of considerable extent and unusual fertility. But he went further. Not content with building the Peribleptos church, he adorned St Sophia with costly decorations in gold and silver, while at Jerusalem he began the rebuilding of the church of the Holy Sepulchre, which was not finished till 1048.

In 1030 or 1031, from purely political motives, Romanus III, having no children of his own, arranged marriages for two of his nieces. One of them, Helena, was married to Parakat IV, King of Iberia, and the other to John-Sempad, King of Greater Armenia. The former of these marriages gave occasion for a visit to Constantinople of Queen Mariam, Parakat's mother, and for a treaty of alliance between the two sovereigns, a treaty, however, which proved of small importance, for Romanus at the first opportunity tore it up; Helena, in fact, had died not long after her marriage.

The chroniclers preserve the remembrance of another embassy which also made its appearance in 1031. This was the Saracen mission, headed by the son of the Mirdāsid Emir of Aleppo, Shibl-ad-daulah. He, also, came to request the renewal by treaty of peaceful relations. His proposal, which was accepted, was to go back to the convention signed after the victories of Nicephorus Phocas, in fact to the payment of a tribute. A treaty on much the same lines resulted, also at this date, from a visit paid by the Emir of Tripolis to Constantinople.

When Zoë ascended the throne, it necessarily happened that her younger sister Theodora was left somewhat neglected and forgotten in the women's apartments of the palace. This did not suit her at all, however devout she may have been, and, debarred from ruling, she betook herself to plotting. Even in 1031 a first conspiracy broke out against Romanus III, the moving spirit of which, Fruyin, or Prusianus, was no other than the eldest son of the last Bulgarian sovereign. He was accused, and apparently the charge was proved, of having had designs upon the throne of Constantinople and perhaps upon the hand of Theodora. In any case, it is fairly plain that the future Empress took a hand in the game. But the plot was discovered, and Prusianus was blinded. Theodora, on this first occasion, was not proceeded against, but her immunity did not last long, for soon afterwards another affair arose which led to more serious consequences. This was the conspiracy of Constantine Diogenes, Romanus III's own nephew. We know nothing of this plot except its results. Some of the highest personages in the State were so deeply implicated in it that they were subjected to the worst outrages, and then imprisoned for the remainder of their lives. Nor did Theodora herself go unpunished. She was sent to expiate her guilt at the convent of Petrion.

Meanwhile Zoë was pursuing her new way of life without measure or restraint at the palace. Romanus III, when he had to give up all hope of children, began to neglect his wife and turn his attention to the government, while Zoë rushed from one adventure to another. Friction soon made itself felt between the elderly couple. Zoë was exasperated by the Emperor's neglect, by the strong influence which his sister Pulcheria exercised over his mind, and by the limits set to her mad extravagance. She found the means of vengeance by attracting the love of a younger brother of the man whose name was soon to become famous throughout the Empire, John the Orphanotrophos, a Paphlagonian eunuch of low birth, who had become the friend, confidant, and only favourite of Romanus. The brother's name was Michael; he was young and handsome. Thanks to his elder brother, Michael had exchanged his business of a money-changer, perhaps a coiner, for the post of "Archon of the Pantheon." He soon, in his turn, became a special favourite with Romanus, and was even more acceptable to Zoë. In course of time the disgraceful passion of Michael and the Empress became public property, and Zoë herself ventured to predict the speedy elevation of her lover to the throne.

Her prophecy was verified on 12 April 1034. Romanus was in his bath when in the night of 11–12 April he was murdered, apparently by some of his suite. Exactly what took place was never known. After having probably been poisoned, he was in some mysterious fashion drowned. However this may have been, no one at Constantinople doubted that Zoë and Michael were indirectly the chief movers in a crime which was to give the imperial crown to Michael IV, the Paphlagonian.

Zoë and Michael IV (1034–1041).

The Empress Zoë's satisfaction was brief. In gaining her new husband by a crime she had at the same time found a master. Cunningly acted upon by John Orphanotrophos, who was already the real ruler of the Empire, she determined to have Michael proclaimed at once, and, within a few hours of her husband's death, to marry him publicly. The Patriarch was hastily summoned to the palace, where he learned at one and the same time the death of Romanus and the service expected of him. It was no light thing. It was in fact that he should proceed without parley to bless the union, on a Good Friday, of a woman stained with crime, fifty-four or fifty-five years of age, and widowed only a few hours, with a young man of no family, thirty years her junior. How came the Patriarch Alexius to lend himself to the accomplishment of anything so infamous? We cannot tell. Scylitzes only relates that he was won over by bribes to do the will of the Empress. At all events, no one at Constantinople made any protest against this exhibition of imperial morals. The city, it appears, was delighted to greet the new sovereign, and on the day of Romanus' funeral there were no lamentations for the dead Emperor, who had not been popular with the inhabitants of Constantinople.

And yet, strange to relate, once seated upon the throne, this untrained man, with no claims to govern, and already tormented by the epileptic fits which a few years later were to carry him off in his turn, proved a good ruler, careful of the public interest, attentive to the defence of the Empire, and courageous when the situation in Bulgaria made demands upon his energy. The character given of him by one who knew him personally and intimately, Psellus, should be studied in order to gain an idea of what Michael was upon the throne. "Such was the conduct of the Emperor," he says, "that setting aside his crime against Romanus III, his treasonable adultery with Zoë, and the cruelty with which he sent several illustrious persons into exile on mere suspicion, and setting aside, further, his disreputable family, for whom after all he was not responsible, one cannot do otherwise than place him among the elect of sovereigns in all ages." He wisely declined to make any hasty innovations, any sweeping changes in the imperial administration. If there was favouritism, if the Senate found itself invaded by the creatures of the new régime, this was the doing of Michael's brother. But there is more to be said. Michael proved to be extremely devout; hardly was he seated on the throne when he began to realise the crime he had committed, to regret it, and to do penance. He would now have no companions but monks, and no anxiety save to do good and to expiate his sins. His life was that of an ascetic, and the whole of the imperial treasure went to build convents, a home for the poor, the *Ptochotropheion*, and even a refuge for fallen women.

Meanwhile, what was Zoë doing? She had not taken long to realise how grossly she had deceived herself. Devoid of gratitude towards a woman whom he had never really loved, Michael broke off relations with the Empress and refused to see her. Under the influence of his brother and of his religious impressions, dreading too lest he should meet with the fate of Romanus, he kept her in retirement and had her carefully watched. All her attendants were changed, officials devoted to the Emperor were introduced into her service, and she was forbidden to go out unless with Michael's permission. Zoë bore with these fresh humiliations patiently until, weary of her servitude, she attempted to poison John. It was labour lost. She met with no success, only causing an increase in the rigour of her confinement. It was the just reward of her crime, and lasted up to the death of Michael IV.

On Michael's accession, his whole family took up their abode in the palace and obtained high offices in the Empire. John Orphanotrophos, the eldest, became chief minister; Nicetas, Constantine, and George became respectively, commander at Antioch with the title of Duke,

Domestic of the Oriental Scholae, and Protovestiary. This latter office, which fell to the youngest, was one of the great dignities of the court. The family were all thoroughly corrupt and as uninteresting as they were uncultivated. They were to prove the ruin of their nephew the next Emperor. The only exception was the famous John Orphanotrophos. Beneath his monk's frock, which he always retained, he was fully as corrupt as his brothers. Though a confirmed drunkard, he had nevertheless remarkable talents for government. He was an able financier, unrivalled as an administrator, and an astute politician. He was, moreover, absolutely devoted to his family and to the Emperor, and, despite his serious faults, his falseness, cynicism, and coarseness, he was in truth, as Psellus somewhere calls him, the bulwark of his brother Michael. He it was who had found means to advance him in Zoë's good graces, and he it was who later contrived to make the fortune of his nephew, Michael the Calaphates, from whom he was in the end to receive no reward but exile.

The powerful eunuch's government was energetic, if not uniformly successful. His untiring activity embraced all the foreign affairs of the Empire, and Byzantine armies were again sent forth to strive for the supremacy and safety of the Empire in Asia Minor against Saracens, Iberians, and Armenians, as well as in Italy and Sicily (where the situation was further complicated by the arrival of the Normans), and also, towards the end of the reign, in Bulgaria. Certainly John could claim brilliant successes from time to time, especially in Sicily, where Syracuse was temporarily re-taken in 1038. Men of a different stamp, however, would have been needed to restore to Constantinople her former prestige, and, in a word, from the reign of Michael must be dated a widespread decline in the strength of the Empire.

As to home affairs, they seem to have been less creditably managed. John hoped to see a new Paphlagonian dynasty founded, and with this object, after having reduced to penury and thrust into prison those who, like Constantine Dalassenus, had fallen under his suspicion, he made it a point of conscience to enrich his own family beyond measure. The people were ground down by taxes. Money was wanted for the war; it was wanted for the absurd and ruinous charities of the Emperor, who, more and more broken down by illness, thought of nothing but distributing *solidi aurei* as a means of regaining health; it was wanted, above all, for the Emperor's relations. Their rapacity was indeed the prime cause of the intense unpopularity which before long was to sweep away the whole tribe of these detested eunuchs. But John imagined himself safe from attack, and in order to establish his authority more firmly he made a momentary attempt, like Photius and Cerularius, to bring about the abdication of Alexius, and have himself nominated Patriarch in his place, thus getting the entire control of affairs, religious as well as political, into his own hands. The manoeuvre was only defeated by the energy of Alexius, and fear of the complications which might ensue.

While his brother and minister John Orphanotrophos was thus governing the Empire, Michael, more and more affected by his epileptic fits, and suffering besides from dropsy, paid scant attention to anything beyond his charitable and devotional employments. He usually spent his time at Salonica, at the tomb of St Demetrius, and from what Psellus tells us only military matters could rouse his interest during his lucid intervals. His state gave some anxiety to the chief minister. Every contingency must be prepared for, if Constantinople, as he hoped, was to be endowed with a new dynasty. Therefore, in the course of the year 1040, he decided on striking a decisive blow. As neither he nor his brothers, who were all eunuchs, could perpetuate their name, he contrived to persuade Michael IV to nominate as Caesar a very young nephew, son of their sister Mary. Further, what seems almost incredible, in spite of the rigorous treatment which both brothers had meted out to Zoë, John and Michael, to ensure the success of their designs, prevailed on the Empress to become a party to them, and suggested to her the idea, to which she cheerfully acceded, of adopting the young man. This was duly carried out. Magnificent fêtes were given at Constantinople, in the course of which Michael V, surnamed the Calaphates, was proclaimed Caesar and adopted son of the imperial couple.

It was in these circumstances that at the end of the year 1040 news came of a rising in Bulgaria. By a supreme effort of will the Emperor put himself at the head of his troops and, without hesitation, marched into Bulgaria. A fierce struggle followed. For a moment the worst disasters seemed to threaten the Empire. Finally, however, Michael triumphed, and suppressed the revolt. But this burst of energy destroyed him. He was still able to be present at the triumph decreed him by his capital. His government even succeeded at this time in foiling a conspiracy, formed no doubt in consequence of the adoption of Michael V, one of the moving spirits in which was that very Michael Cerularius who was soon to become Patriarch. Then the end came. On 10 December 1041 he quitted the imperial palace without even taking leave of Zoë, and betook himself to the monastery of the Holy Argyri, which was his own foundation. There, laying aside his royal robes, he had himself clothed in a serge frock, and thus as a monk he died on the same day, having reigned seven years and eight months over the Empire.

Michael V (1041–1042).

The project which John Orphanotrophos had formed in inducing Zoë to adopt his nephew Michael was not destined to succeed. Indeed it was to lead to the ruin of the whole egregious family. The young man, as it proved, had none of the strong points of his uncles, though he shared in all their defects. Son of a sister of the Paphlagonians, and of Stephen, a plain artisan employed in careening ships in the port of Constantinople,

Michael, when fortune began to smile on his relations, had been appointed commander of the imperial guard, while his father, suddenly placed at the head of the fleet, set out to distinguish himself in Sicily by memorable and grievous defeats. It was from his functions in the palace that John took his nephew to have him proclaimed Caesar and adopted as heir to the throne. Unfortunately for both parties, Michael was an exceedingly worthless young man, vicious, cruel, hypocritical, and ungrateful, though not wanting in cleverness or shrewdness. An unfortunate tension soon made itself felt in the relations between uncles and nephew. Michael detested John, and despised his uncle the Emperor. John began to distrust the Caesar, and Michael IV to be estranged. The result of this was the rapid fall of the adopted son from favour, and his banishment beyond the walls of the city. There he remained until the death of Michael IV, and there he would no doubt have been left, had he not been necessary to the vast schemes of the Paphlagonians. In order to secure the continuance of the family the plan set on foot must be carried out, and it was thus that Zoë, alone and abandoned without defence to the faction of her brothers-in-law, was forced to allow Michael to be consecrated, crowned, and proclaimed Emperor of Constantinople.

At first everything seemed to go smoothly. Michael appeared as the humble servant of the Empress and the docile pupil of his uncle. Honours were distributed to the nobles, and alms to the people. But this was merely an attitude temporarily taken up. In reality, there were serious dissensions between the brothers and the nephew. For a long time Michael had been acting with his uncle Constantine against John, whom they both detested. Thus the first care of the young Emperor was to raise Constantine to the rank of *nobilissimus*, and his second to find an opportunity to get rid of the Orphanotrophos. He took advantage of a debate, at the end of which the old eunuch had retired in great dudgeon to his estates, to have him suddenly carried off and deported to the monastery of Monobatae at a great distance. This was Michael's first victim; his second was to cost him his throne and his life.

Thus left master of the situation by the banishment of the Orphanotrophos, who naturally seems to have disappeared unregretted by anyone at Constantinople, Michael's one idea was to make use of the power that he had acquired. Psellus tells us that, as a base upstart, he bore a deadly hatred to the aristocracy and to all in whom he could trace any marks of distinction. No one, as the historian says, could live in peace or feel safe in the possession of his wealth and honours. It was only the lowest of the populace who were in favour and who seemed well-affected to the Emperor. Nevertheless, as Professor Bury has aptly pointed out, it was he who restored to liberty and to his offices and honours the great general, George Maniaces, who had been imprisoned during the late reign, as also Constantine Dalassenus, one of the greatest nobles of the time. He it was, too, who founded the fortunes of Constantine Lichudes, the future Patriarch and a statesman of distinction. But besides this, another Byzantine historian, Michael Attaliates, has left these words upon Michael V, which as it were fill in the sketch of Psellus. "He conferred honours and dignities upon a great number of good citizens, and also gave proof of great zeal for the maintenance of order and the rigorous administration of justice."[1]

In truth, the most serious blunder of Michael was his attack upon Zoë. From the first he consigned her to the gynaeceum, denying her even necessaries and subjecting her to close supervision. Then, imagining his position securely established at Constantinople and being urged on by his uncle Constantine, suddenly, on 18 April 1042, he had the old Empress torn from the palace, and having ordered a summary trial at which she was found guilty of poisoning, without further formalities he banished the lineal descendant of the Macedonian House to the convent of Prinkipo, first having her hair cut off. The Patriarch Alexius, at the same time, received orders to withdraw to a monastery.

In order to legalise his summary action, Michael V on 19 April caused to be read to the Senate and the assembled people a message in which he explained his conduct and accused the Empress and the Patriarch of having plotted against his life. He felt himself sure of the good effect of his message and of the general approbation. But in this he was grossly deceived.

As soon as the populace learned the exile of its sovereign, there burst forth almost instantly a perfect explosion of fury against the Emperor. The Prefect of the City narrowly escaped being lynched. Meanwhile, as the historian Ibn al-Athīr relates, the Patriarch, thanks to money gifts judiciously administered to the soldiers sent to murder him, contrived to escape and to return in hot haste to Constantinople, where he caused all the bells in the city to be rung. This was probably about mid-day on Monday 19 April, for at that moment the revolution broke out with terrific violence round the palace. The army itself soon joined with the mob to liberate Zoë and kill the Calaphates. The prisons were broken open, and the whole flood of people rushed to set the imperial palace on fire and to pillage and destroy the houses of the Paphlagonian family. Michael and Constantine quickly realised the seriousness of the revolt, and felt that they had only one chance of escape, namely, to recall Zoë and endeavour to defend themselves meanwhile. But even this last shift failed. Zoë indeed arrived at the palace and shewed herself to the people; but it was too late. The revolution, under the leadership of the aristocracy and the clergy, was thoroughly organised, was bent on having the Emperor's life, and dreaded the feeble Empress' perpetual changes of purpose.

[1] Quoted by Schlumberger, *Epopée byzantine*, III. p. 383.

It was at this moment that the mob, under the skilful guidance of some of its leaders, suddenly bethought itself that there still existed in the person of Theodora, forgotten in her convent at Petrion, a genuine princess, born in the purple, daughter of Constantine VIII and sister of Zoë. It was instantly resolved to go in search of her, and to have her crowned and associated in the government. During the evening of 19 April the Patriarch, who was probably the moving spirit in the whole affair, officiated at St Sophia, and there he received and at once proceeded to anoint this elderly woman, who probably hardly understood the transaction in which she appeared as a chief figure. Meanwhile the Emperor was declared to be deposed, and all his partisans were removed from their offices.

The Emperor felt at once that all was lost, and had only one wish left, to fly; but, urged on by his uncle the *nobilissimus*, he was obliged to agree to defend himself in his palace, which was still surrounded and besieged by the crowd. About three thousand men perished in the assault, which finally, after a siege of two days and two nights, was successful. The insurgents then made their way into the Sacred Palace, in the night between Tuesday and Wednesday, smashing and plundering right and left, but the man whom they sought was no longer there. He had fled with his uncle and taken refuge in the Studion, where he precipitately had himself tonsured and clothed with the monastic habit.

This radical solution of the question did not avail to save Michael V or Constantine. As soon as the mob learned the place of their retreat, it rushed thither, bent on dragging them from the altar of the church in which they had taken sanctuary and on putting them to death. Throughout Wednesday the revolutionaries thundered outside the monastery whither they had now hurried, but none dared violate the sacred precincts. It was now that Theodora, from this time onward acting as sovereign, ordered that both uncle and nephew should be removed and their eyes put out. Surrounded by a mob mad with excitement, the two Paphlagonians were brought to the Sigma, frightfully mutilated, and finally condemned to banishment. Michael withdrew to the monastery of Elcimon, the *nobilissimus* we know not where. The revolution was accomplished on 21 April 1042.

Theodora and Zoë (*April–June* 1042).

On the morrow of Michael's disappearance, the two sisters confronted one another, each with her own partisans. Zoë was the elder, and might be supposed by many to be more capable of carrying on the imperial administration than Theodora, who had only just taken leave of her convent. She thus had claims to the chief share of power. Theodora, for her part, had the advantage in that she was the younger, and that not having, like her sister, been twice married already, she might without raising a scandal provide the Empire with a master capable of defending it effectively. In any case, she must be immediately admitted to a share in the government.

This was the solution finally decided on. The two sisters were reconciled—or made a show of it—and it was agreed that Zoë should take precedence of Theodora, but that the two should govern the Empire jointly. The government, in the hands of these two aged women, who were popular with their subjects, lasted for a few weeks and seems to have been fortunate. Except in the case of Michael V's family and his declared partisans, who were deprived of their offices, no change was made in the administration or in the *personnel* of the higher imperial officials. The two sisters presided at the councils, which were managed by the leading ministers, and distributed pardons, favours, and money to great and small. Several wise edicts were issued against the traffic in judicial posts; vacant offices were filled up with a view to the best interests of the State. Maniaces, the famous general, was sent back to Italy to take up the supreme command of the Byzantine troops in the West.

In spite of these things, however, this strange government could not last. The sovereigns were too unlike each other in character, too disunited at heart, too old and too weak, to accomplish anything durable or fruitful. Furthermore, faction was busy all around them. It was absolutely necessary to have a man at the head of affairs, who would attend to the finances with an object other than of depleting them, as Zoë unceasingly did, and to the army, so as to keep at a distance foes ever on the watch to take advantage of Byzantine weakness.

It was owing to this need that marriage schemes at once began to be canvassed. As Theodora positively refused to take any husband whatsoever, the court fell back upon Zoë who, despite her sixty-two years, resolutely demanded a third partner. After several projects had ended in nothing, the choice of Zoë and the court fell upon Constantine Monomachus, who espoused his sovereign on 11 June 1042. On the morrow he was crowned Emperor of Constantinople.

Zoë, Theodora, and Constantine IX Monomachus (1042–1055).

Up to the moment of his accession the new Emperor had led a somewhat stormy life. The son of a certain Theodosius, Constantine was the last representative of one of the most illustrious Byzantine families. Having lost his first wife, he had married as his second the daughter of Pulcheria, the stately sister of Romanus Argyrus, and in this way had acquired an important social position. A great favourite at court, it is said that even as such he had made early advances to Zoë, not without success. Unfortunately the rise of the Paphlagonians had blighted his hopes of a great future, and John Orphanotrophos had banished him to Mitylene. It was there that news was brought him that Zoë had made choice of him for her husband, and he returned in triumph to Constantinople for the celebration of the marriage which was to seat him upon the throne.

Constantine was thus by no means an upstart; he was, moreover, a man of keen intelligence, cultivated, fond of luxury and elegance, but unfortunately not a little given to debauchery. It has been said that after a government of women came a government of loose livers and men of pleasure, but it was, nevertheless, a government fairly fortunate for Constantinople. At all events, it was more representative than the Paphlagonian régime, and was even, in its happier hours, as skilful as it was enterprising.

Constantine had been accustomed to lead a dissolute life, and his first thought was to enjoy his new position of power to the full. Among his mistresses were two who have left a name behind them, Sclerena, and an Alan princess whom we shall meet again later. Sclerena was a niece of Pulcheria and a grand-daughter of Bardas Sclerus. Being left a widow, she lost no time in attaching herself to Constantine, and so strong had been the feeling between them that Sclerena had followed her lover to his exile at Lesbos. Then when he reached supreme power Constantine could not rest until he had recalled her to his side. Soon, under the benevolent patronage of Zoë, Sclerena appeared as *maîtresse en titre*, had her own apartments at the palace, and received the title of Sebaste or Augusta. Stranger still, she contrived to live on excellent terms with Theodora, who also dwelt at the palace, and divided her time between her devotions and attention to her fortune, accumulating money to her heart's content. The system amounted to something like a government by four, and it narrowly escaped causing the Empire a fresh dynastic crisis. For though the four heads of the government regarded each other's amusements with much complaisance and joined in princely depredations on the exchequer, the public quite rightly considered that the scandal had gone far enough, and was not quite easy as to the safety of the two aged sovereigns. This opinion was conveyed to Constantine by the popular support given to a revolt of 9 March 1044, during which it would have gone hard with him but for the intervention of Zoë and Theodora. Strong measures were taken, the foreigners, "Jews, Musulmans, and Armenians," being driven from Constantinople, but, in spite of this rigorous repression, the revolt would doubtless have burst forth anew and for the same reasons, had not Sclerena very opportunely died, no doubt soon after the rising of 1044.

If at the palace nothing was thought of but amusement, it must be allowed that, in contrast with what had been the case at other periods, Constantine and his female colleagues had been careful to surround themselves with distinguished men, capable of managing public affairs efficiently. From the beginning of his reign the new Emperor had had recourse to the wisdom of the famous Michael Cerularius, and when in 1043 Cerularius became Patriarch, his former office was given to a man of great talent, Constantine Lichudes. Besides these valuable ministers, men of solid culture and integrity, there were employed a whole crowd of clerks, notaries, and minor officials, such as Psellus, Xiphilin, and others, who certainly were not chosen at haphazard.

As always happened on the accession of a new Emperor, the court, in order to gain the support of all classes, made lavish distributions of honours to the great and of money to the populace, turned out certain office-holders, and made certain political changes. Constantine IX, we know not why, sent John Orphanotrophos to Mitylene where he put him later to a violent death; Michael V he sent to Chios, and Constantine the *nobilissimus* to Samos. On the other hand, he raised Romanus Sclerus, Sclerena's brother, to the highest dignities. This was the beginning of a very serious revolt, which was not without influence upon Sclerena's unpopularity.

Romanus Sclerus had within the Empire a formidable and powerful foe in the person of that Maniaces whom the ephemeral authority of Michael V had sent back to Italy. In his new position of favourite, Romanus desired above all things to make use of his influence to avenge himself. He prevailed upon Constantine to recall his enemy, and in the meantime ravaged Maniaces' estates and offered violence to his wife. Maniaces was not of a temper to submit to such usage. Supported by his troops he raised the standard of revolt against the Emperor, and caused his own successor, sent out by the Emperor, to be assassinated. He then began his campaign by marching upon Constantinople, there to have himself proclaimed Emperor. But he met with a check at Otranto, and in February 1043 he embarked, landing soon afterwards at Dyrrhachium, whence he advanced upon Salonica in the hope of drawing after him Bogislav's Serbs, who had recently defeated some Byzantine troops in 1042 near Lake Scutari. But, unfortunately for him, his successes soon came to an end. At Ostrovo he encountered the army sent against him by Constantine. He was defeated and killed. The Empire was saved.

At about the same time the chroniclers Scylitzes and Zonaras speak of another revolt, hatched this time in Cyprus by Theophilus Eroticus, which, however, does not appear to have involved the government in serious danger. Such did not prove to be the case with a rising which broke out in September 1047, and for three months threatened to deprive Constantine of the throne. Its leader was Leo Tornicius. Constantine IX in his heart cared little for the defence of the Empire, and consequently neglected the army; the depredations on the treasury went on apace; there were pressing dangers on the eastern and western frontiers; and, because of all this, malcontents were numerous. The rising broke out at Hadrianople, among military commanders who had been displaced or passed over, and Tornicius put himself at its head. This man was of Armenian origin and traced his descent from the

Bagratid kings. Besides all the wrongs which he shared with the other generals, he had special grievances of his own: in the first place, Constantine's policy in Armenia; then, probably, a love-affair which the Emperor had broken off. Tornicius, who was a cousin of the Emperor, was on very intimate terms with a sister of his, named Euprepia. Now between Constantine and Euprepia relations were somewhat strained, and it was to punish his sister as well as his cousin, for whom, be it said, he had no liking, that he sent him to the provinces in honourable exile as strategus, and later compelled him to become a monk. It was this which led Tornicius to resolve upon rebellion, and to take the leadership of a movement which had long existed in the army. On 15 June the whole body of conspirators met at Hadrianople, and soon afterwards Leo was proclaimed Emperor. Thereupon the insurgents set out for Constantinople with the army corps from Macedonia. In these circumstances, Constantine shewed remarkable energy. In spite of the illness by which he was just then tormented, he set to work to arm the troops in Constantinople, who barely numbered a thousand, and gave orders to summon the imperial army by forced marches from the depths of Armenia. If Tornicius, who had reached the walls of Constantinople, had made the smallest exertion, he would have had the Empire in his grasp, but hoping to be acclaimed by the people and unwilling to shed blood, he remained inactive beneath the ramparts of the town. Meanwhile, Constantine on the other hand was acting. He scattered money among the enemy's troops, won over officers and men, and could then await the army from the East and the Bulgarian contingents which he had demanded. Matters were at this point when, in the beginning of October, Tornicius left Constantinople to take up a position on the road from Hadrianople to Arcadiopolis, and to engage in a fruitless siege of the little town of Rhaedestus. After this he relapsed into inactivity. It was then, in the month of December, that the army from Armenia reached Constantinople. Constantine, feeling himself sure of ultimate victory over a foe so strangely passive, was reluctant to shed blood. The hostile army was gradually overcome by bribes, hunger, and promises, and Tornicius soon found himself, with his lieutenant Vatatzes, practically deserted. Both were made prisoners, their eyes were put out on 24 December 1047, and a little later they suffered death.

While within the borders of his empire Constantine's government was disturbed by the revolts of Maniaces and Tornicius, outside it the enemies of Byzantium were also on the alert. In 1043 it became necessary to take arms against the Russians, who were defeated. As a result of this campaign and in order to seal the peace which followed, a Greek princess was married to Yaroslav's son, Vsévolod. Next year, in 1044, there broke out the war with Armenia which ended in the complete and lamentable overthrow of that ancient kingdom, and the appearance on the frontiers of the Empire of the Seljūq Turks. Ani was betrayed to the Greeks, and the last King of Armenia, Gagik II, went forth to live in gilded exile at Bizou. The Katholikos Petros, who had engineered the surrender of Ani, was also deported, first to Constantinople and later to Sebastea, where he died some years afterwards. To the misfortune of both, Armenia was made into a Byzantine province, so that the Empire, without a buffer-state, from this time onwards had to encounter single-handed the race who, in the end, were one day to conquer it. To complete the picture, it will be shewn elsewhere that Asia Minor was not the only ground on which the Byzantine troops were to measure their strength during the reign of Monomachus. With varying success, their generals were obliged to confront Arabs, Patzinaks, Lombards, and Normans. Every frontier was threatened, South Italy was lost, and as a final calamity Michael Cerularius was about to make a complete and definitive breach with the Roman Church, which alone might perhaps have been able to save the ancient Greek Empire.

On the death of the Patriarch Alexius on 22 February 1043, Constantine's government raised to the Patriarchal throne, with circumstances of considerable irregularity, the first minister of the Empire, the man who was to be famous as Michael Cerularius. His consecration took place on 25 March. Cerularius' ordination was merely an incident in his career. In 1040, as a result of the conspiracy which he had organised against the Emperor Michael with a view to taking his place, he had been condemned to deportation and had been forced to assume the monastic habit. Still, if Michael found himself on the patriarchal throne merely through a chapter of accidents, he brought to it, not indeed any striking virtues, but a fine intellect, wide culture, and iron will. And, moreover, in all that he did he had a definite aim. Now that he had reached the highest ecclesiastical position in the Empire and was second only to the Basileus, he attempted to set up on the shores of the Bosphorus a Pontificate analogous to that of the Pope at Rome, so that he would have been in fact Emperor and Patriarch at the same time. This was, indeed, the real cause of the Schism and of his conduct towards Constantine IX. It was at the very close of the reign of Constantine Monomachus, when the Emperor was well known to be ill and near his end, that Cerularius threw down the brand of discord.

Throughout the pontificate of Alexius relations with Rome had been excellent, and there were no signs whatever of a conflict when in 1053 it suddenly burst forth. Cerularius had chosen his opportunity with skill. The Emperor had grown old and seemed to have no energy left; the Pope, Leo IX, was unfortunately placed in Italy under the yoke of the Normans. That Leo, in spite of his misfortunes, should have attempted to extend his authority over the Greek sees in southern Italy is possible, and indeed probable enough, for the authority of Constantinople had sunk extremely low in the West. Nevertheless, the provocation came from Cerularius. Through the medium of Leo, Archbishop of Ochrida, Cerularius wrote to John of Trani a letter, which was really intended for the Pope and the West generally. In this letter he attacked the customs of the Latin Church, particularly the use of unleavened bread and the observance of Saturday as a fast. At the same time a violent composition by the monk Nicetas Stethatus was circulated in the Byzantine Church, in which these two charges were taken up afresh, and an attack was also made on the celibacy of the clergy. These usages were declared to be heretical. Questions of dogma were not touched upon. Finally Cerularius of his own authority closed all those churches in Constantinople which observed the Latin ritual.

Leo IX replied at once; without discussing the trivial charges of the Patriarch, he removed the controversy to its true ground, namely, the Roman claim to primacy of jurisdiction, and demanded, before entering on any discussion, the submission of the Patriarch. The latter at first yielded, and wrote to the Pope a letter respectful in tone and favourable to union. It is certain, however, that he was compelled to take this step by the Emperor, who was himself urged on by the Greeks living in Italy, among others by the Catapan Argyrus. Leo IX wrote in January 1054 to Constantine, entrusting his letter to three legates who arrived in April, bearing also a letter to Cerularius very sharp and harsh in tone and deeply irritating to the Patriarch, as was also the attitude assumed towards him by the three legates[1]. On the other hand, Constantine was won over to the Roman cause by the very affectionate epistle addressed to him by Leo IX, and immediately proceeded to carry out the Pope's wishes. Unfortunately at this juncture Leo IX died, on 19 April, and his successor was not chosen until April 1055. The legates no longer had sufficient authority to enable them to act, and Cerularius, taking advantage of his position, began to write and intrigue, with a view to winning over Eastern Christendom to his cause, beginning with Peter, Patriarch of Antioch. The legates, for their part, in spite of their diminished authority, solemnly excommunicated Cerularius and his supporters. The step turned out a mistake on the Latin side. The Patriarch was only waiting for this opportunity to shew himself in his true colours. He demanded, indeed, an interview with the legates, who had already quitted Constantinople on 17 July 1054, but were recalled by the Emperor's orders. Suddenly, however, suspicions of Cerularius arose. The Emperor, fearing an ambush, again sent off the legates, for it was rumoured that the Patriarch intended to stir up the people to assassinate them. It was upon the Emperor that the brunt of Cerularius' anger fell. At his instigation a rising was let loose in Constantinople, and Constantine was forced to abase himself before the victorious Patriarch. With the Emperor's sanction, he at once held a synod in St Sophia on 20 July, the Roman bull was condemned, an anathema was pronounced,

[1] See *infra*, Chapter IX. pp. 268–69.

and a few days later the bull was burned. The separation was an accomplished fact. Its unhappy consequences were to make themselves soon and lastingly felt.

From the point of view of civilisation, the reign of Constantine Monomachus must be considered one of the most fortunate, for a true literary renaissance flourished at Constantinople under the auspices of the Emperor. Though not himself learned, Constantine was a man of taste, and liked to surround himself with cultivated people. His court was the resort of the most intellectual men of the day, and it was owing to their entreaties that he decided to re-open the University of Constantinople. The most distinguished scholars at that time were John Xiphilin, Constantine Lichudes, Cerularius, John Mauropus, Psellus, and Nicetas Byzantius. They were all bound together by friendship, all loved and pursued letters and jurisprudence, and some, like Xiphilin, Lichudes, and Cerularius, were destined to reach the highest positions in Church and State. The first foundation of Constantine goes back to 1045. With the help of his friends, he began the restoration of the science of jurisprudence, founding a School of Law by his Novel *περὶ τοῦ Νομοφύλακος*. Then he decided that in the new University all branches of learning should be taught. Psellus was entrusted with the teaching of philosophy, Nicetas Byzantius and Mauropus with that of grammar, rhetoric, and orthography. Thus was formed the School of St Peter, so called from the place where the new "masters" lectured. Law was lodged at St George of Mangana, the faculty took the name of the School of the Laws, and Xiphilin became its head. A library was added to the school. It was there that the historian Michael Attaliates taught. In these schools of higher learning law was taught in the first place, but the other branches of humane learning were not neglected. Plato, Homer, the ancient historians, and theology found their commentators. Psellus was undoubtedly the most conspicuous of the professors, the most applauded and discussed. Unfortunately these *savants* were not endowed only with learning and virtues. They had also defects, of which vanity and arrogance were not perhaps the worst. Before long, quarrels broke out between them and the courtiers, then disputes arose among the learned themselves, then difficulties grew up even with the Emperor to such an extent that by about 1050 the enterprise was ruined. Constantine IX was forced to close his University, and to disgrace Lichudes and Mauropus. Xiphilin became a monk, and Psellus joined him at Olympus, only, however, to return before long on the death of Monomachus.

From the artistic standpoint, the reign of Constantine Monomachus is memorable for that stately building, St George of Mangana, which made heavy demands upon the treasury. The Emperor also beautified St Sophia, and enriched it with precious objects intended to serve for divine worship. We also know that he built several hospitals and refuges for the poor.

Life in the women's apartments of the palace remained throughout the reign what it had been at the beginning, that is to say very far from edifying. Zoë, as she grew old, devoted herself to distilling perfumes, and flinging away public money on innumerable absurd caprices. Theodora, a good deal neglected, spent her time in devotion, and in counting her fortune which she hoarded up with care. Constantine fell under the dominion of a dwarf, at whose hands he narrowly escaped assassination, and was then subjugated by a young Alan princess, whom he loaded with presents and looked forward to marrying at some future time. Meanwhile Zoë died in 1050, and Constantine it appears greatly lamented the aged Empress. By rights Theodora should now have regained power. But she never thought of doing so, and the only concession which Constantine made to her feelings was to refrain from marrying the Alan princess. "The aged sovereign," says Psellus, "would never have endured to be at once Empress and first subject of an upstart." He contented himself, as in Sclerena's case, with bestowing on his mistress the title of Augusta, indulging in countless acts of insensate prodigality for her and her family, and putting himself thus in the most ridiculous position to the delight of his enemies and the grief of Psellus.

In the early days of 1055 the Emperor, whose health was failing more and more and who had besides broken with his sister-in-law and caused her to quit the palace, retired to his favourite monastery, St George of Mangana. Feeling himself dying, he summoned a council to his side to choose his successor, regardless of Theodora. The choice fell on an obscure man named Nicephorus, at that time in Bulgaria. But there still existed in the capital a party which had remained loyal to the princess born in the purple. It was this party which, without waiting for the arrival of Nicephorus or the death of the Emperor, proclaimed Theodora afresh as the sole Empress of Constantinople, and sent orders to have the pretender arrested at Salonica. He was then deported to the interior of Asia Minor. Constantine IX died on 11 January 1055, and was solemnly buried besides Sclerena in the monastery of Mangana. Once again Theodora, now aged seventy-five, was momentarily to resume the government of the Empire.

Theodora (1055–1056).

With this aged virgin the glorious history of the Macedonian House comes to an end. Founded in blood in the ninth century, it dies out in the eleventh in barrenness, weakness, and shame, the wretched but just reward of a long series of moral iniquities. We know not with what feelings the Byzantines watched its extinction, nor what presentiments visited them as to the future of the State. One fact alone is known to us, that Theodora supported and favoured Cerularius and his faction, and that it was owing to this party of intriguers that she again took up the government. It is probable that the Patriarch had views of his own, and was awaiting the propitious moment when he might quietly pass from the patriarchal palace to the imperial. But, in the first place, Theodora's reign proved a very brief one. It did not last eighteen months. And, besides, strange to relate, when Cerularius put himself forward to "give the law," he found that Theodora stood her ground, resisted, and in the end disgraced the Patriarch. With him were dismissed several of the great generals, among them Bryennius and Comnenus, and the reign of the eunuchs began. If this was a misfortune for the Empire, it proved at least that the Empress had a will of her own and meant to be obeyed.

As might have been expected, the court immediately began to urge projects of marriage on Theodora, but the Empress was no more disposed at the close of her life than in earlier days to accept an expedient which had turned out so ill in the case of her sister Zoë. Without any support or counsel but such as she could obtain from her eunuchs, she took up the task of governing, and of holding in check the whole military party whose two chief leaders had been disgraced. At the head of affairs she set an ecclesiastic, Leo Paraspondylus, the protosyncellus, a man of great merit, upright, honest, and intelligent, but abrupt and dictatorial to a degree, which accounts for the unpopularity he soon incurred. In addition to this, the Empress' parsimony and the intrigues of Cerularius helped to cool the attachment which the Byzantines had shewn for their sovereign. A seditious outbreak was plainly imminent when Theodora died, rather unexpectedly, on 31 August 1056. As soon as the first symptoms of her malady appeared, there was great agitation among the palace eunuchs. The party in power was by no means ready to throw up the game. Leo Paraspondylus therefore hastily summoned a council to meet around the dying Theodora's bed and provide for the succession. They made choice of an old patrician, who had spent his life in camps, Michael Stratioticus, who seemed to have the qualities requisite for letting himself be governed and at the same time commanding the support of the army. Cerularius was at once consulted, and after some hesitation, before the closing eyes of the sovereign and authorised by a faint sign of consent from her, he crowned and proclaimed Stratioticus Emperor.

Michael VI Stratioticus (1056–1057).

Michael VI, the poor old man who was now to affix his trembling signature to the last page of the history of the Macedonian family, belonged to the aristocracy of Constantinople and was descended from that Joseph Bringas who had been chief minister under Romanus II. To the clique who hoped to govern in his name he was a mere figurehead. His age, his want of capacity, the weakness of his position, unsupported by any party in the State, were for the eunuchs and especially for Leo Paraspondylus so many pledges that they would be confirmed in all their authority. By way of precaution, however, the court, on raising him to the throne, exacted from him an oath that he would never act contrary to the wishes of his ministers. It is plain that they were counting without the strength of the great feudal families, every one of which aspired to sovereign power, and also without the popular outbreaks which they expected to crush without difficulty. In reality the eunuchs were grossly deceived in their calculations.

On the very morrow, indeed, of Michael's proclamation Theodosius, the president of the Senate, attempted to organise an outbreak. He was a cousin of Constantine IX, and in this capacity fancied that he had rights to the succession. But he had no supporters either in the army or the palace or among the clergy. At the head of a troop of dependents, the most he could do was to break open the prisons and to appear in front of the palace and St Sophia. The doors were shut against him; no difficulty was found in arresting him and he was sent into exile at Pergamus. Michael VI and his court fancied that their troubles had ended with this slight attempt at a revolt; they were already distributing profuse gifts to the Senate and the people and planning some few changes in the official staff, when, in rapid succession, the Emperor quarrelled with some of the most popular commanders in the army, with Catacalon Cecaumenus whom he dismissed, with the "Francopol" Hervé whom he ill-treated, with Nicephorus Bryennius to whom he refused the restoration of his estates formerly confiscated by Theodora, and, above all, with Isaac Comnenus. On Easter Day 1057 he denied to all of them the favours which they came to ask, and by the advice of his minister launched out into a flood of invective against each of them. It was the divorce of the court from the army which he so unthinkingly pronounced. There was only one sequel to so sinister a beginning, and that was revolt.

The conspirators immediately gathered at St Sophia, and in concert with the Patriarch deliberated how they might best get rid of the Emperor and his eunuchs. Without further delay they hailed Isaac Comnenus as the future Emperor, afterwards returning to their estates in Asia Minor to prepare for war. It was on 8 June 1057 in the plain of Gunaria in Paphlagonia that Isaac was proclaimed Emperor. Immediately afterwards the rebel army began its march upon Constantinople and reached Nicaea. Everywhere the pretender was recognised, the Asiatic themes submitting to his authority. Michael VI for his part, as soon as he learned what had taken place, attempted to organise the defence. Unfortunately he had no commanders of any capacity on his side, though on the other hand his army was more numerous than that of his opponents. The imperial troops set forth, led by a certain Theodore, and made their way towards Nicaea. At Petroë they halted, not far from the camp of Comnenus, and here it was that the battle took place on 20 August. It was waged with fury, and degenerated into a massacre. Though at first defeated, in the end Isaac Comnenus was the victor, thanks to Catacalon, who came up in time to reinforce the wavering centre and left wing of the rebels.

Even after the battle of Petroë, the unfortunate Michael still hoped to save his crown by winning over the Senate and the populace of Constantinople. Unluckily for himself, the poor Emperor had now contrived to fall out with Michael Cerularius, who for his part was busy plotting against him. Though feeling at heart that all was lost, Michael VI nevertheless tried to negotiate with Comnenus. Through Psellus and two other senators, he offered Isaac the title of Caesar, engaging also to adopt him and name him his successor, as well as to pardon all the rebels. This was on 24 August. The revolted troops were already at Nicomedia, and the embassy sent in Michael's name had been secretly won over to the cause of Comnenus. After an exchange of views had taken place, and some counter-proposals had been made on behalf of Isaac, the envoys returned to Constantinople. There, while ostensibly rendering an account of their mission to the Emperor, in reality during the whole of 29 August they were, with Cerularius, organising the revolt and weaving the conspiracy which ended in the abdication of Michael VI.

As soon as all was completed, Michael VI's embassy, consisting of the same men as before, set out again for Comnenus' camp, and on the same day, 30 August, the revolt broke out at Constantinople. The struggle was not a bloody one, but was marked by the personal intervention of the Patriarch, who suddenly at St Sophia openly ranged himself on the side of the rebels, sanctioned the proclamation of Comnenus as Emperor, and took the direction of the revolutionary movement into his own hands. His first care was to send a number of bishops to the palace with instructions to tonsure the Emperor at once, to clothe him with the monastic habit, and to send him to a convent in Constantinople, where soon afterwards he died. On 31 August 1057 amid indescribable enthusiasm Comnenus made his triumphal entry into the Sacred Palace. The next day, or the day after, he was crowned by the Patriarch. Thus was the dynasty of the Comneni solemnly inaugurated. That of the Macedonians had become extinct.

CHAPTER V.

(A)

THE STRUGGLE WITH THE SARACENS (717–867).

At the accession of Leo III (25 March 717), when the great Arab army was encamped in western Asia Minor and the Anatolic troops had gone to Constantinople to place their strategus on the throne, the position of the Empire seemed almost desperate; and the Arab commander, Maslamah, having some understanding with Leo, was confident of reducing it to subjection. During the spring he took Sardis and Pergamus; and, when it became clear that no assistance was to be expected from Leo, he advanced to Abydos, crossed to Thrace, destroyed the forts on the road, and encamped before Constantinople (July). On 1 September a fleet under a certain Sulaimān joined him, and was followed by another under Omar ibn Hubaira; but, while the ships were sailing round the city, twenty of them became separated from the rest and were destroyed by fire-ships (3 September). After this the fleet was content with inactivity and safety; but an offer of ransom was refused, and in the severe winter the army lost heavily in horses and camels. In the spring fresh ships came from Egypt and Africa besides military reinforcements, and an attack by Slavs was repulsed; but Omar was defeated by the Bulgarians whom Leo had called to his assistance, and in Bithynia a foraging party was routed. Moreover, the Egyptian sailors deserted, and through information obtained from them Leo destroyed with Greek fire many newly-arrived ships. After this the blockade on the sea side was practically raised, while the besiegers were starving. Accordingly Omar II, who succeeded the Caliph Sulaimān in September 717, recalled the Muslim armament (15 August 718); but many ships were destroyed by a storm or captured on the retreat, and only a few reached Syria. The garrison of Taranta, which was thought to be too much exposed, was then withdrawn, and no more expeditions were made while Omar lived. To prevent a recrudescence of the Arab sea-power, after the accession of the Caliph Yazīd II (February 720) a Roman fleet sailed to Egypt and attacked Tinnis. The expedition of 716–718 was in fact the last attempt upon Constantinople, and the neglect of the fleet which followed the removal of the capital from Damascus to Babylonia in 750 made a repetition impossible; hence the war was reduced to a series of plundering raids, until the occupation of Crete and Sicily by western Arabs caused the naval warfare to revive under new conditions. The character of these incursions was so well understood on the Arab side that in the ninth century it was an accepted rule that two raids were made each year, one from 10 May to 10 June when grass was abundant, and, after a month's rest for the horses, another from 10 July to 8 September, with sometimes a third in February and March; and the size of the forces may be gauged from the fact that a commander was once superseded for retreating when he had still 7000 men. Longer expeditions were often made; but even these rarely had any object but plunder or blackmail. A frontier fortress was indeed occasionally occupied, but it was often recovered after a short interval, and more frequently forts were taken only that they might be destroyed and the enemy thereby deprived of a base; and the whole result of 150 years of war was only the annexation by the Arabs of the district between the Sarus and the Lamus, which however included the important towns of Tarsus and Adana and the strong fortress of Lulum. Raids through the Cilician Gates were signalled to Constantinople by a chain of beacons, and a cluster of fortresses was erected on the heights of the Taurus range; but the Romans were generally content to hold the strong places, and, when opportunity offered, overwhelm parties of marauders. Occasionally they made counter-raids; but these had even less permanent result than those of the Arabs, until under the rule of the energetic Caesar Bardas a blow was dealt after which the decaying Caliphate never recovered its offensive power, and the way was laid open for a Roman advance.

Under Yazīd only sporadic raids were made, with little result. Omar ibn Hubaira won a victory in Armenia Quarta (721), and a fortress in Cilicia was taken (723); but ʿAbbās ibn al-Walīd after taking a fort in Paphlagonia allowed his men to scatter, and most of the parties were annihilated (722). After Caliph Hishām's accession, however, more systematic plans were adopted. In 724 his son Saʿīd and his cousin Marwān with the combined forces of Syria and Mesopotamia, coming from Melitene, stormed a fort and massacred the garrison, though a detachment under Kathīr[1] was cut to pieces; and this was followed by the capture of the great fortress of Camacha on the Euphrates (which the Romans must have recovered since 711); and in 726 Maslamah took Neo-Caesarea. After this a series of raids was carried out by Hishām's son Muʿāwiyah, who in 727 took Gangra, which he demolished, and Tataeum[2], and with naval assistance besieged Nicaea. In 728 he took Semaluos in the Armeniac theme; in 729 he raided northern Asia Minor, while Saʿīd, coming from the south, reached Caesarea, and an Egyptian fleet harried the coast. In 730 Muʿāwiyah took the fortress of Charsianum; in 731 he found the frontier too well guarded to cross in force, and his lieutenant, Baṭṭāl, was routed; but in 732 he plundered Paphlagonia and penetrated to Acroïnon (Prymnessus), though on the retreat his rearguard was annihilated, while his brother Sulaimān reached Caesarea. In 733 the two brothers joined forces

[1] Theoph. Χθη (corrupt); corr. from Mahbūb Χεθηρ.

[2] Theoph. Ἀτεοῦς, Arab. 'Taiba.' See Ramsay, *Hist. Geogr.*, pp. 143, 439.

and their vanguard under Baṭṭāl captured a general; in 734 Mu'āwiyah reached the west coast, plundering proconsular Asia as he went; in 735 he returned by way of the north, while Sulaimān raided Cappadocia. In 736 on another joint expedition Mu'āwiyah was killed by a fall from his horse, but Sulaimān after wintering in Roman territory invaded Asia and carried off a Pergamene who claimed to be Justinian's son Tiberius and was granted imperial honours by Hishām. In 738 he took a fort in Pontus and captured a patrician's son, who with other prisoners was put to death in 740 on a report that Leo had killed his Muslim prisoners; and in 739 his brother Maslamah, coming from Melitene, seized some of the subterranean granaries that were numerous in Cappadocia. Assistance by sea was prevented by the activity of the Roman fleet, which in 736 captured part of a fleet returning from a raid and in 739 attacked Damietta in great force and carried off many captives.

For 740 a great invasion was planned. Sulaimān crossed the frontier in May and encamped before Tyana, sending his cousin Ghamr to Asia and Malik and Baṭṭāl to Phrygia, where they took Synada and besieged Acroïnon; but these last were routed by Leo himself and both killed, after which the whole army returned to Syria. Not this victory, however, so much as the internal troubles of the Caliphate caused in the following years the slackness of the Arab offensive.

In 742 Sulaimān marched into the heart of Asia Minor, and Constantine V, who had succeeded Leo in June 741, left his capital on 27 June and came to Crasus in Phrygia to meet him; but Artavasdus' rebellion forced him to flee to the Anatolics at Amorium, leaving the road open to the enemy. However, Hishām's death (February 743) and the accession of the incapable Caliph Walīd II prevented the Arabs from making the most of this opportunity, and in 743 the Romans destroyed the fortress of Sozopetra south-west of Melitene.

After the murder of Walīd (April 744) the Caliphate fell into anarchy; and, order having been restored in the Empire by Artavasdus' overthrow (November), the advantage lay with the Romans. Constantine again destroyed Sozopetra, which had been insufficiently restored, and threatened Perrhe (Ḥiṣn Manṣūr), where the fortifications had been repaired and a strong garrison posted. He forced Germanicea (Mar'ash) and Doliche to capitulate; allowing the garrisons to march out, he removed the inhabitants to Roman territory and demolished the fortifications (746). After this a great outbreak of plague prevented him from pursuing his advantage, and in 748 Walīd ibn Hishām restored Germanicea. In 747 however an Egyptian squadron which had come to Cyprus was unexpectedly attacked in harbour and almost annihilated; and from this time the Egyptian fleet disappears for 100 years.

In June 751 Constantine set out to recover Camacha, but sent the Armenian Khushan, who had fled to the Romans in 750, against the fort, while he himself besieged Melitene. Mesopotamia being in revolt, its

Emir could not bring help, and the place capitulated; the inhabitants with their portable property were then escorted to a place of safety, after which the town was demolished. Thence Constantine went on to Claudias, which he also took, removing the population of the district to Roman territory; but at Arsamosata he failed. Meanwhile Khushan, having taken Camacha and placed a garrison in it, advanced to Theodosiopolis (Erzerūm), which he took and destroyed, making the garrison prisoners and deporting the inhabitants. The merciful treatment which Constantine accorded to his enemies and to the civil populations is a bright spot among the atrocities of these wars. The Romans were never as cruel as the Arabs, but this striking leniency may fairly be set against the character which anti-Iconoclast writers draw of this Emperor.

By the Caliph Marwān II's death (July 751) the new Abbasid dynasty was firmly established, but many revolts followed. When in 754 'Abdallāh, Emir of Syria, had started to invade the Empire, he heard of the death of his nephew, the Caliph Saffāḥ (19 June), and returned to make an unsuccessful bid for the Caliphate. His successor in Syria, his brother Salīḥ, in 756 entered Cappadocia through the pass of Adata, but on hearing that Constantine was about to march against him returned home. Thereupon followed an exchange of prisoners. In 757 Salīḥ began to rebuild the walls of Mopsuestia, which had been overthrown by an earthquake in 756; and 'Abd-al-Wahhāb, who had been made Emir of Mesopotamia by his uncle the Caliph Manṣūr, rebuilt Claudias and began to rebuild Melitene. To prevent this Constantine marched to the Pyramus (758); but the army at Melitene, reinforced by some Persians, the best troops of the Caliphate, under Ḥasan was too strong to attack, and the rebuilding of Melitene and Mopsuestia was completed. In 759, while the Emperor was engaged with Slavonic enemies, Adana, abandoned by the Romans, was occupied by Salīḥ, a garrison, partly of Persians, being placed there, and a fort erected on the Sarus opposite it. In 760, while Constantine was fighting the Bulgarians, the Caliph's brother 'Abbās defeated the Armeniac strategus Paul on the Melas between Melitene and Caesarea with great loss, Paul himself being killed and 42 high officers captured.

For the next five years both sides were occupied, Manṣūr with insurrections and Chazar invasions, and Constantine with Bulgarian wars, and in 766 there was an exchange of prisoners. This year a strong force of Arabs and Persians under 'Abbās and Ḥasan besieged Camacha (August); but, well defended by its commandant, it resisted all their efforts, and on the approach of winter they retired. Some of the army, however, who had separated from the rest for a pillaging expedition, penetrated beyond Caesarea, avoiding roads and towns, but were attacked on their return and fled in confusion to Melitene and Theodosiopolis. The Arabs then set themselves to restore the fortifications of Arsamosata; but in 768 an army which had been ravaging Armenia Quarta crossed the Arsanias and destroyed the works, though after their retreat the task was completed. The citizens were however suspected of collusion with the enemy and removed to Palestine, a fate which also befel the inhabitants of Germanicea (769), which was re-fortified and garrisoned.

In 770 Laodicea Combusta was taken, and in 771 some of the Armenians who had fled to the Romans with Khushan set out to return to their old homes, and a force under the commandant of Camacha which pursued them was surprised and cut to pieces. In 775 Thumāma marched along the Isaurian coast, supported by a fleet, and besieged Syce. Constantine thereupon sent the Anatolics, Armeniacs, and Bucellarii, who occupied the only pass by which Thumāma could retreat, while the Cibyrrhaeots anchored in the harbour and cut off his communications with the ships; but by a desperate attack he cut his way through the cavalry and returned with many prisoners from the neighbourhood, while the fleet sailed to Cyprus and captured the governor. Constantine, wishing to be free to deal with the Bulgarians, now made proposals for peace, but these were rejected.

The deaths of Emperor and Caliph in 775 were followed by greater activity on both sides. Constantine had recently given his chief attention to the Bulgarians and had been content with merely checking Arab inroads; but in 776 Leo IV, who, though from ill health unable to lead armies, was an able and vigorous ruler, sent an expedition to Samosata which carried off many captives. The Muslims were ransomed by the Caliph Mahdī, who on his side prepared a larger force than had been seen since 740 with many of the best Persian troops under 'Abbās, which took the underground granary of Casiṇ with the men in it and reached but did not take Ancyra. In 777 Thumāma made an expedition by land and Ghamr by sea; but Thumāma quarrelled with the Emir 'Īsa, the Caliph's great-uncle, and so in 778 no raid took place. In these circumstances Leo sent the five Asiatic themes to Cilicia and Syria, and they besieged 'Īsa in Germanicea without opposition from Thumāma, who was at Dābiq. Failing to take Germanicea, they plundered the country, and the Thracesian strategus, Michael Lachanodraco, was attacked by a force sent by Thumāma, but defeated them with heavy loss, after which the whole army returned with many captives, largely Syrian Jacobites, and laden with spoil. In 779 Thumāma again remained inactive, though ordered to make an invasion, and the Romans destroyed the fortifications of Adata. The veteran Ḥasan was then appointed to command, and with a large force from Syria, Mesopotamia, and Khurāsān entered the Empire by the pass of Adata. Leo ordered his generals not to fight, but to bring the inhabitants into the fortresses and send out parties of picked men, to prevent foraging and to destroy the fodder and provisions. Ḥasan therefore occupied Dorylaeum without opposition, but after fifteen days lack of fodder for the horses forced him to retreat.

The Caliph now determined to take the field himself, and on 12 March

780 left Baghdad with an even larger army and marched through Aleppo to Adata; here by Ḥasan's advice he ordered the fortifications to be restored (they were completed in 785), and advanced to Arabissus, whence he returned, leaving the command to his son Hārūn, afterwards known as ar-Rashīd, supported by Ḥasan and other capable advisers. This expedition was however hardly more successful than the last. Thumāma, since 'Īsa's death no longer disaffected, being sent westwards, reached Asia, but was there defeated by Lachanodraco, his brother falling in the battle; afterwards Rashīd marched towards the north and besieged Semaluos for thirty-eight days, during which the Arabs suffered heavy loss, and the garrison then surrendered on condition that their lives were spared and that they were not separated from one another. The army thereupon returned to Syria. After this expedition Tarsus, which had been abandoned by the Romans, was occupied and rebuilt by the Arabs.

In September 780 Leo died; and, under the female rule which followed, Asia Minor was again laid open to the enemy. In June 781 the Asiatic themes were sent to the frontier, commanded not by a soldier but a eunuch, the treasurer John. The separate themes, however, retained their strategi, and 'Abd-al-Kabīr, who had invaded by the pass of Adata, was defeated by Lachanodraco and the Armenian Tadjat, strategus of the Bucellarii, who had gone over to the Romans in 780. After this 'Abd-al-Kabīr abandoned the expedition, for which he was imprisoned. The Caliph now made a great effort, and on 9 February 782 Rashīd left Baghdad at the head of a larger force than any that had been sent in the previous years, in which contingents from Syria, Mesopotamia, Arabia, and Khurāsān were included; and, the Empress Irene having just sent an army to Sicily against the rebel Elpidius, the invaders had an easier task. Entering by the Cilician Gates, Rashīd took the fortress of Magida and advanced into Phrygia, where he left Rabī' to besiege Nacolea and sent Yaḥyà the Barmecide to Asia, and after defeating Nicetas, Count of Opsicium, he reached Chrysopolis. Yaḥyà inflicted a crushing defeat on Lachanodraco, but on his way to join Rashīd found his road blocked on the Sangarius by Anthony the Domestic of the Scholae, whom Irene had sent by sea from Constantinople; but Tadjat from hostility to Irene's chief minister, the eunuch Stauracius, opened communications with Rashīd, and on promise of pardon and reward returned to the Arabs. By his advice Rashīd proposed peace; but, when Stauracius, Anthony, and Peter the magister came to discuss terms, he treacherously made them prisoners. Irene, wishing to recover Stauracius and crippled by the loss of Tadjat and Anthony, was forced to accept his conditions. A three years' truce was then made on condition that she paid tribute, ransomed the prisoners, supplied guides and markets for the army on its retreat, and surrendered Tadjat's wife and property. After mutual presents the Arabs returned laden with spoil (31 August). Mopsuestia and the fort opposite Adana were then rebuilt by the Arabs.

In 785 the rebuilding of Adata was finished; but the work was faulty, and the walls were soon so much damaged by the wet winter that early in 786 the Romans easily took and destroyed the town, which was evacuated by its garrison; they also overthrew the fortifications of Sozopetra. Both these frontier places were immediately rebuilt.

In 786 Irene, to carry out her religious policy, changed the composition of the themes and probably deposed the iconoclast strategi[1], thereby impairing the military strength of the Empire, which, while she ruled, was unable to cope with the Arabs; and in September 788 the Romans were defeated in the Anatolic theme with heavy loss. In 790 some soldiers who were being conveyed by sea from Egypt to Syria were captured by the Romans, but an Arab fleet sailed to Cyprus and thence to Asia Minor, and, meeting the Cibyrrhaeots in the bay of Attalia, captured Theophilus the admiral, who was offered rich gifts by Rashīd, now Caliph, to join the Arabs, but on his refusal beheaded[2].

In September 791 Constantine VI, having now assumed the government, marched through Amorium to attack Tarsus, but had only reached the Lycaonian desert when, perhaps from scarcity of water, he returned (October). In 792 he restored his mother to her rank and place, and, having driven the Armeniacs, who had caused her downfall, to mutiny, overcame them by the help of some Armenian auxiliaries (793), who, not having received the expected reward, betrayed Camacha to the lieutenant of ʿAbd-al-Malik, Emir of Mesopotamia (29 July). The same year Thebasa in Cappadocia from lack of water surrendered to ʿAbd-al-Malik's son ʿAbd-ar-Raḥmān on condition that the officers were allowed to go free (October). In the autumn of 794 Sulaimān invaded northern Asia Minor, accompanied by Elpidius, who had fled to the Arabs and received recognition as Emperor; but many men perished from cold, and a safe retreat was only obtained by making terms (January 795).

In the spring of 795 Faḍl led a raid, but Constantine himself marched against him (April) and defeated a party which had nearly reached the west coast (8 May). In 796 he was occupied with the Bulgarians, and Mahomet ibn Muʿāwiyah reached Amorium and carried off captives. In 797 Rashīd in person invaded the Empire by the Cilician Gates, and Constantine, accompanied by Stauracius and other partisans of Irene, again took the field (March); but Stauracius, fearing that success might bring the Emperor popularity, spread a report that the enemy had retreated, and Constantine returned to lose his throne and his sight (19 August). Meanwhile Rashīd took the fort known to the Arabs as aṣ-Ṣafṣāf (the willow)[3] near the Cilician Gates, while ʿAbd-al-Malik plundered the country as far as Ancyra, which he took, and then rejected

[1] Bury, *Later Roman Empire*, II. p. 485.

[2] In such cases the prisoners were probably held as hostages or to ransom, and, if their lives were forfeited, they were spared if they apostatised or turned traitors.

[3] This seems to be Andrasus, but must be a different place from Adrasus in Isauria.

Irene's proposals for a truce. In 798 'Abd-al-Malik extended his ravages to Malagina, where he carried off the horses and equipment from Stauracius' stables, while 'Abd-ar-Raḥmān made many captives in Lydia and reached Ephesus, and in the autumn another party defeated Paul of Opsicium and captured his camp.

In 799 the Chazars invaded Armenia, and so this time Rashīd accepted Irene's offers of tribute and made peace[1]; but her successor Nicephorus refused payment (803). Accordingly in August 803, while he was occupied with Vardan's rebellion, the Caliph's son Qāsim, who had just been named Emir of al-'Awāṣim (the defences), a province in North Syria instituted in 789, entered Cappadocia by the Cilician Gates and besieged Corum, while one of his lieutenants besieged a fort which the Arabs call Sinān; but, being distressed by lack of food and water, he agreed to retire upon 320 prisoners being released. In 804 Rashīd himself advanced through the same pass to Heraclea (Cybistra) in April, while another party under Ibrāhīm took aṣ-Ṣafṣāf and Thebasa, which they dismantled. Nicephorus started in person to meet Ibrāhīm (August); but on hearing that the Caliph's vanguard had taken and dismantled Ancyra turned back and, having met the enemy at Crasus, suffered defeat; but the lateness of the season made it difficult to maintain the army, and Rashīd accepted tribute and made peace, the Emperor agreeing not to rebuild the dismantled fortresses. An exchange of prisoners was also arranged and took place during the winter. In 805 the Caliph was occupied in Persia, and Nicephorus, contrary to the treaty, rebuilt Ancyra, Thebasa, and aṣ-Ṣafṣāf. He also sent an army into Cilicia, which took Tarsus, making the garrison prisoners, and ravaged the lands of Mopsuestia and Anazarbus; but the garrison of Mopsuestia attacked them and recovered most of the prisoners and spoil. Accordingly in 806 Rashīd, with a large army from Syria, Palestine, Persia, and Egypt, crossed the frontier (11 June) and took Heraclea after a month's siege (August) and Tyana, where he ordered a mosque to be built, while his lieutenants took the Fort of the Slavs by the Cilician Gates, Thebasa, Malacopea, Sideropalus (Cyzistra)[2], aṣ-Ṣafṣāf, Sinān, and Semaluos, and a detachment even reached Ancyra. Nicephorus, threatened by the Bulgarians, could not resist, and sent three clerics by whom peace was renewed on the basis of an annual tribute and a personal payment for the Emperor and his son, who thereby acknowledged themselves the Caliph's servants. Since Nicephorus again bound himself not to rebuild the dismantled forts, Rashīd undertook to restore Semaluos, Sinān, and Sideropalus uninjured. As soon, however, as the Arabs had withdrawn, Nicephorus, presuming on the lateness of the season, again restored the forts, whereupon the Caliph unexpectedly returned and retook Thebasa.

[1] The peace is nowhere recorded, but seems to follow from the absence of hostilities and the action ascribed to Nicephorus.

[2] I identify this with Dhū'l Kilā' (*E.H.R.*, 1901, p. 86, n. 195).

The neutralisation of Cyprus, effected in 689, was considered as still in force; but after the breach of the treaty of 804 a fleet under Ḥumaid in 805 ravaged the island and carried 16,000 Cypriots, among whom was the archbishop, as prisoners to Syria (806), but on the renewal of peace they were sent back. In 807 Ḥumaid landed in Rhodes and harried the island, though unable to take the fortified town; but after touching at Myra on the way back many of his ships were wrecked in a storm.

Early in 807 the Romans, who must previously have recovered Tyana, occupied the Cilician Gates, and, when the Arab commander tried to pass, defeated and killed him. Rashīd himself then came to the pass of Adata, and sent Harthama with a Persian army into Roman territory; but he effected nothing and his force suffered severely from hunger. The Romans failed to take Germanicea and Melitene, and the Caliph after assigning to Harthama the task of rebuilding Tarsus returned to Syria (14 July), recalled probably by the news of disturbances in the East. In 808 an exchange of prisoners was effected at Podandus.

During the civil war which followed Rashīd's death (March 809) the Romans recovered Camacha, which was surrendered by its commandant in exchange for his son, who had been captured; but wars with Bulgarians and Slavs prevented them from taking full advantage of the situation. It was fortunate for them that during the terrible years 811—814 the Arabs were unable to organise a serious attack.

In 810 Faraj rebuilt Adana and the fort opposite, and in 811 another leader invaded the Armeniac theme and defeated Leo the strategus at Euchaita, capturing the soldiers' pay and making many prisoners (2 March); but in 812 Thābit, Emir of Tarsus, having crossed the frontier in August, was defeated by the Anatolic strategus, another Leo, afterwards Emperor, and lost many horses and waggons. After 813, though no peace was made, other occupations on both sides prevented active hostilities; but about 818 Leo V, now delivered from the Bulgarians, took advantage of the disturbances in Egypt to send a fleet to Damietta.

In September 813 Ma'mūn became sole Caliph; but, Syria and Mesopotamia being almost wholly in the hands of rebels, he could not engage in foreign war, and in 817 a new rival arose in his uncle Ibrāhīm. On his submission (819) the Syrian rebel Naṣr asked help of the Anatolic general, Manuel, and Leo sent envoys to treat with him; but the indignation of Naṣr's followers at a Christian alliance forced him to put them to death, while Ma'mūn prevented interference by sending the exile Thomas into Asia Minor with Arab auxiliaries, who after the murder of Leo (December 820) was joined by most of the Asiatic themes and remained in arms till 823. During these troubles 'Abdallāh ibn Ṭāhir recovered Camacha (822), and some adventurers who had been expelled from Spain and occupied Alexandria ravaged Crete and the Aegean islands. After the overthrow of Thomas, Michael II proposed a definite peace (825); but Ma'mūn, having just then been delivered from Naṣr, refused to tie his hands and sent raiding parties into the Empire, who were defeated at Ancyra and at another place and lost one of their leaders.

In December 827 the Spanish adventurers were expelled from Alexandria and established themselves in Crete. The Cibyrrhaeot strategus Craterus gained a victory over them (828), but waited to give his men a night's rest; and, as he kept no watch, his force was surprised and cut to pieces, and his ships were captured. He himself escaped in a trading-vessel to Cos, but was pursued, taken, and crucified. In 829 the corsairs annihilated the Aegean fleet off Thasos, and the islands lay at their mercy; but Ooryphas collected a new naval force, and for some time checked their ravages.

Ma'mūn had been hindered from pursuing the war by the rebellion of the Khurrami sectaries under Bābak in Azarbā'ījān and Kurdistān; and about 829 some of these, under a leader who took the name of Theophobus, joined the Romans. Thus strengthened, Theophilus, who succeeded Michael in October 829, crossed the frontier and destroyed Sozopetra, killing the men and enslaving the women, whereupon Ma'mūn started for Asia Minor (26 March 830). Having received a welcome ally in Manuel, who, having been calumniated at court, had fled to save his life, he sent his son 'Abbās to rebuild Sozopetra and passed the Cilician Gates (10 July), where he found no army to oppose him. Magida soon capitulated, and Corum was taken and destroyed (19 July), but the lives of the garrison were spared, while Sinān surrendered to 'Ujaif and Soandus to Ashnās. After taking Semaluos the Caliph returned to Damascus.

Early in 831 Theophilus entered Cilicia and defeated a local force, after which he returned in triumph with many prisoners to Constantinople. But the position in Sicily caused him to use his success in order to obtain peace, and he sent the archimandrite John, afterwards Patriarch, with 500 prisoners and an offer of tribute in return for a five years' truce, but with instructions to promise Manuel free pardon if he returned. Ma'mūn, who had started for another campaign, received the envoy at Adana and refused a truce; but with Manuel John had more success, for, while accompanying 'Abbās in an invasion of Cappadocia the next year, he deserted to the Romans. Meanwhile Ma'mūn crossed the frontier (26 June)[1], besieged Lulum, and received the surrender of Antigus and Heraclea, while his brother Mu'taṣim took thirteen forts and some subterranean granaries, and Yaḥyà took and destroyed Tyana. Failing to take Lulum, Ma'mūn, having heard of the revolt of Egypt, left 'Ujaif to continue the siege and returned to Syria (end of September). The garrison of Lulum succeeded in taking 'Ujaif prisoner, but, after an attempt at relief by Theophilus had failed, released him on condition of his obtaining them a favourable capitulation, and the place was annexed, whereby the command of the pass fell into the hands of the Arabs (832). Meanwhile Ma'mūn returned from Egypt (April), and Theophilus again sent to offer tribute;

[1] I have made a slight emendation in Ṭabarī's text in order to bring the day of the month into accord with the day of the week.

but Ma'mūn refused accommodation and entered Cilicia, where he received an impostor claiming imperial descent, whom he had crowned by the Patriarch of Antioch. After a halt at Adana he again crossed the frontier, obtained the surrender of some forts, ordered Tyana to be rebuilt as a Muslim colony, and returned to Syria (September). In 833 he came to Tarsus, and sent 'Abbās to superintend the rebuilding of Tyana (25 May), himself following on 9 July. Soon afterwards he was seized with illness and died at Podandus (7 August), after rejecting the Emperor's offer to pay the war-expenses and compensation for damage done in Arab territory and to liberate all Muslim prisoners in return for peace. Peace was, however, practically obtained, for, in consequence of the spread of the Khurrami rebellion under Bābak, Ma'mūn's successor, the Caliph Mu'taṣim, abandoned Tyana and ceased hostilities.

In 835 the rebels were defeated, and Omar, Emir of Melitene, was able to invade the Empire. Theophilus himself met the marauders and was at first victorious, but in a second battle he was put to flight and his camp was pillaged. In 836, however, the imperial forces were increased by the adhesion of another party of Khurramis under Naṣr the Kurd; and, the Arabs having just then been defeated by Bābak, Theophilus invaded Armenia, where he massacred many of the inhabitants, and after exacting tribute from Theodosiopolis returned, bringing many Armenian families with him; but a force which he left behind was routed in Vanand. In 837, urged by Bābak, he again crossed the frontier and for the second time destroyed Sozopetra, where Naṣr's Kurds perpetrated a general massacre among the Christian and Jewish male inhabitants. Theophilus then pillaged the district of Melitene, passed on into Anzetene, besieged Arsamosata, which, after defeating a relieving force, he took and burned, carried off captives from Armenia Quarta, which he laid waste, and returned to Melitene; but, expecting another attack, he accepted hostages from the garrison with some Roman prisoners and presents and withdrew. 'Ujaif, whom the Caliph sent against him, overtook him near Charsianum, but the small Arab force was almost annihilated.

This summer Bābak was finally defeated, and soon afterwards taken and beheaded; and Mu'taṣim, now free to pursue the war with vigour, started with a larger force than had yet followed a Caliph to invade the Empire. He left Sāmarrā on 5 April 838, and at Batnae (Sarūj) sent Afshīn through the pass of Adata, while the rest of the army went on to Tarsus, where he again divided his forces, sending Ashnās through the Cilician Gates (19 June), while he himself followed two days later, the destination of all three divisions being Ancyra. Afshīn took the longer road by Sebastea in order to effect a junction with the troops of Melitene and those of Armenia, which included many Turks and the forces of the native princes. Mu'taṣim, having heard that Theophilus was encamped on the Halys, ordered Ashnās, who had reached the plain, to await his own arrival. The Emperor, however, had gone to meet Afshīn, and in the battle which followed near Dazimon on the Iris (24 July) the Romans were at first successful; but heavy rain and mist came on, most of the army, unable to find the Emperor, left the field, and Theophilus, persuaded that the Persians meant to betray him, with a few followers cut his way through the enemy and escaped, while those who remained lit fires to deceive the Arabs and retired. Ancyra having been evacuated on the news of the battle, Theophilus ordered his forces to concentrate at Amorium under the Anatolic strategus Aëtius, while he himself, having received information of a conspiracy, returned to Constantinople. Meanwhile Ashnās occupied Corum, and, after destroying Nyssa and learning from fugitives of the Emperor's defeat, entered Ancyra. Here Mu'taṣim and Afshīn joined him, and, having destroyed Ancyra, the united forces advanced to Amorium, the chief city of the Anatolic theme and the birthplace of Theophilus' father (2 August). Here a stubborn resistance was offered, but an Arab captive, who had turned Christian and was known as Manicophagus, showed them a weak spot; the main attack was directed against this point, until Boiditzes, who commanded in this quarter, finding resistance hopeless, admitted the enemy (13 August). The town was then destroyed, and a massacre followed. Meanwhile Theophilus, who was at Dorylaeum, sent presents to Mu'taṣim with a letter in which he apologised for the slaughter at Sozopetra, saying that it was committed without his orders, and offered to rebuild it and release all prisoners in return for peace; but the Caliph would not see the envoy till Amorium had fallen, and then refused terms unless Manuel and Naṣr were surrendered, returning the presents. On 25 September he began his retreat by the direct road through the desert, where many perished from thirst; and many prisoners who were unable to march, and others who killed some soldiers and fled, were put to death. The chief officers were preserved alive; but Aëtius was crucified on reaching Sāmarrā, and about forty others suffered death seven years later (5 March 845)[1].

After this the Caliph was occupied with the conspiracy of 'Abbās, who had been in correspondence with Theophilus; but Abū-Sa'īd, who was appointed Emir of Syria and Mesopotamia, sent the commandant of Mopsuestia on a raid, in which he carried off prisoners and cattle. He was then attacked by Naṣr, who recovered the prisoners but was shortly afterwards defeated by Abū-Sa'īd and killed, whereupon the Kurds dismounted and fought till all were killed. On the other hand a Roman fleet pillaged Seleucia in Syria (839). Abū-Sa'īd, having fortified Seleucia, in 841 made another invasion and carried off captives, but the Romans pursued him into Cilicia and recovered them. In a second inroad he fared no better, and the Romans took Adata and Germanicea and occupied part of the territory of Melitene. Theophilus now again sent presents and asked for an exchange of prisoners; Mu'taṣim, while refusing a formal exchange, sent richer presents in return, and promised, if the prisoners

[1] See *supra*, p. 125, n. 2.

were released, to release double the number. On these terms a truce was made.

In January 842 both sovereigns died; the Empire passed to a woman and a child, and the Caliphate to a man of pleasure; and for some time few serious operations were undertaken, though in 842 a fleet under Abū-Dīnār sailed for the Aegean, but it was shattered by a storm off Chelidonia in Lycia, and few ships returned. The Cretan pirates were, however, a constant menace; in 841 they were ravaging the Asiatic coast when a party which had landed near Ephesus was annihilated by the Thracesian strategus Constantine Contomytes. In 843 Theodora's chief minister Theoctistus, who knew nothing of war, sailed with a large fleet to expel them from Crete (March), and by force of numbers was on the point of succeeding, when on a report that Theodora had proclaimed a new Emperor he returned, and his men, left without a leader, were cut to pieces. In 844 Omar of Melitene made an inroad as far as Malagina; Theoctistus, who again took command, was defeated on the Mauropotamus[1], and many of his men deserted to the enemy. An exchange of prisoners was then effected on the river Lamus (16 September 845). After the truce had expired (26 October) Aḥmad, Emir of Tarsus, made an invasion by the Cilician Gates; but heavy snow and rain came on; many men died from exposure, some were drowned in the Podandus, others captured, and Aḥmad retreated before the enemy; whereupon his officers forced him to leave the province, and the Caliph Wāthiq appointed Naṣr to succeed him (17 January 846). After this we hear of no invasions till 851; and the raids on the Cilician frontier were henceforth of small account. The disuse of the suburban fire-signals (ascribed to Michael III's fear of their spoiling the circus-games) was therefore of little importance. In 851 an Armenian revolt enabled the Romans to recover Camacha. Theodosiopolis and Arsamosata they failed to take, but with Armenian help defeated and killed Yūsuf, Emir of Armenia, in Taron (March 852), retreating, however, on the arrival of reinforcements sent by the Caliph Mutawakkil.

After Mu'taṣim's death the disintegration of the Caliphate, which had already begun, rapidly advanced. Owing to the hatred in Baghdad for the large Turkish guard instituted by Mu'taṣim, that Caliph removed (836) to the petty town of Sāmarrā, where his Turks were free from all restraint. He was strong enough to control them; but his feeble successors became the puppets of these mercenaries, who cared little for imperial interests, while the Emirs paid small respect to a government directed by Turks. Hence the central authority grew continually weaker, and the local governors became semi-independent rulers, each looking after the affairs of his own province with little interference from the central power. Moreover a system had been introduced of breaking up the great provinces and placing the frontier-districts under separate

[1] Probably the Bithynian Melas (Vasil'ev, I. p. 55, n. 2).

governors. Besides that of al-ʻAwāṣim, Cilicia, perhaps for a time attached to it, was, probably in 808, made a province under the name of Thughūr-ash-Shām (frontiers of Syria) with its capital at Tarsus, and before 820 we find a province of Thughūr al-Jazīra (frontiers of Mesopotamia), extending from Kaisum and Germanicea to the northern Euphrates, with its capital at Melitene. These two provinces contained fifteen fortresses occupied by military colonies, of which that of Tarsus amounted to 5000 men, and those of Adata and Melitene to 4000 each; and behind these in case of necessity lay the six fortresses of al-ʻAwāṣim. This system, probably founded on the Roman themes and clisurae, was intended to provide a special frontier force under commanders whose sole business was to carry on the war against the Empire and to defend the frontier; but in consequence of the weakening of the central power the result was that they had to do this almost entirely out of their local resources. Muʻtaṣim indeed on his return from the campaign of 838 gave the command to Abū-Saʻīd by special commission; but under his successors the frontier governors were left to themselves, and enjoyed so much independence that Omar of Melitene held office at least twenty-eight years and ʻAlī of Tarsus at least eleven. Moreover, Omar spent much time and weakened his forces by fighting with a neighbour or rival. Thus the Romans had only petty disunited chiefs with whom to contend, and henceforward the war went more and more in their favour.

In 853 they sailed to Damietta, probably in order to prevent the sending of supplies to Crete, burned the town, killed the men, carried the women, Muslim and Christian, into captivity, and seized a store of arms intended for Crete (22 May). Simultaneously two other squadrons attacked Syrian ports; and it was perhaps in connexion with these operations that the Anatolic strategus Photinus was transferred to Crete, where he effected a landing, but, though reinforced from Constantinople, was finally defeated and with difficulty escaped. This event caused Mutawakkil to re-create an Egyptian fleet and fortify Damietta; it was probably in order to hinder these operations that in 854 the Romans came again to Damietta, where they remained plundering for a month. The new fleet was, however, of small account, and Egyptian warships really play little part in history till the Fāṭimite period. In 855 a Roman army destroyed Anazarbus, which had been lately re-fortified, and carried off the gipsies who had been settled there in 835. Theodora then asked for an exchange of prisoners, and the Caliph, after sending (December) Naṣr the Shīʻite to discover how many Muslim prisoners there were, agreed, and the exchange took place on the Lamus (21 February 856).

In the summer of 856 the Romans marched from Camacha by Arsamosata to the neighbourhood of Amida and returned by way of Tephrice, the new stronghold of the Paulicians, who, when persecuted by Leo V, had sought the protection of the Emir of Melitene and had been settled in Argaus. They had increased in numbers during the persecution of Theodora, and were now useful auxiliaries to the Arabs. Omar of Melitene and the Paulician Carbeas pursued the invaders on their retreat, but without success. After this Omar was for some years detained by dissensions at home; but in 858 Bugha marched from Damascus in July and took Semaluos.

The Empire was now under the rule of the capable and energetic Bardas, who had ousted Theodora from power in 856. He realised that under the new conditions a vigorous effort might rid Asia Minor of the standing scourge of the raids. In 859 therefore, while a fleet attacked Pelusium (June), a large army under Michael in person, accompanied by Bardas, besieged Arsamosata[1]; but on the third day, a Sunday, when the Emperor was at the Eucharist, a sortie was made by the garrison, and the besiegers retreated in confusion; they abandoned the imperial tents, but were able to return with captives from the country-side.

On 31 May Constantine Triphyllius had reached Sāmarrā with 77 prisoners and a request for a general exchange, and after the retreat Naṣr was sent to Constantinople to discuss the matter; but the negotiations were delayed by an event at Lulum, where the garrison, not having received their pay, excluded their commandant from the town and, when Michael sent to offer them 1000 denarii apiece to surrender the fortress, sent two hostages to Constantinople with an expression of willingness to accept Christianity (November). On receiving the arrears, however, they handed over the envoy to 'Alī's lieutenant, who sent him to the Caliph (March 860). He was ordered to accept Islām on pain of death, and the result of Michael's offer of 1000 Muslims for him is unknown. On the news reaching Constantinople negotiations were resumed, and the general exchange took place at the end of April.

In 860 a still more formidable force, which included the Thracian and Macedonian as well as the Asiatic themes, set out under the Emperor himself to meet Omar and Carbeas, who had reached Sinope; but Michael was recalled by the news that a Russian fleet had come to the mouth of the Mauropotamus[2] on its way to Constantinople. After the retreat of the Russians (June) he rejoined the army and overtook the enemy at Chonarium near Dazimon, but was defeated and was glad even to secure a safe retreat. The same year a fleet under Faḍl took Attalia. In 863 Omar with a large force sacked the flourishing city of Amisus, and Bardas, who was himself no general, placed his brother Petronas at the head of a vast army which comprised the Asiatic and European themes and the household troops. Omar marched south, intending to return by way of

[1] Genesius says 'Samosata'; but he states that the invasion was made to stop Omar's raids, and Omar had nothing to do with Samosata, which was in neither of the frontier provinces. Also to reach it they would have had to pass many strong places. The MSS. of Ṭabarī have 'Arsamosata,' 'Samosata' being an emendation from Ibn al-Athīr and Abū'l Maḥāsin.

[2] This must be the meaning of the Greek (*Th. Mel.*, p. 158). The name Mauropotamus (*supra*, p. 131, n. 1) perhaps covers the lower course of the Sangarius.

Arabissus; but at Poson near the right bank of the Halys, probably not far from Nyssa, the Arabs found the surrounding hills occupied and were almost annihilated (3 September). Here the old Emir fell fighting, while his son with 100 men escaped over the Halys, but was captured by the clisurarch of Charsianum. The Romans then advanced into Mesopotamia, where 'Alī, who had been transferred to Armenia in 862, came from Martyropolis (Mayyāfarīqīn) to meet them, but he also was defeated and killed. After this, insignificant raids continued to be made from Tarsus, and some more serious inroads by the Paulicians; but the Emir of Melitene could only defend the frontier, and in the next reign the Roman boundary began to advance, and with the exception of a short interval under the weak rule of Leo VI the process continued without serious check till under Nicephorus II North Syria and West Mesopotamia were restored to the obedience of the Emperor. Having thus crushed the raiders from Melitene, Bardas set himself to crush those from Crete, who had extended their ravages to Proconnesus, and in 866 he and Michael marched to the mouth of the Maeander to cross to the island; but he was foully assassinated (21 April) and the expedition abandoned. Crete therefore remained a pirates' nest for nearly 100 years longer.

Meanwhile another struggle had been for many years going on in Sicily. Since an attack upon Sicily did not involve immediate danger to the heart of the Empire, its affairs were treated as of secondary importance; and, as no fleet was stationed there, it was always open to attack from the African Arabs, and in such cases the Emperor could only either send a special force, if eastern affairs allowed him to do so, or beg the help of the Italian republics which still retained a nominal allegiance to the Empire. In 752 the Arabs had raided Sicily and forced Sardinia to pay tribute, and the attack was repeated in 763. In 805 Ibrāhīm ibn al-Aghlab (since 800 practically independent Emir of Africa) made a ten years' truce with the patrician Constantine; but nevertheless in 812 the Arabs attacked some islands off Sicily. To meet these enemies, Gregory was sent with a fleet by Michael I and obtained help from Gaeta and Amalfi. Seven of his ships were captured off Lampedusa and the crews massacred, but with the rest he lay in wait for the enemy and destroyed their whole fleet. The Arabs then apologised for the breach of peace, and another ten years' truce was made (813); but this was as little regarded as the previous one, for in 819 the Emir Ziyādatallāh sent his cousin Mahomet to raid Sicily; after which the peace was again renewed.

In consequence of the distance of Sicily from the seat of government, and the little attention paid to its affairs by the Emperors, it was easy for a usurper to start up there; and such a usurper could always, like Elpidius, in case of necessity find a refuge with the Arabs. About 825 the turmarch Euphemius rose against the patrician Gregoras, defeated and killed him, and made himself master of Sicily; and in 826 Constantine was sent as patrician with fresh forces, but he too after a defeat at Catania was taken and put to death. A successful resistance was however offered by an Armenian whom the Arabs call Balāṭa[1], and Euphemius fled to Africa to ask not merely a refuge but the help of the Emir. Then, charges having been made against the Romans of detaining Muslim prisoners, the treaty was declared to have been broken and an expedition resolved upon, at the head of which was placed the judge Asad, the chief advocate of war. On 15 June 827 the Arabs landed at Mazzara and defeated Balāṭa, who fled to Enna (Castrogiovanni) and thence to Calabria, where he soon afterwards died. After the invaders had seized some forts, the Sicilians sent envoys and paid tribute; but, hearing that they were preparing for an attack, Asad continued his march, and, when reinforced by ships from Africa and Spain, besieged Syracuse. A relieving force from Palermo was defeated (828); but the Arabs suffered severely both from famine, which caused discontent in the army, and from plague, which carried off Asad himself (July), to succeed whom they chose Mahomet ibn Abī' l-Jawārī. Theodotus now came with a fleet as patrician, and the Venetians, at the Emperor's request, sent ships. The Emir being occupied with a Frankish invasion, the Arabs were forced to raise the siege, and, unable in face of the hostile fleet to return to Africa, burned their ships and retreated.

Marching north-west, they forced Mineo to surrender after three days; and then the army divided, one detachment occupying Girgenti while the other besieged the strong fortress of Enna. During this siege Euphemius, who had accompanied the invaders, was assassinated by some citizens who obtained access to him on pretence of saluting him as emperor. Theodotus came from Syracuse to relieve Enna and entered the town, but he was defeated in a sortie, while a Venetian fleet sent to attack Mazzara returned unsuccessful. Soon afterwards Mahomet died, and under his successor Zuhair fortune turned against the Arabs. After a foraging party had been defeated, Zuhair next day attacked in force, but was routed and besieged in his camp, and soon afterwards, while trying a night surprise, was caught in an ambush and again routed. He then retired to Mineo, where the Arabs were besieged, and, being reduced to great straits by hunger, at last surrendered[2]. The garrison of Girgenti on hearing the news destroyed the town and retired to Mazzara.

The invaders were, however, relieved by the arrival of some adventurers from Spain, who in 830 began to ravage Sicily, but agreed to work with the Africans on condition that their leader Aṣbagh had the command. The combined force marched into the interior. Mineo was taken and destroyed (August), and Theodotus soon afterwards defeated and killed; but the plague again broke out and caused the death of Aṣbagh, after which the Arabs retreated, suffering much from the attacks of the Romans

[1] Perhaps κουροπαλάτης.

[2] This I infer from the facts that the *Cambridge Chronicle* places the Arab capture of Mineo in 830/1, and that we hear no more of Zuhair.

on the way. Most of the Spanish Arabs then returned; but on account of the eastern war Theophilus could not send reinforcements, and, when early in 831 the Emir's cousin Mahomet arrived with new forces to take command, the Arabs were able to besiege Palermo, which, reduced to extremities, surrendered on condition that the commandant with his family and property, the bishop-elect, and a few others were allowed to retire by sea (September). Palermo was henceforth the Arab capital.

Dissensions between African and Spanish Arabs for a time prevented an advance; but early in 834 the Arabs attacked Enna, and in 835 Mahomet himself assaulted the town and captured the commandant's wife and son; but on his return to Palermo he was murdered by some conspirators, who fled to the Romans. His successor, Faḍl ibn Ya'qūb, raided the district of Syracuse, and another force, finding its road blocked by the patrician, won a victory, in which the Roman commander was wounded and with difficulty rescued. On 12 September, however, Mahomet's brother Abū' l-Aghlab arrived with a fleet as governor, after some of his ships had been wrecked and others captured; he immediately sent out a squadron which took some Roman vessels and another which captured a fire-ship at Pantellaria. The crews of these were all beheaded. In 836 Faḍl raided the Aeolian islands, took some forts on the north coast, and captured eleven ships. On the other hand, an Arab land-force was defeated and its commander made prisoner, but afterwards ransomed, and another suffered a reverse before Enna. Early in 837, however, on a winter night the Arabs entered Enna, but, unable to take the citadel, accepted a ransom and returned with spoil. The same year they besieged Cefalù; but a stubborn resistance was made, and in 838 reinforcements from the East under the Caesar Alexius, whom Theophilus had sent with a fleet to command in Sicily, forced them to retreat, pursued by the Romans, who inflicted several defeats on them. In 839, however, the birth of an heir caused the Emperor to recall and degrade his son-in-law.

The death of the Emir Ziyādatallāh (10 June 838) and consequent uncertainty as to affairs in Sicily caused operations to be suspended for some months; but in 839 his successor Aghlab sent ships which raided the Roman districts, and in 840 Caltabellotta, Platani, Corleone, and Sutera were forced to pay tribute. Theophilus, unable to withdraw forces from the East, had in 839 asked help of the Venetians and even of the Franks and of the Emir of Spain; and in 840 sixty Venetian ships attacked the Arab fleet, then at Taranto, but these were nearly all taken and the crews massacred. In 841 the Arabs sacked Caltagirone; in 843 a fleet under Faḍl ibn Ja'far, assisted by the Neapolitans, who for protection against the Duke of Benevento had allied themselves with the Arabs, attacked Messina, and after a long resistance took it by an unexpected attack from the land side; and in 845 Modica and other fortresses in the south-east were taken.

During the armistice in the East the troops of the Charsianite clisura were sent to Sicily; but towards the end of 845 ʻAbbās ibn al-Faḍl ibn Yaʻqūb defeated them with heavy loss, and in 847 Faḍl ibn Jaʻfar besieged Leontini, and after inducing the garrison by a trick to make a sortie caught them in an ambush, whereupon the citizens surrendered on condition that their lives and property were spared. In 848 the Roman ships landed a force eight miles from Palermo; but the men missed their way and returned, and seven of the ships were lost in a storm. The same year Ragusa near Modica surrendered and was destroyed (August).

On 17 January 851 Abū'l-Aghlab died after a government of fifteen years, during which (probably on account of dissensions such as those which had caused his predecessor's death) he had never left Palermo. His successor, ʻAbbās ibn al-Faḍl, was a man of very different character. As soon as his appointment was confirmed by the Emir Mahomet, he himself took the field, sending his uncle Rabbāh in advance to Caltavuturo, which submitted to pay tribute[1], while the prisoners were put to death by ʻAbbās, who himself ravaged the territory of Enna but failed to draw the garrison out to battle. He repeated the raid in 852 and defeated a hostile force, sending the heads of the slain to Palermo. Then in 853 he made a great expedition by way of Enna to the east coast, where he raided Catania, Syracuse, Noto, and Ragusa (this had been re-occupied by the Romans), and after a siege of five months forced Butera to capitulate on condition that 5000 persons were handed over as slaves. In 856 he took five fortresses, and in 857 harried Taormina and Syracuse and compelled another place to surrender after two months' siege on the terms that 200 of the chief men were allowed to go free; the rest he sold as slaves, and he destroyed the fort. The same year Cefalù capitulated and was destroyed; but, as being on the coast it was more easily defended, he was obliged to allow all the inhabitants their freedom. In 858 he again raided Enna and Syracuse and took Gagliano, returning in the winter to Enna; here he took a prisoner of note, who to save his life showed him a way into the fortress, which after a resistance of 30 years fell (26 January 859). All fighting men were put to death and a mosque built.

This event led Bardas to take vigorous measures; and in the autumn, while negotiations were proceeding with the Caliph, he sent his connexion by marriage, Constantine Contomytes, to Sicily with large reinforcements. ʻAbbās met them with an army and fleet, defeated them near Syracuse, drove them back to their ships, some of which were taken, and returned to Palermo for the winter. They had, however, suffered little; and, when in 860 Platani, Sutera, Caltabellotta, Caltavuturo, and other towns revolted, an army came to support them. ʻAbbās defeated the Romans and besieged Platani and another fort, but was compelled to return northward by the news that another army was marching towards Palermo.

[1] This seems to follow from its revolt in 860.

Having met these new enemies near Cefalù, he forced them to retreat in disorder to Syracuse; the revolted towns, without hope of succour, submitted; and the governor gave orders to re-fortify and garrison Enna, so that the road to the west might no longer be open to the enemy. In 861 he raided Syracuse, but on his return fell ill and died (15 August). The Romans with mean revenge afterwards dug up and burned his body. He was the real conqueror of Sicily.

The Aghlabid Emirs, probably from fear of an independent power arising in Sicily, had been in the habit of appointing princes of their house to the governorship. To this 'Abbās had been a notable exception, having been chosen by the officers in Sicily; and, if a similar appointment had been made after his death, the conquest would have been soon completed. But the Emir Aḥmad reverted to the earlier practice; instead of confirming two temporary governors who had been appointed locally, he sent his kinsman Khafāja (July 862). The new governor was for a time detained by troubles among the Saracens; but in February 864 Noto was betrayed to him, and soon afterwards he took Scicli. In 865 he marched by Enna, ravaging the country, to Syracuse, where a fleet joined him, but on four ships being captured he despaired of taking the city and returned; and his son, whom he sent with a small force to harass the enemy, lost 1000 men in an ambush and retreated. In 866 he again came to Syracuse, and thence to the district of Mt Etna, where he accepted an offer of tribute from Taormina. He then marched against Ragusa, which submitted on condition that the inhabitants were allowed to go free with their goods and animals; but these he nevertheless seized. After more successes he fell ill and returned. Meanwhile Taormina revolted.

Thus the Muslim conquest was complete but for Taormina and Syracuse and a few other places on the east coast, which still owned allegiance to the Byzantine Empire. Syracuse only fell in 878, Taormina not till 902; nevertheless Sicily may now already be called a Muslim outpost.

(B)

THE STRUGGLE WITH THE SARACENS (867–1057).

The struggle with the Saracens constituted the chief problem with which the foreign policy of Basil I had to deal. The circumstances were as favourable as they could possibly be, because during his reign the Empire lived in peaceful relations with its other neighbours: in the east with Armenia, in the north with young Russia and Bulgaria, and in the west with Venice and Germany.

The favourable conditions in which Basil I was placed in his relation with the Eastern and Western Saracens become clearer when we bear in mind the following considerations.

1. Owing to the rapidly increasing influence of the Turks at the Caliph's court, internal dissensions were continually breaking out in the Eastern Caliphate.

2. Egypt became independent in 868, owing to the fact that a new dynasty, that of the Ṭūlūnids, had been founded there.

3. Civil war had broken out among the North African Saracens.

4. The relations of the Spanish Umayyads with the local Christian population were beset with difficulties.

Basil I was occupied during the first four years of his reign with military operations against the Western Saracens, for during this time peace was not violated on the eastern frontier. The help which the Byzantine fleet in 868 gave to Ragusa, which at that time was being besieged by the Saracens, forced the latter to withdraw and was thus the means of strengthening the Byzantine influences on the shores of the Adriatic.

The troubles in South Italy compelled the intervention of the Western Emperor Louis II, who, having concluded an alliance with Basil I and with the Pope, took Bari on 2 February 871. Of the important places in South Italy only Taranto now remained in the hands of the Saracens. The position of Byzantium was not improved during these four years in Sicily, where only Taormina and Syracuse remained in her power; the occupation of the island of Malta by the Saracens in August 870 completely surrounded Sicily with Saracen possessions, for all the other islands in that region already belonged to them.

In the east Basil I, wishing to re-establish peace and union with the Paulicians, who had been severely persecuted by the Empress Theodora, sent to them in 869–870 Peter the Sicilian as his ambassador, but his mission was not successful, and the extravagant demands of Chrysochir, the leader of the Paulicians, led to war.

The campaigns of 871 and 872 gave Tephrice, the chief town of the Paulicians, into the power of Basil, and also a whole chain of other fortified places. In one of the battles Chrysochir himself was slain. The fugitive Paulicians found a ready welcome from the Saracens.

This war with the Paulicians extended the Byzantine frontier as far as the Saracen Melitene (Malaṭīyah), and set Basil free to advance against the Eastern Saracens. In 873 war was declared, and Basil captured Zapetra (Sozopetra) and Samosata, but in the end he was totally defeated near Malaṭīyah.

From 874 to 877 was a period of calm. In the east and in Sicily, we do not hear of any military operations. In Italy, after the death of the Emperor Louis II, the Byzantine troops occupied the town of Bari at the request of the inhabitants, and apparently at this time, in the years

874–877, the Byzantine fleet captured Cyprus; but it remained in the possession of the Greeks only for seven years.

The year 878 was disastrous to the military policy of Byzantium: on 21 May the Saracens took Syracuse by assault after a siege of nine months. Thus the only town in Sicily remaining in the hands of the Greeks was Taormina. The loss of Syracuse was the turning-point in the history of Basil's foreign relations. His foreign policy proved a complete failure, and the last eight years of his reign were occupied in casual and comparatively small encounters. In the east there were frequent conflicts, but of an undecided character; success alternated sometimes in favour of one side and sometimes of the other, but in no case to the glory of the Byzantine arms.

From 886 Basil was in friendly relations with the Armenian King, Ashot I, the Bagratid, whose State formed a useful buffer against the Eastern Saracens. In Sicily the usual skirmishes went on, and it was only in South Italy that the Byzantine troops began to gain victories, more especially after the arrival of Nicephorus Phocas[1] in command. But in this year Basil died (29 August 886).

During his reign the Empire had lost much in the west, but in Asia Minor, notwithstanding some failures, the frontier was considerably advanced eastwards, and thus the Byzantine influence, which had been somewhat weakened, was to a great extent restored.

If Basil I lived in peace with his neighbours, with the exception of the Saracens, it was very different with his successor Leo VI the Wise (886–912). Immediately after his accession to the throne, military operations began in Bulgaria, and this war, which terminated with the peace of 893, brought much humiliation upon the Empire. The peace lasted about twenty years. In connexion with the Bulgarian war, for the first time the Hungarians enter into the history of Byzantium, and towards the end of the reign of Leo the Russians appeared before Constantinople. Armenia, which was in alliance with Byzantium, during the whole of Leo's reign was subjected to Arabian invasions, and the Emperor of Byzantium had not the strength to help the Armenian King Sempad (Smbat); it was only at the end of his reign that Leo went to the aid of Armenia, but he died during the campaign. The question about the fourth marriage of the Emperor caused great division in the Empire. It was thus evident that the conditions of the struggle between the Byzantine Empire and the Saracens were becoming more difficult.

During the first fourteen years of the reign of Leo VI, from 886 to 900, the Greeks suffered frequent defeats in the east, at the Cilician Gates and in the west of Cilicia, where the Saracens successfully advanced along the coast as well as into the interior of the country. The failures

[1] The grandfather of the future Emperor of the same name. See *supra*, Chapter III, p. 69.

on land and the naval defeat of Rāghib in 898 off the coast of Asia Minor compelled the Byzantine government to recall the energetic Nicephorus Phocas from Italy, and about 900 he arrived in Asia Minor. Affairs in Sicily grew worse and worse with every year. In 888 the imperial fleet suffered a severe defeat at Mylae (now Milazzo); but the Byzantines were somewhat helped by the fact that the Saracens were at that time occupied with their own internal dissensions and in conflicts with the African Aghlabids. Some successes gained by the Byzantine arms in Italy had no influence on the general conditions of the struggle between Leo VI and the Saracens. In the east, Nicephorus Phocas by his victory at Adana in 900 justified the hopes that had been placed in him; but the success of the Byzantines came with this nearly to a standstill.

The first years of the tenth century were signalised by a whole series of misfortunes for the Byzantine Empire, in the west as well as in the east. In the west, the Saracen chief Abū'l-'Abbās took possession of Reggio in Calabria on 10 June 901, and the Aghlabid Emir Ibrāhīm captured on 1 August 902 Taormina, the last fortified place of the Greeks in Sicily.

With the fall of Taormina, Sicily was entirely in the power of the Saracens. It is true that several unimportant points, as for instance Demona, still remained in the hands of the Greeks, but this had no importance whatever for the future history of Byzantium. From 902 onwards Sicilian events do not exercise any influence on the course of Byzantine political affairs. In the second half of Leo's reign, the eastern policy of the Empire is quite independent of his relations with the Sicilian Saracens.

The first years of the tenth century were also signalised by important events on sea. At the end of the ninth century the Saracens of Crete had already begun their devastating attacks on the coast of the Peloponnesus; indeed, they held in their power the whole of the Aegean Sea. We possess information about their attacks on the islands of Naxos, Patmos, Paros, Aegina, and Samos. But it was during the first years of the tenth century that these maritime invasions of the Saracens became especially threatening. Their two strong fleets—the Syrian and the Cretan—frequently acted together. In 902 the Saracen fleet laid waste the islands of the Aegean Sea, and destroyed the rich and populous town of Demetrias on the coast of Thessaly. In the summer of 904, another Saracen fleet, under the command of the Greek renegade, Leo of Tripolis, made an attack on the south coast of Asia Minor, and, in the month of July of the same year, took possession of the important town of Attalia. Leo then had the intention of going towards Constantinople, the town "preserved by God." But having entered the Hellespont and captured Abydos, the chief custom-house port for ships going to Byzantium, he suddenly departed, and then, coasting round the peninsula of Chalcidice, approached Thessalonica. Himerius, who was sent against him, did not dare to engage the Saracen fleet in battle.

The Saracen ships approached Thessalonica on 29 July 904, and made an unexpected assault upon it. The story of the siege, which lasted from 29 to 31 July, is well known to us from a work of John Cameniates. Thessalonica passed into the power of the Saracens on 31 July 904, but they shortly afterwards departed for Syria with many prisoners and rich booty. It was only after this misfortune that the Byzantine government began to fortify Attalia and Thessalonica.

The naval failures of 902–904 induced the Emperor Leo to give greater attention to the fleet, which was so quickly and greatly improved that in 906 Himerius was enabled to gain a brilliant victory over the Saracens, and in the summer of 910 he was therefore placed at the head of a large naval expedition, directed against the allied Eastern and Cretan Arabs. Detailed accounts of the composition of this expedition are preserved in the *Ceremonies* of Constantine Porphyrogenitus.

However, the result of the expedition did not correspond to all these great preparations, for after some success at Cyprus Himerius suffered a severe defeat near the isle of Samos in October 911 and lost the greater part of his fleet. On the death of Leo VI, Himerius returned to Constantinople, and was shut up in a monastery by the Emperor Alexander.

In the east, on land, from 900, the usual military operations were carried on with varying success.

Byzantine policy, in its relation to the Saracens, proved a complete failure under Leo VI: in the west, Sicily was definitely lost; in the south of Italy, after Nicephorus Phocas had been recalled, the success of the Byzantine arms was brought to a close; on the eastern frontier, the Saracens were still steadily, if slowly, advancing, especially in Cilicia; on sea, Byzantium met with a whole series of most ruinous disasters.

The reign of Constantine VII Porphyrogenitus is divided into three periods: 1. From 913 to 919—the government of his mother Zoë, who acted as regent during his minority. 2. From 919 to 944—the government of Romanus Lecapenus. 3. From 945 to 959—the absolute government of Constantine himself.

The period down to 927 was occupied with the obstinate and unhappy war with the Bulgarian King Simeon, during which Byzantium was obliged to concentrate all its efforts against this terrible enemy. At this time it was impossible even to think of any regular organised action against the Saracens. It was a happy circumstance for Byzantium that the Caliphate itself was passing at the same time through the epoch of its dissolution, which was caused by internal dissensions and the rise of separate independent dynasties. Consequently, down to 927 the encounters with the Saracens were of the usual harassing and monotonous character, and generally resulted to the advantage of the Saracen arms. It was only in 921 or 922 that the Byzantine fleet gained a great naval victory near the island of Lemnos over the renowned hero of 904, Leo of Tripolis. In 927 Byzantium concluded peace with the Bulgarian King Peter, who had succeeded Simeon, and was thus free to turn her attention towards the Saracens.

In the time of Romanus Lecapenus, eminent leaders arose in the armies of both adversaries; in that of the Greeks, the Domestic John Curcuas, who, after some defeats in Saracen Armenia, fought with success in the frontier province of Mesopotamia, and in 934 captured Melitene (Malaṭīyah). The new Saracen leader was Saif-ad-Daulah, sovereign of Aleppo and chief of the independent dynasty of the Ḥamdānids. He strengthened himself at the expense of the Caliph of Baghdad, and began successful military operations in the regions of the Upper Euphrates. This induced the Emperor to enter into friendly negotiations with the Caliph of Baghdad and with the Egyptian sovereigns, the Ikhshīdids. But disturbances in the Eastern Caliphate and other difficulties drew the attention of Saif-ad-Daulah away from the Byzantine frontier, and this explains why John Curcuas, in the fourth decade, gained a series of easy victories in Armenia and Upper Mesopotamia, and in 942–3 captured the towns of Mayyāfarīqīn (Martyropolis), Dara, and Nisibis. In 944 Edessa, after a severe siege, succumbed to the Greeks, and was obliged to deliver up her precious relic, the miraculous image of the Saviour (*τὸ μανδίλιον*, or *μανδήλιον*), which was with great solemnity transferred to Constantinople.

In 945 Constantine Porphyrogenitus became absolute ruler of the Byzantine Empire. Down to the very year of his death (959) military operations did not cease in the east, where his chief adversary was the already famous Saif-ad-Daulah, who, having settled in 947 his difficulties with the Egyptian Ikhshīdids, turned against Byzantium. In the beginning the advantage was with the Greeks. In 949 they seized Mar'ash (Germanicea); in 950 they totally defeated Saif-ad-Daulah in the narrow passage near the town of Ḥadath; and in 952 they crossed the Euphrates and took the Mesopotamian town of Sarūj. But in 952 and 953 Saif-ad-Daulah defeated the Greeks not far from Mar'ash and took the son of the Domestic prisoner. In 954 Saif-ad-Daulah gained a fresh victory over the Domestic Bardas Phocas near Ḥadath, and in 956 the future Emperor John Tzimisces was defeated by him in the province of the Upper Euphrates near the fortress of Tall-Baṭrīq. Only in 957 did success turn to the side of the Greeks. In this year Ḥadath surrendered to them. In 958 John Tzimisces defeated the Arabs in Northern Mesopotamia and took Samosata. During the life of Constantine Porphyrogenitus, Saif-ad-Daulah was unable to avenge himself upon the Greeks for these last failures.

If the fighting on the eastern frontier was difficult for Byzantium and was far from being always successful, the maritime operations of the Byzantine fleet ended in total disaster. In 949 a great naval expedition was undertaken against the Cretan Arabs, who, as was always the case, were greatly feared, and were desolating the coast of Greece and the islands of the Aegean Sea. To further the success of the enterprise, the Emperor entered into friendly relations with their enemies the Spanish Saracens. The Emperor has left in his *Ceremonies* a detailed account of the composition and equipment of this expedition[1]. The incompetent patrician Constantine Gongylas, who had been given the chief command of the Byzantine fleet, landed troops at Crete, but suffered a terrible defeat and lost the greater part of his vessels.

The monotonous conflicts of the Greeks with the Saracens in the west, in Italy and in Sicily, did not have any influence on the general course of events.

It is true that the military operations in the east, during the reign of Constantine, were not always successful for the Byzantine Empire; but the advance of the last years in removing the frontier beyond the Euphrates laid the foundation for the brilliant triumphs of his successors.

The reign of the weak Emperor Romanus II is distinguished by great victories of the Byzantine arms over the Saracens, thanks to the talents and energy of Nicephorus Phocas, the future Emperor.

This great general captured the island of Crete in March 961, and thus destroyed the nest of pirates who had struck terror into the inhabitants of the islands and of the always open shores of the Mediterranean Sea. After having enjoyed a triumph in Constantinople, Nicephorus Phocas was removed to the eastern frontier and he began there also a successful war with Saif-ad-Daulah. At the end of 961 or in the beginning of 962 he seized Anazarbus; in 962 he captured Mar'ash, Ra'bān, and Dulūk (Doliche); in the vicinity of Manbij he took prisoner the famous poet Abū-Firās, the governor of the town; and, at last, in December of the same year, he took possession of Aleppo, the capital of the Ḥamdānid Emirs, after a difficult siege. All these places, however, did not remain in the hands of the Greeks, for Nicephorus Phocas retired to the Byzantine territory.

Less successful were the military operations of the Byzantine troops in the west, and especially in Sicily. Taormina, as it is well known, was taken by the Saracens in 902, but was again lost by them. And now, on 24 December 962, after a siege of seven months, the Saracens captured it once more; and there remained in the hands of the Greeks only the inaccessible Rametta, situated in the eastern part of the island.

The reigns of Nicephorus Phocas, John Tzimisces, and Basil II Bulgaroctonus, the three next successors of Romanus II, when viewed from the side of the military successes of the Empire in its fight with the Saracens, form the most glorious and successful period of Byzantine history.

After the death of Romanus, 15 March 963, his brilliant general

[1] *De Ceremoniis*, II. 45, pp. 664–678.

Nicephorus Phocas, who was adored by his troops, was proclaimed Emperor by them on 2 July of that year, at Caesarea in Cappadocia. Upon arriving at Constantinople he quickly overthrew Joseph Bringas, who had been all-powerful at court, and was then crowned on 16 August. To consolidate his power he married Theophano, the late Emperor's widow, who had been regent of the Empire.

The new Emperor turned his chief attention to the east, although he was drawn away at times by his hostile relations with the Bulgarians. His policy towards Bulgaria brought about the intervention of the Russian Prince Svyatoslav, and caused conflicts in Italy with the Western Emperor Otto the Great.

In the summer of 964 Nicephorus Phocas arrived in Cilicia, and since Adana had been abandoned by its inhabitants, he concentrated his energies upon Mamistra (Mopsuestia) and Tarsus. While his armies were besieging these towns, the lighter detachments devastated the north and south of Cilicia, took Anazarbus, and even advanced to the boundaries of Syria, where they took possession of the seaport town of Rhosus. In the meantime the sieges of Mamistra and Tarsus were so unsuccessful that the Emperor returned to Cappadocia for the winter, leaving a detachment of sufficient strength to watch the besieged towns. At the renewal of military operations in 965, Mamistra and Tarsus were so greatly exhausted by famine and disease that they were incapable of holding out any longer; on 13 June 965 Mamistra was taken, and on 16 August Tarsus surrendered.

In this year, 965, in connexion with the campaign on land, we may mention the conquest of Cyprus by the patrician Nicetas Chalcutzes, about which only very meagre accounts have been preserved. The Egyptian fleet, which was ordered to convey provisions to the besieged Tarsus and to recover Cyprus from the Greeks, appeared in August 965 off the southern coast of Asia Minor and suffered defeat. The conquest of Cyprus gave into the hands of Byzantium dominion over the north-eastern shore of the Mediterranean Sea, and the general results of the campaign of 965 were such that the possession of Cilicia and the island of Cyprus opened for Nicephorus the road to Syria.

On 23 June 966, near Samosata on the Euphrates, an exchange of prisoners took place, and the Arab poet Abū-Firās, already known to us, obtained his freedom. Fighting, however, was renewed in the autumn, when Nicephorus Phocas appeared in the east and invaded the districts surrounding Amida and Dara, and besieged Manbij (Hierapolis) in north-east Syria, from whose inhabitants he demanded and received one of the Christian relics belonging to the town, a brick on which the image of the Saviour was impressed. Advancing far over the borders of Syria, he drew near to the accomplishment of his chief design, the conquest of Antioch. He began to besiege the city in October 966, but it was so well fortified that Nicephorus Phocas could not at this time capture it, and so, raising the siege, he returned to Constantinople by way of Tarsus.

In January 967 the chief antagonist of Nicephorus Phocas in the east, Saif-ad-Daulah, died after a prolonged illness, and was succeeded by his son Sa'd-ad-Daulah. The war with Bulgaria and disturbances inside the Empire did not allow Nicephorus to profit by the difficulties arising from the succession to the throne of the Ḥamdānids, and consequently the year 967 is only marked by insignificant conflicts with the Saracens, which did not always end to the advantage of the Byzantine troops. Only in the latter half of 968 was the Emperor free to depart again to the east. The chief aim of this campaign was the conquest of the two most important towns of Syria, Antioch and Aleppo. Before beginning a regular siege of these towns, he made devastating incursions into Syria; towns one after another succumbed to his attacks. Emesa, Tripolis, Arca, Ṭaraṭūs (Tortosa), Marāqīyah, Jiblah (Byblus), Laodicea also, suffered much from the Byzantine troops.

Nicephorus began now to besiege Antioch in earnest, but was again unsuccessful. Leaving Peter Phocas, the *stratopedarch*, with the army at Antioch, the Emperor returned to the capital. During his stay there important events were happening near Antioch. Dissensions and disturbances broke out there, and profiting by these quarrels Peter Phocas and Michael Burtzes, the commander of the garrison of the fortress of Baghras, took possession of Antioch on 28 October 969. The chief object was now obtained; the city was in the hands of the Byzantine Emperor. An enormous booty fell to the share of the conquerors. Soon after this the Byzantine troops advanced against the Syrian town of Aleppo, which, at the end of 969 or in the beginning of January 970, after a siege of twenty-seven days, also passed into their hands.

The curious text of the treaty concluded by Peter Phocas with Qarghūyah, who was at that time in possession of Aleppo, is still preserved. By this treaty the boundaries in Syria were accurately fixed and a list of localities was drawn up, some of which passed into the possession of the Greek Emperor and others into feudal dependence. Antioch, the most important of the conquered towns, was annexed to the Empire; but Aleppo only became a vassal. The population was subjected to taxation for the benefit of Byzantium; the Christians living under Muslim rule were, however, freed from all imposts. The Emir of Aleppo was obliged to assist the Emperor in case of war with the non-Musulman inhabitants of these provinces. The restoration of the destroyed churches was guaranteed to the Christians. The Emir of Aleppo was also obliged to give protection to the Byzantine commercial caravans when entering his territory. It was agreed that, after the deaths of the ruler of Aleppo, Qarghūyah, and his successor Bakjūr, the new governor of Aleppo could only be appointed by the Emperor from the nobility of Aleppo. Rules were even prescribed about the surrender of run-away slaves, and so on. This treaty was only ratified after the death of Nicephorus Phocas, who fell by the hands of assassins on the night of 10–11 December 969. We can say that never before were the Saracens subjected to such humiliation as during the reign of Nicephorus Phocas. Cilicia and a part of Syria were taken away from them, and a great part of their territory acknowledged itself as being in vassal dependence upon the Empire.

The military operations of the troops of Nicephorus in Sicily did not correspond with his successes in the east. In Sicily, as we have said, only one town, Rametta, remained in the hands of the Greeks, and this was besieged by the Saracens in 964. To help the besieged town, a great fleet was despatched under the command of Manuel. But the troops which had been landed were defeated, and in 965 Rametta was taken by assault. The whole of Sicily thus passed into the hands of the Saracens. In 967 a durable peace was concluded between Nicephorus Phocas and the Fāṭimite Caliph Muʿizz, to whom Sicily was in subjection.

During the first years of his reign, John Tzimisces was unable personally to take part in the military operations on the eastern frontier. The wars with the Russian Prince Svyatoslav and with Bulgaria, and the revolt of Bardas Phocas, required his unremitting attention. But the wars finished successfully and the revolt of Bardas Phocas was crushed. The dissensions which had broken out in Italy found a happy solution in the marriage of the Byzantine Princess Theophano with the heir to the German throne, the future Emperor Otto II. It was only when these questions had been settled that John Tzimisces was able to turn to the east.

In the meantime, a difficult problem arose there, namely, how to retain all the new acquisitions which Nicephorus Phocas had won in Cilicia and Syria. In 971 the Egyptian Fāṭimite Muʿizz despatched one of his commanders into Syria for the purpose of conquering Antioch. The city was subjected to a severe siege, and was only saved by an unexpected attack by the Carmathians on the Egyptian troops, who were compelled to raise the siege and to retire hurriedly to the south. At the news Tzimisces, who was at that time in Bulgaria, immediately sent Michael Burtzes to the assistance of Antioch; and he at once rebuilt the town-wall, which had suffered much. In 973 Mleh (Melchi) an Armenian, who commanded the Greek troops, invaded the north of Mesopotamia, devastated the provinces of Nisibis, Mayyāfarīqīn, and Edessa, and captured Malaṭīyah, but he suffered a severe defeat near Amida and died in captivity.

These successes of the Greeks angered the Saracens to such an extent that a revolution broke out in Baghdad, and the people demanded an immediate declaration of a holy war (*jihād*) against the victorious Empire. So far as we can judge from the fragmentary and confused accounts of the sources, in 974 John Tzimisces himself set out to the east. He there concluded an alliance with Armenia and victoriously passed along the route of the campaign of 973, *i.e.* through Amida, Mayyāfarīqīn, and Nisibis. Special significance attached to his campaign in the east in 975, concerning which a very valuable document in the form of a letter by the

Emperor to his ally, the Armenian King Ashot III, has been preserved by the Armenian historian, Matthew of Edessa. The plan of this campaign is striking owing to its very audacity: the Emperor aimed at freeing Jerusalem from the power of the Saracens, and thus he undertook an actual crusade.

On leaving Antioch, the Emperor passed Emesa and turned to Baalbek, which was taken after a vain resistance. Damascus also voluntarily surrendered, and promised to pay tribute and to fight for the Byzantines. Turning to the south, the Emperor entered north Palestine, and the towns of Tiberias and Nazareth as well as Caesarea on the coast voluntarily surrendered to him; from Jerusalem itself came a petition to be spared a sack. But apparently he was not in sufficient strength to advance further, and he directed his march along the sea-coast to the north, capturing a whole series of towns: Beyrout (Berytus), Sidon, Jiblah (Byblus), Balanea, Gabala, Barzūyah (Borzo); but at Tripolis the troops of the Emperor were defeated. "To-day all Phoenicia, Palestine, and Syria," says the Emperor with some exaggeration in his letter to Ashot, "are freed from the Saracen yoke and acknowledge the dominion of the Romans, and in addition the great mountain of Lebanon has become subject to our authority." In September 975 the imperial troops retired to Antioch, and the Emperor himself returned to his capital, where he died on 10 January 976.

After the death of John Tzimisces, the two young sons of Romanus II, Basil and Constantine, succeeded. Basil became the head of the government. The first three years of their reign were occupied with quelling the rebellion of Bardas Sclerus on the eastern frontier, among whose troops were not a few Saracens. This revolt was suppressed by the Greek commander Bardas Phocas in 979, but only with much difficulty. Bardas Sclerus escaped to the Caliph of Baghdad, who welcomed a useful prisoner. Bardas Phocas remained in the east and fought the Saracens, especially the weakened Ḥamdānids, with alternating success, and he endeavoured to counteract the rapidly increasing influence of the Egyptian Fāṭimites in Syria.

In 986 began the famous Bulgarian war, which lasted for more than thirty years and ended in 1019 with the destruction of the Bulgarian kingdom of Samuel. Such an arduous and prolonged war might naturally have turned the attention of Basil II completely away from the eastern frontier of the Empire, but in fact he was compelled to intervene, through serious complications which were taking place there. Bardas Phocas, the victor over Bardas Sclerus, having fallen into disgrace at court, was proclaimed Emperor by his troops in 987, and Bardas Sclerus, having escaped from captivity in Baghdad, also appeared in Asia Minor. Bardas Phocas, however, captured him by a stratagem, and then crossed Asia Minor to the Hellespont. The condition of Byzantium was at this time very difficult: from the east the troops of Bardas Phocas were advancing to the capital, and from the north the Bulgarians were pressing on. To this time we must refer the negotiations of Basil II with the Russian Prince Vladímir and the consequent appearance at Byzantium of a Russian contingent of 6000 men. Basil II did not lose his presence of mind. With fresh forces he fought Bardas Phocas in 989, and in this battle the latter was slain. The Empire was thus freed from one of its dangers. In the same year a new insurrection of Bardas Sclerus was crushed.

During this time Syria was subjected to attacks by the troops of the Egyptian Fāṭimites, who several times assaulted Aleppo. Aleppo begged the Greeks for help and the Emperor sent Michael Burtzes, the governor of Antioch, to its assistance; but he suffered a severe defeat on the river Orontes in 994. This petition for help from Aleppo and the news of the defeat of Michael Burtzes reached Basil II when campaigning in Bulgaria. Notwithstanding the Bulgarian war, which was fraught with so much danger to the Empire, the Emperor decided to go personally to the east in the winter of 994–995, especially as danger was threatening Antioch. He unexpectedly appeared under the walls of Aleppo, which was being besieged by the Egyptian troops, and was successful in freeing the former capital of the Ḥamdānids from the enemy; he also captured Raphanea and Emesa; but having fought unsuccessfully under the walls of the strongly-fortified Tripolis, he returned to Bulgaria. In 998 the Greek troops under Damianus Dalassenus were severely defeated near Apamea. In 999 we meet Basil II again in Syria, at the towns of Shaizar and Emesa; but he was once more unsuccessful at Tripolis. Having spent some time in arranging affairs in Armenia and Georgia (Iberia), the Emperor returned to Constantinople in 1001.

In the same year a peace for ten years was concluded between the Emperor and the Egyptian Fāṭimite Ḥākim. Down to the very year of his death, there were no more encounters between him and the Eastern Muslims.

In the west, the Sicilian Saracens made yearly attacks on South Italy, and the imperial government, being occupied in other places, could not undertake expeditions against them. Its forced inactivity gave a welcome opportunity to the Western Emperor Otto II to attempt the expulsion of the Saracens from Sicily. Desiring to obtain a firm point of support in South Italy, he occupied some fortified Byzantine places, as for instance Taranto. But his chief aim was not reached, for in 982 the Saracens severely defeated him at Stilo. After his death in 983, the authority of the Greeks was somewhat restored, and the Byzantine governor occupied Bari, which had revolted. But the attacks of the Saracens on Southern Italy continued, and Bari was only saved by the intervention of the Venetian fleet. At the end of his reign Basil planned a vast expedition for the purpose of winning back Sicily, but during its preparation he died in 1025.

The death of Basil II, that terrible scourge of the Eastern Saracens, gave fresh heart to these enemies of the Empire. The Saracens, with great success, availed themselves of the weakness of the successors of Basil II and of the disturbances which broke out in the Empire, and they quickly took the offensive. Under Romanus III Argyrus (1028–1034), the Emir of Aleppo defeated the governor of Antioch, and the campaign, undertaken in 1030 after long preparation under the personal command of the Emperor, ended in a signal defeat near Aleppo, after which the Emperor quickly returned to Constantinople. In this campaign the young George Maniaces, who later on played a very important part in Byzantine history, distinguished himself for the first time.

The defeat of 1030 was to some degree mitigated by the capture of the important town of Edessa by George Maniaces in 1031, and by his seizing there the second relic of the town[1], the famous letter of Jesus Christ to Abgar, King of Edessa. This letter was sent to Constantinople and solemnly received by the Emperor and the people.

During the reign of the next Emperor, Michael IV the Paphlagonian (1034–1041), the usual collisions went on in the east, sometimes at Antioch, sometimes at Aleppo, whilst at the same time the Saracen corsairs devastated the southern coast of Asia Minor and destroyed Myra in Lycia.

In the west, the object of the imperial government was to recapture Sicily from the Saracens. The internal quarrels among the Sicilian Muslims made the intervention of the Greeks easy, and during the reign of Michael IV they undertook two expeditions. The first, under the command of Constantine Opus in 1037, was unsuccessful, but the second, in which the army was composed of different races, such as the "Varangian-Russian Druzhina" (detachment), and in which the Norse prince Harold Fairhair distinguished himself, was despatched in 1038 under the chief command of the brilliant young Maniaces. The beginning of the expedition was fortunate. Messina, Syracuse, and the whole eastern coast of the island passed into the hands of the imperial troops. But George Maniaces fell into disgrace, and being recalled to Constantinople was put into prison. With his removal, all the Byzantine conquests, with the exception of Messina, passed again into the power of the Saracens.

During the reign of Constantine IX Monomachus (1042–1054), almost complete peace reigned on the frontier of Syria and Mesopotamia; but on the other hand, from 1048 the Byzantine troops were obliged to fight, especially in Armenia, with the Seljūq Turks, who from this time forward appear as a new and formidable enemy on the eastern frontier.

[1] For the first relic of the town, the miraculous image of the Saviour, see *supra*, p. 143.

(C)

SUMMARY

It will be seen from the foregoing pages that, ever since Leo the Isaurian saved Constantinople from the formidable attack of the Saracens in A.D. 717, there was continuous warfare between the Empire and the Caliphate, for three hundred years. Its history is for the most part a monotonous and barren chronicle of raids to and fro across the Taurus mountains, truces, interchanges of prisoners, briefly registered in Greek and Arabic annals. Only occasionally have we a description of events full enough to excite some interest, like the campaign of the Caliph Muta'ṣim (A.D. 838) or the siege of Thessalonica. Successes varied, but few were decisive until Nicephorus Phocas definitely turned the tide in favour of the Empire and reconquered long-lost provinces. After his victories the Abbasid power, which had seen its best days before the end of the ninth century[1], declined rapidly till the Caliphate passed under the control of the Seljūqs. So long as the struggle lasted, the Eastern war had the first claim on the armies and treasury of the Empire, and these were not sufficient to enable the Emperors to deal at the same time effectively with their European enemies, the Slavs and Bulgarians, and to maintain intact their possessions in Sicily and Southern Italy. It was only when the Saracen danger in the east had been finally averted by the army of Nicephorus that his successors were able to recover some of the European provinces which had been lost.

If the Caliphs had a more extensive territory under their rule than the Emperors, it is not certain that they had larger revenues even when they were strongest. Their State was very loosely organised, and it was always a strain on them to keep its heterogeneous parts together. The Empire, on the other hand, was kept strictly under central control; it might be conquered, but it could not dissolve of itself; and the event proved that it had a much greater staying power.

It is to be observed that throughout the period the hostilities which were the order of the day do not seem to have interfered very seriously with the commercial intercourse between the peoples of the two states,

[1] The decline is evident, and may be illustrated from the revenue figures which are recorded. Under Rashīd, apart from contributions in kind, the taxes yielded a sum equivalent to about £21,000,000. In Ma'mūn's reign there was a considerable decline, and early in the tenth century the revenue was less than a twentieth of what it had been in Rashīd's reign. (See Kremer, *Kulturgeschichte* 376, and *Budget Haruns* in the *Verh. des vii intern. Orientalisten-Congresses, semitische Section*, Vienna 1888; Bury, *Eastern Roman Empire*, 236–7.) The Roman treasury was sometimes in great straits, but there was never any falling-off like this.

and reciprocal influences of culture flowed constantly between them. Through educated captives, who were often detained for four or five years and were generally well treated, knowledge of the conditions and features of the Byzantine world passed to Baghdad, and reversely. The capitals of the two Empires vied with each other in magnificence, art, and the cultivation of science. For instance, there cannot be much doubt that Theophilus was stimulated in his building enterprises by what he had heard of the splendour of the palaces of Baghdad. Oriental influences had been affecting the Roman Empire ever since the third century, through its intercourse with the Sasanid kingdom of Persia; they continued to operate throughout the Abbasid period, and were one of the ingredients of Byzantine civilisation.

CHAPTER VI.

ARMENIA.

Lying across the chief meeting-place of Europe and Asia, Armenia suffered immeasurably more from the conflict of two civilisations than it profited by their exchange of goods and ideas. If the West penetrated the East under pressure from Rome, Byzantium, or crusading Europe, if the East moved westwards, under Persian, Arab, Mongol, or Turk, the roads used were too often the roads of Armenia.

This was not all. East and West claimed and fought for control or possession of the country. Divided bodily between Rome and Persia in pre-Christian times, an apple of discord between Persia and the Byzantine Empire during the early part of the Middle Ages, Armenia for the rest of its national history was alternately the prey of Eastern and Western peoples. When the Armenian kingdom was strong enough to choose its own friends, it turned sometimes to the East, sometimes to the West. It drew its culture from both. But, belonging wholly neither to West nor to East, it suffered consistently at the hands of each in turn and of both together.

The stubborn pride of the Armenians in their national Church prevented them from uniting permanently either with Christendom or with Islām. Though driven by eastern pressure as far west as Cilicia, where it was in touch with the Crusaders, Armenia never held more than a doubtful place in the state-system of medieval Europe. Sooner than sink their identity in Greek or Roman Church, the Armenians more than once chose the friendship of infidels. On the other hand, whether as neighbours or as enemies, as allies or as conquerors, the races of the East could never turn the Armenians from their faith. When Armenia ceased to exist as a State, its people kept alive their nationality in their Church. As with the Jews, their ecclesiastical obstinacy was at once their danger and their strength: it left them friendless, but it enabled them to survive political extinction.

Isolated by religion, Armenia was also perpetually divided against itself by its rival princes. Like the Church, the numerous princely houses both preserved and weakened their country. They prevented the foundation of a unified national State. But a large Power stretching perhaps from Cappadocia to the Caspian borders, and disabled by ill-defined frontiers, could never have outfaced the hostility of Europe and

Asia. A collection of small principalities, grouped round rocky strongholds difficult of access, had always, even after wholesale conquest, a latent faculty of recovery in the energy of its powerful families. The Arabs could have destroyed a single royal line, but, slaughter as they might, Armenia was never leaderless: they could not exterminate its nobility. The political history of Armenia, especially during the first half of the Middle Ages, is a history of great families. And this helps to explain the puzzling movement of Armenian boundaries—a movement due not only to pressure from outside, but also to the short-lived uprising, first of one prince, then of another, amidst the ruin, widespread and repeated, of his country.

During the triumph of Rome and for many generations of Rome's decline Armenia was ruled by a national dynasty related to the Arsacidae, kings of Parthia (B.C. 149–A.D. 428). The country had been for many years a victim to the wars and diplomacy of Persia and Rome when in A.D. 386–7 it was partitioned by Sapor III and the Emperor Theodosius. From 387 to 428 the Arsacid kings of Armenia were vassals of Persia, while the westernmost part of their kingdom was incorporated in the Roman Empire and ruled by a count.

The history of the thousand years that followed (428–1473) is sketched in this chapter. It may be divided into five distinct periods. First came long years of anarchy, during which Armenia had no independent existence but was the prey of Persians, Greeks, and Arabs (428–885). Four and a half centuries of foreign domination were then succeeded by nearly two centuries of autonomy. During this second period Armenia was ruled from Transcaucasia by the national dynasty of the Bagratuni. After 1046, when the Bagratid kingdom was conquered by the Greeks, who were soon dispossessed by the Turks, Greater Armenia never recovered its political life.

Meanwhile the third period of Armenia's medieval history had opened in Asia Minor, where a new Armenian State was founded in Cilicia by Prince Ruben, a kinsman of the Bagratuni. From 1080–1340 Rubenian and Hethumian princes ruled Armeno-Cilicia, first as lords or barons (1080–1198), then as kings (1198–1342). During this period the Armenians engaged in a successful struggle with the Greeks, and in a prolonged and losing contest with the Seljūqs and Mamlūks. Throughout these years the relations between the Armenian rulers and the Latin kingdoms of Syria were so close that up to a point the history of Armeno-Cilicia may be considered merely as an episode in the history of the Crusades. This view is strengthened by the events of the fourth period (1342–1373), during which Cilicia was ruled by the crusading family of the Lusignans. When the Lusignan dynasty was overthrown by the Mamlūks in 1375, the Armenians lost their political existence once more. In the fifth and last period of their medieval history (1375–1473), they suffered the horrors of a Tartar invasion under Tamerlane and finally passed under the yoke of the Ottoman Turks.

When Ardashes, the last Arsacid vassal-king, was deposed in 428, Armenia was governed directly by the Persians, who already partly controlled the country. No strict chronology has yet been fixed for the centuries of anarchy which ensued (428–885), but it appears that Persian rule lasted for about two centuries (428–633). Byzantine rule followed, spreading eastward from Roman Armenia, and after two generations (633–693) the Arabs replaced the Greeks and held the Armenians in subjection until 862.

In this long period of foreign rule, the Armenians invariably found a change of masters a change for the worse. The Persians ruled the country though a succession of Marzpans, or military commanders of the frontiers, who also had to keep order and to collect revenue. With a strong guard under their own command, they did not destroy the old national militia nor take away the privileges of the nobility, and at first they allowed full liberty to the Katholikos and his bishops. As long as the Persians governed with such tolerance, they might fairly hope to fuse the Armenian nation with their own. But a change of religious policy under Yezdegerd II and Piroz roused the Armenians to defend their faith in a series of religious wars lasting until the end of the sixth century, during which Vardan with his 1036 companions perished for the Christian faith in the terrible battle of Avaraïr (454). But, whether defeated or victorious, the Armenians never exchanged their Christianity for Zoroastrianism.

On the whole, the Marzpans ruled Armenia as well as they could. In spite of the religious persecution and of a dispute about the Council of Chalcedon between the Armenians and their fellow-Christians in Georgia, the Armenian Church more than held its ground, and ruined churches and monasteries were restored or rebuilt towards the opening of the seventh century. Of the later Marzpans some bore Armenian names. The last of them belonged to the Bagratuni family which was destined to sustain the national existence of Armenia for many generations against untold odds. But this gleam of hope was extinguished by the fall of the Persian Empire before the Arabs. For when they conquered Persia, Armenia turned to Byzantium, and was ruled for sixty years by officials who received the rank of Curopalates and were appointed by the Emperor (633–693). The Curopalates, it appears, was entrusted with the civil administration of the country, while the military command was held by an Armenian General of the Forces.

Though the Curopalates, too, seems to have been always Armenian, the despotic yoke of the Greeks was even harder to bear than the burden of religious wars imposed by the Persians. If the Persians had tried to make the Armenians worship the Sacred Fire, the Greeks were equally bent on forcing them to renounce the Eutychian heresy. As usual, the

Armenians refused to yield. The Emperor Constantine came himself to Armenia in 647, but his visit did nothing to strengthen Byzantine authority. The advance of the Arabs, who had begun to invade Armenia ten years earlier under ʻAbd-ar-Raḥīm, made stable government impossible, for, sooner than merge themselves in the Greek Church, the Armenians sought Muslim protection. But the Arabs exacted so heavy a tribute that Armenia turned again to the Eastern Empire. As a result, the Armenians suffered equally from Greeks and Arabs. When they paid tribute to the Arabs, the Greeks invaded and devastated their land. When they turned to the Greeks, the Arabs punished their success and failure alike by invasion and rapine. Finally, at the close of the seventh century, the Armenian people submitted absolutely to the Caliphate. The Curopalates had fled, the General of the Forces and the Patriarch (Katholikos) Sahak IV were prisoners in Damascus, and some of the Armenian princes had been tortured and put to death.

A period of unqualified tyranny followed. The Arabs intended to rivet the chains of abject submission upon Armenia, and to extort from its helplessness the greatest possible amount of revenue. Ostikans, or governors, foreigners almost without exception, ruled the country for Baghdad. These officials commanded an army, and were supposed to collect the taxes and to keep the people submissive. They loaded Armenia with heavy imposts, and tried to destroy the princely families by imprisoning and killing their men and confiscating their possessions. Under such treatment the Armenians were occasionally cowed but usually rebellious. Their national existence, manifest in rebellion, was upheld by the princes. First one, then another, revolted against the Muslims, made overtures to the enemies of Baghdad, and aspired to re-found the kingdom of Armenia.

Shortly after the Arab conquest, the Armenians turned once more to their old masters, the Greeks. With the help of Leo the Isaurian, Smbat (Sempad) Bagratuni defeated the Arabs, and was commissioned to rule Armenia by the Emperor. But after a severe struggle the Muslims regained their dominion, and sent the Arab commander Qāsim to punish the Armenians (704). He carried out his task with oriental ferocity. He set fire to the church of Nakhijevan, into which he had driven the princes and nobles, and then pillaged the country and sent many of the people into captivity.

These savage reprisals were typical of Arab misrule for the next forty years, and after a peaceful interval during which a friendly Ostikan, Marwān, entrusted the government of Armenia to Ashot Bagratuni, the reign of terror started afresh (758). But, in defiance of extortion and cruelty, insurrection followed insurrection. Local revolts, led now by one prince, now by another, broke out. On one occasion Mushegh Mamikonian drove the Ostikan out of Dwin, but the Armenians paid dear for their success. The Arabs marched against them 30,000 strong; Mushegh fell in battle, and the other princes fled into strongholds (780). Though in 786, when Hārūn ar-Rashīd was Caliph, the country was for the time subdued, alliances between Persian and Armenian princes twice ripened into open rebellion in the first half of the ninth century. The Arabs punished the second of these unsuccessful rebellions by wholesale pillage and by torture, captivity, and death (*c.* 850).

As the long period of gloom, faintly starred by calamitous victories, passed into the ninth century, the Arab oppression slowly lightened. The Abbasid Empire was drawing to its fall. While the Arabs were facing their own troubles, the Armenian nobility were founding principalities. The Mamikonian family, it is true, died out in the middle of the ninth century without founding a kingdom. Yet, because they had no wide territories, they served Armenia disinterestedly, and though of foreign origin could claim many of the national heroes of their adopted country: Vasak, Mushegh, and Manuel, three generals of the Christian Arsacidae; Vardan, who died for the faith in the religious wars; Vahan the Wolf and Vahan Kamsarakan, who fought the Persians; David, Grigor, and Mushegh, rebels against Arab misrule. The Arcruni and the Siwni, who had also defended Armenia against the Arabs, founded independent states in the tenth century. The Arcruni established their kingdom (Vaspurakan) round the rocky citadel of Van, overlooking Lake Van (908). Later, two different branches of their family founded the two states of the Reshtuni and the Antsevatsi. The Siwni kingdom (Siunia) arose in the latter half of the century (970). Many other principalities were also formed, each claiming independence, the largest and most important of them all being the kingdom of the Bagratuni.

Like the Mamikonians, the Bagratuni seem to have come from abroad. According to Moses of Chorene, they were brought to Armenia from Judaea by Hratchea, son of Paroïr, in B.C. 600. In the time of the Parthians, King Valarsaces gave to Bagarat the hereditary honour of placing the crown upon the head of the Armenian king, and for centuries afterwards Bagarat's family gave leaders to the Armenians. Varaztirots Bagratuni was the last Marzpan of the Persian domination, and the third Curopalates of Armenia under the Byzantine Empire. Ashot (Ashod) Bagratuni seized the government when the Arabs were trying to dislodge the Greeks in the middle of the seventh century, and foreshadowed the later policy of his family by his friendliness towards the Caliph, to whom he paid tribute. He fell in battle, resisting the Greeks sent by Justinian II. Smbat Bagratuni, made general of the forces by Justinian, favoured the Greeks. Escaping from captivity in Damascus, it was he who had defeated the Arabs with the help of Leo the Isaurian, and governed the Armenians from the fortresses of Taïkh. In the middle of the eighth century, another Ashot reverted to the policy of his namesake, and was allowed by Marwān, the friendly Ostikan, to rule Armenia as "Prince of Princes." In consequence he refused to rebel with other Armenian princes when the Arab tyranny was renewed, and for his loyalty was blinded by his compatriots. Of his successors, some fought against the Arabs and some sought their friendship; Bagratuni princes took a leading part on both sides in the Armeno-Persian rebellions suppressed by the Arabs in the first half of the ninth century.

The Bagratuni were also wealthy. Unlike the Mamikonians, they owned vast territories, and founded a strong principality in the country of Ararat. Their wealth, their lands, and their history made them the most powerful of Armenian families and pointed out to them a future more memorable than their past. Midway in the ninth century, the power of the Bagratuni was inherited by Prince Ashot. The son of Smbat the Confessor, he refounded the ancient kingdom of Armenia and gave it a dynasty of two centuries' duration. Under the rule of these Bagratuni kings Armenia passed through the most national phase of its history. It was a conquered province before they rose to power, it became more European and less Armenian after their line was extinct. Like Ashot himself, his descendants tried at first to control the whole of Armenia, but from 928 onwards they were obliged to content themselves with real dominion in their hereditary lands and moral supremacy over the other princes. This second and more peaceful period of their rule was the very summer of Armenian civilisation.

Ashot had come into a great inheritance. In addition to the provinces of Ararat and Taïkh, he owned Gugarkh and Turuberan, large properties in higher Armenia, as well as the towns of Bagaran, Mush, Kolb, and Kars with all their territory. He could put into the field an army of forty thousand men, and by giving his daughters in marriage to the princes of the Arcruni and the Siwni he made friends of two possible rivals. For many years his chief desire was to pacify Armenia and to restore the wasted districts, and at the same time to earn the favour of the Caliphate. In return, the Arabs called him "Prince of Princes" (859) and sent home their Armenian prisoners. Two years later Ashot and his brother routed an army, double the size of their own, led into Armenia by Shahap, a Persian who was aiming at independence. Ashot's politic loyalty to the Arabs finally moved the Caliph Muʿtamid to make him King of Armenia (885–7), and at the same time he likewise received a crown and royal gifts from the Byzantine Emperor, Basil the Macedonian. But Armenia was not even yet entirely freed from Arab control. Tribute was paid to Baghdad not immediately but through the neighbouring Ostikan of Azarbāʾījān, and the coronation of Armenian kings waited upon the approval of the Caliphs.

During his brief reign of five years, Ashot I revived many of the customs of the old Arsacid kingdom which had perished four and a half centuries earlier. The crown, it seems, was handed down according to the principle of primogeniture. The kings, though nearly always active soldiers themselves, do not appear to have held the supreme military command, which they usually entrusted to a "general of the forces," an ancient office once hereditary in the Mamikonian family, but in later times often filled by a brother of the reigning king. In Ashot's time, for instance, his brother Abas was generalissimo, and after Ashot's death was succeeded by a younger brother of the new king.

The Katholikos was, after the king, the most important person in Armenia. He had been the only national representative of the Armenians during the period of anarchy when they had no king, and his office had been respected by the Persians and used by the Arabs as a medium of negotiation with the Armenian princes. Under the Bagratid kings, the Katholikos nearly always worked with the monarchy, whose representatives it was his privilege to anoint. He would press coronation upon a reluctant king, would mediate between kings and their rebellious subjects, would lay the king's needs before the Byzantine court, or would be entrusted with the keys of the Armenian capital in the king's absence. Sometimes in supporting the monarchy he would oppose the people's will, especially in a later period, when, long after the fall of the Bagratuni dynasty, King and Katholikos worked together for religious union with Rome against the bitter hostility of their subjects.

Ashot made good use of every interval of peace by restoring the commerce, industry, and agriculture of his country, and by re-populating hundreds of towns and villages. For the sake of peace he made alliances with most of the neighbouring kings and princes, and after travelling through his own estates and through Little Armenia, he went to Constantinople to see the Emperor Leo the Philosopher, himself reputedly an Armenian by descent. The two monarchs signed a political and commercial treaty, and Ashot gave the Emperor an Armenian contingent to help him against the Bulgarians.

Ashot died on the journey home, and his body was carried to Bagaran, the old city of idols, and the seat of his new-formed power. But long before his death, his country's peace, diligently cherished for a life-time, had been broken by the Armenians themselves. One after another, various localities, including Vanand and Gugarkh, had revolted, and although Ashot had been able to restore order everywhere, such disturbances promised ill for the future. The proud ambition of these Armenian princes had breathed a fitful life into a conquered province only to sap the vitality of an autonomous kingdom.

Under Smbat I (892–914) the lesser princes did more mischief than under his father Ashot because they made common cause with the Arabs of Azarbā'ījān, who hated Armenia. For more than twenty years Smbat held his kingdom against the persistent attacks, now separate, now connected, of the Ostikans of Azarbā'ījān and of the Armenian princes, and for more than a generation he and his son looked perforce to the Greeks as their only source of external help.

As soon as Smbat had defeated his uncle Abas, who had tried to seize the throne in the first year of his reign, he turned to face Afshīn, Ostikan of Azarbā'ījān. Afshīn protested against the renewal of the Greco-Armenian alliance and twice invaded Armenia. On the first occasion Smbat not only forced the Arabs to retire by a display of his strength, but made conquests at their expense. He seized Dwin, the capital of the Arab emirs, and sent the Musulman chiefs captive to the Emperor Leo (894). A year later Dwin was almost entirely destroyed by an earthquake. The second time the Arabs invaded Armenia, Smbat, though taken by surprise, cut their army to pieces at the foot of Mount Aragatz (or Alagöz). Afshīn then provoked rebellion among the Armenian princes, but without seriously weakening Smbat. At last, through Armenian treachery, Smbat was defeated by Aḥmad, Ostikan of Mesopotamia, who had invaded the province of Taron. Afshīn took advantage of this reverse to invade Armenia for the third time. Smbat retired to Taïkh, but Kars, the refuge of the queen, capitulated to Afshīn, who took Smbat's son as hostage and his daughter as wife. Not long after, Afshīn died, and the hostages were given back (901). Smbat took this opportunity to obtain from the Caliph both exemption from the authority of the Ostikan of Azarbā'ījān and also permission to pay the annual tribute direct to Baghdad (902).

Afshīn's feud with Armenia was renewed by his brother Yūsuf. Urging that the separation of Armenia and Azarbā'ījān gave dangerous liberty to the Armenians, he invaded the country. Smbat's troops frightened him into retreat before he had struck a blow, but he soon obtained help from some Armenian princes who were restive under heavy taxation. Constrained to retire into the "Blue Fortress" with a handful of men, Smbat assaulted the Muslim and Christian besiegers with great success, and after withstanding a year's siege he capitulated only on receiving a promise that the lives of the garrison should be spared (913). Yūsuf broke his promise. He tortured Smbat for a year, and finally put him to death (914). The Armenian princes retired into fortresses, and Armenia fell once more under the Arab yoke. For several years Yūsuf sent fresh troops into Armenia and organised the devastation of the country from his headquarters at Dwin. No crops were sown, and a terrible famine resulted. It is reported that parents even sold their children to escape death and that some ate human flesh (918).

But the triumph of Yūsuf was short. In the first year of the Arab occupation, Smbat's son, Ashot II, surnamed Erkath, the Iron, had already avenged his father's death by routing the invaders and reconquering the fortresses they held. In 915 the Armenian princes had issued from their strongholds to declare him king. Several years later he visited Byzantium, where the Katholikos had interested the court in the troubles of Armenia, and returned home with a force of Greek soldiers. His reign was one of incessant struggle against the Arabs and the Armenian princes (915–928).

To thwart the new-born power of Armenia, Yūsuf crowned a rival king and provoked a fierce civil war, which was finally ended through the mediation of John, the Katholikos. Many other internal revolts followed, but Ashot suppressed them all, and Yūsuf turned aside to attack the peaceful kingdom of Van. Here, too, he was unsuccessful, but he appointed a new Ostikan of Armenia. The purpose of this new Ostikan and of his successor Bêshir was to capture the Armenian king and the Katholikos. But Ashot retired to the island of Sevan, and built ten large boats. When Bêshir marched against him with a strong army, he manned each boat with seven skilled archers and sent them against the enemy. Every Armenian arrow found its mark, the Arabs took to flight, and were pursued with slaughter as far as Dwin by Prince Gêorg Marzpetuni, Ashot's faithful supporter. After this epic resistance, Ashot left Sevan in triumph, and took the title "King of the Kings of Armenia" in token of his superiority to the other Armenian princes. He died in 928.

Two reigns of perpetual warfare were followed by nearly a century of comparative peace (928–1020). Ashot's successors were content with more modest aims. At home they confined their real rule to their own patrimony and exercised only a moral sway over the other Armenian States. Abroad they sought the favour of the Arabs, rather than that of the Greeks. In this way alone was it possible to secure a measure of peace.

Ashot II was succeeded by his brother Abas (928–951), who concluded a treaty with the Arabs of Dwin and exchanged Arab for Armenian prisoners. He restored towns and villages and built churches. But when he built the cathedral of Kars, he brought not peace but a sword to his countrymen. Ber, King of the Abasgians (Abkhaz), wanted the cathedral to be consecrated according to Greek rites. On the banks of the Kūr, Abas defeated him twice to cure him of error, and then blinded him for having looked on the building with impious eyes.

Ashot III (952–977) adopted a conciliatory policy. When his rebellious brother Mushel founded a kingdom in Vanand with Kars for its capital (968), Ashot entered into friendly relations with him. He earned the good will of Baghdad by defeating a rebel who had thrown Azarbā'ījān and Mesopotamia into confusion. Side by side with a prince of the Arcruni family he faced the Emperor John Tzimisces, who came eastward to fight the Arabs and who seemed to threaten Armenia by pitching his camp in Taron. Baffled by the bold front of Ashot's army, eighty thousand strong, the Emperor demanded and received an Armenian contingent, and then marched away from the frontier.

By such circumspect action, Ashot III gave peace to Armenia. He reorganised the army and could put into the field a host of ninety thousand men. Surpassing his predecessors in the building of pious foundations, he bestowed great revenues on convents, churches, hospitals, and almshouses. He made Ani his capital and laid the foundations of its greatness. He was known as Olormadz, the Pitiful, for he never sat down to meals without poor and impotent men about him.

Ashot's son Smbat II (977–990) was a lover of peace and a great builder like his father. But he was forced into war with his rebellious uncle Mushel, King of Vanand, and before his death he angered the Church by marrying his niece.

Under his brother and successor, Gagik I (990–1020), the Armenians enjoyed for a whole generation the strange experience of unbroken prosperity. Gagik was strong enough to prevent foreigners from attacking him, and to gain the friendship of the other Armenian princes. Free from war, he used all his time and energy to increase the moral and material welfare of his people. He enriched the pious foundations that dated from the time of his brother and father, and appropriated great revenues to churches and ecclesiastics, taking part himself in religious ceremonies. In his reign the civilisation of Armenia reached its height. Flourishing in the unaccustomed air of peace, convents and schools were centres of light and learning; commercial towns such as Ani, Bitlis, Ardzen, and Nakhijevan, became wealthy marts for the merchandise of Persia, Arabia, and the Indies. Agriculture shared in the general prosperity. Goldsmiths, much influenced by Persian models, were hard at work, and coppersmiths made the plentiful copper of the country into objects of every description. Enamelling flourished in neighbouring Georgia, but no Armenian enamel survives to tell whether the art was practised in Armenia itself.

Armenian culture was pre-eminently ecclesiastical. Its literature did include chronicles and secular poems, but was overwhelmingly religious as a whole. Armenian manuscripts, famous alike for their antiquity, their beauty, and their importance in the history of writing, are nearly all ecclesiastical. Most interesting of all in many ways (especially for the comparison of texts and variant readings) are the numerous copies of the Gospels. The Moscow manuscript (887) is the earliest Armenian manuscript actually dated, and two very beautiful Gospels of a later date are those of Queen Melkê and of Trebizond. A collection of theological and other texts executed between 971 and 981 is their earliest manuscript written on paper. Other important writings were dogmatic works, commentaries, and *sharakans* or sacred songs composed in honour of church festivals. Armenian art, again, was mainly ecclesiastical, and survives, on the one hand in the illuminations and miniatures which adorn the sacred texts, and, on the other, in the ruined churches and convents which still cover the face of the country. Architecture was military as well as ecclesiastical, but it is hard not to believe that the people of Ani were prouder of their galaxy of churches than they were of their fortress, their walls, and their towers.

In the tenth century, especially after a branch of the Bagratuni had founded an independent State in Vanand (968), the intellectual focus of Armenia seems to have been Kars, with its crowd of young Armenian students who came there to study philosophy, *belles-lettres*, and theology. But the true centre and most splendid proof of Armenian civilisation was

Ani, city of forty keys and a thousand and one churches. In the eighth century no more than a village, it slowly grew larger and more populous. Ashot I and Ashot III were crowned at Ani, and there Ashot III established the throne of the Bagratuni dynasty. He defended the city with a fortress, and his queen enriched it with two fine convents, but the most splendid buildings were added by Smbat II, who also fortified Ani on the north with a double line of walls and towers and a great ditch of stone. The citadel was defended on the east and south by the river Akhurian, and on the west by the Valley of Flowers. Among the magnificent palaces and temples, richly adorned with mosaics and inscriptions, stood the cathedral, masterpiece of the famous architect Trdat (Tiridates), built on Persian and Byzantine lines.

This mixture of architectural styles is typical of the national art of Armenia, which betrays a subtle mingling of Persian, Arab, and Byzantine influences. The churches of Sevan, of Digor, of Keghard near Erivan, even the Armenian church of Paris in the Rue Jean-Goujon[1], still symbolise the desperate battle the Armenians had to fight against the foreigner, and still suggest that the only way of maintaining the unequal struggle was to turn the encroaching elements to the service of the Armenian Church, dearest and most inviolable stronghold of Armenian nationality.

Under Gagik I that nationality seemed safe. His reign proved Armenia's capacity for quick recovery, and promised the country a fair future if peace could be kept. But the universal grief at Gagik's death was unconscious mourning for the end of prosperity. It presaged the slow declension of Armenia from national pride to servitude, and the gradual passing of the royal house from kingly power to exile and extinction.

Two generations of misfortune (1020–1079) opened with civil war. Gagik had left two sons. His successor John-Smbat (1020–1040), timid and effeminate, was attacked and defeated by his younger and more militant brother Ashot, who was helped by Senekherim Arcruni, King of Vaspurakan (Van). Peace was concluded through the mediation of the Katholikos Petros Getadartz and Giorgi, King of the Georgians, but only by a division of territory. John-Smbat kept Ani and its dependencies, while Ashot took the part of the kingdom next to Persia and Georgia (Iberia). On the death of either brother the country was to be re-united under the survivor.

But Ashot was discontented. He roused the King of Georgia to attack and imprison John-Smbat, who escaped only by yielding three fortresses to Giorgi. Still unsatisfied, Ashot feigned mortal illness and begged his brother to pay him a last visit. Once by Ashot's bedside, John-Smbat saw the trap and begged for his life. Ashot, deceitful to the end, freed him merely to hand him over to Prince Apirat, who

[1] A copy of the church (still standing) of Aghthamar.

promised to kill him at a secret spot. But, visited by sudden remorse, Apirat restored the king to Ani and his throne, and fled himself to Abū'l-Aswār, governor of Dwin, to escape the wrath of Ashot.

While Ashot schemed against his brother, Armenia was threatened on both sides by different enemies, one old, the other new. The new assailants were the Seljūq Turks, led against Vaspurakan at the opening of John-Smbat's reign by Ṭughril Beg, whose precursor Ḥasan had already wasted Mesopotamia. When they had overcome the resistance of Vaspurakan, they advanced into John-Smbat's territory. At the beginning of his reign John-Smbat had had an army of 60,000, but the Armenian generalissimo, Vasak Pahlavuni, had to meet the Turks with a bare five hundred men. Climbing Mount Serkevil to rest, he died there, whether by his own hand, or by treason, or by a rock falling from the mountain while he prayed, is unknown. Meanwhile, Ṭughril Beg left Armenia for the time and conquered the whole of Persia.

On the west, Armenia was threatened once again by the Byzantine Empire. The Turkish advance, instead of inducing the Greeks to help Armenia, revived in them their old ambition of conquest, with fatal results not only to the Armenians but to themselves. During the reign of John-Smbat this ambition was twice fed by Armenian policy. Conquered and then left by Ṭughril Beg, Senekherim of Vaspurakan gave up his kingdom to Basil II (1021) in exchange for the town of Sebastea (Sīwās) rather than wait to offer a second vain resistance to the Turks on their inevitable return[1]. Two years later Basil entered Georgia to repress a revolt in which John-Smbat had been secretly implicated. In fear of the Emperor's wrath John-Smbat violated the treaty he had made with his brother, and through the agency of the Katholikos Petros Getadartz he gave in writing a promise that after his own death Basil should inherit Ani. Basil was well pleased. But some years later his successor Constantine VIII summoned to his death-bed an Armenian priest named Kirakos, and handed him the inequitable document, saying: "Bear this letter to thy king and tell him from me that like other mortals I find myself on the threshold of Eternity, and I would not extort the possession of another. Let him take back his kingdom and give it to his sons." The mischief might have ended here but for the treachery of the priest, who kept the letter in his own possession and finally sold it for a large sum to Michael IV (1034). Much as his dishonesty cost the Emperor, it was to cost Armenia more.

As soon as John-Smbat was dead, Michael sent an embassy to claim Ani and its dependencies. His chance of success was good, because Ani was divided by two factions. One, led by the generalissimo Vahram Pahlavuni, wished to crown Gagik, the fourteen-year-old nephew and heir of John-Smbat; the other intended to give the crown to Vest Sarkis

[1] See Macler, F., *Rapport sur une mission scientifique en Arménie russe et en Arménie turque...*, Paris 1911, p. 46.

Siwni, the regent, or failing him to the Emperor Michael. For the moment, party differences were sunk in unanimous denial of Byzantine claims, but Vest Sarkis destroyed this short-lived amity by seizing the State treasure and several strongholds. Vahram's party won a fairer renown by defeating the Greeks, who were sent by the Emperor to take by force what his embassy had failed to win by persuasion. One after another three Greek armies invaded Armenia; each spread desolation far and wide without conquering Ani. Michael then sent a fourth army to besiege Ani while the King of the Albanians (Aluans) invaded the north-east province of Armenia on behalf of the Greeks. Vahram broke up the invading army by a bold attack. The Greeks, terrified by the fury of the Armenians, fled in disorder, leaving twenty thousand dead and wounded beneath the walls of the town. This victory enabled Vahram to crown Gagik II (1042–1046). With a mere handful of men the boy-king recovered the State treasure and the citadel of Ani from Vest Sarkis, whom he cast into prison. Unhindered for the moment by Greek interference or Armenian treachery, Gagik drove out the Turks and began to restore order in the country. But unfortunately for himself and for his people, he was generous enough to forgive Vest Sarkis and to raise him to honour. Posing as the king's friend, this traitor worked to alienate the Armenian princes from Gagik and to encourage the hostile intention of Constantine Monomachus, successor to Michael V.

Constantine copied the Armenian policy of Michael. Failing to secure Ani by negotiation, he sent an army to seize it. Gagik defeated the Greeks and forced them to retire. Like Michael, Constantine then sent a larger army, and at the same time urged Abū'l-Aswār, governor of Dwin, to harass the Armenians on the east. But Gagik disarmed Abū'l-Aswār by gifts, and after a short battle put to flight the confident Greeks.

Still Constantine would not give up hope. Where peace and war had failed, trickery might succeed. Inspired by Vest Sarkis, he asked Gagik to come to Constantinople to sign a treaty of perpetual peace, swearing on the cross and the gospels in the presence of Gagik's delegate that he would be true to his word. Unwilling to go himself, and discouraged by the Vahramians, the king ultimately yielded to the evil counsel of Vest Sarkis and passed out of Armenia to his ruin. Before he had spent many days in Constantinople, the Emperor demanded Ani of him, and, when he refused it, imprisoned him on an island in the Bosphorus.

When the Armenians heard of this disaster, there was much division among them. Some wanted to deliver Ani to David Anholin of Albania, others to Bagarat, King of Georgia and Abasgia, but the Katholikos Petros, to whom Gagik had entrusted the keys, informed the Emperor that Ani should be his for a consideration. Once assured of a good price for his shameful merchandise, Petros sent the forty keys of the bartered city to Constantine.

Gagik rebelled against the accomplished fact, but finally abdicated his throne, receiving in exchange the town of Bizou in Cappadocia. Here he married the daughter of David, King of Sebastea, and led the wandering life of an exile. After many years, he learnt one day that the Metropolitan, Mark of Caesarea, had named his dog Armên in mockery of the Armenians. Gagik could not stomach the insult, steep it as he must in the bitterness of exile, in hatred of a rival Church, in contempt for a people he had never encountered but as conqueror until they overcame him by guile. To avenge the honour of his country's name, he caused the dog and the ecclesiastic to be tied up together in a sack, and had the animal beaten until it bit its master to death. For this crime against their metropolitan, three Greek brothers seized Gagik by treachery and hanged him in the castle of Cyzistra (1079). He left two sons and a grandson, but they did not long survive him. When the last of them had died in prison, the Bagratuni line was extinct.

During the exile of their king, the Armenians fell a prey to Greek and Turk. At first, not knowing of his abdication, they resisted the Greeks and dispersed the army sent under the command of the eunuch Paracamus to take possession of Ani. But on hearing that Gagik was never again to enter the country, the Armenians lost all heart, and allowed Paracamus to possess the city. Once masters of Armenia, the Greeks committed atrocious cruelties. They exiled or poisoned the princes, replaced Armenian troops by Greek garrisons, and worked for the utter destruction of the country.

But they had reckoned without the Turk. Learning of Armenia's weakness, Ṭughril Beg returned, and spread ruin and desolation far and wide for several years. He sacked the fortified town of Smbataberd and tortured the inhabitants. The rich commercial town of Ardzen shared the same fate (1049). The Greeks at last determined to make an end of his savagery. Together with Liparid, King of Georgia, their general Comnenus offered battle to the Turks near Bayber. But owing to disagreement among the Christians, the Turks were victorious and carried the King of Georgia into captivity. With no one now to oppose him, Ṭughril overran most of Armenia except Ani. Vanand resisted in vain, but their failure in the siege of Manzikert forced the Turks to retire. Ṭughril fell back, only to wreak his vengeance upon Ardskê. His death, like that of the Arab Afshīn long before, brought no relief to Armenia, for like Afshīn, he left a brother, Alp Arslān, to complete his work of destruction. Alp Arslān besieged Ani unsuccessfully for a time, but finally overcame its resistance and sacked the city with unimaginable fury. The river Akhurian ran red with blood; palaces and temples were set on fire and covered thousands of corpses with their ruins (1064). The Turks then invited Vanand to submit. Gagik, the king, feigned friendship and made an alliance with Alp Arslān. But like Senekherim of Van before him, he gave his kingdom to the Eastern Empire in exchange for a stronghold farther west. In 1065 he transported his family to the castle of Dzmndav in Little Armenia. The Greeks, however, could not save Vanand from the Turks, who pushed their conquests as far as Little Armenia. Kars, Karin, Bayber, Sebastea, and Caesarea had submitted to Alp Arslān, when the Emperor Romanus Diogenes opposed him at Manzikert in 1071. The Greeks were defeated, and the Turks led the Emperor into captivity.

By the end of the eleventh century not a vestige remained of Byzantine dominion over Armenia. The Greeks saw too late the fatal consequences of their selfish hostility towards a country which on south and east might have served them as a rampart against their most dangerous foe.

The national history of Greater Armenia ended with the Turkish conquest and with the extinction of the Bagratuni line. Little by little, numbers of Armenians withdrew into the Taurus mountains and the plateau below, but though their country rose again from ruin, it was only as a small principality in Cilicia. The fruits of Armenian civilisation—the architectural splendour of Ani, the military strength of Van, the intellectual life of Kars, the commercial pride of Bitlis and Ardzen—were no more.

Greater Armenia had been eastern rather than western, coming into contact with race after race from the east; with Byzantium alone, half eastern itself, on the west. But the civilisation of Armeno-Cilicia was western rather than eastern: its political interests were divided between Europe and Asia, and its history was overshadowed by that of the Crusades. To the Crusades the change was pre-eminently due. Crusading leaders stood in every kind of relationship to the new Armenian kingdom. They befriended and fought it by turns. They used its roads, borrowed its troops, received its embassies, fought its enemies, and established feudal governments near it. For a time their influence made it a European State, built on feudal lines, seeking agreement with the Church of Rome, and sending envoys to the principal courts of Christendom.

But the Armenian Church, which had been the inspiration and mainstay of the old civilisation, and the family ambitions, which had helped to destroy it, lived on to prove the continuity of the little State of Armeno-Cilicia with the old Bagratid kingdom. Nationalist feeling, stirred to life by fear of religious compromise and by the growth of Latin influence at court, was to provoke a crisis more than once in centuries to come.

Among the Armenian migrants to the Taurus mountains, during the invasions that followed the abdication of Gagik II, was Prince Ruben (Rupen). He had seen the assassination of Gagik to whom he was related, and he determined to avenge his kinsman's death on the Greeks. Collecting a band of companions, whose numbers increased from day to day, he took up his stand in the village of Goromozol near the fortress of Bardsrberd, drove the Greeks out of the Taurus region, and established his dominion there. The other Armenian princes recognised his supremacy and helped him to strengthen his power, though many years were to pass before the Greeks were driven out of all the Cilician towns and strongholds which they occupied.

Cilicia was divided into two well-marked districts: the plain, rich and fertile but difficult to defend, and the mountains, covered with forests and full of defiles. The wealth of the country was in its towns: Adana, Mamistra, and Anazarbus, for long the chief centres of hostility between Greeks and Armenians; Ayas with its maritime trade; Tarsus and Sis, each in turn the capital of the new Armenian State; Germanicea or Mar'ash, and Ulnia or Zeithun. The mountainous region, difficult of approach, and sprinkled with Syrian, Greek, and Armenian monasteries, easily converted into strongholds, was the surest defence of the province, though in addition the countryside was protected by strong fortresses such as Vahka, Bardsrberd, Kapan, and Lambron.

When Ruben died, after fifteen years of wise rule (1080–1095), he was able to hand on the lordship of Cilicia to his son Constantine (1095–1100), who first brought Armeno-Cilicia into close contact with Europe. Constantine continued his father's work by capturing Vahka and other fortresses from the Greeks and thus increasing his patrimony. But he broke new ground by making an alliance with the Crusaders, who in return for his services in pointing out roads and in furnishing supplies, especially during the siege of Antioch, gave him the title of Marquess.

If the principality thus founded in hostile territory owed its existence to the energy of an Armenian prince, it owed its survival largely to external causes. In the first place, the Turks were divided. After 1092, when the Seljūq monarchy split into rival powers, Persia alone was governed by the direct Seljūq line; other sultans of Seljūq blood ruled parts of Syria and Asia Minor. Although the Sultans of Iconium or Rūm were to be a perpetual danger to Cilicia from the beginning of the twelfth century onwards, the division of the Turks at the close of the eleventh century broke for a time the force of their original advance, and gave the first Rubenians a chance to recreate the Armenian State. In the second place, the Crusades began. The Latin States founded in the East during the First Crusade checked the Turks, and also prevented the Greeks, occupied as they were with internal and external difficulties, from making a permanent reconquest of Cilicia. The Latins did not aim at protecting the Armenians, with whom indeed they often quarrelled. But as a close neighbour to a number of small states, nominally friendly but really inimical to Byzantium, Armenia was no longer isolated. Instead of being a lonely upstart principality, it became one of many recognised kingdoms, all hostile to the Greek recovery of the Levant, all entitled to the moral sanction and expecting the armed support of the mightiest kings of Europe.

For about twenty-five years after Constantine's death, his two sons, Thoros I (1100–1123) and Leo I (1123–1135), ruled the Armenians with great success. As an able administrator Thoros organised the country, and would have given his time to building churches and palaces if his enemies had left him in peace. But he had to fight both Greeks and Turks. He took Anazarbus from the Greeks and repulsed an invasion of Seljūqs and Turkomans. In his reign the death of Gagik II was at last avenged: Armenian troops seized the castle of Cyzistra and put to death the three Greek brothers who had hanged the exiled king. Leo I, who succeeded Thoros, had not the administrative gifts of his predecessors, but like them he was a brave soldier. He captured Mamistra and Tarsus, the chief towns still in Greek hands, and was for a time unquestioned master of all Cilicia.

But the Greeks were not permanently ousted from Cilicia until 1168. Leo's dominion was short-lived, owing to the failure of his diplomacy. He wove his political designs round the Christian principality of Antioch. At first he joined with Roger of Antioch against the Turks; then, quarrelling with Roger, he joined the Turks against Antioch (1130). In revenge, Roger's successor Bohemond II allied with Baldwin, Count of Mar'ash, seized Leo by a trick (1131), and as the price of freedom extorted from him the towns of Mamistra and Adana, a sum of 60,000 piastres, and one of his sons as hostage. Leo paid the price demanded, but afterwards re-took by force what he had been compelled to yield to treachery.

Meanwhile Antioch attracted the envious eye of the Emperor John Comnenus. First, he tried to gain it for the Empire by a marriage project. Failing in this, he fought for it. This time Leo joined with Antioch against the Greeks, but again he suffered for his choice. While he was encamped before Seleucia at the head of Latin and Armenian troops, the Emperor invaded Cilicia, took Tarsus, Mamistra, and Adana, and had already begun to attack Anazarbus when Leo hurried back to relieve the city. The Emperor despaired of capturing it until his son Isaac advised him to cover his engines of war with clay to prevent them from being broken. This device succeeded. Leo retired to the castle of Vahka, and in spite of help from Antioch was forced to surrender (1135). Antioch recognised the Emperor's supremacy, and Leo was put into chains and sent to a Byzantine prison, where he died six years later (1141). Two of his sons were imprisoned with him. The elder was tortured and put to death, but Thoros, the younger, survived to deliver his country.

Before deliverance came, the Armenians were tormented for nine long years by their old enemies, the Greeks and the Turks. Leo's misfortune gave Cilicia to the Greeks, who pillaged and destroyed strongholds and towns, convents and churches. The Turks and even the Latins joined in demolishing the laborious work of the first Rubenians. But when the Turkish Emir Aḥmad Malik had seized Vahka and Kapan, the Emperor returned to Cilicia, bringing with him Thoros, son of Leo I. In this campaign, however, the Emperor was killed while hunting, and the Greek army retreated, while Thoros managed to escape and disclosed his identity to an Armenian priest.

Thoros II (1145–1168) had to reconquer his kingdom from the Greeks before he could rule it. At the head of ten thousand Armenians and with the help of his brothers, Stephanê (Sdephanê) and Mleh, who had been at the court of Nūr-ad-Dīn, Sultan of Aleppo, he recaptured the fortresses of Vahka, Simanakla, and Arindz. One by one all the great cities of the plain opened their gates. Manuel Comnenus hastened to bring his Hungarian war to a close and to send his cousin the Caesar Andronicus to oppose Thoros, who retired to Mamistra on the approach of the Greek army. The town was without ammunition, and Thoros undertook to recognise the supremacy of the Greeks if they would respect his paternal rights. Andronicus refused, and threatened to bind Thoros with his father's fetters. But on a dark, rainy night Thoros breached the walls of the town and surprised the enemy at their revels. Andronicus escaped with a handful of men, but Thoros pursued him as far as Antioch, and then returned to Mamistra. He held to ransom the Greek nobles he had captured, and divided the money among his soldiers, telling the wondering Greeks that he did so in order that his men might one day recapture them. Among the prisoners was Oshin, Lord of Lambron, father of the famous Nerses Lambronatsi. Oshin paid twenty thousand pieces of gold as half his ransom, and for the second half left his son Hethum (Hayton) as hostage. Thoros had later so great an affection for Hethum that he gave him his daughter in marriage, and regarding the payment of Oshin's debt as the girl's dowry he sent them both to Lambron, hoping thus to win the friendship of Oshin and his family. This hope was not fulfilled, for Lambron, with its leanings towards Byzantium, was destined to give much trouble to future rulers of Armenia.

Manuel's next step was to induce other rulers to attack Thoros. First he bribed Mas'ūd I, Sultan of Iconium, to oppose him. The Sultan twice invaded Cilicia, only to be repulsed, once by the sight of Thoros' preparations, once by plague (1154). The Emperor then turned to the Latins, and excited Reginald of Chatillon, regent of Antioch, to fight against Armenia. Thoros and Reginald fought a bloody but doubtful battle at Alexandretta, but Reginald, not receiving the Emperor's promised help, made peace with Thoros and marched against the Greeks. He made a naval attack on Cyprus and inflicted great injury on its defenceless people. This diversion enabled Thoros to consolidate his power and even to extend it in the mountainous districts of Phrygia and Isauria.

Manuel was greatly dissatisfied with the unexpected result. He sent against Thoros another army, which failed like the first, and then came to Cilicia in person. Warned in time by a Latin monk, Thoros put his family and his treasure in the stronghold of Tajki-Gar (Rock of Tajik), and hid himself in the mountains while the Emperor deprived him of his hardly-won cities. When peace was finally made through the mediation of Baldwin III, King of Jerusalem, Thoros was restored to power under the title of *Pansebastos* and Manuel kept the two towns of Anazarbus and Mamistra (1159).

But the barbarity of the Greeks provoked fresh hostilities which resulted in their expulsion from the country. While Thoros helped the crusaders against the Sultan of Aleppo, his brother Stephanê (Sdephanê) re-took the towns which the Sultan of Iconium had captured from the Christians. Jealous of Stephanê's success, the Emperor's lieutenant, Andronicus Euphorbenus[1], invited him to a feast and cast him into a cauldron of boiling water (1163). Once more a powerful Greek army was sent to Cilicia, but Thoros determined to avenge his brother's death, and, by defeating the invaders in a great battle near Tarsus, brought to a successful close his life-long struggle against Byzantium. Greek domination in Cilicia was at an end.

Thoros died regretted by all, leaving a child, Ruben II, to succeed him, and a brother to undo his work. This brother, Mleh, had been a Templar and a Catholic, and then became a leader of Turkoman nomads. He spread destruction wherever he went. The young king took refuge with the Katholikos at Romkla, where he soon died. Mleh openly joined the Sultan Nūr-ad-Dīn, invaded Cilicia, and did great harm to the Armenians. But he made himself so unpopular by his cruelty that his own soldiers killed him (1175).

After his death the Armenians filled his place by his nephew Ruben III (1175–1185), the eldest son of the Stephanê who had been cast into boiling water by the Greeks. Of peaceful disposition, Ruben none the less freed his country from external attack; but from his Armenian enemies he was only saved by his brother Leo.

Although the Greeks had been driven out of Cilicia, some of the Armenian principalities, Lambron among them, still looked upon the Emperor as their suzerain. Hethum of Lambron was related to the Rubenians by marriage, but he preferred Byzantine to Armenian supremacy, and asked Bohemond III of Antioch to help him against Ruben III. Bohemond seized Ruben by treachery, imprisoned him at Antioch, and marched against the Armenians, hoping to conquer Cilicia, not for Hethum or the Emperor, but for himself. Leo, however, repulsed him, and forced him and Hethum to make peace with Ruben. On his release, Ruben devoted himself to the welfare of his people, who loved him for his liberality and wise administration. He built towns and convents, and finally retired into a monastery.

Ruben's successor was his brother Leo II (1185–1219), surnamed the Great or the Magnificent, already known as his country's defender, and destined to raise the lordship or barony of Armeno-Cilicia to the status

[1] In another view this atrocity is attributed to Andronicus Comnenus. See *infra,* Chapter XII, p. 375.

of a kingdom. His long reign of thirty-four years fully justified his change of style, for he gave his country a stability and prosperity that were unparalleled in its annals.

His first work was to free the Armenians from Muslim pressure. He conquered Rustam, Sultan of Iconium, who suddenly invaded Cilicia, and two years after his accession he drove back the united forces of the Sultans of Aleppo and Damascus (1187). When he was once more at peace he built fortresses on the frontiers and filled them with well-trained garrisons. With Cilicia he incorporated Isauria, which had been seized by the Seljūqs of Rūm.

In diplomacy, his sovereign purpose was to obtain the help of Western Europe against the Greeks and Muslims. He sought the friendship of the European princes by means of marriage-alliances. His niece Aliza was married to Raymond, son of Bohemond of Antioch; and he himself married Isabella of Austria. Later, he repudiated Isabella and married Sibylla, daughter of Amaury of Lusignan, King of Cyprus. Long before his second marriage he had made a friend of Frederick Barbarossa, who at the outset of his ill-starred Crusade asked for Leo's help in return for the promise of a crown. Leo quickly sent abundant provisions and ammunition to the Crusaders, and when the imperial army entered Isauria he himself went with the Katholikos to greet the Emperor. They never met, for Barbarossa had been drowned on the way, bathing in the Calicadnus.

After some years, Frederick's son Henry VI and Pope Celestine III sent the promised crown to Leo, and, at the feast of the Epiphany in 1198, he was consecrated in the cathedral of Sis[1] by the Katholikos Grigor VII Apirat in the presence of the Archbishop of Mayence, Conrad of Wittelsbach, Papal legate and representative of the Emperor[2]. The Eastern Emperor Alexius Angelus also sent Leo a crown in confirmation of Armenian authority over Cilicia, so long disputed by the Greeks.

Leo was anxious to include the Pope among his European friends. Many letters passed between the Popes on the one side and the Katholikos and King of Armenia on the other with a view to uniting the Roman and Armenian Churches. But the Armenian authorities, willing themselves to make concessions to Rome, were opposed by the Armenian people, who strenuously defended their Church against the authority of the Papacy. In the end, the sole result of attempted reconciliation was an embitterment of religious feeling.

King by the consent of Europe, Leo made his country a European State. He chose a new seat for his government, removing it from Tarsus to Sis, where he entertained German, English, French, and Italian captains, who came to serve under the Armenian banner. In defining the relations

[1] Some historians say Tarsus.

[2] A list of the prelates, lords, and ambassadors who attended the ceremony will be found in the Chronicle of Smbat.

of the princes to the royal house, in establishing military and household posts, in creating tribunals, and in fixing the quota of taxes and tribute, he copied to a great extent the organisation of the Latin princes of Syria. One of the fruits of his alliance with Bohemond of Antioch was the adoption of the Assises of Antioch as the law of Armeno-Cilicia.

In addition, Leo encouraged industry, navigation, and commerce. He cultivated commercial relations with the West, and by granting privileges to Genoese and Venetian merchants he spread Cilician trade throughout Europe. Mindful, too, of the good works of his forefathers, he founded orphanages and hospitals and schools, and increased the number of convents, where skilled calligraphists and miniaturists added lustre to the prosperity of his reign.

Leo's reputation, founded on peaceful achievement, is all the greater because he attained it in spite of intermittent wars. Of his own will he entered on a long succession-struggle in Antioch to defend the rights of his young kinsman, Ruben-Raymond, against the usurpation of an uncle, Bohemond IV the One-Eyed, Count of Tripolis, who had seized the government of Antioch with the help of Templars and Hospitallers. Leo recaptured Antioch and restored Ruben-Raymond to power. Bohemond returned, drove out his nephew a second time, and bribed the Sultan of Iconium, Rukn-ad-Dīn, to invade Cilicia. Though deserted at the last minute by the Templars, for whose services he had paid twenty thousand Byzantine pounds, Leo forced the Seljūqs to retire with serious losses, and turned again to Antioch. While he was preparing to besiege the town, he referred the succession question to Innocent III, who entrusted its solution to the King of Jerusalem and the Patriarchs of Jerusalem and Antioch. The dispute seemed about to end peacefully when one of the cardinals sent by the Pope was corrupted by the enemy to anathematise Leo and Armenia. The anathema was publicly repelled by John Medzabaro the Katholikos; and Leo, too furious to wait for the decision of the arbitrators, continued the siege of Antioch and captured the town (1211). After a triumphal entry, he reinstated Ruben-Raymond once more, and left Antioch for Cilicia, where he sequestrated the property of the Templars and drove them out of the country.

The other wars of Leo's reign were not of his choosing. Without provocation, the Sultan of Aleppo, Ghiyāth-ad-Dīn Ghāzī, son of Saladin, sent an embassy to demand that Leo should do homage or fight. Leo had the envoys taken for diversion into the country for a few days while he marched on the sultan, who was peacefully awaiting the return of his embassy. The sultan's army fled before the sudden attack of the Armenians, and he was obliged to pay Leo a larger tribute than he had hoped to extort for himself.

Leo's last war, waged against his other old enemy, Iconium, was not so successful. Too ill to fight himself, he sent the *baïle* Adam and the grand-baron Constantine against 'Izz-ad-Dīn Kai-Kā'ūs I, who had laid siege to the fortress of Kapan. Adam withdrew from the campaign after a quarrel with his colleague, and, by a feigned retreat and sudden *volte face*, the Turks defeated the Armenians and continued their interrupted siege of Kapan. But on hearing that Leo was ravaging Iconian territory, the sultan made haste to return to his own country and to make peace with Armenia (1217).

Two years later Leo died, to the sorrow of his people. He had made Armenia strong and respected, but even in his reign the old ambitions of the princes were abreast of opportunity. When Leo was away in Cyprus, visiting the relatives of his queen, Hethum of Lambron revolted and invaded the king's territory. Leo was strong enough to seize and imprison the rebel and his two sons on his return, but the revolt shewed that Leo's power rested on the perilous foundation of his own personality, and could not withstand the strain applied to it immediately after his death.

Leo left no son. He had once adopted Ruben-Raymond of Antioch as heir to the Cilician throne, but he repented of his choice on proving the youth's incapacity. In the end, he left the crown to his daughter Zabel under the regency of two Armenian magnates. One of the regents was soon killed, but his colleague, the grand-baron Constantine, became for a time the real ruler of the country. Though never crowned himself, he made and unmade Armenian kings for the next six years (*c.* 1220–1226).

His first act was to discrown Ruben-Raymond of Antioch, who with the help of crusaders had entered Tarsus and proclaimed himself king. Constantine defeated the invaders at Mamistra, and imprisoned Ruben at Tarsus, where he died. He then gave the crown to Philip of Antioch (1222), to whom, with the consent of the Armenian princes and ecclesiastics, he had married Zabel. But the new king was a failure. He had promised to conform to the laws and ceremonies of Armenia, but on the advice of his father, Bohemond the One-Eyed, Prince of Antioch, he soon broke his word, and began to favour the Latins at the expense of the Armenians. He sent in secret to his father the royal ornaments of Armenia and many other national treasures, and then tried to flee with Zabel. Constantine caught and imprisoned him, and demanded the return of the stolen heirlooms from Bohemond as the price of Philip's safety. Bohemond preferred to let his son die in a foreign prison.

For the third time Constantine decided the fate of the Armenian crown. With the approval, not of the lady but of the Armenian magnates, he married Zabel to his own son Hethum (Hayton). After founding a dynasty of his own blood, he discrowned no more kings, but with Hethum's consent he undertook to reorganise the Cilician State, deeply rent by the succession question and shorn of part of Isauria by watchful Iconium. Nevertheless, for the sake of peace, Constantine made an alliance with the Sultan of Iconium, and conciliated the principality of Lambron which had revolted in the reign of Leo the

Great. Later on in Hethum's reign Constantine again governed Cilicia in his son's absence.

The change of dynasty brought with it a change in policy. Cilicia was no longer molested by the Greeks; and the Seljūqs of Iconium, though troublesome for some years to come, were losing power. The paramount danger to the Armenians, as to the Seljūqs themselves, came from the Mamlūks of Egypt, and the crucial question for Armenian rulers was where to turn for help against this new enemy. After more than a century's experience the Armenians could not trust their Latin neighbours as allies. Hethum I (1226–1270), though anxious to keep their good will, and with his eyes always open to the possibility of help from the West, put his trust not in the Christians but in the heathen Mongols, who for half a century were to prove the best friends Armenia ever had.

At the beginning of Hethum's reign, the Mongols were overrunning Persia, Armenia, and Asia Minor, but they did good service to the Armenians by conquering the Seljūqs of Iconium and depriving them of most of their Syrian and Cappadocian territories. Hethum made a defensive and offensive alliance with Bachu, the Mongol general, and in 1244 became the vassal of the Khan Ogdai. Ten years later he did homage in person to Mangu Khan, and cemented the friendship between the two nations by a long stay at the Mongol court.

Meanwhile the Seljūqs, who had incited Lambron to revolt early in the reign, took advantage of Hethum's absence to invade Cilicia under the Sultan 'Izz-ad-Dīn Kai-Kā'ūs II. Hethum defeated the Turks on his return, seized several important towns, and recovered the whole of Isauria.

His triumph gave him brief leisure. The rest of his reign was filled with a struggle against the Mamlūks, whose northward advance was fortunately opposed by the Mongols. Hethum and the Khan's brother Hūlāgū joined forces at Edessa to undertake the capture of Jerusalem from the Mamlūks. The allies defeated Nāṣir, Sultan of Aleppo, and divided his lands between themselves, but all hope of further success vanished with the Khan's death. Hūlāgū hastened back to Tartary on receiving the news, leaving his son Abāghā in charge of an army of 20,000 (1259). Baibars, Sultan of Egypt, took the opportunity to enter Syria, and defeated the Mongols more than once. He seized Antioch from the Christians and invaded Armenia with a large army. One of Hethum's sons was slain, the other (afterwards Leo III) was taken captive. The Mamlūks wasted part of Cilicia, disinterred the bones of Armenian kings, and retraced their steps with numerous captives and much plunder. All that Hethum could do was to ransom his son by sacrificing the castle of Derbessak and by dismantling two other fortresses on the frontier. He entrusted to Leo the government of the country, and after a turbulent reign of forty-four years retired into a monastery.

Leo III (1270–1289) had to face the same problems that had troubled his father—internal revolt and the enmity of Egypt and Iconium. In addition he was scourged by personal illness and by a visitation of plague and famine. Taking advantage of disaffection among the Armenian princes, who had revolted unsuccessfully against Leo, Baibars invaded Cilicia with an army of Turks and Arabs. Leo was deserted and fled to the mountains, leaving the country defenceless. Sis repulsed the invaders, but Tarsus capitulated. Its magnificent buildings were set on fire, thousands of its people were massacred, and thousands more led into captivity (1274). This disaster was followed by famine and plague. Leo himself fell ill; his two sons died.

Scarcely healed of his sickness, the king had to face a second Mamlūk invasion. But this time the Armenian princes rallied to him, and as usual saved their country from final catastrophe. The Mamlūks were caught in a trap, and suffered losses so great that the corpses of the dead prevented the living from taking flight. Baibars, gravely wounded by an arrow, reached Damascus to die (1276).

The Khan Abāghā sent delegates to congratulate Leo on his victory, and to propose that he should add Turkey (Rūm or Asia Minor) and several Mesopotamian towns to his Cilician kingdom. Leo wisely refused this offer of a vast realm, but he agreed to the Khan's other proposal of addressing letters to the Pope and the kings of the West to ask them to join the Mongols for the capture of the Holy Land from the Mamlūks. On 25 November 1276 John and James Vassal, the messengers of Abāghā Khan, announced to Edward I of England their approaching arrival in the West with letters from the Mongol Emperor and the King of Armenia.

After defeating the Seljūqs of Iconium (1278), who had invaded Armenian territory while the Armenians were repulsing the Mamlūks, Leo was bound by his alliance to go to the help of the Mongols, who were again at war with the Mamlūks. The Armenians joined the Mongol army under Mangū Tīmūr without mishap, and met the Mamlūks, led by Saif-ad-Dīn Qalā'ūn al-Alfī, at Ḥimṣ on the Orontes (1281). The Mamlūks would have been defeated but for the inexplicable conduct of Mangū Tīmūr, which gave the day to the sultan, already at the point of flight. As a result, Leo barely escaped to Armenia with thirty horsemen. The Mongols returned to face the anger of their Khan, who beheaded both the generals and forced the soldiers to wear women's clothes. After this disaster the Mongols were hostile to Armenia for two years, because Abāghā's successor hated the Christians. But on the accession of another Khan in 1284, the Mongols resumed their old friendship with the Armenians, and Leo was able to spend the last five years of his reign in works of peace.

Prosperity vanished with Leo's death. Under his son Hethum (Hayton) II the One-Eyed (1289–1305), Armenia was in a peculiarly difficult position. The Mamlūk rulers of Syria and Palestine were bent on annihilating Armenia, the last bulwark of Christendom. Hethum had no reliable allies. The Mongols were not only losing power, but were turning towards Islām. The Christians of the West were broken reeds, for the time of great impulses and united effort was past, even if the Armenian people had not opposed religious agreement with Rome.

Hethum himself weakened Cilicia by his fitful sovereignty. The author of a national chronicle in verse, he preferred the part of monk to that of king, and long refused to be crowned. He abdicated three times, once to enter a monastery, once to turn Franciscan, once to become "Father of the King" to his nephew Leo IV. At a fourth juncture abdication was thrust upon him. As a result he ruled Cilicia for little more than half the time that elapsed between his accession in 1289 and his death in 1307. From 1290 to 1291, and again from 1294 to 1296, he entrusted the government to his brother Thoros III. Thoros in his turn became a monk, and when Hethum went with him to Constantinople to see their sister Ritha he left a third brother Smbat (Sempad) to rule Armenia in his absence (1296–1297). This time he did not intend to abdicate, but Smbat had himself crowned at Sis with the consent of Ghāzān Khān, the Mongol ruler of Persia, and married a Tartar princess. On Hethum's return, Smbat drove him and Thoros out of Cilicia. They appealed in vain to the khan and to their kinsfolk in Cyprus and Constantinople. Smbat seized them near Caesarea in Cappadocia and imprisoned them in the High Fortress (Bardsrberd), where Thoros was put to death and Hethum blinded and left in chains (1298). This *coup d'état* was reversed by a fourth brother Constantine, who dethroned and imprisoned Smbat. When, however, the Armenians wished to reinstate Hethum, who was slowly recovering his sight, Constantine repented of his loyalty and tried to release Smbat. But, with the help of Templars and Hospitallers, Hethum in his turn seized his brothers and sent them to Constantinople (1299). After this experience he did not abdicate again for six years.

Such unstable government did not help the Armenians to resist the Mamlūks. But Hethum was a good soldier when the militant side of his nature was uppermost, and until 1302, when the Tartar alliance was lost, he defended Cilicia with moderate success. It was the threat of invasion by Ashraf, the successor of Qalā'ūn, that finally decided him to be crowned (1289). He sent troops to guard the frontiers and appealed for help to Arghūn Khān and to Pope Nicholas III. Nothing but vague promises from Philip the Fair came of these appeals, but indirectly Cilicia was saved by the Christians, who at the Pope's instigation laid siege to Alexandria. After taking Romkla, the seat of the Katholikos, and massacring its inhabitants, the sultan hurried back to Egypt with the Katholikos in his train, and Hethum gained peace and the release of the Katholikos at the price of several fortresses (1289–1290).

Some years later, during the contention between Hethum and his brothers, Susamish, viceroy of Damascus, prepared to invade Cilicia at the head of a Mamlūk army. Hethum scattered his troops and handed him over to Ghāzān Khān. After this success, Hethum and the khan took the offensive, and tried to seize Syria and Palestine from the Mamlūks. But the khan suddenly returned to Persia to repress the revolt of his kinsman Baidū, and left his troops under the command of Quṭlughshāh. Although Hethum and Quṭlughshāh were at first successful, they were finally, after losing many men in the Euphrates, compelled to retreat.

Ghāzān Khān had promised on leaving Hethum that he would come back to undertake the conquest of the Holy Land for the Christians, but in 1302 he died. His successor, Uljāitū, far from fulfilling that promise, turned Musulman and forswore the ancient alliance with Armenia. The Mongols made war on the Armenians and spent a year reducing Cilicia to a heap of ruins. Turks and Mamlūks then invaded the country three times, and levelled the ruins left standing by the Mongols. Again Hethum was roused to action. As the enemy were about to depart laden with plunder, he attacked them and killed or captured nearly seven thousand of their men. The Sultan of Egypt made peace; and for a time the Turks disappeared from Cilicia.

All through Hethum's reign, the defence of Cilicia depended upon the military qualities of himself and of his people alone. He made the most of his diplomatic opportunities, but with no appreciable result. He tried hard to keep the Mongol alliance, but even before 1302 the khan could not help him against Ashraf and would not help him against his brother Smbat. He made marriage alliances with Constantinople and Cyprus, giving his sister Mariam in marriage to Michael IX, son of the Emperor Andronicus, and marrying another sister Zabel to Amaury, brother of the King of Cyprus. After the loss of the Mongol alliance, he redoubled the efforts of his predecessor to earn Western help by religious concession. The Katholikos Grigor VII Anavarzetsi prepared a profession of faith in nine chapters, and proposed to introduce into the Armenian Church various changes of ritual conforming to the Roman usage. Before anything further was done, the Katholikos died and Hethum resigned the crown to his nephew Leo IV (1305–1307). In 1307 Leo and his uncle summoned the princes and the ecclesiastics to the First Council of Sis. There, owing to the king's insistence, the profession of faith drafted by the late Katholikos was read and adopted. But when the people knew of it, their fury overleapt the bounds of loyalty and patriotism. In their anger they roused Bilarghu the Mongol against Hethum and Leo. Already in Cilicia, Bilarghu treacherously invited the king and his uncle to Anazarbus, where he put them to death with the princes of their persuasion (13 August 1307).

All hope of gaining Western aid in return for religious concession was once more deferred. The only tangible fruit of Hethum's advances to the Latins had been the help given him by the Templars and Hospitallers against his rebellious brothers. Tried and found wanting time after time, the rulers of the West were nevertheless Armenia's only possible friends. Like Hethum, his successor Oshin[1] (1307–1320) worked steadily for their co-operation. Like Hethum, he made marriage alliances, sought religious accommodation, sent despairing appeals for help. And like Hethum he was left to defend Armenia himself.

Isabel of Lusignan, daughter of King Hugh III, was his first wife, and her successor was Joan of Anjou, niece of King Robert of Naples and daughter of Philip I of Anjou-Taranto, known as Philip II, Latin Emperor of the East. Besides marrying into two Western families, Oshin tried to solve the religious problem. In 1316 he summoned to Adana an assembly which examined and adopted the ecclesiastical settlement made at Sis nine years before. The king and the Katholikos Constantine II had the dogma of the Procession of the Holy Ghost proclaimed in conformity with Catholic teaching. But once more the angry people frustrated the will of their rulers, and only the overwhelming peril from the Mamlūks could dull the edge of religious discord. As appeals for help sent to John XXII and to Philip of Valois were fruitless, the burden of defending Cilicia fell upon Oshin. He had expelled Bilarghu and his Mongols from the country at the beginning of his reign, avenging on them the death of his kinsmen. After this he had found time to build strongholds and churches, especially in Tarsus, where he restored and strengthened the famous ramparts, and built the magnificent church now known as Kilīsa-jāmiʻ (= church-mosque). But in the middle of his religious troubles the Mamlūks again threatened Cilicia, and he spent the last years of his reign defending the country single-handed. For twenty years after his death (1320–1340) Armenia struggled unavailingly against the rising power of the Mamlūks.

The minority of Oshin's son Leo V (1320–1342) produced a nationalist crisis. The long-continued friendship of Armenian rulers with the Latins, their adoption of Latin institutions, and their intermarriage with Latin families, had made their court more Latin than Armenian; while their friendly discussions with the Papacy had strengthened the cause of the Uniates, who worked for a complete union of the Armenian Church with Rome. But Leo's minority gave the nationalists their chance. The government was in the hands of a council of regency composed of four barons, Leo himself being under the guardianship of Oshin of Gorigos. Oshin married Leo's mother, exiled the king's Lusignan cousins, and married him to his own daughter in order to counteract Latin influences. When Leo came to power, however, he undid Oshin's work. He married a Spanish wife connected with the Lusignans (Constance of Aragon, widow of Henry II of Lusignan), recalled his cousins, and finally put Oshin to death. During his reign Cilicia was confined to its ancient boundaries, but though the country's defences were in ruins and the

[1] Probably the brother of Leo IV, and not, as some writers say, of Hethum.

princes were occupied with political and ecclesiastical disputes, Leo immersed himself in religious discussions.

Meanwhile Nāṣir, Sultan of the Mamlūks, on hearing that Europe was preparing for a new crusade, made an alliance with the Tartars and Turkomans for the conquest of Armenia. Devastated and plundered by successive armies of Tartars, Turkomans, and Mamlūks, Cilicia was once more saved from complete destruction by a few heroic Armenians. They hid in passes through which the enemy had to march, and massacred several thousand Mamlūks. The sultan agreed to a fifteen years' truce on condition that the Armenians paid to the Egyptians an annual tribute of 50,000 florins, half the customs and revenue from the maritime trade of Ayas, and half the sea-salt. In return, the sultan undertook to rebuild Ayas and the other fortresses at his own expense, and not to occupy any stronghold or castle in Cilicia with his troops.

At last, about 1335, Philip VI of France decided to go to the help of the Armenians, and Nāṣir resolved to conquer them. The net result of the two decisions might have been foreseen. On the one hand, Leo received 10,000 florins from Philip with a few sacks of corn from the Pope; on the other, Armenia was invaded and conquered by the Mamlūks. Leo fled to the mountains (1337); but after forcing him to swear on Bible and Cross never again to enter into relations with Europe, Nāṣir left him to rule what was left of his country until his death in 1342. He was the last of the Rubenian-Hethumian rulers, who thus left Armenia as they had found it, a prey to the foreigner.

For a generation after Leo's death (1342–1373), Armenia was ruled by Latin kings. Two of them were Lusignan princes connected by marriage with the Hethumian dynasty, and the other two were usurpers not of royal blood.

The Lusignans derived their claim to the Armenian crown from the marriage of Zabel, sister of Hethum II, to Amaury of Tyre, brother of Henry II of Cyprus (1295). John and Guy, two sons of this marriage, were in the service of the Emperor at Constantinople when Leo V died. Some months after Leo's death, John, the younger, was called upon to administer the Cilician kingdom, not as king, but as *baïle* or regent. At his suggestion, the elder brother Guy left Constantinople and accepted the crown of Armeno-Cilicia in 1342.

Crowned by the Katholikos according to Armenian rites, Guy acted at first as an Armenian patriot, refusing to pay tribute to the Sultans of Egypt and Turkey. But when Egyptian invasions followed, Guy not only adopted the time-honoured custom of appealing for help to the Pope (Clement VI) and of promising to effect if possible the union of the Armenian Church with Rome, but surrounded himself with Latin princes to whom he entrusted the defence of towns and fortresses. The Pope actually sent a thousand horsemen and a thousand pieces of Byzantine silver, but the Armenians, resenting Guy's Latinising policy, assassinated him with his brother Bohemond and the Western knights who had come to his aid (1344). His other brother John had died a natural death a few months earlier.

The next king, the usurper Constantine IV, son of Baldwin, marshal of Armenia, was more successful (1344–1363). With the help of Theodates of Rhodes and Hugh of Cyprus he repulsed an Egyptian invasion with great slaughter, leaving Ayas alone in the enemy's hands. He hoped that the news of his success would move Europe to help him, but when his embassy returned empty-handed from Venice, Paris, London, and Rome, he marched without allies against the Mamlūks, drove them from the country, and captured Alexandretta from them (1357). As a result of his victory and of his efforts to subdue the religious discord, Armenia was at peace for the rest of his life.

Constantine IV was succeeded by a second usurper, Constantine V, son of a Cypriot serf who had become an Armenian baron. Elected king because of his wealth, he offered the crown to Peter I, King of Cyprus, but when Peter was assassinated in 1369 Constantine kept the throne himself. Four years later, the Armenians put him to death, and during the anarchy which followed they entrusted the government to the widow of Constantine IV, Mary of Gorigos, who had already played an active part in Armenian politics before the king's assassination.

The last King of Armenia was Leo VI of Lusignan (1373, d. 1393). His father was John, brother of King Guy, and his grandmother was Zabel, sister of Hethum II. He himself had been imprisoned with his mother Soldane of Georgia by Constantine IV, who had wished to destroy the royal Armenian line. His reign was not a success. All his efforts to avert the long-impending doom of Cilicia were powerless. He fought energetically against the Mamlūks, but was led captive to Cairo (1375). There he appointed as almoner and confessor John Dardel, whose recently-published chronicle has thrown unexpected light upon the last years of the Cilician kingdom. In 1382 the king was released and spent the rest of his life in various countries of Europe. He died in 1393 at Paris, making Richard II of England his testamentary executor, and his epitaph is still preserved in the basilica of Saint-Denis. After his death, the Kings of Cyprus were the nominal Kings of Armenia until 1489, when the title passed to Venice. Almost at the same time (1485), by reason of the marriage (1433) of Anne of Lusignan with Duke Louis I of Savoy, the rulers of Piedmont assumed the empty claim to a kingdom of the past.

During the exile of Leo VI, Greater Armenia was enduring a prolonged Tartar invasion. After conquering Baghdad (1386), Tamerlane entered Vaspurakan. At Van he caused the people to be hurled from the rock which towers above the city; at Ernjak he massacred all the inhabitants; at Sīwās he had the Armenian garrison buried alive. In 1389 he devastated Turuberan and Taron; in 1394 he finished his campaign at Kars, where he took captive all the people whom he did not massacre, and passed on into Asia Minor. By the beginning of the fifteenth century the old Armenian territory had been divided among its Muslim conquerors—Mamlūks, Turks, and Tartars. Yūsuf, Sultan of Egypt, ruled Sassun; the Emir Erghin governed Vaspurakan from Ostan; and Tamerlane's son, Mīrān Shāh, reigned at Tabrīz. These Musulman emirs made war upon one another at the expense of the Armenian families who had not migrated to Asia Minor on the fall of the Bagratid kingdom. By the close of the fifteenth century Cilicia, too, was finally absorbed into the Ottoman Empire.

Kings and kingdom had passed, but the Armenians still possessed their Church. In the midst of desolation, schools and convents maintained Armenian art and culture, and handed on the torch of nationality. Some of the Armenian manuscripts which exist to-day were written in the fourteenth and fifteenth centuries. The long religious controversy, of which the Uniates were the centre, survived the horrors of the period, and continued to agitate the country. Among the protagonists were John of Khrna, John of Orotn, Thomas of Medzoph, Gregory of Tathew, and Gregory of Klath. In 1438 Armenian delegates attended the Council of Florence with the Greeks and Latins in order to unify the rites and ceremonies of the Churches.

The most important work of the Church was administrative. During Tamerlane's invasion the Katholikos had established the pontifical seat among the ruins of Sis. But towards the middle of the next century Sis rapidly declined, and it was decided to move the seat to Echmiadzin in the old Bagratid territory. As Grigor IX refused to leave Sis, a new Katholikos, Kirakos Virapensis, was elected for Echmiadzin, and from 1441 the Armenian Church was divided for years between those who accepted the primacy of Echmiadzin and those who were faithful to Sis. Finally, the Katholikos of Echmiadzin became, in default of a king, the head of the Armenian people. With his council and synod he made himself responsible for the national interests of the Armenians, and administered such possessions as remained to them. After the Turkish victory of 1453, Mahomet II founded an Armenian colony in Constantinople and placed it under the supervision of Joakim, the Armenian Bishop of Brūsa, to whom he afterwards gave the title of "Patriarch" with jurisdiction over all the Armenians in the Ottoman Empire. From that time to this, the Armenian Patriarch of Constantinople has carried on the work of the Katholikos and has been the national representative of the Armenian people.

CHAPTER VII.

(A)

THE EMPIRE AND ITS NORTHERN NEIGHBOURS.

WHILE the Germans impressed their characteristic stamp on both the medieval and modern history of Western Europe, it was reserved for the Eastern Slavs, the Russians, to build a great empire on the borderlands of Europe and Asia. But the work of civilisation was far more difficult for the Russians than for the German race. The barbaric Germans settled in regions of an old civilisation among the conquered Romans and Romanised peoples, whereas the geographical and ethnical surroundings entered by the Eastern Slavs were unfavourable, in so far as no old inheritance existed there to further any endeavours in civilisation; this had to be built up from the very foundations. Boundless forests, vast lakes and swamps, were great obstacles to the colonisation of the immense plain of eastern Europe, and the long stretch of steppes in southern Russia was for many centuries the home of Asiatic nomads, who not only made any intercourse with Greek civilisation impossible but even endangered incessantly the results of the native progress of the Russian Slavs.

The growth of the Russian empire implies not only the extension of the area of its civilisation but also the absorption of many elements belonging to foreign races and speaking foreign tongues, and their coalescence with the dominant Russian nation.

It was only the southernmost parts of the later Russian empire that had from time immemorial active connexions with the several centres of ancient Greek civilisation. In the course of the seventh century B.C. numerous Greek colonies were founded on the northern shore of the Black Sea, such as Tyras, Olbia, Chersonesus, Theodosia, Panticapaeum (now Kerch), and Tanais. These towns were the intermediaries of the commerce between the barbaric peoples of what is now Russia and the civilised towns of Greece. They were at the same time centres of Greek civilisation, which they spread among their nearest neighbours who inhabited the southern steppes of Russia and were known in history first under the name of *Scythians* and then of *Sarmatians*. Of what race these peoples were, is not clearly established.

The ancient historians mention several tribes who lived to the north and north-west of the Scythians and Sarmatians, and were in all probability Slavs or Finns.

The Scythian and Sarmatian nomads were a continuous danger to the security of the Greek colonies; they extorted from them regular yearly tributes. Still the chief towns to the north of the Black Sea did succeed though with difficulty in maintaining their existence during the whole period of the Scythian and Sarmatian dominion. These towns in course of time exchanged Greek independence for a Roman protectorate.

After the Sarmatians there appeared new enemies of the Greek colonies along the northern littoral of the Black Sea. Already in the first century of our era the name of the Sarmatians is superseded by that of Alans, which new generic name, according to the explanation of ancient historians, comprehends several nomadic races, mainly Iranian.

In the second and third centuries A.D. new immigrants poured in to the northern shores of the Black Sea. The western part of the steppes was occupied by German races, especially by the Goths, the eastern part by Asiatic Huns. The Goths remained more than two centuries in the steppes of southern Russia and the lands bordering the Black Sea, whence they made incursions into the Roman Empire. By the inroad of overwhelming masses of the Huns the Gothic state was subverted in A.D. 375, and the Goths disappeared slowly from the borders of the Black Sea. Only a small part of them remained, some in the Caucasus and others till much later in the Crimea. The other Goths acquired new homes in other lands of Europe. Of the Greek colonies on the north of the Black Sea only those in the Crimea outlived the Gothic period.

With the expansion of the power of the Huns a new period begins in the history of Eastern and Central Europe. Hitherto Asia sent its nomads only as far as the steppes of southern Russia. The Huns are the first nomads who by their conquests extend Asia to the lands on the central Danube. Like a violent tempest their hordes not only swept over the south Russian steppes but also penetrated to Roman Pannonia, where Attila, their king, in the first half of the fifth century founded the centre of his gigantic but short-lived empire. After Attila's death his empire fell to pieces, and the Huns disappeared almost entirely among the neighbouring nations. Only a small part fled to the Black Sea, where they encountered the hordes of the nomadic Bulgars, a people in all probability of Finnish (Ugrian) origin, but mixed with Turkish elements. The Bulgars were originally settled in the lands between the rivers Kama and Volga, where even later the so-called Kama and Volga Bulgars are found, but part of them moved at an unknown time to the south-west, and when the Huns had migrated to Pannonia came to the Black Sea, where they appear already in the second half of the fifth century. Before they arrived there they had lived under so strong a Turkish influence that they could easily blend with the remnants of the Huns. The Greek authors of the sixth century especially mention in these regions two Bulgarian tribes, the Kutrigurs or Kuturgurs and the Utigurs or Utrigurs. The Kutrigurs roamed as nomads on the right bank of the Don to the west, the Utigurs from the Don to the south, eastwards of the Sea of Azov. After the departure of the other Bulgarian hordes in the second half of the seventh century only the Utigurs remained in the lands near the Black Sea; they are later known as the Black Bulgars.

Like other barbarians the hordes of the Bulgars were an unceasing source of trouble to the Eastern Roman Empire. Justinian was forced to pay a yearly tribute to the Kutrigurs. But, as even this subsidy did not restrain them from frequent invasions, he made use of the common Byzantine policy, bribing the Utigurs to be their enemies.

The Utigurs violently attacked the Greek colonies situated on both shores of the Cimmerian Bosphorus. Panticapaeum, better known to the Byzantine authors as Bosphorus, resisted only a short time, and finally had to acknowledge the Utigurs' supremacy in order to save some sort of autonomy. In 522, during Justinian I's reign, Bosphorus had a Greek garrison.

Immediately after the Huns other nomads from Asia thronged to Europe. They were part of a people named by the Chinese Yuan-Yuan but calling themselves Yü-küe-lü, who in Europe became known by the name of Avars. This nation appeared in the territory of the empire of the T'o-pa, founded by a secession from the Chinese Empire.

The empire of the T'o-pa was short-lived. The Yuan-Yuan revolted against their masters and founded on a part of their territory a separate state, for a time under the supremacy of the T'o-pa, but in the second half of the fourth century they rose to such power that they tried to gain their independence. They succeeded in this endeavour under their chief Shelun (402–410), who assumed the title of Khagan. From that time down to the sixth century the Yuan-Yuan became the foremost people in Central Asia. They ruled over Eastern Turkestan, and over the present territories of Mongolia and Manchuria as far as Korea. But from the end of the fifth century the empire of the Yuan-Yuan was already in decline.

The subdued races took advantage of this weakness and endeavoured to shake off their yoke. The Chinese call these hordes T'u-küe, the nearest they could get to Turks. The Chinese knew of a long series of Turkish hordes and counted them among their tributary tribes. Some of these hordes were also under the dominion of the Huns. In the middle of the sixth century the half mythical chieftain T'u-mên united the numerous Turkish tribes and rose to the leadership of the whole

Turkish nation in northern and central Asia, whereupon the Turks allied themselves with the T'o-pa against the Yuan-Yuan. These succumbed, their Khagan A-na-kuei (Anagay) in 552 committed suicide, and their empire came to an end.

That part of the Turks which formerly was under the dominion of the Yuan-Yuan remained in their homes and acknowledged the supremacy of T'u-mên, but the other part migrated to the west into the steppes of southern Russia and further into Pannonia. These new nomadic hordes appear in Europe under the name of Avars. But according to Theophylact Simocatta the European Avars were not the genuine Avars but Pseudo-avars. In any case they, like the other Asiatic nomads, were not an ethnically pure race but a mixed people.

During the migration the number of the Avars increased considerably, since other tribes, kindred as well as foreign, joined them, and among these was also a part of the Bulgars. Soon after their arrival in Europe in 558 the Avars encountered the Eastern Slavs, called Antae in the ancient histories, the ancestors of the later South Russian Slavonic races. The Avars repeatedly invaded the lands of the Antae, devastating the country, dragging away the inhabitants as prisoners, and carrying with them great spoils.

A few years later, in 568, they appear in Pannonia, which they selected as the centre of their extensive dominion, and where they roamed for two centuries and a half. From there they made their predatory incursions into the neighbouring lands, especially into the Balkan peninsula, often in company with the Slavs. The worst period of these devastations by the Avars lasted no longer than about sixty years, for they soon experienced several disasters. From the western Slavonic lands they had been driven by Samo, the founder of the first great Slavonic empire (623–658), and in the East the Bulgarian ruler Kovrat, who was in friendly relations with the Greeks, shook off their yoke. After 626, when the Avars beleaguered Constantinople in vain, the Balkan peninsula remained unmolested by their inroads, their last hostile incursion being the aid they gave to the Slavs in their attack on Thessalonica. Moreover there began in their dominion internal disorders which were in all probability the principal cause of the downfall of their power. In 631 there arose a severe conflict between the genuine Avars and their allied Bulgarian horde, because the chieftain of the Bulgarians had the courage to compete with an Avar for the throne. A fight arose between the two contending parties, which resulted in the victory of the Avars. The vanquished Bulgarian and 9000 of his followers with their families were driven from Pannonia.

During the period in which the dominion of the Avars reached from the middle course of the Danube almost to the Dnieper, there flourished between the Sea of Azov and the Caspian the dominion of the Chazars, nomads of another Turkish race, which in course of time became a half-settled nation. The Chazars formed one of the best-organised Turkish states and their dominion lasted several centuries. Their origin is entirely unknown.

The history of the Chazars becomes clearer with the beginning of the sixth century, when they made repeated inroads into Armenia, crossed the Caucasus, and extended their dominion to the river Araxes. The Chazar warriors not only devastated Armenia, but pushed their inroads even into Asia Minor. Kawad (Kobad), King of Persia, sent an army of 12,000 men to expel them, and conquered the land between the rivers Cyrus and Araxes. Having moreover occupied Albania (Shirvan), Kawad secured the northern frontier of the land by a long wall stretching from the sea to the Gate of the Alans (the fortress of Dariel) and containing three hundred fortified posts. The Persians ceased to keep this wall in good repair, but Kawad's son Chosroes I Nūshirwān (531–578), with the consent of the ruler of the Chazars, had erected the Iron Caspian Gate, from which the neighbouring town near the Caspian Sea was called in Arabic Bāb-al-abwāb, Gate of Gates, and in Persian Darband (gate). The ramparts, however, erected by Chosroes near Darband and running along the Caucasian mountains for a distance of 40 parasangs (about 180 miles) were of no great use, as the Chazars forced their way by the Darband gate into Persia and devastated the land.

In the last quarter of the sixth century the Chazars were a part of the great Turkish empire, founded by T'u-mên. His son, whose name is given in the Chinese annals as Sse-kin and by the Greek authors as Askin or Askil (553–569), ruled over an immense territory stretching from the desert of Shamo as far as the western sea, and from the basin of the river Tarim to the tundras near the river Kien (Kem or Yenisey). The Turkish empire was further extended by his successor Khagan Dizabul, named also Silzibul, in Turkish Sinjibu. During his reign also the Chazars belonged to the Turkish empire.

The Persian empire was a great obstacle to the tendency of the Turks to expand, and as the Byzantines were also the enemies of the Persians, the Turks sought to conclude alliances with them against the common foe. Khagan Sse-kin in 563 was the first to send an embassy to the Byzantines to negotiate a treaty of alliance, and under Justin II in 568 another mission was sent by the Turks to Constantinople. In return the Greeks also sent their ambassadors to the Turks; and in 569 Zemarchus journeyed from Cilicia to Central Asia as Justin II's envoy.

Among other embassies of the Greeks to the Turks should be mentioned that of Valentinus in 579, which was to notify the accession of the new Emperor Tiberius II to the throne. On Valentinus' second journey he had 106 Turks among his retinue. At that time there lived a considerable number of Turks in Constantinople, principally those who had come there as attendants of Byzantine envoys on their return journey. After a long and arduous journey, Valentinus arrived at the seat of Khagan Turxanth in the steppes between the Volga and the Caucasus, evidently one of the khagans subordinate to the supreme khagan who ruled over the Chazars, and from here the Byzantine embassy continued its way into the interior of the Turkish empire to reach the supreme khagan. During their stay there Turxanth acted in open enmity against the Byzantines, assaulting their towns in the Crimea, assisted by Anagay, prince of the Utigurs and vassal of the Turks.

The power of the Turks declined during the reign of Sinjibu's successors. At the end of the sixth century there began contests for the khagan's throne. Although the supreme khagan was able in 597 to subdue the revolt with the aid of the three other khagans, the disturbances were soon renewed, and the horde of Turks dwelling between the Volga and the Caspian Sea, the Chazars, freed themselves from the power of the supreme Turkish khagan in the early years of the seventh century.

During the seventh, eighth, and ninth centuries the empire of the Chazars was very powerful. As soon as the Chazars became independent of the supremacy of the Turkestan Turks, they expanded their dominion in all directions to the injury of the Black Sea Bulgars (Utigurs), the Crimean Greeks, and other peoples. The Bulgarians were for a long period in the seventh century the allies of the Byzantines. In 619 Organas, lord of the "Huns" (obviously the Utigurs), came with his magnates and their wives to Constantinople and embraced with them the Christian faith. In like manner Kovrat, Khan of the Bulgars, having freed himself from the power of the Avars (635), became an ally of the Byzantines. But when Kovrat died and his sons had divided his realm between them, Batbayan, the youngest of them, who remained near the Sea of Azov, was compelled to acknowledge the supremacy of the Chazars and to pay them a tribute.

When in the second half of the seventh century the Arabian Caliphate succeeded the Persian empire, the Chazars waged wars with the Arabs. Their relations with the Byzantines did not change. They had been the steady allies of the Greeks against the Persians, and remained their allies also against the Arabs, in spite of frequent conflicts due to their opposing interests in the Crimean peninsula.

During the reign of the third Caliph, Othman, the Arabs consolidated their power in Armenia and even took a part of their lands from the Chazars. After 683 Armenia was again menaced by the Chazars, but in 690 they were severely defeated and many were burned in churches where they had sought shelter. According to Makīn, the Arabs passed the Caspian gate and killed many Chazars; those who survived were compelled to embrace Islām.

At the beginning of the eighth century the Chazars already ruled over a part of the Crimea, and conquered almost the whole of the peninsula before the end of the century; only the town of Cherson kept its independence, although for a short time it fell under their rule. Towards the end of the seventh century Justinian II, the dethroned Emperor (685–695), was sent there into exile. Some time later he tried to regain his throne, but when the inhabitants of the city attempted to hinder his design, he fled to the Gothic town of Doras in the Crimea, whence he sent to the Khagan of the Chazars, Vusir (*Wazir*) Gliavar, asking for a hospitable reception. This the khagan accorded him with much kindness, and gave him his sister Theodora in marriage. Justinian then lived some time in Phanagoria or Tamatarcha (on the peninsula now called Taman), which at that time belonged to the Chazars. But the Emperor Tiberius Apsimar induced the khagan by incessant bribes to turn traitor and to send him Justinian either dead or alive. The khagan ordered his *tuduns* (lieutenants) in Phanagoria and Bosphorus to slay Justinian. The plans for the execution of the treachery were ready, but Theodora warned her husband in time, and he fled to the Bulgarian prince Tervel, who even aided him to regain his throne in 705.

Justinian now turned all his thoughts to wreaking his revenge on the inhabitants of Cherson. Three times he sent fleets and troops to the Crimea, but no sooner did the third army begin to beleaguer Cherson with some success than the forces of the Chazars arrived and relieved the town. Cherson retained thereafter its autonomy under an elected administrator (*proteuon*) until the time of the Emperor Theophilus, that is for more than a century.

From Byzantine sources we learn that the Emperor Leo the Isaurian sent an ambassador to the Khagan of the Chazars to ask the khagan's daughter as a bride for his son Constantine, who was then in his fifteenth year. The Chazar princess was christened and named Irene (732). In 750 she became the mother of Leo, surnamed the Chazar. She introduced into Constantinople the Chazar garment called *toitzakia*, which the Emperors donned for festivities.

In the eighth century the Chazars had wars with the Arabs with alternating success. Georgia and Armenia were devastated by these wars during a period of eighty years. In 764 the Chazars again invaded these territories, but after that they are not mentioned by the Arabian authors before the end of the eighth century. The Khagan of the Chazars then made an inroad into Armenia in 799 with a great army and ravaged it cruelly, but finally he was expelled by the Caliph Hārūn ar-Rashīd. This was, as far as we know, the last predatory expedition of the Chazars into a land south of the Caucasus.

The organisation of the imperial power of the Chazars is very interesting. At the head of the State was the supreme khagan (*ilek*), but his power was only nominal. The real government was in the hands of his deputy, called *khagan bey* or even simply *khagan* and *isha.* He was the chief commander of the forces and chief administrator. The supreme khagan was never in touch with his people; he lived in his harem and appeared in public only once every four months, when he took a ride accompanied by a bodyguard which followed him at a distance of a mile. His court numbered four thousand courtiers and his bodyguard twelve thousand men, a number which was always kept undiminished.

The supreme Khagan of the Chazars practised polygamy, having twenty-five legal wives, who were every one of them daughters of neighbouring princes. Moreover he kept sixty concubines. The main force of the Chazar army was formed by the bodyguard of 12,000. These troops are called by the Arabian writers *al-arsīya* or *al-lārisīya*, which Westberg says should be *karisiya*, because the overwhelming majority of them were Muslim mercenaries from Khwārazm, the Khiva of our days. In addition to these, men belonging to other nations (Mas'ūdī mentions "Russians" and Slavs) were also taken into the bodyguard or other service of the khagan. This Musulman bodyguard stipulated that it should not be obliged to take part in a war against co-religionists, and that the vizier must be chosen from its ranks.

An ideal tolerance in religion was exercised in the dominions of the Chazars. The Chazars proper (Turks) were originally all heathen and Shamanists. But in course of time Judaism began to spread among the higher classes. Further, some of the nations subdued by the Chazars were heathen, while others professed Christianity. The bodyguard, as we have seen, was almost entirely composed of Muslims, and part of the inhabitants of the capital, Itil, as well as some foreign merchants, were also adherents of Islām. The ruler and his courtiers professed Judaism about the middle of the eighth century (according to other authorities not earlier than the end of the eighth or the beginning of the ninth century).

Judaism and Christianity could spread among the Chazars from two quarters, from the Caucasus and from the Crimea. The existence of Jewish communities is attested by inscriptions dating from the first to the third century of our era in the towns of Panticapaeum, Gorgippia (now Anápa) at the north-western end of the Caucasus, and Tanais. In the eighth century Phanagoria or Tamatarcha was the principal seat of the Jews of the Cimmerian Bosphorus; and in the ninth century it is even called a Jewish town, the Samkarsh of the Jews.

Islām did not predominate among the Chazars before the second half of the tenth century. It seems that Christianity did not find many followers. It was the religion only of some Caucasian tribes subdued by the Chazars, and probably of some foreign merchants who visited the Chazar towns for their business. St Cyril endeavoured to convert the Chazars to Christianity but with no considerable result, for we learn from a legend of the saint that only two hundred Chazars were christened[1].

All religions were ideally tolerant towards each other in the Chazar lands, so that this half-barbarian state could serve as an example to many a Christian state of medieval and even modern Europe. The courts of justice were organised in the capital town of the ruler according to religions. Seven or, according to Ibn Faḍlan, nine judges held courts to administer justice; two of them were appointed for the Muslims, two for the Jews, two for Christians, and one for the heathen. If the judges of their own religion were unable to decide a complicated controversy, the litigants appealed to the *cadis* of the Muslims, whose administration of justice at that time was considered as the most perfect.

But in spite of religious tolerance, it was a great drawback to the Chazar state that there existed within it so many different religions, and, in all probability, it suffered much harm from the adoption of the Mosaic faith by the rulers and their courtiers. The inhabitants of the Chazar empire could not coalesce into one nation, and the Chazar realm continued until its downfall to be a conglomerate of different ethnic and religious elements. The state was upheld by artificial means, especially by the foreign Musulman mercenaries. Although the downfall of the empire did not begin in the ninth century, yet in the tenth it certainly was in rapid decline.

That the Chazar civilisation attained a high development is apparent from the flourishing commerce of a part of the inhabitants and from the existence of several great towns in the empire. The authorities mention principally the towns Itil, Balanjar, Samandar, and Sarkel. Balanjar was a more ancient capital of the Chazars; some ancient authors wrongly assert that it is identical with Itil or Atel.

The oriental historians give us a better knowledge of the later residence of the Chazar khagans, the town Itil or Atel, than we have of Balanjar. It was the greatest town of the Chazars, situated some miles from the estuary of the river Volga (by the Turks named also Itil or Atel), to the north of the present town of Astrakhan. The ancient Arab authors call this town Al-Baidā (The White City), which corresponds with the later name Sarygshar (Yellow City), as the western part of the town of Itil was called. The Arabian geographers relate that the town of Itil was composed of two (according to Mas'ūdī of three) parts separated by the river Itil. The western part situated on the river was the greater, where the supreme khagan resided. The ruler's palace was the only building constructed of brick; the other houses were either of timber or clay. The eastern part of the town was probably the business centre of the Chazars. But according to Ibn Rusta the Chazar inhabitants lived in this twin-town only in winter, moving in spring to the steppes. This led Marquart to the opinion that Itil was the winter

[1] *Cf. infra,* Chapter VII (B), pp. 219–20.

resort (*kishlak*) of the Chazars and Balanjar their summer dwelling (*yaylak*). Later writers, beginning with the twelfth century, give the name Saksin to the town of Itil.

On the river Don was an important town of the Chazars, Sarkel (White Town, a name which the Greeks translated correctly Ἄσπρον ὅσπίτιον, and the Russians *Bêlavêzha*). According to Constantine Porphyrogenitus, this town was built in the reign of the Greek Emperor Theophilus (829–842) at the request of the Khagan of the Chazars. The Emperor is said to have sent there Petronas, who built the city for the Chazars about 835 and was at the same time made an imperial governor, strategus of the city of Cherson, which had hitherto enjoyed full autonomy, being governed by a *proteuon* elected by the citizens.

The Emperor Constantine does not say against whom Sarkel was built, but according to Cedrenus (eleventh century) it was against the Patzinaks. Uspenski tries to prove that the town of Sarkel was founded at the initiative of the Greeks, to secure the Greek territory on the north shores of the Black Sea and at the same time to protect the Chazars, their allies.

To the Chazar empire belonged, according to Ibn Rusta, a people called *Burdas* or *Burtas* by the orientals. Their territory extended along the Volga at a distance of a fortnight's journey from the territory of the Chazars proper. The Burdas disposed of an army of 10,000 horse. Their limited political capacity prevented them from founding an independent state. In fact Ibn Rusta narrates that they had no other chieftains than the elders of their communes. Their territory was rich in forests. They reared cattle, were hunters, and practised a little agriculture and commerce. They raided the neighbouring Bulgars and Patzinaks. They practised the vendetta in sanguinary feuds. The ethnical affinity of the Burdas is still a matter of dispute; according to Mas'ūdī they were a people of a Turkish race, settled along the banks of a river called also Burdas (according to Marquart, the Samara). They exported great quantities of black and brown fox-hides, generally called *burtasians*.

To the north of the Burdas the Bulgars were settled. Their land extended over the regions of the central Volga to the river Kama, and was full of swamps and dense forests. They are the so-called Volga and Kama Bulgars, White or Silver Bulgars, who remained in their original homes when part of the nation emigrated to the Black Sea. They were divided into three tribes, the Barsuls, the Esegels, and the Bulgars proper. They also belonged to the most advanced Ural-Altaic peoples. They very early began to till their lands, and were good hunters and shrewd tradesmen as intermediaries of the commerce between the Swedes ("Russians"), Slavs, and Chazars. The southern boundaries of their lands were only a three days' journey distant from the territory of the Burdas.

The Volga Bulgars often made predatory invasions on their swift horses into the lands of the Burdas and carried the inhabitants into captivity. Among themselves they used fox-hides instead of money, although they obtained silver coins (*dirhem, i.e. drachma*) from the Muslim countries. These silver coins were used by the Bulgars as money when trading with foreigners, the Swedes and Slavs, who did not exchange wares except for money. The great number of foreign coins found in the present government of Perm near the river Kama is the best proof of the brisk trade the Bulgars already drove in the fifth century with foreign lands, especially with the far Orient, the coins being Sasanian and Indo-Bactrian of the fifth century.

To supply the increasing need for specie, the Bulgars began to coin their own money in the tenth century. Three Bulgarian coins of native origin, struck in Bulgary in the towns of Bulgar and Suvar under the rulers Talib and Mumin, have been preserved from the years 950 and 976.

Trade drew members of very different nations to the Bulgarian cities—Chazars, Swedes, Finns, Slavs, Greeks, Armenians, and Khwārazmians. The principal commercial route of the Bulgars was the Volga; by this river merchandise was carried to the west, and southwards to the Caspian Sea, for several centuries called the Chazar Sea. Two waterways led to the west, one to the Western Dvina and the Dnieper, the other by the Oka upstream to its sources and thence by land to the river Desna to reach Kiev downstream. Merchandise was also shipped southwards to the Sea of Azov. The ships went down the Volga to the point opposite to where the Don bends farthest eastward. From here the wares were transported by land to the Don and then shipped to the Sea of Azov. There was moreover another trade route by land to the south.

The centre of the Volga-Bulgarian realm was situated in the country where the river Kama joins the Volga. North and south of the confluence of the Kama and along its upper course were the principal Bulgarian towns. The capital, called Bulgar by the Arabian writers, was situated at a distance of about 20 miles to the south of the junction of the Kama, and about four miles from the Volga, between the present towns of Spassk and Tetyushi. In the Russian annals of 1164 it appears under the name of "the great town," and not earlier than 1361 it is for the first time called Bulgary. The advantageous situation near the Volga was the cause of its rapid growth, and its extensive trade made it famous all over the Orient. The best proof of the great size of the city is perhaps the narrative of Ibn Haukal, an author of the second half of the tenth century, who tells us that even after the devastation of the town by the Russians it contained 10,000 inhabitants. It was only after the invasion of the Mongols that the town of Bulgar declined; it decayed considerably during the second half of the fourteenth century owing to the ravages of Tamerlane, and was completely destroyed by the Golden Horde.

The first beginnings of the political life of the Bulgars are unknown to us. The history of the Volga-Bulgars becomes somewhat clearer when the Russian annals and the Arabian writers give some notices of them in the tenth century. The advantageous situation of the land was favourable to the formation of a state. The north and east were inhabited by the inert Ugrian tribes of the Eastern Finns, who were no menace to their neighbours. To the south lived the Chazars, powerful indeed but remote, and separated by the territory of the Burdas from the Bulgars. It was not until the ninth century that a dangerous neighbour arose on their western borders in the Russian state. The expeditions of the Russians against the Bulgars will be mentioned later. The Ugrian tribes, settled to the north and east of the Bulgars, were partly under the dominion of the Bulgars and partly retained their independence, such as the Permyaks, Yugers, Votyaks, and Cheremises. All these peoples had their own tribal princes, and their submission to the Bulgars consisted only in the payment of a tribute chiefly of furs.

We get some information of the political organisation of the Bulgars from Ibn Faḍlan, who in June 921 was dispatched by the Caliph Muqtadir of Baghdad to the ruler of the Bulgars to instruct them at his request in Islām; he built a mosque, and for the Bulgarian ruler a castle where he could resist the attacks of hostile princes. Ibn Faḍlan arrived at Bulgar in the early summer of 922, and accomplished his task. We learn from his description of the journey, preserved by the geographer Yāqūt, that the throne of the Bulgarian rulers was hereditary and their power limited by that of the princes and magnates. As a proof of this, four princes, subject to the Bulgarian king, are mentioned, who went with their brothers and children to meet the embassy led by Ibn Faḍlan. They were probably tribal chieftains, although we are informed by other authors that there were only three Bulgarian tribes.

With the ninth century we get a clearer insight into the history of the Magyars, another Ural-Altaic nation, which began to play its part in history within the territory of the later Russian empire, on the northern coasts of the Black Sea. There are but few nations of whose origin and original settlements we know so little as we do of the Magyars. The majority of writers contend that they are a nation of Finnish origin, which only at a later period was under the influence of the Turks and Slavs. The principal champion of this theory is Hunfalvy. Vámbéry on the contrary thinks that the Magyars are a Turkish race, which inhabited the northern and north-eastern border-lands of the Turco-Tartar tribes and was in touch with the Ugrian tribes. To Vámbéry the language is not of such decisive weight as the social life and civilisation. The whole mode of living, the first appearance in history, the political organisation of the Magyars, shew clearly that they belong in origin to Turco-Tartar races. According to Vámbéry, even the names by which the Magyars are called by foreigners are of considerable moment. Not only the Byzantines but also the Arabo-Persian writers called them "Turks." Vámbéry therefore is of the opinion that the Magyars originally belonged to the Turco-Tartar peoples, and that they in course of time adopted in their vocabulary Finno-Ugrian words. The ethnical blending of the two races began in times so remote that it escapes historical observation.

Winkler found in the Magyar language a yet greater mixture. The Finnish foundation was influenced, as he thinks, by the Turkish, Mongol, Dravidian, Iranian, and Caucasian languages.

By far the majority of scholars accept Hunfalvy's theory. But, although Vámbéry's fundamental opinion may not be quite correct, it must be conceded that the cultural influence of the Turks on the Finno-Ugrian Magyars was so strong that they thoroughly changed their former mode of life, and that from hunters they became a nomadic people, one of the most warlike of nations.

The oriental authors give us the first mention of the Magyars. Although they wrote in the tenth century and later, the first original source from which they derived their information comes from the second quarter of the ninth century. Ibn Rusta locates the territory of the Magyars between the Patzinaks, who lived as nomads in the Ural-Caspian steppes, and the Esegelian Bulgars, *i.e.* in the territory of the Bashkirs, called by the Arabian authors Bashgurt and the like. It seems that Ibn Rusta confounds the Bashkirs with the Magyars, which can be easily explained by the kinship of the two nations. According to Pauler they were one nation, of which the lesser part, the Bashkirs, remained in their original territory, later on called Great Hungaria, whereas the greater part, the Magyars, migrated about the beginning of the ninth century in a south-westerly direction to the Black Sea. But this was not the first Magyar wave flowing from north to south. Constantine Porphyrogenitus, who also gives us important information regarding the Magyars, says that only a part of the new immigrants remained near the Black Sea, whereas another branch called Σαβάρτοι ἄσφαλοι moved farther to the east into Persia, where these Eastern Magyars lived even in his time in the tenth century.

At first the Magyars occupied the lands near the Black Sea between the rivers Don and Dnieper. Ibn Rusta and Gurdizi very clearly mention two great rivers to which they give different names. Constantine Porphyrogenitus calls this first territory of the Magyars near the Black Sea Lebedia. Many writers have tried to explain this word, but without success. Constantine speaks of a river Chidmas or Chingylus, which watered the territory of the Magyars.

The lands between the rivers Don and Dnieper belonged to the Chazars at the beginning of the ninth century. The Magyars therefore must have fought them to get possession of their new home. Constantine Porphyrogenitus says indeed that the Magyars were the allies of the Chazars, and that they were their neighbours during three years (which some authors correct to 200 or 300 years or at least to 30 years), but an alliance seems to have been impossible, at least at the beginning of the settlement of the Magyars near the Black Sea. The existence of an alliance between the two nations is further made improbable by another report of Constantine that the Kabars (which means, according to Vámbéry, insurgents), a part of the Chazars who were in revolt, joined seven Magyar tribes, becoming thus the eighth tribe. Even if we do not take into account that the Magyars occupied lands belonging to the Chazar empire, they could not at the beginning have been the friends of the Chazars, because they received among them the insurgent Kabars.

Besides a part of the Chazars a certain number also of Black Bulgars, living near the Don, joined the Magyars, for all the nomadic hordes absorbed the different foreign elements barring their way. And so the Magyars, too, were a motley ethnical conglomerate when they settled on the banks of the Black Sea.

Constantine Porphyrogenitus has preserved for us the names of the seven tribes composing the Magyar people. The principal tribe, Μεγέρη, in all probability gave its name at that time to the whole nation; the Musulman writers at least know this name (Majghariyah, Majghariyan), whereas the Byzantines called the Magyars for a longer period "Turks," evidently considering them, just as the Musulman writers did, to be a nation of Turkish origin.

At the head of the several Magyar tribes were chieftains, called after the Slav fashion *voïvodes* (army-leaders). According to the reports of the Musulman authors, the Magyars like the Chazars had two rulers. One of them was called *kende* (*knda*) and is said to have held the higher rank, but the real government was in the hands of the *jila* (*jele*). Constantine Porphyrogenitus gives a different description of the political organisation of the Magyars, saying that beside the ruling prince there were two judges, one of whom was called *gyla* and the other *karchas*. The dignity of the *gyla* (Magyar, *gyula*) may be identical with that of the *jila* of the Musulman writers. The *jila* was both a judge and a military commander according to Ibn Rusta; but as he was sometimes unable on account of old age to perform the duties of a military chieftain, the Magyars elected besides him a deputy called *kende*. This prominent dignity, combined with its outer splendour, could easily be mistaken by foreigners for that of the chief ruler. Pauler thinks that Constantine Porphyrogenitus, who certainly used some Chazar writings, meant by the word *karchas* the dignity of the *kende*. It seems, at any rate, that the dignities of *karchas* and *kende* were copied by the Magyars from the institutions of the Chazars. These words are Turkish, whereas *gyula* is Magyar. The offices disappeared in the Christian period, but during a heathen reaction the Magyars reinstated that of the *karchas*, as appears from the decree (III. 2) of King Ladislas the Saint, dating from the year 1092.

According to Ibn Rusta, the Magyars in their new homes lived during the summer on the steppes, moving with their tents wherever they found a better pasture for their horses and cattle. They even tilled some land. But with the coming of winter they went to the river to live by fishing. Besides that, they made predatory raids into countries inhabited by the Russian Slavs. They led the captive Slavs to the town of Karkh, and bartered them there to Greek merchants for Byzantine gold, brocade, carpets, and other Greek merchandise.

It is difficult to say how long the Magyars lived in their original territory (the so-called Lebedia) by the Black Sea. Pauler thinks that they lived in the lands between the Don and the Dnieper for about sixty years, starting thence for their predatory raids to even more distant countries. In 862 they reached the kingdom of Louis the German, and devastated it. They again penetrated into the lands along the Danube about 884, during the lifetime of St Methodius. That the Magyars lived for a considerable period in Lebedia may be inferred from their changed relations with the Chazars; an alliance was by now concluded, and that could not have been accomplished in a short time.

To the north-east of the Chazars, between the rivers Atel (Volga) and Yaik (Ural), the Turkish nation of the Patzinaks led, according to Constantine Porphyrogenitus, a nomadic life. The Greeks called them Patzinakitai, the Arabs Bajnak, the Latin medieval authors Pezineigi, Picenati, Bisseni, or Bessi, and the Slavs Pechenêgs.

According to the statements of Oriental writers, the territory of the Patzinaks in the middle of the ninth century seems to have been wider than it was later when described by Constantine Porphyrogenitus. It comprised the lands between the rivers Yaik and Don, a distance of one month's journey, reaching on the west to the Slavs, on the south or south-west to the Chazars, and on the east and north to the Kipchaks (Cumans, in Russian Polovtzi) and Guzes (in Russian Torki).

Like other Turco-Tartar hordes, the Patzinaks during a period of several centuries troubled the various nations of south-eastern Europe, until at last they disappeared among them, absorbed by or making room for the Cumans.

Vámbéry is of the opinion that the Patzinaks and the Cumans were one and the same nation, which under different names and at different periods played its part in the history of the peoples of south-eastern Europe. This opinion may not be quite correct, but nevertheless it cannot be doubted that the Patzinaks were closely related to the Cumans. The common original home of all these Turkish races was the boundless steppes of central Asia. From these steppes whole groups of kindred hordes poured into the steppes of southern Russia. The westernmost of these hordes was that which in Europe was given the name of Patzinaks. While they roamed as nomads in the steppes near the Aral and the Caspian Seas the Chinese called them K'ang-li, in which name all the other kindred hordes were comprised before they were perhaps differentiated in Europe. According to Constantine Porphyrogenitus, the hordes of the Patzinaks were driven from their original seats in Europe between the Volga and the Ural about 55 years before he wrote (*c.* 950–2) Chapter 37 of the *De administrando imperio*. This would mean that the Patzinaks crossed the Volga as late as the very end of the ninth century. In conflict with this statement other evidence about the Magyars and the Russians leads us to suppose that the Patzinaks expelled the Magyars from the territory between the Don and the Dnieper as early as the seventh or at the latest the eighth decade of the ninth century.

Constantine also informs us of the reason why the Patzinaks left their original seats in Europe. They were pressed on by the Guzes (or Ghuzz). The majority of the Patzinaks therefore moved to the west beyond the river Don, expelling the Magyars. Only a small part of the Patzinaks remained in the east and blended with the Guzes. The Magyars did not go far from their original seats. They occupied territories hitherto inhabited by Slavs, especially the Tivertsy: this territory comprised the lands to the northwest of the Black Sea and was watered by the rivers Bug, Dniester, Pruth, and Seret. Constantine calls it Atelkuzu, which was until recent times explained as the Magyar Atelköz, *i.e.* the land between the rivers. Westberg, however, sees in the Byzantine form Kuzu the oriental name of the river Dnieper (Kotsho of Moses of Chorene). The new home of the Magyars therefore consisted of the lands of south-western Russia, Bessarabia, and Moldavia. Pauler puts their arrival in these lands in the year 889, following Regino of Prüm, while the narrative of Constantine Porphyrogenitus would date it 896–897.

From Atelkuzu the Magyars went on with their predatory raids into the neighbouring countries, and certainly gained in a short time a good acquaintance with their future home, Hungary. When the German King Arnulf in 892 waged a war against Svatopluk, Prince of Great Moravia, a Magyar horde, at that time in Hungary, joined with the Germans and devastated Great Moravia. Two years later (894) the Magyars came again in considerable numbers to the Danube, but this time they allied themselves with the Moravians and with them invaded Pannonia and the German march or borderland.

But Balkan Bulgaria was far nearer to the Magyars than Hungary, the distance between the two nations being not greater than half a day's journey. The Bulgars in 894 were at war with the Greeks. The Emperor Leo allied himself at that time with the Magyars. While the patrician

Nicephorus Phocas (895) led an army from the south against the Bulgars, the patrician Eustathius sailed with a fleet to bring the Magyar forces. But the Bulgarian Tsar Simeon hired the Patzinaks against the Magyars. The Magyar army was led by one of the sons of the supreme ruler Árpád. As soon as they had crossed the Danube they ravaged the land terribly and vanquished Simeon in two consecutive battles. It was not until the third conflict that Simeon gained a victory and destroyed the greater part of their army. Only a few Magyars saved themselves by flight, to find their land absolutely ruined and depopulated, as the Patzinaks had killed all the inhabitants who remained in Atelkuzu. This national catastrophe induced the Magyars to migrate under the leadership of Árpád into Hungary about the year 895–896.

Their territory near the Black Sea was henceforward completely occupied by the Patzinaks, who now wandered as nomads on the great plains between the Don and the estuary of the Danube. They numbered eight hordes living separately, each probably having its own centre like the Avars, who lived in their *hrings*.

The relations of the Patzinaks to their neighbours and to surrounding nations are interesting. The Greeks, endeavouring to restrain them from invading their colonies in the Crimea, sent them valuable gifts, and bought their assistance against their enemies, such as the Magyars, Danubian Bulgars, Russians, and Chazars. In times of peace the Patzinaks furthered the commercial intercourse between the Russians and Cherson (Korsun) by transporting their merchandise. In times of war they not only robbed the Russian merchants but penetrated with their predatory expeditions even as far as the dominions of Kiev. The princes of Kiev preferred therefore to be on friendly terms with the Patzinaks, and when they had a war with other Russian lands they often won them over to be their allies.

As yet our attention has been engaged with the history of the steppes of southern Russia. Now we must turn to the history of the Slav tribes, who laid the foundations of the later Russian Empire. Even to recent times there prevailed in Russian literature the opinion, defended by the German scholar A. Schlözer, that the Russian empire was founded as late as the middle of the ninth century by Northman (Swedish) immigrants, who united under their dominion numerous Slav and Finnish tribes, losing in course of time their own nationality, and finally becoming blended with the Slav elements. This is the theory of the Varangian origin of the Russian Empire, which was accepted even by the foremost Russian historians, Karamzin, Pogodin, and Solov'ëv. The Russian scholars were misled by the report of their own native annalist, that the first Russian princes were called to the throne from foreign lands and not earlier than the latter half of the ninth century. Just a few scholars tried to prove that the Russian Empire originated by its own innate vitality, without any external assistance. The historical truth lies between the two extreme theories. It was expounded by the late Professor V. Klyuchevski. While the name Rus no doubt belongs to the Swedes and the dynasty which ruled till Fëdor Ivanovich descended from Rurik[1], the legend that in 862 three Swedish brothers Rurik, Sineus, and Truvor were called by the Slav and Finnish tribes to rule over them, only recounts a single incident in the formation of a great state in what is now Russia.

By the authors of the sixth century a southern division of the eastern group of Slavonic tribes is sometimes mentioned, which they call the Antae[2]. These are the tribes which we now call Little Russians or Ukrainians. The Avars tried to subdue the Antae, who in 602 were allied with the Byzantines, but without success. From the seventh century onwards we have no information at all of this branch of the Eastern Slavs. This is explained by the circumstance that Byzantine historiography in these times had considerably declined. But nevertheless we can propound a probable supposition as to the history of the Antae from the latter half of the seventh to the ninth century. As early as the second quarter of the seventh century the dominion of the Avars was on the decline, and when in 679 the principal part of the Bulgars departed from the lands near the Black Sea to the Balkan peninsula, a favourable time opened for the Antae. They were free from the hostile nomadic hordes, who marred any peaceful existence, until the ninth century, when the Magyars appeared near the Black Sea. We must suppose that the Antae spread very far to the east during this period of peace. We learn from Procopius that Slav colonisation had already approached the Sea of Azov in the first half of the sixth century. The Antae were at this time settled to the north of the Utigurs. Afterwards, up to the tenth century, they probably occupied the whole northern borderland of the steppes of southern Russia as far eastward as the river Don, but were driven out of these countries by the later arrival of new nomadic hordes.

We have no reports of the names of the several tribes of the Eastern Slavs of that period. The Russian annals enumerate them only according to their position in the eleventh century. But at that time the Russian peoples had already a history of several centuries; they began at the end of the sixth or at the beginning of the seventh century to spread over Russian territory from the south-west, especially from the south-eastern slopes and spurs of the Carpathian mountains. At that time the Russian Slavs already had a nucleus of political organisation. Masʽūdī mentions a once powerful Slavonic race, the Walinana, who lived on the western banks of the Bug and were once oppressed by the Avars. The Walinana were probably the first East Slavonic tribe to become the centre of some state organisation; they founded a small federation of Slavs.

[1] *Cf.* Vol. III. chapter XIII, pp. 327–8.

[2] See *supra*, p. 186.

From this south-western corner of modern Russia the Slavonic colonisation spread in an eastern and north-eastern direction. In the wild and boundless forests of Russia the Slavonic immigrants hunted wild animals, kept bees, and soon tilled the land in clearings, founding there small solitary homesteads not only surrounded by the forest but also secured on every side by ditches and mounds. In course of time these settlements of single farms developed into hamlets or villages of several farms[1].

Besides the villages there soon arose along the Dnieper, the greatest river in western Russia, several commercial centres, the kernels of future commercial towns. The Greek colonies on the Black Sea had given the impulse to these commercial relations with the more distant Russian countries long before the Christian era. This connexion did not cease even when some Greek cities on the Black Sea were destroyed during the migrations of the nations. The Slavonic colonists thus found a market for various products of their forest industry. Furs, honey, and wax were the principal wares exported from Russia. The development of the Russian trade was also favoured by the circumstance that, just at the time when the Eastern Slavs began to occupy the wooded plains of Russia, the dominion of the Chazars was organised in the southern steppes between the Caspian and the Black Sea, a dominion which performed a rather important cultural mission in the territories of the later south-eastern Russia. Through the Chazar lands passed important commercial routes, partly by land, partly by the rivers connecting Mesopotamia and Central Asia with Eastern Europe, and *vice versa.* In the second half of the seventh or in the first half of the eighth century the Chazars further extended their empire over the lands of the central Dnieper, subduing and making tributary the Slavonic tribe settled around Kiev and subsequently called Polyans. The subjection of the Polyans to the Chazars was not a hard one, and indeed brought eminent advantages to the Polyans. The Slavs along the Dnieper were guarded against the inroads of the nomadic hordes of Asia and had therefore free commercial relations with the Black Sea, while new roads to the East through the dominion of the Chazars were opened to them.

The Arabian author Ibn Khurdādhbih, in the first half of the ninth century, gives us good information on the early and great development of the Russian trade with the Byzantine Empire and the Orient. Russian merchants not only sailed on the Black and Caspian Seas but brought their wares even to Baghdad, to which in the middle of the eighth century the centre of the Arabian Caliphate was transferred. The frequent finds of Arabian coins in the territories of Russia are an important proof of the development of this trade. Most of these coins date from the ninth and tenth centuries, when the trade with the Orient flourished best, but some of them belong to the beginning of the eighth century.

The Dnieper connected the Slavonic colonies of western Russia not

[1] *Cf.* Vol. II. Chapter XIV, pp. 422–3.

only with the south but also with the north. It was possible to journey from the Dnieper to the river Lovat', and to penetrate thence by Lake Ilmen', the river Volkhov, the Ladoga lake, and the river Neva to the Baltic Sea. Another route to this sea from the Dnieper was by the river Dvina. Along both branches of this "route from the Varangians to the Greeks" arose the oldest commercial towns of Russia: Kiev, Smolensk, Lyubech, Novgorod, Polotsk, and others. Besides these towns situated directly on the Varangian-Greek trade route, there were a great number of other towns which formed the connexion between this route and the affluents of the Dnieper as well as the connexion by water with the Volga, by which likewise passed the commercial route to the Orient through the Volga-Bulgars.

As long as the steppes of southern Russia between the Don and Dnieper were not occupied by the Magyars, no obstacles hindered the Russian commerce with the Byzantines. But as soon as the Magyars began to endanger the route, the several towns had to provide for the security of their commerce. From that time the towns of Russia began to fortify themselves and to organise a military force. The commercial centres developed into fortresses offering their protection against hostile attacks.

At this very time, the beginning of the ninth century, there began to appear on the Russian rivers greater numbers of enterprising Swedish companies, the so-called Varangians, travelling in armed bands to Byzantium for commercial purposes. It seems that only a part of the Varangians reached their goal, whereas the majority remained in the Russian commercial towns, especially in Novgorod and Kiev. Here the inhabitants employed them not only for their business but principally for their defence. The Varangians therefore entered the military service of the Russian towns, and also formed mercenary guards of the Russian commercial caravans.

The fortified Russian towns which could command some military force developed in course of time into centres of small states. The inhabitants of the neighbouring smaller towns and villages began to gravitate towards the greater towns, and in this wise arose the first Russian town-states, the *vólosti*. At first all of them were probably republics, but later some of them became principalities. These principalities probably developed in those towns where the Varangian companies were led by a powerful *konung*, who succeeded in seizing the government. But some volosti certainly had princes of Slavonic origin.

These city-states were not founded on a racial basis. The majority of them were composed of different tribes or parts of tribes; in others one whole tribe was joined by parts of other tribes. From these fusions towns arose amongst the populations settled near the principal streams, the Dnieper, the Volkhov, and the western Dvina. But the tribes which were too far from the main routes of commerce never combined to form townships, much less states; they formed part of the territories of other tribes.

The volost of Kiev very soon played the most important part of all these volosti. It grew to be the centre of the Russian trade. It was the meeting-place of all the merchant-ships of the Volkhov, the western Dvina, the upper Dnieper, and its tributaries.

The germs of the state of Kiev are old. Hrushevsky puts the organisation of a strong army and the power of the princes of Kiev as early as the beginning of the eighth century or even earlier, which seems to be an over-estimate if we consider that the Polyans were tributary to the Chazars. But we cannot doubt that the independent state of Kiev already existed in the beginning of the ninth century. At this time the Russians, evidently those of Kiev, made predatory invasions to the shores of the Black Sea, and not only to the northern coasts, reports of which have been preserved in the biography of St Stephen of Surozh (Sugdaea), but also to Asia Minor on the southern shores, as mentioned in the biography of St Gregory of Amastris. An accurately dated report of the existence of the Russian state is found in the Annals of St Bertin, which inform us that the Greek Emperor Theophilus in 839 included in an embassy to Louis the Pious members of a nation called "Rhos," who had been sent to Constantinople as representatives of their lord, called "chacanus," to conclude a treaty of friendship with the Emperor; fearing the barbarians who barred their way (evidently the Magyars), they wished to return by way of Germany. There can be no doubt that by the khagan of the nation called Rhos is meant the Prince of Kiev. The name Russia was given first to the land of Kiev, and later to all the lands (*vólosti*) united under the sceptre of the Prince of Kiev.

Another exact date in the history of Kiev is the year 860. According to a Byzantine chronicle, the Russians made a predatory invasion as far as Constantinople in the summer of that year. Taking advantage of the fact that the Emperor Michael had marched with his army to Asia Minor, they sailed with 200 ships against the imperial city. The Russian chronicle puts this event erroneously in the year 866, and says that it happened under Askol'd and Dir, Princes of Kiev.

If the Princes of Kiev were able in the ninth century to venture on such distant military expeditions beyond the sea, their state must have already existed for many years. Certainly the period of the small principality was at an end; the territory of the state was extended over a greater number of volosti, which were now under the sceptre of a ruler who later assumed the title of Great Prince.

In the foregoing account we have given a short outline, after Klyuchevski and Hrushevsky, of the history of the remotest times of Russia. Although the descriptions of the oldest phase of the political life of the Russian Slavs presented by both these historians are on the whole in harmony, there is nevertheless a great difference between them in their estimate of the influence of the Varangians on the beginnings of Russian state organisation. These Northmen until the middle of the ninth century undoubtedly lived in great numbers among the East Slavonic races, especially among the Slovêns, Kriviches, and Polyans, and they helped the princes to extend their territories and to domineer over the subjected inhabitants. Klyuchevski, in acknowledging the weight of the evidence brought forward, and especially the Swedish character of the names of the first Russian princes and the members of their retinue (*druzhina*), does not object to the assertion that among the founders of the small Russian states there were, besides the Slavs, also Varangians *i.e.* Swedish *konungs*, chiefs of Swedish companies, who came to Gardarik (Russia) in the course of their adventurous travels. Hrushevsky, on the contrary, directly denies the account given by the Russian Chronicle of the Varangian origin of the Russian state and the princely dynasties. But nevertheless even he acknowledges a certain influence of the Varangian companies in the building-up of the Russian state during the ninth and tenth centuries.

Although Hrushevsky defends his opinion very ingeniously, it seems to us that Klyuchevski is nearer the truth. We believe that the Varangians, not only the retinue but also the princes, settled at first in the volost of Novgorod, and only after having gained a firm hold there, went farther to the south and conquered the volost of Kiev. We believe also that by the name Russian or Rus just these Swedish companies with their chiefs were originally meant, although later the Polyans and the country of Kiev and at last all the inhabitants of the great Russian state were designated by this name. The oriental sources undoubtedly mean the Swedes when they use the word Rus, and the "Russian" names of the rapids of the Dnieper, reported by Constantine Porphyrogenitus, are evidently of Swedish origin.

The physical conditions forced the Varangians of Novgorod to look for a way to the Dnieper, to Kiev. Commercial interests also demanded it. The once small state spread southwards to the regions of the Dnieper. The Varangians were assisted in these efforts by the Slavs and Finns over whom they ruled. We see by the history of the state of Smolensk, formed by a part of the Kriviches, and that of the state of the Sêveryans, with its capital of Lyubech, that, besides the Varangian, Slavonic states also developed in Russia, for Oleg became ruler of both these states when he went from Novgorod to Kiev.

Oleg, who appears in history according to the Russian chronicles for the first time in 880, is a half-legendary person. Foreign authors do not even mention his name. Oleg's first care, after having gained possession of Kiev, was to build new fortified places, "castles," against the Patzinaks, and to bring the neighbouring Slavonic tribes under his dominion.

After having secured his power at home, Oleg undertook in 907 a great military expedition against Constantinople. The Greeks bound themselves to pay subsidies to several Russian towns, for "in these towns resided princes, who were under Oleg," as the Chronicle puts it. Moreover a commercial treaty was concluded with the Greeks, by which great advantages were conceded to Russian merchants in Constantinople.

Although this treaty between Oleg and the Greeks is the first Russo-Greek treaty the content of which is given us by the sources, it is evident that such treaties must have been concluded as early as the ninth century. One of them is mentioned in 839; the expedition of the Russians against Constantinople was afterwards undertaken in 860 because the Greeks had violated the agreement.

In 911, after many verbal negotiations, additional clauses were introduced bearing on civil and penal law and the rules of procedure in the courts. The text of this treaty is preserved in the Russian Chronicle, and it has a special interest, for it contains the names of Oleg's envoys, which are all of them Scandinavian.

The first historical Russian prince who appears in contemporary foreign sources is Igor. According to the Russian Chronicle, he began to reign in 913, but Hrushevsky thinks that he ascended the throne much later. Ilovayski puts Igor, not Rurik, at the head of the Russian dynasty.

Igor, too, undertook a military expedition against Constantinople in the summer of 941. The reason probably was that the Greeks had ceased to pay to the Russians the subsidies which they had promised to Oleg. We are informed of Igor's expedition not only by the Russian Chronicle but also by foreign sources. The Russians again chose a time when the Greek fleet was employed against the Saracens. Igor landed first on the shores of Bithynia, and cruelly ravaged the land as far as the Thracian Bosphorus. Driven from Constantinople by Greek fire, he returned again to Bithynia. Meanwhile the Greek army began to rally. Frosts, want of food, and the losses sustained from the Greek fire, compelled Igor to return to Russia. He is said to have escaped with only ten ships to the Cimmerian Bosphorus.

The war lasted for three years more, and was ended in 945 by the conclusion of another treaty between Russia and Byzantium, in which not only the former treaties with Oleg were confirmed with some modifications and additions, but both parties also undertook not to attack the lands of the other party, and to assist each other. We learn from this treaty that the great principality of Kiev was divided, not only among the members of the dynasty but also among the foremost chiefs of the companies, and that even women had their apportioned territories. The whole state was administered from the standpoint of civil law in a business-like manner. Oleg had already in his treaty of 907 agreed with the Greeks what subsidies were to be paid to the several Russian towns, or rather to his deputies residing there (in Russian *posádniki*). Whereas in Western Europe officials were remunerated by fiefs, in Russia they had territories upon which they imposed taxes on their own behalf, and to collect these was their principal care. The taxes were paid in money, probably Arabian, as well as in kind, especially in furs. Either the subject tribes brought their dues to Kiev or the princes rode to the territories to receive them.

Constantine Porphyrogenitus describes the second manner of levying the taxes. In the early days of November the Russian princes and all their retinues started from Kiev to the territory of the Derevlyans, Dregoviches, Kriviches, and other subject tribes, and lived there all the winter, returning by the Dnieper to Kiev in April, when the ice had floated down to the sea. Meantime the Slavs built during the winter boats, hollowed from one piece of timber, and in spring floated them down-stream to Kiev, where they sold them to the retinue of the prince on their return from winter quarters in the lands of the subject tribes. The courtiers shipped their wares, evidently furs and other taxes in kind gathered from the tribes, and in June they proceeded by the Dnieper to the castle or fortress of Vitichev, and thence to Constantinople.

Professor Klyuchevski very acutely recognised that the imposts which the Prince of Kiev levied as a ruler were at the same time the articles of his trade. "When he became a ruler as a *konung*, he as a Varangian (*Varyag*) did not cease to be an armed merchant. He shared the taxes with his retinue, which served him as the organ of administration and was the ruling class. This class governed in winter, visiting the country and levying taxes, and in summer trafficked in what was gathered during the winter."

The oriental authors give us reports of predatory expeditions of the Russians to the shores of the Caspian Sea. From the first, undertaken in 880, all these raids ended in disaster. A particularly audacious one took place in 944. The Russians arrived with their ships by the Caspian Sea at the estuary of the river Cyrus, and sailing upstream invaded the land called by the Arabs Arran (the ancient Albania), which belonged to the Caliphate. Their first success was the conquest of Berdaa, the capital of Arran, situated on the river Terter, a southern tributary of the Cyrus. From Berdaa they ravaged the surrounding country. The governor of Azarbā'ījān levied a great army which beat the Russians after losing a first battle, but this defeat was not decisive enough to induce them to leave the country. Dysentery, however, spreading rapidly among the Russian army, delivered the Albanians from their enemies. After depredations which lasted six months the Russians left the land, returning home with rich spoil.

It is strange that the Russian chronicles are silent about these invasions of the shores of the Caspian Sea, since there is no reason to doubt their reality. They are an evidence that the state of Kiev was already strong enough in Oleg's time—for the earliest expeditions undertaken in the tenth century were certainly his—to venture on war not only against Constantinople but also against the East. The easier therefore was it for Igor to undertake such a campaign.

After Igor's death his widow Olga ascended the throne, the first Christian princess in Russia. Christianity had begun to spread in the principality of Kiev soon after the first expedition of the Russians against Constantinople in 860. It is probable that the Prince of Kiev himself at this time embraced the Christian faith. During Oleg's reign Christianity suffered a decline, although it did not disappear, as can be inferred from the register of the metropolitan churches subordinated to the Patriarch of Constantinople published by the Emperor Leo VI (886–911). In the treaty of Igor with the Greeks in 945 heathen and Christian Russians are mentioned, and the Russian Chronicle calls the church of St Elias (Ilya) in Kiev a cathedral, which implies that there were other churches in the city. But it seems nevertheless that the Christian faith did not take strong root among the Russians, and there was hardly an improvement when the Princess Olga embraced Christianity, which happened probably in 954, three years before her voyage to Constantinople. The purpose of this visit is not known. Former writers thought Olga went there to be baptized, but it seems to be nearer the truth that her journey had only diplomatic aims.

A true type of the adventurous viking was Prince Svyatoslav, son of Igor and Olga, the first prince of the Varangian dynasty to bear a Slavonic name. The Chronicle describes him as a gallant, daring man, undertaking long expeditions to distant lands and neglecting the interests of his own country. His mind was filled with the plan of transferring the centre of his state to the Balkan peninsula. He spent the greater part of his time in foreign lands. He was the first of the Russian princes who forced the Vyatiches to pay him tribute, whereas they had formerly been tributary to the Chazars. But before that he tried to break the power of the Chazars, which from the beginning of the ninth century had been continually declining. They were pressed in the south by the Arabs and the Transcaucasian tribes, in the north by the Patzinaks, and in the west by the Russians. Some tribes had already thrown off their yoke.

Igor himself had cast an eager gaze on the Crimean peninsula and on the shores of the Sea of Azov, where he would have liked to found a Russian dominion. His political aims were followed by his successors. The Chazars hindered these efforts. Svyatoslav therefore in 965 undertook an expedition against them, and conquered their town Sarkel (Bêlavêzha, White Town). After the defeat of the Chazars, Svyatoslav attacked the Ossetes (remnants of the Alans) and the Kasogs (Cherkesses) and subdued them. By this expedition against the Chazars and the tribes belonging to their dominion, Svyatoslav laid the foundations of Tmutorakanian Russia, which derived its name from its capital Tmutorakan, the ancient Tamatarcha.

In 967 Svyatoslav undertook an expedition against the Greeks. The Byzantine Emperor Nicephorus, indignant that the Bulgarian Tsar Peter had not hindered the Magyars from invading the Balkan peninsula, waged war against the Bulgars and sent the patrician Calocyrus to Prince Svyatoslav for assistance. Calocyrus turned traitor. He concluded on his own account with Svyatoslav a treaty for mutual support. The Russian prince was to get Bulgaria, and Calocyrus the imperial throne. Svyatoslav marched into Bulgaria, conquered it, and remained in Pereyaslavets (Prêslav), the residence of the Tsar. During his absence in 968 the Patzinaks attacked the land of Kiev, and only a ruse induced them to leave the beleagured city. Being informed of this menace by the inhabitants of Kiev, Svyatoslav returned and expelled the Patzinaks, but he remained at home only to the end of 970, his mother Olga having died meanwhile in 969. Then he again went to Bulgaria, leaving his sons as governors, Yaropolk in Kiev and Oleg among the Derevlyans. When the inhabitants of Novgorod also demanded a prince of their own, he gave them his natural son Vladímir. But the government was in the hands of the boyars, as all the sons were minors.

In his war with the Greeks Svyatoslav was unfortunate, although he hired Magyar and Patzinak troops. In a short time he was forced to make peace with Byzantium (971) and to renew the former treaties, to which a new clause was added: the Russian prince bound himself not to encroach on the Greek possessions in the Crimea (opposite the territory of Cherson) or Bulgaria.

On his return home to Russia Svyatoslav perished (972) in a sudden attack by Kurya, Prince of the Patzinaks.

The sons of Svyatoslav quarrelled. When Oleg was killed by Yaropolk, Vladímir, fearing a similar fate, fled to the Swedes, but returned after three years (980), and getting rid of Yaropolk by the treason of one of his retinue ascended the throne of Svyatoslav.

Vladímir's retinue composed of heathen Varangians had the principal share in the victories of their lord. Vladímir therefore manifested his heathenism with the greatest zeal and erected idols on the hills of Kiev. He himself also lived the life of a heathen; besides five legal wives he had many concubines—the annals report 800. He very adroitly got rid of the turbulent Varangians who had supported him; the more prominent he won over to his party, the others were dismissed to Constantinople.

His principal aim was to extend and to consolidate the Russian empire, which since Svyatoslav's time threatened to be dismembered into minute principalities. In 981 he undertook an expedition against the Vyatiches, conquered them, and forced them to pay tribute. They again revolted in 982 but were subdued once more. In 984 Vladímir took the field against the Radimiches, subdued them, and forced them to pay tribute. The next year he marched against and defeated the Bulgars, and then concluded a treaty of peace with them. In the last decade of the tenth century he once more waged a victorious war against the Bulgars. In 1006 he concluded with them a commercial treaty, by which the merchants of either state were allowed to carry on their trade in the dominions of the other if they were provided with an official seal.

The statement of the Chronicle that Vladímir in 981 took the Polish castles of Red Russia (the present eastern Galicia) is doubtful, but it is certain that he fought a war with the Polish King Boleslav the Mighty (982), which was ended by a treaty, as Boleslav was engaged in a war with Bohemia. The peace was moreover secured by the marriage of Svyatopolk, son of Vladímir and Prince of Turov, with a daughter of Boleslav.

The incessant raids of the Patzinaks were very troublesome to Vladímir. We read now and again in the annals that the Patzinaks invaded the Russian country, so that there was constant war with them. These unceasing inroads of the nomads led Vladímir to build strong fortresses on the east and south of his territory, and to garrison them with the best men of the Slavs (of Novgorod), the Kriviches, Chudes, and Vyatiches. The Russian princes as a rule subdued the southern tribes by means of the northern peoples; with their assistance they defended themselves also against the barbarians of the steppes.

Under Vladímir friendly relations with Byzantium were again inaugurated. The first step was made by the Greek Emperor Basil II, who (in 988) asked Vladímir to assist him against the anti-Emperor Bardas Phocas. Vladímir promised his help on condition that the Emperor would give him his sister in marriage. Basil accepted this condition if Vladímir consented to be baptised. The Russian prince agreed and sent his army in the spring or summer of 988 to Basil. This army of 6000 infantry remained in Greece even after Phocas had been killed, and took part in the Byzantine wars in Asia in 999–1000. From that time to the last quarter of the eleventh century the Varangians formed the bodyguard of the Byzantine Emperors. Later on they were replaced by soldiers from Western Europe, principally Englishmen.

When the Emperor Basil had been delivered from peril, he hesitated over the fulfilment of his promise to give his sister Anne to Vladímir to wife. The Russian prince, offended by this delay, attacked the Greek possessions in the Crimea. He succeeded (989) in taking Cherson after a long siege. But meanwhile the Greek Emperor was again in difficulties in his own lands, especially in consequence of a revolt in Bulgaria, so that he was obliged to regain Vladímir's good will and to send him his sister Anne, who received Cherson for her dower.

At that time Vladímir was already a Christian, having been baptised about the beginning of 988. The long intercourse of Russia with Constantinople had prepared a favourable ground for the Christian faith. Various missionaries came to the prince at short intervals to explain the advantages of their religion. Finally, he declared for Christianity, and, having received baptism, he had his twelve sons christened also, and encouraged the spread of Christianity among the boyars and the people. Some districts of the Russian empire nevertheless still remained heathen for a long time. There were pagans among the Vyatiches and Kriviches in the beginning of the twelfth century, and in Murom even in the thirteenth century.

During Vladímir's reign an attempt was also made to win the Russians over to Rome. With the daughter of Boleslav the Mighty, Reinbern, Bishop of Kolberg, arrived at the court of Vladímir's son Svyatopolk at Turov, and tried to sever the young Russian Church from the Eastern Church. Vladímir, as soon as he was informed of the plans of Reinbern, imprisoned Svyatopolk, his wife, and the bishop. Thereupon a war broke out with Boleslav, who hastened to make peace with the Germans (1013), and having hired troops from them and the Patzinaks set out against Vladímir. He only devastated the land without gaining further results. Vladímir died in 1015.

The importance of Vladímir in Russian history is enormous. He subdued the tribes which had gained their independence under his predecessors; he defended the empire against the barbarians of the steppes; he accepted Christianity and introduced Christian reforms. He successfully closed the tenth century, the heroic period of Russian history; his reign was famous for the maritime expeditions against the Greeks, the inroads beyond the Danube, the occupation of Bulgaria, and the expeditions against the Chazars and Bulgars.

We have yet to say something of the Magyars in their new home in Hungary.

About the year 895 or 896 the Magyars crossed the northern Carpathian Mountains, and endeavoured in the first place to occupy the lands near the upper course of the river Theiss. The progressive occupation of the territories of later Hungary was made easy to the Magyars by the circumstance that the new political formations, which had begun to arise here, were feeble and of no long duration. The north-western part of later Hungary, inhabited at that time by Slovaks, was a constituent part of the Great Moravian realm, which extended as far as the river Theiss and probably some distance to the south between this river and the Danube. After the death of Svatopluk (894), the Magyars had nothing to fear from the Great Moravian state, which was now governed by his discordant sons. During their quarrels it was an easy matter for the Magyars to occupy the northern part of the territory between the Theiss and the Danube. This is the only possible explanation of their being able to penetrate without opposition into Pannonia, and to undertake their predatory invasions into Italy. In Lower Pannonia there arose by the first half of the ninth century the Slavonic principality of Pribina (840) under the suzerainty of the Franks, with his capital of Blatno (*Urbs paludum*, Mosaburch) near where the river Zala flows into the lake of Blatno (Balaton). The limits of Pribina's principality can only be given approximately. To the north-west it extended to the river Raab, to the south-west to Pettau, to the south as far as the Drave, and to the north and east about to the Danube. With the Slavs there also lived German colonists from Bavaria in scattered settlements in this principality. The country between the Danube and the Raab was settled by Germans, who there formed the majority of the population. In ecclesiastical affairs Pannonia was divided after 829 between the bishoprics of Salzburg and Passau. During the reign of Kocel (861–874), Pribina's successor, the Moravo-Pannonian Slavonic archbishopric was founded about 870 and St Methodius installed in the see. After Kocel's death Lower Pannonia was again governed by German officials. Only after the arrival of the Magyars in Hungary, King Arnulf in 896 invested the Croatian prince Braslav, reigning between the rivers Drave and Save, with the south-western part of Pannonia as a fief.

The most ancient Hungarian chronicler, the so-called *Anonymus regis Belae notarius*, gives us some, not altogether reliable, accounts of the political divisions in the other parts of Hungary and in Transylvania. If we supplement the account of the *Anonymus* with those of the Frankish authors, we can conclude that in the eastern half of Hungary beyond the river Theiss, and perhaps in Transylvania, there were at the end of the ninth century some feeble principalities probably tributary to the Bulgars, and that these were neither old enough nor sufficiently developed to stop the progress of the warlike Magyar tribes. It is certain that in the lands beyond the Theiss as well as in the so-called Black Hungary (Transylvania) there were numerous Slavonic inhabitants, and even now we can find traces of them in the place-names.

We have hardly any other accounts of the Magyars, during the first fifty years after the occupation of Hungary, than that they raided the neighbouring countries. As early as 898 a scouting party of Magyars came into north-eastern Italy to the river Brenta, and the following year the Magyars made a new invasion, and overflowed the plain of Lombardy, plundering and burning the land. For a whole year, until the spring of 900, they devastated Italy, and King Berengar only induced them to leave the country by presents, even giving hostages. On their return they devastated the greater part of Pannonia belonging to the German kingdom, and immediately afterwards, in the middle of the year 900, the whole Magyar nation crossed the Danube and occupied Lower Pannonia as far as the river Raab. That it was possible to do so without serious opposition from the Germans may be explained by the foolish policy of Bavaria. Liutpold of Bavaria, founder of the dynasty of Wittelsbach, preferred to be at enmity with the Great Moravian state rather than to oppose the Magyars. But no sooner had the Magyars conquered Pannonia, than they appeared in Bavaria beyond the Inn. The Bavarians only succeeded in destroying a part of the Magyars; the others escaped with a rich booty. The Bavarians did not make peace with Moravia until 901, when it had become too late.

In 906 the Magyars overthrew the Great Moravian state. The Bavarians in 907 invaded the Magyar territory, but were defeated, and after that Upper Pannonia was also conquered by the Magyars. Under Árpád's successors the Magyars constantly made predatory incursions, and penetrated still farther to the west. Nobody opposed their progress, because the former provinces of the Frankish Empire were in decline. The weapons of the Germans were clumsy: heavy armour, a heavy helmet, a great shield, and a long sword. The Magyars on the contrary appeared suddenly on their swift horses and poured showers of arrows upon their enemies, causing great disorder among them and turning them to flight. The foe seldom succeeded in surprising the Magyars before they had arrayed themselves for battle, because their scouts were exceedingly wary and vigilant. A frequent military ruse of the Magyars was to feign a flight in order to entice the enemy into pursuit. Suddenly they would turn and frighten the pursuers so thoroughly by a flood of arrows that it was an easy matter for their reserves to attack and destroy the baffled foe. The Magyars lacked skill only in taking castles and fortresses; in Germany and Italy therefore the inhabitants began quickly to fortify their towns.

The history of these western invasions, ending with the decisive defeat (955) on the Lechfeld, has been told in the preceding volume of this work. The turn of the Balkan peninsula came comparatively late. It was after their defeat in Saxony in 933 that the Magyars turned their attention in this direction. In the spring of 934 they invaded Thrace in company with Patzinaks with a force which penetrated to Constantinople. Mas'ūdī gives us a somewhat confused report of this incursion, declaring that four tribes were allied against the Greeks, although it seems that only the Magyars with the Patzinaks were the invaders. Marquart thinks that by the town Walandar, conquered at this time by the barbarian armies, Develtus near the modern Burgas is meant. It seems that since 934 the Magyars regularly demanded tribute from the Greeks, at first every nine and later on every five years. In 943 they came again, and the Emperor Romanus Lecapenus appointed the patrician Theophanes, as he had done in 934, to negotiate with them. Theophanes succeeded in concluding a truce for five years, for which both parties gave hostages. It is probable that about this time the Byzantines tried, but in vain, to gain the Magyars for allies against the Patzinaks. After that the Magyars invaded the Balkan peninsula several times, especially in 959 and 962. In 967 a band of Magyars joined the Russian prince Svyatoslav when he attacked Bulgaria.

After the Lechfeld, however, the aggressiveness of the Magyars considerably declined. Western Europe now remained safe from their predatory inroads, and at last even the expeditions against the Balkan peninsula ceased. During the three-quarters of a century in which the Magyars had occupied their new homes in Hungary, political and other conditions had greatly changed. In the first place the neighbours of the Magyars had grown much stronger. This is true principally of the Germanic Empire, which, under the dynasty of Saxon kings, was far more powerful than under the later Carolingians. In the south the Greek Empire stretched as far as the Danube, and completely checked any new Magyar expeditions to the Balkan peninsula. In course of time even the mode of life of the leading Magyars had somewhat changed. Not only Prince Géza but also several chieftains ceased to live in tents, preferring castles for their abodes. This change was caused by the Christian religion, which in the meanwhile had spread in the neighbouring countries and extended its influence also among the inhabitants of Hungary, especially in ancient Pannonia, where a great portion of the Germans and Slavs were Christians. Through these Christian inhabitants the Magyars became acquainted with a peaceful manner of life, with agriculture and trade. During the three-quarters of a century even the ethnic character of the inhabitants underwent a great modification. The Magyars, who were not very numerous even at the time of their occupation of Hungary, did not increase considerably because of their frequent predatory expeditions into foreign lands. Only the first generation was able to gain victories abroad, in fact while the military tactics of the Magyars were unknown. The second generation met with repeated calamities. Many Magyars perished in these expeditions; only a small band returned from the battle of the Lechfeld. The decrease of the Magyar element was unavoidably followed by a great intermixture of the remaining population, which also caused a change in the character of the nation.

In short, since the accession of Géza as Prince of the Magyars, about 970, there begins a radical change in the history of the Magyars. Géza was the first ruler who was judicious enough to see that his people could hold its own among other nations if it would live with them in peace and if it would accept Christianity. Immediately after his accession to the throne he sent messengers to the Emperor Otto I in 973 to initiate friendly relations with Germany. That he resolved on this course of action must be attributed to the influence of his wife Adelaide, a princess of Polish blood and a fervent Christian. By her recommendation St Vojtěch (Adalbert), Bishop of Prague and a distant relative of hers, was called to Hungary. About 985 he converted to the Christian faith not only Géza but also his ten-year-old son Vajk, to whom the name Stephen was given in baptism. Ten years later (995) Benedictine monks from

Bohemia came to Hungary and settled, as it seems, in the monastery of Zobor upon the Nyitra. This Christianisation was moreover very much furthered by Géza having chosen Gisela, a princess of the German imperial dynasty, as a bride for his son Stephen (996). The work begun by Géza was brought to a good end by Stephen, who was canonised for his apostolic zeal. Stephen, immediately after his accession to the throne (997), ordered his subjects to accept Christianity. To set a good example he liberated his slaves. He visited his lands and everywhere preached the new religion. He called in foreign priests, especially Slavs, to assist him. Etymological researches have proved that the ecclesiastical terminology of the Magyars is to a considerable degree of Slavonic origin. This alone would lead to the indubitable conclusion that the first missionaries of the Gospel among the Magyars were to a great extent Slavs belonging to the Roman obedience. And the accounts of the conversion witness to the same fact.

Bohemian priests took a prominent share in the spreading of the Christian faith in Hungary. In the first place Radla, the former companion of St Vojtěch, must be named, who worked in the Hungarian realm from 995 to about 1008; then Anastasius, formerly Abbot at Břevnov near Prague in Bohemia, later of St Martin's in Hungary, and finally Archbishop of Gran (Esztergom) from 1001–1028. Also Astrik, Abbot of Pécsvárad and later Archbishop of Kalocsa, who had been at first one of the priests of St Vojtěch and then an abbot in Poland, excelled among the Slav preachers of the faith in Hungary. Further, St Gerard, tutor of Stephen's son Emeric, and later Bishop of Csanád, was a signal propagator of Christianity in Hungary. St Stephen himself founded several bishoprics and monasteries: besides the archbishoprics of Esztergom and Kalocsa, he instituted the bishoprics of Veszprém, Pécs (Fünfkirchen), Csanád, Vácz (Waitzen), Raab (Györ), Eger (Erlau), and Nagy-Várad (Grosswardein) and Gyulafehérvár (Karlsburg) in Transylvania.

It was the greatest political success of St Stephen that he secured for his lands a complete independence in their ecclesiastical and secular relations. He sent an embassy to Pope Sylvester II to obtain for the Hungarian ruler a royal crown and papal sanction for the ecclesiastical organisation. The Pope complied with both requests, and sent to St Stephen not only the royal crown but also an apostolic cross. Stephen had himself solemnly crowned as king in 1001.

St Stephen only succeeded with difficulty in controlling the refractory chieftains of the tribes. One of them, for instance, Kopány, chief of Somogy (Shümeg) and cousin to St Stephen, headed a revolt in favour of heathenism, but was defeated. Prokuy also, a maternal relative of St Stephen, prince in the territories on both sides of the Theiss, belonged to the turbulent element which hated Christianity. St Stephen subdued him too, and removed him from his government. In Hungary itself, in the south-eastern corner of the land bordered by the rivers Maros, Theiss, and Danube, and by Transylvania, there lay the principality of Aytony (Akhtum). This small principality was also overthrown by St Stephen about 1025.

St Stephen also organised the administration of the land after foreign models, partly German and partly Slav. He arranged his court after the German fashion, and divided his lands into counties (*comitatus*), appointing as their governors officials called in Latin *comites*, in Magyar *ispanok* (from the Slavonic *župan*). He likewise followed foreign and especially German examples in legislative matters, endeavouring to remodel his state entirely in a European fashion, and to make it into an orderly land. He died in 1038. His fame as the second founder and moulder of the Magyar kingdom is immortal. By bringing his savage barbaric nation into the community of Christendom, he saved the Magyars from a ruin which otherwise they could not have escaped.

(B)

CONVERSION OF THE SLAVS.

In the numerous records of missionary activity in the Christian Church of Eastern and Western Europe there is one chapter which, owing to special circumstances, has attained the greatest importance in the history of the world. It deals with an incident which happened more than a thousand years ago, the consequences of which have endured to this day, and it reveals the characteristic features of Christianity in the East and South-East of Europe. It arose in connexion with two brothers, Cyril and Methodius, who lived in the ninth century at Salonica, and are still venerated by more than a hundred million Slavs as apostles to their race and as creators of the language of their ritual, the language which was for many centuries the medium of literary activity, of the public life of the community, as well as of Church functions.

According to the point of view of individual scholars this historical event has been very differently criticised and appreciated. Some modern writers condemn it because it was chiefly the predominance of the language of the Slav Church, based on a Byzantine model, that separated Eastern Europe from the civilisation of Western Europe, and was principally to blame for the unequal progress in the development of Eastern civilisation in comparison with Western. Other writers cannot praise it sufficiently because, as it led to the separation of the Slavonic East and South-East of Europe from the Latin West, they recognise it as one of the chief causes of the preservation of national characteristics, even indeed of political independence.

Much has been written in modern times concerning Cyril and Methodius. There exists a rich literature concerning them in all Slavonic languages, in German, French, Italian, and recently also in English.

Our view of the career of the Brothers, especially of their activity among the Slav peoples, depends on the degree of credence to be attached to the sources. The chief sources are the various Slav, Latin, and Greek legends, the critical examination of which offers many difficulties. So far, at least, no results have obtained general acceptance. Most scholars, however, are of opinion that the two Slav (the so-called Pannonian) Legends, *Vita Cyrilli* and *Vita Methodii*, are of great historical importance and credible in a high degree. Where they agree with the ancient but shorter Latin legend, the so-called *Translatio S. Clementis*, no doubt is cast on the double tradition. This is the view we shall follow in this chapter. Of utmost importance, of course, are the statements of the Popes and of Anastasius, the librarian of the Vatican, but unfortunately they only refer to single incidents in the life and work of Cyril and Methodius.

All sources agree in giving Salonica as the birthplace of the two brothers, who were of distinguished lineage. The name of their father was Leo. He held the appointment of Drungarius. We only meet with their mother's name, Mary, in later sources. According to the Pannonian Legend, Constantine is said to have been the youngest of seven children. As he was forty-two years old when he died (869), we must place his birth in the year 827. Of Methodius we only know that he was the elder, but no mention is made of his age in the Pannonian *Vita Methodii* when the year of his death (885) is referred to. Bearing in mind the subsequent events of his life and his relations to his younger brother, we might be inclined to allow a difference of ten years between the two brothers, which would therefore make 817 the year when Methodius was born. With regard to the younger brother, all information points to the belief that he only assumed the name of Cyril shortly before his death at Rome. It is, however, a moot point whether Methodius did not also bear a different name at first, which he only changed to that by which he is known to us, when he retired into the monastery on Mt Olympus in Bithynia.

The Latin *Translatio*, which treats only of Constantine, relates but little concerning his youth. He is said to have exhibited marked talent and as a boy to have been taken by his parents to Constantinople, where he excelled in piety and wisdom and became a priest. We learn a great deal more concerning the two brothers from the Pannonian Legends which, with the exception of a few decorative details, appear quite credible, and to be based in every particular upon an intimate knowledge of the circumstances[1].

The *Vita Methodii* tells us that he at first devoted himself to a secular career. Of stalwart build, benefiting by the universal admiration of his fellow-citizens for his parents, he is said to have gained great esteem among the lawyers of the town of his birth, probably as a clever jurist. In consequence of his talent in this practical direction, he attracted the attention of the Emperor Michael III and of Theodora, who entrusted him with the administration of a Slavonic "principality." The Slavonic word *knęzĭ* (prince) corresponds with the Greek ἄρχων, and Methodius was thus appointed an archon, but it is unknown where his Slavonic government (ἀρχοντία) was situated, whether in Macedonia or Thessaly. It cannot have been an important one. According to the Legend, he administered this office for "many years"; if he received it when he was twenty-eight years of age and occupied it ten years, we might assume that he was archon between 845 and 855, which is consistent with what comes later. The reason given for his resolve to abandon the secular career was that he experienced numerous difficulties. Tired of office, he retired into a monastery on Mt Olympus in Bithynia, as is now generally accepted, and became a monk[2].

Quite different, however, according to the Pannonian Legend devoted to the life of Constantine, was the youth of the younger brother. In this legend his preference for the study of philosophy was clothed in the form of a poetical account of a dream he had in his seventh year, according to which the strategus of his native town brought before him the most beautiful maidens of Salonica, from whom he was to select a bride, and he gave the preference to "Sophia," *i.e.* philosophy; that is why he was called ὁ φιλόσοφος—a title he probably received subsequently in Constantinople as professor of philosophy. Legend states that he was the best scholar in the school and conspicuous by his extraordinary memory. Another poetic story marks his love of solitude. Once when out hawking, the wind carried the falcon away from him. This he interpreted as an intimation from Heaven to abandon all worldly pleasures and devote himself entirely to study. It sounds quite credible that in his earliest youth he preferred to read the works of Gregory Nazianzen, in which, however, he lacked the instruction of a master. If the Legend is correct, his father died when Constantine was fourteen; that would be in 841–842. If this bereavement did not actually cause the youth to go to Constantinople to pursue higher studies, it at least hastened his decision. The

[1] It is difficult to sustain the opinion that Clement the Slav is the author of these two legends. See my notes in the *Archiv für slav. Philologie,* Vol. XXVII. 1905, pp. 384–395.

[2] See Malyszevski, pp. 441–479, concerning Olympus in Asia Minor and the sojourn there of the two brothers. This happened, as before stated, in the year 855. If we knew that Theoctistus the Logothete was the patron of Methodius also, we could connect his retirement from office with the death of Theoctistus in 856.

legendary narrative connects it with his call to the capital by Theoctistus the Logothete. Here he was to be associated with the young Emperor Michael III; but the idea of an actual joint education is scarcely reasonable in view of the difference in their ages of about twelve years. Among the best masters in Constantinople are enumerated Leo and Photius, and the chief subjects were grammar, rhetoric, dialectic, arithmetic, geometry, astronomy, philosophy, and music. Homer is also said to have been read. Constantine's modesty was coupled with quickness of perception and intense diligence. By means of these rare qualities he is said to have gained the confidence of the Logothete to such an extent that he introduced him into the imperial palace. The Logothete, in fact, wanted him to marry his god-daughter and held out to him the prospect of a brilliant career, that of strategus. But the pure asceticism of Constantine's nature found its worthy object in a spiritual vocation. He was ordained priest. In order, however, to chain him to Constantinople, he was appointed librarian of St Sophia, under the Patriarch, possibly Ignatius; but this post, which brought him into intimate relations with the Patriarch, was too public for him. According to the Legend, he fled to a neighbouring monastery, where he is said to have remained concealed for six months. When he was discovered he was made professor of philosophy. Possibly all this happened in the year 850, or even later, as Constantine was then only twenty-three. This is also supposed to be the date of the discussion which Constantine is said to have had with John, who was deprived of his patriarchal dignity on account of his iconoclastic views. This John, the Grammaticus, was deposed in 843, but he was certainly alive in 846. In the Legend he is represented, during his dispute with Constantine, as an old man opposed to a young one. It is doubtful whether the disputation took place at the request of the Emperor and many patricians in so solemn a form as recounted in the Legend, since the latter always emphasises Constantine's intellectual superiority in argument. As a matter of fact, shortly afterwards, in the twenty-fourth year of his life, that is in 851–852, according to the Legend, a new burden was imposed upon this zealous fighter for the Orthodox faith.

This time it was a mission to the Saracens. The *Translatio S. Clementis* knows nothing of it. However, although the Pannonian Legend does not say from whom the invitation emanated and what was the destination of the journey, whether to Melitene or to Baghdad, still it gives some very precise particulars which seem to have an historical basis. It alleges that Constantine was invited by the Emperor to defend the doctrine of the Trinity in a disputation with the Saracens, and was accompanied on the journey by two men, Asicritus and George. No other evidence of this legendary disputation is known, but in Arabic sources (Ṭabarī) mention is made of an embassy of the Byzantines to the Saracens for the purpose of an armistice and exchange of prisoners, at the head of which was a certain George, who was accompanied by many patricians and servants, numbering nearly fifty persons. This embassy, it is true, only took place in 855, but it is nevertheless possible that the story in the Legend refers to this fact; only the Legend made Constantine, accompanied by George, the principal figure and, in the interest of the disputation, entirely omitted all the other particulars[1].

On his return to Constantinople, Constantine, following the bent of his ascetic inclinations, retired to some solitary spot and then into the monastery on Olympus, where his brother had already taken up his abode as a monk. Thus the brothers after long separation met under one and the same roof in 856-858, both devoted to their pious inclinations. It is noticeable that the Legend refers in both cases to their preference for religious books and intellectual occupation. Concerning Constantine, who was an old friend of Photius, an episode is related by Anastasius, the Roman librarian, which happened about this time; indeed, some believe that Photius was really Asicritus who, together with George, according to the Legend, accompanied Constantine on his journey to the Saracens. In this case, the episode related by Anastasius might have happened about this date. Constantine criticised some remarks of Photius, chiefly directed against the Patriarch Ignatius.

It is impossible to say how long Constantine lived in the monastery with his brother. He now proposed to undertake a new missionary journey, this time in the company of Methodius. Not only the Pannonian Legend and the *Translatio S. Clementis*, but also Anastasius the librarian, confirm the statement that the new journey was to be into the land of the Chazars. They also agree that an embassy had come from that country to Constantinople with a specific request for help in their predicament. It appears that they believed in God but were otherwise pagans, and were being urged on the one hand by the Jews on the other by the Saracens to accept their faith. They therefore prayed for an able missionary to explain the Christian faith to them. The Pannonian Legend, which again lays stress on Constantine's dialectical powers, adds at the same time the promise that, if the Christian missionary proved victorious over the Jews and Muslims, all the Chazars would become Christians. The *Translatio* only states the final result of the mission, that Constantine was in fact successful, and that he gained over the Chazars to the Christian faith. The *Translatio* does not go into details, while in the Pannonian Legend the principal subject is the very detailed report of the disputation. It is said that Constantine himself wrote a treatise in Greek on the whole of the polemical interview, and his brother is said to have divided it into eight parts (λόγοι) and to have translated it into Slavonic. We know

[1] This is the version of the *Archiv für slav. Philologie,* xxv. 549, in which, however, if we believe it all, there is much of the fantastical connected with the journey. For reference to the Greek embassy, see Vasil'ev, *Vizantiya i Araby,* St Petersburg, 1900, pp. 179-180.

neither the Greek original nor the Slavonic version, and yet it is difficult to regard it all as an invention. Perhaps the full text as preserved to us in the Legend is actually an extract from the Slavonic version.

Whilst the disputation with the Jews and the Muslims takes up very considerable space in the Pannonian Legend, the discovery of the relics of St Clement is only mentioned with a reference to the story of their discovery as narrated by Constantine. This reference lends additional credibility to the Legend, as we know now from the letter of Anastasius to Gauderic that Constantine himself really did write a *brevis historia* of the incident in Greek. A full account of the discovery of the relics is given by the *Translatio S. Clementis*[1].

The marked importance attached to the participation of Constantine in the mission to the Chazars explains why the Legend has introduced into the narrative all manner of incredible features to shew the ease with which he acquired foreign languages, the irresistible power of his eloquence, and his success in conversions. The author of the Legend in singing the praises of his hero was led into great exaggerations. Constantine is said to have acquired not less than four languages during his short stay in Cherson—Hebrew, Samaritan, Chazar, and Russian. From the fact that the last-named language is mentioned, some Russian authorities have been led to make very bold inferences, as if Constantine in the Crimea had not only become acquainted with Russian (*i.e.* the Slavonic language) but had even derived from it his Glagolitic alphabet. The language of the *Translatio S. Clementis* is more moderate on this point, and only refers to his learning one language, that of the Chazars.

The journey to the Chazars took place probably about the year 860–861, since he must have returned home, as the Legend also says, to make his report to the Emperor; at that time he must have written the *Brevis Historia*, the λόγος πανηγυρικός (*Sermo Declamatorius*), and the Canon consisting of tropes and odes in honour of the discovery of the relics of St Clement, all in Greek and mentioned by Anastasius in his letter to Gauderic. There is some ground for believing that the Legend preserved in the Slavonic language[2] concerning the translation of the relics of St Clement is in some way connected with the *Brevis Historia* and *Sermo Declamatorius* mentioned by Anastasius. In addition to these subjects, he was also engaged in learned archaeological questions, as is proved by the interpretation, referred to in the Legend, of the Hebrew inscription on a valuable cup in the cathedral of St Sophia. The statement also seems credible that Methodius, as a reward for services rendered to his brother on the journey, was appointed Igumen (abbot) of the rich

[1] There is a considerable literature on the question. Cf. Dr Franko, *St Clement in Cherson* (in Little Russian), Lemberg, 1906, and also *Archiv für slav. Philologie*, vol. XXVIII., who minimises unduly the credibility of the Legends and even of Anastasius.

[2] *See* Bibliography to this Chapter, *Sources*.

and important monastery of Polychronium, after having declined the dignity of a proffered archbishopric.

The activity of the two brothers so far had no influence at all upon the Slav peoples, except perhaps when Methodius in his younger days was an archon. The history of the Church and civilisation of the Slavs is affected only by the last stage of Constantine's life. The Pannonian Legend (*Vita Cyrilli*), dedicated to his memory, is so little national or Slavophil in character that it devotes only the last quarter of the whole book to the description of a period fraught with such consequences for the Slavs. In order correctly to gauge the historical value of the Legend we should not lose sight of the foregoing fact. The author of the Legend is full of admiration for Constantine as a man of great Byzantine learning, of enthusiasm and zeal for his faith, especially in the direction of missionary activity, and devoted to the glory of the Byzantine Empire; he does not present him as a conspicuous Slavophil. That is also the reason why this legend is to be preferred to many later ones which, influenced by later events, divert the activities of the two brothers from the very beginning into Slav and especially Bulgarian channels; such are the so-called Salonica Legend and the *Obdormitio S. Cyrilli* and some others.

The Pannonian Legends place the next sphere of activity of the two brothers in Moravia, that is to say in a Slav land in which the missionaries from the neighbouring German dioceses of Salzburg and Passau had already sown the first seeds of Christianity, although perhaps without much success as yet. Indeed, according to the *Translatio S. Clementis*, the Moravian prince received the news of Constantine's great success in the land of the Chazars, and was thereby induced to address his petition to Constantinople for a capable missionary for his own country. The Pannonian Legend does not insist on this connexion of events, and modern historians associate the decision of the Moravian Prince Rostislav with the political situation of his state; after having attained political independence, it was essential for him to avoid the influence of his powerful East Frankish neighbour in Church matters also. According to the text of a letter, not preserved in the original, of Pope Hadrian to the Moravo-Pannonian princes, it would appear that before Rostislav turned to Constantinople he had made overtures to Rome, but apparently without success. If we are not to ignore the statement of the Pope entirely, we may be able to explain the failure of Rostislav in Rome by the preoccupation of Pope Nicholas with events in Constantinople and Bulgaria. All the more willing was the far-seeing Photius, who was then Patriarch of Constantinople, and whose advice to comply with the wishes of the Moravian prince was followed by the Emperor Michael III. All legends agree that the Emperor induced Constantine to undertake the new mission. The choice is well explained by his successful missions hitherto and by his intimate relations with Photius. It must have been mooted not long after Constantine's return from his mission to the Chazars, because he himself speaks of his fatigue from that journey. We must place this mission in the year 861, or at the latest in the spring of 862. The Pannonian Legend relates the event in a very dramatic manner, and gives some not unimportant details. Amongst other things, the Emperor Michael is said to have been asked by Constantine whether the Moravian Slavs possessed letters of the alphabet, *i.e.* a script for their language. To this the Emperor is said to have replied that his father and grandfather had already made the same inquiry, but in vain. From this anecdote we may at least infer that previous to that time a special Slav script was unknown. This point of view is also confirmed by the statement of the learned monk Chrabr, who expressly declares that, prior to the invention of the Slav script by Constantine, the Slavs were compelled to use Greek and Latin letters when they wanted to write. In the well-known polemic against Methodius of the year 870–871, *Libellus de conversione Bagoariorum et Carantanorum*, occurs the phrase *noviter inventis Sclavinis litteris*, which does not necessarily mean that Methodius had invented them, but that they were certainly new in his time.

To sum up, we must accept the almost contemporary tradition, ignoring the changes introduced by later events, to the effect that Slavonic script originated with and was fixed by Constantine. And the concrete occasion, the expressed wish of the Byzantine Emperor and his Court that Constantine should go to Moravia, is by no means inconsistent with the fact that he invented an alphabet for this particular purpose. He not only wanted to preach the Christian faith to the Moravians, but also to offer them the written Word of God in their own language. According to Byzantine conceptions, and in view of the many instances of Oriental Christians who used their own language and alphabet, it was a necessary and preliminary condition that the Slavs should in the first place possess a script of their own. The statement, supported by the *Translatio*, is also important, namely, that the translation of the Gospels took place at this time also. So we must allow for a period of at least one or two years between the arrival of Rostislav's embassy at Constantinople and the departure of Constantine, his brother Methodius, and the others who were to take part in the new mission. The basis of the future work of the two brothers was thus laid before they left Constantinople.

Although Constantine was the leading spirit, the Pannonian Legends also speak of others who collaborated with him. The invention of this script may reflect the personality and learning of Constantine, but in the work of translation it is easy to imagine that he had others to help him, who must have been in the first instance people of native Slav origin with a Greek education. If we examine the oldest translations, especially the pericopes of the Epistles and Gospels, we have the best proof of a highly developed Slavonic sense of language, which must be attributed to collaborators who were themselves Slavs. In all probability

Constantine must from the very beginning have contemplated establishing Christianity in Moravia on the basis of a Slavonic liturgy. Independently of many Oriental parallels, this is also confirmed by the Pannonian Legend and the *Translatio*, both of which state that the immediate task of the two brothers on their arrival was to instruct the younger generation in the reading of the Word of God and the Slavonic liturgical texts which had been translated from the Greek.

That this purpose of his was recognised at the time is shewn by the opposition raised in Moravia, at the very outset, by those who were hostile to the employment of the Slavonic language for the purposes of the liturgy. The protest emanated as a matter of course from the advocates of the Latin liturgy, who to all appearances were numerous. But the Legends and the *Translatio* further prove, the former with miraculous details, that the brothers had also to fight against various pagan superstitions. There can be no question of a complete Church organisation during the first period of their stay in Moravia. Constantine, compelled to bow to the inevitable, began by educating in the first instance a sufficient number of youths in the Slav liturgy, both written and spoken. The next step was to obtain Slav priests. Up to this moment there was really no one but himself to conduct the divine service in Slavonic, unless he had been able to induce any of the priests of Slav origin, ordained before his arrival, to go over from the Latin rite to the Slavonic-Eastern liturgy.

It was the natural desire to obtain priest's orders for their young followers that induced the two brothers to leave Moravia. It is curious how the various sources differ on this point. According to the *Translatio*, both brothers departed from Moravia and left behind them liturgical books, without saying whither they were going. The *Vita Methodii* only mentions their departure after they had instructed their pupils, without giving their destination. The narrative interpolated in the most ancient Russian chronicle only mentions that Constantine came home in order henceforward to work in Bulgaria, whilst Methodius remained behind in Moravia. This statement has the appearance of a subsequent invention in order not to leave Bulgaria out of the story. But the return home, if by it we are to understand Constantinople, is also impossible to reconcile with their subsequent careers. The reason given by the *Vita Cyrilli*, that it was a question of obtaining ordained priests, gives sufficient ground for their departure from Moravia.

The indefinite mode of expression used by the other sources may perhaps be explained by the fact that Constantine himself did not know for certain where he would succeed in obtaining ordination for the elect of his young pupils. It was out of the question to think of Passau or Salzburg, and it may have been the internal discord of the Greek Church which decided him against Constantinople[1].

[1] There is certainly no evidence that he contemplated a breach with Constantinople.

The nearest sees were Aquileia and Grado, but legend speaks instead only of their sojourn in Venice. The object of the intercalated disputation (which is another proof of the tendency of the author of the *Vita Cyrilli* to attribute such disputations to Constantine[1]) was to point to the fact that Constantine was unable to attain his desire to secure ordination of Slav priests. But there is another conspicuous discrepancy here between the two Pannonian Legends; while the *Vita Methodii* does not say a single word concerning the sojourn of Constantine and Methodius in the territory of Kocel, the *Vita Cyrilli* cannot sufficiently praise the friendliness of Kocel towards the two brothers. The events which followed the death of Constantine in 869 support the credibility of the *Vita Cyrilli*, as Kocel's petition to the Pope to send Methodius into his country makes it natural to assume a previous personal acquaintance. The *Vita Methodii* also knows nothing of the disputation at Venice, but only briefly refers to one at Rome. Both the Pannonian Legends and the *Translatio* agree generally that Pope Nicholas called the brothers to Rome, but his letter, mentioned in the *Translatio*, has not been preserved. According to the text, it must have reached them in Moravia or at least in Pannonia. It would agree better with the circumstances and with the *Vita Cyrilli* to assume that the news of the summons to Rome only reached them on Italian soil, at Grado or Venice.

Curiously enough, the Pannonian Legends entirely ignore the death of Pope Nicholas I, which happened in the meantime (13 November 867); it is only mentioned in the *Translatio*, which also adds the correct date on which the two brothers arrived in Rome with the relics of St Clement—after the election of the new Pope Hadrian II (14 December 867), either at the end of 867 or the beginning of 868. On their arrival in Rome they were received in state by the new Pope, but, according to the *Translatio*, the honours were, as was natural, only shewn to the relics of St Clement.

The real object which Constantine had in view is only mentioned in the *Translatio*, in which we read that the Pope sanctioned the ordination of the young men as priests and deacons. As all these aspirants were intended for the performance of the Slavonic liturgy, their ordination clearly shews the Pope's approval of the innovation. But the further statement of the *Translatio* that the Pope made bishops of Constantine and Methodius is contrary to all other information, although it is accepted as true by some historians. The Pannonian Legends, which contain markedly detailed information concerning the honours shewn in Rome to the Slavonic books and appear to be derived here from eye-witnesses, would scarcely have omitted to report the personal honours shewn to Constantine and Methodius, had they actually taken place. The *Vita Methodii* only states that Pope Hadrian gave the Slavonic books his blessing and priest's orders to Methodius; and, notwithstanding the

[1] The whole story of the great disputation at Venice is merely legendary padding.

opposition of some Roman bishops to the Slavonic liturgy, he selected one of them to ordain three of the young men as priests, and two as anagnosts (lectors).

According to the exact statement in the *Vita Cyrilli*, Constantine died on 14 February 869. Both Pannonian Legends and the *Translatio* state that shortly before his death he assumed the name Cyril and the monastic garb. In close agreement with one another, the *Vita Cyrilli* and the *Translatio* relate that Methodius first wanted to carry the corpse to a monastery in Constantinople in order to comply with his mother's wish. This surely implies that it was now his own intention to go to Constantinople and withdraw into a monastery. According to the *Vita Methodii*, Constantine was afraid of this wish of Methodius and therefore begged of him before his death to abandon it. When the Pope declined to grant Methodius' petition, it was eventually agreed that Cyril should be buried in state in the Basilica dedicated to St Clement.

According to all credible information, Constantine's literary activity consisted first in the invention of a script for a certain definite Slavonic tongue. He chose the Macedo-Bulgarian dialect, called locally Slovenian, and the script had to be accurately fitted, as it were, to this tongue; he had a wonderful ear for phonetics, and contrived to provide a letter for each sound in the dialect. Of the two known Slavonic scripts, that which is recognised as the invention of Constantine by the majority of linguists and historians is the Glagolitic script, which was formed on the model of the Greek minuscules of the ninth century in a manner exhibiting originality and individuality. In all probability recourse was also had to some Latin and Hebrew (or Samaritan) signs. That the South Slavonic dialect was used as the basis of the script is clearly apparent from the employment of a special sign for *dz* as opposed to *z*, and of a single sign for the vowel e^{a} or *ä*, which in the Pannonian-Moravian group of dialects had developed into two separate sounds, *e* or ^{i}e and *ya*.

There is one obvious objection. Why was the script based on a South Slavonic dialect, while its use was intended for a totally different area and tongue in North Slavonia? But this objection may be answered by the following considerations. In the first place, the Slavonic tongues in the ninth century were more nearly related to one another than in the nineteenth; secondly, it is quite possible that Constantine may have discovered from the members of Rostislav's embassy that the South Slavonic dialect he knew was easily intelligible to the Moravians; finally, he may have convinced himself by the comparison of the language of Byzantine literature with the spoken language of the Greek populace that a distinction between the literary language and the dialects of the people constituted no obstacle to success.

The next stage in Constantine's literary activity began before his departure for Moravia. It was in the first instance limited to the translation of the lections from the Gospels and St Paul's Epistles, with the help of his collaborators; and in Moravia, if not earlier, translations were added from the Greek of whatever was indispensable for divine service, especially the Psalms, the pericopes of the Old Testament, and finally a short prayer- and hymn-book. Attempts have already been made to separate in point of language the portions due to Constantine's initiative from the continuations supplied by Methodius and his pupils, but the results are not satisfactory.

While it is a matter of comparative ease to write the life of Constantine or Cyril, the subsequent course of his brother's life has given rise to many controversies, chiefly because, for the purposes of his biography, there is no parallel source by which to test the Pannonian Legend. It is true that we are considerably assisted during this period by the statements of the Papal Curia, but however important this historical source may be, it does not afford sufficient indications of the later life of this great man. A recent discovery, however, of papal documents has been very helpful in establishing the credibility of the Legend. The persecution to which Methodius was exposed at the time when he was already archbishop, and which is mentioned in the Legend without comment, has now been strikingly confirmed by the newly discovered London *Register* of papal letters. This important evidence for the credibility of the Legend in connexion with the later life of Methodius prevents us from being biased against it by the legendary padding in the form of miracles and prophecies.

Whilst Methodius remained at Rome after the death of his brother, Pope Hadrian, according to the Legend, received Kocel's request to send Methodius to him as a teacher. The Pope complied, and addressed to all three princes Rostislav, Svatopluk, and Kocel, a circular letter, the original of which has not been preserved, though the Legend reproduces its contents at length. The genuineness of its contents has been disputed; but a forgery to support the Slavonic liturgy, which we know to have been tolerated in Rome by the Pope, would probably be totally different in character from this simple papal epistle, in which the facts of Constantine's life are referred to, first, to recommend Methodius to continue the work already begun by his brother, and then to authorise the Slavonic Mass, with the express stipulation that the Gospel must first be read in Latin. Why should one not believe the further narrative of the Legend that Methodius first did yeoman's work with his pupils as priest, preacher, and teacher in Pannonia, and only returned to Rome afterwards at the request of Prince Kocel, accompanied by a deputation of the nobility, to receive the bishop's mitre at the hands of the Pope for the restored see of St Andronicus in Pannonia?

It was only now that the dissatisfaction of Salzburg was aroused, for Pannonia had been within its jurisdiction since the days of Charlemagne. They did not confine themselves to polemics such as the *Libellus de conversione Bagoariorum et Carantanorum*, but Methodius was cited before an assembly of secular and ecclesiastical dignitaries, presided over by Louis the German, among whom was probably Svatopluk also, and as he boldly defended himself against the accusation of exercising episcopal rights in another's diocese, he was sent to Swabia and kept there in prison for a year and a half.

We now know from the papal *Register* found in London that all this is true, and that Methodius was actually treated worse than one would imagine from the Legend. As Methodius obtained his freedom in the year 873 by the energetic intervention of the new Pope, John VIII, this violence to his person must have taken place in the years 871–873. Consequently he did not long enjoy in peace the episcopal dignity conferred upon him by the Pope. According to the Legend, the powerful enemies of Methodius, immediately after his expulsion from Pannonia, threatened his former patron Kocel with their displeasure if he ever received him back again. As a matter of fact, Kocel must have recognised the supremacy of the Salzburg Church as soon as Methodius had been removed, for it is known that by 874 a church had been already consecrated in Pettau by Archbishop Theotmar; whether Kocel was then alive we do not know.

The papal legate, Bishop Paul of Ancona, who was entrusted with the settlement of Methodius' case, was, on the one hand, to do his utmost to take him to Moravia to Svatopluk, and, on the other, to return to Rome with him, together with Hermanric, Bishop of Passau, who had treated Methodius in a particularly harsh and cruel manner. Was Methodius at this moment in Rome? According to the text of the Legend it is quite possible, for it relates that the news of his liberation created such a reaction in Moravia that the Latin-German priests were driven out and a petition was addressed to the Pope to give them Methodius as their archbishop. The Pope complied and sent Methodius to Moravia, where he was received with enthusiasm by Svatopluk and all the Moravians, and took over the ecclesiastical administration of the whole country. There is no reason to doubt the correctness of this sequence of events.

In this period, which the Legend describes as the most flourishing in the history of the Church, the baptism of the Bohemian Prince Bořivoi may have taken place on the occasion of Methodius' stay with Svatopluk. Curiously enough, the Legend narrates much less concerning the subsequent activity of Methodius in Moravia than do papal documents. All it says is that a party arose against him, and his removal was expected, but the Moravian people assembled to listen to a letter from the Pope, which placed them in mourning because it was supposed to be unfavourable to Methodius. But suddenly their mourning was changed into great joy; when the papal letter was opened it was found to vindicate the orthodoxy of Methodius and to declare that all "Slovenian lands" were delivered by God and the Apostolic See to his ecclesiastical authority.

This narrative is obscure, and it is particularly surprising that no mention at all is made of the crux of the whole situation, the use of the Slavonic language in the liturgy. Only the omission of the *filioque* clause from the Nicene Creed is hinted at as the reason for the accusation of unorthodoxy brought against him by the Latin party[1]. Is it not possible that this obscurity in the narrative of the Legend is intentional? For we know that in June or July of the year 879 Pope John cited Methodius to Rome on account of the two-fold suspicion which had fallen upon him, first, that he was unsound in dogma in preaching the faith, and, secondly, that notwithstanding the express order of the Pope, communicated to him once before by Bishop Paul of Ancona, forbidding him to sing Mass in the Slavonic language, he had continued to do so. This is contained in the letter of the Pope addressed to Methodius. In a simultaneous second letter addressed to Svatopluk, the Pope only refers to the suspicion cast on Methodius' orthodoxy, no mention being made of the language used in the liturgy. The archbishop obeyed the papal summons, and succeeded not only in convincing the Pope of his orthodoxy but also in obtaining his authority to use the Slavonic language for divine service, which was solemnly expressed in a letter to Svatopluk in July 880: "Litteras denique Sclaviniscas a Constantino quondam philosopho reppertas, quibus Deo laudes debite resonent, jure laudamus et in eadem lingua Christi domini nostri preconia et opera enarrentur jubemus." Thus ran the principal passage in the letter, which clearly refers to the Mass, as it goes on: "nec sane fidei vel doctrinae aliquid obstat sive missas in eadem Sclavinica lingua canere sive sacrum evangelium vel lectiones divinas novi et veteris Testamenti bene translatas et interpretatas legere aut alia horarum officia omnia psallere." There follows Hadrian's express reservation to the effect that "propter majorem honorificentiam evangelium latine legatur et postmodum Sclavinica lingua translatum in auribus populi, latina verba non intelligentis, adnuntietur."

The difficulties of Methodius were, however, by no means at an end. Clearly he could look for no reliable support from Svatopluk, and in his suffragan Wiching, Bishop of Nyitra, he had an uncompromising opponent who sought by various means to undermine Methodius' reputation and activity, both in Moravia with Svatopluk and in Rome with the Pope. This is apparent from the Pope's letter of 23 March 881, in which he consoled Methodius. The Legend here tells of a journey made by Methodius after 881, as we may certainly date it, to the Emperor Basil I at Constantinople. According to the Legend, the visit to Constantinople originated with Basil. This may not be correct, but it is very difficult to ascertain the true reasons which would tempt an aged man to a long and fatiguing journey. It was certainly not a mere ordinary visit. As it is related that the Emperor Basil had kept back a Slavonic

[1] No doubt Methodius, being a Greek, did not use the *filioque* clause. Possibly there was at this time an attempt to Latinise the Slavonic liturgy, while preserving its Slavonic tongue.

priest and a deacon, as well as certain Slavonic church books, it is quite possible for Methodius' arrival in Constantinople to have some connexion with the Slavonic liturgy, either in the interest of the Slavs who were under the rule of Constantinople, or of the Bulgarians who had again sided with Constantinople in ecclesiastical matters.

According to the Legend, Methodius also continued the literary work begun by his brother, especially completing the translation of the Old Testament, with the exception of the Book of the Maccabees. The time given by the Legend for this undertaking (seven months) is, however, far too short, and modern philological investigation does not bear out the statement that the translation was carried through at one time. The report that he also translated a *Nomokanon*, by which is probably meant the digest of the Canon Law of John Scholasticus, and provided reading-matter of an edifying character by translating a *Paterikon*, appears quite worthy of credence.

Little as we know of Methodius' daily life, or of the place where he usually resided—only later sources mention Velehrad in Moravia—we know no more of the place of his death, which is said to have happened on 6 April 885. The Legend relates that his pupils buried him with solemn rites in three languages—Latin, Greek, and Slavonic.

It is certain from the Legend that he designated Gorazd to succeed him, as Gorazd was a Moravian, a fluent Latin speaker, and at the same time orthodox. This is also confirmed by the Greek *Vita Clementis*, which, however, mentions Svatopluk as an unquestioned opponent of Methodius, at least in his last years, so that they could not reckon on his approval of Gorazd's candidature. But at this time a change had taken place on the pontifical throne. The new Pope, Stephen V (VI), was induced, probably by very unfavourable news from Moravia about Methodius, to send a bishop (Dominicus) and two priests (John and Stephen) to the Slavs, *i.e.* to Moravia, with definite orders, one of which was to forbid distinctly the Slavonic Mass (regardless of the concession of John VIII in the year 880), the other requiring Gorazd, who had been appointed by Methodius as his successor, to come to Rome under temporary suspension of his episcopal powers. This was clearly due to Svatopluk and Wiching.

The Slavonic liturgy could not withstand in Moravia the attack of the Latin liturgy, which was supported by Church and State, but the followers of Methodius carried it to the South Slavs, where it took firm hold in Bulgaria, Serbia, and Croatia. After the separation of the Churches, it gave strength to the Eastern Church. In Croatia, which was Catholic, it has remained, but only under strong opposition, until this day, in a few dioceses of Croatia, Istria, and Dalmatia. The chief legacy of the two brothers—of which they had no idea themselves—fell to Russia, in whose many libraries are preserved the richest treasures of Slavonic ecclesiastical literature.

CHAPTER VIII.

THE RISE AND FALL OF THE FIRST BULGARIAN EMPIRE (679–1018).

LIKE the Serbs, but unlike the Albanians, the Bulgarians are not autochthonous inhabitants of the Balkan country to which they have given their name. It was not till 679[1] that this Finnish or Tartar race, after numerous previous incursions into the Balkan provinces of the Byzantine Empire, definitely abandoned the triangle formed by the Black Sea, the Dnieper, and the Danube (the modern Bessarabia), and settled between the Danube and the Balkans (the ancient Moesia). Thus, the first Bulgarian state practically coincided with the Bulgarian principality created 1200 years later by the Treaty of Berlin. The Finnish or Tartar invaders found this country already peopled with Slavs, immigrants like themselves but of different customs and language. As time went on, the conquered, as so often happens, absorbed the conquerors; the Bulgarians adopted the Slav speech of the vanquished; the country received the name of the invaders, and became known to all time as "Bulgaria." Still, after the lapse of more than twelve centuries, the "Bulgarians," as this amalgam of races came to be called, possess qualities differing from those of their purely Slav neighbours, and during the recent European war Bulgarian political writers reminded the world that the Bulgarian people was not of Slavonic origin.

The Patriarch Nicephorus has left the earliest account of this Bulgarian invasion and settlement. He tells how the Bulgarians originally lived on the shores of the Sea of Azov and on the banks of the river Kuban; how their chief, Kovrat (identified with the "Kurt" of the earliest list of Bulgarian rulers), left five sons, the third of whom, Asparuch (or Isparich), migrated to Bessarabia. There he and his Bulgarians might have remained, had not the Emperor Constantine IV Pogonatus undertaken an expedition for the purpose of punishing them for their raids into the borderlands of his dominions. The strength of the Bulgarian position in a difficult country and an attack of gout obliged the Emperor to retire to Mesembria. A panic seized the troops left behind to continue the siege; the Bulgarians pursued them across the Danube as far as Varna. Neither Greeks nor Slavs offered resistance; the Emperor had to make peace and pay a tribute, in order to save Thrace from invasion.

[1] Professor Bury believes that the migration occurred earlier, during the reign of Constans II (641–668). *The Chronological Cycle of the Bulgarians* (*BZ.* XIX. 1910).

The Bulgarians established their first capital in an entrenched camp at Pliska, the modern Turkish village of Aboba to the north-east of Shumla. Recent excavations have unearthed this previously unknown portion of Bulgarian history, and have laid bare the great fortifications, the inner stronghold, and the palace of the "Sublime Khan," as the primitive ruler was called. Unlike modern Bulgaria, early Bulgaria was an aristocratic state, with two grades of nobility, the *boljarin* and the *ugain*, but leading nobles of both orders bore the coveted title of *bagatur* ("hero"). As in Albania to-day, the clan was the basis of the social system. The official language of the primitive Bulgarian Chancery was Greek, but not exactly the Greek of Byzantium—a native tribute to the far more advanced culture of the Empire. The first two centuries of Bulgarian history down to the introduction of Christianity are an almost continuous series of campaigns against the Byzantine Empire, for which, with scarcely an exception, our sources are exclusively Greek or Frankish. Justinian II began these Greco-Bulgarian wars by refusing to pay the tribute to Isparich, and narrowly escaped from a Bulgarian ambuscade. Yet this same Emperor, after his deposition and banishment to the Crimea, owed his restoration to the aid of Isparich's successor Tervel. Escaping to Bulgaria, he promised his daughter to Tervel as the price of his assistance, and bestowed upon his benefactor a royal robe and the honorary title of "Caesar." Three years later, however, in 707, he so far forgot the benefits received as to break the peace and again invade Bulgaria, only to receive a severe defeat at Anchialus, whence he was forced to flee by sea to Constantinople. Once more we find him appealing, not in vain, for Tervel's assistance, and during the brief reigns of Justinian II's three successors hostilities were spasmodic. But when Leo the Isaurian had firmly established himself on the throne, Tervel found it useless to renew the part of king-maker and attempt to restore the fallen Emperor, Anastasius II. Indeed, after Tervel's day and the reigns of two shadowy rulers, the overthrow of the Bulgarian reigning dynasty of Dulo (to which Kurt and his successors had belonged) by the usurper Kormisosh of the clan of Ukil, led to civil war, which weakened the hitherto flourishing Bulgarian state at the time when an energetic Emperor, Constantine V Copronymus, sat upon the Byzantine throne.

In the intervals of his struggle with the monks, the Iconoclast Emperor conducted seven campaigns against the Bulgarians, whom he had alarmed by planting Syrian and Armenian colonists in Thrace. He took vengeance for a Bulgarian raid to Constantinople by invading Bulgaria, but on a second invasion suffered a severe defeat at Veregava (now the Vrbitsa pass between Shumla and Yamboli). Another dynastic revolution prevented the victors from reaping the fruits of their victory. The usurper disappeared from history, but the old dynasty did not profit by his removal from the scene. On the contrary, a general massacre of the house of Dulo ensued, and a certain Telets of the clan of Ugain was proclaimed Khan. Telets was, however, defeated by the Emperor near Anchialus, and his disillusioned countrymen put him to death, and restored the dynasty of Kormisosh in the person of his son-in-law Sabin. The latter's attempt to make peace with the Emperor was followed, however, by his deposition, and it was reserved for his successor, Bayan, to come to terms with Byzantium, where Sabin had taken refuge. But Bayan had a rival in his own country, Umar, Sabin's nominee, and to support him the Emperor invaded Bulgaria, and defeated Bayan's brother and successor Toktu in the woods near the Danube in 765. Both brothers were slain, most of the country was plundered, and the villages laid in ashes. Next year, however, the Greek fleet was almost destroyed by a storm in the Black Sea, but the Emperor routed the Bulgarians at Lithosoria during a further punitive expedition known as "the noble war," because no Christians fell. These sudden reverses of fortune are characteristic of Bulgarian history. The next Bulgarian Khan, Telerig, warned by these events of the existence of a Byzantine party in Bulgaria, obtained by a ruse from the Emperor the names of the latter's adherents, whom he put to death. Constantine was in an ecstasy of rage, but died in the course of a fresh expedition against the barbarian who had outwitted him. Telerig, however, was obliged to seek refuge with the next Emperor, Leo IV, who conferred upon him the rank of patrician and the hand of an imperial princess, besides acting as his godfather when he embraced Christianity. Telerig's successor, Kardam, after defeating Constantine VI, wrote to him an insolent letter, threatening to march to the Golden Gate of Constantinople unless the Emperor paid the promised tribute. Constantine sarcastically replied that he would not trouble an old man to undertake so long a journey, but that he would come himself—with an army. The Bulgarian fled before him, and for ten years there was peace between the Greeks and their already dangerous rivals.

In the first decade of the ninth century the first striking figure in Bulgarian history mounted the throne of Pliska. This was Krum—a name still familiar to readers of Balkan polemics. Krum, whose realm at his accession embraced Danubian Bulgaria and Wallachia, "Bulgaria beyond the Danube," coveted Macedonia—the goal of so many Bulgarian ambitions in all ages. He invaded the district watered by the Strymon, defeated the Greek garrisons, and seized a large sum of money intended as pay for the soldiers. More important still, in 809 he captured Sardica, the modern Sofia, then the northernmost outpost of the Empire against Bulgaria, put the garrison to death, and destroyed the fortifications. The Emperor Nicephorus I retaliated by spending Easter in Krum's palace at Pliska, which he plundered; he foresaw Bulgarian designs upon Macedonia and endeavoured to check the growth of the Slav population there by compulsory colonisation from other provinces. He then resolved to crush his enemy, and, after long preparation, marched against him in 811. Proudly rejecting Krum's offer of peace, he again occupied Pliska, set his seal on the Bulgarian treasury, and loftily disregarded the humble petition of Krum: "Lo, thou hast conquered; take what pleaseth thee, and go in peace." Krum, driven to desperation, closed the Balkan passes in the enemy's rear, and the invaders found themselves caught, as in a trap, in an enclosed valley, perhaps that still called "the Greek Hollow" near Razboina. Nicephorus saw that there was no hope: "Even if we become birds," he exclaimed, "none of us can escape!" On 26 July the Greek army was annihilated; no prisoners were taken; for the first time since the death of Valens four centuries earlier an Emperor had fallen in battle; and, to add to the disgrace, his head, after being exposed on a lance, was lined with silver and used as a goblet, in which the savage Bulgarian pledged his nobles at state banquets. Yet the lexicographer Suidas[1] would have us believe that this primitive savage was the author of a code of laws—one of which ordered the uprooting of every vine in Bulgaria, to prevent drunkenness, while another bade his subjects give to a beggar sufficient to prevent him ever feeling the pinch of want again. To complete the disaster, Nicephorus' son, the Emperor Stauracius, died of his wounds.

This was not Krum's only triumph over the Greeks. In 812 he captured Develtus and Mesembria, as the war party at Constantinople, headed by Theodore of Studion, declined to renew an old Greco-Bulgarian commercial treaty of some fifty years earlier, which had permitted merchants duly provided with seals and passports to carry on trade in either state, and under which the Bulgarian ruler was entitled to a gift of clothing and 30 lbs. of red-dyed skins. The treaty also fixed the Greco-Bulgarian frontier at the hills of Meleona, well to the south of the Balkans, and stipulated for the extradition of deserters. When the Emperor Michael I marched against him in 813, Krum inflicted a severe defeat at Versinicia near Hadrianople, and the rare circumstance of the Bulgarians defeating the trained hosts of Byzantium in the open country led to the suspicion of treachery on the part of the general, Leo the Armenian. At any rate, he profited by the disaster, for he supplanted Michael on the throne, and thus the rude Bulgarian could boast that he had slain one Roman Emperor and caused the death of another and the dethronement of a third. He now burned to take the Imperial city; but this was a task beyond his powers. His strange human sacrifices before the Golden Gate, his public ablutions, and the homage of his harem, did not compensate for lack of experience in so formidable a siege. He then claimed to erect his lance over the Golden Gate, and, when that insolent request was refused, demanded an annual tribute, a quantity of fine raiment, and a certain number of picked damsels. The new Emperor, Leo V, offered to discuss these last proposals, in order to set an ambush for his enemy. Krum unsuspectingly accepted the offer, and narrowly

[1] Suidas, ed. Gaisford, I. 761–62; Cedrenus, II. 41–42; *BZ.* XVI. 254–57.

escaped assassination, thanks, so a monkish chronicler expresses it, to the sins of his would-be assassins. The smoking suburbs of Byzantium were the testimony of his revenge; the palace of St Mamas perished in the flames; the shores of the Hellespont and the interior of Thrace were devastated. Exactly a thousand years later, another Bulgarian army reached Chatalja, the last bulwark of Constantinople, and the Bulgarian siege of 813 was exhumed as an historical precedent.

Hadrianople succumbed to hunger; its inhabitants and those of other Thracian towns were carried off to "Bulgaria beyond the Danube," among them the future Emperor, Basil I. But, by one of those sudden changes of fortune with which recent Bulgarian history has familiarised us, Leo inflicted such a crushing defeat upon the Bulgarians near Mesembria, that the spot where he had lain in wait was long pointed out as "Leo's hill." To avenge this disaster, Krum prepared for another siege of Constantinople, and this time intended to appear with a complete siege train before the walls. But, as in the case of the great Serbian Tsar, Stephen Dušan, death cut short the Bulgarian's enterprise. On 14 April 814 Krum burst a blood-vessel. After a brief period of civil war, Krum's son, Omurtag, became "Sublime Khan," and concluded a thirty years' peace with the Empire, of which a summary has been preserved. By this treaty Thrace was partitioned between the Greeks and the Bulgarians, and the frontier ran from Develtus to the fortress of Makroliváda, between Hadrianople and Philippopolis, whence it turned northward to the Balkans. It was not a paper frontier such as diplomacy loves to trace on maps, but consisted of a rampart and trench, known to Byzantine historians as "the Great Fence" and to the modern peasants, who still tell strange stories of how it was made, as the *Erkesiya*, from a Turkish word meaning a "cutting in the earth."[1]

Thus guaranteed against a conflict with the Greeks, the Bulgarians turned their attention westward, and for the first time came into touch with the Frankish Empire, which had established its authority as far south as Croatia. In 824 a Bulgarian embassy appeared at the court of Louis the Pious, in order to regulate the Franco-Bulgarian frontiers, which marched together near Belgrade. The Western Emperor, knowing nothing about the Bulgarians and their geographical claims, sent an envoy of his own to make inquiries on the spot, and, after keeping the Bulgarian mission waiting at Aix-la-Chapelle, finally sent it back without any definite reply. Omurtag, anxious to maintain his prestige over the Slavs beyond the Danube, who had shewn signs of placing themselves under the protection of his powerful neighbour, invaded Pannonia and set up Bulgarian governors there. In fact, Syrmia and eastern Hungary remained Bulgarian till the Magyar conquest.

A Greek inscription on a pillar of the church of the Forty Martyrs at Trnovo commemorates the works of "the Sublime Khan Omurtag"—

[1] Bury in *EHR.* (1910), xxv. 276–87.

the "house of high renown" which he "built on the Danube," and the "sepulchre" which he "made mid-way" between that and his "old house" at Pliska. Of these two constructions the former has been identified with the ruined fortress of Kadykei near Turtukai on the Danube (the Bulgaro-Roumanian frontier according to the Treaty of Bucharest of 1913), the latter with a mound near the village of Mumdzhilar. Another Greek inscription, recently discovered at Chatalar, records a still more important creation of this ruler—"a palace on the river Tutsa," intended to overawe the Greeks. This "palace," founded, as the inscription informs us, in 821–22, was none other than the future capital of Bulgaria, Great Prêslav, or "the Glorious," a little to the south-west of Shumla. Despite the prayer uttered in this inscription that "the divine ruler may press down the Emperor with his foot," Omurtag, so far from attacking the Greek Empire, actually aided Michael II in 823 against the rebel Thomas, who was besieging Constantinople. Thus Byzantium, besieged by one Bulgarian ruler, was, ten years later, relieved by another. There is little continuity of policy in the Balkans.

Omurtag, who was still alive in 827, was succeeded by his son Presiam, or Malomir as he was called in the increasingly important Slavonic idiom of Bulgaria[1]. His reign is important historically because it was unfortunately marred by the first of the long series of Serbo-Bulgarian wars, of which our own generation has seen three. Characteristically it seems to have arisen out of the Bulgarian occupation of western Macedonia. The Serbian prince, Vlastimir, during a three years' struggle, inflicted heavy losses on the Bulgarians. Presiam's nephew and successor, the famous Boris, who began his long reign in 852, was again defeated by Vlastimir's three sons, and his own son Vladimir with twelve great nobles was captured. Boris had to sue for peace to save the prisoners; he was no more fortunate in his quarrel with the Croats, and he maintained towards the Greeks the pacific policy of Omurtag.

The name of Boris is indelibly connected with the conversion of the Bulgarians to Christianity. Sporadic attempts at conversion had already been made, and with sufficient success to provoke persecution by Omurtag, whose eldest son is even said to have become a proselyte. But in the time of Boris Christianity became the State religion. In the Near East politics and religion are inextricably mingled, and it is probable that political considerations may have helped to influence the Bulgarian ruler. Boris, placed midway between the Western and the Eastern Empire, had played an equivocal part between Louis the German and Rostislav of Moravia, now supporting the German, now the Slav. The Moravian prince pointed out to Byzantium the danger to the whole Balkan peninsula of a Bulgaro-German alliance, especially if Boris, as his German ally desired, adopted the Western faith. Michael III at once saw the gravity of the situation; he made a hostile demonstration against Bulgaria,

[1] Bury, *A History of the Eastern Roman Empire*, Appendix X.

whose ruler submitted without a blow, agreed to accept the Orthodox form of Christianity, thus becoming ecclesiastically dependent on the Ecumenical Patriarch, and received, as a slight concession, a small rectification of his frontier in the shape of an uninhabited district. Boris was baptised in 864–65, the Emperor acted as his sponsor, and the convert took his sponsor's name of Michael. Other less mundane reasons for his conversion are given. It is said that, during a severe famine, he was moved by the appeals of his sister (who had embraced Christianity during her captivity in Constantinople) and by the arguments of a captive monk, Theodore Koupharas, to become a Christian. Another story represents him as terrified into acceptance of the faith by the realistic picture of the Last Judgment painted for him by a Greek artist, Methodius. His attempt, however, to force baptism upon his heathen subjects led to a revolt of the nobles. He put down this insurrection with the utmost severity; he executed 52 nobles with their wives and families, while sparing the common folk. The celebrated Patriarch Photius sent a literary essay to his "well-beloved son" on the heresies that beset, and the duties that await, a model Christian prince, and missionaries—Greeks, Armenians, and others—flooded Bulgaria. Perplexed by their different precepts and alarmed at the reluctance of the Patriarch to appoint a bishop for Bulgaria, Boris craftily sent an embassy to Pope Nicholas I, asking him to send a bishop and priests, and propounding a list of 106 theological and social questions, upon which he desired the Pope's authoritative opinion. This singular catalogue of doubts included such diverse subjects as the desirability of wearing drawers (which the Pope pronounced to be immaterial), the expediency of the sovereign dining alone (which was declared to be bad manners), the right way with pagans and apostates, and the appointment of a Bulgarian Patriarch. Nicholas I sent Formosus, afterwards Pope, and another bishop as his legates to Bulgaria with replies to these questions, denouncing the practice of torturing prisoners and other barbarous customs, but putting aside for the present the awkward question of a Patriarch; Bulgaria was, however, to have a bishop, and later on an archbishop. Photius in reply denounced the proceedings of the Roman Church in Bulgaria, and the reluctance of the new Pope Hadrian II to nominate as archbishop a person recommended by Boris made the indignant Bulgarian abandon Rome for Byzantium, which gladly sent him an archbishop and ten bishops. The Archbishop of Bulgaria took the next place after the Patriarch at festivities; Boris' son, the future Tsar Simeon, was sent to study Demosthenes and Aristotle at Constantinople. One further step towards the popularisation of Christianity in Bulgaria remained to be taken—the introduction of the Slavonic liturgy and books of devotion. This was, towards the end of Boris' reign, the work of the disciples of Methodius, one of the two famous "Slavonic Apostles," when they were driven from Moravia. Boris in 888 retired into a cloister, whence four years later he temporarily emerged to depose his elder son Vladimir, whose excesses had endangered the state. After placing his younger son Simeon on the throne in 893, Boris lived on till 907, and died in the odour of sanctity, the first of Bulgaria's national saints.

With Simeon began again the struggle between Greeks and Bulgarians. Two Greek merchants, who had obtained from the Emperor Leo VI the monopoly of the Bulgarian trade, diverted it from Constantinople to Salonica, and placed heavy duties upon the Bulgarian traders. The latter complained to Simeon, and Simeon to the Emperor, but backstairs influence at the palace prevented his complaints from being heard, and forced him to resort to arms. He defeated the imperial forces, and sent back the captives with their noses cut off. Leo summoned the Magyars across the Danube to his aid; Simeon was defeated and his country devastated up to the gates of Prêslav. But, when the Magyars withdrew, he defeated a Greek army at Bulgaróphygos near Hadrianople and ravaged the homes of the Magyars during their absence on a distant expedition. An interval of peace ensued, during which the classically educated ruler endeavoured to acclimatise Byzantine literature among his recalcitrant subjects. Simeon collected and had translated 135 speeches of Chrysostom; Constantine, a pupil of the "Apostle" Methodius, translated another collection of homilies, and, at Simeon's command, four orations of St Athanasius; John the Exarch dedicated to Simeon his *Shestodnev* (or "Hexameron"), a compilation describing the creation from Aristotle and the Fathers; a monk Grigori translated for him the chronicle of John Malalas with additions; while several unknown writers drew up an encyclopaedia of the contemporary knowledge of Byzantium. There was nothing original in this literature; but, if it was not the natural product of the Bulgarian spirit, it diffused a certain culture among the few, and reflected credit upon the royal patron, whom his contemporaries likened to the Ptolemies for his promotion of learning. Simeon had learned also at Constantinople the love of magnificence as well as of literature. If we may believe his contemporary, John the Exarch, his residence at Great Prêslav, whither the capital had now been removed from Pliska, was a marvel to behold, with its palaces and churches, its paintings, its marble, copper, gold, and silver ornaments. In the palace sat the sovereign "in a garment studded with pearls, a chain of coins round his neck and bracelets on his wrists, girt about with a purple girdle, and with a golden sword at his side." Of all this splendour, and of a city which Nicetas in the thirteenth century described as "having the largest circuit of any in the Balkans," a few scanty ruins remain.

Alexander, the successor of Leo VI, mortally offended Simeon by rejecting his offer to renew the treaty concluded with his father. The accession of the child Constantine Porphyrogenitus gave him his opportunity for revenge. In 913, a century after Krum, he appeared with an army before Constantinople; next year he obtained Hadrianople by treachery; and, on 20 August 917, he annihilated the Byzantine army at Anchialus[1], where half a century later the bones of the slain were still visible. Bulgaria by this victory became for a brief period the dominant power of the Balkan peninsula. Simeon's dominions stretched from the Black to the Ionian Sea, except for a few Byzantine fortresses on the Albanian coast; Niš and Belgrade were Bulgarian; but the Aegean coast remained Greek. In 923 Simeon besieged Constantinople, and Hadrianople again surrendered to the Bulgarians. The title of "Sublime Khan" or even that of "Prince" seemed inadequate for the ruler of such a vast realm; accordingly Simeon assumed the style of "Tsar of the Bulgarians and Greeks," receiving his crown from Rome, while, as a natural concomitant of the imperial dignity, the head of the Bulgarian Church became "Patriarch of Prêslav," with his residence at Silistria.

Simeon's career closed in the midst of wars against the Serbs and Croats, in the course of which he had laid Serbia waste but had been defeated by the Croats. He died in 927, and, like most strong Balkan rulers, was succeeded by a weak man. He had excluded his eldest son Michael from the succession and confined him in a monastery; but his second son, Tsar Peter, had the temperament of a pacifist. His first act was to marry the grand-daughter of the Byzantine co-Emperor, Romanus I Lecapenus, thus introducing for the first time a Greek Tsaritsa into the Bulgarian court. He obtained by this marriage the recognition of his imperial title and of the Bulgarian Patriarchate. But the war-party in Bulgaria, headed by the Tsar's younger brother John, revolted against what they considered a policy of concession to the Greeks; and, when John was defeated, Simeon's eldest son emerged from his cell to lead a fresh rebellion. Upon his death, a far more serious opponent arose in the person of the noble, Shishman of Trnovo, and his sons. Shishman separated Macedonia and Albania from old Bulgaria, and established a second Bulgarian Empire in the western provinces. Torn asunder by these rivalries, Bulgaria was also menaced by her neighbours, the Serbs, the Patzinaks, and the Magyars, while the Bogomile heresy spread through the land from the two parent Churches of the Bulgarians proper and of the Macedonian or Thracian Dragovitchi. In Bulgaria, as in Bosnia, the Bogomile tenets aroused vehement opposition, the leader of which was the presbyter Cosmas. Apart from their beliefs, the Bogomiles, by the mere fact of dividing the nation into two contending religious factions, weakened its unity and prepared the way for the Turkish conquest. Even to-day the name of the *Babuni*, as the Bulgarian Bogomiles were called, lingers in the Babuna mountains near Prilep, the scene of fighting between the Bulgarians and the Allies in the late war. Simultaneously with this important religious and social movement there arose a race of ascetic hermits, of whom the chief, John of Rila, became the patron saint of Bulgaria.

[1] Leo Diaconus, 124. Gibbon confused the site of this battle with the classic river Achelous.

Native of a village near Sofia and a simple herdsman, he lived for twenty years now in the hollow of an oak, now in a cave of the Rila mountains, an hour's climb above the famous monastery which bears his name. Here the pious Tsar Peter visited him, and here he died in 946. His body was removed by Peter to Sofia, but restored to Rila in 1469.

The last years of Peter's weak reign coincided with the great revival of Byzantine military power upon the accession of Nicephorus II Phocas. The Bulgarians had the tactlessness to demand from the conqueror of Crete, just returned from his triumphs in Asia, "the customary tribute" which Byzantium had paid to the strong Tsar Simeon. The victorious Emperor—so the historian of his reign[1] informs us—"although not easily moved to anger," was so greatly incensed at this impertinent demand that he raised his voice and exclaimed that "the Greeks must, indeed, be in a sorry plight, if, after defeating every enemy in arms, they were to pay tribute like slaves to a race of Scythians, poor and filthy to boot." Suiting the action to the word, he ordered the envoys to be beaten, and bade them tell their master that the most mighty Emperor of the Romans would forthwith visit his country and pay the tribute in person. When, however, the soldierly Emperor had seen with his own eyes what a difficult country Bulgaria was, he thought it imprudent to expose his own army to the risks which had befallen his namesake and predecessor in the Balkan passes. He therefore contented himself with taking a few frontier-forts, and invited the Russians, on payment of a subvention, to invade Bulgaria from the north and settle permanently there. Svyatoslav, the Russian Prince, was only too delighted to undertake this task. He landed in 967 at the mouth of the Danube, drove the Bulgarians back into Silistria, and took many of their towns. This Russian success made Nicephorus reflect that a Russian Bulgaria might be more dangerous to Constantinople than a weak native state—the same argument led to the Berlin treaty—so he offered to help the Bulgarians to expel his Russian allies, and requested that two Bulgarian princesses should be sent to Byzantium to be affianced to the sons of the late Emperor Romanus, one of whom was destined to be "the slayer of the Bulgarians." Peter sent the princesses and his two sons as hostages, but his death, the assassination of Nicephorus, and the withdrawal of the Russians in 969, menaced by the Patzinaks at home, ended this episode. The biblically-named sons of Shishman—David, Moses, Aaron, and Samuel—endeavoured to avail themselves of the absence of the lawful heir, Boris II, to reunite eastern and western Bulgaria under their dynasty, but the arrival of Boris frustrated their attempt. It was reserved for the new Byzantine Emperor, John I Tzimisces, to end the eastern Bulgarian Empire.

Svyatoslav had been so greatly charmed with the riches and fertility of Bulgaria that he returned there, no longer as a Byzantine ally but on his own account, preferring, as he said, to establish his throne on the

[1] Leo Diaconus, 61–63, 77–80; Cedrenus, II. 372.

Danube rather than at Kiev. He captured the Bulgarian capital and the Tsar, crossed the Balkans, took and impaled the inhabitants of Philippopolis, and bade the Greek government either pay him compensation or leave Europe. The warlike Armenian who sat on the Greek throne invaded Bulgaria in 971, traversed the unguarded Balkan passes, took Great Prêslav, and released Boris and his family from Russian captivity, saying that he had "come to avenge the Bulgarians for what they had suffered from the Russians." But when Silistria, the last Russian stronghold, fell, and the Russians had evacuated Bulgaria, Tzimisces deposed Boris and the Bulgarian Patriarch, and annexed eastern Bulgaria to the Byzantine Empire. Boris was compelled to divest himself of his regalia, and received a Byzantine court title; his brother was made an eunuch. Great Prêslav was rebaptized Ioannoúpolis after its conqueror; the eastern Bulgarian Empire was at an end. Western Bulgaria under the sons of Shishman remained, however, independent for 47 years longer. Of these four sons, the so-called *Comitopouloi* (or "Young Counts"), David was killed by some wandering Wallachs, Moses was slain while besieging Seres, and Aaron with most of his family was executed for his Greek sympathies by his remaining brother Samuel, who thus became sole Bulgarian Tsar. His realm, at the period of its greatest extent (before the Greek campaigns of 1000–1002), included a considerable part of Danubian Bulgaria, with the towns of Great Prêslav, Vidin, and Sofia, and much of Serbia and Albania, but was essentially Macedonian, and his capital, after a brief residence at Sofia, was moved to Moglena, Vodená, and Prespa (where an island in the lake still preserves the name of his "castle"), and finally to the lake of Ochrida, the swamps of which he drained by 100 canals into the river Drin.

Upon the death of Tzimisces in 976, the Bulgarians rose; both Boris II and his brother, Roman, escaped from Constantinople, but the former was shot by a Bulgarian in mistake for a Greek, while the latter, being harmless, received a post from Samuel, who overran Thrace, the country round Salonica, and Thessaly, and carried off from Larissa to his capital at Prespa the remains of St Achilleus, Bishop of Larissa in the time of Constantine the Great. The ruined monastery of the island of Ahil in the lake still preserves the memory of this translation. Samuel even marched into continental Greece and threatened the Peloponnese, but was recalled by the news that the young Emperor Basil II had invaded Bulgaria. The first of his Bulgarian campaigns, that of 981, ended, however, ingloriously for the future conqueror of the Bulgarians. Whilst on his way to besiege Sofia, he was defeated at Shtiponye near Ikhtiman and with difficulty escaped to Philippopolis. Fifteen years of peace between the hereditary enemies ensued, which Samuel employed in making war upon John Vladimir, the saintly Serbian Prince of Dioclea, in ravaging Dalmatia, and in occupying Durazzo. Bulgaria thus for a brief space—for Durazzo was soon recovered by the Greeks—became an

Adriatic power. The Serbian prince, carried captive to Prespa, won the heart of Samuel's daughter Kosara, who begged her father to release him and allow her to marry him. Samuel not only consented, but allowed him to return and rule over his conquered land.

In 996 began the second war between Basil II and the Bulgarians. Basil, free at last from the cares of the civil wars, had appointed Taronites governor of Salonica for the special purpose of checking Samuel's raids. The new governor, however, fell with his son into a Bulgarian ambush and was killed; whereupon Basil sent Nicephorus Uranus to take his place. Meanwhile Samuel, elated at his success, had marched again through the vale of Tempe as far as the Peloponnese, ravaging and plundering as he went. But this time he was not to return unscathed. On his way back Uranus waited for him on the bank of the swollen Spercheus, and, crossing in the night, fell upon the sleeping Bulgarian soldiers, who had believed it impossible to ford the river. Samuel and his son, Gabriel Radomir Roman, were wounded and only escaped capture by lying as if dead among the corpses which strewed the field, fleeing, when it was dark, to the passes of Pindus. From that moment Samuel's fortune turned. His next loss was that of Durazzo, betrayed to the Greeks by his father-in-law, the chief man of the place, and by the captive son of Taronites, who had obtained the affections of another of the Tsar's susceptible daughters, and had been allowed to marry her and had received a command at that important position. The Greeks everywhere took the offensive. In 1000 they entered and again subdued Danubian Bulgaria, taking Great and Little Prêslav and Pliska, which is now mentioned after a long interval. Next year Basil cleared the Bulgarian garrisons out of the south Macedonian towns of Berrhoea, Servia, and Vodená, and out of the Thessalian castles, removing them to Voleros at the mouth of the Maritza. To this campaign we owe the first description, which enlivens the prose of Cedrenus[1], of the waterfall of Vodená—the Tivoli of Macedonia. In 1002 Vidin and Skoplje fell, and Samuel, believing that the Vardar could not be crossed, once again nearly became the prisoner of the Greeks. Hostilities dragged on, and Basil for the next twelve years annually invaded the western Bulgarian Empire, which was now reduced to part of Macedonia, Albania, and the mountains round Sofia. But in 1014 the third and last Bulgarian war of the reign broke out. On 29 July Nicephorus Xiphías turned the strong Bulgarian position of Kleidíon ("the key") in the Struma valley, near the scene of King Constantine's victories over the Bulgarians 900 years later. Samuel escaped, thanks to his son's assistance, to Prilep, but Basil blinded the 15,000 Bulgarian captives, leaving one man in every hundred with one eye, so that he might guide his totally blinded comrades to tell the tale to the fugitive Tsar. Samuel fainted at the ghastly sight and two days later expired.

The western Bulgarian Empire survived him only four years. His

[1] II. 436, 447, 449–56.

son, Gabriel Roman, by a captive from Larissa succeeded him, but excelled him in physique alone. Barely a year later Gabriel was murdered by his cousin John Vladislav, Aaron's son, whose life he had begged his father to spare when Aaron and the rest of his family were put to death. The ungrateful wretch likewise assassinated his cousin's wife, blinded her eldest son, and invited the Serbian Prince, John Vladimir, to be his guest at Prespa and there had him beheaded. Having thus removed all possible rivals in his own family, the new Tsar began to treat with Basil, whose vassal he offered to become. Basil, mistrusting the murderer, marched upon his capital of Ochrida, blinding all the Bulgarians whom he took prisoners on the way. He captured Ochrida and was on his way to relieve Durazzo, which was invested by the Bulgarians, when a sudden defeat, inflicted upon a detachment of his army by the Bulgarian noble, Ivats, caused him to retire on Salonica. The Bulgarians continued to make a vigorous defence of their difficult country; Pernik successfully resisted a siege of 88 days; the Tsar even endeavoured to make an alliance with the Patzinaks from beyond the Danube against the Greeks. But he fell by an unknown hand while besieging Durazzo in 1018. Bulgaria, left without a head, was divided into two parties—one, headed by the widowed Tsaritsa Maria, the Patriarch David, and Bogdan, "the commander of the inner fortresses"; the other and weaker party, led by the late Tsar's son Fruyin, and the soldierly Ivats. Upon the news of the Tsar's death, Basil marched into Bulgaria to complete the subjection of the country. At Strumitsa the Patriarch met him with a letter from the Tsaritsa, offering on certain conditions to surrender Bulgaria. Bogdan was rewarded with a Byzantine title for his treachery, and then the Emperor proceeded to Ochrida, where he confiscated the rich treasury of the Tsars. In his camp outside there waited upon him the Tsaritsa with her six daughters and three of her sons, a bastard son of Samuel, and the five sons and two daughters of Gabriel Radomir Roman. The conqueror received her kindly, as well as the notables who made their submission. Her three other sons, however, of whom Fruyin was the most prominent, had fled to Mt. Tomor near Berat, where they endeavoured to maintain the independence of Bulgaria in the Albanian highlands, while Ivats held out in his castle of Pronishta in the same mountainous region. The young princes, however, were forced to surrender and compensated with court titles; the brave Ivats was treacherously seized and blinded. The last two nobles who still held out then surrendered. After nearly 40 years of fighting, Bulgaria was subdued.

The "Bulgar-slayer," as Basil II is known in history, celebrated his triumph in the noblest of all existing churches, the majestic Parthenon, then Our Lady of Athens. On his march he gazed upon the bleaching bones of the Bulgarians who had fallen by the Spercheus twenty-two years before, and upon the walls erected in the pass of Thermopylae to repel their invasions. The great cathedral he enriched with offerings out of the Bulgarian treasury, and 900 years later the Athenians were reminded of his triumph there. Thence he returned to Constantinople, where the ex-Tsaritsa, Samuel's daughters, and the rest of the Bulgarians were led through the Golden Gate before him.

BULGARIA A BYZANTINE PROVINCE (1018–1186).

Bulgaria remained for 168 years a Byzantine province. Her nobles had lost their leaders, her princes and princesses had disappeared amidst the pompous functionaries of the Byzantine Court. Only her Church remained autonomous, but that only on condition that the Patriarchate, which during the period of the western Bulgarian Empire had had its seat successively at Vodená, Prespa, and finally at Ochrida, was reduced to the rank of an Archbishopric. In 1020 Basil II issued three charters[1] confirming the rights of "the Archbishop of Bulgaria"—the additional title of "Justiniana Prima" was added in 1157—whose residence continued to be at Ochrida, whither it had been moved by Simeon. He expressly maintained intact the rights and area of its jurisdiction as it had been in the times of both Peter and Samuel, which therefore included 30 bishoprics and towns, such as Ochrida, Kastoria, Monastir, and Skoplje in Macedonia; Sofia and Vidin in old Bulgaria; Belgrade, Niš, Prizren, and Rasa in what is now Jugoslavia; Canina (above Avlona), Cheimarra, Butrinto, and Joánnina in South Albania and Northern Epirus; and Stagi (the modern Kalabaka) in Thessaly. We may therefore safely assume that in the palmy days of Peter and of Samuel these places were included within their respective Empires. In 1020 these thirty bishoprics contained 685 ecclesiastics and 655 serfs. But after Basil II's reign the number of the suffragans was reduced practically to what it had been in the time of Samuel, and after the first archbishop no more Bulgarians were appointed to the see of Ochrida during the Byzantine period. The head of the autonomous Bulgarian Church was always a Greek and often a priest from St Sophia itself, except on one occasion when a Jew was nominated, and the list includes the distinguished theologian and letter-writer, Theophylact of Euboea, who felt as an exile his separation from culture in the wilds of Bulgaria, and John Camaterus, afterwards Ecumenical Patriarch at the time of the Latin conquest of Constantinople. The Bogomile heresy made great progress during this period, especially round Philippopolis, despite its persecution by the Emperor Alexius I. For the civil and military administration of Bulgaria a new (Bulgarian) theme was created under a Pronoetes[2] and also a duchy of Paristrium, while the neighbouring themes had their territory enlarged. The various governors, holding office usually for only a year, made as much out of their districts as possible in the customary Oriental fashion; but the local communities retained a considerable measure of autonomy, and we

[1] *BZ.* II. 40–72. [2] Cf. *infra*, Chapter XXIII, p. 733.

are expressly told that Basil left the taxes as they had been in the time of Samuel, payable in kind.

The Bulgarians did not, however, remain inactive during this long period of Byzantine rule. A succession of weak rulers and court intrigues followed the death of Basil "the Bulgar-slayer." The Bulgarian prince Fruyin, and his mother the ex-Tsaritsa, were mixed up in these intrigues, both imprisoned in monasteries, and the former blinded. In 1040 a more serious movement arose. Simultaneous insurrections broke out among the Serbs of what is now Montenegro and the Bulgarians, who found a leader in a certain Peter Delyan, who gave himself out to be a son of the Tsar Gabriel Radomir Roman. Greeted enthusiastically as Tsar, he had the country at his feet, so lively was the memory of the old dynasty. But a rival appeared in the person of the warlike Tikhomir, who was acclaimed Tsar by the Slavs of Durazzo. Delyan invited his rival and the Bulgarians that were with him to a meeting, at which he told them that "one bush could not nourish two redbreasts," and bade them choose between Tikhomir and the grandson of Samuel, promising to abide loyally by their decision. Loud applause greeted his speech; the people stoned Tikhomir and proclaimed Delyan their sole sovereign. He marched upon Salonica, whence the Emperor Michael IV the Paphlagonian fled, while his chamberlain, Ivats, perhaps a son of the Bulgarian patriot, went over with his war chest to the insurgents. One Bulgarian army took Durazzo; another invaded Greece and defeated the imperial forces before Thebes; the entire province of Nicopolis (except Naupactus) joined the Bulgarians, infuriated at the exactions of the Byzantine tax-collector and at the substitution, by the unpopular finance minister, John, the Emperor's brother, of cash payments for payments in kind. But another Bulgarian leader now appeared in the person of Alusian, younger brother of the Tsar John Vladislav, and Delyan's cousin, whom the grasping minister's greed had also driven to revolt. Delyan wisely offered to share the first place with this undoubted scion of the stock of Shishman—for his own claims to the blood royal were impugned. But a great defeat of the Bulgarians before Salonica, which was ascribed to the intervention of that city's patron saint, St Demetrius, led to recriminations and suspicions. Alusian invited his rival to a banquet, made him drunk, and blinded him. The double-dyed traitor then betrayed his country to the Emperor, the revolt was speedily crushed, and Delyan and Ivats were led in triumph to Constantinople.

Another Bulgarian rising took place in 1073, and from the same cause—the exactions of the imperial treasury, which continued to ignore the wise practice of Basil II and the lessons of the last rebellion. Having no prominent leader of their own to put on the throne, the Bulgarian chiefs begged Michael, first King of the Serbian state of Dioclea, to send them his son, Constantine Bodin, whom they proclaimed "Tsar of the Bulgarians" at Prizren under the popular name of Peter, formerly borne by Simeon's saintly son. But there was a party among the Bulgarians hostile to what was doubtless regarded as a foreign movement; the insurgents made the mistake, after their initial successes, of dividing their forces, and were defeated at Paun ("the peacock" castle) on the historic field of Kossovo, where Bodin was taken prisoner. Frankish mercenaries in Byzantine employ completed the destruction by burning down the palace of the Tsars on the island in the lake of Prespa and sacking the church of St Achilleus. Worse still were the frequent raids of the Patzinaks and Cumans, while Macedonia was the theatre of the Norman invasion. But, except for occasional and quickly suppressed risings of Bulgarians and Bogomiles, there was no further serious insurrection for over 100 years. Under the Comnenian dynasty the Bulgarians were better governed, and they lacked local leaders to face a series of energetic Emperors.

CHAPTER IX.

THE GREEK CHURCH: ITS RELATIONS WITH THE WEST UP TO 1054.

After the festival in honour of the restoration of the images (11 March 843), the last religious differences between the East and West seemed to have disappeared, and yet the course of events during the Iconoclast controversy had seriously modified the conditions under which the relations between Rome and Constantinople had been hitherto maintained.

The Papacy emerged from that long dispute completely emancipated politically from the Byzantine Empire. After the accession of Paul I (757) the Pope no longer applied to the Emperor of Constantinople for the ratification of his election but to the King of the Franks, and after the year 800 to the Emperor of the West. After Pope Hadrian the year of the reign of the Eastern Emperors no longer appears in the papal bulls, and nothing is more significant than this breaking with an ancient tradition[1].

It cannot be disputed that after the second Council of Nicaea (787), held in the presence of the papal legates, relations had been renewed between Rome and Constantinople, which continued until the second abolition of image-worship (815). But neither the Empress Irene nor her successors dreamt of revoking the edict of Leo the Isaurian which had deprived the Roman Church of its patrimony in the East and of its jurisdiction over Southern Italy and Illyricum. A still more illuminating fact is that, when the Empress Theodora restored image-worship in 843, she did not treat with the Pope as Irene had done, and the new Patriarch Methodius ordered the anathema to be launched against the iconoclasts without the co-operation of Rome.

Two distinct and opposed attitudes towards the Pope may, in fact, be seen in the Greek Church. On the one hand the superior clergy, largely recruited from among laymen, ex-governors or high officials, steeped in the doctrines of Caesaropapism, could not shew much enthusiasm and indeed felt considerable misgivings towards a pontiff who, since the events of the year 800, had been the mainstay of the Emperors of the West,

[1] Kleinclausz, *L'empire carolingien, ses origines et ses transformations*, Paris, 1902, p. 165.

regarded at Byzantium as usurpers. A large number of these prelates had adhered to iconoclast doctrines, and in 843 many of them tried to obliterate this past by a reconciliation with orthodoxy.

On the other hand, these high official clergy were confronted by the monks, and especially the Studites, who had defended image-worship even to martyrdom, and were resolute opponents to the interference of the Emperors in the affairs of the Church. Their fundamental doctrine was complete liberty as against the State in matters of dogma no less than of discipline. But the one effective guarantee of this liberty for them was the close union of the Greek Church with Rome. They recognised in the successor to St Peter the spiritual authority denied to the Emperor. Theodore of Studion, in his correspondence with the Popes and sovereigns, emphasises the necessity of submitting to the arbitration of the Pope all the difficulties which may perplex the Church[1], and for a long time the monastery of Studion was considered the stronghold of the Roman party at Byzantium.

For these reasons the restoration of image-worship in 843, even if it was an undeniable victory for the Studites, was not so complete a success as they had wished, and the Patriarch Methodius, himself formerly a monk but animated by a conciliatory spirit and desirous above all things of restoring peace in the Church, made several vigorous attacks on their uncompromising policy. On the other side, the elevation to the Patriarchate in 846 of Ignatius, son of the Emperor Michael Rangabé, who during his brief reign had been the protector and almost the servant of the Studites, seemed to assure definitely the triumph of their doctrines. Brought up in exile on Princes Islands, Ignatius was a true ascetic and had fervently embraced all the principles of Studite reform. Friendly relations with Rome seemed therefore assured, but a significant incident shewed that the new Patriarch, however well disposed he might be towards the Pope, did not propose to abandon one jot of his autonomy. Gregory Asbestas, Archbishop of Syracuse, having taken refuge at Constantinople, was condemned by a synod for certain irregularities. He appealed to Pope Leo IV, who commanded Ignatius to send him the acts of the synod; the Patriarch refused, and the matter remained unsettled. Benedict III, who succeeded Leo IV in 899, refused to confirm the deposition of Gregory Asbestas and contented himself with suspending him until he had seen the evidence[2]. Thus, though the relations between Rome and Constantinople had once more become normal and the good will of Ignatius and the Studites towards the Pope was manifestly great, the long separation due to the Iconoclastic dispute had borne fruit; the Greek Church had become accustomed to complete autonomy, so far as Rome went, and its bishops, who fostered feelings of distrust and even hostility against her, only awaited an opportunity to shew them. The crisis in

[1] MPG, XCIX. cols. 141, 1017, 1020, 1192, 1332.

[2] Bury, *History of the Eastern Roman Empire*, pp. 184–185.

the Patriarchate, which was the result of the deposition of Ignatius, soon supplied them with the desired opportunity.

Ignatius had made many enemies for himself by his uncompromising character and his unbending austerity, which did not spare those who held the highest places. In 858 he dared to attack the Caesar Bardas, whose profligacy was a public scandal, and refused to administer the sacrament to him. Bardas avenged this insult by banishing Ignatius to the island of Terebinthus, after having implicated him in an imaginary plot against the Emperor (27 November 858). Then, being unable to extort from him an act of abdication, and without even waiting for the result of the trial which was pending, Bardas raised to the patriarchal throne a layman, the *protoasecretis* Photius, one of the most renowned teachers in the University of Constantinople.

Photius, if we can believe his letters[1], appears to have hesitated at first to accept the post, but ended by allowing himself to be persuaded, and within six days was professed a monk and received all the ecclesiastical orders. On 25 December 858 he was consecrated Patriarch in St Sophia. He represented the party of the high clergy which had adopted once more the tradition of Tarasius, Nicephorus, and Methodius, and he met at once with violent opposition from the monks, especially from the Studites, whose Abbot Nicholas of Studion refused to take the communion with him, and was banished[2]. He therefore thought it expedient to consolidate his power by a reconciliation with Rome. In 860 a solemn embassy, consisting of four bishops and a high lay official, was sent to Pope Nicholas. Its object was to invite the Pope to assemble a council to settle the dispute as to image-worship, and more especially to obtain the papal recognition of Photius as lawful Patriarch. This step in itself shews that Photius at that time accepted generally the jurisdiction of the Pope.

But Nicholas I refused to recognise the election of Photius without fuller information, and, after protesting against the deposition of Ignatius, he despatched to Constantinople two legates, Radoald, Bishop of Porto, and Zacharias, Bishop of Anagni, with instructions to hold an inquiry and to treat Ignatius provisionally as lawful Patriarch. No efforts were spared at Constantinople to conceal this news. The legates as soon as they arrived (February 861) were secluded and prevented from communicating with Ignatius and his partisans. Pressure was brought to bear on them by threats and even by bribes. They allowed themselves to be persuaded and, contrary to their instructions, they consented to preside at a council which was convened at the Holy Apostles (May 861), and pronounced the deposition of Ignatius, after suborned witnesses had been

[1] Loparev, *Byzantine lives of the saints of the eighth and ninth centuries* (*Vizantiyski Vremennik*, XVIII. 1913, p. 49).

[2] *Vita S. Nicolai Studitae* (MPG, CV. col. 863; cf. Loparev, *Vizantiyski Vremennik*, XVII. p. 189).

produced to affirm that the accused had been elected contrary to the canons[1].

But when the legates returned to Rome, loaded with presents from Photius, the Pope received them with indignation and repudiated all their acts. In an encyclical addressed to the three Eastern Patriarchs he declared that the deposition of Ignatius was illegal and that Photius improperly held the see of Constantinople. In answer to a letter from Photius, brought by an imperial secretary, in which the Patriarch seemed to treat with him on equal terms, the Pope reminded him that the see of Rome was the supreme head of all the Churches. Finally, at the request of some partisans of Ignatius, including the Archimandrite Theognostus, who had succeeded in escaping to Rome, he called a council at the Lateran palace (April 863), which summoned Photius to resign all his powers on pain of excommunication; the same injunction was laid on all the bishops consecrated by Photius[2].

The dispute thus entered the domain of law, and the issue at stake was the jurisdiction of the Pope over the Church at Constantinople. Before taking the final step and embarking on schism, Photius seems to have hesitated and to have adopted diplomatic means at first. He induced the Emperor Michael to write a letter to the Pope, which was in the nature of an ultimatum. The Emperor threatened to march on Rome in the event of Nicholas refusing to revoke his sentences, and repudiated the doctrine of the supreme jurisdiction of the papacy. Nicholas, making the widest concessions, offered to revise the judgment of the council if Ignatius and Photius would consent to appear before him at Rome[3]. Photius, on his side, was fully posted in Western affairs, and knew that the uncompromising character of Nicholas roused keen opposition in those parts. He had favourably received a memorandum from the Archbishops of Cologne and Trèves, who had been deposed by the Pope for having consented to the divorce of Lothar II. In the course of the year 863 Photius addressed letters to the Western clergy and to the Emperor Louis II to demand the deposition of Nicholas by a Council of the Church[4]. This was not yet rupture with the West, since by acting as he did he hoped to find a more conciliatory Pope than Nicholas. Nevertheless, when he learned of the arrival of Roman legates in Bulgaria, considering their interference with this newly-founded Church as an encroachment on the rights of the Patriarchate, he convoked a synod (867), which formally condemned the Latin uses introduced into the Bulgarian Church, and more particularly the double procession of the Holy Ghost. This was the first step in an antagonism which was destined to end in schism.

[1] Mansi, *Concilia,* xv. 179–202. *Vita Ignatii* 19–21 (MPG, cv. col. 488).

[2] Nicolaus, *Epist.* 7 (Mansi, *Concilia,* xv. col. 178–183).

[3] Nicolaus, *Epist.* 8 (Mansi, *Concilia,* xv. 187–216).

[4] Bury, *Eastern Roman Empire,* p. 200. Gay, *L'Italie méridionale et l'empire byzantin,* pp. 80–82.

Matters came rapidly to a head. In November 866 the Pope resolved to address a final appeal to Constantinople, and despatched fresh legates with orders to put letters into the hands of the Emperor and principal personages of the court. Photius then took the decisive step, and it is possible that this decision was influenced by the raising of Basil to the imperial throne as colleague to Michael after the murder of Bardas. He wished to confront the future Emperor, whose hostility he anticipated, with an accomplished fact. In the course of the summer of 867 a council presided over by the Emperor Michael pronounced the excommunication of Pope Nicholas, declared the practices of the Roman Church to be heretical as opposed to Greek use, and stigmatised the intervention of that Church in the affairs of Constantinople as unlawful. The resolutions of the council were sent by Photius to the Eastern Patriarchs in the form of an encyclical, in which he bitterly condemned all the peculiar usages of the Western Churches: the addition of the *Filioque* to the creed, the Saturday fast, the use of eggs in Lent, the custom of the clergy of shaving the beard, and others. Two bishops went to take the acts of the council to Italy. The Pope, desirous of justifying Western uses, commanded Hincmar, Archbishop of Rheims, to convoke provincial councils in order to answer the objections of the Greeks[1].

The split between the East and the West was thus effected. It is clear that the differences in the uses quoted by Photius were not the real cause of the schism. From the dogmatic point of view the East and the West participated in the same faith, that of the Ecumenical Councils. The addition of the *Filioque* to the creed modified in appearance the idea which was formed of the relations between the Persons of the Trinity, but in no respect changed the dogma itself. It was not impossible, as indeed subsequent events shewed, to come to some agreement as to Church discipline and the liturgy. At the close of the year 867 the two apostles of the Slavs, Constantine (Cyril), a pupil of Photius, and his brother Methodius, arrived at Rome, bringing with them the relics of St Clement. Pope Nicholas was dead and it was his successor Hadrian II who consecrated them bishops (5 January 868) and, by giving the name of Cyril to Constantine, paid homage to the great Patriarch of Alexandria who had formerly been the connecting link between the East and Rome. He further approved the translation of the Scriptures made by the two apostles, as well as their liturgy in the Slavonic tongue[2]. No act shews more clearly the conciliatory spirit of the two Churches in the matter of uses. The cause of the separation cannot therefore be found here, but must be attributed to the regard for its autonomy which inspired

[1] Among the answers are quoted those of Odo, Bishop of Beauvais, and Aeneas, Bishop of Paris. Text of the Encyclical of Photius, MPG, CII. cols. 724–731. See Hefele, *Histoire des Conciles* (French translation by Leclercq, 1911), vol. IV. pp. 442–449.

[2] Leger, *Cyrille et Méthode*, pp. 100–103. Cf. *supra*, Chapter VII(B), pp. 224–5.

the Church of Constantinople. Photius, by championing this cause, easily led with him the bishops who, like himself, refused to admit the supreme jurisdiction of the Pope in disciplinary matters. We shall further see that even on this question the Greeks were far from being obstinate, and admitted the intervention of the Pope when it served their interests. Their attitude towards Rome was, in reality, always dependent on the vicissitudes of their own disputes.

It was a palace revolution in the end which overthrew Photius and revived relations with Rome. Some months after the council held by the Patriarch, the murder of Michael III brought Basil the Macedonian to the throne. The new Emperor disliked Photius, possibly because he had been a favourite of Bardas. He saw also that the re-instatement of Ignatius, whom the people esteemed a martyr, would conduce to his own personal popularity. The very day after his accession (25 September 867) he had Photius imprisoned in a monastery, and with great ceremony re-instated Ignatius in the patriarchal chair (23 November 867). All the bishops and archimandrites exiled by Photius were recalled[1].

Thus to obtain his political ends Basil formally recognised a jurisdiction in the Pope by sending him a double embassy composed of partisans of Ignatius and of Photius, with instructions to ask him to re-establish peace in the Church of Constantinople by calling a council and effecting a reconciliation with the bishops consecrated by Photius. In a synod held at St Peter's, at the close of the year 868, Pope Hadrian II, the successor of Nicholas I, solemnly condemned the council of 867 and convoked a council at Constantinople. Stephen, Bishop of Nepi, Donatus, Bishop of Ostia, and a priest, Marinus, were chosen to represent him there.

After a difficult journey the legates entered Constantinople by the Golden Gate on 29 September 869. Basil received them with the greatest honours, and testified in their presence to his veneration for the Church of Rome, "the mother of all the other Churches." But it was manifest from the very first sittings of the Council, which opened on 9 October 869 and took the title of Ecumenical, that a misunderstanding existed between the Emperor and the legates. The Emperor, solicitous for the interests of the State, wished first and foremost to re-establish peace in the Church. He had been surprised to see that, differing from Nicholas I, Pope Hadrian II had condemned Photius unheard and on the sole evidence of the partisans of Ignatius. In order that the peace might be permanent, and to prevent Photius and his followers from being able to plead an abuse of justice, it was necessary that the Council should revise the sentence and deliver a full and detailed judgment. This was the purport of the instructions given to the Patrician Baanes, president of the lay commission which represented the Emperor at the Council. The Pope's standpoint was quite different. His legates had only been instructed by him to

[1] Vogt, *Basile I*, pp. 210–212. Loparev, *Byzantine lives of the saints of the eighth and ninth centuries* (*Vizantiyski Vremennik*, vol. XVIII. p. 61).

publish the sentence against Photius, pronounced by his predecessor and confirmed by him. They had the further duty of reconciling with the Church those bishops, followers of Photius, who should consent to sign the *libellus satisfactionis* brought by them. The jurisdiction of the Pope, differently understood in the East and the West, was the real matter at issue[1].

Baanes won an initial success by demanding that Photius and his followers should be brought before the Council to tender their defence there. On 20 October Photius appeared, but remained mute to all interrogations. His condemnation was then renewed, but the legates observed that they were not re-trying the case but were merely publishing the sentence already formulated. Basil accepted this compromise, which was tantamount to a defeat for him, and came in person to preside at the concluding sessions of the Council, which broke up on 28 February 870.

Thus the Ecumenical Council, which was intended to smooth all the religious difficulties, only ended in increasing the distrust between Rome and Constantinople. Basil certainly lavished friendly words and assurances of orthodoxy on the legates at the ceremony which marked the closing of the Council, but his acts discounted his speeches. Some days previously, to gratify the old partisans of Photius who regretted having signed the *libellus satisfactionis*, he had seized all the copies of that document at the house of the legates in spite of their protests but then consented to allow them to be deposited with Anastasius the Librarian, ambassador of the Emperor Louis II at Constantinople. Further, this scholar was requested by the legates to compare the Greek and Latin texts of the acts of the Council, when he perceived with astonishment that a letter of Pope Hadrian had been tampered with, and that the compliments which he paid to the Emperor Louis II had been suppressed[2].

The most grave incident occurred three days after the close of the Council. The Bulgarians had received baptism from the Greek missionaries sent by Photius, but their Tsar Boris, whose ambition was to see an ecclesiastical hierarchy founded in Bulgaria with a Patriarch at its head, being unable to obtain it from Constantinople, had applied to Rome. Nicholas I had sent a mission to Bulgaria under the direction of Formosus, Bishop of Porto, who replaced the Greek ritual everywhere by the Latin, and Photius had on other occasions protested against this interference. But when Boris called upon the Pope to create Formosus Patriarch, he met with a flat refusal. Then it was that, turning to Constantinople, he sent an embassy to implore the Council to decide to which Church Bulgaria should belong.

The Emperor assembled once more the fathers of the Council and tried to obtain from the legates the formal recognition of the jurisdiction of the Patriarch of Constantinople over Bulgaria. The legates protested

[1] Vogt, *Basile I*, pp. 215–218.
[2] Vogt, *op. cit.* pp. 218–227.

vehemently that they had not received any instructions on this point, and that Bulgaria was besides directly amenable to the see of Rome. Hardly, however, had the legates left when the Patriarch Ignatius consecrated an archbishop and ten bishops for Bulgaria. Photius would not have acted otherwise, and nothing shews more clearly than this affair the inherited misunderstanding which separated the leaders of the two Churches[1].

When the legates took leave of the Emperor, so strained were the relations that Basil was mean enough not to make any arrangements for facilitating their return. Their journey, which lasted nine months, was most arduous: they were captured by Slav pirates and lost all their archives, and only reached Rome on 22 December 870. By good fortune Anastasius the Librarian, who had embarked for the same destination, had safely brought the acts of the Council and the copies of the *libellus satisfactionis*. Hadrian II wrote an indignant letter to Basil, in which he complained of the manner in which his legates had been treated on their return and also of the interference of Ignatius in Bulgaria; but nothing came of it, and the Bulgarian Church remained definitely attached to Constantinople. Finally, as a mark of his dissatisfaction, the Pope refused to pardon the followers of Photius for whom the Emperor had interceded.

But soon, by the usual reversal of Byzantine opinion, Photius, who had been imprisoned in a monastery, succeeded in regaining the good graces of Basil and was recalled to Constantinople[2]. Ignatius continued to govern the Church, but three days after his death, which took place on 23 October 877, Photius was re-instated on the patriarchal throne, and, according to the *Vita Ignatii*, he began by banishing and ill-treating the principal adherents of Ignatius. But what was to be his attitude towards Rome? Logically he ought to have refrained from any relations with the Pope. He did nothing of the kind, and asked Pope John VIII to recognise his re-instatement. The Emperor, who supported this request, had evidently no wish for a rupture with Rome, and placed at the same time his fleet at the disposal of the Pope to defend Italy against the Saracens.

The circumstances were therefore favourable for the union. John VIII consented to recognise Photius as Patriarch on condition that he should ask pardon before a synod for his past conduct and should abstain from any interference in Bulgaria. A council then opened at Constantinople in November 879, but Basil, overwhelmed with sorrow at the loss of his only legitimate son, Constantine, was not present and did not even send a representative. Photius, having thus a free hand, easily outwitted the legates, who were ignorant of Greek and were unaware that the Pope's

[1] Vogt, *op. cit.* pp. 223–230.

[2] According to the *Vita Ignatii*, 52 and *Symeon Magister*, VII. 752, he won the favour of the Emperor by forging a genealogy which connected the family of Basil with the Armenian dynasties.

letter, translated into that language, had been garbled. The Patriarch gave a lengthy defence of his conduct and was rapturously applauded by the 383 bishops present. The question of the Bulgarian Church was referred to the decision of the Emperor; the council refused to admit the prohibition, desired by the Pope, of nominating laymen to the episcopate; finally, by pronouncing the anathema against all who should add anything to the faith of Nicaea, it once more brought up the question of the *Filioque*[1].

Photius had triumphed; it was only three years later, in 882, that the Pope, thanks to an inquiry made by a new legate, Marinus, who was sent to Constantinople, learned what had really happened at the council. John VIII in indignation declared the legates of 879 deposed, and excommunicated Photius. The rupture was complete, and the two Churches were thus separated by a new schism, which persisted under John's successors, Marinus, Hadrian III, and Stephen V, who exchanged letters full of recriminations with Basil.

The death of Basil in 886 was followed by an astonishing *coup de théâtre*, and Photius was once more disgraced. Leo VI, the heir to the throne, who passed for an illegitimate son of Michael III and Eudocia Ingerina, was fired with an intense hatred of Photius. Although he had been his pupil, he had quarrelled with him. He charged him with having intrigued with Basil to deprive him of the throne, and there was even talk at Byzantium that the ambitious Patriarch had contemplated either himself assuming the imperial throne or giving it to one of his relations[2]. The fact remains that Leo VI had hardly attained to power before he pronounced the deposition of Photius. The strategus Andrew and the superintendent of the posts, John Hagiopolites, were commanded to go to St Sophia, where the synod had been assembled. They read out a long recital of all the crimes of which Photius was accused; the Patriarch was then stripped of his episcopal vestments and conducted to a monastery, where he lived for another five years (886–891). An assembly of bishops elected Stephen, the Emperor's brother, as Patriarch[3].

At the same time one of Photius' principal followers, Theodore Santabarenus, was arrested in his diocese of Euchaita, conducted to Constantinople, and put into solitary confinement. The Emperor tried to induce him to accuse Photius of plotting against him, but when confronted with the ex-Patriarch the abbot revealed nothing. Leo VI was furious and ordered him to be scourged and banished first to Athens, where his eyes were put out, and thence to the eastern frontier.

Photius thus came out of the struggle apparently defeated, and left the Greek Church more rent asunder than at his accession. Some hagiographic documents drawn up at this period throw strong light on the

[1] Vogt, *op. cit.* pp. 239–244.
[2] Vogt, *op. cit.* p. 249.
[3] Mansi, *Concilia,* XVIII. 201.

divided attitude of the Greek clergy towards the question of relations with Rome. The author of the life of St Joseph the Hymn-writer, Theophanes the Sicilian, who wrote in the last years of the ninth century, when nearing the end of his work, prays the saint to ask Christ for the cessation of the disputes and for the restoration of peace in the Church, and later he vehemently urges Joseph to obtain by his prayers the boon that orthodoxy remain inviolate[1]. Such was indisputably the desire of a large part of the Greek clergy, and of the monks of Studion in particular, whose *Igumen*, Anthony, had passed almost the whole patriarchate of Photius in exile.

On the other hand, the life of St Euthymius the Younger of Thessalonica strikes a somewhat different note. The author, Basil, Archbishop of Thessalonica, admittedly a supporter of Photius, gives a brief but very partisan account of the vicissitudes of the struggle between Photius and Ignatius, and throws all the responsibility for the schism onto the imperial policy. If he abstains from attacking Ignatius, he none the less considers Photius to be a saint. "The Iconoclast heresy," he says, "was already extinct. St Methodius after having governed the Church for five years had returned to the Lord. Ignatius the Holy had been raised to the episcopal throne of Constantinople. He governed it for ten years.... In consequence of the persecutions of those who then reigned he left his throne and his Church, the one voluntarily, the other under compulsion. He retired to a monastery and published an act of abdication....The news of this forced abdication soon spread, and in consequence many refused to take communion with the new Patriarch. The very holy Nicholas [of Studion], not wishing to have any dealings with him, preferred to leave his monastery, the new Patriarch being orthodox and invested with all virtues. This was the blessed Photius, the torch (τοῦ φωτός) whose rays illuminated the ends of the earth".[2] Then follows a eulogy of Photius and his incomparable life, and an account of his miracles.

This curious testimony gives us the version of the events which had been prepared by the adherents of Photius. It shews us the deep impression which this man, who had nothing of the apostle in him but was first and foremost a politician and a diplomatist, had produced by his intrepidity. He had posed as a champion of orthodoxy against Rome, and had thus bequeathed to his successors a formidable weapon which was destined to render any new agreement between the two Churches unstable and precarious.

Immediately after the deposition of Photius, Leo VI had opened negotiations with the Pope for the re-establishment of religious union, but it was only twelve years later, in 898, that any agreement was reached. The chief difficulty was the question of the bishops consecrated by Photius,

[1] Loparev, *Byzantine lives of the saints of the eighth and ninth centuries* (*Vizantiyski Vremennik*, vol. XVIII. p. 6).

[2] *Ib.* vol. XIX. pp. 101–102.

whose powers the Popes refused to recognise. The Popes, Stephen V (885–891), Formosus (891–896), Boniface VI, Stephen VI, Romanus, Theodore II, all refused any concession. In the end an agreement was reached between Pope John IX and the Patriarch Anthony Cauleas, a former monk of Olympus in Bithynia (898). A general amnesty was proclaimed and concord reigned once more in the Church. Normal relations revived between Rome and Constantinople[1]. Important evidence on this point is supplied by Philotheus the *atriclines* in the work which he has left on the ceremonial of the imperial court under the title of *Kleterologion*. He mentions the arrival at Constantinople in 898 of the papal legates, Bishop Nicholas and Cardinal John, and he gives the interesting detail that in the course of the ancient ceremonies they took precedence of the first order of civil dignitaries, the magistri[2]. Another passage of the same work proves that a permanent papal embassy was re-established at Constantinople. The order of precedence at the imperial table was fixed thus: after the magistri comes the "syncellus of Rome," then that of Constantinople, followed by those of the Eastern Patriarchs[3].

Peace seemed therefore definitely restored, but Leo VI intended to employ this alliance with Rome for the furtherance of his personal aims, and thus to violate the conditions of the agreement. As had already happened under Constantine VI, it was the private conduct of the Emperor which stirred up new dissensions in the Church.

After divorcing Theophano in 893, Leo VI married Zoë, daughter of Stylianus; then on the death of Zoë he married Eudocia Baiane in 889. This third marriage was disapproved by the clergy, since the laws against third marriages, sanctioned even by Leo himself in his Novels, were very strict. But the crowning scandal was when, after the death of Eudocia in 901, it was rumoured that the Emperor proposed to take as his fourth wife his mistress Zoë, "the black-eyed." So great was the indignation that plots were hatched for dethroning the Emperor, and in 902 he narrowly escaped assassination in the church of St Mocius. The Patriarch Nicholas Mysticus was consulted, but flatly refused his approval. When, however, Zoë gave birth to a son, the future Constantine Porphyrogenitus, the Patriarch and the bishops consented to baptise the child, if the Emperor undertook not to live any longer with the mother. The baptism took place with much ceremony in St Sophia on 6 January 906; three days later Leo VI violated his promise and had his marriage with Zoë celebrated by a clerk of his chapel. The bishops immediately forbade Leo to enter the churches, and he appealed to the judgment of the Pope and the Eastern Patriarchs.

Sergius III, who then occupied the pontifical throne, an unworthy creature of Theophylact and of Theodora, returned a favourable answer

[1] Mansi, *Concilia*, vol. XVIII. col. 101.
[2] *De Cerimoniis*, II. 52 (MPG, CXII. col. 1293–1299).
[3] *Ib.* (MPG, CXXII. col. 1341).

to Leo VI. On these tidings the Patriarch Nicholas Mysticus, who appeared at first to have sought some means of solving the difficulties, openly declared against the Emperor. On Christmas Day, in the presence of the whole court, he forbade the Emperor to enter St Sophia (25 December 906).

Leo VI lost no time in revenging himself on Nicholas Mysticus, implicated in the conspiracy of Andronicus Ducas, who had fled to the Saracens. Secret correspondence between the Patriarch and the rebel was seized. On 6 January 907, the Feast of the Epiphany, when the Patriarch had once more forbidden the Emperor to enter the church, Leo yielded, but at the imperial banquet which followed the ceremony he violently harangued Nicholas Mysticus, and in the presence of all the metropolitans taxed him with treason. At that moment the Roman legates arrived at Constantinople. Nicholas refused any dealings with them, but a considerable section of the bishops abandoned him. The synod released the Emperor from all ecclesiastical penalties, and Nicholas Mysticus, compelled to abdicate his office, was sent to a monastery in Asia. Euthymius was appointed Patriarch, and the rival headship divided the Greek Church; several bishops were banished or imprisoned. On 9 June 911 Euthymius anointed the son of Zoë, Constantine Porphyrogenitus, Emperor.

Seized with remorse in his last moments, Leo VI reinstalled Nicholas Mysticus on the patriarchal throne, and gave orders that Euthymius should be deposed (911). His brother Alexander now became sole Emperor, and chafing at the obscurity in which he had been kept, did his best also to reverse all that had been done in the previous reign. Zoë was driven from the palace, Euthymius struck in the face in the presence of the Emperor, and Nicholas Mysticus solemnly re-instated. His first care was to send to Pope Anastasius a memorandum in which he traduced the character of Leo VI, blamed the weakness of Sergius III, whom his legates had misled, and claimed reparation for the scandal. On the death of Alexander, 6 June 912, the Patriarch, being marked out as head of the council of regency for the young Constantine Porphyrogenitus, was all-powerful for several months. In October 913 Zoë succeeded in ousting him from the government, but could not induce Euthymius to resume his office.

Subsequent events in which Byzantium was engrossed for seven years, war with the Bulgarians, the revolt and coronation of Romanus Lecapenus, caused the affair of Leo's fourth marriage to sink into the background. It was only in 920 that Nicholas Mysticus, probably instigated by Romanus Lecapenus, petitioned Pope John X to send new legates to Constantinople. The *entente* with Rome was restored. The memory of Euthymius, who had died in the interval, was vindicated. In the presence of the Emperors Romanus and Constantine, Nicholas Mysticus solemnly promulgated a *tomus unionis*, reconciling the two parties. Leo's good name was sacrificed for this agreement; he was declared absolved on special conditions, and the Church stigmatised in severe terms the fourth and even the third marriage[1].

Peace then seemed to reign once more between Rome and Constantinople, and the Greek Church had again accepted the arbitration of the Pope. But the excessive leniency of the Court of Rome towards Leo VI by no means increased its prestige. On the other hand the Emperor had set an example which could not be lost on his successors. The alliance with the Pope had only been a device for calming the agitation produced by his fourth marriage. The same Emperor who had written letters to Rome emphasising his zeal for the See of St Peter, had addressed to his people veritable homilies in which he savagely attacked the doctrine of the double Procession of the Holy Ghost[2], a policy hardly likely to conduce to a lasting peace. And so it turned out; the relations between the two Churches were constantly dominated by the political affairs of Byzantium at home and abroad.

Except for the ephemeral schism of Sergius, concord existed officially between the two Churches for 134 years, from 920–1054. It must be added that this concord was real. This is the impression produced, if the official relations are neglected and only those of the ordinary members of the two Churches are considered. It may safely be said that the large majority of the Westerners and of the Greeks dreaded schism, and that the two parties, far from mutual hatred and excommunication, considered themselves members of the same Church. The influx of Eastern monks into Rome, Italy, and the entire West at this period, episodes such as the reception of St Nilus at Monte Cassino and his establishment at Grotta Ferrata (1004), the numerous Western pilgrims passing through Constantinople and the cordial welcome they received there, shew conclusively that the faithful of the two cults were animated with a true spirit of charity one towards the other and did not attach too great importance to the difference in their customs[3]. Neither of them desired schism; it was their pastors and princes, not they themselves, who were solely responsible for it.

But however favourable the circumstances were for the union, it was during this period that the definitive separation was prepared. Not that the causes of divergence were multiplied, but historic events modified the situation and favoured the rupture.

First of all, there was the diminishing prestige of Rome. After the end of the ninth century feudal anarchy attacked the Church and did not spare even the throne of St Peter. The Papacy became a fief for which the barons of the Roman Campagna disputed. It was the sinister epoch

[1] Hergenröther, *Photius*, vol. III. p. 684; *Epistolae Nicolai Mystici*, MPG, CXI. col. 276.

[2] Leo VI, *Oratio de Spiritu Sancto*, MPG, CVII. col. 131.

[3] L. Bréhier, *Le Schisme Oriental du XIe siècle*, pp. 18–34.

of an Alberic, a Theodora, a Marozia, and a Crescentius. Then, dating from the coronation of Otto (962), the Popes were creatures of the Germanic Emperors. Rome became a field for intrigues, and the Byzantine Emperors, rivals in Southern Italy of the Germanic Emperors, naturally sought to win partisans for themselves there and to influence the election of the Popes. The Papacy, become a tool of the temporal princes, was on the verge of seeing the catholic character of its power disappear. It had lost all moral authority, and events were destined to disappoint sadly the reliance of the Studites on Roman supremacy.

At this moment, with the Papacy weakened, the Patriarch of Constantinople saw his influence increase. That was the inevitable consequence of the policy of victorious expansion which the Macedonian dynasty followed. It was not merely the victories of Nicephorus Phocas, of John Tzimisces, and of Basil II, but also the success of the missions to Slav countries, and in particular the conversion of the Russians, which helped to spread the jurisdiction of the Patriarchate of Constantinople. The recovery of Southern Italy was followed by the reconstitution of a Greek ecclesiastical hierarchy in Apulia and in Calabria, where colonies of Basilian monks were founded. After the baptism of Vladímir (989), the clerics of Constantinople had organised the Russian Church, whose metropolitan bishop was strictly subordinated to the Patriarchate. Similarly Basil II, after terminating the independence of Bulgaria (1018), substituted an archbishop, a suffragan of Constantinople, for the Patriarch of Ochrida. The military and diplomatic successes of the same Emperor in Armenia, and later the annexation of that country by Constantine IX, resulted in drawing more closely and more cordially the bonds of union between the Greek and Armenian Churches. Finally, in Palestine the protectorate over the holy places and the Christian inhabitants passed at the beginning of the eleventh century from the Franks to the Byzantine Emperors[1].

While the Roman Church was ravaged by schism, simony, and nepotism, the Patriarch of Constantinople bulked more and more as the spiritual head of the East. Although many of the Patriarchs had been monks and some had issued even from the monastery of Studion, they had been accustomed to despise the Papacy. Enjoying virtual autonomy as regards Rome, they actually tried to obtain official recognition of the fact.

The Emperors far more than the Patriarchs maintained unbroken relations with Rome, and for them it was always political interests, internal or external, that were at stake. Thus when Romanus Lecapenus, desirous of placing his power on a secure basis and assuring the future of his dynasty, undertook to raise his son Theophylact, a mere child, to the patriarchal dignity, he applied to Rome. On their side, Pope John XI, son of Marozia, and his brother Alberic, Prince of the Romans, sought his

[1] L. Bréhier, *L'Église et l'Orient au moyen âge. Les Croisades*, pp. 38–39.

alliance. The young Theophylact, aged sixteen years, was consecrated Patriarch on 2 February 933, in the presence of four papal legates. To arrive at this result Romanus Lecapenus had extorted an act of abdication from the Patriarch Tryphon, but there is no indication that this scandalous act raised the slightest protest from the clergy[1]. Theophylact, devoid of the slightest ecclesiastical vocation, led an absolutely worldly life while filling the patriarchal chair, trafficking in dispensations and bishoprics, surrounding himself with pantomimists and dancers, and shewing a consuming passion for horses, which he bred at great cost. He survived the palace revolution which overthrew his father (944), and died in 956 owing to a fall from his horse.

After the middle of the tenth century a strong current of asceticism swept through the Greek Church. This was the epoch when St Athanasius, the spiritual director of Nicephorus Phocas, founded the convent of St Laura on Mount Athos (961), which was to become the most important monastic centre of the East. All the successors of Theophylact in the Patriarchate, Polyeuctes (956–970), Basil the Scamandrian (970–974), Anthony of Studion (974–980), were monks of great austerity, whose uncompromising attitude led often to conflicts with the imperial power. It does not appear that in these disputes the Court of Rome ever tried to arbitrate or that it was ever asked to do so. The relations between Rome and Constantinople seem under Constantine VII, Nicephorus Phocas, and John Tzimisces to have been exclusively political. Constantine Porphyrogenitus, allied with King Hugh of Italy, sent a fleet to his help to protect Provence and Central Italy against the Saracens. Under Nicephorus Phocas, Southern Italy was the debateable point, and the unfortunate embassy of Liudprand, Bishop of Cremona, sent by Otto I in 968, illustrates the barrier of misunderstanding and prejudice which separated the Greeks from the Westerners.

In purely religious questions, on the contrary, where the authority of the Pope was concerned, the Emperors and Patriarchs took the most important steps without paying any attention to Rome. In 964 Nicephorus Phocas published his celebrated Novel on the monasteries, which aroused violent opposition amongst the clergy, without its opponents even attempting to support their cause by calling in Rome, as the Studites had formerly done. Similarly, without consulting the Pope, Nicephorus Phocas altered the ecclesiastical divisions of Southern Italy by creating the province of Otranto and by attempting to hellenise Apulia. No protests were raised by Rome, but we have the testimony of Liudprand to shew what dissatisfaction was caused among the Latin clergy by this act[2].

The feeling which seemed to dominate more and more the Greek

[1] Gay, *L'Italie méridionale et l'empire byzantin,* p. 221.

[2] *Liudprandi Legatio,* 62 (MGH, *Script.* III. pp. 361–63). Gay, *op. cit.* pp. 351–353.

Church was a certain contempt for these Latins, whom it considered mere barbarians, while the Patriarch of Constantinople, whose authority had been founded by the Ecumenical Councils, had been able to keep inviolate the orthodox faith entrusted to him. This is shewn by the curious conversation which the Patriarch Polyeuctes held with Liudprand at the imperial table on 6 July 968, and by the contemptuous tone in which he questioned him on the number of councils held in the West. He spoke scoffingly of the Saxon Council, "too young yet to figure in the canonical collections."[1]

Nothing, however, shews more clearly the way in which the authority of the Papacy was despised than the incident caused by the arrival of the legates, whom Pope John XIII had sent to support the negotiations of Liudprand with a view to an alliance between the two Empires (19 August 968). Nicephorus Phocas had just started for the army in Asia, but when his cabinet dealt with the Pope's letter it discovered with indignation that Otto had been designated in it as "august Emperor of the Romans" and Nicephorus as "Emperor of the Greeks." This was a gross blunder which might well be taken for an insult. The Byzantine Emperors proudly vaunted the tradition which connected them with the Caesars of ancient Rome, and the term "Hellenes" had acquired at Constantinople the sense of "Pagans." The hapless legates were thrown into prison pending the decision of the Emperor, and Liudprand himself, held responsible for this wanton affront, was forced to promise formally that the objectionable words should be corrected at Rome[2].

At the end of the tenth century proofs of the enmity of the Patriarchs of Constantinople towards Rome grew more numerous. Whatever their origin, whether laymen elected to the patriarchate like Sisinnius, physician and magister (996–998), or monks like Sergius, *Igumen* of the monastery of Manuel (998–1019), they shew the same hostility. In 997 Sisinnius published a regulation against unlawful marriages, which condemned by implication the authorisation granted by the Popes to Leo VI to contract a fourth marriage. In an encyclical to the bishops of Asia Minor the same Patriarch revived the already ancient dispute about the double Procession of the Holy Ghost[3].

His successor, Sergius, went a step farther. In 1009 he assembled a synod at Constantinople, confirmed the ordinances of Photius against Latin usages, and erased the name of the Pope from the diptychs. It must be borne in mind that at this moment the organisation of a Greek hierarchy in Russia had singularly increased the power of the Patriarchate. This extraordinary increase of prestige may possibly have stimulated the Patriarch to claim for himself entire freedom from any spiritual

[1] *Liudprandi Legatio,* 21, 22 (MGH, *Script.* III. pp. 351–52). Seemingly the Council of Frankfort held in 794.

[2] *Liudprandi Legatio,* 47 (MGH, *Script.* III. pp. 357–58).

[3] Schlumberger, *Epopée byzantine,* vol. II. pp. 119–120.

jurisdiction of the Papacy. This may be inferred from the subsequent course of events[1].

The act of Sergius does not seem to have effected a schism in the proper sense, and it may even be doubted whether it came to the notice of Rome. Further, we do not know at what moment the name of the Pope was restored to the diptychs. In his letter addressed in 1054 to Michael Cerularius, Peter, the Patriarch of Antioch, states that forty-five years previously, on his way to Constantinople in the time of the Patriarch Sergius, he had heard the name of the Pope in the liturgy with those of the other Patriarchs[2]. But this journey of Peter to Constantinople was in 1009, the very year in which Sergius had, probably some months previously, ordered the name to be struck out.

The proof that this act was after all not followed by any lasting rupture is the step taken by Sergius' successor, the Patriarch Eustathius, at the Court of Rome in 1024. It is only from Western sources that we learn of this curious attempt[3].

Pope John XIX, who, although a layman, had just succeeded his brother Benedict VIII, received an embassy sent by the Emperor Basil and the Patriarch Eustathius. Its aim was to obtain from the Pope a declaration that "the Church in Constantinople should be styled universal in its sphere, just as the Church of Rome was in the universe." The question at issue was to obtain from the Pope *autocephalia*, that is the complete autonomy of the Greek Church, over which he would cease to exercise his jurisdiction. A compromise accepted by both parties was preferred to a violent rupture like that of Photius. The occasion seemed favourable; the embassy brought splendid presents which were not without their effect upon John XIX. He looked round, therefore, for a method of giving satisfaction to the Greeks without arousing attention abroad.

But the news of the scandal rapidly spread in Italy and through the entire West. At this moment the powerful congregation of Cluny had begun to push triumphantly forward the principles of the reform of the Church. Many of its chief adherents came to Rome, as did Richard, Abbot of St Vannes, or wrote, like William of Volpiano, Abbot of St Benignus of Dijon, indignant letters to the Pope. They felt more than John XIX himself that it was the very unity of the Church that was imperilled, and the Pope, intimidated by their angry protests, dared not grant the Greek embassy what it asked.

This curious episode throws vivid light on the religious policy of the Emperors and Patriarchs of Constantinople in the tenth century. The Greeks had no wish for a schism which they knew to be unpopular, but

[1] L. Bréhier, *Le Schisme Oriental*, pp. 6–7.

[2] MPG, cxx. col. 795.

[3] Radulphus Glaber, IV. 1 (MGH, *Script.* VII. p. 66). Hugh of Flavigny (MGH, *Script.* VIII. p. 392).

they hoped to profit by the weakness of the Papacy and by the anarchy prevailing at Rome, in order to build up new legal foundations for the patriarchal power. The actual phrase of Radulphus Glaber: "quatinus cum consensu Romani pontificis liceret ecclesiam Constantinopolitanam in suo orbe, sicuti Roma in universo, universalem dici et haberi," certainly appears to shew that the primary object was to obtain from the Pope that title of "Ecumenical," which had hitherto been refused to the Patriarch of Constantinople, and which denoted full legal autonomy. It seems, then, that there may have been a connexion between the erasure of the Pope's name from the diptychs ordered by Sergius in 1009 and the step taken in 1024. Unfortunately, the available sources only supply some fragmentary details.

A new fact, at any rate, the consequences of which were to be important, emerges from their evidence. For more than a century, ever since the reign of Leo VI, the Emperors and the Patriarchs met with nothing but friendliness at Rome. Thanks to their alliances with the all-powerful members of the Roman nobility, they obtained nearly all that they wished from the weak Popes, who only held office at the bidding of an Alberic or a Crescentius. It was in 1024, therefore, that the Court of Constantinople encountered an unexpected resistance, that of the party of ecclesiastical reform, finding a centre in Cluny, whose doctrines were then beginning to spread over the entire West. These reformers, realising more clearly than John XIX the true interests of the Church, defended the Pope against himself by forcing him to resist the Byzantine claims. This was only a preliminary skirmish between the spirit of the Western Reform and the Patriarchate of Constantinople, but it was significant and forecasted the stubborn disputes which followed soon after.

The embassy of 1024 would not appear to have been entirely fruitless in results for the Greek Church, if it is correct that John XIX consented to recognise the title of metropolitan assumed by the Bishop of Bari, the capital of the Byzantine possessions in Italy[1]. At this juncture the catapan Basil Boioannes re-organised the civil and religious administration of the Italian conquests. John XIX, by recognising the ecclesiastical province of Bari with its twelve suffragan bishoprics, appeared to sanction the religious constitution established in Southern Italy by the Greek Emperors.

The prestige of the Byzantine Emperors was now at its zenith. Basil II, having conquered the Bulgarians and having nothing more to fear from the Arabs and Russians, may have contemplated the re-establishment of his imperial authority at Rome and in the West. Such a contingency would have been of incalculable consequence for the relations

[1] The fact is known from a bull of John XIX preserved in the archives of the Cathedral at Bari. As to its authenticity *vide* Gay, *L'Italie méridionale et l'empire byzantin*, p. 427.

between the two Churches, but these plans were frustrated by the death of the Emperor in 1025. On his death-bed Basil had designated, as successor to Eustathius in the Patriarchate, Alexius, Abbot of Studion, who governed the Church of Constantinople until 1042. There are no signs of any hostility towards the Popes evinced by this Patriarch, although their names had not been restored on the diptychs of the Church of Constantinople. It may at least be said that there was no official schism between East and West before 1054. In 1026 the Emperor and the Patriarch offered the most cordial welcome to Richard, Abbot of St Vannes, the very man who two years previously had wrecked the attempt of the Greek Church to win recognition of its autonomy. Churches of the Latin rite existed at Constantinople, such as St Mary of the Amalfitans, founded by the famous family of the Mauro; St Stephen, due to the munificence of the King of Hungary; and finally the church of the Varangian guard, composed of Scandinavians and Anglo-Saxons. There is no evidence that these had been more disturbed than the churches of the Greek rite which existed at Rome.

Still less was there any desire on the part of the other Eastern Patriarchs to break with Rome. Only two years before the definitive rupture with Rome, in 1052, Peter, elected Patriarch of Antioch, sent, in accordance with traditional custom, his *synodica*, his profession of faith, to Pope Leo IX. This letter, entrusted to a Jerusalem pilgrim, was slow in reaching its destination, but the answer dated 1059 is extant, in which Leo IX, after congratulating the Patriarch on his election and approving his profession of faith, sent him in return his own[1].

The agreement concluded in 898 and renewed in 920 between the two Churches had on the whole been observed, and, if the opinion of the large majority of the ordinary members of the two communities had found means of expression, schism would have been permanently averted. But during this long period, which was a period of eclipse for the papal power, the Patriarchs of Constantinople, whose influence had been strengthened by the external successes of the Empire, had grown accustomed to an almost absolute independence of Rome. Far from repudiating the tradition of Photius, they had continued to manifest their hostility to the Latin usages. Peace prevailed officially, but in reality the champions of the two rituals were secret enemies. The Greek missionaries, who instructed Vladímir in the faith at Cherson in 989, were solicitous to warn him against Latin errors, and went the length of forging, for the purpose of explaining them, a veritable romance, full of calumnies as hateful as they were coarse[2]. Finally, even if the attempt made in 1024 by Eustathius to obtain official recognition of the autonomy of the Greek Church had miscarried, it shews that on this question

[1] L. Bréhier, *Le Schisme Oriental*, pp. 16–18.

[2] *Chronique de Nestor* (French translation by Leger), p. 96.

as on others the Patriarch had remained loyal to the programme of Photius.

This peace, equivocal as was its nature, might have lasted longer had not fresh historical conditions at the middle of the eleventh century tended to modify the character of the relations between the Patriarch and the Pope and to accelerate the rupture.

The schemes of the Patriarch of Constantinople had encountered in 1024 the resistance of the Western party of ecclesiastical reform. This party had for the first time a champion on the Papal throne in Leo IX (1049). In his diocese of Toul he had already favoured reform; and when made Pope he determined to extend it to the Church and to claim vigorously the rights of the Papacy to universal jurisdiction.

Precisely when Leo IX was thus proposing to restore the pontifical authority, the patriarchal throne of Constantinople was occupied by a man whose character was as inflexible as his own. Michael Cerularius, who had succeeded the Patriarch Alexius in 1043, belonged to a family of bureaucratic nobility long established at Constantinople. Destined to fill, as his ancestors had done, some high civil post, he as well as his brother had been carefully educated. But in 1040 he was entangled in a conspiracy against Michael IV and John Orphanotrophos. Denounced and arrested with his brother, he suffered close confinement on Princes Islands. His brother, unable to endure prison, committed suicide, and as a result of this tragic event Michael became a monk. Recalled to Byzantium after 1041, he won the favour of Constantine IX, a former conspirator like himself, and became one of his counsellors. Having been for some time syncellus of the Patriarch Alexius, he was selected by the Emperor to succeed him, and was consecrated Patriarch on 29 March 1043[1].

His contemporaries, and especially Psellus, represent him as a man of strong and haughty character, ambitious of playing a prominent part in the Church and even in the State. Of an unforgiving nature, he had his ancient persecutor John Orphanotrophos deprived of his sight in his prison (1043). "The anger and the spite of the Patriarch pursued any man who had once resisted him, at an interval it might be of ten years or more, and even if submerged among the masses".[2] From the first days of his government he assumed towards the Emperor an attitude by no means customary with the Patriarchs. He was not so much a submissive subject as a power who was on an equal footing with the Emperor. Constantine seems to have been afraid of him, and it is noteworthy that after the death of the Empress Zoë he did not venture on a fourth marriage, in spite of the senile affection which he shewed for his Alan favourite. Fear of the Patriarch no doubt restrained him.

[1] L. Bréhier, *Le Schisme Oriental*, pp. 52–81.

[2] Psellus, *Accusation de l'archevêque devant le Synode*, 63, *Revue des Études Grecques*, XVII. 1904. (Extrait L. Bréhier, *Un discours inédit de Psellos*. Paris, 1904, p. 74.)

Such was the man who was destined to face Leo IX. It required the contact of two characters so headstrong and so unyielding to kindle the conflict.

The occasion for schism was found when the two powers met in Southern Italy. The Norman adventurers, who had first of all supported the revolt of the Lombards against the Empire, were not slow to work for their own hand and ruthlessly ravaged the rich country of Apulia. Desirous of ending their pillaging, Leo IX, after vain recourse to spiritual arms, set about enrolling bands of soldiers and took the offensive against the Normans. But his interests here coincided with those of the government of Constantinople. So at the close of 1051 a military alliance was concluded between the Pope and the Lombard Argyrus, who, at first chief of the Normans, had entered the service of the Empire and received the command of the imperial armies in Italy.

Now this alliance had been concluded against the will of the Patriarch, who was eager to uphold the jurisdiction of Constantinople over Southern Italy, and feared to see Leo IX restore the authority of Rome over the bishoprics of Apulia. This same year, 1051, the inhabitants of Benevento had driven out their prince and had submitted themselves to the Pope, who had sent them two legates, Cardinal Humbert and the Patriarch of Grado[1].

Thus the interests of the Empire were in formal contradiction with those of Michael Cerularius, and it was at the very moment when the imperial government needed the support of the Pope that the Patriarch shewed his enmity to the Roman Church.

The course of events can be pieced together from the actual correspondence of the Patriarch and the Pope. Argyrus left Italy in 1046 and came to Constantinople, where he stayed until 1051. He was well received by the Emperor and was a member of his council at the moment of the revolt of Leo Tornicius (1047). It was then that he quarrelled with the Patriarch as a result of the dispute with him about the Latin ritual, and in particular on the use of unleavened bread in the Eucharist. When it is borne in mind that, even if Calabria was completely hellenised, Apulia had remained to a large extent faithful to the Latin ritual, the cause of this controversy is explicable. Argyrus had come to Constantinople to inform the Emperor of the state of Southern Italy and to urge him to conclude an alliance with Leo IX. His duty then was to defend a policy of conciliation and prudence towards the Latin ritual prevailing in Apulia. He himself, besides being by birth a Lombard, belonged to this ritual, and as he declined to be convinced Michael Cerularius boasted of having refused him the sacrament more than four times[2].

In spite, however, of the Patriarch, Argyrus returned to Italy in 1051 with a mandate for the signature of a treaty of alliance between the

[1] Gay, *L'Italie méridionale et l'empire byzantin*, pp. 469, 482 ff.

[2] Gay, *op. cit.* p. 471. L. Bréhier, *Le Schisme Oriental*, pp. 92–93.

Empire and Leo IX. But at the very time when this alliance was going to produce its effect Michael Cerularius commenced hostilities against Rome. It cannot be denied that he had adopted a policy in contradiction to that of the Emperor.

In 1053, indeed, he writes to the new Patriarch of Antioch, Peter, expressing surprise that the name of the Pope is always mentioned in the liturgy of Antioch. He falsely declares that this name did not appear in the diptychs of Constantinople after the council of 692; but Peter, who had just submitted his profession of faith to Leo IX, had no difficulty in pointing out the intentional inaccuracy[1]. In the same letter Michael Cerularius related his dispute with Argyrus about unleavened bread.

At the same moment a former cleric of Constantinople, Leo, Archbishop of Ochrida in Bulgaria, addressed to an Apulian Bishop, John of Trani, a letter which was a veritable indictment of Latin uses. It was no longer, as in the time of Photius, a question chiefly of the double Procession of the Holy Ghost, but of ritual and discipline. The use of unleavened bread for the Eucharist and the Saturday fast were quoted as regrettable instances of persistence in the Mosaic law[2]. Through the agency of the Bishop of Trani, a rival of the Archbishop of Bari who was devoted to the Holy See, Michael Cerularius tried to draw the other bishops of Apulia into a dispute with the Pope[3]. The letter was communicated by John to Cardinal Humbert, who had it translated into Latin and forwarded to Leo IX[4].

Cerularius further took care that a treatise written in Latin by a monk of the monastery of Studion, Nicetas Stethatus (Pectoratus), was circulated. The attacks on the Latins were presented in it under a more violent form than in the letter of Leo of Ochrida. He not only denounced the use of unleavened bread and the Saturday fast, but, and this point must have gone home to Leo IX and the Western reformers, he condemned the celibacy of priests as contrary to ecclesiastical tradition. These charges, interspersed with coarse insults, were bound to cause keen irritation to the Westerners and to embitter the quarrel[5].

Finally, to cut short any attempt at conciliation, the Patriarch took a decisive step. On his own initiative he ordered the closing of the churches of the Latin rite which existed at Constantinople. The abbots and monks of the Greek monasteries grouped round these churches were commanded henceforward to follow the Greek ritual, and on their refusal were treated as "Azymites" and excommunicated. Some of them resisted, and scenes

[1] L. Bréhier, *Le Schisme Oriental,* p. 92. *Vide* the two letters in Will, *Acta et scripta, quae de controversiis ecclesiae graecae et latinae saeculi XI composita exstant,* pp. 178 and 192.

[2] L. Bréhier, *op. cit.* pp. 93–94.

[3] Gay, *L'Italie méridionale,* p. 495.

[4] Wibert, *Vita Leonis,* IX. II. 11 (Muratori, III. p. 296).

[5] L. Bréhier, *op. cit.* pp. 94–96.

of violence ensued in the course of which Nicephorus, the *sacellarius* of the Patriarch, trod under foot the consecrated host[1].

While Michael Cerularius was thus entering on the contest, the alliance between the Pope and the Emperor had met with a decisive check. Argyrus, defeated by the Normans (February 1053), had been forced to abandon Apulia and to fly northwards. Some months later Leo IX in his turn was defeated and made prisoner at Civitate, and it was no other than John, Bishop of Trani, whom Argyrus dispatched to Constantinople to ask fresh help against the Normans.

These events naturally led to correspondence between the Pope and the Patriarch; and pontifical legates were sent to Constantinople, but opinions differ as to the exact order of the facts. According to some authorities, even before Leo IX had replied to the attacks of the Archbishop of Ochrida, that is to say after the close of 1053, Michael Cerularius wrote the Pope a letter, very conciliatory in tone, in which he protested his zeal for unity and proposed a new alliance against the Normans. By so acting he demonstrated his goodwill towards the political alliance between Pope and Emperor, but he remained obdurate on the matter of the customs which he condemned as heretical. It was not until after he had sent this appeal for conciliation that Michael Cerularius received the two letters addressed to him by the Pope. The first was an indignant refutation of the attacks of Leo of Ochrida on the Roman uses. In the second the Pope accepted the proposed alliance, but refused to treat with the Patriarch as an equal, and reminded him that every Church which broke with that of Rome was only "an assembly of heretics, a conventicle of schismatics, a synagogue of Satan".[2]

But this manner of presenting the facts does not at all explain the express contradiction which exists between the violently aggressive acts of Michael Cerularius against Rome and the extremely conciliatory letter which he wrote to the Pope. The text of this letter, it is true, is no longer extant, but the purport of it can easily be gathered from the answer of Leo IX and the allusions which Michael Cerularius himself makes to it in his correspondence with Peter of Antioch. It is hard to believe that the Patriarch, who had wished to break with Rome in so startling a manner, wrote it of his own free will. Further, the position of the imperial army in Italy at the end of 1053 was so desperate, and the cementing of the alliance with Leo IX appeared so necessary, that we are led to believe in some governmental pressure being brought to bear on the Patriarch. It was almost certainly by order of the Emperor and at the instigation of Argyrus that he consented to this effort at conciliation[3].

But no compromise was possible between the obduracy of Leo IX

[1] Letter of Leo IX (Will, *op. cit.* p. 801), L. Bréhier, *op. cit.* pp. 96–97.

[2] Gay, *L'Italie méridionale*, pp. 492–494.

[3] L. Bréhier, *op. cit.* pp. 97–109.

and that of Michael Cerularius. Determined to obtain the submission of the Patriarch, the Pope sent to Constantinople three legates whom he chose from among his principal counsellors, Cardinal Humbert, Frederick of Lorraine, Chancellor of the Roman Church, and Peter, Bishop of Amalfi. Before departing they had an interview with Argyrus, who posted them up in the political situation at Constantinople; and this fact was made use of later by the Patriarch, who alleged that these legates were mere impostors in the pay of Argyrus.

The legates arrived at Constantinople towards the end of April 1054, and were given a magnificent reception by the Emperor, who lodged them in the Palace of the Springs outside the Great Wall. They visited the Patriarch, but this first meeting was the reverse of cordial. Michael Cerularius was deeply affronted to see that they did not prostrate themselves before him according to Byzantine etiquette. At the ceremonies they claimed to take precedence of the metropolitans, and, contrary to custom, appeared at the Palace with staff and crozier[1].

This attitude conformed to the tone of the two letters which they brought from the Pope. We know already that, in the letter intended for the Patriarch, Leo IX, while thanking him for the desire for unity which he expressed, sharply reproved him for his attacks on the Roman Church. The letter addressed to Constantine IX was, on the contrary, couched in deferential terms. With consummate skill he contrasted the project of alliance against the Normans with the attitude of Michael Cerularius towards him. After enumerating his principal grievances, he threatened to break with the Patriarch if he persisted too long in his obstinacy. In conclusion, he adjured the Emperor to help his legates to restore peace in the Church. It was clear, therefore, that the Pope looked only to the authority of the Emperor to get the better of the Patriarch[2].

Discussions were opened. The legates Humbert and Frederick wrote rejoinders to the treatise of Nicetas Stethatus on the question of unleavened bread. While defending the Roman Church, they vigorously attacked certain uses of the Greek Church, but the treatise, especially addressed to Nicetas, was written in coarse and violent language. The ill-starred monk was overwhelmed with epithets such as Sarabaita, veritable Epicurus, forger.

Then, on 24 June 1054, the Emperor and the legates went across to the monastery of Studion. After the treatise of Nicetas, translated into Greek, had been read, a discussion followed, as a result of which the monk declared himself vanquished. He himself anathematised his own book and all those who denied that the Roman Church was the Head of all the Churches. The Emperor then ordered the treatise to be committed to the flames. The next day Nicetas went to visit the

[1] L. Bréhier, *Le Schisme Oriental,* pp. 105–107.
[2] Will, *op. cit.* pp. 85–88.

legates at the Palace of the Springs. They received him cordially, and removed his remaining doubts by answering all his questions. After he had renewed his anathema against all the enemies of Rome, the legates declared that they received him into communion[1]. The Patriarch naturally did not take any part in these steps, which constituted an absolute defeat for him. The monastery of Studion became once more, as of old, the stronghold of the Roman party.

Michael Cerularius shrank from this open attack and declined to meet the advances of the legates, protesting that they had not the requisite authority for treating with him. Pope Leo IX died on 19 April 1054 and the Papal See remained vacant for a year, as Victor II was only elected in April 1055. The fact of Leo's death was known at Constantinople, as is shewn by the first letter of Michael Cerularius to Peter, Patriarch of Antioch, in which he represented the legates as forgers in the employ of Argyrus[2].

The tactics of the Patriarch of Constantinople were obvious. By refusing to recognise the powers of the legates he protracted the negotiations, and was preparing against the Roman Church a manifesto from all the Eastern Bishops. "Ought those," he wrote to the Patriarch of Antioch, "who lead the same life as the Latins, who are brought up in their customs, and who abandon themselves to illegal, prohibited, and detestable practices, to remain in the ranks of the just and orthodox? I think not".[3] Nothing demonstrates better than this text the real wish of the Patriarch for final schism.

The legates then decided to take the decisive action for which Michael Cerularius was waiting. On Saturday, 15 July 1054, at the third hour, they repaired to St Sophia at the moment when all the congregation was assembled for the celebration of the daily service. After haranguing the crowd and denouncing the obstinacy of Michael Cerularius, they deposited a bull of excommunication on the altar, and then left the church, shaking the dust off their feet[4].

In this bull, which the Patriarch caused to be translated into Greek and inserted in his Synodal Edict, the legates said that they had received from the Roman Church a mission of peace and unity. They rejoiced at having found at Constantinople, as well in the Emperor as among the clergy and people, perfect orthodoxy. On the other hand, they had detected in the Patriarch ten heretical tendencies. In virtue of their powers, therefore, they pronounced the anathema against the Patriarch Michael Cerularius, against Leo, Archbishop of Ochrida, and against the *sacellarius* Nicephorus and their followers. Thus the legates, unable to induce the Patriarch to submit, and not venturing to take steps to depose

[1] L. Bréhier, *op. cit.* pp. 109–113.

[2] Will, *op. cit.* pp. 175 *et seq.*

[3] *Ib.* p. 183.

[4] "Commemoratio brevis rerum a legatis apostolicae sedis Constantinopoli gestarum." (Will, *ib.* pp. 151, 152.)

him, appealed to public opinion. In order to render their triumph more complete, they consecrated, before leaving, some churches of Latin ritual. Constantine IX continued to give proofs of his goodwill and heaped splendid presents upon them[1].

The triumph of the legates was, however, short-lived. Hardly had they started on 17 July for their return journey to Rome, when the Patriarch asked for an interview with them. They had already reached Selymbria (Silivri) on 19 July, when a letter from the Emperor recalled them. They turned back and reached the Palace of the Springs, where they attended the imperial orders. Constantine IX, however, distrusting the intentions of the Patriarch, did not consent to authorise the interview of Michael Cerularius and the legates in St Sophia except in his presence. The Patriarch refused this condition and the Emperor ordered the legates to continue their journey. Subsequently Cardinal Humbert asserted that Michael Cerularius wanted to draw the legates into a snare and assassinate them[2].

However that may be, the Emperor's answer exasperated the Patriarch. Enjoying unbounded popularity at Constantinople, he seems to have had at this epoch a devoted party. A riot soon broke out in the streets of the town. Constantine IX in alarm sent to the Patriarch a veritable embassy of the principal dignitaries of the palace, who were charged to appease him and to represent to him that the Emperor could not offer any violence to the legates on account of their ambassadorial rights. This answer did not satisfy the Patriarch, for soon a second mission, in which the "consul of the philosophers," Psellus, figured, arrived with a new message from the Emperor. Constantine made truly humble excuses for what had occurred and threw the blame on Argyrus. Two citizens, Paulus and Smaragdus, guilty of having translated the bull into Greek and of having circulated it, were handed over to him, after having been scourged. The Emperor affirmed that he had given the order to burn the bull and had committed to prison the son and the son-in-law of Argyrus[3].

By this *volte-face* the Emperor surrendered to the will of the Patriarch and gave him a free hand for the future. It only remained for Michael Cerularius to consummate his triumph by a sensational rupture with Rome. With the authorisation of the Emperor he convened a council on which were represented all the provinces of the Greek Church. Twelve metropolitans and two archbishops signed the acts of it. The opening sections of the Synodal Edict, published in connexion with this assembly, contained a reproduction of the Encyclical sent by Photius to the Eastern bishops. Michael Cerularius recapitulated in it all the grievances of the Greeks against the Roman Church: the double Procession of the Holy Ghost, use of unleavened bread, the Saturday fast,

[1] L. Bréhier, *Le Schisme Oriental,* pp. 118–119.
[2] *Ib.* pp. 120, 121.
[3] *Ib.* pp. 121–124.

celibacy of priests, shaving the beard, etc. He then complained of the profanation of the altar of St Sophia by the legates, gave a biased account of their stay at Constantinople, transcribed their bull of excommunication, fulminated an anathema against them, and lastly produced, as a trophy of victory, the pitiable letter which the Emperor had addressed to him.

Finally, on 20 July 1054, at the patriarchal tribunal, in the presence of seven archbishops or bishops and of the imperial delegates, judgment was pronounced not only "against the impious document but also against all those who had helped in drawing it up, whether by their advice or even by their prayers." Five days afterwards all copies of the bull were solemnly burned before the eyes of the people; one copy only was preserved in the archives of the Patriarchate[1].

By the solemn ceremonial with which he had invested these proceedings, Michael Cerularius had wished to shew that it was no longer the question of a temporary schism like that of Photius but of a final rupture. This schism was indeed his personal achievement and due to his strong and domineering character, but it also reflects the opinion of the Greek episcopate, which lent little support to the power of supreme jurisdiction claimed by a bishop foreign to the Empire, and had only an intolerant contempt for the peculiar uses of the Latins.

This separation was, as we have seen, rendered possible by the weakening of the prestige of Rome in the East in the course of the tenth century. Directly after the dispute about image-worship, there had been in Constantinople an ecclesiastical party which saw no salvation for the Eastern churches except in communion with Rome. This party had been strong enough to resist Photius himself, and upon it the Emperors had relied to re-establish unity. But a century later this Roman party was non-existent in Constantinople. The scandals of which Rome had continuously been the theatre during this period, and the equivocal decisions on the marriage of Leo VI, had discouraged its supporters. Michael Cerularius did not meet with the opposition that had checked Photius.

Notwithstanding wide divergencies, the mass of the faithful followers of the two Churches shrank from schism, and were satisfied with compromises which guaranteed the maintenance of normal relations between Rome and Constantinople. Nevertheless, after the events of 1054, although outside Constantinople no act of religious hostility between Greek and Latins can be shewn, the members of the two Churches soon regarded each other as enemies, and from this epoch dates the definitive rupture between the Churches of East and West.

The results of this schism could not but be disastrous to the Byzantine Empire. It took place precisely when the West was beginning to

[1] L. Bréhier, *Le Schisme Oriental,* pp. 124–125.

lay aside barbarism. The highly-organised States, which were being formed there, lost no time in turning these religious divergencies to profit against the Byzantine Empire. The first consequence of the schism was the final loss of Southern Italy. The Papacy, no longer able to reckon upon the Byzantine Empire, made terms with the Normans[1].

But this schism was fated to have far more widely-reaching effects, and, when the Empire fell on evil days, it was to prove a heavy burden and a constant check on the goodwill of the West. For the Patriarch of Constantinople the schism had been unquestionably a great victory. His authority had been established without dispute over the Slav world and the Eastern Patriarchates. Liberated from fear of subordination to Rome, he had finally defended the *autocephalia* of his own Church. But this victory of the Byzantine clergy was in reality a check for the statesmen who, like Argyrus, looked solely to the interests of the Empire. After this epoch there are clear traces of that antinomy, which was henceforward to dominate all the history of Byzantium, between the political and the religious interests of the Empire. It was the schism which, by rendering fruitless all efforts at conciliation between the Emperors of Constantinople and the West, paved the way for the fall of the Empire.

[1] At the Council of Melfi. Gay, *L'Italie méridionale*, pp. 516–519 (1059).

CHAPTER X.

(A)

MUSLIM CIVILISATION DURING THE ABBASID PERIOD.

When the Abbasids wrested from the Umayyads in 750 the headship of the Muslim world, they entered into possession of an empire stretching from the Indus to the Atlantic and from the southern shore of the Caspian Sea to the Indian Ocean. It had absorbed the whole of the Persian Empire of the Sasanians, and the rich provinces of the Roman Empire on the eastern and southern shores of the Mediterranean; but though Constantinople itself had been threatened more than once, and raids into Asia Minor were so frequent as at certain periods to have become almost a yearly occurrence, the ranges of the Taurus and the Anti-Taurus still served as the eastern barrier of Byzantine territory against the spread of Arab domination. In Africa, however, all opposition to the westward progress of the Arab arms had been broken down, and the whole of the peninsula of Spain, with the exception of Asturia, had passed under Muslim rule. For ninety years Damascus had been the capital of the Arab Empire, and the mainstay of the Umayyad forces in the time of their greatest power had been the Arab tribes domiciled in Syria from the days when that province still formed part of the Roman Empire; but the Abbasids had come into power mainly through support from Persia, and their removal of the capital to Baghdad (founded by Manṣūr, the second Caliph of the new dynasty, in 762) on a site only thirty miles from Ctesiphon, the capital of the Sasanian Shāhanshāh, marks their recognition of the shifting of the centre of power.

From this period Persian influence became predominant and the chief offices of state came to be held by men of Persian origin; the most noteworthy example is that of the family of the Barmecides (Barmakids), which for half a century exercised the predominant influence in the government until Hārūn destroyed them in 803. It was probably due to the influence of the old Persian ideal of kingship that under the Abbasids the person of the Caliph came to be surrounded with greater pomp and ceremony. The court of the Umayyads had retained something of the patriarchal simplicity of early Arab society, and they had been readily accessible to their subjects; but as the methods of government became more centralised and the court of the Caliph more splendid and awe-striking, the ruler himself tended to be more difficult of access, and the presence of the executioner by the side of the throne became under the Abbasids a terrible symbol of the autocratic character of their rule.

A further feature of the new dynasty was the emphasis it attached to the religious character of the dignity of the Caliph. In their revolt against the Umayyads, the Abbasids had come forward in defence of the purity of Islām as against those survivals of the old Arab heathenism which were so striking a feature of the Umayyad court. The converts and descendants of converts, whose support had been most effective in the destruction of the Umayyads, were animated with a more zealous religious spirit than had ever found expression among large sections of the Arabs, who, in consequence of the superficial character of their conversion to Islām, and their aristocratic pride and tribal exclusiveness, so contrary to the spirit of Islāmic brotherhood, had been reluctant to accord to the converts from other races the privileges of the new faith. The Abbasids raised the standard of revolt in the name of the family of the Prophet, and by taking advantage of the widespread sympathy felt for the descendants of 'Alī, they obtained the support of the various Shī'ah factions. Though they took all the fruits of victory for themselves, they continued to lay emphasis on the religious character of their rule, and theologians and men of learning received a welcome at their court such as they had never enjoyed under the Umayyads. On ceremonial occasions the Abbasid Caliph appeared clad in the sacred mantle of the Prophet, and titles such as that of Khalīfah of Allāh (vicegerent of God) and shadow of God upon earth came to be frequently applied to him. As the power of the central authority grew weaker, so the etiquette of the court tended to become more elaborate and servile, and the Caliph made his subjects kiss the ground before him or would allow the higher officials either to kiss his hand or foot or the edge of his robe.

The vast empire into the possession of which they had entered was too enormous and made up of elements too heterogeneous to be long held together under a system, the sole unifying principle of which was payment of tribute to the Caliph. A prince of the Umayyad family, 'Abd-ar-Raḥmān, who had succeeded in escaping to Spain when practically all his relatives had been massacred, took advantage of tribal jealousies among the Arab chiefs in Spain to seize this country for himself, and to detach it from the empire, in 756. North Africa, which had been placed by Hārūn under the government of Ibrāhīm ibn al-Aghlab, became practically independent under this energetic governor, who established a dynasty that lasted for more than a century (800–909); though his successors contented themselves with the title of emir, the Caliph in Baghdad appears to have been powerless to interfere with their administration. Hārūn himself seems to have realised that the break-up of the Arab empire was inevitable, since in 802 he made arrangements for dividing the administration of it between his sons Amīn and Ma'mūn. But on the death of their father in 809 civil war broke out between the two brothers.

The Arabs lent their support to Amīn, and under his leadership made a last effort to regain for themselves the control of the Caliphate; but in 813 Ṭāhir, Ma'mūn's brilliant Persian general, defeated him, and as a reward for his successful siege of Baghdad was appointed by Ma'mūn to the government of Khurāsān, where he and his descendants for half a century were practically independent. Egypt broke away from the empire when a son of one of Ma'mūn's Turkish slaves, Aḥmad ibn Ṭūlūn, having been appointed deputy-governor of Egypt in 868, succeeded in making himself independent not only in Egypt but also in Syria, which he added to his dominions, and ceased sending money contributions to Baghdad. This breaking away of the outlying provinces of the empire was rendered the more possible by the weakness of the central government. Ma'mūn's brother and successor, Mu'taṣim (833–842), made the fatal mistake of creating an army composed almost entirely of Turkish mercenaries. Their excesses made life in Baghdad so intolerable that the Caliph, in order to be safe from the vengeance of the inhabitants of his own capital, moved to a site three days' journey up the Tigris to the north of Baghdad, and from 836 to 892 Sāmarrā was the Abbasid capital where nine successive Caliphs lived, practically as prisoners of their own Turkish bodyguard. While the Turkish officers made and unmade Caliphs as they pleased, the country was ruined by constantly recurring disorders and insurrection. In 865, while rival claimants were fighting for the crown, Baghdad was besieged for nearly a year, and the slave revolt for fourteen years (869–883) left the delta of the Euphrates at the mercy of undisciplined bands of marauders who terrorised the inhabitants and even sacked great cities, such as Baṣrah, Ahwāz, and Wāsiṭ, shewing the weakness of the central power even in territories so close to the capital. A further disaster was soon to follow in the great Carmathian revolt, which takes its name from one of the propagandists of the Ismā'īlī Shī'ah doctrine in 'Irāq during the latter part of the ninth century. His followers for nearly a century (890–990) spread terror throughout Mesopotamia, and even threatened Baghdad. They extended their ravages as far as Syria, murdering and pillaging wherever they went. In 930 they plundered the city of Mecca, put to death 30,000 Muslims there, and carried off the Black Stone together with immense booty.

These movements represent only a part of the risings and revolts that brought anarchy into the Caliph's dominions and cut off the sources of his revenue. In the midst of this period of disorder the Caliph Mu'tamid, shortly before his death in 892, transferred the capital once more to Baghdad, but the change did not bring the Caliphs deliverance from the tutelage of their Turkish troops, and they were as much at their mercy as before.

Deliverance came from Persia where the Buwaihids, who claimed descent from one of the Sasanian kings, had been extending their power from the Caspian Sea southward through Persia, until in 945 they entered Baghdad, nominally as deliverers of the Caliph from his rebellious Turkish troops. For nearly a century from this date the Caliphs were mere puppets in the hands of successive Buwaihid emirs, who set them upon the throne and deposed them as they pleased. The Caliph Mustakfī, whose deliverance from his mutinous Turkish soldiery had been the pretext for the Buwaihid occupation of Baghdad, was in the same year dragged from his throne and cruelly blinded. So low had the office of Caliph sunk by this period that there were still living two other Abbasid princes who like Mustakfī had sat upon the Abbasid throne, but blinded and robbed of all their wealth were now dependent upon charity or such meagre allowance as the new rulers cared to dole out to them. His cousin Muṭī' was set up to succeed him, but though he held the office of Caliph for twenty-eight years (946–974) he had no voice in the administration, and could not even nominate any of the ministers who carried on the business of the state in his name; helpless in the hands of his Buwaihid master, he lived upon a scanty allowance. He was compelled to abdicate in favour of his son Ṭā'i', after a riotous outburst of religious intolerance in Baghdad, and Ṭā'i' for seventeen years (974–991) suffered similar humiliations. He was deposed at last in favour of his cousin Qādir (991–1031), of whose reign of forty years hardly any incident is recorded, because political events pursued their course without any regard to him.

Meanwhile in Upper Mesopotamia an Arab family, the Ḥamdānids, at first governors of Mosul, extended their authority over the surrounding country, and one member of the family, Saif-ad-Daulah, made himself master of Aleppo and brought the whole of Northern Syria under his rule in 944. In North Africa a rival Caliphate had arisen under the Shī'ah Fāṭimids, who annexed Egypt in 969, and after more than one attempt occupied Syria in 988. By the beginning of the eleventh century the power of the Buwaihids was on the decline and they had to give way before the Ghaznawids and the Seljūqs, the latter a Turkish tribe which made its first appearance in history about the middle of the tenth century. In 1055 the Seljūq chief, Ṭughril Beg, after having conquered the greater part of Persia, entered Baghdad and delivered the Caliph from subservience to the Buwaihids. From Baghdad Ṭughril Beg marched to the conquest of Mosul and Upper Mesopotamia, and when he died in 1063 he left to his successor, Alp Arslān, an empire which eight years later stretched from the Hindu Kush to the shores of the Mediterranean.

Alp Arslān died in 1072 and his son, Malik Shāh, still further extended the empire by the conquest of Transoxiana. One of the Seljūq generals, Atsiz, drove the Fāṭimids out of Syria and Palestine, and occupied Jerusalem in 1071 and Damascus in 1075. Under the protection of the Seljūqs, the Caliph in Baghdad enjoyed at the hand of these orthodox Sunnīs a certain amount of respect such as he had failed to receive at the hand of the Shī'ah Buwaihids, but his political authority hardly extended beyond the walls of the city.

The death of Malik Shāh in 1092 was followed by a period of confusion, during which his four sons fought one another for the succession, but in 1117 the supreme authority passed to his third son, Sanjar, the last of the Great Seljūqs to exercise a nominal sovereignty over the whole empire; before his death in 1155 it had split up into a number of separate principalities, some of them ruled over by Seljūq princes, others by officers who, acting first as guardians (or Atābegs) to minors, later assumed the reins of power and founded dynasties of their own.

One permanent result of the rise of the Seljūq empire was that the way had been opened for Muslim domination in Asia Minor. During the whole of the Abbasid period the ranges of the Taurus and Anti-Taurus had formed the frontier line between the Roman and the Arab Empires, and though incursions had frequently, and during certain periods annually, been made by the Muslim troops into Anatolia, no permanent result of these military expeditions into the great plateau of Asia Minor had been achieved beyond the temporary occupation of some fortresses. But the Seljūqs made their way into Asia Minor from Northern Persia through Armenia, and before the end of the eleventh century had occupied all the centre of Asia Minor, leaving only the kingdom of Lesser Armenia and the coast-line which was held by Byzantine troops. This western movement of the Seljūqs and the consequent alarm of the Emperor of Constantinople who appealed for help to the Christian powers of Europe, were among the causes of the Crusades.

When the crusaders entered Syria in 1098, the Seljūq empire had already begun to break up; the greater part of Mesopotamia and Syria had been parcelled out into military fiefs in which the military officers of the Seljūqs had made themselves independent. The political situation of the Muslim world was but little affected by the establishment of the Kingdom of Jerusalem in 1099, and the most important effect of the Crusades upon Muslim history was the rise of the Ayyūbid dynasty, established by Saladin in his long conflict with the crusaders culminating in the battle of Ḥiṭṭīn and the conquest of Jerusalem in 1187.

Farther east, the fratricidal struggle still went on between rival Muslim houses fighting one another for the possession of the fragments of the Seljūq empire. For a brief period the Caliph in Baghdad succeeded in exerting some authority in the neighbourhood of his capital, and Nāṣir (1180–1225), freed from the tutelage of the Seljūqs, restored to the Caliphate some of its old independence, though the narrow territory over which he ruled extended only from Takrīt to the head of the Persian Gulf. His most formidable rival was the Khwārazm Shāh, whose kingdom, founded by a descendant of one of the Turkish slaves of the Seljūq Sultan Malik Shāh, had been gradually extended until it included the greater part of Persia. Under 'Alā-ud-Dīn (1199–1220) the kingdom of Khwārazm embraced also Bukhārā and Samarqand, and in 1214 Afghanistan; but his career of conquest was short-lived, for on his eastern border appeared the Mongol army of Jenghiz Khān which soon involved in a common devastation and ruin the greater part of the various Muslim kingdoms of the East. Muslim civilisation has never recovered from the destruction which the Mongols inflicted upon it. Great centres of culture, such as Herāt and Bukhārā, were reduced to ashes and the Muslim population was ruthlessly massacred. With the Mongol conquest of southern Russia and of China we are not concerned here, but their armies after sweeping across Persia appeared in 1256 under the command of Hūlāgū before the walls of Baghdad, and after a brief siege of one month the last Caliph of the Abbasid House, Musta'ṣim, had to surrender, and was put to death together with most of the members of his family; 800,000 of the inhabitants were brought out in batches from the city to be massacred, and the greater part of the city itself was destroyed by fire. The Mongol armies then moved on into Syria, where first Aleppo and then Damascus fell into their hands, but when they advanced to the conquest of Egypt they met with the first check in their westward movement. Egypt since 1254 had been under the rule of the Mamlūk sultans, and the Egyptian army in 1260 defeated the Mongols at 'Ain Jālūt in Palestine, and following up this victory drove them out of Syria altogether. After the death of Jenghiz Khān in 1227, the vast Mongol empire had been divided among his four sons; of Muslim territories, Transoxiana fell to the lot of his second son Jagatai; one of his grandsons, Hūlāgū, the conqueror of Baghdad, founded the Īl-khān dynasty of Persia and included in his kingdom the whole of Persia, Mesopotamia, and part of Asia Minor. The Seljūqs of Asia Minor had managed to maintain a precarious existence as vassals of the Mongols by making a timely submission; and, under the rule of the Mamlūk Sultans of Egypt, Syria kept the Mongols out. Such remained the general condition of the eastern provinces of what had once been the empire of the Abbasid Caliphs, during the remainder of the thirteenth century.

The Abbasid epoch has dazzled the imagination of the Muslim world with the vision of a period of great wealth and splendour, and the degradation of its latter days was blotted out by the remembrance of its earlier glories, though these lasted barely 83 years. The shadowy Abbasid Caliphate of Cairo bore witness for two centuries and a half (1261–1517) to the impressive character of the ideal of a united Muslim Empire, under the leadership of the Imām-Caliph, regarded as the source of all authority, in spite of the fact that the disruptive influence of national movements and the self-assertion of provincial groups had irremediably destroyed the reality centuries before. As the rule of the Caliph was an absolutism, tempered only by the divinely-inspired law, to which he with every other Muslim had to submit, the state perished with him. For Muslim political theory contained no principle of growth, to provide for the development of self-governing institutions; no attempt had been made to widen the basis of government, or train the subjects to co-operate with the state, and the continuity of city life—so characteristic a feature of political life in the West—was unknown in the Muslim East.

By its elaboration of systems of law, however, the Abbasid period bequeathed to succeeding generations authoritative codes which are still in operation in various parts of the world, but the theocratic origin of this law, based as it is on the unalterable, eternal Word of God, has continuously hampered its adjustment to the changing conditions of political and social life. In other branches of intellectual activity, notably mathematics and medicine, permanent results were attained, of which some account is given in the following sections.

The foundation for the political theories that find embodiment in the organisation of the Abbasid Empire was laid during the period of the Umayyads. These theories were in the main the outgrowth of two definite factors. In the first place, the conquering Arabs were faced with the problem of administering the vast Empire that, in the brief space of a few decades, had fallen into their hands, while their past history had given them no experience of organised methods of government and administration, and their tribal system had ill prepared them for any large outlook upon material problems. But they found in Palestine, Syria, and Egypt, a large body of trained officials, accustomed to the smooth working of the traditional method of administration in the Roman Empire, and familiar with the departmental routine of bureaux of government. Similarly, within the Persian empire, in spite of the anarchy that had prevailed after Chosroes II, the administrative machinery of the Sasanids, with its large body of officials for the collection of taxes, was still available. There is abundant evidence to shew that in the provinces of both these Empires the Arabs made very little change in the methods of administering the country. Accordingly, at a time when Muslim theory was formless and inchoate, it came under the powerful influence of one of the greatest attempts to systematize social and political life that the world has ever seen, and just as Muslim law bears the imprint of the Roman legal system, and the earliest systematic treatises of Islām appear to have been modelled on catechisms of Christian doctrines, so the fiscal system of the Arabs followed the lines that had been laid down centuries before by Roman administrators.

On the other hand, during the whole of the Umayyad period, there had been living in Medina the representatives of the apostolic age of Islām, engaged in attempts to reduce to order the incoherent materials for a Muslim theory of life based upon the ordinances of the Koran (Qur'ān) and the traditionary sayings of the Prophet. As these legists and theologians viewed with horror the heathenish ideals and manners of the Umayyad court, and accordingly kept aloof from practical concern with the details of political life, the theories of the state and of legislation which they worked out very largely ignore the more stable development of the Arab state. Muslim political and legal theories have consequently never been able wholly to shake themselves free from the unreality that marked their beginnings in the rarified atmosphere of speculation in which early Muslim thinkers lived in Medina. When the Abbasids came into power, largely with the help of an orthodox reaction against the alleged heathenism of the Umayyad house, and with the support of Persian converts whose theological zeal was unknown to the latitudinarian Arabs, they attracted to their new capital, Baghdad, the legists and theologians of Medina and lavished a generous patronage on students of theology; at the same time they exercised control over these thinkers and, while helping orthodoxy to triumph in the state, the Abbasids took care to make use of it for their own selfish ends.

According to Islāmic theory, religious dogma, maxims of statecraft, legal ordinances, and the details of the social life of the believer, all have their source in the revealed text of the Koran and in the traditionary sayings and practices of the Prophet; where these fail to provide the required guidance, the consensus of the community is decisive, and most Muslim thinkers have allowed also an analogical deduction from the first two sources to particular cases not expressly mentioned in either of them. During the third century of the Muslim era were compiled the six great collections of traditions that are held to be authoritative in the Sunnī world. These fix definitely the theories that had grown out of the experience of preceding generations of Muslims. These traditions gave final expression to the theory of the Caliphate, according to which the head of the Muslim community, as successor (Khalīfah) of the Prophet, carried on the same functions that he had performed, with the exception of the exercise of the prophetic office which was held to have come to an end with him. Accordingly the Caliph was supreme administrator, judge, and general. The legists summed up his functions as comprising the defence and maintenance of the faith; war against those who refused to accept Islām or submit to Muslim rule; the protection of the country of Islām and the provision of troops for guarding the frontiers; the decision of legal disputes and the punishment of wrongdoers; the collection and disbursement of taxes; the payment of salaries and the appointing of competent officials. The holder of the office had to be a member of the tribe of the Quraish, to which the Prophet himself had belonged, and had to possess the physical and intellectual qualities necessary for the performance of the duties above mentioned. In theory the office was elective, but the first Caliph of the Umayyad dynasty had made it hereditary, and generally each Caliph nominated his successor during his life. It was not necessary that the succession should follow in the direct line. Of the fourteen Umayyad Caliphs only four were succeeded by a son, and of the first twenty-four Caliphs of the Abbasid dynasty only six had a son as his successor; and though, later, direct succession became more common, out of the total number of thirty-six the office passed from father to son in sixteen cases only. The fiction of election was kept up by the institution of the oath of allegiance which was taken by the highest officials and great nobles of the state to the Caliph on his succession and sometimes also to the heir apparent.

The Caliph was also at the same time Imām or leader of the faithful in public worship, and, though he often delegated this religious function to any ordinary Imām, there were even up to the latter days of the Abbasid dynasty solemn occasions on which the Caliph came forward as leader of the faithful in this public act of divine worship. The last Abbasid Caliph who kept up this practice was Rāḍī (934–940). Though the Sunnī doctrine never attached such mysterious significance to the office of the Imām as was characteristic of the Shī'ah sect, yet a certain degree of reverence became attached to this office even among the Sunnīs, and the theorists maintained the necessity of an Imām as leader of the whole body of believers; it was he alone who could declare a general Jihād, calling upon all the faithful, both men and women, to join in war against the unbelievers, and he was held to be the source of all legitimate authority, both in the state and in the administration of justice. In theory every governor was appointed by the Imām-Khalīfah, and even when the separate provinces of the empire had become independent and the Caliph was a helpless puppet, this fiction was still maintained, and a sultan or emir, though he might have carved out a kingdom for himself by force of arms, would apply to the Abbasid Caliph for a diploma of investiture.

The organisation of the administrative machinery is traditionally attributed to Omar (634–644), who established a Dīwān or public register of income and expenditure, the original purpose of which was the division of the revenues of the state among the various members of the Muslim community. But Omar's fiscal system soon broke down, and the machinery of government gradually became more complicated by the establishment of separate administrative departments, the number and designation of which during the Abbasid period varied from time to time. Among the most important were the Treasury (Dīwān al-Kharāj), which kept an account of the taxes, and the State Chancery (Dīwān at-Tauqī'), which issued the decrees of the Caliph and exercised control over provincial governors. There were also separate departments for official correspondence, for the administration of the crown lands, for the army, for the postal service, for accounts, for general expenditure, and for the freedmen and slaves of the Imperial House.

In the centralisation of government so characteristic of the new dynasty, the institution of the Wazīr (Vizier) came into prominence. Whereas the Umayyads, following the traditionary methods of primitive Arab society, were surrounded by an aristocracy made up of chiefs of their own race whom they would consult on special occasions, the more autocratic government of the Abbasids placed the great army of officials under the control of a minister, the Wazīr, to whom the Caliph delegated a large portion of the details of administration. When the Caliph (as was often the case) did not wish to be disturbed in his pleasures by the cares of state, the Wazīr acquired almost autocratic powers and could amass immense wealth; all officials, even the great provincial governors, owed their appointment to him, and he controlled the whole machinery of the state. But his was a perilous position, and the annals of the Abbasid dynasty are full of stories of the sudden ruin that destroyed great and prosperous ministers.

One of the most important departments was that of the State Post (Dīwān al-Barīd), an institution that the Arabs took over from the Romans, as the very designation indicates, *barīd* being a loan-word from the Latin *veredus*; but the story that Hārūn's great Persian minister, the Barmecide Yaḥyà, reorganised the postal system on a new basis, probably indicates that the Arabs incorporated also into their system the old organisation of the Persian Empire. Like the Roman *cursus publicus*, this department was designed only to serve the interests of the state, by keeping the central government in touch with the outlying provinces and providing secret information of the doings of the various governors. Relays of swift mounts were kept at post stations on the great highways, and made possible the rapid communication of information and official orders. In every large province the postmaster had to keep the Caliph informed of every event of importance, to report on the state of the finances and the administration of the crown lands, the behaviour of the officers of the state, and the condition of agriculture and the peasantry. The cost of keeping up this large establishment of postal officials, together with the various stations and the camels and horses required, was very heavy, but as it constituted the only possible means of controlling the administration of such a vast Empire, the Caliphs rightly attached much importance to it, and the Chief Postmaster at the capital had to communicate despatches to the Caliph immediately on their arrival. Pigeons also appear to have been used for transmitting news. Further, this organised control of the great highways, where these postal stations were established, facilitated the movements of the high officials and of the troops.

In addition to this department there was a large force of detective police, and an elaborate system of espionage became a characteristic feature of the administration, whereby a Caliph set spies to watch his officials and even the members of his own family, while they in return employed their own spies to report upon his movements and utterances. For this purpose, in addition to regular members of the postal service, persons of every social grade, merchants, pedlars, physicians, and slave girls, were employed.

It was in harmony with this inquisition into the affairs of private persons that the Muḥtasib, or Prefect of Police, should not only be concerned with preventing breaches of the civil and religious law but also act as a censor of morals. One of his most important duties was to inspect weights and measures, and control commercial transactions by preventing fraud in sales and the counterfeiting of goods or the making of extortionate charges. He forbade the public sale of wine and the playing of musical instruments in public places. In regard to the practices of religion it was his duty to see that the correct ritual observances were followed, for instance, to prevent the utterance of religious formulae not sanctioned by authority, or the repetition in a loud voice of those that were to be uttered in low tones; he could stop a man from taking part in public worship who had not performed the prescribed rites of ablution, or had not carried them out according to the strict prescriptions of the ritual law; he could also punish a man who was detected breaking the fast of Ramaḍān. He found suitable husbands for widows and took care that no divorced women married before the expiration of the legal period. He protected slaves from having tasks imposed upon them that they were not strong enough to perform, and punished the owners of beasts of burden if they did not provide their animals with sufficient provender or overworked them. His authority even extended to the inspection of dolls, to see whether they bore any resemblance to idols or served any other purpose than that of accustoming little girls to the care of infants. Unless he had received express authority, the Prefect of Police could not interfere with the office of the magistrate, for if an accused person denied his guilt the matter had to be brought before the judge.

The judges were appointed either directly by the Caliph or an official, such as his Wazīr, or by a governor to whom authority had been delegated. In the appointment of a judge the locality in which he could exercise jurisdiction had to be expressly stated, and his authority was either general or restricted. In the former instance he not only tried cases but, among other duties, appointed guardians for minors, lunatics, and others who could not manage their own property, administered religious endowments, and saw that wills were carried out according to the directions of the testator. There was a special court of appeal in which were heard complaints of the miscarriage of justice in the administrative or judicial department; the earlier Abbasid Caliphs received such complaints in public audience, but after the reign of Muhtadī (869-870) this office was put into commission and a special officer appointed as president of the Board for the investigation of grievances. In the reign of Muqtadir (908-932), his mother, who controlled the administration, appointed to this post her Mistress of the Robes.

The organisation of the army varied at different times in Muslim history. By the Abbasid period the troops were divided into two classes: the regular Arab army kept on a permanent footing and paid out of the State Treasury, and the volunteers who were not entered on the register and received no fixed pay. The latter received grants out of the poor tax, and took part in the annual raids into Byzantine territory or into the neighbouring countries of the unbelievers. As the Abbasids came into power largely through the assistance of troops from Khurāsān, these formed a separate division of the army recruited from that part of their dominions. Later on, Mu'taṣim (833–842) added another separate army corps made up of Turks, and also enrolled a contingent of slaves mainly from North Africa. The favour which Mu'taṣim extended towards these foreign troops, and the disaffection excited by the excesses they committed on the citizens of Baghdad, was one of the reasons that determined him to transfer his capital to Sāmarrā in 836. Here he built enormous barracks for his Turkish troops and encouraged Turkish chieftains to come and live under his protection; he assigned separate sections of the vast city that grew up around his palace to the Turkish troops according to their tribes and their original habitat, and, in order to keep them apart from the surrounding population, he purchased numbers of Turkish slave girls whom he compelled his troops to marry; fixed stipends were assigned to these slave girls and registers were kept of their names. These Turkish guards came gradually to outnumber every other section of the army, and they grew in wealth and influence as the number of posts conferred upon them increased, until gradually the administration passed from the hands of the Persians into those of the Turks, and the Caliph became quite at the mercy of his Turkish guard. Things came to such a pass that more than one Caliph was put to death by his own troops, and the election of his successor was determined by his Turkish officers. Still greater confusion arose when rival factions among the Turks themselves came to blows with one another: the administration fell into disorder, the provinces ceased to remit revenue to the capital, and the troops mutinied and clamoured for their arrears of pay. It was to escape from such an intolerable position that the Caliph Mu'tamid in 892 abandoned Sāmarrā as a capital.

As the central authority declined and the Empire broke up into a number of independent states and fiefs, the character of the military organisation changed, and in place of the great standing army under a single command a system of military fiefs grew up, according to which different members of a ruling house or separate chiefs were given charge over a town or a district, on condition that they paid an annual tribute and supplied at their own cost a fixed number of troops to their overlord. But in all these separate bodies of troops the presence of Turkish soldiers became a common feature, since fresh accessions to their number were continuously coming from the East as the Turkish troops learned of the wealth and power that their fellow-tribesmen could gain by service within the Muslim Empire.

Many of these Turkish soldiers were slaves, and one reason for the dependence of the Caliphs upon them was the belief that security could be obtained by the possession of a bodyguard entirely dependent on the favour of the sovereign without any ties of family or relationship with the rest of the population. When the Caliphs became disillusioned of the notion that loyalty could be purchased in this manner from the Turks, they still continued to place reliance upon their slaves, and Muqtadir (908–932) in his desire to maintain his authority against the troublesome Turkish troops acquired as many as 11,000 slaves, some of whom he promoted to high office and placed in command of his army.

Slavery from the outset had been a recognised institution of Muslim society, but from the reign of this Caliph the tenure by slaves of some of the highest offices of the state became an increasingly characteristic feature of the social organisation. Conquests and raids had from the earliest days of the expansion of the Arab Empire added to the slave population of the great cities, but a constant supply was kept up later through the well-organised slave-trade, which brought such enormous numbers of black slaves from Africa that their armed risings were at times a source of serious disorder. The white slaves were brought in thousands from various Turkish tribes in Central Asia, and also from Mediterranean ports, especially from Spain and Italy. Many of these slaves were employed by their masters in trade and commercial enterprises of various kinds.

The transference of the capital to 'Irāq by the Abbasid Caliphs was followed by a period of great commercial expansion. Not only did the possession of enormous wealth create a demand for costly articles, such as silks from China and furs from northern Europe, but trade was promoted by certain special conditions, such as the vast extent of the Muslim empire, the spread of Arabic as a world-language, and the exalted status assigned to the merchant in the Muslim system of ethics; it was remembered that the Prophet himself had been a merchant and had commended trading during the pilgrimage to Mecca. Not only did the great trade routes through the empire facilitate commercial relations, but under the Abbasids navigation received a great impulse; for the Eastern trade, Baṣrah, a Muslim creation, was one of the most flourishing ports; in the West, the Arabs entered into the inheritance of the great Mediterranean ports of the Roman Empire. To the sea-faring inhabitants of the coasts of Syria and Egypt the Arabs were indebted also for the building up of their fleet, which became so formidable a rival of the Byzantine navy.

The theory of the Arab State was that of a community of believers holding the primitive faith revealed by God to Adam and successive prophets, and occupying the heritage of the earth that God had given to Adam and his descendants; but from the very outset there was a recognition of persons who did not accept the faith of Islām, and the Koran enjoins toleration towards the "people of the Book," *i.e.* the Jews and the Christians, who are looked upon as professing a religion that is a corrupted form of God's original and oft-repeated revelation.

According to the theory of the Arab legists based on the practice of the Prophet and his immediate successors, religious toleration was granted to the Jews, Christians, and Zoroastrians, on condition that they paid tribute. The non-Muslim living under Arab rule was technically called Dhimmī (literally, one with whom a compact has been made), and the theory was that agreements were made by the Arab conquerors as they extended their authority over different cities and districts. The Arab historians record several examples of such agreements, but by the Abbasid period the actual practice appears to have become uniform, modified only by the idiosyncracies of local governors. Under the influence of the communistic theory of the young Muslim community, in accordance with which the immense wealth poured into the Public Treasury, as the Arab conquests were extended in the Roman and Persian Empires, was divided among the faithful, some attempt appears to have been made to prevent the Arab Muslims from settling down in conquered territory, with the intention that they might constitute a permanent army. Consequently the payers of taxes were the original inhabitants of the conquered territories, and recent investigations go to prove that the taxes they paid to the Arabs were much the same as those they had been accustomed to pay the former governments. But, according to the theory of the legists, the non-Muslims paid *jizyah* as a poll tax, in return for which they received protection for life and property and exemption from military service. The system broke down when the first conquests were followed by the conversion to Islām of large sections of the newly-acquired subjects; their claim to be exempted from the land-tax they had been accustomed to pay threatened the state with financial ruin, and the government was compelled to levy land-tax from Muslims and non-Muslims alike. The *jizyah* in some form or another continued to be levied upon the members of the protected religious communities that refused to accept Islām; it is very doubtful, however, whether the accounts given in legal treatises on the subject correspond to the actual practice followed in the collection of this tax.

In the Koran the only "people of the Book" expressly mentioned were the Jews and the Christians. When the conquest of Persia brought a large Zoroastrian population under Arab rule, it was conveniently remembered that the Prophet had given orders that the Zoroastrians were to be treated just like the "people of the Book" and that *jizyah* might be taken from them also. A similar policy of religious tolerance was extended to the heathen Ḥarrānians and Mandaeans, though, according to the strict letter of the law, they should either have been put to death or compelled to embrace Islām. The Manichaeans likewise were not entitled to toleration according to Muslim law, but they survived as a separate sect up to the tenth century, and during the reign of Ma'mūn (813–833) the leader of this sect held a public disputation with the Muslim theologians in Baghdad in the presence of the Caliph himself; but even on this occasion the Caliph had to furnish this religious teacher with a bodyguard to prevent his being exposed to insult from the fanatical populace, and in later reigns the persecution of the Manichaeans became so severe that those who escaped fled into Turkestan.

During the period of the Umayyads the religious indifference that characterised most of the rulers of this dynasty, with the exception of Omar ibn 'Abd-al-'Azīz (717–720), lent support to this theory of toleration, and the condition of the Christians and the Jews appears to have been tolerable, except, of course, that like all the subject peoples, they were always exposed to the exactions of rapacious taxgatherers. There was a change for the worse with the advent of the Abbasids, in consequence of the emphasis that this dynasty laid upon religious considerations and its zealous patronage of orthodoxy. Hārūn (786–809) passed an edict compelling Jews and Christians to adopt a different costume to that of the Muslims, but it appears to have been put into force only in the capital and even there to have soon ceased to be applied. This temporary change of attitude was very possibly the result of the treachery which the Emperor Nicephorus shewed in his dealings with this Caliph. A more serious persecution broke out in the reign of Mutawakkil (847–861). This fanatical Caliph lent the support of the state to the strong orthodox re-action that had set in against the rationalistic tendencies which had had free play under former rulers, and he came forward as the champion of the extreme orthodox party to which the mass of the Muslim population belonged. He persecuted the Mu'tazilites, whose doctrines had been in the ascendancy in the court during the reign of Ma'mūn, and branded with ridicule their doctrine that the Koran was created. He shewed a similar persecuting zeal against the Shī'ah sect, the members of which were imprisoned and scourged, and he pulled down the tomb of the martyred Ḥusain at Karbalā and forbade pilgrimages to its site. The Christians suffered equally during this period of intolerance. They were ordered to wear a distinctive dress, dismissed from their employments in government offices, forbidden to ride on horses, and harassed with several other restrictions. The churches that had been built since the Arab conquest were ordered to be pulled down, and the dwellings of some of the wealthier Christians were turned into mosques. To the reign of this fanatical ruler belongs the restrictive ordinances which were traditionally ascribed to Omar, the companion and successor of the Prophet; but these intolerant regulations appear to have been in force spasmodically only, and during the confusion into which the administration fell it was not possible to put them into force any more than any other statutes. After each fanatical outburst of persecution the Christians returned to their posts in the government offices; indeed the administration could not do without them, for it had depended upon their special knowledge and skill from the very beginning of the Arab conquest. Despite the complaints repeatedly made by fanatics, the Caliphs persisted in bestowing high offices on non-Muslims. On one occasion when objections were made to the Caliph Mu'taḍid (892–902) against a Christian being governor of the important city of Anbār (on the Euphrates about forty-two miles from Baghdad), he claimed the right to appoint a Christian to any office for which he might be fitted, and added that such a man might be more suitable than a Muslim since the latter might possibly shew undue consideration to his co-religionists.

That such a high administrative office should have been entrusted to a Christian was probably a rare occurrence, but the ministry of finance seems to have been generally filled with them. As physicians too, the Christians exercised great influence at court and acquired considerable wealth. Gabriel, the personal physician to the Caliph Hārūn, was a Nestorian Christian and is said to have amassed a fortune of more than three and a half million pounds sterling.

In trade and commerce too the Christians attained considerable affluence; indeed it was frequently their wealth that excited against them the jealous cupidity of the mob. The wealth possessed by the Christians may be estimated by the magnificent churches erected under Muslim rule, though according to the theory of the legists it was not permissible to build any new churches in Muslim territory after the conquest. In addition to the record of the building of many churches under the Umayyads, several such foundations are mentioned in the Abbasid period, for instance, in 759 the Nestorian Bishop Cyprian completed a church in Nisibis, on which he had expended the sum of 56,000 dīnārs. In the reign of Mahdī (775–785) a church was built in Baghdad for the use of the Christian prisoners taken captive during the numerous campaigns against the Byzantine Empire, and his son Hārūn gave permission for the erection of new churches, including a magnificent building in which the Jacobite Bishop of Mārdīn enshrined the bodies of the prophets Daniel and Ezekiel. The Christian prime minister of the Buwaihid prince Aḍud-ud-Daulah (949–982), who administered Southern Persia and 'Irāq, also built a number of new churches, and the building of churches and monasteries is recorded as late as the reign of Mustaḍī (1170–1180). Some evidence of the wealth in Christian hands is given by the large sums which were expended in bribes, *e.g.* in 912 the Nestorian Patriarch in Baghdad spent 30,000 dīnārs (gold coins) in intrigues against a rival patriarch of the Orthodox Church; the Nestorian Patriarch, Īsho'yabh, in 1190 secured his appointment by means of a bribe of 5,000 dīnārs; a century later, another patriarch spent 7,000 dīnārs for a similar purpose, and his successor did the same.

Of the literature produced during the Abbasid period it is only possible to give a brief sketch here. Not only was the number of individual authors very great, and the output of many of them enormous (*e.g.* as many as 70 works by Ghazālī are recorded and of the writings of Avicenna 99 have survived to us), but they left hardly any subject of human interest untouched. Some estimate of the immense literary activity of this period may be formed from the "Index," compiled in 988 by an-Nadīm, of the Arabic books on every branch of knowledge extant in his day[1]. It was in this period also that Arabic began to take on the characteristics of a world-literature, and became the literary medium ot expression for others besides the Arabs themselves. Some of the most noteworthy contributions to this literature were made by Persians, and the decline of Syriac literature marks the ascendancy of Arabic. Not only did the Nestorian and Jacobite Christians tend more and more to prefer Arabic to Syriac as a literary language, but the heathen of Ḥarrān translated into Arabic much of the wisdom of the Greeks, and nearly all the scientific and philosophic works by Jews between the ninth and thirteenth centuries were written in the same language.

Of the poetry of the Abbasid period, only brief mention is possible here. While some poets continued to imitate the ancient models set in the pre-Islāmic odes and followed by writers of the Umayyad period, there were many more who grew weary of these antiquated conventions and poured scorn on what they considered to be the barbarisms of the desert. The most famous representative of the new school of poetry was Abū Nuwās (*ob. c.* 810), one the court poets of Hārūn; his poems in praise of love and wine made him notorious, and he took the lead among the licentious poets of that reign. In striking contrast to his rollicking contemporary was another poet who enjoyed the patronage of Hārūn, Abu' l-'Atāhiyah (*ob.* 828), whose poetry is marked by a profound scepticism and a philosophic spirit of asceticism. The growing interest in religious and ethical problems and the encouragement given by the Abbasids to theological studies were not without their influence on poetry, and a great quantity of pietistic verse was produced; but with the widening of intellectual interest, poetry came indeed to reflect every aspect of the many-sided culture of this period. Two more names must be mentioned, that of Mutanabbi (*ob.* 965), in the judgment of most of his fellow-countrymen the greatest of the Muslim Arab poets, who was the panegyrist of the Ḥamdānid prince, Saif-ad-Daulah, the generous patron of Abu' l-Faraj Isfahānī, Fārābī, and many other writers; and that of Abu' l-'Alà al-Ma'arrī (*ob.* 1058), the sceptical blind poet, to whom Dr Nicholson has devoted an erudite and illuminating monograph[2].

Of the vast literature of the Abbasid period a large part is connected with those various branches of study that grew out of the efforts to elucidate the Koran. Tradition ascribes the composition of the earliest work on Arabic grammar to the fact that a learned scholar heard a man, quoting a verse of the Koran, make such a gross grammatical blunder as to turn the sense of the passage into blasphemy. But apart from the need of a scientific exposition of the language for an intelligent understanding of the Koran, Arabic was rapidly adopted, at least for purposes

[1] E. G. Browne, *Literary History of Persia,* I, 383 sqq.

[2] *Studies in Islamic Poetry,* chap. II. Cambridge. 1921.

of literary expression, by the subject races, and even the Arabs themselves, belonging to different tribes and speaking varying dialects in a foreign country, were in need of guidance if the purity of their speech was to be preserved. A school of grammarians sprang up during the Umayyad period in Baṣrah, which had been founded just after the conquest of 'Irāq as a great military station to command the approach from the sea, and a rival school arose later in the city of Kūfah, founded about the same time as a permanent camp on the desert side of the Euphrates. Two representatives of these schools may be mentioned here. Sībawaihi (*ob.* 793) wrote the first systematic exposition of Arabic grammar and had a long line of imitators in the Baṣrah school; to the school of Kūfah belonged Kisā'ī (*ob.* 805), whom Hārūn appointed tutor to his sons; both he and Sībawaihi were Persians by birth, and there is a record of their having met in controversy on points of grammar. By the early part of the ninth century these rival schools had lost their importance, and the leading grammarians were to be found in Baghdad.

The study of the Koran also gave a stimulus to the study of history, pre-eminently the life of the Prophet, and then of earlier prophets mentioned in the sacred text; to law, the primary source of which was the Koran; and to other branches of learning. The exegesis of the text of the Koran itself began as a branch of the science of tradition, and the oldest systematic collections of traditions, such as those of Bukhārī (*ob.* 870) and Tirmidhī (*ob.* 892), contain comments on the subject-matter of the Koran. Ṭabarī's (*ob.* 923) monumental commentary was epoch-making; it not only embodies the work of its predecessors in an exhaustive enumeration of traditional interpretations and lexicographical notes on the text, supported by quotations from pre-Islāmic poetical literature, but discusses difficulties of grammar and deals with questions of dogma and law. The commentaries produced by succeeding generations are without number, but among these special mention must be made of the *Kashshāf* of Zamakhsharī (*ob.* 1143), one of the greatest Arabic scholars of his time, though by birth a Persian; his work was exploited by succeeding generations of commentators, and their tribute to his erudition was the more remarkable since the author was a Mu'tazilite and had embodied in his work some of the heretical opinions of his sect. This great work formed the basis of the most widely studied commentary in the Muslim world to the present day, that of Baiḍāwī (*ob.* 1286).

The Muslim system of law claimed to be based on the Koran, but owing to the scarcity of material provided by the sacred text a distinct branch of Muslim study with an enormous literature of its own grew up, technically known as *Fiqh*. This deals not only with legal matters in the narrower sense of the term, *i.e.* criminal and civil law, the law of property and inheritance, constitutional law, and the principles of administration of the state and the conduct of war, but also with ritual and religious observances and the innumerable details of the daily life falling under the consideration of a legal system that makes no distinction between the civil and the religious life of the believer. This system of law was developed largely under the influence of the Roman law which the Arabs found operative in Syria and Mesopotamia; in matters of ritual there were borrowings also from the Jewish law.

The religious character of the Abbasid dynasty gave an impulse to the systematic codification of Muslim law, and produced a vast literature embodying the different standpoints of the various schools of legists that grew up within the Sunnī sect to which the government belonged. By the end of the Abbasid period these had become narrowed down to the four that survive to the present day, but there had been others which became obsolete. These various schools differed mainly according to the place the legists allowed to independent judgment and the use of analogical deduction. In addition to the Sunnī schools, the other sects, particularly the Shī'ahs, developed legal systems of their own.

Dogmatic literature as distinct from exegesis and *fiqh* appears first to have grown up in connexion with the problems of the divine unity and its harmony with the attributes of God, and of the divine justice in relation to the problem of the freedom or determination of the human will. This dogmatic literature tended more and more to take on a metaphysical form as Muslim thinkers came under the influence of Greek thought, brought to their knowledge through versions of Neoplatonic and Aristotelean treatises translated into Arabic either from Syriac or directly from Greek. The writings of the earliest school of speculative theologians, the Mu'tazilites, have almost entirely perished, but the teachings of another liberal movement in theology which endeavoured to harmonise authority with reason and seems to have been connected with the Isma'īlian propaganda, have been preserved to us in the treatises of the so-called Brethren of Sincerity (made accessible to the European reader by Dieterici). They wrote towards the end of the tenth century and put forth an encyclopaedic scheme of human knowledge, dividing learning into three branches—the preliminary, the religious, and the philosophic studies; under the last heading they grouped propaedeutics (consisting of arithmetic, geometry, astronomy, and music), logic, physics, and theology.

This group of thinkers appears to have been obliged to meet in secret, for the orthodox reaction, which received the support of the government under Mutawakkil (847–861) and found expression in the writings of Ash'arī (*ob.* 933), the founder of orthodox scholasticism, effectually crushed liberal movements in theology. Ash'arī had been brought up as a Mu'tazilite, but when he became converted to orthodoxy he adapted the dialectic methods of the philosophers to the defence of the orthodox position. A more popular exposition of the Ash'arite system of theology was given by Ghazālī (*ob.* 1111) who, in the reaction from arid scholasticism, took refuge in Sufiism and gave mystical experience a place in his reasoned exposition of orthodox doctrines. His literary activity was enormous, his best-known works being the autobiography of his spiritual experience in his *Deliverer from Error*, and the vast compendium of his religious system, *The Revivification of the Sciences of the Faith.*

Mysticism in Islām had had a long history before Ghazālī embodied it in a system of orthodox theology. Beginning as a purely ascetic movement, it came under foreign influences, notably Neoplatonic and Gnostic, and so took on more theosophic forms of expression. The teachings of the early Sufis were expressed in sayings handed down by their disciples; one of the oldest systematic treatises was the *Sustenance of the Souls* by Abū Ṭālib al-Makkī (*ob.* 996), which was followed by a vast number of writings too numerous to be recorded here.

Historical literature had its origin in biographies of the Prophet and his companions. The foundations of this literature were laid in the Umayyad period, but the oldest extant biography of the Prophet, written by Ibn Isḥāq, who died in 768 during the reign of the second Abbasid Caliph, has only survived to us in a recension of it made by Ibn Hishām (*ob.* 834), a distinguished grammarian. Another biographer of the Prophet, Wāqidī (*ob.* 822), enjoyed the patronage of Hārūn and wrote *The Book of the Wars*, a detailed account of the campaigns of the Prophet and the early successes of the Arab conquerors. His contemporary, Ibn Sa'd (*ob.* 844), wrote an immense biographical work containing a life of the Prophet and of the various classes of his companions and those who immediately followed them. Balādhurī (*ob.* 892) also wrote an account of the early Arab conquests, which is one of the most valuable sources for this early period, and began a vast biographical work on the life of the Prophet and his kinsmen, among whom the Abbasids are reckoned. Other historians took a larger range. Dīnawarī (*ob.* 895) in his *Book of the Long Histories* paid especial attention to the history of Persia, and Ya'qūbī, his contemporary, wrote a manual of universal history; but all these works were surpassed in extent by the monumental *Annals of the Apostles and the Kings* by Ṭabarī, whose commentary on the Koran has already been mentioned, a history of the world so far as it was of interest to a Muslim historian, from the creation to the year 915. His work was abridged by a later writer, Ibn al-Athīr (*ob.* 1234), who likewise wrote a history of the world, but from the beginning of the tenth century gives an independent record; he also wrote a history of the Atābegs of Mosul and an alphabetical dictionary entitled *Lions of the Jungle*, biographies of 7,500 companions of the Prophet.

Other biographers confined their attention to limited groups, *e.g.* the philosophers, scientists, physicians, or distinguished citizens of particular cities; but none of these equal the interest that attaches to the *Book of Songs* composed by Abu'l Faraj Iṣfahānī (*ob.* 967); beginning merely with a collection of songs composed by the most famous musicians at the court of the Caliph Hārūn, it contains not only detailed and graphic accounts of poets and singers, but incidentally is one of the most important of our sources for the history of the culture of the Muslim world up to the ninth century.

An entirely new form of literary activity was introduced in a highly artificial form of rhymed prose, known as the Maqāmah. The use of rhyme is characteristic of the earliest work in Arabic prose known to us, the Koran, and as a literary device it runs through Arabic prose literature, finding special expression in pulpit oratory and the elevated epistolary style of official correspondence; but this style of composition gave rise to a distinct department of literature when Badī'-uz-Zamān Hamadhānī (*ob.* 1007) conceived the idea of popularising it in a narrative of the adventures of a vagabond scholar, who suddenly appears in gatherings of wealthy persons and learned assemblies and by the display of his erudition gains for himself ample reward. The author makes such compositions an occasion for displaying his erudition by an abundant use of rare and obsolete words and recondite phrases, illustrating now the idiom of the Bedouins of the desert and now that of typical examples of the townsfolk; though clad in a garb of out-of-the-way learning, these compositions are full of humour and pointed satire against various classes of contemporary society. The fame of this work was, however, eclipsed by that of Ḥarīrī (*ob.* 1122), whose Maqāmāt are regarded as a masterpiece of Arabic literary style, full of all manner of rhetorical devices, verbal conceits, and verbal puzzles, intelligible only to trained students of grammar and philology. Ḥarīrī recounts the wanderings of a learned knave who also suddenly appears in all kinds of unexpected circumstances, and after a witty declaration, often in verse, as mysteriously disappears again. Ḥarīrī claimed that his work was not intended merely to amuse but had also a deeper moral purpose, and there are indeed passages in which his hero utters sentiments of the loftiest morals in language of great dignity and beauty.

Prose literature developed also in various other forms of *belles lettres*, notably in translations, such as the stories of Kalīlah and Dimnah, largely under the stimulus of the varied foreign influences that met in the cultured society of Baghdad. Intellectual interest was widened until men of letters left no subject untouched; typical of such a wide intellectual outlook is the Mu'tazilite theologian Jāḥiẓ (*ob.* 869) who, in his numerous writings, ranged over such subjects as theology, rhetoric, natural history (as in his *Book of Animals*), anthropology (in treatises that discussed the relative merits of the Arabs and the Turks), and studies of contemporary society (as in his *Book of Misers*, *of Young Gallants*, *of Scribes*, *of Singers*, etc). The influence of Jāḥiẓ on Arabic prose literature was considerable; his pupil Mubarrad (*ob.* 898) collected in his Kāmil historical notices and examples of early poetry and prose, and such compilations became a recognised form of literary activity to which several writers of genius devoted themselves. Akin to such writers in their wide intellectual outlook were the encyclopaedists, of whom Mas'ūdī (*ob.* 956) may be taken as an example. He spent a large part of his life in travel, and visited almost every part of Muslim Asia from Armenia to India and from the Caspian to Zanzibar. Everything that he saw interested him, and his reading was extensive and profound. In his latter years he composed a universal history from the Creation up to his own period, but his range was not confined to the conventional circle of Islāmic learning, for he studied the beliefs of rival creeds and the wisdom of the Indians, and enquired into puzzling problems of natural history, such as the source of the Nile and the phenomena of tides, and described the sea-serpent and the rhinoceros.

Mas'ūdī is typical of the mental curiosity which produced a rich scientific literature during the Abbasid period. The practical needs of administrators gave an impulse to the scientific study of geography, and the oldest geographical work in Arabic that has survived is an official handbook of *Roads and Countries* by a Persian postmaster, Ibn Khurdādhbih, who lived in the first half of the ninth century. The geographical literature that followed forms an important section of Arabic literature written by eager and close observers. Maqdisī, who wrote in 985, embodied in an attractive style the accumulated experience of twenty years of travel from Sind and Sīstān in the East to Spain in the West. But the greatest of the Arab geographers was Yāqūt (*ob.* 1229), a Greek slave whose master had him educated in Baghdad; he lived a wandering life, finally settling down in Aleppo; among his other writings, he wrote a vast geographical dictionary and a biographical dictionary of learned men. Zakarīyā of Qazwīn (*ob.* 1283) summed up the geographical knowledge of his time in a comprehensive cosmography, a kind of geographical encyclopaedia that deals not only with geography proper but also with astronomy, anthropology, and natural history; this book, translated into Persian, Turkish, and Urdu, was held to be the standard work on geographical sciences until a knowledge of Western learning penetrated the Muslim world.

Philosophy, as distinguished from theological scholasticism, begins with Kindī (*ob. c.* 873), one of the few writers of pure Arab descent who acquired distinction in letters during this period; but he was a translator rather than a constructive thinker, and among the two hundred treatises he wrote on such different subjects as astronomy, geometry, music, politics, and medicine, there are translations of parts of Aristotle's works and abridgments of others. For his pupil Aḥmad, a son of the Caliph Mu'taṣim, he prepared a version of the first work of Greek philosophy translated into Arabic; though this was actually made up of portions of the *Enneads* of Plotinus, it bore the misleading title of the *Theology of Aristotle*, and this absurd designation is responsible for much of the confusion prevailing in Arabic philosophy when attempts were made to expound Aristotelean and Platonic doctrines. A more permanent influence on Muslim philosophic thought was exercised by Fārābī (*ob.* 950), a Turk, who pursued his studies in medicine, mathematics, and philosophy in Baghdad, but spent the last years of his life in Aleppo under the tolerant patronage of the Ḥamdānid prince, Saif-ad-Daulah. Like Kindī, his literary activity was enormous, and included a number of commentaries upon Aristotle as well as independent expositions of metaphysical problems. He certainly presented a fuller exposition of Aristotelean doctrine than had hitherto been available in the Arabic language, but, as he, like Kindī, believed in the authenticity of the *Theology of Aristotle* and wrote several books to establish the agreement between the doctrines of Aristotle and Plato, his exposition of Aristotle is often incorrect. The brief aphoristic form in which he composed many of his treatises, and the mysticism that interpenetrates his thought, makes his system somewhat obscure. The Aristotelean doctrine received a much clearer and more methodical exposition in the writings of Ibn Sīnā (Avicenna) (*ob.* 1037), whose philosophical development was first stimulated by the study of one of Fārābī's works. He was more concerned than his predecessor to attempt to reconcile the Aristotelean metaphysic with Muslim theology. The philosophy of Avicenna, however, belongs almost as much to Western medieval thought as to that of the Muslim East, and will be dealt with in another part of this work.

Henceforth, two distinct streams of philosophic thought manifest themselves; the Spanish philosophers Ibn Bājja (Avenpace) (*ob.* 1138), Ibn Tufail (Abubacer) (*ob.* 1185), and Ibn Rushd (Averroes) (*ob.* 1198), continued to work out philosophic problems in the West, but their influence was more profoundly felt in Christian Europe than in the Muslim East. Here, particularly in Persia, under the stimulus given to speculation by Ghazālī, the philosophers tended more and more to become orthodox; they studied Greek philosophy assiduously and were profoundly influenced by Greek logic, but they carried on a persistent attack upon separate Aristotelean doctrines in their defence of Muslim dogma. Fakhr-ud-Dīn Rāzī (*ob.* 1209), the author of the great commentary on the Koran, *The Keys of the Unseen*, was interpenetrated with Greek ideas, but both here and in his numerous philosophical works he developed the orthodox Ash'arite doctrines with a strong element of mysticism.

A strain of mysticism also characterises the idealistic philosophy of Shihāb-ud-Dīn Suhrawardī (*ob.* 1191), who attacked the position that truth could be attained by pure reason in his *Unveiling of the Greek Absurdities*, and in his philosophy of Illumination sought to reconcile with the theology of Islām the ancient Persian doctrine that identified light and spiritual substance. He founded a school of Persian metaphysics in which speculation and emotion were united and harmonised.

During the next century Naṣīr-ud-Dīn Ṭūsī (*ob.* 1273) also expounded Greek philosophy in the spirit of orthodox Muslim dogma, and had numerous commentators who followed him in making similar use of Greek metaphysics and psychology. His contemporaries, Khawinjī (*ob.* 1248), Abharī (*ob.* 1264), and Kātibī (*ob.* 1276), wrote compendiums of logic, which have been text-books for centuries and have been commented upon by generations of scholars.

In the science of medicine also the Arabs were the pupils of the Greeks. The medical system of the Greeks had been studied in the great school of Jundī-Shāpūr during the Sasanian period, and from the day when the second Abbasid Caliph summoned Georgios, the son of Bukhtyishū‘, from Jundī-Shāpūr to Baghdad in 765, this Nestorian Christian family remained in high favour at the court for more than two centuries and a half. Either from Syriac or the original Greek, Christian physicians translated into Arabic the works of Hippocrates, Galen, Dioscorides, and other authorities on medicine. Of these translators one of the most active was Ḥunain ibn Isḥāq (*ob.* 873), known to medieval Europe as Johannitius; he belonged to a Christian Arab tribe, and studied first in Baghdad and later in Jundī-Shāpūr. Another city that produced translators from the Greek was Ḥarrān, the seat of a sect known as Sabaeans, to which belonged an active translator Thābit ibn Qurrah (*ob.* 901), whose sons and grandsons were also men of learning. Some knowledge of the Hindu system of medicine also appears to have reached Baghdad, and a summary of the Indian medicine is given by ‘Alī ibn Rabban, who in 850 compiled one of the earliest comprehensive works on medical science in Arabic, *The Paradise of Wisdom.* Arabic medical literature, however, is by no means limited to translations, and one of the most prolific contributors to this literature, Rāzī, who died in the early part of the tenth century, was a skilled clinical observer, and made distinctly original contributions to medical science. Out of the fifty works from his pen that are known to us, representing less than half of his writings, two were translated into Latin during the Middle Ages under the titles of the *Continens* and *Liber Almansoris*; the first, the *Ḥāwī*, is a work so enormous that only wealthy persons could afford to have copies made of it, and it consequently became rare; the other book takes its name from his patron, one of the Sāmānid princes of Khurāsān, to whom it was dedicated.

Another comprehensive system of medicine, known to the Middle Ages as the *Liber Regius* of Haly Abbas, was written by ‘Alī ibn al-‘Abbās, a Persian, for the Buwaihid prince ‘Aḍud-ud-Daulah (949–982). It was diligently studied until its fame was eclipsed by the Qānūn (Canon) of Avicenna, who was as great a physician as he was a philosopher, and out of his 99 works that have survived this was the one most widely studied, not only in the East but also in the West, since Gerard of Cremona translated it in the twelfth century. Professor Browne says of this book: "Its encyclopaedic character, its systematic arrangement, its philosophic plan, perhaps even its dogmatism, combined with the immense reputation of its author in other fields besides medicine, raised it to a unique position in the medical literature of the Muslim world, so that the earlier works of ar-Rází and al-Majúsí, in spite of their undoubted merits, were practically abrogated by it, and it is still regarded in the East by the followers of the old Greek medicine, the *Ṭibb-i-Yúnání*, as the last appeal on all matters connected with the healing art."[1] From the tenth century onward Spain produced a number of great physicians, who, of course, wrote in Arabic; while in Persia, the birth-place of the Arabic authors above mentioned, Rāzī, 'Alī ibn al-'Abbās, and Avicenna, a vast medical literature in the Persian language began with an encyclopaedia by a physician named Zain-ud-Dīn Ismā'īl, entitled the Dhakīra-i Khwārazmshāhī, in honour of his patron who was governor of Khwārazm (or Khiva) under the Seljūq Sultan Sanjar.

In the Middle Ages students of science often endeavoured to be encyclopaedic, and several of the philosophers and physicians mentioned above devoted their attention to other branches of learning. As in the case of philosophy and medicine, the first impulse came from translations. These were for the most part made from Greek writings by Syrian Christians or by the so-called Sabaeans of Ḥarrān; but Sanskrit literature provided the earliest material, for an Indian in 771 brought to Manṣūr, the founder of Baghdad, a work on astronomy, which this Caliph ordered to be translated into Arabic, and shortly afterwards astronomical tables compiled under the Sasanians were translated from the Pahlavi. A great impulse to this work of translation was given by the Caliph Ma'mūn (813–833), who organised it by establishing a special translation bureau, to which skilled translators were attracted by offers of large salaries and were employed in rendering into Arabic works on geometry, astronomy, engineering, music, and the like. The names of several of the translators who worked for him are known; among them was Muḥammad ibn Mūsà al-Khwārazmī, one of whose works translated into Latin at the beginning of the twelfth century under the title *Algoritmi de numero Indorum* introduced the Arabic numerals into Europe, while his treatise on algebra was in use in the West up to the sixteenth century. These men were not translators merely; their own writings gave an impulse to mathematical and astronomical studies, which produced fruitful results in the advancement of these branches of knowledge. Astronomy especially was zealously studied, not only for its own sake but because of its connexion with astrology, and astronomers continued to enjoy the patronage of the more barbarous Turkish and Mongol dynasties that dispossessed the Arab Caliphate; among these may be mentioned Omar Khayyām, known in modern times for his Persian poetry, who reformed the calendar in 1079, while as an astronomer he was in the service of the Seljūq Sultan Malik Shāh. Among astronomers may also be mentioned one of the greatest intellects of the eleventh century, Berūnī (*ob.* 1048); he dedicated to

[1] *Arabian Medicine*, p. 62. Cambridge. 1921.

the Sultan Mas'ūd ibn Maḥmūd of Ghaznah a complete account of the science of astronomy, and wrote a number of smaller astronomical treatises dealing with the astrolabe and the planisphere. His profound knowledge of astronomy also reveals itself in his work on the calendars of different nations. But perhaps the greatest monument of his erudition that this remarkable man has left is his book on India, in which he gives an account of the religion, philosophy, astronomy, and customs of the Hindus, based upon a wide acquaintance with Sanskrit literature and upon his own personal observations. Naṣīr-ud-Dīn Ṭūsī, to whom reference has already been made as a philosophical writer, was in charge of an observatory at Marghah, several of the instruments in which he himself had invented; in 1270 he dedicated to his patron the Mongol prince Hūlāgū astronomical tables based on observations of the planets for twelve years, for in the midst of the appalling devastation that the Mongols inflicted upon Muslim culture—a ruin from which it has never recovered—they extended their patronage to one science at least, astronomy.

(B)

THE SELJŪQS.

THE rise of the Seljūq power and the history of the various dynasties which were established by princes of that family deserve attention for more than one reason. Not only were the Seljūqs largely responsible for the consolidation of Islām during the later days of the Abbasid Caliphate, but it is from this revival of power, which was, in no small degree, due to their efforts, that the failure of the Crusaders to make any lasting impression on the East may be traced. Further, it is not alone in politics and warfare that the Seljūqs achieved success: they have laid mankind under a debt in other spheres. Their influence may be observed in religion, art, and learning. Their love of culture was shewn by the universities which sprang up in their cities and in the crowds of learned men fostered at their courts. Under them appeared some of the shining lights of Islām. The philosopher and statesman Niẓām-al-Mulk, the mathematician-poet Omar Khayyām, warriors like Zangī, sultans like Malik Shāh, Nūr-ad-Dīn, and it is right to include Saladin himself, were the product of the Seljūq renaissance. To the Seljūq princes there can be ascribed, to a great extent, not only the comparative failure of the Crusades, but an unconscious influence of East upon West, springing from the intercourse between Frank and Saracen in the holy wars. The rise of the Seljūq power imparted fresh life to the Orthodox Caliphate, with which these princes were in communion, ultimately re-united the scattered states of Islām, and laid the foundations of the Ottoman Turkish Empire at Constantinople. It is impossible to give more than an outline of the important events and characters. The object of the present pages is merely to sketch the rise of the Seljūq power and to mention the states and dynasties by which the territories under Seljūq sway were ultimately absorbed. So numerous were the various Atābegs who supplanted them that sufficient space could not be allotted to their enumeration, which would in most cases prove both wearisome and superfluous.

The period covered by these dynasties lies between the eleventh and thirteenth centuries; the territory in which their rule was exercised extends over large districts of Asia, chiefly Syria, Persia, and Transoxiana. The name by which they are known is that of their first leader, from whose sons the different rulers were descended. This leader, Seljūq ibn Yakāk, is said to have sprung in direct line from Afrāsiyāb, King of Turkestan, the legendary foe of the first Persian dynasty, but this descent is not historical. Seljūq was one of the chiefs under the Khan of Turkestan, and with his emigration from Turkestan to Transoxiana and the subsequent adoption of Islām by himself and his tribe, his importance in history may be said to begin.

At the time of the appearance of the Seljūqs, Islām had completely lost its earlier homogeneity. The Umayyad Caliphate had been succeeded in 750 by the Abbasid, a change of power marked by the transference of the capital from Damascus to Baghdad. The latter Caliphate actually survived until the Mongol invasion under Hūlāgū in 1258, but at a very early period schism and decay had set in. Already in 750, when the Abbasids ousted the Umayyads, Spain became lost to the Caliphate, for 'Abd-ar-Raḥmān, escaping thither from the general slaughter of his kinsfolk in Syria, made himself independent, and his successors never acknowledged the Abbasid rule. The establishment of the Idrīsid dynasty in Morocco (788) by Idrīs ibn 'Abdallāh, of the Aghlabids in Tunis (800) by Ibrāhīm ibn Aghlab at Qairawān, the supremacy of the Ṭūlūnids (868–905) and Ikhshīdids (935–969) in Egypt, were severe losses to the Caliphate in its Western dominions. Nor was the East more stable. In Persia and Transoxiana, as a consequence of the policy pursued by the Caliph Ma'mūn (813–833), there arose a great national revival, resulting in the formation of several quasi-vassal dynasties, such as the Ṣaffārid (867–903) and the Sāmānid (874–999); from the latter the Ghaznawids developed, for Alptigīn, who founded the last-named line, was a Turkish slave at the Sāmānid court. Many of these dynasties became extremely powerful, and the ascendancy of the heterodox Buwaihids cramped and fettered the Caliphs in their own palaces. All these kingdoms nominally acknowledged the spiritual sovereignty of the Caliph, but in temporal matters they were their own masters. The chief visible token of the Caliph was the retention of his name in the Khuṭbah, a "bidding prayer" recited on Fridays in the mosques throughout Islām, and on the coins. It is extremely probable that even this fragment of authority was only allowed to survive for reasons of state, principally to invest with a show of legitimacy the claims of the various rulers who were, theoretically at least, vassals of God's vicegerent on earth, the Caliph at Baghdad.

It was not alone in politics that the decay of the Caliphate was manifest; in religion also its supremacy was assailed. The unity of Islām had been rent by the schism of "Sunnah" ("Way" or "Law") and "Shī'ah" ("Sect"). The former was the name adopted by the orthodox party, the latter the title which they applied to their opponents. The Shī'ites believed in the divine Imāmship of 'Alī, the son-in-law of Mahomet and the fourth Caliph after him. In consequence they rejected all the other Caliphs and declared their succession illegitimate. But they did not, on this account, support the Abbasids, although at first they sided with them. The Abbasids made skilful use of the Shī'ite 'Alids in undermining the Umayyad throne; indeed, by themselves the Abbasids could scarcely have hoped to succeed. Once in power, the allies fell apart. The Shī'ite doctrine contained numerous elements repugnant to a Sunnī, elements which may be regarded as gnostic survivals perhaps, but certainly borrowed from non-Semitic sources. Many held the Mu'tazilite opinion, which denied the fundamental proposition that the Koran is eternal and uncreated. They were noted for the number of their feasts and pilgrimages and for the veneration with which they practically worshipped 'Alī, since they added to the profession of Faith "There is no God but God and Mahomet is his apostle" the words "and 'Alī is his vicegerent (*walī*)." In course of time numerous sects grew out of the Shī'ah, perhaps the most famous being the Ismā'īlīyah, the Fāṭimids, the Druses of the Lebanon, and, in modern times, the Bābī sect in Persia. The kingdom of the Ṣafavids (1502–1736), known to English literature as "the Sophy," was Shī'ite in faith, and Shī'ite doctrines found a fertile soil in India and the more eastern provinces of Islām. On the whole it may be said roughly that the Turks were Sunnīs and the Persians Shī'ites.

At the time of the Seljūqs, when the political authority of the Caliphate was so much impaired, two of the most important Muslim kingdoms subscribed to the Shī'ite tenets. Of these kingdoms, one was that of the Buwaihids, who ruled in Southern Persia and 'Irāq. The dynasty had been founded in 932 by Buwaih, the head of a tribe of mountaineers in Dailam. The Buwaihids rose in power until the Caliphate was obliged to recognise them. In 945 the sons of Buwaih entered Baghdad and extracted many concessions from the Caliph Mustakfī. In spite of their heterodoxy they soon gained control over the Caliph, who became absolutely subject to their authority.

The other Shī'ite kingdom, to which reference has been made, was that of the Fāṭimids in Egypt (909–1171). As their name implies, these rulers claimed descent from Fāṭimah, the daughter of the Prophet, who married 'Alī. It is therefore easy to understand their leanings towards the Shī'ah. The dynasty arose in North Africa where 'Ubaid-Allāh, who claimed to be the Mahdī, conquered the Aghlabid rulers and gradually made himself supreme along the coast as far as Morocco. Finally, in 969 the Fāṭimids wrested Egypt from the Ikhshīdids and founded Cairo, close to the older Fusṭāṭ of 'Amr ibn al-'Āṣ. By 991 they had occupied Syria as far as and including Aleppo. Their predominance in politics and commerce continued to extend, but it is unnecessary to trace their development at present. It is sufficient to recall their Shī'ite tendencies and to appreciate the extent to which the Caliphate suffered in consequence of their prosperity.

It will thus be seen that at the end of the tenth century the position of the Caliphate was apparently hopeless. The unity of Islām both in politics and in religion was broken; the Caliph was a puppet at the mercy of the Buwaihids and Fāṭimids. The various Muslim states, it is true, acknowledged his sway, but the acknowledgment was formal and unreal. It seemed as though the mighty religion framed by the Prophet would be disintegrated by sectarianism, as though the brotherhood of Islām were a shattered ideal, and the great conquests of Khālid and Omar were destined to slip away from the weakening grasp of the helpless ruler at Baghdad.

In such a crisis it would seem that Islām was doomed. It is useful also to recollect that within a very few years the Muslim world was to encounter the might of Europe; the pomp and chivalry of Christendom were to be hurled against the Crescent with, one would imagine, every prospect of success. At this juncture Islām was re-animated by one of those periodical revivals that fill the historian with amazement. The Semitic races have proved to be endowed with extraordinary vitality. Frequently, when subdued, they have imposed their religion and civilisation on their conquerors, imbued them with fanaticism, and converted them into keen propagators of the faith.

Islām was saved from destruction at the hands of the Crusaders by one of these timely ebullitions. The approach of the Seljūqs towards the West produced a new element in Islām which enabled the Muslims successfully to withstand the European invaders; their intervention changed the subsequent history of Asia Minor, Syria, and Egypt. The Seljūqs crushed every dynasty in Persia, Asia Minor, Mesopotamia, and Syria, and united, for certain periods, under one head the vast territory reaching from the Mediterranean littoral almost to the borders of India. They beat back successfully both Crusader and Byzantine, gave a new lease of life to the Abbasid Caliphate which endured till its extinction by the Mongols in 1258, and to their influence the establishment of the Ayyūbid dynasty in Egypt by Saladin may be directly traced.

It has already been stated that the Seljūqs derived their name from a chieftain of that name, who came from Turkestan. They were Turkish in origin, being a branch of the Ghuzz Turks, whom the Byzantine writers style Uzes. An interesting reference is made to the Ghuzz in the famous itinerary of Benjamin of Tudela, whose extensive travels in the Orient took place about 1165. Benjamin speaks of the "Ghuz, the Sons of the Kofar-al-Turak," by which description he means the Mongolian or infidel Turks, as the title Kuffār (plural of Kāfir, heretic), implies. He says: "They worship the wind and live in the Wilderness. They do not eat bread nor drink wine but live on uncooked meat. They have no noses. And in lieu thereof they have two small holes, through which they breathe. They eat animals both clean and unclean and are very friendly towards the Israelites[1]. Fifteen years ago they overran the country of Persia with a large army and took the city of Rayy [Rai]: they smote it with the edge of the sword, took all the spoil thereof and returned by way of the Wilderness." Benjamin goes on to describe the campaign of Sanjar ibn Malik Shāh against the Ghuzz in 1153, and his defeat.

Seljūq had four sons, Mīkā'īl, Isrā'īl, Mūsà (Moses), and Yūnus; the names are recorded with certain variants by different writers. They came from the Kirghiz Steppes of Turkestan to Transoxiana, and made their winter quarters near Bukhārā and their summer quarters near Sughd and Samarqand. They thus came under the suzerainty of Maḥmūd of Ghaznah (998–1030), and they embraced Islām with great fervour. The Ghaznawid dynasty was then at the zenith of its power, chiefly through the genius and success of the great Maḥmūd. He was the son of Sabaktagīn, who ruled under the sovereignty of the Sāmānid dynasty. Maḥmūd asserted his independence and established himself in undisputed supremacy over Khurāsān and Ghaznah, being recognised by the Caliph. A zealous follower of Islām, he made twelve campaigns into India and gained the title of the "breaker of idols." But it is as a pātron of learning that he is best known. He established a university at Ghaznah and fostered literature and the arts with a liberal hand. Under him Ghaznah became a centre to which the learned flocked; the poet Firdausī wrote his *Shāhnāma* under the auspices of Maḥmūd.

The migration of the Seljūqs took place at a somewhat earlier period. It is clear that they were already employed in military service by Sabaktagīn (976–997), the father of Maḥmūd, and before the accession of the latter (about 998) they had begun to play an important part in the political life of the neighbouring Muslim states. Finally, they entered into negotiations with Maḥmūd in order to receive his permission to settle near the frontier of his kingdom, on the eastern bank of the Oxus. According to Rāwandī, Maḥmūd unwisely gave the required permission and allowed the Seljūqs to increase their power within his dominions. The emigrants were then under the leadership of the sons

[1] A circumstance also mentioned by Rāwandī.

of Seljūq. Ultimately Maḥmūd became alarmed at their growing strength, and seizing Isrā'īl the son of Seljūq, caused him to be imprisoned in the castle of Kālanjar in India, where he died in captivity. Qutalmish, the son of Isrā'īl, escaped to Bukhārā and instigated his relatives to avenge his father's death. Accordingly they demanded leave from Maḥmūd to cross the Oxus and settle in Khurāsān. Against the advice of the governor of Ṭūs this was accorded, and during the lifetime of Maḥmūd there was peace with the Seljūqs. Before the death of the Sultan, Chaghrī Beg and Ṭughril Beg were born to Mīkā'īl, the brother of Isrā'īl. Maḥmūd was succeeded by his son Mas'ūd, who was very different from his father in character. The conduct of the Seljūqs caused him serious alarm. Presuming on their strength they made but slight pretence to acknowledge his sovereignty, their independence was thinly veiled, and many complaints against them poured in on the Sultan from his subjects and neighbours.

They defeated the governor of Nīshāpūr and forced the Sultan, then engaged in an expedition to India, to accept their terms. Afterwards Mas'ūd decreed the expulsion of the tribe, and the governor of Khurāsān was instructed to enforce the command. He set out with a large force but met with a crushing defeat, and the victorious Seljūqs, entering Nīshāpūr in June 1038, established themselves in complete independence and proclaimed Ṭughril Beg their king. In the previous year, the name of his brother Chaghrī Beg had been inserted in the Khuṭbah or bidding prayer, with the title of "King of Kings." From this time forward the tide of Seljūq conquests spread westward. The Ghaznawids expanded eastward in proportion as their western dominions were lost. The Seljūq brothers conquered Balkh, Jurjān, Ṭabaristān, and Khwārazm, and gained possession of many cities, including Rai, Hamadān, and Ispahan. Finally in 1055 Ṭughril Beg entered Baghdad and was proclaimed Sultan by the Caliph.

Shortly after the defeat of Mas'ūd near Merv (1040), dissension broke out among the Seljūq princes. While Ṭughril Beg and Chaghrī Beg remained in the East, Ibrāhīm ibn Īnāl (or Nīyāl) went to Hamadān and 'Irāq 'Ajamī. Ibrāhīm became too powerful for Ṭughril Beg's liking, and his relations with the Caliph and with the Fāṭimids in Egypt boded no good to Ṭughril Beg. Ṭughril Beg overcame Ibrāhīm, but the latter was incapable of living at peace with his kinsmen. The affairs of the Caliphate were controlled by the Isfahsālār Basāsīrī, who was appointed by the Buwaihid ruler Khusrau Fīrūz ar-Raḥīm. The Caliph Qā'im was forced to countenance the unorthodox Shī'ah, and when Ṭughril Beg came to Baghdad in 1055 his arrival was doubly welcome to the Caliph. Before the approach of Ṭughril Beg, Basāsīrī fled. He managed to prevail on Ibrāhīm ibn Īnāl to rebel, and receiving support from the Fāṭimids marched to Baghdad, which he re-occupied in 1058. Ṭughril Beg overcame his foes and freed the Caliphate; Ibrāhīm was strangled and Basāsīrī beheaded. The grateful Caliph showered rewards on Ṭughril Beg and finally gave him his daughter in marriage; but before the nuptials could take place Ṭughril Beg died (1063). He had received from the Caliph, besides substantial gifts, the privilege of having his name inserted in the Khuṭbah, the title Yamīnu 'Amīri'l-Mu'minīn (Right hand of the Commander of the Faithful), which was used by Maḥmūd of Ghaznah himself, and finally the titles Rukn-ad-Daulah and Rukn-ad-Dīn. These decorations from the Caliph were of the greatest value. They added legitimacy to his claim and stability to his throne. From being the chief of a tribe Ṭughril Beg became the founder of a dynasty.

Ṭughril Beg, having left no children, was succeeded by Alp Arslān, the son of his brother Chaghrī Beg. For nearly two years before the death of Ṭughril, Alp Arslān had held important posts, almost tantamount to co-regency. He was born in 1029, and died at the early age of forty-three in the height of his power. The greatness that he achieved, though in some degree due to his personal qualities and the persistent good fortune that attended him in his career, was in the main to be ascribed to his famous Vizier Niẓām-al-Mulk. As soon as he was seated on the throne, Alp Arslān dismissed the Vizier of Ṭughril Beg, Abū-Naṣr al-Kundurī, the 'Amīd-al-Mulk, who was accused of peculation and other malpractices. The 'Amīd had exercised great influence in the previous reign; both the Sultan and the Caliph held him in high esteem. He was extremely capable, and the sudden change in his fortunes is difficult to explain. Alp Arslān was not given to caprice or cruelty, at all events in the beginning of his reign, and whatever may be urged against the Sultan there is little likelihood that Niẓām-al-Mulk would have acquiesced without reasonable grounds. According to Rāwandī, Niẓām-al-Mulk was the real author of the overthrow of the 'Amīd, having instigated Alp Arslān. He states that Alp Arslān carried the 'Amīd about with him from place to place, and finally had him executed. Before his death he sent defiant messages to the Sultan and to his successor in the Vizierate, Niẓām-al-Mulk.

Niẓām-al-Mulk was one of a triad of famous contemporaries who were pupils of the great Imām Muwaffaq of Nīshāpūr. His companions were Omar Khayyām, the poet and astronomer, and Ḥasan ibn Ṣabbāh, the founder of the sect of the Assassins, one of whom ultimately slew Niẓām-al-Mulk. The Vizier was noted for his learning and his statesmanship. A work on geomancy and science has been attributed to him, but his most famous literary achievement was his *Treatise on Politics* in which he embodied his wisdom in the form of counsels to princes. Niẓām-al-Mulk gathered round him a large number of savants and distinguished men. Under his influence literature was fostered and the sciences and arts encouraged. In 1066 he founded the well-known Niẓāmīyah University at Baghdad. To this foundation students came from all parts, and many great names of Islām are associated with this college as students or teachers. Ibn al-Habbārīyah the satirist (*ob.* 1110), whose biting sarcasm neither decency could restrain nor gratitude overcome, was tolerated here on account of his wit and genius by Niẓām-al-Mulk, who even overlooked most generously a satire directed against himself. Among the students were: the famous philosopher Ghazālī (1049–1111) and his brother Abū'l-Futūḥ (*ob.* 1126) the mystic and ascetic, author of several important works; the great poet Sa'dī, author of the *Gulistān* and of the *Bustān* (1184–1291); the two biographers of Saladin, 'Imād-ad-Dīn (1125–1201), in whose honour a special chair was created, and Bahā-ad-Dīn (1145–1234), who also held a professorial post at his old university; the Spaniard 'Abdallah ibn Tūmart (1092–1130), who proclaimed himself Mahdī and was responsible for the foundation of the Almohad dynasty. Mention must also be made of Abū-Isḥāq ash-Shīrāzī (1003–1083), author of a treatise on Shāfi'ite law called *Muhadhdhab*, of a *Kitāb at-Tanbīh*, and of other works. He was the first principal of the Niẓāmīyah, an office which he at first refused to accept. Another noted lecturer was Yaḥyà ibn 'Alī at-Tabrīzī (1030–1109).

Such are a few of the names that rendered illustrious not only the Niẓāmīyah University at Baghdad but its founder also. At Nīshāpūr Niẓām-al-Mulk instituted another foundation similar to that at Baghdad, and also called Niẓāmīyah, after the Vizier. It will be easily understood that, with such a minister, the empire of the Seljūqs was well governed. Not only in the conduct of foreign affairs and military expeditions but in internal administration was his guiding hand manifest.

Alp Arslān, on embracing Islām, adopted the name of Muḥammad, instead of Isrā'īl by which he had formerly been known. Alp Arslān signifies in Turkish "courageous lion"; the title 'Izz-ad-Dīn was conferred on him by the Caliph Qā'im. Alp Arslān ruled over vast territory. His dominions stretched from the Oxus to the Tigris. Not content to rule over the lands acquired by his predecessors, he added to his empire many conquests, the fruits of his military prowess and good fortune. As overlord his commands were accepted without hesitation, for he united under his sway all the possessions of the Seljūq princes and exacted strict obedience from every vassal. The first of his military exploits was the campaign in Persia. In 1064 he subdued an incipient but formidable rebellion in Khwārazm, and left his son Malik Shāh to rule over the province. Shortly after, he summoned all his provincial governors to a general assembly, at which he caused his son Malik Shāh to be adopted as his successor and to receive an oath of allegiance from all present.

The next exploit of the Sultan was his victory over the Emperor Romanus Diogenes (1071). The Byzantines had gradually been encroaching on the Muslim frontiers. Alp Arslān marched westwards to meet the enemy and fought with Romanus, who had a great numerical preponderance, at Manzikert. The Byzantines sustained a crushing defeat and the Emperor was taken captive. Alp Arslān treated his royal prisoner with kindness, though at first he ordered rings to be placed in his ears as a token of servitude. After a short period Romanus was released on promising to pay tribute and to give his daughter in marriage to the Sultan. To this victory is due the establishment of the Seljūq dynasty of Rūm; while, in the loss of provinces which provided the best recruits for its armies, the Byzantine Empire experienced a calamity from which it never recovered.

Finally, in 1072 Alp Arslān undertook a campaign against the Turkomans in Turkestan, the ancient seat of the Seljūqs, in order to establish his rule there. It was in this campaign that he met his end. An angry dispute took place between the Sultan and Yūsuf Barzamī, the chieftain of a fortress captured by the Seljūqs. Stung by the taunts of the Sultan, Yūsuf threw himself forward and slew him in the presence of all the guards and bystanders, whose intervention came too late to save Alp Arslān.

Malik Shāh succeeded his murdered father. He was known by the titles Jalāl-ad-Dīn and Mu'izz-ad-Dunyà-wa'd-Dīn. He ascended the throne, which he occupied for twenty years, when he was eighteen, being born in 1053 and dying in 1091. The great Vizier Niẓām-al-Mulk remained in power and for long maintained his influence. As soon as Alp Arslān died Malik Shāh was recognised by the Caliph as his successor, and invested with the title of 'Amir-al-Mu'minīn (Commander of the Faithful), hitherto jealously preserved by the Caliphs for themselves.

Malik Shāh had left Khurāsān on his way to 'Irāq when he was met by the tidings that his uncle Qāwurd had raised a revolt against him and was on his way from Kirmān. Malik Shāh promptly set out to meet him, routed his army, and took Qāwurd captive. As his own troops shewed signs of disaffection and preference for Qāwurd, Malik Shāh, on the advice of his Vizier, had him put to death in prison, either by poison or by strangling. The execution was announced to the populace as a suicide, and the troops returned to their loyalty. Soon after this Malik Shāh sent his cousin Sulaimān ibn Qutalmish on an expedition into Syria, and Antioch was captured. Subsequently (1078) the Sultan himself captured Samarqand. This expedition was marked by an incident which shews how greatly Niẓām-al-Mulk was imbued with the imperial idea. After Malik Shāh had been ferried over the Oxus, the native ferrymen received drafts on Antioch in payment of their services. When they complained to the Sultan, who asked the Vizier why this had been done, the latter explained that he had taken this course in order to afford an object-lesson in the greatness and unity of the Sultan's realms. At this time Malik Shāh espoused Turkān Khātūn, daughter of Ṭamghāj Khān. She became, later on, an implacable foe to the Vizier.

Thus Malik Shāh extended his dominions to the north and west. He rode his horse into the sea at Laodicea in Syria, and gave thanks to God for his wide domain. It is related that, during one of his progresses in the north, he was, while hunting, taken prisoner by the Byzantine Emperor, by whom however he remained unrecognised. Malik Shāh contrived to send word to Niẓām-al-Mulk, who adroitly managed to rescue the Sultan without revealing his master's rank. Soon afterwards the tide turned and the Byzantine Emperor was a captive in the Muslim camp. When brought into the presence of Malik Shāh he remembered his late encounter and made a memorable reply, when the Sultan asked him how he wished to be treated. "If you are the King of the Turks," returned the Emperor, "send me back; if you are a merchant, sell me; if you are a butcher, slay me." The Sultan generously set him at liberty. Peace was made and lasted until the death of the Byzantine Emperor, when, after hostilities, Malik Shāh made Sulaimān ibn Qutalmish ruler over the newly conquered territory.

Malik Shāh appointed a commission of eight astronomers, among whom was Omar Khayyām, to regulate the calendar, and a new era was introduced and named Ta'rīkh Jalālī, or Era of Jalāl, after the title of Malik Shāh. Similarly the astronomical tables drawn up by Omar were called Zījī-Malikshāhī in honour of the Sultan. Malik Shāh was noted for the excellent administration of justice that prevailed in his reign, for his internal reforms, for his public works such as canals and hostels and buildings, for the efficiency in which he maintained his army, and for his piety and philanthropy. To his nobles he made liberal grants of estates. He undertook the pilgrimage to Mecca, and his wells and caravanserais for pilgrims are abiding memorials of his good works. He made even his pleasures productive of charity, for whenever he engaged in the chase, to which he was passionately addicted, he made it a rule to give a dinner to a poor man for every head of game that fell to him.

Towards the end of his reign Niẓām-al-Mulk began to decline in favour. This was due to the intrigues of the Turkān Khātūn, who desired to secure the succession for her son Maḥmūd, while the Vizier favoured the eldest son Barkiyāruq, who was not only entitled to be recognised as heir apparent on the ground of birth but, moreover, was far better fitted to rule. The constant efforts of the Khātūn, coupled with the fact that Niẓām-al-Mulk had placed all his twelve sons in high offices in the State, for which indeed they were well qualified, had their effect on the Sultan. He dismissed the aged Vizier who had served both him and his father before him, and installed in his stead a creature of the Khātūn, Tāj-al-Mulk Abu'l-Ghanā'im. Shortly afterwards Malik Shāh went on a visit to the Caliph, and Niẓām-al-Mulk followed his court at a distance. At Nihāwand, Niẓām-al-Mulk was set upon and murdered by one of the Assassins, instigated by Tāj-al-Mulk. The late Vizier lingered long enough to send a message to the Sultan, urging his own loyalty in the past and offering that of his son for the future. He was buried at Ispahan. He may probably be considered as the most brilliant man of his age.

Shortly afterwards the Sultan himself died, at Baghdad. He was one of the greatest of the Seljūqs, and the policy by which he placed his kinsmen over conquered territories is in keeping with his private liberality. He was succeeded, after a civil war, by his son Barkiyāruq.

This Sultan received the name of Qāsim at circumcision, and the title of Rukn-ad-Daulah-wa'd-Dīn (Column of the State and the Faith) from the Caliph Muqtadī. He was born in 1081, succeeded to the throne at the age of thirteen in 1094, and died in 1106. During his reign he experienced a series of vicissitudes of fortune, being sometimes at the height of power and once at least in imminent danger of execution, when a captive in his rival's hands. The unexpected death of his father at Baghdad and the presence of his enemies at the Caliph's court were serious obstacles to his accession. His chief partisan, Niẓām-al-Mulk, had been murdered; his stepmother the Khātūn was importuning the Caliph to alter the succession in favour of her son Maḥmūd; the newly-appointed Vizier was a supporter of the Khātūn; Barkiyāruq himself was away in Ispahan, and the Caliph was wavering in his decision. Finally, Muqtadī was won over by the Khātūn and declared Maḥmūd, then aged four, successor to Malik Shāh. At the same time Barkiyāruq proclaimed himself at Ispahan. Within a week, the envoys of the Khātūn arrived in order to seize Barkiyāruq, who was, however, saved by the sons of Niẓām-al-Mulk. The sons of the late Vizier were, like their father, pledged to Barkiyāruq's cause, and their own safety was bound up with his. They escaped with the lad to Gumushtagīn, one of the Atābegs appointed by Malik Shāh, who offered generous protection and help. At Rai he was crowned by the governor, Abū-Muslim, and 20,000 troops were enrolled to protect him. Turkān Khātūn had by this time seized Ispahan and she, with Maḥmūd, was besieged by Barkiyāruq. After some time peace was made. The Khātūn and her son were to be left in possession of Ispahan on giving up half of the treasure (one million dinars) left by Malik Shāh. Barkiyāruq retired to Hamadān. Within a few months, however, war again broke out. Hamadān was then ruled by Ismā'īl, the maternal uncle of Barkiyāruq, and the Khātūn opened negotiations with him, proposing to marry him if he would overcome her stepson. The governor agreed and marched against Barkiyāruq, by whom, however, he was defeated and slain. Nevertheless the Sultan had no respite from his enemies, for another uncle, Tutush, the son of Alp Arslān, rose against him and pressed him hard (1094). Barkiyāruq had the Turkān Khātūn executed, but eventually was forced to surrender to his uncle and to Maḥmūd his step-brother. At this stage his life was in great peril. Maḥmūd, who had received Barkiyāruq with every appearance of friendship, soon had him imprisoned. His life hung by a thread. Finally, Maḥmūd gave orders to put out his eyes, in order to render him permanently incapable of ruling. This command would have been carried out but for the sudden illness of Maḥmūd, who caught the smallpox. Thereupon the sentence was suspended while the issue of the llness was in doubt. In point of fact Maḥmūd died and Barkiyāruq was restored to the throne, only to be attacked by the same malady. The Sultan, however, recovered and at once proceeded to restore his authority. He made Mu'ayyid-al-Mulk, a son of Niẓām-al-Mulk, Vizier, and led an army against his uncle Tutush, who was beaten and slain (1095). Barkiyāruq was attacked by one of the Assassins, but the wound was not fatal, and the Sultan led an expedition to Khurāsān, where his uncle Arslān Arghūn was in revolt. The latter was murdered by a slave, and the Sultan, victorious over the enemy, placed his brother Sanjar in authority over Khurāsān.

The next struggle that awaited Barkiyāruq arose from the intrigues of Mu'ayyid-al-Mulk. The latter, who had been replaced in office by his brother Fakhr-al-Mulk, prevailed on one of the late Turkān Khātūn's most powerful supporters, the Isfahsālār Unrū Bulkà, to rebel. The plot came to nothing as Unrū Bulkà met his death at the hands of an Assassin emissary. Mu'ayyid-al-Mulk fled to Barkiyāruq's brother Muḥammad, and renewed his intrigues there. Finally, in 1098 war broke out between the two brothers. Barkiyāruq was weakened by a serious outbreak among his troops and had to flee to Rai with a small retinue, while Muḥammad and Mu'ayyid-al-Mulk reached Hamadān, where Muḥammad was acknowledged as king. Barkiyāruq was driven into exile, but at length succeeded in raising a force and captured Muḥammad and Mu'ayyid-al-Mulk. The latter actually proposed that Barkiyāruq should accept a fine and reinstate him in his office, and at first the Sultan consented; but, when he heard that this leniency was the subject of ridicule among his domestics, he slew the traitor with his own hand. Peace was made with Muḥammad and the empire divided. Muḥammad received Syria, Babylonia, Media, Armenia, and Georgia, while Barkiyāruq retained the remaining territories.

In 1104 Barkiyāruq was travelling to Baghdad in order to confer with Ayāz, whom Malik Shāh had previously appointed governor of Khuzistān. Ayāz had helped Barkiyāruq during his misfortunes and he was now supreme at Baghdad, the Caliph having lost all power. On the way Barkiyāruq was taken ill and died. He declared his son Malik Shāh as his successor and left him under the guardianship of Ayāz and Ṣadaqah. As soon as the death of Barkiyāruq became known, Muḥammad, who now became the chief among the Seljūq princes, seized Malik Shāh and deprived him of his dominions.

Muḥammad, son of Malik Shāh, was born in 1082 and died in 1119. His undisputed reign really began with the death of Barkiyāruq in 1104 and with the seizure of his nephew Malik Shāh at Baghdad. Ayāz and Ṣadaqah, the adherents of Barkiyāruq and his successor, met their death and their armies surrendered to the new Sultan. Muḥammad received the support of the Caliph Mustaẓhir, who granted him the titles of Ghiyāth-ad-Dunyà-wa'd-Dīn and 'Amīr-al-Mu'minīn. The Sultan was noted for his orthodoxy. He reduced the castle of Dizkūh near Ispahan. The Malāḥidah

(Assassins) had seized this fortress, which had been built in order to overawe Ispahan, and having established themselves in safety began to make extensive propaganda for their heretical doctrines, gaining many adherents to their cause. The outrages of the Assassins were fearful; Sa'd-al-Mulk, the minister, was among the disaffected, and so deeply had their intrigues permeated the government that it took Muḥammad seven years to reduce the sect. During this period he was in great danger of death, as the Vizier conspired with the Sultan's surgeon and prevailed on him to use a poisoned lancet. The plot was discovered and the guilty persons punished. It is said that Muḥammad sent an expedition into India to destroy idols. His religious zeal was great. He is also accused of having been unduly economical, even to the point of avarice, but on the whole he was a prudent and beneficent prince. Before his death he designated his son Maḥmūd as his successor, but the power passed to his brother Sanjar.

Sanjar was the last Sultan of a united Seljūq Empire; after his death the various provincial kings and rulers ceased to acknowledge a central authority. His reign was marked by brilliant conquests and ignominious defeats. Although he extended the boundaries of his dominions, his administration was ill-adapted to conserve their solidarity. Yet the break up of the imperial power must not be entirely attributed to him; for this result other causes also are responsible.

Sanjar's other titles were Mu'izz-ad-Dunyà-wa'd-Dīn and 'Amīr-al-Mu'minīn. He was born in 1086 (according to Bundārī in 1079) and he died in 1156. For twenty years previous to his accession he had been king in Khurāsān, to which office he had been appointed by Barkiyāruq, and he ruled the whole of the Seljūq Empire for forty years. He was the last of the sons of Malik Shāh, son of Alp Arslān. His conquests were numerous. He waged a successful war with his nephew Maḥmūd, the son of the late Sultan, in 'Irāq Ajamī, and wrested the succession from him. Maḥmūd was overcome and offered submission. Sanjar received him with kindness and invested him with the government of the province, on the condition that Maḥmūd should recognise his suzerainty. The visible signs of submission were the insertion of Sanjar's name in the Khuṭbah before that of Maḥmūd, the maintenance of Sanjar's officials in the posts to which they had been appointed, and the abolition of the trumpets that heralded the entry and departure of Maḥmūd from his palace. Maḥmūd accepted the terms eagerly and thenceforward devoted his life to the chase, of which he was passionately fond.

In 1130 Aḥmad Khān, the governor of Samarqand, refused tribute. Sanjar crossed the Oxus, invaded Mā-warā-an-Nahr (Transoxiana), and besieged Samarqand. Aḥmad submitted and was removed from his post. Sanjar also made himself supreme in Ghaznah, where he seated Bahrām Shāh on the throne, as a tributary, in Sīstān, and in Khwārazm. His nominal empire was much wider. It is said that "his name was recited in the Khuṭbah in the Mosque from Káshgar to Yaman, Mecca and Ṭā'if, and from Mukrán and Ummán to Ádharbayjàn and the frontiers of Rúm and continued to be so recited until a year after his death: yet he was simple and unostentatious in his dress and habits....He was, moreover, virtuous and pious, and in his day Khurásán was the goal of the learned and the focus of culture and science."

The most eventful wars that occupied Sanjar were those against the Khaṭà (heathen from Cathay) and the Ghuzz. In 1140 Sanjar set out from Merv to Samarqand, and was met by the news that the Khaṭà had invaded Transoxiana and defeated his army. Sanjar himself was routed and his forces nearly annihilated. The Sultan fled to Balkh and rallied his troops at Tirmidh, a strong fortress. Meanwhile Tāj-ad-Dīn, King of Nīmrūz, after a protracted resistance had been overcome and captured by the Khaṭà. Sanjar was beset with other troubles also, chiefly due to the rising of Atsiz, the third of the Khwārazm Shāhs. His grandfather Anūshtigīn, from Ghaznah, had been a Turkish slave, and finally was advanced by Sultan Malik Shāh to be governor of Khwārazm. Anūshtigīn was succeeded in 1097 by his son Qutb-ad-Dīn Muḥammad, who was known by the title of the Khwārazm Shāh and who was followed in 1127 by his son Atsiz. This Shāh greatly extended his dominions, partly at the expense of Sanjar. The dynasty came to an end about a century later when Shāh Muḥammad and his son Jalāl-ad-Dīn were overthrown by the Mongols. At the time of Sanjar, Atsiz was sparing no effort to obtain independence. He stood high in Sanjar's favour on account of the services that he and his father had rendered. When Sanjar made his expedition against Aḥmad Khān, Atsiz rescued him from a band of conspirators who had seized his person while hunting. As a reward Sanjar attached Atsiz to his person and loaded him with honours and marks of distinction, till he roused the jealousy of the court. So strong did the opposition of his enemies become that Atsiz had to ask leave to retire to his governorship at Khwārazm, professing that disorders there required his presence. Sanjar allowed him to depart most unwillingly, for he feared that Atsiz would fall a victim to the hatred of his enemies. But the subsequent conduct of Atsiz was quite unexpected. Instead of quelling the disorders, he joined the malcontents and rebelled against Sanjar. In 1138 the Sultan took the field against Atsiz and his son Ilkilig, who were routed, the latter being slain. Sanjar restored order and, having appointed Sulaimān his nephew to govern the province, returned to Merv. Atsiz was roused to fresh endeavours in spite of the defeat which he had sustained. Rallying his army and collecting fresh forces, he attacked Sulaimān and forced him to abandon his post and flee to Sanjar, leaving Khwārazm open to the mercy of Atsiz. Finally, in 1142 Sanjar led a second expedition against this rebellious vassal and besieged him. Atsiz, reduced to despair, sent envoys to Sanjar with presents and promises of fidelity if spared. The Sultan, who was of a benevolent disposition, and, in addition, was sensible of the debt of gratitude which he owed Atsiz, again accepted his submission and left him in possession of his office. But again was his generosity ill requited. On all sides reports reached Sanjar that Atsiz was fomenting disloyalty and preparing trouble. In order to find out the truth he sent a notable poet, 'Adīb Ṣābir of Tirmidh, to make enquiries in Khwārazm. He found that Atsiz was despatching a band of assassins to kill Sanjar. He succeeded in sending warning, for which act he paid with his life, and the plot was detected at Merv; the traitors were executed. So, in the end, Sanjar had to march against Atsiz for the third time (1147), and again exercised his forbearance and generosity when Atsiz was nearly in his power. Hereafter Atsiz remained loyal, though practically independent. He extended his empire as far as Jand on the Jaxartes, and died in 1156.

In 1149 Sanjar recovered the credit which his defeat by the Khaṭà had lost him. He gained a great victory over Ḥusain ibn Ḥasan Jahānsūz, Sultan of Ghūr, who had invaded Khurāsān. Ḥusain was joined by Falak-ad-Dīn 'Alī Chatrī, Sanjar's chamberlain; both were taken captive and the latter executed. Ultimately, Ḥusain was sent back to his post by Sanjar as a vassal.

In 1153 came the invasion of the Ghuzz Turkomans. An interesting account, to which allusion has been made above, is that of Benjamin of Tudela, almost a contemporary visitor to the East. These tribes were goaded into rebellion by the exactions of one of Sanjar's officers. When the Sultan marched against them, they were seized with fear and offered to submit. Unfortunately Sanjar was persuaded to refuse terms and give battle, in which he was utterly defeated and captured. The Ghuzz came to Merv, plundered it, and killed many of the inhabitants. Then they marched to Nīshāpūr, where they massacred a large number of persons in the mosque. The chief mosque was burned and the learned men put to death. All over Khurāsān the Ghuzz ranged, killing and burning wherever they went. Herat alone was able to repulse their attack. Famine and plague followed them to add to the misery of the land. For two years Sanjar was a prisoner, and was then rescued by some friends. He reached the Oxus, where boats had been prepared, and returned to Merv, but he died soon after reaching his capital, of horror and grief (1156).

Sanjar was the last of the Seljūqs to enjoy supreme imperial power. For a considerable time previously the various provincial governors had acquired practical independence, and if, after the time of Sanjar, the reins of central authority were loosened, this change was effected by no violent rupture. It was the outcome, first of the steady rise on the part of the vassals and viceroys to autonomy, and, secondly, the necessary consequence of the Atābeg system. A certain ambiguity in the method of succession frequently caused strife between uncle and nephew for the right of inheritance. Often, as for example in the case of Niẓām-al-Mulk, the office of Vizier was practically hereditary. Hence the Vizier developed into the position of tutor or guardian to the royal heir, thereby acquiring much influence and consolidating his position for the next reign. The name Atābeg or Atābey ("Father Bey") denotes this office. In many cases the Atābeg forcibly secured the succession and displaced the prince. The reason for their employment and power—which is comparable to that of the Egyptian Mamlūks—was the desire of the kings to possess, as their ministers, such officials as could be trusted implicitly, for reasons not only of loyalty, a quality not invariably present, but also of self-interest. So slaves and subordinates were raised to high positions, in lieu of the nobility. The Seljūq public life was a *carrière ouverte aux talents*. A Vizier chosen from the grandees might have so much influence through descent, wealth, or family as to make his allegiance to the king a matter of choice. In the case of a slave or subordinate, loyalty was a matter of necessity, for such an official could not possibly stand on his own merits. If, on the other hand, the subordinate supplanted his master, as was often the case, this was due to the lack of discrimination displayed by the latter in the choice of his instruments. Frequently also an official who had been kept in check by a strong Sultan succeeded, if the Sultan's successor were weak, in becoming more powerful than his master and ultimately in displacing him. The Atābeg system was only possible when the head of the State was a strong man. By the end of Sanjar's reign the weakness of this policy became manifest. From this time onward the history of the Seljūqs becomes that of the groups into which the empire was now split: four of these groups need attention.

(I) In Kirmān a line of twelve rulers (including contemporary rivals) held sway from 1041 to 1187. This province, which lies on the eastern side of the Persian Gulf, was one of the first occupied by the Seljūqs. 'Imād-ad-Dīn Qāwurd, who was the son of Chaghrī Beg and thus great-grandson to Seljūq, was the first ruler, and from him the dynasty descended. Qāwurd carried on war with Malik Shāh, at whose hands he met his death (1073). For a century the province was tolerably peaceful until the death of Ṭughril Shāh in 1167, when his three sons, Bahrām, Arslān, and Tūrān brought havoc to the land by their disputes and warfare. Muḥammad II was the last of his line; the invading hosts of Ghuzz Turkomans and the Khwārazm Shāhs displaced the Seljūq rulers in Kirmān.

(II) The Seljūqs of Syria are chiefly important for their relations with the Crusaders, on which subject more will be said later. The period of their independence was from 1094 to 1117. Tutush, the first of this branch, was the son of Alp Arslān, the second Great Seljūq. He died in 1094 at Rai, being defeated by his nephew Barkiyāruq. His two sons Riḍwān and Duqāq ruled at Aleppo and Damascus respectively. They were succeeded by Riḍwān's sons Alp Arslān Akhras (1113) and Sulṭān Shāh (1114). After this the dynasty was broken up and the rule passed into the hands of the Būrids and the Urtuqids. The former dynasty were Atābegs of Damascus and were descended from Ṭughtigīn, a slave of Tutush, who rose to power and was appointed Atābeg of Duqāq. From Būrī, the eldest son and successor of Ṭughtigīn, the line takes its name. Eventually the Būrids were supplanted by the Zangids. Of the Urtuqids more will be said hereafter.

(III) The Seljūqs of 'Irāq and Kurdistān consisted of a dynasty of nine rulers, and were descended from Muḥammad ibn Malik Shāh. Four of Muḥammad's five sons, four of his grandsons, and one great-grandson, formed this line of rulers, beginning with Maḥmūd in 1117, and ending with Ṭughril II in 1194, after which the Khwārazm Shāhs became supreme.

(IV) The Seljūqs of Rūm or Asia Minor are perhaps the most important to the Western historian, on account of their relations with the Crusaders and the Eastern Emperors, and their influence on the Ottoman Empire. The first of these rulers was Sulaimān ibn Qutalmish, a son of Arslān ibn Seljūq. This branch of the Seljūq family is thus distinct from the Great Seljūqs, the Seljūqs of 'Irāq, Syria, and Kirmān. From the time of Sulaimān I (1077) until the period of the Ottoman Turks (1300) seventeen monarchs ruled, subject at certain periods to the dominion of the Mongols. The second of this line, Qilij Arslān ibn Sulaimān (1092–1106), made Nicaea his capital, and defeated the earliest crusaders under Walter the Penniless (1096). In the next year he was twice defeated by Godfrey of Bouillon, and Nicaea was captured. Iconium then became the Seljūq capital. In 1107 he marched to the help of Mosul, which was besieged by a rebel; after raising the siege he met with an accident while crossing the Khabur and was drowned. But the dynasty was consolidated by his successors and played an important part in the Crusades, for, in addition to the bravery of their forces, the Seljūqs possessed sufficient political skill to take advantage of the mutual animosity existing between the Greeks and the Crusaders and to utilise it for their own purposes. They also succeeded in supplanting the Dānishmand, a minor Seljūq dynasty of obscure origin. It is said that the founder, Mahomet ibn Gumishtigīn, was a schoolmaster, as the title Dānishmand denotes, but everything connected with this line, which ruled from about 1105–1165, is doubtful. Their territory lay in Cappadocia and included the cities of Sīwās (Sebastea), Qaiṣarīyah (Caesarea), and Malaṭīyah (Melitene). Mahomet defeated and captured Bohemond in 1099, as the latter was marching to help Gabriel of Melitene against him. When Bohemond ransomed himself and became tributary to Mahomet, the two rulers formed an alliance against Qilij Arslān and Alexius, the Emperor of Constantinople, one of the instances which shew that political considerations were more important than religious differences, not only among the Crusaders but also among the Muslims.

Besides the Seljūqs proper, mention must be made of their officers, the Atābegs, whose functions have been described. The power wielded by these vassals was very great, and in the course of the twelfth and thirteenth centuries many established themselves in virtual independence. The most powerful of these were the Zangids or descendants of Zangī, and the Khwārazm Shāhs. They deserve attention for their relations with the Crusaders, but details of their history, apart from this connexion, cannot be given here.

It now remains to deal with the relations between the Seljūqs and the Crusaders. In no small degree the origin of the Holy Wars was due to the expansion of the Seljūq Empire, for as long as the Arabs held Jerusalem the Christian pilgrims from Europe could pass unmolested. The Christians were, to all intents, left undisturbed and the pilgrimages continued as before. The outbreak of persecution (1010) under the insane Egyptian Caliph, Ḥākim, was temporary and transitory, and but for the coming of the Seljūqs popular indignation in Europe would have slumbered and the Crusades might never have taken place.

The first of the Syrian Seljūqs, Tutush the son of Alp Arslān, who ruled at Damascus, captured Jerusalem and appointed as its governor Urtuq ibn Aksab, who had been one of his subordinate officers. Urtuq was the founder of the Urtuqid dynasty. His sons Sukmān and Īl-Ghāzī succeeded him. The Seljūq power, which had been growing rapidly until the Caliph was completely in their hands, was somewhat weakened. After the death of Malik Shāh the Great Seljūq in 1092, in the dissension which ensued, Afḍal, the Vizier of the Egyptian Fāṭimid Caliph, was enabled to capture Jerusalem from Sukmān (1096), who retired to Edessa while his brother returned to 'Irāq. During the Seljūq domination, the Christians, both native and foreign, had suffered greatly, and the reports of their ill-treatment and of the difficulties placed in the way of pilgrimages, kindled the zeal which so largely stimulated the Crusades. When however the first band of Christian warriors reached Asia Minor after leaving Constantinople, they were completely routed by Qilij Arslān on the road to Nicaea (1096). It has already been described how the Seljūqs pushed forward, step by step, until their expansion brought them into conflict with the Byzantine Empire. It was only the enmity between East and West and the scandalous behaviour of the Crusaders that hindered a combined attack on the Seljūqs. Although the Seljūqs and the Emperor were mutually hostile, and for the best of reasons, there was less ill-feeling between them than between the Christian hosts, which, nominally allies, in reality regarded each other with scarcely concealed suspicion. When Godfrey of Bouillon reached Constantinople in 1096, he found a cold welcome at the court; no sooner had he crossed the Bosphorus than the feuds developed into open antagonism. When Nicaea was invested (1097) and it was found that no hope remained for the city, the garrison succeeded in surrendering to Alexius rather than to the Crusaders, and thus avoided a massacre. Qilij Arslān retired to rouse the Seljūq princes to their danger.

At the capture of Antioch, interest is centred on Qawwām-ad-Daulah Karbuqā or Kerbogha, Prince of Mosul, who, in 1096, had wrested Mosul from the 'Uqailids and founded a Seljūq principate there. He and Qilij Arslān were the most noteworthy of the earlier opponents of the Crusaders. The line of Urtuq ibn Aksab produced many heroes beginning with his sons Sukmān and Īl-Ghāzī; the former, who founded the Kaifā branch of the Urtuqids (1101–1231), was famous for his wars with Baldwin and Joscelin. This branch became subject to Saladin and was ultimately merged in the Ayyūbid Empire. Īl-Ghāzī was made governor of Baghdad by the Great Seljūq Muḥammad in 1101, and captured Aleppo in 1117. His descendants were the Urtuqids of Māridīn (1108–1312).

Several of the officers of the Great Seljūq Malik Shāh rose to fame during the Crusades. Of these the most important were Tutush and 'Imād-ad-Dīn Zangī. The latter was made governor of 'Irāq, and after conquering his Muslim neighbours became a dreaded foe to the Christians. He found the Muslims dispirited and completely prostrate. At his death he had changed their despair to triumph. He took Aleppo in 1128, Hamāh in 1129, and then began his wars against the Franks. In 1130 he took the important fortress of Atharib, and in 1144 achieved his greatest glory by capturing Edessa. He followed this up by taking many important towns in Northern Mesopotamia, but in 1146 he was murdered. He had turned the tide of victory against the Franks, and his capture of Edessa called forth the Second Crusade. His son Nūr-ad-Dīn succeeded to his Syrian dominions and was also prominent in the battles against the Crusaders. Among his officers was Ayyūb (Job), whose son Ṣalāḥ-ad-Dīn (Saladin) became the great protagonist of the Crescent against the Cross.

The Seljūq power began and ended gradually. Seven Great Seljūqs are usually reckoned as constituting the dynasty, ruling over a united empire in Persia, Transoxiana, Mesopotamia, and Syria; after Sanjar disintegration set in, but although the empire was split into small parts the separate kingdoms preserved in many cases their power and authority. The empire of the Khwārazm Shāhs encroached on the east and gradually absorbed the Seljūq territory. The centre was divided among the Atābegs, whose various destinies cannot be treated here, and in the west the Seljūqs of Rūm remained in power until the rise of the Ottomans.

CHAPTER XI.

THE EARLIER COMNENI.

ISAAC I (1057–1059). ALEXIUS I (1081–1118).

Among the great families of the aristocracy whose names recur on every page of Byzantine history in the eleventh century, that of the Comneni was destined to be the most illustrious. In all probability we should reject the comparatively recent hypothesis connecting the family with an ancient Roman house which had followed Constantine to Byzantium, and abide by the testimony of the Byzantine chroniclers who represent the Comneni as coming originally from the little village of Comne, in the valley of the Tunja, close to Hadrianople. At a later time large possessions acquired in Asia Minor in the Castamon district secured to the Comneni an important place among the nobility of Asia Minor.

The name Comnenus makes its first appearance in the writings of the Byzantine historians during the reign of Basil II (976–1025). Two personages bearing the name are mentioned by the chroniclers, Nicephorus, governor of Vaspurakan (*i.e.* district of Van), and Manuel. The latter, the servant and friend of Basil II, is often spoken of under the name of Eroticus. He left two sons, Isaac and John, the former of whom was to lay the foundations of the future greatness of his house.

In order to understand the causes of the military revolution which in 1057 raised Isaac Comnenus to the Byzantine throne, it is necessary to go back to the events which followed the death of Basil II. His successor Constantine VIII (1025–1028) dismissed the greater number of the imperial officials, and put the administration in the hands of a new set of functionaries, chosen from among the companions of his debauches, freedmen, eunuchs, and foreigners. Thenceforward the whole business of governing was in the hands of the palace officials, who retained a position of preponderating importance up to the end of the eleventh century. Two classes were equally hateful to the new staff of administrators, the heads of the aristocratic families and the military leaders, whose ambition they feared, and both found themselves entirely excluded from the government. The ministers were enabled the more easily to carry out this definitely anti-militarist policy, as for a considerable time the Empire had had no attacks to fear from its neighbours. Besides, when the latter grew too presumptuous, the central authority always preferred to buy a peace rather than encounter the risks of a war which might enable some military leader to increase his prestige and popularity.

The generals, drawn for the most part from the nobility of Asia Minor, whose power had been markedly increased by the war with the Muslims, endured for many years the ill-will shewn them by the imperial court. The reason for their patience may be found in the fact that legitimist ideas were rapidly making way in the public mind. The people of Constantinople were deeply attached to the Macedonian family; because she was the legitimate heiress the Empress Zoë was suffered to place the supreme power in the hands of her three husbands successively—Romanus Argyrus (1028–1034), Michael IV the Paphlagonian (1034–1041), Constantine IX Monomachus (1042–1054)—and in those of her adopted son Michael V Calaphates (1041–1042). When the last attempted a sudden overthrow of the aged Empress by force, and sent her into exile in one of the Princes Islands, after having caused her to take the veil, rebellion thundered through the streets of the capital, nor were the people pacified until the legitimate heiress was recalled. The state of feeling which this reveals made it particularly difficult for the military chiefs to attempt a revolt.

During the brief reign of Zoë's sister, Theodora (1054–1056), the influence of the palace functionaries grew even greater, and with it their fear that the army would become too powerful. While engaged on an expedition, Isaac Comnenus received letters from the Court ordering him to halt and recommending him to be on his guard against the arrogance of a victorious army. The future Emperor, then Domestic of the Scholae of the East (*i.e.* Commander-in-Chief of the troops in Asia), found himself deprived of this post by the suspicious advisers of the Empress.

The Macedonian dynasty came to an end with Theodora. Michael Stratioticus, her successor, was appointed heir by the Empress on her death-bed. Before being chosen, he was obliged to bind himself by a solemn oath to do nothing against the will and counsel of the ministers and other advisers of the Empress.

The new Emperor, who was much advanced in years, was not long in making himself unpopular by the unfortunate measures which he adopted, and also in raising up powerful enemies for himself, chief among whom must be placed the Patriarch, Michael Cerularius. The Patriarch, whose prestige had been enormously increased by the events of 1054, had only sought in the breach with Rome the means of rendering the Church independent. He now dreamed of placing the State under the yoke of the Church. Around him, drawn together by common interests and forming a powerful party, stood the clergy and the monks. Theodora had already had reason to dread the secret influence of Cerularius. She had not dared to attack him openly, but had attempted to destroy his popularity by throwing suspicion upon his orthodoxy, and by having some of his most notorious partisans proceeded against for heresy. Michael VI and his counsellors continued to exclude him from the business of the state. The Patriarch did not forgive the Emperor for adopting this attitude, and on a favourable opportunity shortly afterwards presenting itself, he determined to make his power felt.

The number of the discontented was increased by the fact that men of senatorial rank found themselves excluded from the greater and more lucrative financial posts, which were thenceforward reserved for professional officials. But it was the openly anti-militarist position taken up by the Emperor and his advisers which brought about the catastrophe in which his power finally disappeared. Angry at having had no part in the shower of favours which had followed the accession of the new sovereign and sore at seeing the palace officials preferred to them in the distribution of high commands, the leaders of the army, during the Easter festival of 1057, tried the effect of making united representations to the Emperor. Chief among them were Catacalon Cecaumenus, the Duke of Antioch, Isaac Comnenus, Constantine and John Ducas, and Michael Burtzes. Admitted by the Emperor to an audience, the generals made their wishes known. The Emperor refused all their requests and violently denounced Catacalon Cecaumenus. The latter's comrades having attempted to raise their voices in his defence, the Emperor silenced them with an intemperance of language in which he spared nobody.

The chief officers of the Byzantine army went out from the interview with bitterly wounded feelings. Nevertheless, before proceeding to an open breach, they tried the effect of an application to the Patriarch's vicar, Leo Paraspondylus, the chief counsellor of Michael VI. This step had no better success than the former. On this fresh failure the generals decided upon enforcing their demands by violence and overthrowing the Emperor. Supported in secret by Michael Cerularius, who thought the opportunity favourable for attempting to carry out his ambitious projects, the military leaders met in the church of St Sophia, and, after the crown had been offered in vain to Catacalon, the choice of the assembly fell upon Isaac Comnenus. As soon as the final arrangements had been made, the conspirators left Constantinople and crossed over into Asia Minor. The arrest and execution of one of their number, Nicephorus Bryennius, after he had been suddenly deprived of his command in Cappadocia, accelerated the course of events. Hastily, and in fear lest their conspiracy had been discovered, the plotters gathered their contingents together and joined Isaac Comnenus, who had fled for refuge to his estates in Paphlagonia. On 8 June 1057 on the plain of Gunaria Isaac Comnenus was proclaimed Emperor, and soon after, the rebel forces having been increased by the arrival of Catacalon and his troops, the usurper set out on his march towards the Bosphorus. He captured Nicaea without much difficulty, and his authority was promptly recognised throughout the eastern part of the Empire. The pretender made steady progress, the discipline and order which he always maintained among his troops winning him many supporters. The soldiers, though in revolt, never behaved like revolutionaries, and, as it has been said with perfect justice, the proclamation of the new Emperor was generally regarded not as a usurpation but as the setting up of a genuine imperial government basing itself upon the support of the army in contradistinction to the civil elements of the capital.

To make head against the rebels, Michael VI hastily collected all the troops at his disposal in the European provinces of the Empire, and despatched them to Asia Minor under the command of the eunuch Theodore and Aaron the Bulgarian. On 20 August 1057 at Hades, not far from Nicaea, the imperial troops were defeated by those of Isaac Comnenus. The news of the disaster soon reached the Sacred Palace, where it spread terror. Michael VI, panic-stricken, exacted from the Senators a written promise never to recognise Isaac Comnenus as Emperor. At the same time he himself opened negotiations with him.

The history of the negotiations is chiefly known to us through the deliberately obscure account left by one of the ambassadors, Michael Psellus. One thing alone seems certain, that from the very beginning of the transaction Michael VI was betrayed. The imperial ambassadors, who reached Nicomedia, where Isaac Comnenus then was, on 24 August, were charged to offer him the title of Caesar with the promise of succeeding to the throne. The better to hoodwink his opponent and give time for his own partisans to take action in Constantinople, Isaac spun out the negotiations tediously, and then pretended to accept the proposals of Michael VI, to whom the ambassadors returned to give an account of their mission. During their stay at Constantinople they came to an understanding with the partisans of the pretender, among the most important of whom were the Patriarch and a certain number of great personages. When Psellus and his colleagues again set out bearing fresh proposals from their master, the conspiracy had been fully organized. On 30 August an outbreak took place at Constantinople. The ringleaders complained of the conduct of Michael VI who, after having forced them to take the oath not to acknowledge Isaac Comnenus, had turned them into perjurers by his own offer in the negotiations. They seized the Patriarch, who in reality was in sympathy with the leaders of the movement, and demanded that he should reclaim the written oaths which the Emperor had exacted from the Senators. Then soon after, by the advice of Cerularius, the rioters burst out in acclamation of Isaac Comnenus. In a few hours they were masters of the capital. The Patriarch sent orders to the Emperor to cut off his hair and put on the monastic habit. Michael VI made no resistance, and thus, thanks to the intervention of Cerularius, who had undertaken the direction of the movement, the capital acknowledged Isaac Comnenus.

The news of the success of the rising was brought by messengers to the camp of the rebels. Isaac Comnenus, who had reached Chrysopolis, made his solemn entry into Constantinople and at St Sophia received the imperial crown from the hands of the Patriarch (1 September 1057).

Born early in the eleventh century (*c.* 1005), the new Emperor was about fifty years old when he mounted the throne. By his marriage with Catherine, daughter of the Bulgarian prince, John Vladislav, he had had two children who died before him.

There is little to be said as to the foreign policy of Isaac Comnenus; an attack by the Turks upon Melitene and Sebastea, uninterrupted progress made by the Normans in Italy, an attack by the Hungarians, a Patzinak invasion which required the Emperor's presence on the Danubian frontier (1059)—such are the principal external events of the reign, the chief interest of which centres in home policy.

The reign of Isaac Comnenus, raised to the throne as he was by the army, was a period of reaction against the reigns that had gone before it. From his first reception of the great officials the Emperor treated them with marked coldness, and instead of making them the usual speech conveyed his orders to them by his secretaries. The army was handsomely rewarded for the help it had afforded the Emperor, who, however, was careful to avoid committing affairs of state to his soldiers, and hastened to send them back to their garrisons. To shew plainly the character which he intended to impress on his government, the Emperor caused himself to be represented on the gold coinage holding in his hand not the *labarum* (the imperial standard) but a drawn sword. Isaac Comnenus was not wanting in the qualities which go to make a ruler. "He was prudent in conception" says an anonymous chronicler, "but more prompt in action; he was devoid of credulity and desired to judge of men rather by experience than by their flatteries." Psellus writes of him: "Like a lofty and unshakeable column he, in a fashion hitherto unknown, bore on his shoulders the burden of power committed to him."

Isaac brought to the business of State administration the military methods to which he was accustomed. The situation of the Empire, the treasury being exhausted by the preceding reigns, necessitated financial measures of such a character that universal clamour quickly arose against the new sovereign. The payment of taxes was exacted with merciless rigour. The allowances attached to official posts were cut off, the donations bestowed by the last Emperors were re-examined, and many confiscations decreed. Finally, the convents were deprived of a large part of their property. All these measures gave offence to so many different interests that they made the new Emperor thoroughly unpopular and created a large body of disaffected subjects. These soon found a leader in the Patriarch.

Michael Cerularius had taken a decisive part in the revolution which raised Isaac Comnenus to the throne. The latter shewed himself grateful, and made an important concession to the Patriarch, giving up to him the nomination of all the officials of St Sophia, which up to this time the Emperors had kept in their own hands. By so doing the Emperor, as Michael of Attalia expresses it, "renounced all rights over the ecclesiastical affairs which up to then had come within the imperial province. From thenceforth the Palace was completely excluded from ecclesiastical administration. Neither the post of treasurer, nor the care and expenditure of the Church's landed property, came for the future within the jurisdiction of the imperial agents; they depended on the will of the Patriarch, who now obtained the right both of the nomination of persons and of the administration of affairs." It would be impossible to lay too much stress on the importance of these measures, for it was by means of them that the Patriarch, "already the Emperor's superior from the spiritual point of view, attained to temporal independence."

These advantages did not satisfy the Patriarch, who dreamed of uniting the spiritual and temporal power in his own hands, of being at once Patriarch and Emperor. The more Cerularius saw his position grow in importance, the more he sought to interfere in the business of the State, and the less he concealed his pretensions. Before long he openly proclaimed them by adopting the purple buskins which at Constantinople formed a part of the imperial costume.

Isaac Comnenus was not a man to allow his rights to be encroached upon and he pushed matters to the point of an open struggle with the Patriarch. The relations between them soon became so strained that the Emperor saw that he would risk his crown if he did not reduce Cerularius to impotence. He therefore decided on the arrest of the Patriarch—a measure not easy to carry out, for Michael had the support of a strong party and was besides very popular. The Emperor was taxed with ingratitude in thus persecuting the man to whom he owed his crown. It was to be feared that the Patriarch's arrest would be the signal for a riot.

Isaac Comnenus accordingly waited until Cerularius had gone into retreat in November 1058 at the convent of the Nine Orders, situated outside the capital close to the gate of the Holy Angels, and then caused him to be arrested by the Varangians of his body-guard. Michael was at once imprisoned at Proconnesus in the Propontis and thence was transferred to the island of Imbros. Despite his captivity he was still the rightful Patriarch. A rising of the people of Constantinople in his favour was always to be dreaded. Comnenus therefore endeavoured to induce his adversary to abdicate. He failed, and Michael remained unshakable. Isaac then determined to procure his deposition. Psellus was charged with drawing up his indictment, which was to be read at a synod convoked to meet at a town in Thrace. The Patriarch was accused of the heresies of Hellenism and Chaldaïsm, of tyranny, sacrilege, and finally of unworthiness for his office. Michael never appeared before his judges, for he died on the way at Madytus. The Emperor thus found himself delivered from the most formidable of his adversaries. Yet in spite of all, the popularity of Cerularius still remained so great that Comnenus, fearing an outbreak at Constantinople, expressed the profoundest veneration for the dead man, going to weep before his tomb and to implore his pardon for the rigorous measures which had been taken against him. The successor of Cerularius was a creature of Isaac, Constantine Lichudes (February 1059).

The victory of Isaac Comnenus over Cerularius led to no results, and a few months after his adversary's death the Emperor was to lay down his power under circumstances which have always remained full of mystery.

In the early months of 1059 Isaac had set out on a march to drive back the Hungarians who had invaded the imperial territory. Having reached Sardica, he found their ambassadors there and peace was arranged. In the course of the summer he marched to the Danube to fight against the Patzinaks who had crossed the river. The expedition was not a fortunate one, and Isaac was obliged to return precipitately to Constantinople on a false alarm that the Turks had made an attack in Asia Minor. During November he fell ill after a hunting-party, and, in spite of the Empress, resolved to abdicate in order to take the monastic habit and retire to the convent of Studion. After having vainly offered the crown to his brother John Comnenus, he named as his successor one of his brother-officers, Constantine Ducas, President of the Senate.

Whatever were the reasons for this decision, we are absolutely ignorant of them. Psellus, who had a considerable share in these occurrences, has thought fit not to leave us too precise information. There is some reason to think that the opposition which Isaac Comnenus encountered did not come to an end on the disappearance of Cerularius, and that the Emperor must have found himself unable to cope successfully with the obstacles raised up against him. As has been very truly said, "the situation was such that the different parties, applying pressure in different directions, paralysed one another and stopped the wheels of the chariot of state." Seeing no way out of the difficulties with which he was struggling, Comnenus preferred placing the imperial power in other hands and succumbed to the opposition of the bureaucracy.

On the accession of Constantine Ducas (1059–1067) the civil element regained all its old influence. The enterprise of Isaac Comnenus had laid the army more than ever open to suspicion. Thus it became the policy of the government systematically to diminish the military forces of the Empire. The "army estimates" were considerably reduced, the number of effective troops was cut down, and it was soon known that a military career no longer offered a man any chance of attaining to the higher administrative posts. Under this *régime* the military system broke down, and the army was soon thoroughly disorganised. The result of this egregious experiment in statesmanship was quickly apparent, and under

Constantine Ducas and his successors, Romanus Diogenes (1067–1071), Michael VII (1071–1078), and Nicephorus Botaniates (1078–1081), the Empire, attacked all along its frontiers, was everywhere obliged to fall back before its enemies.

In Italy, the Normans put a complete end to Byzantine influence. With the fall of Bari in 1071 the Empire was to lose its last foothold there, and before long Guiscard was to be powerful enough to meditate the subjugation of Constantinople. On the other side of the Adriatic, Croatia succeeded in gaining her independence, which was formally consecrated on the day when the legates of Gregory VII set the crown upon the head of Svinimir. Dalmatia, too, profited by the course of events to secure practical independence, while soon afterwards the town of Ragusa was to ally itself with Robert Guiscard.

Serbia was endeavouring to shake off Byzantine suzerainty, and the great rising of 1071 reduced Greek authority there to a very precarious position. In Bulgaria, which was only half subdued, the Greeks and the natives were violently at enmity. Here again the Normans were to find support in their attempt to conquer the Empire.

On the Northern frontier, the Hungarians took advantage of the difficulties with which the Emperors had to struggle, to begin those profitable incursions into Greek territory whence they used to return loaded with spoil. The wandering tribes along the Danube also went back to their old custom of making expeditions across the river, and their undisciplined bands even advanced as far as the suburbs of the capital. The Uzes and the Patzinaks took their share of the spoils of the Empire, which, in order to purchase peace, was forced to pay them a tribute.

In Asia, the situation was far more seriously compromised by the conquests of the Turks. From 1062 onwards, the Musulmans made steady progress. The Byzantine Empire lost Armenia and the Eastern provinces, while Syria was threatened. The Turks, already masters of Ani, Melitene, and Sebastea, ravaged the region about Antioch. To attempt to check their advance, Eudocia Macrembolitissa, widow of Constantine Ducas, sent against them her co-regent Romanus Diogenes, whom she had just married. Despite the low level to which the Byzantine army had sunk, the Emperor at first succeeded in driving back the enemy, but the Turks retaliated, and in the disastrous battle of Manzikert (1071) his forces were destroyed. Thereupon, from all quarters arose pretenders to the imperial purple. Eudocia, who had shared her office with her son Michael VII, looked on helplessly at the ruin of the Empire. The forward movement of the Muslims became irresistible, and soon the conquerors reached the western shores of Asia Minor.

Nor was the situation within the Empire any more hopeful. The army, neglected by the government, was discontented; the aristocracy bore with impatience its exclusion from power. Thence arose a whole series of outbreaks. Never, perhaps, were attempts at a *pronunciamento* more numerous, but the nobility of Europe and that of Asia Minor, between whom was a deadly hatred, so neutralised each other as to hinder the majority of these attempts from coming to any result.

It was at this moment, when the whole structure of the State seemed to be cracking in every direction and on the point of falling in ruins, that Alexius, nephew of Isaac Comnenus, acquired supreme power.

After the abdication of his brother, John Comnenus had retired into obscurity. By his prudent conduct he was able to avoid the perils which in Constantinople usually threatened the members of a family which had occupied the throne. He died about 1067, leaving five sons and three daughters by his marriage with Anna Dalassena. This lady had seen with regret her husband's refusal of the crown, and when the responsibility for the family interests fell upon her she used every effort to obtain a repetition of the lost opportunity. In her eyes the Ducas family, who had profited by the retirement of Isaac Comnenus, were the enemies of her house; her hatred of them dictated her political attitude. A friend and relation of the Empress Eudocia Macrembolitissa, Anna Dalassena attached herself to the fortunes of Romanus Diogenes, whose son Constantine married her daughter Theodora. Manuel, the eldest of the children of John Comnenus, received a command in the army. On the fall of Romanus Anna's position was shaken, and she was for a short time exiled; but she regained favour under Michael VII, who perhaps stood in dread of the support which the Comneni, with their large estates in Asia Minor, might furnish to the Turks. Her son Isaac, now become the eldest by the death of his brother Manuel, married an Alan princess, a cousin of the Empress Maria, wife of Michael VII. The Comneni then found themselves supported in their position by the eunuch Nicephoritza, who relied upon their help to destroy the influence of the Caesar John Ducas, uncle of Michael VII. Isaac was employed in the war against the Turks and in suppressing the insurrection raised by the Norman leader, Roussel de Bailleul. His brother Alexius made his first essay in war under his command, winning great distinction. Being charged a little later with the task of resisting Roussel, Alexius succeeded in making him prisoner. The fortunes of the Comneni rose steadily; honours and dignities fell to their share. The Caesar John Ducas, by this time fallen into disgrace and become a monk, realising the advantages which an alliance with this powerful family would procure for his house, arranged a marriage between his grand-daughter Irene and Alexius Comnenus. The court opposed the match, which by uniting two of the most powerful families of the aristocracy would make their interests thenceforth identical. The marriage nevertheless took place about the end of 1077 or the beginning of 1078.

On the abdication of Michael VII, Alexius Comnenus, being charged with the defence of the capital, made his submission to the new Emperor, Nicephorus Botaniates, who rewarded him by appointing him Domestic of the Scholae and by entrusting him with the suppression of the revolts of Bryennius and Basilaces.

The methods of government employed by the two ministers, Borilus and Germanus, to whom Nicephorus handed over the exercise of power, aroused general discontent. The treasury was empty; the Varangian guard, being unpaid, mutinied; the army was dissatisfied and protested against having the eunuchs of the palace set over it. Among the people the Emperor was unpopular, for he had come into collision with the generally accepted ideas of legitimism by not associating with himself in his office Constantine, the son of Michael VII. Besides this he caused great scandal by contracting a third marriage with Maria, wife of Michael VII who was still alive.

Alexius Comnenus, who had become popular on account of his successes, was exposed to the dislike and distrust of the party in power. On the other hand, besides his own family connexions, he had the support of the Ducas family, which brought with it that of the clergy. He himself had contrived to gain the favour of the Empress, who was perhaps in love with him. In her eyes he appeared as the champion of Michael VII's son Constantine, and he succeeded in persuading her to adopt him. Thenceforward his rights and Constantine's were merged.

It was not without disquiet that the Court watched the progress made by the Comnenian party. The situation became more and more strained, and soon it was apparent to everyone that the breaking-point must before long be reached. Alexius determined to be first in the field, and under the pretext of repelling the Turks, who were occupying Cyzicus, he assembled troops at Chorlu (Tzurulum) on the road to Hadrianople. Divining the intentions of the Comneni, the ministers of Botaniates resolved on their arrest. Alexius, informed of their design through the Empress, hastily fled from the capital (14 February 1081). At Chorlu he was joined by his partisans, chief among them the Caesar John Ducas, who had quitted his monastery. Once assembled, the rebels seem to have been doubtful as to what their course should be. It is almost certain that rivalries arose, and that a party among them wished to proclaim, not Alexius but his brother Isaac. If, finally, Alexius carried the day, he owed it to the intervention of the Ducas family in his favour.

Alexius, having been proclaimed by the army, marched upon Constantinople, the gates of which were opened to him by treachery. The victorious army pillaged the capital, while Nicephorus Botaniates, not seeking to prolong a useless struggle, divested himself of the imperial robes and put on the monastic habit. Soon after, an agreement made between the new Emperor and Nicephorus Melissenus, who had been proclaimed by the troops in Asia Minor, left Alexius sole occupant of the throne.

The early days of the new reign were taken up with intrigues which are only imperfectly known to us. The Ducas family, to whom Alexius largely owed his success, were fearful for a moment that the Emperor would repudiate his wife. And indeed it appears that for a short time he entertained this project, and had decided to marry the Empress Maria. The firmness of Cosmas, the Patriarch, prevented the Emperor from carrying out his purpose. In her hostility to the house of Ducas, Anna Dalassena urged his resignation, in order that Eustratius Garidas might be chosen in his place. Cosmas refused to retire until he had crowned Irene. It was found impossible to overcome his resistance, and Irene was crowned seven days later than her husband. There is no doubt that Alexius' inclinations were all in favour of Maria, but from the point of view of policy it would have been ill-judged to alienate a faction so powerful as that of the Ducas. Cosmas prevented Alexius from committing this blunder. The Empress Maria was obliged to leave the palace. She took care first to have her son Constantine appointed joint Emperor. The young prince, who was betrothed later on to Anna Comnena, daughter of Alexius, remained heir presumptive until in 1088 the birth of the Emperor's son John enabled Alexius to set him aside.

At the time of his accession Alexius was about thirty-three years old. In person he was short and rather stout, deep-chested and broad-shouldered. Of cultivated mind and supple intellect, he had been very thoroughly educated. Passionately fond of philosophy and theology, he enjoyed taking part in the discussions on these subjects which were so frequent during his reign. Accustomed to court life from his youth, he was well acquainted with men and knew how to make use of them. Very steady in pursuing his ends, he gave all possible care to elaborating his plans and made a point of never leaving anything to chance. Of a mild disposition, his reign was not stained by cruelties. With regard to religion, the Emperor looked upon himself as entrusted with the duty of safeguarding the orthodox faith handed down to him, which he felt bound to hand on intact to his successors, and more than once he personally took a share in the conversion of heretics. Comnenus was perfectly aware of the general decadence of the Empire. He exerted himself to remedy it by reforming the clergy, secular and regular, by founding and encouraging schools, and by re-organising the army and the fleet. In addition to this, it must be said that Alexius was a diplomatist of the first order. Thoroughly conversant with the political state of the surrounding countries, he knew how to profit by their divisions, and had a peculiar gift for inducing the enemies of his enemies to enter into alliance with him.

Immediately upon his accession Alexius had to meet a formidable danger, even more pressing than the Turkish peril. The Normans of Italy were preparing to invade the imperial territory, and the Duke of Apulia, Robert Guiscard, meditated no less an enterprise than an advance upon Constantinople itself. As early as the capture of Bari, which marked the definitive expulsion of the Byzantines from Italy, Guiscard had conceived the idea of assuming the imperial crown. Amid the dangers that threatened the Empire, Michael VII had thought of a Norman alliance, and a daughter of Guiscard had been sent to Constantinople to marry Constantine, the heir to the throne. When Botaniates became Emperor, Guiscard took up the *rôle* of champion of the deposed ruler, and in order to win the goodwill of the Greek populations he spread abroad the rumour that Michael had come to seek help of him. A Greek named Rector posed as the dethroned Emperor. At the same time the Duke of Apulia was seeking to win over supporters, even in Constantinople. The invaders were already at work when Alexius ascended the throne, and Bohemond, Guiscard's son, had occupied Avlona, Canina, and Hiericho.

In May 1081 the bulk of the Norman army crossed the Adriatic and concentrated at Avlona. Guiscard began by reducing Corfù, and thence proceeded to the siege of Durazzo.

Though without money or troops, Alexius contrived to meet the danger. He came to an understanding with certain Norman lords, who had been driven from Italy by Guiscard and had taken refuge at Constantinople, and sent them to Italy to re-kindle the spirit of revolt among the vassals of the Duke of Apulia. At the same time Alexius tried, but in vain, to treat with Gregory VII, and entered into negotiations with Henry IV of Germany. To the latter he promised enormous subsidies if he would make a descent upon Apulia and attack Guiscard. The support of the Venetian fleet was secured by a commercial treaty, opening a long series of Greek ports to the merchants of the republic. Finally, a treaty of peace was concluded with Sulaimān, who in the name of the Seljūq Sultan, Malik Shāh, was leading the Musulman troops to the conquest of Asia Minor, and had obtained possession of Nicaea. This allowed the Emperor to devote his whole attention to the war with the Normans.

The campaign began with a victory won by the Venetian fleet over the Normans at Cape Palli, but the Greek army under the Emperor's command was beaten before Durazzo (Oct. 1081), and Guiscard shortly afterwards became master of the whole of Illyria, for Durazzo fell into his hands. Recalled to Italy in the spring of 1082 by a revolt among his vassals, engineered by the agents of Alexius, Guiscard handed over the command of the expeditionary force to his son Bohemond, who occupied Castoria, besieged Joannina, and defeated Alexius. Ochrida, Scopia (Skoplje), Veria, Servia, Vodena, Moglena, and Trikala thus fell into the hands of the Normans, who pushed on into Thessaly as far as Larissa.

Reduced to the necessity of confiscating Church treasure in order to raise money, Alexius with indefatigable patience got together a new army, and while his allies the Venetians were retaking Durazzo, he succeeded in driving the enemy from Thessaly, and recaptured Castoria (October or November 1083). Negotiations with Bohemond, begun through the mediation of the Patriarch of Jerusalem, Euthymius, led to no result.

The year 1084 brought a fresh endeavour on the part of the Duke of Apulia, who, having restored order in his own dominions, renewed operations against Constantinople. He completely defeated the Venetian fleet off Corfù, and in the beginning of 1085 despatched his son Robert to take Cephalonia. He himself was about to take the field, when he was suddenly overtaken by death. The disturbances which consequently broke out in Italy for a time diverted the Norman danger from the Byzantine frontier.

Hardly was the Empire freed from the presence of the Normans, when a new peril arose in the neighbourhood of the Danube. The military contingents supplied by the Manichaean colony of Philippopolis having proved treacherous during the campaign against Guiscard, Alexius had attempted to punish the offenders. A mutiny had broken out, the leader of which, Traulus, appealed for help to the Patzinak tribes. Though at first repulsed (1086), the Patzinaks returned to the charge the following year. Again defeated, they were pursued by the Greek army, which, however, they put to rout near Dristra (Silistria). It was only by a war which broke out between the Cumans and the Patzinaks that the latter were prevented from profiting by their victory to invade the imperial territory. And, in fact, the struggle was merely postponed. During the years 1088–1090 the Patzinaks settled down on Greek territory and occupied the country between the Danube and the Balkans. Thence they spread into the region around Philippopolis and Hadrianople. It took Alexius several years before he could set on foot an army capable, with any chance of success, of undertaking the struggle with the barbarous tribes which threatened Constantinople. Finally, in the spring of 1091, the Emperor, having called in the help of the Cumans, inflicted a severe defeat upon the Patzinaks by the river Leburnium, which for a time freed the Empire from barbarian incursions (29 April 1091).

However, Alexius had not done with the nomad tribes living to the north of the Danube, and in 1094–1095 he was obliged to repel an attack by his late allies the Cumans, who under the command of a self-styled son of Romanus Diogenes named Leo, had advanced as far as Hadrianople. Leo was taken prisoner and blinded.

A little before the time of the Cuman invasion, Alexius had succeeded in asserting his authority over the Serbs. Theoretically these were vassals of the Empire, to which they were obliged to furnish certain military contingents. At the time of Guiscard's expedition, the Serbian prince, Constantine Bodin, had deserted Alexius, and had drawn off with his troops just as battle was joined. Since that date he had made use of the difficulties with which the Emperor had to struggle to extend his borders and make himself independent. His example had been followed by Bolkan, the Župan of Rascia. In 1091 and 1094 Alexius was obliged to interfere in Serbia, but the mountainous character of the country made military operations difficult, and the Emperor, having taken hostages, contented himself with a submission which was rather apparent than real.

In Europe Alexius had successfully beaten off the attacks of the enemies of the Empire. In Asia Minor the state of things was also improved, although the last remnants of the Byzantine possessions in the Antioch province had fallen into the hands of Malik Shāh. The death of Sulaimān (1085) left Asia Minor divided between a number of emirs, whose rivalries made them likely to play into the Emperor's hands. Sulaimān's dominions had been partitioned between Abu'l-Qāsim, Emir of Nicaea, Tzachas, Emir of Smyrna, formerly a favourite of Nicephorus Botaniates, and Pulchas, Emir of Cappadocia. Alexius tried to profit by the internal dissensions of the Mohammedan rulers to re-open the struggle in Asia, and to protect the last remaining possessions of the Empire. He built the fortress of Civitot on the gulf of Nicomedia, placing in it as garrison a body of soldiers of English origin. At some unspecified period Nicomedia again fell into the power of the Greeks.

The relations between Constantinople and the Turkish emirs are very confusing. It appears that a common fear of Tzachas, Emir of Smyrna, drew together Alexius and Abu'l-Qāsim. As to Tzachas, who had succeeded in creating a fleet, he dreamt of no less an enterprise than the conquest of Constantinople, and with this end in view had allied himself with the Patzinaks. The battle on the Leburnium destroyed his hopes, and he was himself defeated by Constantine Dalassenus, an officer of Alexius. When Malik Shāh sent his captain, Būzhān, to reduce the emirs of Asia Minor to obedience, this general began negotiations with Alexius. The Emperor, while continuing the discussions till they were interrupted by the death of Malik Shāh, remained constant to his alliance with Abu'l-Qāsim. When the latter had been defeated and slain by Būzhān, Alexius allied himself with his successor, Qilij Arslān, son of Sulaimān, and together they fought against Tzachas. The Emperor profited by the general scramble which took place among all the vassals of Sulaimān to attempt the recapture of Apollonia and Cyzicus, which the Greek general Opus succeeded in taking. At this time, with the exception of the coast towns, Alexius possessed nothing in Asia Minor besides the region lying between the Sangarius, the Black Sea, the Bosphorus, and the Propontis. Towards the south a natural frontier was supplied by Lake Sophon and by a wide fortified fosse which supplied Nicomedia with water from the lake.

While he was still fighting with the Turks, Alexius was called on to suppress a dangerous insurrection. Fiscal burdens had led to simultaneous revolts in Cyprus and in Crete, and two chiefs, Charices and Rapsomates, declared their independence. Order was restored by the Grand Drungarius Ducas, and Alexius formed in Cyprus a base of operations for the Greek fleets. The Stratopedarch Eumathius Philocales was entrusted with the carrying-out of the Emperor's plans.

For the first eighteen years of his reign, Alexius had been obliged to maintain incessant warfare, and during the same period the situation in the interior had also presented great difficulties.

Alexius, being held responsible for the complications bequeathed him by his predecessors, was for a time extremely unpopular. A large section of the clergy, in spite of the penance afterwards imposed on him, had never forgiven him the pillage of the churches which had followed the capture of the metropolis at the time of the fall of Botaniates. While the Norman war was in progress, Anna Dalassena, who acted as regent during the absence of Alexius with the army, had, in order to replenish the imperial treasury, confiscated the wealth of the churches. This measure caused universal discontent, which was utilised by the enemies of the dynasty for their own purposes. In order to pacify public opinion, Alexius was obliged to pledge himself to make reparation, and assured to the churches a certain sum of money, to be a yearly charge upon the revenue. In 1086, at the time of the struggle with the Patzinaks, Alexius attempted to have recourse to a similar measure to relieve the pressure on the imperial exchequer. But a considerable body of the clergy, strong in the support of public opinion, with Leo the Metropolitan of Chalcedon at their head, prevented the Emperor from carrying out his project. Alexius never forgave the leader of the resistance, and soon afterwards contrived to have him deposed. However, the affair did not end there, and in 1089, at a time when the exterior enemies of the Empire were becoming bolder than ever, the Emperor was obliged in some sort to make the *amende honorable* for the way in which he had dealt with Church property. He promulgated a Novel forbidding his successors to dip their hands into the Church treasuries. It is probable that the Emperor's action was dictated not only by genuine scruples but also by the necessity of satisfying public opinion, which looked upon the Byzantine defeats as a chastisement from Heaven for the sacrilegious acts which had been committed.

Persons with their own interests to serve attempted to profit by the unpopularity of Alexius to overthrow him, and the Emperor had a whole series of plots to circumvent. Among the conspirators we find generals like the Armenian Ariebes and the Norman leader Humbertopulus (*c.* 1090), besides members of the imperial family such as the Emperor's nephew John Comnenus, son of the Sebastocrator Isaac and governor of Durazzo, who engaged in an intrigue with the Serbs (*c.* 1092). But soon a much more serious conspiracy came to light. Alexius, after the birth of his son in 1088, had gradually deprived the young Constantine Ducas of his prerogatives, and had finally forbidden him to wear the purple buskins which were an essential part of the imperial costume. For some time Alexius remained sole Emperor, and it was only in 1092, after his victories over the Patzinaks, that he felt strong enough to associate his son John with him in the imperial dignity, and to have him recognised as heir to the throne. These measures greatly irritated the Ducas family and their supporters. The discontented drew together round the Empress Maria, mother of Constantine, and a plot was formed with the object of assassinating the Emperor. The conspirators occupied the highest posts about the Court. Their leaders were Nicephorus, a son of the Emperor Romanus Diogenes, Catacalon Cecaumenus, and Michael Taronites, brother-in-law of Alexius. The Emperor escaped on several occasions when attempts were made upon his life, and in February 1094, during his expedition against the Serbs, he decided to have Nicephorus Diogenes, Catacalon, and Taronites arrested at his camp at Seres. As to the other culprits, he chose to ignore them, whether because he was unwilling to compromise the Empress Maria, or because they were too highly placed for him to touch them without endangering himself.

It was just when the victories won by Alexius over domestic as well as foreign enemies seemed to promise a breathing-space to the Empire, that the First Crusade came to plunge it into fresh uncertainties, by the complete change which it brought about in the position of the states of the East.

For long years historians have indulged in cheap denunciations of the ingratitude and perfidy of Alexius Comnenus, who, after having (particularly by a letter addressed to Robert, Count of Flanders) solicited help from the Western nations against the Turks, ceased not, throughout the Crusade, to throw all kinds of obstacles in their way, so that his false and treacherous conduct was the cause of all the evils which fell upon the first crusaders. A closer examination of the sources allows us, partially at least, to acquit the Emperor of the charges brought against him, and to assert that Urban II in preaching the Crusade by no means did so in response to a desire expressed by Alexius Comnenus. The Pope's action, in fact, had not been suggested to him by anyone, and had been inspired solely by a wish to secure the safety of Christianity in the East.

It is no doubt true that during the early part of his reign Alexius had sought for allies in the West. At the time of the Norman invasion he had entered into diplomatic relations with Gregory VII; later, in 1089, in connexion with the measures taken against the Latin inhabitants of Constantinople, Pope Urban II had had some correspondence with the Emperor. The relations between Rome and Constantinople had been becoming less strained, as is proved by the "Discourse upon the Errors of the Latins" by Theophylact, Archbishop of Bulgaria, which was composed about this time. Embassies had been exchanged, the reunion of the Churches had been discussed, the Pope had relieved the Emperor from the sentence of excommunication, so that in 1090 or 1091, during the struggle with the Patzinaks, Alexius begged Urban II to help him to raise mercenaries in Italy. About the same time he addressed a similar request to Robert, Count of Flanders, praying him to despatch to Constantinople the corps of cavalry which Robert had promised to send him when, on his way back from the Holy Land in 1087, he had had a meeting with Alexius at Eski-Sagra[1]. It was in these requests that the legend originated according to which the Crusade was preached in response to the demands for help made to the Western princes by Alexius Comnenus. The letter supposed to have been addressed with this object to the Count of Flanders is admittedly to a great extent apocryphal. It was very possibly composed with the help of the letter written by Alexius to Robert about 1089, at a time when no Crusade was in contemplation. The legend circulated rapidly. The fact is that when the Western peoples came to know the difficulties of every kind which the crusaders had had to overcome, when they saw how few returned of those who had gone forth in such numbers, when they learned how large a proportion had left their bones strewn along the road to Palestine, they refused to believe that incapacity and rivalry on the part of the leaders and total lack of generalship had been the cause of all the evils encountered by the army, and preferred to cast the whole responsibility on the head of the Greek Emperor. The relations between the Latins and the Greeks, having been on the whole unfriendly, contributed to the growth of a tradition damaging to the Emperor. This notion of Byzantine perfidy fitted in quite easily with all that was known of what had passed between the Emperor and the Westerns, and of the support lent him by the Pope and the Count of Flanders in previous years. From thence to the idea of ingratitude there was but a step, and it was soon taken.

From the very beginning violent disputes took place between the Latins and the Greeks, and it may fairly be said that neither side was blameless. The undisciplined masses of crusaders, above all those who accompanied Peter the Hermit, behaved on their journey through the imperial territory like mere brigands, plundering, burning, and sacking wherever they went. Thus the Greeks looked upon them much as they did upon the Patzinaks or the Cumans who, a few years before, had devastated the European provinces. The object of the expedition and its character as a religious undertaking were completely overlooked by the Byzantines, who only saw its political side. To them it seemed an attempt at conquest much like that of Guiscard. The crusaders themselves went out of their way to justify this estimate. "There were two parties among the crusaders, that of the religiously-minded, and that of the politicians." This statement of Kugler's[2] is absolutely true. There is no denying that religious feeling played a large part in the First Crusade, but it was to be found chiefly among the rank and file, among humbler knights, among the less important leaders. If the principal barons were concerned for the interests of religion at the outset, such feelings had disappeared as

[1] According to H. Pirenne, *A propos de la lettre d'Alexis Comnène à Robert le Frison, comte de Flandre*, in the *Revue de l'instruction publique en Belgique*, Vol. L. (Brussels, 1907, p. 224), this interview did not take place before 1089.

[2] Kugler, *Kaiser Alexius und Albert von Aachen, Forsch. z. deutsch. Geschicht.* XXIII. p. 486.

soon as the various bands of crusaders were united. Then Bohemond as well as Baldwin, the Count of Toulouse and Godfrey of Bouillon alike, forgot the religious side of their enterprise to dwell solely on their private interests. One idea alone remained in their minds, that of carving out principalities for themselves. One need only recall Baldwin's settlement at Edessa and Tancred's at Tarsus, the rivalries of Bohemond and Raymond of Toulouse at Antioch, and finally Godfrey's refusal to continue the march upon Jerusalem, "conduct very little deserving of the laurels that have been wreathed for him."

Face to face with the powerful forces which from every side streamed in upon the territories of the Empire, Alexius found the part he had to play all the more difficult, inasmuch as at that moment the Greek troops were dispersed along the frontiers and could not be recalled without danger. Constantinople was absolutely ungarrisoned. Moreover, the whole Byzantine army would have been quite unable to make head against the innumerable multitude of crusaders. Thus incapable of repelling the Latins by force, Alexius sought to turn them to account as mercenaries for the recovery of the Asiatic provinces which the Empire had lost. He made no difference between the Latin princes and those barons who had come on various occasions to serve with their troops in his army. It was natural that this should be his opinion of them, when he found Bohemond, one of the chief leaders of the Crusade, asking for the office of Grand Domestic of the Scholae.

Alexius shared with his subjects the belief that anything might be obtained of the Latins by plying them with money, their obedience being merely a matter of barter and sale. He had greatly at heart the recovery of the former provinces of the Empire in Asia, and the restoration of Byzantine authority as far as Antioch. Chance had supplied him with an army the like of which the Empire had never seen; the only question was, by what means he could attach it to his service. To induce the Latins to acknowledge him as their lord, and to make use of them as mercenaries, such was the Emperor's plan. In order to bind the Latins more closely to him, the Emperor adopted their customs and caused them to take the oath of fealty to him. It is fair to state, besides, that Alexius believed that by the considerable sums which he disbursed for the crusaders he had acquired certain rights over them, and the behaviour of the leaders encouraged him in this belief. The haughtiest of the chiefs gave an eager welcome to Byzantine gold, which soon overcame their early reluctance to comply with the Emperor's wishes. Their submission was rendered the easier by the conviction which very soon took possession of them, that their undertaking could not possibly succeed unless by the help of the Emperor.

In order to carry out his designs, Alexius employed all his skill as a politician; to attain his ends he took advantage of all the faults and weaknesses of the Latins; and to bring them over to his views he spared neither money nor promises. But once the treaty was concluded, by which he promised his support and a supply of provisions, on condition that the leaders of the Crusade did homage and swore fealty to him and engaged to restore to the Empire any towns which had formerly belonged to it, Alexius observed his engagements. The Latins made it a special reproach against him that he did not follow up the Crusade with an army as he had pledged himself to do. This complaint is not justified; Alexius did march upon Antioch, and if he stopped short it was because he had been dissuaded from continuing his advance by those crusaders who, thinking all lost at the time of the attack on the town by the Turks, had shamefully taken to flight and informed the Emperor that the Christian army had been wiped out. On looking into the question more closely, we find that all the difficulties arose from Bohemond's refusal to restore Antioch to the Emperor as he had promised. Bohemond was the only crusader with whom Alexius broke off friendly relations; we can see that he remained on the best of terms with others of the leaders, notably with Raymond of Toulouse. But the purely political dispute which Alexius carried on with the Prince of Antioch resulted in the Emperor appearing to Western eyes as the enemy of the crusaders in general, for it was thus that Bohemond, on his visit to France in 1106, represented him to the knights who thronged to take service under him. By making out the Greek Emperor to be the enemy of all Latins, instead of what he really was, his own private enemy, Bohemond, more than anyone else, helped to create a tradition adverse to Alexius.

The first of the crusaders to reach Greek territory were the companions of Peter the Hermit. Having quitted Cologne in the latter half of April 1096, these undisciplined bands gained the Greek frontier towards the end of June. At Niš a collision took place with the Byzantine troops despatched to keep down the excesses of the crusaders, who, having acquired a taste for plunder by the sack of Semlin, were ravaging in all directions. In excuse for the Latins it must be said that pillage was almost forced upon them. For as a matter of fact no measures had been taken for the victualling of this multitude, and they were obliged to live upon the districts through which their march lay. After the encounter at Niš, Peter the Hermit entered into communications with the envoys of Alexius, and the crusaders resumed their march upon Constantinople, where they arrived by 1 August 1096. Peter the Hermit had an interview with the Emperor, who recommended him to wait outside Constantinople for the other crusaders and caused money and provisions to be distributed to the Latins. But at the sight of the pillage in which the crusaders indulged in the neighbourhood of the capital, Alexius changed his mind and determined to transport them across the Bosphorus. The passage began on 5 August. Instead of remaining at Civitot to await the arrival of the bulk of the crusading army, Peter the Hermit's bands penetrated into the interior of the country and began ravaging. When they had pillaged all around them, they were obliged to extend the scope of their operations and advanced as far as Nicaea. They there came into collision with the Turks who, after defeating them at Xerigordon, on the banks of the Dracon, pursued them to Civitot itself. Here the Hermit's companions met with a fearful disaster; the greater number of them perished, and few indeed re-crossed the Bosphorus in the ships sent by the Emperor to bring them help. The wretched remains of these first bands awaited the arrival of the rest of the crusaders at Constantinople, which had been fixed upon as the point of concentration by the Pope's legate, Ademar of Puy.

With regard to the Crusade under the leadership of the barons, Alexius took steps to secure some measure of order. He sent officers to meet each band, with promises of supplies during its march through the European provinces, and at the same time he posted troops so as to form as it were a channel to drain off the crusading torrent upon Constantinople. Thus the pilgrims, it was hoped, would be prevented from straying from the route marked out for them, and so from pillaging. Between these Greek troops and the Latins fighting several times occurred, and in spite of the precautions taken the districts traversed suffered severely.

Hugh, Count of Vermandois, brother of Philip I, King of France, was the first of the leaders to reach Constantinople. Having come through Italy, he landed at Durazzo, after losing the greater part of his vessels. He was received with the more honour because the sorry plight in which he arrived made him less of a danger. Alexius, notwithstanding, detained him for some time as a hostage.

At the end of 1096 Godfrey of Bouillon arrived at Constantinople with a numerous following. We have no precise information as to his journey through the European provinces of the Empire, for the narrative of Albert of Aix, our only authority, is on many points of a biased and legendary nature. Alexius opened communications with Godfrey through the mediation of the Count of Vermandois. From the very first, however, relations were unsatisfactory. The Emperor, whose great fear was lest the crusaders should concentrate outside his capital, did his utmost to persuade them to cross the Bosphorus. Godfrey, on the other hand, was at first quite determined to wait at Constantinople for Bohemond, who was on his way from Italy. He remained encamped in front of the capital up to the beginning of April 1097. To overcome the resistance of the Duke of Lorraine to his will, Alexius several times tried to cut off the food-supply which he furnished to the crusaders. But nothing had any effect until the Emperor succeeded in inducing Godfrey of Bouillon to take the oath of fealty.

Some time after the departure of Godfrey's troops, Bohemond, son of Guiscard, reached Constantinople. Since the death of his father, Bohemond had found Italy too restricted a field for his ambition. He enthusiastically welcomed the idea of the Crusade, and set out with the plan of creating a principality for himself in the East, but at first he designed to do this with the help of the Greeks. Bohemond's army landed at Avlona, and on its way to Constantinople was guilty of a certain amount of violence which was avenged by the Greek troops. On arriving at Rusa, Bohemond, leaving his nephew Tancred in command, went forward alone to Alexius. He took the oath of fealty, was loaded with presents, and asked to be appointed Grand Domestic for the East. When Raymond of Saint-Gilles, Count of Toulouse, arrived at Constantinople by way of Dalmatia and Serbia and refused to take the oath of fealty, Bohemond acted the part of mediator. Raymond persisted in his refusal, and would only consent to swear not to undertake anything against the life or honour of the Emperor. Alexius, much irritated, bestowed few presents on him. With the other leaders Alexius experienced no kind of difficulty; Tancred alone crossed into Asia unfettered by any oath.

A formal treaty was concluded between the Emperor and the crusading chiefs. Alexius pledged himself to take the Cross and place himself at the head of the crusaders, to protect the pilgrims during their journey through his dominions, and to furnish a body of troops to the expedition. The crusaders in return promised to restore to Alexius any towns they should take which had formerly made part of the Greek Empire. This treaty was concluded in May 1097 through the mediation of Bohemond, who had for this purpose remained behind while the bulk of the crusading army, as early as the month of April, had set out to besiege Nicaea.

On the surrender of Nicaea, the crusaders faithfully carried out the treaty and left the town to the Emperor. Alexius then had a fresh interview at Pelecanum with the leaders, who, Tancred excepted, renewed their oaths. The expedition then resumed its march towards Jerusalem, accompanied by a corps of Greek troops under the command of Taticius. Once Iconium was reached, the greater part of the army pressed on towards Antioch by way of Caesarea and Mar'ash (Germanicea), while Tancred and Baldwin reached Cilicia, where they disputed for the possession of Tarsus, which they ought to have handed over in due course to the Emperor.

As far as Antioch the Greek troops had remained in company with the Latins. It was during the siege of that town, begun at the end of October 1097, that the rupture between them took place. This was due to the machinations of Bohemond, who, displeased at having failed to obtain the help of Alexius in carrying out his projects, did not scruple in order to get possession of Antioch to intrigue with Taticius, whom he persuaded to withdraw. Once the Greek contingent was gone, Alexius was accused of having failed to keep his engagements, and on the fall of Antioch the town was handed over to Bohemond, to the great displeasure of the Count of Toulouse, who had been ambitious of securing it for himself.

While these events were taking place, Alexius was preparing to march to the help of the crusaders. A preliminary expedition, commanded on land by John Ducas and on sea by Caspax, was winning back for the Empire Smyrna, Ephesus, and the whole territory belonging to the ancient Thracesian theme. Alexius himself was setting out for Antioch at the head of considerable forces. He had reached Philomelium when he was joined by a certain number of crusaders, among whom were men of importance, such as William of Grantmesnil and Stephen of Blois. These leaders, on the occasion of the Emir Karbuqā's attack upon Antioch, had judged it prudent to take to flight. The picture which they drew for Alexius of the state of the crusading army was no doubt made more gloomy to provide some reasonable excuse which their conduct needed. They convinced the Emperor of the uselessness of the succour which he was bringing to the besieged, and Alexius ordered a retreat to Constantinople.

The fugitives' forebodings were not realised, and the Emir Karbuqā was defeated by the crusaders. Alexius received the news in a letter from the leaders brought to him by Hugh of Vermandois. The message must have caused the Emperor keen annoyance, for, from the moment that he learned that the town had been handed over to Bohemond, he cannot have been under much illusion as to the manner in which the crusaders would fulfil their promises. Alexius immediately made advances to the Caliph of Egypt, and tried also to arrange an understanding with Raymond, Count of Toulouse, who had been openly at feud with Bohemond since the failure of his designs upon Antioch. Apparently the alliance between Alexius and the Count of Toulouse was brought about during the autumn of 1098. It first came to light when in November of the same year Raymond demanded of the council of the crusaders that Antioch should be handed over to the Emperor. The proposal was rejected. At the beginning of 1099 the Count of Toulouse transferred to the Greeks the towns of Laodicea, Maraclea, and Bulunyās (Balanea) on the Syrian coast which had been occupied by his troops.

In the early months of 1099 Alexius replied to the message which the Count of Vermandois had brought him, by a letter which reached the council of the crusaders about Easter (10 April). The Emperor announced that he would arrive by St John's Day (24 June) and that he was ready to keep his engagements provided that Antioch was surrendered to him. In spite of the Count of Toulouse, the crusaders, who had just wasted six months in barren discussions, refused to wait for the Greek army, and resumed their march upon Jerusalem without concerning themselves about Alexius. The rupture was thus definite and complete. It is noteworthy that the Emperor held Bohemond alone responsible for this breach of plighted faith. The latter, moreover, as early as the summer of 1099, was to begin hostilities against the Greeks by attacking Laodicea. He was assisted by a Pisan fleet, on its way to the Holy Land under the command of Daimbert, Archbishop of Pisa. During the voyage the Pisans attacked and pillaged several islands, dependencies of the Greek Empire. The Byzantine fleet pursued them in vain. However, they were repulsed from Cyprus, where they had attempted to land by force in spite of its duke, Eumathius Philocales. One of the commanders of the Greek fleet, Eustathius, then occupied the Isaurian towns of Gorigos and Seleucia, and perhaps also Tarsus, Adana, and Mamistra.

After the fall of Jerusalem, the *rapprochement* between Alexius and Raymond grew still more pronounced. The Count of Toulouse, who, since the army left Antioch, had been the real leader of the Crusade, not only failed to obtain the crown as he had hoped, but was also refused Ascalon by Godfrey of Bouillon. No other means remained to him of forming a principality for himself in the East than to ask help of Alexius. And this course he took, making a journey to Constantinople during the summer of 1100. He there learned that Godfrey of Bouillon had died (18 July 1100) and that Bohemond, who had been made prisoner by the Dānishmandite Emir Malik Ghāzī, was temporarily replaced at Antioch by his nephew Tancred.

Alexius was unable to turn these incidents to account, for he was detained at Constantinople by the coming of fresh bodies of crusaders. At the news that Jerusalem had been taken, the impulse which was carrying the West towards the East had become stronger than ever, and during the winter of 1100–1101 the Lombard crusade, its numbers presently swelled by the followers of Stephen of Blois, exposed the Greeks to the same dangers that had resulted from the first expeditions. With regard to these new crusaders, Alexius took up the same attitude as he had towards the bands under Godfrey of Bouillon. He exacted the oath of fealty from the leaders, and in exchange he furnished them with provisions. The same untoward incidents occurred between the Greeks and the crusaders, the same acts of violence were committed as in 1096. The Emperor would have preferred that this expedition should take the same road as the first. The crusaders refused, and marched towards the dominions of the Great Seljūq, wishing, they said, to liberate Bohemond. They were shattered on the way between Amasia and Sebastea. Their defeat was not due to the treachery of the Count of Toulouse who had taken the command, nor, as some have claimed, to Alexius. The real cause of their ill-success must be sought for elsewhere. The arrival of these fresh bands of crusaders brought about that union among the Turks which up to then had proved impossible of attainment. The Musulmans understood that, if they suffered these reinforcements to reach Syria, their own power there would be at an end. The united forces of Malik Ghāzī, Qilij Arslān, and the Emir of Aleppo, Riḍwān, cut the crusaders to pieces. The survivors of the expedition reached Constantinople with difficulty in 1101. The failure of this expedition caused Alexius to be gravely suspected in the West, although he was not responsible, since the leaders had refused to follow out his plans. In 1102, at the Council of Benevento, very unfavourable reports were for the first time circulated with regard to him.

The expedition of William, Count of Nevers, who was on the best of terms with Alexius while he was passing through Constantinople, proved no more fortunate. The Latins, attacked by Qilij Arslān and Malik Ghāzī, met with a crushing defeat at Heraclea. A similar fate awaited William IX of Aquitaine and Welf, Duke of Bavaria, who were defeated by Qilij Arslān and Qāraja, the Emir of Ḥarrān, as they were endeavouring to reach Cilicia.

In 1102 Constantinople saw the arrival of a new expedition, that of the Scandinavians under Eric the Good, and in the same year Alexius despatched the remains of the Lombard contingent to the port of Antioch (Saint-Simeon), with Raymond of Toulouse at their head.

At this time there was perfect harmony between the Count of Toulouse and the Emperor, and it was with the help of the Duke of Cyprus that Raymond (as soon as he had been set free by Tancred, who on his landing kept him for some time a prisoner) undertook the siege of Tripolis.

About the same time Bohemond returned from his captivity. Being again called upon by Alexius to fulfil the treaties which had been concluded, he declined. Alexius then decided upon an open struggle. He sent to Cilicia Monastras and Butumites who occupied Mar'ash, but next year this place was taken from the Greeks by Joscelin, Count of Edessa. The disaster which the crusaders met with at Ḥarrān (1104) gave the Greeks an opportunity of occupying Tarsus, Adana, and Mamistra. Bohemond, busy with the struggle against the Turks, was unable to hinder the advance of the Byzantines. The commanders of Alexius' fleet, Cantacuzene and Landolf, in a short time took Laodicea and the places along the coast as far as Tripolis.

Closely hemmed in between the Turks and the Greeks, Bohemond saw that he could not escape from the double pressure. To defend Antioch against the Turks, he would need to be free from molestation by the Greeks; while to crush Alexius he would need to strike, not in the East, but at Constantinople itself. The Prince of Antioch therefore decided on a journey to Europe to ask for help and to organise an expedition against the Byzantine Empire. In January 1105 he landed in Apulia, and soon after, accompanied by a papal legate, he passed through Italy and France preaching a crusade against Alexius, whom he painted in the darkest colours.

The Emperor attempted to prove to the Latins by his actions that Bohemond's representations were unworthy of credence. He wrote to the Republics of Pisa, Genoa, and Venice to put them on their guard against the son of Robert Guiscard. At the same time he was negotiating with the Caliph of Egypt for the ransom of the Latin captives.

During the two years spent by Bohemond in preparing for his

expedition (1105–7), Alexius, while organising the defence of his dominions, did not lose sight of affairs in Asia. Thus, Raymond of Toulouse having died in February 1105, the Emperor made great efforts to win over to his side William-Jordan, Count of Cerdagne, who was disputing the succession with Raymond's illegitimate son, Bertrand. In another quarter Comnenus gained an important advantage, getting into his power Gregory Taronites, Duke of Trebizond, who had broken out into revolt, and was now made prisoner just as he was turning for help to Malik Ghāzī.

At about the same time Alexius discovered that a vast plot was brewing at Constantinople, to take advantage of the difficulties created for him by Bohemond and to depose him. At the head of the conspirators were the brothers Anemas, of Turkish origin, and also the representatives of a large number of noble families, Castamunites, Curticius, Basilacius, Sclerus, and Xerus, who was then Prefect of Constantinople, as well as Solomon, one of the leaders in the Senate. All the culprits were arrested and condemned to be blinded, but were pardoned at the intercession of the Empress.

In the autumn of 1107 Bohemond's preparations were complete, and on 9 October the disembarkation of his army, which was 34,000 strong, began at Avlona. The plan of campaign adopted was that of Guiscard, but on this occasion the fate of the expedition was to be very different.

When the enemy appeared, Alexius was ready. Having learned experience by the earlier warfare, he had determined not to fight a battle. He contented himself with enclosing the Norman army in a ring of steel, while at the same time the Byzantine fleet prevented their obtaining supplies by sea. Bohemond succeeded in holding out up to the spring of 1108, but by that time the sufferings of his army were so severe that, after having vainly attempted at Hiericho and at Canina to break through the circle which confined him, he was forced to admit himself worsted. Divisions were also rife in his ranks, for Alexius had arranged that certain compromising letters should fall into the hands of the Prince of Antioch which might be understood as replies addressed by Alexius to overtures from the principal Norman commanders. Thenceforward Bohemond was suspicious of everyone. At the interview which he had with Alexius at Deabolis he was forced to accept very hard terms. In the first place, the compact of 1097 was annulled, and Bohemond, recognising himself the liegeman of Alexius and his son, bound himself not to take arms against them, to serve them personally or by deputy against all their enemies, to undertake nothing against the imperial dominions, and to retain for himself only certain districts enumerated below. He promised to restore to the Empire all such of his conquests as had formerly belonged to it, not to make any treaty engagements detrimental to the Emperor or the Empire, to send back any subjects of Alexius who should desire to enter his service, and to cause any barbarians whom he should subdue to take the oath of allegiance to the Emperor and his son. All conquests which he might make from the Turks or Armenians, though not formerly belonging to the Empire, should be held by him in fief from the Emperor. All his vassals were to take the oaths to Alexius, and, in case of treason on his part, should have the right, after forty days, of going over to the Emperor. The Patriarch of Antioch was to be of the Greek Church, and to be chosen by the Emperor from among the clergy of St Sophia. Alexius, on his part, made over to Bohemond Antioch, Suetius, Cauca, Lulum, Teluseh, Mar'ash, Baghras, and Balitza, a part of the Amanus mountains, and the valley of the Orontes. On the other hand, the following were restored to the Empire: the theme of Podandus, Tarsus, Adana, Mamistra, Anazarbus, Laodicea, Gabala, Bulunyās, Maraclea, and Tortosa. The Emperor also promised to Bohemond two hundred talents in michaelites, and granted him a certain number of towns in the interior of Syria and in the neighbourhood of Edessa. Finally, Bohemond obtained the right of naming his heir.

As soon as the treaty had been signed the Emperor loaded Bohemond with gifts and named him Sebastos, but the Prince of Antioch was crushed by the failure of his hopes. He left abruptly for Italy, where he died not long after (1111 ?).

The treaty which ended the Norman war was a substantial victory for the Emperor. The principality of Antioch was no longer a danger to the Empire, for the passes of the Amanus and Cilicia were now in the hands of the Greeks, who also commanded the sea-ports. Thus, for the future, assistance from Europe could only reach Antioch by permission of the Greeks. The treaty, however, was only of value in so far as its provisions were duly carried out; and when, upon the death of Bohemond, Alexius called upon Tancred to observe the convention made with his uncle, the Prince of Antioch refused. The Emperor either would not or could not embark upon a war with Tancred; he confined himself to attempting to win over the Latin princes of Syria to support his cause. Butumites, despatched with large supplies of money, negotiated fruitlessly with Bertrand, Count of Tripolis, and later with his son Pons. Nor was he more successful with King Baldwin. But, in spite of everything, the treaty of 1108 remained of essential importance, for it was the standard by which the relations of Antioch and Constantinople were regulated, and it was to securing its observance that all the efforts of Alexius, his son, and his grandson, were directed.

The last years of Alexius were to be occupied with fresh struggles against the Turks. The latter had for some years ceased to invade Greek territory, for nearly all the emirs were engaged in the struggle which took place between the two sons of Malik Shāh, Barkiyāruq and Muḥammad. Upon the victory of Muḥammad, the country gradually settled down, and when one of the sons of Qilij Arslān, Malik Shāh, had obtained possession of Iconium, war again began between the Turks and the Greeks.

About 1109 Alexius ordered Eumathius Philocales, who was appointed Governor of Attalia, to relieve Adramyttium and to drive out the Turkish tribes from the neighbourhood. The governor attacked the Musulmans settled in the region of Lampe, and immediately Ḥasan, Emir of Cappadocia, set out to ravage the Greek territories. Philadelphia, Smyrna, Nymphaeum, Chliara, and Pergamus were threatened, and once again the fruitful valleys along the coast of Rūm were traversed by the swift Musulman squadrons dealing terror and destruction as they went. Though repulsed, they soon returned. After 1112 their incursions become continual. In that year Alexius awaited them at Adramyttium, Constantine Gabras at Philadelphia, and Monastras at Pergamus and Chliara, the Turks being defeated by Gabras. In 1113 Nicaea was besieged, and Prusa, Apollonia, and Lopadium taken from the Greeks; the Emir Manalugh ravaged Parium and Abydos, and the Greek troops with difficulty drove back the enemy.

Next year, 1114, an invasion by the Cumans summoned Alexius to the northern frontier. From Philippopolis, where he spent his leisure time in discussions with the Manichaeans who were numerous in that district, he kept watch upon the enemy and succeeded in driving them back, but of the circumstances of his victory little is known.

Returning to Constantinople, Alexius again prepared to do battle with the Musulmans, whose bands continued to harass the Greek frontiers. Alexius gathered a considerable force, and decided on undertaking police operations on a large scale and on driving off the Turkish tribes as far as Iconium. Having repulsed the enemy, the Emperor pushed on to Philomelium and Amorium. During his retreat the Sultan of Iconium attacked the Greeks, but he was beaten near Ampûn, and obliged to make peace. According to Anna Comnena, he conceded the old frontier-line of the Empire as it had been in the time of Romanus Diogenes. This is highly doubtful, and it does not appear that the Greek possessions (with the exception of Trebizond and that part of the Armeniac theme which bordered upon the Black Sea) included anything except the country lying west of a line drawn along Smyrna, Gangra, Ancyra, Amorium, and Philomelium. To this must be added the coast towns as far as the borders of the principality of Antioch. The chief result of this expedition of the Emperor was the liberation of a throng of captives, whom he brought back to Greek territory.

The Musulman war did not monopolise the attention of Alexius during the last years of his life, for we find him attempting to play a part in the affairs of Italy. From this arose the treaty with Pisa in 1111, by which Alexius agreed no longer to interpose obstacles to the crusades set on foot by the Pisans, and to present rich gifts every year to the Archbishop and cathedral of Pisa. The Emperor also made important commercial concessions to the Pisans, to whom were allotted a wharf and a residential quarter at Constantinople.

It is very probable that this agreement with Pisa was part of a project formed by Alexius to secure for Constantinople a preponderating influence in Italian affairs. The death of Roger Borsa, Duke of Apulia, left the Pope without a protector, just as he had embarked on a more violent contest than ever with the Emperor Henry V. It will be remembered that Paschal II, taken prisoner by the Emperor, conceded to him the right of investiture, but repudiated his concession as early as March 1112, acknowledging his weakness. In January 1112 Alexius wrote to Gerard, Abbot of Monte Cassino, expressing his regret at the Pope's captivity, and at the same time he entered into communication with the Romans, whom he congratulated on their resistance to the Emperor. He informed them that if they were still in the same mind as had been reported to him, he would accept the imperial crown for himself or his son. In reply to this message, the Romans in May 1112 despatched a numerous embassy to the Emperor in order to arrange an agreement with him. Alexius had to promise to come to Rome in the course of the summer, but he fell ill and was unable to fulfil his engagement. It is evident that Paschal II only continued these negotiations in the hope of bringing about the re-union of the Churches and the ending of the schism. With regard to this, a letter written to Alexius by the Pope towards the end of the year is of the greatest importance. The Pope thanks Heaven which has inspired Alexius with the idea of this much-desired union, but he does not conceal the difficulties which the scheme will have to encounter; the Emperor, however, has the easier task, for he is in a position to command both clergy and laity. The Pope recognises with pleasure the good faith of Alexius and of his envoy, Basil Mesimerius, but from the outset he makes a point of stating that there is but one means of reconciling all differences, and that is for the Patriarch of Constantinople to acknowledge the primacy of the see of Rome, and for the metropolitan sees and provinces which had formerly been subject to the Papacy to return to their obedience and place themselves at its disposal.

In conclusion, the Pope proposes the assembling of a Council, and makes no allusion whatever to the projects of the Emperor regarding the imperial crown. It is plain that in his mind these projects are dependent upon the recognition by the Church of Constantinople of the primacy of Rome. We know nothing of the further progress of these negotiations, which may, in all probability, be connected with the journey of the Archbishop of Milan, Peter Chrysolanus, to Constantinople in 1113. During his visit he had a discussion with Eustratius, Bishop of Nicaea, on the subject of the errors of the Greek Church. This attempt by Alexius to restore the unity of the Empire, although we know so little of it, is none the less curious. We shall find his idea taken up later by his grandson Manuel.

The last days of Alexius were saddened by quarrels and divisions in his family. The Emperor at one time had reason to fear that his life-work would be destroyed by his nearest relatives. In the early part of his reign Alexius had been under the influence of his mother Anna Dalassena, but by degrees she had rendered herself unendurable to her son, and perceiving this had not waited to be driven from court, but had retired of her own accord to the monastery of Pantepoptes, where she died (*c.* 1105?). Her daughter-in-law Irene succeeded to her influence. She had borne the Emperor seven children—four daughters, Anna, Maria, Eudocia, and Theodora, and three sons, John, Andronicus, and Isaac. The eldest of these children, Anna, a highly cultivated woman, mistress of all the learning to be acquired in her day, to whom we owe the *Alexiad*, having been for a moment heiress to the throne at the time of her betrothal to the son of Michael VII, was inconsolable for the frustration of her hopes by the birth of her brother John. Being very ambitious, she succeeded, with the help of her mother and her brother Andronicus, in forming a considerable party for herself at court, and strong in its support she endeavoured to prepare the way for the succession to the throne of her husband, the Caesar Nicephorus Bryennius, as soon as her father's death should take place. John, whose rights were thus directly threatened, made every effort to gain over the people and the Senate. For several years an underground struggle went on between the two parties. The Empress, whose influence over Alexius had grown to such a height that she accompanied him even on his campaigns, worked unceasingly to bring him to share her ill-opinion of her son John, whom she represented as hopelessly dissolute. Alexius, however, held out against the insinuations of his wife, though, by constantly postponing his decision, he led her to hope that it might prove to be in accordance with her views.

In the beginning of 1118 the Emperor fell seriously ill, and the intriguing around him redoubled. In spite of all her efforts Irene could not prevail upon her husband to sacrifice the son's rights to the daughter's. The Emperor's dream had always been to found a dynasty, and he could not but see that his work would be ephemeral, and that his house would not long retain power, if he himself set the example of undermining the right of succession. His sickness increasing, Alexius was carried to the palace of Mangana. Feeling himself near his end, he summoned his son, and giving him his ring charged him to have himself proclaimed Emperor. John, in obedience to his father's orders, hastily had himself crowned in St Sophia. Then, surrounded by his partisans, he occupied the Sacred Palace, the thick walls of which would enable him to defy the outbreak which his adversaries were likely to stir up. When the Empress and her daughter learned what had happened, they gave way to an explosion of wild rage. Irene renewed her efforts to wring from the dying Emperor the recognition of Bryennius. She hoped that the news of John's action would induce his father to disinherit him. But, far from shewing anger, Alexius, on hearing of his son's success, lifted his hands to Heaven as though to give thanks to God. On this Irene, perceiving that she had been duped, overwhelmed her husband with reproaches. "All your life," she said, "you have done nothing but deceive and use words to conceal your thoughts, and you have remained the same even on your death-bed." Alexius expired during the night of 15–16 August 1118; his body, abandoned by all, was hastily buried without the usual ceremonies at the monastery of Christos Philanthropos.

Up to his last moments Comnenus had fought to defend the rights of his son. Thanks to the resistance which he maintained to the will of his wife and daughter, he succeeded in securing those rights, and all their web of intrigue fell to pieces when confronted with the accomplished fact.

From the administrative point of view, the reign of Alexius is of real importance. Comnenus, in fact, successfully carried out a heavy task by reconstructing the fleet and the army which his predecessors had allowed to fall into decay. We have hardly any information as to the navy. When the reign began, the Byzantine fleet had ceased to exist, and in order to repel the Normans Alexius had been obliged to appeal for help to the naval force of the Venetians. Anna Comnena on several occasions mentions the building of ships by her father's orders. As the history of the reign proceeds, we can see the gradual development of the Greek fleet and the part which it plays. In particular, we find it policing the Archipelago, which was infested with Turkish pirates, and finally it took its share in the war against Bohemond.

The re-organisation of the army always absorbed a large part of Alexius' attention, for the position of the Empire, threatened as it was on all its frontiers, demanded a strong and well-trained army. At the same time the Emperor was always under the apprehension that the weapon which he was forging might one day be turned against him. Thus he always kept the command of important expeditions in his own hands, and carefully avoided giving his generals any opportunity of thrusting themselves into the foreground. Alexius made special efforts to secure two main points. Firstly, he took every precaution that all those who were under the obligation of military service should steadily fulfil the duties laid upon them, and more than once he himself superintended the checking of the military register, resisting all attempts of the great landowners to absorb the small fiefs, granted on condition of service in the army, and to reduce their holders to the status of *coloni*. In the second place, the Emperor tried by constant manœuvring to train his troops and to establish some degree of solidarity among the diverse elements of which they were formed. For at that time the Byzantine army was an absolute mosaic. Alongside of the native troops furnished by the themes and by the holders of military fiefs, we find contingents recruited from among the barbarian peoples who had settled within the Empire, and again from foreign mercenaries, Russians, Colbigni (Patzinaks or Germans?), Turks, Alans, Englishmen, Italian Normans, Germans, and Bulgarians. Alexius' efforts were not thrown away, as the history of his reign attests. At first his inexperienced and ill-organised army was almost invariably defeated, but as the organisation was gradually improved we find victory returning to the Byzantine standards, and at his death Alexius was to leave behind him the admirable machine which was to enable his son to undertake his campaigns in Cilicia and Syria.

The reign of Alexius was a time of extreme wretchedness to the inhabitants of the Empire. Setting aside the disasters which overwhelmed the provinces of Asia Minor, where more than once the Turks carried off whole populations, the material condition of the European provinces was appalling. The rural districts were wasted by continual wars, and on account of the insecurity there a continual movement towards the towns went on among the peasants, who were anxious to escape from the taxes and from military service. What was the pressure of the financial burdens on the country parts will be understood when we learn that a standard conversion-table, drawn up under Alexius, provides for the original sum due by a taxpayer two years in arrear to be multiplied by 28 (56 nomismata instead of 2). This increase is explained by the disturbance in financial administration brought about by Alexius' debasement of the coinage. Since the disaster of Manzikert (1071) the financial difficulties of the Empire had led the sovereigns of Byzantium to issue debased money. Alexius carried the new practice to extremes: Zonaras tells how the Emperor struck copper coins which he used for his own payments, while he insisted that the taxes should be paid mainly in gold, accepting the copper money for only a part of the sums due. The chronicler's evidence is confirmed by numismatics, for there are no less than seven types of the *nomisma* struck by Alexius; some are of gold, but the most common types are of bronze, of electrum, of billon, of silver much debased, or of an alloy of gold and electrum or of gold and billon. This variety of coins bearing the same name, although differing in standard and value, brought confusion into business, as is shewn by the standard conversion-table mentioned above.

The issue of debased coinage was not indeed peculiar to Alexius, and his successors followed his example. If John Comnenus seems to have made an effort to improve the coinage (three out of seven types of *nomisma* bearing his effigy are usually of gold), Manuel Comnenus reverted to the practices of his grandfather: not one of the types of *nomisma* struck by him is of gold; out of the thirteen known types five are of bronze and the others of a very pale electrum which is hard to distinguish from silver.

In dealing with the nobility and clergy, the government used equal rigour in its endeavours to reform abuses. If we have but little information as to the nobility, we have more as regards the clergy, and it is highly probable that measures analogous to those taken against that class were also adopted against the aristocracy. A large part of ecclesiastical property was exempt from the land-tax, but in the imperial charters granting this exemption care had usually been taken to stipulate the number of *paroikoi* and *klerikoi* who were not to be subject to the tax. The clergy shewed a marked tendency to attract to their estates a larger number of *paroikoi* and *klerikoi* than they were entitled to, and the exchequer suffered in proportion. To remedy these abuses Alexius had the number of Church tenants and estates verified afresh with the utmost strictness. The treasury then pitilessly exacted the tax from all men and lands not entitled to exemption.

Another financial expedient, revived by Alexius, did considerable injustice to the monasteries. Not having money enough to reward those who had been faithful to him, nor to provide the different members of his family with large estates, Alexius had recourse to the lands of the monasteries and bestowed them as though they had been fiefs. The beneficiaries, who were called *charistikarioi*, enjoyed the monastic revenues, an infinitesimal part of which went to the support of the monks and the convent. These donations to private persons brought great disorganization into the monastic life. No doubt the number of the convents had at that time grown immensely, and the wealth of the monks was excessive. Some intervention by the central power was a necessity. Alexius, by these donations to lay persons, avoided the difficulty of regulating the whole system anew.

But it would be wrong to conclude from what has been said that Alexius was a persecutor of the clergy. The monastic system was at that time declining rapidly; the monks were constantly quarrelling with their superiors, or becoming tired of their convents and going off to wander about the country or make visits to the capital or the great provincial towns. These were abuses which Alexius undertook to correct both by diminishing the wealth of the monasteries and by reforming the conduct of the monks. This reform of the institution of monasticism was one of the projects nearest to the Emperor's heart, and he gave special encouragement to the great reformer St Christodulus, lavishing privileges on his monastery at Patmos. In the same way the monks entrusted with the care of the hospital and orphanage of St Paul at Constantinople restored by Alexius were overwhelmed with imperial favours, but their administration was narrowly supervised.

The same anxiety for the moral uplifting of the clergy is traceable in the course which Comnenus took with regard to the seculars, whom he accused of sloth and ignorance. To remedy these evils, Alexius limited the number of the priests of St Sophia, and organised a whole system of examinations dealing at once with morals and with learning. The clergy were divided into classes, and were precluded from promotion or from any share in the imperial bounty, except in so far as they satisfied the conditions laid down by Alexius. In order to avoid disputes between the monks and the secular clergy, Alexius by a Novel defined the rights of the Patriarch and bishops over the monasteries.

All these measures shew the interest which Alexius Comnenus felt in religious questions. This interest was further shewn by his intervention in various controversies as to heresy in which he zealously played his part as the defender of orthodoxy. Comnenus had, besides, a marked aptitude for theology, and Anna Comnena depicts her father and mother holding discussions at table on the doctrine of the Fathers. In the greater number of the religious controversies which agitated the Empire during his reign Alexius took a share himself. He did so, for instance, in 1082, in the case of Italus, "Consul of the Philosophers," whose teaching, inspired by Greek philosophy and especially by Platonist conceptions, was solemnly condemned. In the same way Alexius intervened in the condemnation of the heresy of Nilus, whose ideas, no doubt, on many points were akin to the teaching of the Oriental sects at that time widely diffused through the Empire. Not satisfied with combating heresy and disputing with the Armenians and Bogomiles, whom he endeavoured down to the end of his life to bring back to orthodox views, Alexius desired to leave a permanent memorial of his theological zeal, and at his request the monk Euthymius Zigabenus drew up a treatise, the Πανοπλία δογματική, which in the Emperor's judgment contained all the scientific proofs fitted to refute the arguments of the heretics and to shew their emptiness.

Whoever desires to come to a fair estimate of Alexius Comnenus must recognise that his reign marks a temporary arrest in the decline of Constantinople. In Europe, as in Asia, he succeeded in beating back the attacks of the enemies of the Empire. During his reign the Crusade forced new problems upon Byzantine diplomacy. It must be acknowledged that Alexius was able to discern the solutions which most tended to advance the interests of the Empire, and that he traced out the road which his successors were to follow.

If at home his administration weighed heavily on his subjects, the Emperor, none the less, has the credit of having restored peace and tranquillity to the factions which, up to his time, were bringing ruin on the State. It may be said that he was one of those men of talent whom fortune so often gave to the Byzantine Empire in its hour of need, and that he succeeded in arresting for a season the slow dissolution of the Empire into the very diverse elements of which it was compounded.

CHAPTER XII.

THE LATER COMNENI.

JOHN (1118-1143). MANUEL (1143—1180). ALEXIUS II (1180-1183). ANDRONICUS (1183—1185).

JOHN COMNENUS was one of the best Emperors that ever reigned at Constantinople. Of a lofty and generous temper, severe but not cruel, and prompt to forget injuries, the son of Alexius succeeded in gaining the respect of his adversaries. Even the Latins, ill-inclined as they generally were to the Emperors, were forced to bear testimony to his virtues. Upright and austere, John presents a strong contrast to his son and successor Manuel.

Our knowledge of his reign is very scanty, for the two Greek chroniclers who have related the history of Constantinople in the twelfth century, Cinnamus and Nicetas Acominatus, are tantalisingly brief in their notices of him, nor can the gaps in their narratives be at all satisfactorily filled by the help of Oriental or Latin records. Thus we know almost nothing of all that concerns the domestic policy of the reign.

The boldness and decision shewn by the son of Alexius during his father's last hours baffled the conspiracy to bring about the succession of the Caesar Nicephorus Bryennius, the husband of Anna Comnena, and for some time peace appeared to reign at Constantinople. The new Emperor, however, suspected his adversaries of meditating fresh attempts, and, fearing that even his life was in danger, lived for some time in retirement in his palace. His fears gradually died away, and yet, before a year had passed, events fully justified all his apprehensions. Anna Comnena wove a new conspiracy, and, in order to realise her dream of wearing the imperial crown, resolved to procure her brother's assassination. The unwillingness of the Caesar Nicephorus to take the course urged upon him by his wife led to the failure and discovery of the plot. The chief conspirators were arrested. John contented himself with confiscating their property, and before long even pardoned his sister Anna, who having failed to realise her ambitious projects went into retirement for the rest of her life, and endeavoured in recording her father's exploits to console herself for her ill-success and for the oblivion into which she had fallen.

The moderation which John shewed towards those who had attempted to deprive him of his crown was due to the inspiration of his friend Axuch, the companion of his childhood. Of Musulman origin, this man had been made prisoner at the capture of Nicaea by the crusaders and handed over to Alexius. Having been brought up with John Comnenus, Axuch succeeded in gaining his friendship and confidence; he received the office of Grand Domestic and to the end retained the favour of his master. Together with him should also be mentioned, as having had a large share in the government of the Empire, Gregory Taronites, and the Logothete Gregory Camaterus. During the early part of John's reign, his brother Isaac the Sebastocrator also enjoyed immense favour, of which, as we shall see, he was later to prove himself unworthy.

The reign of John Comnenus bore in a marked degree a military stamp. The army was the chief care of the Emperor, who throughout his life paid special attention to the training and discipline of his troops. His efforts were rewarded with success, and he was able to organise his army on a strong and sound basis; but the obligation of serving in it was a heavy burden to that part of the population on which it fell, and at times produced among them considerable discontent. Apparently the Emperor's reign was not marked by any considerable building operations; but he completed and richly endowed the monastery of the Pantokrator, founded by his wife.

As regards foreign policy, John was in no respect an innovator. All the great European or Asiatic questions which concerned the Empire had already taken definite shape during the reign of his father. Alexius had given to Byzantine policy the direction which he judged likely to lead to the most advantageous results, and so sagacious had been his judgment that it may be said that his son and grandson had merely to carry on his work. This continuity of policy on the part of the various sovereigns who succeeded one another during a century is extremely remarkable and much to their credit.

Two great questions of foreign policy predominated throughout the reign of John, that of the kingdom of Sicily and that of the principality of Antioch. If, owing to events which took place in the Norman states of Southern Italy, the former question slumbered for the first few years of the reign, it was not so with the latter, which claimed the constant attention of John Comnenus. With unwearied persistence, the Emperor, in his dealings with the principality of Antioch, pressed for the execution, not of the treaty concluded with the leaders of the First Crusade at the time of their passing through Constantinople, but of the convention which in 1108 had put an end to the war with Bohemond. By this agreement the former duchy of Antioch had been restored to Alexius, who had thereupon granted it in fief to the son of Guiscard. It took eighteen years for John to bring the Princes of Antioch to submit to his claims, the validity of which candid Latins could not but acknowledge. These eighteen years were largely taken up with the preliminary campaigns which the Emperor's designs upon the principality of Antioch necessitated. In fact, it is worthy of remark that the wars of John Comnenus against Europeans were purely defensive. The Emperor took the offensive only against the Musulmans in Asia, and these wars themselves were a necessary prelude to any expedition into Syria. It was impossible for John to contemplate so distant an undertaking until he had put a stop to the advance of his Muslim neighbours, the boldest of whom were thrusting their outposts westward almost as far as the coast, or were even attacking the Byzantine possessions in Cilicia.

The maintenance of order along the frontier in Asia Minor was, in fact, one of the chief tasks laid upon John Comnenus. After the last campaign of Alexius against the Musulmans, changes had taken place in the political situation of the states along the Byzantine frontier. Shāhinshāh, Sultan of Iconium, son of Qilij Arslān, had been overthrown by his brother Mas'ūd, with the help of the Emir Ghāzī, the Dānishmandite prince, who some years before had succeeded in subduing a large number of independent emirs. Indeed, for several years Asia Minor was divided between Mas'ūd, the Emir Ghāzī, and another son of Qilij Arslān, Ṭughril Arslān, Emir of Melitene. While the last-named was attacking the Byzantine possessions in Cilicia, Mas'ūd was pushing his way down the valley of the Maeander, and the Emir Ghāzī was attempting to capture the towns held by the Emperor on the coast of the Black Sea.

Of these various enemies the Musulmans of Iconium were the most formidable. Their unceasing attacks are to be attributed to the nomad tribes dependent on the Sultan of Iconium, who were under the necessity of securing pasture for their flocks. The Maeander valley and the district about Dorylaeum were the two regions the fertility of which gave them a special attraction for the nomads. Their continual advance towards the west and north, apart from the material damage involved, brought with it another danger. The Emperor, if he left the way open to the invaders, risked the cutting of his communications with his possessions on the Black Sea coast, as well as with Pamphylia and Cilicia. Of the three main roads which led to Cilicia two were already in the power of the Turks, and the Byzantine troops could only control the route through Attalia. What has been already said as to the designs of Greek policy upon Antioch is sufficient to explain the stress laid by the Emperor upon maintaining free communication between the various Byzantine possessions in Asia.

The first expedition of John Comnenus to Asia Minor in 1119 seems to have taken the form of a double attack[1]. In the north the Duke of Trebizond, Gabras, attempted to take advantage of the divisions among the Musulman princes, and relied on the support of Ibn Mangū,

[1] The date is that given by Nicetas Choniates (Acominatus), *De Johanne Comneno*, 4, p. 17, CSHB., 1835.

son-in-law of the Emir Ghāzī. He was, however, defeated and taken prisoner. John Comnenus, with better fortune, succeeded first in clearing the valleys of the Hermus and the Maeander, and then a little later occupied Sozopolis, and re-took a whole series of places in the district round Attalia. He thus secured for a time freedom of communication with Pamphylia.

Events in Europe were the cause of an interruption in the war in Asia. For nearly a year (1121–1122)[1] John was occupied with an invasion by certain Patzinak tribes which had escaped the disaster of 1091. The barbarians had succeeded in forcing the passes of the Haemus, and had overflowed into Macedonia and devastated it. After long negotiations the Emperor succeeded in gaining over the chiefs of certain of the tribes; he then marched against such of the barbarian bands as had refused to treat. Preceded by a picture of the Blessed Virgin, the Byzantine troops attacked in the neighbourhood of Eski-Sagra, and inflicted a defeat upon the barbarians, who sought in vain to take refuge behind the waggons which formed their laager. After this defeat the Patzinaks negotiated with the Emperor, to whom they agreed to furnish troops.

About the same time (1122) an attack was made on the Empire by the Venetians. In order to secure the support of the Venetian fleet against the Normans of Italy, Alexius had granted the republic a large number of commercial privileges. On his death, the Doge Domenico Michiel requested John to renew the treaties. But at that moment the Empire had less to dread from the Normans, as they were weakened by the internal dissensions which followed the death of Robert Guiscard in 1085 and broke forth with increased violence on the death of Duke Roger in 1118. John therefore considered that he was paying too dearly for services of which he no longer stood in need, and refused the request of the Venetians for a renewal of the treaties. The doge in revenge attempted in 1122 at the head of a numerous fleet to obtain possession of Corfù. He was unsuccessful. Being urgently entreated to come to the help of the Latins in Palestine, the Venetians broke off hostilities, only to renew them on the return of their fleet from the Holy Land. On this occasion they pillaged Rhodes, occupied Chios, and ravaged Samos, Lesbos, Andros, and Modon (1125). Next year they occupied Cephalonia. Confronted with these attacks, John decided to negotiate, and in 1126 he restored to the Venetians the privileges granted them by his father.

About the same time negotiations were begun with the Papacy. The offers formerly made by Alexius to Paschal II had been by no means forgotten at Rome, and Pope Calixtus II, during his struggle with Henry V, sought to obtain the help of John Comnenus. The question of the

[1] For date see E. Kurtz, *Unedierte Texte aus der Zeit des Kaisers Johannes Komnenos*, BZ. Vol. xvi, p. 88.

re-union of the Churches was again brought up, and letters were exchanged. On the death of Calixtus, negotiations were continued with Honorius II; in 1126 John wrote to the Pope, but while agreeing to re-open the question staunchly maintained the imperial claims. The discussion does not appear to have been carried further at this time. Later on the claims of John Comnenus upon Antioch were to excite displeasure at Rome, and by a bull of 28 March 1138 Innocent II ordered all Latins serving in the Byzantine army to leave the Emperor's service should he attack the principality of Antioch.

Two years after the conclusion of peace with Venice, the Greek Empire had to repel an attack by the Hungarians. Hungarian affairs had never ceased to arouse interest at Constantinople; on the extension of his territories by Koloman, Alexius I, being anxious in case of need to have the means of intervening in the affairs of his powerful neighbours, had married his son to a Hungarian princess named Piriska, who on taking possession of the women's apartments in the imperial palace had assumed the name of Irene. Since that time the Empire had not had occasion to take any part in the affairs of Hungary, but when its King, Stephen II (1114–1131), put out the eyes of his brother Almos, the blinded prince took refuge at Constantinople, where he was well received[1]. Doubtless the ties of relationship and the pity inspired by the hapless victim sufficiently explain the hospitable reception of Almos, but to these reasons must be added the Emperor's desire to have within reach a candidate to oppose in case of need to the ruler of Hungary. Stephen II shewed great displeasure at the hospitality extended to the victim of his brutality, and demanded that the Emperor should expel his guest from the imperial territory. John Comnenus refused to comply with this demand, and Stephen, irritated by his refusal, seized upon the first pretext that offered to declare war against the Greek Empire. The desired excuse was found in the ill-treatment of some Hungarian traders near Branichevo, and hostilities began. Apparently the Hungarians surprised the garrisons of the frontier posts, and succeeded in taking Branichevo and reaching the neighbourhood of Sofia (1128). They then fell back without being molested. To punish them John Comnenus carried the war into Hungary and won a victory near Haram (Uj Palanka), not far from the junction of the Nera with the Danube. But on the withdrawal of the Byzantine troops the Hungarians re-took Branichevo, and the Emperor in order to drive them off returned to the Danube. During the winter, having learned that the enemy was again advancing in force, he succeeded in avoiding an action and withdrawing his troops safely. Such at least is the account given in the Byzantine records; according to the Hungarian, the troops of Stephen II were defeated, and in consequence

[1] The exact date of the arrival of Almos is not known; he was perhaps received at Constantinople as early as Alexius' reign.

of this check the king was compelled to treat. Probably the death of Almos, which took place soon after the outbreak of the war, removed an obstacle to peace.

Towards the end of the reign of Stephen II, John Comnenus, faithful to the policy which had so far been followed, entertained another possible claimant to the Hungarian throne, Boris, the son of Koloman and of Euphemia, daughter of Vladímir Monomachus. Euphemia, accused of adultery, had been banished, and her son had been born in exile. Returning to Hungary, Boris, a little before the death of Stephen, had attempted to usurp the throne. He failed, and took refuge in Constantinople, where John gave him a wife from the imperial house. Later on, in the time of Manuel Comnenus, Boris was to prove a useful instrument of Byzantine policy.

About the time of the war with Hungary, perhaps indeed while hostilities were still going on, the Serbian vassals of the Empire rose in rebellion and destroyed the castle of Novibazar. In considering what were at this time the relations between the Serbs and Constantinople, we touch upon one of the most obscure questions of Byzantine history in the twelfth century. After the death of the prince Constantine Bodin, who for the moment had made the unity of Serbia a reality, the descendants of Radoslav, whom he had dethroned, disputed for power with his heirs. Serbia then passed through a time of inconceivable anarchy. For several years the various rivals succeeded one another with bewildering rapidity. The Župan of Rascia, Bolkan, taking advantage of the confusion to extend his power, succeeded momentarily in imposing his candidate upon the coast districts of Serbia. This claimant however died. The widow of Bodin, Jaquinta, daughter of Argyrus of Bari, now contrived to secure the throne for her son George. It was probably at this juncture that John intervened and set Grubessa on the throne (1129?). When Grubessa died, George succeeded in regaining power, which brought about an intervention of the Greeks, George being taken prisoner and sent to Constantinople. As his successor they set up Gradicna.

Two points stand out in this confused narrative. In the first place, it is plain that the influence of Constantinople in Serbia is small; the Empire contents itself with having a pretender at hand to put forward in case the reigning prince should give cause for displeasure. In the second place, the Župans of Rascia come to play a more and more important part. After Bolkan we find Uroš Župan of this region. One of his daughters married Béla II the Blind, a future King of Hungary. The other, Mary, became the wife of the Moravian prince Conrad, while a son, Béla, took up his abode at the Hungarian court, where later he was to become prominent, and married his daughter to the Russian Prince, Vladímir Mstilavich. These alliances were to prove extremely useful to the sons of Uroš when, under Manuel, they were to attempt to cast off the suzerainty of Constantinople.

About 1130 John Comnenus was again able to turn his arms against the Musulmans of Asia Minor. The fruits of the previous campaigns had not been lost. As far as Iconium was concerned, the position had remained satisfactory. Mas'ūd, being dethroned by his brother, 'Arab, had even come to Constantinople to ask help of the Emperor, who had supplied him with subsidies to oppose the usurper. These disputes among the Musulman rulers had lessened their strength, and for a time the principality of Iconium was less formidable to the Empire. Far different was the position of the Emir Ghāzī. In 1124 he had seized upon the principality of Melitene, and then conquered Ancyra and Comana, and occupied some of the Byzantine strongholds on the coast of the Black Sea. In 1129, on the death of the Armenian prince Thoros, he had turned towards Cilicia, and there was every sign that he was about to contend with his co-religionist, the Atābeg of Mosul, for his share of the spoils of the Latin princes of Syria. Thus a new enemy threatened Antioch, and from this time we may discern the reasons which urged John Comnenus to attempt the overthrow of the Dānishmandite ruler.

The first expedition of John Comnenus proved abortive; the Emperor had hardly crossed into Asia when he learned that a conspiracy against him had been hatched by his brother Isaac. On receiving this news he resolved to return to Constantinople. Isaac the Sebastocrator succeeded in avoiding punishment and escaped into Asia, where he attempted to draw into the struggle against his brother not only the Musulman princes, but also the Armenian Thoros and Gabras, Duke of Trebizond, who had shortly before secured his independence. Isaac met with but partial success, and only the Emir Ghāzī lent him support. Even at a distance the Sebastocrator continued his intrigues; he maintained communications with various personages at the Court of Constantinople; and when in 1132 John entered upon a campaign against the Emir Ghāzī, he was soon forced to return to his capital, where a fresh plot, the result of Isaac's intrigues, had been discovered. As soon as order was restored the Emperor renewed the campaign, and during the winter of 1132–1133 he took from the Emir Ghāzī the important fortress of Castamona, which, however, was soon afterwards recovered by the Muslims.

On the death of Ghāzī, which took place next year (1134), the Emperor decided to profit by the quarrels which immediately arose among the Mohammedan princes to try his fortune in the field. An expedition was set on foot against Mahomet, son and heir of Ghāzī, to which Mas'ūd sent a contingent of troops in the hope of having his share in the dismemberment of the Dānishmandite state. No advantage accrued to the Empire from this alliance; the Muslim troops played false during the siege of Gangra, and John was forced to fall back. Next year, however, he was more fortunate, and Gangra and Castamona fell into his hands (1135).

This success at last enabled the Emperor to attempt the realisation of his designs upon Antioch. A series of negotiations with the Western Emperor and with Pisa prepared the ground for this new campaign. It was apparently not before 1135 that John Comnenus entered into diplomatic relations with the Emperor Lothar who, while he was staying at Merseburg, gave audience to a Byzantine embassy bearing instructions from the Greek Emperor to request help against Roger II, King of Sicily. During the last few years the position of the Norman states in Italy had sensibly altered. Not only had the Count of Sicily, Roger II, added the duchy of Apulia to his dominions, but he had raised his possessions to the rank of a kingdom, and since 1130 had, to the great indignation of the Byzantines, assumed the title of King. The new king, intensely ambitious and more powerful than any of his predecessors, did not confine himself to attacking the coasts of the Greek Empire, but set up claims to the Latin states of the Holy Land, and in particular to Antioch. Accordingly John Comnenus found it necessary, before his departure for Syria to try his fortune in arms, to secure himself against a fresh invasion of his dominions by the Normans of Italy during his absence. It was with this object in view that he had recourse to the Emperor Lothar, whom he urged to make a descent upon Italy in order to oppose the new king, and to whom for the furtherance of this design he promised considerable subsidies. Lothar responded to the Byzantine embassy by sending Anselm of Havelberg to Constantinople. An agreement was arrived at, and Lothar pledged himself to undertake an expedition into Italy. He proved as good as his word, and we know that in 1137, while still in Southern Italy, he received a Greek embassy bringing him gifts from the Emperor. The negotiations of John Comnenus with the Pisans were in the same way dictated by a wish to detach them from the Norman alliance, and ended in 1136 in a renewal of treaty engagements.

Having thus secured his dominions against a possible attack by the Normans, John Comnenus could at last undertake the long-meditated expedition to restore Antioch and its surrounding territory to the Empire (1137). But before invading the principality the Byzantine army had another task to accomplish. The territory of the Empire no longer actually extended as far as the frontier of Antioch, from which it was now separated by the dominions of the Armenian Leo. This prince (a descendant of Rupen, one of those Armenian rulers who, fleeing before the advance of the Muslims, had established themselves in the Taurus and in the neighbourhood of the Euphrates) had in 1129 succeeded his brother Thoros. After an open breach with the Empire, he had made himself master of the chief towns of Cilicia—Tarsus, Adana, and Mamistra. His possessions thus barred the path of John's army, and the conquest of Cilicia was the necessary prelude to the siege of Antioch.

In the early part of the campaign the Emperor met with unbroken success. Tarsus, Adana, and Mamistra were quickly captured, and then came the turn of Anazarbus and the surrounding district. Leo, with his two sons, Rupen and Thoros, was obliged to seek safety in the mountains. Without stopping to pursue them, John at once took the road to Antioch, for at that moment circumstances were eminently favourable to the Greeks.

When John appeared before the city (end of August 1137) Raymond of Poitiers, who, by his marriage with Constance daughter of Bohemond II, had become Prince of Antioch, was absent from his capital. Although aware of the impending attack by the Byzantines, Raymond had not hesitated to go to the help of the King of Jerusalem, who had just suffered a serious defeat at the hands of the Atābeg of Mosul, 'Imād-ad-Dīn Zangī, at Ḥārim. When Raymond returned, the siege of Antioch had already begun. The besieged, owing to the disaster which had just befallen the Latins in their struggle with the Mohammedans, despaired of receiving succour, and from the first a considerable party of them had contemplated negotiations with the Emperor. Certain of the records make it appear probable that the King of Jerusalem, on being consulted, had admitted the validity of the Greek Emperor's claims, and had recommended negotiation. Whatever may be the truth about these *pourparlers*, it is plain that Raymond, threatened with the loss of his dominions, preferred treating with John Comnenus. At the moment the Emperor was bent above all on obtaining a formal recognition of his claims, while for Raymond the main desideratum was the withdrawal of the Byzantines. Once this point had been gained, other matters might be arranged as circumstances should dictate. After some negotiation the Prince of Antioch consented to take the oath of fealty to John Comnenus, and, as a sign of his submission, to hoist the imperial banners on the walls of the city. The Emperor in exchange bound himself to help the Latins the next year in their struggle with the Muslims, but it was stipulated that if by the help of the Basileus Raymond should recover Aleppo, Shaizar, Emesa, and Ḥamāh, he should restore Antioch to the Greek Empire.

This agreement being concluded John returned to Cilicia. It seems probable that it was on this occasion that he succeeded in capturing the Armenian prince, Leo, who with his two sons was sent prisoner to Constantinople, where not long afterwards he died.

Faithful to his engagements, John opened the campaign in the spring of 1138. The Byzantine army, swelled by the Latin contingents, took in succession Balat (between Antioch and Aleppo) and Bizā'a. The allies, however, failed to surprise Aleppo, and turned to besiege Shaizar on the Orontes on 29 April 1138. Before long serious dissensions broke out between the Latin princes and the Emperor. John, indignant at the suspicious behaviour of the Prince of Antioch and of Joscelin, Count of Edessa, seized upon the first pretext he could find to raise the siege and grant the defenders conditions which they had never hoped for.

Returning northwards by the valley of the Orontes, the army fell back upon Antioch, John making a solemn entry into the city. During his stay there, the Emperor, in virtue of the feudal rule obliging a vassal to hand over his castle to his suzerain whenever he was required by him to do so, demanded possession of the citadel. The Latin rulers, not daring a direct refusal, got out of the difficulty by stirring up a riot in the city. In the face of the menacing attitude of the populace, John for the time being ceased to urge his claims and quitted Antioch. The Emperor once gone, the Latins again offered to treat. The result was a hollow reconciliation.

The Greek army then set out on its return. While, on its march towards Constantinople, it was securing the safety of the frontier by police operations against brigands, Isaac Comnenus came to make submission to his brother and received his pardon. The sole result of the campaign was the recognition of the imperial rights over Antioch, whereby the prestige of the Emperor was strikingly increased, not only in the eyes of his subjects but also in those of the Musulmans and Latins. No practical advantage, however, was obtained.

In 1139 the war against the Musulmans was resumed. The Dānishmandite prince Mahomet had taken several places in Cilicia from the Byzantines, and then proceeded to ravage the country as far as the Sangarius. John drove off these invading bands, and during the winter of 1139–1140 laid siege to Neo-Caesarea. In this campaign John, son of Isaac Comnenus, deserted to the enemy[1]. On his return to Constantinople (15 January 1141) the Emperor planned a new campaign, the object of which was Antioch.

A series of diplomatic operations was again undertaken in order to hold the King of Sicily in check during the Emperor's absence. Lothar had died on returning from his Italian campaign, and had been succeeded by Conrad III. In 1140 John asked Conrad to renew the alliance made with his predecessor, and in order to set a seal upon the friendship requested the hand of a princess of the imperial house for his youngest son Manuel. Conrad in reply offered his sister-in-law Bertha, daughter of the Count of Sulzbach. In 1142 another Byzantine embassy was despatched with instructions to treat of the question of a descent upon Italy. Conrad in return sent his chaplain Albert and Robert, Prince of Capua, to Constantinople. A Greek embassy carried John's reply, and brought back the future Empress. These negotiations were disquieting to the King of Sicily, who, in order to break up the league between his enemies, sent an embassy at the beginning of 1143 to propose an alliance with John.

[1] He became a Musulman and married a daughter of the Sultan of Iconium. Bāyazīd I claimed to be descended from this marriage. Cf. Du Cange, *Familiae byzantinae* in the *Historia byzantina duplici commentario illustrata*, Paris 1680, p. 190.

While the negotiations with Conrad were going on, the Emperor again set out for Antioch. The whole of the early part of the campaign was devoted to police work in the neighbourhood of Sozopolis. The army then marched to Attalia, and here a double blow fell upon the Emperor. Within a short interval he lost, first his son Alexius, whom he had associated in the government, and then another son Andronicus. This twofold bereavement did not turn the Emperor from his purpose, and on leaving Attalia the army took the road to Syria.

Since 1138 the position of the Latin states harassed by the Muslims had only altered for the worse. During the last few years they had repeatedly begged help from the Byzantines. Having learned by past experience, John Comnenus did not trust to the promises which had been made to him, and above all he resolved to make himself secure of the fidelity of the Latin rulers by exacting hostages from them. He took pains to conceal the object of his expedition by giving out that he intended only to put into a state of defence the towns in Cilicia which he had taken from Leo. Thanks to these precautions the Emperor was enabled to descend upon the Latin territory in a totally unexpected manner. John had not forgotten the behaviour of Joscelin during the last campaign; so the first attack was made on him, the Emperor appearing suddenly in front of Turbessel. The Count of Edessa, taken by surprise, was obliged to give up his daughter as a hostage, and from Turbessel the Emperor marched to the castle of Gastin (1142). There he demanded of Raymond the fulfilment of his promise to surrender Antioch. Raymond thus driven into a corner took up a pitiful attitude, sheltering himself behind the wishes of his vassals. An important part in the matter was played by the Latin clergy, to whom it was a source of annoyance that the progress of the Greek clergy proceeded *pari passu* with that of the Byzantine armies. The demands of the Basileus were rejected in the name of the Pope and of the Western Emperor.

John Comnenus had certainly foreseen this refusal and had determined to take Antioch by force. This siege was in his eyes only a prelude to the campaign which he intended to wage against the Musulmans—a campaign which, if his views were realised, would be crowned by the entrance into Jerusalem of the Byzantine troops. But having been delayed, doubtless by the death of his sons, the Emperor reached Antioch too late in the season to begin a siege which could not fail to be a long one. He resolved therefore to postpone the renewal of hostilities, and led his troops into Cilicia where he intended to winter. It was there that an accidental wound from a poisoned arrow, received during a hunting party, carried him off on 8 April 1143, at the moment when he was looking forward to the attainment of the object which had been the goal of his entire policy. On his deathbed John named as his successor Manuel, the youngest of his sons, and procured his recognition by the army.

Manuel when he ascended the throne was about twenty years old. For the first few years of his reign he continued the confidence which his father had placed in Axuch and John Puzes, and it was only little by little that the young Emperor's personality developed and made its mark by the direction that he gave to his policy. Manuel's disposition shewed a singular mixture of qualities in the most marked contrast to one another. While on the one hand he has some of the most characteristic traits of the Byzantine type, other sides of his nature seem to mark him out as a product of Western civilisation. He is the typical knight-king, and in courage might compare with Richard Coeur-de-Lion. Even on the first campaign in which he accompanied his father, Manuel shewed himself a bold and courageous warrior, ever a lover of the brilliant bouts and thrusts of single combat. It may be that in his campaigns he proved himself rather a valiant knight than a great general, that he sought too eagerly after those successes, rather showy than permanent, which evoke the plaudits of women and the encomiums of court poets. He constantly sought opportunity to display his skill in riding and fencing, hunting and tournaments, and evidently looked upon it as his vocation to repeat the exploits of the paladins. Hence it is that Manuel is open to the reproach of having cared less for realities than for show, of having attempted to carry out simultaneously projects on a gigantic scale, any single one of which would have taxed the resources of the Empire. This is the weak side of his policy. Manuel attempted to get others to carry out the tasks which he could not himself accomplish; hence arose the failures he met with. It would appear further that Manuel was fitted only for success, and was incapable of bearing misfortune. At his only defeat, the disaster of Myriocephalum, when he saw that he was beaten and in danger of being slain by the enemy with the poor remains of his army, his one idea was to take to flight without giving a thought to his soldiers. Only the opposition of his captains prevented him from carrying out this disgraceful intention.

Manuel's devotion to the ideals of chivalry and his two marriages with Western princesses fostered in him a strong preference for the Latins. Men of Western race, whether Germans, French, Normans, Italians, or English, were sure of his eager welcome, and of finding posts about his court or in his army. Though ignorant of the Greek language, these foreigners who "spat better than they spoke" contrived, nevertheless, to fill considerable administrative offices, to the great disgust of the Emperor's subjects. Nor were they any better pleased to see the Venetians, Pisans, and Genoese settle down at Constantinople. This policy on the part of Manuel led to the accumulation of the national hatred against the Latins which was to burst forth in the reign of Andronicus.

Manuel, like his grandfather Alexius, brought a keen interest to theological questions. He prided himself on being a theologian and took pleasure in theological discussions, as the Patriarch Cosmas found, who was deposed in 1147 for his adhesion to the doctrines of Niphon, a Bogomile monk. Manuel considered himself to possess inspired knowledge, and was in the habit of imposing his decisions upon the clergy. In the cases of Soterichus Panteugenus, of Basilaces, and of Michael of Thessalonica (the representatives of a little group of priests charged with holding views inspired by Platonic philosophy), the Emperor's sentence was decisive (1157). Later on, towards the close of the reign, in the teeth of the opposition of the clergy and the Patriarch, Manuel imposed his own view in a discussion which brought up afresh the doctrine promulgated by the Councils of Nicaea and Constantinople regarding the relation between the Father and the Son. Manuel decided the question in a sense opposite to the traditional doctrine. Finally, we must note the attempt made by Manuel in 1170 to bring about the re-union of the Armenian and Greek Churches. Despite the skill of Theorianus, who was entrusted by the Emperor with the duty of carrying on the negotiation with the Katholikos Nerses, the discussions led to no result.

In contrast to Manuel the theologian there was another Manuel, a dabbler in astrology. Astrologers enjoyed great prestige at the imperial court. The Basileus consulted them upon all important expeditions, and forbade his generals to give battle unless the stars were propitious. Manuel was a believer in magic and in spells. Even on his deathbed his confidence in all the charlatans who surrounded him remained unskaken.

Theological and scientific questions, however, did not engross the Emperor's interest. Manuel, and following his example the whole court, took a pride in shewing a taste for letters; the literary revival initiated in the preceding century in the time of Psellus was continued during this reign. The princesses of the imperial family encouraged authors; the Empress Irene accepted the dedication of the *Chiliads* of Tzetzes, and another Irene, wife of Andronicus, Manuel's brother, was the acknowledged patroness of literary men. A little court of the learned gathered round her, among the ornaments of which were Tzetzes, Constantine Manasses, and one of the Prodromoi. Manuel's niece and mistress, Theodora, was the correspondent of Glycas. Other court ladies took to writing themselves, and it was at this time that Anna Comnena finished her *Alexiad*, the continuation of Bryennius' work in honour of Alexius. Her example was followed by Zonaras and Glycas, the compilers of chronicles, and at the same time Cinnamus and Nicetas Acominatus collected the materials for their works.

Rhetoric also had its representatives, and one of the best judges of classical antiquity, Eustathius, Archbishop of Thessalonica, pronounced some of his orations during this reign. He was one of the most distinguished members of the learned and scholarly group of clergy, devoted to philosophical speculation, several of whom have already been mentioned in dealing with the theological controversies of the day.

The arts were not neglected at Manuel's court. If he took pleasure in re-building the palace of the Blachernae, which he decorated with mosaics commemorating his exploits, and in erecting sumptuous villas on the coast of Asia Minor and on the islands in the neighbourhood of Constantinople where he could go for relaxation after his military exertions, he did not forget public edifices. He had the walls of Constantinople repaired, spent money freely on constructing aqueducts, and undertook operations to make the closing of the harbour possible. On the other hand he did little in the way of ecclesiastical building. He used to rally his courtiers on the vanity which urged them to build monasteries or churches on purpose to erect their tombs there, and used to declare that he only approved of monks in solitary places, and looked with horror on the turbulent monks dwelling in towns and devoting themselves solely to increasing the possessions of their monasteries. By way of setting an example he built a monastery near the entrance to the strait of the Bosphorus, to which he made no donation of lands, confining himself to a yearly grant out of the public treasury sufficient for the maintenance of the monks. Manuel's legislation as to ecclesiastical property is inspired by the same spirit. The imperial Novels forbid churches and monasteries to add to the lands already in their possession, but on the other hand legalise the ownership of those actually held, even when the title could not be shewn or was defective. In this way a general settlement was arrived at, but at the expense of the lay owners, who now saw a legal sanction given to all the usurpations of which they had been victims.

The foreign policy of Manuel was carried out at enormous expense, and was extremely burdensome to the imperial treasury. In order to fill it the Emperor was forced to use great severity in the collection of the taxes and to have recourse to all kinds of financial expedients. The most important seems to have been the converting of the obligation to maintain the navy, which was laid upon certain themes, into a tax—a measure analogous to that formerly resorted to by Constantine IX with regard to service in the army. In conjunction with this measure should be noted the novel distributions of land on condition of military service, grants made for the most part to prisoners of war or to barbarian tribes. These measures caused great disturbances in the provinces and brought about a strained situation there, chiefly known to us through the efforts made later by Andronicus Comnenus to find a remedy.

John Comnenus, in choosing his youngest son to succeed him, had set aside the rights of the elder, the Sebastocrator Isaac. If the young Emperor had the army on his side his brother had the advantage of being in the capital. In order that a conflict might be avoided, Manuel must at all costs make himself master of Constantinople before the news of John's death was known there. The business was entrusted to Axuch, who successfully carried out the task confided to him. He contrived to seize both Isaacs, uncle and nephew, and with no great difficulty defeated a plot to set the crown on the head of the Caesar John-Roger, Manuel's brother-in-law. When the Emperor appeared before his capital, peace was already established; he reached his palace easily enough, and largess, distributed on a lavish scale to clergy and people, secured his popularity.

On the death of John Comnenus the Latins of Antioch had again taken the offensive, and even while Manuel was still in the East had begun hostilities and occupied several places in Cilicia. This provocation had been keenly resented by Manuel, who made it his first care to send troops to Cilicia to deal with the Latins. The Greek arms were victorious, and in 1145 Raymond of Poitiers had to submit to the humiliation of coming to Constantinople to ask mercy of Manuel; he was compelled to visit the church of the Pantokrator and make the *amende* at the dead Emperor's tomb.

While the Byzantine army was on its way back from Cilicia, the troops of the Sultan of Iconium had carried off several persons of importance at court; further invasions had then taken place, the Muslim bands advancing as far as Pithecas near Nicaea; the whole of the Byzantine possessions in Asia Minor were devastated, ruins were heaped up on every side, and the luckless populations were forced to leave their villages and seek refuge in the towns along the coast. Thus one of the first tasks with which Manuel was faced was to secure his frontier in Asia by the erection of a series of fortified posts, intended to check the invaders. This was his main work, and he pursued it to the end of his reign. At the same time he attempted to strike at the heart of the Musulman power, more than once endeavouring to reduce Iconium. At the opening of his reign he was aided in his struggle against Mas'ūd by the divisions among the Muslim leaders which had followed upon the death of the Dānishmandite prince Mahomet (1141). His lands were divided between his son, Dhū'l-Nūn, who obtained Caesarea, and his brothers, Ya'qūb Arslān and 'Ain-ad-Daulah, whose shares respectively were Sīwās and Melitene. Threatened by Mas'ūd, Ya'qūb Arslān, the most powerful of the heirs of Mahomet, treated with Manuel who helped him with subsidies. During the years 1146–1147 the Greeks fought with no great measure of success; Manuel got as far as Iconium, but failed to take it. At the moment when the crusaders appeared before Constantinople, Manuel had just concluded a truce with Mas'ūd.

During this period the policy of Manuel in the West had yielded no striking results. For a short time the Emperor seemed to be meditating a league with the King of Sicily, but he soon returned to the idea of a German alliance, and in January 1146 took to wife Bertha of Sulzbach, sister-in-law of Conrad. But at the very time when this marriage seemed to have set a seal upon his friendship with Germany, all that had been gained by it was lost by the opening of the Second

Crusade, the Greek Empire being left to confront the Norman power in a state of complete isolation.

Learning of the new Crusade by letters from Louis VII and the Pope, Eugenius III, Manuel immediately set himself to obtain guarantees against all eventualities by demanding of the Pope that the crusaders should bind themselves to him by engagements similar to those taken by the leaders of the First Crusade to Alexius. In return he promised that on payment being forthcoming provisions should be supplied. At the assembly of Étampes (February 1147) Manuel's envoys met those of Roger II, who had been instructed to bring about the diversion of the Crusade to their master's profit by promising large advantages. The influence of Conrad, who had only joined in the project for a Crusade at the end of 1146, was certainly not without its weight in the decision to go by Constantinople. The fact that not only the King of France but also the King of Germany was to take part in the expedition made the position of Manuel with regard to the crusaders all the more perilous. He was haunted by the fear that, if the Western troops collected outside his capital, they might be tempted to an assault upon Constantinople. He made every effort to avoid this danger, his task being rendered easier by the ill-feeling of Conrad towards the French.

The measures taken with regard to the crusaders were of the same kind as those employed by Alexius in the case of the First Crusade. The Byzantine troops were disposed so as to confine the streams of pilgrims in a single channel and to prevent the pillaging bands from wandering too far from the prescribed route. The elements of which the crusading army was composed made these precautions necessary. Not only were there warriors on the march; the bulk of the army consisted of pilgrims and of a rout of adventurers ready for any mischief.

The Germans were first to pass through the imperial territory. Their relations with the Greeks were as bad as possible, outrages being committed on both sides which generated violent excitement. Hadrianople was especially the scene of bloodshed. Manuel made a last effort to divert the crusaders from the route through Constantinople and to persuade them to pass through Sestos, but his suggestions were listened to with suspicion and were rejected. Many disasters would have been avoided if his advice had been taken, and it was the route recommended by him which Louis VII took after the destruction of the German army.

Little is known of the relations between Manuel and Conrad during the time that the crusading army remained before Constantinople. It is probable that the two Emperors did not meet; at the same time they appear to have come to an agreement. The news of the arrival of Louis VII decided Conrad upon crossing over into Asia Minor—a step which all the urgency of Manuel had not availed to secure. The march of the German army upon Iconium ended in disaster. The crusaders, although aware of the length of the journey, had not brought a sufficient quantity of provisions; famine soon made its appearance, whereupon the Greek guides were alarmed by accusations of treachery, which caused them to abandon the army and take to flight. The crusaders were forced to fall back upon Nicomedia, harassed as they marched by the Turks who slew them in thousands; as many perished by famine. At Nicomedia the remnants of Conrad's army found the French.

The journey of the French across the Greek territories was equally accompanied by acts of violence; but a Latin eye-witness admits that up to their arrival before Constantinople the Franks did as much injury to the Greeks as they received from them, and that the wrongs were on both sides. Manuel welcomed Louis VII, but made every effort to induce him to cross at once to the coast of Asia Minor. The apprehension which the Greek Emperor shewed is justified by the known fact that there was a regular party in the King of France's council urgent for the taking of Constantinople.

The French once across the Bosphorus, new difficulties arose. Manuel demanded that the barons should do homage and swear fealty to him, and after long parleying Louis ended by yielding. Having joined the wrecks of the German army, the French gave up the idea of marching upon Iconium and took the road for Attalia. At Ephesus Conrad fell ill, and abandoned the Crusade. The march of the crusaders through the Asiatic provinces of the Byzantine Empire was marked by similar acts of violence to those committed in Europe; this explains the fighting which took place between the Greeks and the Latins. The chief accusation brought against the Greeks is that they did not supply provisions and that they charged too dear for such as they did supply. The vast numbers of the crusaders made provisioning a matter of great difficulty, and the presence of unnumbered multitudes in one place is a sufficient explanation of the dearness of commodities.

The army of Louis VII, thus ill-provided, suffered greatly on the march from Laodicea to Attalia. The Musulman bands had appeared, and their unceasing attacks added to the difficulties of the mountain route. The army reached Attalia in a deplorable state. Here provisions were still lacking. Louis VII and the chief lords hired ships of the Greeks and departed, forsaking the mass of the pilgrims. The leaders left in charge abandoned them in their turn. The wretched people fell a prey to the Turks, and to the Greeks who were exasperated at the acts of pillage which the famished multitude had committed.

Manuel has been held responsible for the failure of the Second Crusade. Such accusations are now to a large extent discredited by historians. The ill-success of the Crusade was due to defective organisation, to the want of discipline among the crusaders, and to their obstinate persistence, in spite of the Emperor's advice, in following the road taken by Godfrey of Bouillon and his companions.

Conrad, who had been left behind sick at Ephesus, was received by Manuel, who brought him to Constantinople and loaded him with attentions. The fact was that Manuel was just then threatened by a danger which made the prospect of help from the German King of great value to him. Profiting by the difficulties into which the Basileus was thrown by the coming of the crusaders, Roger II of Sicily had in the autumn of 1147 directed a naval attack upon the coast of the Empire. Corfù had fallen into his hands; Negropont and Cerigo had been ravaged. The Normans then sailed up the Gulf of Corinth and took Thebes and Corinth (centres of the silk-trade and two of the most important commercial towns in the Empire), their rich warehouses being given up to pillage. In order to resist this aggression, Manuel, while the crusaders were still on the Asiatic shore of the Bosphorus, had in vain begged for help from Conrad and Louis. He was obliged to meet the Normans with his own forces, for which however he had secured the support of the Venetian fleet.

Being detained by an invasion of the Cumans (1148), Manuel sent the Grand Domestic Axuch and the Grand Duke Alexius Contostephanus to occupy the places taken by the Normans and to besiege Corfù. It was during the winter of 1148–1149 that Manuel received Conrad, who was returning from the Holy Land, and concluded a treaty with him, by which the German king bound himself to make a descent upon Italy in order to attack Roger II (1149).

Corfù having been re-taken (summer of 1149), Manuel resolved to organise an expedition to punish Roger II. A revolt among the Serbs, supported by the King of Sicily, prevented him from carrying out his plan. Roger II, threatened by the Germano-Byzantine alliance, created difficulties for them both which hindered them from carrying out their project of an invasion of Italy. While Welf, thanks to supplies furnished by Roger, fomented an agitation which detained Conrad in Germany, the Sicilian king was launching the Serbs and Hungarians against the Greek Empire. Hungary and Constantinople were at that time on very bad terms owing to their pursuing a diametrically opposite policy in Russia. While Géza, King of Hungary, maintained the claims of his brother-in-law Izyaslav to the throne of Kiev, Manuel gave his support to George Dolgoruki, son of Vladímir Monomachus, who was also favoured by Vladimirko, Prince of Halicz. At the instigation of the King of Sicily, Géza encouraged the Župan of Rascia, Pervoslav Uroš, to revolt, and the disturbance which broke out in Serbia in the autumn of 1149 kept Manuel occupied until 1150. The Serbs having been subdued, Manuel, eager to punish their Hungarian supporters, took advantage in 1151 of the absence of Géza, who was maintaining Izyaslav's cause in Russia against Vladimirko, to take Semlin and ravage the country between the Save and the Danube. Peace was signed the same year, but in 1152 hostilities broke out again, and Géza formed a connexion with Manuel's cousin, Andronicus

Comnenus, the future Emperor. This treason was discovered and Andronicus was arrested. The struggle lasted until 1155, when peace was signed. The only appreciable result of the campaigns seems to have been the conquest of Semlin.

Roger II had not been satisfied with stirring up the Serbs and Hungarians against Manuel; he had at the same time made use of the failure of the Crusade to attempt the organisation of a European coalition against him. Louis VII sympathised with these projects, but Conrad's fidelity to the Byzantine alliance, and the rupture which took place in 1150 between Pope Eugenius III and Roger, prevented the latter's designs from taking effect. Finally in 1152 the death of Conrad delivered the Norman King from the peril of a Germano-Byzantine alliance.

With Conrad's successor, Frederick Barbarossa, Manuel was never able to come to an understanding. From the beginning of his reign Barbarossa refused to countenance any territorial advantage which might be gained by the Basileus in Italy—a concession which Conrad had made. From 1152 to 1158 numerous embassies came and went between the two Emperors, but it was found impossible to arrange an alliance. Wishing to take advantage of the death of Roger II in 1154, Frederick Barbarossa made a descent upon Italy. Manuel, fearing that this expedition having been made without reference to him might prove to have been made against him, decided to try his fortune single-handed and to make his profit out of the unsettled conditions which had followed on the death of Roger II. He dispatched to Italy Michael Palaeologus, who in the course of 1155, thanks to the support of Robert of Loritello, a revolted vassal of the Norman King William I, and his fellow-rebels, achieved unlooked-for success. In a few months the Greek Emperor's authority was recognised from Ancona to Taranto. This success turned Manuel's head, and was chiefly instrumental in giving a new direction to his policy. At the very time when in 1155 the German Emperor, forced to own himself unable to maintain order in Italy and to play the part he had assumed of protector of the Papacy, abandoned the idea of invading the Norman Kingdom, the Basileus was enforcing the recognition of his own imperial authority in all that part of Italy which had formerly been in the possession of the Greek Emperors. Hence arose in Manuel the desire to restore the Eastern Empire to what it had been in the time of Justinian, and to obtain from the Pope the re-establishment of imperial unity in exchange for the reunion of the Greek Church with the Church of Rome. The first negotiations with this object were begun with Hadrian IV, and the rupture which took place at this time between the Papacy and the Western Emperor seemed to Manuel likely to further the accomplishment of his dream.

The counter-strokes of William I, which in a short time demolished the frail edifice of Byzantine conquest, did not avail to dissuade Manuel from his project. Southern Italian questions became of secondary importance to him in comparison with the schemes he was caressing, and he made no difficulty in 1158 in complying with the suggestions of the Papacy, which, leaning as it did on the support of the kingdom of Sicily and of the Greek Empire, desired to see peace restored between its two allies.

From 1157 onwards Byzantine policy is governed wholly by the idea of restoring the unity of the Empire. For the sake of clearness we will consider in order the relations of Manuel with Italy and Frederick Barbarossa, with the Hungarians and Serbs, and finally with the Muslims and the Latins of the East.

It was natural that Manuel should shew himself favourable to the Pope, Alexander III. During the years from 1161 to 1163 long negotions went on between the Emperor, Alexander III, and Louis VII concerning a coalition to be formed against the Western Emperor. Three years later Manuel judged that the Pope was sufficiently in need of his help to make it safe to acquaint him completely with his desire to re-establish the unity of the Empire under his sceptre. Negotiations about this project went on for several years, Manuel remaining the ally of Alexander until the preliminaries of the Peace of Venice (1177). Although his name does not appear as one of the signatories of the peace, the connexion between the Papacy and Constantinople lasted as long as Manuel reigned.

If the understanding between the Pope and the Greek Emperor led to nothing, one of the chief causes of this was the opposition maintained by the King of Sicily to the Byzantine policy. It will readily be understood that neither William I nor William II looked with favour on the attempts of Manuel to gain a footing in Italy, but that both on the contrary offered a vigorous resistance. Manuel tried every means of overcoming their opposition; he had recourse to Louis VII, and on two occasions he endeavoured to arrange for the marriage of his daughter Mary with William II. But just as matters seemed to be finally settled, the match was broken off, Barbarossa having made overtures to Manuel which seemed to him to promise a more brilliant future to his daughter than alliance with William of Sicily could offer.

Manuel's attitude towards the Italian cities was a natural result of his policy with regard to Alexander III. He endeavoured by every possible means to attach to his interest a group of dependent Italian towns, or at least to be able to rely on the support of a party in the more important cities. Milan was encouraged by him in her struggle with Barbarossa, and Byzantine gold helped to rebuild her streets. Cremona and Pavia had their share of the Greek subsidies. Once already Ancona had given itself up to Palaeologus, and later on, about 1166, its population embraced the Greek cause, won over by the gold of Manuel's emissaries. In 1167 Barbarossa was only able to win a partial advantage over them.

With Pisa Manuel in 1161 entered into negotiations which lasted until 1172. Dragged in different directions by their Ghibelline sympathies and their desire to take advantage of the commercial privileges offered by the Basileus, the Pisans pursued an indecisive policy. The Genoese in the same way treated with the Greek Emperor in 1155, but also with Barbarossa in 1162. Though intercourse between them and Constantinople was broken off in 1162, it was resumed in 1164, and went on until 1170. Manuel was never able to bring the Genoese to the point of breaking with Barbarossa.

The Greek occupation of Ancona and the recapture of the Dalmatian towns gave some anxiety to the Venetians, who had very nearly come to a breach with Manuel at the time of the siege of Corfù, as the result of an unpleasant incident which occurred between the troops of the two nations. Things reached such a point that in 1167 relations between the two countries were completely broken off. The doge even recalled all those of his nation who had settled upon Greek territory. Diplomatic intercourse, resumed at the request of Manuel who drew the Venetians into a veritable snare, was again definitively broken off on 12 March 1171. On this date Manuel ordered the arrest of all Venetians settled in his dominions and the confiscation of their goods. Enormous damage was thus inflicted upon Venice. In revenge the republic during the winter of 1171–2 pillaged the coasts of the Empire and ravaged Negropont, Chios, and Lesbos. In the course of the campaign negotiations were initiated in which the Venetians were duped. These were continued without result up to 1175. At this date Venice made an alliance with William II, King of Sicily. Thus directly threatened, Manuel decided upon concessions. He set at liberty the prisoners arrested in 1171, restored their goods to them, and granted to Venice the privileges enjoyed under former treaties of commerce. In the interval, in 1173, Venice had given help to the Germans in their attempt to take Ancona from the Greeks.

The policy which Manuel pursued in Italy naturally reacted upon the relations between the Greek Empire and the Germans. The attitude which he took up there would naturally have as its first consequence a complete rupture with Barbarossa. This, however, was postponed for some time owing to the secrecy with which the Greek Emperor contrived to cover up his intrigues. It was only when the occupation of Ancona took place in 1166 that Manuel's hostility to Barbarossa shewed itself clearly. From 1159 to 1165 several embassies were exchanged between the two Emperors, and in 1166 Henry, Duke of Austria, made a useless journey to Manuel's court to attempt to bring about an understanding. Just at that time Manuel's occupation of Ancona had opened Barbarossa's eyes, and he was determined to avenge himself on the earliest opportunity. However, the progress made by Manuel in Italy, marked by the treaties with Genoa in 1169 and with Pisa in 1170, decided Barbarossa on attempting a reconciliation. From 1170 to 1172 proposals were discussed for the marriage of Manuel's daughter with Barbarossa's son. They led to nothing, and in 1173 Barbarossa was engaged in the siege of Ancona (which had given itself up to the Greeks), and was also trying to negotiate an alliance with William II, evidently directed against Manuel. At the same time the Western Emperor was attempting in his turn to create difficulties for his adversary, and was treating with the Sultan of Iconium. Manuel took no share in the Treaty of Venice (1177) and, as we shall see, continued the struggle with the Western Emperor up to the last day of his life.

His Italian policy, being based wholly on diplomacy, always left the greater part of the military forces of the Empire free, a circumstance which enabled the Emperor at the same time to pursue a more active and warlike course in two other quarters, Hungary and Asia. Since the peace signed with Géza, Manuel had played a waiting game in Hungary, content with giving a refuge at Constantinople to two of the king's brothers, the future Stephen IV and Ladislas. At the death of Géza (1161), Manuel had made use of the pretenders whom he had at hand in order to interfere in the concerns of the Hungarian succession, calculating thus to secure some advantage for the Empire. The laws of succession were not yet fully fixed in Hungary, and Stephen IV could plead in his favour the ancient usage by which the brother of a dead king was to be preferred to the son, in order to put forward a claim to the throne to the prejudice of his nephew Stephen III. Manuel supported the claims of his *protégé* by Byzantine troops. A strong party grew up in Hungary hostile to the claims of Géza's son, but refusing to admit those of Stephen IV, who was looked upon as too much the vassal of Constantinople. The Hungarians feared that by giving the crown to Stephen IV their country might become a mere satellite of Constantinople, and to avoid this danger made choice of Ladislas, brother of Stephen IV, whom they regarded as less submissive to the influence of the Byzantine court. Ladislas was barely seated on the throne when he died (1162). The struggle between the two Stephens then recommenced, Manuel still giving support to his candidate. To bring the contest to an end, the counsellors of the young King Stephen III offered to hand over to Manuel another son of Géza's named Béla, who was recognised as the future heir to the crown of Hungary and granted a considerable appanage which included Dalmatia. As the appanage of Béla, who would be brought up in Constantinople, Dalmatia practically fell back into the hands of the Byzantines, and the result of Manuel's Hungarian policy was an important territorial acquisition. To make his success the surer, Manuel, who as yet had no son, decided to betroth his daughter Mary to the Hungarian prince, whom he destined for his successor. By this means Hungary would have been united to the Greek Empire.

It was not without difficulty that the Greeks entered into possession of Dalmatia. As the position of Stephen III grew stronger, the Hungarians came to regret the sacrifice they had agreed to, and for several years the war was renewed. Manuel, having become master of Dalmatia in 1166, remained in the end the victor. The birth of a son to him in 1169 caused him to alter his arrangements. Béla ceased to be heir presumptive and, his betrothal to Mary having been set aside, he was married to the Emperor's sister-in-law, a daughter of Constance of Antioch. On the death of Stephen III, Béla with the aid of Byzantine troops mounted the throne of Hungary. As the price of his support Manuel kept his hold on Béla's appanage. Béla always remained devoted to him, although it was only after his patron's death that he recovered Dalmatia.

The continual wars which were waged during this period on the Danube frontier kept up a state of unrest among the Serbs, who were vassals of the Empire. Manuel was repeatedly obliged to intervene. He deposed Pervoslav Uroš, replacing him by his brother Béla (1161?). Then, Béla having retired from power, Manuel set up as his successor Dessa, another son of Béla Uroš (*c.* 1162). Dessa, who a few years later took the name of Stephen Nemanja, attempted to throw off the Byzantine suzerainty. More than once Manuel was forced to interfere to restore order; finally he seized Stephen Nemanja, whom he kept prisoner for some time in Constantinople. It is not known exactly at what date Stephen regained his liberty. He took advantage of the disorder which followed the death of Manuel to secure the independence of his country.

It was not until about 1150 that the affairs of the East called for the intervention of Manuel. At that time the situation of the Byzantine possessions had become critical. Thoros, son of the Armenian prince Leo, had escaped from captivity, and had succeeded in taking from the Greeks a large part of Cilicia. At the same time the Muslim conquest had made a great step in advance by the capture of Edessa, and the position of the Latin states in Palestine was rendered even more precarious by the entrance into the contest of the Musulmans of Iconium, who with Qilij Arslān, son of Mas'ūd, wished to have their share in the dismembering of the Latin principalities. In the extreme peril in which they stood the Latins asked for help from the West, but the danger was so threatening that they had recourse to the Emperor of Constantinople. Manuel ordered his troops in the East to support the Latins. About the same time he bought from the wife of Joscelin II, Count of Edessa, all that remained in her hands of the possessions of her husband. Constance, Princess of Antioch, having become a widow, also turned to the Emperor for protection. The position of things thus favoured Greek intervention. Manuel charged his cousin, Andronicus Comnenus, with the task of reducing Thoros, and sent also his brother-in-law the Caesar John-Roger whom he proposed to Constance as a husband. This projected marriage never took place, and Andronicus only succeeded in getting himself defeated before Mamistra.

Manuel then changed his policy and attempted to secure the submission of Thoros by means of Mas'ūd. The latter accepted Manuel's offers all the more willingly as he had himself subjects of complaint against Thoros. The Armenian prince had pillaged Cappadocia, taking advantage of the struggle between Mas'ūd and the Dānishmandite rulers, Ya'qūb Arslān and Dhū'l-Qarnain, son and heir of 'Ain-ad-Daulah. The result of this experiment did not correspond to Manuel's hopes. On a first occasion Mas'ūd treated with Thoros but at Manuel's expense; on a second the Musulman troops were thoroughly beaten. Profiting by the inaction of Manuel, who was detained by affairs in Italy, Thoros approached Reginald of Chatillon who had become Prince of Antioch through his marriage with Constance, and the two set on foot an expedition against the island of Cyprus, where immense booty was obtained (1155 or 1156).

This aggression against the Byzantines greatly displeased the King of Jerusalem, Baldwin, for, confronted by the growing success of the Atābeg Nūr-ad-Dīn, the master of Damascus, he was meditating a *rapprochement* with Manuel, to whom he had applied for the hand of a princess of the imperial family. The request of Baldwin came just as the imperial idea was beginning to take shape in Manuel's mind. The Emperor, whose Oriental policy, like that of his predecessors, was dominated by the wish to regain Antioch for the Empire, eagerly welcomed the proposal of Baldwin, which would give him an opportunity of posing as the protector of the Holy Places. He gave the King of Jerusalem the hand of his niece Theodora, daughter of his brother Isaac, and as soon as peace had been concluded with the King of Sicily (1157) he organised a great expedition for the East.

By about the month of September 1158 Manuel had arrived in Cilicia at the head of a very considerable force. None of his adversaries dared to stand against him, and in succession Reginald of Chatillon and Thoros were obliged to come in penitential garments and submit themselves to his mercy. The Emperor consented to pardon them. Reginald was obliged to acknowledge himself the vassal of the Empire, engaging to supply a strong contingent of troops whenever required to do so by the Emperor. Ambassadors from most of the Oriental princes were to be found hastening to the imperial camp before Mamistra. The Latins themselves, the King of Jerusalem first among them, sought help of Manuel in whom they now placed all their hopes; Baldwin himself entered into a treaty, he also being obliged to furnish troops to the Greek Empire.

In April 1159 Manuel left Cilicia to make his solemn entry into Antioch, escorted by the Latin princes on foot and unarmed, and followed by the King of Jerusalem on horseback but without weapons. Passing through streets adorned with carpets and hangings, to the sound of drums and trumpets and to the singing of triumphal hymns, the Emperor was brought in procession to the cathedral by the Patriarch in his pontifical robes, while the imperial banners were hoisted on the city walls.

His stay at Antioch marks the highest pitch of glory to which Manuel attained throughout his reign. He took pleasure in the pomp with which he surrounded himself, and in the largess which he distributed to dazzle the Latins and Orientals. For a week feasts and shows followed each other rapidly, and on one day the Emperor might be seen descending into the lists to measure himself against Reginald of Chatillon, while the officers of the imperial army contended with the Frankish knights.

Towards the end of May the Emperor left Antioch with all the materials for a siege, taking the road to Edessa, but after a few days' march the army halted, for the negotiations with Nūr-ad-Dīn had just reached a conclusion. Manuel procured the liberation of all the captives held in the Atābeg's prison, the number of whom reached six thousand. The abandonment of the campaign which had been begun caused the deepest disappointment to the Christians of the East. To justify the retreat of the Greeks, a rumour was circulated that a conspiracy had been discovered at Constantinople. There is perhaps no need to lay stress on the explanations put forward at the time. May it not be supposed that Manuel entered into the treaty because he had no kind of interest in the destruction of the power of Nūr-ad-Dīn? It was to the struggle of the Atābegs and the Christians that the Empire owed the advantages which had been won in the East. Had he subjugated Nūr-ad-Dīn, Manuel would have delivered the Latins from their dread of the Musulman peril, and they as soon as the danger was removed would, as they had done before, make haste to forget their engagements to the Empire. In order that the suzerainty of Constantinople might be recognised by the Latins, it was necessary that the Musulman peril should continue to exist. This appears to give the most reasonable explanation of Manuel's conduct.

On his return to Constantinople Manuel, who had been left a widower, meditated drawing closer the bonds between himself and the Latins of Palestine by marrying a Latin princess. He requested the King of Jerusalem to grant him the hand of Millicent, sister of Raymond III, Count of Tripolis. But, the marriage being once agreed upon, the negotiations were drawn out for more than a year, until at last Manuel suddenly broke them off and transferred his choice to Mary, daughter of Constance, Princess of Antioch. The chief result of the marriage was to bring Antioch more decidedly within the sphere of Byzantine influence, which was now exerted energetically on the side of the Latins against the Turks. At the battle of the Bukaia (1163) and at Ḥārim (1164) the Greeks fought side by side with the Latin lords. After the defeat at Ḥārim the Emperor sent reinforcements to Cilicia, but he made the mistake of committing the province to his cousin Andronicus as governor. Andronicus ruined the imperial policy by procuring the murder of Sdephanê, the brother of Thoros, who was thus alienated from the Empire. Then, having fallen in love with Philippa, Manuel's sister-in-law, Andronicus deserted his post as governor in order to fly with the object of his passion. In spite of these incidents Constantinople and Antioch remained on excellent terms. Manuel came to the help of his brother-in-law Bohemond III with financial support, and obtained from him permission for the Greek Patriarch to return to Antioch. While Amaury, the Latin Patriarch, departed hurling anathemas against the city, the Greek, Athanasius, took possession of the see. This supplies a fresh proof of the influence exercised over Antioch by the Greek element. There was then in this quarter substantial progress on the part of the Byzantines.

Such was not the case in Cilicia. Thoros having died (*c.* 1167), his son Rupen II succeeded him, but after a short time was robbed of his crown by his uncle Mleh, who in order to seize power had allied himself with Nūr-ad-Dīn. With the latter's help Mleh succeeded in maintaining his position until the death of his patron, when he was overthrown and, Rupen II being dead, was replaced by Rupen III, son of Sdephanê, the victim of Andronicus. Throughout these struggles Constantinople seems to have played a very secondary part in Cilicia. It is only the attempt by Manuel to bring about the union of the Greek and Armenian Churches which shews that Constantinople had not yet lost interest in Armenian affairs. It is quite probable that the object aimed at by the Emperor was at least as much political as religious, and that the opposition offered by the Armenian clergy, which caused the failure of the negotiations, was also political in character.

Baldwin's successor on the throne of Jerusalem, Amaury, after having at the opening of his reign sought in vain for help from the West, turned decidedly from 1165 onwards towards Constantinople. He asked for the hand of a princess of the imperial family, and on 29 August 1167 his marriage took place at Tyre with the daughter of the Protosebastos John Comnenus, a nephew of the Emperor, the son of his brother Andronicus. Through this new connexion the ties between Constantinople and the kingdom of Jerusalem became closer, and Manuel agreed to lend his help to King Amaury, who, in order to prevent Nūr-ad-Dīn from occupying Egypt, where the Caliphate had fallen into utter decadence, wished to annex the country himself. Several attempts by the King of Jerusalem had failed; it was now decided that in 1169 the Greeks and Latins should try to effect a joint conquest of Egypt. Delays on the part of Amaury caused the expedition to fail, for the provisions of the Greeks, calculated to last for three months, had been already largely consumed when their fleet quitted Acre.

The Greek fleet under the command of the Grand Duke Alexius Contostephanus had a strength of 150 biremes and 60 transport ships. It left the port of Coela near Sestos in July. But the expedition, instead of setting out in August as had been agreed, only left Syria to besiege Damietta in October. The siege lasted for two months, at the end of which the town made terms with Amaury. The campaign had failed, and the Greeks, who were suffering greatly from want of provisions, were in haste to depart. Their return journey was disastrous, a large number of their vessels being lost at sea, and the Empire derived no advantage whatever from the expedition.

Manuel, however, was not discouraged by this want of success, and in 1171 he gave a favourable reception to Amaury, who had come to Constantinople to ask for his support. A treaty was signed by which Manuel pledged himself to assist the King of Jerusalem in a renewed attempt upon Egypt. According to a Greek chronicler, Amaury at this time acknowledged himself the vassal of the Emperor, but as the statement cannot be verified it is impossible to speak decidedly on the point. As to the proposed expedition, we know that Manuel urged Amaury's successor, Baldwin IV, to march upon Egypt (1177). The opposition of Philip, Count of Flanders and Vermandois, who was then in Palestine, was fatal to the plan which had been agreed on, its execution being deferred to some unspecified date.

It remains for us to consider the relations of Manuel with the Sultan of Iconium. Mas'ūd had died (*c.* 1155) and had been succeeded at Iconium by Qilij Arslān, and at Gangra and Ancyra by another of his sons, Shāhinshāh. On its return from Antioch in 1159 the Greek army was attacked near Cotyaeum by Musulman bands, and next year Manuel undertook a campaign in order to chastise Qilij Arslān. In this struggle he relied on the support of other Mohammedan princes, Ya'qūb Arslān, Dhū'l-Nūn, Mahomet, son of Dhū'l-Qarnain, and also on Shāhinshāh, brother of Qilij Arslān. In 1160 Ya'qūb Arslān was attacking Qilij Arslān, while on all sides the Greeks were falling upon such Turkish tribes as were to be found in the neighbourhood of the frontier. In consequence of this general onslaught Qilij Arslān treated for peace during the winter of 1161. The negotiations fell through, and war was resumed at the beginning of spring. Manuel, by way of Philadelphia, invaded the dominions of the Sultan, who retorted by attacks upon Phileta and Laodicea.

In 1162 Manuel called upon all his vassals to strike a decisive blow. Finding himself seriously menaced, Qilij Arslān made friends with Ya'qūb Arslān and Shāhinshāh, and then negotiated with Manuel, with whom he finally concluded a treaty of alliance. Soon after, Qilij Arslān appeared at Constantinople, where he remained for more than three months. He departed loaded with presents, having made the Emperor the fairest of promises for the future. He had pledged himself to restore to the Empire a number of towns which had been taken by the Musulmans. Not one of these promises was ever carried out.

The years from 1162 to 1174 were occupied by perpetual strife among the Musulmans of Asia Minor, the Greeks being thus allowed some respite. In the end Qilij Arslān was left victor over his chief adversaries. His brother Shāhinshāh and Dhū'l-Nūn then sought refuge at Constantinople.

In order to be able to pursue his European policy undisturbed, Manuel had since his treaty with Qilij Arslān supplied the latter with heavy subsidies as the price of peace. In proportion as his power increased, the Sultan of Iconium, urged on perhaps by Frederick Barbarossa, assumed a more independent attitude towards the Empire, while the incursions of the nomad tribes of Turks were renewed with greater frequency than ever. To secure his frontier, Manuel repaired the fortifications of a certain number of strongholds, notably Pergamus and Chliara. He then fortified the two lines of defence supplied by the rivers Maeander and Hermus.

It was not till 1175 that a definitive rupture took place between Manuel and the Sultan of Iconium. The former insisted that Qilij Arslān should fulfil his promise to restore to the Empire certain towns which he had taken from it. Supported by Frederick Barbarossa, Qilij Arslān refused to comply with the Emperor's demands, and Manuel decided upon war, counting upon the support of all the remaining partisans of Shāhinshāh and Dhū'l-Nūn among the Musulmans. While a detachment of Greek troops was sent under Gabras and Shāhinshāh to occupy Amasia, which was still in the hands of the latter's supporters, Manuel carried out the fortification of a whole series of towns, Dorylaeum, an important strategic point on the road to Iconium, Lampe, and Sublaeum (1175). Next year the Emperor resolved to attack Iconium. With this object he preached a regular crusade, calling upon all his vassals for help. While Andronicus Vatatzes went to attack Neo-Caesarea, Manuel himself took command of the army which was to march upon Iconium. The fate of both expeditions was equally disastrous. Vatatzes failed before Neo-Caesarea and was killed, his army being routed. Manuel himself became entangled with his whole army in the mountainous region to the east of Sublaeum (Homa). He had neglected to explore the country-side with scouts during his march, and was caught by the Muslims in the narrow defiles at Myriocephalum. The Greeks met with a complete disaster, in which the finest of the imperial troops were slaughtered by the Musulmans. Manuel himself compared his defeat to that of Romanus Diogenes at Manzikert. For reasons unknown to us Qilij Arslān used his victory with moderation, and offered peace on honourable terms, stipulating only for the destruction of the fortifications at Dorylaeum and Sublaeum. Manuel agreed to the conditions proposed, and led the wreck of his army back to Constantinople.

With the disaster of Myriocephalum all enterprises on a large scale in the East came to an end. Though broken by his defeat, the Emperor did indeed renew the war during the latter part of his reign; but the Greek generals had to confine themselves to the defence of the frontier, and all idea of an advance upon Iconium, to attack the central seat of the Musulman power, was abandoned. In fact, the battle of Myriocephalum sealed the fate of the Comnenian dynasty, if not of the Byzantine Empire.

As a result of his defeat Manuel met with a mortification from Frederick Barbarossa which he must have felt keenly. The Western Emperor wrote to the Basileus, and remembering old scores himself spoke of the unity of the Empire. In his letter he clearly asserts the superiority of the Emperor of the West, sole heir of the Roman Emperors, over all other sovereigns, in particular, over the *King* of the Greeks.

Manuel, who feared that the Westerns might profit by his defeat to attack his Empire, strove by all the means which he had before found successful to paralyse Barbarossa's forces. He supported William, Marquess of Montferrat, when he raised a revolt in Italy, and, in order to set a seal on the alliance, married his daughter Mary to Renier, one of William's sons. Again it was Byzantine gold that helped to equip the troops that defeated Frederick's Arch-Chancellor, Christian of Mayence, near Camerino. Manuel was trying to arrange for the purchase of Christian, whom Conrad of Montferrat had made prisoner, when his own death put a stop to the negotiations. Thus after lasting twenty years the struggle between the two Empires came to an end—a struggle in which diplomacy counted for more than armies. Manuel's policy with regard to Barbarossa was very burdensome to the imperial treasury, for money was the weapon with which he chiefly carried on the contest. If his policy seems to have yielded no very striking results, it must be remembered that Manuel was successful in keeping the forces of his enemy in a state of inaction, and was thus able to pursue his policy of conquest in Hungary and the East unhindered.

The only success which sweetened the bitterness of Manuel's last years was the marriage of his son Alexius with Agnes, the daughter of Louis VII of France. This match had been arranged at the Emperor's request by Philip, Count of Flanders, who on his return from an expedition to the Holy Land had passed through Constantinople in 1178. The little princess, who reached Constantinople in a Genoese vessel, was married to the heir of the Empire on 2 March 1180. On 24 September in the same year the Emperor died after a long illness, during which, confident in the predictions of astrologers, he never ceased to nurse illusions as to his prospect of recovery. This conviction that he would recover prevented him from making any arrangements for the organisation of the government during the minority of his son.

Alexius II, son and successor of Manuel Comnenus, was twelve years old at the time of his father's death. Naturally therefore he had no share in state affairs, the regency being in the hands of his mother Mary of Antioch, whose charm and beauty the chroniclers vie in celebrating. Every man about the court, convinced that the Empress could be wooed and won, endeavoured to attract her attention. For some time the court was the scene of all manner of intrigues, and, in order to gain favour with the Empress, young and old rivalled one another in the elegance and splendour of their attire and in their jewels and perfumes, each hoping to be the lucky man on whom her choice would fall. Mary made the double mistake, first, of allowing herself to make a choice among the crowd of gallants who surrounded her, and, secondly, of distinguishing with her favour the vain-glorious and incapable Protosebastos Alexius Comnenus, son of Manuel's elder brother Andronicus. All power was soon exercised by the favourite, who by his childish pride, his contemptuous treatment of the chief officials, and the pretensions which he ostentatiously put forward, excited a general hatred in which the Regent was naturally included. The favour which she shewed to the Latins who filled the chief posts in the army and the administration, and on whose support she came naturally to rely, completed the exasperation of the public mind, which was besides excited by the courtiers. Before long the "foreign woman" as the Empress was called was detested in Constantinople, and a plot was set on foot against the all-powerful favourite. In order to kindle the indignation of the populace, it was given out that Alexius Comnenus intended to marry the Empress and to arrange for the disappearance of the young Emperor in order to seize the throne himself.

The leading spirit in the plot was Mary daughter of Manuel, with her husband the Caesar Renier. Having been for a short time heiress to the throne, Mary was inconsolable for the loss of her prospects, and she heartily detested her step-mother. A great many of the members of the imperial family gathered round her—Alexius Comnenus, illegitimate son of Manuel, John and Manuel Comnenus, the sons of Andronicus the future Emperor; and to these were added some of the chief officials, notably John Camaterus, prefect of the city. The assassination of the favourite was resolved on, but the stroke miscarried and the plot was discovered. Mary and her fellow-conspirators at once took refuge in St Sophia, which they turned into a fortress. Although the people shewed themselves clearly in favour of the conspirators, who also had the support of the Patriarch Theodotus and the higher clergy, the Protosebastos did not scruple to order an assault upon the church, thereby causing immense scandal (May 1182). This profanation, which finally alienated the public mind from him, in no way benefited Alexius Comnenus, whose troops were unable to take St Sophia. The Empress-Regent, reduced to treat with the besieged, was compelled to pardon them and to promise the leaders their lives and dignities. Nor was it long before the favourite met with a further rebuff. He attempted to depose the Patriarch and to constrain him to retire into a monastery. But Theodotus was brought back in triumph by the populace. The Regent, feeling herself in danger from the general hostility that surrounded her, sought help from outside, and petitioned her brother-in-law Béla III, King of Hungary, to come to her aid.

Meanwhile events at Constantinople were being watched from a distance with passionate interest by a man whose supporters were constantly stirring up the hostility of the populace against the Regent and her favourite. His name began to pass from mouth to mouth; he was the only person capable of saving the situation; the people of the capital and the malcontents of the Court rested all their hopes on Andronicus Comnenus.

This son of Isaac Comnenus was a strange being. His father was a brother of the Emperor John, and in the son the populace of Constantinople saw its future deliverer. Learned, eloquent, and witty, he had for a long time been the arbiter of fashion and taste in the capital, and the magnificence of his dwelling had become famous. The exquisiteness of his dress shewed off his handsome features—handsome enough to befit a throne, says a chronicler. A man of personal courage, Andronicus, like Manuel, had distinguished himself in single combat, but his cool and ready audacity delighted above all things in political intrigue. Full of ambition, he meditated unceasingly on the means of reaching the throne; of debauched life, the court rang with stories of his various scandalous amours. His vices were paraded with astonishing cynicism. While the lover of his cousin Eudocia, Andronicus had been appointed Duke of Cilicia, and on his defeat by Thoros II had hastened back to his mistress. He had then entered into a conspiracy with Géza, King of Hungary, and when arrested in 1153 was plotting the assassination of Manuel. He made several unavailing attempts to escape, but in the end after many changes of fortune succeeded in gaining a refuge at the court of Yaroslav, Prince of Halicz (1164). Manuel, uneasy that so restless a brain should be intriguing among the Russians, had pardoned his cousin and had then re-appointed him Duke of Cilicia. While residing in his province Andronicus conceived a passion for the Emperor's sister-in-law Philippa, daughter of the Princess of Antioch, who yielded to his solicitations. Quickly forsaking her, Andronicus set out for the Holy Land, where he carried off his cousin Queen Theodora, widow of Baldwin of Jerusalem. The couple for several years led a wandering life, going from court to court in the Muslim East, and finally establishing themselves near Colonea in a citadel presented to them by a Musulman emir. Andronicus made use of his position, which was close to the frontier of the Empire, to keep up incessant warfare against his cousin. Excommunicated by the Patriarch for his relations with Theodora, he nevertheless continued to live with her. It was, however, on her account that he was at last reduced to sue for pardon. In order to get the better of his cousin, Manuel had his mistress carried off by the Duke of Trebizond. Andronicus, incapable of dispensing with her society, resolved upon making his submission. After a solemn reconciliation with Manuel, in which he proved his talents as an actor, he retired into private life at Oenaeum on the shores of the Black Sea.

It was from this retreat that for more than a year he followed the course of events at Constantinople. Increasing age had taught him prudence, and he fully realised that if he did not succeed in reaching the throne this time all his hopes would be at an end. Affecting complete indifference to all the rivalries which surged round Alexius II, Andronicus was meanwhile setting in motion partisans who kept him informed of the state of opinion. The moment came when his daughter Mary gave him the signal for action. He marched without hesitation upon Constantinople at the head of his tenants and of some of the troops in Paphlagonia whom he had seduced from their allegiance, declaring his object to be the liberation of the Emperor. His march across Asia Minor was a triumph; not only did he defeat the loyal troops, but their general, Andronicus Angelus, declared for him. His victorious army encamped upon the Asiatic shore of the Bosphorus, and before long the very sailors of the fleet, on whom lay the duty of barring his passage, came to make their submission to him. The population of the capital rushed to greet its darling, who took up the rôle of champion of the Greeks against the foreigners.

The Empress-Regent and her favourite no longer received any support except from the Latins, who alone staved off the entry of Andronicus into the capital. To overcome this obstacle a formidable outbreak was engineered in Constantinople; the populace, goaded on to attack the Latin quarters, indulged in the most shameless excesses and even massacred the sick in the hospitals. Many Latins perished; at the same time a large number succeeded in getting on board some fifty vessels, and by the ravages they committed in the islands of the Propontis and along the coast exacted a heavy penalty from the Greeks for the treacherous onslaught which they had made.

Once her Latin supporters had been massacred, all was over with the Regent. Giving himself out as the liberator of Alexius II, Andronicus entered Constantinople. He began by banishing the Empress from the palace, and then arranged for the disappearance of such members of the imperial family as were likely to oppose any obstacle to his plans. Mary and the Caesar Renier died in a manner unknown; the Empress-mother was condemned to death, and her son forced to sign her sentence himself. In the face of these atrocities the Patriarch Theodotus withdrew. In September 1183 Andronicus became joint Emperor with Alexius II, whom he murdered in November of the same year, and thereupon married Agnes, who had been his victim's wife.

The reign of Andronicus presents a series of unparalleled contrasts. So far as the administration of the provinces is concerned, Andronicus shewed great and statesmanlike qualities; on the other hand his government at Constantinople was that of the most hateful of tyrants.

The provincial population had much to bear both from the imperial functionaries and from the great feudal lords. Andronicus exacted from the latter class an unfailing respect for the property and rights of the peasants, and treated with extreme severity such as were reported to him as having abused their power. As to the officials, he made a point of choosing them carefully and paying them liberally, so that they should have no need to oppress the peasants in order to recoup themselves for the price paid for their appointments. To all he guaranteed rigid justice. Such as were convicted of peculation were severely punished. "You have the choice," the Emperor used to say, "between ceasing to cheat and ceasing to live." Short as was the reign of Andronicus, these measures had their effect; order and prosperity returned to the provinces, and some of them which had been deserted by their inhabitants again became populated. Finally, one of the happiest measures introduced by the Emperor was the abolition of the rights of wreck and estray.

Andronicus was a lover of literature and of the arts. He surrounded himself with jurists, and took pleasure in beautifying Constantinople. The repairing of aqueducts and the restoration of the church of the Forty Martyrs were the two chief works which he carried out. In one of the additions made to the church of the Forty Martyrs he had a series of mosaics executed representing his adventures and his hunting exploits.

But this bright side of Andronicus' reign is defaced by the ferocious cruelty with which he treated his opponents. The aristocracy opposed him violently. At Philadelphia, at Nicaea, at Prusa, at Lopadium, and in Cyprus, risings took place organised by the representatives of the greatest families among the nobility. At this juncture the Empire was being attacked on all sides: the Sultan of Iconium had re-taken Sozopolis and was besieging Attalia, Béla III had crossed the Danube, and finally in 1185 the King of Sicily, William II, was invading Byzantine territory. In face of all these dangers Andronicus, fearing to lose the power so long coveted, determined to maintain himself by terror. The noblest Byzantine families saw their most illustrious members put to death or horribly mutilated. At Constantinople as in Asia Minor the work of repression was terrible; even the Emperor's own family was not spared. In the capital, terror had bowed the necks of all, and Andronicus seemed to have nothing left to fear when the Norman invasion came and brought about his fall.

During the summer of 1185 the Normans, having taken Thessalonica, advanced upon Constantinople. At their approach a panic fell upon the city; the population, in terror of their lives, complained that Andronicus was making no preparations for resisting the enemy. The Emperor's popularity, already impaired by his cruelties, crumbled away under the fear of invasion. Sullen disaffection was muttering in the capital, and Andronicus again had recourse to violence; large numbers were arrested on the pretext of punishing those secretly in league with the Normans, and the Emperor contemplated a general massacre of the prisoners. The arrest of a man of no great importance, Isaac Angelus, was the last drop that made the cup run over. Escaping from the soldiers sent to arrest him, Isaac took refuge in St Sophia; the people at his summons gathered in crowds, and before long rebellion thundered around him and burst out with terrific force. Isaac Angelus was proclaimed Emperor. Andronicus in vain attempted to resist; he was beaten and took to flight, but was stopped, and soon after given up to the fury of the people. The rabble tore out his beard, broke his teeth, cut off one of his hands, put out one of his eyes, and then threw him into a dungeon. On the morrow his tortures began afresh. He was led through the city on a mangy camel, while stones and boiling water were thrown at him. Finally, he was brought to the Hippodrome, where the soldiers, having hung him up by the feet, amused themselves by cutting him in pieces. Throughout these hideous tortures Andronicus shewed superhuman courage. Raising his mutilated arm to his lips he constantly repeated "Kyrie eleison! wherefore wilt thou break a bruised reed?"

Such in September 1185 was the end of the last Emperor of the house of the Comneni, who for more than a century had arrested the ruin of their country. With his great qualities of statesmanship, the last of the dynasty might have helped to regenerate the Empire. Unfortunately the evil elements in his character had the mastery, and contributed to hasten the hour of that decadence which no member of the house of the Angeli was to prove capable of retarding.

The reign of Isaac II (1185–1195) was indeed a succession of misfortunes, converted by incapacity into disasters. Cyprus remained in revolt under an Isaac Comnenus until it was conquered by Richard Coeur-de-lion in 1191; and the great nobles of the Empire were so much out of hand as to be almost independent. The Bulgarians rose; the Serbs had thrown off (1180) their vassalage. If the Byzantines were able to throw back the invasion of William II of Sicily, Isaac II's alliance with Saladin, and his resistance to Frederick Barbarossa's transit through the Balkans on the Third Crusade confirmed the growing enmity of the West. Frederick forced his way to the Bosphorus, ravaging the country and sacking Hadrianople. He compelled the transport of his troops to Asia from Gallipoli, and the delivery of provisions, but not before he had mooted the proposal of a crusade being preached against the Greeks. When in 1195 Alexius III took advantage of the general discontent to blind and depose his brother, no improvement came about. Rather, the anarchy became worse, while the government's incompetence and oppression remained glaring. The thirteenth century was to shew that there were sound elements and great men still in the Empire, but before they could gain control there fell upon it the shattering disaster of the Fourth Crusade.

CHAPTER XIII.

VENICE.

During the period covered by this chapter the State of Venice did not reach maturity. She did not become a world-power till after the Fourth Crusade, nor was it till a full century later that she finally developed her constitution. But the germs of her constitution and the seeds of her sea-power are both to be found in these earliest years of her existence. The problems which dominate these years are the question of immigration, when and how did the inhospitable islands of the lagoons become settled; how did the community develop; how did it gradually achieve its actual and then its formal independence of Byzantium; how did it save itself from being absorbed by the rulers of the Italian mainland, Charles the Great, Otto II, and Frederick Barbarossa.

The earliest authentic notice we have of the lagoon-population is to be found in the letter addressed (*c.* 536) by Cassiodorus, in the name of Witigis, King of the Goths, to the *Tribuni Maritimorum*, the tribunes of the maritime parts. The letter, written in a tone between command and exhortation, is highly rhetorical in style, but gives us a vivid picture of a poor though industrious community occupying a site unique in the world.

This community, in all probability, formed part of the Gothic Kingdom, for it seems certain that the *Tribuni Maritimorum* whom Cassiodorus addresses were officers appointed by the Goths. The chief characteristics of this people are that they were salt-workers and seamen, two points highly significant for the future development of Venice. No doubt the population here referred to was largely augmented, if not actually formed, by the refugees who sought safety in the lagoons from the ever recurrent barbarian incursions on the mainland, Attila's among the number; but it is not till the Lombard invasion in 568 that we can begin to trace the positive influence of the barbarian raids and to note the first signs of a political constitution inside the lagoons themselves.

The campaign of Belisarius (535–540) brought Venetia once more under the Roman Empire (539); and, when Narses the Eunuch undertook to carry out Justinian's scheme for the final extermination of the Goths (551), he was forced to recognise the importance of the lagoons. His march upon Ravenna by way of the mainland was opposed by the Franks and by the Goths under Teias. In these circumstances John, the son of Vitalian, who knew the country well, suggested that the army should take the lagoon and *lidi* route, through which it was conducted by the lagoon-dwellers with their long ships and light ships (νῆες καὶ ἄκατοι), thereby enabling the Greek army to reach Ravenna and incidentally leading up to the final victories of Busta Gallorum (552) and Mons Lactarius (553); after this the coast districts (τὰ ἐπιθαλασσίδια χωρία) became definitely and undisputedly parts of the Roman Empire once more.

But the hold of Byzantium upon Italy generally was weak. The Persian war absorbed the imperial resources. There was little to oppose Alboin and his Lombards when in the spring of 568 they swept down from Pannonia and within the year made themselves lords of North Italy. Then began a general flight from the mainland; and the process was renewed during the next hundred years down to the second sack of Oderzo (667). Throughout this period the settlement of the lagoons definitely took place, and we find the first indication of a constitution in those obscure officials, the *Tribuni Majores* and *Minores* of the earliest chronicles. Paulinus, Patriarch of Aquileia, fled from his ruined diocese bearing with him the treasury and the relics. He was followed by his flock, who sought refuge in Grado. The refugees from Concordia found an asylum in Caorle; Malamocco and Chioggia were settled in 602, and possibly some of the Rialto group of islands, the site of the future City of Venice, received inhabitants for the first time. The final peopling of Torcello, with which the earliest Venetian chronicles are so much concerned, took place in 636, when Altino, one of the last remaining imperial possessions on the mainland, fell. Bishop Maurus and Tribune Aurius settled in the Torcello group of islands, and built a church. The tribune assigned certain islands as church-lands, and appointed, as his tribune-delegate in the island of Ammiana, Fraunduni, who likewise built a church and apportioned certain lands to furnish the revenue thereof. Twelve lagoon-townships were settled in this manner, Grado, Bibiones (between Grado and Caorle), Caorle, Heraclea, Equilio Jesolo (now Cavazuccherina), Torcello, Murano, Rialto, Malamocco, Poveglia, Clugies minor (now Sottomarina), and Clugies Major (now Chioggia). If, as is probable, a process similar to that which took place in the settlement of Torcello went on in the case of these other townships, then we find a solution of the vexed question as to the exact nature of the major and minor tribunes, the former being, like Aurius, the leaders of the immigrants, the latter, like Fraunduni, delegates in the circumjacent islands.

In the confusion and obscurity of the early chronicles it is difficult to arrive at a clear idea of the political conditions in the lagoon-townships. In the structure of the Empire, Venetia formed part of the province of Istria. We know from the inscriptions of Santa Eufemia in Grado that the Greeks maintained a fleet in the lagoons down to the sixth century; but as they gradually lost ground on the mainland before the Lombard invaders, they withdrew their forces, leaving the islanders of the lagoons to defend themselves as best they might. The lagoon-dwellers gathered round their leading men or tribunes; but their powers of defence were feeble, as is proved by the raid of Lupus, Duke of Friuli, upon Grado (630), and it was probably only the intricate nature of their home-waters which saved them from absorption by the barbarian. These tribunes wielded both military and civil authority, and in theory were undoubtedly appointed by and dependent on the Exarch of Ravenna as representing Byzantium in Italy. The office tended to become hereditary and gave rise to the class of tribunitian families. Side by side with the secular power, as represented by the tribunes, grew the ecclesiastical power centring round the patriarchate of Grado (568), and the lagoon sees of Caorle (598), Torcello (635), Heraclea (640), Malamocco (640), Jesolo (670), Olivolo (774). The Arianism of the Lombards drove the orthodox bishops from their mainland churches to seek asylum in the lagoons. The clergy as was natural, thanks to their education, played a large part in the developing life of the lagoon communities; but, if we may draw a conclusion from the instance of Torcello, it would seem that the secular power reserved a kind of superiority or patronage over the ecclesiastical: a fact significant in the future development of ecclesiastico-political relations in Venice. Besides the leading, or "noble," families represented by the tribunes, and the clergy gathered round their bishops, we find that there was a general assembly of the whole population which made its voice heard in the choice of both tribunes, priests, and bishops, but otherwise appears to have been of little weight.

Throughout the seventh century the imperial possessions on the mainland were gradually shorn away by the Lombard kings. The second sack of Oderzo (667), which had been the seat of an imperial Magister Militum, seems to have caused the rise of Heraclea, the lagoon-township where the refugees from Oderzo found asylum, to the leading place among the twelve tribunitian centres. So great was the number of the fugitives that they overflowed into the neighbouring township of Jesolo, and its population was soon large enough to demand a separate bishopric (670). The collapse of the Roman Empire on the mainland led to the severing of all land-communication between the lagoons and Istria, of which they had hitherto formed a part. It seems that either directly and deliberately by the will of the imperial authorities, or by the will of the lagoon-dwellers with a view to their better protection, Sea-Venice was separated from Istria and erected into a distinct *ducatus* (after 680). The Venetian chronicler, John the Deacon, represents the creation of the first doge in the following terms: "In the times of the Emperor Anastasius and of Liutprand, King of the Lombards, the whole population of Venice, along with the Patriarch and the bishops, came together and by common accord resolved that it would be more honourable for the future to live under dukes than under tribunes; and after long debate as to whom they should elect to this office, at length they agreed upon a capable and illustrious man named Paulitio."

The date usually given for the choice of the first doge is 697, but if John the Deacon be right it cannot be placed earlier than 713, the year in which Anastasius came to the throne. The question has been raised as to whether the lagoon population independently elected their first doge, or whether he was appointed by the imperial authorities. Both may be true in the sense that he was chosen by the community, as in all probability were the tribunes, and confirmed by the exarch or the imperial authority. In any case it is certain that there was no question of the lagoon population claiming formal independence of Byzantium at that time nor for long after; but, as a matter of fact, a very few years later (726), at the time of the Italian revolt against the iconoclastic decrees of Leo the Isaurian, the population of the lagoons undoubtedly made a free and independent election of their doge in the person of Orso, the third holder of that title.

The election of the first doge, Paulutius Anafestus, a "noble" of Heraclea, marks the close of the earliest period in Venetian history; the second period is concerned with the events which led up to the concentration of the lagoon-townships at Rialto, the city we now call Venice, in 810. The notes of the period are: first, the development of the dukedom as against the older order of the tribunes and against the ecclesiastical power of the Patriarchs of Grado; second, the internal quarrels between rival townships, Heraclea, Jesolo, Malamocco, which largely contributed to the final concentration at Rialto; third, the question of self preservation, the maintenance of such practical, *de facto*, independence of Byzantium as the community had acquired through the weakness of the Empire, and the struggle to avoid absorption by the powerful barbarian rulers of the mainland, Lombard and Frank.

The dependence of Venice on Byzantium has been maintained by modern historians, and it cannot for a moment be disputed that, in theory, it existed; as late as 979 we find public documents dated by the year of the imperial reign. But in practice it is the population of the lagoons which elects the doge, and murders, deposes, blinds, or tonsures him if dissatisfied with the tendency of his policy, while no one brings them to account for such acts of independence. An explanation of the frequent revolutions and ducal downfalls has been suggested in the jealousy of the various tribunitian families reduced in importance by the creation of the dukedom; but if it be permissible to consider the lagoon-dwellers as an individual community and to talk of the spirit of a race, viewed by the light of events as they occurred, it looks as though the Venetian population was inspired by an instinct towards independence and deliberately worked towards that goal.

The earliest and most important act of Paulutius was the conclusion of a treaty (713–716) with Liutprand, the powerful King of the Lombards.

The treaty is lost, but we can gather its terms from the reference to it in subsequent *pacta* with the kings of Italy. It consisted of two parts: the first a guarantee of security for Venetian traders on the mainland; protection of Venetian flocks and horses; right to cut wood in Lombard territory; in return for these privileges the doge agreed to pay an annual tribute. The second part contained a definition of boundaries on the mainland. This second part is said to have been "concluded in the days of King Liutprand, between the Duke Paulutio and the Magister Militum Marcellus." Of this difficult passage three explanations have been suggested. It is said that Marcellus was the Magister Militum (the chief imperial authority) of Istria, and that it was he who concluded the treaty with the consent of the doge. But Istria and Sea-Venice were by this time separated; "Dux" is superior in rank to "Magister Militum," and as a matter of fact the doge's name comes first; finally the agreement is said to be not between Marcellus and Liutprand but between (*inter*) Paulutio and Marcellus. The second theory is that Marcellus was Magister Militum in Venice and associated himself with the doge in treating with Liutprand; but here again the word *inter* seems fatal. The third and most plausible theory is that Marcellus was the imperial Magister Militum in Venice, and that acting on imperial orders he and the doge delimited the territory of Heraclea and obtained from Liutprand a confirmation of the same, as is proved by the "precept" of 25 March 996. Whichever view be correct, the treaty with Liutprand is of the highest importance as shewing us the Venetian community under its first doge securing treaty rights from the masters of the mainland.

It is certain that the early doges did not exercise a wide or undisputed power in the lagoon community. Not until the ninth century, after the concentration at Rialto, did they assume the unchallenged headship of the State. The office of tribune persisted long after the creation of the dukedom; as late as 887 we hear of the Tribune Andrea rescuing the body of the Doge Peter I Candianus from the Slavs. But the establishment of the dogeship roused jealousy among the tribunitian families, and the choice of Heraclea for the ducal seat stirred the envy of other lagoon-townships and so began the long series of struggles between the rival centres in one of which the first doge lost his life (717).

He was succeeded by Marcellus Tegalianus, whose identification with Marcellus, Magister Militum of Istria, is by no means certain. He was probably appointed or confirmed by the imperial authorities. During his reign Serenus, Patriarch of Aquileia, supported by Liutprand, attacked Donatus, Patriarch of Grado. The doge, afraid of drawing down on the lagoons the wrath of the Lombards if he employed Venetian arms in support of the lagoon Patriarch, contented himself with an appeal to the Pope, who sharply reprimanded Serenus. Subsequently the Lateran Council (732) formally decreed the separation of the two jurisdictions, declaring Grado to be the metropolitan see of Istria and the lagoons, thereby conferring definite form on the lagoon patriarchate. Marcellus died in 726, at the moment when Italy, following the lead of Pope Gregory II, was in open revolt against the iconoclast decrees of the Emperor Leo III. The various districts expelled or slew the imperial officers and elected dukes for themselves. The bolder spirits even talked of electing a new Emperor and marching with him on Constantinople. Venice shared in the general movement, and, whether Marcellus' death was due to the revolutionary party or not, his successor Ursus was undoubtedly elected by the lagoon population without consulting the imperial authorities.

The Italian revolt of 726 brought to light the difficulty in which the growing lagoon community found itself between east and west. The Pope in his hostility to Leo invited Liutprand to invade the Exarchate and expel the Greeks. The Lombard king was nothing loth, seeing in the request an opportunity for extending his domains. In a first attack on Ravenna, Paul the Exarch was slain. The Emperor despatched Eutychius with gold and troops to take his place. The new exarch came to terms with Liutprand and assisted him to subdue the revolted Dukes of Benevento and Spoleto. But when Gregory III came to the papal throne in 731 he arrived at an understanding with Eutychius which resulted in a fresh revolt of the Duke of Spoleto. Liutprand at once attacked the Exarchate (739). Ravenna fell to Duke Hildebrand and Duke Peredeo. Eutychius fled to the lagoons and summoned the Venetians, by their allegiance to the Emperor, to lend aid in restoring him. They obeyed. The Venetian fleet replaced the exarch in his capital (741).

In the meantime the doge, whose loyalty to Byzantium had been rewarded with the title of *Hypatos* or Consul, had died (737). Both he and his two predecessors were nobles of Heraclea, belonging to the aristocratic or Byzantine party, and ruling in Heraclea. Local jealousy between the rival townships combined with the hostility of the revolutionary party, whose policy was anti-Byzantine and ranged with the Pope for the freedom of Italy from Byzantine suzerainty, led, as the chronicles tell us, to an attack by Jesolo upon Heraclea, and in the fighting the doge fell. Whether the story be strictly true or not, the episode is of importance as shewing us the formation of two distinct parties inside the lagoons, and in its bearing upon the election of the next doge which took place not in Heraclea but at Malamocco, an important step towards the final concentration at Rialto. The reigns of the first three doges had yielded results not altogether satisfactory, and on the death of Ursus, the imperial authorities, or, according to the Venetian tradition, the population of the lagoons, resolved to substitute for the dogeship the yearly office of Magister Militum. The new magistracy was of short duration (737–741), and was marked by the continued violence of party strife. The last Magister Militum, Fabriacus, was blinded and, in 742, the community returned to the system of ducal government, electing

Deusdedit, son of the late Doge Ursus, to that office. But the seat of government was removed from Heraclea—not only the scene of violent faction-fights, but also accessible from the mainland and therefore exposed to the influence of the mainland rulers—to Malamocco, a township on the *lido* which divides the lagoon from the open sea. The choice of Malamocco was a compromise, preluding the final compromise at Rialto, and was determined by the anti-Byzantine party; but the new doge was still an Heracleote and member of the Byzantine party, though no longer ruling in Heraclea.

During the reign of Deusdedit the pressure of external events was never relaxed; the danger that the lagoons might be absorbed by the lords of the mainland was ever present. The remains of Greek lordship in North Italy had all but disappeared; the lagoons were almost all that survived. In 751 Aistulf, the Lombard king, finally captured Ravenna, and so imminent seemed the threat from the south-west that the doge undertook the building of a strong fort at Brondolo to protect his frontiers. Aistulf, however, did not prove hostile; he was at the moment engaged with his scheme for reducing the Papacy to the position of a "Lombard bishopric," and could afford to wait as far as the lagoons were concerned. He therefore willingly renewed the treaty made with Liutprand. But a greater power than that of the Lombards was about to appear on the scene, a power destined to act with decisive effect on the development of Venice. The Pope, alarmed at the threatening attitude of the Lombard sovereign, and unable to claim aid from the weak, distant, and also iconoclastically heretical Emperor, turned to the Franks for protection. Pope Stephen II in 754 made a personal appeal to Pepin, son of Charles Martel. That same year the Franks entered Italy by the Fenestrelle pass. They immediately proved their superiority over the Lombards. Aistulf was defeated and only saved a remnant of his territory through Papal mediation (756). His son Desiderius saw the destruction of the Lombard Kingdom, and by 774 Pavia was in the hands of the Franks.

The Venetians, meanwhile, had been profiting by the disturbed state of the mainland; the decline of Ravenna, in particular, allowed them to extend their trade, which was now beginning to assume its prominent characteristic of a carrying-trade between East and West. We hear of Venetian merchants in Constantinople sending valuable political information to the Papal authorities in Ravenna; and possibly about this period Torcello began to assume its position of ἐμπόριον μέγα, the "great emporium," as Constantine Porphyrogenitus styles it. But prosperity did not allay the internal jealousies of the lagoon-townships. Jesolo still nursed her ancient hatred of Heraclea. The Jesolans, headed by Egilius Gaulus, attacked the Heracleote noble Deusdedit, the Doge. They blinded and deposed him, and their leader seized the ducal chair, only to be blinded and banished, in his turn, within the year (755). The point of the struggle for supremacy between the various townships is emphasised by the fact that the next doge, Dominicus Monegarius, was not an Heracleote but a native of Malamocco, the seat of the government. Either the Venetian population or the imperial authorities seem to have thought that these perpetual revolutions were due to the fact that the doges enjoyed too free a hand. The ducal independence of action was therefore curtailed by the appointment of two tribunes to act in concert with the doge. The effort to shake himself free of these trammels cost Monegarius his throne. He was deposed and blinded and, perhaps by a reaction of party feeling, an Heracleote, Mauritius, was elected in 764. The election of Mauritius has, however, been taken as a proof and a result of a movement which had undoubtedly been going on for some time. The internecine quarrels of Heraclea and Jesolo, ending in the removal of the capital to Malamocco, had seriously injured both townships; a general exodus took place from both into the new capital, where the Heracleotes were soon in sufficient numbers to secure the election of one of themselves to the ducal chair. However that may be, the fact remains that both Heraclea and Jesolo ceased to be of great importance among the lagoon-townships, and their territory was assigned to the fisc, forming the origin of what afterwards became the domain-lands of the Ducatus.

The reign of Mauritius is marked by two points of importance: first, the beginning of the custom of appointing a doge-consort, naturally, as the appointment lay with the doge, a member of his own family, thereby paving the way for the establishment of the dynastic principle which was to play so large a part in the early history of Venice; secondly, the founding of the bishopric of Olivolo. The influx of Heracleotes and Jesolans, which we have already recorded, proved to be so abundant that the immigrants overflowed to Rialto, and so great were their numbers that they soon demanded and obtained a see of their own (774), with its cathedral on the island of Olivolo, one of the north-eastern islets of the Realtine group, afterwards known, and known to this day, as Castello. The foundation of the see of Olivolo may be taken as the first step in the formation of the city of Venice.

Difficult times were at hand for the lagoon-community. Pepin, son of Charles Martel, in the course of his campaign against the Lombards had captured Ravenna and the Pentapolis. These he presented to his ally the Pope. Pepin's son, Charles the Great, after the final destruction of the Lombard kingdom, confirmed his father's donation. In considering his new kingdom he must have observed that Maritime-Venice and the lagoon-townships alone in North Italy still owned allegiance to Byzantium. He probably resolved to bring them within the bounds of his new territory, all the more so that, in the almost inevitable clash with the Greek Empire, Venice alone seemed able to furnish a fleet and a sea-base. In any case Charles ordered the expulsion of Venetian traders from the Pentapolis (784) and took Istria (787), thus enclosing the lagoons in an iron circle. These actions opened the eyes of the lagoon-population to the approaching crisis.

The situation was complicated by the attitude of the Patriarchs of Grado, who, as good Churchmen, favoured the Pope's allies, the Franks. Thus two parties were clearly defined inside the lagoons: the party of the doges, the Byzantine party which clung to its allegiance to the Empire as its safeguard against the danger of being absorbed by the Franks; and the party of the Patriarchs, the party of the Church, the Francophil party which seemed willing to carry the whole community over to Charles, rather than risk the loss of commerce on the mainland which would be entailed by a rupture with the Franks. How far there was a third party, a Venetian party, determined to save the State from the Franks while preserving its *de facto* independence of Byzantium, is not clear. Inside the lagoon the crisis was brought to an issue and the party positions defined over the newly-created see of Olivolo. The Doge John, son of Mauritius, who had first been doge-consort to his father (778) and then reigning doge (787), nominated to the see a young Greek, named Christopher, only sixteen years old. The Patriarch of Grado refused to consecrate him (798). A little later it was known that the Patriarch was urging Charles' son, Pepin of Italy, to form a navy in Ravenna for the subjugation of the lagoons. The doge sent his son, Mauritius the younger, to attack Grado, and the Patriarch was flung from the highest tower of his palace and killed (802).

But this high-handed act made no difference in the policy of the patriarchal see. The murdered John was succeeded by his nephew Fortunatus, a restless, capable, enterprising man, of Francophil leanings even more pronounced than those of his uncle. Fortunatus received the pallium in 803 and at once set to work to develop the Frankish party. Along with others of the faction, Obelerius and Felix the Tribune, he formed a plot against the doge. It was discovered, and the conspirators fled to Treviso, whence Fortunatus proceeded alone to the court of Charles at Seltz. He brought the Emperor many and costly presents, and found him in a mood to listen to his plans for the expulsion of the Byzantine doges and their party, as the Frankish embassy to the court at Constantinople (803), commissioned to secure recognition of Charles' new imperial title, had just been haughtily repulsed.

Meanwhile, encouraged no doubt by news from Fortunatus, the Francophil conspirators in Treviso elected Obelerius as doge (804). He made a dash for the lagoons, entered his native town of Malamocco amid popular acclaim, and the Doges John and Mauritius were forced to fly along with their creature Christopher, Bishop of Olivolo.

This revolution of 804 meant the complete triumph of the Francophil party. How complete that triumph was is proved by the fact that the Doge Obelerius and the Doge-consort, his brother Beatus, paid a visit to the court of Charles at Thionville (Theodonis Villa) about Christmas 805, and early in the next year the Emperor made an *ordinatio* or disposition for the government of the doges and populace of Venice as well as for Dalmatia. Venice, Istria, and Dalmatia were declared to be parts of Pepin's kingdom of Italy.

This deliberate challenge to Nicephorus and the Eastern Empire was at once taken up. In 807 the patrician Nicetas appeared in the Adriatic with the imperial fleet. Charles and Pepin were possessed of no sea-power capable of offering resistance, and Nicetas met with none. If Charles had counted on the Venetians for support he was deceived. Dalmatia returned to its allegiance, as did the doges. Obelerius was rewarded with the title of Spatharius, but Beatus was sent to Constantinople as a hostage for Venetian loyalty. Nicetas made a truce with Pepin and withdrew his fleet in the autumn of 807. The truce came to an end in the autumn of 808, and the patrician Paul appeared with the Greek fleet in the Adriatic. After wintering in Venetian waters, he attacked Comacchio and was repulsed. The Frankish party in the lagoons was strong enough to render his position insecure. He withdrew his fleet down the Adriatic (809), leaving Venice to the wrath of Pepin, who was resolved to make good his claims to the lagoons and to punish the doges for their perfidy in violating the *ordinatio* of Thionville. In the autumn of 809 the attack was delivered from north and south, by land and by sea. The lagoon-dwellers offered a vigorous resistance, and the king's progress was slow. What remained of Heraclea fell; so did Brondolo, Chioggia, Pelestrina, Albiola, and even the capital Malamocco; both doges were taken prisoners; but the lagoons were not conquered. The population of Malamocco withdrew to the central group of islands, called Rialto, and thence defied the conqueror. In vain he attempted to reach and capture the core of the lagoons; the intricate channels through the mud banks baffled him; he was eventually forced to withdraw in 810; and he died in July of the same year.

Recent historians, relying on the testimony of Einhard, claim that this event was a Venetian defeat, a Frankish victory. But Einhard, though a contemporary, was far away from the scene of action, and was moreover in the service of the Carolingians. Though there can be no doubt that Pepin captured the *lidi* up to Malamocco, the capital, and made the doges prisoners, compelling them to consent to a yearly tribute, yet the fact remains that he did not conquer Rialto, the heart of the lagoons, and that the lagoon-population compelled him to abandon his enterprise and to retire. It is not surprising that Constantine Porphyrogenitus in the next century, and the Venetians ever after, should have looked upon the repulse of Pepin as the cardinal point in their early history and have eventually surrounded it with a mass of patriotic legend.

Pepin's attack on the lagoons, and the large measure of success which crowned it, alarmed Constantinople; and in 810 Arsafius, the Spatharius, was sent to negotiate with the king, but finding him dead the envoy proceeded direct to Charles at Aix-la-Chapelle. In the spring of 811 Arsafius left Aix on his return to Constantinople, bearing Charles' terms, which were that he would surrender Venice, Istria, Liburnia, and Dalmatia in return for recognition of his imperial title. It may be observed that, even if Charles considered that Pepin had conquered Venice, Dalmatia certainly was in no sense his, as Pepin's fleet had immediately retired before the fleet of Paul, the Praetor of Cephalonia. More probably Charles based his claim to Venice on the *ordinatio* of Thionville. Arsafius on his way through Venice nominated an Heracleote noble, Agnellus Particiacus, to the vacant dogeship. The Doges Obelerius and Beatus were both in the custody of Arsafius, the former to be consigned, as Charles had ordained, to his lawful sovereign (*ad dominum*), the Emperor Nicephorus, a phrase which can hardly be reconciled with the claim that Venice and the Venetians were Frankish territory and people. By the summer of 812 the treaty of Aix-la-Chapelle was signed, and Venice returned to her ancient position as vassal of the Eastern Empire. The result of the whole episode, as far as Venice was concerned, was that internally a concentration of all the lagoon-townships took place at Rialto, which now became the capital. The rivalries and jealousies between the lagoon-centres came to an end. Further, the new city emerged from Pepin's attack Byzantine in sympathies, and with an Heracleote Byzantine noble as doge. And, with the failure of the Francophil policy of the Patriarch Fortunatus, the power of the Church as an independent political element in Venice began to decline, and Grado slowly waned in power and influence. Externally Venice remained Eastern not Western, aloof from the rest of Italy, looking eastward for the most part, a fact of the highest importance in determining the subsequent character and career of the race.

We are now entering on a new period of Venetian history which goes down to the reign of Peter II Orseolo (991–1009). It is possible now to talk of Venice as a city-state. The characteristic notes of the period are: firstly, the development of the dukedom with its growing dynastic tendencies; the accumulation in single houses of dignities and wealth, thanks to private trading by the doges under special privileges; and the revolt of the Venetian people against these dynastic tendencies. Secondly, we note the relations of the state with the Western Empire, the effort to maintain its independence and to extend its commerce, which are revealed in the series of *pacta* and *praecepta*. And thirdly, the relations of the state with the East; the gradual loosening of the formal bonds which bound it as a vassal to the Eastern Empire, and the extension of its trading privileges in the Levant. For many years to come (down to 979 at least) the formal dependence on the Eastern Empire was fully recognised by the use of the imperial date in public documents, by public prayers for the Emperor, and by the obligations of transport, affirmed and acknowledged in the various imperial bulls; but in fact, owing to the growing sea-power of the Venetians, the relations gradually became rather those of allies. The final note of the period is the growth and the embellishment of the new capital.

The young state soon began to display those commercial instincts which were destined to mark its whole career. Either by a separate treaty—a theory strenuously combated by recent historians—or at least by a special clause in the Treaty of Aix, Charles renewed the privileges, endorsed the tribute, and confirmed the frontiers established by the treaty with King Liutprand. This treaty formed the charter of Venetian trading rights on the mainland, and was frequently rehearsed and re-confirmed during the ninth and tenth centuries.

The valley of the Po formed the natural trade-route from the head of the Adriatic to Lombardy, France, and West Germany; but for the command of this route the lagoon-city of Comacchio was an active competitor, lying as it did near the mouth of that river. At Pavia, the capital of the Italian kingdom, two great trade-routes converged, the Po-valley route, and the route from Rome across the Apennines. Already in the days of Charles, the monk of St Gall reports, Venetian merchants frequented the markets of Pavia, bringing with them "from over seas all the wealth of the orient," chiefly, it seems, silks, spices, golden pheasant and peacock feathers. The life of St Gerald of Aurillac shews us how a Venetian merchant at Pavia acted as expert-adviser on the current prices of silk webs in the markets of Constantinople. The trade of Comacchio was chiefly confined to salt, but we shall presently see how Venice went to war with her rivals in order to secure a monopoly of this commodity.

As regards relations with the East we naturally find no treaties during the ninth century. The formal position of vassal and suzerain was fully recognised; the Emperors, through their officers and bulls, sent their orders, as, for example, those forbidding the Venetians to trade with enemies of the Empire in arms and timber; these orders were obeyed as long as the interests of Venice and of the East were identical. We have a proof that Venetians were already trading far afield in the Levant, for in 829 the body of St Mark was brought from Alexandria to Venice by Venetian merchants on board their own ship; and by 840, on the request of the Emperor Theophilus, Venice was able to send sixty ships to sea. Indeed we find that from the reign of Michael II (820–829) onwards the Emperors made frequent calls on the naval power of Venice. The claim was, no doubt, a right (see the chrysobull of 991), but it gradually assumed the aspect of an appeal to an ally, until it definitely took that form in the dogeship of Peter II Orseolo.

The city itself, during the reigns of the first three doges of the house of Particiacus, shewed a rapid extension in buildings. Agnellus began the first ducal palace, a wooden structure; his son Justinian founded the first church of St Mark, a small basilica, with apse and crypt, occupying the site of the present Capello Zen. The basilica was built to receive the body of St Mark, the translation of whose remains from Alexandria to Venice is an essential point in the ecclesiastical history of the City; for by the possession of the Saint's body the Venetians, in a manner, asserted their superiority to Aquileia and also to Grado, a superiority which was finally confirmed in 1445 by the removal of the patriarchal see of Grado to Venice. By his will (June 829) the Doge Justinian left instructions that the stones of the house of a certain Theophylact of Torcello were to be used in the construction of the Church. During this same period the famous monastery of Sant' Ilario on the Brenta, the convent of San Zaccaria near the ducal palace, and the cathedral church of San Pietro at Olivolo, came into being and received large endowments from members of the ducal family.

As to the constitution of the new state we have little information; we know that Agnellus had two tribunes appointed as assessors in the interests of the Greek Empire, but we hear nothing of their action. The doge seems to have had the sole disposal of the treasury and to have been, for administrative purposes, quite uncontrolled. The tribunes still existed in the various lagoon-townships, but after the concentration at Rialto they possessed but restricted powers. The national assembly seems to have been of vital significance only on the occasions when it was convened. Its voice was heard in the election of the doge, and the doges seem to have called it to confirm their public acts; for example, in May 819, the Doges Agnellus and Justinian Particiacus, who in a possibly spurious passage are styled *per divinam gratiam duces*, declare that, in a donation to the Abbot of San Servolo, they are acting in concert *cum universis Venecie populis habitantibus*.

The dynastic tendency in the dukedom was clearly marked under the first three doges of the house of Particiacus. We find the system of appointing a doge-consort from the reigning family in full force, while the important see of Olivolo-Castello was filled for the long period of thirty-two years (822–854) by Ursus, son of John. Resentment at this tendency to concentrate the supreme power in a single house took definite shape in two conspiracies against the Doge John Particiacus; the first, in 835, headed by the Tribune Carosus, failed after a brief success; the second, under the leadership of the noble family of the Mastalici, deposed the doge (836) and compelled him to retire to a monastery near Grado. The choice of the Venetians then fell upon Peter Tradonicus, a man of noble blood, strong and vigorous, but illiterate—he could not even sign his name. His long reign of twenty-eight years (836–864) was signalised by unsuccessful sea-campaigns against the Slav pirates of the Dalmatian coast, who had already begun to harass the rich and growing trade of Venice in the Adriatic, and against the Saracens in the south of Italy. At the request, or order, of the Emperor Theophilus, conveyed by the patrician Theodosius, the doge fitted out sixty ships for the unlucky expedition to Taranto (840). Unfortunate as were these earliest naval enterprises of the growing State of Venice, they were fruitful in calling out the energy and resolution of the people and in leading to a revolution in Venetian ship-building. It was under Tradonicus that the first great ships[1] were built in Venetian docks, and the type established which was to serve both for trade and war.

A second important point in the reign of Tradonicus, a point which bears upon Venetian relations with the West, was the conclusion of the *pactum*, or treaty, with the Emperor Lothar in 840, the very year in which the Emperor of the East had summoned the Venetians to his aid against the Saracens. This remarkable document, the earliest extant monument of Venetian diplomacy, was prepared during preliminary negotiations in Ravenna, but was signed on 22 February 840 at Pavia. It undoubtedly referred to and recited the terms of the special Venetian clauses in the Treaty of Aix (812), of the *ordinatio* of Thionville (806), and of King Liutprand's treaty of 713. It was to last for five years, and as a matter of fact we find it being renewed every five years down to the Treaty of Mülhausen (19 July 992). It stipulated for the payment of fifty librae of Venetian coinage (*parve*), equal to twenty-five librae of the Pavese coinage, as an annual tribute from Venice, due in March each year. But the payment of this tribute is not to be taken as in any sense a token of vassalage; it was merely a return for the privileges conceded by the *pactum*; peace and good friendship are to exist between Venice and various neighbouring districts inside the kingdom of Italy; these districts are specified and include Istria, Friuli, the Trevisan Marches, Vicenza, Monselice, Ravenna, and the ports on the Adriatic down to Fermo. Neither party is to injure the other. Venetian fugitives inside the kingdom are to be extradited; envoys and couriers are to be protected. The confines of Venetian territory as defined in the treaty with Liutprand are recognised. The Venetians may trade freely in the kingdom, except for the customary dues of water and land transit, and Italian subjects are to enjoy a like privilege by sea. The subjects of the Empire are to lend no aid to enemies of Venice, while Venice is to lend her aid by sea against all Slav freebooters. The importance of the document lies in the fact that it is an independent contract between the Doge of Venice and the rulers of the mainland, and that it confirms and extends existing trading privileges, which were subsequently still further enlarged. At Thionville, by a *praeceptum* dated 1 September 841, the Emperor formally recognised Venetian possessions inside the Empire.

The Doge Tradonicus did not escape the dynastic ambitions which were common to all the earlier holders of the ducal throne. He sur-

[1] Biremes with a crew of 150 men. The proper name for this vessel was Chelandia (Χελάνδια). Johannes Diaconus (ed. Monticolo, *Chron. Venet. Ant.* in Fonti, p. 115) calls it Zalandria. Thietmar (*Chronicon*, SGUS, p. 62) says: "salandria...est...nauis mirae longitudinis et alacritatis." See also *infra*, Chapter XXIII, p. 743.

rounded himself with a body-guard of foreign soldiers, Croats, devoted to his service. This, and his attempt to raise his relative, Dominicus, to the bishopric of Olivolo-Castello, gave the Particiaci faction, which was still strong, the desired opportunity. The doge was murdered on his way from the palace to San Zaccaria (13 September 864).

The murder of Tradonicus cannot be considered as a popular demonstration against the dynastic principle; it was carried out by a group of nobles instigated by the Patriarch of Grado who was a Particiacus, and in the interest of that family. Tradonicus was succeeded by Ursus Particiacus and subsequently by three other members of his house before the Particiaci gave way to the powerful family of the Candiani.

With the Western Empire Ursus maintained friendly relations and on 11 January 880 the *pactum* of Lothar was renewed with Charles the Fat in Ravenna. The modifications in the terms prove the extent to which Venice was growing in power and importance. It is no longer the case of certain specified places inside the kingdom entering on a treaty with Venice, but the Emperor himself treats on behalf of his whole kingdom (*etiam tocius regni nostri*). The slave trade is again to be condemned by a decree signed by doge and patriarch, and, most important of all, the doge's personal merchandise, his private trading stock, was to go free of customs dues. Ursus was further successful in a sharp encounter with the Patriarch of Grado, the upshot of which was to demonstrate and establish the supremacy of State over Church in Venice. The doge insisted on raising to the see of Torcello a eunuch named Dominicus. The Patriarch Peter Marturius refused to consecrate him as being canonically unfit, but had to fly before the doge's wrath. He appealed to the Pope, who summoned Dominicus and the Bishops Peter of Jesolo and Felix of Malamocco to Rome; in obedience to the doge they did not respond. The Pope convened a council in Ravenna (22 July 877), but the Venetian bishops did not appear till it was closing. Finally the Patriarch of Grado came to terms with the doge; he permitted Dominicus to reside at Torcello and to enjoy the revenues of the see, but the bishop was only consecrated by Marturius' successor. The whole episode, however, was a triumph for the doge and the secular authority.

Ursus was succeeded by his son John (881–887), in whose reign Venice embarked on her first aggressive commercial war. Comacchio, lying in its lagoons, near the mouth of the Po, was a serious commercial rival, both on account of its commanding position on the great trade-route and because of its salt industry which brought it into contact with the whole of North Italy. John made an effort to secure by diplomacy the lordship of Comacchio. He sent his brother Badoero to Rome to beg the Pope to grant him investiture. But on his way Badoero was wounded and captured by Marinus, Count of Comacchio, who was alive to the danger. Badoero returned to Venice and there died of his wounds. The doge and the whole population seized the opportunity to sack Comacchio and to establish Venetian officials in the town. Charles III, no more than the Pope, seems to have taken notice of this high-handed attack, and at Mantua (10 May 883) he confirmed by a *praeceptum* the Ravenna *pactum* of 880 with several important additions: the private goods of the doge and his heirs were exempt from the ordinary dues of *teloneum* and *ripaticum* (land and water transit) which other Venetians had to pay; conspiracy against the life of any prince, and therefore of the doge, on the part of any subject of the Empire was a crime; the doge was to enjoy full judicial powers over Venetian subjects in the Empire.

John and his brother and doge-consort resigned their offices in 887, and the choice fell upon Peter Candianus, member of a family destined to play a prominent part in the ensuing years of Venetian history. Peter's brief reign of a few months (April to September 887) at once indicated the lines along which the other doges of his house would move. He immediately undertook an expedition against the Slav pirates of the Dalmatian coasts, a proof that the security of the sea route down the Adriatic was becoming an imperative necessity for the growing state of Venice. The expedition was a failure. The doge fell, and was buried in the church of Santa Eufemia at Grado. The next two reigns, those of Peter Tribunus (888–911) and Ursus (Paureta) Particiacus (911–932), proved to be a long period of quiet and growth for Venice, except for the terror of the Hungarian raid in 900. Venice was threatened by the Magyar hordes who came down the Piave in their coracles of osier and hides and devastated the territories of Heraclea and Jesolo. The alarm at their coming led to the fortification of the city by the construction of a great wall along the line of the present Riva degli Schiavoni, from Castello to St Mark's, which was surrounded, and thence as far as Santa Maria Zobenigo, whence a strong chain was stretched across the mouth of the grand canal to San Gregorio. The doge is said to have defeated the Magyars at Albiola. Whether that be so or not, the fact remains that they never occupied the city of Venice.

The distracted state of the Western Empire, torn in pieces between competing princes, gave Venice an opportunity for renewing and enlarging her treaty rights. The series of *pacta* and *praecepta* is continued under the reigns of Berengar, Guy, Rodolph, and Hugh. In the Berengar *pactum* (7 May 888), signed at Olona, the sea-power of Venice is recognised, and she is entrusted with the policing of the Adriatic for the suppression of the Dalmatian pirates; in return, the duty on goods bartered in the kingdom of Italy was fixed at two and a half per cent., instead of being arbitrary as heretofore. The *praeceptum* of Rodolph (29 February 924), signed at Pavia, recognised in Venice "the ancient right" to coin money for circulation in the kingdom (*secundum quod eorum provinciae duces a priscis temporibus consueto more habuerunt*). That Venice had coined money for home circulation at least as early as the middle of the ninth century is proved by the *pactum* of Lothar (840), in which the annual tribute is made payable in Venetian librae (*libras suorum denariorum quinquaginta*). The exemption of ducal goods from payment of dues was extended from the doge personally to his agents (*proprii negociatores*) to the great enrichment of the family estate, as we shall presently see in the case of Peter IV Candianus who employed it to support a private army.

We now come to the period of the dynastic supremacy of the Candiani (932–976). With the brief exception of three years (939–942) when the last of the Particiaci, Peter Badoero, occupied the throne, Peter II, Peter III, and Peter IV, of the Candiani were supreme. They were a fighting race, and the question of Venetian relations with Istria and Dalmatia, and her position in the Adriatic, gave them full employment. We have seen how the first doge of their house, Peter I, had already fallen in battle with the Slavs. Marquess Gunter (Wintker) of Istria, resenting the steady growth of Venetian commercial importance in the peninsula, had resorted to the confiscation of ducal and episcopal property in Istria and had forbidden his subjects to pay their just debts to Venetian merchants. Peter II, instead of resorting to the costly method of arms, which would have implied an attack on a province of the Italian kingdom with risks to Venetian commerce in Italy, reduced Marquess Gunter to sign a humiliating treaty of peace (12 March 933) by the simple process of boycotting Istria: a striking demonstration of the commanding position of Venice as an emporium. By this treaty, which was renewed in 977 and enlarged in 1074, Venice established her supremacy in Istria and took her first step down the Adriatic and towards her complete dominion in that sea.

The next Candiani Doge, Peter III (942–959), applied the system of boycott with equal success against Lupus, Patriarch of Aquileia, who had attacked Grado, and compelled him to sign a treaty (13 March 944), by which he confirmed the clauses of the treaty with his predecessor Walpert, including the exemption of the doge from all customs dues in his territory.

Peter III died and was succeeded by his son Peter IV (959–976), the most remarkable of the Candiani doges. In him the intention of converting the dukedom into an hereditary monarchy is at once made clear. One of his earliest steps was to employ the family funds, accumulated through the personal private trading of the doges, for the creation of a small standing army in his own pay. But the conditions in both Eastern and Western Empires had undergone a remarkable change. In the West the strong dynasty of the Saxon Ottos had raised the imperial prestige once more, while in the East the Emperor Tzimisces was about to revive the ancient supremacy of Byzantium. It seemed likely that the East and West would once again clash and that, as in 800–810, Venice would find her existence threatened by the conflict between the two great powers. Her position, however, was far stronger now than then. Her wealth was great, her importance as an emporium of necessities established, her sea-power recognised and respected. It was clearly the keystone of Venetian foreign policy to stand well with both East and West, and Peter IV applied himself to the task.

On the fall of Berengar II (961) and the coronation of Otto I, the doge hastened to secure the confirmation of the Venetian treaties. By the terms of the *pactum* signed in Rome on 2 December 967, there seems to have been a certain shrinkage in the privileges which Venice and her doges had gradually acquired during the period of disturbance in the kingdom of Italy. The judicial rights of the doge over all Venetians resident in the kingdom were not confirmed, nor was the exemption of ducal goods from taxation. On the other hand the treaty was now declared to run not for five years only but for all time (*per cuncta annorum curricula*), though in fact it required to be renewed on the accession of each new sovereign. The yearly tribute still remained at its normal fifty librae "*nostrae monetae*," as fixed by the Treaty of Aix-la-Chapelle (812), and for the first time we hear of *unum pallium*, though it is probable that this obligation figured in earlier *pacta*. In any case the *pallium* and the tribute cannot in any sense be taken as an indication of vassalage; the *pallium* here referred to was a web of silk, a rich specimen of Venetian wares. The terms of this *pactum* were renewed in 983, and an attempt has been made to prove that from that date down to 1024 Venice acknowledged the suzerainty of the Western Empire. But the evidence seems to shew that her formal allegiance to the Eastern Empire was still recognised.

The imperative orders of the Emperor Tzimisces, forbidding, under penalty of confiscation and death, the lucrative traffic of Venice with the Saracens, may have helped to throw Peter IV more and more into the arms of the Emperor Otto, who was only too ready to secure Venetian sea-aid in the clash with the Eastern Empire which seemed inevitable if he were to carry out his policy of making all Italy part of his domains. In any case Peter divorced his wife Giovanna and married Gualdrada, daughter of Hubert, Marquess of Tuscany, granddaughter of King Hugh of Provence and niece of Adelaide, wife of Otto I. She brought with her a large dower in money and lands in the Trevisan Marches, in Friuli, and in the territory of Adria; and her husband the doge now began to assume regal state. He increased his private army and undertook military expeditions on the mainland on the plea of protecting his wife's possessions. Feeling rose high in Venice against the obviously monarchical tendencies of the doge. In a general tumult Peter was besieged in the palace; his guards offered resistance; the palace was fired, the doge slain. The conflagration was not stopped till it had destroyed the palace, part of St Mark's, and three hundred houses as far as Santa Maria Zobenigo (11 August 976). The act seems to have been the violent protest of the Venetian people against the attempt to convert the dukedom into a monarchy.

The murder of Peter Candianus placed Venice in a difficult position towards the Emperor Otto II. His hold on the lagoons and their sea-power was shaken; his cousin Gualdrada, wife of the late doge, claimed his defence of her rights. The task of meeting the dangerous situation fell chiefly upon the Orseoli, the third, and most distinguished, of the dynastic ducal families which governed Venice from 810 to 1009.

The day after the murder of Candianus the choice of the electors fell on Peter Orseolo, the first of the new dynasty, a man of saintly character, but, like all his race, possessing higher qualities of statesmanship than we have met with hitherto in his predecessors in the ducal chair. His first care was to repair the damage wrought by the fire. He began the building of a new palace and church. He renewed the treaty with Istria, the original of which had been burned along with the rest of the public documents. But his great service to the state lay in this, that he met and settled, to the nominal satisfaction of Otto II, the claims of the widowed dogaressa Gualdrada. Under his guidance the general assembly agreed to restore to her her *morganaticum* (400 pounds) and also the portion of the late doge's property which fell by right to her son, who had shared the fate of his father. On these terms Gualdrada signed a quittance of all claims against the State of Venice.

The danger was past for the moment. But the doge, obeying his pious instincts, resolved to retire from the world. On the night of 1 September 978 he secretly left Venice and fled to the monastery of Cusa in Aquitaine. Possibly with a view to appeasing Otto further, a member of the house of Candiani, Vitalis, brother of the murdered Peter, was elected, but reigned little more than a year (September 978–November 979). He was succeeded by Tribunus Menius (Memmo) (979–991), during whose reign the question between Otto II and the Venetian State was brought to a crisis.

The murder of Peter Candianus had not only exposed Venice to the wrath of Otto II; it had also created inside the state two factions, the Caloprini who espoused the policy of the Candiani and leaned towards the Western Empire, and the Morosini whose sympathies were with the Orseoli and the Byzantine allegiance as a means of saving the state from absorption by the West. By 980 the Western Emperor was in Italy. The great Emperor of the East, John Tzimisces, had died in 976. The south of Italy, the theme of Longobardia, seemed likely to fall a prey to the Saracens. Otto resolved to seize the opportunity to render Southern Italy a part of his Empire. Towards this object the possession of Venice and her fleet seemed of prime importance, but since the murder of Candianus Otto's party was no longer in the ascendant, especially after the failure of the Caloprini plot to murder all the Morosini. Without waiting to secure Venetian aid, the Emperor pushed south. His expedition failed, and in

983 he was back again in Verona, and there the ambassadors of Venice came to seek renewal of their treaties. By the terms of the new treaty the burdensome dues for river traffic (*ripatica*) were removed, to the great advantage of Venice, but the exemption of ducal goods from customs and the ducal judicial rights over Venetians in the kingdom were not restored. A special clause permitted the subjects of the Empire, who after the murder of Peter Candianus had been forbidden to trade with Venice, to frequent Venetian ports once more (*per mare ad vos*), a phrase which the Venetians subsequently amplified into *per mare ad vos et non amplius*, thereby attempting to concentrate all Italian traffic in the Adriatic at Venice and implicitly establishing a claim on those waters. The favourable conditions of this treaty were probably intended to secure Venetian assistance for the Emperor's future schemes in South Italy. But at this juncture Stefano Caloprini, leader of the Venetian faction, appeared at Verona and offered the Emperor a more speedy method for attaining his ends. He promised that he and his party would assist in reducing Venice if the Emperor would invest him with the dukedom and grant him a yearly pension. The Emperor agreed. The method adopted was a rigid blockade of the lagoons from the mainland. Venice was only saved from starvation and surrender by the friendly offices of the Saracen fleet; but the situation was more serious than it had been even at the time of Pepin's attack. The mainland, under the Bishops of Treviso, Ceneda, and Belluno, was entirely against the sea-city. Its subjects of Cavarzere and Loreo revolted. But on 7 December 983 the Emperor died, and the whole Caloprini scheme fell to pieces. Apart from the grave menace to Venetian independence, the significance of the episode lies in the fact that it illustrates the growing importance of Venetian sea-power.

Tribunus Menius had seen his country safely through the external crisis, but was powerless to repress the bloody faction-fights between the Caloprini and the Morosini. He was deposed and compelled to retire to the monastery of San Zaccaria. The greatest doge that Venice had as yet seen, Peter Orseolo II, succeeded to the throne (991–1009). His chaplain, friend, and biographer, John the Deacon, pictures him as a man of culture, refinement, even imagination, coupled with the statesman's instincts, a strong will, and military energy. His first step was to allay all internal tumults. In the interests of the country he exacted an oath and the signature of ninety-one nobles to a pledge that they would not stir tumult nor draw weapon inside the ducal palace under a penalty of twenty pounds of fine gold or, in default of payment, loss of life (February 997). His next care was to establish the Orseoli family in a commanding position in the State. He chose his son John as doge-consort, and on John's death his third son Otto; his second son Orso was Bishop of Torcello, and subsequently Patriarch of Grado.

Peter's foreign policy was crowned with complete success. In 992 he concluded the first Venetian treaty with the East—the chrysobull of Basil II (March, *indictione quinta*). By the terms of the deed, which was rather a declaration of ancient rights than a bestowal of new ones (*quod ab antiquo fuit consuetudo*), Venetian ships, provided they bore Venetian not Amalfitan or other cargoes, were to pay a fixed sum of two soldi for each ship entering and fifteen soldi for each ship clearing a Greek port, irrespective of the ship's burden and cargo; no ship might be detained by the Greek authorities longer than three days against its will; Venetians were placed under the jurisdiction of the *Λογοθέτης τῶν οἰκειακῶν*, a high official in whose court procedure was more rapid than in the lower courts. In return, Venice was pledged to furnish transport and warships for the defence of the theme of Longobardia, that is of Southern Italy. The chrysobull of 992 is of importance in the commercial history of Venice: it gave Venetians trading in the East valuable advantages over their rivals, Amalfitans, Jews, and others, while the uniform tax on ships irrespective of burden and cargo soon induced the Venetians to increase the size of their build. The consequences will be seen presently in the development of Venetian trade on the mainland of Italy.

In the same year, 992, Peter renewed the treaties with the Western Empire by the *pactum* (*praeceptum*) of Mülhausen. Here again Venetian diplomacy was entirely successful. Venetian rights and privileges were restored to the position they occupied in 961, at the fall of Berengar and before the breach with the Saxon Emperors; the territories of Cavarzere and Loreo, which had seceded to the Emperor at the time of Otto's blockade, were now returned to Venice; and the encroaching Bishops of Treviso and Belluno were ordered to evacuate the lands they had seized in the diocese of Heraclea, though it was not until the doge had applied the blockade that the stubborn John of Belluno made submission to Otto's orders after the *placitum* of Staffolo (998).

The growing importance of Venetian commerce, chiefly in oriental goods, is proved by Peter's request that Otto would allow him to open three markets (*in tribus locis sue ditioni subditis*) in the Italian kingdom, at San Michele del Quarto, on the Sile, and on the Piave, a request which was granted (Ravenna, 1 May 996) and marked a stepping-stone in the history of Venetian western trade.

The new palace, begun under the first Orseolo, was now approaching completion; Venice as a city was rapidly expanding under the cultured guidance of the second Orseolo. Peter was anxious to shew the glories of his capital to his friend the Emperor; Otto was nothing loth to take a romantic journey to the city of the lagoons. The invitation was conveyed through John the Deacon to the Emperor at Como in June 1000. It was agreed that a secret visit should be paid on the Emperor's return journey from Rome. In March 1001 Otto was at Ravenna. Announcing that he was going into retreat in the abbey of Pomposa, he left Ravenna. At Pomposa he found John the Deacon with a boat, and the same evening he set out for Venice. After travelling all night he reached the island of San Servolo the following day about sunset. The doge met him; they embraced, and, waiting till it was quite dark, they rowed into Venice, and the Emperor was lodged in San Zaccaria. Otto granted his every wish to the Doge Peter; he stood sponsor to a daughter, and remitted the yearly tribute of the *pallium* and any monetary tribute beyond the ancient statutory sum of 50 Venetian librae. Otto returned to Ravenna, and three days later Orseolo told his people who his guest had been.

But between the issue of the invitation and the visit of the Emperor, Peter had carried to a successful conclusion the greatest enterprise of his reign. The growing Venetian factories down the Dalmatian coast had been in the habit of paying tribute to the Serbs and Croats for the preservation of their right to trade. Orseolo resolved to put an end to these levies of blackmail. At the beginning of his reign he refused to pay tribute, and on the Dalmatians assuming a threatening attitude he at once prepared a naval expedition. He sailed on 9 May 1000, and made for Istria, where he learned the value of the Candiani's Istrian policy and achievements, in finding Istrian ports open to his fleets. Zara, Veglia, Arbè, and Traù submitted. Spalato was taken. An oath of allegiance was exacted and a formal recognition that the waters of the Adriatic were open to Venetian traffic. The victorious doge returned to Venice and assumed the title of *Dux Dalmatiae*, a title which was recognised by the Western Empire in the treaty of 16 November 1002. We must bear in mind, however, that centuries passed before Dalmatia became definitely Venetian. Zara was always in revolt down to the fourteenth century. Nevertheless Peter's expedition was of the highest importance; it raised the prestige of the Venetians, it opened to them a long line of factories down the Dalmatian coast, and it advanced their claim to free trade in the Adriatic.

Two years later, in 1002, Orseolo was called on to fulfil his obligations to the Eastern Empire under the chrysobull of 992. The Saracens of Sicily had attacked and besieged Bari, the capital of the theme of Longobardia. On 10 August the Venetian fleet, under the command of the doge, set sail, and by 18 October Bari was relieved by a brilliant Venetian victory. This victory led to a marriage-alliance between John, the eldest son of Peter, and the Princess Maria, the niece of Basil II; John's younger brother Otto married the sister-in-law of the Emperor Henry II, thus connecting the family of the Orseoli with both imperial houses. But in 1005 the plague carried off John and Princess Maria as well as their son. The doge never recovered from the blow; he lost his interest in worldly matters, led a claustral life at home, and died in 1009.

Peter's death closed a reign which had a profound significance in Venetian history. A new Venice, the *aurea Venetia* of the chronicler John the Deacon, came into being on the ruins left by the fire which destroyed Peter Candianus; a new palace and a new St Mark's, adorned with the finest workmanship of Byzantine masters, took the place of the older buildings. The doge's taste was shewn in the gifts he presented to his *compater* Otto, an ivory chair elaborately carved and a silver bowl of rich design. It is a new Venice, too, we now find in its relations to the great world-powers, to Eastern and Western Empire alike. Neither Imperial Court refused an alliance with the Doge of Venice, and the Venetian fleet had made its strength felt down both shores of the Adriatic.

But inside Venice there was a party strongly opposed to the dynastic and monarchical tendencies of the Orseolo family. Peter's son and successor Otto (1009–1026), whose elder brother Orso was translated from Torcello to Grado, and whose younger brother Vitalis succeeded to the vacant see, found that jealousy of his family's supremacy had gradually undermined his position. The open hostility of Conrad the Salic, and his refusal to renew the *pacta*, led eventually to the expulsion of the doge. The fall of the Orseoli marked the end of the dynastic system in the dukedom. During the rule of the three great families, the Particiaci, the Candiani, and the Orseoli, the reigning doge had been, to all intents and purposes, an absolute monarch; the fisc was in his sole administration, the popular assembly was summoned merely to sanction his decrees; a recognised constitution cannot be said to have existed. After the fall of the Orseoli we find ourselves dealing with a new kind of doge; the germs of a constitution begin to shew themselves. In 1032, the first year of Domenico Fabiano's reign (1032–1043), the appointment of a doge-consort was declared illegal. This appears to have been an act of the popular assembly, proving that this body was beginning to assume a more prominent place. It is also said that the same body appointed two councillors to assist the doge in current matters, and enjoined him on graver occasions to consult the more prominent citizens, possibly a foreshadowing of the council which eventually developed into the *Pregadi* or Senate of Venice.

The period upon which we are now entering, from the fall of the Orseoli to the opening of the Crusades (1026–1096), is chiefly concerned with the resistance of Grado against the attacks of Poppo, the turbulent Patriarch of Aquileia, supported by Conrad the Salic; with the campaigns against the Normans at the mouth of the Adriatic; and with the expansion of Venetian commercial privileges in Constantinople. Conrad came to Italy in March 1026. He was embittered against the Italians generally by their obvious desire to throw off the German yoke. As regards Venice in particular, he shared the views and aspirations of Otto II; he regarded the Venetians as rebellious subjects, and refused to renew the *pacta*. This, as we have seen, led to the fall of the Orseoli and a weakening of the Venetian State. Poppo, Patriarch of Aquileia, a devoted adherent of Conrad, seized the opportunity to carry out his design of enforcing the decree of the Synod of Mantua (827), which gave the supremacy to Aquileia over Grado. He attacked and sacked Grado twice, once in 1024 immediately after Conrad's accession to the crown of Germany, when he plundered the church and palace and carried off the treasury to Aquileia, and once again in 1044. But Rome was steadily against him, and in 1053 the "Constitution" of Leo IX definitely declared Grado to be "the Metropolitan Church of Venice and Istria." The see of Grado maintained its hierarchical pre-eminence, but the town itself was hopelessly ruined. The growing importance of Venice drew the patriarchs to longer, and eventually continuous, sojourn in that city, bringing with them for the benefit of Venice the prestige of their metropolitan see, till it was finally transformed into the Patriarchate of Venice (1445).

On the death of Conrad relations between Venice and the Western power became easier. During the reign of Domenico Contarini (1042–1071), Henry III renewed the ancient treaties (probably 1055). Contarini's successor, Domenico Silvio (1071–1084), proved once again that a doge of Venice was a fit mate for an imperial princess by marrying Theodora, sister of the Emperor Michael Ducas, a lady to whose oriental luxury and refinement[1] the rougher Venetians attributed the loathsome malady of which she died. During this doge's reign Venice was called upon to play a more prominent part in world-history than she had hitherto done. A new power now appeared at the mouth of the Adriatic. The Normans, after making themselves masters of Sicily and South Italy (Bari fell in 1071 and Palermo in 1072), stretched across to the eastern side of the Adriatic and threatened to advance on Constantinople itself. Under their leader, Robert Guiscard, they laid siege to Durazzo, which commanded the western end of the Via Egnatia, the great Roman road which led by Thessalonica to the capital. Alexius Comnenus had been called to the imperial throne (8 April 1081) on purpose to replace the incompetent bureaucratic government of Michael Ducas and Nicephorus Botaniates. He saw at once that Durazzo must not be allowed to fall. He appealed to Henry IV, but that sovereign was too deeply involved in the struggle with the Pope to be able to lend aid, and he turned to request the aid of Venice. The Venetians could not view with indifference the success of the Normans, which threatened to make them masters of both sides of the Adriatic, and thus to close the mouth of the water avenue which led to and from Venice. Moreover, the Amalfitans, the vigorous commercial rivals of the lagoon-state, were actively supporting Robert. All her interests induced Venice to lend a willing ear to Alexius' appeal. A bargain was soon struck (1081), and in June of that year a fleet of sixty Venetian ships, under the command of Doge Silvio, set sail to relieve Durazzo.

The battle which followed was remarkable both for the tactics developed by the Venetian commander—the fleet drawn up in half-moon

[1] Among other luxuries she used a fork, *quibusdam fuscinulis aureis et bidentibus*, S. Petrus Damianus, *Instit. Monialis*, Cap. XI, *Opera*, Vol. III.

formation, the vessels lashed together with the lighter craft between the horns—and for the ingenious engineering device by which iron-pointed balks of timber were either launched against the enemy's hulls or dropped on his decks from overhanging yards. The upshot was a complete victory for the Venetians and the relief of Durazzo. But in a land battle which took place in October of this year the Greeks were utterly beaten; Durazzo fell into the hands of the Normans, and the Venetian fleet sailed home. In May of the following year (1082) Venice received the rewards for which she had stipulated. The chrysobull of Alexius conferred on Venetians the privilege of trading free of dues throughout the whole Eastern Empire, including the capital, and placed all Venetian merchants under the jurisdiction of the doge, privileges which at once gave Venice an advantage over her rival Amalfi. In return for these concessions Venice was still pledged to support Alexius at sea. In the next three years (1083–1085) the Venetian fleet carried on campaigns against the Normans with varying fortune. At first (spring of 1084) they captured Corfù and in the autumn of the same year they won a great victory at Cassiopo. But at length Robert succeeded in breaking up their strong formation, and the result was a crushing and bloody defeat. The blame was laid at the door of the doge, who was compelled to abdicate and retire to a monastery. It remained for his successor, Vitale Falier (1084–1096), to witness the final freeing of the Adriatic from the Norman fleet, thanks partly to a brilliant victory at Butrinto (1085), partly to sickness which drove the Normans back to Italy. Robert Guiscard died in July of that year.

But though Robert's plans were shattered and the Normans failed to hold the mouth of the Adriatic, Venice was still compelled to fight for her right to free passage in that sea, which was threatened by the appearance of the Hungarian sovereign upon the coast of Dalmatia. By 1097, however, the principal towns were once more in the hold of Venice.

We are now approaching the period of the Crusades, throughout which Venice plays a prominent but distinctly self-interested part, deliberately building up her commercial status until, with the Fourth Crusade, she emerges as the greatest sea-power, the most flourishing commercial community, in the Mediterranean. As yet the state had developed no fixed constitution, nor did she until the close of the thirteenth and the opening of the fourteenth century, when the constitution received its rigidly oligarchical form by the closing of the Great Council (1296) and the creation of the Council of Ten (1310). But during the period with which we have now to deal (1096–1201) we shall find the germs of several departments which went eventually to create the Venetian constitution. These, and the further development of her sea-power, so vigorously displayed during the Norman campaigns, form the chief points of interest in Venetian history during the twelfth century.

The position of Venice as regards the Crusades was by no means easy.

On the one hand, if she joined with vigour she risked her flourishing trade with the Saracens, and she would have to face the hostility of the Eastern Emperors, who disliked and suspected the Crusades. Moreover her sea-route down the Adriatic was far from secure; the Hungarians were a standing menace to Dalmatia, while the Normans had not abandoned their designs on both shores of the Adriatic mouth. All these considerations led Venice to desire a neutral place: she wished to trade with the Crusaders and their enemies alike; she was prepared to supply transport and provisions but not to draw her sword against the infidel. On the other hand, the frank espousal of the Crusades by the commercial rivals of Venice, Genoa and Pisa, threatened to give them such overwhelming advantages in the East that the republic found herself forced to abandon her neutral attitude.

In 1095 the Council of Clermont proclaimed the First Crusade. The question of transport immediately presented itself. Of the three maritime powers of Italy—Genoa, Pisa, and Venice—the latter undoubtedly offered the greatest advantages both in geographical position and in strength of armament. But Venice was the last of the sea-states to move. It was not until Jerusalem fell (1099) that she made up her mind in view of the growing importance of Genoa and Pisa. Under the Doge Vitale Michiel I (1096–1101), the first Venetian fleet with crusaders on board sailed for the Holy Land (1099). It wintered in Rhodes, and there almost immediately revealed the true object of its presence in the Levant by coming to blows with the Pisans who were also wintering in the harbour. In the following spring the Venetians set sail for the Holy Land, plundering as they went, notably at Myra where they broke up the church in their search for the bones of St Nicholas. They arrived in time to take part in the siege of Ḥaifa, which fell in October 1100. The Venetians at once claimed and received a trading quarter in the town and thereby opened the long list of their factories in the Levant, but also by their new possession committed themselves to all the complications of the Levant. The fleet returned home in 1100.

A long pause ensued. Venice was chiefly occupied with the effort to secure her sea-route down the Adriatic and to settle the question of Dalmatia with the Hungarians.

On the mainland of Italy too she was surely consolidating her trade. In 1102 she had the satisfaction of seeing the rival city of Ferrara reduced by the troops of Countess Matilda, and of establishing trading rights there under the protection of a Visdomino or Consul.

During the reign of Ordelafo Falier (1101–1118), Venice continued to prepare steadily for the part she was destined to play in the Levant. The necessity for maintaining her sea-route, and the certainty that she would be called on to fight in the Eastern Mediterranean, compelled the State to turn its attention to its fleet. In 1104 the Arsenal was founded.

When Domenico Michiel came to the throne (1118–1130), the affairs of the Levant began to assume a prominent place once more in Venetian history. Baldwin I died in the year of the doge's accession. Baldwin II, threatened by Musulman power, appealed to the Italian sea-states for help. The doge convened the general assembly in St Mark's, laid the situation before it, and insisted on the danger of allowing Pisa and Genoa to reap all the advantage in the Levant. An expedition was voted, though the dangers from the insecure sea-route and the hostility of the new Emperor of the East, John Comnenus, who had refused to renew the ancient privileges, were not overlooked. The pressure of Genoese and Pisan rivalry in fact forced the hand of Venice. The splendid fleet of one hundred ships, ablaze with colour (*naves coloribus variis picturate erant*), set sail on 8 August 1122. The expedition assumed the aspect of a marauding enterprise. Under cloak of wintering there the Venetians tried to seize Corfù but failed. By 29 May 1123 the Venetians were at Jaffa. The doge immediately attacked and defeated the Egyptian fleet off Ascalon. The question now arose as to which of the two cities, Tyre or Ascalon, the allies should besiege. The lot decided it in favour of Tyre, but not until the doge had secured for his nation the promise of extensive trading rights throughout the whole Latin kingdom: exemption from dues, a church, a quarter, a bakery, and a bath, in each city. The siege lasted from 16 February till 7 July 1124. On the fall of the city Venice exacted the fulfilment of her bargain, and with the capture of Tyre laid the solid foundation of her great Levantine trade.

The success of Venice in Palestine, and the numbers, wealth, and arrogance of the Venetians in Constantinople (it seems that the male Venetian population between twenty and sixty years of age residing in the capital was no less than 18,000 towards the close of the twelfth century), coupled with the dislike and suspicion of the crusaders generally, rendered the Greek Emperors hostile on the whole towards the republic. Circumstances, however, such as the need for Venetian assistance against the Normans, prevented the unrestrained display of their animus. On the fall of Tyre the Emperor John forbade all Venetians in Constantinople to leave the city—they were to remain as hostages—while he refused to renew Venetian privileges. The doge replied by plundering Rhodes, Chios, Cos, Samos, on his triumphant journey home, and crowned his glories by recovering Spalato, Traù, and Zara Vecchia from the Hungarians on his way up the Adriatic. The Emperor was without a fleet; he was entirely dependent on the Venetians for help at sea; the rupture of commercial relations proved a serious loss to his capital. Willingly or unwillingly he came to terms and in 1126 he renewed the treaties.

But Venice was presently called upon to face anew a complicated situation between East and West. On Christmas Day 1130 Duke Roger was crowned King of Sicily. The danger of a Norman power blocking the mouth of the Adriatic was still alive; while the menace to the Eastern Empire, developed by Robert Guiscard, was renewed by King Roger. In April 1135 ambassadors from Venice and Constantinople appealed to the Emperor Lothar, who seized the occasion to form a combination against the Normans. In May 1137 the fleet of King Roger suffered defeat off Trani, probably owing to the Venetians. But the Norman power remained a standing menace to both Venice and Constantinople. The Emperor Manuel, impotent at sea without a fleet, was forced by circumstances to approach the sea-power which had saved Constantinople in the days of Robert Guiscard and Alexius. The Venetians, as usual, made a bargain. The Emperor renewed the Golden Bull, enlarged the Venetian quarter in Constantinople, conferred the title of Protosebastos upon the doge in perpetuity, and confirmed the annual tribute to the church of St Mark. The commercial supremacy of the Venetians was asserted in the clearest terms (1147).

The bargain struck, the doge set sail to attack the Normans, but died at Caorle. He was succeeded by Domenico Morosini (1148–1156). The fleet pursued its course under the command of John Polani, effected a junction with the imperial squadron, and beleaguered Corfù. The siege lasted a year. But during the course of it the Greeks and Venetians came to loggerheads. In derision the Venetian sailors dressed up a negro slave as the Emperor and paid him mock homage. Manuel Comnenus never forgave the insult and treasured its memory till his day for vengeance arrived.

A new trend in Greek imperial politics was laid bare in 1151 by the capture of Ancona. It was clear that Manuel contemplated the revival of the Exarchate and possibly the recovery of Italy. Such a policy was, of course, a peril for Venice, a menace to the supremacy in the Adriatic which she was so carefully building up by her treaties with Fano (1141) on the one coast, and Capo d' Istria (1145), Rovigno, Umago, Parenzo on the other. In Dalmatia, too, the same object was steadily pursued by the appointment of Venetian "counts" in Zara (1155) and other Dalmatian cities. In fact the supremacy of Venice in the northern Adriatic was officially recognised by the treaty of peace between William, King of Sicily, and the republic (1154), which brought the war with the Normans to a close, and that supremacy was threatened by Manuel.

To the west too, from the mainland of Italy, the independence, the very existence of Venice, were likewise menaced. The appearance of Frederick I Barbarossa in Italy, his declared hostility to the communes and to the Italian aspirations towards independence, warned the republic of what might be in store for her. She espoused the cause of Alexander III, the anti-imperial Pope, drawing down upon herself the wrath of the Emperor, who stirred her neighbours, Padua, Verona, Ferrara, and the Patriarch of Aquileia, against her. In 1167 the Lombard League was formed and Venice was forced to join it.

The confusion in Italy now seemed to the Emperor Manuel to offer the opportunity for realising his dream of regaining the whole country for the Eastern Crown. The assistance of Venice, powerful in the Adriatic, was essential to his scheme. He approached the republic on the subject but met with no encouragement. His accumulated hatred of Venice, caused by the part she had played in the Crusades, the insult her sailors had offered him at Corfù, the arrogance and wealth of Venetians in Constantinople, suddenly blazed out. In 1171 every Venetian in the capital was arrested and his property confiscated.

When the news reached Venice there was a unanimous cry for war. One hundred and twenty ships were soon ready, and in September 1171 the doge set sail. On his way he attacked Ragusa, which surrendered and received a "count." At Negropont the Emperor began to open negotiations and kept them dragging on till the fleet was obliged to go into winter quarters at Chios. There the plague broke out, some said from poisoned wells. The whole force was decimated, and when spring came it was only just able to struggle home; here the doge fell a victim to popular indignation (28 May 1172).

This disastrous close to the expedition against Manuel led to a reform in the constitution. Events seemed to have proved that the doge was too independent, and that the popular assembly was too liable to be swept away by a storm of passion. To correct these defects a body of four hundred and eighty leading citizens was elected, for one year, in the six districts (*sestieri*) into which the city had lately been divided; this body was consultative and elective, and in it we doubtless get the germ of the Great Council (Maggior Consiglio). The doge, for the future, was required to take a coronation oath, the *promissione ducale*, by which he bound himself to observe certain constitutional obligations. To the two existing ducal councillors were added four more; the duties of the new body were to act with the doge, and to supervise and check his actions. The doge was absolutely forbidden to trade on his own account. In return for these restrictions he was now surrounded with increased pomp. The Lombard League, for which Venice acted as banker, and the war with Manuel, proved a severe strain on the treasury and compelled the state to have recourse to a forced loan (1171). The loan bore interest at four per cent., and was secured on the whole revenue of the state; the exaction and administration of the fund was entrusted to a body called the Chamber of Loans (*Camera degli imprestidi*). The amount of the loan was one per cent. of net incomes. The bonds could be devised, sold, or mortgaged; and here we find, perhaps, the earliest example of national obligations, or consols.

Other important magistracies such as the *Quarantia*, or supreme court, the *Giudice del Proprio*, or judge in commercial suits, and the *avogadori del Comun*, or procurators fiscal, were created about this time. The campanile was completed as far as the bell chamber, the Piazza was enlarged and paved, the twin columns of San Teodoro and San Marco erected. In short, it is clear that in the latter half of the twelfth century Venice was rapidly developing as a constitutional state, though the completion of her growth took place in a period beyond the limits of this chapter.

The affairs of the Lombard League had now reached a crisis. The final issue was decided by the battle of Legnano (1176), in which the communes were victorious. Frederick resolved to make peace. He expressed a desire to meet Pope Alexander III, and Venice was chosen as the scene of the conference, where the Peace of Venice was signed.

The advantages which accrued to the republic were great. All Europe was assembled within her walls; she appeared as the equal and the friend of Emperor and Pope alike; her independent position was apparently unchallenged. Moreover by a special treaty (17 August 1177) the Emperor renewed all previous privileges and declared that subjects of the kingdom of Italy might trade "as far as Venice but no farther" (*usque ad vos et non amplius*), a restriction which looks very much as if Venice had established her claim to dominion in the upper Adriatic. From the Pope Venice received the ring with which her doge wedded the Adriatic, and, more important still, a final settlement of the long-standing quarrel between Aquileia and Grado.

During the reign of the Doge Orio Mastropiero (1178–1192), the position of Venice in the East was threatened once more and the seeds of the Fourth Crusade were sown. Andronicus attacked the Latins in Constantinople (1182) and sacked their quarters. The refugees appealed to William, King of Sicily, and he and the Venetians set out to avenge the massacre of Constantinople. Their approach caused the fall of Andronicus, to whom succeeded Isaac Angelus, favourably disposed towards Venice, ready to renew the chrysobulls and to compensate for damage, in return for which Venice pledged herself to supply from forty to one hundred warships at the imperial request.

During the Third Crusade Venice played her usual *rôle*: that is to say, she transported the crusaders, took a part in their sieges, and exacted trading privileges as her recompense.

In fact the commerce of Venice was steadily expanding under the vigilant care of her rulers. She was now about to set the seal to her commercial supremacy by her acquisitions after the Fourth Crusade, under her great Doge Enrico Dandolo (1193–1205). Early in his reign, though not without considerable trouble, the doge secured the renewal and enlargement of the Venetian privileges in Constantinople, where their quarter became as it were a little semi-independent state inside the Empire.

In 1201 the ambassadors from the French crusaders appeared at Venice, begging, as usual, for transport. The bargain was struck. Venice pledged herself to carry and to victual for a year four thousand five hundred horses, nine thousand esquires, and twenty thousand foot soldiers; the price was to be eighty-five thousand silver marks of Cologne. The republic was to furnish for her own part fifty galleys on condition that half of all conquests by sea or land should belong to her. It is a proof of the great sea-power of Venice that she could undertake the transport of so large an army. The last clause of the bargain left little doubt as to her real intentions in the Fourth Crusade, which forms the subject of the following chapter.

CHAPTER XIV.

THE FOURTH CRUSADE AND THE LATIN EMPIRE.

On 28 November 1199 some great nobles of Champagne and Picardy, who had assembled in the castle of Ecri-sur-Aisne for a tournament, resolved to assume the Cross and go to deliver the Holy Land. They elected Theobald (Thibaut) III, Count of Champagne, as leader. The suggested expedition coincided so entirely with the desires of Pope Innocent III that he encouraged it with all his might. At his call, Fulk, parish priest of Neuilly in France, and Abbot Martin of Pairis in Germany, began a series of sermons, which by their fervour easily persuaded the mass of the faithful to enlist in the Crusade. No doubt the Western sovereigns intervened only indirectly in the preparation and direction of the expedition, Philip Augustus being engaged in his struggle with John Lackland, and Philip of Swabia entirely engrossed in disputing the Empire with Otto of Brunswick; the Crusade was essentially a feudal enterprise, led by an oligarchy of great barons, and, even at first, partly inspired by worldly aspirations and material interests. In this particular the fourth Holy War differed greatly from the previous ones. "For many of the crusaders," says Luchaire, "it was above all a business matter." And this consideration will perhaps help us to a better understanding of the character which this undertaking quickly assumed.

For the transport of the crusaders to the East a fleet was necessary. In February 1201 the barons sent delegates, of whom Villehardouin was one, to Venice to procure the requisite naval force from the mighty republic. After somewhat troublesome negotiations, recorded for us by Villehardouin, a treaty was concluded in April 1201, whereby in return for a sum of 85,000 marks of silver the Venetians agreed to supply the crusaders by 28 June 1202 with the ships and provisions necessary for the transport of their army overseas; Venice moreover joined in the enterprise, astutely realising the advantage to be gained by guiding and directing the expedition. The Doge, Enrico Dandolo, solemnly assumed the Cross at St Mark's, and in return the crusaders promised to assign half of their conquests to Venice.

Most of the knights regarded Syria as the goal of the expedition and cherished the ambition of reconquering the Holy Land. The great barons, on the other hand, wished to strike at the heart of the Muslim power, *i.e.* Egypt. And this divergence of views heavily handicapped the whole Crusade. It has been asserted that the Venetians, who were bound by treaties with the Sultan of Egypt and did not wish to compromise their commercial interests, were from the first hostile to the expedition, and sought means of diverting the crusaders from their path, thus betraying Christendom. There is nothing to prove that they planned this deliberately, but it is obvious that the stiff contract of April 1201 rendered the Christian army dependent on the republic.

The crusaders slowly prepared to cross the Alps. Meanwhile the death of Theobald of Champagne had obliged them to find another leader. On the recommendation of the King of France, an Italian baron was chosen, Boniface, Marquess of Montferrat, whose brothers had played a great part in the East, both Latin and Byzantine. At Soissons on 16 August 1201 he was acclaimed by the barons, after which he betook himself to Germany, where he spent part of the winter with Philip of Swabia, his intimate friend; and to this visit great importance for the ultimate fate of the Crusade has sometimes been attributed. Meanwhile the army was mustering at Venice, where it was assembled in July-August 1202. But the crusaders had only paid the Venetians a small part of the sum agreed upon as payment for the voyage, and it was impossible for them to collect the remainder. Interned in the island of St Niccolò di Lido, harassed by demands from the Venetian merchants and threats that their supplies would be cut off if the money were not forthcoming, the crusaders were finally obliged to accept the doge's proposal that they should be granted a respite if they helped the republic to reconquer the city of Zara, which had been taken by the Hungarians. In spite of the indignant protests of Innocent III and his legate at an attack directed against a Christian city and a crusading ruler, the enterprise had to be undertaken in order to satisfy the Venetian demands. The barons unwillingly agreed to engage in it (September 1202); and on 8 November 1202 the fleet sailed amidst general rejoicings. On 10 November Zara was attacked, and surrendered in five days, when the Venetians destroyed it utterly. It was in vain that Innocent III threatened and excommunicated the Venetians. The crusaders were now preoccupied by considerations of greater importance, which diverted the Crusade to a new objective. It had been undertaken with the object of delivering Jerusalem, or attacking Egypt; it ended in the conquest of Constantinople.

For over a century the West had for many reasons been casting looks of hate and envy towards Byzantium. The Norman Kings of Sicily and their German successor, the Emperor Henry VI, had several times directed their dreams of conquest towards the Greek Empire. The leaders of the various crusades, indignant at the treachery and ill-will of the Byzantines, had more than once contemplated taking Constantinople and destroying the monarchy. Finally the Venetians, who had for a century been masters of the commerce with the Levant and were anxious to keep for themselves the fine markets of the East, were becoming uneasy, both at the increasing animosity displayed by the Greeks, and at the rivalry of the other maritime cities of Italy. In the course of the twelfth century they had several times been obliged to defend their position and privileges by force of arms; therefore their politicians, and especially the Doge Enrico Dandolo, were considering whether the easiest way of resolving the problem and securing the commercial prosperity of the republic in the East would not be to conquer the Byzantine Empire and establish on its ruins a colonial Venetian empire. All these various causes, unrealised ambitions of conquest, old accumulated grudges against the Greeks, threatened economic interests, almost inevitably led to the diversion of the Fourth Crusade to Constantinople; all that was necessary was that an opportunity should offer itself.

This opportunity occurred in the course of 1202. The Basileus reigning in Constantinople, Alexius Angelus, had dethroned his brother Isaac in 1195, and had cast the deposed monarch and his young son Alexius into prison. The latter succeeded in escaping and came to Germany, either at the end of 1201 or else in the spring of 1202, to seek the help of his brother-in-law, Philip of Swabia, husband of his sister Irene. But Philip had no means of giving direct support to the young prince. Did he arrange with Boniface of Montferrat, or with the Venetians, who were interested in re-opening the Eastern question, that the crusading army, then inactive at Venice, should be utilised against Byzantium? Scholars of to-day have devoted much discussion to this very obscure historical point. It has been suggested that Philip of Swabia, deeply interested in his young brother-in-law, and moreover cherishing, like his brother Henry VI, personal ambitions with regard to the East, immediately on the arrival of Alexius agreed with Boniface of Montferrat that the Crusade should be diverted to Constantinople. It has been suggested that he hoped by this means to checkmate the Papacy, and, by threatening to ruin the projected Crusade, force Innocent III to seek a reconciliation with him. The question has also been raised whether the Venetians had long premeditated their attack on Zara, and whether or not they had agreed with the Marquess of Montferrat that the fleet should next set sail for Byzantium; in a word, whether the diversion of the Crusade sprang from fortuitous causes, or was the result of deep intrigues and premeditated designs. "This," says Luchaire wisely, "will never be known, and science has something better to do than interminably to discuss an insoluble problem." All that can be said is that the arrival of young Alexius in the West suited the policy of the Doge Enrico Dandolo admirably, and that the latter used it with supreme ability to insist on an attempt upon Byzantium against the wishes of some of the crusaders, thereby ensuring enormous advantages to his country.

Even before leaving Venice in September 1202 the leaders of the Crusade had received messengers from the Greek claimant, and had entered into negotiations with Philip of Swabia. After the capture of Zara, envoys from the German king and his young brother-in-law brought them much more definite proposals. In return for the help to be given him in recapturing Constantinople, Alexius promised the crusaders to pay the balance still owing to the Venetians, to provide them with the money and supplies necessary for conquering Egypt, to assist them by sending a contingent of 10,000 men, to maintain five hundred knights to guard the Holy Land, and, finally, to bring about religious reunion with Rome. It was a tempting offer, and, under pressure from the Venetians and Montferrat, the leading barons decided to accept it. No doubt a certain number of knights protested and left the army, starting for Syria direct. It was represented to the majority that the expedition to Constantinople in no way superseded the original plan, that, in fact, it would facilitate its execution, that moreover it would be a meritorious act and one pleasing to God to restore the legitimate heir to the throne; it is also clear that at this time no one contemplated the destruction of the Greek Empire. Whatever their real wishes, the majority allowed themselves to be persuaded. On 25 April 1203 Alexius joined Montferrat and Dandolo at Zara, and at Corfù in May was signed the definitive treaty which established the diversion of the great enterprise. The Pope, solicitous as always that the Crusade should not fall to pieces, allowed matters to go their own way. On 25 May the crusading fleet left Corfù, and on 24 June 1203 it appeared outside Constantinople.

Every one knows the celebrated passage in which Villehardouin describes the impressions which the crusaders experienced at first sight of the great Byzantine city. "Now wit ye well that they gazed at Constantinople, those who had never seen it; for they had not dreamed that there was in all the world so rich a city, when they beheld the high walls and the mighty towers by which she was enclosed all round, and those rich palaces and those great churches, of which there were so many that none might believe it if he had not seen it with his own eyes, and the length and breadth of the city, which was sovereign among all. And wit ye well that there was no man so bold that he did not tremble; and this was not wonderful; for never was so great a matter undertaken by any man since the world was created."[1]

The crusaders had expected that the Greeks would welcome with enthusiasm the monarch whom they had come to restore. But on the contrary every one rallied round Alexius III, who was regarded as the defender of national independence. The Latins were therefore obliged to resort to force. They stormed the tower of Galata, forced the chain across the harbour, and entered the Golden Horn; then on 17 July 1203 they assaulted the town by land and sea. Alexius III, realising his defeat, fled; his victims, Isaac and the young Alexius, were restored to the throne; on 1 August they were solemnly crowned at St Sophia in the presence of the Latin barons.

[1] Villehardouin, ed. Wailly, N. de, ch. 128.

The new sovereigns received the Latins "as benefactors and preservers of the Empire"; they hastened to carry out the promises they had made, and lavished on them the wealth of the capital, thereby only increasing the covetousness of the crusaders, which was already excited. This friendship did not last long. Torn between the demands of his allies and the hostility of the national party, which accused him of having betrayed Byzantium to aliens, the young Alexius IV was soon unable to fulfil his promises. Urged by the Venetians, the Latins had decided to pass the winter season in Constantinople, but they had made the mistake of evacuating the capital after an occupation of a few days, and the insolence of the Greeks had been thereby greatly increased. Finally Dandolo, who during the temporary absence of Montferrat was in command, seized the opportunity of multiplying difficulties and preparing a breach by his unreasonableness. In these circumstances a catastrophe was inevitable. There were affrays and riots, followed by a revolution. In February 1204 the son-in-law of the Emperor Alexius III, Alexius Ducas, nicknamed Mourtzouphlos, the leader of the national party, caused the downfall of the two weak Emperors who were incapable of resisting the demands of the crusaders; and a few days later Alexius IV was strangled in prison. Henceforth any agreement was impossible. The only means of realising the great hopes inspired by the capture of Constantinople, ensuring the success of the Crusade, and attaining the union of the Churches, was to seize Constantinople and keep it. The Venetians especially insisted on the necessity of finishing the work and founding a Latin Empire; and in the month of March 1204 the crusaders agreed on the manner in which they should divide the future conquest. The French and the Venetians were to share equally in the booty of Constantinople. An assembly of six Venetians and six Frenchmen were to elect the Emperor, to whom was to be assigned a quarter of the conquered territory. The other three quarters were to go, half to the Venetians, half to the crusaders. Dandolo succeeded in arranging everything to the advantage of Venice. The city of St Mark obtained a promise that she should receive the lion's share of the booty by way of indemnity for what was due to her, that all her commercial privileges should be preserved, and that the party which did not provide the Emperor (a privilege to which Venice attached no importance) should receive the Patriarchate of Constantinople and should occupy St Sophia. Moreover the doge arranged matters so that the new Empire, feudally organised, should be weak as opposed to Venice. Having thus ordered all things "to the honour of God, of the Pope, and of the Empire," the crusaders devoted themselves to the task of taking Constantinople.

The first assault on 9 April 1204 failed. The attack on 12 April was more successful. The outer wall was taken, and while a vast conflagration broke out in the town, Mourtzouphlos, losing courage, fled. On the morrow, the leaders of the army established themselves in the imperial palaces and allowed their soldiers to pillage Constantinople for three days. The crusaders treated the city with appalling cruelty. Murder, rape, sacrilege, robbery, were let loose. "These defenders of Christ," wrote Pope Innocent III himself, "who should have turned their swords only against the infidels, have bathed in Christian blood. They have respected neither religion, nor age, nor sex. They have committed in open day adultery, fornication, and incest. Matrons and virgins, even those vowed to God, were delivered to the ignominious brutality of the soldiery. And it was not enough for them to squander the treasures of the Empire, and to rob private individuals, whether great or small. They have dared to lay their hands on the wealth of the churches. They have been seen tearing from the altars the silver adornments, breaking them in fragments over which they quarrelled, violating the sanctuaries, carrying away the icons, crosses, and relics." St Sophia was the scene of disgraceful proceedings: a drunken soldiery might be seen destroying the sacred books, treading pious images underfoot, polluting the costly materials, drinking from the consecrated vessels, distributing sacerdotal ornaments and jewels torn from the altars to courtesans and camp-followers; a prostitute seated herself on the throne of the Patriarch and there struck up a ribald song. The most famous works of art were destroyed, bronze statues melted down and used for coinage, and, among so many horrors, the Greek historian Nicetas, who in an eloquent lament described and mourned the ruin of his country, declared that even the Saracens would have been more merciful than these men, who yet claimed to be soldiers of Christ.

The Latins themselves at last experienced some feelings of shame. The leaders of the army took severe measures to restore order. But pillage was followed by methodical and organised extortion. Under pain of excommunication all stolen objects must be brought to a common store; a systematic search for treasure and relics was instituted, and the spoils were divided between the conquerors. "The booty was so great," writes Villehardouin, "that no man could give you a count thereof, gold and silver, plate and precious stones, samite and silks, and garments of fur, vair and silver-gray and ermine, and all the riches ever found on earth. And Geoffrey de Villehardouin, marshal of Champagne, truly bears witness, according to his knowledge and in truth, that never, since the world was created, was so much taken in a city."[1] The total share of the crusaders—three-eighths—seems to have amounted to 400,000 marks of silver. The churches of the West were enriched with sacred spoils from Constantinople, and the Venetians, better informed than the rest as to the wealth of Byzantium, knew very well how to make their choice.

After the booty, there was still the Empire to be divided. On 9 May 1204 the electoral college assembled to elect the new sovereign. One man seemed destined to occupy the throne: the leader of the Crusade,

[1] Villehardouin, ch. 259.

the Marquess Boniface of Montferrat, who was popular with the Lombards because of his nationality, with the Germans because of his relationship to Philip of Swabia, and even with the Greeks because of the marriage he had recently contracted with Margaret of Hungary, widow of Isaac Angelus. But for these very reasons, Montferrat was likely to prove too powerful a sovereign, and consequently a source of uneasiness to Venice, which meant to derive great advantages for herself from the Crusade. Boniface was therefore passed over in favour of a less important noble, Baldwin, Count of Flanders. On 16 May the latter was crowned with great pomp in St Sophia. And those who admired the magnificent ceremonial displayed in these festivities might well believe that nothing had changed in Byzantium since the glorious days of the Comneni.

But this was only a semblance, as was obvious a little later when the final division of the Empire took place. As his personal dominions, the new Emperor was awarded the territory which stretched west and east of the sea of Marmora, from Tzurulum (Chorlu) to the Black Sea in Europe; and, in Asia Minor, Bithynia and Mysia to the vicinity of Nicaea; some of the larger islands of the Archipelago were also assigned to him, Samothrace, Lesbos, Chios, Samos, and Cos. This was little enough, and even in his capital the Emperor was not sole master. By a somewhat singular arrangement he only possessed five-eighths of the city; the remainder, including St Sophia, belonged to the Venetians, who had secured the lion's share of the gains. They took everything which helped them to maintain their maritime supremacy, Epirus, Acarnania, Aetolia, the Ionian islands, the whole of the Peloponnesus, Gallipoli, Rodosto, Heraclea in the sea of Marmora and Hadrianople in the interior, several of the islands in the Archipelago, Naxos, Andros, Euboea, and finally Crete, which Boniface of Montferrat relinquished to them. The doge assumed the title of "despot"; he was dispensed from paying homage to the Emperor, and proudly styled himself "lord of one fourth and a half of the Greek Empire." A Venetian, Thomas Morosini, was raised to the patriarchate, and became the head of the Latin Church in the new Empire. Venice, indeed, was not to hold in her own hand all the territory granted to her. In Epirus she was content to hold Durazzo, and, in the Peloponnesus, Coron and Modon; she granted other districts as fiefs to various great families of her aristocracy; Corfù and most of the islands of the Archipelago thus became Venetian seigniories (the duchy of Naxos, marquessate of Cerigo, grand-duchy of Lemnos, duchy of Crete, etc.). But, by means of all this and the land she occupied directly, she secured for herself unquestioned supremacy in the Levantine seas. The Empire was very weak compared with the powerful republic.

Nor was this all. Some compensation had to be given to Boniface of Montferrat for having missed the imperial dignity. He was promised Asia Minor and continental Greece, but finally, despite the Emperor, he exchanged Asia Minor for Macedonia and the north of Thessaly, which formed the kingdom of Thessalonica held by him as vassal of the Empire. The counts and barons had next to be provided for, and a whole crop of feudal seigniories blossomed forth in the Byzantine world. Henry of Flanders, the Emperor's brother, became lord of Adramyttium, Louis of Blois was made Duke of Nicaea, Renier of Trit Duke of Philippopolis, and Hugh of St Pol lord of Demotika. On one day, 1 October 1204, the Emperor knighted six hundred and distributed fiefs to them. Some weeks later other seigniories came into being in Thessaly and the parts of Greece conquered by Montferrat. The Pallavicini became marquesses of Boudonitza, the La Roche family first barons, and subsequently dukes, of Athens; Latin nobles settled in Euboea, over whom Venice quickly established her suzerainty; finally, in the Peloponnesus, William of Champlitte and Geoffrey of Villehardouin, the historian's nephew, founded the principality of Achaia.

In this new society, the crusaders introduced all the Western institutions to the Byzantine East. The Latin Empire was an absolutely feudal State, whose legislation, modelled on that of the Latin kingdom of Jerusalem, was contained in the *Assises of Romania*. Elected by the barons, the Emperor was only the foremost baron, in spite of the ceremony with which he had surrounded himself and the great officers of his court. To render the Empire, thus born of the Crusade, living and durable, a strong government and a perfectly centralised State were necessary, whereas Baldwin was almost powerless. Boniface of Montferrat in particular was a most unruly subject, and, to impose on him the homage due to his suzerain, Baldwin was obliged to make war on him and to occupy Thessalonica for a while (August 1204); and in these civil disorders there was danger, for, as is said by Villehardouin, "if God had not been pitiful, all that had been gained would have been lost, and Christendom would have been exposed to the peril of death." Matters were arranged more or less satisfactorily; but the emergency had clearly demonstrated the Emperor's weakness. As to the vassals of the outlying parts of Greece, the dukes of Athens and princes of Achaia, they generally took no interest in the affairs of the Empire. The position with the Venetians was even more difficult, engrossed as they were in their own economic interests and impatient of all control. Romania was their chattel, and they meant to keep the Emperor dependent on them. By the agreement of October 1205, a council was established, in which sat the Venetian podestà and the great Frank barons, to assist the Emperor; it combined the right of superintending military operations with judicial powers, and had the privilege of controlling the sovereign's decisions. A High Court of Justice composed of Latins and Venetians similarly regulated everything which affected the relations between vassals and suzerain. Furthermore the Venetians were exempted from all taxation.

Thus the "new France," as it was called by the Pope, which had come into being in the East, was singularly weak owing to the differences between the conquerors, and Innocent III, who at first hailed with enthusiasm "the miracle wrought by God to the glory of His name, the honour and benefit of the Roman See, the advantage of Christendom," very soon experienced a grave disillusion. Many other difficulties, indeed, endangered the new Empire. The manner in which the Latins had treated Constantinople was ill adapted to gain the friendship of the Greeks; the fundamental misunderstanding between victors and vanquished could not fail to become intensified. It was impossible to establish agreement between the two races, the two Churches, the two civilisations. The brutal methods of conquest and the inevitable confiscations (from the first the Latins had seized all the property of the Greek Church) did not conduce to settle difficulties and to quell hatred.

There were, indeed, some Latin princes of greater political insight,—Montferrat in Thessalonica, Villehardouin in Achaia, and Baldwin's successor, Henry of Flanders—who sought to conciliate the vanquished by assuring them that their rights and property would be respected. But, except in the Peloponnesus, the results obtained were disappointing. With the exception of some great nobles, such as Theodore Branas, who adhered to the new government, the great mass of the Greek nation remained irreconcilable, and the patriotic party felt deep contempt for those "servile souls whom," as Nicetas wrote, "ambition armed against their country, for those traitors, who to secure some territory, had submitted to the conquerors," when they should have wished to remain eternally at war with the Latins.

The principal effect of the taking of Constantinople by the crusaders was to arouse patriotic sentiment in the Greeks and to re-awaken in them the sense of nationality. Round the son-in-law of the Emperor Alexius III, Theodore Lascaris, had collected any of the Byzantine aristocracy and leading Orthodox clergy that had escaped disaster, and in 1206 the Greek prince caused himself to be solemnly crowned as Emperor of the Romans. Other Greek states rose from the ruins of the Empire. Some princes of the family of the Comneni founded an Empire at Trebizond, which lasted until the fifteenth century. In Epirus, a bastard of the house of Angelus, Michael Angelus Comnenus, established a "Despotat" which reached from Naupactus to Durazzo; and other seigniories were founded by Gabalas at Rhodes, by Mankaphas at Philadelphia, and in Greece by Leo Sgouros. Of these States, two were specially formidable, Epirus which threatened Thessalonica, and Nicaea which aspired to conquer Asia Minor preparatory to regaining Constantinople.

Herein were many sources of weakness for the Latin Empire. The Bulgarian peril added yet another cause for uneasiness. Since the end of the twelfth century an independent state had arisen in Bulgaria, at whose head was the Tsar Kalojan, or Johannitsa (1197–1207), who styled himself Tsar of the Wallachians and the Bulgars. He was hostile to the Byzantines and quite disposed to be friendly with the Latins. He was also on good terms with Rome, and had even been crowned by a legate of Innocent III. When, therefore, he heard of the taking of Constantinople, he was quite ready to come to terms with the crusaders. But they took a high hand, and summoned the Bulgarian Tsar to restore the "portion of the Greek Empire unjustly retained by him." This was a grave mistake, and was recognised as such by Pope Innocent III. Had the Latins been on peaceful terms with the Bulgars, they might have had some chance of opposing the Greeks, but their methods were such as to unite all their adversaries against them.

Without money, without authority, almost without an army, what could the weak sovereign of the new Latin Empire do, when faced by the hostility of his Greek subjects and of the external enemies, Byzantines and Bulgars, who were threatening him? It was in vain that he posed as the successor of the Basileus, and sometimes caused uneasiness to the Pope by his daring claims on Church property; his position was precarious. The Latin Empire, offspring of the Fourth Crusade, lasted barely half a century (1204–1261), and this short-lived and fragile creation embittered yet more the antagonism which separated the Greeks and the Latins.

Nevertheless, in the first period of confusion which followed the taking of Constantinople, the Latins met with success everywhere. Boniface of Montferrat made a magnificent sally across Thessaly and Central Greece which carried him to Athens and to the very walls of Corinth and Nauplia (the end of 1204–May 1205). About the same time Henry of Flanders undertook the conquest of Asia Minor (November 1204). With the assistance of the Comneni of Trebizond, who were jealous of the new Empire of Nicaea, he defeated the troops of Theodore Lascaris at Poimanenon (December 1204), and seized the most important cities of Bithynia—Nicomedia, Abydos, Adramyttium, and Lopadium. The barely-established Greek State seemed on the point of destruction, when suddenly the Frank troops were recalled to Europe by a grave emergency, and Theodore Lascaris was saved.

The Greek population of Thrace, discontented with the Latin rule, had revolted, and, at their call, the Bulgarian Tsar Johannitsa had invaded the Empire. The Emperor Baldwin and the aged Doge Dandolo advanced boldly with the weak forces at their disposal to meet the enemy. On 14 April 1205, in the plains of Hadrianople, the Latin army was defeated. Baldwin, who was taken prisoner by the Bulgars, disappeared mysteriously a few weeks later, and Dandolo led all that remained of the army back to Constantinople, where he died and was buried with solemnity in St Sophia, his conquest. It seemed as though in this formidable crisis the Empire must perish, but it was saved by the energetic measures of Henry of Flanders, Baldwin's brother.

Chosen by the barons first as regent of Romania, then crowned as Emperor on 21 August 1206, Henry of Flanders, by his courage, energy, and intelligence, was quite equal to the task imposed on him. He was able not only to encounter the Bulgarian invasion and repel it, but also to restore unity among the Latins, and even to secure the submission of the Greeks; during his ten years' reign (1206–1216) he was the real founder of the Latin Empire.

The Greeks, indeed, began to be uneasy at the violence and brutality of their terrible Bulgarian ally. Johannitsa pillaged everything, burnt everything, and massacred every one, in his path. He longed to avenge the defeats which in bygone days Basil II had inflicted on his nation, and, just as the Byzantine Emperor had styled himself the "slayer of Bulgars" (*Bulgaroctonos*), so he proudly flaunted the title of "slayer of Romans" (*Romaioctonos*). The horrified Greeks therefore soon reverted to the side of the Latins. The Emperor Henry knew how to profit by these sentiments. He secured the assistance of Theodore Branas, one of the great Byzantine leaders, by granting him Demotika and Hadrianople as fiefs (October 1205). In person he waged victorious warfare with the Bulgars. He relieved Renier of Trit, who was besieged in Stenimachus, and retook Hadrianople (1206). Finally, to the great advantage of the Empire, he became reconciled with Boniface of Montferrat, whose daughter Agnes was betrothed to him. Undoubtedly the death of the marquess-king, killed in battle in 1207, and the Bulgarian attack on Thessalonica, were fresh causes of disquietude. Fortunately for the Latin Empire, Johannitsa was assassinated outside the city he was besieging (October 1207). The Greek legend assigns the credit for his death to the saintly patron of the city, St Demetrius, who, mounted on his war-horse and armed with his invincible spear, is said to have stricken down the terrible enemy of Hellenism in his own camp. It is unnecessary to add that it happened in a less miraculous manner. But the death of the Bulgarian Tsar delivered the Empire from a great danger. His successor, Boril, after his defeat in 1208 at Philippopolis, soon made peace, which was sealed in 1215 by the marriage of the Emperor Henry with the Tsar's daughter.

About the same time matters improved in Asia Minor. In 1206, at the instigation of David Comnenus, Emperor of Trebizond, who was uneasy at the aggrandisement of Theodore Lascaris and wrathful at the imperial title recently assumed by the Despot of Nicaea, the Latins resumed the offensive in Asia Minor and seized Cyzicus and Nicomedia, which they retained until 1207. But the Bulgarian danger necessitated the concentration of all the forces of the Empire; in order to be able to recall all his troops from Asia Minor, Henry concluded a two years' armistice with Lascaris. The struggle was resumed as soon as the Bulgarian peril had been averted. Lascaris, having vanquished the Turks on the Maeander (1210), became a source of uneasiness to the Latins, as he contemplated attacking Constantinople. The Emperor boldly took the offensive, crossed to Asia, and on 13 October 1211 overwhelmingly defeated the Nicaean sovereign on the river Luparkos (Rhyndakos). Lascaris determined to make peace. By the treaty of 1212 he relinquished to the Latins the north-west of Asia Minor, all the western part of Mysia and Bithynia.

While Henry thus waged victorious warfare with his external enemies, he also strengthened the imperial authority at home. On the death of Boniface of Montferrat, the throne of Thessalonica passed to his infant son Demetrius, in whose name the government was carried on by the Queen-regent, Margaret of Hungary, and Count Hubert of Biandrate, *Baile* or guardian of the kingdom. The Lombard party, whose leader Hubert was, was unfriendly to the queen-regent, and even more hostile to the French and the Emperor, whose suzerainty they wished to repudiate. Henry had no hesitation in marching on Thessalonica, and in spite of Biandrate's resistance he succeeded in occupying the city; then, supported by the queen-regent, he enforced the recognition of his suzerainty, settled the succession which had been left open by the death of Boniface, and caused the young Demetrius to be crowned (January 1209). Henry, indeed, had still much to do in combating the intrigues of Biandrate, whom he arrested, and in neutralising the hostility of the Lombard nobles of Seres and Christopolis, who intended to bar the Emperor's return to Constantinople. He had, however, solidly established the prestige of the Empire in Thessalonica. Thence he proceeded to Thessaly, and, after having crushed the resistance of the Lombard nobles at Larissa, at the beginning of 1209 in the parliament of Ravennika he received the homage of the French barons of the south, above all of the *Megaskyr* of Athens and of the Prince of Achaia, who since the death of Boniface wished to be immediate vassals of the Empire because of their hatred of the Lombards. Henry displayed no less energy in religious matters, and his anti-clerical policy, whereby he refused to return ecclesiastical property seized by laymen, caused displeasure to Innocent III more than once. The concordat signed at the second parliament of Ravennika (May 1210) seemed for a time to have arranged matters. The barons undertook to return any Church property illegally detained by them; the clergy promised to hold these from the civil State, and to pay the land-tax for them. But this attempt at an agreement led to no lasting results. Henry also insisted on opposing the claims of the Patriarch Morosini to govern the Latin Church despotically, and at Morosini's death in 1211 he secured the election to the patriarchate of a candidate chosen by himself. He was equally careful to protect his Greek subjects against the demands of the Latin Church. Unfortunately this monarch, the best of the Emperors whom fate gave to the Latin Empire of Constantinople, died, perhaps of poison, on 11 June 1216, when he was still under forty. This was an irreparable loss for the Empire;

henceforward, under the weak successors of the Emperor Henry, the State founded by the crusaders moved slowly towards its ruin.

Yolande, sister of the two first Latin Emperors, was married to Peter of Courtenay, Count of Auxerre, and he was elected Emperor by the barons in preference to Andrew, King of Hungary, a nephew by marriage of Baldwin and Henry. Peter set out for Constantinople. But in the course of an expedition which he undertook in Epirus, with the object of re-conquering Durazzo which had been taken from the Venetians by the Greeks, he was betrayed into the hands of Theodore Angelus, Despot of Epirus, and died soon afterwards in his prison (1217). The Empress Yolande, who had reached the shores of the Bosphorus in safety, then assumed the regency provisionally in the name of the missing Emperor, and, with the help of Conon of Béthune, one of the heroes of the Crusade, she governed for two years (1217–1219). But a man was needed to defend the Empire. The barons elected Philip, the eldest son of Peter and Yolande, who declined the honour offered to him. His younger brother, Robert of Courtenay, was then chosen in his place; he set out in 1220, and was crowned by the Patriarch on 25 March 1221. He reigned for seven years (1221–1228); after him his throne passed to his brother, Baldwin II, a boy of eleven, during whose minority (1228–1237) the government was entrusted to John of Brienne, formerly King of Jerusalem, a brave knight but an absolutely incapable statesman. Under these feeble governments which succeeded each other for twenty years, Greeks and Bulgars found an easy victim in the exhausted Latin Empire.

In 1222 a grave event took place. The Latin kingdom of Thessalonica succumbed to the attacks of the Despot of Epirus. Theodore Ducas Angelus had succeeded his brother Michael in 1214, and by a series of successful undertakings he had, at the expense of both the Greeks and Bulgars, greatly augmented the State he had inherited. He had retaken Durazzo (1215) and Corfù from the Venetians, and occupied Ochrida and Pelagonia; he appeared to the Greeks as the saviour and restorer of Hellenism. In 1222 he attacked Thessalonica, where the youthful Demetrius, son of Boniface of Montferrat, was now reigning; he took the city easily, and was then crowned Emperor by the Metropolitan of Ochrida. In the ensuing years (1222–1231) the new Basileus extended his sway at the expense of the Bulgars to Macedonia and Thrace, to the neighbourhood of Hadrianople, Philippopolis, and Christopolis. In 1224 he attacked the Latin Empire, and defeated Robert of Courtenay's troops at Seres.

At the very time when the peril which threatened it in Europe was thus increasing, the Latin Empire lost Asia Minor. When Theodore Lascaris (1206–1222), first Emperor of Nicaea, died, he left a greatly increased and solidly established State to his son-in-law, John Vatatzes.

He had, by victories over the Comneni of Trebizond and over the Seljūq Turks, advanced his frontiers to the upper streams of the Sangarius and the Maeander. Vatatzes, who was as good a general as he was an able administrator, during his long reign (1222–1254) completed the work of Lascaris, and bestowed a final period of prosperity on Greek Asia Minor. By 1224 he had recaptured from the Latins almost all the territory they still held in Anatolia, and in a fierce battle at Poimanenon he defeated their army commanded by Macaire of St Menehould. At the same time his fleet seized Lesbos, Chios, Samos, Icaria, and Cos, and compelled the Greek ruler of Rhodes to recognise Vatatzes as suzerain. Before long the Emperor of Nicaea, who was jealous of the success of the new Greek monarch of Thessalonica and suspicious as to his aims, despatched troops to Europe; Madytus and Gallipoli were taken and sacked, and, at the call of the revolted Greeks in Hadrianople, the army of the Nicaean sovereign occupied the city for a time (1224). There they encountered the soldiers of the Emperor of Thessalonica, to whom they had to yield the city. Unfortunately, the Latins were incapable of profiting by the quarrels of the two Greek Emperors, who fell out over their spoils.

They were no better able to profit by the chances offered them by Bulgaria. Since 1218 John Asên had been Tsar at Trnovo (1218–1241). He had married a Latin princess related to the Courtenay family, and, like Johannitsa in bygone days, was quite disposed to side with the Latins against the Greeks; when the Emperor Robert was deposed in 1228, he would gladly have accepted the office of regent during the minority of Baldwin II, as many wished, and he promised to help the monarchy to regain from Theodore Angelus all that had been lost in the West. The foolish obstinacy of the Latin clergy, who were violently opposed to an Orthodox prince, wrecked the negotiations. Thus vanished the last chance of salvation for the Latin Empire.

The Bulgarian Tsar, justly indignant, became a relentless enemy to the Latins, to the great advantage of the Greeks of Nicaea, to whom he rendered yet another service; he conquered their European rival, the Emperor of Thessalonica, whose ambition was becoming a source of uneasiness to Bulgaria. In 1230 he attacked Theodore Angelus, defeated him, and took him prisoner in the battle of Klokotinitza, forcing him to renounce the throne. As is recorded in a triumphal inscription engraved in this very year 1230 on the walls of the cathedral of Trnovo, he annexed "all the country from Hadrianople to Durazzo, Greek territory, Albanian territory, Serbian territory." The Empire of Thessalonica was reduced to modest proportions (it only included Thessalonica itself and Thessaly), and devolved on Manuel Angelus, Theodore's brother.

Thus all-powerful in Europe, John Asên joyfully accepted the proposals of an alliance against the Latins made by John Vatatzes (1234). The two families were united by the marriage of John Asên's daughter to Vatatzes' son; and the two sovereigns met at Gallipoli, which the Nicaean Emperor had taken from the Venetians in 1235, to arrange the division of the Frank Empire. Encompassed on all sides, Constantinople nearly succumbed in 1236 to the combined attack of its two adversaries. But this time the West was roused by the greatness of the danger. The Pisans, Genoese, and Venetians all sent their fleets to succour the threatened capital; Geoffrey II, Prince of Achaia, brought a hundred knights and eight hundred bowmen, and lent an annual subsidy of 22,000 *hyperperi* for the defence of the Empire. Thanks to these aids, Constantinople was saved, and the Latin Empire survived another quarter of a century. But it was a singularly miserable existence. During the twenty-five years of his personal reign (1237–1261), Baldwin II, last Latin Emperor of Constantinople, who had already visited Rome and Paris in 1236, had to beg all over the Western world for help in men and money, which he did not always get. To raise funds he was reduced to pawning the most famous jewels in Constantinople, the crown of thorns, a large piece of the true cross, the holy spear, the sponge, which St Louis bought from him. And such was the distress of the wretched Emperor that for his coinage the lead roofing had to be used, and to warm him in winter the timbers of the imperial palace were chopped up. Some rare successes indeed prolonged the life of the Empire. The Greco-Bulgarian alliance was dissolved; in 1240 Baldwin II recaptured Tzurulum from the Greeks, and thus cleared the approaches to the capital to a certain degree; in 1241 the death of John Asên began the decay of the Bulgarian Empire. Nevertheless the days of the Latin State were numbered. One question remained: would the Greek Empire of Epirus or that of Nicaea have the honour of reconquering Constantinople?

It was secured by Nicaea. While the Latin Empire was in its last agony, John Vatatzes was succeeding in restoring Byzantine unity against the aliens. He drove the Latins from their last possessions in Asia Minor (1241); he gained the powerful support of the Western Emperor Frederick II, whose daughter Constance he married (1244), and who, out of hatred for the Pope, the protector of the Latin Empire, unhesitatingly abandoned Constantinople to the Greeks; he deprived the Franks of the support of the Seljūq Sultan of Iconium (1244); and he seized the Mongol invasion of Asia Minor as an opportunity of enlarging his state at the expense of the Turks. He was specially active in Europe. Since the year 1237, when Michael II Angelus (1237–1271) had founded the despotat of Epirus in Albania at the expense of the Empire of Thessalonica, anarchy had prevailed in the Greek States of the West. In 1240, with the help of John Asên, the aged Theodore Angelus had taken Thessalonica, overthrown his brother Manuel, and caused his son John to be crowned as Emperor (1240–1244). Vatatzes took advantage of this weakness. In 1242 he appeared outside Thessalonica and forced John to renounce the title of Emperor, to content himself with that of Despot, and to become vassal of Nicaea. In 1246 he returned to the attack; this time he seized Thessalonica and expelled the Despot Demetrius. Then he fell on the Bulgarians and took from them a large part of Macedonia—Seres, Melnik, Skoplje, and other places—and the following year he deprived the Latins of Vizye and Tzurulum; finally, a family alliance united him to the only Greek prince who still retained his independence in the West, Michael II, Despot of Epirus. This ambitious and intriguing prince was doubtless about to go to war with Nicaea in 1254. Nevertheless, when on 30 October 1254 Vatatzes died at Nymphaeum, the Empire of Nicaea, rich, powerful, and prosperous, surrounded the poor remnants of the Latin Empire on all sides. Only Constantinople remained to be conquered.

The final catastrophe was delayed for seven years by discords between the Greeks. Theodore II Lascaris (1254–1258) had at one and the same time to carry on war with the Despot of Epirus and to fight with the Bulgars, who after the death of Vatatzes had considered the time favourable for avenging their defeats. Theodore Lascaris routed them at the pass of Rupel (1255); but it was only after the assassination of their King Michael (1257) that he succeeded in imposing peace on them. On the other hand, in spite of his great military and political qualities, the new Greek Emperor was of a delicate constitution. The field was therefore clear for the intrigues of ambitious men, and especially for Michael Palaeologus, who, having married a princess of the imperial family, openly aspired to the throne.

When by Theodore's premature death the throne passed to a child, Michael had no difficulty in seizing the real power after the assassination of Muzalon the regent, nor a little later in superseding the legitimate dynasty by causing himself to be crowned Emperor at Nicaea on 1 January 1259. He soon justified this mean usurpation by the victories he achieved.

He first brought the war with Michael II, Despot of Epirus, to a successful conclusion. Michael II was a formidable enemy: he was the ally of Manfred, King of Sicily, and of William of Villehardouin, Prince of Achaia, who had both married daughters of the despot; he was supported by the Albanians and the Serbs, and was very proud of the successes he had secured; since the capture of Prilep (1258) he was master of the whole of Macedonia, and was already threatening Thessalonica. Michael Palaeologus boldly took the offensive, reconquered Macedonia, and invaded Albania. In spite of the help brought by the Prince of Achaia to his father-in-law, the army of Michael II was overwhelmingly defeated at Pelagonia (1259). William of Villehardouin himself fell into the hands of the Byzantines; and the Emperor seized the opportunity to recover a part of the Peloponnesus. Henceforth the despotat of Epirus was swallowed up by the Empire of Nicaea. The time had come when Michael Palaeologus was to restore Hellenism by reconquering Constantinople.

In 1260 he crossed the Hellespont, took Selymbria and the other strongholds still retained by the Latins outside the capital, and threatened Galata. At the same time he very astutely utilised the rivalry of the Venetians and Genoese to gain the alliance of the latter. On 13 March 1261, by the Treaty of Nymphaeum, he promised that, in return for their help against Venice and their support against his other enemies, he would grant them all the privileges enjoyed by the Venetians in the East. The Genoese secured counting-houses at Thessalonica, Adramyttium, Smyrna, Chios, and Lesbos; they were to have the reversion of the Venetian banks at Constantinople, Euboea, and Crete; the monopoly of commerce in the Black Sea was assigned to them. At this price they consented to betray Western Christendom.

Venice had realised, rather late in the day, the necessity of defending the Latin Empire; since 1258 she had maintained a fleet of some importance at Constantinople. But in July 1261 it happened that the fleet had temporarily left the Golden Horn to attack the neighbouring town of Daphnusia. One of Michael Palaeologus' generals, the Caesar Alexius Strategopulus, seized the opportunity; on 25 July 1261, by a lucky surprise, he captured the capital of the Latin Empire, almost without resistance. Baldwin II had no alternative but to take to flight, accompanied by the Latin Patriarch, the podestà, and the Venetian colonists; on 15 August 1261 Michael Palaeologus made his solemn entry into Constantinople, and placed the imperial crown on his head in St Sophia.

Thus, after an existence of half a century, fell the State established in Constantinople by the Fourth Crusade. Even though the Empire had only an ephemeral existence, yet the East remained full of Latin settlements. Venice, in spite of the efforts of her enemies, retained the essential portions of her colonial empire in the Levant, Negropont, and Crete, and the strong citadels of Modon and Coron; her patrician families kept most of their seigniories in the Archipelago. So also did the other Latin States in Greece born of the Crusade. Under the government of the La Roche family, the duchy of Athens lasted until 1311; and although the disastrous battle of the Cephisus then transferred it to the hands of the Catalans (1311–1334), who were superseded by the Florentine family of Acciajuoli (1334–1456), the Byzantines never regained possession of it. The principality of Achaia, under the government of the three Villehardouins (1204–1278), was even more flourishing. These settlements were really the most lasting results, within the Latin Empire of Constantinople, of the Crusade of 1204.

CHAPTER XV.

GREECE AND THE AEGEAN UNDER FRANK AND VENETIAN DOMINATION (1204–1571).

At the time of the Latin conquest of Constantinople, the Byzantine Empire no longer comprised the whole of the Balkan peninsula and the Archipelago. A Serbian state, a Bosnian *banat*, and a revived Bulgarian Empire had been recently formed in the north, while two of the Ionian Islands—Cephalonia and Zante—already owned the Latin sway of Matteo Orsini, an Apulian offshoot of the great Roman family, and Corfù was threatened by the Genoese pirate, Leo Vetrano. In the Levant, Cyprus, captured from the Greeks by Richard I, was already governed by the second sovereign of the race of Lusignan, while Rhodes, amidst the general confusion, was seized by a Greek magnate, Leo Gabalâs. All the rest of South-Eastern Europe—Thrace, Macedonia, Epirus, Greece proper, Crete and the islands of the Aegean—remained to be divided and, if possible, occupied by the Latin conquerors of Byzantium.

While the newly-created Latin Empire was formed almost wholly outside the limits of Greece, the Greek lands in Europe were partitioned, with the exception of three islands, between the Crusaders, whose leader was Boniface, Marquess of Montferrat, and the Venetian Republic. The marquess received Salonica, the second city of the Byzantine world, with the title of king; and his kingdom, nominally dependent upon the Latin Empire, embraced Macedonia, Thessaly, and much of continental Greece, including Athens. The Venetians, with a keen eye to business, managed to secure a large part of the Peloponnese and Epirus, the Cyclades and Euboea, the Ionian Islands, and those of the Saronic Gulf, and had purchased from the marquess on 12 August 1204 the great island of Crete, which had been "given or promised" to him by Alexius IV in the previous year. Such was, on paper, the new arrangement of the classic countries which it now remained to conquer.

The King of Salonica set out in the autumn of 1204 to subdue his Greek dominions and to parcel them out, in accordance with the feudal system, among the faithful followers of his fortunes. In northern

Greece he met with no resistance, for the only man who could have opposed him, Leo Sgourós the *archon* of Nauplia, fled from Thermopylae before the harnessed Franks, and retreated to the strong natural fortress of Acrocorinth. Larissa with Halmyrus became the fief of a Lombard noble, Velestino that of a Rhenish count; while the commanding position of Boudonitza above the pass of Thermopylae was entrusted to the Marquess Guido Pallavicini, whose ruined castle still reminds us of the two centuries during which Italians were wardens of the northern March of Greece. Another coign of vantage at the pass of Graviá was assigned to two brothers of the famous Flemish house of St Omer, while on the ruins of classic Amphissa Thomas de Stromoncourt founded the barony of Sálona, so called from the city which had given to Boniface his royal title. Neither Thebes nor Athens resisted the invaders; the patriotic Metropolitan, Michael Acominatus, unable to bear the sight of Latin schismatics defiling the great cathedral of Our Lady on the Acropolis, withdrew into exile; a Latin archbishop ere long officiated in the Parthenon; a Burgundian noble, Othon de la Roche, who was a trusted comrade of Boniface, became *Sire*, or, as his Greek subjects called him, *Megaskyr* or "Great Lord," of both Athens and Thebes, with a territory that would have seemed large to the Athenian statesmen of old. Then the King of Salonica and the *Sire* of Athens proceeded to attack the strongholds that still sheltered Sgourós in the Peloponnese.

A large portion of that peninsula had been assigned, as we saw, to the Venetians. But, with two exceptions, "the Morea," as it had begun to be called a century earlier, was destined to fall into the hands of the French. A little before the capture of Constantinople, Geoffrey de Villehardouin, nephew of the delightful chronicler of the conquest, had been driven by stress of weather into the Messenian port of Modon. During the winter of 1204 he had employed himself by aiding a local magnate in one of those domestic quarrels which were the curse of medieval Greece, and thus paved the way for a foreign occupation. Struck by the rich and defenceless character of the land upon which a kind fortune had cast him, Villehardouin no sooner heard of Boniface's arrival in the peninsula than he made his way across country to the Frankish camp at Nauplia, and confided his scheme of conquest to his old friend, William de Champlitte, whose ancestors came from his own province of Champagne. He promised to recognise Champlitte as his liege lord in return for his aid; and the two comrades, with the approval of Boniface, set out with a hundred knights and some men-at-arms to conquer the Morea. One pitched battle decided its fate in that unwarlike age, when local jealousies and the neglect of arms had weakened the power of resistance, and a tactful foreigner, ready to guarantee local privileges, was at least as acceptable a master as a native tyrant and a Byzantine tax-collector. One place after another surrendered; the little

Frankish force completely routed the Moreote Greeks and their Epirote allies in the Messenian olive-grove of Koúndoura; here and there some warrior more resolute than his fellows held out—Doxapatrês, the romantic defender of an Arcadian castle; John Chamáretos[1], the hero of Laconia; Sgourós in his triple crown of fortresses, Corinth, Nauplia, and the Larissa of Argos; and the three hereditary *archons* of the Greek Gibraltar, isolated and impregnable Monemvasía; but Innocent III could address Champlitte, ere the year was up, as "Prince of all Achaia." The prince rewarded Villehardouin, the real author of his success, with the Messenian seaport of Coron. But Venice, if she was not strong enough to occupy the rest of the Peloponnese, was determined that neither that place nor Modon, stepping-stones on the route to the East, should fall into other than Venetian hands. In 1206 a Venetian fleet captured both stations from their helpless garrisons, and the republic thus obtained a foothold at the extreme south of the peninsula which she retained for well-nigh three centuries. In the same year the seizure and execution of Vetrano enabled her to make good her claim to Corfù, where ten Venetian nobles were settled in 1207 as colonists. At this the Count of Cephalonia and Zante thought it prudent to recognise her suzerainty, for fear lest she should remind him that his islands had been assigned to her in the partition treaty.

In the rest of the scattered island-world of Greece, Venice, as became an essentially maritime state, acquired either actual dominion or what was more profitable—influence without expensive administrative responsibility. Crete furnished an example of the former system; Euboea, or Negropont, and the Cyclades and northern Sporades were instances of the latter. For "the great Greek island" the Venetians had to contend with their rivals, the Genoese, who had already founded a colony there, and at whose instigation a bold adventurer, Enrico Pescatore, landed and forced the isolated Venetian garrison to submit. It was not till 1212 that Pescatore's final defeat and an armistice with Genoa enabled the Venetians to make their first comprehensive attempt at colonising Crete. The island was partitioned into 132 knights' fiefs—a number subsequently raised to 230—and 408 sergeants' fiefs, of which the former class was offered to Venetian nobles, the latter to Venetian burgesses. The administrative division of Crete into six provinces, or *sestieri*, was based on the similar system which still exists at Venice, and local patriotism was stimulated by the selection of colonists for each Cretan *sestiere* from the same division of the metropolis. The government of the colony was conducted by a governor, resident at Candia, with the title of duke, who, like most colonial officials of the suspicious republic, held office for only two years, by two councillors, and by a greater and lesser council of the colonists. But the same year that witnessed the

[1] Pitra, *Analecta sacra et classica,* VII. 90—91.

arrival of these settlers witnessed also the first of that long series of Cretan insurrections which continued down to our own time. Thus early, Venice learnt the lesson that absolute dominion over the most bellicose Greek population in the Levant, however imposing on the map, was in reality very dearly bought.

The north and south of Negropont had fallen to the Venetians in the deed of partition. But a soldierly Fleming, Jacques d'Avesnes, had received the submission of the long island when the Crusaders made their victorious march upon Athens, building a fort in midstream, without, however, founding a dynasty on the shore of the Euripus. Thereupon Boniface divided Negropont into three large fiefs, which were bestowed upon three gentlemen of Verona—Ravano dalle Carceri, his relative Giberto, and Pegoraro dei Pegorari—who assumed from this triple division the name of *terzieri*, or triarchs. Soon, however, Ravano, triarch of Kárystos, the southern and most important third, which seems to have included the island of Aegina, became sole lord of Negropont, though in 1209 he thought it prudent to recognise Venice as his suzerain. The republic obtained warehouses and commercial privileges in all the Euboean towns; a Venetian bailie was soon appointed to administer the communities which sprang up there; and this official gradually became the arbiter of the whole island. Upon Ravano's death in 1216 the bailie seized the opportunity of conflicting claims to weaken the power of the Lombard nobles by a re-division of the island into sixths, on the analogy of Crete. The capital remained common to all the hexarchs, while Ravano's former palace there became the official residence of the bailie. A large and fairly harmonious Italian colony was soon formed, and the pleasant little town of Chalcis has probably never been a more agreeable resort than when noble Lombard dames and shrewd Venetian merchants danced in the Italian palaces and took the air from the breezy battlements of the island capital.

Venetian influence in the archipelago took a different form from that which it assumed in Corfù, Crete, and Euboea. The task of occupying the numerous islands of the Aegean was left to the enterprise of private citizens. In truly Elizabethan style, Marco Sanudo, a nephew of the old Doge Dandolo, descended upon the El Dorado of the Levant with a band of adventurous spirits. Seventeen islands speedily submitted; of the Cyclades Naxos alone offered resistance, and there, in 1207, the bold buccaneer founded a duchy, which lasted for more than three centuries. Keeping Naxos for himself, he assigned other islands to his comrades. Thus Marino Dandolo, another nephew of the great doge, became lord of well-watered Andros, the family of Barozzi obtained the volcanic isle of Santorin, the Quirini associated their name with Astypálaia, or Stampalia, while the brothers Ghisi, with complete disregard for the paper rights of the Latin Emperor to Tenos and Scyros, acquired not only those islands but the rest of the northern Sporades. Lemnos, another portion of the imperial share, became the fief of the Navigajosi, who received from the Emperor the title of Grand Duke, borne in Byzantine times by the Lord High Admiral. While the Greek *archon* of Rhodes, Leo Gabalâs, maintained his position there with the barren style of "Lord of the Cyclades," the twin islands of Cerigo, the fabled home of Venus, and Cerigotto, which formed the southern March of Greece, furnished miniature marquessates to the Venetian families of Venier and Viaro. But the Venetian nobles, who had thus carved out for themselves baronies in the Aegean, were not always faithful children of the republic. Sanudo did homage not to Venice but to the Latin Emperor Henry, the over-lord of the Frankish states in the Levant, and did not scruple to conspire with the Cretan insurgents against the rule of the mother-country, when self-interest suggested that he might with their aid make himself more than "Duke of the Archipelago"—"King of Crete."

While the knightly Crusaders and the practical Venetians had thus established themselves without much difficulty in the most famous seats of ancient poetry, there was one quarter of the Hellenic world where they had been forestalled by the promptitude and skill of a Greek. Michael Angelus, a bastard of the imperial house, had attached himself to the expedition of Boniface in the hope of obtaining some advantage on his own account. On the march the news reached him that the Greeks of the province of Nicopolis were discontented with the Byzantine governor who still remained to tyrannise over them. Himself the son of a former governor of Epirus, he saw that with his name and influence he might supplant the official representative of the fallen Empire and anticipate the establishment of a foreign authority. He hastened across the mountains to Arta, found the unpopular officer dead, married his widow, a dame of high degree, and with the aid of his own and her family connexions made himself independent Despot of Epirus. Soon his dominions stretched from the Gulf of Corinth to Durazzo, from the confines of Thessaly to the Adriatic, from Sálona, whose French lord fell in battle against him, to the Ionian Sea. Treacherous as well as bold, he did homage, now to the Latin Emperor Henry and now to Venice, for his difficult country which neither could have conquered. But the mainland of Greece did not suffice for his ambition. He aided the Moreote Greeks at the battle of Koúndoura; his still abler brother, Theodore, accepted for him the Peloponnesian heritage of Sgourós, when the Argive leader at last flung himself in despair from the crags of Acrocorinth; the Ionian island of Leucas, which is practically a part of continental Greece, seems to have owned his sway; and, before he died by an assassin's hand in 1214, he had captured from Venice her infant colony of Corfù. Under him and his brother and successor Theodore, the Epirote court of Arta became the refuge of those Greeks who were impatient of the foreign rule in the Morea, and the base from which it was fondly hoped that the redemption of that fair land might one day be accomplished.

The Franks had scarcely occupied the scattered fragments of the Hellenic world when they began the political and ecclesiastical organisation of their conquest. We may take as the type of Frankish organisation the principality of Achaia, the most important of their creations and that about which we have most information. Alike in Church and State the Latin system was simple. These young yet shrewd nobles from the West shewed a capacity for government which we are accustomed to associate with our own race in its dealings with foreign populations; and, indeed, the parallel is close, for in the thirteenth and fourteenth centuries Greece was to them what our colonies were to younger sons in the nineteenth. They found to their hands a code of feudalism, embodied in the "Assises of Jerusalem," which Amaury de Lusignan had recently adopted for his kingdom of Cyprus, and which later on, under the title of the "Book of Customs of the Empire of Romania," served as the charter of Frankish Greece. Champlitte himself, recalled home by the death of his brother, died on the journey before he could do more than lay the foundations of his principality, which it was reserved for Villehardouin, acting as the bailie of the next-of-kin, to establish firmly on approved feudal principles. Twelve baronies of different sizes were created, whose holders formed the temporal peerage of Achaia; seven lords spiritual, with the Latin Archbishop of Patras as their Primate, received sees carved out of the existing Greek dioceses; and the three great military orders of the Teutonic Knights, those of St John, and the Templars, were respectively settled at Mostenitsa, Modon, and in the rich lands of Achaia and Elis. There too was the domain of the prince, whose capital was at the present village of Andravída, when he was not residing at La Crémonie, as Lacedaemon was then called. Military service, serfdom, and the other incidents of feudalism were implanted in the soil of Hellas, and the dream of Goethe's *Faust*, the union of the classical with the romantic, was realised in the birthplace of the former. The romance was increased by the fatal provision—for such it proved to be—that the Salic law should not apply to the Frankish states. Nothing contributed in a greater degree to the ultimate decline and fall of Latin rule in Greece than the transmission of important baronies and even of the principality of Achaia itself to the hands of women, who, by a strange law of nature, were often the sole progeny of the sturdy Frankish nobles. Ere long feudal castles rose all over the country, and notably in the Morea and the Cyclades, where the network of chivalry was most elaborate. Sometimes, as at Boudonitza, Sálona, and Paroikía, the medieval baron built his keep out of the fragments of some Hellenic temple or tower, which the local tradition believed to have been the "work of giants" in days gone by; sometimes his donjon rose on a virgin site; but in either case he chose the spot with a view to strategic conditions. The Church, as well as the baronage, made its mark upon what was for it a specially uncongenial soil. The religious Orders of the West followed in the wake of the fortunate soldiers, who had founded a "new France" in old Greece. The Cistercians received the beautiful monastery of Daphní, on the Sacred Way between Athens and Eleusis, destined to be the mausoleum of the last Burgundian Duke of Athens; the "Crutched Friars" of Bologna had a hospice at Negropont; the emblem and the name of Assisi still linger in the Cephalonian monastery of Sisia; and the ruins of the picturesque Benedictine abbey of Isova still survey the pleasant valley of the Alpheus. As for the Orthodox bishops, they went into exile; when, towards the end of the fourteenth century, they were again allowed to reside in their ancient sees, they became the ringleaders of the revived national party in the struggle against the rule of a foreign garrison and an alien Church. For in the Near East religion and nationality are usually identical terms.

The wisdom which Villehardouin had shewn in his treatment of Greeks and Franks alike now received its reward. Self-interest and the welfare of the State combined to indicate him as a better ruler of Achaia than any young and inexperienced relative of Champlitte who might, by the accident of birth, be the rightful heir. Youthful communities need able princes, and every step that he took was a fresh proof of Villehardouin's ability. He did homage to the Emperor Henry, and received in return the office of Seneschal of Romania; he won the support of Venice by relinquishing all claim to Modon and Coron; and he thereby induced the doge to assist him in his wily scheme for detaining the coming heir on his journey from France, so that he might arrive in the Morea after the time allowed by the feudal code for his personal appearance. When young Robert arrived with still a few days to spare, the crafty bailie avoided meeting him till the full period had elapsed. Then a parliament, summoned to examine the claimant's title, decided against the latter; Robert returned to France, while Geoffrey remained lord of the Morea. Poetic justice in the next century visited upon his descendants this sin of their ancestor. Meanwhile, Innocent III hastened to greet him as "Prince of Achaia"—a title which he did not consider himself worthy to bear till he had earned it by the capture of the still unconquered Greek castles of Corinth, Nauplia, and Argos. In 1212 the last of them fell; Othon de la Roche, as a reward for his aid, received the two latter as fiefs of the principality of Achaia, thus inaugurating the long connexion of the Argolid with Frankish Athens; while Corinth became the see of a second Latin archbishop. Geoffrey I crowned his successful career by negotiating a marriage between his namesake and heir and the daughter of the ill-fated Latin Emperor, Peter of Courtenay, during a halt which the damsel made at Katákolo on her way to Constantinople. When he died, in 1218, "all mourned, rich and poor alike, as if each were lamenting his own father's death, so great was his goodness."

His elder son and successor, Geoffrey II, raised the principality to a pitch of even greater prosperity. We are told of his wealth and of his care for his subjects; he could afford to maintain "80 knights with golden spurs" at his court, to which cavaliers flocked from France, either in search of adventures abroad or to escape from justice at home. Of his resolute maintenance of the State against the Church the Morea still preserves a striking monument in the great castle of Chloumoûtsi, which the French called Clermont and the Italians Castel Tornese, from the *tornesi* or coins of Tours that were afterwards minted there for over a century. This castle, on a tortoise-shaped hill near Glaréntza, was built by him out of the confiscated funds of the clergy, who had refused to do military service for their fiefs, and who, as he pointed out to the Pope, if they would not aid him in fighting the Greeks, would soon have nothing left to fight for. Alike with his purse and his personal prowess he contributed to the defence of Constantinople, receiving as his reward the suzerainty over the Duchy of the Archipelago and the island of Euboea. The Marquess of Boudonitza and the cautious Count of Cephalonia and Zante, the latter ever ready to worship the rising sun, became the vassals of one who was acknowledged to be the strongest Frankish prince of his time. For, if Athens had prospered under Othon de la Roche, and sea-girt Naxos was safe under the dynasty of Sanudo, the Latin Empire was tottering already, and the Latin kingdom of Salonica had fallen[1] in 1223—the first creation of the Fourth Crusade to go—before the vigorous attack of Theodore Angelus, the second Despot of Epirus, who founded on its ruins the Greek Empire of Salonica. This act of ostentation, however, by offending the political and ecclesiastical dignities of the Greek Empire of Nicaea, provoked a rivalry which postponed the Greek recovery of Byzantium. The fall of the Latin kingdom of Salonica and the consequent re-conquest of a large part of northern Greece for the Hellenic cause alarmed the Franks, whose possessions lay between Thessaly and the Corinthian Gulf. Of these by far the most important was Othon de la Roche, the "Great Lord" of Athens, who had established around him alike at Thebes and Athens a number of his relatives from home, attracted by the good luck of their kinsman beyond the seas. But, as the years passed, the Burgundian successor of the classic heroes and sages, whom the strangest of fortunes had made the heir alike of Pindar and Pericles, began to feel, like several other Frankish nobles, a yearning to end his days in the less famous but more familiar land of his birth. In 1225, after twenty years of authority, he left Greece for ever with his wife and his two sons, leaving his Athenian and Theban dominions to his nephew Guy, already owner of half the

[1] Pitra, *op. cit.*, VII. 335—338, 577—588.

Boeotian city. The descendants of the first Frankish *Sire* of Athens became extinct in Franche-Comté only as recently as the seventeenth century, and the archives of the Haute-Saône still contain the seal and counter-seal of the *Megaskyr*. No better man than his nephew could have been found to carry on the work which he had begun. Under his tactful rule his capital of Thebes became once more a flourishing commercial city, where the silk manufacture was still carried on, as it had been in Byzantine times, where the presence of a Jewish and a Genoese colony implied that there was money to be made, and where the Greek population usually found a wise protector of their customs and their monasteries, diplomatically endowed by Vatatzes, the powerful Greek Emperor of Nicaea[1], in their foreign yet friendly lord. Policy no less than humanity must have led Guy I to be tolerant of the people over whom he had been called to rule. It was his obvious interest to make them realise that they were better off under his sway than they would be as subjects of an absentee Greek Emperor, who would have ruled them vicariously in the old Byzantine style, from Macedonia or Asia Minor. Thus his dominions, if "frequently devastated" by the Epirote Greeks, remained undiminished in his hands, while his most dangerous neighbour, Theodore, the first Greek Emperor of Salonica, became, thanks to his vaulting ambition, the prisoner of the Bulgarians at Klokotinitza, and the short-lived Greek Empire which he had founded, after the usurpation of his brother Manuel, was reduced in the reign of his son John to the lesser dignity of a Despotat, and was finally annexed, in that of John's brother Demetrius, to the triumphant Empire of Nicaea in 1246. Another and very able member of the family of Angelus, the bastard Michael II, had, however, made himself master of Corfù and Epirus ten years earlier, and there held aloft the banner of Greek independence, as his father, the founder of the Epirote dynasty, had done before him.

In the same year that witnessed the annexation of Salonica, the second Villehardouin prince of Achaia died, and was succeeded by his brother William. The new prince, the first of the line who was a native of the Morea—for he was born at the family fief of Kalamáta—was throughout his long reign the central figure of Frankish Greece. Crafty and yet reckless, he was always to the front whenever there was fighting to be done, and his bellicose nature, if it enabled him to complete the conquest of the peninsula from the Greeks, tempted him also into foreign adventures, which undid his work and prepared the way for the revival of Greek authority. At first, all went well with the soldierly ruler. The virgin fortress of Monemvasía, which had hitherto maintained its freedom, yielded, after a three years' siege, to the combined efforts of a Frankish force and a Venetian flotilla, and the three local *archons*—Mamonâs, Daimonoyánnes, and Sophianós—were obliged to acknow-

[1] Sáthas, Μεσαιωνικὴ Βιβλιοθήκη, VII. 509.

ledge the Frank as their lord. To overawe the Slavs of Taygetus and the restive men of Maina, the prince built three castles, one of which, Mistrâ, some three miles from Sparta, was destined later on to play a part in Greek history second to that of Byzantium alone, and is still the chief Byzantine glory of the Morea. At this moment the Frankish principality reached its zenith. The barons in their castles lived "the fairest life that a man can"; the prince's court at La Crémonie was thought the best school of chivalry in the East, and was described as "more brilliant than that of a great king." Thither came to learn the noble profession of arms the sons of other Latin rulers of the Levant; the Duke of distant Burgundy was a guest at the prince's table; King Louis IX of France, most chivalrous sovereign of the age, might well esteem the tall knights of Achaia, who came with their lord to meet him in Cyprus, who helped the Genoese to defend Rhodes against the Greeks. Trade flourished, and such was the general sense of security that people gave money to the merchants who travelled up and down the country on their simple note of hand, while from the King of France the prince obtained the right to establish his own mint in the castle of Chloumoûtsi in place of the coins which he seems to have struck previously in that of Corinth.

Unfortunately the prince's ambition plunged the Frankish world of Greece into a fratricidal war. On the death of his second wife, a Euboean heiress, in 1255, he claimed her ancestral barony in the northern third of that island; and when the proud and powerful Lombards, aided by their Venetian neighbours, repudiated his claim, not only did hostilities break out in Euboea, but also extended to the mainland opposite. William had summoned Guy I of Athens, his vassal for Argos and Nauplia, and, as was even pretended, for Attica and Boeotia as well, to assist him in the struggle. The *Megaskyr*, however, not only refused to aid his nominal lord, but actively helped the opposite party. Practically the whole of Frankish Greece took sides in the conflict, despite the wise warnings of the Pope, anxious lest the cause of the Church should be weakened by this division among its champions at a time when their national enemy had grown stronger. In 1258, at the pass of Mt Karýdi, between Megara and Thebes, Frankish Athens first met Frankish Sparta face to face. The battle of "the Walnut Mountain" was a victory for the latter; the Athenian army retreated upon Thebes, before whose walls the prayers of his nobles prevailed upon the victor to make peace with their old comrades. Guy of Athens, summoned to appear before the High Court of Achaia at Níkli near Tegea for his alleged breach of the feudal code, was sent by the Frankish barons before the throne of Louis IX of France, whose authority they recognised as supreme in a case of such delicacy. The question was referred by the king to a parliament at Paris, which decided that Guy had been, indeed, guilty of a technical offence in taking up arms against his lord, but that, as he had never actually paid him homage, his fief could not be forfeited. His long journey to France was considered sufficient punishment for his disobedience. Guy did not return empty-handed; asked by the king what mark of royal favour he would prefer, he begged, and obtained, the title of Duke, which would raise him to the heraldic level of the Duke of Naxos, and for which, he said, there was an ancient precedent at Athens. The style of "Duke of Athens" was not only borne by his successors for two centuries, but has been immortalised by Dante, Boccaccio, Chaucer, and Shakespeare, who by a pardonable anachronism transferred to Theseus the title of the French, Sicilian, Aragonese, and Florentine rulers of the medieval city.

The history of Frankish Greece is full of sudden reverses of fortune, by which the victor of one day became the vanquished of the next. Guy I had left his country a defeated and an accused man, while his successful rival was the practical leader of the Latin Orient; he returned with the glamour of the ducal title to find his conqueror and feudal lord a prisoner of the Greeks. During Guy's absence, William of Achaia, by his third marriage with Anna, daughter of the Despot Michael II of Epirus, had become involved in the tortuous politics of that restless sovereign. It was Michael's design to anticipate the Greeks of Nicaea in their projected re-conquest of Constantinople, and he was anxious to secure his position by marrying one of his daughters to the powerful Prince of Achaia and another to Manfred, the ill-fated Hohenstaufen King of Sicily. This latter alliance by making Corfù a part of the Epirote princess's dowry led to the subsequent occupation of that island by the Angevin conquerors of Naples. But the plans of the crafty despot met with a serious obstacle in the person of Michael VIII Palaeologus, who had usurped the Nicene throne and intended to make himself master of Byzantium, and who ordered his brother to punish the insolence of his Epirote rival. In 1259 the hostile Greek forces met on the plain of Pelagonía in Western Macedonia; William of Achaia with a chosen band of Franks and a contingent of native troops was among the despot's allies. At a critical moment, a private quarrel between the despot's bastard John and the Frankish prince led the indignant Epirote to desert to the enemy; the despot, warned of his son's intention, fled in the night, and the Franks were left to meet the foe's attack. Despite their usual prowess in the field, the battle was lost; the prince, unhorsed and hiding under a heap of straw, was recognised by his prominent teeth and taken prisoner with many of his nobles. Michael VIII saw at once that the capture of so distinguished a man might be made the means of re-establishing Greek rule in the Morea, and offered him and his fellow-prisoners their liberty and money for the purchase of other lands in France in return for the cession of Achaia. The prince, however, replied in the true spirit of feudalism, that the land conquered by the efforts of his father and his father's comrades was not his to dispose of as if he were an absolute monarch. For three years he remained in captivity, while the Latin Empire fell. Michael VIII restored the seat of his government to Constantinople, and the Duke of Athens acted as bailie of the widowed principality of Achaia. It was, indeed, a tragic moment in the history of Greece when there devolved upon the Duke of Athens the task of receiving the fugitive Latin Emperor Baldwin II as his guest in the castle of the Cadmea at Thebes and upon the sacred rock of the Athenian Acropolis.

Master of Constantinople, Michael VIII was more than ever anxious to obtain a foothold in the Morea. He moderated his demands, in the hope of exhausting the patience of his wearied captives, and he professed that he would be content with the surrender of the three castles of Monemvasía, Maina, and Mistrâ, which had been either captured or built by the prince himself, and which were therefore his to bestow. The question, vital for the future of the Frankish principality, was referred to the high court at Níkli—a parliament consisting, with two exceptions, of ladies only, for the fatal day of Pelagonía had left most of the baronies in the possession of either the wives of the prisoners or the widows of the slain. In an assembly so composed, reasons of state and the scriptural argument employed by the Duke of Athens, that "it were better that one man should die for the people rather than that the other Franks of the Morea should lose the fruits of their fathers' labours," had naturally less weight than sentiment and the voice of affection. In vain Guy offered to pledge his own duchy to raise the ransom, or even to take the prince's place in prison. The three castles—with the doubtful addition of Geráki, which in any case soon became Greek—were surrendered; the prisoners were released; the noble dames were sent as hostages to Constantinople; and a Byzantine province, based on the ceded Frankish quadrilateral, was established in the south-east corner of the Morea, whose capital was Mistrâ, the seat of the "Captain of the Territory in the Peloponnese and its Castles." From the date of this surrender in 1262 began the decline of Frankish power; thenceforth friction between the rival elements in the population was inevitable; and while the discontented Greeks of the still Frankish portion of the peninsula found a rallying-point at Mistrâ, the Greek Emperor gained an excellent recruiting-ground for his light troops and his marines. In a word, the Ladies' Parliament of Níkli by destroying the unity of the State paved the way for the Turkish conquest.

The solemn vow that William had taken never again to levy war against the Greek Emperor was soon broken; hostilities inevitably followed the proximity of the rival residences of Mistrâ and Sparta, and weary years of warfare depopulated the peninsula. One woman, we are told, lost seven husbands one after the other, all killed in battle; such was the drain upon the male portion of the inhabitants. The Greeks imported Turkish mercenaries to aid them against the Frankish chivalry, and thus the future masters of the peninsula made their first appearance there. But the Turks, unable to obtain their pay, deserted to the Franks, whom they helped to win the battle of Makryplági on "the broad hillside" now traversed by the railway to Kalamáta, receiving as a reward lands on which to settle. Had the pride of the Franks then allowed them to accept Michael VIII's proposal for a marriage between his heir, the future Emperor Andronicus II, and the prince's elder daughter Isabelle, the future of the Morea might have been different; the two races might have been welded together; Eastern and Western Christendom might really have met in a firm alliance at Mistrâ; and the Morea might perhaps have resisted the all-conquering Turks. But racial prejudice would not have it so; and Isabelle was made the instrument of uniting the fortunes of the principality with those of the Neapolitan Angevins, whose founder, Charles I, in 1267, received from the exiled Latin Emperor by the treaty of Viterbo the suzerainty of Achaia—the beginning of many unsuspected woes for that beautiful land.

From the first, William, who had welcomed this new feudal tie with the brother of the King of France, found that it constituted an obligation rather than a benefit. He was summoned to the aid of his Angevin suzerain against Conradin at the battle of Tagliacozzo, and when his daughter espoused the second son of Charles I the marriage contract stipulated that, whether the Prince of Achaia left heirs or not, the principality should belong to the house of Anjou, which since 1267 likewise held Corfù and aspired to be the dominant factor in south-eastern, as it already was in southern, Europe. It was true that Neapolitan troops assisted him in the desultory warfare against the Greeks which, together with feudal disputes, occupied the rest of his reign. But when in 1278 the third Villehardouin prince was laid to rest beside his father and brother in the church of St James at Andravída, and the male stock of the family thus came to an end, the evils of the Angevin connexion began to be felt.

Elsewhere also the Greek cause had prospered at the expense of the Latins. In the north, it was true, Hellenism had split up into three divisions, for on the death of Michael II of Epirus his bastard, John I, had established himself as independent ruler of Neopatras—a splendid position on a spur of Mt Oeta, which commands the valley of the Spercheus and faces the barrier of Mt Othrys, while the snows of Tymphrestós bound the western horizon, beyond which lay the Epirote dominions of the lawful heir, Nicephorus I. As the champion of Orthodoxy at a time when Michael VIII was coquetting with the Papacy in order to avert the Angevin designs on Constantinople, the "Duke" of Neopatras, as the Franks called John Ducas Angelus, was a formidable adversary of the restored Greek Empire. When the imperial forces were sent to besiege his capital, he escaped by night and fled to Duke John of Athens, who in 1263 had succeeded his father

Guy, and who assisted his namesake to rout them. But the imperial commander inflicted a crushing defeat off Demetriás in the Gulf of Volo upon a flotilla equipped by the Lombard barons of Euboea, while in that and the other islands of the Aegean the meteoric career of Licario, a knight of Kárystos, caused serious losses to the Latins. Mortally offended by the proud Lombards, this needy adventurer, whose family, like theirs, had come from Northern Italy, gratified his vengeance by offering to subdue the long island to the Emperor's authority. Michael VIII gladly welcomed so serviceable a henchman; Licario's capture of Kárystos proved that he was no vain boaster after the manner of the Franks; he received from his new master the whole of Euboea as a fief, and soon one Lombard castle after another fell into his hands. Knowing full well the rashness of his fellow-countrymen, he easily entrapped one of the triarchs and Duke John of Athens, the victor of Neopatras, outside the walls of Negropont, and had the satisfaction of dragging them in chains to Constantinople. One of the most dramatic scenes in Byzantine history is the passage which describes the triumph of the once despised knight over his former superior, the rage and fury of the triarch and his sudden death of chagrin at the spectacle of the Emperor and Licario in confidential conversation. Ere long, Licario became Lord High Admiral, and spread devastation throughout the archipelago. Already the supposedly impregnable rock of Skópelos, whose Latin lord had believed himself to be beyond the reach of malicious fortune, had surrendered to the traitor of Kárystos; the rest of the northern Sporades, and Lemnos, the fief of the Navigajosi, shared its fate, and thenceforth remained in Greek hands till the fall of Constantinople. Ten other Latin islands were lost for twenty years or more, and two dynasties alone, those of Sanudo and Ghisi, survived this fatal cruise in the Aegean, while the two Venetian Marquesses of Cerigo and Cerigotto were driven from the southern March of Greece, and one of the three Monemvasiote *archons*, Paul Monoyánnes, received the island of Venus as a fief of the Greek Empire. Licario disappeared from history as rapidly as he had risen; we know not how he ended; but his career left a permanent mark on Greek history. Thus Michael VIII had obtained extraordinary success over the Franks. He had destroyed the Latin Empire, recovered a large part of Negropont and many other islands; as early as 1256 his brother, as governor, had replaced the independent Greek dynasty of Gabalâs in Rhodes[1]; another viceroy was established at Mistrâ; and both a Prince of Achaia and a Duke of Athens had been his prisoners at Constantinople. But John of Athens was released on much easier terms than William of Achaia; for Michael VIII feared to provoke the Duke of Neopatras, who was bound by matrimonial ties to the ducal house of Athens and by those of

[1] Miklosich and Müller, *Acta et diplomata*, VI. 198.

commerce to the royal house of Naples, the dreaded enemy of the restored Greek Empire. Soon afterwards the gouty Duke of Athens died, and William, his brother, reigned in his stead. A new era had begun all over the Frankish world. The house of Anjou was now the dominant factor in Greece. Isabelle de Villehardouin had been left a widow before her father died, and by virtue of her marriage contract Charles I of Naples and Sicily was now Prince as well as suzerain of Achaia, and governed that principality, as he governed Corfù, by means of deputies. While these two portions of Greece were his absolute property, he was acknowledged as suzerain of both the Athenian duchy and the palatine county of Cephalonia and Zante, and considered himself as the successor of Manfred in Epirus as well as in the Corfiote portion of the latter's Greek possessions. Alike in Corfù and Achaia his early governors were foreigners, and the Corfiotes for the first time found their national Church degraded and their metropolitan see abolished by the zeal of the Catholic Angevins. In Achaia, where the Frankish nobility was strongly attached to its privileges and looked upon newcomers with suspicion, the rule of the Angevin bailies was so unpopular that Charles was obliged to appoint one of the local barons, and almost the first act of the regency which followed his death was to confer the bailiwick upon Duke William of Athens, whose riches were freely expended upon the defences of Greece. Upon his death in 1287 he was succeeded at Athens by his infant son Guy II, under the regency of the duchess, a daughter of the Duke of Neopatras and the first Greek to hold sway over the Athenians since the conquest, while in the Morea a great Theban magnate, Nicholas II de St Omer, governed for Charles II of Anjou. This splendour-loving noble, then married to the widowed Princess of Achaia, had built out of the dowry of his first wife, a Princess of Antioch, the noble castle of St Omer, of which one tower alone remains, on the Cadmea of Thebes. An Emperor and his court could have found room within its walls, which were decorated with frescoes representing the conquest of the Holy Land by the ancestors of the Theban baron. Similar frescoes of the tale of Troy existed a century later in the archiepiscopal palace of Patras, and may still be seen, on a smaller scale, in the churches of Geráki. Besides the castle of St Omer, Nicholas built that of Avarino on the north of the famous bay of Navarino, the "harbour of rushes" as the Franks called it. And in the north-west of the peninsula the mountains and castle of Santaméri still preserve the name of this once-powerful family.

The barons soon, however, longed for a resident prince. In the eleven years that had elapsed since the death of William of Achaia, they had had six bailies—two foreigners, two of their own order, and two great Athenian magnates. At last they represented to Charles II that he should marry Princess Isabelle, "the Lady of the Morea," who was still living in widowhood at Naples, to Florent d'Avesnes, a young

Flemish nobleman, brother of the Count of Hainault and great-nephew of the conqueror of Euboea. Florent was already a favourite of the king, who accordingly consented to the marriage, on condition that, if Isabelle should survive her husband, neither she nor her daughter nor any other of her female descendants should marry without the royal consent; the penalty for so doing was to be the reversion of the principality to the Neapolitan crown. This harsh stipulation was in the sequel twice enforced; but in the meanwhile all were too well satisfied with the alliance to consider its disadvantages. In 1289 Florent married and became Prince of Achaia, and for seven years the country had peace. The ravages of the Angevin bailies were repaired, and in the words of the *Chronicle of the Morea*, "all grew rich, Franks and Greeks, and the land waxed so fat and plenteous in all things that the people knew not the half of what they possessed." But the insolence of the Flemings, who had followed their countryman to the Morea, another Epirote campaign, and a raid by Roger Loria, the famous Admiral of Aragon, marred this happy period of Moreote history. Unfortunately, in 1297, soon after the peace with the Greeks of the Byzantine province had expired, Florent died, leaving Isabelle again a widow with one small daughter, who was affianced to Guy II, the young Duke of Athens, and rightly regarded as "the best match in all Romania."

The pen of the contemporary Catalan chronicler, Ramón Muntaner, who was personally acquainted with Guy, has left us a charming picture of the Theban court at this period. Muntaner, who had seen many lands, described him as "one of the noblest men in all Romania who was not a king, and eke one of the richest." His coming of age was a ceremony long remembered in Greece, for every guest that came to do him honour received gifts and favours from his hand, and his splendid munificence to Boniface of Verona, a young cavalier from Euboea, who was chosen to dub him a knight, struck the shrewd Catalan freebooter as the noblest gift that any prince made in one day for many a long year. Jongleurs and minstrels enlivened the ducal leisure; in the noble sport of the tournament the young duke knew no fear, and in the great jousts at Corinth, in which more than a thousand knights and barons took part, he did not shrink from challenging a veteran champion from the West. Now for the first time we find the "thin soil" of Attica supplying Venice with corn, while the Theban looms furnished the Pope with silken garments. The excellent French that was spoken at Athens struck visitors from France, while long ere this the foreign rulers of Greece had learned the language of their Greek subjects. One Duke of Athens had even quoted Herodotus; one Archbishop of Corinth had actually translated Aristotle. In short, the little Frankish courts at the end of the thirteenth century were centres of prosperity, chivalry, and a large measure of refinement, while the country was far more prosperous than it had been in the later centuries of Byzantine rule, or than it was either beneath the Turkish yoke or in the early years of its final freedom under Otto of Bavaria. Unhappily, the Athenian duchy had scarcely reached its zenith, when the French dynasty fell for ever beneath the blows of another and a ruder race.

The same year 1294 that made the young Duke of Athens his own master strengthened the hold of the Angevins upon Greece. The ambitious plans of Charles I for the conquest of Epirus and the restoration of the Latin Empire at Constantinople had been baffled by the defeat of his forces amid the mountains of the Greek mainland, and by the Sicilian Vespers and the consequent establishment of the rival house of Aragon on the throne of Sicily. Charles II attempted to recover by diplomacy what his father had lost by arms, and in 1294 he transferred all his claims to the Latin Empire, the actual possession of Corfù with the castle of Butrinto on the opposite coast, as well as the suzerainty over the principality of Achaia, the duchy of Athens, the kingdom of Albania, and the province of Vlachia (as Thessaly was still called), to his second son, Philip, Prince of Taranto. This much-titled personage, who thus became the suzerain of all the Frankish states in Greece, thereupon married, after the fashion of the luckless Manfred, whose sons were still languishing in an Angevin dungeon, a fair Epirote princess, daughter of the Despot Nicephorus I, who promised to give him as her dowry the castle of Lepanto with three other fortresses, and, if the heir apparent died, to make Philip Despot of Epirus, if the heir apparent lived, to make him its suzerain. Philip of Taranto by these extraordinary arrangements became the most important figure, at least on paper, in the feudal hierarchy of medieval Greece. In this capacity he was called upon to give his consent to the third marriage of Princess Isabelle of Achaia, who, during the Papal Jubilee of 1300, had met in Rome Philip, a young scion of the house of Savoy, and desired to wed so likely a defender of her land. The Savoyard was reluctantly invested with the principality by Charles II on behalf of his son, and thus inaugurated the connexion of his famous family with the Morea. But Philip of Savoy, though a valiant knight, looked upon his Greek principality as a means of making money against the evil day when the Angevins, as he felt convinced, would repent of having appointed him and when Philip of Taranto would desire to take his place. He and his Piedmontese followers became very unpopular; for, while they occupied the chief strategic positions, he extorted loans and forced presents from his subjects. Before long Charles II revived the legal pretext that Isabelle's third marriage had been against his consent, and that she had therefore forfeited her principality; and Philip's refusal to assist in furthering the Angevin plans of conquest in Epirus gave him an excuse for releasing the Achaian barons from their allegiance to one who had broken the feudal law. Philip and Isabelle left the Morea for ever; an estate on the Fucine lake was considered adequate compensation for the loss of Achaia; and, in 1311, the elder daughter of the last Villehardouin prince, after having been the tool of Angevin diplomacy ever since her childhood, died in Holland far from the orange-groves of Kalamáta. Her husband remarried, and his descendants by this second union continued to bear the name of "Achaia," and, in one case, endeavoured to recover the principality which had for a few brief years been his. Philip of Taranto, the lawful suzerain, became also the reigning prince, but, after a short visit, he resorted to the old plan of governing the Morea by means of bailies. Of these the first was Guy II, "the good Duke" of Athens, whose wife, the elder daughter of Isabelle, might be regarded by the old adherents of the family as the rightful heiress of Achaia.

Guy had latterly become more influential than ever; for death had left his mother's old home of Neopatras in the hands of a minor, John II, and the Duke of Athens had been appointed as regent there. Thus Athenian authority extended from the Morea to Thessaly; the Greek nobles of the North learnt French, and the coins of Neopatras bore Latin inscriptions in token of the Latinisation of the land. Alas! the duke was suffering from an incurable malady; he had no heir; and, when in 1308 he was laid to rest in the abbey of Daphní, the future destroyers of the French duchy were already at hand. For the moment, however, the future of Athens seemed to be assured. Guy's mother had married, after his father's death, a member of the great crusading family of Brienne, which had already provided a King of Jerusalem and Emperor of Romania and held the less sonorous but more profitable dignity of Counts of Lecce. By a previous marriage with an aunt of the duke, his stepfather had had a son Walter, who now succeeded to his cousin's dominions. Walter of Brienne possessed all the courage of his race; but he lacked the saving virtue of caution, and his recklessness at a critical moment destroyed in a single day the noble fabric which the wise statesmanship of the house of De la Roche had taken a century to construct. So dramatic are the vicissitudes of the Latin Orient: the splendid pageants of chivalry one day, absolute ruin the next.

The new conquerors of Athens came from an unexpected quarter. During the struggle for Sicily between the houses of Aragon and Anjou, Frederick II, the Aragonese king of the island, had gladly availed himself of the support of a band of Catalans, whose swords were at the disposal of anyone who would pay them. When the peace came, they found it necessary to seek employment elsewhere. At that moment the Greek Emperor, Andronicus II, hard pressed by the growing power of the Turks in Asia, was glad of such powerful assistance, and, to the detriment of Greece, took the Catalans into his service. In the East they repeated on a much larger scale their performances in the West; the Emperor, like the King of Sicily, found them valuable but dangerous allies, who quarrelled with his subjects, plundered his cities, and defied his orders. At last they constituted themselves into an organised society, and set out to ravage Macedonia and Greece on their own account. When they had exhausted one district they moved on to another, and by this locust-like progress they and some of their converted Turkish auxiliaries entered the great Thessalian plain in 1309. The young Duke of Neopatras, now emancipated by the death of Guy, was too feeble to oppose them till an imperial force compelled them to move on towards the Eden which awaited them in the Duchy of Athens. Walter of Brienne was at first by no means displeased with their appearance. He knew their language, which he had learnt as a child in Sicily, and he thought that he might use them for the accomplishment of his immediate object—the restoration of Athenian influence over the moribund principality of the Angeli at Neopatras. The Catalans accepted his proposals, and in six months they had captured more than thirty castles of northern Greece for their new employer.

Having thus rapidly obtained his end, Walter wished to dispense with his instrument. He picked out the best of the Catalans for his future use and then peremptorily bade the rest begone without the formality of payment for their recent services. The Catalans, thus harshly treated, remonstrated; Walter vowed that he would drive them out by force, and took steps to make good his threat. In the spring of 1311, at the head of such a force as no Athenian duke had ever led before, a force recruited from the baronial halls of the highlands and islands of Hellas, he rode out to rout the vulgar soldiers of fortune who had dared to defy him. Once again, after the lapse of many centuries, the fate of Athens was decided on the great plain of Boeotia. The Catalans, who knew that they must conquer or die, prepared the battlefield with consummate skill. They ploughed up the soft ground in front of them, and irrigated it from the neighbouring Cephisus; nature herself assisted their strategy, and, when the armies met on 15 March, the quaking bog was concealed with an ample covering of verdure. Walter, impetuous as ever, charged across the plain with a shout, followed by the flower of the Frankish chivalry. But, long before they could reach the Catalan camp, they plunged into the quagmire. Their heavy armour and the harness of their horses made them sink yet deeper, till they stood imbedded in the marsh, as incapable of motion as equestrian statues. The Catalans plied them with missiles; the Turks completed the deadly work; and such was the carnage of that fatal day, that only some four or five of the Frankish knights are known to have survived. The duke was among the slain, and his head, severed by a Catalan knife, was borne to rest in his good city of Lecce long years afterwards. His duchy lay at the mercy of the victors, for there was none left to defend it save the heroic duchess. But, finding resistance vain, she escaped with her little son to France, and thus avoided the fate of many another widowed dame of high degree who became the wife of some rough Catalan, "unworthy," in the phrase of Muntaner, "to bear her wash-hand basin." As for the Greeks, they made no effort to rise in defence of the old order against their new masters; so shallow were the roots which French rule had struck in that foreign land. Nor have the Burgundian Dukes of Athens left many memorials of their sway. A few coins, a few arches, a few casual inscriptions—such is the artistic patrimony which Attica and Boeotia have preserved from this brilliant century of Latin culture.

The victors of the Cephisus were in one respect embarrassed by the completeness of their victory. They realised that they had no one in their own ranks of sufficient standing to become their ruler in the new position which their success had thrust upon them. They accordingly adopted the strange plan of offering the leadership to one of their prisoners, Boniface of Verona, the favourite of Guy II, and a great man in Euboea. Boniface was ambitious, but he felt that he could not, with his wide connexions in the Frankish world, commit such an act of baseness. He, therefore, declined; but his fellow-prisoner, Roger Deslaur, a knight of Roussillon who had already acted as intermediary between the late Duke and the company, had no such obligations, and accepted the post with the castle of Sálona and the hand of its widowed lady. A year later, however, the Catalans realised that their precarious situation (for all the Powers interested in Greece regarded them as interlopers) required to be strengthened by the invocation of some powerful and recognised sovereign as their protector. Their eyes naturally turned to their old employer, Frederick II of Sicily, and they begged him to send one of his sons to rule over them. Frederick gladly consented to a proposal which would add lustre to his house, and for the next 65 years the royal family of Sicily provided absentee dukes for the Catalan duchy of Athens, while the real political authority was always wielded by a vicar-general whom they appointed to represent them at the capital of Thebes. A marshal for long existed by the side of this official, till the two offices were first combined in the same person and then that of marshal was allowed to drop. An elaborate system of local government was created; representative institutions were adapted from Barcelona, whose "Customs" supplanted the "Assises of Romania," and whose language became the official as well as the ordinary idiom. The Greeks were, till towards the close of Catalan rule, treated as an inferior race, while the Orthodox Church occupied the same humble position that it had held in the Burgundian times. Feudalism lingered in a modified form; but it had lost its glamour, and the court of the Catalan vicar-general must have been a very drab and prosaic affair after the magnificent pageants of the splendour-loving Dukes of Athens, whose flag still floated over the Argive fortresses that had been granted to Othon de la Roche a century before.

Having thus established a connexion with one of the acknowledged states of Europe, the Catalan Grand Company began to extend its operations in Greece. A Catalan claim to the Morea furnished it with a plausible pretext for a raid. Two years after the battle of the Cephisus, Philip of Taranto had conferred that principality on Matilda of Hainault, the daughter of Isabelle and widow of Guy II of Athens, on condition that she married and transferred the princely dignity to Louis of Burgundy. The object of this manœuvre was to compensate his brother the Duke of Burgundy for losing the hand of the titular Latin Empress of Constantinople, whom Philip, then a widower, had resolved to marry himself. But before Louis of Burgundy had taken possession of his Achaian principality, another claimant had appeared there. Besides Isabelle, William of Achaia had left another daughter, the Lady of Akova, who was regarded by some as the lawful representative of the Villehardouin dynasty, on the ground of a supposed will made by her father. With the object of securing her claims for her posterity, if not for herself, she married her danghter to the Infant Ferdinand of Majorca, who had at one time played an adventurous part in the career of the Catalan Company and was well known in Greece. Both the Lady of Akova and her daughter died before these claims could be realised, but her daughter left a baby behind her, the future King James II of Majorca; and, on behalf of this child, Ferdinand landed in the Morea to receive the homage of the principality. His usurpation was at first successful; he even coined his own money at the mint of Glaréntza, while the Catalans of Athens set out to aid their old comrade against the Burgundian party. A battle in the forest of Manoláda, in 1316, proved fatal, however, to the Infant's cause; and his head, severed on the field, was displayed before the gate of Glaréntza. The Athenian Catalans turned back at the sad news, but Louis of Burgundy did not long enjoy the fruits of this victory; barely a month afterwards he died, poisoned, so it was said, by the Italian Count of Cephalonia, a medieval villain believed to be capable of every crime. Louis' widow, the Princess of Achaia, was forced against her will by the crooked diplomacy of Anjou to go through the form of marriage, in 1318, with John of Gravina, brother of Philip of Taranto. Matilda stoutly refused to be this man's wife, and when at last pressure was put upon her by the Pope to make her consent she replied that she was already another's. This confession proved to be her ruin. The crafty Angevins appealed to the clause in her mother's marriage contract which declared the principality forfeit should one of Isabelle's daughters marry without her suzerain's consent. While John of Gravina governed as Prince of Achaia, she languished in the Castel dell' Uovo at Naples, till at last, in 1331, death released her from the clutches of her royal gaoler. Thus closed the career of the Villehardouin family; thus, in the third generation, was the deceit of Geoffrey I visited upon the unhappy daughter of the unhappy Isabelle. Two years later, John of Gravina exchanged the Morea for the duchy of Durazzo, the kingdom of Albania, and the

Angevin possessions in Epirus; while the titular Empress Catherine of Valois, acting for her son Robert of Taranto, whose father Philip was then dead, combined in her own person the suzerainty and actual ownership of Achaia, as well as the claim to the defunct Latin Empire. This arrangement had the advantage of uniting in a single hand all the Angevin dominions in Greece—the principality of Achaia, the castle of Lepanto, the island of Corfù, and the island-county of Cephalonia, which last had been conquered from the Orsini by John of Gravina in 1324.

If the Catalans had failed to found a principality in the South, they were much more successful in the North. The feeble Duke of Neopatras had died, the last of his race, in 1318, and the head of the Company, at the time Alfonso Fadrique, a bastard of King Frederick II of Sicily, conquered the best part of the former dominions of the Thessalian Angeli. At Neopatras itself he established a second Catalan capital, styling himself Vicar-General of the Duchies of Athens and Neopatras. The Sicilian Dukes of Athens assumed the double title, and, long after the Catalan duchies had passed away, the Kings of Aragon, their successors, continued to bear it. Venice profited by the dismemberment of this Greek state to occupy Ptéleon at the entrance to the Pagasaean Gulf, her first acquisition on the Greek mainland since Modon and Coron. On the other side of Greece the principal line of the Angeli had also been extinguished in 1318 by the murder of the Despot Thomas, a victim of Count Nicholas of Cephalonia, another member of that unscrupulous family. The assassin soon perished by the hand of his brother John II, who thus continued the traditions of the Hellenised Orsini. But the new ruler of Epirus was a patron of Greek letters; at his command a paraphrase of Homer was written; while the famous church of Our Lady of Consolation at Arta still contains an inscription recording the Orsini and the two bears[1] which were the emblems of their house—one of the most curious and least-known monuments of the Latin domination in Greek lands.

Meanwhile, the house of Brienne had not abandoned the idea of recovering the lost duchy of Athens. Young Walter had grown up to manhood, and, in 1331, landed in Epirus to reconquer his father's dominions. Once again, however, the brilliant qualities of chivalry were seen to be inferior to the less showy strategy of the Catalans. The Greeks remained unmoved by the appearance of this deliverer from the "extreme slavery" which a contemporary described as their lot, and the only lasting result of this futile expedition was the destruction by the Catalans themselves of the noble castle of St Omer, for fear lest it should fall into the invader's hands. The abode of the Theban barons is connected with literature as well as art, for the original of one of the

[1] See the author's article on the old Epirote capital in the *Morning Post* for 16 May 1908.

most valuable memorials of Frankish rule, the French version of the *Chronicle of the Morea*, was found within its walls—a proof of culture among its inmates. Walter's subsequent career was connected with Florentine and English history rather than with Athens, for he became tyrant of Florence, and died, fighting against our Black Prince, at the battle of Poitiers. The family of Enghien, into which his sister had married, succeeded to his Argive castles and his Athenian claims.

While the titular Duke of Athens thus retired to rule over Florence, a Florentine family, destined ultimately to succeed to his Greek duchy, established itself in the Morea. Of the numerous visitors who have journeyed from Florence to see the famous Certosa, few realise that it was constructed out of the Greek revenues of its founder. Niccolò Acciajuoli had made the acquaintance of the titular Empress Catherine of Valois at the Neapolitan Court, whither he had gone to seek his fortune; he became her man of business and the director of her children's education, and, when she and her son Robert obtained through his negotiations the principality of Achaia, he received his reward in the shape of broad estates in that land. He gradually increased his stake in the country, and in 1358 was invested by his old pupil, the Emperor Robert, with the town and castle of Corinth, whence the Acropolis of Athens can be seen, and whence, thirty years later, it was to be conquered. At the other end of the Corinthian Gulf, the archbishopric of Patras was occupied by three members of the Acciajuoli clan, which thus continued to prosper while the feeble rule of an absentee prince and another disputed succession on his death in 1364 weakened the hold of the Angevins upon the principality. Philip II[1] of Taranto, the brother, and Hugh of Lusignan, Prince of Galilee, the stepson, of the titular Emperor Robert, then contended for the possession of the Morea till the latter abandoned the struggle for another similar contest in Cyprus. During these internal convulsions, the Byzantine province had grown stronger and was better governed than the neighbouring Frankish principality. The imperial viceroys of Mistrâ had been appointed for much longer periods than had been the case before; and, in 1348, the Emperor John Cantacuzene had sent his son Manuel as Despot for life to the Morea. Thenceforth, as the seat of a younger member of the imperial family, Mistrâ became more and more important; and its splendid Byzantine churches still testify to the value which, as the Greek Empire declined, the Emperors attached to this isolated fragment of Greece. It is a curious freak of history that, in the last as in the early days of Greek freedom, the two most flourishing cities of Hellas were once more Athens and Sparta—the Athens of the Acciajuoli, the Sparta, as Mistrâ was often pedantically styled, of the Palaeologi.

The peril that was to prove fatal alike to the medieval Athens and

[1] Philip III on the list of titular Emperors of Romania.

the medieval Sparta had ere this appeared on the horizon of Greece. The growing Turkish danger had at last induced the Papacy to recognise the Catalan conquest of Attica, and extend its benediction over those whom it had hitherto described as "sons of perdition." But the new generation of Catalans that had succeeded to the sturdy conquerors of the Cephisus was a degenerate race, given to drink and divided by quarrels, which led to the introduction of the Turks, by this time established in Europe. For the moment, however, the north of Greece had been annexed to the ephemeral empire of the great Serbian Tsar, Stephen Dušan; and, even after his death in 1355, Serbian rule lingered on for a time and provided a more or less feeble barrier between the duchy of Athens and the Ottoman power. On the other side of continental Greece, the tottering Greek despotat of Epirus, long disputed between the Byzantine and the Serbian Empires, had finally perished in 1358 with the Despot Nicephorus II, becoming partly Serb and partly Albanian, while the former island-domain of the Orsini, the county palatine of Cephalonia, had been conferred by the Angevins upon Leonardo Tocco of Benevento, who united four out of the seven Ionian islands in his hand, adopted from one of them the style of "Duke of Leucadia," and founded a family which, after over a century's rule in Greece, has only become extinct at Naples in our own time. Elsewhere, in Chios and Lesbos, two other fresh Italian factors had appeared in the many-coloured map of the Levant: the Genoese families of Zaccaria and Gattilusio. The rule of the Zaccaria in the former island lasted only from 1304 to 1329, but in 1346 Chios was re-conquered by a band of Genoese, who formed a chartered company, or *maona*, which, reconstituted some years later under the title of the "*Maona* of the Giustiniani," held the island till the Turkish conquest in 1566. Lesbos, in 1355, was bestowed by the Greek Emperor, John V, upon his brother-in-law, Francesco Gattilusio, whose dynasty survived by nine years the fall of Constantinople, while in 1374 Genoa obtained Famagosta in pledge from King Peter II of Cyprus. Yet another bulwark of Latin rule had been created in the Aegean by the capture of Rhodes from the Seljūqs, the successors of the Greek governors, by the Knights of St John in 1309. But, if Latin Christendom was as strong as ever in the islands of the Aegean and the Ionian seas, it was weaker in the continental states that lay between them.

The death of Frederick III, King of Sicily and Duke of Athens, in 1377, was a severe blow to the two Catalan duchies, for the claims of his daughter and heiress, Maria, were disputed by Pedro IV of Aragon, who found support with the clergy, the leading nobles, and the burgesses of Athens and Neopatras. Another competitor, however, appeared upon the scene, and repeated on a smaller scale the history of the Catalan Company seventy years earlier. During the struggle between the Kings of France and Navarre, the latter had been assisted by a body of Navarrese of good family, who, at the peace, had offered their services to their sovereign's brother for the conquest of Durazzo, and were at this time lying idle in the south of Italy. Meanwhile, the principality of Achaia, on the death of the childless Philip II in 1373, had been offered to Queen Joanna I of Naples, conferred by her upon one of her numerous husbands, Otto of Brunswick, and then pawned in 1377 for five years to the Knights of St John. All the time, however, the lawful heir was the nephew of Philip and last titular Emperor of Constantinople, Jacques de Baux, who thought that in the disturbed condition of Greece the moment had arrived to make good his claim to Achaia, and that the Navarrese Company would be the best means of doing so. The Company entered his service, captured Corfù from the Neapolitan officials, and in 1380 entered Attica, of which Baux as Prince of Achaia might claim the suzerainty, and as the uncle of Maria of Sicily might desire the conquest. The Navarrese, under the leadership of Mahiot de Coquerel, and Pedro de S. Superan, known as "Bordo" or the "bastard," were aided by the Sicilian party against the mutual enemy, and the important castle of Livadia, a town which had attained great prominence under Catalan rule and had received special privileges at the Catalan conquest, fell into their hands. Sálona and the castle of Athens, however, held out, and their defenders expected their duke, the King of Aragon, to reward their loyalty by signing two series of capitulations which their envoys presented to him. Pedro IV granted many of their requests, and shewed his appreciation of the glamour which must ever attach to the sovereign of the Acropolis by describing that sacred rock as "the most precious jewel that exists in the world, and such that all the kings of Christendom together could in vain imitate." But so great had been the ravages of civil war in the duchy, that he was forced to invite Greeks and Albanians to settle there, the beginning of the Albanian colonisation of Attica and Boeotia. As for the Navarrese, they marched into the Morea in 1381, came to terms with the Knights of St John, already weary of their bargain, and occupied the principality in the name of Jacques de Baux. When the latter died in 1383, they became practically independent, despite the protests of rival claimants. Androûsa, in Messenia, was the Navarrese capital; Coquerel, and, after him, S. Superan, ruled with the title of Vicar, which the latter in 1396 exchanged for that of Prince. Thus, at the end of the fourteenth century, a Navarrese principality was carved out of Achaia, just as at its beginning a Catalan duchy had been created in Attica.

The existence of the latter was now drawing to a close. While the Duke of Athens remained an absentee at Barcelona, Nerio Acciajuoli, the adopted son of the great Niccolò, was watching every move in the game from the citadel of Corinth. Like a clever diplomatist, he prepared his plans carefully; and, when all was ready, easily found his *casus belli*. The important castle of Sálona was at this time in the possession of a woman, and her only daughter, the young countess, was the greatest heiress of the Catalan duchies. Nerio applied, on behalf of his brother-in-law, for her hand; the offer was scornfully refused, and a Serbian princeling preferred to the Florentine upstart's kinsman. The choice of a Slav offended Franks and Greeks alike; Nerio invaded the duchies by land and sea, and in 1387 was master of the city of Athens. The Acropolis, however, held out under the command of a valiant Spaniard, Pedro de Pau, and John I of Aragon, who had by that time succeeded Pedro IV as Duke of Athens and Neopatras, wrote as late as 22 April 1388 to the Countess of Sálona, offering her the "Castle of Athens," if she could succour its garrison[1]. Ten days later, the Acropolis was Nerio's; Catalan domination was over. Two Catalan fiefs alone, the county of Sálona and the island of Aegina, remained independent, but memorials of Catalan rule may still be seen in the castles of Livadia and Lamia and in a curious fresco at Athens. Otherwise, the Catalans melted away, as if they had never been masters of the city of the sages, till at last the title of Athens and Neopatras in the style of the Kings of Spain was the sole reminder of the Greek duchies that had once been theirs.

The epoch that had now been reached was one of change all over Greece. Two years before Nerio hoisted his flag on the Acropolis, another Florentine, Esau Buondelmonti, had put an end to Serbian rule at Joánnina by marrying the widow of Thomas Preljubović, the former ruler of Epirus, while Esau's sister was regent of Cephalonia. Venice, as well as Florence, had increased her Greek possessions. In 1363 a Cretan insurrection, more serious than any that had yet occurred because headed by Venetian colonists, involved Tito Venier, the Marquess of Cerigo, whose family had recovered their island by intermarriage with its Greek lords. Thenceforth Cerigo remained either wholly or partially a Venetian colony. In 1386 Venetian replaced Neapolitan rule at Corfù, and in 1388 the republic purchased Argos and Nauplia, the ancient fiefs of the French Dukes of Athens, from their last representative, Marie d'Enghien. Two years later, the islands of Tenos and Myconus became Venetian by bequest of the Ghisi. In 1383 the murder of Niccolò dalle Carceri, a great Euboean baron who was also Duke of Naxos, and the usurpation of Francesco Crispo, a Lombard of Veronese origin, had installed a new dynasty in the archipelago, which not only allowed two Euboean baronies to come under Venetian influence but also made the duchy of Naxos more dependent upon the goodwill of the republic. Thus, if Florence was predominant at Athens, in Epirus, and in the county palatine, Venice was stronger than ever in Negropont and Crete, held the Argive castles as well as Modon and Coron in the Morea, and was mistress of Corfù and Cerigo. As Ptéleon was a

[1] *Institut d'Estudis Catalans: Anuari* (1907), p. 253.

Venetian colony, and as the Marquess of Boudonitza had long belonged to the Venetian family of Zorzi, both the northern and the southern Marches of Greece were in Venetian hands. Athens itself was soon to follow.

Nerio's ambition had not been appeased by the acquisition of that city; he coveted the Argive appurtenances of the Athenian duchy in its palmy days. Accordingly, he instigated his son-in-law, the Despot Theodore Palaeologus, who then ruled at Mistrâ, to seize Argos before the Venetian commissioner could arrive. On this occasion, however, the wily Florentine over-reached himself; he became the prisoner of the Navarrese Company, acting on behalf of Venice, and had to strip the silver plates off the doors of the Parthenon and rob the treasury of that venerable cathedral in order to raise his ransom. In 1393 the Turks, by the conquest of Thessaly and Neopatras, became his neighbours on the north, and it became evident that the Turkish conquest of Athens, which he avoided by the payment of tribute, was only a question of time. Before the year 1394 was many weeks old, the Catalan county of Sálona had become Turkish, the Dowager Countess had been handed over to the insults of the soldiery, and her daughter sent to the harem of the Sultan, who ere long was reported to have murdered the ill-fated heiress of the Fadriques. The memory of her tragic fate still lingers round the castle rock of Sálona, and the loss of this western bulwark of Athens sounded like a death-knell in the ears of Nerio. King Ladislas of Naples might confer upon him the coveted title of Duke of Athens—a name to conjure with in the cultured world of Florence—but when, a few months later, the first Florentine wearer of the title lay a-dying, he foresaw clearly the fate that was hovering over his new-won dominions.

Nerio left no legitimate sons; but he had a bastard, Antonio, the child of a fair Athenian, and to him he left Thebes and Livadia, while he bequeathed the city of Athens and his valuable stud to the Parthenon, in which he desired to be buried. It was not to be expected that the Orthodox Greeks, who had recently been allowed for the first time since the Frankish conquest to have their own metropolitan resident at Athens, and had thereby recovered their national consciousness, would permit their city to become the property of a Roman Catholic cathedral. While, therefore, Nerio's two sons-in-law, the Despot Theodore I and Carlo I Tocco, were fighting over the possession of Corinth, the Metropolitan of Athens called in the Turks. The Acropolis, however, held out, and its governor, one of Nerio's executors, offered to hand over Athens to the Venetian bailie of Negropont for the republic, on condition that the ancient privileges of the Athenians should be respected. The bailie dispersed the Turks, and the home government decided to accept Athens, but on one ground alone: its proximity to the Venetian colonies, which might be injured if it were allowed to fall into Turkish or other hands. A governor, styled *podestà* and captain, was appointed, and so little desirable did the position seem that four months elapsed before any Venetian noble could be found to accept it. Nor need this reluctance surprise us. Athens at the close of the fourteenth century, as we know from the contemporary account of an Italian visitor, could not have been a very desirable residence. The city contained "about a thousand hearths" but not a single inn; Turkish pirates infested the coast, and Antonio Acciajuoli harried the countryside. Still, the "Church of St Mary" was the wonder of the pious pilgrim, just as the relics which it contained had been the envy of Queen Sibylla of Aragon. Twenty of the columns of the "house of Hadrian," as the temple of the Olympian Zeus was popularly described, were then standing, and the remains of the Roman aqueduct marked, according to the local *ciceroni*, "the study of Aristotle." Venice, however, was not long concerned with the care of this glorious heritage which she so lightly esteemed. The bastard Antonio routed her forces in the pass between Thebes and Negropont, and after a long siege forced the gallant defenders of the Acropolis to surrender from sheer starvation. To save appearances the shrewd conqueror, having obtained all that he wanted, agreed to become the nominal vassal of the republic for "Sythines," as Athens was then called, while the Venetians compensated themselves for its actual loss by the acquisition of the two keys of the Corinthian Gulf—Lepanto, in 1407, from Paul Boua Spata, its Albanian lord, and Patras from its Latin archbishop on a five years' lease. The former of these places remained Venetian for over ninety years; the latter, with an interval, till 1419, when it was restored to ecclesiastical rule, and consequently lost. Four years later the republic purchased Salonica.

The Turkish defeat at Angora in 1402 gave Greece, like the other Christian states of the Near East, a brief respite from her doom, and the tide of Turkish conquest temporarily receded. The Despot Theodore I of Mistrâ, who had endeavoured to strengthen the fighting forces of the Morea by the admission of a large Albanian immigration, and by handing over Corinth to the Knights of St John, now urged the latter to occupy the county of Sálona instead. Turkish rule was, however, soon restored there; and in 1414 the sister creation of the Crusaders, the historic marquessate of Boudonitza, finally disappeared from the map. Meanwhile, in the Frankish principality of Achaia a new and vigorous prince, the last of the line, had arisen. On the death of S. Superan in 1402, his widow had succeeded him, but the real power was vested in her nephew Centurione Zaccaria, a member of the Genoese family which had once ruled over Chios. Centurione, following the precedent of the first Villehardouin, deprived S. Superan's children of their birthright and, by the same legal quibble, received in 1404 the title of Prince of Achaia from the King of Naples. But the Frankish portion of the peninsula was dwindling away before the advancing Greeks. The young

Despot Theodore II, who had succeeded his namesake in 1407, was a son of the Emperor Manuel II, who therefore took a double interest in a part of his diminished Empire which seemed best able to resist a Turkish attack. Manuel visited the Morea, rebuilt the six-mile rampart across the Isthmus, and reduced the lawless Mainates to order. Nor was he the only Greek who occupied himself in the welfare of the Peloponnese. It was at this time that the philosopher George Gemistòs Pléthon, who was teaching the doctrines of Plato at Mistrâ, drew up his elaborate scheme for the regeneration of the country. If Pléthon was an idealist, the other side of the picture is supplied by the contemporary satirist Mázares, who described in dark colours the evil qualities of the seven races then inhabiting the peninsula, the insecurity of life and property, and the faithlessness and craft of the Greek *archons*. Unfortunately, the last period of Moreote history before the Turkish conquest proved that the satirist was nearer the truth than the philosopher.

It was soon obvious that neither ramparts across the Isthmus nor Platonic schemes of reform could save the disunited peninsula. In 1423 the great Turkish captain Tura-Khān, accompanied by the Sultan's frightened vassal, Antonio of Athens, easily demolished the Isthmian wall, and only evacuated the Morea on condition that the rampart should be left in ruins and an annual tribute should be paid to his master. But, before the end came, it was fated that the Greeks should first realise the aspirations of two centuries, and annex all that remained of the Frankish principality. This achievement, which threw a final ray of light over the darkness of the land, was the work of Constantine Palaeologus, destined to die the last Emperor of the East. The necessity of providing this prince with an appanage in the Morea outside of his brother Theodore's possessions, was the occasion of the Greek re-conquest. Constantine first obtained Glaréntza by a politic marriage, and took up his residence in the famous castle of Chloumoûtsi. There he prepared, with the aid of his confidential agent, the historian Phrantzes, his next move against Patras. The folly of the Church in insisting on the restitution of that important city to the archbishop was now demonstrated; the citizens opened their gates to the Greek conqueror, and the noble castle, still a splendid memorial of Latin rule, was forced by lack of provisions to surrender in 1430. Meanwhile, Constantine's brother Thomas, who had also come in quest of an appanage in the Peloponnese, had besieged Centurione at Chalandrítza with such success that the Prince of Achaia was compelled to bestow upon his assailant the hand of his daughter with the remains of the principality as her dowry, reserving for himself nothing but the family barony of Kyparissía and the princely title. Two years later, in 1432, the last Frankish Prince of Achaia died, leaving a bastard behind him to dispute later on the Greek title to his dominions. For the time, however, this man was a fugitive, and the whole peninsula was at last in Greek hands, save where the lion of

St Mark waved over Nauplia and Argos in the east, and over the ancient colonies of Modon and Coron, recently extended to include Navarino, in the south-west. The three brothers divided the rest of the Morea between them; Theodore II continued to reside at Mistrâ, Constantine removed his abode to Kalávryta, and Thomas received in exchange Glaréntza as his capital.

The triumph of the Greeks in the Morea was contemporaneous with two far more lasting Turkish conquests in the north. The year 1430, fatal to the Franks of Achaia, saw the fall of both Salonica and Joánnina. Salonica had been for seven short years a Venetian colony, while Joánnina with Epirus, seized by an Albanian chief after Esau Buondelmonti's death in 1408, had been conquered by Esau's nephew and rightful heir, Carlo I Tocco of Cephalonia, who had thus revived the former dominion of the Orsini over the islands and the mainland of north-western Greece. "In military and administrative ability, he was," according to the testimony of Chalcocondyles, "inferior to none of his contemporaries," while his masterful consort, a true daughter of the first Florentine Duke of Athens, was regarded as the most remarkable woman of the Latin Orient. Froissart extolled her magnificent hospitality, and described her island-court as a sort of fairyland. But Carlo's death without legitimate sons in 1429 exposed his hitherto compact state to the dissensions of his five bastards and his nephew Carlo II. One of the former had the baseness to invoke the aid of the Turks, and the surrender of Joánnina was the result of his selfishness. Carlo II was allowed to retain the rest of Epirus, with Acarnania and his islands, but from that day till 1913 the city of Joánnina with its beautiful lake never ceased to be a part of the Ottoman Empire—another example of Christian jealousies.

Meanwhile, amidst the fall of principalities and the annexation of flourishing cities, the statesmanlike policy of Antonio Acciajuoli had maintained the practical independence of the Athenian duchy. An occasional Turkish raid, such as that which had forced him to accompany the Ottoman troops to the Morea, reminded him that diplomacy must sometimes bow to force; and once, the claim of Alfonso V of Aragon and Sicily to this former Catalan colony gave him momentary alarm. But, with these exceptions, his long reign was a period of almost unbroken prosperity. Himself an honorary citizen of his family's old home of Florence, he encouraged Florentine trade, and welcomed Florentine families at his court, now established in the Propylaea instead of at Thebes. The Athenian history of the time, interspersed with such names as Medici, Pitti, and Machiavelli, reads like a chapter of the Tuscan annals, and the life of the Florentine family party which assembled there was almost as agreeable as it would have been by the banks of the Arno. Good shooting and good mounts from the famous Acciajuoli stable were to be had, and one of the visitors wrote with enthusiasm that "fairer land nor fairer fortress" than Attica and the Acropolis could nowhere else be seen. Nor did the Acciajuoli forget to strengthen the fortifications of their capital; for to them may be ascribed the "Frankish tower" which once stood on the Acropolis, and perhaps the so-called "wall of Valerian" which may still be seen in the city. Even culture began to shew signs of life in Florentine Athens; it was under Antonio that Laónikos Chalcocondyles, the last Athenian historian, and his scholarly brother Demetrius, were born, and a young Italian sought at Athens and Joánnina a chair of any science that would bring him in an income.

When, however, in 1435 Antonio I was one morning found dead in his bed, two parties, one Latin, one Greek, disputed the succession. The Latin candidate to the ducal dignity, young Nerio Acciajuoli, whom the childless duke had adopted as his heir, occupied the city, while the dowager duchess, a noble Greek dame, and her kinsman, the father of the historian Chalcocondyles, held the castle. The Greek party entered into negotiations with the Sultan on the one hand and with Constantine Palaeologus on the other, offering a bribe to the former and the duchy to the latter. Both schemes failed, and peace was secured by the marriage of Antonio's widow with his heir. But Nerio II soon made himself unpopular by his arrogance, and was deprived of the throne by his brother Antonio II. On the death of the latter, however, in 1441, he returned to his palace on the Acropolis, where he received a visit from Cyriacus of Ancona, the first archaeologist who had set foot in Athens since the conquest. But Nerio had occupations more serious than archaeology. In the year of this very visit the Despot Constantine threatened the existence of his tottering state. Theodore II had by that time retired from Mistrâ to the Sea of Marmora, so as to secure the succession to the imperial throne, while Constantine and Thomas divided the Morea between them. At this moment, the news of Hunyadi's successes over the Turks encouraged Constantine to ravage Boeotia and occupy Thebes. A large part of northern Greece declared for the Greek prince, and Cardinal Bessarion dreamed of a resurrection of the ancient glories of Hellas. Nerio escaped destruction by promising tribute, but thereby called down upon himself the vengeance of the Turks, who, after the rout of the Christian forces at Varna, were able to turn their attention to Greece. Placed between Turk and Greek, the wretched puppet on the Acropolis threw in his lot with the former, and joined the Sultan in invading the Morea. In 1446 Murād II stormed the restored Isthmian wall, ravaged the country behind it, and retired to Thebes with a vast train of captives and the promise of a tribute. All Constantine's recent conquests in the north were lost again, and the death of the Emperor John VI in 1448 ended that adventurous prince's direct connexion with Greece proper. On 6 January 1449 the last Emperor of the East was crowned at Mistrâ; upon his brother Demetrius he bestowed his own previous government, and in vain bade both him and Thomas live in unity and brotherly love, the sole means of saving the Morea. Scarcely had he been crowned than the Christian rulers of Greece received another warning of their fate, the annexation by the Turks of all the continental dominions of the Tocco dynasty save three fortresses. Four years later came the awful news that Constantinople had fallen and that the Emperor was slain. The terrified Despots of the Morea, whose first impulse had been flight to Italy, purchased a reprieve by the promise of tribute, while the Albanian colonists, under the leadership of Peter Boua, "the lame," rose against their feeble rulers, and Giovanni Asan, the bastard son of the last Prince of Achaia, raised the standard of a second revolt. Turkish aid was required to suppress these insurrections, for it was the policy of Mahomet II to play off one Christian race against the other, and so weaken them both, till a suitable moment should arrive for annexing Greek and Albanian, Orthodox and Roman Catholic, to his Empire. Giovanni Asan died in Rome, a pensioner of the Pope, like the Despot Thomas whom he had sought to dethrone. For a few more years, however, the two despots remained in possession of their respective provinces, which they might have retained for their lives had they not allowed the promised tribute to fall into arrears. At last Mahomet's patience was exhausted; he sent an ultimatum; and when Thomas refused to pay, he entered the Morea in 1458 at the head of an army. The despots fled at his approach; Acrocorinth surrendered after a gallant resistance; and the cession of about one-third of the peninsula, including Corinth, Patras, and Kalávryta, as well as an annual tribute, were the conditions under which alone Mahomet would allow the two brothers a further respite. Then the conqueror set out for Athens, the city which he longed to visit, and which the governor of Thessaly, Omar, son of Tura-Khān, had captured two years before the campaign in the Morea.

Florentine rule at Athens had ended in one of those domestic tragedies of which the history of the Franks in Greece was so productive. Nerio II, left a widower, had married a beautiful Venetian, daughter of the baron of Kárystos, by whom he had a son Francesco. When his father died in 1451, this child was still a minor, and his mother assumed the regency with the consent of the Sultan. But the duchess had other passions besides the love of power. She became enamoured of a young Venetian noble, Bartolomeo Contarini, who chanced to visit her capital, and bade him share her couch and throne. Contarini had a wife at home, but poison freed him of that encumbrance, and he returned to the palace on the Acropolis to wed the tragic widow. But the Athenians were not minded to support this Venetian usurpation. They complained to Mahomet, who cited Contarini and his stepson to appear before his court, where a dangerous rival awaited them in the person of the former Duke Antonio II's only son Franco, a special favourite of the Sultan.

The real master of Athens ordered the deposition of the duchess and her husband; Francesco disappeared, and Franco ruled, by Mahomet's good pleasure, at Athens. The first act of the new ruler was to throw the duchess into the dungeons of Megara, where she was mysteriously murdered by his orders. Contarini, enraged at her loss, begged Mahomet to punish his puppet, and the Sultan, thinking that the time had come to make an end of Latin rule at Athens, ordered Omar to march against that city. On 4 June 1456 the lower town fell into the hands of the Turks; but the Acropolis, where Franco lay, held out until Omar offered him, in the name of his master, Thebes with the rest of Boeotia, if he would surrender. Then the last duke who ever held court in the Propylaea and the last Latin archbishop who ever performed Mass in the Parthenon left the castle for ever, and when Mahomet returned in triumph from the Morea in the autumn of 1458, he received from the Abbot of Kaisarianè the keys of the city. The Athenians obtained humane treatment and various privileges, thanks to the respect which the cultured conqueror felt for their ancestors and the interest which he shewed in their monuments, while in Boeotia Franco lingered on a little longer as "Lord of Thebes."

Scarcely had Mahomet left Greece than the two despicable Despots of the Morea, whom no experience could teach that honesty and unity constituted their sole hope of safety, resumed their quarrels and intrigues. The inability of Thomas to raise the stipulated tribute was the final stroke which made the Sultan resolve to have done once and for all with both these faithless rulers. In 1460 he a second time entered the Morea; Mistrâ, with Demetrius inside it, surrendered; but the impregnable rock of Monemvasía defied the Turkish menaces, while Thomas, its absent lord, sailed with his wife and family for Corfù and thence to Italy. At this the Monemvasiotes invited first a Catalan corsair and then the Pope to take them under his protection; till in 1464 they found salvation by becoming subjects of Venice, the sole Christian state whose colours broke the monotony of Turkish rule in the Morea. Only one man worthy of the name, Graítzas Palaeologus, was found there to keep flying the flag of Greek independence over the mountain-fortress of Salmenikón, and when he at last capitulated in 1461, the last vestige of Greek rule disappeared from the peninsula. As for the two Despots, Thomas died in Rome in 1465; while Demetrius, after receiving the islands of Imbros and Lemnos and the mart of Aenus, the former dominion of the Gattilusi, as compensation for the loss of his province in the Morea, fell into the disfavour of his master, and finished his days in 1470 as a monk. Thomas' elder son Andrew, after a career of dissipation, married a Roman prostitute, and died in abject poverty in 1502, while the younger accepted the charity of his father's conqueror. Such was the inglorious end of the last Greek princes of the Morea.

The annexation of the last fragments of the Athenian duchy

followed the conquest of the two Greek principalities in the Peloponnese. On his way home Mahomet revisited Athens, where he was informed of a plot to restore Franco. The Sultan thereupon ordered Zagan, his governor in the Morea, to kill the "Lord of Thebes." The order was promptly executed, and the Turkish guards strangled the unsuspecting Franco on his way back from the pasha's tent; Thebes and the rest of Boeotia became Turkish, and the sons of the last Florentine ruler were enrolled among the janissaries. Finally, two of the three continental fortresses held by Leonardo III Tocco were captured, and in 1462 the rule of the Gattilusi ceased to exist in Lesbos. Of all the Latin lords of the Levant this Genoese family had been perhaps the most distinguished for its toleration and its culture. Even Francesco, the founder of the dynasty, had come among the islanders not in the guise of a foreign conqueror but as the brother-in-law of the Greek Emperor. Speaking the language of his subjects[1], he allowed the national Church, which was that of his consort, to retain its local hierarchy, and his successors followed his example. The marriages of ladies of the family with Byzantine, Trapezuntine, and Serbian[2] princes maintained this tendency, while the love of archaeology displayed by Dorino Gattilusio aroused the admiration of Cyriacus of Ancona; and also the historian Ducas was the secretary of his son Domenico. Their abundant coinage proves the commercial prosperity of the little state ruled by the lords of Lesbos and their relatives. Besides Lesbos, its original nucleus, it included at its zenith in the fifteenth century the islands of Lemnos, Imbros, Thasos, and Samothrace, as well as Aenus on the mainland. By 1456, however, Mahomet II had captured all these places except Lesbos, and six years later that island was taken and its last princeling was strangled, as he had likewise strangled his brother. Thus poetic justice closed the career of the Lesbian Latins.

After these sweeping Turkish conquests the only Latin possessions left on the mainland of Greece were the four groups of Venetian colonies —Coron, Modon, and Navarino in the south, Argos and Nauplia on the west, Lepanto at the mouth of the Corinthian, and Ptéleon at that of the Pagasaean Gulf—the Papal fortress of Monemvasía (soon likewise to become Venetian); and the castle of Vónitza on the Gulf of Arta, the last possession of Leonardo Tocco on the continent. But in the islands there was still much Latin territory. While Venice held Corfù and Cerigo, Crete and Negropont, Tenos and Myconus, she had succeeded the Catalan family of Caopena in Aegina in 1451, and had occupied the northern Sporades in 1453. The Genoese still administered Chios and Famagosta, the latter soon to be restored to the still existing kingdom of Cyprus. The Knights of St John were still unconquered in Rhodes; the Dukes of the Archipelago were still secure in Naxos; and Leonardo

[1] Servion, *Gestez et Chroniques de la Mayson de Savoye*, II. 138—139.
[2] Constantine the Philosopher, "Life of Stephen Lazarević." *Glasnik*, XLII. 279.

Tocco still governed the old county palatine of Cephalonia. It now remains to describe the fate of these outworks of Christendom.

A long war which broke out in 1462 between Venice and the Turks led to the temporary conquest of a large part of the Morea by the Venetians, of the islands that had so lately belonged to the Gattilusi, and of the city of Athens. But these exploits of Victor Cappello had no permanent effect; whereas in 1470 Venice lost, through the culpable hesitation of Canale, another of her admirals, the city of Negropont and the rest of that fine island. The heroism of Erizzo, its brave defender, sawn asunder by order of Mahomet II, afforded a splendid but useless contrast to the incapacity of his fellow-officer. Venice emerged in 1479 from the long war with a diminished colonial empire; she ceded all her recent conquests, and by the loss of Argos, Ptéleon, and Negropont was poorer than when she began the contest. The acquisition of Cyprus in 1489 was some compensation for these misfortunes. There James II, having driven the Genoese from Famagosta, had married Caterina Cornaro, an adopted daughter of the Venetian republic. After the death of his posthumous son, James III, the Queen-Dowager continued for a time to govern the island under the guidance of Venice; then, like a dutiful daughter, she gave the real sovereignty to her mother-country, while her rival, Queen Charlotte, left nothing save the barren title of "King of Cyprus" to the house of Savoy.

Meanwhile, another Latin dynasty, that of Tocco, had disappeared from the Ionian Islands, at that time both populous and fertile. Wedded to a niece of King Ferdinand I of Naples, Leonardo III had thereby become an object of suspicion to Venice, and the republic accordingly sacrificed him to the Turks by leaving him out of the treaty of peace which had ended the long war. Accordingly, in 1479, the Turks, seizing upon a slight to one of their officials as a pretext, annexed all the four islands and the mainland fortress of Vónitza, which then comprised this ancient Italian state. Like most of the princely exiles from the Near East, Leonardo and his family found refuge in Italy, whence his brother Antonio succeeded in making a successful raid upon Cephalonia and Zante. Once again, however, the Tocco dynasty had to reckon with Venice. The jealous republic, long mistress of Corfù, Paxo, and Cerigo, coveted the "flower of the Levant" and its big neighbour. Both islands were occupied by the Venetians who, though forced to cede Cephalonia to the Sultan, managed, on payment of a tribute, to keep Zante from that time down to the fall of the republic. The Tocco family long flourished at Naples, almost the sole example of medieval rulers of Greece who prospered in exile, if such it could be called, and the last representative of the honours and titles of this ancient house, the Duke of Regina, died only in 1908.

A twenty years' peace followed the disastrous Turco-Venetian war, but when in 1499 hostilities were resumed, the Turks made further gains in Greece at the republic's expense. Lepanto was lost in that year, and Modon and Coron with Navarino in the following, and great was the lamentation at home when it was known that Modon, the half-way house between Venice and the East, had fallen. While Zante took its place as a port of call, the republic in the same year recovered and thenceforth permanently kept Cephalonia, and temporarily obtained Santa Mavra. The final blow to her colonies in the Morea was dealt by the next Turco-Venetian war, which lasted from 1537 to 1540. Corfù successfully resisted the first of her two great Turkish sieges, but the war cost the republic Nauplia and Monemvasía, Aegina, Myconus, and the northern Sporades. Thenceforth till the time of Morosini she ceased to be a continental power in Greece; but she still retained six out of the seven Ionian Islands, as well as Crete, Cyprus, and Tenos. Moreover, in the Aegean, the duchy of Naxos, founded but no longer ruled by her adventurous sons, lingered on, the last surviving fief of the long extinct Empire of Romania, while the Genoese Company still managed Chios.

The history of the Duchy of the Archipelago, perhaps the most romantic creation of the Middle Ages, is largely personal and centres in the doings of the dukes and the small island-barons. Several of the latter, whom Licario had dispossessed, recovered their lost islands about the beginning of the fourteenth century, while new families arrived at the same time and settled there. The islanders, however, suffered severely from Turkish raids, which grew increasingly frequent, while, under the Crispo dynasty, Venice became more and more predominant in their affairs, twice taking over the government of Naxos, Andros, and Paros in the fifteenth and sixteenth centuries. But the republic was not always able to aid her distant children, who, after the Turkish capture of Rhodes and the departure of the Knights on New Year's Day 1523, were deprived of another bulwark against the Asiatic invasion. The war, which broke out between Venice and the Sultan fourteen years later, involved the downfall of three insular dynasties, those of the Michieli, the Pisani, and the Quirini, while the Duke of the Archipelago, Giovanni IV Crispo, only saved his tottering throne at Naxos from the blows of the terrible Khair-ad-Dīn Barbarossa, who commanded the Turkish fleet, by the humiliating payment of a tribute. The peace of 1540 left only three families, the Crispi, the Sommaripa, and the Gozzadini, still reigning in the Aegean, and it is remarkable that not one of the three was of Venetian origin. This fact and the loss of all the Venetian colonies except Tenos in the Archipelago thenceforth naturally diminished the political interests of the republic in that sea. In vain the duke addressed a solemn appeal to the princes of Christendom to forget their mutual differences and unite against the Turks, emphasising his arguments by a quotation from his great "ancestor," Sallustius Crispus, a proof alike of his literary culture and of his family pride.

Fortunately for himself he ended his reign, the longest of any duke of Naxos, before the final catastrophe. In 1566, however, his son and successor, Giacomo IV, a feeble debauchee, so disgusted the Greeks, who formed the overwhelming majority of his subjects, that they invited the Sultan to depose him. Piale Pasha thereupon occupied Naxos without opposition, and the Latin Duchy of the Archipelago ceased to exist. Selīm II bestowed this picturesque state upon his Jewish favourite, Joseph Nasi, who never visited his insular dominions, but governed them through his deputy, a Spanish Jew, Francesco Coronello. With Nasi's death in 1579 the Hebrew sway over the Cyclades ended, and the duchy was annexed to the Turkish Empire. One petty Latin dynasty, however, that of the Gozzadini of Bologna, which had been restored in 1571, the year of Lepanto, continued to rule far into the seventeenth century. This curious survival of Italian authority in seven small islands ended in 1617, but Tenos remained a Venetian colony for nearly a hundred years longer.

Genoese domination over Chios terminated in the same year as the Latin duchy of Naxos, and by the same hand. The trading company of the Giustiniani managed at its zenith both Chios and the islands of Psará, Samos, and Icaria (this last entrusted to one of its members, Count Arangio) as well as the two towns of Phocaea on the coast of Asia Minor with their rich alum mines. For a long time the payment of a tribute secured immunity from a Turkish invasion, and the chief events of Chiote history were the declaration of independence in 1408, when Genoa became French, and a war with Venice. But Mahomet II was anxious for an excuse to annex this little state; in 1455 the Turks took both the Phocaeas; in 1475 the Company abandoned Psará and Samos, and in 1481 allowed the Knights of St John to occupy Icaria, the neglected county of the Arangio family. Thus reduced to the island of Chios alone, the *maona* merely survived by the prompt payment of what the Sultans chose to demand, till at last its financial condition made it no longer in a position to raise the amount of the tribute. In 1566 Piale descended upon the island and added it to the empire of his master. Genoa struck not a blow in defence of her sons, nor did she ever pay the sum which she had guaranteed to them in the event of the loss of Chios.

Five years after the fall of Chios and Naxos, Cyprus was lost. The history of this island was throughout the Frankish period so completely detached, save at rare intervals, from that of the rest of the Hellenic world, that it seems most convenient to treat it separately. It falls naturally into three sharply-defined epochs: that of prosperity under the Lusignan dynasty down to the death of Peter I in 1369, that of decline under the remaining princes of that house, and that of colonial dependence upon the Venetian republic. Guy de Lusignan, ex-King of Jerusalem, having lost all chance of recovering that dignity, gladly purchased Cyprus from Richard I in 1192, after the *gran rifiuto* of the Templars, and in his short reign laid the foundations of the feudal system in the island. The Franks naturally became, as in Greece, predominant alike in Church and State; the well-to-do Greeks were reduced to the condition of vassals, the peasants remained serfs. His brother and successor Amaury completed his work, organising the Latin Church of Cyprus with its hierarchy dependent upon the Archbishop of Nicosia, introducing the feudal code of Jerusalem, and striving to weaken the power of the Cypriote nobles, none of whom had the right, exercised by some of the Frankish barons in Greece, of coining money for their own use. Anxious to increase his authority, he exchanged the title of "Lord of Cyprus," borne by his brother, for that of "King," which he persuaded the Western Emperor to bestow upon him in 1197, and in the following year added to it the coveted but empty honour of King of Jerusalem. This double accession of dignity proved, however, to be detrimental to the interests of Cyprus; for the former distinction involved the suzerainty of the Western Emperor over the island and led to the subsequent civil war, while the latter diverted the attention of Amaury to Syrian affairs. Another event of lasting influence upon the country was the privilege granted in 1218 to the Genoese, who thus began their connexion with the island. A time of much trouble began in 1228, when the Emperor Frederick II, then on his way to the Holy Land, landed in Cyprus, and claimed suzerainty over the young King Henry I. A long struggle, known as "the Lombard war," ensued between the National party under John of Ibelin, the Regent, and "the Lombards," as the imperialists were called. The Nationalists were at last successful, and the imperial suzerainty was destroyed for ever. After the close of this conflict the island became very prosperous, and the loss of St Jean d'Acre, the last stronghold of the Crusaders in Syria, in 1291, was really a benefit to the Cypriotes, because their sovereigns need no longer concern themselves with the affairs of the phantom kingdom of Jerusalem. From 1269, however, down to the end of their dynasty, the sovereigns of Cyprus continued to bear the title of "King of Jerusalem," and it became the custom to hold a double coronation, one at Nicosia, the Cypriote capital, and the other at Famagosta as representing the Holy City. Thus isolated from the continent, the Cypriote court became, in 1306, a prey to the ambition of Amaury de Lusignan, titular Prince of Tyre, who deposed his brother Henry II, the "beast" of Dante[1], and drove him into exile. This brief usurpation of the regency (for he was assassinated in 1310) was remarkable for the commercial concessions made to the Venetians, who thus became the rivals of the Genoese and established a basis for their future dominion over the island.

The accession of Peter I in 1359, the most valiant and adventurous

[1] *Paradiso,* XIX. 145—148.

of the Lusignan kings, a man who should have been born in the days of the Crusades, plunged Cyprus into a vigorous foreign policy, which contrasted with the concentration of the last two generations in internal politics. The small Turkish princes of Cilicia became his tributaries, and the Cilician fortress of Gorigos remained in Cypriote hands till 1448. Flushed by these successes, he dreamed of recovering the Holy Land, and undertook two long European tours for the purpose of exciting interest in this new crusade. But, although he journeyed as far as London, he received no real support save from the Knights of Rhodes, with whose aid he took Alexandria. In 1368 he was offered the crown of Lesser, or Cilician, Armenia, but was assassinated in the following year on his way to take it—the victim of conjugal infidelity and aristocratic intrigues. With his death the kingdom of Cyprus began to decline, and the two rival Italian republics, Genoa and subsequently Venice, became the real powers behind the throne.

The coronation of Peter II as King of Jerusalem at Famagosta on 2 October 1372 marked the first downward step. A foolish question of precedence between the Genoese consul and the Venetian bailie led to the sack of the Genoese warehouses by the mob. A Genoese fleet under Pietro di Campofregoso arrived off Famagosta; the two coronation cities and the king were captured. Peter II had to purchase his freedom on 21 October 1374 by promising to pay a huge indemnity and by ceding Famagosta, the commercial capital of the island, to his captors until this sum should be paid. In Genoese hands the city became the chief emporium of the Levantine trade, and a clause in the treaty prevented the Kings of Cyprus from creating another port which might interfere with the Genoese monopoly. When Peter II died, circumstances enabled the astute merchant-republic to obtain a confirmation of this humiliating convention from his uncle and successor, James I, then still a hostage at Genoa. The new king was not released till he had paid up his predecessor's arrears and guaranteed to the Genoese the possession of Famagosta, nor was his acquisition of the barren title of King of Armenia by the death of Leo VI, the last native sovereign, in 1393, any real compensation for the loss of the richest city in Cyprus. Thenceforth all his successors wore the three crowns of Cyprus, Jerusalem, and Armenia, although of the former Armenian kingdom they held nothing except the castle of Gorigos. His son Janus, whose name denoted his humiliating birth as a captive at Genoa, tried in vain to drive the foreigners out of Famagosta, with the sole result that he was forced in 1414 to sign another onerous treaty. But this was not the only misfortune of this rash prince. By his encouragement of Christian pirates, who preyed upon the Egyptian coast, he so greatly irritated the Sultan of that country, that the latter, probably instigated by the Genoese, landed in Cyprus, burnt Nicosia, and captured Janus at the battle of Choirokoitía in 1426. An annual tribute to Egypt was one of the conditions of his ransom and thenceforth formed a constant charge upon the Cypriote revenues.

The next reign, that of the feeble John II, marked the further decline of Latin authority and the revival of Hellenism, phenomena which we observed in the contemporary history of the Morea. Indeed, the influence of the Moreote court of Mistrâ then made itself felt in Cyprus also, for the real power behind the throne was Queen Helen, daughter of the Despot Theodore II, a masterful woman, who naturally favoured the claims advanced by the clergy of her own race and creed to supremacy over the hitherto dominant Church. The loss of Gorigos in 1448 was a smaller misfortune than her quarrel with the most dangerous man in the kingdom, the bastard James, himself the offspring of a Moreote mother, who had been compelled as a boy to accept the archbishopric of Nicosia. On the death of John II in 1458, his daughter, the brave young Queen Charlotte, feebly supported by her husband, Louis of Savoy, in vain attempted to combat the rival forces of the bastard, seconded by the Sultan of Egypt. By 1460 her ruthless adversary had already occupied most of the island and assumed the royal style of James II, but the strong castle of Cerines held out for the queen three years longer. Charlotte then withdrew to her husband's land, while the bastard acquired popularity by achieving, in 1464, the ardent wish of his last four predecessors, the recapture of Famagosta, held since 1447 by the Bank of St George, and the consequent abolition of the Genoese monopoly of Cypriote commerce. With characteristic cruelty he completed this conquest by the massacre of the Mamlūks, who had assisted him in his campaign and for whom he had no further use. But if it had been reserved for this bold and unscrupulous usurper to end the galling commercial predominance of one Italian republic, it was also his fate to prepare the way for the political hegemony of another. He had rid his country of Genoa, only by his marriage with Caterina Cornaro, niece of a wealthy Venetian sugar-planter resident in Cyprus, to place it under the influence of Venice, whose adopted daughter his consort was. His premature death, in 1473, followed by that of his posthumous child, James III, a year later, left his widow queen in name but the republic regent in fact, till at last, in 1489, Venice acquired the nominal as well as the actual sovereignty of the coveted island.

The prosperity of Cyprus had, however, begun to wane before the island became a Venetian colony. It was still saddled with the Egyptian tribute; except for the revenues of its salt-pans it yielded little; and a traveller who visited it at this period described its barrenness and depopulation, which the Venetians in vain tried to remedy by colonisation. The republic exacted a hard measure of tithes and forced labour from the people, while to the last there lingered on the descendants of the French nobles, whose serfs were little better than slaves. In these circumstances, it cannot be considered as remarkable that the Greeks should have welcomed the Turks as deliverers, although they found when too late that Turkish officials were more rapacious than Venetian governors. Selīm II, whose bibulous propensities led him to desire the conquest of an island famous for its rich vintage, had promised to bestow on his favourite Nasi, the Jewish Duke of Naxos, the crown of Cyprus, of which he might claim to be suzerain in virtue of the Turkish annexation of Egypt and the consequent transference of the tribute to the Porte. While the ambitious Jew painted in anticipation the arms and title of King of Cyprus in his house, he urged his willing patron to perform his promise by the conquest of this Venetian colony. Accordingly, in 1570, a Turkish fleet appeared off the island; Nicosia, the residence of the Venetian governor, was taken on 9 September, most of the other towns surrendered, but Famagosta held out till, on 1 August 1571, famine forced its heroic defender Bragadino to yield. The name of this brave officer, flayed alive at Famagosta, will ever be remembered, with that of Erizzo, sawn asunder a century earlier at Negropont, as a splendid example of that devotion to duty which Venice demanded from the defenders of her colonial Empire.

Even after the loss of Cyprus, the republic still retained for nearly a century more her much older colony of Crete. The Cretan insurrection of 1363 had been followed by a long period of peace; but after the Turkish conquest of Negropont the Venetians became alarmed for the safety of their other great island. When Cyprus became also Venetian it served as an outpost of Candia, and its capture was therefore felt to have weakened the republic's position in Crete. It was at this period that Venice set to work to restore the fortifications of the island, and sent Foscarini on his celebrated mission to redress the grievances of the islanders. The old feudal military service, which had fallen into abeyance, was revived; exemptions were curtailed; the Jews regarded the commissioner as their enemy, the peasants looked on him as their friend. But vested interests and the fanaticism of the Orthodox clergy proved stubborn obstacles to the reformer. The population diminished, the island cost more than it yielded, and the Cretans avowed their preference for the Turkish rule which was destined to be their lot. In 1669, after a war that had lasted well-nigh a quarter of a century, "Troy's rival," Candia, fell, and only the three fortresses of Grabusa, Suda, and Spinalonga remained in Venetian hands—the first till 1691, the two last till 1715, when Tenos also, the last Venetian island in the Aegean, was lost. Venice, however, still retained the Ionian Islands, including Santa Mavra, reconquered by Morosini in 1684, down to the fall of the republic in 1797, when the career of Franks and Venetians in Greek lands, which had begun six centuries earlier, ended with the short-lived triumph of Bonaparte, the self-constituted heir of both.

The Frankish domination in Greece is certainly the most romantic period of her history. The brilliant courts of Thebes and Nicosia, the gaieties of Naxos and Negropont, the tournament of Corinth, the hunting parties of Attica, Cyprus, and the Morea, and the pleasaunces of Elis, were created by the Franks and perished with them. The grass-grown ruins of Glaréntza were then a flourishing mart with its own weights and measures, the residence of Italian bankers, and known all over the Mediterranean; the palace of Mistrâ, now the haunt of tortoises and sheep, was then a princely residence, second to Constantinople alone. Splendid castles in marvellous sites, like Passavâ, Chloumoûtsi, and Dieu d'Amour, remind us how the Frank nobles lived and fought, while dismantled abbeys by fair streams or above azure seas, like Isova and Bella Paise, tell us how the Latin monks fared in these lands of their adoption. But, except in the Cyclades and the Ionian Islands, the Frankish conquest has left little mark upon the character and institutions of the people. With the exception of the half-castes, a despised breed which usually sided with the Greeks, the two races had few points of contact and never really amalgamated. They differed in origin, in creed, in customs, and, at first, in language, and the tact of many Frankish rulers did not succeed in bridging the impassable chasm which Nature has placed between East and West. In a word, the Frankish conquest of Greece did not succeed in becoming a permanent factor in Greek life, because it was unnatural. Here and there, especially in the case of the Cephalonian Orsini, Latin princes became hellenised, adopting the religion and language of their subjects, only in such cases, as is usual, to assimilate their vices without their virtues. Even in the Cyclades, where the Latin element is still considerable and the Roman Church is still powerful, the picturesque adventurers who built their castles above marine volcanoes or out of classical temples were to the last a foreign garrison, while in Crete the existence, much rarer elsewhere, of a considerable native aristocracy furnished leaders for that long series of revolts against foreign authority which was a peculiar feature of Cretan history. One lesson, however, the Greeks of the Morea learnt from the Franks, a lesson to which they owe in some measure their later independence—that of fighting. For, if the Frankish conquest found the Greeks an unwarlike race, the Turkish conquest was disturbed by continual insurrections. Of the influence of the Latin domination upon the common language of the country there is abundant evidence, especially in the islands, where Venetian authority lingered longest. Frankish Greece has bequeathed to us in literature the curious *Chronicle of the Morea*, a work extant in four languages and even more valuable for social and legal than for political history; while Crete and Corfù produced romances drawn from Western models. In art the influence of Venice may still be seen at Monemvasía, Andros, and Zante, whereas Crete gave birth to a native school of painting which owed nothing to foreign influence, and in the frescoes of Geráki we have perhaps the sole surviving portraits of Frankish nobles on the soil of Greece. That the

Latin masters of the country were not indifferent to culture, we know, however, from several instances. An Orsini patronising a vernacular version of Homer, a Giustiniani and a Gattilusio interested in archaeology, a Sommaripa excavating statues, a Tocco facilitating a foreign savant's search for inscriptions, a Crispo quoting Sallust, a Ghisi studying the *Chronicle of the Morea*, an Archbishop of Corinth translating Aristotle—such are a few of the figures of this by no means barbarous epoch, to which we owe some of the best Byzantine historians—the Athenian Chalcocondyles, the Lesbian Ducas, the Imbrian Critobulus, the Monemvasiote Phrantzes, men not only of letters but of affairs. Even under the Catalans at Athens we find a bishop possessed of a library, while Mistrâ in the time of the Palaeologi was a centre of philosophic culture as the residence of Pléthon. "New France" was therefore, especially at its zenith, a land more brilliant and more prosperous than either the Byzantine provinces out of which it was formed or the Turkish provinces which succeeded it. But the Franks, like their successors, could neither absorb nor suppress that marvellous Greek nationality which has survived through the vicissitudes of more than twenty centuries. Thus the motley sway of Frenchmen and Italians, Catalans and Navarrese, Flemings and Germans, over the classic home of literature and the arts has remained save in a few cases merely a long episode in the long history of Greece, but still an episode curious above all others from its strange contrasts, its unexpected juxtapositions of races and civilisations, its dramatic surprises, and its sudden and tragic reverses of fortune.

TABLES OF RULERS.

PRINCES OF ACHAIA.

William de Champlitte 1205.
Geoffrey I de Villehardouin. Bailie 1209; prince 1210.
Geoffrey II de Villehardouin 1218.
William de Villehardouin 1246.
Charles I of Anjou 1278.
Charles II of Anjou 1285.
Isabelle de Villehardouin 1289.
With Florent of Hainault 1289.
With Philip of Savoy 1301.
Philip I of Taranto 1307.
Matilda of Hainault 1313.
With Louis of Burgundy 1313.
John of Gravina 1318.
Catherine of Valois } 1333.
Robert of Taranto }
Robert of Taranto 1346.
Marie de Bourbon 1364.
Philip II of Taranto 1370.
Joanna I of Naples 1374.
Otto of Brunswick 1376.
[Knights of St John—1377-81.]
Jacques de Baux 1381.

Mahiot de Coquerel, vicar 1383.
Bordo de S. Superan. Vicar 1386; prince 1396.
Maria Zaccaria 1402.
Centurione Zaccaria 1404-32.

DUKES OF ATHENS.

Othon de la Roche, *Megaskyr* 1205.
Guy I. *Megaskyr* 1225; duke 1260.
John I 1263.
William 1280.
Guy II 1287.
Walter of Brienne 1309.

Roger Deslaur, chief of the Catalan Company 1311.
Manfred 1312.
William 1317.
John of Randazzo 1338.
Frederick of Randazzo 1348.
Frederick III of Sicily 1355.
Pedro IV of Aragon 1377.
John I of Aragon 1387.

Nerio I Acciajuoli. Lord of Athens 1388; duke 1394.
[Venice—1394–1402.]
Antonio I 1402.
Nerio II 1435.
Antonio II 1439.
Nerio II (restored) 1441.
Francesco 1451.
Franco 1455–6; "Lord of Thebes" 1456–60.

DESPOTS OF EPIRUS.

Michael I Angelus 1204.
Theodore 1214. Emperor of Salonica 1223.
Manuel 1230. Emperor of Salonica 1230.
Michael II 1236.
Nicephorus I 1271.
Thomas 1296.

Nicholas Orsini 1318.
John II Orsini 1323.
Nicephorus II 1335–58. [Byzantine 1336–49; Serbian 1349–56.]

Simeon Uroš 1358.
Thomas Preljubović 1367.
Maria Angelina 1385.
Esau Buondelmonti 1386–1408.
[Albanians—1408–18; then united with Cephalonia.]

DUKES OF NEOPATRAS.

John I Angelus 1271.
Constantine 1295.
John II 1303–18.
[United with Athens.]

PALATINE COUNTS OF CEPHALONIA.

Matteo Orsini 1194.
Richard. Before 1264.
John I 1303.
Nicholas 1317.
John II 1323.
[Angevins (united with Achaia)—1324–57.]
Leonardo I Tocco 1357.
Carlo I. Before 1377.
Carlo II 1429.
Leonardo III 1448–79.
Antonio 1481–3.

DUKES OF THE ARCHIPELAGO.

Marco I Sanudo 1207.
Angelo *c.* 1227.
Marco II 1262.
Guglielmo I 1303.
Niccolò I 1323.
Giovanni I 1341.
Fiorenza 1361.
With Niccolò II Sanudo "Spezzabanda" 1364.
Niccolò III dalle Carceri 1371.

Francesco I Crispo 1383.

Giacomo I 1397.
Giovanni II 1418.
Giacomo II 1433.
Gian Giacomo 1447.
Guglielmo II 1453.
Francesco II 1463.
Giacomo III 1463.
Giovanni III 1480.
[Venice—1494–1500.]
Francesco III 1500.
[Venice 1511–17.]
Giovanni IV 1517.
Giacomo IV 1564–6.

———

Joseph Nasi 1566–79.

LORDS OF CORFÙ.

[Venice—1206–14.]
Despots of Epirus 1214–59.
Manfred of Sicily 1259–66.
Chinardo 1266.
Charles I of Anjou 1267.
Charles II of Anjou 1285.
Philip I of Taranto 1294.
Catherine of Valois, Robert of Taranto } 1331.
Robert of Taranto 1346.
Marie de Bourbon 1364.
Philip II of Taranto 1364.
Joanna I of Naples 1373.
Jacques de Baux 1380.
Charles III of Naples 1382–86.
[Venice—1386–1797.]

VENETIAN COLONIES.

Crete. [Genoese occupation 1206–10] 1204–1669. (Two forts till 1715.)
Modon, Coron } 1206–1500; 1685–1715.
Argos 1388–1463.
Nauplia 1388–1540; 1686–1715.
Monemvasía 1464–1540; 1690–1715.
Lepanto 1407–99; 1687–99.
Negropont 1209–1470.
Ptéleon 1323–1470.
Ægina 1451–1537; 1693–1715.
Tenos 1390–1715.
Myconus 1390–1537.
Northern Sporades 1453–1538.
Corfù 1206–1214; 1386–1797.
Cephalonia 1483–5; 1500–1797.
Zante 1482–1797.
Cerigo 1363–1797.

———

Sta. Mavra 1502–3; 1694–1797.
Athens 1394–1402; 1466; 1687–88.
Patras 1408–13; 1417–19; 1687–1715.
Naxos 1494–1500; 1511–17.
Andros 1437–40; 1507–14.
Paros 1518–20; 1531–36.
Maina 1467–79.
Vostitza 1470.
$\frac{1}{4}$ Amorgos 1370–1446.
Lemnos 1464–79.
Cyprus 1489–1571.

EPIROTE EMPERORS OF SALONICA.

Theodore Angelus. Emperor 1223.
Manuel. Emperor 1230.
John. Emperor 1240; Despot 1242.
Demetrius. Despot 1244–46.
[Annexed to Nicaea 1246.]

KINGS OF CYPRUS.

Guy de Lusignan. Lord of Cyprus 1192.
Amaury de Lusignan. Lord of Cyprus 1194; King 1197; King of Jerusalem 1198.
Hugh I de Lusignan. King of Cyprus 1205.
Henry I de Lusignan 1218.
Hugh II de Lusignan 1253.

Hugh III de Lusignan 1267; Titular King of Jerusalem 1269.

John I de Lusignan 1284; Titular King of Jerusalem.

Henry II de Lusignan 1285; Titular King of Jerusalem.

[Amaury de Lusignan: Regent 1306–10.]

Hugh IV de Lusignan 1324; Titular King of Jerusalem.

Peter I de Lusignan 1359; Titular King of Jerusalem; King of Armenia 1368.

Peter II de Lusignan 1369; Titular King of Jerusalem.

James I de Lusignan 1382; Titular King of Jerusalem; King of Armenia 1393.

Janus de Lusignan 1398; Titular King of Jerusalem; King of Armenia.

John II de Lusignan 1432; Titular King of Jerusalem; King of Armenia.

Charlotte de Lusignan 1458; †1487; Titular Queen of Jerusalem; Queen of Armenia.

James II de Lusignan 1460; † 6 July 1473; Titular King of Jerusalem; King of Armenia.

[Caterina Cornaro Regent 1473–4.]

James III de Lusignan, b. 27 August 1473; Titular King of Jerusalem; King of Armenia.

Caterina Cornaro 1474–89; †1510; Titular Queen of Jerusalem; Queen of Armenia.

[Venice—1489–1571.]

N.B. The Kings of Cyprus also bore the titles of King of Jerusalem 1198–1205, and from 1269 onward, and of King of (Little) Armenia 1368–9, and from 1393 onward.

RHODES.

Leo Gabalâs 1204.

John Gabalâs. Between 1234 and 1248–56.

[Genoese 1248–50.]

[Annexed to Nicaea 1256.]

[Saracens *c.* 1282–1309.]

Knights of St John 1309–1523.

GENOESE COLONIES.

Smyrna 1261–*c.* 1300; 1344–1402.

Foglia (Phocaea) 1275–1340; 1346–48.

„ Vecchia 1358–1455.

„ Nuova 1351–1455.

Chios 1304–29; 1346–1566. [Venetian 1694–95.]

Samos 1304–29; 1346–1475.

Icaria 1304–29; 1346–1481. [Knights of St John 1481–1523; Venetian 1694–95.]

Psará 1346–1475.

Lesbos 1333–36; 1355–1462.

Thasos 1307–13; *c.* 1434 (or ? *c.* 1419)–1455. [Papal 1456–59; Venetian 1464–79.]

Lemnos 1453–56. [Papal 1456–58; Venetian 1464–79; 1656–57.]

Aenus *c.* 1384–1456.

Samothrace *c.* 1431–56. [Papal 1456–59; Venetian 1466–79.]

Imbros 1453–56. [Venetian 1466–79.]

Famagosta 1374–1464.

CHAPTER XVI.

THE EMPIRE OF NICAEA AND THE RECOVERY OF CONSTANTINOPLE.

THE capture of Constantinople by the Latins did not for long leave the Greeks without a centre round which to rally. At Trebizond on the shores of the Black Sea, and at Nicaea, the city of the Nicene creed, two Greek Empires rose out of the fragments of that which had fallen, while a third Hellenic principality was founded in Epirus, which in its turn became for a brief period the Empire of Salonica. It was reserved for the second of these creations to reconquer Constantinople and thus to become merged in the restored Byzantine Empire, while the first survived by a little the Turkish conquest of Byzantium.

Theodore Lascaris, the founder of the Empire of Nicaea, was about thirty years of age at the time of the sack of Constantinople. The scion of a distinguished Byzantine family, he had been considered worthy of the hand of the fair Anna, second daughter of the Emperor Alexius III; he had given proof of his courage during the operations against the Bulgarian traitor, Ivanko, in the mountains of Rhodope, and during the siege of the capital; and, despite his rather insignificant personal appearance, these qualities had led to his election in the great church of the Divine Wisdom to the imperial throne, vacant by the flight of Moúrtzouphlos. Without waiting to assume the imperial symbols, he made a last effort to rally the defenders of the city, and then, seeing that all was lost, fled with his wife and his three daughters across the Sea of Marmora and called upon the people of Nicaea to receive him as their lawful sovereign[1].

The spot which was to be the refuge of fallen Hellenism was well chosen. Nicaea was not then the feverish village which six centuries of Turkish rule have made it, but a great and prosperous city. Situated on the lake of Askania, neither too far from the sea for commerce nor

[1] We may reject the unsupported statement of Albricus Trium Fontium (*M. G. H. Script.*, XXIII. 885) that he first approached Baldwin I with the offer to subdue Asia Minor to the Latins.

too near it for corsairs, it "lacked," in the phrase of a native writer[1], "neither safety, nor grace." The fertile plains of Bithynia provided it with corn and wine; the lake abounded in fish, and the city in excellent water, while cypresses and other trees rendered it a pleasant residence. No wonder, then, that the Byzantine Emperors had chosen it as the chief town of the Opsician province, that the Seljūq Sultans had made it their capital. The natural defence afforded by the lake, which the crusaders had found such a serious obstacle a century before this time, had been further strengthened by art, and its defenders boasted that it was impregnable. Splendid walls with projecting towers, still surviving in their picturesque decay, then protected the circular city, whose fine houses and richly decorated churches attested the wealth and piety of the inhabitants. Two of these churches, that of the Divine Wisdom and that of the Falling Asleep of the Virgin, still remain, and the mosaics of the latter shew that the praises of the local panegyrist were not exaggerated. Well-organised hospitals sheltered the leper, and it was the boast of the citizens that their philanthropic foundations excelled those of other towns. Such was Nicaea in the thirteenth century.

The inhabitants at first declined to receive Lascaris within their walls, and it was only with difficulty that he persuaded them to give shelter to his wife. Doubtless in their eyes his father-in-law, Alexius III, was still the lawful Emperor, and their loyalty may have been stimulated by the remembrance of the siege which they had endured at the hands of Andronicus I twenty years before, when they had committed the mistake of taking the wrong side in a civil war. For a time he wandered about Bithynia, trying in vain to obtain recognition, till the aid of Theodore Angelus[2], brother and successor of the first Despot of Epirus, and an alliance with the Seljūq Sultan, Kai-Khusrū I, enabled him to become master of Prusa and the neighbouring country. He was greeted as Despot by his new subjects, a title which policy and the absence of the Patriarch suggested as wiser for the moment than the dignity of Emperor.

The founder of this new Greek state had, indeed, many rivals to propitiate or subdue. Asia Minor in 1204 was divided between ten rulers of four different nationalities. While the greater part belonged to the Seljūq Sultans of Iconium, the Cilician kingdom of Armenia occupied the south, and a large colony of Armenians was settled in the Troad. At Trebizond, in the same month in which Constantinople fell, young Alexius, grandson of Andronicus I, established himself with the aid of a Georgian contingent, provided by the care of his paternal aunt Thamar. The family of Comnenus was popular on the Black Sea coast, whence it had originally come, and where men still remem-

[1] Theodore Metochítes, Νικαεύς, *apud* Sáthas, Μεσαιωνικὴ Βιβλιοθήκη, I. 140 *et sqq.*

[2] Mustoxidi, *Delle Cose Corciresi*, LV.

bered the residence of the grandfather of Alexius among them, for a tyrant in the capital may often be the idol of the provinces. Accordingly, in the pompous style of that age, he called himself Grand-Comnenus and Emperor[1], and his successors preserved both the adjective and the imperial title for 250 years. While Oenaeum and Sinope, as well as Trebizond, declared for the new Emperor, his brother David pushed the fortunes of the family farther to the west; a body of Georgians and native mercenaries helped him to subdue Paphlagonia, the cradle of his race, and he was soon able to proclaim Alexius at Heraclea and to extend the Trapezuntine Empire to the banks of the Sangarius. But the two brothers were not the only Greek competitors of Lascaris. In the middle of the Black Sea coast their conquests were interrupted by the petty sovereignty of Sábbas at Samsûn; the old rebel Mankaphâs, nicknamed "Mad Theodore," who had assumed the imperial title in the time of Isaac II, had once more made himself master of Philadelphia; while Mavrozómes had secured a strong position on the Maeander by giving his daughter's hand to the Seljūq Sultan. The Latin element was already represented by two Venetian colonies at Lampsacus and at Pegae on the Hellespont, the former a fief of the Quirini; and by a Levantine branch of the great Pisan family of Aldobrandini at Attalia[2].

The partition treaty had assigned large portions of Asia Minor to the Latin Emperor; among them "the provinces of Nicomedia, Tarsia, Paphlagonia, Oenaeum and Sinope, Laodicea and the Maeander with the appurtenances of Samsûn"—in other words practically the whole of the territory occupied by Lascaris and the Grand-Comnenus. In pursuance of this arrangement, Baldwin I granted large territories beyond the Sea of Marmora as fiefs to his faithful followers: Nicaea with the title of Duke, then considered to be one of the greatest dignities of the East, to Count Louis of Blois, a rich and redoubtable noble, who was nephew of the King of England and had held the banner at the coronation of the first Latin Emperor; Philadelphia, likewise coupled with a ducal coronet, to Stephen of Perche. Of the two great religious orders, the Knights of St John received a quarter of the so-called "Duchy of Neokastra"—the "new forts" of Adramyttium, Pergamus, and Chliara; the Templars Aldobrandino's city of Attalia[3]. It was clear from the outset that Lascaris would have to fight for his new dominions against the Latin invader as well as the native enemy.

On 1 November 1204 the French Duke of Nicaea sent two trusty henchmen, Pierre de Bracheuil and Payen d'Orléans, with a force of 120 knights to take possession of his Asiatic fief. Landing at the Latin

[1] Acropolita, I. 12; Bessarion *apud* Fallmerayer, *Geschichte des Kaiserthums von Trapezunt*, 78; Panarétos, in *Νέος Ἑλληνομνήμων*, IV. 256.

[2] Now Adalia. *Fontes Rerum Austriacarum.* Abt. II., B. xiii. 208–10; Nicetas, 795, 842.

[3] Pauli, *Codice Diplomatico*, I. 93; *Epistolarum Innocentii III*, Lib. IX. 180.

colony of Pegae, where they were sure of a welcome, they occupied the now important town of Panderma, and on 6 December met the army of Lascaris beneath the walls of Poimanenón, a strong castle to the south-east. Despite the inequality of numbers, the superior prowess of the armoured Frankish knights decided the fate of the battle; the Greeks fled, and the neighbouring city of Lopadium, now the village of Ulubad, but then one of the fairest towns in the country and the bulwark of Prusa, opened its gates to the clemency of the victors. Prusa, however, protected by its strong natural position and its high walls, resisted their attack, and the abandonment of the siege encouraged the native population to revolt against their rule, which, though admittedly humane, was still that of a foreign race and an alien creed. A second detachment of Franks, under the Latin Emperor's brother, Henry, now accepted the invitation of the Armenians who dwelt in the Troad, and who probably belonged to the Latin faith, to renew the exploits of the Trojan war, one of the few classical memories known to the crusaders. Crossing the Dardanelles to Abydos, Henry traversed the passes of Ida, and established his headquarters at Adramyttium. Thither a second Greek army, under the command of Theodore's brother Constantine, marched to attack him. But this second pitched battle, fought on 19 March 1205, was even more disastrous to the Greeks than the first; they lost many men and much booty, and the people of the country began to pay tribute to the invaders. A third attempt, this time by the "mad" tyrant of Philadelphia, was defeated by the personal courage of Henry and the irresistible rush of the French cavalry. This success was completed by the occupation of Nicomedia by a third detachment of Franks under Macaire de Ste. Menehould, the Lord High Steward. Five brief months had sufficed for the conquest of the entire rich province of Opsicium and more beside; the whole of north-west Asia Minor from Adramyttium to Nicomedia recognised the Latin Empire; Nicaea and Prusa alone held out for Lascaris.

At this moment, however, the Greeks of Asia were saved by the nation which they are wont to consider as their greatest enemy in Europe. Their fellow-countrymen in Thrace had summoned Kalojan, the Bulgarian Tsar, against the Franks, and Baldwin felt compelled to recall his brother and the other French leaders from Asia Minor to his aid against this new foe. Henry and the other two detachments hastened to obey his command; of all their conquests they retained only Pegae, as a military and naval base on the Hellespont; and with them the Armenian colony of the Troad crossed over into Europe, for fear of reprisals from the Greeks. Thus abruptly ended the first attempt of the Franks to conquer Asia Minor. The first and last French Duke of Nicaea fell in a Bulgarian ambuscade before Philippopolis, without ever having set foot in his Asiatic duchy[1].

[1] *Epistolarum Innocentii III,* Lib. VIII. 131. Cf. also *supra,* Chapter XIV, p. 424.

Lascaris availed himself of the departure of the Franks to occupy the places which they had evacuated, and his perseverance seemed to warrant the assumption of the imperial title. It was necessary, however, first to elect a Patriarch; for the Ecumenical throne was vacant. But Nicaea had by this time become the home of all that was most learned in the ecclesiastical world of Greece, so that the election of a Patriarch caused no difficulty. The newly-elected Patriarch hastened to crown Theodore Emperor, and the historian Nicetas composed an address which the monarch was to deliver on this occasion, enforcing the obedience of his subjects and setting forth the reunion of all the Greeks under his sceptre and the recapture of Constantinople as the objects of his reign. Thus, in the spring of 1206, two years after his flight from the fallen city, Theodore Lascaris was crowned at Nicaea[1].

No sooner was he invested with the imperial dignity, than he began to carry out the programme which Nicetas had traced for him. A politic truce with Henry, now Latin Emperor and fully occupied in Europe, set him free to turn his undivided attention to his Greek rivals. "Mad Theodore," Sábbas, and Mavrozómes were driven from their respective possessions; the two former vanished from history; the third, as the father-in-law of so influential a potentate as Kai-Khusrū, with whom Lascaris wished to remain at peace, received back a strip of territory, including Chonae, the birthplace of Nicetas himself. The next blow was dealt at the Empire of Trebizond. Alexius had offended the Seljūq Sultan, who besieged his capital[2]; David, taking advantage of the evacuation of Nicomedia by the French, had sent his young general, Synadenós, to occupy that city. But this inexperienced strategist was surprised by the abler Lascaris, who led his troops through a difficult mountain pass and even wielded the axe himself to remove the trees from his path. Such energy was bound to be successful; Synadenós was taken prisoner; David was forced to restrict the Trapezuntine frontier to Heraclea, and even from there the Emperor of Nicaea threatened to drive him farther eastward. At this, in self-preservation, David called in the Franks to his aid.

The Franks had been ready to ally themselves with the sole remaining Greek rival of Lascaris, for they complained that he had broken his truce with them, and they were anxious to prevent the growth of a Greek naval power, of which he had laid the foundations under the guidance of a Calabrian corsair[3]. Accordingly, towards the end of 1206, Henry sent Pierre de Bracheuil and Payen d'Orléans for the second time to Asia Minor, with the promise that Bracheuil should have Pegae and Cyzicus with the island of Marmora as a fief, while Thierri de Loos,

[1] After March 20, the date of the Patriarch's election. Kállistos *apud* Migne, *P. G.* cxlvii. 465.

[2] *Recueil des historiens des Croisades. Historiens Orientaux,* II. pt i. 101.

[3] Μιχαὴλ Ἀκομινάτου τὰ σωζόμενα, II. 159.

the Seneschal of the Latin Empire, was invested with Nicomedia. This second Frankish invasion repeated on a smaller scale the achievements of the first. From Pegae as a base Bracheuil occupied and refortified the peninsula of Cyzicus, and the Seneschal, sailing direct from Constantinople to Nicomedia, speedily converted its beautiful minster of the Divine Wisdom into his castle. Two other French nobles, Macaire de Ste. Menehould and Guillaume de Sains, established themselves at Hereke to the north of the Gulf of Izmid and at Gemlik, or Civitot, as the crusaders called it, the port of Nicaea and Prusa, thus cutting off both those cities from the sea. Thus hemmed in by the Franks, Lascaris sent envoys to the Bulgarian Tsar, urging him to attack Constantinople. Once again Kalojan created a welcome diversion in Thrace, and once again it was necessary to recall the French to Europe. Only small garrisons were left to hold the Frankish quadrilateral.

Theodore at once proceeded to attack these isolated fortresses. So fierce was the fighting at Civitot, that only five of its brave defenders remained unwounded when Henry arrived in haste from Constantinople to its relief, and such was its condition that he decided to withdraw the garrison and abandon it. Cyzicus was so closely invested by land and sea that a second expedition was required to raise the siege; Thierri de Loos was captured outside the walls of Nicomedia, and its fortified minster would have been taken, had not Henry returned to save it. Then a truce for two years was concluded; the Greeks released their prisoners, the French evacuated Cyzicus and Nicomedia, and their fortifications were destroyed. Pegae seems already to have fallen; only Hereke remained Frankish.

The truce, though equally beneficial to both parties, was soon broken. David, ever on the watch for an opportunity of attacking the rival Emperor of the East, wrote to Constantinople, begging that he might be included among the subjects, and that his land might be considered a part, of the Latin Empire. Thus sure of Henry's support, he crossed the Sangarius, invaded the dominions of Lascaris with a body of Frankish auxiliaries, and at first carried all before him. But Theodore's general, Andronicus Gídos, suddenly fell upon the Franks at a moment when they were isolated in the "Rough Passes" of Nicomedia; scarcely a man survived to tell the tale. Assistance sent by Henry merely postponed the fall of Heraclea, which was annexed with Amastris to the Empire of Nicaea. The only important Frankish success was the recovery of Pegae by its feudal lord, Pierre de Bracheuil. No wonder that Lascaris complained to the Pope of such breaches of the truce, begged his Holiness to induce the Franks to conclude a permanent peace with him, making the sea the boundary between him and them, and threatened, if these terms were refused, to join the Bulgarians against them. Innocent III replied bidding him render homage to the Emperor Henry and obedience to the Holy Father, whose legate might then intervene on his behalf at Constantinople. Theodore's response was an attempt to recapture the imperial city, an enterprise in which he was aided by the French lord of Pegae, turned traitor to his lawful sovereign[1]. Thus early were the Latins divided against themselves, and even men of good family entered the service of the Greeks.

A new enemy, and one of his own household, now arose to disturb the career of Lascaris and the peace of Asia Minor. The fugitive Emperor Alexius III, after wandering about Europe, arrived at the court of Kai-Khusrū, whom, years before, he had sheltered, baptised, and adopted at Constantinople. The dethroned monarch begged the Sultan to obtain for him, as the rightful Emperor of the Greeks, the crown which his son-in-law had usurped. Thinking that his guest might prove a serviceable instrument of his own designs, the ambitious Sultan, who had not forgotten that his predecessors had once ruled at Nicaea, sent an ultimatum to Theodore, offering him the alternative of instant abdication or war. Theodore's reply was to march against him to Antioch on the Maeander, whither he had advanced with Alexius. The battle was at first unfavourable to Lascaris; 800 Latin mercenaries, who, despite the Papal excommunication, accompanied him, were annihilated, and the Sultan struck him a tremendous blow on the head, which caused him to fall from his horse. For a moment the Emperor seemed at the mercy of his opponent; but with great presence of mind he drew his sword, and severed the hind legs of the mare which the Sultan rode. Kai-Khusrū fell; in an instant his head was cut off, and stuck on a spear in full sight of his army[2]. Deprived of their leader, the Seljūqs were glad to make peace; the victor took Alexius with him to Nicaea, blinded him (according to one account[3]), and placed him in the monastery of Hyakinthos, where he died. So dramatic a triumph inspired the imagination, or rather the rhetoric, of the two chief living men of letters. Nicetas composed a panegyric of the victor who had routed the hitherto invincible Turks, and his brother, the ex-Metropolitan of Athens, sent a letter of congratulation from his exile in Ceos, in which he compared Lascaris to Hercules and Basil "the Bulgar-slayer." Lascaris himself issued a manifesto to the Greek world, promising that, if all his countrymen would but help him, he would "soon free the land from the Latin dogs"; and they offered their aid if he would attack Constantinople.

The news had, however, a very different effect upon the Latin Emperor. His comment on the victory was that "the victor had been

[1] Buchon, *Recherches et Matériaux*, II. 211.

[2] Acropolita (17) says that the Sultan was beheaded by an unknown hand; Nicetas (Μεσαιωνικὴ Βιβλιοθήκη, I. 132), in a rhetorical passage, and Abū 'l-Fidā (*Historiens Orientaux*, I. 86), attribute his death to the Emperor.

[3] Sáthas, Μεσαιωνικὴ Βιβλιοθήκη, VII. 457.

vanquished," for he reckoned the loss of the Latin mercenaries as more than counterbalancing the defeat of the Turks. He knew, however, that the Greeks were flushed with their success and meditated an assault upon the imperial city, so he resolved to wait no longer, but attack them first. Accordingly he crossed to Pegae, now the sole possession of the Franks in Asia Minor, and held since Bracheuil's treachery by Henri de Grangerin[1], whereupon Lascaris took to the mountains. The murmurs of his own subjects, whose property was thus exposed to the raids of the Frankish cavalry, forced the Greek Emperor, however, to give battle. The two armies met at the river Rhyndakos on 15 October 1211, and although the Greek host was greatly superior in numbers and was aided by a fresh band of Latin renegades, the victory rested with Henry, who, according to the account which he has left us of this campaign, did not lose a single man. At this the Greeks right up to the Seljūq frontier submitted to the victor, whose kindness to the vanquished was proverbial. A few castles alone held out for Theodore, and Henry announced from Pergamus to all his friends his triumph over the four enemies of his empire, of whom Lascaris was the first and foremost. Ere long his standards had reached as far south as Nymphaeum near Smyrna, as far east as Poimanenón and Lentianá near Prusa. But it was easier to overrun Asia Minor than to hold it, for the Franks were but a handful of men, and Henry appealed in vain for military colonists from the west. He therefore came to terms with his adversary: he was to retain the Troad and north-west Asia Minor as far as Lopadium; to the east of that, and from Adramyttium southward to Smyrna, lay the dominions of Lascaris; a neutral uninhabited zone was left between the two Empires and a strong frontier guard prevented emigration from one to the other. Even this restricted Frankish territory was perforce entrusted to the charge of a Greek garrison under a Greek commander.

Theodore had made what proved to be a durable peace with the Franks, broken only by a raid of the Duke of Naxos which he avenged by the capture of his enemy; but the new Seljūq Sultan, Kai-Kā'ūs I, had not forgotten the death of his father. In 1214 or 1215, a fortunate raid delivered the Greek Emperor into his hand; his first impulse was to kill his prisoner, but he contented himself with a ransom and the cession of several castles and towns. Such sudden reverses of fortune were characteristic of this period of Greek history. Kai-Kā'ūs continued his career of conquest, took Sinope from the Empire of Trebizond, slew David, who commanded there, and compelled the Emperor Alexius to pay tribute and to render him military service[2].

For several years Theodore remained at peace with the Latin Emperor, while the hand of his own sister secured him the friendship of the Duke of Naxos. He had meanwhile been left a widower; and, after

[1] *Recueil des historiens des Croisades. Lois,* II. 470.

[2] Ibid., *Historiens Orientaux,* I. 87; Papadópoulos-Keraméus, *Fontes,* 131.

an unfortunate alliance with an Armenian princess, he married the daughter of the Latin Empress Yolande, Maria de Courtenay, a politic match which might give him a claim to her brother's throne. In fact, during the interregnum which elapsed before the arrival of the Emperor Robert at Constantinople in 1221, he planned a second attack upon that city. His plan was frustrated by a counter-attack; he made peace with his brother-in-law, and was only prevented by death from strengthening their relationship and therewith his own claims by giving the hand of his daughter Eudocia to Robert. He died in 1222, and was laid beside his first wife and her father Alexius III in the monastery of Hyakinthos at Nicaea. He had living one son by his Armenian consort, but as this child was only eight years old, he bequeathed his empire to the second husband of his eldest daughter—John Ducas Vatatzes.

The Greeks, as their historians acknowledged, owed a great debt to Theodore Lascaris as the re-founder of the fallen empire. In the face of great difficulties he obtained recognition as the leader of Hellenism in Asia, and even the Franks admired his courage and his military skill. He was generous to his friends, and if he once, as was said, flayed an enemy alive, the man was a double-dyed traitor and a disgrace to French chivalry. As a diplomatist, he shewed the audacity which the times demanded, and availed himself of those opportunities for playing off one race against another which the Eastern question has always afforded; while he displayed the talent of a constructive statesman in making his new capital the centre of all that was best in the Greek world. From Euboea and Thrace, as well as from Byzantium, the local aristocracy flocked to his court; he and his family were addressed by the begging-letter writers of the Bosphorus; he sheltered the historian Nicetas, who repaid him by three panegyrics, and he tried to attract the historian's brother from his lonely island. Under his auspices, Nicaea became a learned city, where rhetoric and poetry could be studied, while at Smyrna Demetrius Karýkes, called "the chief of philosophers," gave lectures on logic[1]. But the patriotism and common-sense of the sovereign made him discourage those nice theological discussions which were the delight of Byzantine divines, and which might have been expected to find a congenial atmosphere in the city which had witnessed two great Councils of the Church. Theodore was, however, fully alive to the value of the hierarchy as a national and political force. He had established the Patriarchate in his capital, and he supported the efforts of the Patriarch for the Union of the Churches at a synod to be held there. But this scheme failed; both the Greeks of Epirus and the Greeks of Trebizond declined to acknowledge the authority of the Patriarch of Nicaea, whose actual jurisdiction was further restricted by

[1] Blemmýdes, 4.

the creation of an autocephalous Serbian Church and of two Latin bishoprics, one at Nicomedia, the other at Troy[1].

During the later and more peaceful years of his reign, Theodore encouraged trade with the Venetians, to whom he granted freedom from customs' dues throughout his empire, and for this a proper system of coinage was required. Five issues of gold coins bear his image and superscription, while inscriptions on towers at Prusa, at Nicaea, and at Bender-Eregli still preserve his name and serve as an example of the many buildings which he erected.

In the same year as Theodore, died his rival, the first Emperor of Trebizond. Cut off by the Turkish occupation of Sinope from all hope of expansion to the west, he seems to have turned his attention to the northern coast of the Black Sea, and to have made the Crimea tributary to Trebizond. His Asiatic Empire now extended no farther westward than Oenaeum and the river Thermodon, while Savastopoli 18 hours beyond Trebizond was its eastern boundary[2]. But his capital was deemed impregnable, alike by nature and art. Its mild climate, its vineyards and oliveyards, its excellent water, and its abundant supply of wood combined to make it, in the phrase of an enthusiastic panegyrist, "the apple of the eye of all Asia." It had long been under the special protection of St Eugenius, whose monastery, and that of "the Golden-headed Virgin," were already features of the city.

John III Vatatzes, the second Emperor of Nicaea, was not long allowed to occupy the throne unopposed. Two of Theodore's brothers could not brook the succession of this Thracian nobleman, who, if he belonged to a good family and had held high office at Court, was only connected by marriage with the founder of the Empire. By money and promises they raised a Frankish force at Constantinople, and returned at its head to Asia Minor. Vatatzes met them near Poimanenón, the scene of the battle twenty years before, and by his personal courage won a decisive victory. Four neighbouring Frankish fortresses fell into his hands, and in 1225 the Latin Emperor was glad to obtain peace by the cession of Pegae. The Franks, in the words of one of their own chroniclers, lost "nearly all the land which had been won beyond the Hellespont"; they abandoned the Troad, and retained nothing but the territory near Constantinople and Nicomedia. Well might the enthusiastic Patriarch bid them begone to their own country[3]. Even beyond the coasts of Asia Minor the long arm of the Greek Emperor smote them. His fleet not only watched the Dardanelles from the former factory of the Quirini at Lampsacus and intercepted vessels coming from the west to Constantinople, but captured the four islands of Lesbos, Chios, Samos, and Icaria, which had been assigned to the Latin

[1] *VV*, III. 275; *Epistolarum Innocentii III*, Lib. XIV. 90.
[2] Papadópoulos-Keraméus, *Fontes*, 117–8.
[3] *Revue des études grecques*, VII. 76.

Empire by the partition treaty. An expedition in 1233 against Leo Gabalâs, the "Lord of Rhodes and the Cyclades," who bore the proud title of "Caesar," and asserted his independence[1] of the Greek Emperor, failed, however, to take his famous fortress. Another naval undertaking in aid of the Cretans, who had risen against Venice, was equally unsuccessful. The Emperor's troops did, indeed, capture several Cretan fortresses, and a detachment of them held out for some years in the island. But the expedition cost him nearly the whole of his fleet, shipwrecked in a storm off the island of Cerigo.

Vatatzes had defeated the Franks; but he still had enemies to fear within his own court. The capture of the late sovereign's brothers at the battle of Poimanenón, and the loss of their eyesight as the penalty of their treason, had rendered them harmless; but a fresh conspiracy, organised by his first cousin Nestóngos and several other magnates, was discovered at the very moment when he was fighting against his country's foes. The Emperor's clemency towards the principal conspirator, who was merely imprisoned and then allowed to escape, surprised his contemporaries. But from that moment he surrounded himself with guards, and listened to the prayers of his wife that he would be careful of a life so valuable to his country. It was probably about this time that he moved the capital to Nymphaeum, his favourite winter residence, which thenceforth continued to be the seat of government till the recapture of Constantinople, while the fertile plain near Clazomenae was chosen as the imperial *villeggiatura* in spring. Nicaea remained, however, the seat of the Patriarch, and it was there that the Emperors were crowned.

The election of the old warrior John of Brienne as Latin Emperor inspired the Franks with the hope of recovering the territory which they had lost in Asia Minor by the last peace. One of the conditions of his election was that he should have "the Duchy of Nicomedia," and that "the Kingdom of Nicaea with all its appurtenances and all the land that the Latins ever possessed beyond the Hellespont, comprising the Duchy of Neokastra,"[2] should become the domain of Baldwin II. John waited patiently till he had made adequate preparations for the re-conquest of these hypothetical "kingdoms" and "duchies" and till a favourable moment for attack should arrive. The exhaustion of the Greek forces after their unsuccessful expedition against Rhodes in 1233 seemed to be a suitable opportunity, and the Latin Emperor landed at Lampsacus. But Vatatzes, though his forces were diminished in numbers, proved himself so clever a strategist that he compelled his adversaries to hug the shore where their fleet was constantly at hand. One important success, the recapture of Pegae, was the sole result of this long-planned

[1] Blemmýdes, 61–2; Schlumberger, *Numismatique de l'Orient latin*, 215; Pl. viii. 17, 18.

[2] *Fontes Rerum Austriacarum*, Abt. II. xiii. 265.

campaign[1]. John returned to Constantinople, nor did the Franks re-attempt the invasion of Asia Minor. Henceforth it was not they but the rejuvenated Greek Empire which could take the offensive, and it became the object of Vatatzes to carry out the aspirations of his predecessor and drive them from their diminished dominions alike in Europe and in Asia.

With this policy in view, he sought an alliance with the hereditary enemy of his race, the Bulgarian Tsar, John Asên II, whose signal victory over the victorious Greeks of Epirus on the field of Klokotinitza had made him the dominant factor in Balkan politics. The engagement of their children, both still in the schoolroom, seemed to guarantee their co-operation against the Franks, and Vatatzes celebrated the capture of the Venetian colony of Gallipoli and the betrothal of his son Theodore in rapid succession. Thrace was soon almost entirely freed from the Latins, and the Empire of Nicaea for the first time extended into Europe, where the river Maritza became the frontier between the Greek and the Slavonic states. The allies even laid siege to Constantinople "with infinite thousands of armed men,"[2] till the approaching winter of 1235 compelled them to return to their homes. In the following year they renewed the siege by land and sea, but this time the united forces of the Latins repulsed their attack. Had they been successful, the Greeks and the Bulgarians would have quarrelled over the possession of the city which both coveted. As it was, the unnatural alliance grew weaker as one ally realised what he had had to sacrifice and the other what he had assisted to restore. The Greek Emperor could not but regret that the price which he had to pay for the Bulgarian's aid was the recognition of the independence of the Church of Trnovo and its separation from the jurisdiction of the Ecumenical Patriarch. The Bulgarian Tsar could not fail to perceive that he had exchanged a weak and tottering neighbour for a vigorous and powerful prince, and that on the ruins of the alien Latin Empire he was reinstating a national dynasty which would bar the way to Byzantium and the Aegean. Personal and theological influences further combined to break up the alliance. Asên's consort, a Hungarian princess, was connected with the reigning family of Constantinople; while Pope Gregory IX, who had hopes of converting the Bulgarian Tsar to the Roman faith, denounced Vatatzes as "the enemy of God and the Church," and received from him a haughty letter, in which the Greek ruler claimed to be the real Emperor as the heir of Constantine, and plainly told the Pontiff that, if he had yielded to superior force, he had not relinquished his rights, but would never desist from besieging Constantinople[3].

[1] *BZ.*, XIV. 219; *Recueil des historiens des Croisades. Historiens Occidentaux,* II. 382.

[2] *Les Registres de Grégoire IX,* II. 217.

[3] Ibid. II. 512, 659–60, 672–3; Ἀθηναῖον, I. 369–78; *BZ.* XVI. 141–2.

Asên accordingly resolved to abandon his ally; he obtained possession of his daughter on the pretext of a father's natural longing to see her, and then demonstrated his paternal affection by chastising the damsel when she lamented her enforced separation from her youthful husband and his kind parents. The appearance of a new factor in Balkan politics at this moment facilitated the formation of a triple alliance against the Greek Emperor. The Cumans, a horde of savages from the Caspian, driven from their home by the Mongol invasion, had crossed the Danube and penetrated as far south as Thrace. With them and with the Bulgarians the Franks of Constantinople formed a league against Vatatzes, for all three races had a common interest in driving him from his newly-won possessions on Thracian soil. Their first effort was the siege of Tzurulum, the modern Chorlu, between the present railway and the Sea of Marmora, then an important fortress and the key of the Greek position in Europe. The place was defended by one of those generals who are better known for their good luck than for their good strategy. On the present occasion the commander's reputation was once more verified; in the midst of the siege the news reached Asên that his wife, one of his children, and the newly-created Patriarch were dead. This triple calamity dissolved the triple alliance; the pious Bulgarian saw in his affliction the judgment of Heaven for his breach of faith; he sent his daughter back to the court of Vatatzes, and made peace with the Greeks. The Franks and the Cumans, however, only waited for reinforcements to renew the attack; at this second attempt Chorlu fell, and its commander, a better but a less fortunate soldier than his predecessor, was taken a prisoner to Constantinople. So important did the capture of this fortress seem to the Latin Emperor that he wrote a letter to King Henry III of England, setting forth the political results of its submission[1]. It was some compensation for this loss that Vatatzes captured two of the fortresses (Gebseh and Tusla, now stations on the Anatolian railway) which the Franks still possessed between Nicomedia and Constantinople. The Greek frontier was thus little more than twenty miles from the imperial city. But the defeat of the Greek navy, manned by raw sailors and commanded by an inexperienced Armenian, prevented a further advance[2].

Before renewing his attack upon the Latin Empire, Vatatzes resolved to realise the dream of his predecessor and reunite all the Greeks under one sceptre. The Emperors of Nicaea had viewed with suspicion the growth of an independent Greek principality in Epirus under the despots of the house of Angelus; and, when the despotat of Epirus became the Empire of Salonica, this assumption of the imperial title bitterly offended the only true "Emperor of the Romans" at Nicaea. Theological controversies between the ecclesiastical authorities of the two rival Greek states further

[1] Matthew Paris, *Chronica Majora*, IV. 54.
[2] *BZ.* XIV. 220.

envenomed their relations, and the resentment of the Nicene divines was doubtless all the deeper because the logic and the learning of the Epirote party were superior to their own. Accordingly, the Asiatic Greeks had viewed with equanimity the capture of the Emperor of Salonica by the Bulgarians at the battle of Klokotinitza. But although Theodore Angelus was a prisoner and blinded, his brother Manuel continued to rule at Salonica, with the permission of the Bulgarian Tsar, till the latter, smitten with the charms of his blind captive's daughter, made her his wife and set her father free to plot against Manuel. The plot succeeded; incapacitated by the loss of his sight from reigning himself, Theodore placed his son John on the imperial throne of Salonica, while Manuel sought an asylum at the court of Vatatzes, thus providing his diplomatic host with an excuse for intervention in the affairs of the sister-state. He had no difficulty in pleading his cause, for Vatatzes had long had a *casus belli* against the Empire of Salonica. In 1225 Theodore had cheated him out of the good city of Hadrianople, which he had sent his officers, at the invitation of the inhabitants, to occupy in his name. He now avenged himself by furnishing Theodore's exiled brother with the means of taking a large part of Thessaly. But Manuel had no sooner achieved this object than he threw over his benefactor and made his peace with Theodore. Thus the first move failed; Salonica had outwitted Nicaea. Vatatzes, however, could afford to wait.

In 1241 the favourable moment seemed to have arrived. The great Bulgarian Tsar had died, leaving a child as his successor; Manuel had died also; while the Emperor John of Salonica, whom nature had intended for a monk rather than a sovereign, relied upon the advice of his old blind father. A truce with the Latin Empire left Vatatzes at liberty to devote his whole energies to his long-cherished design[1]. He first enticed old Theodore to his court, and flattered the childish vanity of that experienced ruler by calling him "uncle" and giving him a seat at his own table. When all was ready, in the spring of 1242, he crossed over into Europe and began the first fratricidal war between the two Greek Empires of Nicaea and Salonica. Aided by a body of Cuman mercenaries whom he had attracted to his service, he marched along the coast so as not to violate Bulgarian territory, and met with no resistance till he arrived within about eight stades of his rival's capital. The size and strength of Salonica rendered difficult the use of siege-engines; and, while Vatatzes was still ravaging the neighbourhood, the news arrived that the dreaded Mongols had defeated the Seljūqs of Iconium and were threatening his Asiatic dominions. Keeping the fatal secret to himself, he made the best terms he could with the Emperor John through the medium of old Theodore. His vanity was perforce contented with the degradation of his rival to the rank of a Despot, who no longer outraged the Byzantine protocol by wearing the imperial emblems.

[1] Albricus in *M. G. H. Script.* XXIII. 950.

The Mongol peril and internal affairs kept Vatatzes occupied in Asia during the next few years, for he had pledged himself to aid the new Seljūq Sultan, Kai-Khusrū II, against this common enemy of both. But, as soon as the Mongols abandoned their attack on Iconium for other enterprises, he bethought himself once more of his European possessions. John of Salonica was now dead, and his brother, the Despot Demetrius, who had received his title from the Emperor of Nicaea, was a man of loose and vicious habits, which rendered him unpopular. It was therefore obvious that his position was insecure and that Vatatzes only needed a plausible excuse for the annexation of Salonica. His western frontier had now advanced from the Maritza to a place called Zichna near Seres, and only a small strip of Bulgarian territory served as a buffer-state between the two Greek Empires. A coincidence enabled him in the same year to conquer this Slavonic outpost of Salonica and Salonica itself.

In the autumn of 1246 he was returning from a tour of inspection in his European dominions. On the banks of the Maritza he received the news that the young Bulgarian Tsar Kaliman was dead, and that his still younger brother, Michael Asên, had succeeded him. The temptation to attack the Bulgarians at such a moment was great, for Greek rulers have ever been haunted by the vision of Basil "the Bulgar-slayer." Accordingly Vatatzes returned at once to Philippi, and there on the historic battle-field summoned a council of war to consider the question. Some argued against the proposal, on the ground that the army was weak and that the citadel of Seres, the first Bulgarian fortress, was a strong natural position; but Andronicus Palaeologus, father of the future Emperor, whose advice was all the weightier because he held the post of commander-in-chief, urged a forward policy. The governor of Seres speedily capitulated; the citizens of Melnik responded to an appeal to their Greek origin, while the Bulgarian party was reminded that a Bulgarian princess was the wife of the future Greek Emperor. Other places followed their example; the conquests which John Asên II had made at the expense of the Empire of Salonica sixteen years before were restored to the Empire of Nicaea; a treaty of peace was signed with Bulgaria which made the Maritza the northern, as it had once been the western, boundary of Vatatzes; while Köstendil in the modern kingdom of Bulgaria and Skoplje in Serbian Macedonia owned his sway. The days of Basil "the Bulgar-slayer" seemed to have returned. A patriotic historian could truly boast that "the western frontier of Nicaea marched with that of Serbia."[1]

At this moment the discontent at Salonica had reached a climax. The frivolous despot had trampled on the ancient customs and privileges of that city, and a body of leading citizens sent one of their number to Vatatzes' camp at Melnik, praying for a renewal of their charter. The Emperor gladly consented, and resolved to see for himself how matters stood. He ordered Demetrius to present himself before his lawful

[1] Acropolita, II. 18.

suzerain and render the homage due. The foolish youth was persuaded by the conspirators to refuse. A second refusal sealed his fate. The troops of Vatatzes, aided by treachery, entered the city, and thus in December 1246 the last shadow of the short-lived Empire of Salonica ceased to exist. Its last ruler was imprisoned in an Asiatic dungeon; his dominions were annexed to those of his conqueror. Still, however, Vatatzes had not united all the free Greeks beneath his sceptre. Michael II, a bold scion of the house of Angelus, had established himself in Corfù and Epirus and extended his sway as far east as Monastir, while old blind Theodore still exercised his ruling passion for power by the waters of Vodená and on the lake of Ostrovo. For the present, however, the Emperor deemed it wiser to content himself with the organisation of his new and vast possessions. Each of the captured cities received an imperial message; the future Emperor, Michael Palaeologus, was appointed governor of Seres and Melnik, and his father governor-general of the European provinces of the Nicene Empire with residence at Salonica.

Elated with these bloodless triumphs over Bulgarians and Greeks, Vatatzes returned to Europe in the following spring for the purpose of recovering the fortress of Chorlu from the Franks, an undertaking which the growing weakness of the Latin Empire seemed to facilitate. The governor was Anseau de Cayeux, ex-Regent of the Empire, whose wife was sister-in-law of the Greek sovereign. Thinking that the latter would never besiege a place which contained his wife's sister, Anseau left the castle almost undefended. But Vatatzes was not the man to allow his private relationships to interfere with his public policy; he prosecuted the siege, recaptured Chorlu, and cut off the communications of Constantinople with the west by land. But this exploit nearly cost him his life; he rashly approached the walls to parley with the garrison, and was only saved as by a miracle from the well-aimed bolt of a Frankish crossbowman. He did not press further the advantages which he had gained. Probably the fear of the Mongols restrained him from continuing his campaign against Constantinople, for in 1248 we find two Mongol envoys at the Papal court. Innocent IV received them cordially, and did not scruple to suggest that their master should attack the schismatic Vatatzes. But the Mongol emissaries rejoined, with delicate irony, that they could not advise this policy, because they disliked to encourage "the mutual hatred of Christians."[1] Having given the Holy Father this lesson in Christianity, the infidels returned to their own savage country. The reluctance of the Mongols to invade his dominions seems to have reassured Vatatzes, for in 1249 he was once more preparing for an attempt upon Constantinople, with the assistance of his vassal, John Gabalâs, the new ruler of Rhodes, when a sudden revolution in the fortunes of that island caused the postponement of his plans for the annexation of what little still remained of the Latin Empire.

[1] Matthew Paris, *Historia Minor,* III. 38–9; *Chronica Majora,* v. 38.

We saw how Vatatzes had failed, sixteen years before, in his expedition against Leo Gabalâs, the independent "Lord of Rhodes and the Cyclades." Gabalâs had, however, thought it prudent, after that invasion, to become "the man of Venice," the most powerful maritime state of that day, and had promised to assist the Venetian authorities in Crete against Vatatzes during the Cretan insurrection. Soon, however, he seems to have recognised the suzerainty of Nicaea, retaining the title of "Caesar" but adding that of "servant of the Emperor" on his coins, and perhaps receiving as his reward the post of Lord High Admiral[1]. His brother and successor dropped the Caesarean style and described himself as simple "Lord of Rhodes," who, if he were bound to help his suzerain, looked to him for protection. While the two were at Nicomedia, the news arrived that the Genoese, who coveted Rhodes as a commercial centre, had surprised the citadel by a night attack. Vatatzes at once sent one of his best officers to recover the place. But the Genoese received valuable assistance from a body of the famous Frankish cavalry of the Morea, left by Prince William of Achaia on his way through the island. Reinforcements were necessary before the French knights could be annihilated, the Genoese garrison reduced to surrender, and the imperial suzerainty restored.

The last campaign of Vatatzes was directed against his still existing Greek rivals in Europe. Michael II, the crafty Despot of Epirus, had thought it prudent to remain on good terms with the conqueror of Salonica, who was since 1246 his neighbour in Macedonia. He made a treaty with him and even affianced his eldest son and heir, Nicephorus, to the Emperor's grand-daughter Maria. But, before the wedding had taken place, the restless despot, instigated by his uncle, the old intriguer Theodore, invaded the Nicene territory in Europe and thus forced Vatatzes to take up arms for the preservation of his recent conquests. The despot had shown little diplomatic skill in his choice of opportunity, for his rival had nothing to fear from either the Musulmans in Asia or the Bulgarians in Europe. Vatatzes carried all before him. Old Theodore fled from his possessions at Vodená and Ostrovo; one distinguished personage after another deserted the despot's standard, and the latter was compelled to send the Metropolitan of Lepanto to sue for peace. The Nicene envoys, of whom the historian Acropolita was one, met Michael II at Larissa, the ancient Thessalian city, then an important political, ecclesiastical, and even learned[2] centre. There peace was signed; Michael ceded the three Macedonian lakes of Castoria, Prespa, and Ochrida, as well as the historic fortress of Kroja in Albania, to the victor; and the historian returned to his master with the despot's eldest son and the aged schemer Theodore as his prisoners.

[1] Schlumberger, *Numismatique de l'Orient latin*, 216; Pl. viii. 19–20; Miklosich and Müller, *Acta et Diplomata Graeca Medii Aevi*, IV. 254.

[2] Blemmýdes, 36.

Theodore vanishes from history in the dungeons of Vatatzes. For half a century he had disturbed the peace of the Balkan peninsula; he had experienced every change of fortune; he had made and lost an empire; he had been the victor and the captive of an Emperor. Now at last he was at rest.

Meanwhile, the domestic life of the Emperor had been less fortunate than his campaigns against Franks, Bulgarians, and Epirote Greeks. On the death of his first wife, Irene, for whose loss the courtly Acropolita[1], turned poet for the occasion, had expressed the fear that he would never be comforted, Vatatzes had married in 1244 Constance of Hohenstaufen, daughter of the Emperor Frederick II and sister of the luckless Manfred. The union, despite the great discrepancy of age between the two parties, promised considerable political advantages. Both the Emperors hated the Papacy, and while Greek troops were sent to aid Frederick in his struggle against Rome, Frederick asserted the rights of "the most Orthodox Greeks" to Constantinople. Vatatzes, as we learn from his own son[2], was dazzled by the brilliance of a match which made him the son-in-law of the most famous and versatile monarch of the thirteenth century, while the scholars and theologians of Nicaea would not have been Greeks if they had not admired the abilities of a ruler who, if a Frank by birth, yet wrote letters in their beautiful language in praise of their historic Church. The wedding was celebrated at Prusa with all the pomp of a military Empire, a court poet composed a nuptial ode, and Constance took the Greek name of Anna, the more closely to identify herself with her husband's people. On the other hand, the Pope was furious at the marriage, and one of the counts of the indictment drawn up against Frederick II at the Council of Lyons was that he had given his daughter to the excommunicated heretic Vatatzes.

Unfortunately, the young Empress had brought with her from the West a dangerous rival to her own charms in the person of an attractive young Italian marchioness, who was one of her maids of honour. The languishing eyes and the graceful manners of the lady-in-waiting captivated the heart of the susceptible sovereign, and his infatuation for his mistress reached such a pitch that he allowed her to wear the purple buskins of an Empress and gave her a more numerous suite than that of his lawful consort. The ceremonious court of Nymphaeum was scandalised at this double breach of morals and etiquette. Its indignation found vent in the bitter lampoons of Nicephorus Blemmýdes, the Abbot of St Gregory near Ephesus, whose autobiography is one of the most vivid pieces of Byzantine literature. Blemmýdes hated the favourite for her abandoned life and her Italian nationality, for women and foreigners were his pet aversions. Resolved to brave the patriotic

[1] II. 6.

[2] "Satire du Précepteur" (Paris, Bibliothèque Nationale), MS. sup. gr., XXXVII. f. 56 v°.

moralist, she forced her way into his church, in all the pomp of the imperial emblems, at the moment of the consecration. The abbot instantly ordered the service to cease and bade the shameless hussy quit the holy place which she defiled by her presence. Stunned by his rebuke, she burst into tears, while one of her escort attempted to draw his sword to slay the bold monk at the altar. But the weapon stuck in the scabbard; the accident was, of course, ascribed to the black arts of the abbot; and Blemmýdes was accused of *lèse-majesté* and magic by the infuriated woman and her baffled cavalier. The accused defended himself in a violent encyclical[1]; and the Emperor, from qualms of conscience or motives of policy, refused to punish so just a man, who had only spoken the truth, and whose influence was so great with the Puritans and the Chauvinists of the Empire. From this moment the marchioness disappears from the chronicles of the Nicene court; possibly she married an Italian and returned to Italy and respectability[2]. For a time the legitimate Empress gained influence over her husband; she doubtless read with pleasure the rhetorical funeral oration which her stepson, the future Emperor Theodore, composed on the death of her father in 1250; she welcomed her uncle Galvano Lancia and her other relatives, when they were exiled by Frederick's successor; and a special mission under the direction of Berthold of Hohenburg was required to procure their removal from a court at which they had so powerful a protectress[3]. The death of Vatatzes and the accession of her step-son deprived her of her power; but she was still young and attractive, and when Michael Palaeologus usurped the throne, he sought her first as his mistress, then, when she scorned the *liaison* with one who had been her subject, as his wife, although he was already married. Defeated in this object, he sent the ex-Empress back to her brother Manfred; but the latter's fall at Benevento placed her at the mercy of Charles of Anjou. The Angevin conqueror allowed her to seek an asylum at the court of Aragon, where her nephew Peter III granted her and her daughter an annuity. At last, entering a convent, she renounced her claims to the Greek Empire to James II, and died at a great age in the city of Valencia. There, in the little church of St John-of-the-Hospital a wooden coffin still bears the simple epitaph: "Here lies the lady Constance, august Empress of Greece."[4] Even in the strange romance of medieval Greek history there are few stranger pages than the varied career of this unhappy exile, a sacrifice to politics and the sport of chance.

The connexion between Vatatzes and the great enemy of the Papacy in Western Europe did not prevent the astute Emperor from endeavour-

[1] MPG., CXLII. 605–9.

[2] *Les Registres d'Alexandre IV*, I. 88.

[3] N. de Jamsilla *apud* Muratori, *RR. II. SS.* VIII. 506.

[4] Carini, *Gli Archivi e le biblioteche di Spagna*, II. 9, 18, 19, 189; *Revue des deux Mondes*, 15 March 1902; Diehl, *Figures byzantines*, II. 207–25.

ing to secure the support of Rome, when it suited his policy, by holding out hopes of a reunion of the Churches. In 1232 the presence of five Minorites at Nicaea suggested to the Patriarch the despatch of letters to Pope Gregory IX and the Sacred College, advocating an enquiry into the differences between the East and the West. The Pope replied, urging the Greeks to return to the bosom of the Church, and sent four learned theologians to discuss the doctrinal points at issue. The nice points raised by the Latins in support of the *filioque* clause proved too much for the distinguished philosopher whom the Greeks had put forward as their champion. Blemmýdes had to be called in to their aid, and, in the presence of the Emperor, refuted their arguments to his own complete satisfaction. Vatatzes acted throughout like a statesman, seeking to make one of those compromises which are the essence of politics but which are rare in theology. His wise policy failed to appease the celestial minds of the controversialists, and for some time at Nymphaeum it rained treatises on the Procession of the Holy Ghost, till at last the Patriarch excommunicated the Pope. Still, whenever he thought that he could hasten the fall of the Latin Empire, Vatatzes renewed his diplomatic overtures to the Holy See, thus calling down upon his head the reproaches of his father-in-law, who plainly told him that the papal emissaries really aimed, not at uniting the Churches, but at sowing tares between the two affectionate sovereigns of the East and the West. To the very last the Greek Emperor maintained this policy of compromise. Constantinople, he thought, was worth the promise of a mass.

Vatatzes was no more successful in healing the schism which had arisen with the foundation of the despotat of Epirus between the Greek Churches in Europe and Asia. The despots did not go so far as to elect a rival Patriarch; but the bishops in their dominions were consecrated by the local metropolitans instead of going to Nicaea. At first the Metropolitan of Lepanto acted as the head of the Epirote Church; when the political centre of gravity was transferred to Salonica, Demetrius Chomatianós, the learned theologian who held the ancient see of Ochrida, became its primate, and crowned the Emperor Theodore, an act which caused the greatest indignation at Nicaea, as a usurpation of the Patriarch's prerogative. The dispute between the rival ecclesiastical authorities reached its height when the Emperor of Salonica refused to allow the see of Durazzo to be filled by a nominee of the Nicene Patriarch. The schism continued until 1232, when the Emperor Theodore had fallen and his brother Manuel, anxious to secure the favour of Vatatzes, made his submission to the Patriarch, who sent an ecclesiastic from Asia to represent him in Europe[1]. But, even after the annexation of the Empire of Salonica and throughout the rest of this

[1] Miklosich and Müller, *Acta et Diplomata Graeca Medii Aevi*, III. 59–65; *BZ.* XVI. 120–42.

period, the Greek Church in the independent despotat of Epirus remained autocephalous. The only European bishops who took part in the synods of Nicaea were those from the European provinces of the Empire. As both the Serbian and Bulgarian Churches had obtained the recognition of their independence, owing to the political exigencies of the Nicene Emperors, the Ecumenical Patriarch had a very restricted jurisdiction. Even in Asia Minor, Trebizond continued to dispute his authority, while the Manichaean heresy, which has played so important a part in the history of Bosnia and Bulgaria, now crept into the Nicene Empire. It was some compensation, however, that after 1231 no Roman Catholic bishopric survived there.

Like a wise statesman, Vatatzes took pains to cultivate the favour of so powerful a national and political force as the Greek Church, while he was careful to see that the Patriarch should not be too independent. One of his biographers[1] tells us that he was especially good to monks, and that "he spoke to an archbishop almost as if he were in the presence of God." He issued strict orders that the civil authorities should not seize Church property either in the lifetime or on the demise of a bishop, but that an ecclesiastical administrator should take charge of the estate until the vacancy had been filled[2]. He founded or restored the famous monastery of Sósandra near Magnesia—that "wonder of the world" which inspired Blemmýdes to write verses, and which was the mausoleum of the Emperor and his son; he rebuilt and endowed the monastery on Mt Lembos near Smyrna, and erected the church of St Anthony the Great at Nicaea, while his first wife founded that of St John Baptist at Prusa and a convent of Our Lady. But, with a view to the extension of his political influence, he did not confine his munificence to his own dominions. He redeemed many churches in Constantinople from destruction by the Franks, and even in the French *seigneurie* of Athens the Greek monasteries received benefits from his hand[3].

In the intervals of his campaigns Vatatzes devoted himself with conspicuous success to the economic development of his Empire. Under his patriarchal government the land enjoyed great material prosperity. He was so excellent a manager that the produce of the crown lands not only sufficed for the maintenance of his table, but left him a surplus for the foundation of hospitals, workhouses, and asylums for the aged, so that after his time Nicaea was said to have better philanthropic institutions than any other city. He devoted much attention to stock-breeding, after the fashion of modern monarchs, and endeavoured to induce the aristocracy to subsist on their landed estates by practical farming. The Seljūq Empire afforded a ready market for their cattle and corn, owing

[1] Sáthas, Μεσαιωνικὴ Βιβλιοθήκη, VII. 506.

[2] *Revue des études grecques*, VII. 71–80.

[3] Blemmýdes, 112, 115; Ephraemius, 318; Sáthas, *op. cit.*, 509; Nicephorus Gregorâs, I. 44, 50; *BZ.* XIV. 217, 232.

to the devastations committed there by the Mongols, and so great was the demand that the Greek farmers could command fancy prices for their produce. Out of the money obtained from the sale of eggs from the imperial hen-roosts the Emperor was able in a short time to buy his consort a magnificent coronet of pearls. The natural result of this general prosperity was the increase of luxury, and the nobles spent their money in silken garments from Italy and the East. The Emperor resolved to restrain the extravagance of his subjects and at the same time to encourage national industries at the expense of the foreigner, who had profited by the free-trade policy of his predecessor. He therefore forbade them to wear foreign stuffs or to consume foreign products, under pain of losing their position in society. A Greek nobleman should wear, he thought, a Greek costume, a doctrine no longer esteemed by his countrymen. He shewed his sincerity by making his own family conform to the law, and sternly rebuked his son for going out hunting in a rich garment of silk, reminding him that such luxuries were wrung from the life-blood of the Greeks, and should only be displayed when it was necessary to impress foreign ambassadors with the wealth of the nation. Instead of wasting its resources upon court pageants, he devoted what was thus saved to the strengthening of the national defences against the Mongols, forming a central depôt at Magnesia, and accumulating large quantities of corn, which was stored in sealed granaries for use in case of invasion. In short, all his financial arrangements were of the most business-like character; every effort was made to prevent the Oriental vice of peculation on the part of the "dukes" who governed the provinces, and the dilatoriness of an official of the treasury was punished by so severe a flogging that he died.

Although he was a practical man of affairs, Vatatzes shewed the usual Greek desire for the encouragement of learning. The historian Acropolita acted as his secretary and envoy; the austere Blemmýdes and the historian were successively tutors of his son; another historian, George Pachyméres, was born at Nicaea during his reign; one of his Patriarchs, Germanus II, has left behind him some literary remains. Rhetoric and philosophy were cultivated under his auspices; he founded libraries of technical and scientific books in various cities, sent Blemmýdes to collect valuable manuscripts in Thessaly and Macedonia, and expressed the opinion that the king and the philosopher are alone really famous. His first wife, a woman of masculine abilities, shared his literary tastes, and once tried to pose the young Acropolita by asking him the cause of an eclipse, while the Margrave of Hohenburg's mission was made the occasion for a learned competition between the Latins and their Greek hosts, in which the latter were victorious.

Vatatzes did not long survive his campaign against the Epirote Greeks. On his return to Nicaea he was suddenly seized with an attack of apoplexy, which rendered him speechless for thirty-six hours. As soon as he had recovered sufficiently to travel, he ordered his attendants to convey him to his beloved Nymphaeum. The change of climate availed nothing, however, against the return of his malady. He was affected with frequent fainting-fits; his flesh wasted away; and he in vain made a pilgrimage to the miraculous image of Our Lord at Smyrna in the hope of obtaining relief. At length, after his malady had lasted for more than a year, he died at Nymphaeum on 30 October 1254, aged 62 years, nearly 33 of which he had passed on the throne. The faithful Acropolita delivered his funeral oration; a eulogy of his exploits was composed by his son, and future generations looked back upon him as "the father of the Greeks." In the fourteenth century he even attained to the honours of a saint. When the Turks threatened the Sósandra monastery about 1304, his remains were removed for safety to Magnesia. The watchman of the castle, while going his rounds, was struck by the appearance of a strange lamp, which moved about the ramparts as if on a tour of inspection. When the phenomenon was thrice repeated, he reported it to his superiors, and a search was made. For some time the phantom light eluded the investigators, until at last the watchman's deaf brother declared that he had seen a man dressed in imperial robes and had heard him say that he had charge of the watch. The ghostly guardian of Magnesia was at once recognised as none other than that of the dead Emperor John "the Merciful," who had risen from his grave to defend the city. The capture of Magnesia confirmed, instead of diminishing, the fame of his supernatural power; for when the Turks threw his bones over the cliffs, they worked miracles on the faithful, who collected them with pious care and built a shrine above them. Thenceforth St John Vatatzes the Merciful was worshipped as a saint at Magnesia, at Nymphaeum, and in Tenedos; 4 November was celebrated as his festival; and an encomium and a choral service were composed in his honour[1].

Vatatzes had not followed the usual Byzantine custom of proclaiming his successor during his own lifetime, for he was afraid of spoiling the character of the heir-apparent and of offending the susceptibilities of the people. But there was no doubt that his only son Theodore, who bore the name of Lascaris to shew his direct descent from the founder of the dynasty, would be chosen. As soon as his father's funeral was over, he was lifted on a shield and proclaimed Emperor at Nymphaeum. The ceremony was not, however, complete until he had been consecrated by the Patriarch, whose office had just fallen vacant. Theodore accordingly hastened on the election of that official; and, for the sake of form, offered the post to his old tutor Blemmýdes, in the hope that the wilful ecclesiastic would refuse. Blemmýdes knew his former pupil, and did not disappoint him. He declined the honour so insincerely tendered;

[1] Pachyméres, II. 400–2; *BZ.* XIV. 193–233; Agathángelos, *Ἀσματικὴ Ἀκολουθία τοῦ Ἁγίου Βασιλέως Ἰωάννου τοῦ Βατάτση τοῦ Ἐλεήμονος.*

Theodore at once ordered the election of a monk of little culture who in the brief space of a single week was consecrated successively deacon, priest, and Patriarch. Without further delay, on Christmas Day, Theodore II Lascaris was crowned Emperor at Nicaea.

The new Emperor had not completed his thirty-third year when he ascended the throne. Few sovereigns have been more carefully prepared for their duties than the heir of Vatatzes. All that education, in the Byzantine sense of the word, could do, had been done for the future monarch. He had enjoyed the best instruction that his father's Empire could provide; he had studied literature, mathematics, and, above all, philosophy, and he professed the eminently Greek opinion that knowledge was synonymous with virtue. Save for an occasional hunting-party, he had devoted his ample leisure before his accession exclusively to his books, and he early aspired to a place in the gallery of royal authors. He has accordingly left us a voluminous literary legacy, mostly the work of these earlier years. Theology and satire, a prayer to the Virgin and a eulogy of Nicaea, a funeral oration on Frederick II, and no less than 218 letters, are among the varied products of his instructed mind. But as a writer he was too academically educated to be original; his ideas are overwhelmed in a jungle of rhetoric; and his style, on which he prided himself and eagerly sought the judgment of the critics, strikes us, even in his private letters, as frigid and jejune. His correspondence, to which we naturally look for interesting sidelights on his temperament and times, abounds in commonplaces, but, with the exception of the letters written after his accession, is singularly barren of historical facts. Upon his character his studies had made no real imprint; like Frederick the Great, he affected philosophy as a Crown Prince, only to discard it as mere theory when he was brought face to face with the realities of government. Feeble in health and fond of solitude, he had abnormally developed one side of his nature. He was, in a word, a mass of nerves, an "interesting case" for a modern mental specialist. His short reign not only falsified the maxim of Plato that all would be well if kings were philosophers or philosophers kings, but afforded one more instance of the truism that the intellectual type of monarch is not the most successful, even for a nation which, in its darkest hours, by the waters of Nicaea or in the Turkish captivity, has never ceased to cherish the love of learning.

The new Emperor had good reasons for hastening on his coronation. No sooner had the news of Vatatzes' death reached the Bulgarian capital than the Tsar Michael Asên seized this opportunity of recovering his lost provinces, which the Greek Government had not had time to consolidate with the rest of the Empire. The Bulgarian inhabitants welcomed, and the Greek garrisons were not strong enough to resist, the invaders. Rhodope at once rose in rebellion; it was feared that the whole Greek Empire in Europe might become Bulgarian. So pressing was the danger that Theodore crossed the Dardanelles in January 1255, and began, though in the depth of winter, his first Bulgarian campaign. Success crowned his arms; Stara Zagora fell; but the impregnable fortress of Chepina in the hollow between the ranges of Rila and Rhodope, the key of both Sofia and Philippopolis, baffled all his efforts. When ordered to attack it, his generals, one of them Alexius Strategopulus the future conqueror of Constantinople, first fled at the sound of the enemy's approach, and then refused to renew the attempt. Theodore's energy might have shamed these cowardly or treacherous soldiers. Hearing that Melnik was being besieged by the governor to whom it had been entrusted, he marched with extraordinary rapidity from Hadrianople to Seres, forced the narrow defile through which the Struma flows, and saved the threatened citadel, whose garrison hailed him as "the swift eagle." Thence he hastened as far west as Prilep, recovering one place after another from his Bulgarian brother-in-law, till at last Chepina alone remained unconquered. But the season was now far advanced for a Balkan campaign, and Theodore's plucky march against that mountain-girt fortress had to be abandoned. Leaving his forces at Demotika in the charge of two incompetent generals (for, like most speculative statesmen, he was a bad judge of character) the Emperor re-crossed into Asia.

In the following spring he began a second Bulgarian campaign. During his absence, the position had changed for the worse; the Bulgarian Tsar had attracted a force of Cumans to his standards, and the Greek generals, in direct disobedience of their master's orders, had risked an engagement with those formidable auxiliaries, in which one was taken prisoner and the other only escaped thanks to the swiftness of his horse. Theodore's energy and large army speedily restored the prestige of the Greek name. Michael Asên accordingly begged his father-in-law, the Russian prince Rostislav of Chernigov, to mediate between him and his enemy. The Russian prince accepted the office of peace-maker, met the Greek Emperor, and had no difficulty in making a treaty with him on terms which both parties considered favourable. Bulgarians and Greeks received back their ancient frontiers, but the virgin fortress of Chepina was ceded to Theodore. Such was his joy that he loaded the Russian prince with presents, and despatched a dithyrambic proclamation to his Asiatic subjects announcing the signature of peace, and extolling the importance of the cession of Chepina[1]. His nervous system was so much affected by this excitement that the mere suggestion of fraud on the part of the Russian negotiator made him fall upon the luckless Acropolita, who had drafted the treaty, call that rather solemn personage an "ass" and a "fool," and order a sound beating to be given him for his pains. The assassination of Michael Asên and the marriage of the

[1] *Epistulae*, pp. 279–82; *Archiv f. slav. Philol.* XXI. 622–6; *BZ.* IX. 569; XVII. 181.

new Tsar with one of Theodore's daughters confirmed the validity of the peace.

The close of the Bulgarian war made the Despot Michael II of Epirus anxious to conciliate a rival who might now turn his undivided attention to the invasion of that independent Greek state, always an eye-sore of the Nicene Emperors. The long engagement of their children had not yet ripened into marriage; so the saintly consort of the despot was sent with her son Nicephorus to meet the victorious monarch. Theodore on this occasion shewed a lack of chivalry which proved how much his character had materialised since his accession. He took advantage of his visitor's sex and defenceless position to extort from her the two cities of Servia and Durazzo, respectively the keys of the east and the west, as the price of this alliance. Thereupon the marriage ceremony was solemnly performed at Salonica, but the contract which he had been forced to sign rankled in the mind of Michael, and a breach of the peace between Epirus and Nicaea was only a question of time.

Theodore had scarcely celebrated the wedding of his daughter when the arrival of an alarming despatch from his deputies in Bithynia hastened his return to Asia. The news was that Michael Palaeologus, the most ambitious of his officials, had fled to the Seljūq Turks[1]. We have already seen this crafty intriguer, who was destined to play so great a part in Byzantine history, receiving the post of governor of Seres and Melnik from Vatatzes. The family of Palaeologus, according to a legend still preserved on the walls of the Palazzo Municipale at Viterbo, traced its origin to a certain Remigius Lellius of Vetulonia. Historically, however, it is first mentioned towards the end of the eleventh century, and a hundred years later had risen to such eminence that one of its members married the eldest daughter of Alexius III, and was intended by that emperor to be his successor. The daughter of this marriage married another Palaeologus, who held high office at the Nicene court, and the offspring of the latter union was the future Emperor, who was thus "doubly a Palaeologus," alike on his father's and on his mother's side. His direct descent from the Emperor Alexius, combined with his ambitious disposition, made him an object of suspicion and envy. While governor of Melnik he had been accused of high treason, and had only saved himself by the witty offer to submit his innocence to the ordeal of red-hot iron if the holy Metropolitan of Philadelphia would hand him the glowing metal. The embarrassment of the divine, suddenly invited to test in his own person his theory that pure hands would be unscathed by the fiery ordeal, greatly delighted the court; the accused was acquitted, but the suspicions of Vatatzes were only allayed when he had bound his intriguing subject by a fresh oath of loyalty and by a matrimonial alliance with his great-niece still closer to his throne. The rank of Great Constable and the command in

[1] Miklosich and Müller, *op. cit.*, VI. 197–8.

Bithynia might seem sufficient to satisfy even the vaulting ambition of this dangerous noble. But Theodore II, whose policy it was to diminish the influence of the aristocracy and to surround the throne with men of humble origin who owed everything to himself, still nourished suspicions of Palaeologus, and publicly threatened to put out his eyes. This tactless conduct was the immediate cause of the Great Constable's flight to the court of Iconium. The Emperors of Nicaea were always nervous of Seljūq invasions, and Theodore therefore returned to his eastern dominions, leaving Acropolita, once more restored to favour, as his governor-general in the west.

Fortunately the Sultan Kai-Kā'ūs II was at this moment himself threatened with a Mongol attack. Instead of returning at the head of a Seljūq force to usurp the Greek throne, the fugitive, with profuse expressions of loyalty to the Christian Emperor and of devotion to the Christian religion, assisted the Turks to defeat the Mongol hordes. But the advance of the Mongols soon forced the Sultan to implore the aid of Theodore himself against the common enemy, ceding him as the price of his support the cities of Laodicea and Chonae, the latter of which had been abandoned by the first Emperor of Nicaea. The Mongols, however, succeeded in making the Sultan their tributary, and Palaeologus, finding his protector thus reduced, was glad to return to the service of his former master. Theodore again exacted from him the most solemn oaths of fidelity to himself and his son, and restored him to his former office, nor was it long before the state of the European provinces gave him a fresh opportunity of displaying his energies. The appointment of his brother John as governor of Rhodes[1] was doubtless a further part of the imperial policy of giving this dangerous family honourable employment at a distance from the court.

The Despot of Epirus had not forgiven the treachery of Theodore in extorting Durazzo, his chief city on the Adriatic and at that time the port of transit between Macedonia and Italy, from a defenceless woman. The absence of the Emperor in the east and the treachery of one of the imperial governors gave him the opportunity which he sought. The Serbs and Albanians joined his standard against the Greeks of Nicaea, whose conquests in Europe had made them neighbours of those peoples; Acropolita was besieged in the castle of Prilep. Alarmed at this dangerous coalition, the Emperor despatched Palaeologus as commander-in-chief to the west; but his suspicions caused him to cripple the efficiency of his general by giving him an army small in number and poor in quality. Thus handicapped, Palaeologus failed to prevent the capitulation of Prilep, and the unfortunate historian, dragged about in chains from place to place, had at last ample leisure in the prison at Arta for meditating on the practical defects in his old pupil's education. The fall of Prilep was followed by the loss of all

[1] Miklosich and Müller, *op. cit.*, VI. 198.

Macedonia except Salonica; one imperial commander after another deserted to Michael II; and the Emperor, having failed to subdue his rival by force, resorted to theological weapons. At his instigation, the Patriarch excommunicated his fellow-Greeks of Epirus. But the intervention of Blemmýdes, who was a personal friend and correspondent of the despot, prevented the publication of the anathema, and Theodore, who had patiently endured to be lectured by his old tutor on the duties of kingship[1], meekly tore up the document and returned it to the Patriarch. But the loss of his cities and the defection of his generals made the Emperor more than ever suspicious of Palaeologus. He ordered the arrest of the Great Constable, on the pretext that the terrible malady, from which he had now begun to suffer acutely, was due to the incantations of the man in whom he already saw the future usurper of his son's throne.

His theological studies on the Procession of the Holy Ghost did not prevent him from renewing the futile attempts of his father for the Union of the Churches. Two letters[2] are extant, in which Theodore writes to Pope Alexander IV that he desires peace and begs the Most Holy Father with many adjectives to send inspired men to compose the differences between Nicaea and Rome. His wish was heard, and in 1256 envoys from the Pope arrived in Macedonia on their way to his capital. But meanwhile the Emperor had changed his mind. His victorious campaigns had made the support of the Papacy less valuable to him; like his father, he desired union with Rome merely as a step to Constantinople. After a barren interview with the Papal plenipotentiaries, he told Acropolita to get rid of them as best he could[3].

It was not only in theology that his brief taste of power had made Theodore an opportunist. He noticed, like all his friends, the deterioration of his own character. Before his accession he had prized knowledge before riches; now he wrote that he only cared for gold and jewels. His excuse was that he needed money for the defence of the Empire against its many enemies, and for the expenses of representation, so necessary for impressing the Eastern peoples whom he had to fear. It was with this object that he received the Mongol ambassadors in theatrical style, seated on a lofty throne sword in hand; while he held the sound principle, not always remembered by his successors, that the Greek Empire should look for its safety neither to foreign alliances nor to foreign mercenaries, but to a strong Greek army. Accordingly, he left to his successor a well-filled treasury, for he realised that sound finance is the first requirement of a state. But, though his military and financial occupations gave him no time for his old studies after his accession, he did not neglect the patronage of learning in others. He

[1] In his Λόγος, ὁποῖον δεῖ εἶναι βασιλέα, or Βασιλικὸς ἀνδριάς (MPG. CXLII. 611–74).

[2] *Epistulae*, CXLII.–III.

[3] Sáthas, Μεσαιωνικὴ Βιβλιοθήκη, VII. 529.

founded libraries of the arts and sciences in various cities of his dominions, where the intellectual gymnastics of Byzantium continued to be practised. He established and endowed schools of grammar and rhetoric in the precincts of the church of St Tryphon, the martyr and patron of Nicaea, which he erected there, provided six scholarships for the students of the institution out of his privy purse, and conducted the examinations in person. It appears, however, that the results did not come up to the founder's expectation, for the pupils were sent back by the imperial examiner to complete their education[1]. A year or two later, George of Cyprus found that Nicaea was not exactly the Christian Athens that the glowing rhetoric of Theodore had depicted it. No one could instruct him in Aristotle's logic; grammar and poetry were alone taught and those only superficially, and the academic curriculum had not got beyond the legend of Oedipus and the Trojan war[2]. Still there was no lack of literary society at Theodore's court. Acropolita and his anonymous epitomiser[3] were both companions of the monarch on his journeys; the Patriarch Arsenius strove to imitate the measures of Anacreon in a Paschal hymn; Theodore Metochítes vied with his imperial namesake in a panegyric of their native city of Nicaea.

The hereditary malady from which he suffered, aggravated by overwork, now began to tell upon the Emperor's brain. His suspicion of everyone of eminence led him to commit acts of tyranny against the aristocracy, in which he was obsequiously supported by the time-serving Patriarch and by his bosom-friend and old playmate, George Muzalon, a man of humble origin, whom he had raised to the highest offices of state and married to a princess of the imperial house, and who was his most trusted adviser. Soon Theodore's body as well as his brain was affected, he felt that his end was at hand, and he craved from his old tutor Blemmýdes the remission of his sins. The stern monk, who had courageously opposed the Emperor's despotic policy, refused to forgive the dying and repentant sovereign. Theodore then turned to the Metropolitan of Mitylene, fell at his feet in a flood of tears, and implored his pardon and that of the Patriarch. He then exchanged his imperial robes for those of a monk, and soon afterwards, in August 1258, breathed his last, aged 36. His brief reign of less than four years did not enable him to make a great mark upon the history of his time; while his voluminous writings are mainly interesting as a proof of that morbid self-consciousness which was the key of his character and was doubtless the result of disease.

Theodore's only son, John, was not quite eight years old at the death of his father, who in his will had accordingly appointed George Muzalon regent during the minority. Such an appointment was certain

[1] *Epistulae,* XLIV., CCXVII.

[2] MPG. CXLII. 21–5.

[3] Identified by Heisenberg with Theodore Scutariota, *Analecta,* 3–18.

to arouse the indignation of the nobles, who had been proscribed by the low-born favourite and were resolved never to accept his dictatorship. Conscious of the opposition to himself, the regent in vain endeavoured to secure the succession by extracting the most solemn oaths of allegiance to his young charge from the prelates, the senate, the army, and the people, and by removing the child-Emperor to a strong fortress, while he offered to resign his own post to anyone whom the nobles might select. For the moment the conspirators dissimulated, and Michael Palaeologus, the most prominent of them, begged the regent in their name to retain his office. When they had thus succeeded in allaying his suspicions, they made their preparations for his overthrow. The commemoration of the late Emperor in the mausoleum at Sósandra was chosen for the attack; the Frankish mercenaries, who were commanded by Palaeologus, and had been deprived of their pay and privileges during the late reign at the instigation of the all-powerful minister, were ready to assassinate their enemy at a hint from their leader. When the fatal day arrived, the conspirators and the mercenaries took up their places at the church of the monastery. As soon as Muzalon and his two brothers arrived, the soldiers demanded that the young Emperor should be produced. His appearance only increased the uproar; a movement of his hand, in token that the tumult should cease, was taken as a signal for attack; the mercenaries rushed into the church, where the service had already begun, and hacked Muzalon and his brothers to pieces as they crouched at the altar. Even the still fresh tomb of the Emperor was not safe from insult.

It was necessary to appoint a new regent without delay, for the Mongols in the east, the Despot of Epirus in the west, and the lingering Latin Empire in the north were all enemies whom a child could not combat. Of the numerous nobles who had been the victims of Theodore's tyranny, Michael Palaeologus was the ablest and the most prominent. He had been the brains of the late conspiracy; he was affable, generous, and jovial; he was a distinguished officer; he was a direct descendant of the Angeli and connected by marriage with the reigning dynasty; his future greatness had been foretold—and the Nicene Court was very superstitious. All classes of the population, all three races in the army—Greeks, Franks, and Cumans—welcomed his selection; he was appointed guardian, the dignity of Grand-Duke was conferred upon him, and the clergy, obsequious as ever, soothed any qualms of conscience that he might feign and told him that what he had done would be a crown of righteousness at the Day of Judgment. Ere long a mortal crown, that of Despot, was placed by the Patriarch on his head. But nothing short of the imperial title would satisfy his ambition. Possible rivals were driven into exile; promises and a liberal use of the public money, now at his disposal, secured him the support of the Church for his further designs; and the Patriarch, who still felt some scruples at the abandonment of the boy-Emperor's cause, was compelled to perform the coronation ceremony. Oaths were cheap at Nicaea, and the hypocritical Palaeologus found no difficulty in praying that he might be handed over to the devil if he should plan any harm against the lawful heir and successor of the Empire. With equal readiness all ranks of the nation swore, under pain of excommunication, that, if one of the two Emperors were found scheming against the other, they would slay the schemer, and that if the plot were successful, they would kill the usurper and raise some senator to the throne. This done, Michael Palaeologus was, on 1 January 1259, proclaimed[1] Emperor, and a little later crowned at Nicaea. It had been intended by the partisans of the lawful dynasty that the coronation of the two Emperors should take place on the same day, and that John IV should first receive the crown. But, at the last moment, the friends of Palaeologus secured the postponement of the boy's coronation, while the usurper blandly promised to hold the imperial dignity merely as a trust during the minority of the lawful Emperor. His innocent rival, caring for none of these things and heedless of his approaching fate, was sent back to his childish games at Magnesia, and Michael VIII, having secured his position at home, devoted himself to the foreign policy of the Empire, then in need of a firm hand.

His first thought was for the safety of his European provinces. His namesake, Michael II of Epirus, had advanced his eastern frontier to the Vardar, and threatened to become a formidable competitor for the reversion of Constantinople. Even before his coronation, Palaeologus had sent his brother John to attack the despot, while he gave him the option of peace on favourable terms. Strengthened meanwhile by two matrimonial alliances with Manfred of Sicily and William de Villehardouin, Prince of Achaia, the despot replied with insolence to the proposals of the Emperor, who, after futile negotiations at the Sicilian and Achaian courts, ordered his brother to resume his attack. The decisive battle of Pelagonia placed the Prince of Achaia at the mercy of the Emperor, who was thus ultimately able to obtain a permanent footing in the Peloponnese, and the imperial troops entered the Epirote capital of Arta, where the luckless Acropolita was still languishing in prison. The Nicene forces penetrated as far south as Thebes; but these latter successes had little real value, for even the Greek population regarded their compatriots from Nicaea as interlopers. Fresh reinforcements arrived from Italy to aid the native dynasty, and a year after the battle of Pelagonia the despot's son Nicephorus defeated and captured Alexius Strategopulus, the imperial commander and the future captor of Constantinople.

[1] The year is absolutely settled not only by Pachyméres (I. 81, 96) but also by documents signed by Michael VIII as Emperor in 1259. (Miklosich and Müller, *op. cit.*, V. 10–3; VI. 199–202.)

It was against that city that the efforts of Michael VIII were now directed. The Emperor Baldwin II, with naïve ignorance of the relative strength of their respective Empires, had demanded from him the cession of all his European dominions from Salonica eastward, and, when he sarcastically refused this ridiculous demand, professed willingness to be content with an extension of territory to the mouth of the Maritza. Michael VIII at this told the Latin envoys, who had already had some experience of his quality as a soldier during his governorship of Bithynia, that he would remain at peace with their master on condition that he received half the customs' dues and the same proportion of the profits from the mint. His forces were not yet sufficient for the siege of so great a city; but in the spring of 1260 they captured Selymbria, and occupied all the country up to the walls of Constantinople, except the strong fort of Aphameia outside the Golden Gate, a district inhabited by Greek farmers, known as "the Independents" because neither party could depend upon them. The Emperor had been prevented from taking part in these operations by the resignation of his enemy, the Patriarch Arsenius, who regarded himself as the representative of the legitimate Emperor, and whose *gran rifiuto*, as rare in the Eastern as in the Western Church, produced a schism dangerous to the usurper. The election of a new Patriarch favourable to himself demanded his presence at Lampsacus, and it was only after this question had been settled that he felt it safe to join his troops before Constantinople. His hopes of taking the city were based upon the treacherous overtures of one of the garrison. Among the prisoners captured at the battle of Pelagonia was a noble Frank, Ancelin de Toucy[1], who was a cousin of the Greek Emperor. His relationship had procured him his release, and he was at this time living in a house on the wall and had command of certain of the gates. Michael accordingly thought that this man, a kinsman whom he had loaded with presents, might be trusted to betray the city. He therefore amused the Franks by an attack upon the castle of Galata, while he was really all the time awaiting the fulfilment of his correspondent's promises. But time went on, the famous archers of Nicaea continued to display their skill, and yet the gates remained closed. At last, an evasive message came from Ancelin, to the effect that the governor of the city had taken away the keys. The Emperor then withdrew, and accepted the offer of a year's truce with his Latin foes. The only result of this futile attack was the discovery of the remains of Basil "the Bulgar-slayer" in the ruined monastery of St John the Evangelist in the Hebdomon quarter. Michael VIII received the skeleton of his great

[1] Acropolita and the Anonymous Chronicler call him simply Ἀσέλ, adding that he was one of the prisoners of Pelagonia, which points to Ancelin de Toucy, and a cousin of Michael VIII, which might apply to a descendant of A. de Cayeux. But the former was living in Constantinople in the last years of the Latin Empire (Χρονικὸν τοῦ Μορέως, l. 1321).

predecessor with the highest honour, and ordered it to be laid to rest in the monastery of the Saviour in his newly-won city of Selymbria.

Like a cautious diplomatist, the Emperor used the breathing-space that he had obtained by his truce with the Latins to create a political situation favourable to his great design. He sent the serviceable Acropolita on a secret mission to the Bulgarian Tsar, Constantine Asên, doubtless with the object of securing the neutrality of that monarch, whose wife, the sister of John IV, was naturally indignant at her brother's exclusion from his rights by the usurper and was urging her husband to assist him. The Greek envoy was only partially successful; but on the side of his Asiatic neighbours, the Seljūq Turks, Michael was able to feel perfectly secure. With their Sultan he was already on terms of friendship, dating from the time when he had fled to the court of Iconium, and now, by a sudden reverse of fortune, Kai-Kā'ūs II and his brother were glad to find a refuge from the advancing Mongols in the Greek Empire, and Michael to use the Seljūqs as a buffer against those formidable hordes. The wives and children of the Sultan were carefully guarded at Nicaea, while the Sultan accompanied his host on his compaigns as a further hostage for the good behaviour of his people.

Having thus courted the neutrality of the Bulgarians and gained the security of his Asiatic dominions, Michael sought the alliance of some Latin state which might aid him in his designs against the Latin Empire. Of all the Western governments Genoa was most clearly indicated as his ally. The Genoese were a maritime power; they were the rivals of Venice, whose participation in the Latin conquest of Greece had given her an enormous preponderance in the Levantine trade, and whose recent victory in the long-drawn struggle for the church and commerce of Acre rankled in their minds. On the other hand, if they had fought against the Nicene Empire in defence of Constantinople in 1236 and had surprised the vassal island of Rhodes in 1249, and if Vatatzes had once tried to restrict their commercial privileges, he also had endeavoured to make them his allies[1] in 1239, and his successor was now only carrying out his policy. To the shrewd statesmen of Genoa the only obstacle to the suggested alliance was the certainty of incurring the anger of the Pope, the special protector of the Latin Empire. But the prospects of larger profits prevailed over the fear of spiritual punishments. Two Genoese envoys proceeded to Nymphaeum, and there, on 13 March 1261, was signed the memorable treaty[2] which transferred to the Genoese the commercial supremacy in the Levant so long enjoyed by their hated competitor. The concessions granted them by Michael were of two kinds: those within his own Empire, which it was in his power to bestow at once, and those in his prospective dominions, at present

[1] Continuator Caffari *apud* Muratori, *RR. II. SS.* VI. 481.

[2] The best text is in *Atti della Società Ligure di Storia patria,* XXVIII. 791–809.

occupied by the Franks. In the former category were included the absolute possession of Smyrna, already a flourishing port; and the right to an establishment with churches and consuls not only there but at Anaia and Adramyttium, in the islands of Lesbos and Chios, and at Cassandria in the parts of Salonica; in the latter were comprised similar grants at Constantinople and in the islands of Crete and Euboea, together with the confirmation of their old privileges in the imperial city, and the church of St Mary and the site of the Venetian castle there in the event of their sending a naval force to aid in the siege. Free-trade throughout the present and future provinces of the Greek Empire, and the closing of the Black Sea to all foreign ships except those of Genoa and Pisa; an annual present of money and three golden *pallia* to the commune and archbishop of Genoa, in revival of the ancient custom; and war against Venice till such time as both the high contracting parties should decide upon peace: such were the further advantages gained by the Genoese. On their side they promised to grant free-trade to the Emperor's subjects, to allow no hostile force to be equipped against him in their ports, and to arm a squadron of 50 or fewer galleys, if the Emperor demanded it, for his service but at his expense, provided that they were not employed against the Pope, or the friends of the republic in the West or East, among the latter the Prince of Achaia and his successors, the King of Cyprus, and the Knights of St John. On 10 July this treaty was ratified by the republic; fifteen days later, before the Genoese flotilla had had time to arrive[1], Constantinople fell.

In the early part of 1261 Michael VIII had sent his experienced general, Alexius Strategopulus, now released from his Epirote prison, to Thrace at the head of a small force of Greeks and Cumans, with orders to keep that region quiet and the Bulgarians in check. At the same time he was told to make a demonstration before Constantinople, not with any hope of taking the city—for his army was not considered sufficient for such an enterprise—but in order to frighten the Latin garrison. Strategopulus, on reaching the modern village of Kuchuk Chekmejeh, received from the "Independents," who were constantly going to and fro between the city and their farms in the country, information which led him to risk an attempt at capturing the capital of the Latin Empire. He knew that Baldwin II was in desperate straits; his informants told him that the new Venetian *podestà*, Marco Gradenigo, had gone with almost the whole of the garrison to attack the island of Daphnusia, which lies off the south coast of the Black Sea, and then formed part of the Nicene Empire[2]; while his nephew Alexius and an

[1] Cf. Meliarákes, Ἱστορία τοῦ Βασιλείου τῆς Νικαίας, 654–8, where all the authorities for this statement are collected.

[2] *Fragmentum Marini Sanuti* apud Hopf, *Chroniques gréco-romanes*, 172.

"Independent" called Koutritzákes reminded him of a prophecy that three persons of their names should one day take Constantinople. He therefore moved to Balukli, opposite the Selymbria gate, where his confederates shewed him an old aqueduct, through which a body of soldiers one by one could enter the city, underneath the walls. A dark night was chosen for the venture; the band of subterranean invaders emerged safely inside the fortifications, silently scaled the ramparts, hurled the somnolent Latins to destruction below, burst open the gate, and proclaimed the Emperor Michael from the walls, as a signal to their friends to enter. Strategopulus and his troops, not more than 1000 in number, thus obtained possession of Constantinople without striking a blow, in the early morning of 25 July 1261. The cautious general did not advance into the heart of the city till broad daylight enabled him to ascertain the real numbers of the remaining garrison. Indeed, at one moment he had almost given the signal for retreat at the appearance of an armed body of Franks. But the "Independents," who knew that their lives depended on his success, rallied to his aid; panic seized the Latins, who fled to the monasteries for safety; while their Emperor took refuge in the Great Palace above the Golden Horn and then, leaving in his haste the emblems of sovereignty behind him, embarked on a vessel for Greece and the West.

Meanwhile the expedition against Daphnusia, having failed to capture that island, was on its way back when the news reached it that the Greeks were masters of Constantinople. The *podestà* was not the man to abandon the city without a struggle for its recovery; but his followers had left hostages behind them in the persons of their wives and children; and when the Greeks set fire to their homes and they saw their families fleeing in despair across the burning squares which lined the water's edge, they thought only of saving them. They conveyed all whom they could on board their vessels, and followed their fugitive Emperor, leaving Constantinople in the possession of the victorious Greek general, whom an extraordinary accident had enabled unaided to accomplish in a night the dream of fifty-seven years.

Michael VIII was at Meteorion in the Hermus valley, when his sister aroused him from his sleep with the news that Constantinople was his. At first he refused to believe that so small a force could have taken so great a city; indeed, the people would not credit the story until they saw the regalia of the Latin Emperor. But, as soon as the report was confirmed, he set out in haste for his new capital, taking with him his wife and his little son Andronicus, but leaving behind him at Magnesia the legitimate occupant of the throne, whom he was now more than ever anxious to displace. On 14 August he arrived before Constantinople, and, after passing the night in the monastery of Kosmidion, the modern Eyyūb, entered the city on the morrow through the Golden Gate. His entry, by his own special desire, partook of a religious rather than a political character. Special prayers for the occasion were composed by the historian Acropolita, in the absence of Blemmýdes, and recited from one of the towers of the gate by the Metropolitan of Cyzicus—for the widowed Church had no Patriarch. The famous image of the Path-finding Virgin guided the Emperor, as, after many genuflexions, he passed on foot through the Golden Portal to the neighbouring monastery of Studion; and a thanksgiving service in the church of the Divine Wisdom completed the ceremonial. But Michael did not consider the recovery of the ancient seat of Empire duly ratified till he had been crowned Emperor in the imperial city of Constantine. His enemy Arsenius was induced to resume his functions as Patriarch, and to perform this second coronation in Santa Sophia. No mention was made of the legitimate sovereign in the coronation oath, but Strategopulus, the real conqueror of Constantinople, received the honour of a triumph, and his name was ordered to be mentioned for the space of a year in the public prayers throughout the Empire. John IV was blinded and imprisoned in a fortress, where many years later the conscience-stricken successor of the usurper visited him[1].

Thus, after the lapse of fifty-seven years, the Empire of Nicaea merged in the greater glories of Byzantium, and the centre of gravity of Hellenism was removed from Bithynia to the Bosphorus. Amidst the universal rejoicing, we are told that one voice was raised in lament at the return to Constantinople, that of the Emperor's private secretary, who may have foreseen with the eye of a statesman that the coming Turkish peril needed a strong bulwark in Asia Minor, or who may have realised that the past can never be recalled and that the newly-conquered Byzantium would not be the old. But with a patriotism similar to that of the Piedmontese and Florentines in our own day, the people of Nicaea and Nymphaeum acquiesced in an act which, while it redounded to the glory of the Greek name, reduced their cities to the dull level of provincial towns. We are told, indeed, that, though Nicaea "like a mother aided her daughter with all that she had," yet even after this sacrifice she still excelled all other cities, some by her situation, some by her fertile soil, others by her great circumference, others by her beautiful buildings, others again by her philanthropic establishments. But, when every year the great festival of St Tryphon was celebrated in the church which Theodore II had built, the thoughts of the older men may have gone back with regret to the time when the Patriarch resided in their midst, when letters flourished by the waters of the Askanian mere, when the heralds announced the arrival of the Emperor in the holy city from his autumn pleasaunce of Nymphaeum.

The Empire of Nicaea, the chief of the three mainstays of Hellenism after the Frankish Conquest, has left but few tangible memorials behind

[1] But a document of Charles I of Anjou, dated Trani 9 May 1273, states that he has escaped and invites him to Sicily. *ASI,* Ser. III., vol. XXII. 32.

it. A picturesque ruin, however, called by the peasants the "Castle of the Genoese," still marks the site of the imperial palace at Nymphaeum, the scene of the famous treaty. If we have no seals of any of the five Nicene Emperors, there are, at any rate, coins of all of them, except the unhappy John IV, while the elder Sanudo[1] tells us that the latter was portrayed in the gold *hyperperi* of Michael VIII as a child in the arms of his treacherous protector. One extant coin of Michael was undoubtedly minted at Nicaea, for it bears the figure of St Tryphon, the patron of that city. The brief and uncertain tenure of the Franks in Asia Minor accounts for the absence of all Frankish coins, which were doubtless replaced by the money of Venice, the chief Latin mercantile power in the Greek dominions. Irene, Theodore II's daughter, is still portrayed in the church of Boyana near Sofia; portraits of all five Nicene Emperors are to be found in manuscripts; and to the Nicene Empire is ascribed the first modern use of the double-headed eagle as a symbol[2].

But, although Nicaea was now only an appendage of Constantinople, the rival Greek Empire of Trebizond continued its separate existence. From the moment when the Seljūqs occupied Sinope, a wedge was driven between the two Hellenic states, which thenceforth did not come into collision, while Trebizond during the latter years of Alexius I and the reigns of his three immediate successors alternated between an occasional interval of independence and vassalage to the Seljūqs or the Mongols. On the death of the founder of the Empire in 1222, his eldest son John was set aside in favour of his son-in-law Andronicus Gídos, who was perhaps identical with the general of Lascaris—a theory which would account for the selection of an experienced commander in preference to a raw youth as ruler of a young and struggling community. Andronicus I soon justified his appointment. A ship bearing the tribute of the Crimean province of Trebizond, together with the *archon* who collected the annual taxes, was driven by a storm into Sinope. The governor, a subordinate of Malik, the son of the Seljūq Sultan Kai-Qubād I, not only seized the vessel and all its cargo but also sent his ships to plunder the Crimea, in defiance of the treaty recently made by his master with the new Emperor. Andronicus, on receipt of the news, ordered his fleet to retaliate by attacking Sinope; and his sailors not only plundered the district right up to the walls of the "mart," but captured the crews of the ships lying in the harbour, who were exchanged for the captive *archon* and his taxes. Malik now marched upon Trebizond, which was even then strongly fortified, a fact which the astute Emperor contrived to make known to the enemy by pretending to sue for peace and inviting him to send envoys to negotiate it inside the city. The governor of Sinope fell during the siege; Malik was deluded into making another

[1] *Apud* Hopf, *Chroniques gréco-romanes,* 114; P. Lámpros, *Zeitschrift für Numismatik,* IX. 44–6.

[2] Sp. P. Lámpros, *Νέος Ἑλληνομνήμων,* VI. 433–73.

attack by the appearance of a man in his camp, who purported to be the leading citizen and pretended to invite him to enter in the name of his fellows. But a sudden thunderstorm scattered the attacking army, and Trapezuntine piety ascribed the deliverance of the city to the intervention of St Eugenius, who had personated their chief magistrate in order to lure to destruction the infidel who had ordered the destruction of his monastery. Thus baffled, Malik fled, only to fall into the hands of the mountain-folk, who dragged him before Andronicus. The Emperor wisely received him with honour, and released him on condition that the tie of vassalage which had bound Trebizond to Iconium should cease.

But Trebizond did not long remain independent. A new and formidable rival of the Seljūqṣ appeared in the person of Jalāl-ad-Dīn, the Shāh of Khwārazm, who called himself "King of the Globe," and it would appear that Andronicus assisted him against Kai-Qubād at the disastrous battle of Khilat in 1230 and sheltered his flying troops at Trebizond after their crushing defeat. The natural result of this unsuccessful policy was that the Greek Empire on the Euxine, weakened and isolated, once more became a vassal of the Seljūq Sultan, to whom, in 1240, it was bound to furnish 200 lances, or 1000 men[1]. About this time, too, it would seem that the Georgians, who had assisted the formation and had acknowledged the supremacy of the Empire, severed their connexion with it, although long afterwards they continued to be included in the imperial title.

When in 1235 Andronicus I was laid to rest in the church of the "Golden-headed Virgin," which he richly endowed and which in its present form is perhaps a memorial of his reign, the eldest son of Alexius I was old enough to assume his heritage. But John I, or Axoûchos, as he was called, after a brief reign of three years, was killed while playing polo. His son Joannicius was then put into a monastery and his second brother Manuel ascended the throne. Manuel I obtained the names of "the greatest captain" and "the most fortunate"; but his reign of 25 years witnessed the exchange of the Seljūq for the Mongol suzerainty. His lances doubtless served in the Seljūq ranks on the fatal day of Kuza-Dāgh, when the Mongols overthrew the forces of Kai-Khusrū II, and accordingly the friar Rubruquis, who visited the victors in 1253, found him "obedient to the Tartars." In that same year he sent envoys to Louis IX of France at Sidon, begging him to give him a French princess as his wife. The King of France had no princesses with him, but he recommended Manuel to make a matrimonial alliance with the Latin Court of Constantinople, to which the aid of "so great and rich a man" would be useful against Vatatzes[2]. If we may assume that the monastery of the Divine Wisdom, from which his portrait has now

[1] Vincent of Beauvais, *Speculum historiale*, Bk xxx, ch. 144.
[2] Rubruquis, *Voyage*, 3; Joinville, *Histoire de St Louis*, 324.

disappeared, was his work, his riches merited the praise of the saintly French sovereign. Nor can we be surprised that Trebizond was a wealthy state, for at this period it was an important depôt of the trade between Russia and the Seljūq Empire. For the purposes of this traffic a special currency was required, of which specimens have perhaps survived in bronze coins of Alexius I, and in both bronze and silver coins of John I and Manuel I. But no seals of any of these early Trapezuntine Emperors are known to exist.

Nicaea and Trebizond have, however, apart from aught else, a permanent lesson for the historian and the politician; they teach us the extraordinary vitality of the Hellenic race even in its darkest hour.

TABLE OF RULERS.

Empire of Nicaea	French Duchy of Nicaea	Empire of Trebizond
Theodore I Lascaris. Despot 1204–6; Emperor 1206.	Count Louis of Blois and Chartres 1204–5.	Alexius I Grand-Comnenus 1204.
John III Ducas Vatatzes 1222.	**French Duchy of Philadelphia**	Andronicus I Gídos 1222.
Theodore II Lascaris 1254.	Count Stephen of Perche 1204–5.	John I Axoûchos 1235.
John IV Lascaris 1258.		Manuel I 1238–63.
Michael VIII Palaeologus 1259.		

CHAPTER XVII.

THE BALKAN STATES.

I. THE ZENITH OF BULGARIA AND SERBIA (1186–1355).

THE close of the twelfth century witnessed the birth of Slavonic independence in the Balkan peninsula. The death of Manuel I in 1180 freed the Southern Slavs from the rule of Byzantium, and in the following decade were laid the foundations of those Serbian, Bosnian, and Bulgarian states which, after a brief period of splendour acquired at the expense of one or other Christian nationality, fell before the all-conquering Turk to rise again in modified form and on a smaller scale in our own time. As has usually happened in the history of the Balkans, the triumph of the nation was in each case the work of some powerful personality, of Stephen Nemanja in Serbia, of Kulin in Bosnia, and of the brothers Peter and John Asên in Bulgaria.

The founder of the Serbian monarchy was a native of the Zeta, the older Serbian kingdom of Dioclea and the modern Montenegro. Starting from his birthplace on the banks of the Ribnica, Nemanja made Rascia, later the *Sanjak* of Novibazar, the nucleus of a great Serbian state, which comprised the Zeta and the land of Hum, as the Herzegovina was then called, with outlets to the sea on the Bocche di Cattaro and at Antivari, North Albania with Scutari, Old Serbia, and the modern kingdom before 1913 as far as the Morava. Of the Serbian lands Bosnia alone evaded his sway, for there his kinsman Kulin, ignoring the authority alike of the Hungarian crown and of the Byzantine Empire, governed with the title of *ban* a rich and extensive country, then "at least a ten days' journey in circumference," and became the first great figure in Bosnian history, whose reign was regarded centuries afterwards as the golden age. Italian painters and goldsmiths found occupation in his territory, and Ragusans exploited its trade. Miroslav, Nemanja's brother and Kulin's brother-in-law, whom the former made prince of the land of Hum, formed the link between these two separate yet kindred Serbian communities.

Before the time of Nemanja the chiefs of the various Serbian districts, or *župy*, who were thence styled *župans*, had considered themselves as practically independent in their own dominions, merely acknowledging the more or less nominal supremacy of one of their number, the so-called

"Great *Župan*." Nemanja, while retaining this traditional title, converted the aristocratic federation as far as possible into a single state, whose head in the next generation took the corresponding name of king. Further, to strengthen his position with the majority of his people, he embraced the Orthodox faith, and endeavoured to promote ecclesiastical no less than political unity. With this object he laboured to extirpate the Bogomile or Manichaean heresy, which was then rife in the Balkan lands and had attained special prominence in Bosnia. The simple worship of the Bogomiles, the Puritans of south-eastern Europe, was sometimes encouraged and sometimes proscribed by the Bosnian rulers, according as they wished to oppose the pretensions, or invoke the aid, of the Papacy. Thus Kulin at one time found it expedient to join the Bogomile communion with his wife, his sister, and several other members of his family, whose example was followed by more than 10,000 of his subjects; while at another, the threat of Hungarian intervention, supported by the greatest of the Popes, led him to recant his errors. On 8 April 1203 the *ban* and the chief Bogomiles met the papal legate on the "white plain" by the river Bosna, and renounced their heretical practices and beliefs. The oldest Bosnian inscription tells us how Kulin and his wife proved the sincerity of their re-conversion by restoring a church[1]. While Kulin thus ended his career as a devout Roman Catholic, Nemanja, at the instigation of his youngest son, the saintly Sava, retired from the world in 1196 to the monastery of Studenica, which he had founded, leaving to his second son Stephen the bulk of his dominions with the dignity of "Great *Župan*," and to his eldest son Vukan his native Zeta as an appanage, a proof that the unification of the Serbian monarchy was not yet completely accomplished. From Studenica he moved to Mount Athos, where, on 13 February 1200, he died as the monk Simeon in his humble cell at Chiliandarion. After his death he received the honours of a saint, and his tomb is still revered in his monastery of Studenica. Just as the lineage of the *ban* Kulin is said to linger on in the Bosnian family of Kulenović, just as later rulers regarded the customs and frontiers of his time as a standard for their own, so the Serbs look back to Nemanja as the author of the dynasty with which their medieval glories alike in Church and State are indissolubly connected.

Meanwhile, in 1186, a third Slavonic nation had asserted its independence of the Byzantine Empire. The unwise imposition of taxes to furnish forth the wedding festivities of the Emperor Isaac II Angelus aroused the discontent of the Bulgarians and Wallachs (Vlachs) of the Balkans. The rebels found leaders in the brothers Peter and John Asên, descendants of the old Bulgarian Tsars, who summoned the hesitating to a meeting in the chapel of St Demetrius which they had built at Trnovo, and by means of a pious fraud persuaded them that

[1] *Wissenschaftliche Mittheilungen,* VII. 215–20.

the saint had migrated thither from his desecrated church at Salonica, and that providence had decreed the freedom of Bulgaria. Peter at the outset assumed the imperial symbols and the style of "Emperor of the Bulgarians and Greeks"; but his bolder brother soon took the first place, while he contented himself with the former capital of Prêslav and its region, which in the next century still bore the name of "Peter's country." Three Byzantine commanders in vain strove to stamp out the insurrection: John Asên, driven beyond the Danube, returned at the head of a body of Cumans, the warlike race which then occupied what is now Roumania; Nemanja availed himself of the Bulgarian rebellion to extend his dominions to the south; and the Serbian and Bulgarian rulers alike hoped to find in Frederick Barbarossa, then on his way across the Balkan peninsula to the Holy Land, a supporter of their designs. Isaac Angelus barely escaped with his life near Stara Zagora; the victorious Bulgarians captured Sofia, and carried off the remains of their national patron, St John of Rila, in triumph to their capital of Trnovo. Such was the contempt of the brothers Asên for their former masters that they rejected the terms of peace offered them by the new Emperor, Alexius III, and advanced into Macedonia. But, in the midst of their successes, two of those crimes of violence so common in all ages in the Balkans removed both the founders of the second Bulgarian Empire. John Asên I was slain by one of his nobles, a certain Ivanko, after a nine years' reign; the assassin temporarily occupied Trnovo and summoned a Byzantine army to his aid; but Peter associated with himself his younger brother Kalojan, and carried on the government of the Empire until, a year later, he too fell by the hand of one of his fellow-countrymen, and Kalojan reigned alone as "Emperor of the Bulgarians and Wallachs."

The new Tsar continued to extend his dominions at the expense of his neighbours: from the Greeks he captured Varna in the east, from the Serbs, divided among themselves by a fratricidal struggle between the two elder sons of Nemanja, he took Niš in the west; his Empire extended as far south as Skoplje, as far north as the Danube, while his relative, the savage Strêz, held the impregnable rock of Prosêk in the valley of the Vardar as an independent prince. Thus, on the eve of the Latin conquest, Bulgaria had suddenly become the most vigorous element in the Balkan peninsula, while Serbia lay dismembered by the disunion of her reigning family and the foreign intervention which it produced. For Vukan, not content with his appanage in the Zeta, had invoked the aid of the Pope and the Hungarians in his struggle to oust his brother from the Serbian throne; King Emeric of Hungary occupied a large part of Serbia in 1202, with the object of allowing Vukan to govern it as his vassal, while he himself assumed the style of "King of Rascia," as his predecessors had long before assumed that of "King of Rama" from a Bosnian river—two titles which ever since then remained attached to the Hungarian crown. His brother had already made the subsequent Herzegovina a Hungarian duchy, and Bosnia was only saved from premature absorption by Kulin's politic conversion to Catholicism. Even the Bulgarian Tsar was treated as a usurper by the proud Hungarian monarch whose newly-won Serbian dependency he had dared to devastate.

Menaced alike by his Hungarian neighbour and by the new Latin Empire, which had now arisen at Constantinople and which claimed authority over his dominions as the heir of the Greeks, Kalojan thought it prudent, like other Slav rulers, to obtain the protection of the Papacy. He begged Innocent III to give him an imperial diadem and a Patriarch; the diplomatic Pope sent him a royal crown and ordered his cardinal legate to consecrate the Archbishop of Trnovo as "Primate of all Bulgaria and Wallachia"; two archbishops and four bishops completed the Bulgarian hierarchy, and on 8 November 1204 Kalojan was crowned by the cardinal at Trnovo.

But the crafty Bulgarian was not restrained by respect for the Papacy from attacking the Latins as soon as occasion offered. His old enemies the Greeks of Thrace, who had at first welcomed the erection of Philippopolis into a Flemish duchy for Renier de Trit, speedily offered to recognise Kalojan as Emperor if he would aid them against their new masters. He gladly accepted their offer, and soon the heads of some thirty Frankish knights testified to the savagery of the Bulgarian Tsar. The Latin Emperor Baldwin I set out with Count Louis of Blois to suppress the rebellion and relieve the isolated Duke of Philippopolis. On 14 April 1205 a decisive battle was fought before Hadrianople. The Count of Blois was killed; Baldwin fell into the hands of the Bulgarian victor. Even now the end of the first Latin Emperor of Constantinople is not known with certainty. Two months after the battle he was reported to be still alive and treated as a prisoner of distinction. But he soon fell a victim to the rage of his barbarous captor. Nicetas tells us that the desertion of the Greeks of Thrace to the Latins infuriated Kalojan, who vented his indignation on his prisoner, ordered his hands and feet to be cut off, and then cast him headlong into a ravine, where on the third day he expired. A Flemish priest, however, who was passing through Trnovo, heard a Bulgarian version of the story of Potiphar's wife, according to which the virtuous Baldwin was sacrificed to the injured pride of Kalojan's passionate Cuman consort, and cut down in the presence of the Tsar. Twenty years later a false Baldwin was hanged in Flanders, and tradition attaches the name of the first Latin Emperor to a ruined tower of the medieval Bulgarian capital.

Kalojan did not long survive his victim. For a time his career was a series of unbroken successes over Franks and Greeks alike. Renier de Trit was driven from Philippopolis; King Boniface of Salonica was slain in a Bulgarian ambush and his head sent to the Tsar; so fatal were

Kalojan's raids to the native population that he styled himself "the slayer of the Greeks," and they called him "the dog John." He was about to attack Salonica in the autumn of 1207, when pleurisy, or more probably a palace revolution prompted by his faithless wife, ended his life. The popular imagination ascribed the deed to St Demetrius, the patron-saint of the city, but the usurpation of the dead Tsar's nephew Boril and his speedy marriage with the widowed Empress pointed to the real authors of the deed. Kalojan's lawful heir, his son John Asên II, fled to Russia, while Boril reigned at Trnovo. At first he pursued his predecessor's policy of attacking the Franks, only to receive a severe defeat near Philippopolis. Later on, we find him receiving the visit of a cardinal sent him by the Pope, persecuting the Bogomiles as the Serbian and Bosnian rulers had done, doubtless for the same reason, and marrying his daughter to his former enemy, the Latin Emperor Henry, a striking proof of the growing importance of Bulgaria. But there was a large party which had remained faithful to the legitimate Tsar; John Asên II returned with a band of Russians and besieged the usurper in his capital. Trnovo long resisted but, at last, in 1218 Boril was captured while attempting to escape, and blinded by his conqueror's orders.

A year earlier Serbia had been raised to the dignity of a kingdom. The Hungarian monarchs, occupied elsewhere, could no longer interfere in the domestic quarrels of the Serbs. Sava reconciled his brothers and persuaded the ambitious Vukan, the self-styled "King of Dioclea and Dalmatia," to recognise Stephen's right to the position of "Great *Župan*." An Italian marriage, the example of Bulgaria, the desire of papal support, and the absence of the jealous King of Hungary in Palestine, prompted Stephen to ask the Pope once more for a royal crown, an act for which the negotiations of the Serbian ruler of Dioclea with Gregory VII furnished a precedent. In 1217 Honorius III sent a legate to perform the coronation, and the "first-crowned" King "of all Serbia" connected himself with the former royal line by styling himself also "King of Dioclea," adding Dalmatia and the land of Hum as a flourish to his other titles. But it has always been a dangerous experiment for a Balkan ruler to purchase the political support of the Western Church, at the risk of alienating the Eastern, to which the majority of his subjects belong. The King of Serbia recognised his mistake; his brother Sava availed himself of the critical position of the Greek Empire of Nicaea to obtain from the Ecumenical Patriarch, who then resided there, his own consecration in 1219 as "Archbishop of all the Serbian lands" together with the creation of a separate Serbian Church; and on his return home he crowned Stephen in 1222 in the church of Žiča, which the "first-crowned" king and his eldest son had founded, and which remains to our own day the coronation church of the Serbian kings. Thanks to Sava's influence the anger of the King of Hungary at this assumption of a royal crown was averted; and, when Stephen died in 1228, his eldest son Radoslav succeeded to his title. But the second King of Serbia was of weak character and feeble understanding. His next brother Vladislav, a man of more energy, was a dangerous rival; public opinion favoured the latter; Radoslav became a monk, and Vladislav in turn was crowned by the reluctant Sava. Together the new king and the archbishop built the monastery of Mileševo in the *Sanjak* of Novibazar, where their bones[1] were laid to rest. St Sava's memory is still held in reverence by the Serbs as the founder of their national Church; many a pious legend has grown up around his name, but through the haze of romance and beneath the halo of the saint we can descry the figure of the great ecclesiastical statesman whose constant aim it was to benefit the country and the dynasty to which he himself belonged, and to identify the latter with the national religion.

One of Sava's last acts had been to promote a matrimonial alliance between the Serbian and the Bulgarian courts, and it was at Trnovo, then the centre of Balkan politics, that he died. Under John Asên II the second Bulgarian Empire attained its zenith, and became for a time the strongest power in the peninsula. The Latin Empire of Constantinople was already growing weaker; the vigorous Greek Empire of Salonica, which had arisen on the ruins of the Latin kingdom of the same name, received from the Bulgarian Tsar a crushing blow at the battle of Klokotinitza in 1230, and its Emperor, Theodore Angelus, became his captive; the new Emperor Manuel had married one of his daughters; the King of Serbia had married another; his own wife was a daughter of the King of Hungary. Of the two Bulgarian princelings who had made themselves independent of his predecessors in Macedonia, Strêz of Prosêk had long before died a violent death, in which the superstitious saw the hand of St Sava; Slav of Melnik, who had played fast and loose alike with Latins, Greeks, and Bulgarians, had been swallowed up in the Greek Empire of Salonica. On a pillar of the church of the Forty Martyrs, which he built in 1230 at Trnovo, the Tsar placed an inscription, still preserved, in which he boasted that he had "captured the Emperor Theodore" and "conquered all the lands from Hadrianople to Durazzo, the Greek, the Albanian, and the Serbian land." His mild and statesmanlike demeanour endeared him to the various nationalities included in his wide dominions; even a Greek historian admits that he was beloved by the Greeks (a very rare achievement for a Bulgarian), while a Bulgarian monk praises his piety, his generous ecclesiastical foundations, and his restoration of the Bulgarian Patriarchate. During the first Bulgarian Empire the Patriarch had resided first at Prêslav and then at Ochrida. When that Empire fell, the Greeks reduced the Patriarchate to an Archbishopric; and,

[1] Those of St Sava were burned by the Turks at Vračar in 1595 (*Arch. f. slav. Philologie,* XXVIII. 90–93).

when the second Empire arose, the Pope, as we saw, could not be persuaded to grant more than the title of Primate to the Archbishop of Trnovo. In 1235, however, as the price of his aid against the Latins of Constantinople, John Asên II obtained from the Emperor Vatatzes of Nicaea and the Ecumenical Patriarch the recognition of the autonomy of the Bulgarian Church and the revival of the Bulgarian Patriarchate, whose seat thenceforth remained at Trnovo until the Turkish conquest placed the Bulgarian Church once more under the Greeks, from whom the creation of the Exarchate in 1870 has again emancipated it.

But John Asên II did not confine his energies to politics and religion. Like his contemporaries in Serbia, Bosnia, and the adjacent land of Hum, he granted to the Ragusan merchants, who during a large part of the Middle Ages had the chief carrying-trade of the Balkan peninsula in their hands, permission to do business freely in his realm. He called these intermediaries between Italy and the East his "dear guests," and they repaid the compliment by recalling his "true friendship." Gold, silver, richly-worked garments, and salt entered the Bulgarian Empire through the medium of the South Slavonic commonwealth on the Adriatic, while the centralisation of Church and State at Trnovo gave that city an importance which was lacking to the shifting Serbian capital, now at Novibazar, now at Priština, now at Prizren. There was the treasury, there dwelt the great nobles who occupied the court posts with their high-sounding Byzantine names, and there met the synods which denounced the Bogomiles and all their works. The stranger who visited the "castle of thorns" (Trnovo) on the festival of Our Lord's Baptism, when the Tsars were wont to display their greatest pomp, went away impressed with the splendour of their residence on the hill above the tortuous Jantra, a situation unique even among the romantic medieval capitals of the different Balkan races.

The conflict with the Greek Empire of Salonica had been forced upon the Tsar, and it was not till 1235 that he joined the Greek Emperor of Nicaea in an attack upon the Latins of Constantinople, of which the union of their children was to be the guarantee. In two successive campaigns the allies devastated what remained of the Latin Empire in Thrace, where the Frankish duchy of Philippopolis, then held by Gerard de Stroem, fell to the share of Asên, and they advanced to the walls of Constantinople. Defeated in the attempt to capture the Latin capital, the allies drifted apart; Asên saw that it was not his interest to help a strong Greek ruler to recover Byzantium; he removed his daughter from the court of Nicaea, and transferred his support to the Franks against his late ally. Suddenly the news that his wife, his son, and the Patriarch had all died filled him with remorse for his broken vows; he sent his daughter back, and made his peace with Vatatzes, a fact which did not prevent him from giving transit through Bulgaria to a Frankish relief force on its way to Constantinople. His last acts were to marry the fair daughter of the old Emperor Theodore of Salonica, whom he had previously blinded, and then to aid his blind captive to recover Salonica. In the following year, 1241, on or about the feast of his patron saint, St John, the great Tsar died, leaving his vast Empire to his son Kaliman, a lad of seven.

The golden age of Bulgaria under the rule of John Asên II was followed by a period of rapid decline. Kaliman I was well-advised to renew the alliance with the Greek Emperor of Nicaea and to make truce with the Franks of Constantinople. But his youth and inexperience allowed Vatatzes to become the arbiter of the tottering Empire of Salonica, and his sudden death in 1246, at a moment when that ambitious ruler chanced to be in Thrace, tempted the latter to attack the defenceless Bulgarian dominions. Kaliman's sudden end was ascribed by evil tongues to poison; but, whether accidental or no, it could not have happened at a more unfavourable moment for his country. Michael Asên, his younger brother, who succeeded him, was still a child; the Empress-mother, who assumed the regency, was a foreigner and a Greek; and the most powerful monarch of the Orient was at the head of an army on the frontier. One after another John Asên's conquests collapsed before the invading forces of Vatatzes. The Rhodope and a large part of Macedonia, as well as the remains of the Greek Empire of Salonica, formed a European appendage of the Empire of Nicaea, while at Prilep, Pelagonia, and Ochrida, the Nicene frontier now marched with that of another vigorous Greek state, the despotat of Epirus. In the south old blind Theodore Angelus still retained a small territory; thus Hellenism was once more the predominant force in Macedonia, while the new Bulgarian Tsar was forced to submit to the loss of half his dominions.

So long as Vatatzes lived, it was impossible to think of attempting their reconquest. But in 1253 a quarrel between the Ragusans, his father's "dear guests," and the adjacent kingdom of Serbia, seemed to offer an opportunity to Michael Asên for obtaining compensation from his fellow-Slavs for his losses at the hands of the Greeks. A coalition was formed between the merchant-statesmen of Ragusa, their neighbour, the *Župan* of Hum, and the Bulgarian Tsar, against Stephen Uroš I, who had ousted, or at least succeeded, his still living[1] brother Vladislav in 1243. It was agreed that, in the event of a Bulgarian conquest of Serbia, the Ragusans should retain all the privileges granted them by the Serbian kings, while they promised never to receive Stephen Uroš or his brother, should they seek refuge there. The King of Serbia, however, came to terms with the Ragusans at once, and Michael Asên's scheme of expansion was abandoned. One result was the removal of the Serbian ecclesiastical residence to Ipek.

When, however, Vatatzes died in the following year, the young Tsar

[1] Miklosich, *Monumenta Serbica*, 35, 561.

thought that the moment had come to recover from the new Emperor of Nicaea, Theodore II Lascaris, what the Greeks had captured. At first his efforts proved successful; the Slavonic element in the population of Thrace declared for him; and the Rhodope was temporarily restored to Bulgaria. But his triumph over his brother-in-law was not for long; the castles of the Rhodope were speedily retaken; in vain the mountain-fastness of Chêpina held out against the Greek troops; in vain the Tsar summoned a body of Cumans to his aid; he was glad to accept the mediation of his father-in-law, the Russian prince Rostislav[1], then a prominent figure in Balkan politics, and to make peace on such terms as he could. Chêpina was evacuated; the Bulgarian frontier receded to the line which had bounded it before this futile war. The failure of his foreign policy naturally discontented Michael Asên's subjects. His cousin Kaliman with the connivance of some leading inhabitants of Trnovo, slew him outside its walls, seized the throne, and made himself master of the person of the widowed Empress. But Rostislav hastened to the rescue of his daughter, only to find that the usurper, fleeing for safety from place to place, had been slain by his own subjects. With the death of Kaliman II in 1257 the dynasty of Asên was extinct. Rostislav in vain styled himself "Emperor of the Bulgarians."

The nobles, or *boljare*, convoked a council for the election of a new Tsar. Their choice fell upon Constantine, a man of energy and ability settled near Sofia, but descended through the female line from the founder of the Serbian dynasty, whom he vaunted as his grandfather. In order to obtain some sort of hereditary right to the crown, he divorced his wife and married a daughter of Theodore II Lascaris, who, as the granddaughter of John Asên II, would make him the representative of the national line of Tsars. To complete his legitimacy, he took on his marriage the name of Asên. Another competitor, however, a certain Mytzês, who had married a daughter of John Asên II, claimed a closer connexion with that famous house, and for a time disputed the succession to the throne. But his weakness of character contrasted unfavourably with the manly qualities of Constantine; he had to take refuge in Mesembria, and by surrendering that city to the Greeks obtained from them a peaceful retreat for himself and his family near the site of Troy.

Constantine's marriage with a Greek princess had benefited him personally; but it soon proved a source of trouble to his country. The Tsaritsa, as the sister of the dethroned Greek Emperor John IV, nourished a natural resentment against the man who had usurped her brother's throne, and urged her husband to avenge him. Michael Palaeologus had, indeed, foreseen this effect of his policy; and in the winter before the recapture of Constantinople from the Latins, he had sent his trusty agent, the historian Acropolita, to Trnovo with

[1] *Archiv für slavische Philologie*, XXI. 622–6.

the object of securing the neutrality of the Tsar during the accomplishment of that great design. The re-establishment of the Greek Empire at Byzantium, which had been the goal of the Bulgarian Tsars, offended the national susceptibilities of the nobles, and a sovereign who owed his election to that powerful class and who was half a foreigner would naturally desire to shew himself more Bulgarian than the Bulgarians. Thus a conflict with the Greeks was inevitable. Its only result was the loss of all Bulgaria south of the Balkans.

Constantine Asên was also occupied in the early years after the recapture of Constantinople with resisting Hungarian invasions from the north. The Kings of Hungary had always resented the resurrection of the Bulgarian Empire and the independence of Bosnia; and the patronage of the Bogomile heresy by the rulers of both those countries gave them, as the champions of the Papacy, an excuse for intervention. The history of Bosnia during the half-century which followed the death of Kulin in 1204 mainly consists of Hungarian attempts to acquire the sovereignty over the country by means of its theological divisions. First the King of Hungary and the Pope granted Bosnia to the Hungarian Archbishop of Kalocsa, on condition that he purged the land of the "unbelievers" who infested it. Then, when the Bosniaks retorted by making Ninoslav, a born Bogomile, their *ban*, the king took the still stronger step of bestowing their country upon his son Koloman, who in 1237 made himself master of not only Bosnia but of Hum also. The great defeat of the Hungarians by the Tartars four years later temporarily rid Bosnia of Hungarian interference, and the Papacy tried concessions instead of crusades, allowing Ninoslav, now become a Catholic, to reign unmolested, and the priests to use the Slavonic tongue and the Glagolitic characters in the services of the Church. At last, however, in 1254 religious differences and a disputed succession caused both Bosnia and Hum to fall beneath Hungarian suzerainty. Bosnia was then divided into two parts; while the south was allowed to retain native *bans*, the north, for the sake of greater security against Bulgaria and Serbia, was at first entrusted to Hungarian magnates, and then combined with a large slice of northern Serbia, which under the name of the *banat* of Mačva was governed by the Russian prince Rostislav, whose name has been already mentioned in connexion with Bulgaria, and who, as son-in-law of the King of Hungary, could be trusted to carry out his policy. This enlarged (and in 1264 reunited) *banat* or duchy of Mačva and Bosnia, as it was officially called, thus formed, like Bosnia in our own time, an advanced post of Hungary in the Balkan peninsula.

Bulgaria was stronger and less exposed than Bosnia; but it was equally coveted by the Hungarian sovereigns. One of them had already assumed the title of "King of Bulgaria"; another, after a series of campaigns in which the Hungarian armies reached the walls of Trnovo and temporarily captured the "virgin fortress" of Vidin, not only adopted the same style, but handed down to his successors a shadowy claim to the Bulgarian crown. Thus, in the second half of the thirteenth century, the Hungarian monarchs were pleased to style themselves "Kings of Bulgaria, Rascia, and Rama," sovereigns (on paper) of all the three South Slavonic States.

When the Hungarian invaders retired, Constantine Asên bethought him of revenge upon the Greeks. He did not scruple to call the Sultan of Iconium and the savage Tartars to his aid; Michael Palaeologus narrowly escaped capture at their hands, and it was long before the rich plain of Thrace recovered from their ravages. These exhausting campaigns caused the Greek Emperor to propitiate so active an enemy. Constantine's wife was now dead, and Michael VIII accordingly endeavoured to attach the Bulgarian Tsar to the new dynasty at Constantinople by offering him the hand of his own niece Maria, with Mesembria and another Black Sea port as her dowry. No sooner, however, had the marriage been celebrated than Michael refused to hand over those places, on the plea that their inhabitants, being Greeks, could not be fairly transferred to Bulgaria against their will. To his surprise, his niece, as soon as she had become a mother, threw in her lot entirely with her adopted country, and urged her husband to assert his claims. The Greek Emperor only avoided a Bulgarian invasion by another diplomatic marriage, that of his natural daughter to the powerful Tartar chief Nogai Khan, who from the steppes of southern Russia kept Bulgaria quiet.

The great design of Charles of Anjou, now established on the throne of Naples, for the recovery of the Latin Empire, affected both Bulgaria and Serbia. Stephen Uroš I had married a daughter of the exiled Latin Emperor Baldwin II, and Queen Helena, whose name is still preserved in the cathedral at Cattaro and in a ruined church on the river Bojana, played as important a part as the Bulgarian Empress in advocating an attack upon the Greeks. In vain the Greek Emperor tried to win over the Serbian monarch by a marriage between one of his daughters and a son of Stephen Uroš. But the pompous Byzantine envoys, who were ordered to report upon the manners and customs of the Serbian court, were horrified to find "the great" king, as he was called, living in a style which would have disgraced a modest official of Constantinople, his Hungarian daughter-in-law working at her spindle in an inexpensive gown, and his household eating like a pack of hunters or sheep-stealers. The lack of security for property, which was to be characteristic of the Serbian lands under Turkish rule, deepened this bad impression, and the projected marriage was broken off. Negotiations were resumed between Naples and the Serbian and Bulgarian monarchs, and the Greek Emperor sought to save himself by accepting the union of the Churches at the Council of Lyons, and by repudiating the rights of the Bulgarian and Serbian ecclesiastical establishments to autonomy. But here again the crafty Palaeologus over-reached himself. By his concessions to the Ecumenical Patriarch he aroused the national pride of the two Slav States; by his concessions to the Pope he alienated the Orthodox party in his own capital. At the Bulgarian court the Empress Maria, who was in constant communication with the opposition at Constantinople, worked harder than ever against him, and even tried to incite the Sultan of Egypt to attack the Byzantine Empire in conjunction with the Bulgarians.

This ambitious woman now wielded the supreme power in Bulgaria, for the Tsar was incapacitated by a broken leg, and their son Michael, whom she caused to be crowned and proclaimed as his colleague, was still a child. One powerful chieftain alone stood in her path, a certain James Svętslav, who in the general confusion had assumed the style of "Emperor of the Bulgarians." A Byzantine historian has graphically described the sinister artifice by which his countrywoman first deluded, and then destroyed, this possible but ingenuous rival. She invited him to Trnovo, and there, in the cathedral, amidst the pomp and circumstance of the splendid eastern ritual, adopted the elderly nobleman as her son. Svętslav's suspicions were disarmed by this solemn act of adoption, but he found when it was too late that his affectionate "mother" had only embraced him in order the better to kill him. Even this assassination did not, however, leave her mistress of Bulgaria. A new and popular hero arose in the place of the murdered man. Ivailo (such seems to have been his real name) had begun life, like some much more famous Balkan heroes, as a swineherd, and his nickname of "the lettuce," from which the Greeks called him Lachanâs, may have been given him from his habitual diet of herbs. Saintly forms appeared to him in visions as he tended his herd, urging him to seize the throne of the nation which he was destined to rule. His credulous comrades flocked to the side of the inspired peasant; two victories over the Tartar hordes, which were devastating the country with impunity, convinced even the better classes of his mission to deliver their country; and the lawful Tsar, crippled by his malady and deprived by his wife's cruel machinations of his most faithful adherents, fell, in a forlorn attempt to save his crown, by the hand of the triumphant swineherd.

The success of this adventurer disturbed the calculations of the Greek Emperor, whose recent attempts at obtaining influence over Bulgarian policy had so signally failed. His first idea was to attach the peasant ruler to his person by giving him one of his own daughters in marriage. But on second thoughts he came to the conclusion that the swineherd would doubtless fall as rapidly as he had risen, and that it would be therefore wiser to set up a rival candidate to the Bulgarian throne. He readily found an instrument for this purpose in the person of the son of the former claimant, Mytzês, whom he married to his daughter Irene and proclaimed Emperor of the Bulgarians under the popular name of John Asên III. Meanwhile the Dowager-Empress Maria was placed in a position of the utmost difficulty in the capital. Menaced on three sides—by the citizens of Trnovo, by the swineherd, and by the Byzantine candidate—she saw that she must come to terms with one of the two latter. Self-interest suggested Ivailo as the more likely to allow her and her son to share the throne with him, especially if she offered to become his wife. At first the peasant was disinclined to accept as a favour what he could win by force; but he was sufficiently patriotic to shrink from a further civil war, agreed to her proposal, and early in 1278 celebrated the double festival of his marriage and coronation with her at Trnovo. But this unnatural union failed to secure her happiness or that of her subjects. The savage simplicity of the swineherd was revolted by the luxury of the Byzantine princess, and when their conjugal discussions became too subtle for his rude intelligence, he beat her as he would have beaten one of his own class. Another Tartar inroad increased the perils of the situation; the Byzantine claimant, at the head of a Greek army, invested Trnovo; and, though the cruelty of Ivailo struck terror into the hearts of the besiegers, accustomed to obey the recognised rules of civilised warfare, the report of his defeat at the hands of the Tartars in 1279 caused the wearied citizens to deliver both the Empress Maria and her son to the Greeks and to recognise John Asên III as their lawful sovereign. Maria was led away *enceinte* to Hadrianople, and ended her career, so fatal to her adopted country, unlamented and unsung.

But the removal of this disturbing element did not bring peace to Bulgaria. John Asên III ascended the throne as a Greek nominee, supported by a foreign army, while the most popular man in the country was a certain George Terteri, who, though of Cuman extraction, was connected with the native nobility and was well known for his energetic character and shrewd intelligence. Byzantine diplomacy saw at once the danger ahead, and sought to avoid it by the usual method, a matrimonial alliance between the dangerous rival and the reigning Tsar. Terteri consented to wed John Asên's sister, even though he had to divorce his wife, who had already borne him an heir, in order to make this political marriage. But it was not long before circumstances made him the inevitable ruler of Bulgaria. Ivailo, supposed to have disappeared finally from the scene, suddenly reappeared in the summer of 1280 with a Tartar general at his side. In vain the Greek Emperor sent two armies to defend the throne of his minion; two successive defeats convinced John Asên that it was time to flee alike before the enemy outside and the rival within. He took with him all the portable contents of the Bulgarian treasury, including the imperial insignia which the founders of the Empire had captured from Isaac Angelus ninety years earlier, and which thus returned with their unworthy successor to Constantinople. Such was the indignation of Michael VIII at the cowardly flight of the man whom he had laboured to make the instrument of his policy for the reduction of Bulgaria to a vassal state, that he at first refused him admission to the city. Meanwhile, George Terteri was raised to the vacant throne by the general desire of the military and the nobles. Such was his reputation that Ivailo at once retired from a contest to which he felt himself unequal single-handed.

Ivailo betook himself to the court of Nogai Khan, the Tartar chief who had once before been the arbiter of Bulgaria. There he found his old rival, John Asên III, well provided with Byzantine money, and calculating on the fact that the chief's harem contained his sister-in-law. For some time the wily Tartar was equally willing to receive the presents and listen with favour to the proposals of both candidates, till at last one night in a drunken bout he ordered Ivailo to be killed as the enemy of his father-in-law, the Greek Emperor. Asên only escaped a like fate thanks to the intervention of his wife's sister, who sent him back in safety to Constantinople. Thenceforth, he abandoned the attempt to recover the Bulgarian crown, preferring the peaceful dignity of a high Byzantine title and founding a family which played a prominent part in the medieval history of the Morea. His rival, even though dead, still continued to be a name with which to conjure; several years later, a false Ivailo caused such alarm at Constantinople that the Dowager-Empress Maria was asked to state whether he was her husband or no; even her disavowal of his identity availed nothing with the credulous peasants, who regarded him as their heaven-sent leader against the Turks. For a moment Byzantine statecraft thought that he might be utilised for that purpose; but, as his followers became more numerous and more fanatical, caution prevailed, and the pretender vanished in one of the Greek prisons.

Andronicus II, who had now succeeded to the Byzantine throne, realising the hopelessness of any further attempt to restore John Asên, not only made peace with Terteri, but sent back to him his first wife on condition that he divorced his second. Thus, the Tsar was able to pacify the scruples of the Bulgarian hierarchy, which had regarded him as excommunicated, nor could the united efforts of Pope Nicholas IV and Queen Helena of Serbia induce him to abandon the national Church. But the founder of the new dynasty was soon forced to flee before another Tartar invasion. In vain he had tried to prevent that calamity by a matrimonial alliance; Nogai Khan ravaged Bulgaria; and, while the Tsar was a suppliant at the Greek court, one of his nobles, "prince Smilec," was appointed by will of the Tartar chief to rule the country as his vassal. Smilec's reign was, however, brief; upon the death of Nogai, his son Choki claimed Bulgaria as the son-in-law of Terteri and was ostensibly supported by the latter's son, Theodore Svętslav. The allies were successful; Smilec disappeared, leaving as the one memorial of his name the monastery which he founded near Tatar-Pazardzhik; and Choki and Svętslav entered Trnovo in triumph. Then the Bulgarian appeared in his true colours; a sudden stroke of fortune enabled him to spend money freely among his countrymen, who naturally regarded him as the rightful heir to the throne; at last, when he thought that the moment had come for action, he ordered his Tartar ally to be seized and strangled, and the Bulgarian Patriarch, who had long been suspected of intrigues with the Tartars, to be hurled from the cliffs. Two attempts to drive out the new ruler failed. There was a small Grecophil party in Bulgaria which proclaimed Michael, the son of Constantine Asên and the Empress Maria; but the reception with which he met on his arrival convinced him that his cause was hopeless. The Byzantine Court then supported the brother of Smilec, who was in his turn defeated, and the number of Byzantine magnates who were captured on that occasion enabled Svętslav to ransom his father from the custody in which the Greeks had placed him. His filial piety did not, however, so far prevail over his ambition as to make him yield the throne to the founder of his dynasty. He placed him in honourable confinement in one of his cities, where he was allowed to live in luxury provided that he did not meddle with affairs of state.

The Bulgarian Empire no longer occupied the great position in Balkan politics which it had filled half a century earlier. The rivalries of pretenders, foreign intrigues, and the sinister influence of a woman had weakened the fabric so rapidly raised by the energy of the previous Tsars. In contrast with the feverish history of this once dominant Slavonic State, that of Serbia during the same period shews a tranquillity which increased the resources of that naturally rich country and thus prepared the way for the great expansion of the Serbian dominions in the next century. The "great king," Stephen Uroš I, whose simple court had so profoundly shocked the Byzantine officials, after a long and peaceful reign, only disturbed by a Tartar inroad, was ousted from the throne in 1276 by his elder son Stephen Dragutin (or "the beloved"), assisted by the latter's brother-in-law, the King of Hungary. The old king fled to the land of Hum, where he died of a broken heart, but his cruel son did not long wear the Serbian crown. Disabled by an infirmity of the foot from the active pursuits necessary to a Balkan sovereign in the Middle Ages, he abdicated in favour of his brother Stephen Uroš II, called "Milutin" (or "the child of grace"). But, like other monarchs who have resigned, he soon grew weary of retirement, and returned to the throne, till his malady, combined with qualms of conscience, compelled him, at the end of 1281[1], to withdraw definitely from the government of Serbia. As some compensation for this loss of dignity and as occupation for his not too active mind, he received from his brother-in-law, the King of

[1] Miklosich, *Monumenta Serbica*, 54, 55, 561.

Hungary, the Duchy of Mačva and Bosnia, and also governed Belgrade. There he busied himself entirely with religious questions; while he mortified his own flesh, to atone for his unfilial conduct, he and his son-in-law and vassal, Stephen Kotroman, the founder of the subsequent Bosnian dynasty, persecuted the Bogomiles with a zeal which became all the greater after his conversion to the Roman Church. At his request, the Franciscans, who have since played such an important part in Bosnian history, settled in the country; but, even with their aid, the fanaticism of Dragutin could make no headway against the stubborn heretics. At his death in 1316, the bishopric of Bosnia had been "almost destroyed," despite all the efforts of the Popes.

Stephen Uroš II has been judged very differently by his Serbian and by his Greek contemporaries. One of the former, who owed everything to him, extols his qualities as a ruler; one of the latter, who was naturally opposed to him, depicts him as a savage debauchee. The two characters are, however, by no means incompatible; and if this "pious king," the founder of churches and the endower of bishoprics, was anything but an exemplary husband, he left Serbia in a stronger position than she had ever held before. The chief object of his foreign policy was to enlarge his kingdom at the expense of the Byzantine Empire, which, he bitterly complained, had annexed foreign territory without being able to defend its own. Some two years before his accession, the Serbian troops under the guidance of a Greek deserter had penetrated as far as Seres; and the first act of his reign was to occupy Skoplje and other places in Macedonia, an undertaking all the easier in that his father-in-law, the bold Duke John of Neopatras, at that time the leading figure of Northern Greece, was at war with the Byzantine Emperor. Michael VIII died before he could punish the confederates, and his successor contented himself with sending the Tartar auxiliaries whom his father had collected to glut their desire for plunder in Serbia, and thus incidentally to weaken a nation which caused constant vexation to his subjects. The Tartars came and went, but the Serbian raids continued; Serbian standards approached the holy mount of Athos, and the Greek commander of Salonica confessed that his orthodox tactics were no match for the guerrilla warfare of these marauders. He therefore advised the Emperor, especially in view of the Turkish peril in Asia Minor, to make peace with the Serbs. Andronicus II took his advice and, to render the treaty more binding upon the volatile Serbian temperament, resolved to give the hand of one of the imperial princesses to Stephen Uroš. Such marriages were not, as a rule, happy; had not the gossips told how the "first-crowned" king had turned his Greek wife out of doors all but naked? Stephen Uroš II, it was pointed out, had an even worse reputation. That uxorious monarch, the Henry VIII of the Balkans, had already, it was true, had three wives, and had divorced two of them, while the third was still his consort. But

Byzantine sophistry declared the second and third marriages null, as having been contracted during the first wife's lifetime; as she was now dead, it followed that her husband could put away his third wife and marry again without offending the canons of the Church. Stephen Uroš was nothing loth; he wanted an heir, and had no further use for his third wife, a daughter of the dethroned Tsar Terteri; the only difficulty was that the widowed sister of Andronicus vowed that she, at any rate, did not share her brother's views as to the legality of such a second marriage. The Greek Emperor was not, however, discouraged by her refusal; he sacrificed his only daughter Simonis, though not yet six years of age, to the exigencies of politics and the coarseness of a notorious evil-liver who was older than her father and in Greek eyes his social inferior. The scruples of the Ecumenical Patriarch, increased by the theological flirtations of Stephen Uroš with the Roman Church, availed as little as the opposition of the Queen-Dowager Helena, who, as a good Catholic, regarded her son's marriage with abhorrence. The parties met on an island in the Vardar; the King of Serbia handed over his Bulgarian consort together with the Greek deserter who had for so long led his forces to victory, and received in exchange his little bride with all the humility of a *parvenu* marrying into an old family.

This matrimonial alliance with the imperial family suggested to the ambitious mind of Stephen Uroš the possibility of uniting the Byzantine and Serbian dominions under a single sceptre. His plan was shared by his mother-in-law, the Empress Irene, who, as an Italian, was devoid of Hellenic patriotism, and, as a second wife, knew that her sons could never succeed to their father's throne. In the King of Serbia she saw the means of acquiring the Byzantine Empire for her own progeny, if not for the offspring of Simonis, then for one of her own sons. From her retreat at Salonica she made Stephen Uroš the confidant of her conjugal woes, loaded him with presents, and sent him every year a more and more richly-jewelled tiara, almost as splendid as that of the Emperor himself. When it became clear that Simonis was not likely to have children, she persuaded the King of Serbia to adopt one of her two surviving sons as his heir. But the luxurious Byzantine princeling could not stand the hard and uncomfortable life in Serbia, and his brother also, after a brief experience of the Serbian court, was thankful to return to the civilisation of northern Italy. Simonis herself, when she grew up, disliked her adopted country quite as much as her brothers had done. She spent as much of her time as possible at Constantinople; and, when her husband threatened vengeance on the Greek Empire unless she returned to him, she was sent back in tears to his barbarous embraces. Obviously, then, Balkan capitals were even less agreeable places of residence for luxurious persons of culture at that period than they are now.

The Greek connexion had naturally given offence to the national party in Serbia, which was opposed to foreign influence and suspicious of feminine intrigues. Stephen Dragutin protested from his retirement at an arrangement which might deprive his own son Vladislav of the right, which he had never renounced for him, of succeeding to the Serbian throne upon the death of Stephen Uroš. A more dangerous rival was the king's bastard, Stephen, who had received the family appanage in the Zeta, but was impatient of this subordinate position and ready to come forward as the champion of the national cause against his father's Grecophil policy. Stephen Uroš, however, soon suppressed his bastard's rebellion; the rebel fled to the banks of the Bojana, where stood the church which still bears his father's name[1], and begged for pardon. But the king was anxious to render him incapable of a second conspiracy, and his Byzantine associates suggested to him that blinding was the best punishment for traitors of the blood royal. The operation was, however, only partially successful; but the victim had the sense to conceal the fact, and lived unmolested in a monastery at Constantinople, until his father in his old age, at the instigation of the historian Daniel, recalled him to Serbia and assigned him the ancient royal city of Dioclea, whose ruins may yet be seen near the modern Podgorica, as a residence.

The failure of his scheme for the union of the Serbian and Greek realms under his dynasty by peaceful means led Stephen Uroš to enter into negotiations, in 1308, with Charles of Valois, then seeking to recover the lost Latin Empire of Constantinople in the name of his daughter, the titular Empress. In order the better to secure the aid of the West, the crafty Serb expressed to Pope Clement V the desire to be received into that Roman Church of which his mother had been so ardent a devotee, and which could protect him from a possible French invasion. A treaty was then concluded between him and Charles, pledging both parties to render mutual assistance to one another, and securing for the King of Serbia the continued possession of Prilep, Štip, and other Macedonian castles formerly belonging to the Byzantine Empire. A further proposal for a marriage between the two families, contingent on the conversion of Stephen Uroš, fell through, and the feebleness and dilatoriness of the French prince convinced the shrewd Serbian monarch that such an alliance would not further his designs, and that he had nothing to fear from that quarter. He therefore abandoned Western Europe and the Papacy, and was sufficient of a Balkan patriot to assist the Greeks against the Turks.

The death of his brother Dragutin gave Stephen Uroš an opportunity of expanding his kingdom in another direction. He imprisoned his nephew, whom the royal monk had commended to his care, and made himself master of his inheritance in Mačva. Stephen Uroš II was now at the zenith of his power. It was no mere flourish of the pen which made him sign himself "King of Serbia, the land of Hum, Dioclea,

[1] *Wissenschaftliche Mittheilungen,* VII. 231.

Albania, and the sea-coast," for his authority really corresponded with those titles, and under him Serbia had, what she has at last regained, a sea-board on the Adriatic. But his unprincipled annexation of a former Hungarian land brought down upon him the vengeance of the King of Hungary, while his designs against the Angevin port of Durazzo[1], which he had already once captured, aroused the animosity of its owner, Philip of Taranto, now husband of the titular Empress of Constantinople. The Pope bade the Catholic Albanians fight against the schismatic Serb who had played fast and loose with the Holy See, and the league was completed by the adhesion of the powerful Croatian family of Šubić, which had latterly become predominant in Bosnia and would brook no Serbian interference in their domain. Stephen Uroš lost his brother's Bosnian duchy together with Belgrade; but to the last he was bent on the extension of his dominions. Death carried him off in 1321, as he was scheming to make political profit out of the quarrel between the elder and the younger Andronicus.

Stephen Uroš II was an opportunist in both politics and religion. His alliances were entirely dictated by motives of expediency, and he regarded the *filioque* clause as merely a pawn in the diplomatic game. If he delighted the Orthodox Church by his gifts to Mount Athos, and his pious foundations at Salonica, Constantinople, and even Jerusalem; if a chapel near Studenica still preserves the memory of this "great-grandson of St Simeon and son of the great King Uroš"—he was so indifferent, or so statesmanlike, as to permit six Catholic sees within his realm and to allow Catholic bishops and even the *djed*, or "grand-sire," of the Bogomiles to sit in his Council at Cattaro. One of his laws prevented boundary disputes between villages; he was anxious to encourage commerce; and, though he more than once harassed Ragusa, he wrote to Venice offering to keep open and guard the great trade route which traversed his kingdom and then led across Bulgaria to the Black Sea. But in commercial, as in other matters, his code of honour was low, and his issue of counterfeit Venetian coin has gained him a place among the evil kings in the *Paradiso*[2] of Dante.

Upon the death of Stephen Uroš II the crown should have naturally devolved upon his nephew Vladislav, who had now been released from prison. But the clergy, always a dominant factor in Serbian politics, favoured the election of the bastard Stephen, who, during his father's later years, had borne all the royal titles[3] as a designation of his ultimate succession, and had already once championed the national idea. Stephen proclaimed that he was no longer blind, and astutely ascribed to a miracle what was the result of the venality or clumsiness

[1] Angevin 1272, Serbian 1296, Angevin 1305, Serbian 1319, Angevin 1322, Albanian 1368, Venetian 1392, Turkish 1501, Serbian 1912, Albanian 1913.

[2] XIX. 140–1.

[3] *Mon. spect. hist. Slav. Merid.* I. 192.

of the operator. To cover his illegitimacy, he assumed the family name of Uroš, already associated in the popular mind with two successful kings, but posterity knows him by that of Dečanski from the monastery of Dečani in Old Serbia, which he founded. With the ruthlessness of his race, he speedily rid himself of his two competitors, Vladislav and another natural son of the late king, a certain Constantine. Vladislav died an exile in Hungary; Constantine was nailed to a cross and then sawn asunder; while the usurper tried yet further to strengthen his position by wooing a daughter of Philip of Taranto and by obtaining from the Pope a certificate of his legitimacy. To secure these objects he surrendered Durazzo and offered to become a Catholic, only to withdraw his offer when the support of the Orthodox clergy seemed more valuable to him than that of Rome.

The civil war which was at that time threatening the Byzantine Empire involved both the neighbouring Slav states, each anxious to benefit by the struggle, which ultimately resulted in a pitched battle between them. The dynasty of Terteri had become extinct in Bulgaria a year after the accession of Stephen Uroš III to the Serbian throne. Svętslav, although he had domestic difficulties with Byzantium, had kept on good terms with the Serbs, and his warlike son George Terteri II, who succeeded him in 1322, died after a single Greek campaign. Bulgaria was therefore once more distracted by the claims of rival claimants, of whom the strongest was Michael of Vidin, already styled "Despot of Bulgaria," and founder of the last dynasty of Bulgarian Tsars. His father had established himself as a petty prince in that famous Danubian fortress; the son, as was natural in one living so near the Serbian frontier, had married a half-sister of the new King of Serbia and owed his success to Serbian aid. In order, however, to secure peace with the Greeks and at the same time to consolidate his position at home, he now repudiated his consort with her children, and espoused the widow of Svętslav, who was a sister of the younger Andronicus. This matrimonial alliance led to a political treaty between the Bulgarian Tsar and the impatient heir of Byzantium; they met in the autumn of 1326, and came to terms which seemed favourable to both: Michael promised to assist Andronicus to oust his grandfather from the throne; Andronicus pledged himself to support Michael against the natural indignation of the insulted Serbian king, and, in the event of his own enterprise succeeding, to give money and territory to his Bulgarian brother-in-law. On the other side, the elder Andronicus sent the historian Nicephorus Gregorâs on a mission to the Serbian government, with the object of conciliating Stephen Uroš III. The literary diplomatist has left us a comical picture of the peripatetic Serbian court, then in the vicinity of Skoplje, as it struck a highly-cultured Byzantine. The inadequate efforts of his barbarian majesty to do honour to the high-born Greek lady whose daughter he had recently married, seemed ridiculous to a visitor versed in the etiquette of Constantinople. Still, as the historian complacently remarked, one cannot expect apes and ants to act like eagles and lions, and he re-crossed the Serbian frontier thanking Providence that he had been born a Greek. Similar opinions with regard to the Balkan Slavs are still held by many of his countrymen.

After making, however, due allowance for the national bias of a Greek author, it is clear that Serbia, then on the eve of becoming the chief power of the peninsula, was still far behind both the Greek and Latin states of the Levant in civilisation. The contemporary writer, Archbishop Adam, who has left a valuable account of the country at this period, tells us that it contained no walled and moated castles; the palaces of the king and his nobles were of wood, surrounded by palisades, and the only houses of stone were in the Latin towns on the Adriatic coast, such as Antivari, Cattaro, and Dulcigno, the residences of the Catholic Archbishop and his suffragans. Yet Rascia was naturally a very rich land, producing plenty of corn, wine, and oil, well-watered, and abounding in forests full of game. Five gold mines and as many of silver were being constantly worked, and Stephen Uroš II could afford a gift of plate and a silver altar to the church of St Nicholas at Bari. But his subjects were too heterogeneous to be united; the Latins of Scutari and the coast-towns, as well as the Albanians, also Catholics, were oppressed by the Serbs, whose priesthood was debased and whose bishops were often in prison. As against this last statement, obviously caused by the theological zeal of the archbishop, we may set the gloomy account of the abuses in the six Roman churches of Serbia, which we have from Pope Benedict XI some twenty years earlier, while, at the moment when Adam wrote, the Orthodox Archbishop was no less eminent a man than the patriotic historian Daniel. If, then, Serbia was still uncultured, if the manners and morals of her rustic court still left much to desire, she was obviously possessed of great natural energy and capacity, which only awaited a favourable moment and the right man to develop them.

While the Serbian nobles, whose influence was usually predominant in deciding questions of public policy, soon wearied of supporting the elder Andronicus, and plainly said that if their sovereign insisted on fighting he would fight alone, the Bulgarian Tsar suddenly changed sides, warmly espoused the cause of the old Emperor, and sent 3000 horsemen under a Russian general with the object (so it was suspected) of seizing Constantinople for himself and thus realising the dream of his greatest predecessors. Self-interest and patriotism alike urged the younger Andronicus to warn his grandfather of the danger which he would incur if he entrusted the palace to the custody of these untrustworthy allies. Andronicus II acted on this timely hint from his rival; for neither of them could desire to see a Bulgarian conquest of Constantinople as the result of their family disputes. The Russian was alone admitted within the gates, and the reproaches and bribes of the younger Andronicus speedily effected the recall of the Bulgarian force. A few days later Andronicus III entered the city in triumph; Byzantium never again so nearly fell beneath the Bulgarian yoke as in that memorable spring of 1328, until the famous campaign of 1912–13.

The same Bulgarian Tsar, who had thus all but achieved the ideal of every Balkan nationality, was destined to bring his country to the verge of ruin. Stephen Uroš III had never forgiven the insult to his sister, and Michael therefore resolved to forestall a Serbian invasion by acting first. He had no difficulty in forming a formidable coalition against the rising Serbian state. Andronicus III, whose Macedonian frontier near Ochrida had lately been ravaged by the Serbs, joined the league and menaced Serbia from the south; the Prince of Wallachia and 3000 Tartar mercenaries swelled the native army of Bulgaria, already 12,000 strong. At the head of such forces, Michael boasted that he would be crowned in his enemy's land, and set out down the valley of the Upper Struma to cross the frontier a little to the north of Köstendil, then a Serbian but now a Bulgarian town. On 28 June 1330, the most decisive battle in the mutual history of the two Slav states was fought in the plain of Velbužd, as Köstendil was then called. The Tsar was taken by surprise, for he had expected no fighting that day; indeed, it was afterwards stated that his opponent had given his word not to begin hostilities till the morrow. Thus, at the moment when the Serbs charged from a narrow defile into the plain, the bulk of the Bulgarian army was away foraging. Aided by a body of several hundred tall German knights, Stephen Uroš easily routed his distracted foes; Michael himself was unhorsed, and died, either in the battle, or of his wounds a few days afterwards; but the conquerors merely disarmed the fugitives, whom, as men of their own race, it was not lawful to take captive. On the hill where his tent had been pitched, the victor founded a church of the Ascension, the ruins of which still serve as a memorial of this fratricidal war. Bulgaria was now at his mercy, for the rest of the native army had fled at the news of their sovereign's defeat, and Andronicus III at once returned to Constantinople. The proud Bulgarian nobles, who had deemed themselves their Tsar's "half-brothers," came to meet their conqueror and hear his decision. Stephen Uroš might have united the two Slav states under his own sceptre, and thus prevented those further rivalries which have governed Balkan politics in our own time. But he preferred to allow Bulgaria, then more than twenty days' journey in extent, to remain as a dependency of his family; he contented himself with restoring his sister and her young son John Stephen to the throne of the Tsars. The immediate effect of this policy was the expulsion of the late ruler's Greek consort, which gave her brother Andronicus an excuse for annexing a large part of Southern Bulgaria. Thus Greeks and Serbs alike had profited by the victory of Velbužd; Serbia had won the hegemony of the Balkan States.

Stephen Uroš III did not long enjoy the fruits of his triumph. His worst enemies were those of his own household, and he fell a victim to one of those domestic tragedies which were characteristic of his family. He had married a second time, and his eldest son Stephen, then twenty-two years of age but still unprovided with a wife, looked with suspicion on the offspring of his Greek step-mother, a cousin of Andronicus III. He had been carefully educated as a crown prince; indeed, his father had had him crowned with himself, and had promised to make him ruler over half his kingdom. The courtier-like Archbishop Daniel, anxious to please his young master, asserts that Stephen Uroš had not kept this promise; an impartial Greek contemporary says that the prince's suspicions were exploited by those Serbian nobles who were weary of his father's rule and hoped to benefit by a change. They proclaimed him king; he was crowned on 8 September 1331; the flower of the army, attracted by his prowess at Velbužd, flocked to his standard; the old king was easily captured and imprisoned in the castle of Zvečan near Mitrovica. There, two months later, he was strangled, either by the orders[1] or at least with the tacit consent of his son, who durst not oppose the will of his powerful followers[2]; and the name of Dušan, by which Stephen Uroš IV is known in history, is variously derived, according to the view taken of his share in his father's murder, either from *duša* ("soul"), a pet name given him by his fond parent, or from *dušiti* ("to throttle"). The epithet of "strong," which his countrymen applied to him, was fully justified by the masterful character and the great achievements of this most famous of all Serbian sovereigns.

His first care was to secure himself on the side of Bulgaria, where, a few months before, a revolution organised by two court officials had driven the Serbian Empress and her son from the throne, and had placed upon it John Alexander, a nephew of the late Tsar, who assumed the ever popular surname of Asên. Instead of attempting to restore his aunt to Bulgaria against the will of the nobles, Dušan adopted the wiser policy of marrying the sister of the usurper and thus attaching the latter to his side, while John Stephen, after wandering as an exile from one land to another, now a suppliant at Constantinople and now a prisoner at Siena, ended his days at Naples. Thus Bulgaria under John Alexander was practically a dependency of Serbia.

But Dušan by his Bulgarian marriage disarmed the enmity, and gained the support, of another powerful Balkan ruler, the Prince of Wallachia, who was father-in-law of the Bulgarian Tsar, and who had first made the land which was the nucleus of the present kingdom of

[1] Adam (Pseudo-Brochart) in *Rec. hist. Crois., Doc. Armén.* II. 438, 446, who wrote in 1332, thus confirming the date of Dušan's accession (cf. *Rad.* XIX. 180; *Mon. spect. hist. Slav. Merid.* XIII. 337; XXV. 122), which Miklosich (*Monumenta Serbica,* 115) had placed in 1336.

[2] Nicephorus Gregorâs, I. 457.

Roumania a factor in Balkan politics. During the former half of the thirteenth century, while Serbia and Bulgaria were already independent states, the opposite bank of the Danube had been traversed by successive barbarian tribes, the Cumans and the Tartars, who had driven the Roumanian population before them to the mountains. A Slav population dwelt in the plains, the *banat* of Craiova, or "little Wallachia," was Hungarian, while here and there the fortresses of the Teutonic Knights and the Knights of St John availed but little to stem the tide of invasion. But about 1290 the Roumanians descended from Transylvania into Wallachia to escape the religious persecutions of the Catholic Kings of Hungary, and the generally received account ascribes the foundation of the principality to a colony from Fogaras, which, under the leadership of Radou Negrou, or Rudolf the Black, established itself at Campulung, and gave to the essentially flat country of Wallachia the local name of "land of mountains," in memory of those mountains whence the founder came. His successor, Ivanko Basaraba, the ally of the Bulgarians in the campaign of 1330, extended his authority over "little Wallachia," completely routed the Hungarians, and strengthened his position by marrying his daughter to the new Tsar of Bulgaria. About the same time as the foundation of the Wallachian principality, a second principality, dependent however on the Hungarian crown, was created in Moldavia by another colony of Roumanians from the north of Transylvania under a chief named Dragoche. This vassal state threw off its allegiance to Hungary about 1349, and became independent. Such was the origin of the two Danubian principalities, which thenceforth existed under various forms till their transformation in our own day into the kingdom of Roumania.

Thus connected with the rulers of Bulgaria and Wallachia, Dušan was able to begin the realisation of that great scheme which had been cherished by his grandfather of forming a Serbian Empire on the ruins of Byzantium. While his ally, the Bulgarian Tsar, recaptured the places south of the Balkans which Andronicus III had so recently occupied, Dušan, assisted by Sir Janni, a political adventurer who had abandoned the Byzantine for the Serbian court, easily conquered nearly all Western Macedonia. The assassination of Sir Janni by an emissary of the Byzantine Emperor and the threatening attitude of the King of Hungary led him, however, to make peace with the Greeks and even to seek their aid against this dangerous enemy. The Greek and the Serbian monarchs met and spent a very pleasant week in one another's society; and this meeting had important results, because it gave Dušan an opportunity of making the acquaintance of the future Emperor John Cantacuzene, then in attendance on Andronicus. Thus, for the moment, peace reigned between the Greeks and the Balkan Slavs; Dušan was content to bide his time; John Alexander obtained the hand of the Emperor's daughter for his eldest son, and could afford to ignore the appeal which the Pope made to him to join the Church of Rome.

Dušan availed himself of this peace with the Greeks to attack the Angevin possessions in Albania. Durazzo, however, the most important of them, resisted all his efforts, and the Angevin rule there survived the great Serbian conqueror. But this aggressive policy had made him an object of general alarm. The King of Hungary, himself an Angevin, and the powerful Bosnian *ban*, Stephen Kotromanić, who had succeeded the family of Šubić in 1322, regarded him with suspicion, and their attitude so greatly alarmed him that he wrote to Venice in 1340, begging for a refuge there in the event of his being defeated by his numerous enemies, offering to assist the republic in her Italian wars, and guaranteeing her merchants a safe transit across his dominions on their way to Constantinople. Venice bestowed the rights of citizenship upon the serviceable Serbian monarch and his family.

The death of Andronicus III in 1341 and the rebellion of John Cantacuzene against the rule of the young Emperor John V and his mother Anne of Savoy were Dušan's opportunity. He at once disregarded his treaty with the Greeks, and overran the whole of Macedonia. Soon this barbarian, as the elegant Byzantine authors considered him, had the proud satisfaction of receiving at Priština, which, though it had been the Serbian capital, was still only an unfortified village, bids for his alliance from both parties in the struggle for the dominion of the Empire. Cantacuzene, in the hour of need, sought a personal interview with him there; the King and Queen of Serbia welcomed their distinguished suppliant with every mark of respect; but, when it came to business, Dušan demanded as the price of his assistance the whole of the Byzantine Empire west of the pass of Christópolis near Kavala, or, at any rate, of Salonica. Cantacuzene informs us that he indignantly declined to give up even the meanest of Greek cities; the utmost concession which he could be induced to make was to recognise Dušan's rights over the Greek territory which he already held. Anne of Savoy, as a foreigner, was less patriotic; she more than once promised Dušan that, if he would send her Cantacuzene alive or dead, she would give him what her rival had refused, so that the Serbian Empire would stretch from the Adriatic to the Aegean. The matter was referred to the Council of twenty-four officers of State whom the Serbian kings were wont to consult, and this Council, acting on the advice of the queen, repudiated the suggestion of assassinating an honoured guest, and advised Dušan to be content with a formal oath from Cantacuzene that he would respect the territorial *status quo*. Baffled in her negotiations with the King of Serbia, Anne of Savoy did not scruple to purchase the aid of the Bulgarian Tsar by the cession of Philippopolis and eight other places, the last aggrandisement of the Bulgarian Empire. Thus, the divisions of the Greeks benefited Serbia and Bulgaria alike, while both Cantacuzene and his rival found ere long that their Slav allies only looked to their own advancement. In the general confusion, both parties invoked the assistance of the Turks, who had taken Brūsa (Prusa) in 1326 and Nicaea in 1330, and who now appeared sporadically in Europe. Brigand chiefs formed bands in the mountains, changing sides whenever it suited their purpose, and one of these guerrilla leaders, a Bulgarian named Momchilo, not only survives in the pages of the imperial historian but is still the hero of Slavonic ballads.

It was the policy of Dušan to allow the two Greek factions to exhaust themselves, and to strengthen his position at the expense of both. While they fought, he occupied one place after another, till, by 1345, he had acquired all that he had originally asked Cantacuzene to cede, and the whole of Macedonia, except Salonica, was in his power. It was scarcely an exaggeration when he described himself in a letter to the Doge, written from Seres in this year, as "King of Serbia, Dioclea, the land of Hum, the Zeta, Albania, and the Maritime region, partner in no small part of the Empire of Bulgaria, and lord of almost all the Empire of Romania."[1] But for the ruler of so vast a realm the title of King seemed insignificant, especially as his vassal, the ruler of Bulgaria, bore the great name of Tsar. Accordingly, early in 1346, Dušan had himself crowned at Skoplje, whither he had transferred the Serbian capital, as "Emperor of the Serbs and Greeks," soon to be magnified into "Tsar and Autocrat of the Serbs and Greeks, the Bulgarians and Albanians." Shortly before, with the consent of the Bulgarian, and in defiance of the Ecumenical, Patriarch, he had raised the Archbishop of Serbia to that exalted dignity with his seat at Ipek, and the two Slav Patriarchs of Trnovo and Ipek placed the crown upon his head. At the same time, on the analogy of the Western Empire with its "King of the Romans," he had his son Stephen Uroš V proclaimed king, and assigned to him the old Serbian lands as far as Skoplje, reserving for himself the new conquests from there to Kavala. Byzantine emblems and customs were introduced into the brand-new Serbian Empire; the Tsar assumed the tiara and the double-eagle as the heir of the great Constantine, and wrote to the Doge proposing an alliance for the conquest of Constantinople. The officials of his court received the high-sounding titles of Byzantium, and in the papal correspondence with Serbia we read of a "Sebastocrator," a "Great Logothete," a "Caesar," and a "Despot." The governors of important Serbian cities, such as Cattaro and Scutari, were styled "Counts," those of minor places, like Antivari, were called "Captains." In vain did Cantacuzene, as soon as the civil war was over, demand the restitution of the Greek territory which Dušan had conquered since their meeting in 1342. The Tsar had no intention of keeping his word or of returning to the *status quo* of that year.

[1] *Mon. spect. hist. Slav. Merid.* II. 278–9.

On the contrary, he still further extended his frontiers to the south, where they marched with the former despotat of Epirus. That important state, founded on the morrow of the Latin conquest of Constantinople, had maintained its independence till, in 1336, it had been at last re-united with the Byzantine Empire. Cantacuzene had appointed one of his relatives as its governor; but upon his death in 1349 the Serbian Tsar, who had already occupied Joánnina, annexed Epirus and Thessaly, assuming the further titles of "Despot of Arta and Count of Vlachia." His brother, Simeon Uroš, was sent to rule Acarnania and Aetolia as his viceroy, while the Serbian "Caesar," Preljub, governed Joánnina and Thessaly. Thus a large part of northern Greece owned the sway of the Serbs. Cantacuzene resolved at once to punish this culminating act of aggression. The moment was favourable to his plans, for Dušan was engaged on the Bosnian frontier, and several of the Serbian nobles, always intolerant of authority, deserted to the popular Greek Emperor, whom they knew and liked. Such was his success (for even the Serbian capital of Skoplje offered to surrender in the absence of the Tsar) that Dušan hastened back and came to terms with his enemy. The two Emperors met outside Salonica; Cantacuzene reproached the Tsar with his breach of the treaty made between them eight years earlier; and, if we may judge from the speeches which he composed for himself and his opponent, Dušan was completely dumbfounded by his arguments. A fresh treaty was drawn up between them, by which Acarnania, Thessaly, and the south-east of Macedonia as far as Seres, were to be retroceded to the Greeks, and five commissioners were appointed on either side for the transfer of this territory. But the renewal of the unhappy quarrel between Cantacuzene and John V thwarted the execution of this agreement. Emissaries of the young Emperor advised Dušan to resist, telling him that he would obtain better terms by aiding their master against Cantacuzene. The Tsar thereupon repudiated the treaty which he had just signed, promised his assistance to John V, and urged him to divorce Cantacuzene's daughter and marry the sister of the Serbian Empress. Cantacuzene in vain warned his young rival to beware of Serbian intrigues; in vain did Anne of Savoy endeavour to prevent the unholy league; a new triple alliance was formed between John V and the two Serbian and Bulgarian Tsars. Thus Dušan was able to retain his Greek conquests, with a flagrant disregard for the treaty of 1350 which recalls the futility of such instruments in the settlement of Balkan questions.

It was not, however, only the other Christian races of the Near East who profited by the fatal dissensions between the two Greek Emperors. The nation, which a century later was destined to grind them all to powder, owed its first permanent settlement in Europe to their divisions. The Ottoman Turks from their capital of Brūsa could aid either party, according as it suited their convenience, nor did Cantacuzene hesitate to buy the support of the Sultan Orkhān by giving him his daughter to wife. For some years the Turks were content to raid the neighbouring coast; then their marauding bands penetrated farther inland, and so severely devastated Bulgaria that John Alexander complained to Cantacuzene of the depredations of his savage allies. Cantacuzene was sufficient of a statesman to foresee the coming Turkish triumph; he replied by offering to keep up a fleet at the Dardanelles for the protection of the European coast, if the Bulgarian Tsar would contribute towards its maintenance. A popular demonstration at Trnovo in favour of common action against the Turks convinced the Tsar of the wisdom of accepting Cantacuzene's proposal. But at the last moment Dušan wrecked the scheme by remonstrating with his vassal for paying what he scornfully called "tribute" to the Greek Empire. In vain Cantacuzene warned the offended Bulgarian that Bulgaria would one day, when it was too late, rue his decision. Not long after, in 1353 according to the Greek, or in 1356 according to the Turkish account, Orkhān's son crossed the Dardanelles and occupied the castle of Tzympe, the first permanent settlement of the Turks in Europe. Cantacuzene had offered them money to quit, and they were preparing to go when a sudden convulsion of nature tempted them to break their bargain; the great earthquake of 2 March 1354 laid the neighbouring towns in ruins[1]; and Gallipoli, the largest of them, was colonised and re-fortified by these unwelcome guests, who had now come to stay and conquer.

It has been mentioned that Cantacuzene's successes in 1350 were favoured by Dušan's absence in Bosnia. That Napoleonic ruler could not be expected to acquiesce in the co-existence of another Serb state adjacent to, yet independent of, his own. He had an old grudge against Stephen Kotromanić, the Bosnian *ban*, because the latter had annexed, in 1325, the land of Hum, which for the previous two generations had been a dependency of the Serbian crown and furnished one of Dušan's many titles. Kotromanić had further gained for Bosnia what she had never had before, an outlet on the Adriatic, and both Hungary and Venice were glad of the aid of so powerful a ruler, who thus laid the foundations of the future kingdom built up by his successor. As soon as he had sufficient leisure from his Macedonian conquests, Dušan demanded the hand of the *ban's* only daughter for his son and, as her dowry, the restitution of the Serbian territory which his rival had annexed; and, though Venetian intervention prevented an immediate conflict, a collision between the two Serb potentates was clearly inevitable. The Bosnian *ban* thought it wiser to begin the

[1] The Byzantine chronicle (in *Sitzungsberichte der k. Akademie,* IX. 392) gives the date of the earthquake; the Turkish settlement was, according to N. Gregorâs (III. 224) "about two years earlier," and due to Cantacuzene (III. 202); the latter (III. 242, 276) puts it in 1353, and is confirmed by the Bulgarian Chronicle (in *Archiv für slav. Philologie,* XIII. 537) which narrates it immediately after his embassy to John Alexander.

attack; he availed himself of Dušan's Greek campaign of 1349 to invade the Serbian Empire and to menace the town of Cattaro. Dušan, as soon as the subjugation of Epirus and Thessaly was complete, marched into Bosnia, and laid siege to the strong castle of Bobovac, whose picturesque ruins still recall the memory of the many Bosnian rulers who once resided within its walls. The invader found valuable allies in the Bogomiles, whose support Kotromanić had alienated by embracing Catholicism, and who, as has usually happened in the history of Bosnia, flocked to the standard of anyone who would free them from their persecutor. Their power had greatly increased; they possessed a complete organisation; their spiritual head, or *djed*, resided at Janjići in the Bosna valley, and twelve "teachers" formed a regular hierarchy under his orders. Moreover, the conflicts of the Dominicans and Franciscans for the exclusive privilege of persecuting the Bosnian heretics had naturally favoured the growth of the heresy. Bobovac, however, resisted all attacks, for the chivalry of its garrison no less than the zeal of the besiegers was aroused by the presence of the *ban's* beautiful daughter within the castle. Dušan was recalled by the troubles in his own Empire, nor did the few remaining years of his reign leave him time for repeating this invasion. The death of Kotromanić in 1353, and the succession of his young nephew Tvrtko I under the regency of a woman, might otherwise have been the Serbian Tsar's opportunity; for the Bosnian magnates, many of whom were zealous Bogomiles, were contemptuous of a *ban* who was not only a child but a Catholic, nor could his mother have opposed a second Serbian attack. But Dušan was occupied with greater schemes; the moment passed for ever, and it was reserved for the despised Tvrtko to make for himself the greatest name in Bosnian history, to found a kingdom, and to unite Serbia, Croatia, and Dalmatia beneath the sceptre of the first Bosnian king.

At the moment of Tvrtko's accession, Dušan was engaged in war with Hungary. Louis the Great, who now sat on the Hungarian throne, had aided Kotromanić against the Serbs and had married his fair daughter, whose hand Dušan had demanded for his son, and whom he had besieged in Bobovac. The two monarchies had long been rivals, as they were yesterday; the Serbian Tsar marched to the Danube and the Save; Belgrade, the future Serbian capital, lost a generation earlier and already beginning to be an important fortress, was recovered. But in the following year the Catholic king made such formidable preparations for an attack upon the schismatic Tsar, that the latter considered it prudent to revert to the time-honoured diplomacy of his predecessors in such cases, and to affect a desire for conversion to Catholicism, so as to secure the intervention of the Pope on his behalf. He therefore wrote offering to restore to the Catholics of his dominions most of the monasteries and churches which he had taken from them, and begging the Pope to send him some men learned in the Catholic faith. At the same time he asked to be appointed "Captain of the Church" against the Turks. Innocent VI, with the ingenuousness characteristic of the Papacy in its negotiations with the Balkan Slavs, imagined that Dušan was in earnest, and sent two bishops to his court, while he diverted the King of Hungary's projected attack upon so hopeful a proselyte. When, however, the papal legate and his companion arrived in 1355 at the Serbian court, they found that the Tsar had no longer any interest in becoming a Catholic. Cantacuzene had just been deposed; the Byzantine Empire had fallen into the hands of John V; and there was a party among the Greeks themselves who thought that the only way of saving the remnant from the Turks was to invoke the protection of the powerful Serbian Emperor[1], whose chances would naturally be all the greater if he remained a member of the Orthodox Church. Accordingly, when the legate was introduced into the presence of the Tsar, "of all men of his time the tallest, and withal terrible to look upon,"[2] he was expected to conform to the usual custom of the Serbian court and kiss the Emperor's foot. On his refusal, Dušan ordered that none of his Catholic subjects should attend the legate's mass under pain of losing his eyesight; but neither the orders nor the savage mien of the insistent tyrant availed against the fervid faith of his German guard, whose captain, Palmann, boldly told him that they feared God more than they feared the Tsar.

Dušan might well believe that the moment had come for completing his conquests by that of Constantinople, and establishing what a poetic Serbian prince of our own day once called a "Balkan Empire," which should embrace all the races of the variegated peninsula within its borders, and keep the Turks beyond the Bosphorus, the Hungarians beyond the Save. The former were threatening his enemies, the Greeks; the latter were about to attack his friends, the Venetians. On St Michael's Day, 1355, if we may believe the native chronicler, he assembled his nobles, and asked whether he should lead them against Byzantium or Buda-Pesth. To their answer, that they would follow him whithersoever he bade them, his reply was "to Constantinople," from which Thrace alone separated his dominions. But on the way he fell ill of a fever, and at Diavoli, on 20 December, he died[3]. By a strange irony, the very site of his death is uncertain; for, while some think that he had not yet left his own dominions, others place Diavoli within a few leagues of the imperial city. No Serbian ruler has ever approached so near it; possibly, had he succeeded and had another Dušan succeeded him, the Turkish conquest might have been averted.

[1] *Mon. spect. hist. Slav. Merid.* III. 266.

[2] ASBoll., *Januarius*, II. 998.

[3] Miklosich (*Monumenta Serbica*, 155) gives the day. The year must be 1355, *not* 1356, because a Venetian document of 23 Jan. 1356, alludes to his death (*Mon. spect. hist. Slav. Merid.* III. 308). Similarly the Serbian and Bosnian Chronicles in *Arch. f. slav. Philologie*, XIII. 520; XXIII. 631, 633, and in *Wiss. Mitt.* IV. 377.

Great as were his conquests, the Serbian Napoleon was no mere soldier. Like the French Emperor, he was a legislator as well as a commander, and he has left behind him a code of law, the so-called *Zakonnik*, which, like the *Code Napoléon*, has survived the vast but fleeting empire which its author too rapidly acquired. Dušan's law-book consists of 120 articles, of which the first 104 were published in 1349 and the remaining 16 five years later. It is not an original production, but is largely based on previous legislation; the articles dealing with ecclesiastical matters are derived from the canon law of the Greek Church, others are taken from the statutes of the Adriatic coast-towns, notably those of Budua, while the institution of trial by jury is borrowed from Stephen Uroš II. For the modern reader its chief importance lies in the light which it throws upon the political and social condition of the Serbian Empire at its zenith.

Medieval Serbia resembled neither of the two Serb states of our own day. Unlike Montenegro, it was never an autocracy, even in the time of its first and greatest Tsar, but the powers of the monarch were limited, as in medieval Bulgaria, by the influence of the great nobles, a class which does not exist in the modern Serbian kingdom. Society consisted of the sovereign; the ecclesiastical hierarchy, ranging from the newly-created Patriarch to the village priest; the greater and lesser nobles, called respectively *vlastele* and *vlasteličići*; the peasants, some free and some serfs bound to the soil; slaves; servants for hire; and, in the coast-towns, such as Cattaro, and at a few places inland, small communities of burghers. But the magnates were throughout the dominant section; one of them established himself as an independent prince at Strumitsa in Macedonia; on two occasions Dušan had to cope with their rebellions. The leading men among them formed a privy council of twenty-four which he consulted before deciding important questions of policy; his legal code was approved by a *sabor*, or parliament of nobles, great and small, at which the Patriarch and the other chief officials of the Church were present; and its provisions defined their privileges as jealously as his own. Their lands were declared hereditary, and their only feudal burdens consisted of a tithe to holy Church and of military service to the Tsar during their lifetime, a compulsory bequest of their weapons and their best horse to him after their death. If they built a church on their estates, they became patrons of the living; they exercised judicial powers, with a few exceptions, over their own serfs; they enjoyed the privilege of killing their inferiors with comparative impunity, for a graduated tariff regulated the punishment for premeditated murder—hanging for that of a priest or monk, burning for parricide, fratricide, or infanticide, the loss of both hands and a fine for that of a noble by a common man, a simple fine for that of a commoner by a noble. Two days a week the peasant was compelled to work for his lord; once a year he had to pay a capitation-tax to the Tsar. But the law protected him and secured to him the fruits of his labour; no village might be laid under contribution by two successive army corps; and, in case of trial by jury, the jurors were always chosen from the class to which the accused belonged. But the peasant was expressly excluded from all share in public affairs; they were the business of his betters alone; and, if he organised or attended a public meeting, he lost his ears and was branded on the face. For theft or arson the village, for *corveés* or fines the household, of the culprit were held collectively responsible; the provinces had to build the palaces and maintain the fortresses of the Tsar.

Next to the nobles, the Orthodox Church was the most influential class of the community. Though on occasion Dušan coquetted with Rome, his permanent policy was to strengthen the national Church, to which he had given a separate organisation, independent of Constantinople. The early archbishops of Serbia had been drawn from the junior members of the royal family, and their interests were accordingly identified with those of the Crown; their successors were often the apologists and the sycophants of royal criminals, just as, in our own day, we have seen a Metropolitan of Belgrade condone successful regicide. In return for their support, the established Church received special privileges and exemptions: on the one hand, the Tsar protected the new Patriarchate from Greek reprisals by ordering the expulsion of Greek priests; on the other, his code enjoined the compulsory conversion of his Catholic subjects and the punishment of Catholic priests who attempted to propagate their doctrines in Orthodox Serbia. A similar phenomenon, the result of policy not of fanaticism, meets us in the kindred Empire of Bulgaria. There we find John Alexander—a man who was so little of a purist that he sent his Wallachian wife to a nunnery and married a beautiful Jewess—consigning his ecclesiastical conscience to an inspired bigot, half-hermit, half-missionary, and, at his bidding, holding two Church Councils against the Bogomiles and similar heretics, who sought salvation by discarding their clothes, and who paid for their errors by branding or banishment. "The friend of monks, the nourisher of the poor," he founded a monastery at the foot of Mt Vitoš, and gave rich gifts to Rila, where one of Dušan's great officials ended his career and built the tower which still preserves his name. Even the Jewish Tsaritsa, with all the zeal of a convert, restored churches and endowed monasteries, but her munificence could not prevent the restriction of the civil liberties of her own people, from whom the state executioner was selected.

While the great Serbia of Dušan, like the smaller Serbia of our own day, was pre-eminently an agricultural state, whose inhabitants were chiefly occupied in tilling the land and in rearing live-stock, it possessed the enormous advantage of a coastline, which thus facilitated trade. Like the enlightened statesman that he was, Dušan had no prejudices against foreign merchants. He allowed them to circulate freely, and to the Ragusans, who were the most important of them, he shewed marked favours. Thus, while Ragusan chroniclers complain of his father's vexatious policy towards the South Slavonic republic, he vied with the *ban* of Bosnia, in 1333, in giving her the peninsula of Sabbioncello, over which both sovereigns had claims. The possession of this long and narrow strip of land enormously reduced the time and cost of transport into Bosnia, and amply repaid the annual tribute which Ragusa prudently paid to both Serbia and Bosnia to ensure her title, and the expense of the still extant fortifications which she hastily erected to defend it, lest the king should repent of his bargain. He allowed a colony of Saxons to work the silver mines of Novobrdo, and to exercise the trade of charcoal-burners; but a wise regard for his forests led him to limit the number of these relentless woodmen. His guard was composed of Germans, and its captain obtained great influence with him. He guaranteed the privileges of the numerous Greek cities in Macedonia which he had conquered, and endeavoured to secure the support of the natural leaders of the Hellenic element in his composite Empire by including them among the ranks of the nobility. Anxious for information about other, and more civilised, lands than his own, he sent frequent missions to different countries, and sought the hand of a French princess for his son; but this great match was hindered by the difference of religion, and Stephen Uroš V had to content himself with a Wallachian wife. With no Western state were the relations of both Serbia and Bulgaria closer than with Venice. Dušan more than once offered her his aid; she on one occasion accepted his mediation; while John Alexander gave her merchants leave to build a church, and allowed her consul to reside at Varna, whence she could dispute the Black Sea trade with Genoa, whose colony of Kaffa had already brought her into intercourse with Bulgaria. To shew his hospitality to foreigners, Dušan decreed that ambassadors from abroad should receive free meals in each village through which they passed.

Of literary culture there are traces in both the Slav Empires at this period. Dušan, following the example of Stephen Uroš II, the donor of books to the Serbian hospital which he founded at Constantinople, presented the nucleus of a library to Ragusa. John Alexander was, however, a patron of literature on a larger scale. For him was executed the Slav translation of the Chronicle of Constantine Manasses, the copy of which in the Vatican[1] contains coloured portraits: of the Tsar; of his second son, John Asên, lying dead with the Emperor and Empress standing by the bier, and the Patriarch and clergy performing the obsequies; of the boy's reception in heaven; and of the Tsar, this time surrounded by three of his sons. These extremely curious pictures, rougher in design than Byzantine work, are of great value for the

[1] Codice Slavo II.

Bulgarian art and costume of the middle of the fourteenth century, just as the frescoes at Boyana are for those of the thirteenth. Three other treatises of a theological character were copied by order of this same ruler, while his spiritual adviser, St Theodosius of Trnovo, whose life was written in Greek, was the master of a school of literary monks, whose works are the swan-song of the second Bulgarian Empire. Boril, another much earlier Tsar, commanded the translation of a Greek law-book directed against the Bogomiles. But the Serbian sovereigns of the thirteenth and the early fourteenth centuries, more fortunate than their Bulgarian contemporaries, found a biographer in the Archbishop Daniel, whose partiality can only be excused by his dependence upon their bounty, but whose work forms a continuation of the various lives of Nemanja. Of Serbian music the sole contemporary account is from the pen of a Greek, who found the singing of the Easter hymns simply excruciating; but the same author mentions that the Serbs already commemorated the great deeds of their national heroes in those ballads which only attained their full development after the fatal battle of Kossovo. Their best architects came from Cattaro, where was also the Serbian mint in the reigns of both Dušan and his son. It is noticeable that under the former's rival, Stephen Kotromanić, began the series of Bosnian coins, a proof of the growing commercial importance of that third Slav state.

The Serbs look back to the reign of Dušan as the most glorious epoch of their history. But his name is more than a historical memory: it is a political programme. The five centuries and more which have elapsed since his death have seemed but as a watch in the night of Turkish domination to the patriots of Belgrade. They have regarded his conquests as the title-deeds of their race to lands that had long ceased to be theirs, and a Serbian diplomatist has been known to quote him to a practical British statesman, to whom it would never have occurred to claim a large part of France because it had belonged to the Plantagenets in the time of Dušan. But, while the lost Empire of the great Tsar is still a factor in Balkan politics, it must have been evident to those of his contemporaries who were men of foresight that it could not last. Medieval Serbia, like some modern states, was made too fast; at its zenith it comprised five Balkan races—Serbs, Greeks, Albanians, Koutzo-Wallachs, and that aboriginal tribe whose name still survived in Dušan's code in the term *neropch* as a designation for a kind of serf. Of these races, the Greeks were on a higher intellectual plane and were the products of an older civilisation than that of their conquerors, who recognised the fact by imitating the usages of the Greek capital, where Dušan himself passed his boyhood. Moreover, the natural antipathy between the Hellene and the Slav was accentuated by Dušan's creation of a Serbian Patriarchate, a measure which produced similar bitterness to that caused by the erection of the Bulgarian Exarchate in 1870, and which had a similar political object. The Greeks of the Serbian Empire naturally regarded with suspicion and resentment a Tsar who was excommunicated by the Ecumenical Patriarch and who had expelled their priests; and the negotiations of the Serbian government shew the importance which it attached to official Greek recognition of the national Church. The Albanians, again, were first-class fighting men, who then, as now, had little love for the Serbs, from whom they differed in religion, while the hands of the Bogomile heretics were always against the established order in their own country, although they might side with a foreign invader of another faith. Thus, despite Dušan's attempt to enforce theological uniformity, four religious bodies yet further divided the five races of his Empire, and experience has shewn, alike in India and in the Balkans, that such a mixture of nationalities and creeds can only be governed by a foreign race which stands outside them all. The Serbian element, even if united, was not sufficiently numerous to dominate the others, nor did Dušan in all his glory unite the whole Serbo-Croatian nor even the whole Serb stock beneath his sceptre. The one unifying force in the Empire, the monarchy, was weakened by its limitations, which in their turn corresponded with the national traditions and character. Even the strongest of Serbian monarchs was barely equal to the task of suppressing the great nobles, and it was doubtless distrust of the native aristocracy which led him to surround himself with a German guard and to give important posts to foreigners who owed everything to him. While, therefore, Stephen Dušan is justly considered to have been the ablest and most famous of Serbian rulers, the vast Empire which he built up so rapidly was as ephemeral as that of Napoleon. Still, short-lived as was that Serbian hegemony of the Balkan races which was his work, it will be remembered by his countrymen as long as the Eastern Question, in which these historical reminiscences have played such an embarrassing part, continues to perplex the statesmen of Western, and to divide the nationalities of South-Eastern, Europe.

CHAPTER XVIII.

THE BALKAN STATES.

II. THE TURKISH CONQUEST (1355–1483).

THE great Serbian Empire broke into fragments on the death of Dušan. The dying Tsar had made his magnates swear to maintain the rights of his son, then a boy of nineteen. But even the most solemn oaths could not restrain the boundless ambition and the mutual jealousies of those unruly officials. Stephen Uroš V had scarcely been proclaimed when his uncle Simeon Uroš, the viceroy of Acarnania and Aetolia, disputed the succession. Many of the nobles were on the latter's side; the Dowager-Empress, instead of protecting her son's interests, played for her own hand; while the most powerful satraps availed themselves of this family quarrel to establish themselves as independent princes, each in his own part of the country, sending aid to either of the rival Emperors, or remaining neutral, according as it suited their purpose. The civil war in Serbia and the death of Preljub, the Serbian governor of Joánnina and Thessaly, suggested to Nicephorus II, the exiled Despot of Epirus, the idea of recovering his lost dominions. His former subjects received him gladly; he drove Simeon into Macedonia and might have retained his throne, had he not offended the Albanians by deserting his wife in order to marry the sister of the Serbian Empress. An Albanian victory near the town of Achelous in 1358 ended his career and with it the despotat of Epirus. Simeon then returned, and established his authority in reality over Thessaly, in name over Epirus also. Thenceforth, however, he confined his personal attention entirely to the former province, making Trikala his capital and styling himself "Emperor of the Greeks and Serbs," while he assigned Joánnina to his son-in-law Thomas Preljubović, and left the rest of Epirus to two Albanian chieftains, heads of the clans of Boua and Liosa. From that time onward the Serbian possessions in Greece remained separate from the rest of the Empire. Simeon Uroš was succeeded in 1371 by his son John Uroš, who retired from the pomps of Trikala to the famous monastery of Metéoron, where, long after the Turkish conquest of Thessaly in 1393, he died as abbot. At Joánnina Thomas Preljubović, after a tyrannical reign, was assassinated by his bodyguard, and his widow, by marrying a Florentine, ended Serbian rule there in 1386. The four decades of Serbian sway over Thessaly and Epirus in the fourteenth century are now almost forgotten. Its only memorials are an inscription at the Serbian capital of Trikala; the church of the Transfiguration at Metéoron, founded by the pious "King Joseph," as John Uroš was called by his fellow-monks; and perhaps the weird beasts imbedded in the walls of the castle at Joánnina.

The Greek provinces of the Serbian Empire were naturally least attached to Dušan's son. With a certain section of the Serbian nobles John Cantacuzene had always been more popular than the great Tsar himself, and accordingly Voijihna, who held the rank of "Caesar" and governed Drama, invited Matthew Cantacuzene to invade Macedonia, and promised that Seres, which contained the Empress, should be his. Matthew engaged a body of Turkish auxiliaries for this enterprise; but these turbulent irregulars disregarded his orders, and began to attack and plunder his Serbian confederates. The latter retaliated, and Matthew, forced to flee, was captured while hiding among the reeds of the marshes near Philippopolis, and handed over by Voijihna to the Greek Emperor. Seres, meanwhile, continued to be the residence of the Serbian Empress, while from there to the Danube stretched the vast provinces of the brothers John Uglješa and Vukašin, natives of the Herzegovina, of whom the former was marshal, and the latter guardian and cup-bearer, of the young Tsar. Between Seres and the Vardar lay the domain of Bogdan, a doughty warrior whose name is still famous in Serbian ballads. In the Zeta, the cradle of the dynasty, the family of Balša, by some connected with the French house of Baux, by others with the royal blood of Nemanja through the female line, from imperial governors became independent princes, whose territory stretched down to the Adriatic at Budua and Antivari and whose chief residence was Scutari. Various native chiefs held the rest of Albania, most famous among them Carlo Thopia, who in 1368 drove the Angevins, from whom he boasted his descent, out of Durazzo, and whose monument with the French lilies is still to be seen near Elbassan[1]. Finally, Lazar Hrebeljanović, a young noble connected by marriage with the imperial house (according to some he was a natural son of Dušan[2]), administered Mačva on the Hungarian frontier. Central authority there was none save the young and feeble Tsar, a mere figure-head, guided, like Rehoboam of old, by the advice of men as young and inexperienced as himself.

The first result of his weakness was a Hungarian invasion. The two powerful magnates whose provinces adjoined the Danube, Vukašin and Lazar, quarrelled with one another, the latter invoked the aid of the King of Hungary, and a Hungarian army forced the Serbs to retire to the impregnable forests which then covered their mountains. Ragusa,

[1] *Wiss. Mitt.* x. p. 67. [2] Ducas, p. 15.

since 1358 a Hungarian protectorate, was involved in this dispute, with the natural result that Serbian trade suffered. Peace had not long been restored when a revolution broke out in Serbia. Vukašin, a man of boundless ambition and marked ability, was no longer content with the rank of despot, which he had received from his young master, now emancipated from his control. Supported by his brother and a strong party among the nobles, he drove Stephen Uroš V from the throne in 1366, assumed the title of king with the government of the specially Serbian lands whose centre was Prizren, and rewarded Uglješa with the style of "despot" and the Greek districts round Seres, where the latter wisely endeavoured to strengthen his hold upon the Hellenic population in view of the Turkish peril, by restoring to the Ecumenical Patriarch all the churches and privileges which Dušan had transferred to the newly-created Serbian Patriarchate. A later legend makes the usurper complete his act of treachery by the murder of his sovereign during a hunting-party on the plain of Kossovo. But it has now been proved[1] that Stephen Uroš survived his supposed murderer. For the rest of his life, however, he was a mere cypher in the history of his country, glad to accept a present from the Ragusans, who, in spite of his former war with them, alone remained faithful to him and continued to pay him the customary tribute, even suffering losses for his sake.

The Bulgarian Empire was almost as much divided as the Serbian. The Jewish marriage of John Alexander had created bitter enmity between his favourite son, John Shishman, whom he had designed as his successor at Trnovo, and John Sracimir, the surviving offspring of his first wife, to whom he had assigned the family castle of Vidin as an appanage, while on the Black Sea coast an independent prince had established himself and has perpetuated his name, Dobrotich, in the dismal swamps of the Dobrudzha. Thus weakened by internal divisions, Bulgaria was further crippled by the attacks of her Christian neighbours, at a time when all should have united their resources against the Turks. John V Palaeologus invaded the Black Sea coast, and extorted a war indemnity from the Tsar, and when the latter died[2] in 1365 the Hungarians seized Vidin, carried off Sracimir and his wife, and retained possession of that famous fortress for four years. The new Tsar, John Shishman, revenged himself on the Greek Emperor, who had come to ask his aid in repelling the common enemy of Christianity, by throwing him into prison, whence he was only released by the prowess of the famous "green count," Amadeus VI of Savoy. Well might the rhetorician Demetrius Kydónis point out the futility of an alliance with a nation which was so fickle and now so feeble, and which dynastic marriages had failed to bind to Byzantine interests. The Ecumenical Patriarch tried

[1] *Sitzungsberichte der k. böhm. Gesellschaft* (1885), pp. 115, 131, 136–7; *Archiv f. slav. Phil.* II. p. 108.

[2] *Ibid.* XIII. p. 538; XIV. pp. 265–6.

indeed to form a Greco-Serbian league to check the Ottoman advance, but died at the moment when his diplomacy seemed to be successful.

Meanwhile, the Turks were rapidly spreading their sway over Thrace. Demotika, Hadrianople, Philippopolis, marked the progress of their arms; the city of Philip became the residence of the first Beglerbeg of Rumelia, that of Hadrian the capital of the Turkish Empire. In vain the chivalrous Count of Savoy recovered Gallipoli; despite the appeal of Kydónis, that important position was surrendered to the Sultan. One place after another in Bulgaria fell before him; their inhabitants were exempted from taxes on condition that they guarded the baggage of the Turkish army. Popular legends still preserve the memory of the stand made by the imperial family in the neighbourhood of Sofia; the disastrous attempt of the Serbs to repulse the Turks in the valley of the Maritza is one of the landmarks of Balkan history. Alarmed at the progress of the enemy, Vukašin and his brother Uglješa collected a large army of Serbs and Wallachs, which marched as far as Chirmen between Philippopolis and Hadrianople. There, at dawn on 26 September 1371, a greatly inferior Turkish force surprised them; most of the Christians perished in the waters of the river; both the King of Serbia and his brother were slain, and poetic justice made the traitor Vukašin the victim of his own servant. So great was the carnage that the battlefield is still called "the Serbs' destruction." Macedonia was now at the mercy of the conqueror, for the leaders of the people had been killed, and their successors and survivors were compelled to pay tribute and render military service to the Turks. On these ignominious terms "the king's [Vukašin's] son Marko," that greatest hero of South Slavonic poetry, was able to retain Prilep and Skoplje, and his friend Constantine the district round Velbužd, whose modern name of Köstendil contains a reminiscence of the time when the borderland between Bulgaria and Macedonia was still known as "Constantine's country." Even the Bulgarian Tsar could only save himself by promising to follow the Sultan to war and by sending his sister Thamar to Murād's seraglio, where "the white Bulgarian" princess neither forswore her religion nor yet forgot her country.

Two months after the Serbian defeat on the Maritza, Stephen Uroš V died "as Tsar and in his own land," the last legitimate male descendant of the house of Nemanja. The adherents of the national dynasty naturally fixed their eyes at this critical moment upon Lazar Hrebeljanović, who was connected with the imperial family and had led the opposition to Vukašin. Lazar ascended the throne of the greatly diminished Serbian Empire, and either a sense of proportion or his native modesty led him to prefer the style of "Prince" to the title of Tsar which was conferred upon him. But the hegemony of the Southern Slavs now passed from Serbia to Bosnia, whose ruler, Tvrtko, after a long and desperate struggle for the mastery of his own house, had become the leading statesman of the Balkan peninsula. Threatened by Louis the Great of Hungary, who forced him to surrender part of the land of Hum and sought to make him a mere puppet without power; deposed at one moment by his rebellious barons and his ambitious brother, and then restored by Hungarian arms; he was at last able to think of extending his dominions. The moment was favourable to his plans. The King of Hungary was occupied with Poland; the Bosnian nobles were crushed; his brother was an exile at Ragusa; while Lazar was glad to purchase his aid against his own refractory magnates by allowing him to take from them and keep for himself large portions of Serbian territory, which included a strip of the Dalmatian coast from the Cetina to the Bocche di Cattaro and the historic monastery of Mileševo in the district of Novibazar. There in 1376, on the grave of St Sava, Tvrtko had himself crowned with two diadems "King of the Serbs, and of Bosnia, and of the coast." Not a voice was raised against this assumption of the royal authority and of the Serbian title, which he could claim as great-grandson of Stephen Dragutin. All his successors bore it, together with the kingly name of Stephen. Ragusa was the first to recognise him as the rightful wearer of the Serbian crown, and promptly paid him the so-called "Serbian tribute," which the republic had been accustomed to render to the Kings of Serbia on the feast of St Demetrius. Venice followed suit, and the King of Hungary was too busy to protest. Tvrtko proceeded to live up to his new dignities. His court at Sutjeska and Bobovac, where the crown was kept, was organised on the Byzantine model. Rough Bosnian barons held offices with high-sounding Greek names, and the sovereign became the fountain of hereditary honours. Hitherto Bosnian coins had been scarce except some of Stephen Kotromanić, and Ragusan, Hungarian, and Venetian pieces had fulfilled most purposes of trade. But now money, of which many specimens still exist, was minted from the silver of Srebrenica and Olovo, bearing Tvrtko's visored helmet surmounted by a crown of fleur-de-lis with a hop-blossom above it. Married to a princess of the Bulgarian imperial house, representing in his own person both branches of the Serbian stock, Stephen Tvrtko took his new office of king by the grace of God very seriously, for he was animated, as he once wrote, "with the wish to raise up that which is fallen and to restore that which is destroyed."[1]

Tvrtko had gained the great object of all Serbian rulers, medieval and modern—a frontage on the sea. But the flourishing republic of Ragusa interrupted his coast-line, while he coveted the old Serbian city of Cattaro, hidden in the remotest bend of its splendid fiord; both of them were then under Hungarian protection, and the former was too strong to be conquered by one who had no navy. The death of Louis the Great of Hungary in 1382 and the subsequent confusion were his

[1] Miklosich, *Mon. Serb.* p. 187.

opportunity. In the same year he founded the picturesque fortress of Novi, or Castelnuovo, at the entrance of the Bocche, to be the rival of Ragusa and the outlet of all the inland trade, as it is the port of the new Bosnian line. Three years later Cattaro was his. Thus possessed of the fiord which is now a Jugoslav naval station, he sought to make Bosnia a maritime power and thereby conquer the Dalmatian coast-towns. One after another they were about to surrender, and 15 June 1389 had been fixed as the date on which Spalato was to have opened its gates. But when that day arrived, Tvrtko was occupied elsewhere, and the fate of the Southern Slavs for centuries was decided on the field of Kossovo.

The successes of the Turkish arms had thoroughly alarmed the leaders of the Serbian race, for the Turks had been coming nearer and nearer to the peculiarly Serbian lands. In 1382 the divided Bulgarian Empire had lost Sofia, the present capital; in 1386 Niš was taken[1] from the Serbs and Lazar forced to purchase a craven peace by the promise to pay an annual tribute and to furnish a contingent of horsemen to the Sultan. Upon this the Bosnian king made common cause with his Serbian neighbour; a Pan-Serbian league was formed against the Turks, and in 1387 on the banks of the Toplica the allies won a great victory, their first and last, over the dreaded foe. This triumph at once decided the waverers: John Shishman joined the league; Mirčea, the first Prince of Wallachia who received the epithet of "Great," took his share in the defence of the peninsula. Croatians, Albanians, and even Poles and Hungarians, furnished contingents to the army which was intended to save the Balkans for the Balkan peoples. On his side, Murād made long preparations to crush the Christians who had dared to combine against their destined masters.

Bulgaria, being the nearest, received the first blow. The capital of the Tsars offered but a feeble resistance; Shishman, after a stubborn defence of Great Nicopolis between Trnovo and the Danube, obtained peace from the Sultan on condition that he paid his arrears of tribute and ceded the fortress of Silistria. Scarcely had Murād left, when he refused to carry out this humiliating cession; whereupon the Turkish commander captured his castles on the Danube, besieged him again in Great Nicopolis, and forced him a second time to beg for mercy. Murād was long-suffering; he allowed Shishman to retain a throne from which he knew full well that he could remove him at his own good pleasure. Sracimir, too, remained in his "royal city of Vidin" by accepting the suzerainty of the Sultan, instead of signing himself "vassal of the King of Hungary."[2] Having thus disposed of Bulgaria, Murād marched into Old Serbia by way of Köstendil, where his tributary, Constantine, entertained him splendidly and joined his army. Lazar's messenger,

[1] The Serbian is more probable than the Turkish date of 1375.

[2] *Archiv f. slav. Phil.* XVII. pp. 544–7.

the bearer of a haughty message, was sent back with an equally haughty answer. From his capital of Kruševac (for the Serbian royal residence had receded within the recent limits of the modern kingdom) Lazar set out attended by all his paladins to do battle on the field of Kossovo.

The armies met on 15 June 1389. Seven nationalities composed that of the Christians; at least one Christian vassal helped to swell the smaller forces of the Turks. While Murād was arraying himself for the fight, a noble Serb, Miloš Kobilić, presented himself as a deserter and begged to have speech of the Sultan, for whose ear he had important information. His request was granted, he entered the royal tent, and stabbed Murād to the heart, paying with his own life for this act of daring and thereby gaining immortality in Serbian poetry. Though deprived of their sovereign, the Turks, with the perfect discipline once characteristic of their armies on the field of battle, went into action without dismay. At first the Bosniaks under Vlatko Hranić drove back one of the Turkish wings; but Bāyazīd I, the young Sultan, held his own on the other, and threw the Christians into disorder. A rumour of treachery increased their confusion; whether truly or no,[1] it is still the popular tradition that Vuk Branković, Lazar's son-in-law, betrayed the Serbian cause at Kossovo. Lazar was taken prisoner, and slain in the tent where the dying Murād lay, and Bāyazīd secured the succession to his father's throne by ordering his brother to be strangled, thus completing the horrors of that fatal day.

At first Christendom believed that the Turks had been defeated; a *Te Deum* was sung in Paris to the God of battles, and Florence wrote to congratulate Tvrtko on the supposed victory, to which his Bosniaks had contributed. But Lazar's widow Milica, as the ballad so beautifully tells the tale, soon learnt the truth in her "white palace" at Kruševac from the crows that had hovered over the battlefield. The name of Kossovo polje ("the plain of blackbirds") is still remembered throughout the Serbian lands as if the fight had been fought but yesterday. Every year the sad anniversary is solemnly kept, and in token of mourning for that great national calamity (the Waterloo of the Serbian Empire) the Montenegrins still wear a black band on their caps. Murād's heart is still preserved on the spot where he died; Lazar's shroud is still treasured by the Hungarian Serbs in the monastery of Vrdnik; and in many a lonely village the minstrel sings to the sound of the *gusle* the melancholy legend of Kossovo. Kumanovo, 523 years later, avenged that day.

[1] The other versions are that Murād was killed by a wounded Serb on the field, and Lazar in the battle. Stanojević (*Archiv*, xviii. p. 416 *n.* 1) and Jireček (*Gesch. d. Serben*, ii. i, 122) deny the tradition, universal since 1601, of Branković's treachery. *Cf.* Ducas, pp. 15–7; Chalcocondyles, pp. 53–9, 327; Saʿd-ad-Dīn, i. pp. 152–5; Makuscev, *Monumenta*, i. p. 528 (a contemporary document, which makes 12 Serbs force their way to Murād's tent). The form "Kobilić," which appears in the Italian version of Ducas (p. 353), was altered in the eighteenth century to "Obilić," because "Kobilić" (*i.e.* "son of a brood-mare") seemed inelegant.

The Serbian Empire had fallen, but a diminished Serbian principality lingered on for another 70 years. Bāyazīd I recognised Stephen Lazarević, the late ruler's eldest son, a lad not yet of age, on condition that he paid tribute, came every year with a contingent to join the Turkish troops, and gave him the hand of his youngest sister. The Sultan then withdrew, leaving the Serbs weakened and divided. Vuk Branković, likewise his vassal, held the old capital of Priština and styled himself "lord of the Serbs and of the Danubian regions"; the dynasty of Balša ruled over the Zeta. Tvrtko, instead of using this brief respite to concentrate all his energies for the defence of his realm against the Turks, continued his Dalmatian campaign; made himself master of all the coast-towns, except Zara and Ragusa, as well as of some of the islands; and assumed, in 1390, the additional title of "King of Dalmatia and Croatia." The first King of Bosnia had now reached the summit of his power. He had achieved the difficult feat of uniting Serbs and Croats under one sceptre; he had made Bosnia the centre of a great kingdom, which possessed a frontage on the Adriatic from the Quarnero to Cattaro, save for the two enclaves of Zara and Ragusa; he had laid the foundations of a sea-power; and under his auspices Dalmatia, in union with Bosnia, was no longer what she has so often been—"a face without a head." Even thus his ambition was not appeased. He was anxious to conclude a political alliance with Venice, and a matrimonial alliance (for his wife had just died) with the house of Habsburg. Then, on 23 March 1391, he died, without even being able to secure the succession for his son, and the vast power which his country had so rapidly acquired as rapidly waned. The Bosnian kingdom had been made too fast. Its founder had not lived long enough to weld his conquests into an harmonious whole, to combine Catholic Croats with Orthodox Serbs, Bosnian Slavs with the Latin population of the Dalmatian coast-towns, Bogomile heretics with zealous partisans of Rome. The old Slavonic law of succession, which did not recognise the custom of primogeniture, added to these racial and religious difficulties by multiplying candidates to the elective monarchy; and thus foreign princes found an excuse for intervention, and the great barons an excuse for independence. Deprived of all real authority, which lay in the hands of the privy council of nobles, Tvrtko's successors were unable to cope with the Turkish autocracy, while the Kings of Hungary, instead of assisting them, turned their arms against a land which from its geographical position might have been the bulwark of Christendom.

The evil effects of Tvrtko's death were soon felt. His brother, or cousin, Stephen Dabiša, who succeeded him, felt himself too feeble to govern so large a kingdom. The Turks invaded Bosnia; the King of Naples was plotting to obtain Dalmatia and Croatia. Accordingly, at Djakovo in Slavonia, in 1393, Dabiša ceded the two valuable and neighbouring lands, which his brother had so lately won, to King Sigismund of Hungary, who recognised him as King of Bosnia, and to whom he bequeathed the Bosnian crown after his death. A combination of Bosnian magnates and Croatian rebels refused, however, to accept this arrangement, which Dabiša thereupon repudiated. A Hungarian invasion and the capture of the strong fortress of Dobor on the lower Bosna reduced him to submission, and a battle before the walls of Knin in Dalmatia finally severed the brief connexion between that country and the Bosnian crown. On Dabiša's death, in 1395, the royal authority was further weakened by the regency of his widow, Helena Gruba, in the name of his infant son. All power was in the hands of the magnates, who had elected her as their nominal sovereign, but who were practically independent princes in their own domains. One of their number, the Grand-Duke Hrvoje Vukčić, towered above his fellows, and his figure dominates Bosnian history for the next quarter of a century.

Meanwhile the Turks had gained fresh triumphs in the Eastern Balkans. Mirčea of Wallachia, who like his modern representative ruled over the Dobrudzha with the strong fortress of Silistria (a precedent invoked in 1913), was carried off a prisoner to Brūsa and only released on payment of tribute in 1391—the first mention of Wallachia as a tributary province of Turkey. Two years later Bāyazīd resolved to make an end of Bulgaria. On 17 July 1393 Trnovo was taken by storm after a three months' siege; the churches were desecrated, the castle and the palaces were set on fire, the leading nobles were treacherously summoned to a consultation and then butchered; the last Bulgarian Patriarch was stripped of his sacred garb and led to execution on the city wall. At the last moment, however, a miracle (so runs the legend) arrested the headsman's arm; the Patriarch's life was spared; and he lived to conduct a band of sorrowful exiles across the Balkans, where he was ordered to bid his flock farewell. Their path led to Asia Minor, his to Macedonia, where he ended his days; the Bulgarian national Church was suppressed, and from 1394 to 1870 Bulgaria remained under the ecclesiastical jurisdiction of the Ecumenical Patriarch. Thus alike in politics and religion the Bulgars became the slaves of foreigners; the Turks governed their bodies, the Greeks ministered to their souls. It is no wonder that many abjured their faith in order to reap the advantages of the Turkish colony which settled on the castle hill among the blackened walls of the imperial palaces, and offered up prayer in the mosque that had once been the church of the Forty Martyrs, over the graves of the Bulgarian Tsars.

John Shishman had been absent when his capital fell, but he did not long survive its fall. Local tradition connects his death with the mound which still bears his name near Samokov, where seven fountains mark the successive bounds of his severed head. A Bulgarian chronicle[1] states, however, that Bāyazīd killed the captive Tsar on 3 June 1395. One of his sons became a Musulman; another settled in Hungary;

[1] *Archiv f. slav. Phil.* XIII. p. 539.

while Sracimir was allowed to linger as a Turkish vassal in his palace at Vidin—the last remnant of the Bulgarian Empire.

Bāyazīd's next object was to crush Mirčea. Followed by his unwilling Serbian dependents, "the king's son, Marko," and Constantine, he invaded Wallachia, and at Rovine on 10 October 1394 gained a victory with heavy loss of life. Marko Kraljević had said to his friend Constantine that he prayed that the Christians might win and that he himself might fall among the first victims of their swords. Half the prayer was heard; the two comrades perished in the battle. Mirčea fled to Sigismund of Hungary, who restored him to his throne and prepared to recover Bulgaria, which he had demanded from the Sultan as an ancient possession of the Hungarian crown. Bāyazīd's reply was to lead the envoy into his arsenal, and there to shew him hanging on the walls the weapons that were the Turkish title-deeds of Bulgaria.

Sigismund assembled an army of many nationalities, which was to drive the Turk from Europe and revive the memory of the Crusades. The first act of his soldiers in the Balkan peninsula was to attack the Christian vassals of the Sultan, to plunder the Serbs, and to force Sracimir of Vidin to acknowledge for the second time the Hungarian suzerainty. Nicopolis on the Danube[1] resisted for 15 days, until Bāyazīd had time to come up. There, on 25 September 1396, a great battle was fought which sealed the fate of this brilliant but ill-planned expedition. The rashness of the proud French chivalry, the retreat of the Wallachian prince, and the strategy of the Sultan, were responsible for the overwhelming defeat of the Christians, while it was reserved for Stephen Lazarević and his 15,000 Serbs[2], at a critical moment, to strike the decisive blow for the Turks. Immediately after the battle, or at most two years later, the victor ended the last vestige of the Bulgarian Empire at Vidin, and the whole of Bulgaria became for nearly five centuries a Turkish province. The last Tsar's son, like Constantine "the Philosopher" and other Bulgarian men of letters (for the Empress Anne of Vidin had patronised learning[3]), found a refuge at the court of the literary Serbian prince, whose hospitality Constantine repaid by writing the biography which is so valuable a record of this period. Unfortunately South Slavonic literature only began to flourish when the Balkan States were already either dead or dying.

Stephen Lazarević was well aware that he only existed upon the sufferance of the Sultan, and for the first thirteen years of his long reign he thought it prudent to follow a Turcophil policy, even at the cost of his own race and his own religion. Content with the modest title of "Despot," which he received from the Byzantine Emperor, he aimed at the retention of local autonomy by the strict observance of his

[1] *Archiv f. slav. Phil.* XIII. p. 539, XIV. p. 274.
[2] Schiltberger, *Bondage*, p. 3.
[3] *Archives de l'Orient latin,* II. pp. 389–90.

promises to his suzerain. Thus every year he accompanied the Turkish troops; in 1398 his soldiers assisted in the first great Turkish invasion of Bosnia; in 1402 he stood by the side of Bāyazīd at the fatal battle of Angora with 5,000 (according to others 10,000) lancers, all clad in armour. When the fortune of the day had already decided against the Sultan, the Serbian horsemen twice cut their way through the Tartar bowmen, whose arrows rebounded from their iron cuirasses. Seeing that all was lost, Stephen in vain urged Bāyazīd to flee; and, when the latter refused to leave the field, the Serbian prince saved the life of the Sultan's eldest son Sulaimān, and escaped with him to Brūsa. There the Sultan's Serbian wife, whose hand had been the price of Serbian autonomy thirteen years before, fell into the power of Tamerlane. The brutal Mongol, flushed with his victory, insulted both his captives by compelling the Serbian Sultana to pour out his wine in the presence of her husband, no longer "the Thunderbolt" of Islām.

The Turkish defeat at Angora and the civil war between the sons of Bāyazīd which followed it, removed for a time the danger which threatened the Christian states of the Balkan peninsula. It was now the policy of the Serbian Despot to play off one Turkish pretender against another. At first he supported Sulaimān, who had been proclaimed Sultan at Hadrianople; then, like Mirčea of Wallachia, he espoused the cause of Mūsà, only, however, to desert him at a critical moment. But Stephen was not the only Serb who sought to profit by the rivalry of the Turkish claimants. George Branković, the son of the traditional traitor of Kossovo, had succeeded his father in 1398, and, no longer content with the lordship of Priština, had assumed the style of "Prince of Serbia." Branković undermined Stephen's influence at the court of Sulaimān, who despatched him with a Turkish force to make good his pretensions. A second battle on the fatal field of Kossovo, fought on 21 November 1403, resulted in so uncertain a victory for either side that Branković and Stephen concluded peace. The two relatives were temporarily reconciled; Branković contented himself with his paternal heritage and the expectation that one day he might succeed the childless Stephen; Sulaimān was occupied by the civil war in Asia, and sorely-tried Serbia enjoyed, under her benevolent despot, a period of peace, while an attempt of the late Tsar's sons to raise a revolt in Bulgaria failed.

Stephen Lazarević, secure against Turkish and domestic intrigue, devoted his energies to the organisation of his country and the patronage of literature. We are told that he appointed a species of Cabinet, with which he was wont to discuss affairs of state; a second class of officials meanwhile attended in an outer room to receive the orders of his ministers; while a third set of functionaries waited in an ante-chamber to carry them out. Imaginative writers have seen in these arrangements the germs of parliamentary government; but the description rather suggests an elaborate system of bureaucracy. He obtained Belgrade from the Hungarians by diplomacy in 1404, fortified it, and adorned it with churches. But his most celebrated religious foundation was the monastery of Manassia, still one of the glories of Serbia. His own inclinations were in the direction of a monastic life, and he converted his court into an abode of puritanical dullness, whence music and mirth were banished and where literature was the sole relaxation of the pious diplomatist who sat on the throne. Himself an author, he possessed a rich library, and he strove to increase it by the translations of Greek books which were made by his orders. Thus for five years the land had rest.

Serbia had again and again suffered from the quarrels of the reigning family; and even when it should have united to consolidate the state against the inevitable Turkish revival, a fresh pretender arose in the person of Stephen's next brother Vuk, who demanded half of the country as his share and appeared at the head of a Turkish army to enforce his demand. Stephen was compelled to retire to the strong frontier-fortress of Belgrade, and to purchase domestic peace by ceding the south of Serbia to his brother, under Turkish suzerainty, in 1409. Fortunately for the national unity, Vuk did not long survive this arrangement. Summoned to assist Mūsà in the civil war which still divided the Turkish Empire, he played the part of traitor, after the fashion of the day, thinking thereby to obtain the whole of Serbia from the gratitude of Sulaimān. But on his way to seize his reward, he fell into the hands of the Sultan whom he had betrayed. Mūsà sent him and the youngest of the three Lazarević brothers to the scaffold; but, with characteristic diplomacy, he spared the life of George Branković, who had shared the treachery of the others, in order that Stephen might still have a rival, and the Turks an ally, in his own household. Branković at first acted as the Sultan had anticipated, and the latter, at last triumphant over Sulaimān in 1410, invaded Serbia. In order to strike terror into the hearts of the Serbs, the barbarous invader butchered the entire garrison of three castles, and then ordered his meal to be spread upon their reeking corpses. Acts of this kind made Branković revolt from contact with such a monster. He abandoned the camp of Mūsà, was reconciled with Stephen, and thenceforth regarded his uncle as a father whose crown he would one day inherit. Together they aided Mahomet I, the most powerful of the Turkish claimants, to overthrow his brother. At the battle of Chamorlú near Samokov, on 10 July 1413, the fate of the Turkish Empire and with it that of the Balkan Slavs was decided. It was the lot of the two Serbian rulers, Stephen Lazarević and his nephew, to contribute, the one by the assistance of his subjects the other by his personal prowess, on that day to the consolidation of the Ottoman power, and thus inadvertently to prepare the way for the complete conquest of their country later on. Stephen, to whom some have assigned the command of the left wing, is known to have returned home before the battle[1]; but Branković dealt Mūsà the blow which caused him to flee from the field. The conqueror rewarded the Despot of Serbia with an increase of territory, and assured his envoys of his pacific intentions. Mahomet I was as good as his word; for the rest of his reign Serbia remained unmolested. Nor did his warlike successor Murād II attack that country as long as the diplomatic despot lived.

Another, and a Western, Power had now, however, obtained a footing in Serbian lands, thus exciting the protests of the despot in his later years. We saw that some fifty years earlier the family of Balša had established itself in the Zeta, where it had formed an independent state, the germ of the heroic principality of Montenegro, with Scutari as its capital. In 1396, however, George II Balša, hard pressed by the Turks, who had already once captured his residence, sold Scutari with its famous fortress of Rosafa, whose legendary foundation is enshrined in one of the most beautiful Serbian ballads and whose name recalls the Syrian home of SS. Sergius and Bacchus, together with the neighbouring castle of Drivasto, to the Venetian Republic. Three and four years earlier Venice had obtained possession of Alessio and Durazzo respectively; a few years later she occupied the sea-ports of Dulcigno, Antivari, and Budua; in 1420 the citizens of Cattaro, long anxious for Venetian protection against Balša on the one hand and the Bosnian barons, who had for a generation been their lords, on the other, at last induced her to take compassion upon their city; and that year found Venice mistress of practically all maritime Dalmatia, except where Castelnuovo, Almissa, and the republic of Ragusa formed an enclave in her territory. Finally, when in 1421 the last male representative of the Balša family died, Venice declined to recognise his maternal uncle, the Despot of Serbia, as his heir and cede to him the places which had once belonged to that race. Hostilities broke out, but it was finally agreed that Venice should keep Scutari, Cattaro, and Dulcigno, while Stephen should have Drivasto, Antivari, and Budua. The inhabitants of these three places found, however, that the republic could give them support against the Turks, which the Serbian rulers were unable to furnish. One after the other they begged to share the good-fortune of Cattaro, until at last in 1444 we find them all Venetian colonies[2]. In the same year, the tiny republic of Poljica near Spalato, a "Slavonic San Marino," which had been founded by Bosnian fugitives in 944 and had received Hungarian *bans* from about 1350, placed herself under Venetian overlordship.

When Stephen Lazarević saw his end approaching, he recognised the suzerainty of Hungary over his land, as the only means of securing it from the Turks, and obtained from King Sigismund the formal confirmation of his nephew George Branković as his heir. Then, on 19 July 1427, he died, the last of his name. His tombstone at

[1] Gelcich and Thallóczy, *Diplomatarium*, p. 226.

[2] *Mon. spect. hist. Slav. Merid.* XVII. p. 249; XXI. pp. 156–7, 190.

Drvenglave has survived the ravages of the foes whom he had seen divided, but whose power he had unwittingly helped to consolidate; his life is better known than that of far greater Serbian sovereigns, thanks to the fact that he found a biographer among his contemporaries. If, with pardonable exaggeration, the Ragusans[1] wrote of the just-departed despot as "the hammer and bulwark against the enemies of the Christian faith," modern research has shewn him to have been a stronger character than earlier historians had believed.

Meanwhile, the other surviving Slav state of the Balkan peninsula had suffered more than Serbia from the Turks without and also from a civil war within. The great Turkish invasion of 1398, which had "almost entirely ruined Bosnia," had convinced the Bosnian magnates that a woman was unfit to rule over their land. Headed by Hrvoje Vukčić, the king-maker of Bosnian history, they accordingly deposed Helena Gruba and elected Stephen Ostoja, probably an illegitimate son of the great Tvrtko, as their king. As long as Ostoja obeyed the dictates of his all-powerful vassal, who proudly styled himself "the grand *voïvode* of the Bosnian kingdom and vicar-general of the most gracious sovereigns King Ladislas and King Ostoja," he kept his throne. Under Hrvoje's guidance he repulsed the attack of King Sigismund of Hungary, who had claimed the overlordship of Bosnia in accordance with the treaty of Djakovo, and endeavoured to recover Dalmatia and Croatia for the Bosnian crown under the pretext of supporting Sigismund's rival, Ladislas of Naples. But when the latter shewed by his coronation at Zara as King of both those lands that he had no intention of allowing them to become Bosnian possessions, Ostoja changed his policy, made his peace with Sigismund, and recognised him as his suzerain. The puppet-king had, however, forgotten his maker. Hrvoje, the "Bosnian kinglet," aided by the Ragusans, laid siege to the royal castle of Bobovac, where the king was residing; and, when Sigismund intervened on behalf of his vassal, summoned an assembly of the nobles in 1404 to depose Ostoja and choose a new sovereign. The assembled barons unanimously voted the expulsion of Ostoja, and elected Tvrtko's legitimate son, who had been passed over thirteen years before, under the title of Tvrtko II. All real authority, however, lay as before in the hands of Hrvoje, whom the grateful Ladislas had created Duke of Spalato and lord of Cattaro, whom Sigismund regarded as his "chief rival," whom a modern historian[2] has described as "the most powerful man between the Save and the Adriatic," and to whom the shrewd Ragusans wrote that "whatsoever thou dost command in Bosnia is done."[3]

A Hungarian invasion and a civil war followed the election of

[1] Gelcich and Thallóczy, *Diplomatarium*, p. 325.
[2] Klaić, *Geschichte Bosniens*, p. 294.
[3] Pucić, *Spomenici srpski*, I. p. 59.

Tvrtko II, for Sigismund was resolved to restore his influence, while Ostoja still held out in Bobovac. After a first futile attempt, the Magyar monarch entered Bosnia in 1408; once again the walls of Dobor witnessed a Hungarian victory; the yellow waters of the Bosna were reddened by the headless corpses of more than a hundred Bosnian nobles, and Tvrtko II was led a prisoner to Buda. Hrvoje humbled himself before the victor, and Ladislas of Naples sold all his Dalmatian rights to Venice in despair. But Sigismund's schemes for extending Hungarian authority over Bosnia encountered the stubborn resistance of the national party, whose leaders came from the land of Hum, the cradle of so many insurrections against the foreigner. They restored Ostoja to the throne, and in their own stony country and in the south of Bosnia their candidate held out against the Hungarian sovereign, who dismembered the rest of the kingdom, and even bestowed Srebrenica, its most important mining-district, upon the Despot of Serbia, thus sowing discord between the two kindred peoples. Law and order ceased; members of the royal family took to highway robbery, and the Ragusans complained that even among the heathen Turks their traders met with less harm than in Christian Bosnia. The climax was reached when Sigismund, occupied with the religious quarrels of Western Europe, released Tvrtko in 1415, and sent him with a Hungarian army to recover the Bosnian crown. Hard pressed by this formidable combination (for Tvrtko's was a name to conjure with) his rival and Hrvoje, who had now rallied to Ostoja, committed the fatal mistake of summoning the Turks to their aid, thus setting an example which ultimately caused the ruin of Bosnia. The immediate result of this policy was, indeed, successful; the Magyars were routed, but the victors could not rid themselves of their Turkish allies so easily. In the very next year Mahomet I appointed his general Isaac governor of the district of Vrhbosna, which took its name from the "sources of the Bosna," and occupied the heart of the country. From the like-named castle, on the site of the present fortress of Sarajevo, the low-born Turkish viceroy could dominate the plain at his feet and confirm great Bosnian nobles in their fiefs by the grace of his, and their, master, the Sultan.

The joint authors of this Turkish occupation did not long survive the evil which they had inflicted on their country. In the same year that saw the Turkish garrison installed in Vrhbosna Hrvoje died. No Balkan noble is better known to us than this remarkable man. An ancient missal has preserved for us his features, and we are told of his gruff voice and rough manners which so greatly disgusted the courteous magnates of Hungary. The coins which he struck for his duchy of Spalato have survived, and the loveliest town in all Bosnia, the fairy-like Jajce ("the egg" of the Southern Slavs) will ever be connected with his name. There, on the egg-shaped hill above the magnificent waterfall, he had bidden an Italian architect build him a castle on the model of the famous Castel dell' Uovo at Naples, and there he dug out those catacombs which still bear his arms and were intended to serve as his family vault[1]. But the influence of this Bosnian king-maker perished with him; his widow became the wife of Ostoja, who, two years later, died himself; another great noble, the grand *voïvode* Sandalj Hranić of the house of Kosača, once Hrvoje's most formidable rival, for nearly two decades wielded from his stronghold in the land of Hum the predominant authority over the south. He did not scruple, during the brief reign of Ostoja's feeble son and successor, Stephen Ostojić, to increase his estates by the aid of the Turkish garrison in Vrhbosna. Fortunately the death of "king" Isaac on a Hungarian raid ended for the moment the Turkish occupation. Stephen Ostojić did not, however, long profit by the liberation of his country from this terrible foe. Tvrtko II, who had disputed the throne with Ostoja, now once more arose to wrest it from Ostoja's son. His attempt succeeded; in 1421 Ostojić is heard of for the last time. Tvrtko II wore again the crown of his father, a crown which had, however, just lost that bright jewel which the first Tvrtko had added to it, the city of Cattaro and its splendid fiord. Only the "new castle" which the great king had built to command the mouth still remained in Bosnian hands, the powerful hands of Sandalj Hranić, and survived in those of his successors the downfall of the kingdom itself.

Wallachia, like Bosnia, had suffered from the armies of Mahomet I. After the defeat of Mūsà, the victorious Sultan sent an army to ravage the land of Mirčea, who had previously sheltered his rival, and Mirčea was forced to purchase peace by the promise of a tribute. The spirit of the Wallachian ruler chafed, however, at this fresh degradation. He welcomed the advent of a self-styled son of Bāyazīd, who claimed the Turkish throne, and supported his claim. The pretender was defeated, and Mirčea paid for his temerity by a fresh Turkish inroad. In order to have a base for future action against Wallachia, Mahomet occupied the two Roumanian towns, Turnu-Severin and Giurgevo. Not long afterwards, in 1418, Mirčea "the Great," as his countrymen call him, died, the first commanding figure in their troubled history. Unfortunately, "the Great" prince had won his crown by the murder of his elder brother, and his crime was now visited upon his heirs and his country. Wallachia was distracted by the civil wars of the rival cousins, who appealed with success to the jealousies of the nobles and to those misguided feelings of local patriotism which tended towards the separation of the smaller western from the larger eastern portion of the principality. In their eagerness to gain the throne, the hostile candidates called in now the Hungarians and now the Turks to their aid, and thus the resources of the country were weakened by almost constant bloodshed. Meanwhile, the sister-principality of Moldavia, after a number of

[1] *Wiss. Mitt.* II. pp. 94–107.

ephemeral reigns, found in Alexander the Good a prince who managed to maintain himself on the throne, albeit under the suzerainty of Poland, for nearly a whole generation. His administration, which lasted from 1401 to 1433, was devoted to the internal organisation of Moldavia and to the development of its resources. He regulated the tariff, prevented the export of the famous Moldave horses, upon which the defence of the country largely depended, established the official hierarchy of the Moldave nobles, and recognised the long-disputed authority of the Ecumenical Patriarch over the Moldavian Church. Hitherto both the Roumanian principalities had, with rare intervals, depended in ecclesiastical matters upon the ancient Church of Ochrida, an arrangement dating from the time of the first Bulgarian Empire, which had had the natural result of introducing Old Slavonic as the language of the Roumanian church services. Even at a time when Ochrida had long ceased to be Bulgarian and a Patriarchate, the jurisdiction of this archiepiscopal see over the distant Roumanian lands beyond the Danube was revived, and the literature of the Church and the official language of the princely chanceries still remained Slav. After Alexander's time the archbishopric of Ochrida recovered its authority, which Wallachia did not shake off till the end of the fifteenth, and Moldavia till the seventeenth century, when the Roumanian language, alike in Church and State, replaced the archaic idiom of the alien Slavs.

While such was the dubious plight of the Latins of the lower Danube, their neighbours, the Serbs, were being driven back upon that river under the pressure of the Turkish advance to the north. Originally a mountainous, and at its zenith a Macedonian state, Serbia under George Branković, except for a few places on the Adriatic, was essentially a Danubian principality, even to a greater degree than was till lately the case. The new despot, a fine, tall man of sixty when he at last succeeded his uncle, was an experienced diplomatist, whose life had been spent in those tortuous political manœuvres which passed in the Near East for the height of statesmanship. But something more than diplomacy was needed to defend the Balkan Christians from the Turks, now that a warlike Sultan in the person of Murād II directed their undivided forces. As soon as Murād had leisure to attend to Serbian affairs, he sent an embassy to the despot, demanding the whole of Serbia for himself, on the pretext that a sister of the late prince had married his father. George saw that his best policy was to "pacify the dragon" by making some concessions, and thus to save at least a portion of his territory[1]. He promised to sever all connexion with Hungary, to pay an annual tribute (not a difficult undertaking for a man of his great wealth), to furnish the usual military contingent to the Sultan's armies, and to give to the latter the hand of his daughter Maria with a dowry of Serbian land. Delay in the performance of this last condition brought upon Branković a Turkish

[1] Ducas, p. 205.

invasion. Kruševac, the residence of Prince Lazar, fell before the invaders, and ceased to be the Serbian capital; and the despot, when he had secured a respite by the betrothal of his daughter, humbly but astutely asked from her all-powerful suitor permission to build a new fortress at Smederevo, or Semendria, on the right bank of the Danube. The site was well chosen; for, if the Sultan was induced to approve of the construction of Semendria as a bulwark against Hungary, the despot could easily escape thence across the river, should his suzerain attack him there. The noble towers and ramparts of George Branković's castle, thenceforth the Serbian capital till the Turkish conquest, still stand by the brink of the great river; the cross of red brick which the master-builder defiantly built into the walls has survived the long centuries of the Crescent's domination; and the coins which the despot minted there commemorate the foundation of this great Danubian stronghold. In our own day, when Serbia feared the Austrian more than the Turk, it was a disadvantage to have the capital on the northern frontier; in the fifteenth century, when the Hungarian was the only hope of safety, it was the best choice. Branković, in order to secure for himself a comfortable refuge beyond the Danube, did not hesitate to hand over Belgrade itself, which his uncle had rendered even stronger than it was by nature, to the King of Hungary in exchange for a goodly list of towns and estates in that sovereign's territory. This act of enlightened selfishness was a sore blow to the Serbian people; it was a bitter humiliation to them to see "the white city" transferred to the authority of a Magyar commander. Nature herself seemed to protest against the cession of Belgrade; thunder rolled over the betrayed fortress; a tempest swept the roofs off the houses; and the citizens wept at the surrender of their homes to the foreigner from beyond the Save. More serious still, Murād was angry that so valuable a position should be in Hungarian hands. For the present, however, he contented himself with sending for his betrothed, who still lingered at her father's court. Branković, who had just received from the Greek Emperor the dignity and the emblems of despot, gave the bride a splendid outfit worthy of a king's daughter. The charms of the Serbian princess captivated the heart of the Sultan; but this matrimonial alliance, from which the Serbs might have expected much, availed nothing against reasons of state. Branković, as a French traveller[1] who visited him said, was "in daily fear of losing Serbia." His only safeguard was the Sultan's belief that tributary states were more profitable to Turkey than annexation.

Murād had not been many months married to the fair Serbian when one of those fanatics so common in Muslim lands accused him of sinning against Allāh by allowing the unbelievers to live in peace. The building of Semendria, so this man insisted, had been not only a crime but a blunder, for it barred the way to the conquest of Hungary and

[1] Bertrandon de la Brocquière, in *Recueil de voyages et de documents*, XII. 209–10.

of Italy beyond it—the ultimate goal of Musulman endeavour, which might be reached by means of the immense riches of the Serbian Despot. Murād listened to this counsel, and sent an ultimatum to his father-in-law, demanding the surrender of Semendria. Branković left his capital in charge of his eldest son Gregory and one of his Greek relatives, and crossed over with his youngest son Lazar into Hungary to obtain assistance. Semendria, strong as were its defences, had, however, provisions for no more than three months, so that before the pedantic bureaucracy of the Magyar army could be put in motion the garrison was compelled to yield. Gregory and his next brother Stephen, who had been forced to accompany Murād to the siege, were blinded at the instigation of the Sultan's fanatical adviser and deported to Asia Minor. From Semendria, where he left a Turkish guard, Murād marched to the rich mining town of Novobrdo, which a Byzantine historian calls "the mother of cities,"[1] and the minerals of which had been rented by the Ragusans for a large sum. Novobrdo was captured, and nearly all Serbia was in 1439 a Turkish province. Her lawful ruler was forced to seek refuge in the maritime towns of Antivari and Budua, which were still Serbian. Even there, however, the long arm of the Sultan menaced him; he fled with his vast treasures to the neighbouring republic of Ragusa, where he hoped to find a shelter on neutral ground. But Murād was still inexorable; he bade the embarrassed republicans banish their guest, and suggested that they might salve their consciences for this breach of hospitality by appropriating the 500,000 ducats which his father-in-law had deposited for safety in their public coffers. The Ragusans boldly refused to tarnish their honour at the Sultan's bidding, but they none the less hinted to their guest that he had better return to Hungary. Warned by this example, his last possessions on, or near, the Adriatic (Budua, Drivasto, and Antivari) sought and obtained from Venice that protection which he could no longer give them. Many noble Serbs settled at Ragusa, and that artistic city owes one of her most treasured relics, the cross of Stephen Uroš II, to this troubled period of South Slavonic history.

Belgrade, however, with its Hungarian garrison, still rose above the Ottoman flood which had swept over the rest of Serbia, and in 1440 Murād accordingly laid siege to it by land and water. The fortress was commanded by a Ragusan and provided with excellent artillery, which wrought such terrible havoc among the besiegers that neither the Turkish flotilla nor the janissaries could prevail against it. After wasting six months before the town, Murād reluctantly raised the siege with the sinister threat that sooner or later "the white city" must be his. It was not till eighty-one years after this first Turkish siege that his threat was accomplished by one of his greatest successors.

A new figure now arose to check for a time the Ottoman advance.

[1] Ducas, p. 209.

John Hunyadi, "the white knight of Wallachia," a Roumanian in the service of Hungary, began his victorious career with his appointment as *voïvode* of Transylvania in 1441. After several preliminary defeats of the Turks on the slopes of the Carpathians and in the neighbourhood of Belgrade, he undertook with King Vladislav I in 1443 a great expedition across Serbia and Bulgaria. Both Pope Eugenius IV and Branković subsidised the undertaking, Vlad "the Devil" of Wallachia joined his countryman, while the exiled despot placed his local knowledge at the disposition of the dashing Roumanians. The Christian army rapidly traversed Serbia, burning Kruševac and Niš on the way, and entered Bulgaria, whose inhabitants received the Polish King of Hungary and the Slavs in his force as brothers. Leaving Sofia behind him, Hunyadi pressed on with his colleagues towards Philippopolis; but he found the pass near Zlatica already occupied by the janissaries whom Murād had assembled, and he had to retreat. On the return march, the despot, who was in command of the rear, was attacked by the Turks at Kunovica near Niš, but the cavalry came to his aid and completely routed his assailants. Murād, dismayed at this first great Hungarian raid across the Danube, and threatened by troubles in Asia, signed, in July 1444, the humiliating peace of Szegedin, which restored to Branković the whole of Serbia and his two blinded sons, on condition of his handing half the revenue of the land as tribute to the Sultan. Bulgaria remained a portion of the Turkish Empire, and the citizens of Sofia, which ten years earlier had been the most flourishing town in the whole country, lamented among the ashes of their ruined houses the vain attempt of the Christians to set them free. Their city, famous for its baths, became the residence of the "Beglerbeg of Rumelia," the viceroy of the Sultan in the Balkans. Wallachia, under Vlad "the Devil," continued to pay tribute to Turkey while acknowledging the suzerainty of Hungary, whose sovereign pledged himself not to cross the Danube against the Turks, just as the Sultan vowed likewise not to cross it against the Magyars. The only real gainer by the campaign of 1443 was George Branković, who received the congratulations of Venice on his fortunate restoration to the throne of Serbia[1]. Honour and policy alike suggested the maintenance of this solemn treaty with the Turks.

But the parchment bond had scarcely been signed when the evil counsels of Cardinal Julian Cesarini, the papal legate, caused the Hungarian monarch to break it. The moment seemed to the statesmanship of the Vatican to have come for driving the Turks out of Europe. Murād was occupied in Asia, and it was thought that the fleets of the Duke of Burgundy and the Pope could prevent his return. In vain Branković argued against this impolitic act of treachery; Hunyadi, the soul of this new crusade, was eager to free Bulgaria in order to revive in his own person the Empire of the Tsars; the legate was ready to

[1] *Mon. spect. hist. Slav. Merid.* xxi. pp. 186–7; Makuscev, ii. pp. 81–4.

absolve Vladislav from the oath which he had so lately sworn. Not without forebodings of his approaching doom, the perjured King of Hungary re-crossed the forbidden river, set fire to Vidin, and, flushed by easy successes gained at the expense of the helpless peasantry whom he had come to liberate, disregarded the warning of the astute *voïvode* of Wallachia and pushed on to the Black Sea. Thus far his expedition had been a triumphal march; but among the gardens and vineyards of Varna, the district which still preserves the name of the former Bulgarian Despot Dobrotich, he suddenly found himself confronted by the Turkish army. Murād had made peace with his enemies in Asia, and, thanks to a strong wind which had prevented the Christian vessels from leaving the Dardanelles, had crossed over to Europe at his ease where the Bosphorus is narrowest, and had reached Varna by forced marches. The battle which decided the fate of this last attempt of Christendom to free Bulgaria was fought on 10 November 1444. It is only a later, if picturesque, legend that Murād displayed before him on a lance his copy of the broken treaty[1], but when night fell the scattered remnant of the Christian army had good cause to lament alike the perjury and the rashness of its leader. At first the prowess of Hunyadi seemed to have broken the Ottoman ranks; but the young king, envious of the laurels of his more experienced commander, insisted on exposing his valuable life at a critical moment. His death was the signal for the defeat of his army; his evil adviser, the cardinal, perished in the carnage; the survivors fled either across the Danube into Wallachia, or westward to the fastnesses of Albania, where Skanderbeg a year earlier had begun to defy the Turks in his native mountains. Hunyadi was treacherously captured by the Wallachian "Devil," whom he had accused of double-dealing during the campaign, but was released on the arrival of a Hungarian ultimatum. Two years later he wreaked his vengeance upon his captor, whom he deprived of both crown and life, restoring the elder branch of the Wallachian princely house to the throne which Mirčea and his descendants had usurped from his brother and his brother's children.

George Branković, wise in his generation, had refused to take part in the expedition which had ended so disastrously at Varna. Like the shrewd diplomatist that he was, he had made his calculations in the event of either a Hungarian or a Turkish victory. In the former case he relied on his money to shelter him from the consequences of his neutrality; against the latter he made provision by sending news of the Christian advance to the Sultan and by barring the road by which Skanderbeg was to have traversed Serbia on his way to join the Christian forces at Varna. He persisted in the same policy of enlightened selfishness when, four years later, Hunyadi again attacked the Turks. On this occasion, too, Branković betrayed the Christian cause by warning Murād

[1] Zinkeisen, I. p. 702, *n.* 3.

of the coming Hungarian invasion, and refused to participate in an expedition which he considered inadequate for the purpose intended. Hunyadi stormed, and vowed vengeance upon him, but once more facts proved the shrewd old Serb to be right. The armies met on the fatal field of Kossovo on 17 October 1448, while the Serbs lurked in the mountain passes which led out of the plain, ready to fall upon and plunder the fugitives. On the first and second days the issue was uncertain; but, when the fight was renewed on the third, the Roumanian contingent, whose leader owed his throne to Hunyadi, deserted in a body to the Turks. Murād, however, suspecting this movement to be a feint, ordered them to be cut to pieces. Nevertheless, their defection demoralised their chivalrous countryman, who fled for his life towards Belgrade. His danger was great, for Branković, anxious to obtain possession of a man whom he hated and whom he could then surrender to the Sultan, had ordered the Serbs to examine and report to the authorities every Hungarian subject whom they met, while the Turks were also on his track. Once, like Marius, he hid himself among the reeds of a marsh; then he narrowly escaped assassination at the hands of two Serbian guides; at last, driven by hunger, he was forced to disclose his identity to a Serbian peasant. The peasant revealed the secret to his brothers, one of the latter reported it to the local governor, and Hunyadi was sent in chains to Semendria. The despot durst not, however, provoke the power of Hungary by refusing to release so distinguished a champion of Christendom, and his captive recovered his freedom by promising to pay a ransom and never to lead an army across Serbia again. Not only did these promises remain unfulfilled, but, as soon as Hunyadi was free, he revenged himself by seizing the Branković estates in Hungary and by devastating Serbian territory.

But the Serbian Despot's armed neutrality while others fought at Varna and Kossovo was not his only crime against the common cause of the Balkan Christians. Despite his years and the imminent Turkish peril, he did not scruple to extend his frontiers at the expense of Bosnia with the Sultan's permission. Tvrtko II had not long enjoyed in peace his restoration to the Bosnian throne. His title was disputed by Radivoj, a bastard son of Ostoja, who summoned Murād II to his aid, and Tvrtko was forced to purchase peace by the cession of several towns to the Sultan, already the real arbiter of Bosnia. In 1433 the puppet king was overthrown by a combination between Branković and the powerful Bosnian magnate, Sandalj Hranić, who paid the Sultan a lump sum for his gracious permission to partition the Bosnian kingdom. The despot thereupon annexed the district of Usora, watered by the lower Bosna, while the grand *voïvode* ruled over the whole of what was soon to be called the Herzegovina, and a part of what is now Montenegro. Hranić might claim to be *de facto*, if not *de jure*, the successor of the great Tvrtko, for the monastery in which the first Bosnian king had been crowned, and the castle which he had built to command the fiord of Cattaro, were both his. But the opposition of the barons hindered, and his death in 1435 ended, his striving after the royal title. His vast territories passed to his nephew, Stephen Vukčić, the last of the three great Bosnian magnates whose commanding figures overshadowed the pigmy wearers of the crown. His land was now regarded as independent of Bosnia; ere long, despite a Bosnian protest, he received, either from the Emperor Frederick III or from the Pope, the title of "Duke of St Sava," which, in its German form of *Herzog*, gave to the Herzegovina its name[1]. Meanwhile, in 1436, a Turkish garrison re-occupied Vrhbosna, and Tvrtko II, who had sought refuge in Hungary, recovered his throne by consenting to pay a tribute of 25,000 ducats to the Sultan. He had not, however, been long re-installed when the Turkish invasion of Serbia up to the gates of Belgrade seemed to forebode the annexation of Bosnia also. In his despair he implored now Venice, now Vladislav I, the Polish King of Hungary, to take compassion upon him. Venice he begged to take over the government of his dominions, Vladislav he urged to succour a land whose people were also Slavs. But the diplomatic republic declined the dangerous honour with complimentary phrases, while Tvrtko did not live long enough to witness the fulfilment of the Hungarian monarch's promise to aid him. In 1443 he was murdered by his subjects, and with him the royal house of Kotromanić became extinct. In his place the magnates elected another bastard son of Ostoja, Stephen Thomas Ostojić, as their king.

Stephen Thomas began his reign by taking a step which had momentous consequences for his kingdom. Although his predecessor had been a Roman Catholic, his own family was, like most of the Bosnian nobles of that time, devoted to the Bogomile heresy, which had come to be regarded as the national religion. The new king came, however, to the conclusion that he would not only enhance his personal prestige at home, diminished by his illegitimate birth and his humble marriage, but would also gain the assistance of the West against the Turks, if he embraced the Roman Catholic faith. But, although he had none of the fervour of a convert from conviction, he soon found that the erection of Roman Catholic churches did not satisfy the zeal of the Franciscans, of his protector Hunyadi, and of the Pope. Accordingly in 1446 an assembly of prelates and barons met at Konjica,

[1] It is usually supposed that Vukčić received the ducal title either from Frederick III in 1448, or from the Pope in 1449, when he turned Roman Catholic, or else from the King of Aragon (*Wiss. Mitt.* III. pp. 503–9; X. p. 103 *n.*; Klaić, p. 382). But he is styled *dux terre Huminis* as early as 23 August 1445 (*Mon. spect. hist. Slav. Merid.* XXI. p. 226), "Duke of St Sava" in a document of 1446 (Farlati, *Illyricum Sacrum*, IV. p. 68), and "Duke" in a dubious inscription of that year (*Wiss. Mitt.* III. p. 502). A less probable theory (*ib.* I. p. 434) derives the name of the Herzegovina from a Turkish word meaning "the land of stones." Thallóczy (*Studien zur Gesch. Bosniens u. Serbiens*, pp. 146–59) thinks that he took the title himself with the connivance of the Porte.

the beautiful town on the borders of the Herzegovina through which the traveller now passes on the railway from Sarajevo to Mostar. It was there decided that the Bogomiles "shall neither build new churches nor restore those that are falling into decay," and that "the goods of the Catholic Church shall never be taken from it."[1] No less than 40,000 of the persecuted sect emigrated to the Herzegovina in consequence of this decree, and found there a refuge beneath the sway of Duke Stephen, who, although he had allowed his daughter Catherine to embrace Catholicism and marry Stephen Thomas, remained himself a Bogomile. Thus, if the King of Bosnia had, by his conversion, gained a divorce from his low-born consort and had become the son-in-law of the powerful magnate whose sovereign he claimed to be, if he had been taken under the protection of the Holy See and had secured the support of the famous Wallachian hero, he had estranged a multitude of his own subjects, whose defection involved him in a war with his heretical father-in-law, and hastened the downfall of Bosnian independence. Moreover, the old Despot of Serbia continued to harass his eastern frontier, so long a source of discord between the two sister-states; while, as if that were not enough, this embarrassed successor of the great Tvrtko must needs try to make good his mighty predecessor's title of "King of Dalmatia and Croatia," regardless of the hard fact that what should have been in theory the natural sea-frontage of his inland kingdom had become a long and practically unbroken line of Venetian colonies. Such was the behaviour of the Balkan leaders when in 1451 their destined conqueror, Mahomet II, ascended the throne.

It was the policy of the new Sultan to humour the Balkan princes until the capture of Constantinople left him free to subdue them one by one. He not only renewed his father's treaty with Serbia, but sent his Serbian stepmother back to her father with every mark of distinction, assigning her sufficient estates to support her in her widowhood. The consequence was that George Branković assisted him to amuse the Hungarians till the capital of the Byzantine Empire fell, and contributed nothing to the defence of those walls which only five years before he had helped to repair[2]. When the fatal news arrived, the wily despot and the terrified King of Bosnia hastened to send envoys to make the best terms that they could with the conqueror. For the moment Mahomet contented himself with a tribute of 12,000 ducats from Serbia; but he had already made up his mind to put an end to the autonomy which that rich and fertile country, the stepping-stone to Hungary and Wallachia, had been permitted to enjoy for the last two generations. In the spring of 1454 he sent an ultimatum to the despot, bidding him, under threat of invasion, surrender at once the former land of Stephen Lazarević, to which he had no right, and promising him in

[1] Farlati, *l.c.*

[2] Inscription on the walls of Constantinople. Miklosich, *Monumenta Serbica*, p. 441.

return the ancestral territory of the Branković family with the city of Sofia. Only twenty-five days were allowed for the receipt of his answer. George was, however, absent in Hungary when the ultimatum reached Semendria, and his crafty officials managed to detain its bearer until they had had time to place the fortresses on a war footing. Before the Sultan could reach the Serbian frontier, Hunyadi had made a dash across the Danube, had penetrated as far as the former Bulgarian capital, and had retired with his plunder beyond the river. Mahomet's main object was the capture of Semendria, the key of Hungary, but that strong castle resisted his attack, and he withdrew to Hadrianople. In the following year he repeated his invasion, and forced Novobrdo to surrender after a vigorous and protracted bombardment. A portion of the inhabitants he left there to work the famous silver mines, which, as his biographer remarks, had not only largely contributed to the former splendour of the Serbian Empire but had also aroused the covetousness of its enemies. Indeed, the picture which Critobulus[1] has drawn of Serbia in her decline might kindle the admiration of her modern statesmen as they read of the "cities many and fair in the interior of the land, the strong forts on the banks of the Danube," the "productive soil," the "swine and cattle and abundant breed of goodly steeds," with which this little Balkan state, so blessed by nature, so cursed by politics, was bountifully endowed. But the "numerous and valiant youths" who had been the pride of the old Serbian armies had been either drafted into the corps of janissaries to fight against their fellow-Christians, or were helpless, in the absence of their aged and fugitive prince, against the artillery of Mahomet. The summer was, however, fast drawing to a close; Serbia gained another brief respite, and George to his surprise obtained peace on the basis of *uti possidetis* and the payment of a smaller tribute for his diminished territory.

In June 1456 Mahomet appeared with a large park of heavy artillery before the gates of Belgrade, boasting that within a fortnight the city should be his. So violent was the bombardment that the noise of the Turkish guns was heard as far off as Szegedin, and the Sultan hoped that all succour from that quarter would be prevented by his fleet, which was stationed in the Danube. But Hunyadi routed the unwieldy Turkish ships, and made his way into the beleaguered town with an army of peasant crusaders, whom the blessing of Calixtus III and the preaching of the fiery Franciscan Capistrano had assembled for this holy war. Enthusiasm compensated for their defective weapons; when the janissaries took the outer city, they not only drove them back, but, headed by the inspired chaplain, charged right up to the mouths of the Turkish cannon; Mahomet himself was wounded in the struggle, and retreated in disorder to Sofia, while the Serbian miners from Novobrdo fell upon his defeated troops. Unfortunately, the pestilence

[1] II. ch. 7.

that broke out in the Hungarian camp and the death of Hunyadi prevented the victors from following up their advantage. Belgrade was saved for Hungary, but the rest of Serbia was doomed. Even at this crisis, the quarrels of the despot and Hunyadi's brother-in-law Szilágyi, the governor of Belgrade, demonstrated the disunion and selfishness of the Christian leaders. The despot, who tried to entrap his enemy, was himself captured; and, although he was released, died not long afterwards on 24 December 1456, of the effect of a wound which he had received in the encounter. His ninety years had been spent in a troublesome time; his character had been rather of the willow than of the oak, and the one principle, if indeed it was not policy, which he consistently maintained, was his refusal to gain the warmer support of the West by abandoning the creed of his fathers and his subjects, as he had abandoned the cause of the other Balkan Christians to keep his own throne.

George Branković had bequeathed the remnant of his principality to his Greek wife Irene and his youngest son Lazar; for his two elder sons, Gregory and Stephen, had been blinded by Murād II. But the new despot chafed at the idea of sharing his diminished inheritance with his mother; indeed, he had refused to ransom his old father from captivity, in order to anticipate by a few months his succession to the throne. The death of Irene occurred at such an opportune moment and under such suspicious circumstances that it was attributed to poison administered by her ambitious son; and his eldest brother and his sister, the widow of the late Sultan, were so greatly alarmed for their own safety that they fled the selfsame day with all their portable property to the court of Mahomet II. That great man treated the fugitives with generosity; they obtained a home near Seres, where the former Sultana became the good angel of the Christians, obtaining through her influence permission for the monks of Rila to transport the remains of their pious founder from Trnovo to the great Bulgarian monastery which bears his name. Lazar III was now sole ruler of Serbia, for his second brother Stephen soon followed the rest of the family into exile, and became a pensioner of the Pope. But he did not long profit by his cruelty. While he allowed the internal affairs of his small state to fall into confusion, he was lax in paying the tribute which he had promised to his suzerain. Mahomet was preparing to attack this weak yet presumptuous vassal, when, on 20 January 1458, the latter died, leaving a widow and three daughters. Before his death, Lazar had provided for the succession by affiancing one of his children to Stephen Tomašević, son and heir of the King of Bosnia—an arrangement which would have united the two Serbian states in the person of the future Bosnian ruler, and seemed to promise a final settlement of the disputes that had latterly divided them.

Three candidates for the Serbian throne now presented themselves,

Stephen Tomašević, a son of Gregory Branković, and Mahomet II. None could doubt which of the three would be ultimately successful; but at first the Bosniak gained ground. In December 1458 King Matthias Corvinus of Hungary in a parliament at Szegedin formally recognised him as Despot of Serbia, that is to say of as much of that country as was not occupied by the Turks. Meanwhile, in order to strengthen herself, as she thought, against the latter, the widowed princess, a daughter of the Despot Thomas Palaeologus, had offered the principality as a fief to the Holy See. The marriage of the Serbian heiress and the Bosnian crown-prince took place; the commandant of Semendria was sent in irons to Hungary; and Stephen Tomašević took up his abode in the capital of George Branković. But the inhabitants of Semendria regarded their new master, a zealous Catholic and a Hungarian nominee, as a worse foe than the Sultan himself. They opened their gates to the Turks; the other Serbian towns followed their example; and, before the summer of 1459 was over, all Serbia, except Belgrade, had become a Turkish pashalik.

The history of medieval Serbia was thus closed; but members of the Branković family continued, with the assent of the kings of Hungary, to bear the title of despot in their Hungarian exile, whither many of their Serbian adherents had followed them and where their house became extinct just 200 years ago. Belgrade was able, in Hungarian hands, to resist repeated Turkish attacks till 1521, while the Serbian Patriarchs did not emigrate from Ipek to Karlovic till 1690. But from the time of Mahomet II to that of Black George in the early years of the nineteenth century, the noblest representatives of the Serbs were to be found fighting for their freedom among the barren rocks of what is now Montenegro.

The kingdom of Bosnia survived by only four years the fall of Serbia. In 1461 Stephen Thomas was slain by his brother Radivoj and his own son Stephen Tomašević, who thus succeeded to the sorry heritage of the Bosnian throne, of which he was to be the last occupant. The new king depicted to Pope Pius II in gloomy but not exaggerated colours the condition of his country, and begged the Holy Father to send him a crown and bid the King of Hungary accompany him to the wars, for so alone could Bosnia be saved. He told how the Turks had built several fortresses in his kingdom, and how they had gained the sympathy of the peasants by their kindness and promises of freedom. He pointed out that Bosnia was not the final goal of Mahomet's vaulting ambition; that Hungary and the Dalmatian possessions of Venice would be the next step, whence by way of Carniola and Istria he would march into Italy and perhaps to Rome. To this urgent appeal the Pope replied by sending his legates to crown him king. The coronation took place in the picturesque town of Jajce, Hrvoje's ancient seat, whither the new sovereign had transferred his residence from

Bobovac for greater security. The splendour of that day, the first and last occasion when a Bosnian king received his crown from Rome, and the absolute unanimity of the great nobles in support of their lord (for on the advice of Venice he had made peace with the Duke of St Sava, whose son was among the throng round the throne) cast a final ray of light over this concluding page of Bosnia's history as a kingdom. Stephen Tomašević assumed all the pompous titles of his predecessors—the sovereignty of Serbia, Bosnia, the land of Hum, Dalmatia, and Croatia—at a time when Serbia was a Turkish pashalik, when a Turkish governor ruled over the "Bosnian province" of Foča, and when the self-styled "King of Dalmatia" was imploring the Venetians to give him a place of refuge on the Dalmatian coast! There was still, too, one Christian enemy whom he had not appeased. The King of Hungary had never forgiven the surrender of Semendria, and had never forgotten the ancient Hungarian claim to the overlordship of Bosnia. He resented the Pope's recognition of Stephen Tomašević as an independent sovereign, and was only appeased by pecuniary and territorial concessions, and by a promise that the King of Bosnia would pay no more tribute to the Sultan. This last condition sealed the Bosniak's fate.

When Mahomet II learnt that Tomašević had promised to refuse the customary tribute, he sent an envoy to demand payment. The Bosnian monarch took the envoy into his treasury, and shewed him the money collected for the tribute, telling him, however, at the same time that he was not anxious to send the Sultan so much treasure. "For in case of war with your master," he argued, "I should be better prepared if I have money; and, if I must flee to another land, I shall live more pleasantly by means thereof."[1] The envoy reported to Mahomet what the king had said, and Mahomet resolved to punish this breach of faith. In the spring of 1463 he assembled a great army at Hadrianople for the conquest of Bosnia. Alarmed at the result of his own defiant refusal, Tomašević sent an embassy at the eleventh hour to ask for a fifteen years' truce. Michael Konstantinović, a Serbian renegade, who was an eye-witness of these events, has preserved the striking scene of Mahomet's deceit. Concealed behind a money-chest in the Turkish treasury, he heard the Sultan's two chief advisers decide upon the plan of campaign: to grant the truce and then forthwith march against Bosnia, before the King of Hungary and the Croats could come to the aid of that notoriously difficult and mountainous country. Their advice was taken; the Bosnian envoys were deceived; and even when the eavesdropper warned them that the Turkish army would follow on their heels, they still believed the word of the Sultan. Four days after their departure Mahomet set out. Ordering the Pasha of Serbia to prevent the King of Hungary from effecting a junction with the Bosniaks, he marched with such rapidity and secrecy that he found the Bosnian

[1] Laónikos Chalcocondyles, p. 532.

frontier undefended and met with little or no resistance until he reached the ancient castle of Bobovac. The fate of the old royal residence was typical of that of the land. Its governor, Prince Radak, a Bogomile forcibly converted to Catholicism, could have defended the fortress for years if his heart had been in the cause. But, like so many of his countrymen, he was a Bogomile first and a Bosniak afterwards. On the third day of the siege he opened the gates to Mahomet, who found among the inmates the two envoys whom he had so lately duped. Radak met with the fitting reward of his treachery, for when he claimed his price the Sultan ordered him to be beheaded. The giant cliff of Radakovica served as the scaffold, and still preserves the name, of the traitor of Bobovac.

At the news of Mahomet's invasion, Stephen Tomašević had withdrawn with his family to his capital of Jajce, hoping to raise an army and get help from abroad while the invader was expending his strength before the strong walls of Bobovac. But its surrender left him no time for defence. He fled at once towards Croatia, closely pursued by the van of the Turkish army. At the fortress of Ključ (one of the "keys" of Bosnia) the pursuers came up with the fugitive, whose presence inside was betrayed to them. Their commander promised the king in writing that if he surrendered his life should be spared, whereupon Tomašević gave himself up, and was brought as a prisoner to the Sultan at Jajce. Meanwhile, the capital had thrown itself upon the mercy of the conqueror, and thus, almost without a blow, the three strongest places in Bosnia had fallen. The wretched king himself helped the Sultan to complete his conquest. He wrote, at his captor's dictation, letters to all his captains, bidding them surrender their towns and fortresses to the Turks. In a week more than seventy obeyed his commands, and before the middle of June 1463 Bosnia was practically a Turkish pashalik, and Mahomet, with the captive king in his train, was able to set out for the subjugation of the Herzegovina. But the Turkish cavalry was useless against the bare limestone rocks on which the castles were perched, while the natives, accustomed to every cranny of the crags, harassed the strangers with a ceaseless guerrilla warfare. The duke and his son Vladislav, who only a few months before had intrigued with the Sultan against his own father, now fought side by side against the common foe, and Mahomet, after a fruitless attempt to capture the ducal capital of Blagaj, withdrew to Constantinople. But before he left he resolved to rid himself of the King of Bosnia, who could be of no further use and might be a danger. It was true that the Sultan's lieutenant had promised to spare the prisoner's life; but a learned Persian was found to pronounce the pardon to be invalid because it had been granted without Mahomet's previous consent. The trembling captive, with his written pardon in his hands, was summoned to the presence, whereupon the lithe Persian drew his sword and cut off Tomašević's head. The body of the last

King of Bosnia was buried by the Sultan's orders at a spot on the right bank of the river Vrbas only just visible from the citadel of Jajce, where, in 1888, the skeleton was discovered, the skull severed from the trunk. The remains of the ill-fated monarch are now to be seen in the Franciscan church there, his portrait adorns the Franciscan monastery of Sutjeska, but the *fetva*, which was carved on the city gate of Jajce to excuse the Sultan's breach of faith by representing his victim as a traitor ("the true believer will not allow a snake to bite him twice from the same hole") vanished some seventy years ago. The king's uncle Radivoj and his cousin were executed after him; his two half-brothers were carried off as captives; and his widow Maria became the wife of a Turkish official[1]. But his stepmother Catherine escaped to Ragusa and Rome, where she received a pension from the Pope. There, in the midst of a little colony of faithful Bosniaks, she died on 25 October 1478, after bequeathing her kingdom to the Holy See, unless her two children, who had become converts to Islām, should return to the Catholic faith. A monument with a dubious Latin inscription in the church of Ara Coeli and a fresco in the Santo Spirito hospital still preserve the memory of the Bosnian queen, far from the last resting-place of her husband by the banks of the Trstivnica.

Even although Bosnia had fallen, the Turks were not allowed undisturbed possession. In the same autumn the King of Hungary entered Bosnia from the north, while Duke Stephen's son Vladislav attacked the Turkish garrisons in the south. Before winter had begun Matthias Corvinus was master of Jajce, and even the return of Mahomet in the following spring failed to secure its second surrender. Such was the terror of the Hungarian king's arms that the mere report of his approach made the Sultan raise the siege. Matthias Corvinus then organised the part of Bosnia which he had conquered from the Turks into two provinces, or *banats*, one of which took its name from Jajce, and the other from Srebrenik. Over these territories, which embraced all lower Bosnia, he placed Nicholas of Ilok, a Hungarian magnate, with the title of king, not however borne by his successors[2]. Under Hungarian rule, these two Bosnian *banats* remained free from the Turks till 1528 and 1520 respectively—serving as a buffer-state between the Ottoman Empire and the Christian lands of Croatia and Slavonia.

The Herzegovina, which had repulsed the conqueror of Bosnia, did not long maintain its independence. The great Duke Stephen Vukčić, after losing nearly all his land in another Turkish invasion caused by the aid he had given in the recovery of Jajce, died in 1466, leaving all his possessions to be divided equally between his three sons, Vladislav, Vlatko, and Stephen[3]. The eldest, however, whose quarrels with his

[1] Hopf, *Chroniques*, p. 333; *Historia Politica*, p. 83; *Wiss. Mitt.* III. p. 384.
[2] Makuscev, II. p. 95.
[3] *Ibid.* II. p. 104; Hopf, *Chroniques*, pp. 333, 335.

father had wrought such infinite harm to his country, did not long govern the upper part of the Herzegovina which fell to his share; he entered the Venetian service, and thence emigrated to Hungary where he died. Accordingly, the second brother, Vlatko, assumed the title of Duke of St Sava, and re-united for a time all his father's estates under his sole rule, relying now on Venetian and now on Neapolitan aid, but only secure as long as Mahomet II allowed him to linger on as a tributary of Turkey. In 1481 he even ventured to invade Bosnia, but was driven back to seek shelter in his strong castle of Castelnuovo. Two years later Bāyazīd II annexed the Herzegovina, whose last reigning duke died in the Dalmatian island of Arbe. The title continued, however, to be borne as late as 1511 by Vladislav's son Balša[1]. Stephen, the youngest of old Duke Stephen's three sons, had a far more remarkable career. Sent while still a child as a hostage to Constantinople, he embraced the creed and entered the service of the conqueror. Under the name of Aḥmad Pasha Hercegović, or "the Duke's son," he gained a great place in Turkish history, and, after having governed Anatolia and commanded the Ottoman fleet, attained to the post of Grand Vizier. His name and origin are still preserved by the little town of Hersek, on the Gulf of Izmid, near which, far from the strong duchy of his father, he found a grave.

The fall of the Bosnian kingdom is full of meaning for our own time. The country is naturally strong, and under the resolute government of one man, uniting all creeds and classes under his banner, might have held out like Montenegro against the Turkish armies. But the jealousies of the too powerful nobles who overshadowed the elective monarchy, and the still fiercer rivalries of the Roman Catholics and the Bogomiles, prepared the way for the invader, and when he came the persecuted heretics welcomed him as a deliverer, preferring "the mufti's turban to the cardinal's hat." Most of the Bogomiles embraced Islām, and became in the course of generations more fanatical than the Turks themselves; they had preferred to be conquered by the Sultan rather than converted by the Pope; and, when once they had been conquered, they did not hesitate to be converted also. The Musulman creed possessed not a few points of resemblance with their own despised heresy, while it conferred upon those who embraced it the practical advantage of retaining their lands and their feudal privileges. Thus Bosnia, in striking contrast to Serbia, presents us with the curious phenomenon of an aristocratic caste, Slav by race yet Muslim by religion, whose members were the permanent repositories of power, while the Sultan's viceroy in his residencies of Vrhbosna, Banjaluka, or Travnik, was, with rare exceptions, a mere fleeting figure, here to-day and gone to-morrow. In fact, Bosnia remained under the Turks what she had been in the days of her kings, an aristocratic republic with a titular

[1] Orbini, *Il regno degli Slavi*, p. 388; *Mon. spect. hist. Slav. Merid.* VI. pp. 114, 126.

head, who was thenceforth a foreigner instead of a native; while the Bosnian *beys* were in many cases the descendants of these medieval nobles who had lived in feudal state within their grey castle walls, whose rare intervals of leisure from the fierce joys of civil war were soothed by the music of the piper and amused by the skill of the *jongleur*, and who, unlike the rougher magnates of the more primitive Serbian court, received some varnish of western civilisation from their position as honorary citizens and honoured guests of Ragusa, "the South-Slavonic Athens." But, besides these converted Bogomiles, there remained in the midst of Orthodox Serbs and Catholic Croats some who adhered to the ancient doctrines of that maligned sect, and it is said that only a few years before the Austrian occupation a family named Helež, living near Konjica, abandoned the "Bogomile madness" for the Muslim faith. Their bitter enemies, the Roman Catholics, at first emigrated in numbers to the territories of adjacent Catholic Powers, till a Franciscan prevailed upon Mahomet II to stop the depopulation of the country by granting them the free exercise of their religion in what was thenceforth for four centuries the border-land between the Cross and the Crescent, the home of "the lion that guards the gates of Stamboul."

The Turkish conquest of Bosnia was followed, after a desperate struggle, by that of Albania. That mysterious land, whose sons are probably the oldest race in the Balkan peninsula, had been divided upon the collapse of the great Serbian Empire between a number of native chieftains, over whom Carlo Thopia exercised, with the title of "Prince of Albania," a species of hegemony for a whole generation. After his death, Albania was split up among rival clans who acknowledged no common head, and seemed inevitably destined to one of two fates—that of a Turkish province or that of a Venetian protectorate. At first there appeared to be some hope of the latter alternative. The republic began her career as an Albanian power with the acquisition of Durazzo in 1392; Alessio, "its right eye," was annexed as a matter of necessity in the next year; then followed in succession Scutari and Drivasto, Dulcigno and Antivari, all acquisitions from the Balša family, and finally, in 1444, Satti and Dagno on the left bank of the Drin. At that time the whole Albanian coast as far south as Durazzo was Venetian, and the Albanian coast-towns were so many links in the chain which united Venetian Dalmatia with Venetian Corfù. The Adriatic was, what it has never been again, an Italian lake. It was not, however, the policy, nor indeed within the power, of the purely maritime republic to conquer the interior of a country so difficult and so unproductive. It was her object to save expense alike of men and money, and she saved the former by devoting a little of the latter to subsidising the native chieftains in order that they might act as a bulwark against the Turks. But the brute force of the Turkish arms proved to be too strong even for such astute diplomatists as the Venetians and such splendid fighters as the Albanians. As early as 1414 the Turks began to establish themselves as masters of Albania, and for nearly twenty years the castle of Kroja, soon to be immortalised by the brave deeds of Skanderbeg, was the seat of a Turkish governor. The national hero of Albania, whose name is still remembered throughout a land which has practically no national history except the story of his career, was of Serbian origin[1]. His uncle had, however, married an heiress of the great Thopia clan, and had thus acquired, together with the fortress of Kroja, some of the prestige attached to the leading family of Albania. Then came the Turkish invasion, and George Castriota, the future redeemer of his country, was sent as a youthful hostage to Constantinople. The lad was educated in the faith of Islām, and received the Turkish name of Iskander, or "Alexander," with the title of *beg*, subsequently corrupted by his countrymen into the form of Skanderbeg, under which he is known as one of the great captains of history. For many years he fought in the Turkish ranks against Venetians and Serbs, leaving to Arianites Comnenus, a prominent Albanian chief, the futile task of trying to drive out the Ottoman garrisons from his native land. At last, in 1443, while serving in the Turkish army which had been defeated by Hunyadi's troops near Niš, he received the news of a fresh Albanian rising. Realising that his hour had come, he hastened to Kroja, made himself master of the fortress, which was thenceforth his capital, abjured the errors of Islām, and proclaimed a new crusade against the Turks. His personal influence was increased by a marriage with the daughter of Arianites; the other chiefs rallied round him; the Montenegrins flocked to his aid; and at a great gathering of the clans held on Venetian soil at Alessio he was proclaimed Captain-General of Albania. Venice, at first hostile to this new rival of her influence there, took him into her pay as a valuable champion against the common enemy, and soon Christendom heard with delighted surprise that an Albanian chief had forced the victor of Varna and Kossovo to retreat from the castle-rock of Kroja. The Pope and the King of Naples hastened to assist the tribesmen, who were both good Catholics and near neighbours, while the king dreamed of reviving the claims of the Neapolitan Angevins beyond the Adriatic, and even received the homage of Skanderbeg.

Mahomet II was, however, a more formidable adversary than his predecessor. He played upon the jealousy of the other Albanian chiefs, and his troops utterly routed an allied army of natives and Neapolitans. For the moment Skanderbeg seemed to have disappeared, but he soon rallied the Albanians to his side; fresh victories attended his arms, until in 1461 the Sultan concluded with him an armistice for ten years, and the land had at last a sorely-needed interval from war. But the peace had lasted barely two years when Skanderbeg, at the instigation

[1] Hopf, *Chroniques*, p. 334.

of Pope Pius II, broke his plighted word and drew his sword against the Turks. The death of the Pope caused the failure of the projected crusade; and Skanderbeg found himself abandoned by Europe and left to fight single-handed against the infuriated Sultan whom he had deceived. In the spring of 1466 Mahomet himself undertook the siege of Kroja; but that famous fortress baffled him as it had baffled his father, and Skanderbeg journeyed to Rome, where a lane near the Quirinal still commemorates his name and visit, to obtain help from Paul II. With the following spring the Sultan returned to the siege of Kroja, only once again to find it impregnable. But his valiant enemy's career was over; on 17 January 1468 Skanderbeg died[1] in the Venetian colony of Alessio. Thereupon the Turks easily conquered all Albania, with the exception of the castle of Kroja, occupied by Venice after Skanderbeg's death, and of the other Venetian stations. Ten years later, the disastrous war between the republic and the Sultan brought Kroja, Alessio, Dagno, Satti, and Drivasto under Turkish rule until 1912; the peace of 1479 surrendered Scutari; in 1501 Durazzo, and in 1571 Antivari and Dulcigno, the two ports of modern Montenegro, were finally taken by the Turks, and the flag of St Mark disappeared from the Albanian coast. To-day, a part of the castle of Scutari, a mutilated lion there, a Venetian grave and escutcheon at Alessio, and a few old houses and coats-of-arms at Antivari and Dulcigno, are almost the sole remains of that Venetian tenure of the Albanian littoral which modern Italy was anxious to revive. Skanderbeg's memory, however, still lives in his own land. Although his son and many other Albanian chiefs emigrated to the kingdom of Naples, where large Albanian colonies still preserve their speech, a *soi-disant* Castriota has in our own day claimed the Albanian throne on the strength of his alleged descent from the hero of Kroja. If his grave in the castle of Alessio has disappeared, the ruins of the castle which he built on Cape Rodoni still stand to remind the passing voyager that Albania was once a nation. And, even under Turkish rule, the Roman Catholic Mirdites preserved their autonomy under a prince of the house of Doda, still wearing mourning for Skanderbeg, still obeying the unwritten code of Lek Ducagin.

Serbia, Bosnia, and Albania had successively fallen, but there was another land, barren indeed and mountainous, but all the more a natural fortress, which sheltered the Orthodox Serbs in this, the darkest hour of their history, and which the Turks have in vain tried to conquer permanently. We saw how the Balša family had established a century earlier an independent principality in what is now Montenegro, and how upon the death of the last male of that house in 1421 his chief cities had been partitioned between Venice and Stephen Lazarević of Serbia. Even in the time of the Balšas, however, a powerful local

[1] Phrantzes, p. 430; *Mon. spect. hist. Slav. Merid.* xxii. p. 404.

family, that of the Crnojević, derived by some from the royal line of Nemanja itself[1], had made good its claim to a part of the country, and its head, Radič Crnoje, even styled himself "lord of the Zeta." After his death in battle against the Balšas in 1396, the family seems to have been temporarily crushed; but early in the fifteenth century two collateral members of it, the brothers Juraševič, had established their independence in the upper, or mountainous, portion of the Zeta, the barren sea of white limestone round Njeguš, which then began to be called by its modern name of Crnagora[2] (in Venetian, *Montenegro*), perhaps from the then predominant local clan, less probably from the "black" forests which are said to have once covered those glaring, inhospitable rocks. Venice found the brothers so useful in her struggle with the Balšas that she paid them a subsidy, and offered to recognise one of them as "*voïvode* of the Upper Zeta," although they were supposed to be nominally subjects of the Despot of Serbia. A son[3] of this *voïvode*, Stephen Crnojević by name, revolted against the Serbian sovereignty, then weakened by its conflict with the Turks, made himself practically independent in his native mountains, but in 1455 admitted the overlordship of Venice, which had appointed him her "captain and *voïvode*" in the Zeta. A solemn pact was signed, between the republic and the 51 communities which then composed Montenegro, on the sacred island of Vranina on the lake of Scutari: Venice swore to maintain the cherished usages of Balša and to permit no Roman Catholic bishop to rule over the Montenegrin Church; while Stephen Crnojević, victorious alike over Serbs and Turks, hoisted the banner of St Mark at Podgorica, and made his capital in the strong castle of Žabljak[4].

On his death[5] in 1466, his son and successor, Ivan the Black, was confirmed by Venice in his father's command as her "captain and *voïvode*" in the Zeta. In this capacity he assisted with his brave Montenegrins in the defence of the Venetian city of Scutari against the Turks in 1474, an event still commemorated by a monument on a house in the Calle del Piovan at Venice and by a picture by Paolo Veronese in the Sala del Maggior Consiglio. Four years later he again aided the Venetian governor of Scutari and the heroic Dominican from Epirus who was the soul of the defence. But by the peace of 1479 the republic ceded Scutari to the Turks after an occupation of 85 years, and Montenegro lost this powerful obstacle to the Turkish advance from the south, the quarter from which the principality has always been most vulnerable. The conclusion of peace was a severe blow to the Montenegrin chief,

[1] Petrović (*trsl.* Ciàmpoli), *Storia del Montenegro*, p. 23.

[2] First found in a Ragusan document of 1362. (*Mon. spect. hist. Slav. Merid.* XXVII. p. 212.)

[3] *Mon. spect. hist. Slav. Merid.* XXI. pp. 10, 164, 205, 382, 384.

[4] *Ibid.* XXII. pp. 67–8, 153.

[5] *Ibid.* XXII. pp. 364, 383.

especially of a peace on such terms. Abandoned by Venice, Ivan the Black was now at the mercy of the invader. His capital was too near the lake of Scutari to be any longer a safe residence; accordingly, he set fire to Žabljak, and founded in 1484 his new capital at Cetinje, which remained the seat of the Montenegrin government. There he built a monastery and a church, and thither he transferred the metropolitan see of the Zeta, hitherto established in the Craina[1], the piece of the Dalmatian coast between the Narenta and the Cetina. The Turks occupied the lower Zeta; but a national ballad expresses the belief that Ivan the Black would one day awake from his sleep in the grotto of Obod near Rjeka, and lead his heroic Montenegrins to the conquest of Albania. At Obod he erected a fortress and a building to house a printing-press for the use of the church at Cetinje, and under his eldest son George the first books printed in Slavonic saw the light there in 1493, an achievement commemorated with much circumstance four centuries afterwards. But George Crnojević was driven from Montenegro in 1496 by his brother Stephen with the support of the Turks. The exiled prince took refuge in Venice, the home of his wife, whence, after a futile attempt to recover his dominions, he threw himself upon the mercy of the Sultan, embraced Islām, and died, a Turkish pensioner, in Anatolia. Meanwhile, Montenegro was governed by Stephen II till 1499, when[2] it was annexed to the *Sanjak* of Scutari and placed under a Turkish official who resided at Žabljak[3]. But the mountaineers resisted the Turkish tax-gatherers, and in 1514 Stephen II was restored by the Sultan[4]. According to tradition, one of his descendants, married to a Venetian wife who found residence at Cetinje both monotonous and useless, abandoned the Black Mountain for ever and retired to the delights of Venice in 1516, after transferring the supreme power to the bishop, who was assisted by a civil governor chosen from among the headmen of the Katunska district. The prince-bishop, or *Vladika*, was elective, until in 1696 the dignity became hereditary, with one interval, in the family of Petrović. Meanwhile, for some years after the final abdication of the Crnojević family, another brother of George, who had become a Musulman, held, under the name of Skanderbeg, the post of Turkish "governor of Montenegro," a land which, although the Turks have often invaded and overrun it, they never permanently conquered.

While Montenegro, the autonomous Mirdites, and the tiny republic of Poljica alone remained free on the west of the Balkan peninsula, the two Danubian principalities of Wallachia and Moldavia retained a large

[1] *Mon. spect. hist. Slav. Merid.* XXII. p. 67.
[2] Sanudo, *Diarii,* II. pp. 372, 504.
[3] *Ibid.* XII. p. 153.
[4] *Ibid.* XVIII. p. 397.

measure of domestic independence, under the forms of vassalage, on the east. After a long period of civil war between rival claimants, who called in their neighbours and partitioned their distracted dominions, Wallachia acknowledged in 1456 a strong if barbarous ruler in the person of Vlad "the Impaler," and Moldavia in 1457 a vigorous prince in that of Stephen the Great. The Wallach's hideous cruelties do not belie his name; he executed 20,000 of his subjects to consolidate his throne; but he achieved by his savage punishments what his predecessors had failed to obtain, the loyalty of his terrified nobles and the suppression of brigandage. As soon as he felt secure at home, he defied his Turkish suzerain, refusing to send him the contingent of 500 children which Mahomet demanded in addition to the customary annual tribute. He impaled the Sultan's emissaries, and when the Sultan himself marched forth to avenge them in 1462 forced him to retire in disgrace. In the same year, however, "the Impaler" was driven from his throne by his brother, a Turkish puppet, aided by the great Prince of Moldavia. For the rest of the century Stephen overshadowed the petty rulers of the sister-principality, and became the leading spirit of resistance to the Turks in Eastern Europe. His father had, indeed, paid tribute to them as far back as 1456; but he completely routed them at the battle of Racova in 1475, the first time that a Turkish and a Moldavian army had met. Europe applauded his success; but, after in vain trying to form a league of the Christian Powers against the enemy, he realised at the end of his long reign that his efforts had only postponed the necessity of recognising the suzerainty of the Sultan. His son Bogdan in 1513 made his submission and promised to pay tribute, on condition that the Moldaves should retain the right of electing their own princes and that no Turks should reside in their country—a condition modified in 1541 by the imposition of a guard of 500 Turkish horsemen upon the prince of that period. Thus, largely owing to the fraternal quarrels of their rulers, both the principalities had fallen within the sphere of Turkish influence; their constantly changing princes, whether natives or Phanariote Greeks, were the creatures of the Sultan; but, unlike Bulgaria, Serbia, and Bosnia, they never came under his direct rule, were never formally annexed to the Turkish Empire.

The medieval history of the Balkan states and the causes of their fall are full of significance for our own time. In the Near East, and in the Near East alone, the Middle Ages are but as yesterday to the newly-emancipated nations, which look upon the centuries of Turkish domination as a watch in the night, and aspire to take up the thread of their interrupted national existence where it was left by their ancient Tsars, each regardless of the other's overlapping claims to lands which have been redeemed from the Turk. The medieval records of the motley peninsula teach us to regard with doubt, in spite of Turkish vicinity, the prospect of common action between Christian races, which, if small individually, would, if united, have formed a powerful barrier against the foreigner either from the East or from the West. But the greater nations of Christendom cannot afford to criticise too harshly their weaker brethren in the Balkans; for it was quite as much the selfishness and the mutual jealousy of the Western Powers as the fratricidal enmities of the Eastern States which allowed the East of Europe to be conquered by Asia, and which has even in our own day retarded its complete emancipation.

TABLES OF RULERS.

SERBIA.

Stephen Nemanja, "Great *Župan*"	1143 (or 1159)–1196 † 1200
Stephen, "Great *Župan*" ...	1196
King	1217
[Vukan, "King of Dioclea" ...	1195–1207]
Radoslav, King	1228
Vladislav, King	1234–43 † 1263
Stephen Uroš I, King ...	1243
Stephen Dragutin, King	1276–81 † 1316
Stephen Uroš II, Milutin, King	1281
Constantine, King	1321
Stephen Uroš III, Dečanski, King	1322
[Vladislav, King	1321–4]
Stephen Uroš IV, Dušan, King	1331
Tsar	1346
Stephen Uroš V, Tsar ...	1355–1371
[Simeon Uroš, Tsar	1356–71]
[Vukašin, King	1366–71]
Lazar I Hrebeljanović, Prince	1371
Lazar II, or Stephen Lazarević, Despot	1389–1427
[Vuk Branković, Despot ...	1389]
[George Branković, Prince ...	1398]
George Branković, Despot ...	1427
Irene ... ... } Lazar III Branković, Despot ... }	1456
Lazar III ,, alone ...	1457
Stephen Tomašević, Crown Prince of Bosnia, Despot	1458–9

[Turkish: 1459]

BULGARIAN TSARS.

Peter } John Asên I } ...	1186
Peter } Kalojan }	1196
Kalojan alone	1197
Boril	1207
John Asên II	1218
Kaliman I	1241
Michael Asên	1246
Kaliman II	1257
Constantine Asên ...	1258
Ivailo	1277
John Asên III	1279
George Terteri I ...	1280
Smilec	1292
Theodore Svętslav ...	1295
George Terteri II ...	1322
Michael Shishmanich ...	1323
John Stephen	1330 † 1373
John Alexander ...	1331

John Shishman (Trnovo) 1362 or 1365 – 1393 † 1395
[Turkish: 1393]

John Sracimir (Vidin) 1360–5; 1369–98
[Hungarian: 1365–9; Turkish: 1398]

FRANKISH DUKES OF PHILIPPOPOLIS.

Renier de Trit	1204
Gerard de Stroem	1229

[Bulgarian: 1235]

Bosnia.

Borić	*Ban.*	1154–63
[Byzantine Empire:		1166–80]
Kulin	*Ban.*	1180–1204
Stephen	*Ban.* after	1204
Matthew Ninoslav	*Ban.*	1232–37 ; 1240–50
[Kingdom of Hungary:		1237–40]
Prijesda I, "the great"	*Ban.* after	1250–87
Prijesda II and Stephen Kotroman	*Bans.*	1287–90
Stephen Kotroman, alone		1290–1302
Paul Šubić	*Ban.*	1299–1312
Mladen Šubić	*Ban.*	1312–22

Lower Bosnia
[under Hungary]. Hungarian magnates, 1254–64.

Duchy of Mačva and Bosnia

Agnes, Duchess		1264
Béla, Duke		1271–2
Stephen Borić	*Ban.*	1272
Egidius	*Ban.*	1273
Ugrin	*Ban.*	1279
Queen Elizabeth of Hungary, Duchess		1280–84
Stephen Dragutin, ex-King of Serbia		1284–1316

Stephen Kotromanić		1322
Stephen Tvrtko I	*Ban.* 1353, King	1376
Stephen Dabiša, King		1391
Helena Gruba, Queen		1395
Stephen Ostoja, King		1398
Stephen Tvrtko II Tvrtković, King		1404
Stephen Ostoja (2), King		1408
Stephen Ostojić, King		1418
Stephen Tvrtko II Tvrtković (2), King		1421
Stephen Thomas Ostojić, King		1443
Stephen Tomašević, King		1461–3

[Turkish 1463, except *Banat* of Jajce: Hungarian 1463–1528
and *Banat* of Srebrenik: „ 1463–1520]

Hum. (*Herzegovina.*)

Miroslav, Prince	1180–90
[Hungarian:	1198–1202]
Peter, Prince	c. 1220
[Hungarian:	1237]
Tolen, Prince	–1239
Andreas, Prince	1239
Radoslav, *Župan*	1254
[Hungarian:	1254]
[Serbian:	c. 1284–1325]
[Bosnian:	1325–57]
[½ Hungarian:	1357–74]
½ {Vojeslav Vojnov, Count	1357–71
½ {Niccolò Altomanović	1371–4
[Bosnian*:	1374–1435]
Stephen Vukčić	1435
"Duke of St Sava"	1445–66
Vladislav } Vlatko }	1466–7
Vlatko, "Duke of St Sava"	1467–83
[Turkish:	1483]

* Sandalj Hranić-Kosača practically independent 1404–35.

The Zeta (Montenegro).

Balša I ... ... c. 1360
Stracimir 1362
George I 1372
Balša II 1378
George II 1385
Balša III 1405–21

[Part Venetian: 1421–1479]

[Part Serbian: 1421–7]

Radić Crnoje 1392–96
George and Alexius Juraševič 1403–c. 1427

Stephen I Crnojević ... ... c. 1427
Ivan I „ 1466
George I „ ... ... 1490–6 † before 1514
Stephen II „ 1496–9; 1514
Ivan II „ 1515
George II „ 1515–16
[Skanderbeg Crnojević, Turkish "Governor of Montenegro" ... ... 1523–6]

Venetian Colonies in Albania.

Durazzo	1205–15; 1392–1501
Alessio	1393–1478
Drivasto	1396–1419; 1421–3; 1442–78
Scutari	1396–1479
Antivari	1421–23; 1444–1571
Dulcigno	1421–1571
Dagno, Satti	1444–56; 1458–78

The Republic of Poljica.

Founded	944
Under Hungarian *Bans*. ...	c. 1350
Under Venetian suzerainty	1444

Turkish Sultans.

Osmān	1299
Orkhān	1326
Murād I	1360
Bāyazīd I	1389
Sulaimān	1402
Mūsà	1410
Mahomet I	1413
Murād II	1421
Mahomet II	1451
Bāyazīd II	1481

East Roman Emperors from 1261

Michael VIII Palaeologus	1259–82
Andronicus II	1282–1332
Michael IX	1295–1320
Andronicus III	1325(28)–41
John V	1341–76
John VI Cantacuzene	1347–54
Andronicus IV	1376–79
John V (restored)	1379–91
John VII, usurper	1390
Manuel II	1391–1425
John VII, co-regent (restored)	1399–1412
John VIII	1423–48
Constantine XI Dragases	1448–53

Princes of Wallachia.

Radou I Negrou	c. 1290
Ivanko Basaraba	1310
Nicholas Alexander Basaraba	1330
Vladislav I	1364
Radou II	1372
Dan I	1385
Mirčea "the Great"	1386
[First Tributary to Turkey:	1391]
[Vlad I	1394–5]
Michael I	1418
Dan II	1420
Radou III	1422
Dan II (2)	1427
Vlad II "the Devil"	1432
Dan III	1446
Vladislav II	1448
Vlad III "the Impaler"	1456
Radou IV "the Fair"	1462
Laïote Basaraba	1465
Vlad III (2) "the Impaler"	1477
Laïote Basaraba "the Young"	1477
Vlad IV "the Monk"	1481
Radou V "the Great"	1494

Princes of Moldavia.

[Under Hungarian suzerainty:	c. 1288–1349]
Bogdan I	1349
Latzcou	1370
Juga I Coriatović	1374
Peter I Mouchate	1375
Roman I ,,	1390
Stephen I ,,	1394
Stephen II ,, } Peter II ,, }	1395
Roman II ,,	1399
Juga II ,,	1400
Alexander I "the Good"	1401
Elias, alone	1433
Stephen III, alone	1433
Elias (2) } Stephen III }	1435
Stephen III } Roman III } Peter III }	1444
Roman III, alone	1447
Peter III (2) } Alexander II }	1448
Bogdan II	1449
Peter III (3) } Alexander II (2) }	1451
Peter III, alone	1455
[First Tributary to Turkey:	1456]
Stephen IV "the Great"	1457
Bogdan III	1504

CHAPTER XIX.

ATTEMPTS AT REUNION OF THE GREEK AND LATIN CHURCHES.

Between the schism of Michael Cerularius and the capture of Constantinople by the Turks, a period of four hundred years, from 1054 to 1453, some thirty attempts were made to unite the Greeks and the Latins once more in the same communion. At three separate times, in 1204 under compulsion, and in 1274 and 1439 by the terms of an agreement, the union appeared to have been effected; but on each occasion it was inchoate and ephemeral.

It might be said that, from the eleventh to the fifteenth century, the union was the "great ambition" of the Popes and Emperors. It seemed to them the one effective remedy for all the ills of Christendom, which would reconstruct the unity of the Church and re-establish religious concord; strengthened by it, Christendom could resist the attacks of the infidels. Every time that this splendid ideal seemed within grasp, events thwarted its realisation; and the wisest combinations, the most subtle compromises, the fruit of long and laborious negotiations, were powerless before the permanent causes of schism which were destined to render all these efforts abortive. The history therefore of the attempts at union is one of continued mortification, repeated checks, perpetual failures, which militated against religious peace. In point of fact, the union could never be completely attained, and it was the impossibility of achieving this end which brought on the final fall of the Empire.

At the present day the dogmatic and disciplinary divergences which were then separating the two Churches, the double Procession of the Holy Ghost, the dispute as to the pains of purgatory, the use of unleavened bread, and so on, do not appear insuperable difficulties to the union. Agreement on these points was reached several times, and the Popes recognised the right of the Uniate Greeks to preserve their peculiar uses.

But all these questions, which gave birth to countless controversies, were really only an excuse for schism. The fundamental difficulty was the recognition by the Greek Church of the papal supremacy, which was far more wide-reaching in the thirteenth and fourteenth centuries than in the days of Photius and Cerularius. The Greek Church, jealous of her traditions, proud of her history and of the Ecumenical Councils on which orthodoxy was based, and in which she had played so prominent a part, could not accept passively the idea of pontifical monarchy held by a Gregory VII or an Innocent III. She admitted the primacy of the Pope, while the more moderate of her members allowed the Papacy its universal character, but one and all rejected the disciplinary jurisdiction which made all bishops merely delegates and papal vicars.

Two irreconcilable parties were thus opposed, and there was no solution to the dispute on the religious side. The Western conception of the freedom of the Church from the State, for which the supremacy of the Pope was the essential guarantee, was confronted by the Eastern doctrine of the *autocephalous* Church, whose autonomy corresponded to that of the State, to which it was strictly subordinated. It is the rule with the East that an independent sovereign requires an autonomous patriarch, whose relations with the other patriarchs are only spiritual. The one link between the Churches is the participation in orthodoxy established by the Councils. The Patriarch of Constantinople himself was bound, within his own territory, to recognise the *autocephalia* of the island of Cyprus, Bulgaria, Serbia, Russia, and Moldo-Wallachia.

Since no agreement was possible between these two contradictory conceptions, the questions of dogma and discipline were always in dispute. Theologians, far from trying to solve them, took pleasure in complicating them. This is the explanation why that protracted controversy, in which on the Latin side men like St Anselm or St Thomas Aquinas, on the Greek side men like John Beccus (Veccus), Barlaam, Mark of Ephesus, Bessarion, Gemistos Plethon, are found, produced absolutely no results.

It may be said that from 1054 to 1453 the question did not advance one step. Nothing can surpass the monotony of these erudite treatises on the Procession of the Holy Ghost, of these dialogues and contradictory debates, which repeat over and over again the same arguments and appeal continually to the same authorities. Whether at Constantinople in 1054, at Lyons in 1274, or at Florence in 1439, the discussion revolves round the same points and arrives at no result.

One chief hindrance to the establishment of the union was its complication at all times with political interests. It was never desired for its own sake, but for the temporal advantages which the Emperors, Byzantine and Western alike, expected from it. The consequence was that, when the political advantages looked for from the union disappeared, the union itself was abandoned.

From 1054 to 1453 the Emperors always looked to religious union as a means of carrying out their political designs, or of assuring the defence of the Empire. From 1055 to 1071 they, as Constantine IX had done, contracted, by means of the union, a political and military alliance with the Papacy against the Normans of Italy. Then from 1073 to 1099 the union was courted by Michael VII and Alexius Comnenus to assure the defence of the Empire against the Seljūq Turks. In the twelfth century, at the time of the Popes' struggle with the Germanic Emperors, John and Manuel Comnenus had entertained the fond hope of reconquering Italy by means of the union, and assuming at Rome the Western imperial crown. After the conquest of 1204, at the time of the decadence of the Latin Empire, Theodore I Lascaris, John Vatatzes, and Theodore II saw in the union the means of re-entering Constantinople. Michael Palaeologus, master of the capital in 1261, made full use of the union to check the ambitious projects of Charles of Anjou. Finally, in the fourteenth and fifteenth centuries the preliminary negotiations for the union were more or less actively prosecuted according to the advance or the retreat of the Ottomans, and it was not until the danger from them was pressing that this union was finally realised at Florence in 1439.

The Popes, on their side, saw in the union primarily a means of saving Eastern Christendom from the Musulman invasion. Such was the point of view of Gregory VII and of Urban II. Then the Popes of the twelfth century, Paschal II, Calixtus II, Honorius II, Hadrian IV, Alexander III, thought to employ the union to secure for themselves at Constantinople a protector against the schemes of the Germanic Emperors. The series of Popes which starts with Innocent III saw, on the contrary, that the sole chance of success in the Crusades lay in the union, and pursued the policy of making Constantinople a base of operations against the infidels. Finally, in the fourteenth and fifteenth centuries the Ottoman peril which threatened all Europe constituted the chief reason why they sought the union.

The policy of the union, voluntarily adopted, was opposed by that of conquest which was intended to bring about a union by force. The Kings of Sicily—Roger II, William I, William II—being desirous of founding a mighty Mediterranean empire, initiated this policy, which was adopted by such men as St Bernard and Suger. The Hohenstaufen, who were masters of Sicily by inheritance, dreamed of realising this ambition of the Norman kings, and the conquest of 1204 was prepared by an agreement between Philip of Swabia and Venice. The union had been forcibly imposed on the Greek Church, and then, when some years later the collapse of the Latin Empire was apparent, Charles of Anjou and his heirs revived against Constantinople the plans of their predecessors in Sicily.

Such are the different points of view which by their continuous opposition add to the complication of this period of history, but they all have the common characteristic of regarding the union merely as a means of political profit, and this lack of sincerity and altruism on both sides is the ultimate cause of the final failure of all these efforts.

We know that the solidarity, which united the interests of the Pope to that of the Emperor in common cause against the Normans in Italy, had been the principal obstacle to the schism of 1054[1]. It is not surprising then that the first efforts to resume relations were made in that sphere. After 1055 the trusty emissary of the alliance between Pope and Emperor, the Lombard Argyrus, comes once more on the scene. In order to save Byzantine Italy he has recourse to Henry III, to whom he sends an embassy. He himself, taking advantage of the semi-disgrace into which Michael Cerularius fell in the reign of Theodora, went to Constantinople to ask for fresh powers.

One of the legates of 1054, the Chancellor Frederick of Lorraine, elected Pope under the name of Stephen IX (1057), thought the moment had come to resume the policy of Leo IX, and chose Desiderius, Abbot-designate of Monte Cassino, and two other legates to go to Constantinople. But when the legates were on the point of embarking with Argyrus (January 1058), the news of the Pope's death stopped their departure.

This policy was obsolete, and the counsellors of the Papacy, such as Hildebrand, clearly saw that it did not correspond with the actual situation. The treaty of Melfi (1059), by which Nicholas II recognised the sovereignty of the Norman Robert Guiscard over Apulia, Calabria, and Sicily, set the seal to the expropriation of the imperial power in Italy.

The political basis on which the union might have been built up was removed. In 1062 the Emperor Constantine X made a fruitless attempt at Rome to secure the election of a Pope pledged to the alliance with Byzantium. As the result of an intrigue engineered by the Piedmontese Bishop Benzo and Pantaleone, a merchant of Amalfi in high repute at Constantinople, Cadalus, Bishop of Parma, elected Pope under the style of Honorius II, was opposed to the candidate of reform, Alexander II[2]. But in 1064 Cadalus, who had sought asylum in the castle of Sant' Angelo, was driven from Rome, and with him the plan of alliance against the Normans disappeared. In 1071 the capture of Bari by Robert Guiscard completed the fall of the imperial power in South Italy. The time was not far off when, on the very territory of the Empire, the Basileus would have to fight the Normans, now become the allies and protectors of the Pope.

Henceforward, the negotiations towards the union were transacted in another sphere. The victory of the Normans marked the first check to the expansion of Byzantium which had begun at the end of the ninth century. The Empire for the future is on the defensive: it has to face the Normans on the west, the Patzinaks on the north, the Seljūq Turks on the east. The most menacing danger was on the Turkish side; the battle of Manzikert (1071), in which Romanus Diogenes was taken prisoner, shook the Byzantine domination in Asia Minor and even the security of Constantinople. For a long time now bodies of Western

[1] See *supra*, Chapter IX.

[2] Narrative of Benzo, MGH, *Script.* XI. p. 617. Gay, *L'Italie méridionale et l'empire byzantin*, pp. 527–533.

mercenaries, Lombards, Anglo-Saxons, or Normans, had figured in the imperial armies. Confronted by the new dangers which threatened the Empire, the Basileus naturally thought of raising larger levies in the West, and the religious union seemed to him the most effective means of persuading the Popes to uphold their cause among the peoples.

This new policy was entered upon in 1073 by the Emperor Michael VII. On his accession he sent two monks to convey to Gregory VII a letter, in which he expresses his devotion to the Roman Church. The Pope sent him an answer by Dominic, Patriarch of Grado, and informed him of his wish to re-establish "the ancient concord" between the two Churches. As a result of these parleys Gregory VII[1] published on 1 March 1074 a letter addressed to all the faithful, *ad omnes christianos*, in which, after describing the outrages of the Turks, he exhorts them to help the Christians of the East[2]. In his letter of 7 December to Henry IV he announced that he was ready himself to march at the head of 50,000 men to liberate the East and the Holy Sepulchre, and to bring the Oriental Churches back to Christian unity[3]. But circumstances prevented the realisation of this grandiose plan. The Pope was soon involved in the struggle with Henry IV; Michael VII was dethroned by Nicephorus Botaniates, whom the Pope solemnly excommunicated in 1078 as a usurper, and relations were once more broken off between Rome and Constantinople. The close alliance made in 1080 between Gregory VII and Robert Guiscard excluded all possibility of an agreement.

Under Urban II and Alexius Comnenus the conferences were resumed. On his accession (1088) the Pope sent the Emperor two legates, one of whom was the Basilian Abbot of Grottaferrata, in order to ask him to allow the Latin priests to celebrate mass with unleavened bread[4]. The Emperor received the request graciously, and invited the Pope to come to Constantinople to settle the question.

The events of which Rome was then the theatre prevented Urban II from leaving Italy, but towards 1091 the tension between Rome and Constantinople was considerably relieved, as is shewn by a curious treatise of Theophylact, Archbishop of Ochrida, "On the errors of the Latins," written at this period. He twits the Greeks on their craze for finding heresies everywhere, and for blaming the Latin priests because they shaved their beards, wore gold rings, fasted on Saturday, and so on. The only difference which seemed to him important was the addition to the Creed[5].

It appears certain that at the same time levies of troops were being raised in Italy on behalf of the Emperor[6], and a regular correspondence

[1] Mansi, *Concilia*, xx. p. 74. [2] *Reg.* I. 49. Jaffé, *Monumenta Gregoriana*, p. 69.
[3] *Reg.* II. 31. *Ib.* p. 144. On these projects *vide* Riant, *Archives de l'Orient latin*, I. p. 56. [4] Gaufridus Malaterra, IV. 13.
[5] Chalandon, *Essai sur le règne d'Alexis Comnène*, p. 130.
[6] Anna Comnena, *Alexiad*, VIII. 5. CSHB, p. 401.

was established between Urban II and Alexius Comnenus[1], who the whole time continued to be in constant communication with the monks of Monte Cassino[2]. Finally in 1094 Greek ambassadors appeared at the Council of Piacenza to ask the Pope and the faithful to defend Christendom against the pagans. At the request of Urban II many knights pledged themselves by an oath to go to the East[3].

Such was the sequence of events, and it is clear, as has been established by Chalandon[4], that, when asking for extensive reinforcements, Alexius Comnenus did not contemplate the formidable movement of the Crusade, of which the Council of Clermont (18–28 November 1095) was the starting point. It is evident that the idea of proclaiming the Holy War and launching armed multitudes on the East belonged to Urban II, but the Pope was himself supported and probably incited by the mystic impulse which drew the Western peoples to the Holy Sepulchre. The ambitious programme of the Crusade widely surpassed in its scale that of the union between the Churches, which according to the Pope's idea ought to have followed naturally from it. The Crusade was to solve all difficulties, political or religious[5].

We know that the Crusade did not long remain true to this exalted ideal. On the one hand, Alexius Comnenus tried to exploit it for reconquering the territories torn from the Empire by the Turks. On the other hand, the Western barons, become sovereign princes in Syria, were not slow in shewing their hostility to the Empire. The Crusade, far from solving the problems, only increased the misunderstanding between the East and the West. In 1098 the crusaders complained to the Pope, charging Alexius with being the principal obstacle to their march on Jerusalem[6].

The capture of Antioch and of Jerusalem had at any rate the result of bringing two of the ancient Eastern patriarchates, whose holders were henceforward Latins, directly under the authority of the Pope. The councils held by Urban II at Bari (1098) and at Rome (1099) were probably intended to proclaim the religious union with these patri-

[1] Ekkehard, *Hierosolymita*, Ed. Hagenmeyer, v. 3—VI. 1.

[2] Trinchera, *Syllabus graecarum membranarum*, pp. 78–83.

[3] Bernold, MGH, *Script.* v. p. 450.

[4] Chalandon, *Alexis Comnène*, pp. 129 and 155. Louis Bréhier, *L'Eglise et l'Orient*, pp. 60–61.

[5] The predominant idea of Urban II was "liberation of the Eastern Churches." This is confirmed by a very interesting local document, a charge of Stephen, Bishop of Clermont, to the faithful: "cum ad libertatem Orientalis ecclesiae devastandam barbarica persecutio inhorresceret, exhortans decretum a summo pontifice processit ut omnis occidentalium nationum virtus ac fides in auxilium destructae religionis festinaret." *Cartulaire de Sauxillanges*, ed. Doniol, p. 502, No. 697. Clermont-Ferrand, 1864.

[6] MPL, CLI. col. 155. *Vide* also the opinion of Guibert de Nogent on the Greek Church, MPL, CLVI. col. 686.

archates. At Bari there was a debate in the presence of the Pope between St Anselm and the Greek clergy on the Procession of the Holy Ghost[1]; at Rome the Pope published decrees condemning the errors of the Greeks[2]. But this was only a partial union, for the Patriarch of Constantinople does not appear to have been represented at these meetings. A more significant fact is that Pope Paschal II gave his support to Bohemond, Prince of Antioch, in his attempt to conquer the Greek Empire, which failed before Durazzo in 1108. This attack of Bohemond may fairly be regarded as a first attempt to settle the Graeco-Latin dispute by conquest[3].

The negotiations for the religious union were soon placed on another basis, and to achieve this object the Basileus tried to employ the protracted struggle between the Papacy and the Germanic Empire which filled the twelfth century. Alexius Comnenus seems to have initiated this policy. Paschal II having been made prisoner by Henry V in 1111 and forced to crown him Emperor, Alexius wrote, in January 1112, a letter to the Romans, in which he protested against this treatment of the Pope, and professed his readiness to come in person to Rome to assume the imperial crown. The Romans welcomed these proposals, and sent a numerous embassy to Constantinople. An illness prevented Alexius from keeping his promise. But the correspondence between the Pope and the Emperor was continued. At the close of 1112 the Pope signified to Alexius that the first condition of the alliance ought to be the submission of the Greek Church, and suggested the calling of a new council. In 1113 Peter Chrysolanus, Archbishop of Milan, held a public debate with Eustratius, Bishop of Nicaea, but the matter went no further.

Negotiations were again opened between Calixtus II and John Comnenus about 1124. The Pope sent an embassy to Constantinople, and received one from the Emperor. New embassies were exchanged in 1126 between John Comnenus and Honorius II. In 1136 a new controversy was broached at Constantinople between Anselm of Havelberg and Nicetas, Archbishop of Nicomedia[4]. No agreement resulted from it.

Meanwhile the opinion spread more and more widely in the West that conquest alone would put an end to the ill-will of the Greeks, and assure the success of the crusades. The chief mover in this direction was Roger II, King of Sicily, who at the very moment when the Second Crusade was starting had taken the offensive against the Greek Empire (1147). But he tried in vain to induce the King of France, Louis VII, to favour his project, and give permission to use the route through Southern Italy

[1] Mansi, *Concilia,* xx. 950. Speech of St Anselm, *De Processione sancti Spiritus contra Graecos,* MPL, CLVIII. col. 289.

[2] Lambert of Arras, *De primatu sedis Atrebatensis,* MPL, CLXII. col. 644.

[3] W. Norden, *Das Papsttum und Byzanz,* pp. 67–74.

[4] d'Achery, *Spicilegium,* I. 161. Dräseke, *Bischof Anselm von Havelberg* (*Zeitschrift für Kirchengesch.* XXXI. 179).

to gain the East[1]. The crusaders reached Constantinople by the Danube route, but while Louis VII was actually the guest of Manuel Comnenus the Bishop of Langres advised him to open the Crusade by seizing Constantinople[2]. Such a proposal had no chance of being entertained by a King of France, but Roger II returned to the attack when he had an interview with Louis VII at Potenza on his return from the Crusade. The king, passing through Italy, communicated the project to Pope Eugenius III at Tivoli, but the Pope, who feared the ambition of the King of Sicily, did not welcome the idea[3]. Nevertheless, the plan of Roger was approved by highly qualified religious personalities, by Peter the Venerable, Abbot of Cluny, by St Bernard, and above all by Suger, Abbot of St Denis, who in his correspondence with the Pope saw in it the most effective means of consummating the union between the Churches. The plan of a crusade against Constantinople was definitely given to the world.

This danger being temporarily averted, Manuel Comnenus tried to utilise the political rivalries which divided the West to revive the grandiose project of Alexius Comnenus of bartering the religious union for the imperial crown at St Peter's in Rome.

From the very first it was the common hostility of Pope Hadrian IV and the Basileus against William I, King of Sicily, which furnished a basis of negotiations. An alliance was concluded between them at Bari in 1155. This partook of a military character, and the Pope was pledged to raise troops to help the Greek generals to conquer Apulia. But the religious union was not forgotten, and Hadrian IV sent to Constantinople two pontifical notaries to work there. The correspondence which he exchanged on this subject with Basil, Archbishop of Ochrida, shews us how far more difficult the religious agreement was than the political alliance. When the Pope compared the Greek Church to the lost piece of silver or the lost sheep of the Gospel, Basil replied somewhat sharply that the Roman Church, which had herself made an addition to the Creed, was not entitled to accuse the Greeks of having wandered from the fold[4].

Circumstances seemed more propitious when in 1159 Alexander III sent an embassy to Manuel, asking his alliance against Frederick Barbarossa[5]. The struggle between the Pope and the Germanic Empire began afresh with Italy as the stake, but Manuel seemed to hesitate, when in 1161 he received letters from the King of France, Louis VII, and the pontifical legate in France, William of Pavia, which urged him to recognise Alexander III and proposed an alliance. The legate, after censuring

[1] Odo of Deuil, MGH, *Script.* XXVI. 66.

[2] *Ib.* XXVI. 66.

[3] Chalandon, *Jean II et Manuel Comnène,* pp. 334–337.

[4] Mansi, *Concilia,* XXXI. 799. Chalandon, *op. cit.* pp. 358–360. W. Norden, *op. cit.* p. 95. Schmidt, *Des Basilius aus Achrida bisher unedierte Dialoge.*

[5] Chalandon, *op. cit.* p. 558. *Liber Pontificalis,* ed. Duchesne, II. p. 403.

the conduct of the Germanic Emperors, recalled the prosperous times which the Church had known when there was but one Empire in the world. The allusion was clear[1].

Manuel seems to have been favourably disposed towards this idea. On 25 December 1161 he writes to Louis VII that he recognises Alexander III as lawful Pope, and asks the king to send an embassy to Constantinople. He himself sent in 1163 to France three ambassadors[2], whose mission was to communicate a matter of extreme importance, not to be divulged except in the joint presence of the Pope and the king at the same conference[3]. But this preliminary condition could not be carried out, and it would appear from the correspondence exchanged on the matter that it was the hesitation of Louis VII which destroyed the formal conclusion of an alliance. After having seen the king, the ambassadors waited a long time at Saint-Gilles for instructions which never came. It was January 1164 before they once more reached Constantinople[4].

This want of success did not deter Manuel, who now adopted the policy of addressing himself directly to the Pope, and proposed in 1166 the reunion of the Churches in exchange for the imperial crown of the West[5]. The Pope cordially welcomed these overtures and sent to Constantinople Ubaldo, Cardinal-Bishop of Ostia, and Cardinal John[6]. Discussions were held at Constantinople between these legates and the members of the Greek clergy, but they led to nothing. According to Cinnamus[7], the Pope required Manuel to transfer his residence to Rome, and that was the cause of the discontinuance of the negotiations.

In 1170 Manuel made a final attempt with Alexander III, but the favourable moment had passed. The formation of the Lombard League had improved the position of the Pope, who only returned an evasive answer to these overtures, but sent, however, two legates to Constantinople[8]. The relations between the Pope and the Basileus were excellent right up to the last. In 1175 Manuel announced to Alexander III the victory which he had just won over the Turks at Dorylaeum, and invited him to accelerate the departure of the Western crusaders to fight the Turks. The Pope gave instructions to this effect to the legate whom he had sent to France[9]. But notwithstanding sincerely good intentions the Pope and the Emperor had been powerless to triumph over the obstacles which militated against their agreement. The very curious dialogue between the Emperor Manuel and the Patriarch Michael Anchialus

[1] *Recueil des Historiens des Gaules*, xv. 55 and 772.
[2] *Ib.* xvi. 81.
[3] *Ib.* xv. 803–807.
[4] *Ib.* xvi. 56, 57. Chalandon, *op. cit.* pp. 560–562.
[5] *Liber Pontificalis*, ed. Duchesne, ii. p. 415.
[6] Chalandon, *op. cit.* p. 565. Hergenroether, *Photius*, iii. p. 810.
[7] Cinnamus, vi. 4 (CSHB, p. 262).
[8] *Liber Pontificalis*, ed. Duchesne, ii. pp. 419–420.
[9] *Osberti Annales*, MGH, *Script.* xviii. 86. Chalandon, *op. cit.* p. 567.

shews unmistakably that the Greek clergy clung to all their distrust of Rome[1]. On the other hand, the incessant interference of the Comneni in the doctrinal and disciplinary matters of the Greek Church proves that the Basileus would never consent to resign the religious authority which had been transmitted to him from his predecessors[2].

The death of Manuel Comnenus in 1180 was followed by a violent reaction against his Western policy and against the Latins. Andronicus Comnenus, the usurper of the throne, consolidated his power by letting popular hatred work its worst on the Western colonies in Constantinople. The massacre of the Latins in 1182 was an unpardonable act which led to the reprisals of 1204. From this moment it was open warfare between the West and Byzantium, and act upon act of hostility followed. Now it was the aggression of William II, King of Sicily, in 1189, and the sack of Thessalonica; now the alliance of Isaac Angelus with Saladin in 1189; now the hostility which he evinced to Frederick Barbarossa in 1190; now the occupation of the island of Cyprus in 1191 by Richard Coeur-de-Lion. Above all, there were the preparations of Henry VI, heir to the Norman Kings of Sicily, to have done once and for all with the Byzantine Empire: a fleet had already been assembled at Messina, and, in spite of the Pope, the Emperor was on the point of embarking for Constantinople when he died prematurely (28 September 1198).

All these acts intensified bitterness. At the very time when Barbarossa's Crusade was passing through, the Greeks openly treated the Latins as heretics, and the Patriarch in a sermon preached at St Sophia promised indulgences to every Greek who killed a hundred crusaders[3]. The crusade against Constantinople seemed therefore inevitable, and would have taken place sooner had not the death of Henry VI produced a lull which the new Pope, Innocent III, tried to utilise on behalf of the union.

Ever since his accession, in fact, Innocent III had been busy in organising a crusade, and to his mind the realisation of religious union with Constantinople was the postulate of its success. The first step towards agreement was taken by Alexius III, who found he had the same enemy as the Pope in the person of Philip of Swabia, brother of Henry VI and son-in-law of the deposed Emperor Isaac Angelus. He openly proposed to the Pope an alliance against the Hohenstaufen, but Innocent III in his answer brought the question on to the religious plane by intimating to the Emperor that, if he wanted to end the complaints of the Western peoples against him, he ought to lead a crusade to the Holy Land, and work for the union of the Churches. A letter on the

[1] Ed. Loparev, *VV.*, xiv. p. 344.

[2] Oeconomos, *La vie religieuse dans l'empire byzantin au temps des Comnènes et des Anges.*

[3] Letter of Frederick Barbarossa to King Henry, ed. W. Norden, *op. cit.* p. 120; Ansbert, *Historia de expeditione* (*Fontes rerum Austriacarum Scriptores*, v. 32).

necessity of re-establishing the unity of the Church was at the same time addressed to the Patriarch[1]. For more than a year this correspondence was kept up without any result, and in a style which shewed little diplomacy, for the two principals refused to make the slightest concession in fundamentals.

The Pope, while negotiating with Alexius III, was all the time ordering the Crusade to be preached; but the expedition was organised independently of him, and the barons who took the cross were content with asking him to ratify the measures which they adopted. The Pope took no share in the conclusion of the treaty with Venice for free passage (March 1201), nor in the election of Boniface of Montferrat as leader of the Crusade (May 1201). The prince Alexius, son of Isaac Angelus, escaping from his prison, lost little time in coming, first of all, to ask Innocent III to support the restoration of his father, and to undertake the promotion of the religious union; but he next went to Germany to his brother-in-law Philip of Swabia, and it was then probably that, without the cognisance of Innocent III, Philip of Swabia and Boniface of Montferrat decided at the interview at Haguenau (25 December 1201) to divert the Crusade to Constantinople. Boniface of Montferrat, on presenting himself at Rome in May 1202 to propose to Innocent III the restoration of Isaac Angelus with the support of the crusaders, encountered a categorical refusal.

The barons thereupon acted contrary to the wish of the Pope, and the crisis was precipitated. There was, first of all, the diversion to Zara, to which the crusaders consented on the plea of paying their debt to the Venetians. Then, on the Pope's refusal to excuse the capture of Zara, it was determined to confront him with the accomplished fact. The arrival at Zara of embassies from Philip of Swabia (1 January 1203) and from the pretender Alexius (7 April) decided the crusaders to attack Constantinople. The conscience of the crusaders had been salved by most specious promises, union of the Churches, participation of the restored Emperor in the Crusade—the entire programme of the Pope himself.

Innocent III had in vain made the greatest efforts to keep the Crusade on the route to Egypt. The alliance between the Ghibellines, of whom Philip of Swabia was the leader, and the Venetians, which saw in the Byzantine Empire a tempting prey, was stronger than the will of the Pope. Further, Isaac Angelus and his son, once restored, were unable to keep the promises which they had made, and the crusaders were forced to besiege Constantinople a second time. This time it was conquest pure and simple: the sack of the palace, the monasteries, and the churches, the partition of the Empire between the barons and the Venetians. In 1205 the whole East was covered with Latin settlements, and only two centres of resistance were left, the one in Epirus under the dynasty of the Angeli, the other at Nicaea round Theodore Lascaris. The con-

[1] MPL, CCXIV, cols. 326–7.

querors could fondly flatter themselves that, by disobeying the orders of the Pope, they had put an end to the schism of the Greeks, and assured for ever the supremacy of the Roman Church in the East.

According to the principles of the Canon Law, the conquest of the East in no way necessarily involved the absorption of the Greek Church by the Latin Church. To realise the union, it was necessary, first, that the Greeks gave a formal adherence, then, that the Greek Church should return to the conditions previous to 1054, communion with Rome, autonomous institutions, native clergy, national rites. But for this solution to prevail the conquerors, clerics as well as laymen, would have had to shew improbable self-abnegation; the property and revenue of the Greek clergy was too tempting a prey for them.

To do this, these men of the thirteenth century needed a perfect familiarity with history which they could not possess. Between 1054 and 1204 the position of the Papacy had been completely changed; the spiritual supremacy of the Holy See was accepted by all, and many would defend its temporal supremacy. To the West, since the schism of the Greeks, the Roman Church represented the Catholic Church. What she required from the other Churches was no longer merely communion, but submission in matters of dogma and discipline. The Christian republic tended to become a monarchy.

On the side of the Greeks, finally, a spirit of conciliation would have been necessary, but the events of which they had just been victims rendered this impossible. The chronicle of Nicetas echoes the exasperation which the sack of Constantinople roused among them. A contemporary pamphlet, entitled "Our grievances against the Latin Church," enumerates a long list, as absurd as it is spiteful, of the practices with which they charged the Latins, and declares that it is impossible to communicate with men who shave their beards and eat meat on Wednesday and fish in Lent[1]. The more moderate Greeks, in a letter to Innocent III about 1213, declared that they would gladly attempt a conciliation, but on condition that the difficulties were solved by an Ecumenical Council and that no violence should be employed to secure their adhesion[2].

Innocent III, resigned to the conquest of Constantinople, which he had never wished but in the end considered a providential event, resolved at least to turn it to the best advantage of Christendom by realising the religious union and organising the Church of the East. But the crusaders, taking no account of his intentions, had confronted him with actual facts. At the very outset, on their own authority, they placed Latin clergy at the head of the churches and monasteries; their task was lightened by the Greek clergy, of whom many members had fled for refuge to Nicaea or Epirus. On the other hand, agreeably to the bargain struck with Venice, the greater part of the property of the Church was

[1] Luchaire, *Innocent III, La question d'Orient,* pp. 238–243.
[2] *Ib.* pp. 251–257.

secularised. At Constantinople itself the Venetians took possession of the richest monasteries, and installed at St Sophia a chapter of canons, who elected to the Patriarchate a Venetian noble, Thomas Morosini. The Pope, much against his will, was forced to confirm this choice.

The same example was followed in all the states founded by the Latins, the kingdom of Thessalonica, duchy of Athens, principality of Achaia, the Venetian possessions in Crete and the Archipelago. The Latin clergy and the religious or military orders of the West were installed everywhere. Innocent III had no choice but to accept this spoliation of the Greek Church; he did his best, however, to stop it, and to bring the new clergy into strict subordination to the Holy See. His legate, Cardinal Benedict of Santa Susanna, was able to sign a treaty in 1206 with the regent of the Latin Empire, Henry of Flanders, by which the barons relinquished to the Church a fifteenth of their estates and incomes. The same legate was commissioned to obtain the consent of the Greek clergy to the religious union. His instructions were to offer most conciliatory terms. He negotiated with the Greek bishops of one power after another, even treating with those of the Empire of Nicaea, and going so far as to concede the use of leavened bread for the Eucharist. The Pope even allowed the validity of the orders conferred by the Greek prelates. The only obligation which he imposed on them was to recognise formally the authority of the Holy See by means of an oath taken according to the feudal form while clasping the hands of the legate. The bishop must swear fidelity and obedience to the Roman Church, undertake to answer every summons to a council, to make a journey, like the Western bishops, to the threshold (*ad limina*) of the Apostles, to receive the legates with due ceremony, and to inscribe the name of the Pope on the diptychs.

This was in reality a serious innovation, irreconcilable with the system of autonomy which the Greek Church had enjoyed before 1054. Many indeed of the Greek bishops agreed to take this oath, but it was one of the principal obstacles to the duration of the union. In many places resistance was offered to it, and there were even scenes of violence.

The mission entrusted to Cardinal Pelagius in 1213 completed the exasperation of the Greeks. His instructions were far less conciliatory than those of his predecessor, and he went far beyond them. Being commissioned to obtain the submission of all the Greek clergy, he had the recalcitrant thrown into prison, had seals affixed to the church doors, and drove the monks out of their convents. The Emperor Henry was alarmed at these events, and intervened, liberating the prisoners and reopening the churches.

In these circumstances Pelagius, in order to carry out the pontifical instructions, called for the assembling of a conference at Constantinople with the Greek clergy of Nicaea. Nothing could come of this. The delegate of the Empire of Nicaea, Nicholas Mesarites, Metropolitan of Ephesus, was received with honour, but complained of the haughty attitude of Pelagius. Sharp and sarcastic words were exchanged, and, after a week of discussion, the meeting broke up without any results.

At the Lateran Council, in 1215, there was not a single representative of the Greek native clergy, and very few of the Latin bishops of the Eastern Empire took the trouble to attend. The Council proclaimed that the Greeks had come once more under the jurisdiction of the Holy See. They were permitted to preserve their ritual and their peculiar uses, but the hatred which they incessantly shewed towards the Latins, by re-baptising the infants whom they had baptised, and by purifying the altars which had been used by them, was denounced in vigorous terms.

The situation did not improve under the successors of Innocent III, and the relations between the Latin clergy and the natives became worse and worse. The correspondence of the Popes of the thirteenth century is full of expostulations directed against the Latin bishops for their abuse of power and their outrages[1]. Step by step as the Emperor John Vatatzes or the Despot of Epirus reconquered territories, the Latin bishops were compelled to abdicate and make room for Orthodox Greeks. Towards the middle of the thirteenth century the Church of the Latin Empire was, like the Empire itself, plunged into deep distress, and, except in the Morea and in the Venetian possessions, the moment was drawing near when it would disappear. Nothing was destined to remain of the conquerors' exploits but the hatred rankling in the heart of the Greeks.

But for a long time the Popes had come to despair of the safety of the Latin Empire and, being supremely solicitous for the interests of Christendom, they were beginning to welcome the proposals for alliance which came to them from Nicaea.

Theodore Lascaris had indeed thought of regaining Constantinople by peaceable means, through a marriage with the daughter of the Emperor Peter de Courtenay in 1219. This matrimonial policy was intended to be completed by a religious union with Rome. According to a letter of the Patriarch of Nicaea to John Apocaucus, Metropolitan of Naupactus, he contemplated calling a council at Nicaea to put an end to the schism. This project was not carried out, doubtless on account of the opposition of the clergy, sufficiently shewn by the reply of John Apocaucus to the Patriarch[2]. The process was not all on one side, for in 1232, Manuel, Despot of Epirus, became master of Thessalonica, and, seeing his overtures rejected by the Patriarch of Nicaea, made his submission to Pope Gregory IX[3].

At the same time the Emperor of Nicaea, John Vatatzes, sent by the hands of the Patriarch Germanus a letter to the Pope and cardinals

[1] W. Norden, *op. cit.* pp. 274–5.

[2] Ed. Vasil'evski, *VV.*, 1896. W. Norden, *op. cit.* p. 342.

[3] W. Norden, *op. cit.* p. 349. Tafrali, *Thessalonique des origines au* XIVe *siècle*, p. 220.

to propose the union to them. In reality, John Vatatzes was trying in this way to check the offensive which John de Brienne, elected Emperor of Constantinople in 1231, was preparing against Nicaea. Gregory IX was favourably inclined towards these proposals, and sent to Nicaea two Franciscans and two Dominicans who had conversations with the Patriarch and the Holy Synod, but far from ending in harmony the conference terminated in reciprocal anathemas[1]. Vatatzes at least had been able to conclude a suspension of hostilities with John de Brienne.

Gregory IX made another overture to Vatatzes in 1237, but the letter which he sent him was never answered[2]. The Pope then prepared a crusade against him, and the King of Hungary, Béla, consented to direct it (1240). Vatatzes in alarm sent to Béla a promise of religious union with Rome. But, Hungary having been invaded by the Mongols in 1241, Vatatzes, having no cause of anxiety from that quarter, forgot his promise.

Nevertheless with laudable constancy the Popes, who had abandoned the task of supporting effectively the Latin Empire, continued to follow up the religious union with Nicaea. At the Council of Lyons in 1245 Innocent IV reckoned the Greek schism among the five wounds from which the Church was suffering. In 1249 he sent to Vatatzes John of Parma, General of the Franciscans, in order to dissuade him from the alliance with Frederick II, and to gain him over to the union. Conferences followed, but in 1250 Frederick II captured in Southern Italy the ambassadors whom Vatatzes was sending to the Pope. They remained in prison until his death (December 1250). Set free by Manfred, they were able to rejoin the Pope at Perugia in November 1251, but the negotiations came to nothing, and Vatatzes renewed his attacks upon the Latin Empire[3].

It was Vatatzes who resumed the *pourparlers* in 1254. His ambassadors, the Archbishops of Cyzicus and Sardis, were detained like their predecessors in the kingdom of Sicily, but ended by joining Innocent IV at Rome, and accompanied him to Anagni and then to Assisi. Vatatzes demanded the abandonment of Constantinople, the re-establishment of the Greek Patriarch, and the withdrawal of the Latin clergy. In return he undertook to recognise the primacy of the Pope, to replace his name in the diptychs, to obey his decisions in so far as they conformed to the Councils, and to admit his jurisdiction and his right to assemble councils. He even admitted that the Greek clergy should take an oath of canonical obedience to the Papacy. Never had the Greeks up to that time made such liberal concessions, and the matter might perhaps have been settled but for the simultaneous deaths of Innocent IV and John Vatatzes (1254)[4].

[1] Mansi, *Concilia*, XXIII. pp. 47–55.

[2] Ed. Norden in *Papsttum und Byzanz*, p. 751.

[3] *Ib.* pp. 362–366.

[4] *Ib.* pp. 367–378.

The conversations were resumed, however, in 1256 between Theodore II Lascaris and Alexander IV. The Pope sent to Nicaea Orbevieto, Bishop of Civitavecchia; he had instructions to arrange for the assembling of a council, and to ask that Greek clerics should be sent to Rome, but after the interview which he had with Theodore at Thessalonica the preliminaries were broken off[1].

The plan of the Pope had failed, and he had not been able to use for the union the valuable pledge of Constantinople. The Greeks re-entered that city in 1261 without ceasing to be schismatics. The Pope, Urban IV, contemplated at first preparations for a crusade against Michael Palaeologus, but to carry that out he would have been forced to tolerate the alliance of Manfred, whose idea was to restore the Latin Empire for his own advantage. On his side, Michael Palaeologus, having tried in vain to treat with Manfred, had no resource left but to turn to the Pope. It was thus a common hostility against Manfred which decided them to take up the question of the union.

Michael Palaeologus, one of the most practical minds of the thirteenth century and as subtle a diplomat as the Byzantine world ever produced, regarded the union merely as an instrument which would enable him at the same time to gain all the Latin States and hinder the promotion of a new crusade against Constantinople. This is the key to the fluctuating character of his diplomacy. The whole time he was negotiating with the Pope he was continually fighting the Latins, and his zeal for the union varied with his successes and his reverses.

In 1262 Michael sent to Urban IV an embassy which put the question in unequivocal terms. Let the Pope recognise Michael Palaeologus as legitimate sovereign of Constantinople, and the religious union would be easy. Urban answered that he would consent to that, if Michael refrained from attacking the Latin possessions. But at the beginning of 1263 Michael, finding the occasion favourable, attacked the Venetian possessions with the aid of the Genoese fleet. The Pope immediately ordered a crusade against him to be preached and then, in consequence of the ill-success of his appeal, picked up the broken threads of the negotiations. He wrote a conciliatory letter to Michael (28 July 1263), and sent him four Franciscan friars, but these delayed on their route to negotiate at Venice, in Epirus, and in Achaia.

It was only in the spring of 1264, at the moment when the discouraged Pope was preaching the crusade against him, that Michael Palaeologus, whose army had suffered a check in Messenia, once more contemplated the union. The letter which he addressed to Urban IV contains a formal promise of union and of participation in the crusade. The Pope in his answer (June 1264) could not disguise his joy, and he announced the despatch of legates to Constantinople.

But Urban IV died (close of 1264), and at the outset of his pontificate

[1] Papadopoulos, *Theodore II Lascaris*, p. 101.

Clement IV, occupied with the struggle against Manfred, ignored Constantinople. It was probably in 1266 that new embassies were exchanged[1], but at that moment the victory of Charles of Anjou over Manfred at Benevento (February 1266) was a factor which modified and complicated the question. Charles of Anjou, titular defender of the Holy See, lord of the kingdom of Sicily, soon revived the plans of his Ghibelline predecessors against Constantinople. On 27 May 1267, by the treaty of Viterbo, Baldwin II surrendered to Charles of Anjou his rights over the Latin Empire, and the King of Sicily made immediate preparations to start his expedition.

But Clement IV, while seeming to approve them, distrusted the plans of Charles of Anjou, and continued to treat with Michael Palaeologus, who, disturbed by the menaces of the King of Sicily, had sent him another embassy, imploring him to prevent the war between the Greeks and Latins (1267). A characteristic detail, which shews how pressing the danger seemed, is that even the Patriarch wrote to the Pope proposing the union to him. The Pope welcomed these overtures, but, deeming himself master of the situation, insisted in his answer upon a complete submission of the Greek Church without any discussion, undertaking in return to prevent the war. Michael, whose fears were increasing, replied that he could not accept these terms of union without rousing against himself all the Greeks. To testify his goodwill, he actually offered to take part in the coming crusade. The Pope in his answer (17 May 1267) maintained his uncompromising attitude, and refused to give any assurance to the Emperor until the union was accomplished. On 27 May following Clement IV gave his approbation to the Treaty of Viterbo, a clear proof that he counted upon the threat of Charles of Anjou to render the Greeks more tractable.

Clement IV, however, died on 28 November 1268, and in consequence of divisions among the cardinals the papal throne was vacant for three years. Charles of Anjou wished to profit by this circumstance to realise his plans, but, in the absence of a Pope, it was to the King of France, St Louis, that Michael Palaeologus turned in order to avert the danger. He sent two embassies to France (1269) with proposals for religious union. St Louis referred the matter to the college of cardinals, who returned to Michael Palaeologus the ultimatum imposed by Clement IV in 1267. The Emperor had at least attained his object, for Charles by joining his brother St Louis in the crusade of Tunis (1270) was obliged to postpone his attack upon Constantinople[2].

Immediately after the death of St Louis (25 August 1270), however, Charles of Anjou resumed his offensive against the Greek Empire both by diplomacy and by force of arms. It was evident that nothing but the

[1] According to the conjecture of W. Norden, *op. cit.* p. 444.
[2] L. Bréhier, *L'Église et l'Orient*, p. 237.

conclusion of the union would succeed in stopping him. The cause of the union, so much desired by Michael Palaeologus, found a champion in the person of the new Pope, Tedaldo Visconti, elected under the name of Gregory X (September 1271), who was in the Holy Land when he heard of his exaltation. Gregory X, like Innocent III before him, saw in the union the essential condition of success of the crusades. He could not therefore be anything but hostile to the ambitious projects of Charles of Anjou, and as soon as he assumed the tiara he opened relations with Michael Palaeologus.

A series of embassies was exchanged in 1272 and 1273 between Rome and Constantinople. One of the most active emissaries between the two courts seems to have been a Franciscan friar of Greek origin, John Parastron, who could speak both Greek and Latin. During these negotiations Charles of Anjou was hurrying on his preparations, and sent an army to the Morea (May 1273). Michael Palaeologus on his side continued to attack the Latin states.

In spite of these unfavourable circumstances, the Pope and the Emperor had such interests in the union that they ended by achieving their purpose. The embassy sent by the Pope to Constantinople in 1272 announced the assembling of an Ecumenical Council at Lyons for May 1274. Michael Palaeologus then set on foot among the Greek clergy a very clever campaign of propaganda, by emphasising the incalculable benefits which the union would procure for the Empire at the cost of trifling or purely platonic concessions, such as the recognition of the primacy of the Pope and his commemoration on the diptychs. He met with an obstinate opposition headed by the Patriarch Joseph, but he was resolved to have his own way.

In May 1273 Michael sent a new embassy to Rome. Without disguising the difficulties with which he met from the Greek clergy, he declared that the union would shortly be consummated, and he asked the Pope for safe-conducts for the Greek ambassadors who would be sent to the Council. Gregory X immediately took measures to insure the safety of this embassy, and in November 1273 he called on Charles of Anjou to enter into a solemn undertaking on the point. The King of Sicily, who saw himself threatened by a possible rising of the Ghibellines in Italy, complied, sorely against his will, and gave the necessary instructions to his agents.

Michael Palaeologus, meanwhile, had not been inactive at Constantinople, and had continued his propaganda among the clergy. A decisive success for him was the conversion of the *chartophylax* John Beccus to the cause of the union; this example helped to win over several bishops. The most obstinate were sent into exile or imprisoned. Finally, on the assurance that not an iota would be changed in the Creed, the clergy drew up an act by which they agreed to the primacy of the Pope, his mention on the diptychs, and appeals to Rome. The Patriarch Joseph alone remained obdurate. This act was intended to be handed to the

Pope simultaneously with a letter from the Emperor which recognised the Roman doctrines in a much more explicit manner.

Gregory X had opened the Ecumenical Council in the cathedral of Lyons on 7 May 1274. On 24 June following, Germanus, ex-Patriarch of Constantinople, the Archbishop of Nicaea, and the Grand Logothete were received there with great ceremony, and put the letters of the Emperor and the Greek people into the hands of the Pope. On 6 July the Pope read out these letters and, in the name of the Emperor, the Grand Logothete repudiated the schism; the Pope then chanted a *Te Deum*. The union was achieved, and the ex-Patriarch handed to the Pope letters from the Serbian and Bulgarian clergy who formally recognised it.

Thus, according to the plan which had been drawn up by Clement IV, the union had been accomplished without discussion or controversies. The Greek Church had submitted voluntarily, at least in appearance. A new era of peace seemed to dawn for Christendom, but its duration was destined to be brief.

The first tangible result of the union for Michael Palaeologus was the conclusion of a truce with Charles of Anjou, through the mediation of the Abbot of Monte-Cassino delegated by the Pope (1 May 1275). Gregory X had kept his promise. Would Michael Palaeologus be able to keep all of his?

There is evidence that from the very first he continued in 1275 his attacks on the Latin states of Greece. Was he at least going to make a reality of the religious union? On 16 January, the day of the festival of St Peter, he had a solemn service held in the chapel of the imperial palace, and commemorated the name of the Pope. On 25 May following, the Patriarch Joseph, obdurate as ever, was replaced by John Beccus, head of the union-party. But the public ceremony, by which the decisions of the Council of Lyons should have been notified to the people, was continually postponed. In the family of the Emperor his sister Eulogia was at the head of the opponents of Rome. Michael, notwithstanding, continued to make a shew of burning zeal to the Pope, and on 10 January 1276 he announced to Gregory X his intention of taking part in the much talked-of crusade.

Even in Rome the conditions were becoming less favourable to the union. After the death of Gregory X three Popes of the Angevin party followed within a few months of each other. An ultimatum prepared by Innocent V was sent to Michael Palaeologus by John XXI (1277). The Emperor was to swear to the union personally, and to obtain an oath from the Greek clergy, who were to pledge themselves also to teach nothing contrary to the Roman doctrines. The Emperor consented to take the required oath, but the mass of the Greek clergy refused, in spite of excommunications from John Beccus. At the same moment the Despot of Epirus, John the Bastard, held an anti-unionist council, which excommunicated the Emperor, the Patriarch, and the Pope.

John Gaetano Orsini, elected Pope in 1278 under the name of Nicholas III, was, unlike John XXI, an opponent of the Angevins, and he rendered a conspicuous service to Michael Palaeologus when he forbade Charles of Anjou to attack Constantinople. On the question of the union, however, he was more peremptory than his predecessors. The papal nuncios, whom he sent to Michael Palaeologus in October 1278, notified a new ultimatum to him. The Emperor was called upon to send a fresh statement of his adherence to the confession of Lyons, to compel the Patriarch and the clergy also to swear adherence to it, to accept the permanent residence of a papal legate at Constantinople, to introduce the *Filioque* into the Creed, to renounce all uses which the Pope might deem contrary to the faith, and to excommunicate the enemies of the union.

A fresh breach was imminent, and yet Michael Palaeologus struggled to the end to uphold the union. A synod was convened to receive the proposals of the nuncios, and drew up a reply, the exact wording of which is not known, but which appears, without running counter to the Pope's wishes, to have consisted mainly of vague promises. Nevertheless, in order to satisfy the Pope, John Beccus introduced the *Filioque* into the Creed, but by doing so he only supplied new grievances to the opposite party, many of whom were imprisoned by the Emperor.

Nicholas III was succeeded, however, on 22 February 1281 by a Pope of the Angevin party, Martin IV. Charles of Anjou had already sent troops to Epirus, and, with the support of the Pope, was preparing a decisive attack on the Greek Empire. It is not therefore astonishing that the Pope did not receive favourably the embassies which Michael Palaeologus had sent him. So much so that on 18 November 1281 he excommunicated Michael Palaeologus, and threatened to pronounce his deposition if he did not submit before 1 May 1282. Some months previously the Pope had entered into the coalition formed by Venice and Charles of Anjou against Michael (July 1281). The departure of the Crusade was fixed for the month of April 1283. The days of the Byzantine Empire seemed numbered, when the tragedy of the Sicilian Vespers (30 March 1282) wrecked the schemes of the coalition. When Michael Palaeologus died (11 December 1282) he had shaken off the nightmare of Angevin invasion, but the religious union to which he had devoted all his energies was definitely broken.

With the power of Charles of Anjou disappeared the principal political reason which could justify this union in the eyes of the Greeks. The new Emperor, Andronicus II, had no anxieties on the Western frontier. It is not therefore surprising that his reign was marked by a violent reaction against the policy of union. All the clergy condemned by Michael Palaeologus were considered martyrs of Orthodoxy, and were released from their prisons. The Patriarch John Beccus was deposed, exiled to Prusa, and then brought before a synod. A reign of terror prevailed at Constantinople, and the unionist clergy knew in their turn the pains of exile and imprisonment. Even the memory of the late Emperor was condemned. This outburst of fanaticism shews the intense unpopularity of the union at Constantinople. Henceforward the monks dominated the Greek Church, and from this epoch onwards the higher ranks of the clergy were almost exclusively recruited from among them. It was the monks then who fanned the flame of popular hatred against the Westerners. Forced into an attitude of sullen nationalism, they shewed that they preferred the ruin of the Empire to union with Rome.

The check to the union and the attitude of Andronicus II explain why the Crusade against Constantinople was still the order of the day in the West, but there was no prince now in those parts capable of renewing the attempt of Charles of Anjou. Charles of Valois in 1307–1308 and Philip of Taranto (1312–1325), both heirs by marriage of claimants to the Latin Empire, tried in turn, but without success, to invade Greece. The danger to the Empire that was destined to revive the proposals of union lay in a different quarter.

It may be said that it was during the long and disastrous reign of Andronicus II (1282–1332) that the fate of Byzantium was sealed. Religious disputes, ravages by the Catalan Company, Turkish invasions of Asia Minor, civil war, all these calamities burst almost at once over the Empire. Andronicus by his incompetence and invertebrate policy destroyed the fabric reared by his father. It is not then surprising that he could not maintain to the end the uncompromising attitude which he had adopted towards the Latins.

In 1323, learning that a French fleet in the service of the Pope, commanded by Amaury de Narbonne, was on the point of setting sail for Constantinople, he sent to the West the Genoese Bishop of Kaffa to propose a new union. Soon after, in 1326, he commissioned another Genoese to bear a letter on the same subject to the King of France, Charles the Fair. The king sent to Constantinople the Dominican Benedict of Como, but the negotiations were kept secret, and Andronicus was compelled to admit to the ambassador how difficult it would be to propose a new union to the Greeks[1].

Meantime the Ottoman State, which had been allowed to form owing to the weakness of Andronicus II, was becoming more and more a menace to Constantinople. In 1334 Andronicus III became anxious, and sent overtures of union to Pope John XXII by two Dominicans who were returning from the Tartars. The Pope gave them a favourable hearing and sent them back to Constantinople, but they were unable to discuss the matter publicly with the Greek clergy as they demanded.

In 1335, as a proof of his good will, Andronicus III consented to take part in the Crusade organised by Benedict XII under the leadership of the

[1] Paris, Archives Nationales; Trésor des Chartes. See Omont, *Bibliothèque de l'École des Chartes*, 1892, p. 254.

King of France. Finally in 1339 the Emperor sent secretly to Avignon the Venetian Stephen Dandolo, and one of the most celebrated humanists of Constantinople, the Calabrian monk Barlaam, Abbot of the Soter. But these emissaries had not even official letters accrediting them to the Pope. They had the difficult mission of inducing Benedict XII to promise the despatch of prompt aid to the East. It was only subsequently that there could be any question of union. Barlaam pleaded his case eloquently. "That which separates the Greeks from you," he said, not without justification, "is not so much the difference of dogmas as the hatred they feel against the Latins, provoked by the wrongs which they on their side have suffered. It will be necessary to confer some great benefit upon them to change this feeling."[1] He added that the union could not be effected by force; only a General Council could establish it, and if the Greeks had not recognised the Council of Lyons it was because the Greek emissaries had been appointed by the Emperor and not by the Patriarchs of the East[2]. Barlaam had thus outlined the programme of the future council which was intended to effect the union, but this idea was so far premature, and the Pope offered an invincible opposition to every argument. The despatch of Western help must in his view be conditional on the recognition by the Greeks of the Council of Lyons. The whole matter went no further than the exchange of fine promises.

There existed, however, at Constantinople a party favourable to the union, which centred round the Empress Anne of Savoy and the nobles of her country whom she had brought to Constantinople in 1326[3]. Having become regent in the name of her son John V Palaeologus after the death of Andronicus III in 1341, Anne of Savoy sent to Pope Clement VI in the autumn of 1343 a gentleman of Savoy, Philip de Saint-Germain, bearing instructions from the regent and the Grand Duke Alexius Apocaucus. He was commissioned to express to the Pope the attachment of the regent and of her son John V to the Roman Church, and to pray for the despatch of a fleet and an army to defend Constantinople against the attacks of the Turks, as well as against those of their ally John Cantacuzene, who had proclaimed himself Emperor[4].

Clement VI was extremely favourable to the union. In 1343 he was occupied in organising with the help of Venice the naval league which ended in the recapture of Smyrna from the Turks (1344). He wrote to the Latin Patriarch Henry, who resided at Negropont, to the Dominicans of Pera, and to the Venetian and Genoese colonies of Constantinople, to invite them to exert all their efforts towards preparing the union. In spite of his friendly inclinations, the Pope held the same point of view as

[1] Gay, *Le pape Clément VI et les affaires d'Orient*, pp. 49–50.

[2] *Ib.* p. 115.

[3] *Ib.* p. 46.

[4] *Ib.* p. 47. These instructions are known from the answers of Clement VI (21 and 23 Oct. 1342) and from John Cantacuzenus, III. 87, CSHB, p. 359.

his predecessors; the despatch of assistance must be conditional on the abjuration of the schism.

At the time of the ill-starred Crusade of the Archipelago in 1346, the heir to the Dauphiné, Humbert, treated with the regent, and the question between them was the union of the Churches, but nothing occurred beyond conversations, and the occupation of the island of Chios by the Genoese only exacerbated the Greeks.

Meanwhile Western politicians regarded the union as more and more desirable. When the prince Humbert, a disillusioned man, entered the Dominican order, he founded scholarships at the University of Paris, and reserved many of them for students belonging by birth to "Greece and the Holy Land," whom he destined to teach Greek in the convents of the Dominicans (1349)[1]. But these good intentions were powerless before the hatred which divided the Greeks from the Western nations. There were incessant conflicts in the countries still occupied by the Latins. In 1364 the Greeks of Candia rose against the Venetians, who wished to impose the Latin ritual on them, and terrible massacres ensued[2]. The anecdotes related at the same epoch by Petrarch to Urban V leave no doubt about the feeling of the people towards the Latins. Sometimes they riotously interrupted the Latin services, sometimes they fumigated the churches frequented by the Latins, and lost no opportunity of treating them as dogs, "when they could do so with impunity."[3]

John Cantacuzene, now master of Constantinople (February 1347), sought to dissipate the justifiable distrust which his alliance with the Turks had roused against him. Unlike his predecessors, he sent to the Pope an official embassy to persuade him that, far from favouring the Turks, he was prepared to fight them, and also to ask that the leader of the coming crusade might act in concert with him. Clement VI, who was by no means friendly towards Cantacuzene, gave a vague answer and promised to send him an embassy, but three years elapsed before he despatched to Constantinople two Dominicans, one a bishop in Venetia, the other in Crete, with instructions to negotiate the religious union[4].

John VI replied to these overtures by testifying his zeal for the union, at the same time declaring that only a truly Ecumenical Council could render it possible. The Pope, on his side, informed him that he was favourable to holding a council, but that the existing state of Christendom made it impossible to assemble it[5]. Relations, however, still continued between him and the Emperor, but nothing came of them.

[1] Gay, *op. cit.* p. 79.

[2] Gibbons, *The Foundation of the Ottoman Empire*, p. 132. Gregoras, xxv. 17, CSHB, p. 41.

[3] Petrarch, *Senilia*, 7 (Gibbons, *op. cit.* p. 133).

[4] Gay, *op. cit.* pp. 102–109.

[5] Gay, *op. cit.* pp. 110–118. Cantacuzenus, IV. 9, CSHB, pp. 59–60.

Under cover of the civil war between John Cantacuzene and John Palaeologus, the Ottomans had gained a footing in Europe by the capture of Gallipoli (1354), and had lost no time in overrunning Thrace. John V, who held power after the abdication of Cantacuzene (1355), saw no hope of safety except in complete submission to the Pope. In 1356 he sent two ambassadors to Avignon with a document in which he pledged himself to recognise the Pope as head of the Church, to obtain like recognition from his subjects, to receive the pontifical legates with all respect, and to send his son Manuel to Rome as a hostage. In return he claimed prompt aid for Constantinople, of which the Pope would bear the cost for six months. During that period a legate could go to Constantinople, and collate whom he wished to ecclesiastical benefices. As a clearer proof of his zeal the Emperor proposed to found at Constantinople colleges where Latin would be taught, and he recognised the right of the Pope to declare the throne vacant if he failed to execute his promises.

Innocent replied to the Emperor by a gushing letter, writing also to the Patriarch Callistus and the principal bishops, and sent two nuncios to Constantinople. But, when the question of collecting the required fleet was broached, the Pope could not obtain anything from the Latin powers: neither Venice, nor Genoa, nor the King of Cyprus, nor even the Knights of Rhodes, consented to the slightest sacrifice.

Meantime the position of the Ottomans in the Balkan peninsula grew stronger day by day. In 1363 Murād compelled John V to sign a treaty, tantamount to vassalage, which prevented him from lending his help to the effort made by the Hungarians and the Serbs, in response to the Pope's demand, to recapture Hadrianople. In 1366 Murād actually took up his residence at Hadrianople, the first step towards the blockade of Constantinople. At this crisis John V made fresh appeals to the Pope for help, and, while Urban V preached the crusade, he himself paid a visit to the King of Hungary towards the close of 1365, in order to remove the scruples which the king felt in lending his help to schismatics, and to affirm by oath the intention of himself and all his family to embrace the Roman faith.

The Crusade, led by Amadeus VI, Count of Savoy, cousin of the Emperor, succeeded in recovering Gallipoli from the Turks and in rescuing John V, whose return to Constantinople was in danger of being cut off by the Bulgarians. The Archbishop of Smyrna and the Latin Patriarch of Constantinople actually embarked on the fleet of Amadeus VI, which was returning to the West, with orders to announce to Urban V that the Emperor would come and abjure the schism before him in person (1367). Urban V lost no time in writing to the three sons of the Emperor, to the Empress Helena, to John Cantacuzene (who had retired to a convent), to the Patriarch Philotheus, to the people and clergy of Constantinople, to exhort them to favour the union.

On 18 October 1369 John V, received at Rome with the greatest ceremony, presented his profession of faith to the cardinals. On 21 October he solemnly abjured the schism before the Pope on the steps of the basilica of St Peter. But this was only a personal abjuration, and was not binding on the Greeks. Thus the voyage of John V to Italy failed to produce the results anticipated from it. His conduct at Venice ended in his being thrown into prison for debt, and, when after this humiliation he passed once more through Rome in 1370, he could not obtain from the Pope the smallest subsidy.

It was in vain that in 1373 his ambassadors scoured Europe and actually reached France, where Charles V made them vague promises. In vain Pope Gregory XI, fully aware of the danger which the Ottomans were threatening to Europe, wrote urgent letter after letter to the crowned heads, to Louis, King of Hungary (1372 and 1375), to Edward III, King of England (1375). The sovereigns and their knights assumed the cross with stately pomp, for it was a time of splendid festivals and eloquent speeches; but no profitable results followed. John V, abandoned by all, had ended in 1373 by acknowledging himself the vassal of Murād and handing over to him his son Manuel as hostage.

Manuel, who became Emperor in 1391, renewed the same pressing appeals by embassies to the Western sovereigns. This time the King of Hungary, Sigismund, directly threatened by the Turks, backed up the Byzantine demands, and Pope Boniface preached the Crusade which terminated in the disaster of Nicopolis (1396), although its object had been the deliverance of Constantinople. In 1397 Manuel sent his uncle Theodore Cantacuzene to Paris. The King Charles VI refused permission to his brother the Duke of Orleans to start for the East, but he promised 600 men-at-arms, who were placed under the orders of Marshal Boucicaut, and succeeded in clearing the immediate approaches to Constantinople and breaking the blockade.

At the advice of Boucicaut himself, Manuel adopted the policy of visiting the West personally in order to plead more effectually the cause of Constantinople. He set out on 10 December 1399, passed through Venice, Padua, and Milan, made another solemn entry into Paris on 3 June 1400, landed in England, was received in London on 21 December by Henry IV, returned to France in February 1401, and remained in Paris until November 1402. After a stay at Genoa, he went to take ship at Venice (April 1403), and on 15 June following he was back in Constantinople[1].

The Emperor had found everywhere a courteous and splendid welcome. At Paris and at London, in particular, he and his suite owed much to their being objects of public curiosity. He was overwhelmed with banquets; the most complimentary speeches and the fairest promises were lavished on him. During his stay in Paris he even had a controversy on the Procession of the Holy Ghost with a doctor of the

[1] Collected texts by Lambros, *Neoshellenomnemon*, XIII. pp. 132–133.

Sorbonne, but this was only a showy passage of arms without any results. As a crowning misfortune, the West was torn by the Schism, and Manuel appears to have negotiated at the same time with the two Popes, Benedict XIII and Boniface IX. The latter sent on 27 May 1400 an encyclical, exhorting all Christians to arm for the defence of Constantinople, and promising them the same indulgences as for a crusade; but everyone turned a deaf ear to his appeals, and the travels of Manuel were, when all is summed up, as useless for the cause of the union as for that of the crusade.

The salvation of Constantinople came from a wholly unexpected quarter, from the Mongols of Tīmūr. While Manuel was in France the Ottoman power was broken at the battle of Angora (20 July 1402), and the dynastic discord which followed the death of Bāyazīd gave some years of respite to the remnant of the Byzantine Empire. It would have seemed natural to utilise this lull for negotiating the union and preparing a new crusade, but this was the period when the civil wars in France, and even more the Great Schism, distracted the West. Further, it seems that the easily-won successes of Manuel in the midst of the Ottoman intrigues had greatly quenched his zeal for the union. From 1402–1417 he took no action in the West, and did not even send a representative to the Council of Pisa (1409).

It was only when the Turkish menace was renewed that Manuel came once more into touch with the West. In 1417 he sent to Martin V an embassy which appeared at the Council of Constance. After the siege of Constantinople by Murād II (1422) an embassy, headed by John Palaeologus with Francesco Filelfo as interpreter, went the round of the Western courts. The Pope Martin V, who was strongly in favour of the union, proposed that a council should be held in Italy, and offered 100,000 florins to defray the travelling expenses of the Greeks (1423). The same Pope authorised in 1425 marriage between Greeks and Latins, and granted indulgences to those who would go to the aid of the Greeks. Deceived by the friendly attitude of Manuel, he nominated the Cardinal of Sant' Angelo to be legate at Constantinople, and sent two nuncios to inform the Emperor of the fact. Manuel, who had just made terms with Murād II, rejected the proposals of the Pope, and let him understand that no union was possible before the Ecumenical Council was held (1425). It is hard to say whether the cynical words, which Phrantzes attributes to him on his death-bed, can be taken as exact[1]. He is said to have recommended his son not to consider the union as anything except a weapon against the Turks. "Propose," he said to him, "a council; open negotiations, but protract them interminably....The pride of the Latins and the obstinacy of the Greeks will never agree. By wishing to achieve the union you will only strengthen the schism." True or not, these words define excellently the policy which he had himself followed.

[1] Phrantzes, II. 13.

Nevertheless, the union appeared to all who reflected upon the subject as an essential condition of salvation for Christian Europe menaced by the Turks. At Constantinople even, and in the very convents of Mount Athos, a party of resolute unionists was formed, of which the most authoritative representatives were Isidore, Igumen of St Demetrius at Constantinople, and Bessarion, a native of Trebizond, subsequently a monk in the Morea. The idea of an ecumenical council, which would finally solve all dogmatic or disciplinary difficulties and put an end to all misconceptions, is from this time onwards equally popular in the West and in the East.

In 1431 John VIII Palaeologus sent envoys to the Pope in order to come to some agreement with him as to holding the council which had been talked of for more than a century. The Greek clergy would have preferred it to be held at Constantinople, but the Emperor accepted an Italian town on condition that the Pope undertook to defray all the travelling expenses of the Greeks. The envoys on their way learnt of the death of Martin V and retraced their steps, but a new embassy was sent to the new Pope, Eugenius IV.

At this moment an Ecumenical Council, called by Martin V before his death, assembled at Basle to work at the reform of the Church. The Council of Basle took in hand the problem of the Greeks, and on 19 October 1431 asked the Pope to despatch envoys on this subject to Constantinople. But soon a veritable feud broke out between the Fathers assembled at Basle and Eugenius IV. The Pope, under pretext of giving satisfaction to the Greeks, endeavoured to transfer the Council to Italy. In order to render this transference impossible, the Council of Basle tried to bring the Greeks to join with it in order to conclude the union. An embassy from the Council arrived at Constantinople in 1433, charged with informing the Emperor that the Council was superior to the Pope, that it was under the protection of the Emperor Sigismund, and that if the Greeks consented to come to Basle they would receive money and troops for the defence of Constantinople.

The Emperor entertained these proposals favourably, and sent to Basle his brother Demetrius and the Abbot Isidore. But at the same time he was exchanging letters and embassies with Eugenius IV. By a singularly rapid change the legate Christopher Garatoni, sent to Constantinople in 1434, accepted the proposal that the Council should be held in the imperial city. He returned to Italy with two ambassadors of John VIII in 1435, and this decision was at once communicated to the Council of Basle, which formally refused to admit it.

A second deputation, consisting of the Dominican John of Ragusa, a canon of Constance, and a canon of Orleans, left Basle in 1435. It was empowered to offer the Emperor financial help, with a first instalment of 9000 florins in a bill on the banks of the Medici, on the condition that the council was held in the West. After a three months' journey the mission reached Constantinople 24 September 1435. The Pope's legate Christopher Garatoni appeared in his turn (1436). Each party then tried to outbid the other, and to attract the Greeks to its side by offering the greatest advantages. The Emperor, vacillating as ever, sent two ambassadors, one, Manuel Bulotes, to the Pope, the other, John Dishypatus, to Basle.

At the same time the choice of the city where the union was to be concluded roused violent storms in the Council of Basle. The majority had fixed on Avignon, the minority, supported by John Dishypatus, pronounced in favour of Florence or Udine. On the voting-day each party had prepared its decree and the uproar was so great that it almost came to blows. A bishop of the minority forcibly seized the seal of the Council, and, after sealing the decree started off to convey it to the Pope (7 May 1437).

Eugenius IV, considering the decree of the minority as alone valid, appointed an embassy to announce the fact at Constantinople. On the way it took up at Crete 300 archers intended for the defence of the city. The ambassador of Basle, John of Ragusa, was still there. He was speedily ignored, and John VIII concluded a treaty with the Pope, who undertook to put at his disposal the necessary ships and escort.

After six years of wearisome negotiations the Council of Union was finally convened. In order to invest it with a truly ecumenical character the Emperor asked the three Eastern Patriarchs to send representatives to it. The Abbot Isidore, nominated Archbishop of Kiev, was intended to bring over the Great Prince of Russia, and delegations were secured from the Prince of Moldo-Wallachia and the Iberian clergy. Conferences of theologians, in which the partisans and the opponents of the union confronted each other, were assembled in order to discuss the concessions that could be made to Rome.

John Palaeologus, accompanied by his brother the Despot Demetrius, by the Patriarch Joseph, seventeen metropolitans, and a large number of bishops and igumens, left Constantinople on 24 November 1437 and arrived at Venice on 8 February 1438. Pope Eugenius IV awaited him at Ferrara, where the Council was to sit. The most important question, if we leave aside the preliminary difficulties which emerged at the interview of the Pope with the Patriarch, was to determine the procedure to be followed. The Emperor, whose thoughts were mainly fixed on the defence of Constantinople, wished to await the delegates of the princes, in order to settle first of all the political and military question. But the numerous theologians of the rival camps did not agree to this. After the opening of the Council (9 April 1438) commissions were nominated for the purpose of solving the fundamental divergences between the two Churches: the Procession of the Holy Ghost, the use of unleavened bread, the nature of the pains of purgatory, the primacy of the Pope.

The opponents of the union, at whose head was Mark of Ephesus, demanded that it should first be discussed "whether it is permitted to add to the Creed," thinking thus to block the union by this preliminary question. It was in vain that Bessarion asked that the question should be put in this form: "is the *Filioque* lawful?" The point of view of Mark of Ephesus prevailed, and on 14 October began a long series of oratorical sessions, in which Greeks and Latins confuted each other in turn and quite fruitlessly. The form of a debate by picked opponents was then tried, but, after a brilliant oratorical tournament which lasted several days between Mark of Ephesus and Julian Cesarini, the discussion had made little advance. Then the plague, which was raging at Ferrara and had already made several victims in the Council, decided the Pope to remove the Council to Florence (10 January 1439).

Taught by the experience of Ferrara, the Pope and the Emperor resolved to quicken the discussions. It was arranged that there should be a public session three times a week, and that on the other days mixed commissions should transact preliminaries for the union. But fresh and endless debates on the Procession of the Holy Ghost began again for a month between Mark of Ephesus and John of Ragusa. Another change of method was tried. On 30 March it was decided to suppress the open discussions, and to substitute conferences between unionists of both sides. But the negotiations touching the union did not start before 13 April. After a series of preliminaries, the Greeks ended by agreeing on the identity of the formula *qui ex Patre Filioque procedit*, and *qui ex Patre per Filium procedit* (3 June). The union was now in sight.

Concurrently with these theological discussions, political harmony was being promoted. The Pope undertook to preach the crusade for the defence of Constantinople, to maintain permanently a force of 300 soldiers to guard the city, and to supply galleys in event of a siege. Then, in order to accelerate matters, the Pope put into the hands of the Emperor's delegates schedules, on which were noted the doctrines to be accepted on the points in dispute. It was their duty to get the Greeks to subscribe to them.

On 12 June an agreement was reached about the nature of the pains of purgatory, on 15 June about the eucharistic bread, unleavened or leavened, on 20 June about the words of consecration. But when the doctrine of the primacy of the Pope was touched upon, the whole discussion nearly began *de novo*. Heated debates were held, and the Emperor talked of leaving. Finally, on 26 June Bessarion proposed a formula of conciliation, which recognised the universal authority of the Pope as "the representative and vicar of Christ," the rights and privileges of the Eastern Churches being reserved. Nothing now was left but to draw up the decree of union which, translated into Greek, was approved by the Pope and the Emperor on 5 July. The next day, 6 July, in the cathedral of Florence, under the dome completed by Brunelleschi in 1436, the decree was read in Latin by Cardinal Julian Cesarini and in

Greek by Bessarion; the two prelates then kissed each other, and all the members of the Council, the Emperor at their head, bent the knee before the Pope.

Finally, after the close of the Council the union was completed by the declarations of assent which the Eastern Churches sent to the Pope, each like the Greek Church retaining its liturgical and disciplinary uses. On 22 November 1439 the union was accepted by the delegates of Constantine, Patriarch of the Armenians, on 5 February 1441 by the Jacobites of Syria. On 2 September 1441 the Pope received an embassy of Constantine, King of the Ethiopians, and on 25 February 1443 he announced in an encyclical that the Ethiopians had adhered to the union. Finally, on 26 April 1442 Eugenius IV promulgated at St John Lateran the constitutions for the Syrians, the Chaldeans, and the Maronites.

For the first time since 1054 the unity of the Church seemed restored, and even the last scattered remnants of the heretical sects, most of which had been separated from the Church since the fifth century, had ended by returning to the fold. Whereas at the Council of Lyons the union had been imposed upon the Greek clergy by the will of the Emperor, at Florence its representatives had come voluntarily to debate with the Latins. The most obstinate opponents of the union, such as Mark of Ephesus, had been able to bring forward their objections without fear. The question seemed settled for all time to come, and Christendom, united in one and the same communion, would be able to devote itself to the crusade against the Turks. In order to cement this union more closely, on 18 December 1439 the Pope admitted Bessarion, Archbishop of Nicaea, and Isidore, Archbishop of Kiev, to the College of Cardinals.

Unhappily by signing the union at Florence John Palaeologus had only accomplished a part of his task. It was now necessary to make the clergy and the people of Constantinople accept it. On his return to his capital (1 February 1440) the Emperor encountered an obstinate opposition. If Ducas may be believed[1], when the Venetian ships with John VIII and his suite on board entered the Golden Horn, the travellers were greeted with ribaldry and insults. Many bishops who had subscribed to the decree of union protested that their signatures had been extracted from them by force. The Patriarch Joseph had died at Florence, and the Emperor had to exercise great pressure on the clergy of St Sophia to induce them to nominate a unionist successor, Metrophanes, Bishop of Cyzicus.

The opposition was led by the Emperor's own brother, the Despot Demetrius, and notably by Mark of Ephesus, whose submission John VIII, notwithstanding the solicitations of the Pope, had not succeeded in obtaining. Mark soon became very popular and was venerated as a saint. He began a very active campaign against the union in the monasteries of Constantinople and on Mount Athos, where the monks refused to

[1] Ducas, 31 (MPG, CLVII. col. 1013).

communicate with the unionists. In the end Mark was ordered to return to his diocese of Ephesus. Imprisoned in the island of Lemnos, he continued his propaganda and won over to his views the Emperor's private secretary, George Scholarius, who had faithfully served the Council.

In order that the union might triumph at Constantinople, the Western Crusade, on which it had been conditional, ought to have been rapidly organised, and ought to have won sufficiently decisive victories to release Constantinople from the grip of the Turks. In spite of the disturbed condition of the East the Pope tried to keep his promise so far as possible. In 1443 an army commanded by Cardinal Julian Cesarini joined forces with John Hunyadi and Vladislav I, King of Hungary. The Sultan Murād II suffered a sanguinary defeat before Niš. On 24 December 1443 the crusaders entered Sofia: the road to Constantinople was open. Unfortunately the leaders of the Crusade were unable to follow up their victory. On 15 July John Hunyadi signed a truce with Murād. Julian Cesarini refused to recognise it. The crusaders continued their march in Bulgaria, but the disaster that befel them at Varna on 10 November 1444 wrecked all the hopes of Christendom. Constantinople was nearing its death-throes.

This serious defeat and the death of John VIII (31 October 1448) increased the boldness of the opponents of the union. The new Emperor, Constantine XI, brother of John VIII, had been one of its most determined partisans. George Scholarius dared to propose that his coronation should be deferred until he had given pledges for his orthodoxy. Threatened with prosecution, George took refuge in a monastery, and under the name of Gennadius succeeded Mark of Ephesus, who died in 1447, as head of the opponents of the union.

Under his influence an anti-unionist council, at which the three Eastern Patriarchs were present, assembled in St Sophia in 1450[1]. The Patriarch Gregory, elected since 1443, was cited to appear there to justify himself, and on his refusal he was deposed and replaced by the monk Athanasius. Gemistos Plethon violently attacked the Latin doctrine of the Holy Ghost, denounced the pressure which the Emperor had brought to bear on the bishops to force them to admit it, and resisted the ambitious schemes of Bessarion. A list of Latin errors was drawn up in twenty-nine articles and published. The Patriarch Gregory was obliged to fly to Italy.

At the moment when the blockade of Constantinople was tightening again, and on the eve of the accession of Mahomet II, no demonstration could be more inopportune. On 11 October 1451 Pope Nicholas V called upon Constantine XII to proclaim solemnly the union at Constantinople, to bring back the Patriarch Gregory, and to compel the clergy to mention

[1] The exact date is uncertain. Mansi, *Concilia*, XIII, 1365 seq. Vast, *Le Cardinal Bessarion*, p. 133.

the name of the Pope in the liturgy. The decree was brought to Constantinople by Cardinal Isidore of Kiev in 1452. He negotiated with the opposing party, lavished promises and threats, and ended by bringing over part of the superior clergy.

Finally, on 12 December 1452 the union was solemnly proclaimed in St Sophia in the presence of Constantine, the legate, and the Patriarch Gregory, who officiated together with the assistance of 300 priests. But the infuriated populace rushed to the monastery of Pantokrator, where they found written by Gennadius on the door of his cell a prophecy which threatened the Empire with its coming slavery to the Turks. In that fanatical crowd, already attacked by what has been called "siege-fever," the conviction spread that the Panagia (the Virgin) would herself defend her city, as in the times of Heraclius and of Photius. While the crowd was shouting in the streets "Death to the Azymites!" the Grand Duke Lucas Notaras declared that he would rather see the turban at Constantinople than the hat of a Roman cardinal. Henceforward the church of St Sophia, where the union had been proclaimed, was deserted by the people, and remained empty until that gloomy vigil of 28 May 1453 which preceded the capture of Constantinople.

Obliged to choose between the safety of the Empire and the autonomy of their Church, the Greeks resolutely sacrificed their political independence to their hatred of the West and to their antipathy to Rome. There is no doubt that their attitude diminished the good-will of the Western nations, as is proved by a curious question put to the Pope on the point, whether a Christian had the right to go to the assistance of schismatic Greeks[1]. Besides this, the new régime which the Greek Church was about to experience had already been working for many years in the provinces occupied by the Turks. The bishops, nominated by the Patriarchs, were everywhere recognised by the conquerors as the civil and religious heads of the Christian community[2]. Mahomet II therefore had no difficulty in extending this régime to the whole Empire by requiring, immediately after his entry into Byzantium, the election of a new Patriarch; this was Gennadius, the leader of the opponents of the union.

Thus for four centuries the Byzantine Emperors and the Popes indefatigably laboured to stay the schism which divided Christendom since 1054. Whether their object was to conclude an alliance against a common enemy, or to make Constantinople a rampart against Asiatic invasion, the necessity of first attaining religious union always thwarted their wish for agreement.

[1] Jorga, *Notices et extraits pour servir à l'histoire des croisades au* XVe *siècle*, 4th series, p. 46.

[2] Jorga, *op. cit.* pp. 32–34 (extraits d'un rapport daté de 1436 sur les rapports entre les Turcs et l'Eglise grecque).

This much-desired union was, in truth, the ambition of the Christian policy of the last four centuries of the Middle Ages, but to the reasons for its failure, which the analysis of the facts has shewn, we must add a more profound cause. The Christian policy, the European policy we might say, which surpassed in breadth the narrow standpoint of the territorial policy of the various states, was clearly grasped only by the great Popes of the Middle Ages, such as Gregory VII, Innocent III, Gregory X, and by Byzantine Emperors such as Alexius I, Manuel Comnenus, and Michael Palaeologus; but their views were different and their interests irreconcilable. The Caesars of Byzantium, at least until Manuel Comnenus, cherished the illusive hope of regaining the heritage of the Caesars of Rome; for them the union was but a means of rebuilding their sovereignty in the West, or of saving it in the East. The Popes, on their side, saw in the union under them the unity of the restored Church, a Christendom united in one communion and forgetting its private quarrels, which were veritable civil wars, in order to repel the infidel and make the whole world the kingdom of Christ.

Between these two conceptions agreement was impossible, and this explains why the union could only be realised in periods of crisis, whether by violent conquest as in 1204, or in the face of an imminent peril as in 1274 or in 1439. On the contrary, every time the situation improved the pontifical doctrine and the imperial doctrine came into conflict, without any real hope of conciliation.

It is thus easy to see why the union, realised at three separate times, had on each occasion so ephemeral an existence. The abnormal conditions in which it was concluded doomed it to early failure. In 1204 the union imposed by force lighted in the heart of the Greeks an unquenchable hatred. The union of 1274 was tainted in its core by the violent pressure which Michael Palaeologus brought to bear on his clergy. The union of 1439, although debated by an Ecumenical Council, came too late. When the house is blazing it is too late to settle disputes about ways of preventing fire.

CHAPTER XX.

THE MONGOLS.

In attempting to give an account of the Mongols, the historian is confronted with many serious obstacles. At the outset, it would seem as though the stories of these wandering tribes could never be co-ordinated; the incidents of their history are so heterogeneous in character, that it seems an impossible task to pick out a connecting thread running through them all. The internal events, which should assist the historian in tracing the development and confederation of the various tribes, baffle and retard him. The early history is shrouded in myth and mystery. At so late an epoch in the progress of humanity, the student might not unreasonably expect trustworthy evidence and records. But, in reviewing the early period of the Mongolian State, it is a matter of exceptional importance to separate the historical elements from the fictitious, and this is a task involving much discrimination and patience. Every piece of information seems, on its own merits and taken by itself, to be petty and negligible; nor is it easy to discover any positive relation of any consequence between disconnected and sporadic occurrences. There are no central figures, no outstanding personalities, before the time of Jenghiz. The darkness is broken by no brilliant flashes but only by tiny gleams that serve but to intensify the obscurity. We cannot mark cause and effect; we cannot explain, by the recognised canons of historical judgment, the phenomena displayed by the Mongol history. On the other hand, if the events of their internal progress are sporadic and disconnected, if they seem to violate the normal course of national growth, when we come to examine the external events and the expansion of these savage tribes, we find ourselves confronted by facts that are equally inexplicable. Insignificant at home and enormous abroad may be said to sum their salient characteristics, in any case during the earlier periods. It is precisely on account of their foreign relations that a knowledge of the Mongols is essential to the student. Without their effect on the human race outside their borders, the Mongols could be suffered to remain in obscurity.

The difficulties that await the investigator are not exhausted. He has to work with a telescope instead of a microscope. Not only has a vast extent of territory to be kept under constant observation, but movements and actions among neighbouring peoples must be watched closely. The history of the Mongols knows no geographical boundaries. The settled limits of nations were swiftly and ruthlessly overthrown. Unchecked by human valour, they were able to overcome the terrors of vast deserts, the barriers of mountains and seas, the severities of climate, and the ravages of famine and pestilence. No dangers could appal them, no stronghold could resist them, no prayer for mercy could move them. Wherever their fancy roamed, their hordes followed. Flourishing cities perished in a night, leaving no memorial but ruins and mounds of piled-up corpses. The quiet that followed the Mongol invasions was not the calm that settled on a world wearied of strife, eager to foster once again the fruits of civilisation: it was the gasp of expiring nations in their death-agony, before the eternal silence of the tomb. They made their deserts and they called it peace. To follow the destinies of the Mongols, it is necessary to think in continents not in countries, for like an irresistible torrent the armies of the Khans swept over the map of Asia and Europe. A knowledge of no single language will suffice to equip a student for the task of investigating the Mongol races with any profundity. Besides the Tartar languages, some acquaintance is essential with the languages of the peoples with whom the Mongols came into contact. Their armies ranged over all Central Asia, pushing on eastwards to China and westwards to Russia and even to Germany. As a result, the student must be prepared to deal with sources in many tongues, and with more freedom and greater facility than is the case when dealing with other nations.

But if this combination of circumstances invests a study of the Mongols with difficulty, it constitutes an equally potent reason for undertaking the task. We are confronted with a new power in history, with a force that was to bring to an abrupt end, as a *deus ex machina*, many dramas that would otherwise have ended in a deadlock, or would have dragged on an interminable course. The very magnitude of the Mongol influence and the colossal area of their operations should prove an additional incentive to the student, and render an attempt to estimate the nature and scope of the changes which ensued alike attractive and fruitful.

In Europe the Mongols overran Russia, Hungary, and Silesia; to the upheaval which they brought about, the establishment of the Turkish Empire, and consequently the growth of the Renaissance, must be directly attributed. This same upheaval reacted on the contests between Saracen and Crusader and, nearer home, on the antagonism of the Papacy and the Empire. The extermination of the Assassins (1256), a task beyond the power of Europe or Syria, was a matter of comparative ease to the Mongols. Before the terror which their name inspired, Europe seemed utterly demoralised and incapable of resistance, and, had not the Mamlūks intervened (1260) and beaten back the invaders at a critical moment, there is little doubt but that a great portion of Europe would have succumbed to Tartar rule.

The convulsion caused by the Mongols in Europe, great though it was, cannot be compared to that produced in Asia. The destruction of Baghdad and the overthrow of the Caliphate (1258), the annihilation of the Kin or Golden Dynasty which ruled the northern half of China (1234), the conquest of Southern China, of Khwārazm, Persia, and the surrounding countries, the establishment of the rule of the Moguls[1] in India, are some of the events any of which alone would suffice to make a knowledge of the Mongol power indispensable to the general historian. It is not accurate to regard the Mongols merely as a ravaging horde. After sacking Baghdad, Hūlāgū founded an observatory; after conquering China, Kublai established a university at Cambalu (Pekin). The "scourge of God" does not smite blindly. It is a noteworthy phenomenon that a successful barbarian attack on civilisation, however destructive be its ravages at the moment, is ultimately followed by a great revival, and this revival may often be traced to the very catastrophe which seemed destined to overwhelm culture in irretrievable ruin. In the sphere of religion, this may be observed by the Assyrian (B.C. 587) and Roman (A.D. 70) conquests of Judaea, which, in the end, created and strengthened the diaspora and made the outer world acquainted with the moral teachings of the Pentateuch and Prophets. In the spheres of the arts and humanities, the Roman conquest of Greece, the Turkish conquest of the Byzantine Empire, are instances which go to prove how the accumulated stores of learning may be released and rendered accessible to a wider circle. The Arab conquest of Spain gave the light of science, medicine, philosophy, and poetry to Europe in the Dark Ages. The capture of Jerusalem led directly to the establishment of the schools in Jamnia, the ruthless persecution of Hadrian produced the academies of Babylon, and "on the day when the Temple was destroyed, the Messiah was born."

The same statement may be made of the Mongols. The fall of Baghdad transferred the seat of the humanities to Egypt. At the same time it dispersed many scholars and humanists who survived the *débacle*. Their dispersion throughout the Muslim lands brought academic strength to the places where they settled, while the removal of the literary centre of gravity from Baghdad to Cairo facilitated the access of the Western world to the culture of the Orient. But, apart from mere negative results, the growth of the Mongol power was responsible for other developments in the East. The first and foremost of these was the unification of Asia. This must not be interpreted in the modern sense of political unity or homogeneity. The Mongol government secured tranquillity within its vast borders. The roads were open and a traveller could, as things went, count upon a safe journey, unless he had the misfortune to pass within range of the Emperor's funeral *cortège*, in which case his fate was death. There was complete religious toleration, and it is only a superficial judgment that will ascribe this to spiritual indifference on the part of the Mongols. Economic changes were also introduced; thus the service of posts,

[1] The later Mogul Emperors hated, and tried to disown, their Mongol origin.

though utilised by the Arabs previously, was largely increased, and the use of paper money was sanctioned by Gaikhātū Khan in 1294 and previously by Kublai. No nation can claim to excel in every branch of human activity, and the deficiency of the Mongols in the domain of literature was made good in other directions.

It is necessary to begin a sketch of the Mongols with a brief account of their origin, and an explanation or rather an enumeration of the names by which they are known. The name Mongol itself was first applied to certain tribes inhabiting Central Asia. It has come to be a generic name, far more catholic and comprehensive, but it is doubtful whether the various tribes surrendered their own individual names in favour of a uniform imperial designation. "Mongol" as a national name would seem to be more frequent in the mouths of foreigners. It is also known to Europe in the form of Mogul, a title which is more properly restricted to the Mongol rulers of India and which has probably arisen through the Arabic Mughūl[1]. As to the etymology of the name, opinions are divided, the most generally accepted being that of Sanang Setzen (*b.* 1604) who derives the name from the word Mong which, in the Chinese language, has the signification of brave.

The second name, Tartar, should more correctly be spelt Tātār, as in Persian. The first "r" has been inserted in consequence of a fanciful connexion with Tartarus; the paronomasia was attributed variously to Innocent IV and to others (*Ad sua Tartara Tartari detrudentur*)[2]. Various theories were held in the Middle Ages with regard to the origin of the Tartars[3]. According to Roger Bacon, they were the soldiers of Antichrist; Friar John of Pian di Carpine believed them to be remnants of the ten tribes whom Alexander the Great endeavoured to shut up in the mountains by the Caspian. Most, however, of these fanciful speculations were based on the contemporary estimate of the character of the invading hordes, not on geographical or ethnological considerations. Fear, not history, was their source. As a matter of fact the Turkish elements in the Mongol confederacy repudiated the name Tartar which, according to Howorth, "was sometimes applied generically by the Chinese to all their Northern neighbours and it was thus that it came to be applied to the Mongols. But there was a specific race, Tartar, from which the generic term was derived. This we might guess from the fact that the name Tartar was known in the West long before the days of Mongol supremacy and when the Mongols were only an obscure tribe."

Mongol, then, and Tartar were names of two tribes living in the Eastern portion of Central Asia, to the north-west of China, by the river Uldza and

[1] Rubruquis always spells the name Moal; see Rubruquis, p. 112 note (Hakluyt Society's ed.). For the etymology see Howorth, I. p. 27.

[2] For a discussion on the name Tartar see Yule, I. p. 12; Rubruquis, XVII and XVIII (Notes); and Howorth, I. p. 700 note.

[3] See Matthew Paris, *Chronica Majora*, Rolls ed., pp. 76 ff., 386 ff.

by the Kerulen, Orkhon, Onon, and other tributaries to the great river Amur. The origin of these tribes is shrouded in an obscurity which for the present purpose requires no investigation. It is sufficient to pick up the thread of the story at the place where, having formed a powerful confederacy, they proceeded to launch forth their hordes in all directions and play a prominent part on the stage of general history. A brief enumeration of the component elements would resolve itself into a mere list of names, but a few of the more important tribes deserve mention. Of these the chief was that known as the Kipchaks, who ultimately spread over the districts to the north of the Black Sea and the Caspian, practically from the Danube to the Ural. They were one of the five sections of the Turks under Oghuz Khan, whence their later Arabic name of Ghuzz (Uzes, Guzes) is derived[1]. To Europe they were known as Cumans[2], from Comania (Kūmistān) in Persia, a name derived from the river Kuma. In the ninth century their expansion brought them to the Volga, and having conquered territory round the banks of that river they made themselves a thorn in the side of Russia, until their incorporation by the Mongols in the Golden Horde during the thirteenth century.

The Eastern neighbours of the Kipchaks were the Kankali, whose territory lay to the north of Lake Aral, between the Ural river and Lake Balkash. They were also part of Oghuz Khan's Turkish subjects; Rubruquis and other travellers, in the course of their wanderings, visited and mentioned them. Many of the Kankali were in the service of the Khwārazm Shāh until the overthrow of the latter by Jenghiz Khan. Farther eastward, to the south of the Ob and Yenisey rivers, were the Naimans, also Turks, in whose district was the famous town Karakorum, which Ogdai Khan made his capital. In 1211 Kushluk, Khan of the Naimans, usurped the sovereignty of the Kara Khitai. In the time of Rubruquis, the Naimans were, according to that traveller[3], subjects of Prester John, but Mangu Khan claimed their allegiance[4]. To the south of the Naimans, in the western part of Mongolia, stretching towards China were the Uighurs. By the close of the eighth century their power increased and they had diplomatic relations with China. This tribe was one of the centres of Nestorian Christianity. To the north of the Uighurs, beyond the lands of the Keraits, were the Merkits, who have been described by Marco Polo and Rashīd. They were conquered by Jenghiz Khan in 1197. These were the chief tribes in the Mongol Confederacy[5].

As regards the origins of the Mongols, it is not necessary to say much. Many fables are told about the various tribes and their heroes; among the

[1] See John of Pian di Carpine, p. 36, note 2. See also Benjamin of Tudela, ed. Adler, p. 61 and note.

[2] This was first mentioned by Rubruquis, see p. xxxviii. But see *supra,* Chapter VII (A), pp. 197–8.

[3] Rubruquis, p. 162.

[4] *Ibid.* pp. 2 and 9.

[5] For details see Howorth, I. pp. 1–26.

most interesting of these is the story of the ancestral hero, nourished when a child by a wolf, thus furnishing an Eastern parallel to Romulus and Remus. But until the twelfth century the influence exercised on the outside world was insignificant. Mention is first made of the Mongols in Chinese records, in the history of the T'ang Dynasty (618–690), and scattered references occur later, for instance in 984 and in 1180.

Rashīd traces the descent of the Mongols back to Japhet, but of course the greater part of the early period is merely mythical. It is only near the period of Jenghiz Khan that safe ground is reached. During the Kin Dynasty in China, it is known that many Mongols, probably with their Khan, Kabul, became subject to the Chinese Emperor Tai-Tsung from 1123–1137, but rebelled in 1138 after his death. This rebellion marks the beginning of the rise of the Mongols. It was at this period that they suffered from internal dissension; the feud between the Mongol and Tartar tribes was ended by the triumph of the former through the instrumentality of Jenghiz Khan. This hero was the son of Yesukai, who was the grandson of Kabul Khan. While Yesukai in 1154–1155 was ravaging the Tartar lands, his wife Ogelen Eke (or Yulun) gave birth to a first-born son who was called Temujin, after the name of the Tartar chieftain recently slain by Yesukai. The name Temujin is most probably Chinese by etymology and means "excellent steel." The similarity of the Turkish Temurji (smith) is perhaps the origin of the fable that Jenghiz was himself a smith. Temujin, later known by his style of Jenghiz Khan, was born at a place called Deligun Buldagha, near the Onon. The name of the spot has remained until the present time; by Rubruquis it is called Onan Kerule. When he was thirteen years of age, his father Yesukai died, leaving to his son a small nucleus of subjects. At the outset Jenghiz was confronted with many difficulties. The spirit of disaffection which prevailed among his followers soon developed into revolt. A general rising jeopardised the prospects of the youthful chieftain, but the energy and capability of his mother Yulun recovered some of the lost ground for him. A long period of unending strife ensued. With the Naimans, whose centre is said to have been Karakorum, and the Keraits, Jenghiz had to wage war continuously, and with varying success. Once he was captured and tortured, but managed to escape with his life. At length after many years he succeeded in consolidating his position. Finally, after a series of victories Jenghiz overcame his last opponent, Wang Khan, and became supreme over the nucleus of the Mongols. From the date of the Kuriltai, or general convocation, which took place after this event, in 1203, the beginning of the empire is usually considered to date. The title of Khan, was, however, assumed in 1206 at another assembly by the river Onon. The period from this date until 1227, when Jenghiz died, comprises the era of extension and conquest. The first object of attack was China, which consisted of two main divisions: the Northern, with Yenkin (near Pekin) as its capital, and the Southern, the chief town of which was Lingan, also called Hangchow or Kinsai. This Empire was ruled by the Sung Dynasty and the Northern by the Kin. The Kin rulers were supreme over Tartary. Subject to their sway were the Khitans, who had previously been supplanted in the dominion of the Northern Empire. Preliminary invasions of Hia or Tangut, the province to the west of the Yellow River, were successfully undertaken in 1208; the Kin army was defeated and the territory within the great wall reduced to submission. These victories paved the way for an attack on a larger scale, and in 1213 three grand armies were despatched. The main expedition under the command of Jenghiz himself and Tulē, his youngest son, followed a south-eastern direction. He sent his three other sons—Juji, Jagatai, and Ogdai—with another force to form his right wing and operate on the south, while the remainder, under his brothers, were despatched to the east in the direction of the sea. It is unnecessary to follow the steps of these armies in detail; it is sufficient to record their complete success. The subjugation of the Hia occupied him from 1208 to 1212, and the Kin and Kara-Khitai in Eastern Turkestan from 1212 to 1214. Having crushed these foes, Jenghiz turned his ambitions to the western horizon. His dominions now reached as far as the territory of Muḥammad, the Shāh of Khwārazm. This mighty empire was bounded on the west by Kurdistān, Khūzistān, and the Persian Gulf; to the east it reached nearly to the Indus. It included the littoral of Lake Aral, and partly of the Caspian, on the north. It comprised Azarbā'ījān, 'Irāq 'Ajamī, Fārs, Kirmān, Mukrān (Beluchistan), Sīstān, Khurāsān, Afghanistan, the Pamirs, Sughd, and Mā-warā-an-Nahr (Transoxiana) among its main portions. The empire had been originally founded by Anūshtigīn, a slave of Malik Shāh the Seljūq. At the time of Jenghiz, Muḥammad, the Shāh of Khwārazm, was at the height of his power, and it is estimated that he could put into the field an army of half a million soldiers. War was inevitable; the insatiable ambition of Jenghiz supplied the *casus belli*; the execution by Muḥammad of the Mongol envoys was alleged as a pretence. In 1219 Jenghiz left his capital Karakorum with two divisions under his sons Juji and Jagatai. Massacre and pillage were the concomitants of their victories. Piles of corpses and the blackened traces of ruined cities marked their progress. Pity was unknown to them; the most atrocious treachery and disregard of oaths and of promises of quarter were employed to hunt out and extirpate the scattered survivors of their barbarity. The flourishing cities of Tashkent, Nur, Bukhārā, Samarqand, and Balkh were utterly destroyed, and their inhabitants ruthlessly butchered, according to the well-known Mongol principle, "Stone dead hath no fellow." Muḥammad fled to Nīshāpūr, but was pursued to the shores of the Caspian, where he died, leaving a shattered wreck of a kingdom to his son Jalāl-ad-Dīn. Merv and Nīshāpūr shared the fate of the other cities. Finally Jenghiz and Jalāl-ad-Dīn met in battle on the banks of the Indus; the latter was utterly defeated but managed to escape to Delhi, where he found a refuge and peace for a while at the court of the Sultan. The last act of Jenghiz in this campaign was to massacre all the inhabitants of Herat, since they had ventured to depose his nominee from the governorship. According to Douglas, 1,600,000 people were slain within the walls.

Jenghiz returned, but did not long enjoy the fruits of peace. Not even the enormous booty which his victories had brought him could induce the conqueror to spare his neighbours. The death of the last of the Kin Dynasty in 1223 removed the final shadow of autonomy in North China, and Jenghiz was now face to face with the Sung Dynasty in the South. He set out on a fresh expedition, but died in 1227 by the Sale river in Mongolia. The funeral escort that bore his corpse homeward slaughtered every person whom they met, in order to prevent the news of his death from being divulged.

Jenghiz Khan deserves to be remembered as a ruler, not only as a conqueror. In the intervals of bloodshed, he found time to promote the arts of peace and order. He organised a regular service of posts and couriers, and rendered the highways secure for travellers. His tolerance to all religious beliefs was probably due less to superstition than to indifference. Not being deeply attached to any definite faith, he was not anxious that one creed should secure preponderance. Divines, physicians, and learned men were exempted from taxes. Perhaps the only plea by which a captive might save his life was that of learning, though few instances of such clemency are preserved. Jenghiz introduced the use of the Uighur character, and caused his subjects to acquire the art of writing. He compiled a code of laws, or rather authorised the codification of existing tribal customs, which he raised to a legal value, and to which he imparted the sanction of his authority. His personal habits were such as could be expected from his character. The joys of the chase, mingled with frequent drinking-bouts, were the normal relaxations of Jenghiz. His wives and concubines numbered five hundred. But, though he ruled his subjects with an iron hand, his death found him at the zenith of popularity.

The Empire of Jenghiz Khan was the largest that ever fell to one conqueror. The brain reels at the thought of the slaughter by which it was achieved. In China over eighteen millions of human beings were slain by his armies. No plague, no other "Scourge of God," has ever smitten so severely. Howorth[1] would seek to palliate his record, but it is impossible to do so.

The death of Jenghiz was followed by an interregnum of two years. The affairs of state were administered without interruption by the sons of the late chief and by the officers whom he had appointed. At length, in 1229, a Kuriltai was held in order to elect an overlord. It is important to notice the names of four sons of Jenghiz whose claims were considered at this Kuriltai, for their subsequent dissensions contributed in no small

[1] See Howorth, *op. cit.* I. pp. 113 *seqq.*

degree to the disruption of the Empire. Juji, the eldest son, had died during his father's lifetime, but the claims to the succession which were his by right of primogeniture passed, according to Mongol custom, to his family. His three brothers, in order of age, were Jagatai, Ogdai, and Tulē. The pretensions of Juji's family might without injustice have been passed over in favour of Jagatai, but the Kuriltai had no free choice. Jenghiz before his death had settled the destinies of his sons and, although he ventured to break down the regular Mongol ideas of inheritance, the force of his authority remained binding beyond the grave. The Kuriltai, after due deliberation and no little hesitation, carried out the commands of Jenghiz. Ogdai, who was elected chief Khan and successor to his father, retained Tulē near the seat of government, appointing him to various official posts. The family of Juji received possessions in the west, Jagatai in the Uighur country. For the present there was loyal co-operation between the brothers, and with the accession of Ogdai a new stage in the history of Mongol expansion begins.

This expansion proceeded in both directions, towards China and towards Europe. The death of Jenghiz found the Mongol possessions extending "from the China Sea to the Dnieper." In China, the Kin Dynasty had been beaten and reduced to submission. In the west, the kingdom of Khwārazm had been destroyed and its ruler driven far away from his home. Numerous expeditions had spread the fame of the Mongols and shaken Europe with terror. The time was ripe for another ebullition. In China the subjugated Kin were beginning to shew signs of revival. Sporadic hostilities had occurred. In 1228 and again in 1230 the Mongols were defeated; the battles, though by no means serious in character, were sufficient to raise false hopes among the Chinese; the Mongols no longer appeared to be invincible. Eventually Ogdai roused himself to punish the rebels and determined to teach them an enduring lesson. It was not merely the effect of the Kin victories and various incidents of a provocative nature that set the Mongols in motion; it was the prospect of further conquests beyond the territories of the Kin. The Southern division of China under the Sung Dynasty, probably alarmed at the fate of the Kin, had endeavoured to propitiate the Mongols and avoid any collision with them. It is in any case doubtful whether this course would have had any efficacy, but a political error at this juncture gave the Mongols a *casus belli*, which when they had finished with the Kin they were not slow to utilise. The Sung Emperor refused to grant the Mongol armies leave to pass through his dominions, and slew their envoy. This refusal was to cost him dear. Meanwhile Ogdai marched against the Kin from the north; Tulē invaded Honan from Paoki, in the Shensi province. After various campaigns, battles, and massacres, the Kin were finally swept out of existence in 1234, and the descendants of Jenghiz maintained the supreme rule until displaced by the Ming Dynasty in 1368.

The overthrow of the Kin was speedily followed up by an attack on the Sung. The Sung Emperor had ended by assisting the Mongols in their war against the Kin. His reward was to have been the province of Honan. This the Mongols refused to evacuate. Having secured all that they desired from the Sung Emperor, they were in no mood to keep their promise, and alleging as a pretext his former refusal of a passage to the Mongol forces, they despatched an army in 1235.

At this stage it is desirable to turn back to events in the West. The last years of Jenghiz Khan were marked by signs of activity among the conquered cities of Khwārazm. When Muḥammad Shāh, defeated by the Mongol armies, died of illness on the Caspian shore, he left a son Jalāl-ad-Dīn. The destruction of the Khwārazmian empire deprived the latter of a throne. A beaten fugitive from his Mongol pursuers, he reached Delhi. Here the Sultan received him with kindness and gave him his daughter in marriage. Jalāl-ad-Dīn watched for a favourable opportunity, and, with the aid of his father-in-law, succeeded in regaining piecemeal large portions of his lost heritage. He crossed the Indus and marched north. Although his troops were few in number and had suffered severely from the hardships of the journey, he effected the expulsion of his surviving brother Ghiyāth-ad-Dīn, who ruled ʿIrāq ʿAjamī, Khurāsān, and Māzandarān, and seized his dominions. He attacked and defeated the Caliph of Baghdad. In 1226 he captured Tiflis in Georgia, between the Black Sea and the Caspian, and, in the following year, overcame a small Mongol army. The important city of Khilat, in Armenia, now fell into his hands and his power increased on all sides. But vengeance fell upon him swiftly and suddenly. Ogdai sent a large force to reduce him, and before the news of its coming reached Jalāl-ad-Dīn he was surrounded in Diyārbakr. No chance of combat remained, for the Khwārazmian troops were far away. Jalāl-ad-Dīn took refuge in flight but was slain by a Kurd. His death brought an end to the Khwārazm Shāhs and their kingdom. But the Mongols did not cease their campaign. The horror inspired by their name was such that their victims abandoned all thoughts of resistance. It is related that the whole population of a large village obeyed the command of a single Mongol, and stood in a line while he slaughtered them, one by one. Terror and devastation spread all over the country. By 1236 they had overcome Erbil, Diyārbakr, Khilat, Mesopotamia, Azarbāʾījān, Georgia, and Armenia. They made terrible examples of Kars and Tiflis. The Caliph of Baghdad preached a *jihād* (sacred war) against them and won a victory at Jabal Hamrīn on the Tigris. In 1238 he was, however, defeated, and the Mongol armies marched northwards.

The hordes of Mongols seemed as inexhaustible as they were irresistible. In 1235 Ogdai organised three large expeditions: against Korea, the Sung Dynasty, and the country beyond the river Volga. The King of Korea had submitted to Jenghiz Khan in 1218, but subsequently various incidents stirred up discord between vassal and overlord. The murder of a Mongol envoy in 1231 was followed by a victorious invasion, led by Sabutai, who set up Mongol governors in many cities of Korea. In 1232 a popular upheaval resulted in the assassination of many of these officials, and the King of Korea, frightened of the consequences, fled to the island of Siang-Hua on the west coast. Ogdai summoned him to appear before his judgment-seat to answer for these acts; a refusal led to the expedition of 1235. By 1241 the Korean King submitted and gave the required hostages.

The expedition against the Sung Dynasty, though generally successful, effected no permanent conquests, and the Southern Dynasty was not finally reduced until the time of Kublai Khan, the second son of Tulē.

The third army requires further mention, for this force swept down upon the West like an overwhelming avalanche. No crowning mercy, such as the victory of Tours in 732 against the tide of Islām, saved the destinies of Europe. Divided, and distracted by internal strife, the Christian countries could offer no opposition to the invading hordes. The Mongol wave spent its energy and fell back, shattered by no rock or impediment. Had not the death of Ogdai recalled Bātu and his generals, there is little doubt but that Paris and Rome would have shared the fate of Kiev and Moscow.

It was originally the wish of Ogdai to lead the Western army in person, but on reflection he changed his mind and assigned the command to Bātu the son of Juji. With Bātu the renowned Sabutai was associated as adviser. Ogdai's sons and nephews accompanied the expedition. The forces met in Great Bulgaria in 1237. The Mongol onslaught was characterised by its usual speed; indiscriminate slaughter, rape, and destruction, as before, marked their path. A list of Mongol victories resolves itself into a catalogue of doomed towns and ravaged country-sides. Blow after blow followed in quick succession. Bulgar, Ryazan, Moscow, Vladímir, are but a few of the places that succumbed. Princes, bishops, nuns, and children were slain with savage cruelty. It is impossible to describe the barbarities that prolonged the death of the unfortunate inhabitants. None remained to weep or to tell the tale of disaster. Novgorod was saved by a thaw which melted the ice and turned the country into an impassable swamp. Koselsk was the scene of such exceptional severity that the Mongols themselves noted the occasion by calling this place "Mobalig," town of woe. In 1240 the Mongols advanced still further, towards the Dnieper. Pereslavl, Chernigov, Glokhov, and finally the metropolitan city Kiev, were destroyed. The Mongols divided their forces, one part marching against Poland and the other through the Carpathians against Hungary. At Mohi on the Theiss the whole chivalry of Hungary was crushed in an overwhelming defeat. The nobility and clergy shared the fate of the common soldiers, and the King Béla IV escaped as a fugitive to the Adriatic. In the same year (1241) Henry, Duke of Silesia, was overthrown at Liegnitz near Breslau by the Mongols, and the whole of Silesia was given up to slaughter. The area over which the Mongol hordes were spreading seemed limitless; no country was safe.

Bātu followed up the capture of Pesth by crossing the Danube and assaulting Gran, which he took. Europe was now prostrate, and no saviour arose to ward off the Mongols. But the death of Ogdai, in the same year as that of Pope Gregory IX, involved the return of Bātu to Karakorum, in order to assist in the election of a new Khan, and the western portions of Europe were freed from the terror of the Mongol armies.

The coming of the Mongols found Europe utterly unprepared and heedless. The first invasion of 1222, when the forces of Jenghiz Khan crossed the Caucasus and ravaged parts of Russia, created little notice. The west of Europe seems to have been ignorant of the event, but in the years 1235–1238 two circumstances combined to awaken the Christian kings to a knowledge of the perils awaiting them. The first of these was an embassy from the Ismā'īlīyah, and the second was the arrival of the Mongol armies under Bātu and his generals. Those Ismā'īlīyah, or Ishmaelites, who are known to the general historian by the name of "Assassins," were themselves marked out by the Mongols as a prey, but they escaped attention until the time of Hūlāgū. Stirred by premonition, or roused by the fate of their neighbours, they strove to effect a combination against the all-conquering Mongols among all nations, even those mutually hostile, that were confronted by this same foe whose coming would involve them all in common ruin. The efforts of the Assassins were not limited to the rulers in their immediate neighbourhood. In 1238 they sent envoys to the Kings of France and England, asking their aid. The fame of this sect was great among the crusaders. Many distinguished men, Muslim and Christian, had fallen victims to their daggers, and Saladin himself narrowly escaped assassination. It would have been thought that, seeing the terror of their dreaded enemies, the Christian princes would have awakened to a sense of their position and have concluded an alliance, at least until such time as the Mongols had been repulsed. Who knows what the effect of such an alliance might have been? Apart from all military results, it is impossible to estimate the effect on Europe of friendly intercourse and military co-operation on a large scale with the Easterns[1]. But the warning fell on deaf ears. The Emperor Frederick II did indeed realise what was at stake. He wrote an extremely important letter to Henry III urging combined action, and giving what was for that time a fairly accurate account of the Mongols[2].

[1] Hayton, King of Little Armenia (1224–1269), was a friend and ally of the Mongols. He sent missions and himself visited Bātu and Mangu in 1254, after the accession of the latter. An account of his travels was compiled by one of his followers. See *Enc. Brit. s.v.* Cf. *supra*, Chapter VI, p. 175.

[2] Matthew Paris, *Chronica Majora* (Rolls ed.), pp. 112 ff.

Other rulers also bestirred themselves. In 1241, a few weeks before the battle of Liegnitz, the Landgrave of Thuringia appealed for aid to the Duke of Brabant, and the Church assisted in publishing the danger by proclaiming fasts and intercessions. In an often misquoted passage, Matthew Paris relates that in 1238 the fishermen from Friesland and Gothland, "dreading their attacks, did not, as was their custom, come to Yarmouth, in England, at the time of the herring-fisheries, at which place their ships usually loaded; and, owing to this, herrings in that year were considered of no value, on account of their abundance, and about forty or fifty, although very good, were sold for one piece of silver, even in places at a great distance from the sea."

Nevertheless, despite the growing feeling of insecurity, no active steps were taken. The envoys were given empty answers. Nothing but the quarrel between Emperor and Pope occupied men's minds. Some alleged that Frederick II had manufactured the scare in order to help his cause. Others, whose lack of political foresight was only equalled by their ignorance of the Mongols, suggested that, if Europe remained inactive, Mongols and Muslims would destroy one another and the triumph of the Cross would be assured. The mass of the population were too apathetic to be moved: nothing except the thoughts of Crusades could arouse them from their torpor. Pope Gregory IX had written letters of sympathy to the Queen of Georgia and to the King of Hungary, when these rulers had been smitten by the Mongol scourge, but his mind was concentrated on his quarrels with the Emperor. He died shortly after the battle of Liegnitz, when the death of Ogdai recalled the Mongols and gave Europe a breathing-space. The successor to Gregory was Innocent IV, who was elected in 1243. He, as none before him, understood what was at issue, and conceived two main plans for saving Christendom from the Mongols —attack and persuasion. In order to stimulate the former, he ordered a new combination of forces against them, and invested the expedition with the dignity of a crusade by offering to all who fought against the "ministers of Tartarus" spiritual privileges similar to those offered to the crusaders. Little came of these efforts, but the second plan, though equally ineffective, has proved of infinite value to later ages on account of the information thus gleaned concerning the Mongols.

The Pope imagined that, if the Mongols could be converted to Christianity, they would be restrained from attacking Europe through religious fears. Wonderful stories of Prester John filled Europe; it was possible that the Mongols were in some way connected with this strange monarch. There were the legends ascribing to the Mongols Semitic origin: they were the lost ten tribes, shut up by Alexander within impenetrable mountains, from which they had broken forth to ravage the world. In short the soil was ripe for the seed of the gospel, and the monk would succeed where the knight had failed.

This fond hope resulted in the missions of Friars John of Pian di

Carpine and Benedict the Pole in 1245, and of Friar William of Rubruck (Rubruquis) in 1253. The former were envoys of the Pope, the latter of Louis IX. The itineraries of these travellers have been preserved, and can well be ranked with the accounts of Marco Polo and Don Clavijo. The mass of information contained therein constitutes one of the principal sources of extant knowledge concerning the Mongols of this period. Diplomatically and spiritually the mission of Friar William was as unsuccessful as that of his predecessors, but from the point of view of the historian both journeys were signally fruitful.

Ogdai's death, which delivered Europe, occurred in his fifty-sixth year, on 11 December 1241. His comparatively early end was due to excessive intemperance, a fault to which Mongols were prone. His chief pleasure lay in hunting. He built a palace for himself at Karakorum, to which he gave the name of Ordu Balig or City of the Camp. The site of the palace and the marvels that were to be seen there have long been disputed, but the Central Asiatic expeditions of N. Yadrintsev (1889), of the Helsingfors Ugro-Finnish Society in 1890, and of Radlov in 1891, have succeeded in fixing the position. The use of paper currency was known to Ogdai, but it is uncertain whether he actually adopted this expedient. Certain reforms are also ascribed to him, notably the curbing of the extortionate demands and requisitions imposed by the princes and state officials upon the common people. His personal gentleness forms a contrast to the severity of Jagatai; but there was little evidence of tenderness in his government. The policy of rule by brute force was not modified until the later reigns of Mangu and Kublai.

After the death of Ogdai, the succession did not pass to either of his nominees, Kuchu or Shiramun, the son of Kuchu. The former was the third son of Ogdai and had predeceased his father in 1236. Shiramun was kept from the throne by the instrumentality of Turakina, the widow of the late Khan; Kuyuk, the eldest son of Ogdai, was ultimately, in 1246, elected as Khan, as Turakina wished.

The Kuriltai at which Kuyuk was chosen is of interest because of the presence of Friar John of Pian di Carpine, who gives a full description of the ceremony in his itinerary. The ill-will between the houses of Jagatai and Ogdai was all this while increasing, but the dominion of the house of Ogdai was not yet ended. The reign of Kuyuk, on the whole uneventful, is noteworthy on account of various incidents. A Musulman called 'Abd-ar-Raḥmān was allowed to purchase the farming of the taxes; this circumstance was greatly resented, because the efforts to distribute the taxes on a just basis were beginning to bear good fruit. The foreign wars were maintained and armies sent against Korea, the Sung, and Persia. Both in Mesopotamia and in Armenia the conquests and ravages of the Mongols continued. At the court of Kuyuk Nestorian Christians frequently appeared; Islām, Christianity, Buddhism, and Shamanism were tolerated on an equal footing.

At the death of Kuyuk (1248) considerable confusion ensued; Kaidu, grandson of Ogdai, and Chapar, son of Kaidu, successively held the Khanate for short and troublous periods. Discontent among the nobles and rival claims robbed the titular rulers of every shadow of authority, and finally in 1251 Mangu, the son of Tulē, was elected Khan. The feud between the houses of Jagatai and Ogdai was quelled and the house of Ogdai ruled no more. The house of Tulē, youngest son of Jenghiz, now took the lead.

The accession of Mangu brought a settlement to the political strife. A period of prosperity followed. Rubruquis, whose visit happened at this time, bears testimony that the luxury prevalent at Mangu's court was not incompatible with the stability of the State, efficiency in government, order and peace thoughout the Empire. Internal administration was wise and popular. The Mongols were beginning to learn the lesson of ruling as well as of conquering. But fresh conquests were soon undertaken; a new outburst was ready.

Reference has already been made to the Assassins. The Mongols decided that these dangerous foes could no longer be tolerated, and orders for their extermination were given. Hūlāgū, the brother of Mangu, was appointed for this work at the Kuriltai of 1252. He sent his chief general Kitubuka in advance to invade Kūhistān, where the Assassins were strongest, and after various military operations and the capture of important towns and castles laid siege to Maimundiz, a fort of great strength. Rukn-ad-Dīn, the head of the Assassins, surrendered to Hūlāgū. Once in his power, Rukn-ad-Dīn was forced to dismantle all his fortresses and strongholds, the investment of which might have caused the Mongols some trouble. Later on he set out on a journey to Mangu, who refused to receive him, and ultimately Rukn-ad-Dīn was slain on the homeward journey. His end synchronised with the termination of the political power of the Assassins.

Having freed the world from the Assassins, the Mongols advanced against the citadel of Islām. Baghdad, the Rome of the Muslim faith, vied with and surpassed Mecca in importance. The first four Caliphs had ruled from Medina; the Umayyads who rose to power in 661 under Mu'āwiyah transferred the seat of government to Damascus. On the fall of the Umayyads in 750 the capital was again changed, and Baghdad, which was built by Manṣūr in 762, became the centre of empire. The position of the Caliph, or Successor to Mahomet, was in many respects comparable to that of the Papacy. Endowed, at the outset, with temporal as well as spiritual power, the holders of the office were gradually divested of the former. Lieutenants and governors made themselves independent; separate states soon began to break the unity of the Empire of Islām. But the spiritual ascendancy of the Caliphate maintained, to a far higher degree than in the case of the Papacy, both the union of all Muslim states and the authority of the Caliph in politics, international and domestic; it was the destruction of Baghdad by the Mongols that brought the old Caliphate to an end. Resurrected by the Mamlūks of Egypt, it was a shadow and the holder of the office a puppet, maintained in a fettered pomp that scarcely concealed the name of captivity. Sultans such as Baibars found the presence of a Caliph convenient in order to legitimate their claims and procure popular support, but the power of the Caliphate was gone. The Ottoman Turks, who conquered Egypt in 1517, compelled the last Abbasid, Mutawakkil, to resign his claims in their favour. By virtue of this and of the possession of the sacred relics of the Prophet, the Sultans at Constantinople claim to-day to be the vice-gerents of Allāh over all Islām.

Yet in 1250 the Caliphate was still a formidable foe. Musta'ṣim, who held the office, could count on the allegiance of many princes. Egypt, Rūm, Fārs, Kirmān, Erbil, and Mosul were all loyal, although at the time of Hūlāgū's attack several feudatories had accepted the Mongol sway. Nevertheless many internal causes contributed to the downfall of the Caliphate. The feud between Sunnī and Shī'ah sapped the forces of Islām. The Caliph, though devoted to luxury, was a pious recluse who abandoned the affairs of state to his viziers; of these it must be said that their conduct can only be cleared from the blackest treachery to Church and State by the plea of almost incredible folly and ineptitude[1]. Hūlāgū wrote to Musta'ṣim, accusing him of sheltering Mongol enemies and of withholding support from the Mongols when they crushed the Assassins; he also demanded complete submission and the dismantling of the fortifications of Baghdad. To this the Caliph, mainly relying on mistaken ideas of his powers and the amount of help that his vassals would afford, returned a refusal couched in boastful terms. Hūlāgū advanced and laid siege to Baghdad, which fell on 15 February 1258. The Caliph suffered a terrible death; the city was given up to pillage and the inhabitants to slaughter. The massacre exceeded even the usual Mongol limits; 800,000 perished and scarcely a stone remained standing. Horror and woe spread to the confines of Islām; no event in the annals of the Faith roused such consternation. Baghdad was the centre of the arts; literature and science found a home under the aegis of the Caliph. The Muslim rulers fostered and endowed the humanities, and encouraged the progress of civilisation at a time when Europe was swathed in obscurantism. Philosophy and scholasticism flourished; rhetoric and all forms of learning and education were cultivated. In the realms of art, learning, and commerce, no less than in the sphere of religion, Baghdad was the cynosure of all Muslim eyes; its fall brought about a complete re-arrangement in the political world also. Fresh boundaries, alliances, and centres of government had to be found. Yet the great catastrophe had some effects that were beneficial. Cairo, the new focus of Islām, was nearer Europe and more

[1] See Browne, E. G., *Literary History of Persia*, II. pp. 464 ff., 484.

accessible. The scattering of Muslim savants, diffusing learning among many places, gave the impetus to a renaissance in Islām. It gave Egypt a short breathing-space to prepare for the Mongol attack, with the consequence that the victory of Quṭuz at ʿAin Jālūt in 1260, which warded off the danger from Egypt, saved Christendom as well; the signal service that the Sultan of Egypt rendered to Europe was beyond the power of any Western king to accomplish.

The fall of Baghdad was the prelude to the invasion of Syria. Even so great an object-lesson failed to teach the Muslims the necessity of union. The feud between Shīʿah and Sunnī still continued, carefully fostered by the Mongols to their own advantage. Hūlāgū favoured the former, and took precautions to preserve the tomb of ʿAlī from destruction. Some of the princes of Syria submitted. Nāṣir Ṣalāḥ-ad-Dīn Yūsuf, a descendant of the famous Saladin (Ṣalāḥ-ad-Dīn), who was prince of Aleppo and also of Damascus, defied the Mongols and prepared to offer a brave resistance. He sent his wives to Egypt, where the Sultan Quṭuz protected them, and gathered an army for battle, north of Damascus. But under the influence of terror his men fled; Hūlāgū marched to Aleppo, capturing and destroying as he went. The town fell and was razed to the ground; death or captivity was the lot of the victims. Damascus surrendered and was spared. Antioch surrendered but was destroyed. A terrible famine and pestilence broke out and completed the devastation of Syria, Mesopotamia, and the surrounding lands. Hūlāgū meditated a march on Jerusalem and probably after that a campaign against Egypt; but while at Aleppo the news of the death of Mangu reached him. He was obliged to return for the great Kuriltai, just as the death of Ogdai had previously recalled Bātu. The leadership of the Mongol army was given to Ketbogha.

Quṭuz, the Sultan of Egypt at this time, 1260, was a Khwārazmian Mamlūk, who had displaced the son of Aibak and seized the throne. Roused by the approach of the foe, he gathered an army and anticipated their attack. The Mamlūks advanced to Acre, where they reckoned on the support of the Crusaders. The latter were too timid to offer any aid, and the burden of the war lay on Quṭuz alone. At ʿAin Jālūt (1260) the armies met. The bravery of Quṭuz and of Baibars, his general, won the day and Ketbogha was slain. For the first time in history the Mongols were fairly and indisputably beaten in a decisive battle. The effect was magical. Wherever the news of the Mamlūk victory became known, men gave themselves up to the wildest transports of rejoicing. The spell was broken at last, and it was clear that the superhuman power, claimed by Mongol boasts and credited by the fears of their victims, was a myth. Damascus rose and cast off the Mongol yoke. The Mamlūks did not remain satisfied with the fruits of a single victory. The Mongols, broken and crushed, were driven out of Syria beyond Emesa. Quṭuz reinstated, where possible, the former officials as governors under his command and reduced the country to order. His return was a triumphant progress; he was accompanied by prayers and thanksgiving. Wherever he passed signs of popular joy were manifest. Extraordinary preparations were made to welcome the conqueror. As he drew nearer to his own kingdom the celebrations became grander, and the decorations of the towns and villages increasingly costly. All Cairo united to honour its victorious ruler as no other before, but Quṭuz was treacherously robbed of the fruits of his victory. He was stabbed by his general Baibars, who usurped his master's throne and rode into Cairo, a second Zimri, amid the plaudits destined for his murdered lord. The erstwhile Mamlūk slave, who had saved the proud sovereigns of Europe and had succeeded in a task which they dared not undertake, fell a victim in the height of his glory to the dagger of another slave.

The land which Hūlāgū had conquered became his own, and he retained possession of such parts as were not recaptured from him. The dynasty which he founded in Persia ruled for several generations under the title of Īl-khāns, acknowledging the Khan of the Eastern Mongols as their overlord. In 1282 Aḥmad Khān became a Muslim. Islām had entirely permeated Persia by 1295, when Ghāzān Khān succeeded to the throne, but it did not altogether eradicate many superstitions. Ghāzān broke off his allegiance to the Supreme Khan. The inauguration of independence by the Īl-khāns is marked by the alteration in the legend on their coins. Abū-Sa'īd (1316) was the last of the great Īl-khāns, and after his death (1335) the kingdom split into petty states, which by 1400 were incorporated by Tīmūr in his dominions.

In the meanwhile there had been considerable military activity on the eastern borders of the Empire. Reference has been made to the continual hostilities that disturbed the relations between the Sung Dynasty in Southern China and the Mongols. In 1252 the latter ordered a great forward movement. Kublai, the brother of Mangu, was to advance into Yunnan, a province outside the Sung borders to the south-west, and in 1253 he assembled his forces at Shensi as a preliminary step. The Mongols were favoured with their usual success, but Kublai was a man of different temperament from his predecessors. He saw that the policy of wanton destruction and indiscriminate slaughter, though effective for inspiring terror in the foe and thus aiding the conqueror, was inimical to the future government of the captured area. It was easier to rule a settled country than a desert waste. Industry and commerce can be overthrown with ease and speed, but cannot be revived except with infinite trouble and delay. Moreover Kublai's nature was averse to bloodshed. His ambition sought to effect great conquests with the minimum loss of life. Thus Tali, an important city of Nanchao in Yunnan, was taken by him without causing a single death. After this exploit Kublai returned to Mangu, leaving the famous general Uriang Kadai, the son of Sabutai, to continue the campaign. With various intervals the war continued until

1257. The Mongols captured Annam (Tongking) in 1257, and achieved many successes. Kublai, who had been appointed governor at Honan, had not abandoned his policy of conciliation. The popularity which he gained from the wise and considerate treatment of his subjects provoked the jealousy of Mangu, who sent a Mongol called Alemdar from Karakorum to supersede Kublai. The latter, however, returned to Mangu, and by tact and submission recovered the favour of the Khan and the position of which he had been deprived.

In this same year, 1257, Mangu held a Kuriltai and determined to lead the army against the Sung. Kublai accompanied him, and three strong forces invaded the province of Suchuan. Two years were spent in conquests, and in the Mongol operations the gentle spirit of Kublai asserted itself. Finally, in 1259 siege was laid to Hochau at the junction of the Kialing and the Feu, near the point where these rivers join the Yangtse Kiang. The besiegers suffered much from dysentery, and Mangu himself succumbed to the disease. The funeral procession, which bore the dead Khan to his last resting-place at Burkan Kaldun, according to previous custom slew all whom they met *en route*, to prevent the intelligence of the death of the Khan from preceding the bier.

Mangu's sudden death created some difficulty in the appointment of a successor. The vast extent of the Empire prevented a Kuriltai from being summoned at once. According to the Mongol custom, the new Khan should be chosen from among the brothers of Mangu, and of these Hūlāgū was in Syria, Kublai in China. Of Mangu's other brothers, the next in age to Hūlāgū was Arikbuka, who was in command at Karakorum. To him Kublai sent, asking for reinforcements and supplies. Arikbuka complied and sent Kublai an invitation to attend the Kuriltai which had been convoked at Karakorum to elect a new Khan. Kublai, fearing a trap, declined and summoned a Kuriltai of his own at Shangtu. To this assembly neither Hūlāgū nor the descendants of Jagatai were invited, owing to the time which must elapse before they could attend. The conduct of the war rendered it imperative that a new head should be chosen for the state without delay. Kublai was elected for this office with the usual pomp and festivities. The election was scarcely valid, as the entire electorate was not present. Of the absentees, Hūlāgū acquiesced, but Arikbuka and the supporters of the houses of Jagatai and Ogdai were disaffected.

Nevertheless Kublai was on the throne, and his reign lasted thirty-five years. His achievements were considerable, and he ruled over a wider extent than any Mongol or indeed any other sovereign. He was the first to govern by peaceful means. By this time the head of the Mongols had become invested with the state of an Emperor. The splendour of his court and the magnificence of his *entourage* easily surpassed that of any Western ruler. The change though gradual was now accomplished. It was strikingly significant of Mongol development. The rude leader of nomads, governing by the sword, with no thoughts of settlement but only of rapine and conquest, had given place to a cultured monarch, eager for the good government of his subjects and the prosperity of his kingdom.

The beginning of his reign found him assailed by civil war. Arikbuka raised the standard of rebellion and collected a large force. Kublai and his generals were active; their clemency gained over many of Arikbuka's followers, who were enraged at the cruelties that he perpetrated. Arikbuka was defeated in 1261 but spared. Again he rebelled and again he was defeated (1264). He came in utter abasement to Kublai, who pardoned him once more, but soon afterwards he died. At his death all the other rebels submitted, with the exception of Kaidu. The war with the Sung Dynasty was a legacy to Kublai from his late brother. When the news of the death of Mangu reached Kublai, he was besieging Wuchang. The Chinese general concluded a treaty with him but did not inform the Chinese Emperor of the terms of peace. It was agreed that Kublai should retreat, leaving Wuchang seemingly unconquered, on condition that the Emperor paid tribute and acknowledged the Mongol Khan as overlord. In view of Arikbuka's rebellion Kublai accepted the conditions. Later on he sent to demand their fulfilment, but the Chinese Emperor, having no knowledge of any treaty, naturally repudiated Kublai's claims. After various delays, hostilities were resumed in 1267 and continued with great vigour. Finally, in 1279, after many victories and conquests, the whole country was subjugated, the young Emperor being drowned in the last naval battle. The whole of China was now in the hands of the Mongols. They were successful in Korea and in Burma, both of which were subdued, but the expeditions to Java and Japan resulted in failure.

Kublai was a generous patron of literature. The culture and religion of China had great attractions for him. While Islām was making headway among the Western Mongols, Buddhism was encroaching from the East. Hūlāgū became a Muslim and Kublai a Buddhist; thus Shamanism was threatened on both sides. The name of Lama was given by the Mongols to the Buddhist priests. Kublai introduced the Chinese ritual of ancestor-worship, and built a large temple in which Jenghiz, Ogdai, and the other Khans were commemorated and worshipped. He also ordered that the Uighur characters should be discarded, since he deemed it beneath the dignity of the Mongols to use a script borrowed from foreigners. In 1269 a new national mode of writing was invented by the chief Lama and published. Kublai's encouragement of learning was remarkable. He caused Jamāl-ad-Dīn, a Persian astronomer, to draw up a calendar; he founded an academy and schools. The Chinese classics were translated at his bidding, and a history of the Mongols compiled in order to familiarise the young men with the exploits of their ancestors. An administrative council of twelve was set up, with the object of assisting the Khan in state affairs; the vast empire was sub-divided into twelve provinces, so as to secure effective local government by decentralisation. The postal service was maintained with great care; hostelries, horses, couriers, and vehicles were provided throughout the Empire. Perhaps the most abiding memorial to the greatness of Kublai was the new capital that he built near Yenkin, which had been the capital of the Chinese sovereigns. The city that he created was known by the names Tatu (Daitu or Taitu) or "Great Court," Khan Balig (Kambalu, Cambaluk) or "Khan's town," and Pekin. The description of this wonderful town given by Marco Polo seems reminiscent of the marvels of the *Arabian Nights*; he too gave the inspiration of Coleridge's lines, "In Xanadu did Kubla Khan a stately pleasure-dome decree." The currency was reformed, block-printing, far in advance of Europe, being utilised for the paper coinage. The army was re-organised, and a valuable system of roads and canals constructed. Trees were planted in many places for the benefit of the public; the welfare of the subject was now the chief care of the ruler. Every act of Kublai, in politics, government, war, court ceremonial, literature, religion, and personal habits, shews clearly how far the Mongol state had progressed. The nomads had become civilised, but they had abandoned their chief characteristics. Islām on the one hand, Buddhism on the other, Arabic culture and Chinese civilisation, had slowly permeated and transformed them. The establishment of the courts of Hūlāgū and of Kublai marked a great change. Karakorum gave place to Persia and to Pekin. The transfer changed the habits of the Mongols, and this was the beginning of the disintegration of the Empire. Civilisation involved a loss of military power, for the Mongols lost their hardihood with their brutality. The very size of the Empire rendered unity impossible. The nomads settled down and remained savage peasants or became more cultured, according as their geographical position rendered them susceptible to outside influences or not. The barbarian at home was cut off by a growing barrier of civilisation from his fellow-Mongol at the fringe of the Empire. A comparison between the soldiers of Jenghiz and the subjects of Kublai is valuable. Under Jenghiz and his immediate successors, the army was a machine for rapine and destruction. The range of the Mongol arms, the distance from home at which they fought, the long stretch of desert which they had to traverse, their energy and insensibility to the most exhausting hardships, their resolution and inflexible obedience to the plans and commands which, neither deterred by misfortune nor seduced by victory, they invariably carried into execution, cannot fail to impress the student of their history. Yet it cannot be denied that the efficiency of the Mongols as a military organisation was only attained at the expense of their development in other spheres. The progress of civilisation among them was imperceptible until the age of Kublai. The growth of culture and the humane arts can scarcely be traced; in comparison to the high level which existed among their Chinese neighbours and the Muslim nations it is altogether negligible. Neither sporadic instances of luxury at the court of the Khan, the result of the mass of booty, nor the royal patronage and care in fostering scientific institutions, can be taken as indicative of the general Mongol attitude to culture. Military prowess turned the whole nation into a marvellous fighting organisation, brutal, mechanical, but invincible; lacking the brilliancy and dash of Napoleon's armies, animated by the lust for plunder and slaughter, stimulated by blind and terrorised obedience rather than by the call of patriotism. History can furnish many instances of victorious nations being educated by contact with their captives, to whom the conquerors were inferior in culture. But the Mongols were thus influenced to a very small extent, for their wars were outbursts of extermination and desolation; no victims survived their fury to teach them valuable lessons and react on their masters; the civilisation of the conquered lay buried under ghastly corpse heaps and beneath the ashes of ruined cities.

The age of Kublai, as has already been shewn, was different in character. Captives were spared, and conquered provinces were administered with a regard to the well-being of their inhabitants rather than to the mere possibilities of plunder and extortion. Literature and civilisation flourished, and higher forms of religion began to pervade the state. The old Mongol spirit was dead save in Central Asia, and the new Mongol Empire was soon destined to fall in pieces. The estimate of Howorth is well worth citing:

"In reviewing the life of Khubilai, we can hardly avoid the conclusion which has been drawn by a learned authority on his reign, that we have before us rather a great Chinese Emperor than a Mongol Khan. A Chinese Emperor, it is true, wielding resources such as no other Emperor in Chinese history ever did, yet sophisticated and altered by contact with that peculiar culture which has vanquished eventually all the stubborn conquerors of China. Great as he was in his power, and in the luxury and magnificence of his court, he is yet by no means the figure in the world's history that Jingis and Ogotai were. Stretching out their hands with fearful effect over a third of the human race, their history is entwined with our western history much more than his. Big as the heart of the vast empire was, it was too feeble to send life into its extremities for very long, and in viewing the great Khakan at the acme of his power, we feel that we shall not have long to wait before it will pass away. The kingdoms that had been conquered so recently in the West were already growing cold towards him, and were more in form than in substance his own. This was no doubt inevitable, the whole was too unwieldy, its races too heterogeneous, its interests too various. Yet we cannot avoid thinking that the process was hastened by that migration from the desert to the luxurious south, from Karakorum to Tatu and Shangtung which Khubilai effected, and which speedily converted a royal race of warriors into a race of decrepit sensualists."

Kublai died in 1294, at the age of eighty, having reigned thirty-five years. After his death the history of the Mongols ceases to call for much detailed comment. The reigns of his successors are of little interest to the general historian, for the Empire begins to pass from the zenith of its power and it remains but to trace the course of decay. Within fifty years of the death of Kublai the Empire was smitten by a series of floods and earthquakes. The Mongol power weakened and rebellion spread. In 1355 a Buddhist priest raised an army in China to drive out the Mongols. Korea joined in the revolt and Pekin was captured. The Khan fled and made good his escape, but the Mongol troops were driven out. In 1368 the revolution was over. A new dynasty, called the Ming or "Bright," was set up, and the priest who had led the revolt became Emperor (Hung-Wu). The descendants of Jenghiz were driven away for ever. But worse was in store. Hung-Wu carried the campaign beyond his own confines. The Eastern Mongols were vigorously attacked and continually beaten. In the reign of Biliktu (died 1378) the Mongols were expelled from Liau Tung. He was succeeded in the next year by Ussakhal, who was slain after the great disaster that overtook the Mongols at Lake Buyur, when the Chinese completely broke the power of their former conquerors. Hereafter the supremacy passed from one branch of the Mongols to another. They became scattered and autonomous, except in so far as the jurisdiction of the Chinese compelled their obedience. Yet the tale of disruption is illuminated by occasional flashes of the old Mongol greatness. The Mongols, who were driven to the North by the Ming, gradually recovered and measured their strength with the foe. They raided Tibet and China, and one of the results of these expeditions was to bring them more into touch with Buddhism. In 1644 the Ming Dynasty was overthrown by the Manchus, who ruled China until the recent proclamation of the republic; the Manchus effectually subdued the Eastern Mongols, who henceforward are merged in the Chinese Empire.

The Mongol Empire can scarcely be said ever to have formed a homogeneous unity; for this reason it is impossible to deal with all those tribes bearing the common designation Mongol or Tartar as a single corporate body. It is difficult to get a general view and to place isolated incidents in their proper setting. This difficulty in finding a true perspective involves a certain amount of individual treatment of the various tribes, and from the time of Kublai onward the historian is compelled to trace the course of the scattered bodies one by one. The fate of the successors of Kublai has been recounted. It now remains to deal with various other branches of the Mongol Confederacy.

The Khalkhas, or Central Mongols, whose territory was the ancient Mongol home, where Jenghiz had begun his career, after diplomatic relations with Russia and contact with Christianity, were finally merged in the Chinese Empire at the conference of Tolonor. To this great meeting the Emperor Kang-hi summoned the chiefs of the Khalkhas in

1691, and with great ceremony they performed the "kowtow" in the imperial presence; with this act their separate existence as a nation came to an end.

The Keraits and Torgods for a long period were distracted by internal feuds. The kingdom of the mysterious Prester John, who has been identified with Wang Khan, is placed in their land. Later they had diplomatic and also hostile relations with Russia, Turkey, and the Cossacks. Ayuka Khan, one of their great leaders, invaded the Russian territory as far as Kazan, but made peace with Peter the Great at Astrakhan in 1722. After some time, however, fear of the Russians and discontent at their oppressions caused them to adopt the expedient of wholesale emigration. The extraordinary spectacle was witnessed of 70,000 families breaking up their homes and marching away with all their chattels. The old nomad spirit seemed to have revived. They travelled to China where they were most hospitably received, but the price paid for release from Russian tyranny was the surrender of their nationality. China completely assimilated them. Thus China, Russia, and the steppes were absorbing or scattering great divisions of the former Mongol Empire.

Of the western Mongols, importance centres round the descendants of Jagatai, who passed through many vicissitudes until the rise of Tīmūr Leng (Tīmūr the lame), or Timurlane (Tamerlane, Tamburlaine), of Samarqand. In the year 1336, scarcely more than a century after the death of Jenghiz Khan, Tīmūr was born at Kesh in Transoxiana, to the south of Samarqand. The Mongol hold of Central Asia was still firm, but disintegration was spreading rapidly. It was the destiny of Tīmūr to rouse the Mongols to fresh exploits and distant victories. The direct result of his invasion of India was the rise of the Mongol Dynasty at Delhi, better known as the Moguls. Much light is thrown on Tīmūr and his reign by the narrative of Ruy Gonzalez de Clavijo, who came on an embassy to his court in the years 1403–6.

Besides this, there are several accounts of the great conqueror, but they are mostly *ex parte* statements written either by inveterate enemies or flattering court scribes. Yet it is not difficult to form a fair estimate of the man. In his youth he had the benefit of a fair education. He was as versed in literature as he was proficient in military skill. He was a Muslim by faith, but had no scruples about attacking and slaughtering his co-religionists. At the outset of his career, from about 1358 onward, he had to struggle for supremacy among the scattered tribes of the neighbourhood and the hordes to the north of the Jaxartes. In this he may be compared to Jenghiz. By dint of persistence he succeeded in becoming supreme among the Jagatai tribes, and in 1369, having overcome and slain Ḥusain, his brother-in-law and former ally, he was proclaimed sovereign at Balkh and ruled in Samarqand. He was now at the age of thirty-three, and he waged incessant warfare for the next thirty years.

The chief of his exploits was the celebrated invasion of India. Tīmūr was prompted by the double motive of zeal to spread the faith and the prospect of rich plunder. He crossed the Indus in 1398, after having passed the mountains of Afghanistan. Multān was conquered and the Musulman leader Shihāb-ad-Dīn defeated. After other victories, notably the capture of Bhatnir, the road to Delhi lay open. Before the gates the army of Sultan Muḥammad of Delhi was drawn up under the famous general Mallu Khān; against Mongol ferocity the bravery of the Indians was useless, and after a bloody battle Tīmūr entered Delhi on 17 December 1398. The sack of Delhi and the massacre of the inhabitants followed, and utter ruin spread far and wide. It is said that for the next fifty years the country was so impoverished that the mints ceased to issue gold and silver coins; copper currency sufficed for the needs of the miserable survivors.

Tīmūr did not stay long. Passing along the flank of the Himalayas he captured Meerut and returned to Samarqand through Kashmir. In the Khuṭbah, or prayer for the reigning monarch that is recited every Friday in the mosques, the names of Tīmūr and his descendants were inserted, thus legitimising the subsequent claims of Bābur.

From Samarqand Tīmūr soon marched to the west. In 1401 Baghdad was taken and sacked, the horrors almost equalling the scenes enacted under Hūlāgū. The captives were beheaded and towers constructed of the heads as a warning, but mosques, colleges, and hospitals were spared. Karbalā and Aleppo were taken and Damascus destroyed, Persia and Kurdistān were reconquered. He reduced the Mongols round the shores of the Caspian and penetrated to the banks of the Ural and the Volga. Advancing through Asia Minor, he met the Ottoman Sultan Bāyazīd I, then at the height of his power, at Angora in 1402. The Turks were beaten and the Sultan captured. Tīmūr dragged the fallen monarch after him to grace his triumph; according to the story utilised by Marlowe, he was imprisoned in a cage. Tīmūr, now in his seventieth year, next planned a great expedition to China. He actually set out on the march, but died in 1405 at Otrar near Kashgar. His atrocities were enormous but not comparable to those of other Mongol Khans. He made no attempt to consolidate his conquests, and after his death the decay was quick. Samarqand and Transoxiana were ruled by his son and grandson, but the various petty dynasties that soon arose weakened each other by warfare. Finally Muḥammad Shaibānī or Shāhī Beg, the head of the Uzbeg Mongols, captured Samarqand and Bukhārā and between 1494 and 1500 displaced all the dynasties of the Tīmūrids.

Parallel to the advance of Buddhism in the East, was the growth of Islām in the West. Nowhere did the faith of Mahomet find more fruitful soil than among the Īl-khāns of Persia, who traced their descent to Hūlāgū, the conqueror of Baghdad. Between Egypt and the Īl-khāns there was often warfare. In 1303 Nāṣir, Sultan of Egypt, overthrew a Mongol army at Marj-as-Suffar. But the relations between the two powers were sometimes friendly. The same Nāṣir made an extradition treaty with Abū-Saʿīd, the nephew of Ghāzān, whose army had been defeated at Marj-as-Suffar. The smaller states which succeeded the Īl-khāns were finally swept away by Tīmūr before 1400.

The descendants of the victorious general Bātu were the famous Golden Horde or Western Kipchaks. Bātu ruled from Lake Balkash to Hungary. He was succeeded in 1255 by his brother Bereke, in whose reign a crusade against the Mongols was preached by the Pope. But the Mongols carried the war into the enemy's country and invaded Poland and Silesia. Cracow and Beuthen were captured and vast masses of slaves were led away. The result of these operations was that the Mongols maintained a suzerainty over the Russians. Several European princes and princesses intermarried with them; they were on friendly terms with the Sultans of Egypt, perhaps owing to the hostility between the Mamlūks and the Īl-khāns. In 1382 Tuqtāmish sacked Moscow and several important Russian towns, but the campaign of slaughter was resented by Tīmūr his overlord, who utterly crushed him. Gradually all these Mongol tribes were absorbed by Russia or the Ottoman Turks, but from the Uzbegs on the Caspian Bābur set forth on his journey to India and founded the Indian Empire of the Moguls, to which Sir Thomas Roe was sent on an embassy in 1615–1619. The lingering Khanates were crushed by the expansion of Russia, and either as subjects or protectorates have lost all independence.

CHAPTER XXI.

THE OTTOMAN TURKS TO THE FALL OF CONSTANTINOPLE.

It was in 1299 that Osmān (Othmān, ‘Uthmān) declared himself Emir of the Turks, that is, of the tribe over which he ruled. The Seljūq Turks have been treated in a previous chapter; but there were many other Turkish tribes present in the middle and at the end of the thirteenth century in Asia Minor and Syria, and, in order to understand the conditions under which the Ottoman Turks advanced and became a nation, a short notice of the condition of Anatolia at that time is necessary. The country appeared indeed to be everywhere overrun with Turks. A constant stream of Turkish immigrants had commenced to flow from the south-west of Central Asia during the eleventh century, and continued during the twelfth and indeed long after the capture of Constantinople. Some of these went westward to the north of the Black Sea, while those with whom we are concerned entered Asia Minor through the lands between the Persian Gulf and the Black Sea. They were nomads, some travelling as horsemen, others on foot or with primitive ox-waggons. Though they seem to have left Persia in large bodies, yet, when they reached Anatolia, they separated into small isolated bands under chieftains. Once they had obtained passage through Georgia or Armenia or Persia into Asia Minor, they usually turned southwards, attracted by the fertile and populous plains of Mesopotamia, though they avoided Baghdad so long as that city was under a Caliph. Thence they spread through Syria into Cilicia, which was then largely occupied by Armenians under their own princes, and into Egypt itself. Several of these tribes crossed the Taurus, usually through the pass known as the Cilician Gates, and thereupon entered the great tableland, three thousand feet above sea-level, which had been largely occupied by the Seljūqs. By 1150, the Turks had spread over all Asia Minor and Syria. These early Turks were disturbed by the huge and well-organised hordes of mounted warriors and foot-soldiers under Jenghiz Khan, a Mongol belonging to the smallest of the four great divisions of the Tartar race, but whose followers were mainly Turks. The ruin of the Seljūqs of Rūm may be said to date from the great Mongol invasion in 1242, in which Armenia was conquered and Erzerūm occupied. The invading chief exercised the privilege of the conqueror, and gave the Seljūq throne of Rūm to the younger brother of the Sultan instead of to the elder. The Emperor in Constantinople supported the latter, and fierce war was waged between the two brothers. A resident, somewhat after the Indian analogy, was appointed by the Khan of the Mongols to the court of the younger brother. The war contributed to the weakening of the Seljūqs, and facilitated the encroachment of the nomad Turkish bands, who owned no master, upon their territory. The Latin occupation of Constantinople (1204–1261) had the same effect, for the Latin freebooters shewed absolutely no power of dealing with the Turks, their energies being engaged simply in making themselves secure in the capital and a portion of its European territory. Hūlāgū, the grandson of Jenghiz Khan, captured Baghdad in 1258 and destroyed the Empire of the Caliphs. He extended his rule over Mesopotamia and North Syria to the Mediterranean. The dispersion of the new Turkish hordes not only greatly increased the number of nomads in Asia Minor, but led to the establishment of additional independent Turkish tribes under their own rulers, or emirs, and to an amount of confusion and disorder in Asia Minor such as had not previously been seen under the Greek Empire. The chieftain and his tribe usually seized a strong position, an old fortified town for example, held it as their headquarters, refused to own allegiance to the Emperor or any other than their immediate chieftain, and from it as their centre plundered the inhabitants of the towns and the neighbouring country. The tribes shewed little tendency to coalesce. Each emir fought on his own account, plundered on all the roads where travellers passed, or demanded toll or ransom for passage or release. In this want of cohesion is to be found one explanation of the fact that though the Turks were defeated one day, yet they emerge with apparently equal strength a short time after in another place. They had to be fought in detail in their respective centres or as wandering tribes. During the thirteenth century many such groups of Turks occupied what a Greek writer calls "the eyes of the country." Even as far south as Aleppo there was such an occupation by a tribe with a regular Turkish dynasty. Some such chiefs, established on the western shores of the Aegean, not only occupied tracts of country, but built fleets and ravaged the islands of the Archipelago. During the half century preceding the accession of Osmān, Tenedos, Chios, Samos, and Rhodes fell at various times to these Turkish tribes. Some of them, who had occupied during the same period the southern and western portions of the central highland of Asia Minor, met with great success. Qaramān established his rule around the city of Qaramān, whose strongly fortified and interesting castle still stands, a noble ruin, on the plain about sixty-four miles south-east of Qonya. But the same Qaramān ruled over a district extending for a time to the north-west as far as, and including, Philadelphia. Indeed, he and his successors were for perhaps half a century the most powerful Turks in Asia Minor. Other chiefs or emirs ruled in Germiyān, at Attalia (called

Satalia by the crusaders), at Tralles, now called after its emir Aidīn, and at Magnesia. The shores of the Aegean opposite Lesbos and large strips of country on the south of the Black Sea were during the same period under various Turkish emirs. The boundaries of the territories over which they ruled often changed, as the tribes were constantly at war with each other or in search of new pasture. Needless to say, the effect of the establishment of so many wandering hordes of fighting men unused to agriculture was disastrous to the peaceful population of the country they had invaded. The rule of the Empire in such districts was feeble, the roads were unsafe, agriculture diminished, and the towns decayed. The nomad character of these isolated tribes makes it impossible to give a satisfactory estimate of their numbers on the accession of Osmān. The statements of Greek and Turkish writers on the subject are always either vague or untrustworthy.

Three years before Osmān assumed the title of emir, namely in 1296, Pachymer reports that the Turks had devastated the whole of the country between the Black Sea and the territory opposite Rhodes. Even two centuries earlier similar statements had been made. For example, William of Tyre after describing Godfrey of Bouillon's siege of Nicaea in 1097 says the Turks lost 200,000 men. Anna Comnena tells of the slaughter of 24,000 around Philadelphia in 1108; four years later a great band of them were utterly destroyed. Matthew of Edessa in 1118 describes an "innumerable army of Turks" as marching towards that city. It would be easy to multiply these illustrations. The explanation is to be found in the nomadic habits of the invaders, and in the fact already noted that there was a constant stream of immigration from Asia.

The tribe over which Osmān ruled was one which had entered Asia Minor previous to Jenghiz Khan's invasion. His ancestors had been pushed by the invaders southward to Mesopotamia, but like so many others of the same race continued to be nomads. They were adventurers, desirous of finding pasturage for their sheep and cattle, and ready to sell their services to any other tribe. The father of Osmān, named Ertughril, had probably employed his tribe in the service of the Sultan 'Alā-ad-Dīn of Rūm, who had met with much opposition from other Turkish tribes. According to Turkish historians, he had surprised Maurocastrum, now known as Afyon-Qara-Hisār, a veritable Gibraltar rising out of the central Phrygian plain about one hundred miles from Eski-Shehr (Dorylaeum)[1]. Ertughril's deeds, however, as related in the Turkish annals, are to be read with caution. He became the first national hero of the Turks, was a Ghāzī, and the victories gained by others are accredited to him. They relate that he captured Bilijik, Āq-Gyul (Philomelium), Yeni-Shehr, Lefke (Leucae), Āq-Hisār (Asprocastrum), and Gīvē (Gaiucome).

[1] Jorga, *Geschichte des osmanischen Reiches*, I. p. 51.

A romantic story which is probably largely mythical is told of the early development of the tribe of the Ottoman Turks. It relates how Ertughril found himself by accident in the neighbourhood of a struggle going on to the west of Angora (Ancyra) between the Sultan of the Seljūqs, Kai-Qubād, and a band of other Turks who had come in with the horde of Jenghiz Khan, neither of whom were known to him. Ertughril and his men at once accepted the offer of the Seljūqs, who were on the point of losing the battle. Their arrival turned the scale and after a three days' struggle the Seljūqs won. The victors were generous, and the newly arrived tribe received a grant from them of a tract of country around Eski-Shehr, a hundred and ninety miles distant from Constantinople, with the right to pasture their flocks in the valley of the Sangarius eastward towards Angora and westward towards Brūsa.

Whatever be the truth in this story, it is certain that the followers of Ertughril obtained a position of great importance which greatly facilitated their further development. Three ranges of mountains which branch off from the great tableland of western Asia Minor converge near Eski-Shehr. The passes from Bithynia to this tableland meet there. It had witnessed a great struggle against the Turks during the First Crusade in 1097, in which the crusaders won, and again in 1175 in the Second Crusade. Its possession gave the Turks the key to an advance northwards. It commanded the fertile valley of the Sangarius, a rich pasture ground for nomads. Ertughril made Sugyut, about ten miles south-east of Bilijik, now on the line of the Baghdad railway, and about the same distance from Eski-Shehr, the headquarters of his camp.

Ertughril died at Sugyut in 1281, and there too his famous son Osmān was born. The number of his subjects had been largely increased during the reign of his father by accessions from other bands of Turks, and especially from one which was in Paphlagonia. Osmān from the first set himself to work to enlarge his territory. He had to struggle for this purpose both with the Empire and with neighbouring tribes. The Greek historians mention two notable victories in 1301 gained by the Greeks over the Turks, in the first of which the Trapezuntines captured the Turkish chief Kyuchuk Āghā at Cerasus and killed many of his followers, and in the second the Byzantines defeated another division at Chena with the aid of mercenary Alans from the Danube. Neither of these Turkish bands were Ottomans; the second belonged to a ruler whose headquarters were at Aidīn (Tralles) and who had already given trouble to the Empire. One of the last acts of the Emperor Michael Palaeologus (1259–1282) had been to send his son Andronicus, then a youth of eighteen, in 1282 to attack the Turks before Aidīn, but the young man was unable to save the city for the Greek Empire. Andronicus II in his turn despatched his son and co-regent Michael IX (1295–1320) with a force of Alans to Magnesia in 1302 to attack other Turks, but they were in such numbers that no attack was made, and Michael indeed took refuge in that city while the nomads plundered the neighbouring country. To add to the Emperor's difficulties, the Venetians had declared war against him. His mercenaries, the Alans, revolted at Gallipoli, and the Turkish pirates or freebooters, fighting for themselves, attacked and for a time held possession of Rhodes, Carpathos, Samos, Chios, Tenedos, and even penetrated the Marmora as far as the Princes Islands. The Emperor Andronicus found himself under the necessity of paying a ransom for the release of captives. Taking advantage of the preoccupation of the Empire in fighting these other Turks, Osmān had made a notable advance into Bithynia. In 1301 he defeated the Greek General Muzalon near Baphaeum, now Qoyun-Hisār (the Sheep Castle), between Izmid and Nicaea, though 2000 Alans aided Muzalon. After this victory Osmān established himself in a position to threaten Brūsa, Nicaea, and Izmid, and then came to an important arrangement for the division of the imperial territories with other Turkish chieftains. He was now "lord of the lands near Nicaea."

It was at this time that Roger de Flor or Roger Blum, a German soldier of fortune of the worst sort, took service with the Emperor (after August 1302). The latter, was, indeed, hard pressed. Michael had made his way to Pergamus, but Osmān and his allies pressed both that city and Ephesus, and overran the country all round. At the other extremity of what may be called the sphere of Osmān's operations, in the valley of the Sangarius, he ruled either directly or by a chieftain who owed allegiance to him. One of his allies was at Germiyān and claimed to rule all Phrygia; another at Calamus ruled over the coast of the Aegean from Lydia to Mysia. It was with difficulty that Michael IX succeeded in making good his retreat from Pergamus to Cyzicus on the south side of the Marmora. That once populous city, with Brūsa, Nicaea, and Izmid, were now the only strong places in Asia Minor which had not fallen into the possession of the Turks. It was at this apparently opportune moment, when the Emperor was beset by difficulties in Anatolia, that Roger de Flor arrived (autumn 1303) with a fleet, 8000 Catalans, and other Spaniards. Other western mercenaries, Germans and Sicilians, had come to the aid of the Empire both before and during the crusades. But great hopes were built on the advent of the well-known but unscrupulous Roger. His army bore the name of the Catalan Grand Company. Roger at once got into difficulties with the Genoese, from whom he had borrowed 20,000 bezants for transport and the hire of other mercenaries.

One of Roger's first encounters in Anatolia was with Osmān. The Turks were raiding on the old Roman road which is now followed by the railway from Eski-Shehr to Izmid, and kept up a running fight with the imperial troops, and Roger, defeating them near Lefke, in 1305 took possession of that city.

The Catalan Grand Company soon shewed that they were dangerous auxiliaries. Roger at various times defeated detached bands of Turks, and made rapid marches with his band into several districts, but his men preyed upon Christians and Muslims with equal willingness.

The first thirty years of the fourteenth century were a period of chaotic disorder in the Empire, due partly to quarrels in the imperial family and partly to struggles with the Turks and other external foes. But of all the evils which fell upon the state the worst were those which were caused by the Catalan mercenaries. The imperial chest was empty. The Catalans and other mercenaries were without pay, and the result was that, when they had crossed the Dardanelles at the request of the Emperor and had driven back the enemy, they paid themselves by plundering the Greek villagers, a plunder which the Emperor was powerless to prevent. Feebleness on the throne and in the councils of the Empire and the general break-up of the government opened the country to attack on every side. The so-called Empire of Nicaea, which had made during half a century a not inglorious struggle on behalf of the Greek race, had ceased to exist. The city itself, cut off from the resources of the neighbouring country and situated in an almost isolated valley ill-adapted for the purpose of commerce, became of comparatively little importance, though its ancient reputation and its well-built walls still entitled it to respect. The progress of the Ottoman Turks met with no organised resistance.

In 1308 a band of Turks and of Turcopuli, or Turks who were in the regular employ of the Empire, was induced to cross into Europe and join with the Catalan Grand Company to attack the Emperor Andronicus. This entry of the Turks into Europe, though not of the Ottoman Turks, is itself an epoch-making event. But the leaders of the Catalans were soon quarrelling among themselves. Roger had killed the brother of the Alan leader at Cyzicus. He was himself assassinated by the surviving brother at Hadrianople in 1306. The expedition captured Rodosto on the north shore of the Marmora, pillaged it, and killed a great number of the inhabitants, the Emperor himself being powerless to render any assistance. One of the Catalan leaders, Roccafort, however, shortly afterwards delivered it to the Emperor. In the same year Ganos, on the same shore, was besieged by the Turks, and though it was not captured the neighbouring country was pillaged, and again the Emperor was powerless to defend his subjects. In the year 1308 another band of Turks, this time allied with Osmān, captured Ephesus. Brūsa was compelled to pay tribute to the Ottoman Emir. The Turks who had joined the Catalans in Europe withdrew into Asia, while their allies continued to ravage Thrace.

Osmān took possession of a small town, spoken of as Tricocca, in the neighbourhood of Nicaea. In 1310 the first attempt was made by him to capture Rhodes, an attempt which Clement V states to have been due to the instigation of the Genoese. The Knights had only been in possession of the island for two years. It was the first time that the famous defenders of Christendom, who were destined to make so gallant a struggle against Islām, met the Ottoman Turks.

An incident in 1311 shews the weakness of the Empire. Khalīl, one of the allies of Osmān, with 1800 Turks under him, had agreed with the Emperor that they should pass into Asia by way of Gallipoli. They were carrying off much booty which they had taken from the Christian towns in Thrace. The owners, wishing to recover their goods, opposed the passage until their property was restored. Khalīl took possession of a castle near the Dardanelles, possibly at Sestos, and called other Turks to his aid from the Asiatic coast. The imperial army which had come to assist the Greeks was defeated, and Khalīl in derision decked himself with the insignia of the Emperor.

The struggle went on between the Greeks and the Turks with varying success during the next three or four years, the Turks maintaining their position in Thrace and holding the Chersonese and Gallipoli. In 1315 the Catalan Grand Company, after having done great injury to the Empire, finally quitted the country.

The struggle between the young and the old Emperor Andronicus increased in violence and incidentally strengthened the position of Osmān. Both Emperors, as well as Michael IX who had died in 1320, employed Turkish troops in their dynastic struggles. The young Andronicus, when he was associated in 1321 with his grandfather, had the population on his side, the old Emperor having been compelled to levy new and heavy taxes in order to oppose the inroads of the Turks who had joined his grandson's party. Shortly afterwards the partisans of the young Emperor attacked near Silivri a band of Turkish mercenaries and Greeks who were on his grandfather's side. They disbanded on his approach and this caused terror in the capital. The mercenaries refused to defend it, and demanded to be sent into Asia. Chalcondyles states that Osmān slew 8000 Turks who had crossed into the Chersonese. Thereupon the old Emperor sued for peace.

In addition to the dynastic struggles and those with the Turks, the Empire had now to meet the Serbs, Bulgarians, and Tartars. The Tartars made their appearance in Thrace, having worked their way from South Russia round by the Dobrudzha. Young Andronicus III in 1324 is reported to have defeated 120,000 of them.

While in the last years of the reign of Osmān the Empire was unable to offer a formidable resistance, Osmān himself was making steady progress. He never lost sight of his main object, the conquest and occupation of all important places between his capital at Yeni-Shehr (which he had chosen instead of Eski-Shehr) and the Marmora with the straits that lead to it from north and south. Two points are noteworthy in his campaign of conquest: first, that he trusted largely to the isolation of the towns which he desired to capture; secondly, that he made great use of cavalry. Every Turk under him was a fighter. They continued their nomad habits and many of them almost lived on horseback. The result was that they moved much more quickly than their enemies, and this mobility, combined with the simple habits of others who travelled readily on their simple ox-carts, which served them as dwellings, greatly favoured Osmān's method of isolating a town. By pitching their tents or unyoking their oxen in a neighbourhood from which cavalry had driven away the inhabitants, they reduced the town by starvation. Osmān had now during nine or ten years applied this method to the capture of Brūsa. His son Orkhān (born 1288) was in command of his father's army, and in 1326 the position of Brūsa was so desperate that, when the Emperor was unable to send an army to break the blockade, the inhabitants surrendered the city.

The surrender of Brūsa to Osmān's army in November 1326 marked an epoch in the advance of the Ottoman Turks. He had gained a most advantageous position for attacking the Empire from the Anatolian side. Once in the hands of the Turks, who already held the country between it and the passes concentrating near Eski-Shehr, its situation rendered it secure from the south. The Bithynian Olympus immediately in its rear made it inaccessible from that side, while its commanding natural position on the mountain slope rendered it strong against an army attacking it in front. While itself occupying an exceptionally strong natural position, no other place was so good a centre for operations against an enemy on the Marmora. It dominated Cyzicus, and was not too distant to serve as a defensive base against an enemy attempting to cross from Gallipoli to Lampsacus. On the other side it threatened Nicaea and facilitated the capture of Izmid. Henceforth it became the centre of operations for the Ottoman Turks, and when immediately afterwards in November 1326 Osmān died, his historian could truthfully note that while he had taken many strongly fortified places in Anatolia, and in particular nearly every seaport in the region on the Black Sea between Ineboli and the Bosphorus, his greatest success, the most important to the race which history was to call after him Osmanlis or Ottomans, was the surrender of Brūsa.

Osmān was at Sugyut, the capital chosen by his father, when the news was brought to him of the success of his son at Brūsa. He was then near his end and died in November 1326 at the age of sixty-eight. The expression of his desire to be buried in Brūsa marks the value which he attached to its possession. His wish was complied with; and the series of tombs of the early sultans of his race, which are still shewn to visitors to the city, mark its importance during the following century and a half.

Osmān rather than Ertughril is regarded as the founder of the Ottoman nation. His successors on the throne are still girt with his sword. The Turkish instinct in taking him as at once their founder and greatest national hero is right. While rejecting most of the stories regarding him, we may fairly conclude that he was a ruler who recognised that to obtain the reputation of a lover of justice was good policy. His merits as a warrior-statesman rest on a surer foundation. There is reason to believe that the advance of his people from the time he ascended the throne until the capture of Brūsa was in accordance with a general plan. While occasionally finding it necessary to carry on war to the south of the mountain ranges which on his accession formed the southern boundary of his territory, he never lost hope of an advance to the straits and the Marmora. In making an advance in that direction he increased the number of his own immediate subjects by allying himself with other Turks; and, by gaining the reputation of a ruler who might be safely followed, and under whose protection Christians might find security both from other Turks and from the exactions of their own Emperor, he drew even Christians to accept his rule.

ORKHĀN (1326–1359).

Osmān had been a successful conqueror. It remained for his son to extend his father's conquests on the lines which he had laid down, and to organise the administration of his government. Orkhān offered to share the government with his brother 'Alā-ad-Dīn, who refused, but consented to be his Vizier or "burden-bearer." To him quite as much as to Orkhān is due the organisation of the army which is one of the main features of the reign. As the Turkish writers report the matter, while Orkhān occupied himself with the conquest of new territories, 'Alā-ad-Dīn gave a civilised form to the government.

The line of advance of the victorious tribe from Brūsa was clearly indicated. Iznīq, the name by which the Turks know Nicaea, "the city of the creed," is not more than a day's journey for an army from Brūsa. Izmid, or Nicomedia, is only a few hours farther off. It was to these strongholds that the new Emir directed his attention. Nicaea, which had been occupied at least twice by bands of Turks, though not by Ottomans, was attacked by Orkhān. Although surrounded by good walls, its resources would not allow of a long defence, and the inhabitants were about to surrender when they learned that the Emperor, young Andronicus, with Cantacuzene, who afterwards in 1341 was associated as joint-Emperor, were coming to its relief. In the late spring of 1329 they arrived with a hastily-gathered army, met the Turks, and defeated them. But a band of too impetuous Greeks endeavoured to follow up the victory, and the Turks, employing the ruse which continued for centuries to give them success, simulated flight. When the band had thus well separated themselves from the main body of the army, the Turks turned and attacked. The Emperor and Cantacuzene then intervened. In the battle which ensued the Emperor was himself wounded, and the result of the struggle was indecisive. Shortly afterwards, however, a panic followed, and the Turkish troops took advantage of it to capture the city and pillage the imperial camp.

The capture of Nicaea was effected in 1329. Its wealth was probably still great. After the recovery of Constantinople in 1261, its importance had at once lessened, but it was still the store-house of Greek wealth in Asia Minor. Orkhān decreed that tribute should be exacted from every place in Bithynia, and this cause, combined with the knowledge of its wealth, probably led to the pillage of the city by the Turks in 1331.

The next stronghold of the Empire which Orkhān attacked was Izmid, formerly Nicomedia. Situated at the head of the gulf of the same name which stretches forty miles into Asia Minor from Constantinople, its position was always an important one. Diocletian had selected it as the capital of the Empire in the East. Instead of being landlocked as is Nicaea, which at the time of the First Council (325) was for a while its rival, it is on the sea at the head of a noble valley through which the great highway leads into the interior of Asia Minor. In 1329 Orkhān sat down before its great walls. But the Emperor Andronicus III, now the sole occupant of the throne, had command of the sea, and hastened to its relief with so strong a force that Orkhān was compelled to abandon the siege and make terms. A few months passed and Orkhān once more appeared before its walls. Once more the Emperor hastened to its relief and the siege was raised. But Orkhān pursued the plan already mentioned of starving the inhabitants into surrender by devastating the surrounding country. The Emperor was unable to furnish an army sufficiently strong to inflict a defeat upon the elusive hordes who were accustomed to live upon the country, and in 1337 Nicomedia surrendered.

In 1329, and during the next ten years, attacks by the Turks suggest unceasing movement on their part. In that year the Emirs of Aidīn and Caria, jealous of the conquests of the Ottomans, arranged with the Emperor for his support. An army sent by Orkhān against them by sea was destroyed near Trajanopolis. In the following year the Greeks were still more successful: 15,000 Turks were defeated and destroyed in Thrace.

In 1333 Omar Beg, the Emir of Aidīn, sent an expedition to Porus in Thrace, which was defeated and compelled to retire. Another band of Turks was destroyed at Rodosto, and again another at Salonica, both in the same year. In 1335 we hear of the Turks as pirates in various parts of the Mediterranean, and of the Emperor's vain attempts to combine his forces with those of the West to destroy them. His territory on the eastern shore of the Aegean was in constant danger from the Turkish emirs established there. In 1336 Andronicus was compelled to ally himself with the Emir of Magnesia and other local Turkish chieftains in order to save Phocaea. A struggle with the Turks continued in the same neighbourhood for two years. In the spring of 1338 a great invasion of Thrace by the Tartars compelled the Emperor's attention. They attacked the Turks who were still in that province and exterminated them, but as the Emperor was unable to pay for their services they captured 300,000 Christians[1]. Other Turks, however, came the following year, and devastated even the neighbourhood of the capital.

Being now in possession of the chief port in Bithynia, the head of all the great roads from Anatolia to Constantinople, and of Brūsa, well fitted by its natural strength to be the capital of a race of warriors, Orkhān turned his attention to the organisation of his government. He had from his accession been conscious that he had succeeded to the rule of a greatly increased number of subjects and of a larger extent of territory than his father, and judged that he was entitled to abandon the title of Emir and to assume the more ambitious one of "Sultan of the Ottomans." Hitherto the coinage current was either that of Constantinople or that of the Seljūqs; Orkhān with his new sense of sovereignty coined money in his own name.

Besides having greatly increased the number of his Muslim subjects, he had to rule over a large number of Christians. Most of them were the inhabitants of conquered territory. Many of the peasants, however, from neighbouring territories sought his protection; for, as the Greek writers record, his Christian subjects were less taxed than those of the Empire. He saw that it was wise to protect these *rayahs*. He left them the use of their churches, and in various ways endeavoured to reconcile them to his rule. This policy of reconciliation, commenced on his accession, was continued during his reign and did much to set his army free for service in the field. He took a step, however, with regard to his Christian subjects, of which he could not have foreseen the far-reaching results. In this he was at least greatly aided by his brother 'Alā-ad-Dīn and by Khalīl, a connexion of his family. He formed a regiment of Christians who were kept distinct from the remainder of his army. The men were at first volunteers. The inducements of regular pay, of opportunities of loot and adventure, and of a career which was one for life, appealed to many amid a population which had been greatly harassed and impoverished by his army. The experiment was a new one, and when Ḥājjī Bektāsh, a celebrated dervish, was asked to give a name to the new corps, the traditional story is that he laid the loose white sleeve of his coat over the head of one of them, declaring that this should be their distinctive head-dress, and called them New Troops or Janissaries. Under this name they were to become famous in history. The special feature which has attracted the attention of Europeans, namely that they were tribute children, probably did not apply to them in the time of Orkhān. Von Hammer follows the Turkish

[1] In this and other cases I give the numbers captured or slain as they are stated by the writers quoted. Needless to say that they are often greatly exaggerated and incapable of being checked.

authors who claim that Khalīl, called Qara or Black Khalīl, suggested that Christian children taken into military service should be forcibly brought up as Muslims. But the first mention of compulsory service by Christians made in the Greek authors is attributed to the first year of the reign of Orkhān's successor Murād in 1360. They relate that one-fifth of all Christian children whose fathers were captured in battle were regarded as *ipso facto* the property of the Sultan, and that Murād caused his share of the boys to be taken from their parents and brought up as Muslims to become Janissaries. It may be noted, however, that not all Janissaries were soldiers. A large proportion, perhaps even one-half, were educated for the civil service of the State. The seizure and apportionment of the children and other property of Christians in resistance to the Sultan was in accordance with Islāmic law.

Orkhān and his brother 'Alā-ad-Dīn organised the army. In the early stages of their history the Ottomans had possessed only a tribal organisation. Every Turk continued to be a fighter and was always liable to serve, but now classification had become necessary. We have various accounts of how this was accomplished, all agreeing that the army under Orkhān was organised on the basis of a militia associated with land tenure, but that there were, in addition, paid troops who constituted a standing army, of which the Janissaries soon formed the most notable division. The general lines of the organisation of the Ottoman army as laid down in this reign provided that the first and most important portion should consist of men who held their lands from the Sultan and were liable to well-defined military service. The second portion was formed of men who were paid for their services. The first, military tenants, were the "nerves and sinews of the Empire." These tenants received various names in accordance with the rent they paid for the crown lands and the services required of them. The Timariots held lands by title-deeds or *teskeres*, either from the Sultan's land-courts for which they paid any rent up to 20,000 aspers annually, or from a beglerbey on paying annual rent up to 6000 aspers. Each Timariot had to furnish himself with a small tent when on campaign, and was required to carry three or four baskets for making earthworks and trenches. Those who paid rent higher than 20,000 aspers were known as Za'īms. If the rent were above 100,000 aspers the Za'īm became a pasha or sanjakbey, and if above 200,000 he was a beglerbey. The Za'īms had not only to render personal service, to find their own tents, needful utensils for campaigning, stabling etc., but for every 5000 aspers at which the Za'īm was rated he had to bring one horseman into the field. The Za'īm might be called upon to supply up to nineteen men. The organisation recalls the feudal service in Western Europe with its tenants of the crown and their retainers.

The second portion of the army consisted of men who were paid for their services. It consisted first of the Janissaries who served for life, and secondly of Sipāhīs who were cavalry, armourers or smiths, gunners, and mariners. All in this second division were hired for the campaign only, and though, like all Ottoman subjects, liable to serve at all times, in the interval between campaigns they returned to their homes and pasturage. It was in forming an army mostly of infantry and retaining the services of all his male subjects that Orkhān is credited with having formed the first standing army of modern times. The infantry were known as Piyādē. Subsequently the name Piyādē was restricted to such infantry as had lands apportioned to them. Those who had no such lands were known as 'Azabs, and resembled the irregulars who at a later period were known as Bashi-bazuks. Corresponding to them, with the exception that they were cavalry, was a body of light horsemen known as Aqinji, who also were without regular pay and dependent on plunder. It was Orkhān who first gave Turkish soldiers a distinctive uniform. The general remark must, however, be made that modern authors, in describing the organisation of the Turkish army, credit Orkhān with the later organisation. Only the general outlines of this can safely be attributed to Orkhān.

The last twenty years of Orkhān's reign were years of less active aggression. But the Sultan found abundant occupation for his army. The facts justify us in assuming that he never lost sight of his father's intention to extend his empire northwards so as to encroach on that of Constantinople.

The ravages of the Turks who had been called into Thrace to resist the Tartars continued during two years. Then until 1344 we hear of fewer troubles with them in Thrace, though in that year they were before Salonica in the west and before Trebizond in the east of the Empire, while still another band attacked the Knights of Rhodes, who once more defeated them. It was probably shortly after the capture of Nicaea that Orkhān took possession of Gemlik, formerly called Civitot, and of almost all the south coast of Marmora.

In order to attach Orkhān to his side, the Emperor Cantacuzene in 1344 promised his daughter Theodora in marriage to the Ottoman Sultan. The offer was accepted, and Orkhān sent 6000 troops into Thrace. Perhaps the most noteworthy fact during the dynastic struggle, which went on in the imperial family during Orkhān's reign, was that two opposing bands of Turks were preying upon the country and thus impoverishing the Empire.

In the midst of the civil war Cantacuzene gave another daughter in marriage to the young Emperor John Palaeologus, aged fifteen, who had been associated with him. Orkhān came to Scutari to congratulate his father-in-law in 1347 on thus effecting a reconciliation, though Cantacuzene asserts that the object of his visit was to kill the young Emperor, whom he regarded as the rival of Cantacuzene or of a son that he himself might have by his wife Theodora.

The Serbs had now developed into a formidable nation. Orkhān sent 6000 Ottomans against Stephen Dušan. The Turks defeated the Serbs, but then recrossed into Asia with their booty. Two years later, in 1349, Orkhān sent 20,000 of his horsemen against the Serbs, who were attacking Salonica. Matthew, the youngest son of Cantacuzene, was with the Ottomans. In 1352 the Tsar of Bulgaria united with Stephen Dušan to support the young Emperor Palaeologus, who was now quarrelling with his father-in-law. Much of the fighting centred about Demotika, in the neighbourhood of which in the same year Sulaimān, the son of Orkhān, defeated the Serbs. Orkhān himself refused to assist in attacking his brother-in-law.

In these later years also, the struggle between the Genoese and the Venetians disturbed the Empire and assisted in furthering the advance of the Ottomans. On more than one occasion the Venetian fleet had successfully resisted the Turk; for the fleet of the republic, like that of Genoa, often made its appearance in the Aegean, and penetrated even to the Euxine to protect the trade of its subjects. As the two States were at this time almost constantly at war, it was practically inevitable that in the civil war raging during the time of Cantacuzene one or both of them should be invited to take sides. The Genoese were already established in Galata, and they had strongly fortified it with walls which may still be traced. In 1353 fourteen Venetian galleys fought at the entrance to the Bosphorus against the combined Greek and Genoese fleets, and their passage through the Straits was intercepted. In the following year Cantacuzene had to take a decided line between the two powers. He refused to ally himself with the Venetians, who had sent a fleet to invite him so to do, probably because of his unwillingness to give offence to Orkhān. His conduct, however, was of so dubious a character that the Genoese declared war against him. The Venetians and the fleet of the King of Aragon went to his assistance. Fighting took place once more in the Bosphorus, and the Genoese persuaded Orkhān to come to their aid. Thereupon Cantacuzene was compelled to come to terms with the Genoese; he granted them an extension of territory beyond the then existing walls of Galata, doubling in fact its area, and surrendered to them the important towns of Heraclea and Selymbria (Silivri) on the north shore of the Marmora. Cantacuzene, however, had fallen into disfavour with the citizens of his capital, who suspected that he was prepared to hand over Constantinople itself to Orkhān. It was when he proposed to place the fortress of Cyclobium around the Golden Gate in Orkhān's possession, for so went the rumour, that the old Emperor resigned, and assuming the habit of a monk retired to a monastery at Mangana; but a different version is given a century later by Phrantzes.

Orkhān now assumed an attitude of open hostility to the Empire. The year 1356 marks an epoch in the progress of the Ottoman Turks.

They and other Turkish tribes had frequently found themselves in Thrace, either to help one of the parties in the civil war, or to assist the Empire to repel Serb or Bulgar or Tartar invaders. But now Sulaimān, the son of Orkhān, succeeded in crossing the Straits simply with the intention of conquering new territory. A boat was ferried across the north end of the Dardanelles, a Greek peasant was captured who assisted the Turks in making rafts united by bullocks' hides, and on each raft forty horsemen were ferried across to Tzympe, possibly at the foot of the hill on which the castle of Sestos stands. In three nights thirty thousand men were transported to the European shore, either in boats or, as seems more likely, on a bridge supported on inflated skins. This was the real entry of the Turks into Europe.

Shortly afterwards the Ottoman army, now under the command of Murād, the second surviving son of Orkhān, took possession of three of the most important towns in Thrace, Chorlu on the direct line to Hadrianople, Epibatus, and Pyrgus[1]. In 1357 the Ottomans pushed on to Hadrianople, which they captured and held as their European capital until Constantinople fell into their hands. The capture was made by Sulaimān, who, however, died shortly afterwards. A few weeks later Demotika, which had had various fortunes during half a century and which was near the Bulgarian frontier, fell into the hands of the Ottomans. To have obtained possession of Hadrianople and of Demotika, and to be able to hold them, was the greatest Ottoman advance yet made in Europe.

An incident occurred in the last year of Orkhān's life which is instructive as shewing how much influence the fear of his power had in the Empire. His son Khalīl, by Theodora the daughter of Cantacuzene, was taken prisoner by pirates, probably Turks under the Emir of Magnesia, and sent to Phocaea at the head of the Gulf of Smyrna. The Emperor, with whom Matthew the son of Cantacuzene was associated, went himself with a fleet to capture the city, but returned without having accomplished his object. After some weeks spent in the capital, Orkhān insisted that he should return to set Khalīl free. The request was in the nature of a command, and was obeyed. The Palaeologus met his fleet returning. Negotiations went on, but for a while without effect. Finally in 1359 Khalīl was ransomed by the Emperor, brought to the capital, made governor of Bithynia, and took up his quarters at Nicaea. Previous to his arrival the Emperor had agreed with Orkhān to give his ten-year-old daughter to Khalīl. The agreement was made at Chalcedon; the betrothal was celebrated at Constantinople with great pomp and amid the rejoicing of the people, who believed that by the marriage and the signature of a treaty of perpetual peace they would have rest.

Orkhān died a few months afterwards at Brūsa in 1359, two months

[1] Cantemir makes this statement, though there is nothing to shew whether he means the Bulgarian Burgas, or a place of the same name about fifteen miles west of Constantinople but not on the coast.

after the death of his son Sulaimān. He had consolidated the realm over which Osmān had ruled, and had largely extended it. The Turkish writers claim that he had captured nearly every place between the Dardanelles and the Black Sea, including the shores of the gulfs of Gemlik and Izmid. The claim is exaggerated, for though he had harassed all the neighbourhood he had not taken possession of it. If, instead of speaking of his taking possession of these places, it is said that he claimed sovereign rights from the Dardanelles to the Black Sea, the statement would be correct. On the European side also he had acquired many places in Thrace and, most important of all, had captured Hadrianople, which was to serve as the chief centre of attack on the Empire by his successors.

MURĀD I (1359–1389).

The thirty years' reign of Sultan Murād marks a great advance of Ottoman power. On his accession, the Ottomans were already the most powerful division of the Turks in Asia Minor. With two or three exceptions, such as Karamania, little attention had to be given to the Turks in the rear, that is, to the south and east of the territory the Ottomans occupied. The greater body was constantly attracting to itself members of the smaller bodies.

The attention of Murād was devoted at the beginning of his reign mainly to the development of the important territory his people had already acquired, extending from the north of the Aegean eastward to Ineboli on the Black Sea. This territory, though for the most part conquered in the sense that it paid tribute and contained no population able to revolt, was ill-organised, and it was the business of the new sultan to complete its organisation for the purpose of government. But the great object of Murād's life was to make a still further advance into Europe. Indeed the remark may be made once for all that the Ottomans were never prosperous except when they were pushing forward to obtain new territory. Times of peace always shewed the worst side of the race. Inferior in civilisation and intelligence to the races they conquered, they resented their inferiority and became oppressors. Religion at this early stage of their history was not a powerful element in their character, but as they had adopted Islām the difference in religion between the conquerors and conquered tended to become more and more the distinguishing mark between them, with results which became increasingly important as time went on. Various Greek writers note the commencement of a religious persecution by Murād, and attribute it to the influence of a mufti. The Sultan is said to have promised to the 'Ulama one-fifth of the spoils of war.

We have seen that the predecessor of Murād had effected a landing in Thrace, had overrun the country, and claimed sovereignty over several towns. Murād's object was to make such sovereignty real and permanent, and to obtain effectual possession of further territory, and especially of important centres like Hadrianople and Salonica. We have seen that the first of these cities had been taken by his father, but its occupation had been only temporary. The explanation is that, numerous as the hordes of the Ottoman Turks were, they had not sufficient men to hold the cities they conquered.

They were now destined to meet much more formidable enemies than the Greek Emperor. The great Slav nations, Bulgars and Serbs, were strong, and were indeed at the height of their power. They too had taken advantage of the weakness of the Empire, and had strengthened their already powerful kingdoms. The chief struggles of Murād were to be with them, aided as they were by the Magyars and the Roumanians of Wallachia.

Meantime the advance of the Ottomans had aroused some of the nations of the West. England and France were too much occupied with the Hundred Years' War to take an active part in opposing the common enemy of Christendom. But the Pope, who was perhaps the strongest Power in western Europe, had long seen the advance of the Muslims, and accordingly did his utmost to rouse Christian nations to check that advance.

The Greek Empire at this time was in the midst of civil war. Though the fullest account we have of its condition is that written by the Emperor Cantacuzene himself, the picture presented is one of hopeless incompetence. Nor was Asia Minor unmolested. The Mamlūks had invaded Cilicia, and had captured Tarsus, Adana, and other cities. In the following year Attalia was taken by the King of Cyprus with the aid of the Knights of Rhodes. Murād did not trouble himself with the capture of Asiatic territory. The Ottomans were constant to their purpose of extending their conquests in Europe. The rival parties in the Empire were ready to buy their services. Sulaimān, the brother of Murād, had taken Hadrianople. Cantacuzene, after remonstrances based on appeals to the treaties made by Orkhān, was compelled to pay 10,000 crowns to Sulaimān on his promise to abandon his conquests in Thrace and return to Asia. Nevertheless, on the death of Sulaimān, Murād again took possession of Hadrianople. Probably, however, it was not held in permanence until 1366, six years after its occupation by Murād. In the same way and in the same year Gallipoli, which several times was occupied for a short time by the Ottomans, was taken from them by the Count of Savoy and given back to the Emperor within a year of its capture. The Emperor tried to induce the Serbs to join with him to expel the Turks, but this effort failed. After Murād had taken Demotika in 1361, he drove the Serbs out of Seres, and then attacked various claimants to both the Serbian and Bulgarian thrones.

In 1363 Murād was obliged to give his attention to Asia Minor.

So strong was he that he was able, before crossing into Asia, to obtain a treaty from the Emperor that he would not attempt to retake any of the places captured in Thrace, but would send aid to him across the Bosphorus. Returning the same year from his Asiatic territory, Murād made an agreement with the Genoese to transport 60,000 of his followers into Thrace. Proceeding to Hadrianople, we find him attacking and defeating an army composed of Serbs, Bulgarians, and Magyars. Three years later, in 1366, the South Serbs made an effort to capture Hadrianople. Their army of 50,000 men was, however, defeated[1]. To have accomplished this result the number of the Turks in Europe must certainly have been great. Other evidence is to the same effect. Ducas, writing three-quarters of a century later, states his belief that there were more Turks between the Dardanelles and the Danube than in Asia Minor itself. He describes how the Turks from Cappadocia, Lycia, and Caria had crossed into Europe to pillage and ruin the lands of the Christians. A hundred thousand had laid waste the country as far as Dalmatia. Notwithstanding the defeat of the Serbs just mentioned, they again attacked the Turks. In September 1371 Vukašin, King of South Serbia, with an army of 70,000 men, made a desperate stand near the banks of the river Maritza. In this battle the rout of the South Serbs was complete. Two sons of the king were drowned in the river, and Vukašin himself was killed in flight. The kingdom of the South Serbs had perished[2].

It is noteworthy that in the battle of the Maritza the Greeks took no part. It may be said that the impotency of the Empire reached its highest point two years later, in 1373, when Murād was formally recognised as his suzerain by the Emperor, who promised to render him military service, and consented to surrender his son Manuel as a hostage.

John V, the Greek Emperor, was meantime seeking aid from western Europe. In 1366 the Pope, in reply to his request for aid, pressed for the Union of the two Churches as a condition precedent, and urged him to take part in a crusade headed by Louis, King of Hungary. Urban V in the following year wrote to the Latin princes to facilitate the voyage of John and to assist him in raising means to oppose the Turks. In 1369 John visited Venice and thence went to Rome, where he formally professed the Roman faith. Upon such profession he was allowed to collect troops. Meantime the Pope urged Louis and the Voivode of Wallachia to join in attacking the Turks. John went to France, but his mission failed, and he found himself in money difficulties when in 1370 he returned to Venice. A new Pope, Gregory XI, preached once more a crusade with the object of driving the Turks back into Asia, and tried to obtain soldiers for Louis. The effort met with little success,

[1] The most complete study of this campaign yet made is by S. Novakovič, *Die Serben und Turken in XIV und XV Jahrhundert*, chs. VI and VII.

[2] Cf. *supra*, Chapter XVIII, p. 555.

and in 1374 the Pope reproached Louis for his inactivity, ignoring the fact that the task assigned to him was beyond his means. The Union of the Churches had not been completed, and though the Knights of Rhodes were urged to attack the Turks and to send seven hundred knights to attack them in Greece, and although a papal fleet was building, these preparations resulted in very little. In reference to the proposed Union one thing was clear, that, whatever the Emperor and his great nobles were prepared to do in the matter, the majority of his subjects would have none of it[1].

An incident in 1374 is significant of the relations between the chief actors, Murād the Sultan and John Palaeologus the Emperor. In 1373 John had associated his younger son Manuel with him as Emperor. Both father and son loyally fulfilled their obligations to Murād, and joined him in a campaign in Asia. The elder son, Andronicus, was on friendly terms with Sauji, the son of Murād. These two, who were about the same age, joined in a conspiracy to dethrone their fathers. When Murād and John returned from Asia Minor, they found the army of the rebellious sons in great force on the Maritza near Demotika. The most powerful element in the rebel army was Turkish. A bold appeal made in person to them by Murād caused large defections. Though both the rebel sons resisted, Demotika was captured. The inhabitants were treated with exceptional cruelty, which revolted Turks as well as Christians. The garrison was drowned in the Maritza; fathers were forced to cut the throats of their sons. The Sultan and the Emperor, say the chroniclers, had agreed to punish the chief rebels. Sauji was blinded[2].

The disastrous war between members of the imperial family, a war without a single redeeming feature, continued. The chief combatants were the rival sons of John—Manuel and Andronicus—the latter of whom gained possession of Constantinople in 1376, having entered it by the Pege Gate. He imprisoned John, his father, and his two brothers in the tower of Anemas. He had promised the Genoese the island of Tenedos in return for their aid. But the Venetians were in possession, and strongly opposed the attempt of Andronicus and the Genoese fleet to displace them. Amid these family disputes the Turks were steadily gaining ground. The one city in Asia Minor which remained faithful to the Empire was Philadelphia. In 1379, when John V was restored, the Turks, possibly at the instigation of Bāyazīd who later became Sultan, stipulated that the annual tribute paid by the Empire should be 30,000 gold bezants, that 12,000 fighting men should be supplied to the Sultan, and that Philadelphia should be surrendered. The bargain was the harder

[1] Cf. *supra*, Chapter XIX, pp. 617–18.

[2] Chalcondyles, I. p. 44, Phrantzes, I. Ducas, I. 12, says that Murād blinded his son and called on John to blind Andronicus, but though some formality of blinding was gone through by pouring vinegar upon the eyes, it was not effective.

because the Emperor had to send his own troops to compel his subjects to open their gates to the enemy.

The Turks were now waging war in southern Greece and in the Archipelago with great energy and success. Even Patmos had to be surrendered to them in 1381 in order to effect the ransom of the Grand Master of Rhodes. Islands and towns were being appropriated by Turks or Genoese without troubling about the consent of the Emperor. Scio or Chios, however, was given on a long lease by him to a company of Genoese who took the name of Giustiniani. In 1384 Apollonia on the Black Sea was occupied by Murād after he had killed the villagers. Two years later Murād sent two of his generals to take possession of several of the flourishing towns north of the Aegean. Gumaljina, Kavala, Seres, and others farther afield into Macedonia as far as Monastir, fell into Turkish hands.

As we near the end of Murād's reign, the increasing impotency of the Greek Empire becomes more manifest. Almost every year shews also an increase in numbers of the subjects who had come under Ottoman rule, and the wide-spread character of Ottoman conquest. The Muslim flood, which though not exclusively was mainly Ottoman, had spread all over the Balkan Peninsula. Turks were in Greece, and were holding their own in parts of Epirus. West of Thrace the most important city on the coast which had not been captured by the Turks was Salonica. After a siege lasting four years, it was captured for Murād in 1387.

The growth and development of the Bulgars and Serbs during the early part of the fourteenth century forms one of the leading features in the history of Eastern Europe. Their progress was checked by the Ottoman Turks. The Serbs had been so entirely defeated as to accept vassalage at Murād's hands. In 1381 their king was ordered to send 2000 men against the Emir of Karamania (Qaramān). On the return of this detachment the discontent at their subjection to Murād was so great that King Lazar revolted. He was defeated and thereupon set to work to organise an alliance against Murād. In 1389 the decisive battle was fought on the plains of Kossovo; Lazar was taken prisoner, and the triumph of the Ottomans was complete. As the battle on the Maritza had broken the power of the South Serbs and of the eastern Bulgarians in 1371, so did this battle on the plains of Kossovo in 1389 destroy that of the northern Serbians and the western Bulgarians[1].

During or immediately before the battle, there occurred a dramatic incident. A young Serb named Miloš ran towards the Turkish army, and, when they would have stopped him, declared that he wanted to see their Sultan in order that he might shew him how he could profit by the fight. Murād signed to him to come near, and the young fellow did so, drew a dagger which he had hidden, and plunged it into the heart of

[1] Cf. *supra*, Chapter XVIII, pp. 557–58.

the Sultan. He was at once cut down by the guards. Lazar, the captive king, was hewn in pieces.

Murād was the son of a Christian woman, who in Turkish is known as Nīlūfer, the lotus flower. She was seized by Orkhān on the day of her espousal to a Greek husband, and became the first wife of her captor. It is a question which has been discussed[1], whether the influence of the mother had any effect in moulding the character of her distinguished son. Murād seems to have possessed traits quite unlike those of his father or grandfather: a singular independence, a keen intelligence, a curious love of pleasure and of luxury, and at the same time a tendency towards cruelty which was without parallel in his ancestors. In his youth he was not allowed to take part in public affairs, and was overshadowed by his brother Sulaimān. It is claimed for Murād that he was inexorably just, and that he caused his "beloved son Sauji to be executed for rebellion." Von Hammer believes that he had long been jealous of him, but the better opinion would appear to be that Bāyazīd intrigued to have his brother condemned. When this elder brother came to the throne, he put another brother named Ya'qūb to death so as to have no rival.

The reign of Murād is the most brilliant period of the advance of the Ottomans. It lasted thirty years, during which conquest on the lines laid down by his two predecessors extended the area of Ottoman territory on a larger scale than ever, its especial feature being the defeat of the Serbians and Bulgarians with their allies in the two crowning victories of the Maritza in 1371 and Kossovo in 1389. On Murād's assassination it looked as if the Balkan peninsula was already under Ottoman sway. They had overrun Greece, had penetrated into Herzegovina, and had captured Niš, the position which commands the passes leading from Thrace into Serbia. The success of Murād was due to four causes, the impotence of the Greek Empire, the organisation of the Ottoman army, the constant increase of that army by an unending stream of Muslims from Asia Minor, and the disorganised condition of the races occupying the Balkan peninsula. We have already spoken of the impotence of the Empire. Murād and his brothers had developed the organisation of the Ottoman army, had improved its discipline, and had perfected a system of tactics which endured for many generations. It was already distinguished for its mobility, due in great part to the nomad character of a Turkish army. We may reject the stories of Turkish writers that the Christian armies were encumbered with women and with superfluous baggage due to their love of luxury, but, in comparison with the simple requirements of an army of nomads, it was natural and probably correct on the part of the Turks to regard the *impedimenta* of the other armies as excessive and largely useless. The constant stream of Asiatic immigrants is attested by many writers, Muslim and Christian. Moreover, the

[1] By Halil Ganem, *Les Sultans ottomans*, p. 64.

great horde from central Asia under the leadership of Tīmūr was already on the march, and had driven other Turks before it to the west; to them were due the constant accretions to the Ottoman army. The disorganised condition of the races once occupying the Balkan peninsula aided the advance of the Ottomans. The Slavs, as we have seen, were divided. There were Bulgars, Serbs, and inhabitants of Dalmatia; there were also Albanians, Wallachs of Macedonia, and Greeks. In the Ottoman army there was the tie of a common language. Patriotism, that is love of country, did not exist, but its place was taken by a common religion. Among the Christians whom they attacked, though there was unity of religion, patriotism was far from forming a bond of union.

The reign of Murād is important, not merely because of his successes in the Balkan peninsula, but because it was the beginning of an Ottoman settlement in Europe. It is true that the army still marched as a disciplined Asiatic horde, but the soldiers wherever they took possession of territory had lands, or *chiftliks*, granted to them according to their valour and the Sultan's will. Liable as they were at all times to continuous military service, they were always ready on the conclusion of peace to return to their lands, their flocks and herds. The occupation of Hadrianople caused that city soon to be the centre from which further Ottoman conquests were made—so that, while nominally Brūsa remained the capital of the race, Hadrianople soon became a more important city and the real centre of Ottoman rule.

BĀYAZĪD (1389–1403). WARS OF SUCCESSION (1403–1413).

On the assassination of Murād, Bāyazīd succeeded to the Ottoman throne. He was popular with the army because already renowned for his successes as a soldier. He is known as *Yilderim*, or the Thunderbolt, a title conferred upon him on account of the rapidity of his movements in warfare. Regarded simply as a man, he was the most despicable of Ottoman Sultans who had as yet been girded with the sword of Osmān. He alternated periods of wonderful activity with others of wild debauch. He was reckless of human life and delighted in cruelty. Had he possessed the statesmanlike ability of either of his predecessors he might have made an end of the Greek Empire. As it was, he would probably have done so if he had not encountered an opponent even more powerful and ruthless than himself.

Immediately after the victory of Kossovo he led his troops in quick succession against the Bulgars, the Serbs, the Wallachs, and the Albanians, reducing them to submission. He compelled Stephen, the son of Lazar, to acknowledge him as suzerain, and to give him his sister Maria in marriage. To such an extremity was the lingering Empire of Trebizond reduced that its Emperor Manuel in 1390 was compelled to contribute a large subsidy to aid Bāyazīd in a campaign against his father-in-law, the Emir of Germiyān or Phrygia, and to bring a hundred knights to aid in the campaign. Bāyazīd had in the meantime strengthened his fleet, which overran the islands in the Aegean as far as Euboea and the Piraeus. Sixty of his ships burnt the chief town of the island of Chios. A swift campaign in Asia Minor made him complete master of Phrygia and of Bithynia. Then he turned his attention to Constantinople. The Emperor proposed to strengthen the landward walls and to rebuild the famous towers at the Golden Gate. Bāyazīd objected and threatened to put out the eyes of the Emperor's son Manuel, who was with him as a hostage, unless the new buildings were demolished. The old Emperor John had to yield, and the surrender helped to kill him. The towers were shortly afterwards, on the death of Bāyazīd, rebuilt. Simultaneously Bāyazīd demanded payment of tribute, a recognition of the Emperor's vassalage to him, and the establishment of capitulations by which a Muslim cadi should be named in the capital to have jurisdiction over Ottoman subjects. He appears to have waged during 1392 and 1393 a war of extermination throughout Thrace, the subjects of the Empire being either taken captive or killed.

The advance of the Turks was now well known in western Europe, but the efforts made to resist it were spasmodic and shewed little power of coherence between the Christian States. Those who were nearest to the Balkan peninsula naturally were the most alarmed. Venice in 1391 decided to aid Durazzo in opposing Turkish progress. In the following year its senate treated with the King of Hungary for common action. Ten thousand Serbs from Illyria joined Theodore Palaeologus of Mistra, in his attempt to expel the Turks from Achaia. Theodore himself in 1394 was compelled by Bāyazīd to cede Argos. The Sultan later sent his general, Ya'qūb, into the Morea with 50,000 men, who penetrated as far as Methone and Coronea, captured Argos which Theodore had not surrendered, and carried off or killed 30,000 prisoners. The Emperor Manuel, whose rule hardly extended beyond the walls of Constantinople, made a series of appeals to the Western princes. Sigismund, King of Hungary and brother of the Emperor of the West, was the first to respond. He attacked the Turks at Little Nicopolis in 1393, and defeated them. This encouraged the Western powers to come to his aid. The Pope Boniface IX preached a new crusade in 1394, and in 1396 the Duke of Burgundy, at the head of 1000 knights and 9000 soldiers (French, English, and Italian), arrived in Hungary and joined Sigismund. German knights also came in considerable numbers. The Christian armies defeated the Turks in Hungary, and gained the victory in several engagements. The Emperor Manuel was secretly preparing to join them. Then the allies prepared to strike a decisive blow. They gathered on the banks of the Danube an army of at least 52,000 and possibly 100,000 men, and encamped at Nicopolis. The *élite* of several nations were present, but those of the highest rank were the French knights. When they heard of the approach of the enemy, they refused to listen to the prudent counsels of the Hungarians and, with the contempt which so often characterised the Western knights for the Turkish foe, they joined battle confident of success.

Bāyazīd, as soon as he had learned the presence of the combined Christian armies, marched through Philippopolis, crossed the Balkans, made for the Danube, and then waited for attack. In the battle which ensued (1396), Europe received its first lesson on the prowess of the Turks and especially of the Janissaries. The French with rash daring broke through the line of their enemies, cut down all who resisted them, and rushed on triumphantly to the very rearguard of the Turks, many of whom either retreated or sought refuge in flight. When the French knights saw that the Turks ran, they followed, and filled the battlefield with dead and dying. But they made the old military blunder, and it led to the old result. The archers, who always constituted the most effective Turkish arm, employed the stratagem of running away in order to throw their pursuers into disorder. Then they turned and made a stand. As they did so, the Janissaries, Christians in origin, from many Christian nations, as Ducas bewails, came out of the place where they had been concealed, and surprised and cut to pieces Frenchmen, Italians, and Hungarians. The pursuers were soon the pursued. The Turks chased them to the Danube, into which many of the fugitives threw themselves. The defeat was complete. Sigismund saved himself in a small boat, with which he crossed the river, and found his way, after long wandering, to Constantinople. The Duke of Burgundy and twenty-four nobles who were captured were sent to Brūsa to be held for ransom. The remaining Burgundians, to the number of 300, who escaped massacre and refused to save their lives by abjuring Christianity, had their throats cut or were clubbed to death by order of the Sultan and in the presence of their compatriots[1].

The battle of Nicopolis gave back to Bāyazīd almost at once all that the allies had been able to take from him. The defeat of Sigismund, with his band of French, German, and Italian knights, spread dismay among their countrymen and the princes of the West.

Bāyazīd, having retaken all the positions which the allied Christians had captured from him, hastened back to the Bosphorus, his design being to conquer Constantinople. For this purpose, having strengthened his position at Izmid and probably at the strong fortification still remaining at Gebseh, he immediately gave orders for the construction of a fortress at what is now known as Anatolia-Hisār. The fort was about six miles from the capital on the Asiatic side and at the mouth of a small river now known as the Sweet Waters of Asia. The arrival in March 1397 of the great French soldier Boucicaut in the capital probably influenced the design of the Sultan; for although he had defeated the Christian allies at Nicopolis and had made all preparations for the capture of Con-

[1] Cf. *supra*, Chapter XVIII, p. 561.

stantinople, and although the Emperor had been summoned to surrender it, a demand to which he had not replied, the grand vizier represented to him that its siege would unite all Christian Europe against him, and the project was therefore delayed. The construction of Anatolia-Hisār, which was to serve as his basis of attack, was however pushed on and completed[1]. A few months later in 1397, the Sultan endeavoured to accomplish his object by persuading John, the nephew of the Emperor Manuel, to claim the throne, promising that if he did so he would aid him in return by the cession of Silivri. John refused, and when Bāyazīd made further proposals Manuel took a step which suggests patriotism and which Godefroy, the biographer of Boucicaut, attributes to his wise intervention. Manuel agreed to admit John into the city, to associate him on the throne, and then to leave for western Europe to bring the aid so greatly needed (1398). Boucicaut arrived in the following year at the head of 1400 men-at-arms and with a well-manned fleet. At Tenedos he was joined by Genoese and Venetian ships, and became admiral-in-chief. He met near Gallipoli a Turkish fleet of seventeen galleys and defeated them. Then he pushed on to the Bosphorus, and arrived in the Golden Horn just in time to prevent Galata being captured by the Turks. The Emperor appointed him Grand Constable. The French knights under him fought the Turks whenever they could find them, from Izmid to Anatolia-Hisār, defeated them in many skirmishes, and sent many Turkish prisoners to Constantinople. But their numbers were too few to have much permanent value. They harassed Bāyazīd's army at Izmid, but failed to capture the city. They burnt a few Turkish villages; but after a year's fighting Boucicaut left for France in order to obtain more volunteers. He left in Constantinople Chateaumorant with 100 knights and their esquires and servants to assist in defending the city.

The Turks were now spread throughout the Balkan peninsula and claimed to rule over almost all Asia Minor. Western Europe was alarmed at their progress and many attempts were made to resist it. Had their forces been capable of united action under a great general like Boucicaut, they might have succeeded in effecting a check. But while that general was fighting on the shores of the Marmora, destroying many Turkish encampments and greatly harassing the enemy, he was only hopeful of success if he could obtain a larger contingent of French knights. While others, as we have seen, were fighting the battle of civilisation in the Morea, the Knights of Rhodes had captured Budrun, the ancient Halicarnassus, and had already made themselves a strong power in the Aegean and Levant; but they were themselves a cause of weakness to the Empire. Theodore of Mistra, the brother of Manuel, had ceded Corinth to them, but they attempted to obtain other concessions, and

[1] Leunclavius says that the Sultan desisted only on condition that a quarter in the city should be given to the Turks. Chalcondyles says he withdrew because he had had no success. Ducas speaks of the resistance of the citizens as obstinate.

Bāyazīd tempted Theodore with the promise of peace if he would give his aid to expel the Knights. While Bulgarians, Serbs, and Albanians were ready for resistance whenever a favourable opportunity occurred, there was little solidarity between them in their efforts to resist the invaders. Bāyazīd, a ruthless invader with forces ever increasing, was ready everywhere to employ his genius for warfare and the great mobile army whose interest was to follow him; and the result was that the efforts of his disunited enemies hardly impeded his progress.

Boucicaut persuaded the Emperor Manuel to offer to become the vassal of Charles VI of France; and the Venetians, Genoese, and the Knights of Rhodes consented to his doing homage. Venetians and Genoese in the Bosphorus agreed to join forces and work for the defence of the city. The Emperor Manuel and Boucicaut left together for Venice and France. Charles received both with great honours, and consented to send 1200 soldiers and to pay them for a year. In order to avoid the responsibility of giving Manuel the protection of a suzerain, he seems to have refused to accept him as his vassal. Manuel went in 1400 from Paris to England, where Henry IV received him with great honour but gave no assistance. In 1402 he returned to Venice by way of Germany.

In the same year Bāyazīd summoned John to surrender the capital. During three years it had been nearly isolated by the Turks, but now it was threatened by assault. Bāyazīd swore "by God and the prophet" that if John refused he would not leave in the city a soul alive. The Emperor gave a dignified refusal. Chateaumorant, who had been in charge of the defence for nearly three years, waited to be attacked.

At this time, remarks Ducas, the Empire was circumscribed by the walls of Constantinople, for even Silivri was in the hands of the Turks. Bāyazīd had gained a firm hold of Gallipoli, and thus commanded the Dardanelles. The long tradition of the Roman Empire seemed on the eve of coming to an end. No soldier of conspicuous ability had been produced for upwards of half a century, none capable of inflicting a sufficient defeat, or series of defeats, on the Turks to break or seriously check their power. The Empire had fought on for three generations against an ever-increasing number of Muslims, but without confidence and almost without hope. It was now deficient both in men and in money. The often-promised aid from the West had so far proved of little avail. The power of Serbia had been almost destroyed. Bulgaria had perished. From Dalmatia to the Morea the enemy was triumphant. The men of Macedonia had everywhere fallen before Bāyazīd's armies. Constantinople was between the hammer and the anvil. Asia Minor, on the one side, was now nearly all under Turkish rule; Europe, on the other, contained as many Turks as there were in Asia Minor itself.

Bāyazīd passed in safety between his two capitals, one at Brūsa, the other at Hadrianople, and repeated his proud boasts of what he would do beyond the limits of the Empire. It seemed as if, with his overwhelming force, he had only to succeed once more in a task which, in comparison with what he and his predecessors had done, was easy, and his success would be complete. He would occupy the throne of Constantine, would achieve that which had been the desire of the Arab followers of Mahomet, and for which they had sacrificed hundreds of thousands of lives, and would win for himself and his followers the reward of heaven promised to those who should take part in the capture of New Rome. The road to the Elder Rome would be open, and he repeated the boast that he would feed his horse on the altar of St Peter.

When he had sent his insolent message in 1402 to John VII, the answer was: "Tell your master we are weak, but that in our weakness we trust in God, who can give us strength and can put down the mightiest from their seats. Let your master do what he likes." Thereupon Bāyazīd had laid siege to Constantinople.

Suddenly in the blackness of darkness with which the fortunes of the city were surrounded there came a ray of light. All thought of the siege was abandoned for the time, and Constantinople breathed again freely. What had happened was that Tīmūr the Lame, "the Scourge of God," had challenged, or rather ordered, Bāyazīd to return to the Greeks all the cities and territories he had captured. The order of the Asiatic barbarian, given to another ferocious barbarian like Bāyazīd, drove him to fury. The man who gave it was, however, accustomed to be obeyed.

Tīmūr, or Tamerlane, was a Musulman and a Turk[1]. His nomad troops advanced in well-organised armies, under generals who seem to have had intelligence everywhere of the enemy's country and great military skill. After conquering Persia, Tīmūr turned westward. In 1386 he appeared at Tiflis, which he subsequently captured, at the head of an enormous host estimated at 800,000 men. At Erzinjān he put all the Turks sent there by Bāyazīd to the sword.

Bāyazīd seems from the first to have been alarmed, and went himself to Erzinjān in 1394, but returned to Europe without making any attempt to resist the invader, probably believing that Tīmūr had no intention of coming farther west. He soon learned his mistake. Tīmūr was not merely as great and cruel a barbarian but as ambitious as Bāyazīd himself. In 1395, while the Sultan was in the Balkan peninsula, Tīmūr summoned the large and populous city of Sīwās to surrender. The inhabitants twice refused. Meantime, he had undermined the wall. On their second refusal, his host stormed and captured the city. A hundred and twenty thousand captives were massacred. One of Bāyazīd's sons was made prisoner and put to death. A large number of prisoners were buried alive, being covered over in a pit with planks instead of earth so as to prolong their torture. Bāyazīd was relieved when he heard that

[1] Cf. *supra*, Chapter xx, pp. 650–51.

from Sīwās, which had been the strongest place in his empire, the ever victorious army had gone towards Syria.

Tīmūr directed his huge host towards Aleppo, the then frontier city of the Sultan of Egypt, his object being to punish the Sultan for his breach of faith in imprisoning his ambassador and loading him with irons. On his march to that city, he spread desolation everywhere, capturing or receiving the submission of Malaṭīyah, ʻAin Tāb, and other important towns. At Aleppo the army of the Egyptian Sultan resisted. A terrible battle followed, but the Egyptians were beaten, and every man, woman, and child in the city was slaughtered.

After the capture of Aleppo, Ḥamāh and Baalbek were occupied. The last, which, like so many other once famous cities, has become a desolation under Turkish rule with only a few miserable huts amid its superb ruins, was still a populous city, and contained large stores of provisions. Thence he went to Damascus, and in January 1401 defeated the remainder of the Egyptian army in a battle which was hardly less bloody than that before Aleppo. The garrison, composed mostly of Circassian mamlūks and negroes, capitulated, but its chief was put to death for having been so slow in surrendering. Possibly by accident the whole city was burned.

Tīmūr was stopped from advancing to Jerusalem by a plague of locusts, which ate up every green thing. The same cause rendered it impossible to attack Egypt, whose Sultan had refused to surrender Syria.

From Damascus Tīmūr went to Baghdad, which was held by contemporaries to be impregnable. Amid the heat of a July day, when the defenders had everywhere sought shade, Tīmūr ordered a general assault, and in a few minutes the standard of one of his shaikhs, with its horsetail and its golden crescent, was raised upon the walls. Then followed the usual carnage attending Tīmūr's captures. The mosques, schools, and convents with their occupiers were spared; so also were the *imāms* and the professors. All the remainder of the population between the ages of eight and eighty were slaughtered. Every soldier of Tīmūr, of whom there were 90,000, as the price of his own safety, had to produce a head. The bloody trophies were, as was customary in Tīmūr's army, piled up in pyramids before the gates of the city.

It was on his return northward from Damascus that, in 1402, Tīmūr sent the message to Bāyazīd which at once forced him to raise the siege of Constantinople. Contemporaneously with this message Tīmūr requested the Genoese in Galata and at Genoa to obtain aid from the West, and to co-operate with him to crush the Turkish Sultan.

Tīmūr organised a large army on the Don and around the Sea of Azov, in order that in case of need it might act with his huge host now advancing towards the Black Sea from the south. His main body passed across the plain of Erzinjān, and at Sīwās Tīmūr received the answer of Bāyazīd. The response was as insulting as a Turkish barbarian could make it. Bāyazīd summoned Tīmūr to appear before him, and declared that, if he did not obey, the women of his harem should be divorced from him, putting his threat in what to a Musulman was a specially indecent manner. All the usual civilities in written communications between sovereigns were omitted, though the Asiatic conqueror himself had carefully observed them. Tīmūr's remark, when he saw the Sultan's letter containing the name of Tīmūr in black writing under that of Bāyazīd which was in gold, was: "The son of Murād is mad." When he read the insulting threat as to his harem, Tīmūr kept himself well in hand, but turning to the ambassador who had brought the letter, told him that he would have cut off his head and those of the members of his suite, if it were not the rule among sovereigns to respect the lives of ambassadors. The representative of Bāyazīd was, however, compelled to be present at a review of the whole of the troops, and was ordered to return to his master and relate what he had seen.

Meantime Bāyazīd had determined to strike quickly and heavily against Tīmūr, and by the rapidity of his movements once more justified his name of Yilderim. His opponent's forces, however, were hardly less mobile. Tīmūr's huge army marched in twelve days from Sīwās to Angora. The officer in command of that city refused to surrender. Tīmūr made his arrangements for the siege in such a manner as to compel or induce Bāyazīd to occupy a position where he would have to fight at a disadvantage. He undermined the walls and diverted the small stream which supplied it with water. Hardly had these works been commenced before he learned that Yilderim was within nine miles of the city. Tīmūr raised the siege and transferred his camp to the opposite side of the stream, which thus protected one side of his army, while a ditch and a strong palisade guarded the other. Then, in an exceptionally strong position, he waited to be attacked.

Disaffection existed in Bāyazīd's army, occasioned by his parsimony, and possibly nursed by emissaries from Tīmūr. Bāyazīd's own licentiousness had been copied by his followers, and discipline among his troops was noted as far less strict than among those of his predecessor. In leading them on what all understood to be the most serious enterprise which he had undertaken, his generals advised him to spend his reserves of money freely so as to satisfy his followers; but the capricious and self-willed Yilderim refused. They counselled him, in presence of an army much more numerous than his own, to act on the defensive and to avoid a general attack. But Bāyazīd, blinded by his long series of successes, would listen to no advice and would take no precautions. In order to shew his contempt for his enemy, he ostentatiously took up a position to the north of Tīmūr, and organised a hunting party on the highlands in the neighbourhood, as if time to him were of no consequence. Many men of his army died from thirst under the burning sun of the waterless plains, and when, after three days' hunting, the Sultan returned to his camping ground, he found that Tīmūr had taken possession of it, had almost cut off his supply of drinking water, and had fouled what still remained. Under these circumstances, Bāyazīd had no choice but to force on a fight without further delay. The ensuing battle was between two great Turkish leaders filled with the arrogance of barbaric conquerors, each of whom had been almost uniformly successful. Nor were pomp and circumstance wanting to impress the soldiers of each side with the importance of the issue. Each of the two leaders was accompanied by his sons. Four sons and five grandsons commanded the nine divisions of Tīmūr's host. In front of its leader floated the standard of the Red Horsetail surmounted by the Golden Crescent. On the other side, Bāyazīd took up his position in the centre of his army with his sons 'Īsà, Mūsà, and Muṣṭafà, while his eldest son Sulaimān was in command of the troops who formed the right wing. Stephen of Serbia was in command of his own subjects, who had been forced to accompany Bāyazīd, and formed the left wing of the army. The Serbians gazed in wonder and alarm upon a number of elephants opposite to them, which Tīmūr had brought from India.

At six o'clock in the morning of 28 July 1402, the two armies joined battle. The left wing of Bāyazīd's host was the first to be attacked, but the Serbians held their ground and even drove back the Tartars. The right wing fought with less vigour, and when the troops from Aidīn saw their former prince among the enemy, they deserted Bāyazīd and went over to him. Their example was speedily followed by many others, and especially by the Tartars in the Ottoman army, who are asserted by the Turkish writers to have been tampered with by agents of Tīmūr.

The Serbians were soon detached from the centre of the army, but Stephen, their leader, at the head of his cavalry, cut his way through the enemy, though at great loss, winning the approval of Tīmūr himself, who exclaimed: "These poor fellows are beaten, though they are fighting like lions." Stephen had advised Bāyazīd to endeavour like himself to break through, and awaited him for some time. But the Sultan expressed his scorn at the advice. Surrounded by his ten thousand trustworthy Janissaries, separated from the Serbians, abandoned by a large part of his Anatolian troops and many of his leading generals, he fought on obstinately during the whole of the day. But the pitiless heat of a July sun exhausted the strength of his soldiers, and no water was to be had. His Janissaries fell in great numbers around him, some overcome by the heat and fighting, others struck down by the ever pressing crowd of the enemy. It was not till night came on that Bāyazīd consented to withdraw. He attempted flight, but was pursued. His horse fell and he was made prisoner, together with his son Mūsà and several of the chiefs of his household and of the Janissaries. His other three sons managed to escape. The Serbians covered the retreat of the eldest, Sulaimān, whom the grand vizier and the Āghā of the Janissaries had dragged out of the fight.

The Persian, Turkish, and most of the Greek historians say that Tīmūr received his great captive with every mark of respect, assured him that his life would be spared, and assigned to him and his suite three splendid tents. When, however, he was found attempting to escape, he was more rigorously guarded and every night put in chains and confined in a room with barred windows. When he was conveyed from one place to another, he travelled much as Indian ladies now do, in a palanquin with curtained windows. Out of a misinterpretation of the Turkish word, which designated at once a cage and a room with grills, grew the error into which Gibbon and historians of less repute have fallen, that the great Yilderim was carried about in an iron cage. Until his death he was an unwilling follower of his captor.

After the battle of Angora, Sulaimān, the eldest son of Bāyazīd, who had fled towards Brūsa, was pursued by a detachment of Tīmūr's army. He managed to cross into Europe, and thus escaped. But Brūsa, the Turkish capital, fell before Tīmūr's attack, and its inhabitants suffered the same brutal horrors as almost invariably marked either Tartar or Turkish captures. The city, after a carefully organised pillage, was burned. The wives and daughters of Bāyazīd and his treasure became the property of Tīmūr. Nicaea and Gemlik were also sacked and their inhabitants taken as slaves. From the Marmora to Karamania, many towns which had been captured by the Ottomans were taken from them. Asia Minor was in confusion. Bāyazīd's empire appeared to be falling to pieces in every part east of the Aegean. Sulaimān, however, established himself on the Bosphorus at Anatolia-Hisār, and about the same time both he and the Emperor at Constantinople received a summons from Tīmūr to pay tribute. The Emperor had already sent messengers to anticipate such a demand. Tīmūr learned with satisfaction that the sons of Bāyazīd were disputing with each other as to the possession of such parts of their father's empire as still remained unconquered.

In 1402 the conqueror left Kyūtāhiya for Smyrna, which was held, as it had been for upwards of half a century, by the Knights of Rhodes. In accordance with the stipulation of Muslim sacred law, he summoned them either to pay tribute or to become Musulmans, threatening them at the same time that if they refused to accept one or other of these conditions all would be killed. No sooner were the proposals rejected than Tīmūr gave the order to attack the city. With his enormous army, he was able to surround Smyrna on three sides, and to block the entrance to it from the sea. The ships belonging to the Knights were at the time absent. All kinds of machines then known for attack upon walled towns were constructed with almost incredible speed and placed in position. The houses within the city were burned by means of arrows carrying flaming materials steeped in naphtha or possibly petroleum, though, of course, not known under its modern name.

After fourteen days' vigorous siege, a general assault was ordered, and the city taken. The Knights fought like heroes but were driven back into the citadel. Seeing that they could no longer hold out, and their ships having returned, the Grand Master placed himself at their head, and he and his Knights cut their way shoulder to shoulder through the crowd of their enemies to the sea, where they were received into their own ships. The inhabitants who could not escape were taken before Tīmūr and butchered without distinction of age or sex.

The Genoese in Phocaea and in the islands of Mitylene and Chios sent to make submission, and became tributaries of the conqueror.

Smyrna was the last of Tīmūr's conquests in western Asia Minor. He went to Ephesus, and during the thirty days he passed in that city his army ravaged the whole of the fertile country in its neighbourhood and in the valley of the Cayster. The cruelties committed by his horde would be incredible if they were not well authenticated and indeed continually repeated during the course of Tartar and Turkish history. In fairness it must also be said that the Ottoman Turks, although their history has been a long series of massacres, have rarely been guilty of the wantonness of cruelty which Greek and Turkish authors agree in attributing to the Tartar army. One example must suffice. The children of a town on which Tīmūr was marching were sent out by their parents, reciting verses from the Koran to ask for the generosity of their conqueror but co-religionist. On asking what the children were whining for, and being told that they were begging him to spare the town, he ordered his cavalry to ride through them and trample them down, an order which was forthwith obeyed.

Tīmūr, wearied with victories in the West, now determined to leave Asia Minor and return to Samarqand. He contemplated the invasion of China, but in the midst of his preparations he died, in 1405, after a reign of thirty-six years.

Bāyazīd the Thunderbolt had died at Āq-Shehr two years earlier (March 1403), or according to Ducas at Qara-Hisār, and according to another account by his own hand. His son Mūsà was permitted to transport his body to Brūsa.

The next ten years were occupied in struggles among the sons of Bāyazīd for the succession to his throne. These struggles threatened still more to weaken the Ottoman power. The battle of Angora had given the greatest check to it which it had yet received. Tīmūr's campaign proved, however, to be merely a great marauding expedition, most of the effects of which were only temporary. But its immediate result was that the victorious career of the Thunderbolt was brought suddenly to an end. The empire of the Ottomans which he had largely increased, especially by the addition to it of the southern portion of Asia Minor, was for a time shattered. Mahomet of the old dynasty had taken possession of Karamania; Caria and Lycia were once more under independent emirs. The sons of the vanquished Sultan, after the departure of Tīmūr and his host, quarrelled over the possession of what remained. Three of them gained territories in Asia Minor, while the eldest, Sulaimān, retook possession of the lands held by his father in Europe. Most of the leaders of the Ottoman host, the viziers, governors, and shaikhs, had been either captured or slain, and in consequence the sons of Bāyazīd fighting in Asia Minor found themselves destitute of efficient servants for the organisation of government in the territories which they seized on the departure of the great invader.

The progress of the Asiatic horde created a profound impression in Western Europe. The eagerness of the Genoese to acknowledge the suzerainty of Tīmūr gives an indication of their sense of the danger of resistance. The stories of the terrible cruelties of the Tartars lost nothing in the telling. When the news of the defeat at Angora, along with the capture of Brūsa, of Smyrna, and of every other town which the Asiatic army had besieged, and of the powerlessness of the military Knights, reached Hungary, Serbia, and the states of Italy, it appeared as if the West were about to be submerged by a new flood from Asia. Then, when news came of the sudden departure of the Asiatics and of the breaking up of the Ottoman power, hope once more revived, and it appeared possible to the Pope and to the Christian peoples to complete the work which Tīmūr had begun by now offering a united opposition to the establishment of an Ottoman empire. Constantinople itself when Bāyazīd passed it on his way to Angora was almost the last remnant of the ancient Empire. The battle of Angora saved it and gave it half a century more of life.

Sulaimān in 1405 sought to ally himself with the Emperor, and his proposals shew how low the battle of Angora had brought the Turkish pretensions. He offered to cede Salonica and all country in the Balkan peninsula to the south-west of that city as well as the towns on the Marmora to Manuel and his nephew John, associated as Emperor, and to send his brother and sister as hostages to Constantinople. The arrangement was accepted.

Sulaimān attacked his brother ‘Īsà in 1405, and killed him[1]. Another brother, Mūsà, in the following year, attacked the combined troops of Sulaimān and Manuel in Thrace, but the Serbians and Bulgarians deserted the younger brother, and thereupon Sulaimān occupied Hadrianople. Manuel consented to give his granddaughter in marriage to Sulaimān, who in return gave up not merely Salonica but many seaports in Asia Minor, a gift which was rather in the nature of a promise than a delivery, since they were not in his possession. Unhappily Sulaimān, like many of his race, had alternate fits of great energy and great lethargy, and was given over to drunkenness and to debauchery. This caused disaffection among the Turks; and Mūsà, taking advantage of it, led in 1409 an army composed of Turks and Wallachs against him. The Janissaries, who were dissatisfied with the lack of energy displayed by their Sultan, deserted

[1] Chalcondyles, IV. p. 170. Ducas says he disappeared in Karamania; Phrantzes, p. 86, that he was bowstrung.

and went over to the side of Mūsà. Sulaimān fled with the intention of escaping to Constantinople, but was captured while sleeping off a drinking bout and killed.

Then Mūsà determined to attack Manuel, who had been faithful to his alliance with Sulaimān. He denounced him as the cause of the fall or Bāyazīd, and set himself to arouse all the religious fanaticism possible against the Christian population under the Emperor's rule. According to Ducas, Mūsà put forward the statement that it was the Emperor who had invited Tīmūr and his hordes, that his own brother Sulaimān had been punished by Allāh because he had become a *giaour*, and that he, Mūsà, had been entrusted with the sword of Mahomet in order to overthrow the infidel. He therefore called upon the faithful to go with him to recapture Salonica and the other Greek cities which had belonged to his father, and to change their churches into mosques.

In 1412 he devastated Serbia for having supported his brother, and this in as brutal a manner as Tīmūr had devastated the cities and countries in Asia Minor. Then he attacked Salonica. Orkhān, the son of Sulaimān, aided the Christians in the defence of the city, which however was forced to surrender, and Orkhān was blinded by his uncle.

While successful on land Mūsà was defeated at sea, and the inhabitants of the capital, in 1411, saw the destruction of his fleet off the island of Plataea in the Marmora. In revenge for this defeat he laid siege to the city. Manuel and his subjects stoutly defended its landward walls, and before Mūsà could capture it news came of the revolt of his younger brother, Mahomet, who appeared as the avenger of Sulaimān. The siege of Constantinople had to be raised. Mahomet had taken the lordship of the Turks in Amasia shortly after the defeat of his father at Angora, and had not been attacked by Tīmūr. The Emperor proposed an alliance with him, which was gladly accepted, and the conditions agreed to were honourably kept by both parties. Mahomet came to Scutari, where he had an interview with the Emperor. An army composed of Turks and Greeks was led by Mahomet to attack his brother. But Mūsà defeated him in two engagements. Then Manuel, after a short time, having been joined by a Serbian army, attempted battle against him, and with success. The Janissaries deserted Mūsà and went over to Mahomet and Manuel, and his army was defeated. Mūsà was himself captured and by order of Mahomet was bowstrung.

Mahomet was now the only survivor of the six sons of Bāyazīd, with the exception of Qāsim, the youngest, who was still living with Manuel as a hostage; three of his brothers had been the victims of fratricide. In 1413 Mahomet proclaimed himself Grand Sultan of the Ottomans.

MAHOMET I, CALLED THE GENTLEMAN (1413–1421).

Mahomet was a soldier at the age of fifteen and proved himself from the first an able one. After the ten years of civil war already mentioned he was formally recognised as Sultan. Shortly before his accession he charged the representatives of Venice, Serbia, Bulgaria, and Wallachia, who went to offer their congratulations, not to forget to repeat to their masters that he purposed to give peace to all and to accept it from all. He added: "May the God of Peace inspire those who should be tempted to violate it." At his accession the Ottomans had lost nearly all their possessions in Europe except Hadrianople. Bosnia, Bulgaria, and Wallachia had recovered their freedom. In Asia Minor revolts followed each other in rapid succession. According to his promise, Mahomet restored to the Emperor Manuel the strong positions which the Turks had occupied on the Black Sea, on the Marmora, and in Thessaly; and he acknowledged the rule of the Serbians over a considerable portion of the territory they had lost. When the Emperor returned by sea from the Morea, the two rulers had a friendly interview in Gallipoli on an imperial ship. In 1416 Mahomet gave permission to the Knights of Rhodes to build a castle in Lycia as a refuge for fugitives from the Muslims.

In the following year, 1417, he crossed from Hadrianople to Asia Minor and recaptured Smyrna from Junaid, who had declared himself independent during the war of succession.

Venice at this time sent out many rovers who, while owning allegiance to the republic, fought for their own hands, annexed territory to the sovereign city, but were allowed to establish themselves as rulers. They plundered the Turkish coasts and captured Turkish vessels wherever they found them. War with the republic was declared in 1416. The Sultan had so far not sought war with any European State, nor did he now seek war with Venice, the republic indeed forcing it upon him. He fitted out no less than 112 ships, of which thirteen were galleys. The Venetian fleet was under the command of Loredan. The two fleets met off Gallipoli on 29 May 1416, when a bloody encounter took place and the Turks were utterly defeated[1]. Twenty-seven Turkish vessels were captured, and a tower built by the Genoese at Lampsacus to prevent the Turks passing into Europe was rased to the ground[2].

Mahomet did not seek to play the part of a conqueror in his expeditions against Hungary in 1416 and the two following years, but he introduced a better organisation into the places which his predecessor had captured. He erected a series of forts on the frontier of the Danube. One of the most important was at Giurgevo, opposite Ruschuk. Junaid, the former governor of Smyrna, was named to the same post in Nicopolis.

[1] Jorga, p. 372, speaks of the battle as an event of world importance.

[2] Von Hammer, ch. IX, p. 172. The *Rapport de Loredano,* given in full in Laugier's *Histoire de Venise,* I. 5.

Severin, near Trajan's bridge, was fortified. Mahomet endeavoured, but with less success, to introduce better organisation among the Serbs, west and northwest of Belgrade, as far as Styria. Sigismund, however, declared war, and obtained a victory over the Turks between Niš and Nicopolis in 1419. The last years of Mahomet's reign were comparatively peaceful.

Mahomet had to meet a pretender, as he is called by the Turkish historians, who claimed to be Muṣṭafà, brother of the Sultan, who had disappeared after the battle of Angora. He was supported by Junaid, the ex-rebel of Smyrna whom we have seen named governor of Nicopolis, and also by the Wallachs. The rebellion raised by them became more serious in the reign of the following Sultan. Mahomet died from a fit of apoplexy, in which he fell from his horse at Hadrianople, at the end of 1421 or perhaps in January 1422[1].

Halil Ganem claims that Mahomet was the greatest, wisest, noblest, and most magnanimous of the Ottoman conquerors. He was called *Chelebi*, "the gracious lord," "the gentleman." He was renowned for his justice as much as for his courage. He was the rebuilder, the restorer, whose practical wisdom was of as much value to the Ottomans as the military genius of his predecessor. Their empire on his accession appeared as a mass of fragments. The attacks on the Greek Empire almost altogether ceased, because the Sultan considered it was his first duty to undo the mischief following Tīmūr's dislocation of the Ottoman dominions.

The defeat of the Turks by the Venetians and the Sultan's treatment of the Empire led its rulers to hope once more for the recovery of their rule, and enabled them to strengthen their positions in the capital. The story of Mahomet's reign would appear to justify the belief that when he came to the throne he had decided that, instead of seeking for an extension of his dominions, he would consolidate and strengthen those which his predecessors had conquered and he had inherited. While therefore he did not seek war, he not only improved the administration of his government, but also founded mosques and schools in the large towns. Brūsa itself contains the most important of the institutions established by him, and the Yeshil-jāmi', or Green Mosque, of that city is at once the most beautiful specimen of Turkish architecture and decoration and one of the world's artistic monuments.

MURĀD II (1421–1451).

Murād, the lawful heir to the throne, was, on the death of Mahomet, at Amasia. Indeed the death was concealed by Bāyazīd, the faithful vizier, until Murād could be produced. Notwithstanding the comparative calm which characterised the reign of Mahomet, the evidence shews that,

[1] Leunclavius says in A.H. 824 = A.D. 1421. Chalcondyles, ch. v, makes him reign twelve years. Ducas, ch. 22, makes the reign last only eight years. The difference is due to the date fixed on for his accession.

during his reign and during the war of succession which preceded it, the number of Turks, both in Europe and in Asia, was continually increasing. Remembering the huge hordes under Tīmūr, and still more the Turks who had fled westward before his advance, there can be little doubt that this increase in the numbers of invading Asiatics was largely due to the great movement in question. Ducas notes that, after the hordes of Tīmūr left Persia and passed through Armenia, they invaded Cappadocia and Lycaonia, where they received permission to pillage the lands of Christians, and that, without swords or lances, they were in such numbers that they swept the country before them. The invasion, he adds, was so general that it spread all over Anatolia and Thrace, even into the provinces beyond the Danube. They ravaged Achaia and Greece, and while trying to keep on good terms with the Empire attacked the Serbians, Bulgarians, and Albanians; they destroyed all nations except the Wallachs and Hungarians. Ducas believed that there were more Turks between the Danube and Gallipoli than in Asia. When, often to the number of a hundred thousand, they entered the various provinces, they took possession of everything they could find. They desolated the country as far as the frontier of Dalmatia. The Albanians, who were considered innumerable, were reduced to a small nation. Everywhere they obliged Christian parents to give to the Grand Signor one-fifth of the prisoners and booty captured, and the choicest children were taken. From the rest the young and strong were purchased at low prices, and were compelled to become Janissaries. The victims were then compelled to embrace the conqueror's religion and to be circumcised. Everywhere the army formed of tribute children was victorious. Among them, says Ducas, were no Turks or Arabs but only children of Christians—Romans, Serbians, Albanians, Bulgarians, and Wallachs. The statement of Ducas is confirmed by both Turkish and Christian writers.

It was the increased and ever-increasing body of Turks which under the second Murād was destined to carry the Ottoman banner throughout the length of the Balkan peninsula. Murād commenced his reign by an action which shewed, as the Turkish writers insist, that he was a lover of peace. He proposed to the Emperor Manuel to renew the alliance which had existed with his father. The Emperor had supported the claims of the pretender Muṣṭafà, who succeeded in capturing Gallipoli but then refused to surrender it to the Emperor, alleging that it was against the religion of Islām to yield territory to infidels except by force. Shortly afterwards, however, Muṣṭafà was defeated at Lopadium on the river Rhyndakos by Murād, who obtained possession of Gallipoli, followed Muṣṭafà, and hanged him at Hadrianople in 1422. Murād then made war on John, who in 1420 was associated with his father Manuel, and laid siege to Constantinople in June 1422. The siege continued till the end of August and was then abandoned. One of the reasons alleged for so doing was that Murād's younger brother, thirteen years old, named Muṣṭafà, aided by Elias Pasha, had appeared as a claimant to the throne, and was recognised as Sultan by the Emirs of Karamania and Germiyān as well as in Brūsa and Nicaea. The rebellion appeared formidable, and was not ended till 1426, when the boy was caught and bowstrung.

Thereupon in 1423 Murād returned to Hadrianople, and made it his capital. John, who was now the real Emperor, made peace with Murād, but on condition that he paid a heavy tribute and surrendered several towns on the Black Sea, including Derkos. The Turks during the next seven years steadily gained ground. Salonica after various vicissitudes, the chief being its abandonment by the Turks in 1425, was finally captured from the Venetians in 1430, and seven thousand of its inhabitants were sold into slavery. In 1430 Murād took possession of Joannina. In 1433 he re-colonised the city with Turks. He later named a governor at Uskūb (Skoplje), the former capital of Serbia. George Branković bought peace with Murād by giving his daughter in marriage to him with a large portion of territory as dowry. From Serbia the Sultan crossed to Hungary, devastated the country, and retired, but, pushing on to Transylvania, was so stoutly opposed that he had to withdraw across the Danube[1].

In Greece, during the year 1423, the Turks took temporary possession of Hexamilion, Lacedaemon, Cardicon, Tavia, and other strongholds. In 1425 they captured Modon (Methone) and carried off 1700 Christians into slavery. In the same year one of Murād's generals destroyed the fortifications at the Isthmus of Corinth. In 1430 the Sultan granted capitulations to the republic of Ragusa. Three years later a Turkish fleet ravaged the coasts of Trebizond. The Emperor Sigismund, the King of Hungary, with Vladislav, King of Poland, was beaten by Murād on the Danube in 1428.

We are not concerned here with the profoundly interesting negotiations which went on between the Greek Emperors and the Pope, except to note that the price required to be paid for assistance from the West was the acceptance by the Orthodox Church of the supremacy of Rome, that the great mass of the Greek population, owing to many causes, mainly the recollection of the Latin Empire of Constantinople (1204–1261), was bitterly opposed to Union, and that the Emperor and the few dignitaries who were willing to change their creed so as to bring it about had no authority, expressed or implied, to act on behalf of the Orthodox Church. The Union however, such as it was, was accepted in 1430 by the Emperor John, who had gone to Florence for that purpose. Thereupon the Pope undertook to send ten galleys for a year, or twenty for six months, to attack the Turks and give courage to the Christian Powers. Early in 1440 he sent Isidore as delegate to Buda. John, who returned from Italy in February of the same year, finding that Murād had become

[1] Cf. for these events *supra*, Ch. XVIII, pp. 568–70.

restive at the action of the Pope, sent to him to declare that his journey had been solely for the purpose of settling dogmas and had no political object. He was, however, treating already for common action with Vladislav, now also King of Hungary. In the same year Skanderbeg (Skander or Alexander bey), an Albanian who had reverted to Christianity, declared war against the Sultan.

Meantime the Pope had invited all Christian princes, including Henry VI of England, to give aid against the Turks. The King of Aragon promised to send six galleys. Vladislav responded too, and joined George, King of Serbia, in 1441. John Corvinus, surnamed Hunyàdi, who was Voivode of Transylvania, at the head of a Hungarian army drove the Turks out of Serbia. A series of engagements followed, in which the brilliant soldier Hunyadi defeated the Turks. The Emir of Karamania also attacked the Ottomans in his neighbourhood. Murād went in consequence into Asia Minor, but the invasion of the Serbians and Bulgarians compelled him to return. Several engagements took place between the Slav nations and Murād, the most important being in 1443 at a place midway between Sofia and Philippopolis. Three hundred thousand Turks are stated, probably with gross exaggeration, to have been killed[1].

Thereupon a formal truce was concluded for ten years in June 1444 between Murād and the King of Hungary and his allies. Each party swore that his army should not cross the Danube to attack the other. Vladislav swore on the Gospels and Murād on the Koran. Ducas states that Hunyadi refused either to sign or swear. This peace, signed at Szegedin, is regarded by the Turkish writers as intended by Murād to be the culminating point of his career. Murād was a philosopher, a man who loved meditation, who wished to live at peace, to join his sect of dervishes in their pious labour, and to have done with war. But his enemies would not allow him. The treaty thus solemnly accepted was almost immediately broken. The story is an ugly one and, whether told by Turks or Christians, shews bad faith on the side of the Christians. The cardinal legate Julian Cesarini bears the eternal disgrace of declaring that an oath with the infidel might be set aside and broken. Against the advice of Hunyadi, the ablest soldier in the army of the allies, battle was to be joined. The decision was ill-considered, for the French, Italian, and German volunteers had left for their homes on the signature of the treaty. John was not ready to send aid. George of Serbia would have no share in the war. He refused not only to violate his oath but even to permit Skanderbeg to join Vladislav. The place of rendezvous was Varna, but the whole number of the Christians, who gathered there in the early days of November 1444, probably did not exceed 20,000 men. Hunyadi reluctantly joined. To the astonishment of the Christians they found immediately after their

[1] Bartletus, *Vita Scanderbegii*; Ducas, XXXII; Leunclavius, 107; von Hammer, II. 299. Callimachus was present at the battle and describes it.

arrival at Varna that Murād had advanced with the rapidity then characteristic of Turkish military movements, and that he had with him 60,000 men. A great battle followed, during which one of the most notable incidents was that the Turks displayed the violated treaty upon a lance, and in the crisis of the battle, according to the Turkish annals, Murād prayed: "O Christ, if thou art God, as thy followers say, punish their perfidy." The victory of the Turks was complete. The Christian army was destroyed[1]. Murād, who in June 1444 had abdicated in favour of his son Mahomet when the latter was only fourteen years old, again retired after the victory of Varna and fixed his residence at Magnesia. But in 1445 the Janissaries became discontented. His son is reported to have written to him in the following terms: "If I am Sultan I order you to resume active service. If you are Sultan then I respectfully say that your duty is to be at the head of your army." Murād accordingly was compelled to reascend the throne. In 1446 one of Murād's generals desolated Boeotia and Attica. His fleet in the meantime attacked the Greek settlements in the Black Sea. Later in the same year Murād destroyed the fortifications at the Isthmus though he was opposed by 60,000 men. Patras was also taken and burned. Thereupon the Morea was ravaged, and the inhabitants were either killed or taken as slaves. Constantine, afterwards the last Emperor of Constantinople, was compelled to pay tribute for the Morea. During the years 1445–8 a desultory war was being waged against the Albanians under Skanderbeg. In 1447 Murād, having failed to capture Kroja, later called Āq-Hisār, the capital of Albania, withdrew to Hadrianople where, according to Chalcondyles, he remained at peace for a year.

In the autumn of 1448 the war against the Albanians recommenced. George Castriotes, known to us already as Skanderbeg, was still their trusted leader, and now and for many years was invincible. Meantime under the directions of Pope Nicholas V the Hungarians and the Poles were preparing once more to aid in resisting the advance of the Turks. Hunyadi, notwithstanding the defeat at Varna, for which he was not responsible, was named general, and succeeded in forming a well-disciplined but small army of 24,000 men. Of these 8000 were Wallachs and 2000 Germans. As the King of Serbia refused to join, Hunyadi crossed the Danube and invaded his kingdom. While Murād was preparing for a new attack on the Albanians, Hunyadi encamped on the plains of Kossovo, where in 1389 the Sultan's predecessor of the same name had defeated his enemies and had been assassinated. The Turkish army probably numbered 100,000 men[2].

[1] For a full description of this battle see *The Destruction of the Greek Empire*, pp. 161 and 170, by the present writer. Cf. *supra*, Ch. XVIII, pp. 571–72.

[2] Aeneas Sylvius says two hundred thousand, Chalcondyles fifteen hundred thousand, which von Hammer reasonably suggests is an error for a hundred and fifty thousand.

For some unexplained reason Hunyadi did not wait for the arrival of Skanderbeg. A battle ensued on 18 October 1448. It lasted three days. On the second the struggle was the fiercest, but the brave Hungarians were powerless to break through the line of the Janissaries. On the third day the Wallachs turned traitors, obtained terms from Murād, and passed over to his side. The Germans and a band of Bohemians held their ground, but the battle was lost. Eight thousand, including the flower of the Hungarian nobility, were said to have been left dead on the field. During the fight 40,000 Turks had fallen.

The effect of this defeat upon Hungary and Western Europe was appalling. The Ottoman Turks had nothing to fear for many years from the enemy north of the Danube. Skanderbeg struggled on, and in 1449 beat in succession four Turkish armies and again successfully resisted an attempt to capture Kroja. Indeed one author states that the Sultan died while making this attempt. In the autumn Murād returned to Hadrianople, where he died in February 1451.

MAHOMET II (1451-1481).

The great object which Mahomet II had to accomplish to make him supreme lord of the Balkan peninsula was the capture of Constantinople itself. He was only twenty-one years old when he was girt with the sword of Osmān. But he had already shewn ability, and had had experience both in civil and military affairs. The contemporary writers, Muslims and Christians, give ample materials from which to form an estimate of his character. From his boyhood he had dreamed of the capture of New Rome. Ducas gives a striking picture of his sleeplessness and anxiety before the siege of the city. Subsequent events shewed that he had laid his plans carefully, and had foreseen and prepared for every eventuality.

When his father Murād died he was at Magnesia. He hastened to Gallipoli and Hadrianople, and at the latter place was proclaimed Sultan. Though he distrusted Khalīl Pasha, who had prevented him from retaining supreme power when his father had abdicated, he named him again to the post of grand vizier, called him his father, and continued to shew him confidence. He commenced his reign by the murder of his infant brother Aḥmad[1], the only other member of the Ottoman dynasty being Orkhān who was with the Emperor in Constantinople, though in order to avoid public disapprobation for the act he had 'Alī, the actual murderer, put to death[2].

Shortly after his arrival at Hadrianople he received ambassadors with congratulations from Constantinople and the semi-independent emirs of

[1] Von Hammer notes that Turkish historians praise Mahomet for this act of brutality, vol. II. p. 429, note 3.

[2] Filelfo, *De imbecilitate et ignavia Turcorum*, quoted by Jorga, *Geschichte*, vol. II. p. 4.

Asia Minor, but he noted that Ibrāhīm, the Emir of Karamania, was not represented. Mahomet confirmed the treaty already made with Constantine, and professed peaceful intentions to all. His father had failed in 1422 to capture the city because of the rebellion of the Emir of Karamania. To prevent the repetition of such opposition the Sultan crossed into Anatolia and forced the emir to sue for peace.

No sooner had Mahomet left Europe than the Emperor committed the blunder of sending ambassadors to Khalīl Pasha, Mahomet's grand vizier, who had always been friendly to the Empire, with a demand that Orkhān, a pretender to the throne for whose maintenance Murād had paid, should receive double the amount, failing which the ambassadors suggested that Orkhān's claims would be supported by the Empire. Khalīl bluntly asked them if they were mad, and told them to do their worst. Mahomet, when he learned the demand, hastily returned to Europe.

He at once set about preparations for the capture of Constantinople. He concluded arrangements with the Venetians, and made a truce with Hunyadi for three years, the latter step enabling him to arrange peace with Hungary, Wallachia, and Bosnia. He amassed stores of arms, arrows, and cannon balls. He was already master of the Asiatic side of the Bosphorus by means of the castle at Anatolia-Hisār built by Bāyazīd. In order to seize the tribute paid by ships passing through the Bosphorus, and also that he might have a strong base for his attack upon the city, he decided to build a fortress opposite that of Bāyazīd at a place now known as Rumelia-Hisār. The straits between the two castles are half a mile wide. In possession of the two he would have command of the Bosphorus, and could transport his army and munitions without difficulty. When the Emperor, the last Constantine, and his subjects heard of Mahomet's preparations, they were greatly alarmed, and remonstrated. Mahomet's answer was a contemptuous refusal to desist from building a fort; for he knew that the imperial army was so reduced in strength as to be powerless outside the walls.

In the spring of 1452 Mahomet himself took charge of the construction of the fortress, and pushed on the works with the energy that characterised all his military undertakings. Constantine sent food to Mahomet's workmen, with the evident intention of suggesting that he was not unwilling to see executed the work which he could not prevent. Meantime the Turks gathered in the harvest in the neighbourhood of the new building, and seemed indeed to have desired that Constantine should send out troops to prevent them, a step which the Emperor dared not undertake. All the neighbouring churches, monasteries, and houses were destroyed in order to find materials for building the series of walls and castles which formed the fortification. The work was begun in March 1452 and completed by the middle of August. The fortifications still remain to add beauty to the landscape and as a monument of the conqueror's energy. When they were completed, as the Turks seized the toll paid by ships passing the new castle, Constantine closed the gates of Constantinople. Mahomet answered by declaring war and appearing before the landward walls with 50,000 men. But he had not yet completed his preparations for a siege. After three days he withdrew to Hadrianople. The value of his new fortification was seen a few weeks afterwards, for when on 10 November two large Venetian galleys from the Black Sea attempted to pass they were captured, the masters killed, and their crews imprisoned and tortured.

Mahomet now made no secret of his intention to capture Constantinople. Critobulus gives a speech, which he declares was made by the Sultan at Hadrianople, attributing the opposition to the Ottomans from a series of enemies, including Tīmūr, to the influence of the Emperors.

The country around Constantinople was cleared by Mahomet's army. San Stefano, Silivri, Perinthus, Epibatus, Anchialus, Vizye, and other places on the north shore of the Marmora and on the coast of Thrace on the Black Sea were sacked. In November 1452 Cardinal Isidore had arrived in Constantinople with 200 soldiers sent by the Pope, together with a papal letter demanding the completion of the Union of the Churches. In consequence on 12 December a service was held in St Sophia commemorating the reconciliation of the Eastern and Western Churches. Leonard, Archbishop of Chios, had arrived with the cardinal. Six Venetian vessels came a few weeks afterwards, and at the request of the Emperor their commander, Gabriel Trevisan, consented to give his services *per honor de Dio et per honor de tuta la christianitade.* They had safely passed the Turkish castles owing to the skilful navigation of their captain. On 29 January 1453 the city received the most important of its acquisitions, for on that day arrived John Giustiniani, a Genoese noble of great reputation as a soldier. He brought with him 700 fighting men. He was named, under the Emperor, commander-in-chief, and at once took charge of the works for defence. In April a chain fixed upon beams closed the harbour of the Golden Horn, its northern end being fastened within the walls of Galata. Ten large ships, with triremes near them, were stationed at the boom. The Genoese of Galata undertook to aid in its defence.

By the end of March, Mahomet's preparations were nearly completed. Nicolò Barbaro, a Venetian surgeon who was present within the city from the beginning to the end of the siege, states that there were 150,000 men in the besieging army between the Golden Horn and the Marmora, a distance of three miles and three-quarters[1]. Barbaro's estimate is confirmed by that of the Florentine soldier Tedaldi, who states that there were 140,000 effective soldiers, the rest, making the number of

[1] Filelfo estimates 60,000 foot and 20,000 horse. Ducas' estimate is 250,000, Montaldo's 240,000. Phrantzes says 258,000 were present. The Archbishop of Chios, Leonard, with whom Critobulus agrees, gives 300,000, while Chalcondyles increases this to 400,000.

Mahomet's army amount to 200,000, "being thieves, plunderers, hawkers, and others following the army for gain and booty."

In this army the most distinguished corps consisted of at least 12,000 Janissaries, who formed the body-guard of the Sultan. This force had shewn its discipline and valour at Varna and at Kossovo. This, the most terrible portion of Mahomet's force, was derived at that time exclusively from Christian families. It was the boast of its members in after years that they had never fled from an enemy, and the boast was not an idle one. The portion of the army known as Bashi-bazuks was an undisciplined mob. La Brocquière says that the innumerable host of these irregulars took the field with no other weapon than their curved swords or scimitars. "Being," says Filelfo, "under no restraint, they proved the most cruel scourge of a Turkish invasion."

In January 1453 report reached the capital of a monster gun which was being cast at Hadrianople by Urban, a Hungarian or Wallach. By March it had been taken to the neighbourhood of the city. Fourteen batteries of smaller cannon were also prepared, which were subsequently stationed outside the landward walls. Mahomet had also prepared and collected a powerful fleet of ships and large caiques. A hundred and forty sailing-ships coming up from Gallipoli arrived at the Diplokionion south of the present palace of Dolma Bagcha on 12 April[1]. Cannon balls of a hard stone were made in large numbers on the Black Sea coast, and brought to the Bosphorus in the ships which joined the fleet.

The Turkish army with Mahomet at its head arrived before the city on 5 April. The arrangement of the troops was as follows: Mahomet, with his Janissaries and others of his best troops, took up his position in the Lycus valley between the two ridges, one crowned by what is now called the Tōp Qāpū Gate, but which was then known as that of St Romanus, and the other by the Hadrianople Gate. This division probably consisted of 50,000 men. On the Sultan's right, that is between Tōp Qāpū and the Marmora, were 50,000 Anatolian troops, while on his left from the ridge of the Hadrianople Gate to the Golden Horn were the least valuable of his troops, including the Bashi-bazuks, among whom were renegade Christians. With them was also a small body of Serbs.

Two or three days after his arrival Mahomet sent a formal demand for the surrender of the city upon terms which were probably intended to be rejected. Upon their rejection he at once made his dispositions for a regular siege.

For the most part the remains of the walls still exist, so that little difficulty is found in learning what were Mahomet's chief points of attack. The Golden Horn separates Galata and the district behind it, known as Pera, from Constantinople proper, now distinguished as Stamboul, the Turkish corruption of εἰς τὴν πόλιν. Galata was a walled city under

[1] So Barbaro; Phrantzes gives the total number of ships and boats as 480; Ducas as 300; Leonard as 250; Critobulus as 250.

the protection of the Duke of Milan, and ruled under capitulations by the Genoese, and was not attacked during the siege. The length of the walls which gird Constantinople or, to give it the modern name, Stamboul, is about thirteen miles. Those on the Marmora and the Horn are strong but single. Those on the landward side are triple, the inner wall being the loftiest and about forty feet high. The landward walls have also in front of them a foss about sixty feet broad, with a series of dams in every part except about a quarter of a mile of steep ascent from the Horn, where exceptionally strong walls and towers made them impregnable before the days of cannon.

The walls on the two sides built up from the water were difficult to capture, because the attack would have to be made from boats. They therefore required few men for their defence. The landward walls were, in all the great sieges, except that by the filibustering expedition in 1202–4 called the Fourth Crusade, the defence which invaders sought to capture. Some places, notably near the Silivri Gate and north of that of Hadrianople, were weaker than others, but the Achilles' heel of the city was the long stretch of wall across the Lycus valley. About a hundred yards north of the place where the streamlet, which gives the valley its name, flows under the walls to enter the city, stood a military gate known as the Pempton, or Fifth Military Gate, and called by the non-Greek writers who describe the siege the St Romanus Gate. It gave access to the enclosure between the Inner and the Second wall. Mahomet's lofty tent of red and gold, with its *sublima porta*, as the Italians called it, was about a quarter of a mile distant from the Pempton in the valley. The fourteen batteries, each of four guns, were distributed at various places in front of the landward walls. The Emperor Constantine had fixed his headquarters within the city in the vicinity of the same gate.

Under normal conditions a large detachment of the defenders should have been stationed on the city side of the great Inner wall. But the troops for the defence were not even sufficient to guard the second landward wall. Indeed the disparity in numbers between the besiegers and besieged is startling. To meet the 150,000 besiegers the city had only about 8000 men. Nearly all contemporary writers agree in this estimate. Phrantzes states that a census was made and that, even including monks, it shewed only 4983 Greeks. The result was so appalling that he was charged by the Emperor not to let it be known[1]. Assuming that there were 3000 foreigners present, 8000 may be taken as a safe total. The foreigners were nearly all Venetians or Genoese. The most distinguished among them was the Genoese Giustiniani. We have already seen the spirit which actuated Trevisan. Barbaro records the names "for a perpetual memorial" of his countrymen who took part in the defence.

[1] Leonard's estimate was 6,000 Greeks and 3,000 foreigners. Tedaldi says there were between 5,000 and 7,000 combatants within the city "and not more." Ducas says that there were not more than 8,000 all told.

The arrangements for the defence were made by Giustiniani under the Emperor. With the 700 men he had brought to the city he first took charge of the landward walls between the Horn and the Hadrianople Gate, but soon transferred his men with a number of Greeks to the enclosure in the Lycus valley as the post of greatest danger. Archbishop Leonard took the place which he had left. At the Acropolis, that is near Seraglio Point, Trevisan was in command. Near him was Cardinal Isidore. The Greek noble, the Grand Duke Lucas Notaras, was stationed near what is now the Maḥmūdīye mosque with a few men in reserve. The monks were with others at the walls on the Marmora side. The besieged had small cannon, but they were soon found to be useless. The superiority of the Turkish cannon, and especially of the big gun cast by Urban, was so great that Critobulus says: "it was the cannon which did everything."

A modern historian of the siege[1] claims that the population of the city was against the Emperor. This is scarcely borne out by the evidence. It is true that a great outcry had been raised against the Union of the Churches; that the popular cry had been "better under the Turk than under the Latins;" that the demand of the Pope for the restoration of Patriarch Gregory, sent away because he was an advocate of Union with Rome, offended many; that Notaras himself, the first noble, had declared that he "preferred the Turkish turban to the cardinal's hat;" and that the populace had sought out Gennadius because he was hostile to the Union. But when the gates of the city were closed against the enemy, this sentiment in no way interfered with the determination of all within the city to oppose the strongest resistance, and the population rallied round the Emperor.

In the early days of the siege Mahomet destroyed all the Greek villages which had already escaped the savagery of his troops, including Therapia and Prinkipo.

Mahomet's army took up its position for the siege on 7 April. On 9 April the ships in the Golden Horn were drawn up for its defence, ten being placed at the boom and seventeen held in reserve. On the 11th the Turkish guns were placed in position, and began firing at the landward walls on the following day. The diary of the Venetian doctor, Nicolò Barbaro, and the other contemporary narratives shew that the firing of the Turks went on with monotonous regularity daily from this time, and that the three principal places of attack were, first, between the Hadrianople Gate and the end of the foss which terminates a hundred yards north of the palace of the Porphyrogenitus, secondly, in the Lycus valley at and around the Pempton or so-called St Romanus Gate, and thirdly, near the Third Military Gate to the north of the Silivri (or Pege) Gate. The ruined condition of the walls, which have hardly been touched

[1] M. Jorga, *Geschichte des osmanisches Reiches*, vol. II. p. 22.

since the siege, confirms in this respect the statement of contemporaries. The cannon from the first did such damage that Mahomet on 18 April tried a general assault in the Lycus valley. It failed, and Giustiniani held his ground in a struggle which lasted four hours, when Mahomet recalled his men, leaving 200 killed and wounded.

The effect of the cannon in the Lycus valley soon, however, became terrible. In front of the Pempton, the Middle wall, as well as that which formed one of the sides of the foss, was broken down, and the foss in the lower part of the valley had been filled in. Giustiniani therefore constructed a stockade or *stauroma* of stones, beams, crates, barrels of earth, and other available material, which replaced the Outer and Middle walls through a length of 1500 feet.

Probably on the same date as the first general assault, Balta-oghlu, the admiral of Mahomet's fleet, tried to force the boom, but failed. On 20 April occurred a notable sea-fight which raised the hopes of the besieged. Three large Genoese ships in the Aegean, bringing soldiers and munitions of war for the besieged, fell in with an imperial transport. They had been long expected in the capital and also by the Turks. Mahomet's fleet was anchored a little to the south of the present Dolma Bagcha palace. When the ships were first seen Mahomet hastened to the fleet, and gave orders to the admiral to prevent them entering the harbour or not to return alive. The inhabitants of the city crowded the east gallery of the Hippodrome, and saw the fleet of at least 150 small vessels filled with soldiers drawn up to bar the passage. One of the most gallant sea-fights on record ensued. The large ships, having a strong wind on their quarter, broke through the Turkish line of boats, passed Seraglio point and, always resisting the mosquito fleet, fought under the walls of the citadel, when the wind suddenly dropped. The ships drifted northwards towards the shores of Pera and a renewed struggle began, which lasted till sunset, at the mouth of the Golden Horn. It was witnessed by Leonard, the Archbishop of Chios, and hundreds of the inhabitants from the walls of the city, and by Mahomet from the Pera shore. The Christian ships lashed themselves together, while the Turks and especially the vessel containing Balta-oghlu made repeated efforts to capture or burn them. Mahomet rode into the water alternately to encourage and threaten his men. All his efforts, however, failed and, when shortly before sunset a northerly breeze sprung up, the four sailing ships drove through the fleet, causing enormous loss[1]. After sunset the boom was opened and the relieving ships passed safely within the harbour.

The defeat of his fleet was the immediate cause of Mahomet's decision to obtain possession of the Golden Horn by the transport of his ships overland from the Bosphorus to a place outside the walls of Galata.

[1] *The Destruction of the Greek Empire,* by the present writer, gives a full description of the fight.

But preparations for this task had been in hand for several days. He had tried, and failed, to destroy the boom. He was unwilling to make an enemy of the Genoese by trying to force an entrance into Galata, where one end of the boom was fastened. His undisputed possession of the country beyond its walls enabled him to make his preparations for the engineering feat he contemplated without interruption. He had already stationed cannon, probably on the small plateau where the British Crimean Memorial Church now stands, in order to fire over a corner of Galata on the ships defending the boom and to distract attention from what he was doing. Seventy or eighty vessels had been selected, a road levelled, wooden tram-lines laid down on which ship's cradles bearing the ships could be run, and on 22 April the transport was effected[1]. A hill of 240 feet had been surmounted and a distance of a little over a mile traversed. The ships probably were started from Tophana and reached the Horn at Qāsim Pasha[2].

The sudden appearance of 70 or 80 ships in the Golden Horn caused consternation in the city. After a meeting of the leaders of the defence, it was decided to make an effort to destroy them. James Coco, described by Phrantzes as more capable of action than of speech, undertook the attempt. Night was chosen and preparations carefully made, but the plan could not be kept secret. On 28 April the attack was made and failed, the design probably having been signalled to the Turks from the Tower of Galata. Coco's own vessel was sunk by a well-aimed shot fired from Qāsim Pasha. Trevisan, who had joined the expedition, and his men only saved their lives by swimming from their sinking ship. The fight, says Barbaro, was terrible, "a veritable hell, missiles and blows countless, cannonading continual." The expedition had completely failed.

The disadvantages resulting from the presence of the fleet were immediately felt. Fighting took place almost daily on the side of the Horn as well as before the landward walls. The besieged persisted in their efforts to destroy the enemy's ships, but their inefficient cannon did little damage. During the early days of May, a Venetian ship secretly left the harbour in order to press the Venetian admiral Loredan, who, sent by the Pope, was believed to be in the Aegean, to hasten to the city's relief. The Emperor was urged by the nobles and Giustiniani to leave the city, but refused. Meantime Mahomet continued an attack on the ships in the harbour with his guns on the slope of Māltepe. On 7 May a new general assault was made, and failed after lasting three hours. A similar attempt was made on 12 May, near the palace of the Porphyrogenitus, now called Tekfūr Serai. This also failed.

[1] Critobulus says there were 68 ships, Barbaro 172, Tedaldi between 70 and 80, Chalcondyles 70, and Ducas 80.

[2] For a description of the disputed question as to the route followed, see Appendix III of my *Destruction of the Greek Empire*.

After 14 May the attacks on the landward side were concentrated on the stockade and walls of the Lycus valley. Attempts were made to undermine the walls, and failed; and to destroy the boom, and thus admit the great body of the fleet which still remained in the Bosphorus. The latest attempt on the boom was on 21 May. Two days later the Venetian brigantine, which had been sent to find Loredan, returned in safety but with the news that they had been unable to find him. Their return was due to a resolution of the crew which has the best quality of seamanship, "whether it be life or death our duty is to return."

In the last week of May the situation within the city was desperate. The breaching of the walls was steadily going on, the greatest damage being in the Lycus valley, for in that place was the big bombard throwing its ball of twelve hundred pounds weight seven times a day with such force that, when it struck the wall, it shook it and sent such a tremor through the whole city that on the ships in the harbour it could be felt. The city had been under siege for seven weeks and a great general assault was seen to be in preparation. Two thousand scaling ladders, hooks for pulling down stones, and other materials in the stockade outside the Pempton had been brought up, and ever the steady roaring of the great cannon was heard. In three places, Mahomet declared, he had opened a way into the city through the great wall. Day after day the diarists recount that their principal occupation was to repair during the night the damages done during the day. The bravery, the industry, and the perseverance of Giustiniani and the Italians and Greeks under him is beyond question; and as everything pointed to a great fight at the stockade, it was there that the *élite* of the defence continued to be stationed.

Mahomet shewed a curious hesitation in these last days of his great task. The seven weeks' siege was apparently fruitless. Some in the army had lost heart. The Sultan's council was divided. Some asserted that the Western nations would not allow Constantinople to be Turkish. Hunyadi was on his way to relieve the city. A fleet sent by the Pope was reported to be at Chios. Mahomet called a council of the heads of the army on Sunday, 27 May, in which Khalīl Pasha, the man of highest reputation, declared in favour of abandoning the siege. He was opposed and overruled. Mahomet thereupon ordered a general assault to be made without delay.

On Monday Mahomet rode over to his fleet and made arrangements for its co-operation, then returned to the Stamboul side and visited all his troops from the Horn to the Marmora. Heralds announced that every one was to make ready for the great assault on the morrow.

What was destined to be the last Christian ceremony in St Sophia was celebrated on Monday evening. Emperor and nobles, Patriarch and Cardinal, Greeks and Latins, took part in what was in reality a solemn liturgy of death, for the Empire was in its agony. When the service was ended, the soldiers returned to their positions at the walls. Among the defenders was seen Orkhān, the Turk who had been befriended by Constantine. The Military Gates, that is those from the city leading into the enclosures between the walls, were closed, so that, says Cambini, by taking from the defenders any means of retreat they should resolve to conquer or die. The Emperor, shortly after midnight of 28–29 May, went along the whole line of the landward walls for the purpose of inspection.

The general assault commenced between one and two o'clock after midnight. At once the city was attacked on all sides, though the principal point of attack was on the Lycus valley. First of all, the division of Bashi-bazuks came up against the stockade from the district between the Horn and Hadrianople Gate. They were the least skilled of the army, and were used here to exhaust the strength and arrows of the besieged. They were everywhere stoutly resisted, lost heavily, and were recalled. The besieged set up a shout of joy, thinking that the night attack was ended. They were soon undeceived, for the Anatolian troops, many of them veterans of Kossovo, were seen advancing over the ridge crowned by Tōp Qāpū to take the place of the retired division. The assault was renewed with the utmost fury. But in spite of the enormous superiority in numbers, of daring attempts to pull down stones and beams from the stockade, of efforts to scale the walls, the resistance under the brave defenders of the thousand-year-old walls proved successful. The second division of the army had failed as completely as the first.

The failure of the Turks had been equally complete in other parts of the city. Critobulus is justified in commenting with pride on the courage of his countrymen: "Nothing could alter their determination to be faithful to their trust."

There remained but one thing to do if the city was to be captured on 29 May—to bring up the reserves. Mahomet saw that the two successive attacks had greatly weakened the defenders. His reserves were the *élite* of the army, the 12,000 Janissaries, a body of archers, another or lancers, and choice infantry bearing shields and pikes. Dawn was now supplying sufficient light to enable a more elaborate execution of his plans. The great cannon had been dragged nearer the stockade. Mahomet placed himself at the head of his archers and infantry and led them up to the foss. Then a fierce attack began upon the stockade. Volleys were fired upon the Greeks and Italians defending it, so that they could hardly shew a head above the battlements without being struck. Arrows and other missiles fell in numbers like rain, says Critobulus. They even darkened the sky, says Leonard.

When the defenders had been harassed for some time by the heavy rain of missiles, Mahomet gave the signal for advance to his "fresh, vigorous, and invincible Janissaries." They rushed across the foss and attempted to carry the stockade by storm. "Ten thousand of these grand masters and valiant men," says Barbaro with admiration for a brave enemy, "ran to the walls not like Turks but like lions." They tried to tear down the stockade, to pull out the beams, or the barrels of earth of which it was partly formed. For a while all was noise and mad confusion. To the roar of cannon was added the clanging of every church bell in the city, the shouts "*Allāh! Allāh!*" and the replies of the Christians. Giustiniani and his little band cut down the foremost of the assailants, and a hard hand-to-hand fight took place, neither party gaining advantage over the other.

It was at this moment that Giustiniani was seriously wounded. He bled profusely, and determined to leave the enclosure to obtain surgical aid. That the wound was serious is shewn by the fact that he died from it after a few days, though some of his contemporaries thought otherwise and upbraided him for deserting his post. Critobulus, whose narrative, written a few years after the event, is singularly free from prejudice, says that he had to be carried away. It was in vain that the Emperor implored him to remain, pointing out that his departure would demoralise the little host which was defending the stockade. He entered the city by a small gate which he had opened to give easier access to the stockade. The general opinion at the time was undoubtedly that by quitting his post he had hastened the capture of the city[1]. Meanwhile the Emperor himself took the post of Giustiniani, and led the defenders.

Mahomet witnessed from the other side of the foss the disorder caused by the departure of the Genoese leader. He urged the Janissaries to follow him, to fear nothing: "The wall is undefended; the city is ours already." At his bidding a new attempt was made to rush the stockade and to climb upon the débris of the wall destroyed by the great gun.

A stalwart Janissary named Ḥasan was the first to gain and maintain a position on the stockade, and thereby to entitle himself to the rich reward promised by the Sultan. The Greeks resisted his entry and that of his comrades and killed eighteen. But Ḥasan held his position long enough to enable a number of his followers to climb over the stockade. A fierce but short struggle ensued while other Turks were pouring into the enclosure. They followed in crowds, once a few were able to hold their position on the stockade. Italians and Greeks resisted, but the Turks were already masters of the enclosure. Barbaro says that within a quarter of an hour of the Turks first obtaining access to the stockade there must have been 30,000 within the enclosure. The defenders fled in panic. The Turks, according to Leonard, formed a phalanx on the slope of each side of the hill and drove Greeks and Italians before them. Only the small gate into the city was open, and this was soon crowded with dying or dead.

The overwhelming numbers of the invaders enabled them soon to slaughter all opponents who had not escaped into the city. The military

[1] See the statements of contemporaries quoted in my *Destruction of the Greek Empire*, pp. 346–7.

gate of the Pempton was at once opened. Hundreds of Turks entered the city, while others hastened to the Hadrianople Gate and opened it to their comrades. From that time Constantinople was at the mercy of Mahomet. A public military entry followed, probably at about ten in the morning, and then the city was handed over to the army, as Mahomet had promised, for a three days' sack.

In the first struggle within the enclosure and near the Pempton, the Emperor bore a part worthy of his name and his position. The last Constantine perished among his own subjects and the remnant of the Italians who were fighting for the *honor de Dio et de christianitade*. All accounts of his death attest his courage. He refused, says Critobulus, to live after the capture of the city, and died fighting. The manner of his death and the question whether his body was ever found are, however, both doubtful[1].

An incident is mentioned by Ducas, and is incidentally confirmed by other writers, which may have hastened the capture of the city. Whether by accident or by treason a small postern gate near Tekfūr Serai (the palace of the Porphyrogenitus) had been left open, and in the midst of the final struggle a number of Turkish troops entered and obtained possession of the walls between the palace and the Hadrianople Gate, where they hoisted Turkish ensigns. Some even went as far as the mosaic mosque, known as the *Chora*, and plundered it. But an alarm was immediately given, and the Emperor hastened to the Hadrianople Gate and assisted in driving out the intruders. Then as hastily he returned to the stockade, arriving just at the moment when Giustiniani was preparing to leave. The story of Ducas is not mentioned by Critobulus, who either knew nothing of it or regarded the incident as unimportant. Sa'd-ad-Dīn gives a version which, apart from the bombastic fashion in which he wrote his account of the capture of the city, occasionally contains a grain of truth. He says that, "while the blind-hearted Emperor" was busy resisting the besiegers to the north of the Hadrianople Gate, "suddenly he learned that the upraising of the most glorious standard of 'the Word of God' had found a path to within the walls." The entrance into the city at this moment by the sailors opposite the church of St Theodosius, now the Gul-jāmi', may be held to confirm the story of Ducas.

Mahomet's capture of Constantinople was the crowning of the work done by his able predecessors. With the sack of the city and with the further conquests of Mahomet we have nothing to do. His biographers claim that he conquered two empires and seven kingdoms. Cantemir calls him the most glorious prince who ever occupied the Ottoman throne. Halil Ganem is justified in saying that, judged by his military exploits,

[1] See the various contemporaries quoted on pp. 353–4 of *The Destruction of the Greek Empire*.

Mahomet occupies the first place in the Ottoman annals. Responsibility had been thrown upon him by his father while still a boy. Throughout his life he was self-reliant. He cared nothing for the pleasures usually associated with an Asiatic sovereign. As he was, like so many of the earlier Sultans, the son of a Christian mother, he may have derived many of the elements in his character from her. He shewed from the first a dislike for games, for hunting, indeed for amusement of any kind. He kept his designs to himself, and is reported to have said in reply to a question: "If a hair in my beard knew what I proposed I would pluck it out."

He had no court favourites and was a lonely man, though he enjoyed conversation on historical subjects, knew the life of Alexander the Great well, and took interest in the story of Troy. He was careful in the selection of his ministers, and a rigid disciplinarian. The Janissaries had already begun to count upon their strength, and exacted from him a donative on his accession. He never forgave their Āghā for permitting it. Shortly afterwards he degraded and flogged him for not preventing a revolt. At the beginning of his reign he reformed Turkish administration, and increased the revenue by preventing great leakage in the collection of taxes. He is spoken of by the Turks as the *Qanūni* or Lawgiver. Thoughtful as a youth, he continued during his life to take a delight in studies which have not occupied the attention of any other Turkish ruler. Gennadius, the new Patriarch, became so great a favourite with him that some of his subjects spoke of him as an unbeliever. Yet his mind was usually occupied with great projects. He rightly judged what were the obstacles to the Turks' further advance. The phrase "First Rhodes, then Belgrade," is attributed to him as indicating the direction of his ambition. He shewed his intention of making the Turks a European power when he commenced his reign, by laying the foundation of his palace at Hadrianople. He was, moreover, a lover of learning according to his lights, delighted in discussing theology and philosophy, and had acquired five languages. He employed Gentile Bellini, the Venetian painter, and when he left presented him with the arms and armour of Dandolo. The dark side of his character shews him as reckless of human life and guilty of gross cruelty. He made infanticide in the imperial family legal, though it had been commonly practised before his reign. All things considered, we can have no hesitation in pronouncing him the ablest of Ottoman Sultans.

The capture of Constantinople marks not only the end of the Greek Empire but the establishment of that of the Ottomans. After that event, when the world thought of Turks they connected them with New Rome on the Bosphorus. The Ottoman Turks had advanced to be a European nation.

CHAPTER XXII.

BYZANTINE LEGISLATION FROM THE DEATH OF JUSTINIAN (565) TO 1453.

In this long evolution of almost nine hundred years extending from the death of Justinian to the capture of Constantinople by the Turks, it is necessary to distinguish periods. The first period reaches from the death of Justinian to the reign of Basil the Macedonian (565–866); during this time Justinian's codification remained the principal source of law. The second period includes the interval between the accession of Basil the Macedonian and the date when Constantine Monomachus re-established the School of Law in Constantinople (867–1045); its main feature was the publication of a new compilation of laws, the Basilics. The third period stretches from this restoration of the School of Law in Constantinople down to the fall of the Byzantine Empire (1045–1453); this period was marked, at least at first, by a revival in the science of law due to the great event of 1045, and later by the final decadence[1].

In the study of these three periods, it will be necessary to point out what were the new constitutions (Novels) promulgated by the Emperors who succeeded each other on the throne, and also to mention the legal works which, together with Justinianean law, the Basilics, and the Novels, formed the sources of Byzantine legislation, a system as complicated as that of Roman law, but which never attained its perfection.

I.

The study of Byzantine legislation after Justinian cannot be undertaken without a consideration of the works devoted to his codification even during the Emperor's life-time. For at whatever period they may have been written, whether before or after 565, the commentaries on the imperial compilation composed by Greek professors became, in the same way as the work itself, a veritable source of Byzantine law of the very highest value, from which materials for other works or codes were for long derived.

Justinian[2], fearing that freedom of commentary would reduce law to the former confusion and disorder which he had intended once and for all to end, authorised jurisconsults to select one of three methods only in

[1] Some modern authors only distinguish two periods: 565–866, and 867–1453.

[2] In his constitution *Deo auctore,* § 12 and in his constitution *Tanta,* Δέδωκεν, § 21.

explaining his Digest and his Code: (1) τὰ κατὰ πόδας, *i.e.* by giving literal translations of the Latin texts into Greek. (2) Παράτιτλα, *i.e.* either by framing additions to one of the "titles" in the original, in the form of a systematic statement or in the form of extracts from other parts of the text closely related to the subject of the "title" under consideration, or else by drawing up tables of concordance between a given law and other texts (παραπομπαί). (3) Ἴνδικες (Indices), *i.e.* by making abridgments or summaries of the texts. These three methods were employed concurrently in the schools of the East. But a fourth method was tolerated although it was a departure from the imperial injunctions: the use of παραγραφαί or explanatory notes on passages in the legislative work. This was the only fruitful method in common use even before Justinian in the days when legal instruction was concentrated on the sources of classical Roman law; it was by means of this method that the professors of the sixth and seventh centuries still succeeded in making some improvements in the law.

The commentators whose names and places of residence have come down to us are the following:

Under Justinian we find Theophilus, professor in Constantinople, probably the author of the celebrated Greek Paraphrase of the Institutes of Justinian, who also gave lessons on the Digest; Dorotheus, professor in Berytus (Beyrout) (Institutes and Digest); Isidore (Digest and Code); Anatolius, professor in Berytus (Code); Thalelaeus (Code and Digest), author of the most extensive commentary on the Code; Julian, professor in Constantinople, who formed the collection of Novels translated into Latin and called by his name, the *Epitome Juliani*.

Under Justin II and Maurice there are Stephen, an eminent jurisconsult (Digest, Code, Institutes); Cobidas (Digest, τὸ ποινάλιον); Cyril the Younger (Digest); the advocates Athanasius (Novels), Theodore of Hermopolis (Code, Digest?, Novels), Anastasius (Digest), Philoxenus and Symbatius (Novels), and finally an unknown jurisconsult called the Anonymus (Digest).

With the exception of the Paraphrase of the Institutes composed by or attributed to Theophilus, the works of the preceding authors have not been preserved in their integrity. They are only known to us by the extracts which constitute the "ancient scholia" on the Basilics, to which we shall refer later.

After an eclipse of the science of law in the days of Phocas, the reign of the Emperor Heraclius (610–641) witnessed the appearance of some few legal works, two of which still relate to the work of Justinian. (1) The Book of the Antinomies (τὸ τῶν ἐναντιοφάνων μονοβιβλίον) written by an anonymous author, who from the title of his work has received the name of Enantiophanes; only a few fragments have survived in the scholia on the Basilics; (2) Αἱ Ῥοπαί, a collection which was widely known even in the West, and which consisted of classified excerpts of all passages in Justinianean law referring to the legal influence which prescription "up to a hundred years" has on the substance of law. A third work, which is devoted to law-suits (the treatise *De Actionibus*), is the re-issue in a revised form of a treatise prior to Justinian, which in spite of its poor quality had a certain success, for it went through another edition after the publication of the Basilics.

Only a very small number of the Novels promulgated by Justin II, Tiberius, and Heraclius have been preserved. They relate to matters of public, ecclesiastical, or private law (especially marriage). The most celebrated are Novels XXII to XXV of Heraclius on the organisation of the Church, and especially on the *privilegium fori.* The Novels of Tiberius possess an interest of another kind. Under Justin II, the economic situation of the Eastern Empire, already serious in the time of Justinian, had become still worse. The Powerful (*οἱ δυνατοί*), certain of impunity, gave way to excesses which Constantine Manasses chronicles in his emphatic verses. Tiberius, both as co-regent and when reigning alone, tried to counteract this situation by his Novels, which reveal the distress of the small landholders, the gradual disappearance of free labourers, the venal partiality of the governors, and the tyranny of the Powerful. According to Monnier, Tiberius suspended the practice of the ἐπιβολή (*adiectio*, or the compulsory linking of waste lands to adjoining cultivated land, with a view to ensuring the collection of the tax); the ἐπιβολή was not re-established until the reign of Nicephorus I (802–811), and then under a different form.

A fresh eclipse of legislation occurred in the century which intervened between the reign of Heraclius and that of the Iconoclastic Emperor, Leo III. Leo and his son Constantine V have also only left a few Novels. On the other hand, famous in political and religious history for the iconoclastic reform, they have retained the attention of jurists owing to the publication of a very important work, the *Ecloga*, a kind of civil code, to which must be added the three Codes which complete it, the Military Code, the Maritime Code, and the Rural Code[1].

The *Ecloga* (Ἐκλογὴ τῶν νόμων, etc.) was for long ascribed to other Emperors likewise bearing the names of Leo and Constantine, the sons of Basil the Macedonian. Nowadays no one disputes its attribution to Leo III and Constantine V. The *Ecloga* was promulgated by them in March 740. It is a kind of abridged civil code, founded on the Institutes, Digest, Code, and Novels of Justinian, "corrected with a view to improvement," as the very title of the work states, and conceived in a more

[1] Cf. *supra*, Chapter I, pp. 4–5. For a different view as to the date of these Codes see the Introduction to this volume.

Christian spirit. The Preface indicates the purpose of the work. Having recognised that the laws promulgated by their predecessors were dispersed throughout many books, and that their meaning escaped many of their subjects, especially those dwelling in the provinces, the Emperors—according to the version of certain manuscripts—ordered the quaestor Nicetas, another Nicetas, and Marinus, as well as other officials, to collect the ancient books, and to arrange in a clearer and more concise manner the decisions on the more ordinary cases and contracts and on the scale of penalties for crimes. In accordance with this programme, the *Ecloga* is therefore not an exhaustive work; the Emperors did not seek to regulate everything, but only here and there to establish the precision which was needed. It consists of eighteen titles, dealing with the ordinary actions of legal life (betrothal, marriage, dowry, donations, wills, successions and legacies, wardship, enfranchisement), with contracts, with crimes, and finally with the division of the *spolia*. The enactments contained in the work are—as modern scholars have shewn—frequently derived from the popular or vulgar customary law of the East, while other enactments spring from the development of the principles of Justinianean law. Certain provincial Greek institutions, differing from those of Rome, have become legal institutions in the *Ecloga*: thus, among other instances, the distinction between marriage by written contract and marriage without it, to which concubinage was assimilated, the restriction of wardship to minors, the impossibility of emancipating minors, the exercise of the *patria potestas* by the mother and father conjointly, the necessity for the consent of both parents to the marriage of children *alieni* or *sui iuris*, the right of the surviving partner in a marriage to the property of the deceased partner, their two estates being now considered to become one by marriage. In this respect the vigorous judgment of the Iconoclasts, and their lofty conception of family life, made them far exceed the limits of Roman law; community of property and identity of pecuniary interests were to them logical consequences of personal union; breaking here and there through the shackles of the dowry system, there appears a system fully inspired with the Christian ideal of community of goods[1].

The *Ecloga* differs from Justinianean law in the absence of all distinction between the *tutela* and the *cura*, the regulation of intestate estates, the legal conception of the testament, and the law of disinheritance. The influence exercised therein by ecclesiastical law is mainly shewn, as might be expected, in the marriage-laws, in which the Emperors enforced decisions arrived at by the Councils of the seventh century. Finally, the system of punishments, amongst which are found many cruel penalties unknown to the law of Justinian, such as various kinds of mutilation, seems partly to have sprung from the custom by which in practice

[1] So Monnier. Other authors (*e.g.* Schupfer) fail to see any real community in the *Ecloga*, because there is lacking the amalgamation of property between husband and wife.

magistrates inflicted certain arbitrary, but milder, penalties on criminals whom they might have condemned to death.

The authority of the *Ecloga* diminished in course of time under the influence of the reaction against the policy of the Iconoclasts. It was even formally abrogated by Basil the Macedonian, who wished to replace it by his own productions, and in particular by his *Prochiron*. But this abrogation proved of no avail because the *Ecloga* was a convenient manual (Encheiridion), in harmony with provincial customs. It continued all the same its brilliant career, the development of which will be noticed in the course of this sketch. A particular and very striking proof of the favour which it still retained is that certain manuscripts contain both the *Ecloga* and the *Prochiron* of Basil himself.

Three small Codes completed the *Ecloga*: the Military Code (Νόμος στρατιωτικός), the Maritime Code (Νόμος Ῥοδίων ναυτικός), and the Rural Code (Νόμος γεωργικός). The three Codes answer the same purpose as the principal work: to spare jurists lengthy researches in the works of Justinian and to simplify their task. They were compiled in part directly from these works, in part from the private labours of jurisconsults. Of the three the Rural Code is that which supplies historians with the most useful information on the condition of the free and the dependent peasants in the middle of the eighth century, and on the rural police and the penalties applicable to crimes or to involuntary damage committed in the course of agricultural work.

As a whole, the Iconoclastic Emperors displayed as much originality in legislative, as they did in political, matters. In the judgment of legal historians, their legislative experiments prove their understanding of the fact that Justinian's codification could not satisfy practical needs, because this work, considered by many modern authors inferior to the works of Roman jurisconsults during the great classical period, was on the other hand too abstruse for the practitioners of the East. The Iconoclasts wished to rectify this excess of science in a personal manner without interfering with the code itself. In opposition to their methods we shall see that Byzantine legislators and jurists of later ages thought they could attain this object in a totally different way by successive attempts to adapt the code to the increasingly feeble intelligence of men of law in the East.

Only a few Novels issued during the period subsequent to Leo III and Constantine V remain. They are due to Leo the Chazar and Constantine VI, to Irene, Nicephorus I, Leo V, and Theophilus. These Novels are chiefly concerned with political, religious, and canonical legislation.

According to the chroniclers, it was the Caesar Bardas (856–866) who revived profane letters, which had disappeared and been lost for many years through the barbarism and ignorance of the Emperors.

He assigned to each science a school in some fixed spot; he collected scholars in the Palace of Magnaura, he contributed handsomely to their support, and ordered them to give free instruction to their pupils. The chroniclers conclude by saying that the personal action of Bardas did so much good that the laws revived. Although we have no exact information on the form assumed by legal education at this period, it is necessary to mention the initiative of Bardas, because it doubtless contributed to the legal equipment of the men who were themselves to accomplish great things, or to assist the Emperors in accomplishing them, in ensuing years.

In Justinian's reign, the canons of the Eastern Ecumenical Councils were combined with the Constitutions of the Code relating to ecclesiastical matters in the *Collectio XXV capitulorum* (about 535). At an unrecorded date in the sixth century there appeared the *Synagoge canonum* under fifty titles, ascribed either to John Scholasticus (of Antioch) or to other writers. An appendix to this work called the *Collectio LXXXVII capitulorum* includes extracts from some lost Novels of Justinian. From a slightly later period date the *Synopsis Canonum* attributed to Stephen of Ephesus, and the *Collectio constitutionum ecclesiasticarum tripertita*, the manuscripts of which include as an appendix the four Novels of Heraclius already cited, which contain important pronouncements on the organisation of the Eastern Church. To the end of the sixth century belong the three first known *Nomocanones*: the *Nomocanon titulorum* derived from the *Synagoge canonum*, which only assumed its final form in the ninth century; the *Canonicon* of John Nesteutes; and the *Nomocanon XIV titulorum*, which achieved the greatest success. Formerly it was erroneously attributed to Photius (ninth century), but it was really due, according to some, to the Anonymus or to Hieronymus, according to others, to Julian the editor of the Epitome of the Novels of Justinian.

II.

The second period is dominated by the names of two law-giving Emperors: Basil the Macedonian (867–886) and Leo the Wise (886–911), who both lived at its commencement.

Basil, a conqueror on the field of battle, wished likewise to ensure for his subjects the benefits of a system of legislation more practical than that which had existed before him. Two motives urged him to this course. The first, of a legislative kind, is mentioned by his official biographer, the author of the *Vita Basilii*: it was to dissipate the obscurity and unravel the confusion prevailing in civil law as a result of good and bad enactments, and the uncertainty as to which laws had been abrogated and which were still in force. The second motive, of a political order, is referred to in the Prologue to the *Prochiron* itself, and in a passage of the *Epanagoge*, two of his works of which we are about to speak: this was to substitute works edited under his own auspices for the *Ecloga* of the Iconoclasts, against whom Basil had vowed an undying hatred which is betrayed in the unfair judgment he passed on their admirable little book. All Basil's work was thus intended to achieve the rehabilitation of Justinian's legislation, which practising lawyers had been abandoning more and more.

In the first place Basil published an introductory manual to the science of law: the Πρόχειρος νόμος (*lex manualis*) or *Prochiron*, promulgated between 870 and 879 by himself and his two sons, Constantine and Leo (the Wise). This very simple manual consisted of texts which were being continually applied in current usage; it has frequently been compared with the Institutes, and it was founded on Greek translations of, and commentaries on, the works of Justinian. In its second part it also reproduced the provisions of the *Ecloga* in spite of the abuse of its authors in the Prologue. There are few innovations due to Basil. The *Prochiron* is divided into forty titles: betrothal and marriage (titles I to XI), obligations (titles XII to XX), inheritance (XXI to XXXVII), public law (XXXVIII to XL). The *Prochiron* enjoyed a great reputation among civil lawyers, as well as among the canonists of the Greek and Russian Churches, even after the fall of the Eastern Empire. Further on we shall quote some striking proofs of the evident estimation in which it was held.

Basil's second work was likewise a manual of law: the Ἐπαναγωγὴ τῶν νόμων published in the names of Basil, Leo, and Alexander, between 879 and 886. This work only constitutes a draft, without any official character, of a "second edition"—such is the meaning of the Greek title—of the *Prochiron*[1], as well as an introduction to the work which Basil intended to be his masterpiece, the Ἀνακάθαρσις τῶν παλαιῶν νόμων (*Repurgatio veterum legum*), a collection "of pure and unadulterated law, divided into forty books, and prepared like a divine draught," a work to which we shall presently return. As regards the *Epanagoge*, it consists of forty titles corresponding in general to those of the *Prochiron*. Like the latter, it marks a return to the provisions of Justinianean law, although it includes certain later reforms.

There exists great obscurity as to the *Anacatharsis*, to which we alluded above. The most competent students of Byzantine history consider that the work, which has not been preserved, was actually executed in Basil's reign, although there are doubts about its scope, as the *Prochiron* speaks of a work in sixty books, while the *Epanagoge* refers to one in forty. Most probably the *Anacatharsis* was not promulgated by Basil, but served as foundation for the Basilics promulgated by his son, Leo VI.

[1] So Biener and Zachariae.

The Emperor Leo the Wise, or the Philosopher, must be regarded as the most eminent Byzantine legislator after Justinian, for on the one hand he has left the most famous and most extensive monument of post-Justinian Graeco-Roman law (the Basilics), and on the other a great number of Novels.

The Basilics owe their name, not to the Emperor Basil, but to their character as imperial decisions (τὰ βασιλικά, ὁ βασιλικός). They are also called ὁ Ἑξηκοντάβιβλος because they contain sixty books, and ὁ Ἑξάβιβλος because in the manuscripts they form six volumes.

The edict (*Proemium*) which appears at the beginning of the Basilics explains the aim and defines the spirit of the compilation. According to Leo, the error in the method employed by Justinian was that the same subjects were distributed over four different works (Code, Digest, Institutes, Novels); the Emperor Leo, discarding everything contradictory or obsolete, proposed on the contrary to assemble in one single book all previous laws bearing on the same subject, so as to facilitate reference. For this purpose he appointed a commission of qualified jurisconsults, whose names have been lost, except that of the President, the Protospatharius Symbatius. The exact date when the Basilics were promulgated has not been determined; it has been placed by different authorities in 888, 889, or 890.

The sixty books of the Basilics are divided into a varying number of titles supplied with rubrics; the titles are themselves divided into numbered chapters (κεφάλαια), and these, finally, are divided into paragraphs (θέματα).

As there no longer exists in any library a complete manuscript, the general arrangement of the work is only known by the table or *Index* of the manuscript Coislin 151 of the Bibliothèque Nationale in Paris, and by the *Tipucitus*[1]. In some particulars the plan follows that of the Code, in others that of the Digest. The first Book is devoted to the Holy Trinity and the Catholic Faith. In the second are collected the general rules of law drawn from the Digest. Books III to V treat of ecclesiastical law. Books VI to IX deal with magistrates, jurisdictions, and procedure. Books X to LIII are devoted to matters concerning civil law, Books LIV to LVII to public and military law. Book LVIII is occupied with servitudes and the water-system[2], Book LIX with funerary laws, Book LX with crimes and penalties.

Within the titles, the laws (or chapters) are not the personal work of Leo; their text was in no way revised by the commissioners for the Basilics. They were all drawn from earlier works, chiefly from the Code and the Digest, a very few from the Institutes, many from the Novels of Justinian and his successors, a few also from the *Prochiron*. The laws are all given in Greek; when they are derived from the three Latin works of Justinian, they have been extracted not from the originals but from Greek commentaries of the sixth and seventh centuries; for the Code,

[1] See *infra*, p. 722.

[2] See Vol. II. Chapter III, p. 89.

from the Commentary of Thalelaeus and from the *Breviarium* of Theodore; for the Digest, from the commentaries of the Anonymus, Stephen, and Cyril; for the Institutes, from the Paraphrase of Theophilus. The Novels are drawn from the collection called the CLXVIII Novels, in which Justinian's Novels were completed by the addition of the Novels of Justin II and Tiberius, and by the Eparchics (or Edicts of the Praetorian Prefects).

It must be noted that the text of the laws is, in the manuscripts, accompanied by numerous marginal scholia. The most important of these, which constitute the "ancient scholia," are extracts from the Greek commentaries of the sixth and seventh centuries enumerated above; they were probably added to the actual text of the laws, of which they represent a sort of interpretation (*ἑρμηνεία*), between 920 and 945, in the reign of Constantine Porphyrogenitus. To refer the addition of the ancient scholia to his reign is the only way of explaining how Balsamon could have attributed a final *Repurgatio Legum* to Leo's son. The other scholia, "the recent scholia," were introduced subsequently, in the course of the eleventh, twelfth, and thirteenth centuries; they are due to jurisconsults of less weight: John Nomophylax, Calocyrus Sextus, Constantine Nicaeus, Gregory Doxopater, Patzus, Theodorita or Hagiotheodorita, and finally the Anonymus[1].

If we wish to appreciate the value of the Basilics in a few words, it may be said that in themselves they offered to the lawyers of the Greek Empire the great advantage over the Justinianean Code of being a unified work composed in Greek. At the time of their appearance, and for long afterwards, they inspired a respect all the deeper for being the work realised or inspired by the founder of the Macedonian house in continuance of the reforms of the great Emperor Justinian. For modern scholars, the text of the Basilics and the ancient scholia present the advantage of sometimes enabling them to recover the original version of Justinian's works, which has been altered by copyists, or even the original version of the texts of classical jurisconsults altered by the members of Justinian's commission. The closer examination of the ancient scholia has even permitted the recovery of some fragments of pre-Justinian law, whose import and origin are only beginning to be perceived.

The Novels of Leo the Wise are chiefly known by the collection of CXIII Novels, with Preface, a collection of which the Latin translation by Agylaeus is appended to the Novels of Justinian in the complete editions of the *Corpus iuris civilis*. With two exceptions which concern two Novels not appearing in this edition, they are undated. Most of

[1] The chief fault in Heimbach's edition of the Basilics is that he has not been sufficiently careful to preserve the distinction observed in the manuscripts between the scholia of different authors or different ages. The *Supplementum* of Zachariae von Lingenthal does not incur this reproach.

them are later than the Basilics. This collection of CXIII Novels was probably formed previous to Leo's second marriage (894), or at any rate to his third marriage (899). The Preface states that the Emperor has made a selection among the ancient laws, that he has omitted or expressly abrogated useless laws, and that he has converted into laws certain customs deemed worthy of this honour.

The collection of CXIII Novels has been abridged in a work entitled *Ecloga Novellarum Leonis pii Imperatoris in capp. LVI.* The author is possibly identical with that of the *Synopsis Maior*[1]; wishing to preserve only those Novels still in force, he has not kept more than half of the original collection, and has only retained the enactive clauses of the original texts. This *Ecloga Novellarum* was probably compiled towards the middle of the tenth century.

There exist, moreover, seven Novels by Leo which have survived, in addition to the collection of CXIII Novels.

Leo's Novels have been utilised by the principal writers of treatises on Civil or Canon Law subsequent to the tenth century: Psellus, Michael Attaliates, Balsamon, Matthew Blastares, and Harmenopulus. Several of these Novels shew that, in the reign of Leo the Wise, great territorial estates were constantly growing, and that Leo was not strong enough to struggle with the Powerful, who, under the Macedonian dynasty, were developing into real feudal lords.

During the long period which separated Leo's reign from that of Constantine Monomachus, *i.e.* from 911 to 1045, the legislative activity of the Emperors does not appear to have been very fruitful. The manuscripts only provide us with a few Novels by Romanus Lecapenus, Constantine VII Porphyrogenitus, Nicephorus Phocas, John Tzimisces, Basil II Bulgaroctonus, Romanus III Argyrus, and Zoë.

In contrast to the Novels of Basil and Leo which, in completion of their fundamental works, treat various subjects affecting different parts of legislation, the scanty Novels of these Emperors only refer to a few special points. Two subjects in particular are the object of regulations:

1. The law of redemption, preference, or pre-emption (*protimesis, ius protimeseos*), granted to relatives or neighbours in cases of alienation of some estate or house for a pecuniary consideration, was established principally by Novel II of Constantine VII and Romanus Lecapenus in 922. Some writers have conjectured that this law, which had existed since an earlier period of the Roman Empire, was intended to moderate the oppression of small landholders by the Powerful. The Byzantine Emperors were frequently obliged to revive its operation on account of the inefficacy or obscurity of the decrees of their predecessors.

2. The character of military estates which it was necessary to protect so as to safeguard the resources intended to meet the expenses of the army.

[1] See *infra*, p. 717.

Whatever the subject treated, the Novels are above all concerned with custom, either in recording good customs or in attempting to check bad ones. Amongst the most original institutions which they regulate and which arose from ancient popular customs, must be mentioned the *θεώρητρον* referred to for the first time in a Novel of Constantine VII Porphyrogenitus. This was a gift made by the husband to the wife for *ius primae noctis* or *pretium virginitatis*; it was in addition to the *ὑπόβολον* or donation *propter nuptias*.

All official teaching of law in a State school had long disappeared when it was restored by Constantine Monomachus in 1045. It had been replaced, much to the detriment of legal studies, by a purely private system of instruction which is described rather inadequately in broad outline in the *Book of the Prefect* by Leo the Wise (*Λεόντος τοῦ σόφου τὸ ἐπαρχικὸν βιβλίον*), which is an edict on the trade-gilds of Constantinople, discovered by Nicole. From Chapter I of this edict, devoted to the organisation of the notarial profession, we get our information. The twenty-four notaries of the capital formed a corporation. To be eligible for it, young men had to attend the lectures of professors attached to this corporation. These professors were of two kinds, professors of law, *παιδοδιδάσκαλοι νομικοί*, and encyclopaedic professors, *διδάσκαλοι*; they were under the supervision of the Prefect, and after having been elected by co-option they had to be confirmed by that high official. The students subsequently underwent an examination before the whole corporation of notaries. Possibly the same professors also taught the youths who were studying for the bar, who would then have to undergo an examination before the gild of advocates. The programme of studies was amazingly simple: the *Book of the Prefect* states that the candidates "must know by heart the forty titles of the *Prochiron* and be familiar with the sixty books" (of the Basilics), and this was all.

Some historians have thought that control by the Prefect, enjoined by the Edict of Leo, was not of long continuance, and that the organisation of studies by the corporation of notaries became relaxed, so that finally legal education was absolutely uncontrolled; this would give the cause, or one of the causes, for the serious decadence of the science of law between Leo's reign and the reform of 1045. Their hypothesis seems to be absolutely confirmed by the complaints of Constantine Monomachus, when he took steps to end this lamentable state of things.

The *Epitome legum*, or *Ecloga legum in epitome expositarum*, which appeared in 920, the first year of the reign of Romanus Lecapenus, was derived, according to its editor Zachariae, from another *Epitome ex antiquis libris collecta*, consisting of extracts from the Digest (after Stephen and the Anonymus), extracts from the Code (after Theodore and Thalelaeus), extracts from the Novels (after the Breviarium of Theodore), a selection from the texts of the *Prochiron*, with some references to the Basilics and the Novels of Leo. The author—possibly the Symbatius of the Basilics—announces in a Preface full of interesting historical details that he will only record useful regulations. The work consists of fifty titles. This manual enjoyed a great reputation, as may be seen from the numerous copies and revisions of its text.

The *Ecloga* of Leo and Constantine, although condemned by Basil, had nevertheless retained a great practical influence for the reasons already indicated. The influence of this very convenient short manual is shewn by the publication of new works based upon it, which are known as the *Ecloga Privata*, the *Ecloga Privata Aucta*, and the *Ecloga ad Prochiron Mutata*. The *Ecloga Privata* was a re-issue, now lost, of the original with some modifications; Zachariae considers that it is the source of the *Ecloga Privata Aucta*. The *Ecloga Privata Aucta* seems to have been compiled from the *Ecloga Privata* and an *Encheiridion* containing a mixture of Justinianean law and new law. This work expounds the form of Byzantine law prevailing in Southern Italy. Its date is very hard to discover, but possibly it may even be as late as the twelfth century. The *Ecloga ad Prochiron Mutata* in forty titles seems to have been drawn up at the same date and in the same country. It is derived from the *Ecloga Privata*, the *Epitome legum*, and the *Prochiron*. Two of its peculiarities are, first, the presence among its texts of the *Ecloga Legis Mosaicae*, extracted from the Mosaic law in thirty-six short chapters taken from the Pentateuch, and, secondly, the presence of *loci singulares* dealing with penal law, passages of foreign origin alien to Graeco-Roman law, which have given rise to controversy (they are attributed by different writers to a Lombard or to a Norman origin).

The *Synopsis Basilicorum Maior* is a work composed with the help of the Basilics. It opens with a title on the Orthodox faith. It contains twenty-four parts or letters, divided into titles arranged in alphabetical order according to the rubrics of the titles of the Basilics, and includes extracts from the *capitula* of the Basilics. The work, whose author is unknown and is perhaps the same as the compiler of the *Ecloga Novellarum Leonis*, was written towards the middle of the tenth century. It is accompanied by annotations due to various authors. Its success was considerable; it was the foundation of the *Synopsis Minor*[1] and was utilised by the *Prochirum auctum*[2] and by Harmenopulus[3].

The *Prochiron* of Basil only underwent one modification. This was the *Prochiron legum*, which was made up of fragments from the *Ecloga*, the *Prochiron*, the *Epanagoge*, and the *Epitome legum*; these fragments were adapted to contemporary (late tenth century) practice and to the part of Italy in which the compilation was made.

Amongst other revisions of the *Epanagoge*, it will be enough to mention the *Epanagoge aucta*, at the end of the tenth century, a small

[1] See *infra*, p. 722. [2] See *infra*, p. 722. [3] See *infra*, pp. 722–3.

manual which utilises the *Prochiron*, the *Ecloga cum appendice*, the *Epitome Novellarum* of Athanasius, the *Basilics*, and the *Novels* of Leo, as well as the *Epanagoge*.

After all these works, which were in fact only abridgments or revisions of existing works, we come at last to a more original achievement, which possesses the merit of being the result of practical jurisprudence; it is actually the only example of this kind in all the abundance of Byzantine legal literature.

It was called the Πεῖρα or *Practica sive Doctrina ex actis magni viri Eustathii Romani*. It was written by an unknown author employed in the law-courts at Constantinople, who appears to have been subsequently a judge in the same courts, and who was regarded with considerable respect by his colleagues. The seventy-five titles of the treatise consist both of fragments from the Basilics and of reports of cases with reasons for the decisions. These cases extend from the middle of the tenth century (about 950) until the reign of Romanus III Argyrus (1028–1034). According to the title of the work, the author utilised the decisions of the famous jurisconsult, Eustathius Romanus, although we are not certain whether the latter ever drew up a list of legal cases which could have served in the composition of the Πεῖρα. The Πεῖρα is too mediocre a work to be ascribed to Garidas, or to be regarded as an official manual intended for use in the new School of Law of Constantine Monomachus, as has been suggested. Nevertheless it is of sufficient value to supply us with precious details on the jurisprudence and the legal administration, organisation, and procedure of the Greek Empire, at the end of the tenth and beginning of the eleventh century.

In conclusion, and for the sake of completeness, it is necessary to mention some monographs written at various times in the tenth and eleventh centuries: the opusculum of Eustathius and of George Phobenus on the *Hypobolon* (a new name for the donation *propter nuptias*); a short anonymous commentary on the *protimesis* (right of redemption); and finally, the treatises *de peculiis* and *de privilegiis creditorum*.

In the period between 867 and 1045 there appeared only re-issues of canonical collections or *Nomocanones* composed in the sixth century. These were: the re-issue in 883 of the *Nomocanon XIV titulorum* called the *Syntagma* of Photius, but of which Photius, the well-known Patriarch of Constantinople, was probably neither the new editor nor the author[1]; another revision of the same work, which served as a foundation to the work of Theodore Bestes (eleventh century); and a revision of the *Epitome* (*Synagoge*) *canonum* by Simon the Logothete in the reign of Basil II Bulgaroctonus (975–1025).

[1] So Zachariae.

III.

The development of the science of law has, at all times and in all places, a close connexion with the organisation of serious instruction in this science. It seems that the system indicated in the *Book of the Prefect*, which we described in considering the previous period, did not give satisfactory results (if indeed it remained in force). The Novel of Constantine Monomachus in 1045 on the reform of legal education reveals the deplorable results of the system of gild education, and proposes to rectify them by a return to the system of State education. These were the two fundamental ideas developed therein.

The Novel itself states that there were no means of guaranteeing a high standard for professors of law, as these were independent teachers. "The young men," it says, "eagerly seek for some one to teach them the science of law, but, as they find no one with professional authority and supported by the imperial approval, for lack of a better each adopts the teacher whom he meets haphazard." Thereby there arose great confusion in the judgment of cases, and often there were divergencies, or even contradictions, in the sentences pronounced by the judges, who had been trained by teachers holding different opinions; hence also the inferiority of the notaries and advocates. The Emperor was very careful to note that these evils arose from the system of liberty in legal education which prevailed in Constantinople, because, in the first place, other branches of education supported by the State were in successful operation, and, secondly, because certain towns, in which the teaching had remained organised, attracted students to the detriment of the capital. The responsibility for this decadence falls, says the Emperor, on his predecessors, who indeed improved the laws but failed to ensure an official organisation for the Schools of Law.

Constantine Monomachus, a pacific Emperor, was fortunate enough to find two able counsellors, who helped him to start the necessary reforms —Xiphilin and Psellus, the former a judge in the Courts of the Hippodrome, the latter secretary to the Emperor. The drafting of the Novel of 1045 was due to John Mauropus or Euchaïtensis, amongst manuscripts of whose works it was discovered by Cardinal Angelo Mai.

According to the Novel, the school founded by the Emperor was an official and gratuitous State school. The professor-principal (*Nomophylax*) was appointed by the Emperor, was removable by him, and was paid by him. The course of study is defined in the Novel. The diploma on leaving was a State diploma necessary for the exercise of the offices of advocate or notary, or for eligibility for high administrative office. The first Nomophylax was Xiphilin himself. He was no doubt helped in his task by other teachers. The school was established in the buildings of the church of St George.

Notwithstanding the absence of precise information, we must suppose that the school of Constantinople survived at least until the fourteenth century; for the title of Nomophylax was borne, in the twelfth century by Doxopater, Alexius Aristinus, and Theodore Balsamon; in the thirteenth by Michael Chumnus; in the fourteenth by Constantine Harmenopulus; all of whom were jurists or canonists of reputation. Other jurisconsults such as Garidas, the Pseudo-Tipucitus, or Hagiotheodorita, were professors in the same school, but not its principals.

All these men have left legal works of greater or lesser value, and of varying degrees of originality, works which in any case shew the successful result of the reform operated by Constantine Monomachus.

Byzantine legislation, in the strict sense of the word, includes the civil laws (*νόμοι πολιτικοί*), and the Novels (*νεαραί*) of the Emperors.

Up to the eleventh and twelfth centuries the civil laws were still summed up in the two great legislative works of Justinian and Leo the Wise, for Leo, when he promulgated the Basilics, had no intention of superseding Justinian's compilation, to which however the Basilics was to be preferred in cases of disagreement. But at the close of the twelfth entury, during the reign of Manuel Comnenus, Justinian's codification was definitely put aside, although, as we shall see, jurisconsults still studied the works of which it was composed. So much for the legislation of the past.

The Novels of the Emperors, whereby new law was created, were not very numerous between the eleventh and the fifteenth century. Of some Emperors there is only a single Novel extant (Constantine Monomachus, Michael Stratioticus, Isaac Comnenus, Constantine Ducas, Alexius II Comnenus, Michael Palaeologus, Andronicus III). Of others we know only two, three, or four Novels (Michael Ducas, Nicephorus Botaniates, John Comnenus, Isaac Angelus, John Vatatzes, Andronicus II Palaeologus). The only Emperors whose Novels form a more imposing collection are Alexius I Comnenus, twenty-five of whose texts remain, and Manuel Comnenus who left seventeen. Many of these enactments regulated points in religious government or in canon law: for instance, binding force given to betrothal or promise of marriage (1084, 1092), prohibition of marriage on account of consanguinity (1094, 1160), marriage of slaves (1094). The reforms in civil law are generally of little interest; it is only necessary to mention one which also has to do with marriage, the privilege granted by Constantine Ducas to the wife to have priority of the exchequer in the recovery of her dowry in respect of the objects named in the marriage contract. Finally, among the Novels referring to other matters, the most important was the great Novel X of Manuel Comnenus (1166) which constitutes a real system of judicial organisation and procedure, as it deals with assessors, the hearing of cases, the introduction of a suit, with preliminary examinations, advocates, sentences, with summons and appeals, and even with *protimesis* in the case of a mortgage.

The vicissitudes of the Eastern Empire under various dynasties, sometimes Greek, sometimes Latin, were naturally not without their echoes in the development of legal science, in so far as it found expression in treatises of varied nature and diverse scientific import. Several phenomena of legal activity are worthy of note: the manuscripts of Justinian's Novels and the Institutes and Paraphrase of Theophilus were re-copied as frequently as the Basilics themselves and their scholia; later scholia were added to the work of Leo the Wise; the Greek Emperors favoured the composition of treatises on civil or canon law; the earlier sources of Byzantine law, such as the *Prochiron*, *Ecloga*, and *Epanagoge*, continued to serve as nuclei for new commentaries; but the most famous work of this period, the *Promptuarium* of Harmenopulus, only appeared at the close of the Greek Empire.

The earliest productions of legal literature with which we meet are monographs. First, a *Liber de Actionibus* arranged in alphabetical order, only a few extracts from which have been preserved among the later scholia of the Basilics, and which the professor Garidas wrote in the reign of Constantine Ducas (1059–1067); then, by the same author, a short treatise *de homicidiis*, intended to explain Novel XII of Constantine Porphyrogenitus on murder; finally, the *Meditatio de nudis pactis* dating from the middle of the eleventh century, a somewhat brief text, which presents the interesting feature of being an original work without a model. It is probably the *votum* of an assessor of the Supreme Court of the Empire, which was presided over by the Emperor in person, or in his absence by the Drungarius of the watch[1]. It may have been written by John Xiphilin himself, the counsellor of Constantine Monomachus.

After these monographs comes the *Synopsis Legum*, composed in 1406 iambic and "political" verses[2]; it is usually attributed to Michael Psellus and may date from 1070. This attribution is, however, denied by Monnier on account of the weak and childish character of the work. It was compiled by order of Constantine Monomachus with the object of instructing Michael Ducas in some elementary notions of law; it utilises the Code, Digest, and Novels, and the Basilics, reverting to ancient law, making law-suits the starting-point for the discussion of legal matters, and seeking inspiration from various prose treatises and monographs, some still extant, others lost. Among these authorities we find a few works which offer some analogy to certain elements of the *Synopsis*, and which go under the name of Psellus; possibly they also are not his work.

[1] So Monnier and Platon.

[2] The Greek national metre of the Middle Ages, and even of the present day. A "political" verse is an iambic tetrameter catalectic, but depends on stress accent not on quantity.

The Ποίημα νομικόν of Michael Attaliates contains thirty-seven titles and a preface dedicated to Michael Ducas. It is almost entirely derived from the Basilics. It was followed in the original redaction by a supplement containing, among other texts, the Novels of Leo. The aim of Michael Attaliates was to edit a very brief manual of law both practical and theoretical, accessible to all, with some historical notes. The probable date of its composition is 1073 or 1074. The Ποίημα νομικόν was utilised in a few later works, particularly in the *Prochirum auctum*.

To the beginning of the twelfth century belongs the *Tipucitus*, the work of an unknown author. Its title, τιπούκειτος, is an artificial one derived from the words τί που κεῖται; (*quid ubi invenitur?*). The title is appropriate to the character of the book, which is a table of contents of the Basilics, giving the rubrics and most important chapters under each title and indicating analogous passages in all of them. The *Tipucitus* is of undoubted service in reconstructing the lost books of the Basilics[1]. With regard to the Basilics, it is well to recall the fact that it was during this period that they received the addition of the "recent scholia" derived from the works of John Nomophylax, Calocyrus Sextus, Constantine Nicaeus, Gregory Doxopater, Patzus, Theodorita or Hagiotheodorita, and finally an anonymous writer (eleventh or thirteenth century).

The *Synopsis Minor* (τὸ μικρὸν κατὰ στοιχεῖον), which is divided into twenty-four parts or letters of the alphabet, subdivided into titles, has for sources the Ποίημα of Michael Attaliates, the *Synopsis Maior*, the *Epanagoge*, and the *Glossae Nomicae*; its author (according to Zachariae) wrote in Nicaea under John Ducas Vatatzes (1222–1255). It is not a mere reproduction of its authorities, and, notwithstanding the decadent period during which it was written, it constitutes a convenient repertoire of thirteenth-century law.

The *Prochirum auctum* is a *Prochiron* in forty titles, augmented by texts from the Basilics, the *Synopsis Maior*, etc., Imperial Novels, and extracts from works on canon law; the text is followed by thirty-two *Paratitla*, of which No. XXV is the treatise *De Creditis*. This work was written before 1306. It dates about the period of the restoration of the Empire to Constantinople.

The *Promptuarium*, or *Hexabiblos*, of Harmenopulus, Nomophylax and supreme judge at Thessalonica, a friend of Philotheus who was Patriarch from 1354 to 1355 and again from 1362 to 1376, the author of various treatises on canon law, has a history which is told in the preface. Harmenopulus had taken up Basil's *Prochiron*, believing that in accordance with the preface of the book he would find therein collected all provisions of obvious necessity and constant utility. But when he read it he was disappointed to find that some of the most important things had been omitted. Therefore he decided to revise the book, making it complete, as he says, by aid of the *Corpus Legum*, the Basilics, the

[1] The *Tipucitus* has not yet been published in its entirety.

Novels, the Romaics of the Magister, the Eparchics, and the Manuals. In order to distinguish between his texts, he put the *signum solare* at the head of his additions, and the *signum saturninum* before the original text of the *Prochiron.* The sources identified by the modern editor, Gustav Ernst Heimbach, are as follows: the *Synopsis Maior* (not the Basilics), the *Synopsis Minor*, the *Ecloga Novellarum Leonis*, the *Ῥοπαί*, the *Πεῖρα* (referred to under the name of "the Romaics of the Magister"), an appendix to the *Synopsis* whence Harmenopulus derived the Novels up to the days of Manuel Comnenus, the *Epanagoge*, extracts from Julianus Ascalonita (a pre-Justinian writer who described the law which, in Syria and Palestine, governed vicinage, boundaries of property, and the like), the *Ecloga*, and the synodal sentences of the patriarchs. Later interpolations, taken from the same works and added to the manuscripts, attest the success of the *Hexabiblos*, a success which continued in Greece and Russia even after the fall of the Eastern Empire. The six books (whence the name *Hexabiblos*) are concerned with the following subjects:

(I) Law, legal organisation, restitutions, and liberty (18 titles).
(II) Possession, new work, adoption, and maritime law (11 titles).
(III) Sale, deposit, and partnership (11 titles).
(IV) Betrothal and marriage (12 titles).
(V) Wills and wardship (12 titles).
(VI) Crimes and penalties (15 titles).

The six books are followed by four titles on various subjects, and by appendices, containing among other things the rural laws.

The *Promptuarium* is the most complete treatise on civil and criminal law composed during the final period of Byzantine law. An additional merit in the eyes of modern historians is that certain texts which appeared in Justinian's codification have been reproduced by Harmenopulus from pre-Justinian sources; in the *Hexabiblos* they consequently appear untouched by Justinian's commissioners, and give readings free from the interpolations which so often prevent us from knowing the original versions of classical texts.

It was only after the days of the Comneni that the study of canon law became more serious and produced important works, either by order of the Emperors, or at least encouraged by them.

In addition to the revisions of the *Epitome Canonum Antiqua*, which belong to the eleventh and twelfth centuries, we find the *Nomocanon* of Doxopater, which was composed by order of John Comnenus (1118–1143), and presents great analogies with the *Syntagma*, ascribed to Photius. Another *Nomocanon*, on the *Epitome canonum*, is due to the Nomophylax Alexius Aristinus.

The same *Syntagma*, attributed to Photius, which consists of a *Nomocanon* with XIV titles and of the *Collectio Canonum*, was first developed, so to say, by Theodore Bestes, who had been directed by Michael VII before 1080 to transcribe the texts of the civil laws cited in each chapter; this transcription has been utilised by modern editors of Justinian's Code. In the twelfth century the *Syntagma* was not only revised but annotated in the remarkable works of John Zonaras, Grand Drungarius of the watch in the reign of Manuel Comnenus (1159–1169), and of Theodore Balsamon, Nomophylax and Patriarch of Antioch. The *Exegesis Canonum* of Balsamon, undertaken by order of Manuel Comnenus and of the Patriarch Michael Anchialus (1169–1177), acquired in the East a very great reputation which has lasted until the present day. The author proposed to establish a concordance between the civil laws used in the *Nomocanon* ascribed to Photius, as edited by Zonaras, and the texts of the Basilics; for this purpose he employed a twofold method: he reproduced the passages from the Basilics parallel with the civil texts from the *Nomocanon*, and indicated the passages which had not been retained in the Basilics. The work was therefore of the greatest practical utility to contemporaries; it is equally helpful to modern critics of the Justinianean code and the Basilics, as also for the study of Byzantine law in general, for it includes several Novels either by Leo the Wise or the Comneni, as well as sentences passed by synods and patriarchs which are only known to us by this transcription.

From the eleventh, twelfth, and thirteenth centuries there also remain some canonical writings by Michael Psellus, Balsamon, Michael Chumnus, and others, of which it is enough to mention the existence.

Under the Palaeologi there appeared a work as famous as that of Balsamon, and as wide-spread among the clergy as the *Promptuarium* of Harmenopulus was among the world of lay practitioners. This was the *Syntagma Canonum et Legum*, which Matthew Blastares, a monk, completed in 1335. The preface is followed by a history of the sources of the body of Greek Canon law up to 879, and by a history of Roman law up to the Basilics. The *Syntagma* of Matthew Blastares contains three hundred and three titles in twenty-four chapters or letters of the alphabet. The titles are formed of the provisions of canon law and of civil law alternately or separately. The provisions of civil law seem to have been taken from a revision of the *Epanagoge*.

The last work to be mentioned is the *Epitome Canonum* which Harmenopulus placed at the end of his *Promptuarium*; it is divided into six sections and twenty-six titles.

Byzantine legislation shed its lustre throughout Eastern Europe and Asia. Its influence is unmistakable on the ecclesiastical law of the Russians, and on the civil law of the Roumanians, Serbs, and Georgians (Code of Vakhtang).

In the West it likewise exerted its influence on the law of Italy, which was for so long part of the Empire of Constantinople. This is not the place to deal exhaustively with the diffusion of Byzantine legislation in Italy, because the subject seems rather to belong to the history of Italian law. It will be enough to indicate the principal features of this diffusion[1].

The diffusion of Byzantine law in Italy, or more precisely in Southern Italy and Sicily, is shewn first by a phenomenon referred to above: the compilation on Italian soil of legal works on Byzantine law. The *Prochiron legum* (tenth century), the *Ecloga privata aucta* (twelfth century ?), the *Ecloga ad Prochiron mutata* (twelfth century), are works which are very valuable for comparison because they add to their models the modifications arising from local laws, or even *loci singulares* which are not of Graeco-Roman origin.

The influence of Byzantine law in Italy was moreover exercised in another way, as well as in the learned and scientific form: by the rise of customs, which, here as everywhere, constitute popular and vulgar law, customs which are proved by the acts of notarial practice, or which are found codified in numerous municipal statutes in the Middle Ages. But when we examine the details of institutions, there is great difficulty in determining the exact extent of Byzantine influence; as some institution or other existing in Italian law, to which we are tempted to assign a Byzantine origin because the same institution occurs in Byzantine law, may have arisen either by development of the native law, or by contamination from foreign laws possessing similar institutions. Thus, in Sicily, community of property between husband and wife, or between them and their children, may as reasonably have arisen from the development of the vulgar law, or by contamination from Franco-Norman law, as from the direct influence of the *Ecloga*. And the same applies to certain regulations on *protimesis* common alike to Sicilian sources and to Byzantine, such as the *Epanagoge*, the Novels of Leo the Wise, or those of Constantine Porphyrogenitus and Romanus Lecapenus; probably these regulations in Sicily are derived from customs already existing there in the Byzantine period, and confirmed in the East by legislative texts, rather than from these texts themselves. In Southern Italy the *protimesis* is said to be *Graecorum prudentia derivata*; the Byzantine element preponderates in public law and in ecclesiastical matters; in private law, the executors of wills are called *epitropi* (ἐπιτρόποι); but other institutions may have arisen from native development of ancient customs, and not from the diffusion of Byzantine legal works or Byzantine Novels.

[1] Siciliano Villanueva has given a good résumé of the subject (*Diritto Bizantino*, § 4).

CHAPTER XXIII.

THE GOVERNMENT AND ADMINISTRATION OF THE BYZANTINE EMPIRE.

I.

Few States, even in the Middle Ages, possessed so absolute a conception of monarchical authority as the Byzantine Empire. The Emperor, or Basileus as he was officially termed after the beginning of the seventh century, always regarded himself as the legitimate heir and successor of the Roman Caesars; like them he was the *Imperator*, that is, both the supreme war-lord and the unimpeachable legislator, the living incarnation and infallible mouthpiece of the law. Since his contact with the Asiatic East, he had become something more, the master (*despotes*), the autocrat (*autokrator*), the absolute sovereign below whom there existed, not subjects, but, as they humbly styled themselves, slaves (δοῦλοι τῆς βασιλείας); the greatest personages only approached him after prostrating themselves in an actual act of adoration (προσκύνησις). Finally, Christianity had bestowed a crowning attribute on him. He was the elect of God, His Vicar in earth, and, as was said in Byzantium, a prince equal to the apostles (*isapostolos*); by right of which he was regarded as the supreme head and defender of religion, at once king and priest, absolute, and infallible in the spiritual order as he was in temporal matters. And from the combination of these various elements there resulted a despotic and sacred power, whose exercise, at least theoretically, knew no bounds, an authority not only based on political investiture but also consecrated and adorned with matchless lustre by God and the Church[1].

The Roman tradition as accepted in Byzantium placed the Emperor above the law. He thus exercised absolute authority over inanimate objects as well as people, and his competence was universal. "All things depend on the care and administration of the imperial majesty," declared Leo VI in one of his Novels. The Basileus exercised military power, either when he appeared personally at the head of his armies, or when his generals carried off victories in his name. In him was vested the legislative power; he enacted and repealed laws at will. Indeed all the Byzantine Emperors from Justinian to the Comneni were great legislators. He kept a close

[1] On the quasi-sacred position of the Emperor cf. Battifol, P., and Bréhier, L., *Les survivances du culte impérial romain*; and on the support given by provincials to the Emperor because he was Christian, see an excellent paper by Sir W. Ramsay, read at the Berlin International Historical Congress, 1908, and published in the *Expositor*, October, 1908.

supervision over administrative affairs, appointing and dismissing officials at his pleasure, and advancing them in the complicated hierarchy of dignities according to his caprice. He was the supreme judge; the imperial courts of justice, at which he not infrequently presided in person, both tried criminal cases and heard appeals. He watched the financial administration, so essential to the welfare of the Empire, with constant care. His authority extended to morals, which he supervised, and to fashion, inasmuch as he laid down sumptuary laws and imposed limits on extravagance.

The Basileus governed the Church as well as the State. He nominated the bishops to be elected, and conferred investiture on them. He made the laws in religious as in civil matters. He convoked councils, directed their discussions, confirmed their canons, and enforced their decisions. He interfered in theological quarrels, and, priding himself on his skill as a theologian, did not shrink from defining and imposing dogmas. He was the defender of the Church, and it was his duty not only to combat heresy, but to spread the Orthodox faith throughout all the inhabited globe (*οἰκουμένη*), over which God had promised him dominion as a reward for his pious zeal. "Nothing should be done in Holy Church contrary to the opinion and will of the Emperor," declared a Patriarch of the sixth century. "The Basileus," said a prelate in the twelfth century, "is the supreme arbiter of faith in the Churches."

Outward appearances and external forms were carefully designed to increase this absolute power and express the character of this imperial majesty. In Byzantium ostentation was always one of the favourite instruments of diplomacy, magnificence one of the common tricks of politics. For this reason were attached to the name of the Emperor in official language sonorous titles and pompous epithets, originally borrowed from the magnificent titles of the older Roman Emperors, but replaced later by this shorter formula: "N., the Emperor faithful in Christ our God, and autocrat of the Romans" (*πιστὸς ἐν Χριστῷ τῷ θεῷ βασιλεὺς καὶ αὐτοκράτωρ τῶν Ῥωμαίων*). To this end were designed the display of countless and extravagant costumes donned by the Emperor on various ceremonial occasions, the splendour of the imperial insignia, the privilege of wearing purple buskins, and, above all, the ostentatious and somewhat childish ceremonial which in the "Sacred Palace" encompassed the ruler with dazzling magnificence, and which, by isolating him from common mortals, caused the imperial majesty to be regarded with more profound respect. "By beautiful ceremonial," wrote Constantine Porphyrogenitus who in the tenth century took special pleasure in codifying Court ritual, "the imperial power appears more resplendent and surrounded with greater glory; and thereby it inspires alike foreigners and subjects of the Empire with admiration." It was to this end that round the Emperor there were endless processions and a countless retinue, audiences and banquets, strange and magnificent festivals, in the midst of which he led a life of outward show, yet hollow and unsatisfying, from which the great Emperors of Byzantium often succeeded in escaping, but whose purpose was very significant: to present the Basileus in an effulgence, an apotheosis, wherein he seemed not so much a man as an emanation of the Divinity. And to attain this end everything that he touched was "sacred," in works of art his head was surrounded by the nimbus of the saints, the Church allowed him to pass with the clergy beyond the sacred barrier of the iconastasis, and on the day of his accession the Patriarch solemnly anointed him in the ambo of St Sophia. And to this end the official proclamations announced that he reigned by Christ, that by Christ he triumphed, that his person "proceeded from God and not from man," and that to these Emperors, "supreme masters of the universe, absolute obedience was due from all."

Such were the character and the extent of imperial power in Byzantium, and thence it derived its strength. But there were also inherent weaknesses.

In Byzantium, as in Rome, according to the constitutional fiction the imperial dignity was conferred by election. Theoretically the choice of the sovereign rested with the Senate, which presented its elect for the approval of the people and the army. But in the first place the principle of election was often in practice replaced by the hereditary principle, when the reigning Emperor by an act of his will admitted his son, whether by birth or adoption, to share his throne, and announced this decision to the Senate, people, and army. Moreover, the absence of any fixed rule regarding the right of succession paved the way for all kinds of usurpation. For a considerable time there might be in Byzantium neither a reigning family nor blood royal. Anyone might aspire to ascend the throne, and such ambitions were encouraged by soothsayers and astrologers. After the end of the ninth century, however, we notice a growing tendency in favour or the idea of a legitimate heir. This was the work of the Emperors of the Macedonian family, "in order to provide imperial authority," as was said by Constantine VII, "with stronger roots, so that magnificent branches of the dynasty may issue therefrom." The title of *Porphyrogenitus* (born in the purple) described and hallowed the members of the reigning family, and public opinion professed a loyal and constantly increasing devotion to the dynasty. In spite of many obstacles the house of Macedon maintained itself on the throne for over a century and a half; that of the Comneni lasted for more than a century without a revolution; and in the eleventh century usurpation was regarded as a folly as well as a crime, because, says a writer of that period, "he who reigns in Constantinople is always victorious in the end." It is none the less true that between 395 and 1453 out of 107 Byzantine Emperors only 34 died in their beds; while eight perished in the course of war, or accidentally, all the others abdicated, or met with violent deaths, as the result of 65 revolutions in the camp or the palace.

This power, already so uncertain in origin and stability, was further limited by institutions and custom. As in pagan Rome, there were the Senate and the People over against the Emperor. No doubt in course of time the Senate (σύγκλητος βουλή) had become a Council of State, a somewhat limited assembly of high officials, generally devoted to the monarch. It nevertheless retained an important position in the State, and it was the rallying-point of the administrative aristocracy which was still called, as in Rome during the fourth century, the senatorial order (συγκλητικοί), that civil bureaucracy which often derived means of resisting the Emperor from the very offices wherein it served him. The people indeed, who were officially represented, so to speak, by the *demes* or factions in the circus, were now only a domesticated rabble, content if it were fed and amused. But these factions, always turbulent and disaffected, often broke out into bloodthirsty riots or formidable revolutions. Yet another power was the Church. Although so subservient to imperial authority, in the Patriarch it possessed a leader who more than once imposed his will on the Basileus; once at least in the ninth century it sought to claim its liberty, and Byzantium only just escaped a quarrel similar to that of the Investitures in the West. Finally and above all, to keep imperial authority in check there was the army, only too ready to support the ambitions of its generals and constantly shewing its might by insurrections. So that it may fairly be said that imperial power in Byzantium was an autocracy tempered by revolution and assassination.

II.

Round the person of the Emperor there revolved a whole world of court dignitaries and high officials, who formed the court and composed the members of the central government.

Until towards the close of the sixth century, the Byzantine Empire had retained the Roman administrative system. A small number of high officials, to whom all the services were subordinated, were at the head of affairs, and, after the example of Rome, the Byzantine Empire had maintained the old separation of civil and military powers and kept the territorial subdivisions due to Diocletian and Constantine. But during the course of the seventh and eighth centuries the administration of the Byzantine monarchy underwent a slow evolution. Civil and military powers became united in the same hands, but in new districts, the *themes*, which superseded the old territorial divisions. The high officials in charge of the central government became multiplied, while at the same time their individual competence was diminished. And, simultaneously, personal responsibility towards the Emperor increased. It is hard to say by what gradual process of modification this great change took place. The new system made its first appearance in the time of the Heraclian dynasty, and the Isaurian Emperors probably did much to establish it definitely.

In the tenth century, in any case, the administration of the Empire in no way resembled the system which prevailed in the days of Justinian.

Henceforward in Byzantium a twofold and carefully graded hierarchy, the details of which are recorded for us at the beginning of the tenth century by the *Notitia of Philotheus*, determined the rank of all individuals who had anything to do with the court or with public administration. Eighteen dignities, whose titles were derived from the civil or military services of the palace, formed the grades of a kind of administrative aristocracy, a sort of Byzantine *Chin*, in which advancement from one grade to another depended on the will of the Emperor. Of these honorary titles the highest, except those of *Caesar*, *Nobilissimus*, and *Curopalates*, which were reserved for the princes of the imperial family, were those of *Magister*, *Anthypatus*, *Patrician*, *Protospatharius*, *Dishypatus*, *Spatharocandidatus*, *Spatharius*, and so on. Eight other dignities were specially reserved for eunuchs, of whom there were many in the Byzantine court and society. Certain active duties, similarly classified according to a strict hierarchy, were generally attached to these dignities, the insignia (βραβεῖα) of which were presented to the holders by the Emperor. Such were in the first place the high offices at court, whose holders, the *praepositus* or Grand Master of Ceremonies, the *parakoimomenos* or High Chamberlain, the *protovestiarios* or Grand Master of the Wardrobe, and so on, were in charge of the various services of the imperial household (κουβουκλεῖον) and of all that vast body of subordinates, *cubicularii*, *vestiarii*, *koitonitai*, *chartularii*, *stratores* (grooms), etc., whose numbers made the palace seem like a city within a city. Such were also the sixty holders of the great offices of public administration, who occupied the posts of central government and the high military or administrative commands, either in Constantinople or in the provinces, each of whom had a large number of subordinates. Appointed by imperial decree and subject to dismissal at the Emperor's pleasure, they advanced in their career of honours by favour of the ruler. And advancement in the various grades of the hierarchy of dignities generally coincided exactly with promotion to higher administrative office. In order to understand the mechanism of the imperial administration, it must be borne in mind that in Byzantium every official had two titles, one honorary, marking his rank in the administrative nobility, the other indicating the actual office with which he had been invested. And as both dignity and office, and advancement in either, depended entirely on the good will of the Emperor, the zeal of the administrative body was always sustained by the hope of high office, and by the expectation of some promotion which would place the recipient one step higher in the ranks of the Empire's nobility. Never in consequence was any administrative body more completely in the master's hands, more strongly centralised, or more skilfully organised, than that of the Byzantine government.

In the capital near the sovereign, the heads of the great departments, the Ministers, if they may be so called, directed the government from above and transmitted the will of the Emperor throughout all the realm. Since the seventh century the Byzantine Empire had gradually become Hellenised, and the Latin titles which were still borne by officials in the days of Justinian had assumed a purely Greek form: the *praefectus* had become the *eparch*, the *rationalis* the *logothete*, and so on. Among these high officials there were first the four logothetes. The *Logothete of the Dromos* was originally entrusted with the service of transport and the post (*dromos* is the translation of the Latin *cursus publicus*), but gradually became the Minister of Home Affairs and of Police, the Secretary for Foreign Affairs, and the High Chancellor of the Empire; finally after the tenth century he was simply known as the *Grand Logothete*, and became a sort of Prime Minister. Next to him came the Logothete of the Public Treasury (τοῦ γενικοῦ) who managed financial affairs; the Logothete of the Military Chest (τοῦ στρατιωτικοῦ) who was Paymaster-General of the Army; and the Logothete of the Flocks (τῶν ἀγέλων) who managed the studs and crown estates. Other high offices of the financial administration were held by the *chartulary of the sakellion*, who dealt with the patrimony and private fortune of the Emperor, by the *eidikos*, who was in charge of manufactures and arsenals, and above all by the *sacellarius*, who was a kind of Comptroller-General. The *quaestor*, who alone of all these officials retained his Latin title, was Minister of Justice; the *Domestic of the Scholae*, or *Grand Domestic*, was Commander-in-chief of the army; the *Grand Drungarius* was Minister of the Navy. Finally the *Eparch*, or Prefect of Constantinople, had the onerous task of governing the capital and maintaining order in it; he had to supervise the gilds among which Byzantine industries were distributed and to keep an eye on the factions of the circus (*demes*), who officially represented the people; he controlled the city police and the prisons, and had power to try any case affecting public order; finally, he had charge of the food supplies of the capital. All these duties rendered him a person of very great importance, and secured him the foremost rank among civil dignitaries. In the list of the sixty great officials he was eighteenth, while the Sacellarius was only thirty-second, and the Logothete of the Dromos only thirty-seventh. And with regard to this it must be remembered that in the Byzantine Empire, as in all states in the Middle Ages, military officials definitely took precedence of the civil ones; the *Domestic of the Scholae*, or Commander-in-chief of the army, was fifth on the list of great officials, the *strategi*, who were both governors of provinces and commanders of army corps, were placed above the ministers, and the most important of them, the Strategus of the Anatolics, was fourth on the list.

Under the orders of the ministers there existed a large body of employees. These formed the innumerable bureaux which were known as *secreta* or *logothesia*; prominent among them were those of the imperial chancery controlled in the Palace by the First Secretary (*protoasecretis*) and the master of petitions (ὁ ἐπὶ τῶν δεήσεων), and those of the various ministers. It was this skilfully organised bureaucracy which, in Byzantium as in Rome, really assured the firm government and solid foundation of the monarchy; it was this large body of obscure σεκρετικοί, studying affairs in detail, preparing decisions, and conveying to all parts the sovereign pleasure, that supplied the support and strong framework which gave life and endurance to the Byzantine Empire. And at certain periods, as for instance in the eleventh century, this bureaucracy was strong enough even to direct the general policy of the monarchy.

III.

It is obvious that between the fifth and eighth centuries great changes were introduced into the government of the provinces by the administrative reforms of Justinian and his successors. Contrary to the Roman tradition, in some districts the civil and military powers had been amalgamated; soon the necessity of establishing the defence of the territory on a firmer basis led to the appointment of those who held high military command to be civil administrators of the districts in which their troops were stationed. Thus at the end of the sixth century the exarchates of Africa and Italy were created in the West, and during the course of the seventh century the *themes* of the Anatolics, the Armeniacs, the Opsician, the Thracesian, and that of the "sailors" (Carabisiani), in the East[1]. Gradually the civil administration became subordinated to the great military chiefs, and finally lost all importance and nearly disappeared, while the civil provinces, the *eparchies*, into which Rome divided the Empire, were superseded by the *themes*, so called from a word which originally meant army corps and afterwards came to be applied to the district occupied by an army corps. During the course of the eighth century the new system became universal, and was improved by the subdivision of those themes which were too large and by the creation of new themes. This remained the basis of the Byzantine administrative system until the fall of the Empire.

At the beginning of the tenth century there were twenty-six themes, a little later thirty-one. They were divided between the two great departments which existed in the *logothesion of the dromos*, that of the East (Ἀνατολή) and that of the West (Δύσις). Neither the boundaries nor the chief towns are precisely known; and their extent, and even their number, were in the course of centuries modified by somewhat frequent re-adjustments. But we know that until the eleventh century those of the East were the most important; they were indeed the richest and most prosperous districts, fertile and populous, those which, as has been said, "really constituted the Roman Empire." In the hierarchy of officials their governors occupied a much higher position than did those of the provinces in Europe, and their emoluments were much greater. From

[1] Cf. on the origin of the *themes*, Vol. II. pp. 38–39, 226 seq., 395–396.

Asia Minor the Empire drew its best soldiers, its finest sailors, and the treasury derived thence its most certain revenue. It was the strength of the monarchy, and the occupation of its greater part by the Seljūq Turks at the end of the eleventh century was a terrible blow from which Byzantium never recovered.

In the tenth century the themes of Anatolia were as follows: in the western portion of Asia Minor, the Opsician (capital Nicaea), the Optimatan (capital Nicomedia), the Thracesian (south-west of Anatolia), Samos, the Cibyrrhaeot (south coast of Anatolia), Seleucia, and above all the great theme of the Anatolics. Near the Black Sea were the themes of the Bucellarians, Paphlagonia, the mighty theme of the Armeniacs, and that of Chaldia. Along the eastern frontier there stretched the themes of Charsianum, Lycandus, Mesopotamia, Sebastea, and Colonea. All these marches of the Empire were full of fortresses and soldiers, and in the epic of Digenes Akritas Byzantine popular poetry has finely recorded the active and simple, perilous and heroic, life led by the imperial soldiers in their unending warfare with the infidel.

The Western themes were those of the Balkan peninsula, and until the beginning of the eleventh century, as long as the first Bulgarian empire lasted, they occupied only its outskirts. There was the theme of Thrace which contained Constantinople, and that of Macedonia with its capital Hadrianople, both of them rich enough and important enough to enable their governors to rank close after those of the Asiatic themes, whether as to their place in the hierarchy or their emoluments. Then came, stretching along the shores of the Archipelago, the themes of Strymon, Thessalonica (of great importance because of its capital which was justly regarded as the second city of the Empire in Europe), Hellas, the Peloponnesus, and the Aegean Sea. On the shores of the Ionian Sea and the Adriatic were situated the themes of Nicopolis, Dyrrhachium, Cephalonia, and Dalmatia, and in Southern Italy those of Calabria and Longobardia. Finally, on the Black Sea there was the theme of Cherson. During the tenth century the number of provinces in the Empire was increased by the conquests of the Emperor, either by the creation of certain themes which only survived a short time, such as those of Leontokomes, Chozan, Samosata, etc., or by the establishment of other subdivisions of a more lasting character, such as the duchy of Antioch, the government of Bulgaria, which was entrusted to an officer bearing the title of commissioner (προνοήτης), or that of Italy, which combined the two Italian provinces under the authority of a magistrate styled *catapan*. During the days of the Comneni other themes made their appearance. But, whatever the nature of these changes, the principle which guided this administrative system was always the same: the concentration of every sort of power in the hands of the military governor.

At the head of each theme was placed a governor called a *strategus*, generally honoured with the title of *patrician*, whose salary varied according to the importance of his government, from 40 pounds of gold to five pounds. He was appointed by the Emperor and reported directly to him. He not only commanded the military forces of his district, but exercised within it all administrative power, the government of the territory, and the administration of judicial and financial affairs. He was like a vice-emperor; and, especially in early days when the themes were less numerous and of greater extent, more than one strategus was tempted to abuse his excess of power. Under his orders the theme was divided into *turmae*, governed by officers bearing the title of *turmarchs*, while the turma was again subdivided into *lieutenancies* (*topoteresiae*) and *banda*, which were similarly administered by soldiers, *drungarii* and *counts*. Furthermore, the strategus was assisted by an adequate number of officials. There were the *Domestic of the Theme* or Chief of Staff; the *Chartulary of the Theme* who supervised recruiting, commissariat, and military administration; the *count of the tent* (κόρτη), and the *count of the hetairia*, the *centarch of the spatharii*, the *protochancellor*, and the *protomandator*. Most important of all was the *protonotary*, who in addition often bore the title of *Judge of the Theme*. He was at the head of the civil administration; he attended to judicial and financial affairs; and, although subordinate to the strategus, he had the right of corresponding directly with the Emperor. Thus the central power maintained a representative of civil interests to supervise and hold in check the all-powerful governor.

As a variation of this system the governors of certain provinces bore other titles than that of strategus—*Count* in the Opsician, *Domestic* in the Optimatan, *Duke* at Antioch, *Pronoetes* in Bulgaria, and *Catapan* in Italy and elsewhere. Furthermore, at certain strategical points of the frontier there existed, beside the themes, small independent governments centred round some important stronghold; these were called *clisurae* (κλείσουρα means a mountain pass), and their rulers styled themselves *clisurarchs*. Many frontier provinces were originally clisurae before their erection into themes; among these were Charsianum, Seleucia, Lycandus, Sebastea, and others. Here again, as in all degrees of this administrative system, most of the power was in the hands of the military chiefs. And thus, although she derived such strength from the Roman tradition, Byzantium had developed into a state of the Middle Ages.

This administrative body, well trained and well disciplined, was generally of excellent quality. The members of the bureaucracy were usually recruited from the ranks of the senatorial nobility (συγκλητικοί), and were trained in those schools of law which were pre-eminently nurseries of officials (it was specially for this purpose that in 1045 Constantine Monomachus reorganised the School of Law in Constantinople). Kept in close and exclusive dependence on the Emperor, who appointed, promoted, and dismissed all officials at his own pleasure, they were very closely supervised by the central power, which frequently sent extraordinary commissions of inquiry to the provinces, invited the bishops to superintend the acts of the administration, and encouraged subjects to bring their grievances before the imperial court. Thus these officials played a part of the first importance in the government of the Empire. No doubt they were only too often amenable to corruption, as happens in most Oriental states, and the sale of offices, which was for long habitual in Byzantium, led them to oppress those under them in the most terrible manner. As regards the collection of taxes, indeed, this administration, anxious to satisfy the demands of the sovereign and the needs of the treasury, frequently shewed itself both hard and unreasonable, and consequently often hindered the economic development of the monarchy. But it rendered two great services to the Empire. In the first place it succeeded in securing for the government the financial resources necessary for carrying out the ambitious policy of the Basileus. Nor was this all. The Empire had neither unity of race nor unity of language. It was, as has truly been said by A. Rambaud, "an entirely artificial creation, governing twenty nationalities, and uniting them by this formula: one master, one faith." If, after the middle of the seventh century owing to the Arab conquest, and after the eighth owing to the loss of the Latin provinces, the Greek-speaking population held a preponderance in the Empire, many other ethnical elements—Syrians, Arabs, Turks, and above all Slavs and Armenians—were intermingled with this dominant element, and imparted a cosmopolitan character to the monarchy. To govern these varied races, often in revolt against imperial authority, to assimilate them gradually, and to bestow cohesion and unity on this State devoid of nationality, such was the task which confronted the imperial government and which devolved on its administrative agents. And the work achieved by this administration is undoubtedly one of the most interesting aspects of the history of Byzantium, one of the most striking proofs of the power of expansion which was for so long possessed by Byzantine civilisation.

"Every nationality," says Constantine Porphyrogenitus, "which possesses characteristic customs and laws, should be allowed to retain its peculiarities." The Byzantine government did not indeed always apply this rule of perfect toleration to the vanquished; more than once it happened that some small body of people was forcibly removed from one district to another so as to make room for others more amenable to imperial authority. In general, however, it shewed more consideration for those who had been annexed by conquest, endeavouring by calculated mildness to gain their affections and encourage them to adopt the manners and customs of Byzantine society. Thus, in conquered Bulgaria, Basil II decreed "that the old order of things should continue," that taxes should be paid as heretofore in kind, that, subject to the authority of the Byzantine High Commissioner, the country should retain its native officials, and that a Bulgarian prelate should be at the head of the Bulgarian Church, which was to be independent of the Patriarch of Constantinople. By a lavish distribution of titles and honours the Basileus endeavoured to conciliate the Bulgarian aristocracy, and sought, by encouraging intermarriage, to establish friendship between the best elements of both nations, thus leavening the Byzantine nobility with the most distinguished of the vanquished. In like manner in Southern Italy the imperial government very skilfully adapted its methods to local conditions, allowing members of the native aristocracy to share in the government of the province, seeking also to attract them by lavishing on them the pompous titles of its courtly hierarchy, and scrupulously respecting the customs of the country. Elsewhere the vanquished were conciliated by reductions in taxation, or by a system of exemption for a more or less extended period. Thus, little by little, was stamped on these alien elements a common character, that of Hellenism, while moreover they were unified by the common profession of the Orthodox religion.

Greek was the language of the administration and the Church. It was inevitable that by slow degrees all the populations of the Empire should come to speak it. In certain districts colonies were established to secure the predominance of Hellenism; such was the case alike in Southern Italy and in the region of the Euphrates, on the confines of the Arab world. In other parts, by the mere influence of her superior civilisation Byzantium assimilated and modified those elements which were most refractory. Whether she succeeded in merging the best of the vanquished in her aristocracy by their marriages with wives of noble Greek birth, or whether she attracted them by the lure of high command or great administrative office, by the distribution of the sonorous titles of her hierarchy or the bribe of substantial pay, she conciliated all these exotic elements with marvellous ingenuity. The Greek Empire did not shrink from this admixture of barbarian races; by their means it became rejuvenated. Instead of excluding them from political life it threw open to them the army, the administration, the court, and the Church. Byzantium in its time had generals of Armenian, Persian, and Slav origin; Italian, Bulgarian, and Armenian officials; ministers who were converted Arabs or Turks. For all these aliens Greek was the common language in which they could make themselves understood, and thus Greek assumed the spurious appearance of a national language. Speaking the same language, gradually and insensibly adopting the same customs and manners of life and thought, they emerged from the mighty crucible of Constantinople marked with the same character and merged in the unity of the Empire.

It was the great aim of the imperial administration to apply this policy and realise this union by means of Hellenism. The Church helped this work by uniting all the discordant elements which formed the Empire in a common profession of faith. Here again language and race mattered little; it was enough to have been baptised. Baptism admitted the barbarian neophyte to the State as well as to the Church. No doubt this religious propaganda more than once took the form of cruel persecutions, in the ninth century of the Paulicians, in the eleventh of the Armenians, in the twelfth of the Bogomiles. It was generally, however, by shewing a more skilful tolerance that Byzantium gained adherents. She evangelised and made Christians of the dissidents, Slavs of Macedonia and the Peloponnesus, the Turks of the Vardar, the pagan mountaineers of Maina, the Muslims of Crete and the Upper Euphrates, who formed part of the Christian Empire or became subject to it by annexation. Conquest was everywhere followed by religious propaganda, and, to incorporate the vanquished territory more completely in the Empire, the Church multiplied the number of Greek bishoprics, whose incumbents, subject to the Patriarch of Constantinople, were the most faithful and efficient agents for the spread of Orthodoxy. In the regions of Anatolia recaptured from the Arabs, as in Southern Italy regained from Lombards or Saracens, and also in Armenia which was annexed at the beginning of the eleventh century, the first work of the imperial government was to create numerous bishoprics of the Greek rite, which by establishing the predominance of Orthodoxy in the country ensured its moral possession by the monarchy. The monks, especially in Southern Italy, were not the least active agents of Hellenisation. In Calabria, the territory of Otranto, and Apulia, their monasteries, chapels, and hermitages were centres round which the people gathered, and where, by association with the monks, they learnt Greek. Thus religion in combination with Hellenism assured the unity of the Byzantine Empire. "Orthodoxy," says Rambaud, "took the place of nationality."

IV.

The administrative organisation of the Byzantine Empire was founded, as we have seen, on military institutions. In Byzantium, indeed, as in all states in the Middle Ages, an essential place was held by the army, which assured the defence of the territory and formed the strength of the monarchy. "The army," wrote one Emperor, "is to the State what the head is to the body. If great care be not taken thereof the very existence of the Empire will be endangered." Consequently all the rulers who really considered the greatness of the monarchy, alike the Isaurian Emperors, the great military sovereigns of the tenth century, and the *Basileis* of the Comnenian family, exercised a constant and watchful care over their soldiers; and as long as the Byzantine army was steadfast and numerous, devoted to its task and to its master, so long the Empire endured in spite of all difficulties.

At all periods of its history the Byzantine army was partly recruited from the inhabitants of the Empire. In theory every Roman citizen was subject to military service, and those men who rendered it, either by conscription or by voluntary enlistment, were even in administrative language regarded as the real soldiers, the true representatives of the national army; they were always called *οἱ Ῥωμαῖοι*. Actually these levies were of somewhat unequal quality, and for various reasons the imperial government very soon allowed a military tax to be substituted for actual military service. And it gradually came to rely in greater measure on the services of mercenaries, whom it regarded as superior in quality and more constant in fidelity. Since the Emperor paid handsomely, since to those who enlisted under his flag he made liberal grants of land, actual military fiefs, irrevocable, inalienable, and hereditary, he had no difficulty in securing from the neighbouring states a countless number of adventurers ready to barter their services. Thus it was a strange patchwork of nationalities that met under the standards of Byzantium. In Justinian's day there were Huns and Vandals, Goths and Lombards, Persians, Armenians, African Moors, and Syrian Arabs. In the armies of the tenth and eleventh centuries there appeared Chazars and Patzinaks, Varangians and Russians, Georgians and Slavs, Arabs and Turks, Northmen from Scandinavia and Normans from Italy. In the army of the Comneni there were Latins from all the countries of the West, Anglo-Saxons and Scandinavians, Italians and Germans, Frenchmen from France, Normans from Sicily, and representatives of all the races of the East. These aliens were even allowed to enlist in the bodyguard of the Emperor. One of the regiments of this guard, the *hetairia*, was in the tenth century almost exclusively composed of Russians, Scandinavians, and Chazars. And the famous Varangian guard, originally formed of Russians at the end of the tenth century, was successively recruited from among Russian Scandinavians, Northmen of Norway and Iceland, and Anglo-Saxons. In the tenth century Armenian contingents were numerous and highly esteemed in the imperial army; in the twelfth century the Latins were the best of the Byzantine troops. Many of these foreigners achieved brilliant careers in Byzantium, and attained high command and great military honours.

The army thus constituted possessed great qualities of steadfastness and courage. Inured to the profession of arms, capable of bearing every kind of hardship, fatigue, and privation, constantly engaged in strenuous exercises, strengthened by the frequent improvements that were introduced into its methods of warfare, it was a matchless instrument of war which for over six hundred years rendered brilliant services to the monarchy and crowned its banners with a halo of glory. Nevertheless the army was not without grave and formidable defects. The system of regional recruiting resulted in placing the soldiers in too close a personal relation with their leader, generally one of the feudal nobility of the land, to whom the men were closely attached by many ties of dependence, and whom they more readily obeyed than the distant Emperor; so that the monarchy was constantly disturbed by political insurrections, caused by the ambitions of the generals and supported by the fidelity of their men. On the other hand, the mercenaries, homeless adventurers intent only on earning as much as possible, were no less dangerous servants, owing to their want of discipline and their tendency to mutiny. Their leaders were real condottieri, always ready to sell themselves to the highest bidder or to fight for their own hand; and during the latter part of its existence the Empire suffered terribly, alike from their greed and their insurrections. The efficient control of such soldiers depended entirely on the general commanding them, the influence he exercised, and the confidence he inspired. Fortunately for Byzantium it happened that for centuries the Empire was lucky enough to have eminent generals at the head of its army—Belisarius and Narses in the sixth century, the Isaurian Emperors in the eighth, John Curcuas, the Phocas, Sclerus, Tzimisces, and Basil II in the tenth, and the Emperors of the Comnenian family in the twelfth. All these, and especially those of the tenth century, watched over their soldiers with careful solicitude; they lavished on them rewards and privileges, they surrounded them with consideration and recognition, so as to keep them contented and enthusiastic, and to find them always ready to "risk their lives for the sacred Emperors and the whole of the Christian community." By encouraging in them this double sentiment, first that they were the descendants of the invincible Roman legions, and secondly that they were fighting under Christ's protection for the defence of Christendom, the *Basileis* inspired their soldiers with patriotism for Byzantium, a patriotism compounded of loyal devotion and pious enthusiasm which for long made them victorious in every field of battle.

The troops forming the Byzantine army were divided into two distinct groups, the *τάγματα*, who garrisoned Constantinople and its suburbs, and the *θέματα*, who were stationed in the provinces. The first group was chiefly composed of the four cavalry regiments of the Guard, the Scholae, Excubitors, Arithmus or Vigla, and Hicanati, and the infantry regiment of the Numeri. Each of these corps, whose strength was generally quoted, perhaps with some exaggeration, at 4000, was commanded by an officer bearing the title of Domestic; in the tenth century the Domestic of the Scholae was Commander-in-chief of the army. The themes, or provincial army corps (*τὰ ἔξω θέματα, τὰ περατικὰ θέματα*), whose strength varied from 4000 to 10,000 men according to the importance of the province they defended, had at their head a strategus; each theme was divided into two or three brigades or turmae, each turma into three *μοῖραι* or *δροῦγγοι* commanded by a Drungarius, each *μοῖρα* or regiment into ten *banda* commanded by a count. These troops are often referred to in the texts as *τὰ καβαλλαρικὰ θέματα*. The cavalry indeed formed their principal part, for cavalry in Byzantium, as in all states in the Middle Ages, was the most esteemed arm; whether it were the heavy cavalry in armour, the *cataphracts*, or the light cavalry, the *trapezitae*, it formed an instrument of war of admirable strength and flexibility.

Besides these troops, which constituted the actual army in the field, there was the army of the frontiers (τὰ ἀκριτικὰ θέματα), which was formed on the model of the *limitanei* of the fifth and sixth centuries; it occupied military borderlands along the frontier, where in return for their military service the soldiers received land on which they settled with their families. The duties of these detachments were to defend the *limites*, hold the fortified posts, castles, and citadels which Byzantium had established in successive lines along the whole extent of the frontier, to occupy strategic points, hold mountain passes, guard roads, keep a close watch on all preparations by the enemy, repel invasion, and be ready with a counter-offensive. A curious tenth-century treatise on tactics has preserved for us a picturesque account of the strenuous life led on the "marches" of the Empire, on the mountains of Taurus, or the borders of Cappadocia, perpetually threatened by an Arab invasion. It was an arduous and exacting warfare, in which the problem was to contain an enterprising and daring enemy by means of weak forces; a war of surprises, ambushes, reconnaissances, and sudden attacks, in which the *trapezitae*, or light cavalry, excelled. All along the frontier a network of small observation posts was connected with headquarters by a system of signals; as soon as any movement by the enemy was observed, skirmishing parties of cavalry set out, carrying only one day's rations to ensure greater mobility, and with darkened accoutrements and weapons so as to be less visible. Behind this curtain mobilisation proceeded. The infantry occupied the mountain passes, the population of the plains took refuge in the fortresses, and the army concentrated. It is interesting to note in these instructions with what care and forethought nothing is left to chance, either as regards information or supplies, the concentration or movements of troops, night attacks, ambushes, or espionage. Meanwhile the cavalry made daring raids into enemy territory to cause the assailants uneasiness regarding their lines of communication and to attempt a useful diversion, while with his main force the Byzantine strategus sought contact with the enemy and engaged battle, generally by a sudden and unforeseen attack displaying mingled courage and cunning. It was an arduous type of warfare in which it was necessary always to be on the alert to avoid a surprise, to counter blow with blow, raid with raid; a war full of great duels, cruel, chivalrous, and heroic episodes; but a marvellous training for those who took part in it.

The Byzantine epic gives a magnificent picture of the valiant and free life led by these soldiers on the Asiatic marches in the poem of Digenes Akritas, the defender of the frontier, "the model of the brave, the glory of the Greeks, he who established peace in Romania." Nowhere are the qualities of courage, energy, and patriotism of these Byzantine soldiers more clearly shewn than in this poem, wherein also is evident the proud consciousness of independence innate in these hard fighters, great feudal lords, who waged the eternal struggle with the infidel on the frontiers, amid glorious adventures of love and death. "When my cause is just," says the hero of the poem, "I fear not even the Emperor." This characteristic feature betrays, even in an epic which exalts into beauty all the sentiments of the age, the inherent weakness from which the Empire was henceforward to suffer—the insurmountable unruliness of the Byzantine army and its leaders.

It is difficult to calculate exactly the strength of the Byzantine army, but we must be careful not to exaggerate its size. In the sixth as in the tenth century, in the tenth as in the twelfth, armies were not of vast numbers—only about 20,000 to 30,000 men, and often much less, although they achieved the most signal victories and conquered or destroyed kingdoms. Against the Arabs in the tenth century the army in Asia attained a total of some 70,000 men. Including the Guard and the regiments of the army in Europe, the grand total of the Byzantine forces does not seem to have amounted to more than 120,000 men. But handled as they were with a tactical skill the rules of which had been carefully laid down by the Emperors themselves, such as Leo VI and Nicephorus Phocas, fortified by a multitude of ingenious engines of war which were preserved in the great arsenal of Mangana, based finally on the network of strongholds which Byzantine engineers constructed with so consummate a science of fortification, this army, steadfast and brave, full of spirit, enthusiasm, and patriotism, was indeed for long almost invincible.

V.

Owing to the great extent of her coast-line, and the necessity of retaining command of the sea, which formed the communication between the different parts of the monarchy, Byzantium was inevitably a great maritime power. Indeed, in the sixth and seventh centuries, and until the beginning of the eighth, the imperial fleet dominated the eastern seas, or rather it was the only Mediterranean fleet until the Arabs made their appearance halfway through the seventh century. It was thus capable of successfully carrying on the struggle when the Umayyad Caliphs of Syria in their turn created a naval power and assailed Byzantium by sea as well as by land; it was actually the fleet which saved the Empire in the seventh century, and which saved Constantinople in the great siege of 717. After this the navy was apparently somewhat neglected. The war with the Caliphs of Baghdad was mainly on land; and the Isaurian Emperors seem moreover to have felt some uneasiness as regards the excessive power of the Grand Admirals. In the ninth century the monarchy paid dearly for this neglect when the Muslim corsairs, who were masters of Crete, for over a century ravaged the coasts of the Archipelago almost with impunity, and when the conquest of Sicily ensured to the Arab navy the supremacy of the Tyrrhenian sea as well as that of the Adriatic. Towards the close of the ninth century it was decided to reorganise the fleet, and once more, until the beginning of the twelfth century, Byzantium was the great sea-power of the Mediterranean. In the tenth century the Emperor of Constantinople boasted that he commanded the seas (*θαλασσοκρατεῖν*) up to the Pillars of Hercules. Nicephorus Phocas declared that he was the sole possessor of naval power, and even at the end of the eleventh century Cecaumenus wrote: "The fleet is the glory of Romania (*ὁ στόλος ἐστὶν ἡ δόξα τῆς Ῥωμανίας*)". This position was seriously threatened when the Seljūq Turks conquered Asia Minor, because the Empire was thereby deprived of the provinces whence its best crews were drawn. Henceforth Byzantium resorted to the practice of entrusting its naval operations to other navies, those of Pisa, Genoa, and above all Venice; and depending on these allies it neglected naval construction. This was the end of the Byzantine navy. In the thirteenth century the maintenance of a fleet was regarded by the Greeks as a useless expense, and a contemporary writer states with some regret that "the naval power of Byzantium had vanished long ago."

Originally all the naval forces of the Empire were combined under one command; in the seventh century the fleet was the "theme of the sailors" (*τὸ θέμα τῶν καραβισιάνων or τῶν πλωιζομένων*), whose chief, or strategus, generally held the rank of patrician. The Isaurian Emperors divided this great command, and created the two themes of the Cibyrrhaeots (which included all the south-western coast of Asia Minor) and the Dodecanese, or Aegean Sea, whereto was added in the ninth century the theme of Samos. These were the three pre-eminently maritime themes; but naturally the other coastal provinces—Hellas, Peloponnesus, and above all the themes of the Ionian Sea (Nicopolis, Cephalonia)—also contributed somewhat to the formation of the fleet and the provision of crews.

The Byzantine fleet, like the army, partly recruited its men from the population of the Empire; and in return for their services the Empire assigned to the sailors of the Cibyrrhaeot, Samian, and Aegean themes estates which, as with the land forces, were constituted as inalienable and hereditary fiefs. Another part of the personnel was drawn from the Mardaites of Mount Lebanon, whom the Emperors established in the seventh century, some in the region of Attalia where they possessed a special and almost autonomous form of government under their catapan, others in the coastal provinces of the Ionian Sea. Finally, Varangian sailors, whose skill was highly appreciated, were often engaged to serve in the fleet. As in the land forces, the pay was good; consequently the Empire found no difficulty in securing crews for its ships.

Like the army, the navy was divided into two distinct groups. There was in the first place the imperial fleet (τὸ βασιλικοπλόϊμον), commanded by the *Drungarius of the Fleet*, whose importance seems to have increased immensely towards the close of the ninth century. This squadron was stationed in the waters of the capital. There was also the provincial fleet (ὁ θεματικὸς στόλος), composed of the squadrons from the maritime themes, which was commanded by the strategi of these themes. Generally in great naval expeditions both these fleets were united under the command of the same admiral. It is impossible to compute, from the documents extant, the relative strength of these two fleets. The number of ships assembled for the campaign of 907 shews an imperial fleet of 60 dromons in line as opposed to 42 from the maritime themes, and this fact is enough to shew the importance of the squadron entrusted with the defence of the capital.

The Byzantine fleet contained units of various types. There was first the *dromon*, which was a strong and heavy but swift vessel, with a high wooden turret on deck (the *xylokastron*) furnished with engines of war. The crew consisted of 300 men, 230 rowers and 70 marines. Originally, the same men were employed for rowing and for fighting, but soon the drawbacks of this system became apparent, and by the reforms of the ninth century the two groups which formed the crew were separated. Subordinate to the dromon there were lighter vessels, the *pamphylians*, some manned by 160 others by 130 men, and the *ousiai*, which seem to have been built after the model of the large Russian boats, and to have been attached to the dromons at the rate of two ousiai to each larger vessel. Their crews varied from 108 to 110 men. All vessels other than dromons were often referred to under the general name of *chelandia*, some belonging to the pamphylian class, others to that of the ousiai.

What rendered these ships particularly formidable was the superiority which they derived from the use of Greek fire. A Syrian engineer of the seventh century, named Callinicus, had imparted to the Byzantines the secret of this "liquid fire," which could not be extinguished, and which was said to burn even in water. It was thrown on to the enemy ships, either by means of tubes or *siphons* placed in the prow of the Greek vessels, or by means of hand-grenades. The reputation of this terrible weapon, exaggerated by popular imagination, filled all the adversaries of Byzantium with terror. Igor's Russians, who were crushed outside Constantinople in 941, declared: "The Greeks have a fire resembling the lightning from heaven, and when they threw it at us they burned us; for this reason we could not overcome them." In the thirteenth century Joinville speaks of Greek fire with similar emotion. Any man touched by it believed himself to be lost; every ship attacked was devoured by flames. And the Byzantines, conscious of the advantage they derived from this formidable weapon, guarded the secret with jealous care. The Emperors, in their dying recommendations, advised their successors not to reveal it to anyone, and threatened with anathema any impious person who might dare to disclose it.

Like the army, the navy was handled with great tactical skill. In the special treatises of the tenth century which have been preserved, we find the most minute instructions for manœuvring and for boarding, for the use of Greek fire and other weapons of offence, boiling pitch, stones, masses of iron, and the like. There is also evident the same anxiety in maintaining the efficiency of the crews by incessant practice, and the same care with regard to the sailors as to the soldiers. Nevertheless, and in spite of the importance given to the great theme of the Cibyrrhaeots by the proximity of the Arab territory, in spite of the great services rendered by the fleet, in the tenth century the navy was less regarded than the land forces; the strategi of the three maritime themes received much lower salaries (ten pounds of gold) than those of the governors of the great continental themes of Anatolia.

But by all these means, by land and sea, Byzantium was a great power; and, by her wise naval and military organisation, she remained until the end of the twelfth century a great and powerful military state.

CHAPTER XXIV.

BYZANTINE CIVILISATION.

For over a thousand years, from the end of the fourth century to the middle of the fifteenth, the Byzantine Empire was the centre of a civilisation equal to that of any age in brilliancy, certainly the most brilliant known to the Middle Ages, and possibly even the only real civilisation which prevailed in Europe between the close of the fifth century and the beginning of the eleventh. While the barbarian states of the West were laboriously developing the elements of a new culture from the scanty remains of the Roman tradition, Byzantium—Rome's successor, and imbued with the spirit and teachings of Hellenism—never ceased to be the centre of refinement and the home of a great movement in thought and art. Byzantium, indeed, was no mere transmitter of the tradition of antiquity. Contact with the East had modified her, and the influence of Christianity had left a deep imprint; and, contrary to a still widely-spread opinion, she was capable of originality and creation. Hellenism, Christianity, and the East met and combined in forming Byzantine civilisation; and by the characteristic forms it assumed, by its superiority, as well as by the long and profound influence it exercised in both the Eastern and Western world, this civilisation played a prominent part in the history of the Middle Ages, the history of thought, and the history of mankind.

For over a thousand years, Constantinople, the capital of the Empire, was the most brilliant and characteristic expression of this civilisation. For over a thousand years the whole world gazed with feelings of admiration and greed at the city which Byzantines called "the City protected by God," or merely, "the City (πόλις)," the magnificent, mighty, and prosperous city which has been felicitously described as "the Paris of the Middle Ages." The whole medieval world dreamt of Constantinople as a city famous for beauty, wealth, and power, seen through a shimmer of gold. "She is the glory of Greece," wrote a Frenchman in the twelfth century; "her wealth is renowned, and she is even richer than is reported." "Constantinople," said another, "is the peer of Rome in holiness and majesty"; and Benjamin of Tudela adds: "Except Baghdad there is no town in the universe to be compared with her." According to Robert of Clari, it was said that "Two-thirds of the world's wealth were in Constantinople, and the other third was scattered throughout the world." And everyone knows the celebrated passage in which Villehardouin declares: "No man could believe that so rich a city existed in all the world," and asserts that the city was "queen over all others." The fame of the imperial city resounded throughout the whole of the then-known world. Men dreamt of her amid the chilly mists of Norway, and on the banks of the Russian rivers, down which the Varangians sailed towards matchless Tsarigrad; they dreamt of her in Western strongholds, where *trouvères* sang the marvels of the imperial palace, the floating hall swayed by the breezes of the sea, and the dazzling carbuncle which gave light to the imperial apartments during the night. Men dreamt of her alike among the barbarian Slavs and the needy Armenians, who aspired to seek their fortunes in the service of an Emperor lavish of pay. Men dreamt of her in Venice and the commercial cities of Italy, and calculated the magnificent revenues which the Byzantine sovereigns yearly derived from their city. Even up to her final days of decadence, Constantinople remained one of the most beautiful and illustrious cities of the universe, the splendid centre and ornament of the Empire, the home of matchless wealth and culture, the pride and glory of the monarchy.

In order to obtain a clear understanding of Byzantine civilisation, to visualise the mode of life and the dominant tastes in this vanished society, and to realise the mentality of the Greeks in the Middle Ages, we must therefore begin by studying Constantinople. And moreover it is about her that we have most information. At every stage of her history there are valuable documents which describe for us admirably the buildings of the great city, and the appearance she presented: for the fifth century we have the *Notitia* of 450; for the sixth century the book of *Edifices* by Procopius, the poem of Paul the Silentiary, and the description of the church of the Holy Apostles by Nicholas Mesarites; for the tenth century the poem of Constantine the Rhodian on the seven wonders of the capital and the *Ceremonies* of Constantine Porphyrogenitus; finally the narratives of countless travellers,—French, Italians, Spaniards, Russians, and Arabs,—who visited Constantinople from the twelfth to the fifteenth century. Moreover Byzantine literature reflects, as in a magic mirror, the ideas which were familiar and precious to the inhabitants of the capital, and the great currents of thought which prevailed in her. But Constantinople was not the Empire. In contrast to the capital which was luxurious, refined, and elegant, and also turbulent, cruel, and corrupt, there was another Byzantium, simpler and ruder, more robust and more serious, the Byzantium of the provinces, about which we know less than the other, but whose aspect we must nevertheless attempt to reconstruct; for the strength and stability of the monarchy was derived therefrom, no less than from Constantinople, and its study is indispensable if we wish to understand the character of Byzantine civilisation. In this vanished world, Constantinople and the provinces seem like the two opposite leaves of a diptych, and, in spite of the deep contrast offered by these two Byzantiums, it was their union which formed the power and greatness of the Empire.

But before presenting a picture of Byzantine civilisation under this twofold aspect, a preliminary remark is necessary. In the course of a thousand years, between the fourth century when it came into being and the fifteenth when it disintegrated, Byzantine society necessarily underwent profound changes. A historian who seeks to present a picture of the whole runs great risks of completely falsifying the aspect of things if he borrows indiscriminately from authors of widely different ages, if, like Krause who aspired to shew us the "Byzantines of the Middle Ages," he combines facts drawn from sources which are chronologically widely apart. In order to avoid this danger, we shall here note only the most persistent features, those which seem really characteristic of Byzantine civilisation, and, apart from these permanent elements, we shall always be careful to mention the exact date of the social phenomena recorded and to mark their evolution. Thus perhaps will emerge an approximately correct presentment of this vanished world, this infinitely complex society to which the mixture of nationalities imparted so strongly cosmopolitan a character, and which we must study successively in Constantinople and in the provinces so as to arrive at a clear understanding of the soul of Byzantium.

I.

By the general appearance she presented, the splendour of her public buildings, the multitude of ancient statues which adorned her broad squares, the luxury of her palaces and the beauty of her churches, the picturesque animation lent to her streets by a motley and cosmopolitan crowd, Constantinople, even at first sight, produced a powerful impression of wealth and magnificence. By the middle of the fifth century, barely a hundred years after her foundation, the Byzantine capital was already a very large town. Theodosius II was obliged to enlarge the city which had become too narrow for the enormous influx of population, and carried the new enclosure far beyond the wall built by Constantine, thus making her boundaries, except at one point, identical with those of Stamboul in the present day. For her protection he built the admirable line of ramparts from the Sea of Marmora to the end of the Golden Horn, which still exist to-day, and whose triple defences, ranged one behind the other, remain one of the finest examples of military architecture of all time. Against this mighty wall, which rendered Constantinople a great and impregnable fortress, there hurled themselves in succession all the barbarians, Huns and Avars, Bulgars and Russians, Arabs from the East and Crusaders from the West. On the very eve of the final catastrophe in 1453, the great capital still vaunted her military power and "this crown of ramparts, which was surpassed not even by those of Babylon."

Within this vast enclosure there stretched henceforward a magnificent city. Built like Rome on seven hills, she was divided like the former capital of the Empire into fourteen regions, and since the days of Constantine the Emperors had spared no pains to render her equal or even superior to the great city, which for so many centuries had been the heart of Roman power. The *Notitia* of 450 shews us a Constantinople full of palaces—the first region especially was, says this document, *regiis nobiliumque domiciliis clara*—magnificent squares; sumptuous buildings for public utility, baths, underground cisterns, aqueducts and shops; buildings devoted to popular amusement, theatres, hippodromes, and the like. Some figures given in the *Notitia* are significant of the greatness and wealth of the city: without taking into account the five imperial palaces, six *domus divinae* belonging to Empresses, and three *domus nobilissimae*, there were in Constantinople in the fifth century 322 streets, 52 porticoes, 4388 *domus* or mansions, and 153 private baths; and moreover this magnificent city was the finest museum in the world, because of the masterpieces of ancient art which the Emperors had removed from the famous sanctuaries of the Hellenic world to adorn their capital.

But to realise fully the importance of the imperial city, we must consider her as she was in the tenth century, at the moment when, indeed, she attained her apogee of splendour and prosperity. We possess fairly exact information as to her plan and her principal streets at this date, and they can still be traced in the thoroughfares of present-day Constantinople.

Between St Sophia to the north, the imperial palace to the south, and the Senate-house to the east, there stretched the square of the Augusteum, "Constantinople's square of St Mark," all surrounded with porticoes, in the centre of which, on a tall column, towered an equestrian statue of the Emperor Justinian. To the west lay the arcade of the Golden Milestone, whence started the great street of the Mese, which, like all the important thoroughfares of the city, was bordered with arcaded galleries, or ἔμβολοι. Crossing the quarter of the bazaars, and passing the Royal Basilica (Law-courts) and the Praetorium (residence of the Prefect of the City), it led into the Forum of Constantine, one of the handsomest parts of the city. In the centre stood a porphyry column (now called the *burnt pillar*), and all round the square there were palaces with gigantic domes, their walls decorated with mosaics and panels of precious metals; in front of these, under marble porticoes, were ranged the masterpieces of Greek sculpture. Thence, through the quarter of the Artopolia (the bakers), the Mese reached the great square of the Taurus, where in front of the Capitol was erected the lofty column of Theodosius, decorated, like Trajan's column, with spiral bas-reliefs commemorating "the slaughter of the Scythian barbarians and the destruction of their towns." Farther on there were the cross-roads of Philadelphion, where the main street split into three branches. One descended towards the Golden Horn; the second led to the church of the Holy Apostles and the gate of Charisius (Hadrianople Gate); the third and most frequented crossed the squares of Amastrianon and the Bous, whence a street branched off to the right towards the gate of St Romanus (Tōp Qāpū), and finally, after crossing the Forum of Arcadius in which rose a tall column with bas-reliefs representing scenes of war and triumph, it passed in front of the monastery of Studion, and reached the Golden Gate. This was the most famous and most magnificent of all the gates of Constantinople, with its propylaea decorated with ancient bas-reliefs and inlaid with coloured marbles, and the triple bay of its triumphal arch flanked by two massive marble pylons; it was through this gate that the Emperors made their solemn entry into the capital on their days of coronation or triumph, when they went in stately procession through streets hung with tapestry, blazing with lights, and strewn with flowers, amidst the acclamations of the people, and passed along the Mese to St Sophia.

In close proximity to these vast thoroughfares, bordered with long arcaded galleries, decorated with statues, and full of rich palaces, there were naturally to be found in Constantinople narrow streets, dark, muddy, and squalid, infested with dogs and with thieves, who, says one historian, "were almost as numerous as the poor." Often sheltered in cellars, there swarmed a wretched and sordid population in miserable houses. In strong contrast to these noisy, overcrowded quarters where the people huddled together, there were peaceful and deserted districts—such, for instance, as Petrion, on the slopes of the fifth hill, where amid shady gardens there stood monasteries and quiet churches, schools and hospitals. In the tenth century all the outskirts of the city, the district lying between the wall of Constantine and that of Theodosius II, was as yet sparsely inhabited; great open-air cisterns lay there with their still waters; the valley of the Lycus with its meadows was a rural and deserted spot; and there were hardly any buildings in the Blachernae suburb, with the exception of the famous sanctuary of the Virgin. Later, from the twelfth century, when the Emperors transferred their residence to the Blachernae palace, this suburb became fashionable because of its proximity to the Court, and churches and houses sprang up there. The sanctuaries of the Pantokrator (Kilīsa-jāmiʿ), Pantepoptes (Eski-Imaret-jāmiʿ), Pammakaristos (Fetḥīye-jāmiʿ), and the Christ of Chora (Qahrīye-jāmiʿ) date from this period. But in the tenth century fashionable life was elsewhere.

By the contrasts she presented Byzantine Constantinople was truly a great Oriental city. And she offered a magnificent spectacle. All these buildings of which she was full, public buildings of classical architecture and private houses of a more eastern type, palaces and churches, baths and hostelries, underground cisterns and aqueducts, columns and statues, combined to produce an incomparable effect. Constantine the Rhodian, writing in the tenth century, has justly sung the praises of "the famous and venerable city which dominates the world, whose thousand marvels shine with singular brilliancy, with the splendour of her lofty buildings, the glory of her magnificent churches, the arcades of her long porticoes, the height of her columns rising towards the skies." Within her walls Constantinople contained seven wonders—as many as the whole ancient world had known—"wherewith she adorned herself," as was said by one author, "as with so many stars."

In this vast city there dwelt an enormous population whose numbers during the period between the fifth and the thirteenth centuries may be fixed without exaggeration at from 800,000 to 1,000,000. It was a motley and cosmopolitan population in which might be met every type, garb, condition, race. From every province in the Empire and every country in the world men flocked to Byzantium for business, for pleasure, for litigation. There were Asiatics with hooked noses, almond eyes under thick eyebrows, pointed beards, and long black hair falling over their shoulders; Bulgars with shaved heads and dirty clothes, wearing an iron chain round their waists by way of belt; fur-clad Russians with long fair moustaches; Armenian or Scandinavian adventurers, who had come to seek their fortunes in the great city; Muslim merchants from Baghdad or Syria, and Western merchants, Italians from Venice or Amalfi, Pisa or Genoa, Spaniards and Frenchmen; there were Chazars of the Imperial Guard, Varangians "tall as palm-trees," Latin mercenaries with long swords, who in their armour "looked like bronze figures." There was a confusion of every tongue and every religion. And in the midst of this animated and picturesque crowd, the inhabitants of the city might be recognised by the rich silken garments embroidered with gold in which they were clad, the fine horses on which they were mounted, and the exhibition of such luxury as gave them, as was said by a traveller, "the semblance of so many princes." Anyone who visited Constantinople a few years ago will remember the spectacle offered by the Great Bridge at Stamboul. Medieval Byzantium offered a somewhat similar spectacle, and foreigners who visited the imperial city carried away a dazzling picture of the Byzantine streets.

But in this magnificent Constantinople full of splendid sights, where extravagance of costume vied with beauty of architecture, three things were specially characteristic of Byzantine civilisation: the pomp of religious ceremonial as displayed by the Orthodox liturgy on great feast days; the brilliant ostentation of imperial life shewn in the receptions and the etiquette of the Sacred Palace; and the amusements of the Hippodrome where was manifested the mind of the people. "In Constantinople," says A. Rambaud, "for God there was St Sophia, for the Emperor the Sacred Palace, and for the people the Hippodrome." Round these three poles there gravitated a great part of Byzantine life, and in them may best be studied some of the leading features of this society.

II.

Religion held an essential place in the Byzantine world. The medieval Greeks have often been blamed for the passionate interest they took in theological disputes, and the manner in which they neglected the most serious interests and the very safety of the State for apparently futile controversies. There is no doubt that, from the Emperor down to the meanest of his subjects, the Byzantines loved controversies about faith and dogma to distraction. It would nevertheless be foolish to believe that these interminable disputes of which Byzantine history is full, and the profound troubles which resulted from them, were only caused among the masses by the love of controversy, the mania for argument, and the subtlety of the Greek intellect, and, among statesmen, by the empty pleasure of laying down the law. These great movements were determined by deeper and graver reasons. In the Eastern world heresies have often concealed and disguised political ideas and enmities, and the conduct of the Emperors in these matters was often inspired rather by State reasons than by a desire to make innovations in matters of faith. Nevertheless a deep and sincere piety inspired most Byzantine souls. This people which adored pageants loved the sumptuous magnificence of liturgical ceremonies; their pious credulity attributed miraculous virtues to the holy icons, and images "not made by hands" (ἀχειροποιητοί); they devoutly adored those holy relics of which Byzantium was full, treasures a thousand times more dearly esteemed than "gold and precious stones," and which tempted so strongly the covetousness of the Latins. Finally, their superstitious minds sought in every event an indication of the Divine Will; so much so that the Byzantine people, which was singularly impressionable, lived in a constant state of mystic exaltation, which, from the very outset, rendered them very amenable to the all-powerful influence of the Church. In education the study of religious matters held an important place. In society, devotion was closely allied with fashionable life; church and hippodrome were, as has ingeniously been said, the only places of public resort possessed by Byzantine society, and people repaired to the former to meet and to gossip as much as to pray. Finally, the cloister exercised a mystical attraction over many men. The foundation or endowment of monasteries was one of the commonest forms of Byzantine piety. The monks were objects of universal veneration; they were much sought after as directors of conscience by pious persons, and consequently they exerted a profound influence on society. Moved by natural piety, by weariness of the world, or by the need for renunciation and peace, many Byzantines aspired to end their days among these holy men, who by their prayers and mortifications assured the salvation of the Empire and of humanity; and wished to become, like them, "citizens of heaven." The life of the Emperor himself, closely associated with all the religious feasts, was indeed, as has been said, a sacerdotal life; and St Sophia, where the Emperor's coronation took place, and where the ostentatious retinue of the imperial processions was displayed on the innumerable feast-days, St Sophia, the most venerated of sanctuaries, in which the Patriarch could entrench himself as in a citadel, was one of the centres of public life, of the government, and even of the diplomacy of the monarchy.

Ever since it had been rebuilt by Justinian with incomparable splendour, St Sophia had been the wonder of Constantinople. With its lofty dome, so aerial and light that, in the phrase of Procopius, it seemed "to be suspended by a golden chain from heaven," the fine breadth of its harmonious proportions, the splendour of its facings of many-coloured marble, the brilliancy of its mosaics, the magnificent gold and silver work which enriched the iconostasis, ambo, and altar, the church built by Anthemius of Tralles and Isidore of Miletus has throughout centuries excited the admiration of all beholders. If we consider its design, its enormous dome with a diameter of 107 feet, supported by four great arches which rest on four colossal piers, the two semi-domes which abut the central dome and are in their turn supported by three smaller apses, if we study the skilful combinations of equipoise which ensure the success of the work, we are overcome with amazement at this "marvel of stability and daring," this masterpiece of logical audacity and scientific knowledge. The magnificence of the decoration, the beauty of the lofty columns with their exquisite capitals, the many-coloured marbles so skilfully variegated as to give the illusion of Oriental carpets hung on the walls of the apse, and the dazzling effect of the mosaics with their background of dark blue and gold, complete the effect of magic splendour produced by St Sophia. Robbed though it has been since 1453 of its former magnificence, it still justifies the profound admiration which it excited from the time of Justinian until the last days of the Byzantine Empire. "Words worthy of it are not to be found," wrote an author of the fourteenth century, "and after we have spoken of it, we cannot speak of anything else." Another Byzantine writer declared that God must certainly have extended His mercy to Justinian, if only because he built St Sophia. And if we try to picture the great church as it was in former days on occasions of solemn ceremonial, when, amid clouds of incense, glowing candles, and the moving harmony of sacred chants, there was displayed the mystic pageant of ritual processions and the beauty of the Orthodox liturgy, the impression becomes even more marvellous. There is a legend that ambassadors from Vladímir, Great Prince of Kiev, imagined that in a vision they had seen the angels themselves descending from heaven to join with the Greek priests in celebrating Mass on the altar of St Sophia, and they could not resist the attraction of a religion in which such things were to be seen, "transcending, they said, human intelligence." Under the golden domes of Justinian's church, every

Byzantine experienced emotions of the same kind, as deep and as powerful, and his mystic and pious soul became marvellously exalted.

Constantinople, moreover, was full of churches and monasteries. There was the church of the Holy Apostles, with its five domes, an architectural masterpiece of the sixth century, from which St Mark's in Venice was copied at a later date; here were buried ten generations of Emperors in sarcophagi of porphyry or marble. There was the New church (*Nea*), a basilica built in the ninth century by the Emperor Basil I, and the fine churches of the Comneni, the most famous of which, that of the Pantokrator, was from the twelfth century the St Denis of the monarchy. "In Constantinople," wrote one traveller, "there are as many churches as there are days in the year." To mention a few of those that still exist, there were St Irene and Little St Sophia (really the church of SS. Sergius and Bacchus) which date from the sixth century, the church of the Theotokos (Vefa-jāmi'), which appears to date from the eleventh, and also the Pammakaristos (Fetḥīye-jāmi') and the Chora (Qahrīye-jāmi'), built in the twelfth and thirteenth centuries, the latter of which still contains mosaics which are among the masterpieces of Byzantine art.

A singularly active and powerful religious life filled the Byzantine capital with its manifestations. Although in somewhat close dependence on the Emperor who appointed and deposed him at will, the Patriarch, a veritable Pope of the Eastern Church, was a power to be reckoned with in the State, especially when the holder of the office was a Photius, a Cerularius, or even a Polyeuctes or a Nicholas. The power of the Church was further increased by the great development in monasticism. We have already referred to the prominent part played in the Byzantine world by religious houses; Constantinople was full of monasteries; in like manner, outside the capital, in Egypt, in Palestine, and in Sinai during the fourth and fifth centuries, later, on Olympus in Bithynia, and on Latros in Caria, in the solitudes of Cappadocia, and—especially in the tenth century—on the Holy Mount of Athos, there was a marvellous expansion of monastic establishments. We know with what respect Byzantine society regarded the monks, and how great an influence they exercised in consequence. Moreover the monks became a real power, and sometimes one formidable to the State, because of the vast possessions which accumulated in their hands. Against this the Emperors—not only the iconoclasts, but even the orthodox—were obliged to wage a bitter and violent struggle. "The monks," said Nicephorus Phocas in a Novel, "possess none of the evangelical virtues; at every moment of their existence they are only considering how to acquire more earthly possessions." But the monks were too powerful to be easily overthrown; the State had to give way before the strong current, as it had often to yield to the turbulent outbursts organised in the monasteries, which penetrated even to the Sacred Palace, to present the grievances and claims of the Church. Vainly it endeavoured to reform the frequently relaxed discipline of the monasteries; even the Church itself, led by men such as Christodulus of Patmos in the eleventh century, or Eustathius of Thessalonica in the twelfth, failed to attain this object. The Byzantine monks were extremely popular because of the miraculous powers and prophetic gifts which were attributed to them, the holy images and venerable relics of which their monasteries were the pious depositaries; their preaching and moral influence, their works of mercy and the schools clustered round their monasteries. On account of this popularity, of their fanaticism, and their spirit of independence, they were a perpetual source of trouble in Byzantine society, and a double danger—political and social—to the State. The important place held in the Byzantine world by the monastic institution is one of the most characteristic features of this vanished civilisation, and is the best proof of the essential importance within it of everything which concerned religion.

On the side of the hills that slope from the square of Ātmeydān to the Sea of Marmora, close to St Sophia and the Hippodrome, were ranged the innumerable buildings which formed the imperial palace. Of this vast assemblage there now remain only ruins; owing, however, to the descriptions left by Byzantine authors, above all in the *Ceremonies* of Constantine Porphyrogenitus, it is easy to reconstruct its plan and picture its appearance. The Sacred Palace was indeed a city within a city; from its builder, Constantine, until the twelfth century, almost every Emperor took pride in enlarging it, or improving it by some new addition. After the fire which accompanied the Nika riot, the vestibule of Chalce, which opened on the Augusteum, was magnificently rebuilt by Justinian. The Chrysotriclinium, a sumptuous throne-room, was erected in the midst of the gardens by Justin II, and, at the end of the seventh century, Justinian II connected it with the ancient palace by the long arcades of Lausiacus and Justinianus. In the ninth century Theophilus built the palace of Triconchus in imitation of Arab models, surrounding it with gardens and adding a number of elegant pavilions decorated with rare marbles and precious mosaics, which were known by picturesque titles, such as the Pearl, Love, or Harmony. A little later Basil I erected the new palace, or Caenurgium, close to the Chrysotriclinium; Nicephorus Phocas added magnificent decorations to the maritime palace of Bucoleon, his favourite residence. Even in the twelfth century buildings were added within the grounds of the great Palace; from this period dated the pavilion of Mouchroutas, "the Persian house," whose architecture was inspired by Seljūq models.

Thus, within high walls which after the tenth century bore the appearance of a fortress, the work of successive generations had produced a complicated assemblage of all kinds of buildings, great reception rooms and more private pavilions hidden among trees, palaces and barracks, baths and libraries, churches and prisons, long arcades and terraces whence the eye could look far over the Sea of Marmora and the Bosphorus, wide stair-ways and magnificent landing-stages adorned with statues, gardens rich with flowers, trees, and running water, and large open spaces in which the Emperor played polo with his intimates. All this was laid out without symmetry or settled plan, but was full of charming fancy and of unparalleled magnificence. If we wish to form some idea of the Sacred Palace, we must not recall the noble and symmetrical façades of the Louvre and Versailles, but rather some Eastern palace, the Kremlin of the Tsars, or the Old Seraglio of the Sultans.

The resplendent luxury of the imperial apartments has often been described, and it is unnecessary to dwell for long on the precious marbles, mosaics, and gold; the gorgeous processions which passed every day through the lofty rooms hung with tapestries and strewn with flowers; the picturesque and glittering train of court officials, the magnificent ceremonial of the solemn audiences, receptions, and State dinners; and the thousand refinements of the precise and somewhat childish etiquette which regulated every act of the imperial life—the fairy-like setting of this court life, whose brilliant picture, worthy of the Arabian Nights, dazzled all the Middle Ages like a blaze of gold. In this magnificent setting, adorned with all the magic of art, within which passed the ostentatious and complicated life of the Emperor, everything was carefully calculated to enhance the sovereign majesty: whether by the luxury of splendid costumes, which for each fresh feast were of new form and colour, or by the pomp of the ceremonies which from the day of his birth to that of his death accompanied every act in the existence of the Basileus, and which rendered his life, as has been said, "a completely representative and pontifical life." On each of the great feasts of the Church, and on each solemn Saint's Day, the Emperor went to St Sophia, or to some other church in the capital, to be present in great state at the Divine Office. Then there were in the palace the civil festivities, daily processions, receptions, dinners, and audiences in which Byzantium took pride, in order to dazzle visitors and to display all her riches, magnificent jewels, precious tapestries, and splendid mosaics, multiplying lights and flowers, resplendent costumes, and gorgeous uniforms, and seeking even by magical illusions to astonish strangers. There were the feasts of the Dodecahemeron which lasted from Christmas till Epiphany, of the Brumalia, and many others, in which songs, dances, banquets, and performances by buffoons succeeded each other in an exact and complicated etiquette which left nothing to chance or fancy. And if we consider the busy, monotonous, and empty existence led by the Byzantine sovereign, and the crowd of courtiers who from morning till night, from one year's end to the other, seemed to have no object save to participate in this pompous puppet-show, we wonder whether indeed these people did not run a risk of developing, as was said by Taine, "idiot minds," and whether the ruler who submitted to such a life of show was not in danger of losing all capacity and energy. But although there was certainly some monotony in the profusion of purple, precious stones, and gold which illuminated the imperial existence, and a good deal of futility in the etiquette which surrounded him, it must not be forgotten that Byzantium wished thereby to give to the world an impression of incomparable splendour, of dazzling wealth and luxury, and that she thereby succeeded in giving a particular stamp to the civilisation of which she was the brilliant centre.

In the twelfth century the Comneni left the former imperial residence and settled in a new one at the end of the Golden Horn. This was the palace of Blachernae, whose splendour was not less striking than that of the Great Palace. Strangers permitted to visit it have left us dazzling descriptions. Everywhere there were gold and precious stones, goldsmith's work and mosaics, and, writes a contemporary, "it is impossible to say which gave most value and beauty to things, the costliness of the material or the skill of the artist." Round the rulers of the Comnenian dynasty there moved an elegant and worldly court, less ceremonious than the former one, passionately interested in festivities, music, tourneys, art, and letters, full of intrigues and amorous adventures. And all this lent a singular attraction to the city. Travellers who came to Constantinople declared that "nothing like it can be found in any other country." But somewhat grave consequences arose from the essential place held in Byzantine society by the Sacred Palace and court life.

In an absolute monarchy, where everything depended on the ruler's favour, the palace was the centre of everything; and naturally, to gain or retain this favour, there was an atmosphere of perpetual intrigue round the prince. In this court full of eunuchs, women, and idle high dignitaries, there were intrigues incessantly and everywhere, alike in the Gynaeceum, the barracks of the guards, and the Emperor's antechambers; every man fought for himself and sought to overthrow the reigning favourite, and any means were good, flattery or calumny, bribery or assassination. In dark corners was prepared the fall of the minister in power, nay even the fall of the Emperor himself. The history of the Sacred Palace is full of plots, murders, and *coups d'état*. And naturally in this court atmosphere there was scope for every kind of meanness, villainy, surrender of principle, recantation, and treachery. We must not indeed draw too black a picture. There were not only Emperor-drones content to slumber in the ostentatious and empty life of the palace, but also rulers full of energy, determined to carry out their great task as leaders of the State both in the field and in the government; and there were more of the latter than is commonly thought. In strong contrast to the mean and worthless courtiers, there were in this society many worthy men, and alike in the Byzantine aristocracy and the bourgeoisie there was an accumulated treasure of strong qualities and solid virtues. Nevertheless, even in the best of the Byzantines, there is visible a disquieting love for complication, subtlety, and intrigue, a way of contemplating and conducting life which suggests a certain amount of cunning, of prudent cleverness not overburdened with useless scruples, a weakness of character which contrasts with their superior intelligence. Court life greatly helped to develop this background of corruption and demoralisation, and to present a somewhat turbid picture of Byzantium, a picture of gorgeous luxury and excessive refinement, but of refinement in vice as well; shewing us amidst a marvellously enchanting setting a multitude of mediocre and worthless spirits, led by a few superior and evil geniuses.

Finally, in this elegant and ostentatious court, devoted to pleasure and feasting, in which women played a leading part, there was great corruption, and the imperial palace was the home of many startling adventures and wide-spread scandals. In spite of the apparently severe seclusion in which the life of the Empress was passed, in spite of the retinue of eunuchs by which the approaches to the Gynaeceum were guarded, Byzantine history is full of Empresses who played a leading part in State affairs or in society. They were granted a great place in palace festivities by ceremonial custom; the political constitution of the monarchy, which did not exclude women from the throne, bestowed on them an official position in the government at the side of the Emperor; several Byzantine Empresses by their high ability succeeded in gaining powerful influence and playing the part of a statesman. To appreciate the active part they took in directing political affairs, it is only necessary to recall the names of Theodora and Irene, of Theophano and Eudocia Macrembolitissa; or to realise what Byzantine society owed to their luxury, elegance, and spirit of intrigue, we may conjure up the figures of Zoë Porphyrogenita, Mary of Antioch, or the princesses, of such varied character, of the Comnenian family. Their morality was frequently doubtful, but their talent and culture were often eminent; and as they shared all the tastes of the period, alike for religion and for the Hippodrome, as they were as intriguing and ambitious as the men, they helped to bestow a characteristic stamp on Byzantine society. And from the imperial palace this love of intrigue so necessary for success, this openly-flaunted corruption, spread throughout all classes of society.

Round the palace there revolved a whole noble society, powerful alike by the high offices with which its members were invested and the territorial wealth they possessed; from it were drawn the intimates of the Emperor, his counsellors, ministers, officials, and generals; it was called the *Senatorial Order* (συγκλητικοί). We can most easily judge of Byzantine social life and luxury from these great aristocratic families. Though we know little about Byzantine dwellings, it may be said that, up to the time of the Crusades, they were constructed on the plan of the houses of antiquity; those which still exist in the dead cities of Central

Syria contain courts surrounded by porticoes, baths, and large gardens round the central edifice; in miniatures we see buildings of two or three stories, with gabled, terraced, or domed roofs; their façades, decorated with porticoes and flanked by towers or pavilions, were often adorned with balconies or loggias. The internal decorations seem to have been extremely luxurious. The rooms were lined with marble and decorated with mosaics or paintings; they were furnished with sumptuous articles made of wood inlaid with metal, mother-of-pearl, or ivory, covered with magnificent tapestries embroidered with religious subjects or fantastic animals. The luxury of the table was great, and still more that of costume. The forms of classical attire had been retained, but the influence of the East had added great extravagance, and, moreover, certain new fashions had been introduced from neighbouring peoples, which soon lent singular diversity to Byzantine costume. Its characteristic feature was extraordinary magnificence. Only garments of silk or purple were worn, tissues embroidered with gold which fell in stiff, straight folds, and materials embellished with embroideries and priceless jewels. There was no less extravagance in horses and carriages, and moralists such as St John Chrysostom in the fifth century, or Theodore of Studion in the ninth, severely criticised the excessive expenditure of their contemporaries. The period of the Crusades somewhat altered the character of this luxury, without diminishing it. Magnificence was always one of the characteristic features of Byzantine life; it is what strikes us first in the pictures of this vanished world preserved for us in mosaics and miniatures, both in the brilliant pictures which in San Vitale at Ravenna represent Justinian and Theodora in the midst of their court, and in the sumptuous portraits of emperors and empresses, ministers and great dignitaries, which illustrate manuscripts.

It was said for long and is still often repeated that the whole history of Byzantium is summed up in the quarrels of the Greens and Blues. However exaggerated this statement may be, it is certain that up to the twelfth century the games in the circus were among the favourite pleasures of the Byzantine world; so much so that it has truly been said of the Hippodrome that it was indeed "the mirror of Greek society in the Middle Ages." From the Emperor down to the meanest of his subjects, Byzantium devoted a passionate attention to everything which concerned the Circus, and women were no less keenly interested than men in the spectacles of the Hippodrome, the success of the fashionable charioteers, and the struggles between the factions. "The ardour which in the circus inflames men's minds with extraordinary passion is a marvellous thing," says a writer of the sixth century. "Should the green charioteer take the lead, half the people are in despair; should the blue one outstrip his rival, at once half the city is in mourning. Men who have no stake in the matter give vent to frenzied abuse; men who have suffered no hurt feel gravely injured; for a mere nothing people come to blows, as though it were a question of saving the country from danger." The gravest of men declared that without the theatre and the hippodrome "life were totally devoid of joy," and an Emperor who was a good psychologist wrote: "We must have games to amuse the people."

Consequently the societies which organised the games in the Circus, the famous factions of Greens and Blues, were recognised corporations of public utility, with their presidents or *demarchs*, their leaders of the regions, their funds, their places in official ceremonies, in fact a complete organisation—in the form of a kind of urban militia—which put arms in their hands and rendered them powerful and frequently dangerous. The whole people ranged itself on one side or the other, according to the colour favoured, and the Emperor himself took sides passionately in the struggle between the rival factions; so that the rivalries of the Circus very often assumed a political aspect, and spread from the Hippodrome to the State. The Ātmeydān in Constantinople still marks the site and retains the shape of the Byzantine Circus, where, in the magnificent arena, along the *spina* decorated with lofty columns and statues, the charioteers urged their horses down the track, and where the people thrilled with excitement at the thousand spectacles—animal-hunting, combats between men and wild beasts, the feats of acrobats, and the fooling of clowns—lavished by imperial liberality. But the Hippodrome was much more than this. It was also the scene of solemn triumphs, when under the eyes of the people there passed some victorious general, followed by a train of illustrious prisoners and a display of the wealth taken from a conquered world. Here also was the scene of public executions, which gratified the taste for cruelty and blood always existent in the Byzantine populace. But it was still something more. It took the place of the ancient Forum as one of the centres of public life. Here, and here only, the people could give vent to their feelings, their spirit of opposition and discontent, and here they retained their right to hiss or applaud anyone, even the Emperor. In the Circus the new Basileus came for the first time in contact with his people; in the Circus there sometimes occurred—as, for instance, at the beginning of the Nika riot—really tragic scenes, the prelude to mutiny or revolution; in the Circus, amid the execrations of the people, there sometimes closed the existence of the dethroned and tortured Emperor. For over two hundred years, from the fifth to the seventh century, the factions of the Circus maintained a profound and ceaseless agitation in the Byzantine State; they were in the forefront of all the insurrections, all the revolutions, in which the Hippodrome was often the battlefield or the chief fortress. The government indeed gradually succeeded in taming the factions; it appointed as their leaders *democrats*, who were great officers of the crown; and they became more and more official corporations, which on the days of great ceremony lined the streets on the sovereign's way and greeted him with their rhythmic acclamations. But, although less formidable to the State, the games of the Hippodrome were no less dear to the people, and the population of the capital still remained a source of constant preoccupation to the imperial government.

It was not an easy matter to keep the peace in this cosmopolitan multitude, constantly augmented by the undesirables who flocked from the provinces to the capital, an idle populace, impressionable, restless, turbulent, and discontented, which passed with equal facility from cheers to abuse, from enjoyment to mutiny, from enthusiasm to discouragement. Agitators found it easy to exert an influence over this superstitious and devout populace, always ready to believe the prophecies of soothsayers or the miracles of the holy images, and to credit all the rumours, false or true, which were abroad in the city. In a few hours the multitude became excited and infuriated; they were passionately interested in religious and political questions, and under the leadership of the monks who directed them, or of politicians who made use of them, they often imposed their will on the palace. Eager for gossip, they delighted in pamphlets, in abuse, in brawling and idle opposition. Moreover there was much corruption in the city. Houses of ill-fame established themselves at the very church doors; in the police orders are recorded the impious blasphemies, the rage for gambling, the licentious morals, the affrays which constantly took place in drinking-booths, and the consequent necessity of closing the latter at seven o'clock in the evening, the number of thieves, and the insecurity of the streets during the night. "If Constantinople," said a writer of the twelfth century, "surpasses all other cities in wealth, she also surpasses them in vice." Thus it was a hard task for the Prefect of the City, entrusted with the policing of the capital, to maintain order in this fickle, passionate, bloodthirsty, and ferocious crowd, always ready to blame the Emperor when dissatisfied with anything. Exempt from all taxation, the populace were fed by the government, who distributed bread, wine, and oil gratuitously, and it was no small matter to ensure supplies for the enormous capital, to regulate exactly the arrival of wheat from Egypt, as was done by Justinian, to supervise, as is shown by the *Book of the Prefect* at the end of the ninth century, the making of bread and the sale of fish and meat. Then the populace had to be amused by games in the circus, and by dazzling pomps and ceremonies, which thus became means of government. Above all it had to be mastered, sometimes severely, by bloody repression. Nevertheless imperial authority had often to yield when popular fury was unchained. From the twelfth century onwards, we even find the dregs of the Byzantine people, the poorer classes of the great cities, becoming organised to give voice to their demands, and for social struggles; the history of the "Naked" (*γυμνοί*) in Corfù in the twelfth century, and that of the "Zealots" in Thessalonica in the fourteenth, betray a vague tendency towards a communistic movement.

III.

But Constantinople was also a great industrial and commercial town.

Between the square of the Augusteum and that of the Taurus, all along the great street of the Mese, there stretched the quarter of the bazaars. Here were exhibited in great quantity the products of the luxury trades, sumptuous materials in bright colours embroidered richly in gold, a monopoly jealously guarded for themselves by the Byzantines; wonderful specimens of the goldsmith's art; jewels glittering with rubies and pearls; bronzes inlaid with silver; enamels cloisonné in gold; delicately carved ivories; icons of mosaic—in fact everything in the way of rare and refined luxury known to the Middle Ages. There, at work under the porticoes in the open air, might be seen the innumerable craftsmen of Byzantine industry, jewellers, skinners, saddlers, wax-chandlers, bakers, etc., the tables of the money-changers heaped with coin, the stalls of the grocers who sold meat and salt fish, flour and cheese, vegetables, oil, butter, and honey in the street; and the stalls of the perfume-sellers, set up in the very square of the Palace, at the foot of a venerable icon, the Christ of the Chalce, "in order," says a document at the end of the ninth century, "to perfume the sacred image as is fitting, and to impart charm to the palace vestibule." And it is evident how much all this resembles the Eastern colour still apparent in present-day Stamboul. Farther on, close to the Long Portico, between the Forum of Constantine and the Taurus, was the quarter of the silk and linen merchants, where each branch of the trade had its own place. In the Taurus and the Strategion were sold sheep and pigs, in the Amastrianon horses; on the quays of the Golden Horn was the fish-market. And all day long in the bazaars of the main street, an active and incessant movement of business was kept up by an animated, noisy, and cosmopolitan crowd.

The industrial corporations were each hedged round by very strict administrative regulations. Constantinople in the Middle Ages was, as has been said, "the paradise of monopoly, privilege, and protection." There was no liberty of labour. Under the superintendence of the Prefect of the City, the various trades were organised in hermetically closed gilds, minutely regulated in everything concerning membership, wages, methods of manufacture, conditions of work, and prices. Industrial life was watched over in every detail by government officials, often very inquisitorial in their methods. On the other hand, these gilds were protected by severe measures limiting or suppressing foreign competition. In the *Book of the Prefect*, an ordinance dating from the reign of Leo VI, we see the essential features of this economic system, and also the nature of the most important of these gilds, which is worthy of note. Some of them were occupied in provisioning the capital, others in building, as was natural in a great city where many edifices were under construction.

Most were employed in manufacturing articles of luxury, and this was indeed the characteristic feature of Byzantine industry, which was essentially a luxury-industry. Finally, the money market, represented by the very numerous money-changers and bankers, who were highly respected in Constantinople, naturally held a prominent position in a city which was one of the great markets of the world.

By her geographical position, situated as she was at the point of contact between the East and the West, Constantinople was the great emporium in which the commerce of the world became centralised. Through Syria and by the Red Sea the Empire was in communication with the Far East; and either directly, or by way of the Persians, and later of the Arabs, it came into touch with Ceylon and China. Through the Black Sea and the Caspian Sea, spices, aromatic essences, and precious stones reached it from Central Asia. Towards the North trade-routes extended even to the Scandinavians and the Russians, who supplied Byzantium with furs, honey, wax, and slaves. The Byzantine merchants, Syrians, especially in the fifth and sixth centuries, and Armenians penetrated to Africa, Italy, Spain, and Gaul. Until the eleventh century the Byzantine merchant marine, under the protection of the imperial fleet, dominated the Mediterranean. Merchandise from the whole world poured into the markets of the capital. Paul the Silentiary, a poet of the sixth century, pleasantly describes the trading vessels of the universe sailing full of hope towards the queenly city, and even the winds conspiring to bring the goods which enriched her citizens. There was therefore ceaseless activity all day long in the port, alike near the Golden Horn and on the shores of the Propontis. Thither Asiatics from Trebizond and Chaldia brought their spices and perfumes, Syrians and Arabs their sumptuous silken robes and their carpets, merchants from Pontus and Cerasus their cloth, Russians their salt fish, caviar, salt, and furs, and Bulgarians their flax and honey. Western merchants, first of all from Amalfi and Venice, later from Pisa and Genoa, as well as Catalans and "Celts from beyond the Alps," played an ever-increasing part in this great business activity. From the tenth century there were special places reserved for the warehouses and colonies of the Venetians along the Golden Horn, and from the thirteenth century for the Genoese at Galata. By the liberality of the Emperors, they secured substantial reductions on the custom-house dues levied on the ingress and egress to the Dardanelles, as well as important privileges for their compatriots, and thus, from the twelfth century, they gradually became masters of all the trade of the capital, to the great discontent of the Byzantines. The economic policy of the Emperors contributed not a little to this result; Byzantium shewed scanty interest in opening commercial channels and conducting her own export trade, but took pride in seeing all the world meet on the shores of the Bosphorus, to seek precious merchandise and bring their gold. The inevitable consequence was that, in the rich market of the East, Byzantium insensibly allowed herself to be supplanted by younger and more active nations. But, in spite of this mistaken policy, Constantinople nevertheless remained throughout centuries "a great business centre," to quote the expression of Benjamin of Tudela, "whither merchants come from all countries of the world," a marvellously prosperous and wealthy city. It has been calculated that, in the twelfth century, in the city of Constantinople alone, the Emperors received from shop-rents, and market and custom-dues, the enormous annual revenue of 7,300,000 *solidi* of gold.

Finally Constantinople was a great intellectual city.

We have already alluded to the fact that, in spite of all she owed to contact with the East and to the influence of Christianity, Byzantine civilisation had remained imbued with the spirit of antiquity. In no other place in the medieval world had the classical tradition been retained so completely as in Byzantium, in no other place had direct contact with Hellenism been so well maintained. Politically, the Byzantine Empire could indeed claim the name of Rome and to be her heir, intellectually she was firmly rooted in the fertile soil of ancient Greece. In the rest of medieval Europe Greek was a foreign language, which was difficult to learn and which even the most eminent intellects for long found hard to understand. In Byzantium Greek was the national language; and this fact alone was enough to bestow on Byzantine civilisation an absolutely different aspect from that of other medieval civilisations. There, it was never necessary to discover Greek antiquity anew.

The Byzantine libraries were richly endowed with all the wealth of Greek literature, and in them there existed many works of which we have only preserved the title and the bare memory. The nature and extent of reading shewn in the works of Byzantine authors prove no less what close contact Byzantium had kept with the classical masterpieces. Greek literature was the very foundation of Byzantine education. An important place was indeed reserved for the Scriptures, the works of the Fathers, the lives of saints, and sometimes also for mathematics and music; but grammar, rhetoric, dialectic, the perusal and annotation of the classical masterpieces, were its essential features. Every cultivated person had studied Homer, "the all-wise Homer," as he was called by Tzetzes, and not only Homer but Hesiod and Pindar, the tragic poets and Aristophanes, historians such as Thucydides and Polybius, orators such as Demosthenes, the treatises of Aristotle and the dialogues of Plato, as well as Theocritus, Plutarch, Libanius, and Lucian. When we consider the extent of learning shewn by an imperial princess such as Anna Comnena, who prided herself on having studied "Hellenism from end to end," or by a man of high descent such as Photius, or by a lettered member of the middle class such as Michael Psellus, we realise what were the character and extent of this education throughout all classes of society. From the ninth to the fourteenth century the schools of Constantinople were renowned throughout the whole world, in the Arab East as in the Latin West. An author of the thirteenth century has left a picturesque sketch of the eager life led there—very like that led in the Musulman universities of the present day—and of the subtle arguments which went on all day long in the school of the Holy Apostles, between grammarians and dialecticians, doctors, mathematicians, and musicians. But above all the University of Constantinople was the incomparable home of the classical tradition.

Founded in the fifth century by the Emperor Theodosius II, reconstituted in the ninth century in the palace of Magnaura by Caesar Bardas, protected with careful solicitude by the Emperors of the tenth century, the University was an admirable school of philosophy and science. The "masters of the rhetors," who were alike grammarians, philologists, and humanists, lectured on the texts of the poets, historians, and orators of ancient Greece. The "consuls of the philosophers" studied Aristotle and Plato, and from the eleventh century onwards teachers such as Psellus and John Italus preluded that Platonic renaissance which was to be the glory of the fifteenth century in Italy. Men of science, mathematicians, astronomers, and naturalists rendered services comparable, as is declared by a good judge, to those rendered by Roger Bacon in the West. The School of Law, which had been so flourishing in the days of Justinian, was reorganised in the eleventh century. Medicine was the object of learned research. But education was mainly based on the study of the classical masterpieces. In the eleventh century Psellus interpreted the ancient texts with an enthusiasm for Athens which betrayed itself in striking and charming touches. In the twelfth century Eustathius of Thessalonica wrote commentaries on Homer and Pindar. The great professors of the days of the Palaeologi, such as Planudes, Moschopulus, and Triclinius, were admirable philologists inspired already with the spirit of humanism. Round them there flocked students drawn from every part of the Empire, and also from the Arab world and from the distant West; the success of their teaching was prodigious and its influence profound. The whole of Byzantine society in its literary tastes and its writings seems to have been imbued with the spirit of antiquity. The language used by most of the great Byzantine authors is a learned, almost artificial, language, entirely modelled on the classical masterpieces, and quite unrelated to the spoken tongue, which came to approximate more and more to its modern form. And from all this there arose a remarkable movement of thought of which Byzantine literature is the significant expression.

This is not the place in which to write the history of Byzantine literature. To indicate the position it occupied in the civilisation of the Empire, it will be enough to mention its different periods, its principal tendencies, and to describe the general features which characterised it.

In the history of ideas, as in the history of art and in political history, the sixth century was a brilliant and fruitful period, still imbued with Hellenic influence, which in history as in poetry and eloquence still appeared to be continuing the development of classical Greek literature. The grave crisis through which the Empire passed between the seventh and ninth centuries caused a notable slackening in the intellectual movement; literature then assumed an almost exclusively ecclesiastical character; this was undoubtedly the feeblest period in the history of thought in Byzantium. But after the middle of the ninth century, contact being restored with the ancient culture, a renaissance came about, simultaneously with the political renaissance experienced by the Empire under the government of the princes of the Macedonian family, and with the renaissance of art, likewise inspired by the classical tradition. The tenth century appears especially as an era of scientists and learned men, intent on compiling in vast encyclopaedias an inventory of all the intellectual riches inherited from the past. On these foundations later generations were to build. The eleventh and twelfth centuries were a period of extraordinary brilliancy in history, philosophy, and eloquence. And notwithstanding the crisis of 1204, this great activity of thought lasted until the days of the Palaeologi when, during the fourteenth and fifteenth centuries, both Byzantine literature and Byzantine art experienced an ultimate renaissance, as though, on the eve of the final catastrophe, Byzantium had gathered all her energies in a last magnificent expansion.

At every period in this great movement of ideas, history was the favourite form of expression of Byzantine thought, and in this, and in religious poetry, we find the most remarkable manifestation of the Byzantine genius. To shew the prodigious wealth and infinite variety of this class of literature it will be enough to recall the names of its most famous representatives: in the sixth century Procopius, Agathias, and Menander; in the tenth Constantine Porphyrogenitus and Leo Diaconus; in the eleventh Psellus and Michael Attaliates; in the twelfth Nicephorus Bryennius, Anna Comnena, Cinnamus, and Nicetas; in the thirteenth Acropolita and Pachymeres; in the fourteenth Nicephorus Gregoras and John Cantacuzene; and finally, in the fifteenth, Chalcondyles, Ducas, Phrantzes, and Critobulus. In addition there were chroniclers, such as Malalas in the sixth century; Theophanes and Nicephorus at the end of the eighth; George Monachus and Simeon Magister in the tenth; Scylitzes in the eleventh; and Cedrenus and Zonaras in the twelfth. If we compare some of these great historians with their contemporaries in the Latin West, we shall recognise that the Greeks are on an undoubtedly higher intellectual plane, by their political insight, the delicacy of their psychology, their sense of composition, and the quality of their language. And there are some of them, for instance Psellus, who by the picturesque precision of their descriptions, their acuteness of observation, and the raciness and humour of their style, are equal to the greatest in any literature.

This was partly because all these writers had behind them a long tradition by which they were inspired. In Byzantium history was closely allied to the classical past; in like manner theology, which, with history, was the subject which undoubtedly most interested Byzantine thought, was always dominated by the Christian past. Here again, to shew the abundance of their literature, it will be enough to mention a few names: Leontius of Neapolis in the sixth century; John Damascenus and Theodore of Studion in the eighth; Photius in the ninth; Psellus in the eleventh; Euthymius Zigabenus, Nicholas of Methone, and Nicetas Acominatus in the twelfth; during the last centuries of the Empire the great representatives of Eastern mysticism, Palamas and the two Cabasilas, and the followers of Western scholastic philosophy, Gregory Acyndinus, Demetrius Cydones, and Nicephorus Gregoras; and in the fifteenth century the adversaries and the friends of the Latins, Marcus Eugenicus, George Scholarius, and Bessarion. There were also the hagiographic writers whose work was summed up in the tenth century in the vast collection of Simeon Metaphrastes; and the masters of religious eloquence, whose most famous representatives—Photius in the ninth century, Eustathius of Thessalonica and Michael Acominatus in the twelfth—were greatly superior to most of the contemporary Western preachers. And here again it is an undoubted fact that this theological literature was, as a whole, at least until the twelfth century, greatly superior to anything similar produced by the West.

However, the powerful influence exerted on all minds by the classical or Christian past was not without drawbacks. The constant effort to adhere to classical models bestowed a singularly artificial style on historical writing. The incessant fear felt by theologians lest they should depart from the tradition of the Fathers deprived their ideas of much originality and freedom, especially after the middle of the ninth century. In spite, however, of these shackles, Byzantium was sometimes capable of creative work. It is the immortal glory of Michael Psellus that in the eleventh century he restored the Platonic doctrine to its place in education, and he inaugurated a movement of free thought which was a source of serious disquietude to the Church; and it was likewise by means of Byzantines—Gennadius, Gemistus Plethon, and Bessarion—that, in the fifteenth century, the West became acquainted with Platonic thought. It is the immortal glory of Romanus, "*le premier des mélodes*," that, at the dawn of the sixth century, by his hymns full of ardent inspiration, heartfelt sincerity, and intense dramatic power, he created that school of religious poetry which is indeed the most personal expression of the Byzantine genius. It is the glory of the philologists of the fourteenth century that, as we have seen, they initiated the great movement towards humanism. Many other instances might be cited to shew alike the variety and creative power of this literature. It must however be admitted that as a whole, in spite of the real talent of many of its writers, it often lacks freshness, spontaneity, and life, and that, being almost the exclusive property of the learned, it very quickly became more and more unintelligible to the mass of the Greek people.

It was exactly for this reason that, little by little, the spoken language found a place in literature, and here a masterpiece made its appearance. This was the popular epic, a cycle of *chansons de geste*, of which the poem of Digenes Akritas is the most celebrated example, and which about the eleventh century collected round the name of some national hero. In this epic poetry, as in religious poetry, Byzantium owed nothing to ancient models. Its form and language were new, it had its roots in the depths of the Byzantine soul, the Christian soul of the people; thence it derived its freshness of inspiration and of thought. It also proves, with other works, that in spite of its close dependence on the past, in spite of the learned and artificial style which it too often assumed, Byzantine literature, alike by the free circulation of ideas which it exhibits and the creative originality which it often displayed, deserves a place in the history of Byzantine civilisation.

Byzantine art was one of the most brilliant expressions of Byzantine civilisation, and also one of the most characteristic. Everywhere in it we find that love of stupendous luxury and of prodigious splendour which Byzantium displayed at every period of her history. In the decoration of churches and palaces it is always the same story—precious marbles, glittering mosaics, magnificent work in gold and silver, and wonderful hangings, all intended to enhance the beauty of the rites of religion, and the majesty of the imperial person; in public and private life nothing but sumptuous tissues shot with purple and gold, finely carved ivories, bronzes inlaid with silver, richly illuminated manuscripts, enamels cloisonné in resplendent colours, gold and silver plate, and costly jewels. Whether, by decorating the walls of churches with the pageant of sacred history skilfully disposed, this art was intent on glorifying God, on expressing an article of faith, on interpreting the liturgical rites, or whether, to glorify the majesty of the sovereign and to give pleasure to the court and to the grandees, it was depicting in a more profane spirit subjects borrowed from classical history or mythology, picturesque scenes dear to Hellenistic art, as well as historical paintings, representations of imperial victories, and portraits of the princes in their glory, everywhere we find that love of magnificence which even to-day makes us visualise Byzantium in a jewelled iridescence, in a shimmer of gold.

It must not, however, be thought that, as is too often said, this art was a lifeless and monotonous one, incapable of transformation or renewal. Like Byzantine literature it remained, indeed, firmly attached to classical tradition and constantly returned to classical models for fresh sources of inspiration and occasionally for fresh methods. Like the whole of Byzantine civilisation it had, indeed, been greatly influenced by the East, and had thence derived a taste for realism and colour, and it had received an even deeper imprint from Christianity, which, while using it for the service of the Church, also brought it under her guardianship and subjection. Because of all this, and also because it was essentially an official art, Byzantine art often lacked freshness, spontaneity, and life; it was often both an imitation and a copy; in its excessive attachment to tradition, and docility to the Church, it too often and too quickly translated its most fertile discoveries into immutable formulas. Nevertheless the fact remains that this art shewed itself capable of creation, that at least twice in the course of its thousand years' existence it succeeded in regaining a new vigour and experiencing an unlooked-for revival, and that by combining the various tendencies under whose influence it had come it succeeded in assuming an original form "responding to the real genius of the people."

Justinian's reign marks the decisive moment when, after a long period of preparation and experiment, Byzantine art found its definitive formula and at the same time attained its apogee. "At this moment," says Choisy with much discrimination, "the evolution was complete. All the methods of construction were fixed, all types of buildings had been produced and were being applied at the same time, without exclusion or prejudice; the polygonal design found new life in St Sergius at Constantinople and San Vitale at Ravenna; the basilican form recurs in the church of the Mother of God in Jerusalem; the cruciform plan with five domes appears in the reconstruction of the church of the Holy Apostles; St Sophia in Salonica presents the type of a church with a central dome, of which the churches of Athos and Greece are only variants." Finally, St Sophia at Constantinople, a marvel of science and audacity, is the original and magnificent masterpiece of the new style. In these buildings, so varied in type and plan, in which the creative fertility of Byzantine art shews itself, a sumptuous decoration clothes the walls with many-coloured marbles and dazzling mosaics with backgrounds of blue and gold, such as are to be seen in Sant' Apollinare Nuovo or in San Vitale at Ravenna, and at Parenzo in Istria, or such as could be seen at St Demetrius in Salonica before the fire of 1917. These same tendencies—love of luxury, and a combination of the classical spirit and Eastern realism—are revealed in all the works of this period, in the miniatures which illustrate the Genesis and the Dioscorides in Vienna, the Joshua and the Cosmas at the Vatican, the Bible of Florence, the Gospels of Rossano, in the ivories, and in the tissues; everywhere we find this striving after decorative effect, this love for brilliant colours, this eagerness for pomp and majesty, which bestow such imposing beauty on the monuments of this age.

This was the first golden age of Byzantine art. But this great effort was no transitory one. After the iconoclastic crisis, there was a magnificent revival from the tenth to the twelfth century in the days of the Macedonian Emperors and the Comneni. Under the influence of the recovered classical and secular tradition Byzantium then experienced a marvellous efflorescence of art. Unfortunately nothing is left of the Imperial Palace, nor of the *Nea*, the "New" basilica which was one of the masterpieces of the new style. But the little churches in Constantinople, Salonica, and Greece are enough to shew how Byzantine architects succeeded in making charming and ingenious variations on the plan of a Greek cross, and how they sought inspiration sometimes in simple lines, sometimes in harmonious complexity, in the picturesque effects taught by the Hellenistic tradition or in the austere and grave ideal, with large masses and firm lines, derived from the Eastern tradition. The mosaics of St Luke in Phocis and of Daphni in Attica in their admirable blending of colour and decorative effect reveal the skilful arrangement of this iconography, an achievement alike artistic and theological, which devoted profound thought to the inspiration and scheme of the decorations in sacred edifices, and which was one of the most remarkable creations of the Byzantine genius. The same mastery is visible in the beautiful manuscripts illuminated for the Emperors, the Gregory Nazianzene and the Psalter of Paris, the Menologium in the Vatican, the Psalter of Venice, and in all the examples of the minor arts, such as ivory triptychs, reliquaries or bindings set with enamels, the figured or embroidered silken stuffs. No doubt during this second golden age, under the influence of theology, art sacrificed a great deal to decorum, to discipline, and to respect for tradition. Nevertheless there is evident, especially in the imperial and secular art of which there remain only too few examples, a search for the picturesque, an often realistic observation of life, and a feeling for colour, which shew a continual desire for renewal, and foreshadow the evolution whence was derived the last renaissance of Byzantine art during the fourteenth and fifteenth centuries.

The mosaics of Qahrīye-jāmiʻ, the frescoes at Mistra, the churches in Athos, Macedonia, Serbia, and Russia bear witness to the marvellous expansion which Byzantine art experienced in the days of the Palaeologi. Once again Byzantine art was transformed; it became living, picturesque, dramatic, emotional, and charming; its iconography became enriched and renewed itself, more pathetic and more impassioned; its skilful and harmonious use of colour seems almost impressionistic. Schools were formed and works comparable to the creations of the Italian Primitives were produced.

In the course of its thousand years' history, the Byzantine monarchy experienced many unexpected and striking revivals, in which, according to the phrase of one chronicler, "that old mother, the Empire, appeared like a young girl adorned with gold and precious stones." Byzantine art underwent similar experiences; it also became transformed and renovated. And Constantinople, which, as Rambaud has justly remarked, was more than once in the course of her long history herself the whole Empire, and which, on the very brink of the catastrophe which threatened destruction, succeeded in striking out a path of salvation and renewed life, likewise represents by the monuments which are preserved the evolution and greatness of Byzantine art. St Sophia and the other monuments of Justinian's reign, the charming churches of the period of the Macedonians and the Comneni, and the mosaics of Qahrīye-jāmiʻ, testify to the splendour and the transformations of this art, and, in spite of the loss of so many other monuments, are enough to shew what a marvellously artistic city she was, and why for centuries she appeared as the real centre of the civilised world.

IV.

Constantinople was not the only great city in the Empire. All round the shores of the Eastern Mediterranean, at the termini of the known and frequented trade-routes, flourishing towns were to be found, active centres of exchange, at which were gathered the merchants and merchandise of the whole world. Among them, until the seventh century when they were taken from the Empire by the Arab conquest, were Alexandria in Egypt and the Syrian ports. Later there were the great cities of Asia Minor, Tarsus, Ephesus, Smyrna, Phocaea, and Trebizond, which last was from the thirteenth to the fifteenth century to be the capital of a powerful state. In Europe there was Thessalonica, which was, after Constantinople, the most important economic centre of the European provinces and which boasted that it was particularly dear to the Emperor's heart. There, every year at the end of October, on the occasion of the feast of St Demetrius, the patron and celestial protector of the city, was held a famous fair in the plain of the Vardar, to which for business transactions there resorted Greeks and Slavs, Italians and Spaniards, "Celts from beyond the Alps," and men who came from the distant shores of the Atlantic. In this great city of commerce and wealth, sumptuous churches testified to the riches of the inhabitants and their love of magnificence; of these the most famous was the basilica of St Demetrius. In many provinces of the Empire, a flourishing industry was engaged in the manufacture of those articles of luxury which were the glory of Byzantine work-shops. Thebes, Corinth, and Patras were famous for their silks; Thessalonica was renowned for its activity in the arts of smelting and metal-work. Heavy gold brocade, magnificent silken stuffs dyed in dark violet or in bright purple and covered with embroidery, fine linens, marvellous goldsmith's work, cloisonné enamel, elegant glass-work, all came from the hands of Byzantine artisans. And it was to this industrial and commercial activity that the Byzantine Empire, the economic centre of the Eastern world, owed long centuries of prodigious wealth.

This was not, however, the most original and noteworthy feature which Byzantine civilisation presented in the provinces. All through the Empire, but especially in the Asiatic provinces, were to be found vast domains whose proprietors, with their retinue of clients, vassals, and soldiers, led an entirely feudal existence on their estates. Very early, both in the Byzantine East and in the Latin West, a twofold social phenomenon was observable. In the general insecurity of a troubled time the obscure, the poor, and the weak sought the patronage (*patrocinium*) of some powerful and wealthy neighbour, and in return for the advantages they reaped from this protection, they bartered their liberty and became the clients and vassals of the great noble who was to defend them. On the other hand the great landowners, the "powerful" (δυνατοί) as they were called, made use of their power to increase their lands at the expense of the small landholders; and thus small independent holdings disappeared at the same time as the freemen.

On the enormous estates which thus came into existence lived those great feudal families whose names fill Byzantine history. In Asia there were the Phocas, Scleri, Dalasseni, Ducas, Comneni, and Palaeologi; in Europe the Bryennii, Melisseni, Cantacuzenes, and many others. Very rich from the lands they possessed and which they were constantly augmenting by their usurpations, very powerful from the number of clients and vassals whom they collected round them, they added to these causes of influence the prestige of the high offices which the Emperor entrusted to them, and they increased their riches by the salaries and endowments which the government distributed among them. It was amongst these great nobles indeed that the Basileus found his best servants and his most illustrious generals. But, in spite of the services it rendered, this landed aristocracy created a formidable danger for the Empire. A serious social question arose from the ninth century onwards in the Byzantine world confronted by the two classes, the "powerful" (δυνατοί) and the "poor" (πένητες).

The disappearance of the free peasant had the effect of robbing the State of taxable material, necessary for a satisfactory state of the finances; the disappearance of the small freeholds, especially of those military fiefs which the Emperors had established as one of the bases of recruiting, robbed the army, of which the hardy peasants were the essential nucleus, of its best soldiers. To defend the small holdings and the middle class of small peasant proprietors, and to check the usurpations of the "powerful," the Emperors of the ninth and tenth centuries struggled energetically and even violently with the great feudal barons, and for a time, during the reign of Basil II, it seemed as though they had conquered. But it was only in appearance. From the eleventh century the aristocracy raised its head once more and took its revenge. When, at the beginning of the thirteenth century, the Latins conquered the Byzantine Empire, they easily identified the Greek *archon* with the Western baron, and the peasant tied to the land (πάροικος) with the *villeins* they had at home. And indeed the place occupied in this apparently absolute monarchy by feudalism was not the least curious nor the least surprising thing in the history of Byzantium.

Nor was this all. By the fact of regional recruiting, the soldiers who were placed under the command of these great nobles in the army were very often their clients and vassals in civil life; they knew their leaders, their illustrious descent, their wealth, and their exploits; they appreciated their liberality and the value of their protection. These soldiers therefore displayed whole-hearted devotion and fidelity to their generals; they obeyed these leaders whom they admired much more readily than the distant Emperor. Moreover, although the great barons were generally faithful subjects, they were always unruly ones; they treated the Emperor almost as an equal; they considered that they had a right to give him advice, and were very much surprised if he did not follow it in every particular. Finally, a firm solidarity arising from community of interests, reinforced by numerous family marriages and maintained by a common life of exploits and dangers, united the members of this aristocracy. Entrenched in their impregnable castles, proud of their wealth, their popularity, and their prestige, these great feudal lords were therefore quite naturally inclined to lay down the law to the Emperor, to express their dissatisfaction, or to manifest their ambition by formidable insurrections. The second half of the tenth century was full of these great feudal insurrections, with which are associated the names of Bardas Phocas and Bardas Sclerus, and which caused such serious trouble to the Byzantine Empire. There we see what close bonds of devotion and fidelity united the great barons and the men of their native province, how community of interests and of sentiments made all these *archons* into one caste, and what proud and magnificent figures were produced by this aristocratic Byzantine society.

The epic of Digenes Akritas gives a good picture of the life of these great Asiatic barons, a life of luxury, wealth, and splendour; the beauty of their palaces built in the midst of gardens and glittering with jewels and gold and with shining mosaics; the marvellous feasts which were given in these castles, the unparalleled extravagance of costume and arms, the great hunting expeditions, the adventures in love and in war, and the wonderful exploits of which their life was full. There also is shewn the independent temper of these great barons; and above all we realise the violent and brutal, chivalrous and heroic, existence which was led on the frontiers of Asia, subject to the perpetual menace of a Muslim invasion and to the constant care for the defence of the Empire and the Orthodox religion. It was a land of fine feats of arms, of single combats, abductions, pillage, massacres, adventure, war. No doubt the epic has embellished it with a touch of the marvellous; it has adorned with grace and courtesy the real and permanent background of brutality and cruelty which characterised this society. Nevertheless it explains how good a preparation for life and for warfare this rough existence was to these men of the provinces, and how it enabled these indefatigable warriors to become the real strength of the monarchy.

The provinces, and especially the Asiatic provinces, supplied the Empire with its best soldiers and with the greater part of the crews for the fleet. The themes of Anatolia, as has been said, "really formed the Roman Empire." When contrasted with the capital, the Byzantine provinces appear as a hardy element, healthy and strong, with their rough peasants, their tenants of military fiefs (*καβαλλάριοι*), and their great nobles marvellously trained for war from boyhood. These men indeed had their faults and they were often dangerous to the Empire. The curious little book in which one of them, Cecaumenus, towards the middle of the eleventh century summed up the lessons of his long experience, and of his realistic and somewhat disillusioned wisdom, reveals them as rather mistrustful of the capital as too refined, too elegant, and of the court as too fertile in humiliations and disgraces. They lived on their estates and were eager to enrich themselves; as loyal and faithful subjects they served in the army; above all, they wished to remain independent. But such as they were, they were the strength of the Empire. As long as Byzantium was mistress of Asia, she was strong militarily and economically. When, at the end of the eleventh century, she lost the greater part of Anatolia, it was a terrible blow from which the Empire never recovered.

V.

We must now seek to ascertain from the sources at our disposal what was the mentality of the medieval Greeks, and to discover the general character, so complex and complicated, of the Byzantine mind. We have already described some of the dominant tastes of this society, the place held by religion both in public and private life, the love of shows, of ceremonies, of the games in the circus, the taste for intrigue and for magnificence; we have referred to the industrial and commercial activity, the stout military energy, and above all the intellectual superiority which characterised it. To arrive at a complete understanding of the Byzantine character, we must also remember of how many different elements and how many different races this medieval Greek society was composed. Situated on the borders of Asia and Europe, and subject alike to the influences of the Persian and Arabian East and the infiltration of all the Northern barbarians, this society was essentially cosmopolitan. Here Slavs, Thracians, Armenians, Caucasians, Italians, and Arabs met and mingled; certain races, such as Slavs and Armenians, at certain moments exercised a preponderating influence. By the prestige and power of her civilisation Byzantium indeed succeeded in assimilating and transforming these apparently opposed and refractory elements, and such was the strength of the classical tradition with which this society was imbued that Hellenism stamped its impress deep on all these foreigners, and that Greek, the language of the Church, of the administration, and of the literature, acquired, as has been said by Rambaud, "a false air of being the national language" in the Byzantine Empire. But under this common stamp there existed many contrasts, and the Byzantine mind presented a mixture, often contradictory and sometimes disconcerting, of high qualities and startling vices.

In many ways the Byzantine was an Oriental. As we have seen, he delighted in magnificent spectacles; it did not displease him if these spectacles were bloody and savage. We know the atrocity of Byzantine punishments, the refinements of torture with which the people wreaked their anger on their victims. By contact with the East these Greeks acquired a cruel mentality; they were pitiless as they were unscrupulous; they delighted in alternations of bloodshed, sensuality, and death. When their passions were aroused, when their anger was excited, when their religious or political hatred was unloosed, these nervous and impressionable people were capable of all kinds of violence. And like the Turks of the present day, whom they resemble in many particulars, these same men, when cool, shewed themselves to be gifted with strong qualities and real virtues. Among the Byzantine middle class, as depicted by Psellus, and even among the aristocracy, we find charming examples of the close ties of family life. But in these same exquisite minds there was sometimes to be found a singular hardness of heart, and their religious preoccupation encouraged in them a lack of balance and steadiness, and a mystic exaltation, which rendered them dangerous to handle.

But, although they were akin to the East, the Byzantines were also Greeks, keenly interested in all things of the mind, curious about enquiries and subtleties of all kinds, and generally intelligent to a very high degree. Like true Greeks, they delighted in the refinements of argument, applying the methods of ancient sophistry to religious matters with a passionate ardour. They delighted in words; in their eyes eloquence was always the supreme virtue. And they also delighted in gossip, in raillery, and in abuse, whether it were vulgar or witty. But although they were thereby indeed the heirs of the Athenians of Aristophanes, Christianity had given another direction to these tendencies. The Byzantines believed in miracles, in soothsayers, in magic, in astrology; they lived in an atmosphere of exalted mysticism, and when their piety was involved, they were prepared to sacrifice everything, even their country, to their desire to prove their case and triumph in the controversy.

Under this twofold influence a very complex character became formed. In great moments indeed—and these were frequent—the Byzantines were capable of valour, of delicacy, of disinterestedness, of devotion. There were many very worthy men in Byzantine society. Nevertheless the morality of most was indifferent, or even doubtful. In spite of the apparently severe segregation of feminine life, there was great corruption in the Greek world of the Middle Ages. The administration, in spite of the great services it rendered to the State, was honeycombed with vices. As places were sold, so were favours and justice. To make a fortune and gain advancement, merit was of less use than intrigue, and even among the best, by the side of undeniable good qualities, there is visible an eager pursuit of selfish aims, whether of pleasure or of adventure, wealth or power, and a manner of conducting life which left too much scope for skilful acuteness, for successful cunning, and for cleverly calculated treachery. And this explains why these supple and subtle Greeks, in spite of their real virtues, were always regarded with distrust by the blunt and straightforward Latins, and why so many lamentable prejudices arose in the West against Byzantium which have survived to the present day.

What is specially noticeable in the Byzantines, who were as extraordinarily ardent for good as for evil, is a frequent lack of balance and steadiness, and above all a striking discrepancy between their intelligence, which is unquestionable and often admirable, and their character, which was not up to the level of their mentality. We feel that they were overburdened by their past, that their energies were soon exhausted, and that they were wanting in moral principles. Whether we consider Psellus, who was certainly one of the most remarkable men produced by Byzantium, and the most finished type of courtier, or, in a somewhat different social grade, John Cantacuzene, or again Andronicus Comnenus, or a provincial mind such as is revealed in the writings of Cecaumenus—everywhere we find the same characteristics: a prudent cleverness untroubled by idle scruples, a wary caution bordering on cunning, unmeasured ambitions and vile intrigues, a subtle intelligence which is not supported by moral principles. But although demoralisation was undoubted and deep-seated, the Byzantines were always supremely talented. Compared with the barbarians who surrounded them, these ingenious and cultivated Greeks, who reflected on complex and difficult themes and speculations, and who knew how to express their thoughts in fine language, who were capable of comprehending and discussing the most delicate problems, who understood how to resolve all the difficulties of life with elegant ingenuity, and who moreover were not hampered by idle scruples, seem like men of a higher race, like educators and masters. It was for this reason that Byzantine civilisation exercised such profound influence on the whole medieval world, as much by its external splendour as by its innate value, and that it rendered eminent services alike to the Arabs and Slavs in the East and to the Latins in the West.

VI.

To the Slav and Oriental world Byzantium was what Rome has been to the Western and Germanic world, that is to say the great educator, the great initiator, the bringer both of religion and of civilisation. She supplied the Serbs, Croats, Bulgars, and Russians, not only with the Orthodox faith but with all the elements of their future greatness, the conception of government, the principles of law, the forms of more refined life and of intellectual and artistic culture. Byzantium gave the Slavs their alphabet and their literary language on the day when Cyril and Methodius, "the Apostles of the Slavs," translated the Scriptures into a Slavonic dialect for the use of the Moravians whom they were about to convert, and invented the Glagolitic script in which to write their translation. Not only by her missionaries but also by her architects who built churches for the new converts and her artists who decorated them with mosaics and frescoes, Byzantium brought historic life and civilisation to all the Slav nations of the East; over all of these and also over the nations of the Asiatic East, the Armenians and even the Arabs, she exercised supremacy to a greater or lesser degree, by means of her literature, her art, her laws, her religion. To all of them she presented a marvellous model; and thereby Byzantium accomplished a very great work in the general history of civilisation.

To the West she also gave many things. For centuries, as we know, the Greek Empire possessed more or less important parts of Italy, and the imperial government made so great and successful an effort to assimilate its Italian subjects, that even under the Norman and Angevin kings the peninsula seemed like a new Magna Graecia. We have referred to the active relations which Syrian and Byzantine merchants maintained in the Western Mediterranean and the numerous establishments founded there by Greek monks. We have called special attention to the marvellous prestige which the imperial city enjoyed among Western peoples, and how all works of art which were difficult of execution or of rare quality were sought in Constantinople. The close relations established by the Crusades led to yet greater knowledge of the Byzantine world. From this incessant contact the West derived enormous intellectual benefit.

It was from Byzantium that there came the knowledge of the Justinianean Law, and the masters who taught it in Bologna from the close of the eleventh century played no small part in spreading the principles from which jurists derived absolute monarchy and divine right. It was from Byzantium that there came the great artistic movement which, between the fifth and seventh centuries, created the monuments in Ravenna and Rome, and which later, in the eleventh and twelfth centuries, made the splendour of Venice and of Norman Sicily. St Mark's, which is a reproduction of the church of the Holy Apostles in Constantinople, with its five domes, the richness of its marbles, metal-work, and mosaics, the gleam of the purple and gold which illuminate it, offers the most exact picture of Byzantium as she was in the days of the Macedonian renaissance. The mosaics at Cefalù, in the Capella Palatina at Palermo, in the Martorana Church, and at Monreale are admirable examples of the genius of Byzantine artists. For centuries Byzantine art was, as has been said, "the standard art of Europe," and in the Middle Ages only Gothic art was capable of an equally vast and fruitful growth. Both the Carolingian and the Ottonian renaissance were infinitely indebted to Byzantium; Romanesque architecture and decoration were inspired by Byzantine lessons and models far more than is generally believed. No doubt the capture of Constantinople by the Crusaders in 1204 and the half-century of Latin supremacy which followed were a serious blow for the Greek capital and for Byzantine civilisation from which politically the Empire never recovered. But even though under the Palaeologi decadence was evident, Constantinople still remained a wonderful city, and the Greek world still retained part of its intellectual and artistic superiority. The Italian Primitives of the Trecento were in many ways Byzantines. It was in the school of Byzantium that fourteenth-century Italy learnt Greek; the great professors in the days of the Palaeologi were the initiators of the revival of Greek studies, and they contributed in no small measure to prepare the great movement of humanism. Finally, it was from Byzantium, which from the eleventh century had restored it to a place in education, that Italy learnt the Platonic philosophy. And though indeed it is an exaggeration to say, as has been done, that without Byzantium the world would perhaps never have known the Renaissance, it is at least undeniable that Byzantium played a great part in bringing it to pass, and that, by the services it rendered to the European world as well as by its own brilliancy, Byzantine civilisation deserves an eminent place in the history of thought, of art, and of humanity.

LIST OF ABBREVIATIONS OF TITLES OF PERIODICALS, SOCIETIES, ETC.

(1) The following abbreviations are used for titles of periodicals:

AB. Analecta Bollandiana. Brussels.
AHR. American Historical Review. New York and London.
AKKR. Archiv für katholisches Kirchenrecht. Mayence.
AMur. Archivio Muratoriano. Rome.
Arch. Ven. (and N. Arch. Ven.; Arch. Ven.-Tri.). Archivio veneto. Venice. 40 vols. 1871–90. Continued as Nuovo archivio veneto. 1st series. 20 vols. 1891–1900. New series. 42 vols. 1901–1921. And Archivio veneto-tridentino. 1922 ff., in progress.
ASAK. Anzeiger für schweizerische Alterthumskunde. Zurich.
ASHF. Annuaire-Bulletin de la Société de l'histoire de France. Paris.
ASI. Archivio storico italiano. Florence. Ser. I. 20 v. and App. 9 v. 1842–53. Index. 1857. Ser. nuova. 18 v. 1855–63. Ser. III. 26 v. 1865–77. Indexes to II and III. 1874. Suppt. 1877. Ser. IV. 20 v. 1878–87. Index. 1891. Ser. V. 49 v. 1888–1912. Index. 1900. Anni 71 etc. 1913 ff., in progress. (Index in Catalogue of The London Library vol. I. 1913.)
ASL. Archivio storico lombardo. Milan.
ASPN. Archivio storico per le province napoletane. Naples. 1876 ff.
ASRSP. Archivio della Società romana di storia patria. Rome.
BISI. Bullettino dell' Istituto storico italiano. Rome. 1886 ff.
BRAH. Boletin de la R. Academia de la historia. Madrid.
BZ. Byzantinische Zeitschrift. Leipsic. 1892 ff.
CQR. Church Quarterly Review. London.
CR. Classical Review. London.
DZG. Deutsche Zeitschrift für Geschichtswissenschaft. Freiburg-im-Breisgau.
DZKR. Deutsche Zeitschrift für Kirchenrecht. Leipsic.
EHR. English Historical Review. London.
FDG. Forschungen zur deutschen Geschichte. Göttingen.
HJ. Historisches Jahrbuch. Munich.
HVJS. Historische Vierteljahrsschrift. Leipsic.
HZ. Historische Zeitschrift (von Sybel). Munich and Berlin.
JA. Journal Asiatique. Paris.
JB. Jahresberichte der Geschichtswissenschaft im Auftrage der historischen Gesellschaft zu Berlin. Berlin. 1878 ff.
JHS. Journal of Hellenic Studies. London.
JRAS. Journal of the Royal Asiatic Society of Great Britain. London.
JSG. Jahrbuch für schweizerische Geschichte. Zurich.
JTS. Journal of Theological Studies. London.
MA. Le moyen âge. Paris.
MIOGF. Mittheilungen des Instituts für österreichische Geschichtsforschung. Innsbruck.
Neu. Arch. Neues Archiv der Gesellschaft für ältere deutsche Geschichtskunde Hanover and Leipsic.
NRDF. Nouvelle Revue historique du droit français. Paris.
QFIA. Quellen und Forschungen aus italienischen Archiven und Bibliotheken. Rome.
RA. Revue archéologique. Paris.

RBén. Revue bénédictine. Maredsous.
RCHL. Revue critique d'histoire et de littérature. Paris.
RH. Revue historique. Paris.
RHD. Revue d'histoire diplomatique. Paris.
RHE. Revue d'histoire ecclésiastique. Louvain.
Rhein. Mus. Rheinisches Museum für Philologie. Frankfort-on-Main.
RN. Revue de numismatique. Paris.
RQCA. Römische Quartalschrift für christliche Altertumskunde und Kirchengeschichte. Rome.
RQH. Revue des questions historiques. Paris.
RSH. Revue de synthèse historique. Paris.
RSI. Rivista storica italiana. Turin. *See Gen. Bibl.* I.
SKAW. Sitzungsberichte der Kaiserlichen Akademie der Wissenschaften. Vienna. [Philos.-hist. Classe.]
SPAW. Sitzungsberichte der kön. preussischen Akademie der Wissenschaften. Berlin.
TRHS. Transactions of the Royal Historical Society. London.
VV. Vizantiyski Vremennik (Βυζαντινὰ Χρονικά). St Petersburg (Petrograd). 1894 ff.
ZCK. Zeitschrift für christliche Kunst. Düsseldorf.
ZDMG. Zeitschrift der deutschen morgenländischen Gesellschaft. Leipsic.
ZKG. Zeitschrift für Kirchengeschichte. Gotha.
ZKT. Zeitschrift für katholische Theologie. Gotha.
ZMNP. Zhurnal ministerstva narodnago prosvêshcheniya (Journal of the Ministry of Public Instruction). St Petersburg.
ZR. Zeitschrift für Rechtsgeschichte. Weimar. 1861–78. Continued as
ZSR. Zeitschrift der Savigny-Stiftung für Rechtswissenschaft. Weimar. 1880 ff.
ZWT. Zeitschrift für wissenschaftliche Theologie. Frankfort-on-Main.

(2) Other abbreviations used are:

AcadIBL. Académie des Inscriptions et Belles-Lettres.
AcadIP. Académie Impériale de Pétersbourg.
AllgDB. Allgemeine deutsche Biographie. *See Gen. Bibl.* I.
ASBen. *See* Mabillon and Achery *in Gen. Bibl.* IV.
ASBoll. Acta Sanctorum Bollandiana. *See Gen. Bibl.* IV.
BEC. Bibliothèque de l'École des Chartes. *See Gen. Bibl.* I.
BGén. Nouvelle Biographie générale. *See Gen. Bibl.* I.
BHE. Bibliothèque de l'École des Hautes Études. *See Gen. Bibl.* I.
Bouquet. *See* Rerum Gallicarum...scriptores *in Gen. Bibl.* IV.
BUniv. Biographie universelle. *See Gen. Bibl.* I.
Coll. textes. Collection des textes pour servir à l'étude et à l'enseignement de l'histoire. *See Gen. Bibl.* IV.
CSCO. Corpus scriptorum christianorum orientalium. *See Gen. Bibl.* IV.
CSEL. Corpus scriptorum ecclesiasticorum latinorum. *See Gen. Bibl.* IV.
CSHB. Corpus scriptorum historiae Byzantinae. *See Gen. Bibl.* IV.
DNB. Dictionary of National Biography. *See Gen. Bibl.* I.
EcfrAR. Écoles françaises d'Athènes et de Rome. Paris.
EncBr. Encyclopaedia Britannica. *See Gen. Bibl.* I.
Ersch-Gruber. Ersch and Gruber's Allgemeine Encyklopädie. *See Gen. Bibl.* I.
Fonti. Fonti per la storia d'Italia. *See Gen. Bibl.* IV.
Jaffé. *See Gen. Bibl.* IV.
KAW. Kaiserliche Akademie der Wissenschaften. Vienna.
Mansi. *See Gen. Bibl.* IV.
MEC. Mémoires et documents publ. par l'École des Chartes. *See Gen. Bibl.* IV.
MGH. Monumenta Germaniae Historica. *See Gen. Bibl.* IV.
MHP. Monumenta historiae patriae. Turin. *See Gen. Bibl.* IV.
MHSM. Monumenta spectantia historiam Slavorum meridionalium. *See Gen. Bibl.* IV.
MPG. Migne's Patrologiae cursus completus. Ser. graeco-latina. [Greek texts with Latin translations in parallel columns.] *See Gen. Bibl.* IV.

MPL.	Migne's Patrologiae cursus completus. Ser. latina. *See Gen. Bibl.* IV.
PAW.	Königliche preussische Akademie d. Wissenschaften. Berlin.
RAH.	Real Academia de la Historia. Madrid.
RC.	Record Commissioners.
RE^3.	Real-Encyklopädie für protestantische Theologie, etc. *See* Herzog and Hauck *in Gen. Bibl.* I.
Rec. hist. Cr.	Recueil des historiens des Croisades. *See Gen. Bibl.* IV.
RGS.	Royal Geographical Society.
RHS.	Royal Historical Society.
Rolls.	Rerum Britannicarum medii aevi scriptores. *See Gen. Bibl.* IV.
RR.II.SS.	*See* Muratori *in Gen. Bibl.* IV.
SGUS.	Scriptores rerum Germanicarum in usum scholarum. *See* Monumenta Germaniae Historica *in Gen. Bibl.* IV.
SHF.	Société d'histoire française.
SRD.	Scriptores rerum Danicarum medii aevi. *See Gen. Bibl.* IV.

Abh.	Abhandlungen.	mem.	memoir.
antiq.	antiquarian, antiquaire.	mém.	mémoire.
app.	appendix.	n.s.	new series.
coll.	collection.	publ.	published, publié.
diss.	dissertation.	R. / r.	reale.
hist.	history, historical, historique, historisch.	roy.	royal, royale.
Jahrb.	Jahrbuch.	ser.	series.
k.	kaiserlich. / königlich.	soc.	society, société, società.
		Viert.	Vierteljahrschrift.

GENERAL BIBLIOGRAPHY.

I. DICTIONARIES, BIBLIOGRAPHIES, AND GENERAL WORKS OF REFERENCE.

For modern historical works, co-operate or in series, see Section V.

Allgemeine deutsche Biographie (histor. Kommission bei d. kön. Akademie der Wissenschaften zu München). Ed. Liliencron, R. von, and Wegele, F. X. Leipsic. 1875–1910. (AllgDB.)

Allgemeine Geschichte in Einzeldarstellungen. Ed. Oncken, W. Berlin. 1879–93. (Series by various writers, *cf. sub nom.*)

Annuario bibliografico della storia d' Italia. 1902 ff.

Balzani, U. Le cronache italiane del Medio Evo. 3rd edn. Milan. 1909.

Bernheim, Ernst. Lehrbuch der historischen Methode und der Geschichtsphilosophie. (5th and 6th enlarged edn.) Leipsic. 1908.

Bibliothèque de l'École des Chartes. Paris. 1839–1900. (BEC.)

Bibliothèque de l'École des Hautes Études. Paris. 1839 ff. (BHE.)

Biographie nationale de Belgique. Brussels. 1866, in progress. Acad. Roy. des sciences, des lettres, et des beaux arts.

Biographie universelle, ancienne et moderne. (Michaud.) Paris. 1854–65. 45 vols. [Greatly improved edn. of earlier work, 1811–28, and supplement, 1832–62.] (BUniv.)

Cabrol, F. Dictionnaire d'archéologie chrétienne et de liturgie. Paris. 1907 ff., in progress.

Capasso, B. Le fonti della storia delle provincie napolitane dal 568 al 1500. Ed. Mastrojanni, E. O. Naples. 1902.

Ceillier, R. Histoire générale des auteurs sacrés et ecclésiastiques. 23 vols. Paris. 1729–63. New edn. 14 vols. in 15. Paris. 1858–69.

Chevalier, C. U. J. Répertoire des sources historiques du moyen âge. Bio-bibliographie. Paris. 1883–8. Rev. edn. 2 vols. 1905–7. Topo-bibliographie. Montbéliard. 1894–1903.

Dahlmann, F. C. and Waitz, G. Quellenkunde der deutschen Geschichte. 8th edn. Herre, P. Leipsic. 1912.

Dictionary of National Biography. Ed. Stephen, L. and Lee, S. 63 vols. London. 1885–1901. 2nd edn. 22 vols. 1908–9. 1st supplt. 3 vols. 1901. 2nd supplt. 3 vols. 1912. (DNB.)

Du Cange, C. du Fresne. Glossarium ad scriptores mediae et infimae Latinitatis. Edns. of Henschel, 7 vols., Paris, 1840–50, and Favre, 10 vols., Niort, 1883–7.

—— Glossarium ad scriptores mediae et infimae Graecitatis. 2 vols. Lyons. 1688.

Encyclopaedia Britannica. 11th and 12th edn. 32 vols. Cambridge. London and New York. 1910–22. (EncBr.)

Encyclopaedia of Islam. A dictionary of the geography, ethnography, and biography of the Muhammadan peoples. Ed. Houtsma, M. T., Arnold, T. W., and Basset, R. Leiden and London. 1913 ff., in progress.

Ersch, J. S. and Gruber, J. G. Allgemeine Encyklopädie der Wissenschaften und Künste. Berlin. 1818–90. (Ersch-Gruber.) [Incomplete.]

Giry, A. Manuel de diplomatique. Paris. 1894.

Gröber, G. Grundriss der romanischen Philologie. 2 vols. Strasbourg. 1888–1902. 2nd edn. Vol. I. 1904–6.

Gross, C. Sources and Literature of English History from the earliest times to about 1485. London. 1900. 2nd edn. enl. 1915.

Hastings, J. and Selbie, J. A. Encyclopaedia of Religion and Ethics. Edinburgh and New York. 12 vols. 1908–21.

Herre, P., Hofmeister, A., and Stübe, R. Quellenkunde zur Weltgeschichte. Leipsic. 1910.
Herzog, J. J. and Hauck, A. Real-Encyklopädie für protestantische Theologie und Kirche. 3rd edn. 24 vols. Leipsic. 1896–1913. (RE[3].)
Keene, H. G. An Oriental Biographical Dictionary, founded on materials collected by Beale, T. W. New and revised edn. London. 1894.
Krumbacher, K. Geschichte der byzantinischen Literatur. *See below*, v.
Lees, B. A. Bibliography of Mediaeval History. (400–1500.) London. 1917. (Historical Assoc. Leaflet 44.)
Lichtenberger, F. Encyclopédie des Sciences religieuses. 13 vols. Paris. 1877–82.
Maigne d'Arnis, W. H. Lexicon manuale ad scriptores mediae et infimae Latinitatis (publ. Migne). Paris. 1866.
Meister, A. Grundriss der Geschichtswissenschaft zur Einführung in das Studium der deutschen Geschichte des Mittelalters und der Neuzeit. Vol. I (1). Leipsic. 1906. Vol. I (2) and II (1–8). 1907. 2nd edn. 1912 ff., in progress.
Molinier, A. Les Sources de l'histoire de France des origines aux guerres d'Italie (1494). 6 vols. Paris. 1901–6.
Monod, G. Bibliographie de l'histoire de France. 5 vols. Paris. 1901–4.
—— Bibliographie de l'hist. de France depuis les origines jusqu'en 1789. Paris. 1888.
Nouvelle Biographie générale, depuis les temps les plus reculés jusqu'à nos jours, avec les renseignements bibliographiques. Sous la direction de J. Ch. F. Höfer. Paris. 1854–66. 46 vols. in 23. (BGén.)
Oudin, Casimir. Commentarius de scriptoribus ecclesiae antiquae illorumque scriptis tam impressis quam manuscriptis adhuc extantibus in celebrioribus Europae bibliothecis a Bellarmino, etc. omissis ad annum MCCCCLX. 3 vols. Frankfort-on-M. and Leipsic. 1722.
Paetow, L. J. Guide to the study of Medieval History (University of California Syllabus Series, No. 90). Berkeley, California. 1917.
Pastrnek, F. Bibliographische Übersicht über die slavische Philologie, 1876–91. Berlin. 1892.
Paul, H. Grundriss der germanischen Philologie. 2nd edn. 3 vols. Strasbourg. 1896 ff.
Pauly, A. F. von. Real-Encyklopädie der klassischen Alterthumswissenschaft. Vienna. 1837–52. Ed. Wissowa, G. Stuttgart. 1894–1903. New edn. 1904 ff., in progress. (Pauly-Wissowa.)
Pirenne, H. Bibliographie de l'hist. de Belgique. Brussels and Ghent. 1893. 2nd edn. 1902.
Potthast, A. Bibliotheca historica medii aevi. Wegweiser durch die Geschichtswerke des europäischen Mittelalters bis 1500. 2nd edn. 2 vols. Berlin. 1896.
Rivista storica italiana. Rome. Turin. Florence. 1884 ff., in progress. [Up to 1921 contained quarterly classified bibliography of books and articles on Italian history.] (RSI.)
Sophocles, E. A. Greek lexicon of the Roman and Byzantine periods (B.C. 146 to A.D. 1100). Boston. 1870. Ed. Thayer, J. H. New York. 1887 and 1893.
Thompson, E. M. Introduction to Greek and Latin Palaeography. London. 1912.
Vacant, A. Dictionnaire de la Théologie. Paris. 1899 ff.
Waitz. *See above*, Dahlmann.
Wattenbach, W. Deutschlands Geschichtsquellen im Mittelalter bis zur Mitte des XIII Jahrhunderts. Berlin. 1858. 7th edn. Dümmler, E. 2 vols. Stuttgart and Berlin. 1904.
Wetzer, H. J. and Welte, B. Kirchenlexikon oder Encyklopädie der katholischen Theologie. 1847–60. 2nd edn. Kaulen, F. Freiburg-i.-B. 1882–1901. Index, 1903. (Wetzer-Kaulen.) French transl. Goschler, I. 26 vols. 1869–70.

II. ATLASES AND GEOGRAPHY.

Anderson, J. G. C. Asia Minor. (Murray's Handy Classical Maps, ed. Grundy, G. B.) London. 1903.
Banduri, A. Imperium orientale sive antiquitates Constantinopolitanae. 2 vols. Paris. 1711.

Baudrillart-Vogt-Rouziès. Dictionnaire d'histoire et de géographie ecclésiastique. Paris. 1911, in progress.
Bursian, C. Geographie von Griechenland. 2 vols. Leipsic. 1862–72.
Droysen, G. Allgemeiner historischer Handatlas. Bielefeld. 1886.
Du Cange, C. du Fresne. Constantinopolis Christiana. (Historia Byzantina. Pts. II and III. *See below*, v.)
Freeman, E. A. Historical Geography of Europe (with Atlas). London. 1881. 3rd edn. revised and ed. Bury, J. B., 1903.
Kanitz, F. Donau-Bulgarien und der Balkan. 2nd edn. 3 vols. Leipsic. 1880. French transl. Paris. 1882.
Kiepert, H. *Πίναξ τοῦ μεσαιωνικοῦ Ἑλληνισμοῦ κατὰ τὴν δεκάτην ἑκατονταετηρίδα.* Publ. by the Athenian *Σύλλογος πρὸς διάδοσιν τῶν Ἑλληνικῶν γραμμάτων.* Berlin. 1883.
Kretschmer, K. Historische Geographie von Mitteleuropa. 1904. (In Below's Handbuch, *see* v *below.*)
Le Strange, G. The lands of the Eastern Caliphate. Cambridge. 1905.
Mordtmann, A. Esquisse topographique de Constantinopole. Lille. 1892.
Muir, R. Philips' New Historical Atlas for students. 2nd edn. London. 1914.
Poole, R. L. (ed.). Historical Atlas of Modern Europe. Oxford. 1902. [With valuable introductions.]
Putzger, F. W. Historischer Schul-Atlas. Ed. Baldamus, A. and others. 43rd edn. Bielefeld and Leipsic. 1922.
Ramsay, W. M. Cities and bishoprics of Phrygia. 1 vol. (in 2). Oxford. 1895–7. [All publ.]
—— Historical geography of Asia Minor. (RGS., Suppl. papers, 4.) London. 1890.
Saint-Martin, V. de, and others. Nouveau dictionnaire de Géographie Universelle. 7 vols. Paris. 1879–95. Supplement by Rousselet, L. 2 vols. 1895–7. [Contains short bibliographies.]
Schrader, F. Atlas de géographie historique. New edn. Paris. 1907.
Spruner-Menke. Hand-Atlas für die Geschichte des Mittelalters und der neueren Zeit. Gotha. 1880. (3rd edn. of Spruner's Hand-Atlas, etc. Ed. Menke, Th.)
Van Millingen, A. Byzantine Constantinople. London. 1899.

(For place-names:—)

Bischoff, H. T. and Möller, J. H. Vergleichendes Wörterbuch der alten, mittleren, und neuen Geographie. Gotha. 1892.
Deschamps, P. Dictionnaire de Géographie (supplt. to Brunet, J. C. Manuel du Libraire). Paris. 1870. 2nd edn. 2 vols. 1878–80.
Grässe, J. G. T. Orbis Latinus. Dresden. 1861. Ed. Benedict, F. Berlin. 1909. [Part I only.]

III. CHRONOLOGY, NUMISMATICS, AND GENEALOGY.

(Chronology:—)

L'Art de vérifier les dates et les faits historiques. 2e partie. Depuis la naiss. de J.-C. 3rd edn. Paris. 3 vols. 1783 ff., and other edns. and reprints. Also 4th edn. by Saint-Allais. 1818–19. 18 vols.
Bond, J. J. Handybook of Rules and Tables for verifying Dates. London. Last edn. 1875.
Gams, P. B. Series episcoporum ecclesiae Catholicae (with supplement). Ratisbon. 1873, 1886.
Ginzel, F. K. Handbuch der mathematischen und technischen Chronologie. 3 vols. Leipsic. 1906–14.
Grotefend, H. Taschenbuch der Zeitrechnung des deutschen Mittelalters und der Neuzeit. 3rd enlarged edn. Hanover. 1910.
—— Zeitrechnung des deutschen Mittelalters und d. Neuzeit. 2 vols. Hanover. 1891–8.
Ideler, C. L. Handbuch der mathematischen und technischen Chronologie. 2 vols. Berlin. 1825. New edn. Breslau. 1883.

Krug, P. Kritischer Versuch zur Aufklärung der byzantinischen Chronologie. St Petersburg. 1810.
Lane-Poole, S. The Mohammadan Dynasties. London. 1894.
Mas Latrie, J. M. J. L. de. Trésor de chronologie, d'histoire, et de géographie pour l'étude des documents du moyen âge. Paris. 1889.
Muralt, E. de. Essai de chronographie byzantine (395–1057). St Petersburg. 1855.
—— Essai de chronographie byzantine (1057–1453). 2 vols. Basle and Geneva. 1871–3.
Nicolas, Sir H. N. The Chronology of History. Revised edn. London. 1838.
Poole, R. L. Medieval Reckonings of Time. (Helps for Students of History.) S.P.C.K. London. 1918.
Ritter, Carl. Geographisch-statistisches Lexicon. 8th edn. Penzler, J. 2 vols. Leipsic. 1894–5.
Rühl, F. Chronologie des Mittelalters und der Neuzeit. Berlin. 1897.
Schram, R. Hilfstafeln für Chronologie. Vienna. 1883. New edn. Kalendariographische und chronologische Tafeln. Leipsic. 1908.
Stokvis, A. M. H. J. Manuel d'histoire de généalogie et de chronologie de tous les États du globe, etc. 3 vols. Leiden. 1888–93.
Wislicenus, W. F. Astronomische Chronologie. Leipsic. 1895.
(*Note:*—Much information in such works as Le Quien, Oriens Christianus; Gedeon, Πατριαρχικοὶ πίνακες; Ughelli, Italia Sacra; for which see IV.)

(Numismatics:—)

Codrington, O. Manual of Musalman numismatics. (Royal Asiatic Soc.) London. 1904.
Corpus nummorum italicorum. Vols. I–VIII, in progress. Rome. 1910 ff.
Engel, A. and Serrure, R. Traité de Numismatique du Moyen Âge. 2 vols. Paris. 1891–4.
Hill, G. F. Coins and Medals. (Helps for Students of History.) S.P.C.K. London. 1920. [Excellent bibliographical guide.]
Luescher von Ebengreuth, A. Allgemeine Münzkunde und Geldgeschichte des Mittelalters und der neueren Zeit. 1904. (Pt. 5 of Below's Handbuch, *see* v.)
Macdonald, G. The Evolution of Coinage. Cambridge. 1916.
Sabatier, J. Description générale des monnaies byzantines. 2 vols. Paris and London. 1862.
Schlumberger, G. Numismatique de l'Orient latin. (Société de l'Orient Latin.) 2 vols. Paris. 1878, 82.
—— Sigillographie de l'empire byzantin. Paris. 1884.
Wroth, W. Catalogue of the coins of the Vandals, Ostrogoths, and Lombards, and of the Empires of Thessalonica, Nicaea, and Trebizond in the British Museum. London. 1911.
—— Catalogue of the Imperial Byzantine coins in the British Museum. 2 vols. London. 1908.

(Genealogy:—)

Du Cange, C. du Fresne. Familiae Augustae Byzantinae. Familiae Dalmaticae Sclavonicae, Turcicae. (Historia Byzantina. Pt. I. *See below*, v.)
—— Les familles d'outre-mer. Ed. Rey, E. Paris. 1869. (Collection de documents inédits sur l'histoire de France.)
George, H. B. Genealogical Tables illustrative of Modern History. Oxford. 1873. 5th edn., Weaver, J. R. H., rev. and enl. 1916.
Grote, H. Stammtafeln mit Anhang calendarium medii aevi. (Vol. IX of Münzstudien.) Leipsic. 1877.
Hopf, K. Chroniques gréco-romanes. *See below*, IV.
Institut héraldique de France. Le Nobiliaire universel. 24 vols. Paris. 1854–1900.
Litta, P. (and continuators). Famiglie celebri italiane. 11 vols. Milan and Turin. 1819–99. 2nd series. Naples. 1902 ff., in progress.

Moreri, L. Le grand dictionnaire historique. Latest edn. 10 vols. Paris. 1759. English version, Collier, J., with App. London. 1721.
See also L'Art de vérifier les dates (*above*), and Lane-Poole, Mohammadan Dynasties (*above*).

IV. SOURCES AND COLLECTIONS OF SOURCES.

Achery, L. d'. Spicilegium sive collectio veterum aliquot scriptorum. 13 vols. Paris. 1655 (1665)–77. New edn. Barre, L. F. J. de la. 3 vols. Paris. 1723.
Acta Sanctorum Bollandiana. Brussels. 1643–1770. Paris and Rome. 1866, 1887. Brussels. 1894 ff., in progress. (ASBoll.)
Altnordische Saga Bibliothek. Ed. Cederschiöld, G., Gering, H., and Mogk, E. 7 vols. Halle. 1892–8.
Amari, M. *See under* Muratori.
Archivio storico italiano. *Cf. List of Abbreviations* (1). ASI. [Useful Index in Catalogue of The London Library, vol. I, 1913.]
Basilicorum libri LX. Vols. I–VI. Ed. Heimbach, W. E. Leipsic. 1833–70. With 2 supplts. 1. Ed. Zachariae von Lingenthal, K. E. Leipsic. 1846. [Containing books XV–XIX.] 2 (Vol. VII). Ed. Ferrini, E. C. and Mercati, J. Leipsic. 1897.
Biblioteca Arabico-Hispana. Ed. Codera and Ribera. 10 vols. Madrid and Saragossa. 1883–95.
Bibliotheca rerum Germanicarum. Ed. Jaffé, P. 6 vols. Berlin. 1864–73. (Bibl.rer.German.)
Böhmer, J. F. Regesta imperii. (New edn. in several parts by various editors.) Innsbruck. 1877 ff.
I. Regesten d. Kaiserreichs unter den Karolingern, 751–918. Ed. Mühlbacher, E. 2nd edn. Lechner, J. 1908 ff.
II. Regesten d. Kaiserreichs...919–1024. Ed. Ottenthal, E. von. Liefg. I. 1893, in progress.
V. Regesten d. Kaiserreichs...1198–1272. Ed. Ficker, J. and Winkelmann, E. 3 vols. 1881–1901.
VI. Regesten d. Kaiserreichs...1273–1313. Ed. Redlich, O. Abtlg. 1. 1898, in progress.
VIII. Regesten d. Kaiserreichs unter Karl IV, 1346–78. Ed. Huber, A. 1877. Additamentum I. 1889.
XI. Urkunden Kaiser Sigmunds, 1410–37. Ed. Altmann, W. 2 vols. 1896–1900.
Bouquet. *See* Rerum Gallicarum...scriptores.
Brackmann, A. Germania Pontificia. *See under* Kehr, P. F.
Byzantine Texts. Ed. Bury, J. B. 5 vols. London. 1898–1904.
Chartes et diplômes relatifs à l'histoire de France. Publ. AcadIBL. Paris. 1908 ff., in progress.
Collection de chroniques Belges inédits. Publ. par l'ordre du gouvernement. 44 vols. Brussels. 1858–74.
Collection de documents inédits sur l'histoire de France. Paris. 1835 ff., in progress.
Collection de textes pour servir à l'étude et à l'enseignement de l'histoire. Paris. 1886 ff., in progress. (Coll. textes.)
Constantine Porphyrogenitus. De cerimoniis aulae Byzantinae. Ed. Reiske, J. J. De thematibus. De administrando imperio. Ed. Bekker, I. 3 vols. CSHB. 1829–40. Also MPG. CXII–CXIII.
Corpus scriptorum christianorum orientalium. Ed. Chabot, J. B. and others. Paris, Rome and Leipsic. 1903 ff. (CSCO.)
Corpus scriptorum ecclesiasticorum latinorum. Vienna. 1866 ff., in progress. (CSEL.)
Corpus scriptorum historiae Byzantinae. Bonn. 1828–97. (CSHB.)
Fejér, G. Codex diplomaticus Hungariae ecclesiasticus et civilis. (Chronological table by Knauz, F. Index by Czinár, M.) 45 vols. Buda-Pest. 1829–66.
Fonti per la storia d' Italia. Publ. Istituto storico italiano. Genoa, Leghorn, and Rome. 1887 ff., in progress. (Chronicles, 29 vols. Letters, 6 vols. Diplomas, 6 vols. Statutes, 7 vols. Laws, 1 vol. Antiquities, 3 vols.) (Fonti.)
Gedeon, M. J. Πατριαρχικοὶ πίνακες. Constantinople. 1890.

Geschichtschreiber der deutschen Vorzeit, etc. Ed. Pertz, Wattenbach, and others. New series. Leipsic. 1884, in progress. [German translations.]
Graevius, J. G. and Burmannus, P. Thesaurus antiquitatum et historiarum Italiae, etc. 30 vols. Leiden. 1704–25.
—— —— Thesaurus antiq. et histor. Siciliae, Sardiniae, Corsicae, etc. 15 vols. Leiden. 1723–5.
Guizot, F. P. C. Collection des mém. relatifs à l'hist. de France depuis la fondation de la monarchie française jusqu'au 13e siècle. Paris. 1823–35. [French translations.]
Haller, J. Die Quellen zur Gesch. der Entstehung des Kirchenstaates. Leipsic and Berlin. 1907. *In* Quellensammlung zur deutschen Geschichte. Ed. Brandenburger, E. and Seeliger, G.
Historiae patriae monumenta. *See* Monumenta historiae patriae.
Hopf, K. Chroniques gréco-romanes inédites ou peu connues. Berlin. 1873.
Jaffé, P. Regesta Pontificum Romanorum ab condita ecclesia ad annum post Christum natum 1198. Berlin. 1851. 2nd edn. Wattenbach, W., Loewenfeld, S., Kaltenbrunner, F., Ewald, P. Leipsic. 1885–8. 2 vols. (Jaffé.)
—— *See under* Bibliotheca rerum Germanicarum.
Justinian. Codex Justinianus. Ed. Krueger, P. Berlin. 1877. Also ed. Krueger, P. *in* Corpus Juris civilis. Vol. II. 9th edn. Berlin. 1915.
—— Novellae. Ed. Zachariae von Lingenthal, K.E. 2 pts. and appendix. Leipsic. 1881–4. Also ed. Schoell, R. and Kroll, W. *in* Corpus Juris civilis. Vol. III. 4th edn. Berlin. 1912.
Kehr, P. F. Regesta Pontificum Romanorum. Italia Pontificia. Ed. Kehr, P. F. Vol. I. Rome. II. Latium. III. Etruria. IV. Umbria, etc. V. Aemilia. VI. Liguria (Lombardy, Piedmont, Genoa). VII, 1. Venetiae et Histria. Berlin. 1906–23. In progress.
Germania Pontificia. Ed. Brackmann, A. Vol. I, i, ii. Salzburg. Berlin. 1910–11. In progress.
Le Quien, M. Oriens Christianus. 3 vols. Paris. 1740.
Liber Censuum de l'église romaine. Ed. Fabre, P. and Duchesne, L. Vol. I. 1889–1910. Vol. II in progress. EcfrAR.
Liber Pontificalis. 3 vols. Rome. 1724–55. Ed. Duchesne, L. 2 vols. Paris. EcfrAR. 1884–92. Ed. Mommsen, T. Gesta Pontif. Romanorum. Vol. I (to 715). MGH. 1898.
Mabillon, J. Annales Ordinis S. Benedicti. 6 vols. 1703–39. 2nd edn. Lucca. 1739–45.
Mabillon, J. and Achery, L. d'. Acta Sanctorum ord. S. Benedicti [A.D. 500–1100]. 9 vols. Paris. 1668–1701. Repr. Venice. 1733–40. (ASBen.)
Mansi, J. D. Sacrorum conciliorum collectio. 31 vols. Florence and Venice. 1759–98. Repr. Martin, J. B. and Petit, L. (With continuation, vols. XXXII–L.) Paris. 1901 ff., in progress. (Mansi.)
Marrier, M. and Quercetanus (Duchesne), A. Bibliotheca Cluniacensis. Paris. 1614.
Martène, E. and Durand, U. Thesaurus novus anecdotorum. 5 vols. Paris. 1717.
Mémoires et documents publiés par l'École des Chartes. Paris. 1896 ff. (MEC.)
Migne, J. P. Patrologiae cursus completus. Series graeco-latina. Paris. 1857–66. 161 vols. in 166. (MPG.) Indices, Cavallera, F. Paris. 1912. [This is the series containing Greek texts with Latin translations in parallel columns. The so-called Series graeca (81 vols. in 85. 1856–67) contains the Latin translations only.]
—— —— Series latina. 221 vols. Paris. 1844–55. Index, 4 vols. 1862–4. (MPL.)
Miklosich, F. and Müller, J. Acta et diplomata graeca medii aevi sacra et profana. 6 vols. Vienna. 1860–90.
I, II. Acta patriarchatus Constantinopolitani. 2 vols. 1860, 62.
III. Acta et diplomata res graecas italasque illustrantia. 1865.
IV–VI. Acta et diplomata monasteriorum et ecclesiarum. 3 vols. 1870–90.
Mirbt, C. Quellen zur Geschichte des Papsttums und des römischen Katholizismus. 2nd edn. Freiburg, Tübingen, and Leipsic. 1901. 3rd edn. enl. 1911.

Monumenta Germaniae Historica. Ed. Pertz, G. H., Mommsen, T., and others. Hanover. 1826 ff. New edns. in progress. Hanover and Berlin. (MGH.) Index, 1890.

Auctores Antiquissimi. 15 vols. in many pts. 1876 ff. (Auct. ant.) Vols. IX, XI, XIII form Chronica minora (saec. IV, V, VI).

Deutsche Chroniken (Scriptores qui vernac. lingua usi sunt). I–VI. 1892 ff., in progress.

Diplomata imperii. I. 1872. Fol. [All published; contains Merovingian diplomas.]

Diplomata Karolinorum. Die Urkunden d. Karolinger. I. 1906 ff., in progress.

Diplomata regum et imperatorum Germaniae. Urkunden d. deutschen Könige und Kaiser. Vols. I–IV. 1879 ff., in progress.

Epistolae. I–VII 1. 1887 ff., in progress. (III–VII 1 are Epist. Karolini aevi, I–V 1.)

Epistolae saec. XIII e regestis pontificum Romanorum. I–III. 1883–94.

Epistolae selectae. I, III. 1916 ff., in progress. 8°.

Gesta pontificum Romanorum. I. 1898, in progress. [*See above*, Liber Pontificalis.]

Leges. I–V. 1835–89. Fol.

Legum sectiones quinque. 4°.

Sect. I. Legum nationum Germanicarum. I, II 1, V 1. 1902 ff., in progress.

Sect. II. Capitularia regum Francorum. 2 vols. 1883, 1897. Complete.

Sect. III. Concilia. 2 vols. 1893–1908. Complete.

Sect. IV. Constitutiones, etc. I–V, VI 1, VIII. 1893 ff.

Sect. V. Formulae Merovingici et Karolini aevi. 1886. Complete.

Libelli de lite imperatorum et pontificum (saec. XI, XII). I–III. 1891 ff.

Libri confraternitatum. 1884.

Necrologia Germaniae. I–IV, V 2. 1884 ff., in progress.

Poetae Latini medii aevi (Carolini). 4 vols. in 5. 1881–1923. Complete.

Scriptores. 30 vols. in 31. Fol. 1826–96. And 4°. Vols. XXXI, XXXII. 1903, 1913. (Script.) In progress.

Scriptores rerum Germanicarum in usum scholarum. Hanover. 1839 ff. Fresh series. 1890–1920. 8°. (SGUS.) New series under the title of Scriptores rerum Germanicarum. I. Berlin. 1922, in progress. [Contain revised editions of many of Scriptores in Fol. edition.]

Scriptores rerum Langobardicarum et Italicarum. 1878.

Scriptores rerum Merovingicarum. I–VII. 1885 ff., in progress.

Monumenta historiae patriae. 19 vols. Fol. 2 vols. 4°. Turin. 1836 ff., in progress. (MHP.)

Monumenta Hungariae historica. (Published by the Hungarian Academy.) In four series. I. Diplomataria. II. Scriptores. [Vols. XXI and XXII never published. *See below*, V, Krumbacher, K. Geschichte d. byzant. Lit. pp. 310–12.] III. Monumenta comitialia. IV. Acta extera. Buda-Pest. 1857 ff.

Monumenta spectantia historiam Slavorum meridionalium. Agram. 1868 ff. (MHSM.)

Müller, C. Fragmenta historicorum graecorum. 5 vols. Paris. 1841–83.

Muratori, L. A. Rerum Italicarum scriptores. 25 vols. Milan. 1723–51. Supplements: Tartini, J. M., 2 vols., Florence, 1748–70; and Mittarelli, J. B., Venice, 1771; and Amari, M., Biblioteca arabo-sicula, versione italiana, and Appendix. Turin and Rome. 1880–1, 1889. Indices chronolog. Turin. 1885. New enlarged edn. with the chronicles printed as separate parts. Carducci, G. and Fiorini, V. Città di Castello and Bologna. 1900 ff., in progress. (RR.II.SS.)

—— Antiquitates italicae medii aevi. 6 vols. Milan. 1738–42. Indices chronolog. Turin. 1885.

Ouvrages publiés par la Société de l'histoire de France. Paris. 1834 ff., in progress.

Pauler, G. and Szilágyi, S. A Magyar honfoglalás kútfői. (Sources for the occupation of Hungary by the Magyars.) Buda-Pest. 1900.

Pitra, J. B. Juris ecclesiastici Graecorum historia et monumenta. 2 vols. Rome. 1864–8.

Potthast, A. Regesta Pontificum Romanorum inde ab anno 1198 ad annum 1304. 2 vols. Berlin. 1874–5.

Prefect, Book of the. Ed. Nicole, J. Λέοντος τοῦ Σοφοῦ τὸ ἐπαρχικὸν βιβλίον. Le Livre du Préfet. Geneva. 1893. French transl. Nicole, J. Geneva. 1894.

Prochiron. Ed. Zachariae von Lingenthal, K. E. Ὁ Πρόχειρος Νόμος. Imperatorum Basilii, Constantini, et Leonis Prochiron, etc. Heidelberg. 1837. Re-edited Brandileone, F. *in* Fonti. 1895.

Recueil des historiens des croisades. AcadIBL. Paris. 1841 ff. (Rec. hist. Cr.)
  Documents arméniens. 2 vols. 1869, 1906. [Contents given in Bibl. to ch. VI, sect. I.]
  Historiens grecs. 2 vols. 1875, 81.
  Historiens occidentaux. 5 vols. 1844–95.
  Historiens orientaux. 5 vols. 1872–1906.
  Lois. 2 vols. 1841, 43.

Regesta chartarum Italiae. Publ. by K. Preuss. Histor. Instit. and Istituto storico italiano. Rome. 1907 ff., in progress.

Rerum Britannicarum medii aevi scriptores. (Chronicles and Memorials of Great Britain and Ireland during the Middle Ages.) Published under direction of the Master of the Rolls. (Various editors.) London. 1858 ff. (Rolls.) [For convenient list see Gross (Section I, *above*), App. C.]

Rerum Gallicarum et Francicarum scriptores. (Recueil des hist. des Gaules et de la France.) Ed. Bouquet, M. and others. 23 vols. 1738–1876. Vols. I–XIX re-ed. by Delisle, L. 1868–80, and vol. XXIV, 1894. New series. 4°. 1899, in progress. (Bouquet.)

Rhalles, G. A. and Potles, M. Σύνταγμα τῶν θείων καὶ ἱερῶν κανόνων κτλ. 6 vols. Athens. 1852–9.

Sathas, K. N. Μεσαιωνικὴ βιβλιοθήκη. Bibliotheca graeca medii aevi. 7 vols. Venice and Paris. 1872–94.

—— Μνημεῖα Ἑλληνικῆς ἱστορίας. Documents inédits relatifs à l'histoire de la Grèce au moyen âge. 9 vols. Paris. 1880–90.

Scriptores rerum Danicarum medii aevi. Ed. Langebek, I. 9 vols. Copenhagen. 1772–1878. (SRD.)

Scriptores rerum Germanicarum in usum scholarum. *See above*, Monumenta Germaniae Historica. (SGUS.)

Stevenson, J. Church Historians of England. 8 vols. London. 1853–8. [Translations.]

Stritter, J. G. Memoriae populorum olim ad Danubium, Pontum Euxinum, Paludem Maeotidem, Caucasum, Mare Caspium, et inde magis ad septentriones incolentium, e scriptoribus historiae Byzantinae erutae et digestae. 4 vols. St Petersburg. 1771–9.

Stumpf-Brentano, K. F. Die Reichskanzler vornehmlich des X, XI, und XII Jahrhunderts. 3 vols. Innsbruck. 1865–83.

Thallóczy, L. de, Jireček, C., and Sufflay, E. de. Acta et diplomata res Albaniae mediae aetatis illustrantia. Vienna. 1913 ff. [Contains a bibliography.]

Theiner, A. Codex diplomaticus dominii temporalis S. Sedis. 3 vols. Rome. 1861–2.

Trinchera, F. Syllabus Graecarum membranarum. Naples. 1865.

Troya, C. Codice diplomatico Longobardo dal 568 al 774. (Storia d'Italia del Medio-Evo. Vol. IV, pts. 1–5.) 5 vols. and index. Naples. 1852–9.

Ughelli, F. Italia sacra. 2nd edn. Coleti, N. 10 vols. Venice. 1717–22.

Wadding, L. and others. Annales minorum seu trium ordinum a S. Francisco institutorum. 2nd edn. 25 vols. Rome, etc. 1740–1886.

Watterich, J. M. Pontificum Romanorum qui fuerunt inde ab exeunte saeculo IX usque ad finem saeculi XII, vitae. 2 vols. Leipsic. 1862.

Zachariae von Lingenthal, K.E. Collectio librorum juris graeco-romani ineditorum. Ecloga Leonis et Constantini. Epanagoge Basilii, Leonis, et Alexandri. Leipsic. 1852. [Continued by the following.]

—— Jus graeco-romanum. In 7 parts. Leipsic. 1856–84.

V. MODERN WORKS.

Alzog, J. Universalgeschichte der Kirche. Mainz. 1841. Best edn. 10th by Kraus, F. X. 1882. Transl. (from 9th German edn.) Pabisch, F. J. and Byrne, T. S. Manual of Church History. 4 vols. Dublin. 1895–1900.
Baronius, Cæs. Annales Ecclesiasticae una cum critica historica chronologica P. A. Pagii, contin. Raynaldus, O. Ed. Mansi, J. D. Lucca. 34 vols. 1738–46. Apparatus, 1 vol. Index, 4 vols. 1740, 1757–9. New edn. Bar-le-Duc. 1864–83.
Below, G. von, and Meinecke, F. Handbuch der mittelalterlichen und neueren Geschichte. Munich and Berlin. 1903 ff., in progress. *See below*, Redlich, Schaube, *and above* (II) Kretschmer.
Bréhier, L. L'Église et l'Orient au moyen âge. Les Croisades. Paris. 1907. (Bibliothèque de l'enseignement de l'histoire ecclésiastique.) [With bibliography.]
Bresslau, H. Handbuch der Urkundenlehre für Deutschland und Italien. Leipsic. 1889. Vol. I. 2nd edn. enlarged. 1912.
Brockelmann, C. Geschichte d. arabischen Litteratur. 2 vols. Weimar and Berlin. 1898–1902.
Bryce, J. The Holy Roman Empire. Enl. edn. London. 1907.
Bury, J. B. The constitution of the Later Roman Empire. (Creighton memorial lecture.) Cambridge. 1910.
—— History of the Eastern Roman Empire from the fall of Irene to the accession of Basil I (802–867). London. 1912.
—— History of the Later Roman Empire from Arcadius to Irene (395–800). 2 vols. London. 1889. New edn. (to Justinian, 395–565). 2 vols. London. 1923.
—— The imperial administrative system in the ninth century. With a revised text of the Kletorologion of Philotheos. (British Academy. Supplemental papers. I.) London. 1911.
Bussell, F. W. The Roman Empire: essays on the constitutional history... (81 A.D. to 1081 A.D.). 2 vols. London. 1910.
Caetani, L. C. (Duca di Sermoneta). Annali dell' Islam. Vols. I–VII. Milan. 1905–14.
Chalandon, F. Les Comnènes. Études sur l'empire byzantin aux XIe et XIIe siècles. Vol. I. Essai sur le règne d'Alexis Comnène (1081–1118). Vol. II. Jean II Comnène (1118–1143) et Manuel I Comnène (1143–1180). Paris. 1900–13.
Dalton, O. M. Byzantine art and archaeology. Oxford. 1911.
Diefenbach, L. Völkerkunde Osteuropas. 2 vols. Darmstadt. 1880.
Diehl, C. Byzance: grandeur et décadence. Paris. 1919.
—— Études byzantines. Paris. 1905.
—— Figures byzantines. 2 series. Paris. 1906–8.
—— Histoire de l'empire byzantin. Paris. 1919.
—— Manuel d'art byzantin. Paris. 1910.
Dozy, R. P. A. Hist. des Mussulmans d'Espagne de 711–1110. 4 vols. Leiden. 1861. Transl. Stokes, F. G. Spanish Islam: a hist. of the Moslems in Spain. Introd. and notes. London. 1913.
—— Recherches sur l'hist. polit. et litt. de l'Espagne pendant le moyen âge. Vol. I. Leiden. 1849 [all publ.]. 3rd edn. enl. with app. 2 vols. Paris, Leiden. 1881.
Du Cange, C. du Fresne. Histoire de l'empire de Constantinople sous les empereurs françois. Paris. 1657. Ed. Buchon, J. A. 2 vols. Paris. 1826.
—— Historia Byzantina duplici commentario illustrata. 3 pts. Paris. 1680.
Ebert, A. Allgemeine Geschichte der Litteratur des Mittelalters im Abendland. 3 vols. Leipsic. 1874–87. 2nd edn. of vols. I and II. 1889.
England, A History of, in seven volumes. Ed. Oman, C. 7 vols. London. 1905–13.
—— The Political History of. Ed. Hunt, W. and Poole, R. L. 12 vols. London. 1905–10.
Fallmerayer, J. P. Geschichte des Kaiserthums von Trapezunt. Munich. 1827.
Ficker, G. and Hermelinck, H. Das Mittelalter. (Handb. d. Kirchengesch. für Studierende. Ed. Krüger, G. Vol. I, ii.) Tübingen. 1912.

Finlay, G. Ed. Tozer, H. F. History of Greece, B.C. 146 to A.D. 1864. 7 vols. Oxford. 1877.
Fleury, Claude. Histoire ecclésiastique. 20 vols. Paris. 1691–1720. Continued to end of 18th century under Vidal, O. Many editions. [Orig. edn. to 1414. 4 add. vols. by Fleury to 1517, publ. Paris, 1836, 37.]
Gardner, A. The Lascarids of Nicaea. London. 1912.
Gay, J. L'Italie méridionale et l'Empire byzantin. (867–1071.) EcfrAR. Paris. 1904.
Gebhardt, B. Handbuch d. deutschen Geschichte. 2 vols. Stuttgart. 1891–2.
Gelzer, H. Abriss der byzantinischen Kaisergeschichte. *In* Krumbacher, K. Geschichte d. byzant. Literatur. *See below.*
—— Byzantinische Kulturgeschichte. Tübingen. 1909.
Gerland, E. Geschichte des lateinischen Kaiserreiches von Konstantinopel. (Geschichte der Frankenherrschaft in Griechenland. Vol. II, 1.) Homburg v. d. Höhe. 1905.
Geschichte der europäischen Staaten. Ed. Heeren, A. H. L. and Ukert, F. A. Hamburg and Gotha. 1819–98. (Series by various writers, *cf. sub nom.*) Contin. ed. Lamprecht, K. Allgemeine Staatengeschichte.
Gfrörer, A. F. Byzantinische Geschichten. Ed. Weiss, J. B. 3 vols. Graz. 1872–7.
Gibbon, Edward. The History of the Decline and Fall of the Roman Empire. 1776–81. Ed. in 7 vols. by Bury, J. B. London. 1896–1900. Latest edn. London. 1909–14. [Notes essential, especially for bibliography.]
Gibbons, H. A. The Foundation of the Ottoman Empire. Oxford. 1916.
Giesebrecht, W. von. Geschichte der deutschen Kaiserzeit. Vols. I–V. Brunswick and Leipsic. 1855–88. I–III (5th edn.). Leipsic. 1881–90. IV (2nd edn.). Brunswick. 1899. VI (ed. Simson, B. von). Leipsic. 1895.
Gieseler, J. C. L. Lehrbuch der Kirchengeschichte. Bonn. 3 vols. 1824 ff. and 6 vols. in 5, 1828–57. Transl. Davidson, S. 5 vols. Edinburgh, 1854, and Cunningham, Text-book of Ecclesiastical History. Philadelphia. 3 vols. 1836.
Golubinski, E. E. History of the Bulgarian, Serbian, and Roumanian Churches. Moscow. 1871. (In Russian.)
—— History of the Russian Church. Vol. I. Moscow. 1900. (In Russian.)
Gregorovius, F. Geschichte der Stadt Athen im Mittelalter. 2 vols. Stuttgart. 1889. Greek transl., with addns., Lampros, S. P. 3 vols. Athens. 1904–6.
—— Geschichte der Stadt Rom im Mittelalter. 8 vols. Stuttgart. 1859–72. (Translated from 4th edition by Mrs A. Hamilton. London. 1894–1902. 8 vols. in 13.)
Hammer-Purgstall, J. von. Geschichte des osmanischen Reiches. 10 vols. Pest. 1827–35. [With bibliography.] French transl. Hellert, J. J. 18 vols. and atlas. Paris. 1835–43.
Harnack, G. C. A. Dogmengeschichte. Tübingen. 1905. 5th edn. 1914. (Grundriss d. theolog. Wissenschaften, IV, 3.) Engl. transl. Buchanan, N., etc. 7 vols. London. 1894–9.
Hartmann, L. M. Geschichte Italiens im Mittelalter. I–IV 1. Gotha. 1897–1915, in progress. (Geschichte der europäischen Staaten.)
Hauck, A. Kirchengeschichte Deutschlands. 5 vols. Leipsic. 1887–1920. Vols. I–IV. 4th edn. 1906–13. Vol. V. 2nd edn. 1911–20.
Hefele, C. J., contin. Hergenröther, J. A. G. Conciliengeschichte. 9 vols. Freiburg-i.-B. 1855 ff. 2nd edn. 1873 ff. French transl. Delarc, O. 1869. New Fr. transl. Leclercq, H. I–VIII 1. Paris, in progress. 2nd edn. 1914 ff., in progress.
Hertzberg, G. F. Geschichte der Byzantiner und des osmanischen Reiches bis gegen Ende des XVI^en Jahrhunderts. Berlin. 1883. (Allgemeine Geschichte in Einzeldarstellungen.)
—— Geschichte Griechenlands seit dem Absterben des antiken Lebens bis zum Gegenwart. 4 vols. Gotha. 1876–9. (Geschichte der europäischen Staaten.)
Heyd, W. Geschichte des Levantehandels im Mittelalter. Stuttgart. 1879. French transl. Raynaud, F. Histoire du commerce du Levant au moyen âge. 2 vols. Leipsic. 1885, 86.
Hirsch, F. Byzantinische Studien. Leipsic. 1876.

Historia Generale de la España. By members of Real Acad. de la Hist. Ed. Cánovas del Castillo, A. Madrid. 1892 ff., in progress.
Hodgkin, T. Italy and her Invaders. 8 vols. Oxford. 1880–99. Vols. VI (2nd edn. 1916)–VIII.
Hopf, K. Geschichte Griechenlands vom Beginn des Mittelalters bis auf unsere Zeit. (Ersch-Gruber. Vols. LXXXV and LXXXVI.) Leipsic. 1867, 68.
Jackson, T. G. Dalmatia, the Quarnero, and Istria, with Cettigne and Grado. 3 vols. Oxford. 1887.
Jahrbücher der deutschen Geschichte bis 1250. Berlin and Leipsic. 1862 ff., in progress. Kön. Akad. d. Wissenschaften (Munich).
Jahrbücher des deutschen Reiches unter dem sächsischen Hause. (Ed. Ranke, L. v.) 3 vols. Berlin. 1837–40.
Jireček, C. J. Geschichte der Bulgaren. Prague. 1876.
—— Geschichte der Serben. Vols. I, II, 1 [all publ.]. Gotha. 1911–18. (Geschichte der europäischen Staaten.)
Jorga, N. Transl. Powles, A. H. The Byzantine Empire. (Temple Primers.) London. 1907. [Bibliography appended.]
—— Geschichte des osmanischen Reiches. 5 vols. Gotha. 1908–13. (Geschichte der europäischen Staaten.)
—— Geschichte des rumänischen Volkes. 2 vols. Gotha. 1905. (Geschichte der europäischen Staaten.)
Köhler, G. Die Entwicklung des Kriegswesen und der Kriegsführung in der Ritterzeit von der Mitte des 11 Jahrhunderts bis zu den Hussitenkriegen. 3 vols. Breslau. 1886–90.
Kondakoff (Kondakov), N. P. Histoire de l'art byzantin. French transl. Trawinski, F. 2 vols. Paris. 1886–91.
Kraus, F. X. Ed. Sauer, J. Geschichte der christlichen Kunst. 2 vols. in 3. Freiburg-i.-B. and St Louis, Minnesota. 1896–1908.
Kretschmayr, H. Geschichte von Venedig. Vols. I, II. Gotha. 1905 ff., in progress. (Geschichte der europäischen Staaten.)
Krumbacher, K. Geschichte der byzantinischen Litteratur. (527–1453.) 2nd edn. (Handbuch d. klass. Altertums-Wissenschaft. Ed. Müller, I. von. Vol. IX, i.) Munich. 1897.
Lampros (Lambros), Sp. P. Ἱστορία τῆς Ἑλλάδος. Vols. I–VI. Athens. 1886–1908.
Langen, J. Geschichte der römischen Kirche. 4 vols. Bonn. 1881.
Lavisse, E. and others. Histoire de France jusqu'à la Révolution. 9 vols. in 18. Paris. 1900–11. Vols. I–IV.
Lavisse, E. and Rambaud, A. Histoire générale du IVe siècle jusqu'à nos jours. 12 vols. Paris. 1893–1900. Vols. I–III.
Lebeau, C. Histoire du Bas-Empire. Ed. Saint-Martin, J. A. and Brosset, M. F. 21 vols. Paris. 1824–36.
Manitius, M. Geschichte der lateinischen Literatur des Mittelalters. Teil 1. (Handbuch d. klass. Altertums-Wissenschaft. Ed. Müller, I. von. Vol. IX, ii 1.) Munich. 1911.
Marquart, J. Osteuropäische und ostasiatische Streifzüge. Leipsic. 1903.
Meitzen, P. A. Siedelung und Agrarwesen der Westgermanen und Ostgermanen, der Kelten, Römer, Finnen, und Slawen. 4 vols. Berlin. 1893–6.
Meliarákes, A. Ἱστορία τοῦ Βασιλείου τῆς Νικαίας καὶ τοῦ Δεσποτάτου τῆς Ἠπείρου (1204–61). Athens. 1898.
Miller, W. Essays on the Latin Orient. Cambridge. 1921.
—— The Latins in the Levant: a history of Frankish Greece (1204–1566). London. 1908. Enlarged Greek transl. Lampros (Lambros), Sp. P. Ἱστορία τῆς φραγκοκρατίας ἐν Ἑλλάδι. Athens. 1909–10.
—— The Latin Orient. (Helps for Students of History.) S.P.C.K. London. 1920. [Contains a bibliography.]
Milman, H. H. History of Latin Christianity. London. 1854–5. Rev. edn. 9 vols. 1867.
Moeller, C. Hist. du moyen âge depuis la chute de l'empire romain jusqu'à la fin de l'époque franque (476–950). Paris and Louvain. 1898–1905. 2nd edn. with index. Louvain. 1910.

Moeller, W. Hist. of the Christian Church (A.D. 1–1648). Transl. Rutherfurd and Freese. 3 vols. London. 1892–1900.
Mosheim, J. L. von. Institutionum historiae ecclesiasticae antiquae et recentioris libri IV. 4 vols. Helmstedt. 1755. Transl. Murdock, J., ed. Soames, H. 4 vols. London. 1841. 2nd rev. edn. 1850.
Mühlbacher, E. Deutsche Geschichte unter den Karolingern. Stuttgart. 1896. (*In* Zwiedineck-Südenhorst's Bibliothek deutscher Geschichte.)
Muir, W. The Caliphate: its rise, decline, and fall. Revised edn. Weir, T. H. Edinburgh. 1915.
Müller, K. Kirchengeschichte. Vols. I, II. Freiburg-i.-B. 1892.
Muratori, L. A. Annali d' Italia. 12 vols. Milan. 1744–9. Also other editions and reprints.
Murav'ev, A. N. History of the Church of Russia. Engl. transl. Blackmore, R. W. Oxford. 1842.
Neale, J. M. History of the Holy Eastern Church. Pt. I. General introduction. 2 vols. London. 1850.
Neumann, C. Die Weltstellung des byzantinischen Reiches vor den Kreuzzügen. Leipsic. 1894. French transl. Renauld and Kozlowski. Paris. 1905.
Norden, W. Das Papsttum und Byzanz. Berlin. 1903.
Oman, C. W. C. The Byzantine empire. London. 1892.
—— History of the Art of War. The Middle Ages. London. 1898.
Paparrhegopoulos, K. Ἱστορία τοῦ Ἑλληνικοῦ ἔθνους. 4th edn. Ed. Karolides, P. 5 vols. Athens. 1903.
—— Histoire de la civilisation hellénique. Paris. 1878. [Extracted from the preceding.]
Pargoire, J. L'Église byzantine de 527 à 847. Paris. 1905. (Bibliothèque de l'enseignement de l'hist. ecclésiastique.)
Pertile, A. Storia del diritto italiano dalla caduta dell' impero Romano alla codificazione. 6 vols. 2nd edn. Del Giudice, P. Turin. 1892–1902. Index. Eusebio, L. Turin. 1893.
Pirenne, H. Histoire de Belgique. 5 vols. Brussels. 1900–21. 3rd edn. in progress.
Previté-Orton, C. W. Outlines of Medieval History. Cambridge. 1916.
Quentin, H. Les Martyrologes historiques du Moyen Âge. Étude sur la formation du martyrologe romain. Paris. 1908. (Études d'hist. des dogmes et d'ancienne littérature ecclésiastique.)
Rambaud, A. N. Histoire de la Russie. 5th edn. Paris. 1900.
Ranke, L. von. Weltgeschichte. 9 vols. Leipsic. 1881–8. And later edns.
Reddaway, W. F. Introduction to the study of Russian history. (Helps for Students of History.) S.P.C.K. London. 1920. [Contains a bibliography.]
Redlich, O. and Erben, W. Urkundenlehre. Pt. I. 1907. IV, 1 of Below's Handbuch (*see above*).
Richter, G. and Kohl, H. Annalen d. deutschen Gesch. im Mittelalter. 3 pts. in 5. Halle a. S. 1873–98.
Romano, G. Le dominazioni barbariche in Italia. (395–1024.) (Storia polit. d' Italia.) 1909.
Schaube, A. Handelsgeschichte der romanischen Völker des Mittelmeergebiets bis zum Ende der Kreuzzüge. (Below and Meinecke, Handbuch, *see above*.) Munich and Berlin. 1906.
Schlosser, F. C. Geschichte der bilderstürmenden Kaiser des oströmischen Reichs. Frankfort. 1812.
Schlumberger, G. L. Un empereur byzantin au xe siècle: Nicéphore Phocas. Paris. 1890.
—— L'épopée byzantine à la fin du xe siècle. In 3 pts. 1. Jean Tzimiscès, Basile II (969–989). 2. Basile II (989–1025). 3. Les Porphyrogénètes, Zoé et Théodora (1025–57). Paris. 1896–1905.
Schupfer, F. Manuale di storia del diritto italiano. Città di Castello. 1904.
Storia politica d' Italia scritta da una Società di Professori. Vols. I–VIII. Milan, in progress. (By various writers, *cf. sub nom.*)
Strzygowski, J. Die Baukunst der Armenier und Europa. 2 vols. Vienna. 1919.
Temperley, H. W. V. History of Serbia. London. 1917.

Tozer, H. F. The Church and the Eastern Empire. London. 1888.
Überweg, F. Grundriss der Geschichte der Philosophie. 10th edn. Ed. Heinze, M. and Prächter, K. 4 vols. Berlin. 1904–9. [Bibliography.]
Vinogradoff, P. Roman Law in Mediaeval Europe. London and New York. 1909. [Excellent bibliographies.]
Viollet, P. Histoire du droit civil français. 3rd edn. Paris. 1905.
Weil, G. Geschichte der Chalifen. 3 vols. Mannheim. 1846–51.
—— Geschichte der islamitischen Völker von Mohammed bis zur Zeit des Sultans Selim. Stuttgart. 1866.
Weltgeschichte in gemeinverständlicher Darstellung. Ed. Hartmann, L. M.
Vol. IV. Das Mittelalter bis zum Ausgang der Kreuzzüge. Hellmann, S. Gotha. 1920.
Vol. V. Das späte Mittelalter. Kaser, K. Gotha. 1921.
Xénopol, A. D. Histoire des Roumains de la Dacie Trajane... (513–1859). 2 vols. Paris. 1896. [Abridged from the Roumanian edition.]
Young, G. F. East and West through fifteen centuries. Vols. I, II. London. 1916.
Zachariae von Lingenthal, K.E. Geschichte des griechisch-römischen Rechts. 3rd edn. Berlin. 1892.
Zeller, J. Hist. d'Allemagne. Paris. 1872–91. Vols. 1–9. [No more publ.]

CHAPTER I.

LEO III AND THE ISAURIAN DYNASTY.

I. SPECIAL BIBLIOGRAPHIES.

Lombard, A. Constantin V, empereur des Romains. Paris. 1902. [For the reign of Constantine V.]
Vasil'ev, A. A. Lektsii po istorii Vizantii. Vol. I. Petrograd. 1917.

II. ORIGINAL AUTHORITIES.

(a) General.

Anonymus. Ad Constantinum Caballinum. MPG. XCV.
Cedrenus, George. Synopsis historiarum. Vol. II. Ed. Bekker, I. CSHB. 1839.
Codex Carolinus. Ed. Gundlach, W. MGH. Epistolae. Vol. III. 1892.
Ecloga. Ed. Zachariae von Lingenthal, K. E. *in* Collectio librorum juris graeco-romani ineditorum. *See Gen. Bibl.* IV. Also ed. Monferratos, A. G. Athens. 1889.
George of Cyprus. Νουθεσία γέροντος περὶ τῶν ἁγίων εἰκόνων. Ed. Melioranski, B. St Petersburg. 1901.
Georgius Monachus. Chronicon. Ed. Boor, C. de. 2 vols. Leipsic. 1904.
Germanus Patriarcha. Epistolae. MPG. XCVIII.
Gregorius II Papa. Epistolae. MPL. LXXXIX.
Johannes Damascenus. Πρὸς τοὺς διαβάλλοντας τὰς ἁγίας εἰκόνας. Three discourses. MPG. XCIV.
—— Πηγὴ γνώσεως. MPG. XCVI.
Leo Grammaticus. Chronographia. Ed. Bekker, I. CSHB. 1842.
Liber Pontificalis. Ed. Duchesne, L. *See Gen. Bibl.* IV.
Mansi, J. D. Sacrorum Conciliorum Collectio. Vols. XII and XIII. *See Gen. Bibl.* IV.
Narratio de ss. patriarchis Tarasio et Nicephoro. MPG. XCIX.
Nicephorus Patriarcha. Opuscula historica. Ed. Boor, C. de. Leipsic. 1880.
—— Antirrhetici III adversus Constantinum Copronymum. MPG. C; and also ed. Pitra, J. B. *in* Spicilegium Solesmense. Vols. I and IV. Paris. 1852, 58.
—— Apologeticus major pro sanctis imaginibus. MPG. C.
—— Apologeticus minor pro sanctis imaginibus. *Ibid.*
Νόμος γεωργικός. Ed. Ferrini, C. *in* BZ. VII. 1898. pp. 558–72; and also ed. Ashburner, W. *in* JHS. Vols. XXX, XXXII. 1910, 1912.
Νόμος ναυτικός. Ed. Pardessus, J. M. Collection de lois maritimes. Vol. I. Paris. 1828. And also ed. Ashburner, W. The Rhodian sea-law. Oxford. 1909.
Νόμος στρατιωτικός. Ed. Monferratos, A. G. Athens. 1889.
Theophanes. Chronographia. Ed. Boor, C. de. 2 vols. Leipsic. 1883, 85.
Zachariae von Lingenthal, K. E. Jus graeco-romanum. Pt. III. Novellae Constitutiones. *See Gen. Bibl.* IV.
Zonaras. Epitome historiarum. Vol. III. Ed. Büttner-Wobst, T. CSHB. 1897.

(b) Hagiographical.

Acta viginti monachorum S. Sabae. ASBoll. Mart. III. App. 2.
Acts of the Sixty Martyrs of Jerusalem. Ed. Papadopoulos-Kerameus, A. Russian Palestine Society. Fasc. XXXIV. St Petersburg. 1892.

Laudatio funebris Theoctistae. By Theodorus Studita. MPG. xcix.
Vita Andreae in Crisi. ASBoll. 17 Oct. viii. pp. 135–42.
Vita Germani Patriarchae. Ed. Papadopoulos-Kerameus, A. *in* Μαυρογορδάτειος βιβλιοθήκη, Ἀνέκδ. ἑλλην., suppl. to Vols. xv–xvii of the Ἑλληνικὸς Φιλολόγικος Σύλλογος of Constantinople. Also ed. (*sub nom.* Theophanis) Boor, C. de, *in* Theophanes. *See above,* ii(*a*). Vol. ii. pp. 3 ff.
Vita Gregorii Spatharii. ASBoll. 9 Aug. ii. pp. 434–47.
Vita Johannis Damasceni. MPG. xciv.
Vita Johannis Episcopi Gothiae. ASBoll. 26 Jun. v. pp. 190–4.
Vita Nicephori Patriarchae. By Ignatius diaconus. Ed. Boor, C. de, *in* Nicephori opuscula historica. Leipsic. 1880.
Vita Pauli junioris. ASBoll. Jul. ii. pp. 635–9.
Vita Philareti. *In* Izvêstiya russk. arkheol. Instituta v Konstantinopolê. Vol. v. Sofia.
Vita Platonis abb. Saccudii. By Theodorus Studita. MPG. xcix.
Vita Stephani junioris. By Stephanus diaconus of St Sophia. MPG. c.
Vita Tarasii Patriarchae. By Ignatius diaconus. Ed. Heikel, I. A. *in* Acta soc. scient. Fennicae. xvii. Helsingfors. 1889.
Vita Theophanis. Ed. Boor, C. de, *in* Theophanes. Vol. ii. *See above,* ii(*a*).

(*c*) Criticism on Authorities.

Theophanes.
Hubert. Observations sur la chronologie de Théophane. BZ. vi. pp. 471 ff. 1897.
Nicephorus.
Gelzer, H. Sextus Julius Africanus. Vol. ii. Leipsic. 1885.
Hirsch, F. Byzantinische Studien. *See Gen. Bibl.* v.
Hagiographa.
Bréhier, L. L'hagiographie byzantine des viiie et ixe siècles. *In* Journ. des Savants. Aug. and Oct. 1916. Jan. 1917.
Loparev. Vizantiyskiya zhitiya svyatykh viii i ix vêkov. *In* VV. xvii, xviii, xix. 1913–15.

III. MODERN WORKS.

(*a*) General.

Bury, J. B. History of the Later Roman Empire. Vol. ii. *See Gen. Bibl.* v.
Bussell, F. W. The Roman Empire. *See Gen. Bibl.* v.
Lebedev, A. P. Vselenskiye Sobory vi, vii, i viii vêkov. St Petersburg. 1904.
Paparrhegopoulos, K. Ἱστορία τοῦ Ἑλληνικοῦ ἔθνους. Vol. iii. Athens. 1867. *Cf. Gen. Bibl.* v.
Shestakov, S. P. Lektsii po istorii Vizantii. Vol. i. Kazan. 1915.
Vasil'ev, A. A. Lektsii po istorii Vizantii. Vol. i. *See above,* i.

(*b*) Monographs, Biographies, etc.

Andreev. German i Tarasi, patriarkhi konstantinopolskie. 1907.
Bréhier, L. La querelle des images. Paris. 1904.
Diehl, C. Études sur l'administration byzantine dans l'exarchat de Ravenne. Paris. 1888.
—— L'impératrice Irène. Une bourgeoise de Byzance au viiie siècle. *In* Figures byzantines. 1re série. *See Gen. Bibl.* v.
—— Une vie de saint de l'époque des empereurs iconoclastes. *In* Comptes rendus. AcadIBL. 1915.
Gasquet, A. L'empire byzantin et la monarchie franque. Paris. 1888.
Gelzer, H. Die Genesis der byzant. Themenverfassung. *In* Abhand. d. phil.-hist. Klasse d. sächs. Gesellschaft d. Wissensch. Vol. xviii. Leipsic. 1899.
—— Verhältniss von Staat und Kirche in Byzanz. HZ. 1901.
Gfrörer, A. F. Der Bildersturm. *In* Byzantinische Geschichten. Vol. ii. *See Gen. Bibl.* v.

Harnack, A. Lehrbuch der Dogmengeschichte. 4th edn. Vol. II. Tübingen. 1909.
Harnack, O. Das karolingische und das byzantinische Reich in ihren wechselseitigen politischen Beziehungen. Göttingen. 1880.
Hartmann, L. M. Geschichte Italiens im Mittelalter. Vol. II. Heft 2. *See Gen. Bibl.* v.
Hefele, C. J. von. Histoire des Conciles. Transl. Leclercq, H. Vol. III. Pt. II. *See Gen. Bibl.* v.
Langen, J. Johannes von Damaskus. Gotha. 1879.
Lombard, A. Constantin V, empereur des Romains. Paris. 1902.
Marin, E. Les moines de Constantinople. Paris. 1897.
Marx, J. Der Bilderstreit der byzant. Kaiser. Trèves. 1839.
Melioranski, B. George of Cyprus and John of Jerusalem, two little known defenders of orthodoxy in the 8th century. St Petersburg. 1901. (In Russian.)
Pargoire, J. L'Église byzantine de 527 à 847. *See Gen. Bibl.* v.
Phoropoulos, J. D. *Εἰρήνη ἡ Ἀθηναία αὐτοκράτειρα Ῥωμαίων.* Pt. I (769–788). Leipsic. 1887. [diss.]
Preobrazhenski. The struggle over images in the Byzantine Empire. Moscow. 1890. (In Russian.)
Schenk, K. Kaiser Leo III. Halle. 1880.
—— Kaiser Leons III Walten im Innern. BZ. v. pp. 257–301. 1896.
Schlosser, F. C. Geschichte der bilderstürmenden Kaiser. Frankfort. 1812. [Antiquated.]
Schwarzlose, C. Der Bilderstreit, ein Kampf der griechischen Kirche um ihre Eigenart und um ihre Freiheit. Gotha. 1890.
Vasil'evski, V. The legislation of the Iconoclasts. ZMNP. Vols. CXCIX–CCI. 1878. (In Russian.)
Zachariae von Lingenthal, K. E. Geschichte des griechisch-römischen Rechts. *See Gen. Bibl.* v.

CHAPTER II.

FROM NICEPHORUS I TO THE FALL OF THE PHRYGIAN DYNASTY.

I. SPECIAL BIBLIOGRAPHY.

Bury, J. B. History of the Eastern Roman Empire. pp. 493 ff. *See Gen. Bibl.* v. [Very complete.]
Cf. Vasil'ev, A. A. Lektsii po istorii Vizantii. Vol. I. Petrograd. 1917.

II. ORIGINAL AUTHORITIES.

(*a*) General.

Acta concilii A.D. 815. Ed. Serruys, D. *in* Mélanges d'archéologie et d'histoire. (École franç. de Rome.) XXIII. Rome. 1903.
Anastasius bibliothecarius. Praefatio in Concilium Constantinopolitanum IV. *In* Mansi. XVI. *See Gen. Bibl.* IV.
Anonymus. Vita Leonis Bardae Armenii filii. Ed. Bekker, I., *with* Leo Grammaticus. (*See below.*) *Also* MPG. CVIII. col. 1009.
Cedrenus. Synopsis historiarum. Vol. II. Ed. Bekker, I. CSHB. 1839.
Constantine Porphyrogenitus. De cerimoniis aulae Byzantinae. De thematibus. De administrando imperio. *See Gen. Bibl.* IV.
Genesius. Regna. Ed. Lachmann, C. CSHB. 1834.
Georgius Monachus. Chronicon. Ed. Muralt. St Petersburg. 1859. Also ed. Boor, C. de. 2 vols. Leipsic. 1904.
Leo Grammaticus. Ed. Bekker, I. CSHB. 1842.
Liber Pontificalis. Ed. Duchesne, L. Vol. II. *See Gen. Bibl.* IV.
Mansi, J. D. Sacrorum conciliorum collectio. Vol. XVI. *See Gen. Bibl.* IV.
Methodius Patriarcha. Opera. Ed. Pitra, J. B. *in* Juris ecclesiastici Graecorum historia et monumenta. Vol. II. *See Gen. Bibl.* IV. *Also* MPG. C.
Narratio de ss. patriarchis Tarasio et Nicephoro. MPG. XCIX.
Nicephorus Patriarcha. Antirrhetici. *See Bibl.* II (*a*) *to ch.* I.
Nicolaus I Papa. Epistolae. Responsa ad consulta Bulgarorum. MPL. CXVII.
Photius. Epistolae. MPG. CII. Also ed. Papadopoulos-Kerameus, A. St Petersburg. 1896.
—— Opera. MPG. CI–CIV. *Cf.* Hergenröther, J. A. G. Monumenta graeca ad Photium eiusque historiam pertinentia. Ratisbon. 1869.
—— Λόγοι καὶ ὁμιλίαι. Ed. Aristarches. 2 vols. Constantinople. 1900.
Symeon Magister (or Logothetes). Chronicle. Old Slavonic version, ed. Sreznevski. St Petersburg. 1905.
Symeon (pseudo-). Chronicle. Ed. Bekker, I., *with* Theophanes continuatus. *See below.*
Theodorus Studita. Opera. MPG. XCIX.
—— Epistolae. Ed. Cozza-Luzi *in* Mai, A. Nova Patrum bibliotheca. VIII. Rome. 1871.
—— Parva catechesis. Ed. Auvray, E. Paris. 1891.
Theophanes. Chronographia. Ed. Boor, C. de. 2 vols. Leipsic. 1883, 85.
Theophanes continuatus. Chronographia. Ed. Bekker, I. CSHB. 1838.
Zonaras. Epitome Historiarum. Vol. III. Ed. Büttner-Wobst, T. CSHB. 1897.

(*b*) Hagiographical.

Acta 42 martyrum Amoriensium. Ed. Vasil'evski, V. and Nikitin, P. *In* Mém. AcadIP. 8th series. Vol. vii, 2. 1905.
Vita Euthymii junioris. By Basil of Thessalonica. Ed. Petit, L. Revue de l'Orient chrétien. Vol. viii. 1903.
Vita Ignatii Patriarchae. By Nicetas the Paphlagonian. MPG. cv.
Vita Joannicii. ASBoll. 4 Nov. ii.
Vita Josephi hymnographi. Ed. Papadopoulos-Kerameus, A. *in* Sbornik grecheskikh i latinskikh pamyatnikov kasayushchikh Fotiya Patriarkha. ii. St Petersburg. 1901. *Also* MPG. cv.
Vita Methodii Patriarchae. ASBoll. 14 June. ii. *Also* MPG. c.
Vita Michaelis syncelli. *In* Izvêstiya russk. arkh. Instituta v Konstantinopolê. xi. Sofia. 1906.
Vita Nicephori Patriarchae. *See Bibl.* ii (*b*) *to ch.* i.
Vita Nicetae Mediciani. By Theosterictus. ASBoll. 3 April. i. App. xxiii.
Vita Nicolai Papae. MPL. cxvii.
Vita Nicolai Studitae. MPG. cv.
Vita Theodorae Augustae. Ed. Regel, W. *in* Analecta Byzantino-russica. St Petersburg. 1891.
Vita Theodori Grapti. MPG. cxvi.
Vita Theodori Studitae. MPG. xcix.
Vitae Theophanis. Ed. Boor, C. de *in* Theophanes. Vol. ii. *See above,* ii (*a*). And ed. Krumbacher, K. *in* Sitzung. k. Bayer. Akad. 1897.
[For the lives of the "Apostles of the Slavs," Cyril and Methodius, *see below, Bibliography of ch.* vii (b), *and* Bury, *op. cit.* pp. 500, 501.]

(*c*) Oriental Sources.

See below, Bibliography of ch. v (a), *and cf.* Bury, *op. cit.*

(*d*) Criticism on Authorities.

Symeon Magister and Logothetes.
Boor, C. de. Die Chronik des Logotheten. BZ. vi. 1897.
—— Weiteres zur Chronik des Logotheten. *Ibid.* x. 1901.
Bury, J. B. The Chronicle of Simeon, Magister and Logothete. *Op. cit.* Appendix iii.
Constantine Porphyrogenitus.
Bury, J. B. The treatise De administrando imperio. BZ. xv. 1906.
—— The ceremonial book of Constantine Porphyrogennetos. EHR. Vol. xxii. 1907.
Theophanes continuatus, Georgius Monachus, etc.
Hirsch, F. Byzantinische Studien. *See Gen. Bibl.* v.
Leo Grammaticus.
Patzig, E. Leo Grammaticus und seine Sippe. BZ. iii. 1894.
Hagiographa.
Bréhier, L. L'hagiographie byzantine. *See above, Bibl.* ii (*c*) *of ch.* i.
Loparev. Vizantiyskiya zhitiya svyatykh viii i ix vêkov. *See above, Bibl.* ii (*c*) *of ch.* i.

III. MODERN WORKS.

(*a*) General.

Bury, J. B. History of the Eastern Roman Empire. *See Gen. Bibl.* v. [Indispensable.]
Bussell, F. W. The Roman Empire. *See Gen. Bibl.* v.
Lebedev, A. P. Vselenskiye Sobory vi, vii, i viii vêkov. *See above, Bibl.* iii (*a*) *of ch.* i.
Paparrhegopoulos, K. Ἱστορία τοῦ Ἑλληνικοῦ ἔθνους. Vol. iii. *See Gen. Bibl.* v.
Vasil'ev, A. A. Lektsii po istorii Vizantii. Vol. i. *See above,* i.

(*b*) Monographs, Biographies, etc.

Boor, C. de. Der Angriff der Rhôs auf Byzanz. BZ. iv. 1895.
Bréhier, L. La querelle des images. Paris. 1904.
Bury, J. B. The Bulgarian treaty of 814. EHR. xxv. 1910.
—— The identity of Thomas the Slavonian. BZ. i. 1892.
Conybeare, F. C. The key of truth. A manual of the Paulician Church of Armenia. Oxford. 1898.
Diehl, C. La bienheureuse Théodora.
—— Les romanesques aventures de Basile le Macédonien. (*Both in* Figures byzantines. 1re série. *See Gen. Bibl.* v.)
Dobroklonski. Prepodobny Fëdor ispovêdnik i igumen studiyski. Pt. i. Ego epokha. Pt. ii. Ego tvoreniya. Odessa. 1913–14.
Dobschütz, E. v. Methodios und die Studiten. BZ. xvii. 1909.
Gardner, A. Theodore of Studium. London. 1905.
Gasquet, A. L'empire byzantin et la monarchie franque. Paris. 1888.
Gay, J. L'Italie méridionale et l'empire byzantin. *See Gen. Bibl.* v.
Gerland, E. Photios und der Angriff der Russen auf Byzanz, 18 June 860. (*In* Neue Jahrbücher f. d. Klass. Altertum. Ed. Ilberg, J. xi. Leipsic. 1903.)
Goetz, L. C. Geschichte der Slavenapostel Konstantinus und Methodius. Gotha. 1897.
Grossu, N. Prepodobny Fëdor Studit, ego vremya. Kiev. 1907.
Hergenröther, J. A. G. Photius, Patriarch von Konstantinopel. 3 vols. Ratisbon. 1867–9.
Jagić, V. Zur Entstehungsgeschichte der Kirchenslavischen Sprache. *In* Denkschriften d. KAW. phil.-hist. Klasse. Vol. xlvii. Vienna. 1900. Corrected separate edn. Berlin. 1913.
—— Die neuesten Forschungen über die slavischen Apostel Cyrill und Methodius. *In* Archiv für slavische Philologie. iv. Berlin. 1880.
Jireček, C. J. Geschichte der Bulgaren. *See Gen. Bibl.* v.
Lapôtre, A. L'Europe et le Saint-Siège à l'époque carolingienne. Vol. i. Paris. 1895.
Lebedev, A. P. Istoriya razdêleniya tserkvey v ix, x, i xi vêkakh. Moscow. 1900.
Leger, L. Cyrille et Méthode. Paris. 1868.
Marin, E. Les moines de Constantinople. Paris. 1897.
—— Saint-Théodore. Paris. 1906.
Marquart, J. Osteuropäische und ostasiatische Streifzüge. Leipsic. 1903.
Pargoire, J. L'Église byzantine de 527 à 847. *See Gen. Bibl.* v.
—— St Théophane le chronographe et ses rapports avec saint Théodore Studite. *In* VV. ix. 1902.
Preobrazhenski, V. Prepodobny Fëdor Studit i ego vremya. Moscow. 1895.
Schneider, G. A. Der hl. Theodor von Studion, sein Leben und Wirken. (Kirchengeschichtliche Studien. Ed. Knöpfler, A. Vol. v, iii.) Münster. 1900.
Schwarzlose, K. Der Bilderstreit, ein Kampf der griechischen Kirche. Gotha. 1890.
Ter Mkrttschian, K. Die Paulikianer im byzantinischen Kaiserreiche. Leipsic. 1893.
Thomas, C. Theodor von Studion und sein Zeitalter. Osnabrück. 1892.
Tougard, A. La persécution iconoclaste d'après la correspondance de saint Théodore Studite. Paris. 1891. And in RQH. 1891.
Uspenski, F. Ocherki po istorii vizantiyskoi obrazovannosti. St Petersburg. 1892.
Vailhé, S. Saint Michel le Syncelle et les deux frères Grapti. *In* Revue de l'Orient chrétien. vi. 1901.
Vogt, A. Basile Ier. Paris. 1908.

CHAPTERS III AND IV.

THE MACEDONIAN DYNASTY.

I. SOURCES.

(a) Historians and Chroniclers.

[Most of these authorities are reprinted in MPG.]

Attaliates, Michael. Historia. Ed. Bekker, I. CSHB. 1853.
Cedrenus. Ed. Bekker, I. 2 vols. CSHB. 1838, 39.
Chronographica narratio (De Leone Armeno). Ed. Bekker, I., *with* Leo Grammaticus. *See below.* Also ed. Combefis, F. MPG. cviii. col. 1009.
Constantine Porphyrogenitus. Vita Basilii. *See below* (*in* Theophanes continuatus, pp. 211 ff.).
[Georgius Monachus.] Chronicon. (The interpolated Chronicle of George with its continuation.) Ed. Muralt. St Petersburg. 1859.
—— The latter part of the Chronicle in Theophanes continuatus. *See below.*
Glycas, Michael. Chronicle. Ed. Bekker, I. CSHB. 1836.
Joel. Chronographia. Ed. Bekker, I. CSHB. 1837.
Johannes Geometres (Cyriotes). Carmina. MPG. cvi.
Leo Diaconus. Historia. Ed. Hase, C. B. CSHB. 1828.
Leo Grammaticus. Chronographia. Ed. Bekker, I. CSHB. 1842.
Liudprand. Antapodosis, and Relatio de legatione Constantinopolitana. MGH. Script. iii. 1839. Revised edn. Becker, J. SGUS. 1915.
Lupus Protospatarius. Chronicon. MGH. Script. v.
Manasses, Constantinus. Synopsis Historica. Ed. Bekker, I. CSHB. 1837.
Pachymeres, Georgius. Opera. Ed. Bekker, I. CSHB. 1835.
Salernitanum Chronicon. MGH. Script. iii.
Scylitzes, Johannes. Chronicle. (The original text is virtually contained in Cedrenus, who transcribed it. *See above.*) Latin version. Ed. Gabius, J. B. Venice. 1570.
Symeon Magister (or Logothetes). Chronicle. Old Slavonic version, ed. Sreznevski. St Petersburg. 1905. [This chronicle was largely transcribed in the compilations of Leo Grammaticus and Theodosius of Melitene, and in the pseudo-Georgian chronicle (*see above under* Georgius Monachus), ed. Muralt, E. v. St Petersburg. 1859.]
Symeon (pseudo-). Chronicle. Ed. Bekker, I., *with* Theophanes continuatus. *See below.*
Theodosius Melitenus. Chronographia. Ed. Tafel, T. L. F. *In* Monumenta Saecularia. (K. Akad. d. Wissenschaften.) Munich. 1859.
Theophanes continuatus. Chronographia. Ed. Bekker, I. CSHB. 1838.
Zonaras. Epitome Historiarum. Vol. iii. Ed. Büttner-Wobst, T. CSHB. 1897.

(b) Ecclesiastical Documents.

Anastasius Bibliothecarius. Praefatio ad viii Concilium. MPL. cxxix.
Hadrianus II, Papa. Epistolae. MPL. cxxii.
Johannes VIII, Papa. Epistolae. MPL. cxxvi. Ed. Ewald. Neu. Arch. v. (1879.)
Liber Pontificalis. Ed. Duchesne, L. *See Gen. Bibl.* iv.
Life of Athanasius the Athonite. Ed. Pomyalovski. St Petersburg. 1895.

Lives of the Fathers of the Church of Athos. 4th edn. St Petersburg. 1875. (In Russian.)
Mansi. Concilia. Vols. xv–xix. *See Gen. Bibl.* iv.
Meyer, Ph. Die Haupturkunden für die Geschichte der Athos Klöster. Leipsic. 1894.
Monumenta graeca ad Photium ejusque historiam pertinentia. Ed. Hergenröther, J. A. G. Ratisbon. 1869.
Nea Taktika. Ed. Gelzer, H. (*in* George of Cyprus, Descriptio orbis romani). Leipsic. 1890.
Nicetas, David. Vita S. Ignatii, archiep. Constantinopol. MPG. cv.
Nicolaus I, Papa. Epistolae. MPL. cxix. Mansi, *op. cit.* xv.
Nicolaus Mysticus. MPG. cxi.
Office inédit en l'honneur de Nicéphore Phocas. Ed. Petit, L. *in* BZ. xiii (1904). p. 398.
Photius. Epistolae, libri tres. Ed. Valettas. MPG. cii. 1864.
Rhalles, G. A. and Potles, M. Σύνταγμα τῶν θείων καὶ ἱερῶν κανόνων. *See Gen. Bibl.* iv.
Stephanus V, Papa. Epistolae. MPL. cxxix.
Stylianus. Epistolae ad Stephanum Papam. (*In* Mansi, xvi.)
Theognostus. Libellus ad Nicolaum Papam. MPG. cv.
Typika. Ed. Dmitrievski. Kiev. 1895.
Vita Sancti Euthymii. Ed. Boor, C. de. Berlin. 1888.
Vita Sanctae Theodorae imperatricis. Ed. Regel. St Petersburg. 1891.
Vita Sanctae Theophano. Ed. Kurtz. St Petersburg. 1898.

(c) Legal and Administrative Documents.

Basilicorum libri lx. *See Gen. Bibl.* iv.
Constantinus VII. De cerimoniis aulae Byzantinae. De thematibus. De administrando imperio. *See Gen. Bibl.* iv.
Epanagoge. Ed. Zachariae v. Lingenthal (*in* Collectio librorum juris graeco-romani ineditorum). *See Gen. Bibl.* iv.
Juris ecclesiastici Graecorum...monumenta. Ed. Pitra, J. B. *See Gen. Bibl.* iv.
Juris graeco-romani tam canonici quam civilis tomi duo. Ed. Leunclavius. Frankfort. 1596.
Juris orientalis libri iii. Ed. Bonefidius. Paris. 1573.
Jus graeco-romanum. Ed. Zachariae v. Lingenthal. Pt. iii. Novellae imperatorum. *See Gen. Bibl.* iv.
Prefect, Book of the. *See Gen. Bibl.* iv.
Prochiron. *See Gen. Bibl.* iv.

II. MODERN WORKS.

(a) General.

Banduri, A. Imperium orientale. *See Gen. Bibl.* ii.
Bêlyáev, D. F. Byzantina. Vols. i–iii. St Petersburg. 1891–1908. (In Russian.)
Bréhier, L. Le schisme oriental du xie siècle. Paris. 1899.
Bury, J. B. History of the Eastern Roman Empire. *See Gen. Bibl.* v.
Cognasso, F. Partiti politici e lotte dinastiche in Bisanzio. Turin. 1912.
Diehl, C. Histoire de l'empire byzantin. *See Gen. Bibl.* v.
Ebersolt, J. Le grand Palais de Constantinople et le livre des Cérémonies. Paris. 1910.
Finlay, G. History of Greece. *See Gen. Bibl.* v.
Foord, E. The Byzantine Empire. London. 1911.
Gay, J. L'Italie méridionale et l'Empire byzantin. *See Gen. Bibl.* v.
Gelzer, H. Abriss der byzantinischen Kaisergeschichte. *See Gen. Bibl.* v.
Gfrörer, A. F. Byzantinische Geschichten. *See Gen. Bibl.* v.
Gibbon, E. Decline and Fall of the Roman Empire. *See Gen. Bibl.* v.

Hefele, C. J. v. Conciliengeschichte. French transl. New edn. Leclercq. Vol. IV. *See Gen. Bibl.* v.
Hergenröther, J. A. G. Photius, Patriarch von Konstantinopel. 3 vols. Ratisbon. 1867–9.
Hesseling, D. C. Essai sur la civilisation byzantine. French transl. Paris. 1907.
Hirsch, F. Byzantinische Studien. *See Gen. Bibl.* v.
Jorga, N. The Byzantine Empire. *See Gen. Bibl.* v.
Krumbacher, K. Geschichte der byzant. Litteratur. *See Gen. Bibl.* v.
Labarte, J. Le Palais impérial à Constantinople. Paris. 1881.
Lampros (Lambros), Sp. P. Ἱστορία τῆς Ἑλλάδος. Vols. III and IV. *See Gen. Bibl.* v.
Lebeau, C. Histoire du Bas-Empire. *See Gen. Bibl.* v.
Marin, E. Les Moines de Constantinople depuis la fondation de la ville jusqu'à la mort de Photius (330–898). Paris. 1897.
Millet, G. L'art byzantin. (*In* Michel, A. Histoire de l'Art. Vol. I, pt. 1. Paris. 1905.)
Mortreuil, J. A. B. Histoire du droit byzantin. 3 vols. Paris. 1843–7.
Muralt, E. de. Essai de chronographie byzantine. *See Gen. Bibl.* III.
Neumann, C. Die Weltstellung des byzantin. Reiches. *See Gen. Bibl.* v.
Nissen, W. Die Regelung des Klosterwesens im Rhomäerreiche bis zum Ende des IX Jahrh. Hamburg. 1897.
Norden, W. Das Papsttum und Byzanz. *See Gen. Bibl.* v.
Panchenko, B. A. Rural property at Byzantium. The agrarian law and monastic deeds. Izvêstiya russk. arkheol. Instituta v Konstantinopolê. Vol. IX. Nos. 1 and 2. Sofia. 1904. (In Russian.)
Richter, J. P. Quellen der byzantinischen Kunstgeschichte. Vienna. 1897.
Schlumberger, G. L. Les îles des Princes. Paris. 1884.
Sickel, W. Das byzantinische Krönungsrecht bis zum x Jahrh. BZ. VII (1898), p. 54.
Skabalanovich, N. A. The Byzantine Empire and the Church in the eleventh century. St Petersburg. 1884. (In Russian.)
Sokolóv, I. The law of property in the Greco-Roman Empire. Moscow. 1896. (In Russian.)
—— The election of patriarchs at Byzantium from the middle of the ninth to the middle of the fifteenth century (843–1453). St Petersburg. 1907. (In Russian.)
—— The external situation of monasticism in the Byzantine Church from the middle of the ninth to the thirteenth century (842–1204). Kazan. 1894. (In Russian.)
Ter Sahakean. Die armenischen Kaiser von Byzanz. 2 vols. Venice. 1905.
Unger, F. W. Quellen der byzantinischen Kunstgeschichte. Vienna. 1878.
Vasil'ev, A. A. Lektsii po istorii Vizantii. Vol. I. Petrograd. 1917.
Vasil'evski, V. Materials for the internal history of the Byzantine Empire. ZMNP. Vols. 202 and 210. 1879–80. (In Russian.)
Zachariae von Lingenthal, K. E. Geschichte der griechisch-römischen Rechts. *See Gen. Bibl.* v.
Zhishman, J. v. Das Stifterrecht in der morgenl. Kirche. Vienna. 1888.

(*b*) Monographs on Particular Reigns.

On Basil I.
Brooks, E. W. The Age of Basil I. BZ. xx (1911), p. 486.
Der Sahaghian, G. Un document arménien de la généalogie de Basile I. BZ. xx (1911), p. 165.
Kaufmann. Die Chronik des Achimaaz über die Kaiser Basilios I und Leo VI. BZ. VI (1897), p. 100.
Laemmer, H. Papst Nikolaus I und die byzantinische Staatskirche. Berlin. 1857.
Lapôtre, A. L'Europe et le St Siège à l'époque carolingienne. Le Pape Jean VIII. Paris. 1895.
—— De Anastasio bibliothecario. Paris. 1887.
Papadopoulos-Kerameus, A. Ὁ πατριάρχης Φώτιος ὡς πατὴρ ἅγιος τῆς ὀρθοδόξου καθολικῆς Ἐκκλησίας. BZ. VIII (1899), p. 647.

On Basil I. (*cont.*)

Vasil'ev, A. A. The beginnings of the Emperor Basil the Macedonian. *In* VV. xii (1905). (In Russian.)

Vogt, A. Basile Ier et la civilisation byzantine à la fin du ixe siècle. Paris. 1908.

On Leo VI.

Diehl, C. Les quatre mariages de l'empereur Léon le Sage. *In* Figures byzantines. 1re série. *See Gen. Bibl.* v.

Fischer, W. Zu "Leo und Alexander als Mitkaiser von Byzanz." BZ. v (1896), p. 137.

Lampros (Lambros), Sp. P. Leo und Alexander als Mitkaiser von Byzanz. BZ. v (1896), p. 13.

—— Die Abdankungsurkunde des Patriarchen Nikolaos Mystikos. BZ. i (1892), p. 551.

Mitard, M. Études sur le règne de Léon VI. BZ. xii (1903).

Popóv, N. A. The Emperor Leo VI the philosopher and his government from an ecclesiastical standpoint. Moscow. 1892. (In Russian.)

—— On Byzantine history in the tenth century. *In* Odessan Annual. iv. Odessa. 1894.

On Constantine VII.

Hirsch, F. Kaiser Konstantin VII Porphyrogennetos. (Programm der Königstädt. Realschule. Berlin. 1873.)

Rambaud, A. L'Empire grec au xe siècle. Constantin Porphyrogénète. Paris. 1870.

On Nicephorus II Phocas.

Dändliker, K. and Müller, J. J. Liudprand von Cremona und seine Quellen. Leipsic. 1871.

Diehl, C. Théophano. *In* Figures byzantines. 1re série. *See Gen. Bibl.* v.

Fischer, W. Beiträge zur historischen Kritik des Leon Diakonos und Michael Psellos. MIOGF. vii. 1886.

Köpke, R. De vita et scriptis Liudprandi episcopi Cremonensis commentatio historica. Berlin. 1842.

Laurent, J. Skylitzès et Nicéphore Phocas. BZ. vi (1897), p. 318.

Moltmann, J. Theophano, die Gemahlin Ottos II, in ihrer Bedeutung für die Politik Ottos I und Ottos II. Schwerin. 1878.

Schlumberger, G. L. Un empereur byzantin au xe siècle, Nicéphore Phocas. *See Gen. Bibl.* v.

Uhlirz, K. Über die Herkunft der Theophanu, Gemahlin Kaisers Otto II. BZ. iv (1895), p. 467.

Wartenberg, G. Berichtigung einer Angabe des Skylitzes über Nikephoros II Phokas. BZ. iv (1895), p. 478; vii (1898), p. 90.

On John Tzimisces.

Schlumberger, G. L. L'épopée byzantine à la fin du xe siècle. Pt. i. J. Tzimiscès, Basile II (969-989). *See Gen. Bibl.* v.

CHAPTER V.

(A)

THE STRUGGLE WITH THE SARACENS (717–867).

I. SPECIAL BIBLIOGRAPHIES.

In Krumbacher's Geschichte d. byzantinischen Litteratur (*see Gen. Bibl.* v) under each author and at the end of the volume. [For Greek sources.]

In Bury's edn. of Gibbon, vol. v, Appendix (*see Gen. Bibl.* v), and in his Eastern Roman Empire. *See Gen. Bibl.* v. [Very full.]

In Laurent's L'Arménie entre Byzance et l'Islam. *See below,* III (*c*) *Monographs.*

II. AUTHORITIES.

(*a*) CONTEMPORARY.

Acta 42 Martyrum Amoriensium. Ed. Vasil'evski, V., and Nikitin, P. (Mém. AcadIP., Cl. Hist.-phil. VII, No. 2.) 1905.

Dionysius (so-called). Chronicon (Syriac). Ed. with French transl. Chabot, J. B. BHE. 102. 1895. [A work of the year 775, probably by Joshua the Stylite of Zuqnin.]

Georgius Monachus. Historia Chronica. Ed. Boor, C. de. Leipsic. 1904. MPG. cx. (With the interpolations from Symeon Logothetes.)

Ibn Khurdādhbih. Liber viarum et provinciarum (Arab.). Ed. with French transl. De Goeje, M. J. (Bibliotheca Geographorum Arabicorum. VI.) Leiden. 1889. (With extracts from Qudāma; *see below,* (*b*) ii.)

Leontius. Historia Chalifarum (Arm.). Ed. Ezean, K. St Petersburg. 1887. French transl. Chahnazarian, V. Paris. 1856. Russian transl. Patkanian, K. St Petersburg. 1862. Latin transl. (of extracts with commentary) Filler, E. *See below,* III (*b*).

Nicephorus. Historia concisa. Ed. Boor, C. de. Leipsic. 1880.

Theophanes. Chronographia. Ed. Classen, J. and Bekker, I. 2 vols. CSHB. 1839, 41. Also ed. Boor, C. de. 2 vols. Leipsic. 1883, 85.

Ya'qūbī (Ibn Wāḍiḥ). Historiae (Arab.). Ed. Houtsma, M. Th. 2 vols. Leiden. 1883. Relevant parts transl. Brooks, E. W. *in* JHS. 1898 and EHR. 1900 for period 717–813 (*see below,* III (*c*) *Monographs*), and Vasil'ev, A. A. *in* Vizantiya i Araby, vol. I, for 813–867 (*see below,* III (*c*) *Monographs*).

(*b*) LATER.

i. *Greek.*

Cedrenus. Synopsis Historiarum. Ed. Bekker, I. 2 vols. CSHB. 1838, 39.

Chronicon Cantabrigiense. Ed. Cozza-Luzi, G. (Documenti per servire alla storia di Sicilia, ser. 4, vol. II). Palermo. (Soc. Siciliana per la storia patria.) 1890. Ed. Batiffol, P. (Comptes Rendus. AcadIBL. Ser. 4, vol. XVIII.) 1890. (From the Paris MS only.) [This chronicle was first discovered in an Arabic version at Cambridge, which is published with the Greek text with Italian transl. in Cozza-Luzi's edn. The Greek text is reprinted with a Russian transl. of the Arabic in Vasil'ev's Vizantiya i Araby; *see below,* III (*c*) *Monographs.*]

Constantine Porphyrogenitus. De cerimoniis aulae Byzantinae (with the so-called Appendix). *See Gen. Bibl.* iv.
Genesius. Regna. Ed. Lachmann, C. CSHB. 1834.
Leo Grammaticus (so-called). Chronographia. Ed. Bekker, I. CSHB. 1842.
Symeon Logothetes. Chronicle. *See* ii (*a*), Georgius Monachus.
Symeon Magister (so-called). Annales. Ed. Bekker, I. CSHB. 1838.
Theodosius Melitenus. Chronographia. Ed. Tafel, T. L. F. *In* Monumenta Saecularia. (K. Akad. d. Wissenschaften.) Munich. 1859.
Theophanes continuatus. Chronographia. Ed. Bekker, I. CSHB. 1838.
Zonaras. Annales. Ed. Pinder, M. and Büttner-Wobst, T. 3 vols. CSHB. 1841–97.

ii. *Oriental.*

Balādhuri. Liber expugnationis regionum (Arab.). Ed. De Goeje, M. J. Leiden. 1863. English transl. Khūri Ḥitti, P. (Columbia University Studies in History, Economics, and Public Law, vol. lxviii, No. 163.) New York. 1916. (In progress.) German transl. Rescher, O. Leipsic. 1917. (In progress.) [Balādhuri died in 892; but, as his work contains nothing relevant after 838 exc. one Sicilian notice, it is not placed among contemporary sources.]
Chronicon anni 846 (Syr.). Ed. Brooks, E. W., with Latin transl. by Chabot, J. B. (CSCO. Chronica Minora, vol. ii.) 1904. [Contains nothing relevant after 726.]
Elias Nisibenus. Opus chronologicum (Syr. and Arab.). Ed. with Latin transl. Brooks, E. W., and Chabot, J. B. (CSCO.) 1909–10. French transl. Delaporte, L. J. (BHE. 181.) 1910.
Ibn ʿAdhārī. Notitiae Occidentis (Arab.). Ed. Dozy, R. P. A. 2 vols. Leiden. 1848–51. French transl. Fagnan, E. 2 vols. Algiers. 1901–4.
Ibn al-Athīr. Chronicon perfectissimum (Arab.). Ed. Tornberg, C. J. 14 vols. Leiden. 1851–76. Passages relating to Asia Minor for period 717–813 transl. Brooks, E. W. JHS. 1898. (*See below,* iii (*c*) *Monographs.*) Relevant passages from 813 transl. Vasil'ev, A. A. Vizantiya i Araby. (*See below,* iii (*c*) *Monographs.*) Passages relating to Sicily transl. Amari, M. Biblioteca Arabo-Sicula, vers. ital., i, p. 353. *See below,* iii (*b*).
Ibn Kutaiba. Manuale Historiae (Arab.). Ed. Wüstenfeld, F. Göttingen. 1850. Relevant passages from 813 transl. Vasil'ev (*see above*). [The author lived 828–88, but records nothing relevant after 838.]
Johannes Catholicus. Historia Armeniae (Arm.). Ed. Anon. Jerusalem. 1867. French transl. Saint-Martin, J. Paris. 1841.
Kindī. Liber rectorum (Arab.). Ed. Guest, R. (E. J. W. Gibb Memorial, 19.) Leiden and London. 1912. Relevant passages transl. Brooks, E. W. BZ. 1913. *See below,* iii (*c*) *Monographs.*
Liber fontium (Kitāb al-ʿuyūn) (Arab.). Ed. De Goeje, M. J. (Fragm. Historicorum Arabicorum, vol. i.) Leiden. 1871. Relevant passages transl. Brooks. JHS. 1898–9, and Vasil'ev. *See above.*
Maḥbūb (Agapius) of Manbij (Hierapolis). Liber tituli (Arab.). Ed. with French transl. Vasil'ev, A. A. (Patrologia Orientalis, v, p. 561; vii, p. 458; viii, p. 396). 3 pts. Paris and Freiburg. 1910–12.
Malikī. Horti animarum (Arab.). Parts relating to Sicily ed. Amari, M. Biblioteca Arabo-Sicula, p. 176, i vol. and Appendices. Leipsic. (Deutsche Morgenländische Gesellschaft.) 1857–87. Italian transl. Bibl. Arabo-Sicula, vers. ital. (*see below,* iii (*b*)), i, p. 294. Russian transl. Vasil'ev. *See above.*
Maqrīzī. Liber admonitionis et considerationis (Arab.). Ed. ʿAdawi, M. K. 2 vols. Bulak. 1853. Ed. Wiet, G. (Mém. de l'Institut français d'Archéologie Orientale 30, etc.) Cairo. 1911 ff. (In progress.) French transl. Bouriant, U. (Mém. de la Mission Archéologique du Caire, 17.) 2 pts. Paris. 1895–1900. Continued by Casanova, P. (Mém. de l'Inst. fr. d'Arch. Or. 3.) Cairo. 1906. (In progress.) Passage about Mutawakkil's restoration of the Egyptian fleet transl. Rosen, V. R. Imp. Vasili Bolgaroboytsa, p. 274. (Mém. AcadIP. xliv.) 1883. *See also* Vasil'ev, A. A. Vizantiya i Araby. Vol. i, App. p. 124. *See below,* iii (*c*).

Mas'ūdī. Liber commonitionis et recognitionis (Arab.). Ed. De Goeje, M. J. (Bibl. Geogr. Arab. 8.) Leiden. 1894. French transl. Carra de Vaux, B. Paris. (Société Asiatique.) 1896.
—— Prata aurea. Ed. with French transl. Barbier de Meynard, C. A. C. 9 vols. Paris. 1861-77.
Michael Syrus. Chronicon (Syr.). Ed. with French transl. Chabot, J. B. 3 vols. Paris. (AcadIBL.) 1899-1910. [Copies the lost contemporary Chronicle of Dionysius.]
Nuwairī. Encyclopaedia (Arab.). Parts relating to Sicily ed. Amari, M. Bibl. Arabo-Sicula. p. 423. (*See above.*) Italian transl. Bibl. Arabo-Sicula, vers. ital. *See below,* III (*b*), II, p. 110. Russian transl. Vasil'ev. *See above.*
Qudāma. Liber tributi (Arab.). *See* Ibn Khurdādhbih, *sect.* (*a*) *above.* [Important for Arab military organisation.]
Stephanus Taronensis. Historia Armeniae (Arm.). Ed. Malkhasian, S. St Petersburg. 1885. German transl. Gelzer, H., and Burckhardt, A. Leipsic. 1907.
Ṭabarī. Historia populorum et regum (Arab.). Ed. De Goeje, M. J., and others. 15 vols. Leiden. 1879-1901. Relevant parts transl. Brooks. JHS. 1898-9, and EHR. 1900, and Vasil'ev. *See above.*

III. MODERN WORKS.

(*a*) General.

Bury, J. B. A History of the Later Roman Empire. *See Gen. Bibl.* v.
EncBr. (*See Gen. Bibl.* I.) De Goeje, M. J. *s.v.* Caliphate.
Finlay, G. A history of Greece. *See Gen. Bibl.* v.
Gelzer, H. Abriss d. byzantinischen Geschichte. *See Gen. Bibl.* v.
Gibbon, E. The history of the Decline and Fall of the Roman Empire. *See Gen. Bibl.* v.
Holm, A. Geschichte Siciliens im Alterthum. Vol. III. Leipsic. 1898.
Müller, A. Der Islam im Morgen- u. Abendland. 2 vols. (Oncken's Allgemeine Geschichte. Abth. 2. Th. 4.) Berlin. 1885-7.
Weil, G. Geschichte der Chalifen. *See Gen. Bibl.* v.

(*b*) On Authorities.

Arabic authors:
Brockelmann, C. Geschichte d. arabischen Litteratur. 2 vols. Weimar and Berlin. 1897-1902; and in another form in Die Litteraturen des Ostens. Vol. VI. Leipsic. 1901.
EncBr. (*See Gen. Bibl.* I.) De Goeje, M. J., and Thatcher, G. W. *s.v.* Arabia.
Wüstenfeld, F. Die Geschichtsschreiber d. Araber u. ihre Werke (Abh. d. Kön. Gesellschaft d. Wissenschaften zu Göttingen, Hist.-phil. Cl. XXVIII, No. 2, 3; XXIX, No. 1). 1881-2.
Amari, M. Biblioteca Arabo-Sicula, vers. ital. 2 vols. and App. 8vo edn. Turin, Florence, and Rome. 1881, 89. [Introduction on authors dealing with Sicily.]
Notices of the Arabic authorities are also given in the Appendix to Vasil'ev's Vizantiya i Araby. *See below,* III (*c*) *Monographs.*
Chronicon Cantabrigiense:
Cipolla, C. Testi greci della cronaca arabo-sicula di Cambridge. (Atti della R. Accad. delle scienze di Torino. XXVII.) 1892. p. 830.
Cozza-Luzi, G. Sulla scoperta di due cronache greche siculo-saraceniche e loro correlazione coll' arabico di Cambridge. Rome. 1893.
Constantine Porphyrogenitus:
Bury, J. B. The Ceremonial Book of Const. Porphyrogennetos. EHR. 1907. pp. 209, 417.

"Dionysius":
Nau, F. La 4me partie de la chronique de Denys de Tellmahré. (Review of Chabot's edn.) Bulletin Critique. 1896. p. 121.
—— Nouvelle étude sur la chron. attribuée à D. de T. *Ibid.* p. 464.
—— Les auteurs des chroniques attribuées à D. de T. et à Josué le Stylite. *Ibid.* 1897. p. 54.
Nöldeke, Th. La chron. de D. de T. (Review of Chabot's edn.) Vienna Oriental Journal. 1896. p. 160.
Elias Nisibenus:
Baethgen, F. Fragmente syrischer u. arabischer Historiker. (Abh. f. die Kunde d. Morgenlandes. VIII.) Leipsic. (Deutsche Morgenländische Gesellschaft.) 1884.
Georgius Monachus and later Byzantine historians:
Hirsch, F. Byzantinische Studien. *See Gen. Bibl.* v.
Also in Bury's Eastern Roman Empire. App. 2. *See Gen. Bibl.* v.
Leontius:
Filler, E. Quaestiones de Leontii Armenii historia. (Commentationes philologicae Jenenses 7, fasc. 1.) 1903.
Maḥbūb:
Vasil'ev, A. A. Agapi manbidzhski, khristianski arabski istorik x vêka. *In* VV. 1904. p. 574.
Michael and Theophanes:
Brooks, E. W. The Chronology of Theophanes. BZ. 1899. p. 82.
—— The Sources of Theophanes and the Syriac chroniclers. BZ. 1906. p. 578.
Nicephorus:
Burckhardt, A. Der Londoner Codex d. Breviarium d. Nikephoros Patriarcha. BZ. 1896. p. 465.
Symeon Logothetes (source of Leo, Cedrenus, Theodosius, and the interpolator of George):
Boor, C. de. Die Chronik d. Logotheten. BZ. 1897. p. 233.
Patzig, E. Leo Grammaticus u. seine Sippe. BZ. 1894. p. 470.
Serruys, D. Recherches sur l'Épitomé. BZ. 1907. p. 1.
Also in Bury's Eastern Roman Empire. App. 3. *See Gen. Bibl.* v. [The literature of this subject is enormous; see Bury, *op. cit.* p. 502, for other publications.]
Syriac authors:
Duval, R. La Littérature Syriaque. (Bibliothèque de l'enseignement de l'histoire ecclésiastique.) Paris. 1899. 3rd edn. 1907.
Theophanes:
Preobrazhenski, P. G. Lêtopisnoe povêstvovanie Sv. Feofana ispovêdnika. Vienna. 1912.

(c) Monographs and Special Treatises.

Amari, M. Storia dei Musulmani di Sicilia. 4 vols. Florence. 1854–68.
Anderson, J. G. C. The road-system of eastern Asia Minor. JHS. 1897. p. 22. (With map.)
Boor, C. de. Der Angriff der Rhôs auf Byzanz. BZ. 1895. p. 445. [For the chronology of the campaigns of 859–63.]
Brooks, E. W. The Arabs in Asia Minor from Arabic sources. JHS. 1898. p. 200. (Translation of relevant passages with notes.)
—— The campaign of 716–8 from Arabic sources. JHS. 1899. p. 19. (Translation of passages from the Kitāb al-ʿuyūn and Ṭabarī with notes.)
—— Byzantines and Arabs in the time of the early Abbasids. EHR. 1900. p. 728. 1901. p. 84. (Translation of relevant passages with notes and map.)
—— The Arab occupation of Crete. EHR. 1913. p. 431.
—— The relations between the empire and Egypt from a new Arabic source. BZ. 1913. p. 381. (With translation of extracts from Kindī.)
Bury, J. B. Mutasim's march through Cappadocia. JHS. 1909. p. 120.
—— The embassy of John the Grammarian. EHR. 1909. p. 296.

Bury, J. B. The naval policy of the Roman Empire in relation to the Western provinces from the 7th to the 9th century. (Centenario della nascita di M. Amari. Vol. II.) Palermo. 1910.
—— A History of the Eastern Roman Empire. *See Gen. Bibl.* v.
Encyclopaedia of Islam. *See Gen. Bibl.* I. Especially Streck, M. ʿAwāṣim. Baghdād. Zettersteen, K. V. Hārūn al-Rashīd.
Ghazarian, M. Armenien unter d. arabischen Herrschaft bis zur Entstehung d. Bagratidenreiches. Zeitschrift f. armenische Philologie. 1904. p. 149.
Laurent, J. L'Arménie entre Byzance et l'Islam. (EcfrAR. 117.) Paris. 1919. [The best work on this subject with full bibliography and useful map.]
Le Strange, G. The lands of the Eastern Caliphate. *See Gen. Bibl.* II.
Lombard, A. Constantin V, empereur des Romains. (Université de Paris. Bibl. de la Faculté des Lettres 16.) Paris. 1902.
Ramsay, W. M. The war of Moslem and Christian for the possession of Asia Minor. Contemporary Review. 1906. p. 1.
Schenk, K. Kaiser Leon III. Halle. 1880.
Vasil'ev, A. A. Vizantiya i Araby. 2 vols. St Petersburg. 1900–2. [Critical history from 813 with translation of relevant passages from Arabic writers.]
Wellhausen, J. Die Kämpfe d. Araber mit den Romäern in d. Zeit d. Umaijiden. Nachrichten d. K. Gesellschaft d. Wissenschaften zu Göttingen. Phil.-hist. Cl. 1901. p. 414. [Detailed criticism of the records and reconstruction.]

(B)

THE STRUGGLE WITH THE SARACENS (867–1057).

I. SPECIAL BIBLIOGRAPHIES.

In Krumbacher's Geschichte d. byzantinischen Litteratur (*see Gen. Bibl.* v) under each author and at the end of the volume. [For Greek sources.]

II. AUTHORITIES.

(*a*) Greek and Latin.

Annales Beneventani. Ed. Pertz, G. H. MGH. Script. III, p. 173.
Cameniates. De excidio Thessalonicae. Ed. Bekker, I. CSHB. 1838.
Cecaumenus. Strategicon. Ed. Vasil'evski, V., and others *in* Zapiski Ist.-Filol. Fakult. AcadIP. XXXVIII. 1896.
Cedrenus. Synopsis Historiarum. Ed. Bekker, I. 2 vols. CSHB. 1838, 39.
Chronicon Cantabrigiense. *See Bibl. to ch.* v (A), II (*b*) i.
—— Salernitanum. Ed. Pertz, G. H. MGH. Script. III, p. 467.
Constantine Porphyrogenitus. De cerimoniis aulae Byzantinae. De administrando imperio. De thematibus. *See Gen. Bibl.* IV.
Genesius. Regna. Ed. Lachmann, C. CSHB. 1834.
Georgius Monachus (so-called). Historia Chronica. MPG. CX. [This compilation from 843 to 948 is taken from the lost work of Symeon Logothetes, and after that from Zonaras.]
Johannes Diaconus Neapolitanus. Acta translationis S. Severini. Ed. Waitz, G. MGH. Script. Lang. et Ital. pp. 463 ff.
Leo Diaconus. Ed. Hase, C. B. CSHB. 1828.
Leo Grammaticus (so-called). Chronographia. Ed. Bekker, I. CSHB. 1842.
Leo Sapiens. Tactica. MPG. CVII. Also ed. Vári, R. *in* Sylloge Tacticorum Graecorum. Vol. III. (Magyar Tudományos Akadémia.) Buda-Pest. 1917, in progress.
Liudprandus. Relatio de legatione Constantinopolitana. Ed. Becker, J. *in* SGUS. 3rd edn. Hanover. 1915.

Lupus Protospatarius Barensis. Chronicon. *Also* Annales Barenses. Ed. Pertz, G. H. MGH. Script. v, p. 52.
Narratio de imagine Edessena. Ed. Dobschütz, E. von *in* Texte u. Untersuchungen. Neue Folge. III, p. 39**. Leipsic. 1899.
Nicephorus Phocas (so-called). De velitatione bellica. Ed. Hase, C. B. *with* Leo Diaconus. CSHB. 1828.
Nicolaus Mysticus. Epistolae. MPG. CXI. [Epp. 1, 2, addressed to the Emir of Crete, contain valuable information, esp. about Cyprus.]
Petrus Siculus. Historia Manichaeorum. MPG. CIV. [On the Paulicians.]
Psellus. Chronographia. Ed. Sathas, C. (Byzantine Texts.) London. 1899.
Scylitzes. Chronicon. Greek text unpublished. Latin transl. Gabius, J. B. Venice. 1570.
Symeon Logothetes. *See above*, Georgius Monachus.
Symeon Magister (so-called). Annales. Ed. Bekker, I. CSHB. 1838.
Theodosius Melitenus. Chronographia. *See Bibl. to ch.* v(A), II (*b*) i.
Theodosius Monachus. Ep. ad Leonem diaconum de expugnatione Syracusarum. Greek text (imperfect), ed. Zuretti, C. O. Ἰταλοελληνικά. *In* Centenario della nascita di M. Amari. Vol. I, p. 165. Palermo. 1910. Latin version (complete) by Josaphat of Messina *in* RR.II.SS. (1st edn.). Vol. I, pt. II, p. 256. 1725.
Theophanes continuatus. Chronographia. Ed. Bekker, I. CSHB. 1838.
Vita S. Eliae iunioris. ASBoll. 17 Aug. III.
—— S. Pauli iunioris. Ed. Delahaye, H. *in* AB. XI, p. 5. 1892.
Zonaras. Annales. Ed. Pinder, M. and Büttner-Wobst, T. 3 vols. CSHB. 1841–97.

(*b*) Oriental.

Abū'l Fidā. Annales Muslemici (Arab.). Ed. with Latin transl. Reiske, J. J., and Adler, I. G. C. 5 vols. Copenhagen. 1789–94. Ed. Anon. 4 vols. Constantinople. 1870.
Abū'l Maḥāsin. Annales (Arab.). Ed. with Latin transl. Carlyle, J. D. 2 parts. Cambridge. 1792. (From 971.) Ed. Juynboll, T. G. J., and Matthes, B. F. 2 vols. Leiden. 1852–61. Continued by Popper, W. (Univ. of California publications in Semitic philology. II.) Berkeley. 1909, etc. (In progress.) Relevant parts to 959 transl. Vasil'ev, A. A. *in* Vizantiya i Araby. Vol. II. *See below*, III (*c*) Monographs.
ʿAinī. Monile Margaritarum (Arab.). Unpublished. Extract ed. with French transl. Fagnani, E. Nouveaux textes historiques. *In* Centenario della nascita di M. Amari. Vol. II, p. 86. Palermo. 1910. Relevant parts to 959 transl. Vasil'ev. *See above.*
ʿArīb. Chronicon (Arab.). Ed. De Goeje, M. J. Leiden. 1897. Relevant parts transl. Vasil'ev. *See above.* [Continuation of Ṭabarī.]
Aristaces Lastivertensis. Historia Armeniae (Arm.). Ed. Anon. (Mkhitharists). Venice. 1844. French transl. Prud'homme, E. *in* Revue de l'Orient. Vol. XV, p. 343; XVI, pp. 41, 159, 268, 289; XVII, p. 5. (Soc. Orientale de France.) Paris. 1863, 64.
Chronicon ad ann. 1234 pertinens (Syr.). Ed. Chabot, J. B. 2 vols. (CSCO. 81, 82.) Paris. 1917–20.
Ḍahabī. Historia Islamica (Arab.). Unpublished. Relevant parts to 959 transl. Vasil'ev. *See above.*
Elias Nisibenus. Opus chronologicum (Syr. and Arab.). *See Bibl. to ch.* v(A), II (*b*) ii.
Eutychius. Annales (Arab.). Ed. Cheikho, P. L., and others (CSCO.). 2 vols. Beyrout and Paris. 1909–12. Latin transl. Pocock, E. MPG. CXI.
Ibn ʿAdhārī. Notitiae Occidentis (Arab.). *See Bibl. to ch.* v(A), II (*b*) ii.
Ibn al-Athīr. Chronicon perfectissimum (Arab.). Ed. Tornberg, C. J. 14 vols. Leiden. 1851–76. Relevant parts to 959 transl. Vasil'ev. *See above.* Passages relating to Sicily transl. Amari, M. Biblioteca Arabo-Sicula, vers. ital. Vol. I, p. 353. *See Bibl. to ch.* v(A), III (*b*).
Ibn al-Jauzī. Liber speculi temporum (Arab.). Unpublished. Relevant parts to 959 transl. Vasil'ev. *See above.*

Ibn Kathīr. Historia universalis (Arab.). Unpublished. Relevant parts to 959 transl. Vasil'ev. *See above.*
Ibn Khaldūn. Historia Islamica (Arab.). Ed. Anon. 7 vols. Bulak. 1867. Relevant parts relating to Sicily transl. Amari. (*See above.*) Vol. II, p. 161. [The Eastern portions are all taken from existing sources.]
Ibn al-Khaṭīb (Lisān-ad-Dīn). Gesta regum clarorum (Arab.). Ed. Abdul-Wahab, H. H. Contributions a l'histoire de l'Afrique du nord et de la Sicile. *In* Centenario della nascita di M. Amari. Vol. II, p. 427. Palermo. 1910.
Ibn Ẓafīr. Liber de dynastiis praeteritis (Arab.). Unpublished. Relevant parts to 959 transl. Vasil'ev. *See above.*
Johannes Catholicus. Historia Armeniae (Arm.). *See Bibl. to ch.* v(A), II (*b*) ii.
Kamāl-ad-Dīn. Selecta ex historia Halebi (Arab.). Full text unpublished. Portions ed. with Latin transl. Freytag, G. (i) Sel. ex hist. Hal. Paris. 1819. (637–947.) (ii) Regnum Saahd-Aldaulae. Bonn. 1820. (968–991.) (iii) Locmani fabulae et plura loca ex codd....historicis. Bonn. 1823. (991–1002.) Latin transl. (extracts) Müller, J. J. Historia Merdasidarum. Bonn. 1829. (1002–79.) Relevant parts to 959 transl. Vasil'ev. *See above.*
Liber fontium (Kitāb al-ʻuyūn) (Arab.). Ed. De Goeje, M. J. *in* Fragm. Historicorum Arabicorum. Vol. I. Leiden. 1871. Relevant parts to 959 transl. Vasil'ev. *See above.*
Maḥbūb (Agapius) of Hierapolis. Liber tituli (Arab.). This part unpublished. Extracts in Russian transl. Rosen, V. R. ZMNP. CCXXXVII. p. 47. 1884.
Makīn. Historia Saracenica (Arab.). Ed. with Latin transl. Erpenius, T. Leiden. 1625. French transl. Vattier, P. Paris. 1657.
Masʻūdī. Liber commonitionis et recognitionis, and Prata aurea (Arab.). *See Bibl. to ch.* v(A), II (*b*) ii.
Matthaeus Edessenus. Chronicon (Arm.). Full text unpublished. Parts relating to period 963–76 ed. with French transl. Dulaurier, J. P. L. F. E. *in* Rec. hist. Cr., Doc. Armén. Vol. I. 1869. Complete French transl. Dulaurier. Bibl. Hist. Arm. Pt. II. Paris. 1858.
Michael Syrus. Chronicon (Syr.). Ed. with French. transl. Chabot, J. B. 3 vols. (AcadIBL.) Paris. 1899–1910. Arm. version (epitome with additions relating to Armenia) ed. Anon. Jerusalem. 1870–1. French transl. Langlois, V. Venice. 1868.
Miskawaihī. Probationes gentium (Arab.). Ed. with English transl. Amedroz, H. F., and Margoliouth, D. S. *in* The Eclipse of the ʻAbbasid Caliphate. Vols. I, II, IV, V. Oxford. 1920, 21.
Nuwairī. Encyclopaedia (Arab.). *See Bibl. to ch.* v (A), II (*b*) ii.
Rudhrāwarī (Abū Shujāʻ). Historia Islamica (Arab.). Ed. with English transl. Amedroz, H. F. and Margoliouth, D. S. *in* The Eclipse of the ʻAbbasid Caliphate. Vols. III, VI. Oxford. 1920, 21. [Continuation of Miskawaihī.]
Stephanus Taronensis. Historia Armeniae (Arm.). *See Bibl. to ch.* v (A), II (*b*) ii.
Ṭabarī. Historia populorum et regnorum (Arab.). Ed. De Goeje, M. J., and others. 15 vols. Leiden. 1879–1901. Relevant parts transl. Vasil'ev. *See above.*
Yaḥyà of Antioch. Annales (Arab.). Ed. Cheikho, P. L., and others (CSCO.). Beyrout and Paris. 1909. (With Eutychius.) Extracts relating to reign of Basil II ed. with Russian transl. and commentary, Rosen, V. R. Imp. Vasili Bolgaroboytsa (Mém. AcadIP. XLIV). 1883. Relevant parts to 959 transl. Vasil'ev. *See above.*
Yaʻqūbī (Ibn Waḍih). Historia (Arab.). Ed. Houtsma, M. T. 2 vols. Leiden. 1883. Relevant parts transl. Vasil'ev. *See above.*

III. MODERN WORKS.

(*a*) General.

Amari, M. Storia dei Musulmani di Sicilia. 4 vols. Florence. 1854–68.
Bussell, F. W. The Roman Empire. *See Gen. Bibl.* v. [Specialises on Armenian relations.]

Dulaurier, J. P. L. F. E. Recherches sur la chronologie arménienne. Bibl. Hist. Arm. Pt. I. Paris. 1859.
EncBr. (*See Gen. Bibl.* I.) De Goeje, M. J. *s.v.* Caliphate.
Encyclopaedia of Islam. (*See Gen. Bibl.* I.) Especially Streck, M. Armenia. Sobernheim, M. Ḥamdānids.
Finlay, G. History of Greece. *See Gen. Bibl.* v.
Gay, J. L'Italie méridionale et l'Empire byzantin. (867–1074.) *See Gen. Bibl.* v.
Gelzer, H. Abriss d. byz. Geschichte. *See Gen. Bibl.* v.
Gibbon, E. History of the Decline and Fall of the Roman Empire. *See Gen. Bibl.* v.
Hartmann, L. M. Geschichte Italiens im Mittelalter. Vols. III, IV. *See Gen. Bibl.* v.
Holm, A. Geschichte Siciliens im Alterthum. Vol. III. Leipsic. 1898.
Müller, A. Der Islam im Morgen- u. Abendland. 2 vols. *See Bibl. to ch.* v(A), III (*a*).
Oman, C. W. C. A history of the Art of War. *See Gen. Bibl.* v.
Ramsay, W. The historical geography of Asia Minor. *See Gen. Bibl.* II.
Weil, G. Geschichte d. Chalifen. *See Gen. Bibl.* v.

(*b*) On Authorities.

Arabic authors.
See Bibl. to ch. v(A), III (*b*).
Chronicon Cantabrigiense.
See Bibl. to ch. v(A), III (*b*).
Constantinus Porphyrogenitus.
Bury, J. B. The Ceremonial Book of Constantine Porphyrogennetos. EHR. 1907. pp. 209, 417.
—— The treatise De administrando imperio. BZ. 1906. p. 517.
Elias Nisibenus.
See Bibl. to ch. v(A), III (*b*).
Maḥbūb.
See Bibl. to ch. v(A), III (*b*).
Petrus Siculus.
Friedrich, J. Der ursprungliche bei Geo. Monachus nur theilweise erhaltene Bericht über die Paulikianer. *In* Sitzungsberichte d. bayer. Akad. d. Wissenschaften. Philos.-philol. u. hist. Cl. Munich. 1896. p. 67.
Psellus.
Bury, J. B. Roman Emperors from Basil II to Isaac Komnênos. EHR. 1889. pp. 41, 251.
Rambaud, A. N. Michael Psellos *in* Études sur l'histoire byzantine, p. 111. Paris. 1912. (Reprinted from RH. 1877.)
Symeon Logothetes.
See Bibl. to ch. v(A), III (*b*).
Syriac authors.
Baumstark, A. Geschichte d. Syrischen Literatur. Bonn. 1922.
Duval, R. La Littérature Syriaque. *See Bibl. to ch.* v(A), III (*b*).
Theophanes continuatus and other Byzantine historians.
Brooks, E. W. The date of the last two books of the Continuator of Theophanes. BZ. 1901. p. 416.
Hirsch, F. Byzantinische Studien. *See Gen. Bibl.* v.

(*c*) Monographs and Special Treatises.

Anderson, J. G. C. The campaign of Basil I against the Paulicians in 872. CR. 1896. p. 136.
—— The road-system of eastern Asia Minor. JHS. 1897. p. 22. (With map.)
Ghazarian, M. Armenien unter d. arabischen Herrschaft bis zur Entstehung d. Bagratidenreiches. *In* Zeitschrift für armenische Philologie. Marburg. 1904. p. 149.

Laurent, J. L'Arménie entre l'Byzance et l'Islam. (EcfrAR. CXVII.) 1919.
Leonhardt, K. Kaiser Nicephorus II Phokas u. die Hamdaniden. Halle. 1887.
Le Strange, G. The lands of the Eastern Caliphate. *See Gen. Bibl.* II.
Rambaud, A. N. L'Empire grec au xe siècle. Paris. 1870.
Rosen, V. R. Imp. Vasili Bolgaroboytsa. Mém. AcadIP. XLIV. 1883.
Schlumberger, G. L. Un Empereur byzantin au xe siècle. *See Gen. Bibl.* V.
Tomaschek, W. Hist.-topographisches vom oberen Euphrat u. aus Ost-Kappadokien *in* Kiepert-Festschrift. Berlin. 1898. p. 137.
—— Zur hist. Topographie v. Kleinasien im Mittelalter. SKAW. CXXIV (1891). Abhandlung 8.
Vasil'ev, A. A. Vizantiya i Araby. 2 vols. St Petersburg. 1900–2. [Critical history from 813 with translation of relevant passages from Arabic writers.]
Vogt, A. Basile Ier, empereur de Byzance. Paris. 1908.

CHAPTER VI.

ARMENIA[1].

I. COLLECTIONS OF SOURCES.

Collection des historiens anciens et modernes de l'Arménie, ed. Langlois, V. 2 vols. Paris. 1868, 69.
Collection d'historiens arméniens, ed. Brosset, M. F. 2 vols. St Petersburg. 1874, 76.
Rec. hist. Crois. *See Gen. Bibl.* IV. Documents arméniens. Vol. I, ed. Dulaurier, E. Paris. 1869. [Contains: Preface, materials for the history of the kingdom of Little Armenia. Introduction, the kingdom of Little Armenia, or Cilicia, in the time of the Crusades. Genealogical and dynastic tables. Matthew of Edessa. Gregory the Priest. The Doctor Basil. Nerses Shnorhali. Gregory Dgha. Michael the Syrian. Guiragos of Kantzag. Vartan the Great. Samuel of Ani. Hethum the historian, Count of Gorigos. Vahram of Edessa. Ballad on the captivity of Leo, son of King Hethum I. King Hethum II. Narses of Lambron. The Constable Smbat. Martiros of Crimea. The Doctor Mĕkhithar of Tashir. Appendix, continuation of the history of Little Armenia. Armenian Charters.]
Id. Vol. II. Latin and French docs. concerning Armenia, ed. Kohler, C. Paris. 1906. [Contains: John Dardel, Chronique d'Arménie. Hayton, La flor des estoires des parties d'Orient. Haytonus, Flos historiarum terre Orientis. Brocardus, Directorium ad passagium faciendum. Guillelmus Adae, De modo Saracenos extirpandi. Daniel de Thaurisio, Responsio ad errores impositos Hermenis. Les gestes des Chiprois.]
Langlois, V. Le trésor des chartes d'Arménie, ou Cartulaire de la Chancellerie royale des Roupéniens. Venice. 1863.

II.

Period of Anarchy (428–885).

A. *Armenian sources.*

Elisha vardapet. The History of Vardan and his companions. Armenian text publ. at Constantinople 1764, at St Petersburg 1787, at Venice 1827, 1828, 1832, 1838, 1859, 1864, at Moscow 1861, at Theodosia 1861, at Jerusalem 1865, at Tiflis 1879. French transl. Langlois. V. Histoire de Vartan et de la guerre des Arméniens; *in* Collection des historiens anc. et mod. de l'Arm. Vol. II. Paris. 1869. [Relates the first part of the religious war against the Persians under Yesdigerd III.]
Eznik of Kolb. The Refutation of the Sects. Armenian text publ. at Constantinople 1763, at Smyrna 1772, at Venice 1826 and 1863. German transl. Schmid, J. M. Des Wardapet Eznik von Kolb, Wider die Sekten. Vienna. 1900. [Against the heretical doctrines then invading Armenia.]
John the Mamikonian. History of the Province of Taron. Armenian text publ. Constantinople 1708 and 1719, Venice 1832. French transl. Langlois, V. Collection des historiens anc. et mod. de l'Arm. Vol. I. pp. 357–82. Paris. 1868. [Wars of the Mamikonians against the Persians.]

[1] In the bibliography are indicated, not all the works relating to each question and subject treated, but the chief works to be consulted. This bibliography is intended above all to be critical.

Lazarus of Pharpi. History of Armenia. Armenian text publ. Venice 1793, 1807, 1873, Tiflis 1904. French transl. Langlois, V. Collection des historiens anc. et mod. de l'Arm. Vol. II. pp. 253–368. Paris. 1869. [Gives Armenian events 388–485, especially the religious war which ended when Vahan Mamikonian became *marzpan*.]

Levond. History of the Successors of Mahomet. Armenian text publ. Paris 1857. French transl. Chahnazarian, G. V. Paris. 1856. [Continues Sebêos to 788.]

Sebêos the Bishop. History of Heraclius. Armenian text publ. Constantinople 1851 and St Petersburg 1879. French transl. Macler, F. Paris. 1904. [Wars of Heraclius; Arab invasions to 661.]

B. *Modern Authors.*

Aslan, K. Études historiques sur le peuple arménien. pp. 245–98. Paris. 1909. [Many mistakes and misprints.]

Chahnazarian, G. V. Esquisse de l'histoire de l'Arménie. pp. 28–32. Paris. 1856.

Chamich, M. History of Armenia, from B.C. 2247 to the year of Christ 1780...transl. from the original Armenian by Johannes Avdall...to which is appended a continuation...from the year 1780 to the present date. Vol. I. pp. 252–414. Calcutta. 1827.

Gelzer, H. Short History of Armenia...transl. into Armenian by G. V. Galemkhearian. Vienna. 1897.

Palasanian, S. History of Armenia. pp. 177–247. 2nd edn. Tiflis. 1895. (In Armenian.)

Saint-Martin, J. Mémoires historiques et géographiques sur l'Arménie. Vol. I. pp. 320–49. Paris. 1818.

III.

The Bagratids (885–1079).

A. *Armenian Sources, relative to the Bagratids in Western Armenia and to the kingdom of the Arcrunis in Vaspurakan (Van).*

Aristakes of Lastivert (10th–11th centuries). Armenian text publ. Venice 1844. French transl. Prud'homme, E. Histoire d'Arménie, comprenant la fin du royaume d'Ani et le commencement des invasions des Seldjoukides, *in* Revue de l'Orient, de l'Algérie, et des colonies. Paris. 1864. [From *c.* 1000 to 1064.]

George the Priest, *see* Matthew of Edessa.

John VI Katholikos (897–925). History of Armenia. Armenian text publ. Jerusalem 1843 and 1867, Moscow 1853. French transl. Saint-Martin, J. Histoire d'Arménie, par le patriarche Jean VI, dit Jean Catholicos. Ouvrage posthume. Ed. Lajard, F. Paris. 1841. [Arab wars; establishment of Bagratid dynasty at Ani.]

Matthew of Edessa (12th century). History. Armenian text publ. Jerusalem 1862. French transl. Dulaurier, E. Paris. 1858. Also fragments transl. Dulaurier. Rec. Hist. Crois., Doc. Armén. Vol. I. Paris. 1869. *See above*, I. [Of the western provinces, 952–1136; continued to 1168 by the priest George.]

Moses Kalankatuatsi. History of the Aghuans (Albanians of the Caucasus). Armenian text publ. Paris and Moscow 1860. Partial transl. Brosset, M. F. *in* Additions et éclaircissements à l'histoire de la Géorgie. St Petersburg. 1851. Also, Histoire des Aghovans de Moïse de Kalankatoani, extraite et traduite du manuscrit arménien, par E. Boré, avec des annotations de Vivien de Saint-Martin, *in* Nouvelles annales de voyages. Paris. 1848. [Third Part contains events in Albania up to the tenth century.]

Samuel of Ani (12th century) drew up, at the request of the Katholikos Gregory, his researches and chronological tables, extending from the creation to 1179. Anonymous continuation to 1340. Armenian text unpublished. Latin transl. Zohrab and Mai. Milan. 1818. Rome. 1839. French transl. Brosset, *in* Collection d'historiens arméniens. Vol. II. St Petersburg. 1876.

Stephen Asolik of Taron (10th–11th centuries). Universal History. Armenian text publ. Paris 1859 and St Petersburg 1885. Russian transl. Emin. Moscow. 1864.

French transl. (Part I.) Dulaurier. Paris. 1883. (Part II.) Macler. Paris. 1917.
German transl. Gelzer, H. and Burckhardt, A. Leipsic. 1907. [To A.D. 1004.]
Thomas Arcruni (9th–10th centuries). History of the House of Arcruni. Armenian text publ. Constantinople 1852. French transl. Brosset, *in* Collection d'historiens arméniens. Vol. I. St Petersburg. 1874. [From the creation to 936; anonymous continuation to 1326.]

B. *Modern Authors.*

Adonts, N. Nachal'naya istoriya Armenii. *In* VV. Vol. VIII. St Petersburg. 1901.
Aslan, K. Études historiques, etc. pp. 299–339. *See above,* II B.
Chahnazarian, G. V. Esquisse de l'histoire de l'Arménie. pp. 32–52. *See above,* II B.
Chamich, M. History of Armenia. Vol. II. pp. 1–163. *See above,* II B.
Daghbaschean, H. Gründung des Bagratidenreiches durch Aschot Bagratuni. Berlin. 1893. [Litteratur, pp. xiii–xiv. Valuable.]
Gelzer, H. Short History of Armenia. *See above,* II B.
Lynch, H. F. B. Armenia. Travels and Studies. Vol. I. pp. 334–92. London. 1901.
Ormanian, M. L'Église arménienne. Paris. 1910.
Palasanian, S. History of Armenia. pp. 378–451. *See above,* II B.
Saint-Martin, J. Mémoires, etc. Vol. I. pp. 349–76. *See above,* II B.
Ter-Mikelian, A. Die armenische Kirche in ihren Beziehungen zur byzantinischen (vom IV bis zum XIII Jahrhundert). Leipsic. 1892.
Ter-Minassiantz, E. Die armenische Kirche in ihren Beziehungen zu den syrischen Kirchen, bis zum Ende des 13 Jahrhunderts. Leipsic. 1904.
Therdjimanean, H. Short History of Armenia. pp. 244–80. Venice. 1885. (In Armenian.)
Thopdschian, H. Politische und Kirchengeschichte Armeniens unter Ašot I und Smbat I, nach armenischen, arabischen, syrischen, und byzantinischen Quellen bearbeitet. (Mitteilungen des Seminars für orientalische Sprachen zu Berlin, Abt. II [Westasiatische Studien].) Berlin. 1905.
Thopdschian, J. Die inneren Zustände von Armenien unter Ašot I. Berlin. 1904.
Tournebize, F. Histoire politique et religieuse de l'Arménie. Vol. I. pp. 104–38, 138–67. Paris. 1910.

On the art and architecture of the Armenians during the Bagratid period, see especially:

Brosset, M. F. Les ruines d'Ani. With atlas. St Petersburg. 1860.
Dubois de Montpéreux, F. Voyage autour du Caucase (1833–4). 6 vols. and atlas. Paris. 1839–43.
Lynch, H. F. B. *See above.*
Marr, N., Professor at the University of St Petersburg, has devoted several studies, in Russian, to the excavations conducted by himself at Ani, the Bagratid capital.

For the study of Armenian MSS see:

Abdullah, S. and Macler, F. Études sur la miniature arménienne. Paris. 1909.
Dashian, J. Sketch of Armenian palaeography. Vienna. 1898. (In Armenian.)
Finck, F. N. Armenische Paläographie. Erläuterungen zu d. Schriftproben aus d. armenischen Handschriften d. k. Universitäts-bibliothek in Tübingen. *n.d.* (Offprint from Veröffentlichungen d. k. Universitäts-bibliothek zu Tübingen, I, 1–16.)
Macler, F. Rapport sur une mission scientifique en Arménie russe et en Arménie turque. Paris. 1911.
—— L'Évangile arménien. Édition phototypique du MS no. 229 de la bibliothèque d'Etchmiadzin. Paris. 1920.
Neumann, C. F. Versuch einer Geschichte der armenischen Literatur. Leipsic. 1836.
Strzygowski, J. Das Etschmiadzin-Evangeliar. Vienna. 1891.
—— Die Baukunst der Armenier und Europa. *See Gen. Bibl.* V.

For the study of Armenian literature under the Bagratids see:

Zarbhanalian, G. Literary history of ancient Armenia. 3rd edn. Venice. 1897 (In Armenian.)

IV.

Armeno-Cilicia and the Rubenians-Hethumians (1080–1342).

A. *Armenian Sources.*

Gregory Dgha (the child) (1133–90), nephew and successor of Nerses Shnorhali, wrote, among other things, an Elegy on the capture of Jerusalem by Saladin. *See above*, I. Rec. Hist. Crois., Doc. armén. Vol. I.

Hethum II, King of Armenia (1290–1305) composed in verse a little chronicle of the kingdom of Cilicia. Printed in some editions of the Armenian bible: Amsterdam 1666, Constantinople 1705, and Venice 1733. *See above*, I. Rec. Hist. Crois., Doc. armén. Vol. I. pp. 550–5.

Matthew of Edessa. *See above*, III A.

Michael the Syrian (1127–99). Jacobite patriarch of Antioch. Chronicle. Armenian text publ. Jerusalem 1870–1. French transl. Langlois, V. Chronique de Michel le Grand, patriarche des Syriens jacobites. Ischôk. Venice. 1868. The Syriac text, with a French transl., ed. Chabot, J. B. Paris. 1899 ff. [From the creation to 1196. This Syriac chronicle was translated into Armenian by the priest Ishôk, and then continued to 1246. The Syriac text was long lost, and the Armenian thought to be the original. It was a source of Abulpharagius.]

Mkhithar Ayrivanetsi. History, from the creation to 1289. Armenian text publ. Moscow 1860 and St Petersburg 1867. Transl.: Russian, St Petersburg 1869; and French, Brosset, St Petersburg 1869.

Nerses Shnorhali (the graceful) (1102–73). Several works, including two historical compositions in verse: an Elegy on the capture of Edessa by ʿImād-ad-Dīn Zangī in 1144, and a History of Armenia. (*See above*, I. Rec. Hist. Crois., Doc. armén. Vol. I.)

Samuel of Ani. *See above*, III A.

Smbat, constable of the kingdom of Cilicia, brother of King Hethum. Chronicle, 952–1274. Continuation till 1331. Armenian text publ. Moscow 1856 and Paris 1859. French transl. Langlois, V. St Petersburg. 1862.

Stephen (Orbelian) of Siwni, metropolitan of Siwni. History of the Province of Siwni. Armenian text publ. Paris 1859, Moscow 1861. French transl. Brosset. St Petersburg. 1864–6. [Completed in 1297.]

Vahram Rabuni, secretary of King Leo III. History of the Rubenian Dynasty. The narrative extends as far as 1280. Armenian text publ. Madras 1810, Calcutta 1832, Paris 1859. English transl. (partial). Neumann, C. F. London. 1832. French transl. Bedrosian, S. *in* Revue de l'Orient. 1864. [In verse, to 1280.]

B. *Modern Authors.*

[Alishan, L. M.] Sissouan ou l'Arméno-Cilicie. Description géographique et historique, avec carte et illustrations. Traduit du texte arménien et publié sous les auspices de son Exc. Noubar pacha.... Venice. 1899.

Chahnazarian, G. V. Esquisse, etc. pp. 52–96. *See above*, II B.

Chamich, M. History of Armenia. Vol. II. pp. 164–309. *See above*, II B.

Dulaurier, E. Étude sur l'organisation politique, religieuse, et administrative du royaume de la Petite-Arménie. JA. Paris. 1861.

—— L'Histoire des Croisades d'après les chroniques arméniennes. Revue de l'Orient. Paris. 1858.

Farcinet, C. L'ancienne famille de Lusignan. Les premiers sires de ce nom. Fontenay-le-Comte. 1899.

Langlois, V. Chronographie d'Héthoum, seigneur de Gorigos, ouvrage inédit du moine Aithon, auteur de l'histoire des Tatars.... Revue de l'Orient. Paris. 1863.

—— Considérations sur les rapports de l'Arménie avec la France au moyen-âge. Revue de l'Orient. Paris. 1861.

—— Documents pour servir à l'histoire des Lusignans de la Petite-Arménie (1342–94). Revue archéologique. Paris. 1859.

—— Essai historique et critique sur la constitution sociale et politique de l'Arménie sous les rois de la dynastie roupénienne, d'après les documents orientaux et

occidentaux conservés dans les dépôts d'archives de l'Europe.... Mém. AcadIP. 7th series. Vol. III. No. 3. St Petersburg. 1860.
Langlois, V. Essai sur les monnaies des rois arméniens de la dynastie de Roupène. Revue archéologique. 7th year. Paris. 1850.
—— Extrait de la chronique de Sempad, seigneur de Babaron, connétable d'Arménie, suivi de celle de son continuateur et traduit pour la première fois de l'arménien. Mém. AcadIP. 7th series. Vol. IV, 6. St Petersburg. 1862.
—— Inscriptions grecques, romaines, byzantines, et arméniennes de la Cilicie. Paris. 1854.
—— Lettre à M. Brosset, sur la succession des rois d'Arménie de la dynastie de Roupên et de la maison de Lusignan, d'après les sources orientales et occidentales. Mélanges asiatiques tirés du Bulletin de l'AcadIP. Vol. IV. 1861.
—— Mémoire sur les relations de la République de Gênes avec le royaume chrétien de la Petite-Arménie, pendant les XIIIe et XIVe siècles. Mem. della R. Accademia delle Scienze di Torino. Ser. II. Vol. XIX. Turin. 1861.
—— Numismatique de l'Arménie au moyen âge. Paris. 1855.
—— Numismatique générale de l'Arménie. Paris. 1859.
—— Rapport sur l'exploration archéologique de la Cilicie et de la Petite-Arménie pendant les années 1852–3. Paris. 1854.
—— Le trésor des chartes d'Arménie. *See above*, I.
—— Voyage dans la Cilicie et dans les montagnes de Taurus. Le Tour du Monde. Paris. 1852–3.
—— Voyage dans la Cilicie et dans les montagnes du Taurus.... Paris. 1861.
—— Voyage à Sis, capitale de l'Arménie au moyen âge. JA. Paris. 1855.
Ormanian, M. L'Église arménienne. *See above*, III B.
Palasanian, S. History of Armenia. pp. 452–573. *See above*, II B.
Rec. hist. Crois. Documents Arméniens. *See above*, I.
Saint-Martin, J. Mémoires historiques, etc. Vol. I. pp. 387–403, 435–6. *See above*, II B.
Ter-Gregor, N. History of Armenia (illustrated) from the earliest ages to the present time. London. 1897.
Ter-Mikelian, A. Die armenische Kirche. *See above*, III B.
Ter-Minassiantz, E. Die armenische Kirche. *See above*, III B.
Therdjimanean, H. Short History of Armenia. pp. 281–320. *See above*, III B.
Tournebize, F. Histoire politique, etc. *See above*, III B.

V.

Armeno-Cilicia and the Lusignans (1342–1373).

The same Sources and Modern Works as for Section IV. In addition, Modern Works:

Carrière, A. La Rose d'or du roi d'Arménie, Léon V. Revue de l'Orient Latin. Vol. IX. pp. 1–5.
Schlumberger, G. Revue de l'Orient Latin. Vol. I. p. 161. (On the legend of Leo VI's seal.)

CHAPTER VII.

(A)

THE EMPIRE AND ITS NORTHERN NEIGHBOURS.

I. ORIGINAL AUTHORITIES.

Of the first importance are the Byzantine authors; next in value are the Russian and Oriental sources, particularly the Arabian geographers; lastly some information is supplied by the Western sources. No collection of excerpts from Oriental writers has yet appeared; for translations of single works *see* II *below*.

(*a*) Collections of Sources for the Russians.

Ikonnikov, V. S. Opyt russkoy istoriografii (Essay in Russian historiography). 4 vols. Kiev. 1891–1908. [Summarises Byzantine and Russian sources and gives editions.]

Makushev, V. Skazaniya inostrantsev o bytê i nravakh Slavyan (Reports of foreigners on the life and customs of the Slavs). St Petersburg. 1861. [No longer up to date; must be supplemented by recent works.]

Publications of the Russian Imp. Archaeographical Commission; especially
  Polnoe sobranie russkikh lêtopisey. (Complete collection of Russian chronicles.) 1841 ff.
  Shakhmatov, A. Razyskaniya o drevneyshikh russkikh lêtopisnykh svodakh (Researches into the most ancient Russian annalistic compilations). St Petersburg. 1908.

Stritter, J. G. Memoriae populorum olim ad Danubium, Pontum Euxinum...incolentium. *See Gen. Bibl.* IV. [Important though antiquated collection of excerpts from Byzantine writers on the Slavs and neighbouring peoples.]

(*b*) Collections of Sources for the Magyars.

Marczali, H. Ungarns Geschichtsquellen im Zeitalter d. Árpáden. Berlin. 1882.

Pauler, G. and Szilágyi, S. Quellen d. ungarischen Landeseroberung. (A Magyar honfoglalás kútfői, Sources for the occupation of Hungary by the Magyars.) *See Gen. Bibl.* IV. [Gives the earliest authorities.]

II. MODERN AUTHORITIES.

(*a*) Bibliography.

Bestuzhev-Ryumin, K. N. Russkaya istoriya. Vol. I. St Petersburg. 1872. German transl. by Schiemann, T., Geschichte Russlands. Milan. 1874.

For review of more recent works, *see* Hrushevs'ky (*below*). For literature of the early history of the Magyars, *see* Pauler *and* Marczali (*below*).

(*b*) Principal Authors.

Bury, J. B. Hist. of the Eastern Roman Empire. *See Gen. Bibl.* V.

—— Hist. of the Later Roman Empire. *See Gen. Bibl.* V.

Charmoy, F. B. Relation de Masoudy et d'autres auteurs musulmans sur les anciens Slaves. 1833.

Chwolson, D. Izvêstiya o Khazarakh, Burtasakh, Bolgarakh, Mad'yarakh, Slavyanakh, i Russakh Ibn Dasta (Reports of Ibn Rusta on the Khazars, Burtas, etc.). St Petersburg. 1869. [Rusta was misread Dasta.]
Dorn, B. Kaspi, o pokhodakh drevnikh Russkikh v Tabaristan (Caspia: On the military expeditions of the ancient Russians to Tabaristan). German transl. Caspia, über d. Einfälle d. alten Russen in Tabaristan u. ihre sonst. Unternehmungen auf d. Kaspischen Meere. Mém. AcadIP. 7th series. Vol. XXVI (i).
Dümmler, E. Gesch. des ostfränkischen Reiches. 3 vols. Latest edn. Leipsic. 1887–8.
Fessler-Klein. Gesch. v. Ungarn. Vol. I. Leipsic. 1867.
Finlay, G. History of Greece. *See Gen. Bibl.* v.
Fraehn, C. M. De Chazaris excerpta ex scriptoribus arabicis. AcadIP. 1822.
—— Ibn Foszlans und anderer Araber Berichte über die Russen älterer Zeit. AcadIP. St Petersburg. 1823.
Gedeonov, S. Varyagi i Rus' (Varangians and Russians). St Petersburg. 1876.
Gibbon, E. Decline and Fall. Ed. Bury. *See Gen. Bibl.* v.
Golubinski, E. E. Istoriya russkoy tserkvi (History of the Russian Church). Vol. I. *See Gen. Bibl.* v.
Golubovski, P. Pechenêgi, Torki, i Polovtsy (The Patzinaks, Torks, and Polovtsi). Univ. Izvêstiya. Kiev. 1883.
—— Bolgary i Khazary (The Bulgars and Chazars). Kievskaya Starina (Antiquity of Kiev). 1888.
Greben'kov. Drevniya snosheniya Rusi s prikaspiyskimi stranami (Ancient relations between the Russians and the lands of the Caspian Sea). Tiflis. 1896.
Grigor'ev, V. V. Rossiya i Aziya. St Petersburg. 1876.
Grot, K. I. Moraviya i Mad'yary s poloviny IX do nachala X vêka (Moravia and the Magyars, from the middle of the ninth to the beginning of the tenth centuries). St Petersburg. 1881.
Harkavy, A. Skazaniya musul'manskikh pisateley o Slavyanakh i Russkikh (Reports of Musulman writers on the Slavs and Russians). St Petersburg. 1870.
—— Soobshcheniya o Khazarakh (Reports on the Chazars, in "Evreyskaya Biblioteka." VIII). St Petersburg. 1880.
—— Skazaniya evreyskikh pisateley o Khazarakh (Reports of Jewish writers on the Chazars). St Petersburg. 1874.
Howorth, H. H. The Khazars: were they Ugrians or Turks? Third Internat. Congress of Orientalists in St Petersburg. Travaux. Vol. II. 1879.
Hrushevs'ky, M. Geschichte des ukrainischen (ruthenischen) Volkes. Vol. I. Leipsic. 1906.
—— Kievskaya Rus' (The Russia of Kiev). Vol. I. St Petersburg. 1911.
Hunfalvy, P. Ethnographie von Ungarn. Buda-Pest. 1877.
—— Die Ungarn oder Magyaren. Vienna and Teschen. 1881.
Ilovayski, D. Razyskaniya o nachalê Rusi (Researches on the beginnings of Russia). 2nd edn. Moscow. 1882.
—— Istoriya Rossii. Part I. Moscow. 1876.
Jewish Encyclopedia. Article on Chazars. New York and London. 1907.
Karamzin, N. M. Istoriya gosudarstva Rossiyskago (History of the Russian empire). Vol. I. St Petersburg. 1816, and later editions. French transl. by St Thomas and Jauffret, Hist. de l'empire de Russie. 11 vols. Paris. 1819–26. German transl. 11 vols. Riga and Leipsic. 1820–33.
Klyuchevski, V. O. Kurs russkoy istorii. Part I. 3rd edn. Moscow. 1908.
Kulakovski, Y. A. Istoriya Vizantii (History of the Eastern Empire). Vols. I–III. Kiev. 1910–15.
Kunik-Rosen. Izvêstiya Al Bekri i drugikh avtorov o Rusi i Slavyanakh (Reports of Bakri and other authors on the Russians and Slavs). Part I. St Petersburg. 1878.
Kuun, G., Count. Relationum Hungarorum cum Oriente gentibusque orientalis originis historia antiquissima. 2 vols. Claudiopoli. 1893–4.
Lambin, N. Slavyane na sêvernom Chernomorii (The Slavs on the northern shores of the Black Sea). ZMNP. Nos. 5, 6, 12. St Petersburg. 1877.
Laskin, G. Sochineniya Konstantina Bagryanorodnago o Femakh i o Narodakh

(Works of Constantine Porphyrogenitus on themes and nations). Chteniya Imp. Obshchestva Istorii i Drevnostey Rossiyskikh (Lectures of the Imp. Soc. of Russian History and Antiquities). Moscow. 1899.
Lüttich, R. Ungarnzüge in Europa im 10 Jahrhundert. Berlin. 1910.
Makari, Archim. Istoriya khristianstva v Rossii (History of Christianity in Russia). St Petersburg. 1846.
Marczali, H. A vezérek kora és a királyság megalapítása (The time of chieftains and the foundation of the Kingdom), in the first part of A Magyar nemzet története (History of the Magyar nation), ed. Szilágyi, S. Buda-Pest. 1895.
Marquart, J. Osteuropäische und ostasiatische Streifzüge. *See Gen. Bibl.* v.
Neumann, K. F. Die Völker des südlichen Russlands. Leipsic. 1847.
Ohsson, C. de. Les peuples du Caucase. Paris. 1827.
Pauler, G. A Magyar nemzet története Szent Istvánig (History of the Magyar nation to St Stephen). Buda-Pest. 1900.
—— A Magyar nemzet története az Arpádházi királyok alatt (History of the Magyar nation during the Arpad dynasty). Vol. I. Buda-Pest. 1899.
Píč, Jos. Lad. Der nationale Kampf gegen das ungarische Staatsrecht. Leipsic. 1882.
Pogodin, M. P. Izslêdovaniya, lektsii, i zamêchaniya (Investigations, lectures, and observations). 7 vols. Moscow. 1846–59.
Rambaud, A. N. L'empire Grec au xe siècle. Paris. 1870.
—— Histoire de la Russie. *See Gen. Bibl.* v.
Rostovtseff, M. I. Les origines de la Russie Kievienne. Revue des Études Slaves. II. 1922. pp. 1–18.
—— Iranians and Greeks in South Russia. Oxford. 1922. [The ancient history, and pp. 210–22: "The origin of the Russian state on the Dnieper."]
Schlumberger, G. L. Un empereur byzantin au xe siècle: Nicéphore Phocas. *See Gen. Bibl.* v.
—— L'épopée byzantine à la fin du xe siècle. Pt. I. Jean Tzimiscès, Basile II (969–989). *See Gen. Bibl.* v.
Solov'ëv, S. M. Istoriya Rossii. Vol. I. Moscow. 1851.
Szabó, K. A Magyar vezérek kora (The time of the Magyar chieftains). Buda-Pest. 1869.
Thomsen, V. The relations between ancient Russia and Scandinavia, and the origin of the Russian state. Oxford. 1877.
Tomaschek, W. Die Goten in Taurien. (Ethnolog. Forschungen über Osteuropa und Nordasien. I.) Vienna. 1881.
Uspenski, F. G. Rus' i Vizantiya v x vêkê (Russia and the Eastern Roman Empire in the tenth century). Odessa. 1888.
—— Vizantiyskiya vladêniya na sêvernom beregu Chernago morya (The Byzantine dominion on the northern shore of the Black Sea), in the periodical Kievskaya Starina (Antiquity of Kiev). 1889.
Vámbéry, Arminius. Die Ursprung der Magyaren. Leipsic. 1882.
Vasil'evski, V. G. Russko-vizantiyskiya izslêdovaniya (Russo-Byzantine Researches). St Petersburg. 1893.
—— Varyago-russkaya druzhina v Konstantinopolê (The Varangian-Russian Guard in Constantinople). ZMNP. 1874–5.
Westberg, F. Beiträge zur Klärung orient. Quellen über Osteuropa (Bulletin AcadIP. 5th series. Vol. XI. 1899). St Petersburg. 1900.
—— K analizu vostochnykh istochnikov o vostochnoy Evropê (Contributions to the analysis of the oriental reports on Eastern Europe). ZMNP. February, March, 1908. [A revision of the preceding.]

(B)

CONVERSION OF THE SLAVS.

[*Sources and works marked by an asterisk are the more important.*]

I. DOCUMENTARY SOURCES.

*John VIII, Pope. Epistolae. Ed. Caspar, E. MGH. Epist. VII, 1. 1912. (Nos. 200, 201, 225, 276.)

*—— and Stephen V. Register of letters (from MS in the British Museum). Publ. by Miklosich, F. and Rački, F. *In* Starine. Vol. XII. (Jugoslavenska Akademija Znanosti i Umjetnosti.) Agram. *Cf.* Ewald, P. *in* Neu. Arch. V. Also publ. by Pastrnek (*see below under* III).

*Anastasius, Librarian at Rome.

Ein Brief des Anastasius bibliothecarius an den Bischof Gaudericus von Velletri. Newly discovered, and ed. Friedrich, J. *In* Sitzungsberichte der k. bayer. Akad. d. Wissenschaften. Heft 3. Munich. 1892. *Cf.* Jagić, I. V. Vnov' naidennoe svidêtel'stvo o dêyatel'nosti Konstantina filosofa, pervouchitelya slavyan sv. Kirilla. *In* Sbornik, LIV. No. 3. (AcadIP.)

[This is a criticism of the interpretation of the entire material constituting the legend as given by Friedrich.]

For other references to Anastasius and Pope John VIII, *see* Pastrnek (*below under* III), pp. 245, 246.

*Anonymi Salisburgensis Libellus de conversione Bagoariorum et Carantanorum. Ed. Kopitar, B. in his Glagolita Clozianus, pp. LXXII–LXXVI. Vienna. 1836; and ed. Wattenbach, W. *in* MGH. Script. XI. 1854.

II. THE LEGENDS.

*Vita cum translatione S. Clementis. ["The Translatio."] Publ. in ASBoll. 9 Martii. II. pp. 20–22; and elsewhere, for instance, by Ginzel, Bil'basov, Pastrnek (*see below under* III).

Legenda Moravica. (Founded on the Translatio.) Ed. Dobrovský, J. 1826. (Earlier in ASBoll. *Ibid.* pp. 22–24; and elsewhere, for instance, by Ginzel, Pastrnek, Bil'basov.)

Legends concerning Wenceslas, Ludmila, and the so-called "Christianslegende" have now been critically treated by Pekař, J. Die Wenzels- und Ludmilla-Legenden und die Echtheit Christians. Prague. 1906. All these legends contain references to Cyril and Methodius according to the later versions.

*{Vita S. Methodii archiepiscopi. / Vita S. Constantini sive Cyrilli.} "The Pannonian Legends" (in Slavonic).

These two Moravian-Pannonian legends are the principal sources of their class. They were critically edited by Šafařík, P. J. *in* Památky dřevního písemnictví Jihoslovanův. Prague. 1853. New edn. 1873, with separate titles Život sv. Konstantina řečeného Cyrilla. Z rukopisu XV století. Život sv. Methodia. Z rukopisu XVI století.

Bodyanski published both legends singly from different MSS; Vita Constantini, *in* Chteniya of the Imp. Obshchestvo istorii i drevnostey rossiyskikh, Moscow, 1863. Vol. II. Nos. 1–7; 1864. Vol. II. Nos. 8–12; 1873. Vol. I. Nos. 13–16; Vita Methodii. *Ibid.* 1865. Vol. I. Nos. 1–8; The Panegyrics (Encomia) on both saints. *Ibid.* 1865. Vol. II. Nos. 1–6; 1866. Vol. II. Nos. 7–15. Critical edn. with Latin transl. of the legend of Saint Cyril by Dümmler, E.

and Miklosich, F. *in* Denkschriften d. KAW. Phil.-hist. Klasse. Vol. XIX. Vienna. 1870. Do. of the Legend of Methodius with Latin transl., Vita Sancti Methodii Russico-Slovenice et Latine. Ed. Miklosich, F. Vienna. 1870. The Methodius Legend was also ed. by Bil'basov (*see below under* III), and by Lavrov, P. Zhitie sv. Mefodiya. Moscow. 1899. Finally both legends are in Fontes rerum bohemicarum, I. Prague, 1873, and in Pastrnek (*see below under* III). [Pastrnek reconstructed the language in an ideal and grammatical form, which was scarcely justified.]

"Nestor." The old Russian chronicler interpolates a narrative under the year 898. This text, which is identical in the two principal "Nestor" MSS (Laurentian and Hypatian), is dependent on the Pannonian Methodius-Legend, *see above*, but contains modifications of later Bulgarian origin. Published by the Russian Archaeographical Commission, St Petersburg, 1846 and again 1872. French transl. Leger, L. Chronique dite de Nestor. Paris. 1884.

Later Slavonic legends. These are publ. both separately and by Bil'basov (*see below under* III).

Translation of the relics of St Clement. A Slavonic legend translated from the Greek possibly based upon a work by Constantine (Cyril) himself. Publ. in Kirillo-Mefodievski Sbornik. Ed. Pogodin, M. P. Moscow. 1865. It has been discussed by Franko, J., St Clement in the Chersonese, an essay on the early Christian legend, pp. 242–52 (in the language of Little Russia), Lemberg (Lwów), 1906; and by Lavrov, P. *in* Pamyatniki Khristianskago Khersonesa. No. 2. pp. 127–39. Moscow. 1911.

*Vita Clementis. (A Macedonian bishop, pupil of Cyril and Methodius.) Written in Greek, republished by Miklosich, F. after the rare editions of 1741 and 1802 as Vita s. Clementis episcopi Bulgarorum. Vienna. 1847. Re-edited, Moscow, 1855; and by Bil'basov, 1871, *see below under* III; and in Fontes rerum bohemicarum. I. Prague. 1873. A shorter text of the legend was published by Šafařík, P. J. *in* Památky Hlaholského Písemnictví, Prague, 1853, according to the text communicated to him by Grigorovich. Republished by Bil'basov, *op. cit.* and by Balashchev in an old Bulgarian version (1898).

III. MONOGRAPHS ON CYRIL AND METHODIUS.

Bartolini, D. Memorie storico-critiche archeologiche dei SS. Cirillo e Metodio, etc. Rome. 1881.

Bil'basov, B. A. Kirill i Mefodi po dokumental'nym istochnikam. 2 vols. St Petersburg. 1868, 1871. Title of vol. II: Kirill i Mefodi po zapadnym legendam. (A third volume was announced but has not appeared.)

Brückner, A. Die Wahrheit über die Slavenapostel. Tübingen. 1913.

Dobrovský, J. Cyrill und Method. *In* Abh. d. kön. böhmischen Gesellschaft d. Wiss. VIII. Prague. 1823. Also publ. separately. Prague. 1823. Russian transl. Pogodin, M. P. Kirill i Mefodi, slovenskie pervouchiteli. Moscow. 1825. [The last contains valuable supplements.]

—— Mährische Legende von Cyrill und Method. *In* Abh. d. kön. böhmischen Gesellschaft d. Wiss. Neue Folge. I. Prague. 1826. Also publ. separately. Prague. 1826.

Filaret, Bishop of Riga. Kirill i Mefodi slavyanskie prosvêtiteli. Moscow. 1846. (Russian.) German transl. Cyrillus und Methodius. Mitau and Leipsic. 1847. Publ. in Kirillo-Mefodievski Sbornik, ed. Pogodin, M. P. pp. 43–80. Moscow. 1865. (Russian.)

*Ginzel, J. A. Geschichte der Slavenapostel Cyrill und Method. Leitmeritz. 1857. 2nd edn. Vienna. 1861.

*Goetz, L. K. Geschichte der Slavenapostel Konstantinus (Kyrillus) und Methodius, Quellenmässig untersucht und dargestellt. Gotha. 1897.

*Golubinski, E. E., wrote a work before 1870 on Cyril and Methodius which was adjudged Uvarov's prize, but only an extract has been published: Svyatýe Konstantin i Mefodi pervouchiteli slavyanskie. Moscow. 1885.

Gorski, A. Zhitiya sv. Kirilla i Mefodiya. First published in the periodical Moskvityanin. Moscow. 1843. Reprinted in Kirillo-Mefodievski Sbornik, ed. Pogodin, M. P. pp. 1–42. Moscow. 1865. (Russian.)
Gromnicki, T. Swięci Cyryl i Metody. Cracow. 1880. (Polish.)
Hilferding, A. F. *In* Collected Works. Vol. I. pp. 299–340. St Petersburg. 1868. Also publ. in Kirillo-Mefodievski Sbornik. pp. 1–42. Ed. Pogodin, M. P. Moscow. 1865.
*Jagić, V. Zur Entstehungsgeschichte der Kirchenslavischen Sprache. *In* Denkschriften d. KAW. philos.-hist. Klasse. Vol. XLVII. 1900. Corrected separate edn. Berlin. 1913.
—— Konstantin (Ćiril) i Metodye, osnivači slovenske crkve i književnosti. Publ. in Brastvo, XVI. Belgrade. 1921. (Serbian.)
Lapôtre, A. L'Europe et le Saint-Siège à l'époque carolingienne. Part I. Paris. 1895.
Lavrovski, P. Kirill i Mefodi kak pravoslavnye propovědniki u zapadnykh slavyan. Kharkov. 1863. (Russian.)
Leger, L. Cyrille et Méthode. Étude historique. Paris. 1868.
*Malyshevski, J. Svyatye Kirill i Mefodi pervouchiteli slavyanskie. Kiev. 1886.
Pastrnek, F. Dějiny slovanských apoštolů Cyrilla a Methoda, s rozborem a otiskem hlavních pramenů. Prague. 1902. (Czech.)
Potkański, K. Konstantyn i Metodyusz. Cracow. 1905. (Polish.)
*Rački, F. Vijek i djelovanje sv. Cyrilla i Methoda, slovjenskih apostolov. 2 vols. Agram. 1857, 59. (Croatian.)
Rettel, L. Cyryl i Metody. Streszczenie najnowszych poszukiwań. Paris. 1871. (Polish.)
Ritig, S. Povijest i pravo slovenštine u crkvenom bogoslužju, sa osobitim obzirom na Hrvatsku. I sveska; od 863–1248. Agram. 1910. (Croatian.)
Šafařík, P. J. Slovanské starožitnosti (Slavonic Antiquities). Prague. 1837. 2nd edn. 2 vols. Prague. 1862–3. Part II, 488–506. German transl. by Mosig von Aehrenfeld. Slawische Alterthümer. 2 vols. Leipsic. 1843, 44.
Schubert, H. Die sogenannten Slavenapostel Constantin und Methodius. Heidelberg. 1916.
Snopek, F. Studie Cyrillo-Methodějské. Brünn. 1906. (Czech.)
—— Konstantin-Cyrill a Methoděj slovanští apoštolé. Olmütz. 1908. Prague. 1920. (Czech.)
—— Konstantinus-Cyrillus und Methodius die Slavenapostel. Ein Wort zur Abwehr für die Freunde historischer Wahrheit. (Operum Academiae Velehradensis. Vol. II.) Kremsier. 1911.
—— Die Slavenapostel. Kritische Studien, zugleich als Replik gegen meine Rezensenten. (Oper. Acad. Velehr. Vol. V.) Kremsier. 1918.
*Voronov, A. Glavnêyshie istochniki dlya istorii sv. Kirilla i Mefodiya. Kiev. 1877. (Russian.)

IV. SOME IMPORTANT SPECIAL WORKS.

Berčić. Dvie službe rimskoga obreda za svetkovima Cirila i Metoda. Agram. 1870. *Cf.* Jagić, V. Ein fünfter bibliographischer Beitrag der Laibacher Lyzealbibliothek. *In* Anzeiger d. KAW. philos.-hist. Klasse. No. XX. 1899.
Bodyanski. O vremeni proiskhozhdeniya slav. pis'men. Moscow. 1855. (Russian.)
*Brückner, A. Legendy o Cyrylu i Metodym wobec prawdy dziejowej. (Offprint from Rocznik Towarzystwa Przyjaciół Nauk Poznańskiego. Vol. XXX. Posen. 1903.) (Polish.)
*—— Thesen zur Cyrillo-Methodianischen Frage. *In* Archiv für slavische Philologie. Vol. XXVIII. Berlin. 1906.
*Bury, J. B. History of the Eastern Roman Empire (802–867). (*See Gen. Bibl.* V.) pp. 392 ff., 485 ff., 500–1, 506–7. [Contains bibliographies.]
*Dümmler, E. Die Pannonische Legende vom h. Methodius. *In* Archiv f. Kunde österr. Geschichtsquellen. Vol. XIII. Vienna. 1854.
Grivec, F. Pravovernost sv. Cyrila in Metoda. *In* Bogoslovni Vestnik. Ljubljana. 1921. (Slovene.)

Hýbl, F. Slovanská liturgie na Moravě v IX věku. *In* Časopis historický. Vol. XIV. 1908. (Czech.) *Cf.* also *ibid.* Vol. XVII. 1911. pp. 272 ff.

*Jagić, V. Vopros o Kirillê i Mefodii v slavyanskoy filologii. (St Petersburg. 1885. Sbornik otdêleniya russkago yazyka i slovesnosti. Vol. XXXVIII. No. 1.) [Contains a full bibliography on Cyril and Methodius.] (Russian.)

Lavrov, P. Kliment episkop Slovenski. Moscow. 1895. (Appeared in Chteniya of the Imp. Obshchestvo istorii i drevnostey rossiyskikh. Moscow. 1895. Vol. I. No. 172.) (Russian.) *Cf.* the same author's Die neuesten Forschungen über den Slav. Klemens. Archiv für Slavische Philologie. Vol. XXVII. 1909.

Lavrovski, P. Byl li Kirill Solunski episkopom. ZMNP. April. 1885.

*—— Italyanskaya legenda. ZMNP. July–August. 1886. (Russian.)

*Martinov, S. J. Apropos de la légende dite Italique. (RQH. Vol. XLI. 1887. January.)

—— Une lettre d'Anastase bibliothécaire. (Monde latin et Monde slave, 1894. 1 January.)

*—— Saint Méthode apôtre des Slaves et les lettres des souverains pontifes conservées au British Museum. (RQH. Vol. XXVIII. 1880. October.)

Snopek, F. List papeže Hadriana II v pannon. legendě. *In* Sborník Velehradský VI. Olmütz. 1896. (Czech.)

—— Methodius Slavorum apostolus quo sensu orthodoxus declaratus sit. Prague. 1908. (Ex actis I conventus Velehradensis theologorum.)

Vondrák, V. Studie z oboru církevněslovanského písemnictví. Prague. 1903. (Appeared in Rozpravy české Akademie, třída III, č. 20.) [Especially the treatise "O původu obou tak zvaných pannonských legend."]

Wattenbach, W. Beiträge zur Geschichte der christl. Kirche in Mähren und Böhmen. Vienna. 1849. [Based upon Gorski.]

CHAPTER VIII.

THE RISE AND FALL OF THE FIRST BULGARIAN EMPIRE.

I. ORIGINAL AUTHORITIES.

(*a*) Byzantine Writers.

Attaliates, Michael. Ed. Bekker, I. CSHB. 1853.
Cedrenus and Scylitzes. Ed. Bekker, I. 2 vols. CSHB. 1838, 39.
Constantine Manasses. Ed. Bekker, I. CSHB. 1837.
Constantine Porphyrogenitus. Vol. iii. De thematibus et de administrando imperio. Ed. Bekker, I. *See Gen. Bibl.* iv.
Genesius. Regna. Ed. Lachmann, C. CSHB. 1834.
Georgius Monachus. Chronicon. Ed. Boor, C. de. Vol. ii. Leipsic. 1904.
Glycas. Ed. Bekker, I. CSHB. 1836.
Leo Diaconus. Ed. Hase, C. B. CSHB. 1828.
Leo Grammaticus, and Symeon Magister. Ed. Bekker, I. CSHB. 1842.
Nicephorus Bryennius. Ed. Meineke, A. CSHB. 1836.
Nicephorus Patriarcha. *Ἱστορία σύντομος*; and Ignatius. Βίος Νικηφόρου. Ed. Boor, C. de. Leipsic. 1880.
Nicolaus Patriarcha. Epistolae. MPG. cxi.
Photius. MPG. cii. col. 628–96.
Psellus. History. [*Χρονογραφία.*] Ed. Sathas, C. (Byzantine Texts.) London. 1899.
Suidas. Lexicon. Ed. Gaisford, T. Vol. i. Oxford. 1834.
Theodorus Studites. Parva Catechesis. Ed. Auvray, E. Paris. 1891.
Theophanes. Ed. Boor, C. de. 2 vols. Leipsic. 1883, 85.
Theophanes continuatus. Ed. Bekker, I. CSHB. 1838.
Theophylactus, Bulgariae Archiepiscopus. Epistolae. MPG. cxxvi. col. 307–557.
Zonaras. *Ἐπιτομὴ Ἱστοριῶν.* Ed. Dindorf, L. Vols. iii, iv. Leipsic. 1870, 71.

(*b*) Slavonic and Frankish Sources.

Annales Bertiniani. Ed. Waitz, G. SGUS. 1883.
Annales Regni Francorum. Ed. Kurze, F. SGUS. 1895.
List of Ancient Bulgarian Princes to 765. Engl. transl. by Bury, J. B. in his edn. of Gibbon, E., Decline and Fall of the Roman Empire (*see Gen. Bibl.* v). Vol. vi. Appendix 9.
Nestor. Chronica (Russo-Slavonic text and Latin transl.). Ed. Miklosich, F. Vol. i (all publ.). Vienna. 1860. French transl. and commentary. Leger, L. Chronique dite de Nestor. Paris. 1884.
Nicolaus I Papa. Responsa ad consulta Bulgarorum. Mansi. xv. 401 ff. And MPL. cxix. col. 978–1016.

II. MODERN WORKS.

(*a*) Books.

Bury, J. B. History of the Eastern Roman Empire. (802–867.) *See Gen. Bibl.* v.
—— Appendices 8–12 of vol. vi of his edn. of Gibbon, E., Decline and Fall of the Roman Empire. *See Gen. Bibl.* v.
Gelzer, H. Der Patriarchat von Achrida. Leipsic. 1902. Reviewed by Jireček, C. J. *in* BZ. xii. pp. 192–202. 1903.

Golubinski, E. E. History of the Bulgarian, Serbian, and Roumanian Churches. (In Russian.) *See Gen. Bibl.* v.
Hilferding [Gil'ferding], A. F. Geschichte der Serben und Bulgaren. (Transl. by Schmaler, J. E., from the Russian edn. of 1855.) 2 vols. Bautzen, etc. 1856–64.
Jireček, C. J. Geschichte der Bulgaren. *See Gen. Bibl.* v.
—— Geschichte der Serben. Vol. I. *See Gen. Bibl.* v.

(b) Periodical Literature.

Banescu, N. Paristrion, un ducat de graniţă bizantin in Dobrogea de azi. *In* Analeta Dobrogei. II, 3. pp. 313 ff. Constanţa. 1921.
Bury, J. B. The Chronological Cycle of the Bulgarians. BZ. XIX. pp. 127–44. 1910.
—— The Bulgarian Treaty of A.D. 814 and the Great Fence of Thrace. EHR. XXV. pp. 276–87. 1910.
Gelzer, H. Ungedruckte und wenig bekannte Bistümerverzeichnisse der orientalischen Kirche. BZ. I. pp. 256, 57; II. pp. 40–72. 1892, 93. [Contains Basil II's three charters of 1020.]
Kazarow, G. Die Gesetzgebung des bulgarischen Fürsten Krum. BZ. XVI. pp. 254–57. 1907.
Milyukov, P. N. [Monuments of Prespa.] Izvêstiya russkago arkheologicheskago Instituta v Konstantinopolê. IV. pp. 466 ff. 1889.
Uspenski, F., Shkorpil, K., and others. Materialy dlya bolgarskikh drevnostey Aboba-Pliska. Izvêstiya russk. arkheol. Inst. v Konstantinopolê. X. 1905.

CHAPTER IX.

THE GREEK CHURCH: ITS RELATIONS WITH THE WEST UP TO 1054.

I. SOURCES.

1. Collections of Documents.

Mansi. Sacr. Conciliorum collectio. Vols. xv, xvi, xvii, xviii, xix. *See Gen. Bibl.* iv.
Monumenta graeca ad Photium eiusque historiam pertinentia. Ed. Hergenröther, J. A. G. Ratisbon. 1869.
Will, C. Acta et scripta quae de controversiis eccles. graecae et latinae saec. xi composita exstant. Leipsic and Marburg. 1861.

2. Acts of Councils and Synods.

Council of Constantinople (858). Deposition of Ignatius. Mansi. xv. 518–22.
Eighth Ecumenical Council, 4th of Constantinople (869–870). Mansi. xvi. 1–550.
Council of Constantinople (under Photius 879). Mansi. xvii. 365–530.
Synod of Constantinople and Tomus Unionis (920). Mansi. xviii. 331–44.
Synodal Edict of Michael Cerularius (1054) containing legatine bull of excommunication. Will. Acta (*see above*). pp. 55 ff. MPG. xx. 737 ff.

3. Official Letters of Popes, Emperors, Patriarchs, and Bishops.

Letters of Nicholas I (858–867). Mansi. xv. 143–366. *Also* MPL. cxix.
Responsa Nicolai Papae I ad consulta Bulgarorum. Mansi. xv. 401–34.
Letters of Hadrian II (867–872). Mansi. xv. pp. 806–62.
Correspondence of Hadrian II with Basil and Photius, *in* Acts of Eighth Council. *Ibid.* xvi. 1–550.
Letters of John VIII (872–882). *Ibid.* xvii. 1–247.
Correspondence of John VIII and Photius. *Ibid.* pp. 524–6.
Letter of Stephen V to Basil (885). *Ibid.* xviii. 11–13.
Letters of Photius. MPG. cii.
Letters of Nicholas Mysticus (895–925). MPG. cxi.
Correspondence of Leo IX with Peter, Patriarch of Antioch, Michael Cerularius, and Constantine IX. Mansi. xix. Will (*see above*). pp. 168–71. MPL. cxliii. 744–81.
Correspondence of Michael Cerularius with Peter, Patriarch of Antioch. Will (*see above*). pp. 172–228. MPG. cxx. 752–820.
Letter of Leo, Archbishop of Ochrida (Achrida), to John, Bishop of Trani. Will (*see above*). pp. 52–64. MPG. xx. 836–44.
Correspondence of Peter, Patriarch of Antioch, with Dominic, Patriarch of Grado. Will (*see above*). pp. 205, 214. MPG. cxx. 755. MPL. cxli. 1455.

4. Pamphlets, Letters and Speeches.

Anastasius the Librarian. Praefatio in Concilium Constant. iv. Mansi. xvi. 1 ff.
Humbert of Sylva Candida, Cardinal. Adversus Graecos. Will (*see above*). p. 136. MPL. cxliii. Dialogue between a Latin and a Constantinopolitan. Will. p. 93. Adversus Simoniacos. MPL. cxliii.
Nicetas Stethatus (Pectoratus). Treatises against the Azymites. Will (*see above*). p. 127. MPG. cxx. 845–50.

Pavlov, N. Historico-literary sketch of the ancient Russian polemic against the Latins. St Petersburg. 1878. (Text in Greek and Old Russian following MSS in Synodal Library, Moscow.) (In Russian.)
Photius. Works. MPG. CI–CIV. Λόγοι καὶ ὁμιλίαι. Ed. Aristarchos. 2 vols. Constantinople. 1900.
Psellus, Michael. Corresp. and speeches. Sathas, K. N. Bibliotheca graeca medii aevi. Vols. IV, V. *See Gen. Bibl.* IV. *See esp.* Funeral oration on Michael Cerularius. IV. 303–87.
—— Accusation of Patriarch Michael Cerularius before the Synod (1059). Bréhier, L. Un discours inédit de Psellos. Rev. des Études grecques. XVI (1903). 375–416. XVII (1904). 35–76.
Theognostus. Libellus ad Nicolaum papam. Mansi. XVI. 296.

5. HISTORIES.

(*For Byzantine chronicles see special chapters.*)

Special sources for papal relations with Constantinople are:

Commemoratio brevis rerum a legatis apostolicae sedis Constantinopoli gestarum. Will. p. 150. MPL. CXLIII. [Attributed to Cardinal Humbert: a semi-official relation of the legation sent by Leo IX in 1054.]
Liudprand. Legatio. Ed. Pertz. MGH. Script. III. And ed. Becker, J. SGUS. 1915.
Psellus, Michael. Chronographia (976–1077). Ed. Sathas, K. N. Bibl. graeca medii aevi. IV. *See Gen. Bibl.* IV. *Also* London. 1899.

6. HAGIOGRAPHY AND ECCLESIASTICAL BIOGRAPHY.

(*a*) *Greek and Slavonic sources.*

(*See also Bibl. to ch.* VII(B).)

Vita Constantini (St Cyril). (The Pannonian Legend.) Serbo-Slavonic text with Latin transl. Ed. Dümmler, E. L. and Miklosich, F. Vienna. 1870.
Legenda SS. Cyrilli et Methodii. ASBoll. 9 Martii, II. pp. 22 ff. (The Moravian Legend.)
Vita Euthymii. Ed. Boor, C. de. Berlin. 1888. [Written by a contemporary of the Patriarch Euthymius, 907–912. Essential for the history of the struggle of the tetragamia.]
Vita Euthymii junioris. By Basil of Thessalonica. Ed. Petit, L. Rev. de l'Orient Chrétien. 1903. pp. 155 ff.
Vita Ignatii. Attributed to Nicetas of Paphlagonia. Mansi. XV. 209 ff. MPG. CV. 488 ff. [Essential for the history of the rivalry between Ignatius and Photius.]
Vita Josephi hymnographi. By John the Deacon. MPG. CV. 931 ff.
Vita Methodii (The Pannonian Legend). Ed. Miklosich, F. Vienna. 1870.
Vita Nili. (Founder of the monastery of Grottaferrata.) ASBoll. 26 Sept. VII. MPG. CXX. 1 ff.

(*b*) *Latin sources.*

Liber Pontificalis. Vol. II. *See Gen. Bibl.* IV.
Lives of Popes:
Hadrian II. Mansi. XV. 805 ff.
Nicholas I. *Ibid.* pp. 143 ff.
Leo IX. By Wibert. MPL. CXLIII. 465 ff.

II. MODERN WORKS.

1. GENERAL.

Bréhier, L. Normal relations between Rome and the Churches of the East before the schism of the eleventh century. The Constructive Quarterly. New York. 1917.
Gay, J. L'Italie méridionale. *See Gen. Bibl.* V.

Gfrörer, A. F. Byzantinische Geschichten. *See Gen. Bibl.* v.
Guldencrone, D. de. L'Italie byzantine. Étude sur le haut moyen âge, 400–1050. Paris. 1914.
Hefele, C. J. Conciliengesch. French transl. Leclercq, H. *See Gen. Bibl.* v.
Hergenröther, J. A. G. Photius Patriarch von Konstantinopel. 3 vols. Ratisbon. 1867–9. [Continues the history of the relations between Eastern and Western Churches to modern times.]

2. Times of Photius.

Bury, J. B. The relationship of the Patriarch Photius to the Empress Theodora. EHR. 1890. pp. 255–8.
—— History of the Eastern Roman Empire from the fall of Irene. *See Gen. Bibl.* v.
Dobschütz, E. v. Methodios und die Studiten. BZ. xviii. p. 41.
Goetz, L. K. Geschichte der Slavenapostel Konstantinus und Methodius. Gotha. 1897.
Lapôtre, A. L'Europe et le Saint-Siège à l'époque carolingienne. Le pape Jean VIII. Paris. 1895.
Leger, L. Cyrille et Méthode. Étude hist. sur la conversion des Slaves. Paris. 1868.
Loparev. Vizantiyskiya zhitiya svyatykh viii–ix vêkov. *In* VV. xvii, xviii. Petrograd. 1913–15. Grecheskiya zhitiya svyatykh viii i ix vêkov. Petrograd. 1914. (*Cf.* Bréhier, L. L'hagiographie byzantine des viiie et ixe siècles. Journ. des Savants, Aug. and Oct. 1916.)
Marin, E. Les moines de Constantinople, de la fondation de la ville jusqu'à la mort de Photius. Paris. 1897.
Ruinaut, J. Le schisme de Photius. Paris. 1910.
Vogt, A. Basile Ier, empereur de Byzance, et la civilisation byzantine à la fin du ixe siècle. Paris. 1908.

3. From Photius to the schism (895–1054).

Diehl, C. Les quatre mariages de Léon le Sage. *In* Figures byzantines. 1re série. pp. 181 ff. *See Gen. Bibl.* v.
Jugie. La vie et les ouvrages d'Euthyme patriarche de Constantinople. Échos d'Orient. xvi. 1913. pp. 385–95.
Lampros (Lambros), Sp. P. Die Abdankungsurkunde des Patriarchen Nikoläus Mysticos. BZ. i. 1892. pp. 551 ff.
Popóv, N. A. Imperator Lev VI i ego tsarstvovanie. Moscow. 1892.
Schlumberger, G. Un empereur byzantin au xe siècle: Nicéphore Phocas. *See Gen. Bibl.* v.
—— L'Épopée byzantine à la fin du dixième siècle. i. Jean Tzimiscès, Basile II (969–989). ii. Basile II (989–1025). *See Gen. Bibl.* v.

4. The Schism of 1054.

Belin, F. A. Histoire de la latinité de Constantinople. 2nd edn. Paris. 1894.
Bréhier, L. Le Schisme Oriental du xie siècle. Paris. 1899.
Bury, J. B. Roman Emperors from Basil II to Isaac Komnenos. EHR. 1889. pp. 41–64, 251–85.
Delarc, O. Un pape alsacien, saint Léon IX. Paris. 1876.
Dräseke, J. Psellos gegen Michael Keroularios. ZWT. 1905. pp. 194–409.
Ermini. Michele Cerulario e lo scisma di Oriente. Rivista internat. d. scien. soc. xv. 1897.
Rambaud, A. Michel Psellos philosophe et homme d'état. RH. 1877.
Schlumberger, G. L'Épopée byzantine. Pt. iii. Les porphyrogénètes, Zoé et Théodora (1025–57). *See Gen. Bibl.* v.
Skabalanovich, N. A. Vizantiyskoe gosudarstvo i tserkov' v xi vêkê. St Petersburg. 1884.
Suvorov. Le pape byzantin. Relations entre l'Église et l'État à Byzance. Moscow. 1902.

CHAPTER X.

(A)

MUSLIM CIVILISATION DURING THE ABBASID PERIOD.

I. SPECIAL BIBLIOGRAPHIES.

Chauvin, V. Bibliographie des ouvrages arabes ou relatifs aux Arabes publiés dans l'Europe chrétienne de 1810 à 1885. Liège. 1892–1903.
Encyclopaedia of Islam. *See Gen. Bibl.* I.
Friederici, C. Bibliotheca Orientalis. Leipsic. 1877–84.
Gabrieli, G. Manuale di bibliografia musulmana. Rome. 1916.
Islam, Der. Zeitschrift für Geschichte und Kultur des islamischen Orients. Ed. Becker, C. H. Strasbourg, Hamburg. 1910. In progress.
Klatt, J. Orientalische Bibliographie. *In* Literatur-Blatt für orientalische Philologie. Leipsic. 1884–8.
Orientalische Bibliographie. Ed. Müller, A. (1888–92), Kuhn, E. (1892–5), and Schermann, L. (1896–1915). Berlin.
Wüstenfeld, F. Die Geschichtschreiber der Araber und ihre Werke. Abh. d. k. Gesell. d. Wiss. zu Göttingen. 1882.

II. AUTHORITIES.

(*a*) Muslim.

(i) *Arabic.*

(*In chronological order.*)

Aḥmad ibn abī Ṭāhir Taifūr. Sechster Band des Kitâb Baġdâd. Ed. and transl. Keller, H. Leipsic. 1908.
Ibn Qutaibah. Kitāb al-Ma'ārif. Ed. Wüstenfeld, F. Göttingen. 1850.
Ṭabarī. Annales. Ed. Goeje, M. J. de. 15 vols. Leiden. 1879–1901.
Dīnawarī. Kitāb al-akhbār aṭ-ṭiwāl. Ed. Guirgass, V. Leiden. 1888.
Mas'ūdī. Kitāb at-tanbīh wa'l-ishrāf. Ed. Goeje, M. J. de. Leiden. 1894. French transl. Carra de Vaux, A. Paris. 1897.
—— Murūj adh-Dhahab. Ed. and transl. Barbier de Meynard, C. and Pavet de Courteille. 9 vols. Paris. 1861–77.
Abu'l-Faraj Isfahānī. Kitāb al-Aghānī. Cairo. 1867–8, 1905.
Muḥammad ibn Isḥāq an-Nadīm. Kitāb al-Fihrist. Ed. Flügel, G., Roediger, J., and Müller, A. 2 vols. Leipsic. 1871–2.
Abu'l-Muṭahhar. Ḥikāyah Abi'l-Qāsim al-Baghdādī. Ed. Mez, A. Heidelberg. 1902.
Fragmenta Historicorum Arabicorum. Ed. Goeje, M. J. de. 2 vols. Leiden. 1869, 1871.
Miskawaihi, Abū Shujā' Rūdhrāwarī and Hilāl ibn Muḥassin. The Eclipse of the Abbasid Caliphate. Ed. and transl. Amedroz, H. F. and Margoliouth, D. S. 7 vols. Oxford. 1920–1.
Hilāl ibn Muḥassin. Kitāb al-Wuzarā. Ed. Amedroz, H. F. Beyrout. 1904.
Ibn al-Qalānisī. History of Damascus 363–555 A.H. Ed. Amedroz, H. F. Beyrout. 1908.
Anūshirwān ibn Khālid. Histoire des Seldjoucides de l'Irâq par al-Bondari, d'après Imâd addin al-Kâtib al-Isfahâni. Ed. Houtsma, M. Th. Leiden. 1889.

Yāqūt. Dictionary of Learned Men. Ed. Margoliouth, D. S. 5 vols. Leiden and London. 1907–13.
Ibn al-Athīr. Chronicon. Ed. Tornberg, C. J. 14 vols. Leiden. 1862–76.
Sibt ibn al-Jauzī. Mir'āt az-Zamān. Ed. Jewett, J. Chicago. 1907.
Ibn Khallikān. Kitāb wafayāt al-a'yān. 2 vols. Cairo. 1882. Ed. Wüstenfeld, F. Göttingen. 1835–43. Eng. transl. Slane, G. de. Biographical Dictionary. 4 vols. Paris. 1843–71.
Ibn aṭ-Ṭiqṭaqà. Al-Fakhrī. Histoire du Khilafat et du Vizirat. Ed. Derenbourg, H. Paris. 1895. French transl. Amar, E. Paris. 1910.
Ibn Khaldūn. Kitāb al-'ibar. 7 vols. Cairo. 1867. Prolégomènes. Ed. Quatremère, E. M. 3 vols. Paris. 1858. *In* Notices et extraits des manuscrits. xvi, 1; xvii, 1; xviii, 1. French transl. Slane, G. de. 3 vols. Paris. 1862–8. *In* Notices et extraits des manuscrits. xix, 1; xx, 1; xxi, 1.
Suyūṭī. Ta'rīkh al-Khulafā. Cairo. 1888. Transl. Jarrett, H. S. (Bibliotheca Indica.) Calcutta. 1880.
Abū Yūsuf Ya'qūb ibn Ibrāhīm. Kitāb al-Kharāj. Cairo. 1885. Transl. Fagnan, E. Le livre de l'impôt foncier. Paris. 1921.
Yaḥyà ibn Ādam. Kitāb al-Kharāj. Ed. Juynboll, Th. W. Leiden. 1896.
Māwardī. Kitāb al-aḥkām as-sulṭāniyyah. Cairo. 1881. French transl. Fagnan, E. Algiers. 1915.

(ii) *Persian.*

(*In chronological order.*)

Baihaqī. Ta'rīkh-i-āl-i-Subuktigīn. Ed. Morley, W. H. (Bibliotheca Indica.) Calcutta. 1862.
Rāwandī. Rāḥat uṣ-Ṣudūr wa Āyat us-Surūr, being a history of the Saljūqs. Ed. Muḥammad Iqbāl. (Gibb Memorial Series.) London. 1921.
Ibn Isfandiyār. History of Ṭabaristān, abridged transl. by Browne, E. G. (Gibb Memorial Series.) London. 1905.
Minhāj-i-Sirāj al-Jūzjānī. Ṭabaqāt-i-Nāṣirī: a general history of the Muhammadan Dynasties of Asia. Transl. Raverty, H. G. (Bibliotheca Indica.) London. 1873–81.
Juwainī. Ta'rīkh-i-Jahān-Gushā. Ed. Mīrzā Muḥammad. 2 vols. (Gibb Memorial Series.) London. 1912, 1916.
Ḥamdullāh Mustaufī. Ta'rīkh-i-Guzīda. Ed. and transl. Browne, E. G. (Gibb Memorial Series.) London. 1911, 1914.
Mīrkhwānd. Rauḍat uṣ-Ṣafā. Bombay. 1854–5. Lucknow. 1883. Mirchond's Geschichte der Sultane aus dem Geschlechte Bujeh. Ed. and transl. Wilken, F. Berlin. 1835.

(*b*) Christian.

(i) *Syriac.*

(*In chronological order.*)

Thomas of Margā. The Book of Governors: the Historia Monastica. Ed. and transl. Budge, E. A. W. London. 1893.
Dionysius of Tall Maḥray. Chronique de Denys de Tell Mahré, quatrième partie. Ed. and transl. Chabot, J. B. Paris. 1895. (Review by Nau, F. *in* Bulletin Critique de Littérature. Paris. 15 June. 1896.)
Elias bar Shīnāyā. Eliae Metropolitae Nisibeni opus chronologicum. Ed. Brooks, E. W. and Chabot, J. B. CSCO. Series iii. Vols. 7–8. Paris. 1909–10.
—— Fragmente syrischer und arabischer Historiker. Ed. Baethgen, F. Leipsic. 1884.
Michael the Syrian. Chronique de Michel le Syrien, patriarche jacobite d'Antioche (1166–99). Ed. and transl. Chabot, J. B. Paris. 1899–1911.
Barhebraeus. Chronicon Ecclesiasticum. Ed. and transl. Abbeloos, J. B. and Lamy, T. J. Louvain. 1872–7.
—— Chronicon Syriacum. Ed. Bedjan, P. Paris. 1890.

(ii) *Arabic.*

(*In chronological order.*)

Eutychius. [Sa'īd ibn Batrīq.] Annales. Ed. Cheikho, L., Carra de Vaux, A., and Zayyat, H. CSCO. Script. Arabici. Series III. Vols. 6–7. Paris. 1906–9.
Yaḥyà ibn Sa'īd al-Anṭakī. Rosen, V. R. Imperator Vasili Bolgaroboytsa. St Petersburg. 1883.
Barhebraeus. Ta'rīkh mukhtaṣar ad-duwal. Ed. Ṣāliḥānī, A. Beyrout. 1890.
Mārī ibn Sulaimān, 'Amr ibn Mattai, and Ṣalībā ibn Yuḥannā. Maris, Amri et Slibae De Patriarchis Nestorianorum Commentaria. Ed. Gismondi, H. Rome. 1896–9.

III. MODERN WORKS.

(*a*) General.

Arnold, T. W. The Preaching of Islam: a history of the propagation of the Muslim faith. 2nd edn. London. 1913.
Blochet, E. Le messianisme dans l'hétérodoxie musulmane. Paris. 1903.
Bouvat, L. Les Barmécides d'après les historiens arabes et persans. Paris. 1912.
Caetani, L. (Duca di Sermoneta.) Annali dell' Islām. Milan. 1905. In progress.
Defrémery, C. Mémoire sur les Émirs al-Oméra. (Mémoires AcadIBL. Series I. Vol. II.) Paris. 1852.
Dozy, R. Het islamisme. 2nd ed. Haarlem. 1880. French transl. Chauvin, V. Leiden. 1879.
Freytag, G. W. Geschichte der Dynastie der Hamdaniden in Mossul und Aleppo. ZDMG. x, pp. 432 ff.; xi, pp. 177 ff. Leipsic. 1856–7.
Goeje, M. J. de. Mémoire sur les Carmathes du Bahrain et les Fatimides. 2nd ed. Leiden. 1886.
Goldziher, I. Muhammedanische Studien. 2 vols. Halle. 1888–90.
—— Vorlesungen über den Islam. Heidelberg. 1910.
Huart, C. Histoire des Arabes. 2 vols. Paris. 1912–13.
Kremer, A. von. Culturgeschichte des Orients unter den Chalifen. 2 vols. Vienna. 1875–7. Transl. S. Khuda Bukhsh. Calcutta. 1920.
—— Culturgeschichtliche Streifzüge auf dem Gebiete des Islams. Leipsic. 1873. Transl. S. Khuda Bukhsh. Contributions to the History of Islamic Civilization. Calcutta. 1905.
—— Geschichte der herrschenden Ideen des Islams. Leipsic. 1868.
—— Ueber das Einnahmebudget des Abbasiden-Reichs vom Jahre 306 H. (918–19). Denkschriften der KAW., Philos.-hist. Classe, XXXVI, pp. 283 ff. Vienna. 1887.
—— Ueber das Budget der Einnahmen unter der Regierung des Hârûn alraśîd. Verh. d. VII internat. Orientalisten-Congresses. Semit. Section. pp. 1 ff. Vienna. 1888.
Krymski, A. Istoriya Arabov i arabskoy literatury. Moscow. 1912.
Lammens, H. La Syrie. 2 vols. Beyrout. 1921.
Le Bon, G. La civilisation des Arabes. Paris. 1884.
Le Strange, G. Baghdad during the Abbasid Caliphate. Oxford. 1900.
—— Palestine under the Moslems. A description of Syria and the Holy Land from A.D. 650 to 1500. Translated from the works of the mediaeval Arab geographers. London. 1890.
—— The Lands of the Eastern Caliphate. *See Gen. Bibl.* II.
Margoliouth, D. S. The early development of Mohammedanism. London. 1914.
Marrast, A. Bagdad sous les Khalifes. *In* La vie byzantine au VIe siècle. pp. 305 ff. Paris. 1881.
Müller, A. Der Islam im Morgen- und Abendland. 2 vols. Berlin. 1885–7.
Muir, Sir William. The Caliphate: its rise, decline, and fall. Revised edn. Weir, T. H. *See Gen. Bibl.* V.
Nöldeke, Th. Orientalische Skizzen. Berlin. 1892. Transl. Black, J. S. Sketches from Eastern History. London. 1892.
Sédillot, L. A. Histoire générale des Arabes: leur empire, leur civilisation, leurs écoles philosophiques, scientifiques, et littéraires. 2 vols. Paris. 1877.

Vasil'ev, A. Vizantiya i Araby. 2 vols. St Petersburg. 1900, 1920.
Weil, G. Geschichte der Chalifen. *See Gen. Bibl.* v.
Zaydan, J. Ta'rīkh at-tamaddun al-islāmī. 5 vols. Cairo. 1902–6. (Fourth part transl. Margoliouth, D. S. Umayyads and Abbasids. (Gibb Memorial Series.) London. 1907.)

(*b*) Special.

(i) *Condition of non-Muslim subjects.*

Arnold, T. W. Articles on Persecution (Muhammadan), and Toleration (Muhammadan), *in* Hastings' Encyclopaedia of Religion and Ethics. *See Gen. Bibl.* i.
—— The Preaching of Islam. Chaps. iii, vii. London. 1913.
Becker, C. H. Article on Djizya *in* Encyclopaedia of Islam. *See Gen. Bibl.* i.
Belin, F. A. Fetwa relatif à la condition des Zimmis et particulièrement des Chrétiens, en pays musulmans, depuis l'établissement de l'islamisme jusqu'au milieu du viiie siècle de l'hégire. JA. Series iv. Vol. xviii. Paris. 1851.
Benjamin ben Jonah of Tudela. Itinerary. Ed. and transl. Asher, A. (with Essay on the state of the Khalifat of Bagdad during the latter half of the twelfth century, by F. Lebrecht). London. 1840–1.
Bevan, A. A. Article on Manichaeism *in* Hastings' Encyclopaedia of Religion and Ethics. *See Gen. Bibl.* i.
Chwolson, D. Die Ssabier und der Ssabismus. St Petersburg. 1856.
Fortescue, A. The Lesser Eastern Churches. London. 1913.
Gottheil, R. J. H. Dhimmis and Moslems in Egypt. Old Testament and Semitic Studies in memory of William Rainey Harper. Vol. ii. Chicago. 1908.
Haneberg, B. Das muslimische Kriegsrecht. Abh. der k. bayer. Akad. d. Wiss., Cl. i, Bd. xii, Abth. ii. Munich. 1871.
Pethahiah ben Jacob. Travels of Rabbi Petachia. Transl. Benisch, A. London. 1856.
Shedd, W. A. Islam and the Oriental Churches. Philadelphia. 1904.

(ii) *Literature, law, science, commerce, etc.*

Baumstark, A. Geschichte der syrischen Literatur. Bonn. 1922.
Becker, C. H. Christenthum und Islam. Tübingen. 1907. Transl. Chaytor, H. J. London. 1909.
Berchem, Max van. La propriété territoriale et l'impôt foncier sous les premiers califes. Étude sur l'impôt du Kharāg. Geneva. 1886.
Berthelot, M. P. E. Histoire des Sciences. La chimie au moyen-âge. 3 vols. Paris. 1893.
Boer, T. J. de. Geschichte der Philosophie im Islam. Stuttgart. 1901. Transl. Jones, E. R. London. 1903.
Brockelmann, C. Geschichte der arabischen Litteratur. *See Gen. Bibl.* v.
Browne, E. G. Arabian medicine. Cambridge. 1921.
—— A Literary History of Persia. 2 vols. London. 1902, 1906.
Cantor, M. Vorlesungen über Geschichte der Mathematik. 2nd ed. Vol. i, pp. 649 ff. Leipsic. 1894.
Carra de Vaux, A. Les grands philosophes. Avicenne. Paris. 1900.
—— —— Gazali. Paris. 1902.
—— Les Penseurs de l'Islam. Paris. 1921. In progress.
Diercks, G. Die Araber im Mittelalter und ihr Einfluss auf die Cultur Europas. 2nd ed. Leipsic. 1882.
Duval, R. La littérature syriaque. 3rd ed. Paris. 1907.
Gaudefroy-Demombynes, M. Les institutions musulmanes. Paris. 1921.
Goeje, M. J. de. International handelsverkeer in de middeleeuwen. *In* Verslagen en Mededeelingen der K. Akad. van Wet., Afd. Letterkunde. Series iv. Vol. ix, pp. 245 ff. Amsterdam. 1908.
Goldziher, I. Die islamische und die jüdische Philosophie des Mittelalters. *In* Die Kultur der Gegenwart. Ed. Hinneberg, P. Teil i, Abt. v, pp. 301 ff. 2nd edn. Leipsic. 1913.

Goldziher, I. Muhammedanisches Recht in Theorie und Wirklichkeit. Zeitschrift für vergleichende Rechtswissenschaft. VII. Stuttgart. 1888.
—— Die Richtungen der islamischen Koranauslegung. De Goeje-Stiftung. No. VI. Leiden. 1920.
Graf, A. Die christlich-arabische Litteratur. *In* Strassb. Theol. Studien. VII, 1. Freiburg-im-Breisgau. 1905.
Hariz, J. La part de la médecine arabe dans l'évolution de la médecine française. Paris. 1922.
Hartmann, M. Die islamische Verfassung und Verwaltung. *In* Die Kultur der Gegenwart. Ed. Hinneberg, P. Teil II, Abt. II, 1. pp. 49 ff. Leipsic. 1911.
Hauser, F. Ueber das *kitâb al ḥijal*—das Werk über die sinnreichen Anordnungen—der *Benû Mûsâ*. Erlangen. 1922.
Heyd, W. von. Histoire du commerce du Levant au moyen-âge. Transl. Raynaud, F. *See Gen. Bibl.* v.
Horovitz, S. Ueber den Einfluss der griechischen Philosophie auf die Entwicklung des Kalam. Jahresbericht des jüdisch-theologischen Seminars zu Breslau. 1909.
Horten, M. Indische Gedanken in der islamischen Philosophie. Viert. für wiss. Philosophie und Soziologie. XXXIV, pp. 310 ff. Leipsic. 1910.
—— Die philosophischen Ansichten von Rázi und Túsi. Bonn. 1910.
—— Die philosophischen Systeme der spekulativen Theologen im Islam. Bonn. 1912.
Juynboll, Th. W. Handbuch des islamischen Gesetzes. Leiden. 1910.
Leclerc, L. Histoire de la médecine arabe. 2 vols. Paris. 1876.
Macdonald, D. B. Development of Muslim theology, jurisprudence, and constitutional theory. London. 1903.
Massignon, L. La passion d'al-Ḥallâj, martyr mystique de l'Islam: étude d'histoire religieuse. 2 vols. Paris. 1922.
Mez, A. Die Renaissance des Islâms. Heidelberg. 1922.
Neuburger, M. Geschichte der Medizin. Stuttgart. 1908.
Nicholson, R. A. A Literary History of the Arabs. London. 1907.
—— Studies in Islamic Mysticism. Cambridge. 1921.
—— Studies in Islamic Poetry. Cambridge. 1921.
O'Leary, D. L. Arabic thought and its place in history. London. 1922.
Ritter, H. Ein arabisches Handbuch der Handelswissenschaft. Der Islam. (*See above*, I.) VII, pp. 1 ff. Strasbourg. 1916.
Schreiner, M. Beiträge zur Geschichte der theologischen Bewegungen im Islâm. ZDMG. LII, pp. 463 ff.; 513 ff.; LIII, pp. 51 ff. Leipsic. 1898–9.
Snouck Hurgronje, C. Le droit musulman. Revue de l'Histoire des Religions. XXXVII. Paris. 1898.
Steinschneider, M. Alfarabi, des arabischen Philosophen, Leben und Schriften, mit besonderer Rücksicht auf die Geschichte der griechischen Wissenschaft unter den Arabern. Mém. AcadIP. Series VII. Vol. XIII, no. 4. St Petersburg. 1869.
—— Die arabische Literatur der Juden. Ein Beitrag zur Literaturgeschichte der Araber. Frankfort. 1902.
—— Die arabische Uebersetzungen aus dem Griechischen.
I. Philosophie (*in* Beihefte zum Centralblatt für Bibliothekswesen. VII, pp. 51 ff.; XII, pp. 129 ff. Leipsic. 1889, 1893);
II. Mathematik (*in* ZDMG. 50, pp. 161 ff. Leipsic. 1896);
III. Medicin (*in* Virchow's Archiv für Pathologie. CXXVI. Berlin. 1891).
—— Die europäischen Uebersetzungen aus dem Arabischen. SKAW. CXLIX and CLI. Vienna. 1904, 1905.
Suter, H. Die Araber als Vermittler der Wissenschaften in ihrem Übergang vom Orient in den Occident. 2nd edn. Aarau. 1897.
—— Die Mathematiker und Astronomen der Araber und ihre Werke. Leipsic. 1900.
Wiedemann, E. Beiträge zur Geschichte der Naturwissenschaften. X–XXXII. (And numerous other contributions to the history of Arabic science.) Erlangen. 1906–13.
Wüstenfeld, F. Geschichte der arabischen Aerzte und Naturforscher. Göttingen. 1840.
—— Die Uebersetzungen arabischer Werke in das Lateinische seit dem XI Jahrhundert. Abh. Gött. Gesellschaft d. Wiss. XXII. Göttingen. 1877.

(B)

THE SELJŪQS.

I. SOURCES.

Muḥammad an-Nasawī. History of Jalāl-ad-Dīn Mankobirti, prince of Khwārazm. Ed. with French transl. Houdas, O. (Publ. de l'École des Langues Orientales vivantes. Ser. III. ix ff.) Paris. 1891.

Naṣir ibn Khusrau. Safar Nāmah. Ed. with French transl. Schefer, C. Sefer Nameh. Relation du voyage...en Syrie, Palestine, Égypte, Arabie, et en Perse (1035–42). (*Ibid.* Ser. II. Vol. I.) Paris. 1881.

Rāwandī (Najm-ad-Dīn Abū-Bakr Muḥammad ibn ʿAlī). Rāḥatu'ṣ-Ṣudūr (Refreshment of Hearts). Ed. Muḥammad Iqbál. Gibb Memorial Series. New Ser. Vol. II. London. 1921. [Written 1202–3.]

Other important sources for the Seljūqs are contained in

Houtsma, M. T. Recueil de textes relatifs à l'histoire des Seldjoucides. 4 vols. Leiden. 1886–1902.

1. The history of the Seljūqs of Kirmān by Muḥammad Ibrāhīm.
2. The history of the Seljūqs of ʿIrāq by Bundārī, based on the history in Persian by Anūshirwān ibn Khālid translated into Arabic by ʿImād-ad-Dīn al-Iṣfahānī.
3. The history of the Seljūqs of Rūm, abridged from a work of Ibn Bībī.

II. MODERN WORKS.

[*An asterisk is prefixed to the more important works.*]

*Browne, E. G. A rare manuscript history of the Seljúqs. *In* JRAS. July, 1902, pp. 567–610, and October, 1902, pp. 849–87. [Also publ. separately.]

* —— The early Seljúq period. *In* Literary history of Persia. Vol. II, ch. III ff. London. 1906.

*Defrémery, C. Histoire des Seldjoukides. JA. May, 1848, p. 417; September, 1848, pp. 259 ff.; October, 1848, pp. 334 ff.

—— Le règne du Sultan Barkiarok (1092–1104). JA. May, 1853, p. 425; October, 1853, p. 217.

EncBr. *"Seljūks" (with bibliography), and other articles.

Encyclopaedia of Islam. Articles. *See Gen. Bibl.* I.

Guignes, J. de. Histoire générale des Huns, des Turcs, des Mogols, et des autres Tartares. 4 vols. in 5. Paris. 1756–8. [Books X–XI deal with the Seljūqs of Persia, Iconium, and Aleppo, respectively.]

—— Histoire des princes Atabeks en Syrie par Aboulhasan Ali...Azz-ed-dīn. *In* Notices et extraits des MSS de la Bibliothèque du Roi. pp. 542 ff. Paris. 1787.

Herbelot, B. d'. Bibliothèque Orientale. Paris. 1697. Hague. 4 vols. 1777–9.

Houtsma, M. T. Zur Geschichte der Selǵuken von Kirman. ZDMG. 1885. pp. 362–401.

*Lane-Poole, S. The Mohammadan Dynasties. *See Gen. Bibl.* III.

O'Leary, D. L. Short history of the Fatimid Caliphate, ch. XI ff. London. 1923.

Süssheim, K. Prolegomena zu einer Ausgabe der..."Chronik des Seldschuqischen Reiches." Leipsic. 1911.

MAPS.

For maps see Spruner-Menke. Hand-Atlas. No. 83. (*See Gen. Bibl.* II.) And Poole, R. L. Historical Atlas. Nos. 78 and 79. (*See Gen. Bibl.* II.)

CHAPTER XI.

THE EARLIER COMNENI.

I. SPECIAL BIBLIOGRAPHIES.

Bréhier, L. Le schisme oriental du XIe siècle. Paris. 1899.
Chalandon, F. Les Comnènes. Études sur l'empire byzantin aux XIe et XIIe siècles. Vol. I. Essai sur le règne d'Alexis Comnène. *See Gen. Bibl.* V.

On the authorities for the First Crusade, compare:

Molinier, A. Sources de l'histoire de France. Vol. II. pp. 278 ff. *See Gen. Bibl.* I.

II. ORIGINAL AUTHORITIES.

A. Greek.

(1) *Chronicles.*

Attaliates, Michael. Ἱστορία. Ed. Bekker, I. CSHB. 1853.
Bryennius, Nicephorus. Ὕλη ἱστορίας. Ed. Meineke, A. CSHB. 1836.
Cedrenus, Georgius. Σύνοψις ἱστοριῶν. Ed. Bekker, I. 2 vols. CSHB. 1838, 39. (*Cf.* Scylitzes.)
Comnena, Anna. Ἀλεξίας. Ed. Reifferscheid, A. 2 vols. Leipsic. 1884.
Glycas, Michael. Βίβλος χρονική. Ed. Bekker, I. CSHB. 1836.
Psellus, Michael. Βυζαντινῆς ἱστορίας ἑκατονταετηρίς. Ed. Sathas, K. *in* Μεσαιωνικὴ βιβλιοθήκη. Vol. IV. *See Gen. Bibl.* IV. *Also in* The History of Psellus. (Byzantine Texts.) London. 1899.
Scylitzes, Johannes. A part of his chronicle is inserted in that of Cedrenus. The second part of his work is edited by Bekker, I., at the end of the work of Cedrenus. *See above.*
Zonaras, Johannes. Ἐπιτομὴ ἱστοριῶν. Vol. III. Ed. Büttner-Wobst, T. CSHB. 1897.

(2) *Orations, letters.*

Comnenus, Alexius. Λόγος πρὸς Ἀρμενίους *in* Papadopoulos-Kerameus, A. Ἀνάλεκτα Ἱεροσολυμιτικῆς σταχυολογίας. Vol. I. p. 116. St Petersburg. 1891.
Psellus, Michael. Πρὸς τὴν Σύνοδον κατηγορία τοῦ ἀρχιερέως. Ed. Bréhier, L. Un discours inédit de Psellos *in* Revue des études grecques. Vol. XVI. p. 375. Paris. 1903. New edn. in Cozza-Luzi, J. Nova patrum bibliotheca ab Angelo Card. Maio collecta. Vol. X. Rome. 1905.
—— Ἐπιστολαί. Ed. Sathas, K. *Op. cit.* Vol. V.
Theophylactus, Archbishop of Bulgaria. Works. MPG. Vols. CXXXIII–CXXXVI. Paris. 1864.

(3) *Charters.*

Irene, Empress. Typikon. Ed. Montfaucon, B. de, *in* Analecta graeca. Paris. 1688. Also ed. Miklosich, F. and Müller, J., *in* Acta et diplomata graeca medii aevi. Vol. V. p. 327. *See Gen. Bibl.* IV.
Miklosich, F. and Müller, J. *Op. cit.* Vols. V, VI.
Nicole, J. Une ordonnance inédite de l'empereur Alexis Ier Comnène, sur les privilèges du χαρτοφύλαξ. BZ. Vol. III. p. 17. Munich. 1894.

Pacuprianus, Gregory. Typikon. Ed. Petit, L. *in* VV. xi. Suppl. No. 1. St Petersburg. 1904.
Petit, L. Le monastère de Notre Dame de Pitié en Macédoine. *In* Izvêstiya russkago arkheologicheskago Instituta v Konstantinopolê. vi. p. 1. Sofia. 1900. [Contains several diplomas of Alexius and his successors.]
Sakkelion, J. Documents inédits de la Bibliothèque de Patmos. *In* Bulletin de correspondance hellénique. Vol. ii. p. 102. Paris. 1878.
Tafel, G. L. F. and Thomas, G. M. Urkunden zur älteren Handels- und Staatsgeschichte der Republik Venedig. (Fontes Rerum Austriacarum, Diplomata et acta. Vols. xii–xiv.) Vienna. 1856–7.
Uspenski, F. I. Sinodik v nedêlyu pravoslaviya. Odessa. 1893.
Vasil'evski, V. Khrisovul imperatora Alexêya I Komnena. *In* VV. iii. p. 121. St Petersburg. 1896.
Zachariae von Lingenthal, K. E. Jus graeco-romanum. Pt. iii. *See Gen. Bibl.* iv.

B. Oriental.

Chronicles.

Barhebraeus (Abulpharagius). Chronicon syriacum. Ed., with Latin transl., Bruns, P. J. and Kirsch, G. G. 2 vols. Leipsic. 1789.
Michael the Syrian. Chronicle. Ed., with French transl., Chabot, J. B. Paris. 1900–10.
Recueil des historiens des croisades. AcadIBL. Historiens arméniens. 1869–1906. Historiens orientaux. 1874–1906. *See Gen. Bibl.* iv.

C. Western.

(1) *Chronicles for the war with the Normans and relations with Italy.*

Chronicles of Lupus Protospatarius. Ed. Pertz. MGH. Script. v. And of the Anonymus of Bari. Ed. Muratori. RR.II.SS. Vol. v. [Both are annals.]
Guilelmus Apuliensis. Gesta Roberti Wiscardi. Ed. Wilmans. MGH. Script. ix.
Malaterra, Gaufredus. Historia sicula. Ed. Muratori. *Op. cit.* Vol. v.
Petrus Diaconus. Continuator of the Chronica monasterii Casinensis of Leo Ostiensis from lib. iii, c. xxxv. Ed. Wattenbach. MGH. Script. vii.

(2) *Chronicles relating to the First Crusade and to the Latins of the East.*

[The greater number are published in the Recueil des historiens des croisades. AcadIBL. Historiens occidentaux. 1841–85. *See Gen. Bibl.* iv.]
Albertus Aquensis. Liber christianae expeditionis pro erectione, emundatione, et restitutione Sanctae Hierosolymitanae ecclesiae. *In* Hist. occidentaux. v. (*See above.*) [Private information.]
Anonymus. Gesta Francorum et aliorum Hierosolymitanorum. *Ibid.* iii, as Tudebodus abbreviatus; also ed. Hagenmeyer, H. Heidelberg. 1890. [Eye-witness.]
Chanson d'Antioche, La. Ed. Paris, P. 2 vols. Paris. 1848.
Ekkehardus, Abbot of Aura (Uraugiensis). Hierosolymita. Ed. Hagenmeyer, H. Tübingen. 1877. [This and the above give some information on the relations between Greeks and Crusaders.]
Fulcherius Carnotensis. Gesta Francorum Iherusalem peregrinantium. *In* Hist. occidentaux. iii. (*See above.*) [Eye-witness.]
Radulfus Cadomensis. Gesta Tancredi Siciliae regis in expeditione Hierosolymitana ab ipso belli sacri exordio. *Ibid.* iii. [Private information.]
Raimundus of Aguilers. Historia Francorum qui ceperunt Hierusalem. *Ibid.* iii. [Eye-witness.]
Robertus Remensis monachus. Historia Hierosolymitana. *Ibid.* iii.
[Guibert of Nogent and Baldric of Bourgueil (*ibid.* vol. iv) had no original information, nor, for this period, had William of Tyre (*ibid.* vol. i).]

(3) *Letters.*

Hagenmeyer, H. Die Kreuzzugsbriefe aus den Jahren 1088–1100. Innsbruck. 1901.
Riant, P. Alexii Comneni imperatoris ad Robertum I Flandriae comitem epistola spuria. Paris. 1879.
—— Inventaire critique des lettres historiques des croisades. *In* Archives de l'Orient latin. Vol. i. Paris. 1880.

III. MODERN WORKS.

A. General Works.

Except the general histories of the Byzantine Empire, Lebeau, Gibbon, Finlay, Hopf, Hertzberg, there are no works dealing with this period as a whole. Reference may be made, however, to:

Neumann, C. Die Weltstellung des byzantinischen Reiches vor den Kreuzzügen. French transl. by Renauld and Koslowski. *See Gen. Bibl.* v.

B. Monographs.

(1) *On Isaac Comnenus.*

Bréhier, L. Le schisme oriental du xie siècle. Paris. 1899.
Bury, J. B. Roman Emperors from Basil II to Isaac Komnenos. EHR. iv. pp. 19, 41, 251 ff. London. 1889.
Mädler, H. Theodora, Michael Stratiotikos, Isaak Komnenos. Plauen. 1894.
Schlumberger, G. L'épopée byzantine. Pt. iii. *See Gen. Bibl.* v.

(2) *On Alexius I, Comnenus.*

Chalandon, F. Les Comnènes. Études sur l'empire byzantin aux xie et xiie siècles. Vol. i. Essai sur le règne d'Alexis Comnène. *See Gen. Bibl.* v.

C. On Italian Affairs.

Chalandon, F. Histoire de la domination normande en Italie et en Sicile. 2 vols. Paris. 1907.
Deutzer, B. Topographie der Feldzüge Robert Guiscards gegen das byzantinische Reich. *In* Festschrift des geographischen Seminars der Universität. Breslau. 1901.
Heinemann, L. v. Geschichte der Normannen in Unteritalien und Sizilien. Vol. i (all publ.). Leipsic. 1894.
Meyer von Knonau, G. Jahrbücher des deutschen Reiches unter Heinrich IV und Heinrich V. 7 vols. Leipsic. 1890–1909. (Jahrb. d. deutsch. Gesch.)
Schwartz, K. Die Feldzüge Robert Guiscards gegen das byzantinische Reich. Fulda. 1854.

D. On the Crusades.

Bréhier, L. L'Église et l'Orient au moyen âge. Les Croisades. *See Gen. Bibl.* v.
Hagenmeyer, H. Geschichte des ersten Kreuzzuges. Innsbruck. 1901.
—— Chronologie de la première croisade. *In* Revue de l'Orient latin. Vol. vi. pp. 214 ff. Paris. 1898.
Kugler, B. Boemund und Tankred. Tübingen. 1862.
Riant, P. Expéditions et pèlerinages des Scandinaves en Terre Sainte au temps des croisades. Paris. 1865.
Röhricht, R. Geschichte des Königsreiches Jerusalem. Innsbruck. 1898.
Sybel, H. v. Geschichte des ersten Kreuzzuges. Düsseldorf. 1841. 2nd ed. Leipsic. 1881.

E. On Constantinople and its Vassal-states.

Fischer, W. Trapezus im 11 und 12 Jahrhundert. MIOGF. Vol. x. p. 107. Innsbruck. 1889.
Petrov, A. Knez Konstantin Bodin. *In* Sbornik statey po slavyanovêdêniyu sostavlenny i izdanny uchenikami V. Lamanskago. St Petersburg. 1883.
Vasil'evski, V. Vizantiya i Pechenegi. ZMNP. Vol. clxiv. pp. 116 ff. St Petersburg. 1872.

F. On the Internal History of Constantinople.

Renaudin, Dom P. Christodule higoumène de Saint-Jean à Patmos. *In* Revue de l'Orient chrétien. Vol. v. p. 265. Paris. 1900.
Uspenski, F. I. Bogoslovskoe i filosofskoe dvizhenie v Vizantii xi i xii vêkov. ZMNP. Vol. cclxxvii. (1891.) Sept., p. 102, Oct., p. 51. St Petersburg. 1891.
—— Dêloproizvodstvo po obvineniyu Ioanna Itala v eresi. *In* Izvêstiya russk. arkheol. Instituta v Konstantinopolê. Vol. ii. p. 1. Odessa. 1897.
Vasil'evski, V. Materialy dlya vnutrenney istorii vizantiyskago gosudarstva. Pt. iv. ZMNP. Vol. ccx. pp. 355 ff.

G. Criticism of Authorities.

Bury, J. B. Some notes on the text of Anna Comnena. BZ. Vol. ii. p. 76. Munich. 1893.
Dieter, K. Zur Glaubwürdigkeit der Anna Comnena. I. Der Petschenegenkrieg (1084–91). BZ. Vol. iii. p. 386. Munich. 1894.
Dräseke, J. Psellos und seine Anklageschrift gegen den Patriarchen Michael Kerularios. ZWT. Vol. xlviii. pp. 194 ff., pp. 362 ff. Jena. 1905.
Hagenmeyer, H. Der Brief des Kaisers Alexios I Komnenos an den Grafen Robert I von Flandern. BZ. Vol. vi. pp. 1 ff. Munich. 1897.
Krumbacher, K. Michael Glykas. *In* Sitzungsberichte d. philos.-philolog. u. histor. Classe d. k. bay. Akad. d. Wissenschaften. Munich. 1894. p. 891.
Kugler, B. Albert von Aachen. Stuttgart. 1885.
Neumann, C. Griechische Geschichtschreiber und Geschichtsquellen im zwölften Jahrhundert. Leipsic. 1888.
Oster, E. Anna Komnena. 3 vols. Rastatt. 1863–71.
Pirenne, H. À propos de la lettre d'Alexis Ier Comnène à Robert le Frison, comte de Flandre. *In* Revue de l'instruction publ. en Belgique. Vol. 50. pp. 217 ff. Brussels. 1907.
Rambaud, A. Michel Psellos. RH. Vol. iii. pp. 241 ff. Paris. 1877.
Seger, J. Byzantinische Historiker des 10 und 11 Jahrhunderts. I. Nikephoros Bryennios. Munich. 1888.
Vercruysse, F. Essai critique sur la chronique d'Albert d'Aix. *In* Annales de la faculté de philosophie et lettres de l'Univ. de Bruxelles. Vol. i. Fasc. i. No. 2. Liège. 1889.

CHAPTER XII.

THE LATER COMNENI.

I. SPECIAL BIBLIOGRAPHIES.

See Bibliography I of chapter XI.

1. On the Reign of Andronicus Comnenus.

Bibliography in:

Radojcić, M. Dva posljednja Komnena na carigradskom prijestolju. Agram. 1907.

2. On the Second Crusade.

Bibliography in:

Molinier, A. Les sources de l'histoire de France. Vol. II. p. 299. *See Gen. Bibl.* I.

II. ORIGINAL AUTHORITIES.

A. Greek.

1. *Greek Chronicles.*

Cinnamus, John. *Ἐπιτομὴ τῶν κατορθωμάτων τῷ μακαρίτῃ βασιλεῖ καὶ πορφυρογεννήτῳ κυρῷ Ἰωάννῃ τῷ Κομνηνῷ καὶ ἀφήγησις τῶν πραχθέντων τῷ ἀοιδίμῳ υἱῷ αὐτοῦ τῷ βασιλεῖ καὶ πορφυρογεννήτῳ κυρῷ Μανουὴλ τῷ Κομνηνῷ πονηθεῖσα Ἰωάννῃ βασιλικῷ γραμματικῷ τῷ Κιννάμῳ.* Ed. Meineke, A. CSHB. 1836.

Nicetas Acominatus (Choniates). *Χρονικὴ διήγησις.* Ed. Bekker, I. CSHB. 1835.

2. *Letters, Orations, varia.*

Basil of Ochrida (Achrida). Des Basilius von Achrida unedierte Dialoge. Ed. Schmidt, J.; *and in* Vasiliya Okhridskago, arkhiepiskopa solunskago, neizdannoe nadgrobnoe slovo na smert' Iriny pervoy suprugi imperatora Manuila Komnena. *In* VV. Vol. I, p. 55. St Petersburg. 1894.

Demetracopoulos, Andronicus. Bibliotheca ecclesiastica. Leipsic. 1864. [Contains several theological works bearing on the religious disputes under Manuel Comnenus.]

Eustathius of Thessalonica. De Thessalonica a Latinis capta anno 1185 liber. Ed. Bekker, I. CSHB. 1842. Opuscula. Ed. Tafel, G. L. F. Frankfort. 1832. [A German transl. of Eustathius' funeral oration on Manuel Comnenus is in Tafel, G. L. F. Komnenen und Normannen. Ulm. 1852.]

Kurtz, E. Unedierte Texte aus der Zeit des Kaisers Johannes Komnenos. *In* BZ. Vol. XVI. p. 69. Munich. 1907.

Michael Acominatus. *Ἀκομινάτου τοῦ Χωνιάτου τὰ σωζόμενα.* Ed. Lampros, S. 2 vols. Athens. 1879–80.

Michael Italicus. Letters. Ed. Cramer, T. *in* Anecdota graeca e codicibus manuscriptis bibliothecarum Oxoniensium. Vol. III. pp. 156 ff. Oxford. 1836.

Prodromus, Theodorus. Partly publ. in MPG. Vol. CXXXIII.

Regel, W. Fontes rerum byzantinarum. Vol. I. St Petersburg. 1892. [Contains orations by Michael of Thessalonica.]

Theiner, A. and Miklosich, F. Monumenta spectantia ad unionem ecclesiarum graecae et romanae. Vienna. 1872.
Theorianus. Opera. MPG. Vol. cxxxiii.

3. *Charters.*

Bertolotto, G. Nuova serie di documenti sulle relazioni di Genova coll' impero bizantino. *In* Atti d. Soc. ligure di storia patria. Vol. xxviii. Genoa. 1896.
Dmitrievski, A. Typika. Kiev. 1895. [Contains the Typikon of the monastery of the Pantokrator at Constantinople.]
Müller, G. Documenti sulle relazioni delle città toscane coll' Oriente cristiano. Florence. 1879.
Nicetas Acominatus (Choniates). *Θησαυρὸς ὀρθοδοξίας.* An incomplete edn. in MPG. Vol. cxxxix, col. 1101 ff. [Contains a part of the acts of the Councils assembled during the reign of Manuel Comnenus.]
Petit, L. Documents inédits sur le concile de 1166 et ses derniers défenseurs. *In* VV. Vol. xii. pp. 465 ff. St Petersburg. 1904.
—— Le monastère de Notre Dame de Pitié en Macédoine. *In* Izvêstiya russk. arkheol. Instituta v Konstantinopolê. vi. p. 1. Sofia. 1900. [Contains some diplomas.]
Sakkelion, J. Πατμιακὴ βιβλιοθήκη. Athens. 1890.

B. Oriental.

Cf. the Bibliography of the preceding chapter.

Benjamin ben Jonah of Tudela. Itinerary. Ed. with transl. Asher, A. 2 vols. London and Berlin. 1840, 41. Also ed. with transl. Adler, M. N. London. 1907.
Kamāl-ad-Dīn. History of Aleppo. Transl. by Blochet, E. *in* Revue de l'Orient latin. Vol. iii. pp. 509 ff. Vol. iv. pp. 1 ff. Vol. v. pp. 37 ff. Vol. vi. pp. 1 ff. Paris. 1895–8.
Nerses Klaježi (Narses Clajensis). Opera. Ed. Cappelletti, G. Venice. 1833. [On the attempt at reuniting the Greek and Armenian Churches under Manuel Comnenus.]
Usāma ibn Munqiḍ. Autobiography. Ed. Derenbourg, H. *in* Publ. de l'École des langues orientales vivantes. 2nd series. Vol. xii. Part ii. Paris. 1886. [French transl. by Derenbourg, H. *in* Revue de l'Orient latin. Vol. ii. pp. 329 ff. Paris. 1894.]

C. Western.

We can only mention the chief works. The following may be consulted as to the relations of Constantinople with:

1. *Germany.*

Otto of Freisingen. Chronicon. Ed. Wilmans, R. MGH. Script. xx. Revised ed. Hofmeister, A. SGUS. 1912.
—— Gesta Friderici I imperatoris, with continuation by Rahewin, 1158–60, and by an anonymous author to 1170. Ed. Waitz, G. MGH. Script. xx. Revised ed. Simson, B. de. SGUS. 1912.
Wibald, Abbot of Stavelot. Epistolae. Ed. Jaffé, P. Bibl. rerum german. Vol. i. *See Gen. Bibl.* iv. [Most important.]

2. *Italy.*

(*a*) *Venice.*

Annales Venetici breves. Ed. Simonsfeld, H. MGH. Script. xiv.
Dandolo, A. Chronicon. Ed. Muratori. RR.II.SS. Vol. xii.
Historia ducum Veneticorum. Ed. Simonsfeld, H. MGH. Script. xiv.

(*b*) *Pisa.*

Marango. Annales Pisani. Ed. Pertz, K. *Ibid.* xix.

(*c*) *Genoa.*

Cafarus. Annales Genuenses to 1163, with continuations by Osbertus to 1173, and by Ottobonus to 1196. Ed. Pertz, K. *Ibid.* xviii.

(*d*) *Rome.*

Boso. Gesta pontificum Romanorum. Ed. Duchesne, L. Liber pontificalis. Vol. ii. *See Gen. Bibl.* iv.

(*e*) *Kingdom of Sicily.*

Falcandus, Hugo. Ed. Siragusa, G. La Historia o liber de regno Sicilie. (Fonti.) 1897.

Romuald of Salerno. Chronicon. Ed. Arndt, W. MGH. Script. xix.

3. *Hungary and Serbia.*

The Priest of Dioclea. De regno Slavorum. Ed. Lucius, J. De regno Dalmatiae et Croatiae. Amsterdam. 1666; and Schwandtner, J. G. Scriptores rerum Hungaricorum. Vol. ii. Vienna. 1746.

Thomas, Archdeacon of Spalato. Historia Salonitarum pontificum. Ed. Lucius, *op. cit.*; and Schwandtner, *op. cit.* vol. iii; and Rački, F. MHSM. xxvi (Script. iii). Agram. 1894.

Thurocz, John de. Chronica Hungarorum. Ed. Schwandtner, J. G. *Op. cit.* Vol. i. Vienna. 1746.

To these authorities must be added the Lives of St Simeon (Stephen Nemanja) by Stephen "the first-crowned," and of St Sava by Domentijan. Ed. Šafařík, P. J. *in* Památky dřevního pisemnictví Jihoslovanův. Prague, 1873; and Pavlović, Žitie krala srbskih. Belgrade. 1877.

These should be compared with the information, for the most part legendary, supplied by the Serbian Annals. Ed. Šafařík, P. J. *Op. cit.*

Finally, some information is given in the Hypatian Annals (Nestor), publ. by the Russian Imp. Archaeographical Commission of St Petersburg under the title: Povêst' vremennykh lêt', po Ipatskomu spisku. St Petersburg. 1871.

4. *The Latins of the East and the Crusaders of* 1147.

Eudes of Deuil. De Ludovici VII profectione in orientem. MPL. clxxxv. Col. 1205 ff.

William of Tyre. Historia rerum in partibus transmarinis gestarum, 1095–1184. Rec. hist. Crois. Historiens occidentaux. Vol. i. Paris. 1844. *See Gen. Bibl.* iv.

Valuable information may be gained from the Letters of Louis VII and of various personages among the Latins of the East, publ. in Bouquet, vols. xv and xvi.

III. MODERN WORKS.

1. General.

Besides the general histories (*see* Bibl. iii of chapter xi) there is only the obsolete work of

Wilken, F. Rerum ab Alexio I, Joanne, Manuele, et Alexio II Comnenis gestarum. Libri quatuor. Heidelberg. 1811.

2. Monographs.

Chalandon, F. Les Comnènes. Vol. ii. Jean II Comnène (1118–43) et Manuel I Comnène (1143–80). *See Gen. Bibl.* v.

Cognasso, F. Partiti politici e lotte dinastiche in Bizanzio alla morte di Manuele Comneno. Turin. 1912. Reprd. from Memorie della reale Accademia delle scienze di Torino. Series iv. Vol. lxii. 1912.
Diehl, C. Andronic Comnène. *In* Figures byzantines. 2nd ser. *See Gen. Bibl.* v.
Kap-Herr, H. von. Die abendländische Politik Kaiser Manuels. Strasbourg. 1881.
Radojcić, M. *See above*, i.
Uspenski, F. I. Tsari Alexêy II i Andronik Komneny. ZMNP. Vol. ccxii, p. 95, vol. ccxiv, p. 52. St Petersburg. 1880–1.
Wroth, W. Catalogue of the imperial Byzantine coins in the British Museum. *See Gen. Bibl.* iii.

3. Relations of Constantinople with Germany and Italy.

Bernhardi, W. Lothar von Supplinburg. (Jahrbücher d. deutschen Geschichte.) Leipsic. 1879.
—— Konrad III. *Ibid.* Leipsic. 1883.
Chalandon, F. Histoire de la domination normande en Italie et en Sicile. 2 vols. Paris. 1907.
Dräseke, J. Bischof Anselm von Havelberg und seine Gesandtschaftreisen nach Byzanz. ZKG. Vol. xxx. Gotha.
Heyd, W. Geschichte des Levantehandels im Mittelalter. French transl. by Raynaud, F. Revised by the author. Histoire du commerce du Levant au moyen âge. *See Gen. Bibl.* v. [Important for the relations of Pisa, Genoa, and Venice with Constantinople.]
Langer, Otto. Politische Geschichte Genuas und Pisas im xii Jahrhundert. Leipsic. 1882.
Norden, W. Papsttum und Byzanz. *See Gen. Bibl.* v.
Prutz, H. Kaiser Friedrich I. 3 vols. Dantzic. 1871–4.
Reuter, H. F. Geschichte Alexanders des dritten und der Kirche seiner Zeit. 3 vols. Leipsic. 1860–4.
Simonsfeld, H. Jahrbücher des deutschen Reiches unter Friedrich I. Vol. i. Leipsic. 1908. (Jahrbücher d. deutsch. Gesch.)
Streit, L. Venedig und die Wendung des vierten Kreuzzuges gegen Konstantinopel. Anklam. 1877.

4. On the Relations between Constantinople and the Hungarians and Slavs.

Fessler, J. A. Geschichte von Ungarn. 2nd edn. by Klein, E. 4 vols. Leipsic. 1887.
Grot, C. Iz istorii ugrii i slavyanstva v xii vêkê. Warsaw. 1889.
Katona, S. Historia critica regum Hungariae stirpis Arpadianae. Vol. iv. Posonii. 1781.
Thallóczy, Lajos. III Bela és a magyar birodalom. Buda-Pest. 1907.
Vasil'evski, V. Iz istorii Vizantii v xii vêkê. *In* Slavyanski sbornik. Vol. ii. p. 210. 1877.

5. On the Relations with the Second Crusade and the Latins of the East.

Gruhn, A. Die byzantinische Politik zur Zeit der Kreuzzüge. Berlin. 1904.
Horna, K. Das Hodoiporikon des Konstantin Manasses. BZ. Munich. Vol. xiii. pp. 313 ff.
Kugler, B. Studien zur Geschichte des zweiten Kreuzzuges. Stuttgart. 1866.
—— Analekten zur Geschichte des zweiten Kreuzzuges. Tübingen. 1878.
—— Neue Analekten zur Geschichte des zweiten Kreuzzuges. Tübingen. 1883.
Röhricht, R. Geschichte des Königsreiches Jerusalem. Innsbruck. 1898.
Sybel, H. von. Über des zweiten Kreuzzug. *In* Kleine hist. Schriften. Vol. i. pp. 411–51. Munich. 1863.

6. On the Internal History of Constantinople.

Hergès, A. Le monastère du Pantokrator à Constantinople. *In* Échos d'Orient. Vol. II. pp. 70 ff.
Kurtz, E. Die gegen Soterichos gerichtete Synode zu Konstantinopel im Jahre 1157. BZ. Vol. xv. pp. 599 ff. Munich. 1906.
Ter-Mikelian, A. Die armenische Kirche in ihren Beziehungen zur byzantinischen. Leipsic. 1892.

7. Criticism of Authorities.

For Cinnamus, Nicetas Acominatus (Choniates), and the question of the Prodromi, *see* Neumann, C., *op. cit.* in the Bibliography of chapter XI, iii, G.

Dräseke, J. Zu Basilios von Achrida. ZWT. Vol. XLVIII. p. 112. Jena. 1895.
Neumann, C. Über die urkundlichen Quellen zur Geschichte der byzantinisch-venetianischen Beziehungen vornehmlich im Zeitalter der Komnenen. BZ. Vol. I. pp. 366 ff. Munich. 1892.
Papadimitriou, S. Ὁ Πρόδρομος τοῦ Μαρκιανοῦ κώδικος. XI, 22. *In* VV. Vol. x. 1903. pp. 102 ff.; and Theodorus Prodromus (in Russian). Odessa. 1905. See the account by Kurtz, E. BZ. Vol. XVI. p. 289. Munich. 1907.

CHAPTER XIII.

VENICE.

I. BIBLIOGRAPHY.

(a) Collections of Sources.

Archivio storico italiano. *See List of Abbreviations, etc.* (ASI.)
Archivio veneto. (Arch. Ven.) *Contin. as* Nuovo Archivio Veneto (N. Arch. Ven.), *and* Archivio Veneto-Tridentino. *See List of Abbreviations.*
Fonti per la storia d'Italia. *See Gen. Bibl.* iv. (Fonti.)
R. Deputazione Veneta di Storia Patria (R. Dep. Ven.). Monumenti storici. In 4 series. I. Documenti. II. Statuti. III. Cronache. IV. Miscellanea (in 3 series). Venice. 1876 ff.

(b) Special Bibliographies.

Baracchi. Le carte del mille e del millecento che si conservano nel R. Archivio Notarile di Venezia. Arch. Ven. vi–x, xx–xxii.
Cecchetti, B. Delle fonti della storia Veneziana fino al secolo xiii. Venice. 1867.
Cicogna, E. A. Bibliografia Veneziana. Venice. 1847.
Cipolla, C. Fonti edite della storia della regione Veneta dalla caduta dell' Impero Romano sino al fine del sec. x. R. Dep. Ven. Miscel. (Ser. i). Vol. ii. Venice. 1883. *See above,* i (*a*).
Kretschmayr, H. Gesch. von Venedig. Vol. i. Anmerkung i. *See Gen. Bibl.* v.
Lazzarini, V. Originali antichissimi della cancelleria Veneziana. N. Arch. Ven. Nuov. Serie, No. 8.
Monticolo, G. In new edition of Sanudo's Le Vite dei Dogi *in* RR.II.SS. *See below,* ii (*b*).
—— Il patto del Doge Domenico Michiel con Bari. N. Arch. Ven. xviii, pp. 118–20.
Soranzo, G. Bibliografia Veneziana. Venice. 1885.

II. SOURCES.

(a) Unpublished.

Liber Primus pactorum, in the R. Archivio di Stato, ai Frari, Venice.
Liber Albus, containing copies of treaties with the East. *Ibid.*
Liber Blancus, containing copies of treaties with the West. *Ibid.*
Liber Trevisaneus, a series of diplomas and pacts with Popes, Emperors, and other Princes from 700 to 1400. *Ibid.*
Chronicon anon. Marcianum. Bib. Naz. di S. Marco. Lat. x, cod. 137.
Trevisan, Chronicle. Bib. Naz. di S. Marco. Ital. vii, cod. 519.
Dandolo, Chronicle. Museo Civico di Venezia, cod. Cicogna, 3423.
Chronicon anon. Museo Civico, cod. 1499.
Cronicon anon. Bib. Naz. di S. Marco. Ital. vii, cod. 2051.
Dolfin, Chronicle. Bib. Naz. di S. Marco. Ital. vii, cod. 794.
—— Chronicle. Museo Civico, cod. Cicogna, 2608.

(*b*) PUBLISHED.

Andrea Dandolo. Chron. Venetum. Ed. Muratori. RR.II.SS. XII.
Anna Comnena. Alexias. Ed. Schopen, L. and Reifferscheid, A. CSHB. 2 vols. 1839–78.
Annales Venetici breves. MGH. Script. XIV. 1883.
Cassiodorus. Variae. Ed. Mommsen. MGH. Auct. Antiquissimi. XII. 1894.
Chronicon Venetum quod vulgo dicunt Altinate. MGH. Script. XIV.
Cicogna, E. A. Delle Inscrizioni Veneziane. 6 vols. Venice. 1824–53.
Codice Diplomatico Padovano. Ed. Gloria. Vol. I, dal secolo sesto a tutto l' undecimo. Vol. II, dall' anno 1101 alla pace di Costanza, 1183. R. Dep. Ven. Documenti, II, IV and VI. Venice. 1877, 79, 81. *See above*, I (*a*).
Constantine Porphyrogenitus. De administrando imperio. *See Gen. Bibl.* IV.
Corner, F. Ecclesiae Venetae et Torcellanae. 18 vols. Venice. 1749.
Cronache Veneziane antichissime. Ed. Monticolo, G. *in* Fonti. 1890. Contains (1) Cronica de singulis Patriarchis de Nove Aquileie. (2) Chronicon Gradense. (3) Cronaca brevissima di Grado. (4) La cronaca Veneziana del Diacono Giovanni. (5) Scritture storiche aggiunte alla cronaca del Diacono Giovanni.
Einhard. Annales. MGH. Script. I. And in Annales Regni Francorum. Ed. Kurze, F. SGUS. 1895.
Fulcherius Carnotensis. Historia Hierosolymitana. Rec. hist. Cr., Hist. Occident. III.
Gallicciolli, G. Memorie Venete antiche. 8 vols. Venice. 1795.
Guillermus Apuliensis. Gesta Roberti Wiscardi. MGH. Script. XIV
Historia ducum Veneticorum. *Ibid.*
Jaffé. Regesta. *See Gen. Bibl.* IV.
Justiniani Chronicon. MGH. Script. XIV.
Lorenzo de Monacis. Chron. de rebus Venetorum. Ed. Corner, F. Venice. 1758.
Marin Sanudo Torsello. Liber secretorum fidelium S. Crucis. *In* Bongars, J., Gesta Dei per Francos. Hanover. 1611.
Martin da Canal. Cron. des Veniciens. Ed. Rossi. ASI. (Ser. I.) Vol. VIII. 1845.
Pacta and Praecepta relating to the Western Empire are printed in MGH. Legum sect. II (Capitularia), vol. II; Legum sect. IV (Constitutiones), vol. I; and Diplomata, vols. I–V. *See Gen. Bibl.* IV.
Regesta Imperii. Ed. Böhmer, Mühlbacher, and others. *See Gen. Bibl.* IV *under* Böhmer.
Romanin, S. *See below*, IV. Documents in app. to vols. I, II.
Romuald of Salerno. Annales. MGH. Script. XIX.
Sanudo, M. Le Vite dei Dogi di Venezia. Muratori, RR.II.SS. XXII, and in course of publication in the new edition by Monticolo, G. *See Gen. Bibl.* IV.
Tafel, G. L. F. and Thomas, G. M. Urkunden zur älteren Handels- und Staatsgeschichte der Republik Venedig. 3 vols. (Fontes Rerum Austriac. II. Vols. XII–XIV.) Vienna. 1856–7. [A collection of documents relating to the East.]
Ughelli, F. Italia Sacra. Vol. V. *See Gen. Bibl.* IV.
Villehardouin. La Conquête de Constantinople. Ed. Wailly, N. de. Paris. 1872. Also ed. Bouchet, É. 2 vols. Paris. 1891.
William of Tyre. Historia rerum in partibus transmarinis gestarum. Rec. hist. Cr., Hist. Occident. I. *See Gen. Bibl.* IV.

III. CRITICISM OF SOURCES.

Besta, E. Intorno a due opere recenti su la costituzione e la politica Veneziana nel medioevo. N. Arch. Ven. XIV.
Cipolla, C. Ricerche sulle tradizioni intorno alle immigrazioni nelle lagune. Arch. Ven. XXVIII, XXIX, XXXI.
Kretschmayr, H. Gesch. von Venedig. Vol. I. *See Gen. Bibl.* V.
Lenel, W. Die Entstehung der Vorherrschaft Venedigs an der Adria. Mit Beiträgen zur Verfassungsgeschichte. Strasbourg. 1897.
—— Zur älteren Geschichte Venedigs. HZ. 3rd series. III, 3. Munich. 1907.
Monticolo, G. I manoscritti e le fonti della cronaca del diacono Giovanni. BISI. No. 9.

Monticolo, G. La cronaca del diacono Giovanni e la storia politica di Venezia sino al 1009. R. Liceo Forteguerri di Pistoia. 1882. Also *in* Arch. Ven. xxv.
—— Intorno alla cronaca di Giovanni Diacono. Arch. Ven. xv.
—— La cronaca di Giovanni Diacono. Arch. Ven. xvii.
Simonsfeld, H. Andreas Dandolo und seine Geschichtswerke. Munich. 1876.
—— Das Chronicon Altinate. Munich. 1878.
Tafel, G. L. F. and Thomas, G. M. Der Doge Andreas Dandolo und die von demselben angelegten Urkundensammlungen zur Staats- und Handelsgeschichte Venedigs. Munich. 1855.

IV. GENERAL HISTORIES.

Amelot de la Houssaie, A. N. Histoire du gouvernement de Venise. 2 vols. Paris, 1677.
Blondus, Fl. Italia illustrata. Verona. 1481. And *in* Graevius. Thesaurus...Italiae. Vol. i. *See Gen. Bibl.* iv.
Filiasi, G. Memorie storiche de' Veneti primi e secondi. 9 vols. Venice. 1796.
Giustinian, B. Historia de origine urbis Venetiarum. Venice. 1492.
Hartmann, L. M. Geschichte Italiens im Mittelalter. *See Gen. Bibl.* v.
Heyd, W. Le Colonie commerciali degli Italiani in oriente nel medio evo. Ital. transl. Müller, G. 2 vols. Venice. 1866.
Hodgson, F. C. The Early History of Venice from the foundation to the Conquest of Constantinople. London. 1901.
Kretschmayr, H. Gesch. von Venedig. Vol. i. *See Gen. Bibl.* v.
Le Bret, J. F. Staatsgeschichte der Republik Venedig. 3 vols. Leipsic and Riga. 1769–77.
Marin, C. A. Storia civile e politica del commercio de' Veneziani. 8 vols. Venice. 1798–1808.
Molmenti, P. La storia di Venezia nella vita privata. 4th edn. 3 vols. Bergamo. 1905–8. Engl. transl. Brown, H. F. 6 vols. London. 1906–8.
Musatti, E. Storia di un lembo di terra; ossia Venezia ed i Veneziani. Padua. 1886.
Röhricht, R. Geschichte des Königreiches Jerusalem (1100–1291). Innsbruck. 1898.
Romanin, S. Storia documentata di Venezia. 10 vols. Venice. 1853–61.
Sabellico, M. A. Historia Venetiana. Venice. 1487. Also *in* Istorici d. cose veneziane. Vol. i. Venice. 1718.
Sandi, V. Principii di Storia civile della Repubblica di Venezia. 10 vols. Venice. 1700–67. 3 vols. 1769–72.
Tentori, C. Saggio sulla storia della Repubblica di Venezia. 12 vols. Venice. 1785–90.

V. SPECIAL TREATISES.

Armingaud, J. Venise et le Bas-Empire. Paris. 1867.
Baer, A. Die Beziehungen Venedigs zum Kaiserreiche in der staufischen Zeit. Innsbruck. 1888.
Bertaldo, J. Splendor consuetudinum civitatis Venetiarum. Ed. Schupfer. Bologna. 1896.
Besta, E. Il Senato Veneziano. *In* R. Dep. Ven. Miscell. (Ser. ii.) Vol. v. *See above*, i (*a*).
—— Il diritto e le leggi civili di Venezia fino al dogado di Enrico Dandolo. Venice. 1900.
—— Jacopo Bertaldo e lo Splendor consuetudinum civitatis Venetiarum. N. Arch. Ven. xiii.
Bresslau, H. Jahrbücher d. deutschen Reiches unter Konrad II. 2 vols. Leipsic. 1879–84. (Jahrb. d. deutsch. Gesch.)
Cecchetti, B. Il Doge di Venezia. Venice. 1864.
—— La Vita dei Veneziani fino al secolo xiii. Arch. Ven. 1871.
—— La Vita dei Veneziani fino al 1200. Venice. 1870.
De Laigne, R. Les Doges Sébastien et Pierre Ziani. Paris. 1906.
Diehl, C. Études sur l'administration byzantine dans l'exarchat de Ravenna, 568–751. Paris. 1888.

Diehl, C. Études byzantines. *See Gen. Bibl.* v.
Fanta, A. Die Verträge der Kaiser mit Venedig bis zum Jahr 983. MIOGF. Ergänzungbd. I. 1885.
Ficker, J. Forschungen für Reichs- und Rechtsgeschichte Italiens. Innsbruck. 1868–74.
Gfrörer, A. F. Geschichte Venedigs bis zum Jahre 1048. Graz. 1872.
Hain, A. Der Doge von Venedig seit dem Sturze der Orseoler bis zur Ermordung Vitale Michiels. Leipsic. 1883.
Harnack, O. Das karolingische und byzantinische Reich in ihren Wechselbeziehungen. Göttingen. 1880.
Hartmann, L. M. Untersuchungen zur Geschichte der byzantinischen Verwaltung in Italien 540–750. Leipsic. 1889.
Kohlschütter. Venedig unter dem Herzog Peter II Orseolo. Göttingen. 1868.
Lazari, V. Del traffico e delle condizioni degli schiavi a Venezia nel tempo di mezzo. Miscel. di storia italiana. Ser. I. Vol. I. Turin. 1862.
Lenel, W. Die Entstehung der Vorherrschaft Venedigs an der Adria. Strasbourg. 1897.
Lentz, E. Das Verhältniss Venedigs zu Byzanz nach dem Fall des Exarchats bis zum Ausgang des 9 Jahrhunderts. Berlin. 1891.
—— Der allmähliche Uebergang Venedigs von faktischer zu nomineller Abhängigkeit von Byzanz. BZ. II. pp. 64 ff.
Meyer. Die Spaltung des Patriarchates Aquileia. K. Gesell. f. d. Wissensch. Göttingen. 1898.
Monticolo, G. L'Ufficio della giustizia vecchia a Venezia dalle origini fino al 1330. R. Dep. Ven. Miscel. (Ser. I) Vol. XII. 1893. *See above,* I (*a*).
Neumann, C. Zur Geschichte der byzantinisch-venetianischen Beziehungen. BZ. I. 1892.
Papadopoli, N. Sulle origini della Veneta zecca e sulle antiche relazioni dei Veneziani cogli Imperatori. Venice. 1882.
Pasolini, D. Delle antiche relazioni fra Venezia e Ravenna. Florence. 1874.
Schmeidler, B. Venedig und das deutsche Reich im Jahre 983. MIOGF. 1904.
—— Der Dux und das Comune Venetiarum von 1141–1229. *In* Ebering's Historische Studien. Berlin. 1902.
Schulte, A. Geschichte des Levantehandels und Verkehrs zwischen Westdeutschland und Italien mit Ausschluss von Venedig. Leipsic. 1900.
Wüstenfeld, T. Venetorum historia ab antiquissimis temporibus usque ad ducum sedem Rivoalti fixam deducta. Dissertatio inauguralis in Academia Georgia Augusta. Göttingen. 1846.

GEOGRAPHY.

Constantine Porphyrogenitus. De administrando Imperio. *See Gen. Bibl.* IV.
Filiasi, G. *See above,* IV.
Gallicciolli, G. *See above,* II (*b*).
Johannes Diaconus. Cronaca Veneziana. *See above,* II (*b*). Cronache veneziane ant.
Kretschmayr, H. Die Beschreibung der venezianischen Inseln bei Konstantin Porphyrogennetos. BZ. 1904.
Nissen, H. Italische Landeskunde. 2 vols. Berlin. 1883–1902.
Paulus Diaconus. Historia Langobardorum. MGH. Script. rer. Lang. et Ital. 1878.
Procopius. De bello Gothico. Ed. Comparetti, D. (Fonti.) 1895.

ETHNOGRAPHY.

Kretschmer, P. Einleitung in die Gesch. der griechischen Sprache. Göttingen. 1896.
Nissen, H. *See above,* Geography.
Pauli, C. Die Veneter und ihre Schicksale. Leipsic. 1891.
Polybius. Historiae, Bk. II.
Strabo. Geographica, Bks. IV, V.

CHAPTER XIV.

THE FOURTH CRUSADE AND THE LATIN EMPIRE.

I. ORIGINAL SOURCES.

Acropolites, Georgius. Χρονικὴ συγγραφή. Ed. Heisenberg, A. 2 vols. Leipsic. 1903.
Chronicle of Morea. Greek text ed. Schmitt, J. (Byzantine Texts.) London. 1904. French text ed. Buchon, J. A. *in* Recherches historiques sur la principauté française de Morée. Vol. I. *See below*, II. Also ed. Longnon, J. Paris. 1911.
Chronicle of Novgorod. (Chronista Novgorodensis.) Latin transl. Hopf, K. *in* Chroniques gréco-romanes. *See Gen. Bibl.* IV.
Clari, Robert de. La prise de Constantinople. Ed. Hopf, K. *Ibid.*
Devastatio Constantinopolitana. (Annales Herbipolenses 1202–4.) MGH. Script. XVI.
Epistolae ad quartum bellum sacrum pertinentes. MPL. CCIX. col. 924 ff. and CCXIII. col. 1041 ff.
Ernoul and Bernard the Treasurer. Chronique. Ed. Mas-Latrie, L. de. Paris. 1871.
Exuviae sacrae Constantinopolitanae. Ed. Riant, P. 2 vols. Geneva. 1877, 78.
Gesta Innocentii III Papae. MPL. CCXIV.
Gregory IX, Pope. Registres. Ed. Auvray, L. EcfrAR. 3 vols. Paris. 1896 ff.
Günther of Pairis. Historia Constantinopolitana. Ed. Riant, P. Geneva. 1875. MPL. CCXII.
Henry, Emperor. Epistolae. MPL. CCXV.
Henry of Valenciennes. Ed. Wailly, N. de. (With Villehardouin. *See below.*)
Historia ducum Veneticorum. MGH. Script. XIV.
Honorius III, Pope. Regesta. Ed. Pressuti, P. 2 vols. Rome. 1888, 95.
Innocent III, Pope. Epistolae. MPL. CCXIV–CCXVII.
Muratori, L. RR.II.SS. Vol. XII. *See Gen. Bibl.* IV.
Nicetas Acominatus (Choniates). Historia. Ed. Bekker, I. CSHB. 1835.
—— De signis Constantinopolitanis. *Ibid.*
Tafel, G. L. F. and Thomas, G. M. Urkunden zur älteren Handels- und Staatsgeschichte der Republik Venedig. (Fontes Rerum Austriac. II. Vols. XII–XIV.) Vienna. 1856–7.
Villehardouin, Geoffroy de. La conquête de Constantinople. Ed. Wailly, N. de. Paris. 1872. Also ed. Bouchet, É. 2 vols. Paris. 1891.

II. MODERN WORKS.

Bréhier, L. L'Église et l'Orient au moyen âge. Les Croisades. *See Gen. Bibl.* V.
Buchon, J. A. Recherches historiques sur la principauté française de Morée et ses hautes baronnies. Première époque. 2 vols. Paris. 1845.
—— Nouvelles recherches historiques sur la principauté française de Morée. Seconde époque. Paris. 1843.
Diehl, C. Une république patricienne: Venise. Paris. 1915.
Du Cange, C. du Fresne. Histoire de l'empire de Constantinople sous les empereurs françois. *See Gen. Bibl.* V.
Gerland, E. Der vierte Kreuzzug und seine Probleme. *In* Neue Jahrbücher f. d. Klass. Altertum. Ed. Ilberg, J. XIII. Leipsic. 1904.
—— Geschichte des lateinischen Kaiserreiches von Konstantinopel. *See Gen. Bibl.* V.
Hanotaux, G. Les Vénitiens ont-ils trahi la chrétienté en 1202? RH. Vol. IV. 1877.
Heyd, W. Histoire du Commerce du Levant au moyen âge. Transl. Furcy-Raynaud. *See Gen. Bibl.* V.

Hopf, K. Geschichte Griechenlands im Mittelalter: der vierte Kreuzzug. *See Gen. Bibl.* v.
Ilgen, T. Markgraf Conrad von Montferrat. Marburg. 1881.
Klimke. Die Quellen zur Geschichte des vierten Kreuzzugs. Breslau. 1875.
Luchaire, A. Innocent III. La question d'Orient. Paris. 1907.
Manfroni, C. Storia della marina italiana. Pt. I (400–1261). Leghorn. 1899.
Meliarakes, A. Ἱστορία τοῦ βασιλείου τῆς Νικαίας κτλ. *See Gen. Bibl.* v.
Miller, W. Essays on the Latin Orient. *See Gen. Bibl.* v.
—— The Latins in the Levant. *See Gen. Bibl.* v.
Norden, W. Das Papsttum und Byzanz. *See Gen. Bibl.* v.
—— Der vierte Kreuzzug. Berlin. 1898.
Pears, E. The fall of Constantinople: the story of the Fourth Crusade. London. 1885.
Riant, P. Innocent III, Philippe de Souabe, et Boniface de Montferrat. RQH. Vols. XVII, XVIII. 1875.
—— Le changement de direction de la quatrième croisade. RQH. Vol. XXIII. 1878.
—— Des dépouilles religieuses enlevées à Constantinople au XIIIe siècle par les Latins. Paris. 1875.
Romanos, I. A. Περὶ τοῦ δεσποτάτου τῆς Ἠπείρου. Corfù. 1895.
Sayous, E. Les Bulgares, les croisés français de Constantinople, Innocent III. (Séances de l'Acad. des sciences morales. Vol. 1267.)
Schaube, A. Eine bisher unbekannte Regentin des latein. Kaiserreiches. MIOGF. VIII. 1887.
Stevenson, W. B. The crusaders in the East. Cambridge. 1907.
Streit, L. Venedig und die Wendung des vierten Kreuzzuges gegen Konstantinopel. Anklam. 1877.
Tessier, J. La quatrième croisade. Paris. 1884.
Thil-Lorrain. Baudouin de Constantinople, fondateur de l'empire latin d'Orient. Brussels.
Todt, B. Die Eroberung von Konstantinopel im Jahre 1204. Halle. 1878.
Winkelmann, E. Philipp von Schwaben und Otto IV. (Jahrbücher der deutschen Geschichte.) 2 vols. Leipsic. 1873–8.

CHAPTER XV.

GREECE AND THE AEGEAN UNDER FRANK AND VENETIAN DOMINATION.

I. SPECIAL BIBLIOGRAPHIES.

Cobham, C. D. Excerpta Cypria. Materials for a history of Cyprus. Cambridge. 1908.

Hellwald, F. de. Bibliographie méthodique de l'ordre souverain de St Jean de Jérusalem, rédigée et publiée sous les auspices du grand maître. Rome. 1885.

Legrand, É. and Pernot, H. Bibliographie ionienne. 2 vols. Paris. 1910.

Miller, W. The Latins in the Levant. (pp. 655–63.) *See Gen. Bibl.* v. Further enlarged in the Greek translation by Lámpros (Lambros), Sp. P., Ἱστορία τῆς Φραγκοκρατίας ἐν Ἑλλάδι (vol. II, 445–58). Athens. 1909–10.

II. MSS.

Cornaro, Andrea. Historia di Candia. Cod. Marcian. Ital. Cl. vi. No. 286. *In* Marciana. Venice.

Dandolo, Enrico. Cronaca Veneta. Cod. Marcian. Cl. vii. No. 102. [To 1380.] *In* Marciana. Venice.

Lichtle, I. Description de Naxie. MS in Berlin among Hopf's papers, Naxos, Brit. Museum (Addit. 36,538), and in collection of Ἱστορικὴ καὶ Ἐθνολογικὴ Ἑταιρεία at Athens (No. 73). Parts published by Krémos, G. *in* Apóllon. Vols. VII, VIII. Athens. 1891–2.

Raggioni che ha la Ser[ma] Rep[a] di Venezia sopra il Ducato di Nassia coll' Isole del-l' Arcipelago. Cod. Cicogna, 2532, § 34. [Important for history of the Gozzadini.] *In* Museo Correr, Venice.

San Gallo. Notebook. Barberini MSS No. 4424. [Important for Cyriacus of Ancona.] *In* Vatican.

Serra, N. Storia antica e moderna della Città, ed Isola del Zante. 1784. [Translation "with considerable additions" of Remondini, B. M. De Zacynthi antiquitatibus et fortunâ. Part published by Hopf, K. *in* Chroniques gréco-romanes, pp. 341–5. *See Gen. Bibl.* IV.] MS in the possession of the author of this chapter.

Turresanus, A. Elogium historicarum nobilium Veronae propaginum. 1656. At Verona.

Valier, A. Cronaca. *In* Venice.

III. PRIMARY AUTHORITIES.

(*a*) Venetian Documents.

Giomo, G. Le Rubriche dei Libri *Misti* del Senato perduti. *In* Arch. Ven. Vols. VII, 126–40, 251–73; XVIII, 40–69, 315–38; XIX, 90–117; XX, 81–95, 293–313; XXIII, 66–83, 406–24; XXIV, 82–110, 309–28; XXVII, 91–105, 374–94. Venice. 1879–84.

—— Regesto di alcune deliberazioni del Senato *Misti*. *Ibid.* Vols. XXIX, 403–10; XXX, 153–62; XXXI, 179–200. Venice. 1885–6.

—— Lettere di Collegio, rectius Minor Consiglio 1308–10. Venice. 1910.

Jorga, N. Notes et extraits pour servir à l'histoire des Croisades au xve siècle. 5 vols. Paris and Bucharest. 1899–1915.

Lamansky, V. Secrets d'état de Venise. St Petersburg. 1884.
Ljubić, S. Monumenta spectantia historiam Slavorum meridionalium. (MHSM.) Vols. III, IV, IX, XXII. 1872–91. *See Gen. Bibl.* IV, *under* Monumenta.
Mas Latrie, L. de. Documents concernant divers pays de l'Orient latin, 1382–1413. Paris. 1897. (Extrait de la B. de l'École des Chartes, vol. LVIII.)
Miller, W. and Giomo, G. Le Rubriche dei Misti del Senato, Libri XV–XLIV. *In* Δελτίον τῆς Ἱστορικῆς καὶ Ἐθνολογικῆς Ἑταιρείας τῆς Ἑλλάδος. Vol. VII, 69–119. Athens. 1910.
Noiret, H. Documents inédits pour servir à l'histoire de la domination vénitienne en Crète de 1380 à 1485. Paris. 1892.
Predelli, R. Il Liber Communis detto anche Plegiorum. *In* Arch. Ven., Anno Secondo. Venice. 1872.
—— I Libri Commemoriali della Republica di Venezia regesti. 7 vols. Venice. 1876–1907.
Relazioni degli Ambasciatori Veneti. Vols. I–IV. Florence. 1840–63.
Sáthas, K. N. Μνημεῖα Ἑλληνικῆς ἱστορίας (Monumenta Hellenicae historiae). *See Gen. Bibl.* IV.
Tafel, G. L. F. and Thomas, G. M. Urkunden zur älteren Handels- und Staatsgeschichte der Republik Venedig (1204–1300). Fontes Rerum Austriac. Abth. II. Vols. XII–XIV. Vienna. 1856–7.
Thomas, G. M. and Predelli, R. Diplomatarium Veneto-Levantinum (1300–1454). 2 vols. Venice. 1880–99.
—— Der Doge Andreas Dandolo...mit dem Original-Register des Liber Albus, des Liber Blancus, und der Libri Pactorum. Munich. 1855.

(*b*) NEAPOLITAN DOCUMENTS.

Barone, N. Notizie storiche di Re Carlo III di Durazzo. ASPN. Year XII. Naples. 1887.
Del Giudice, G. Codice diplomatico del regno di Carlo I e II di Angiò (1265–70). 3 vols. Naples. 1863–1902.
—— La famiglia di Re Manfredi. 2nd edn. Naples. 1896.
Riccio Minieri, C. Saggio di codice diplomatico. 2 vols. with supplement. Naples. 1878–83.
—— Alcuni fatti riguardanti Carlo I di Angiò dal 6 di Agosto 1252 al 30 di Dicembre 1270. Naples. 1874.
—— Il regno di Carlo I di Angiò negli anni 1271 e 1272. Naples. 1875.
—— Il regno di Carlo I di Angiò, dal 2 Gennaio 1273 al 31 Dicembre 1283. ASI. Series III, vol. XXII–. Series IV, vol. V. Florence. 1875–80.
—— Il regno di Carlo I d' Angiò, dal 4 Gennaio 1284 al 7 Gennaio 1285. *Ibid.* Series IV, vol. VII. Florence. 1881.
—— Studi storici su' fascicoli angioini. Naples. 1863.
—— Della dominazione angioina nel reame di Sicilia. Naples. 1876.
—— Nuovi studii riguardanti la dominazione angioina nel regno di Sicilia. Naples. 1876.
—— Studii storici fatti sopra 84 registri angioini. Naples. 1876.
—— Notizie storiche tratte da 62 registri angioini. Naples. 1877.

(*c*) PAPAL DOCUMENTS.

Epistolarum Innocentii III libri XVI. 2 vols. Ed. Baluze, S. Paris. 1682. *Also* MPL. Vols. CCXIV–CCXVII.
Honorii III Opera. 4 vols. Ed. Horoy. Paris. 1879–80.
Regesta Honorii Papae III. Ed. Pressutti, P. 2 vols. Rome. 1888–95.
Les Registres de Grégoire IX. Ed. Auvray, L. Vols. I, II, and III, pts. 1 and 2. EcfrAR. Paris. 1896–1910.
Les Registres d'Innocent IV. Ed. Berger, É. Vols. I–III. EcfrAR. Paris. 1884–97.
Les Registres d'Alexandre IV. Ed. Bourel de la Roncière, C., de Loye, J., and Coulon, A. Vol. I. EcfrAR. Paris. 1895–1902.

Les Registres d'Urbain IV (1261–4). Ed. Guiraud, J. Vols. I–III, and IV, pt. 1. EcfrAR. Paris. 1901–6.
Les Registres de Clément IV (1265–8). Ed. Jordan, É. Vol. I. EcfrAR. Paris. 1893–1912.
Les Registres de Grégoire X et Jean XXI (1271–7). Ed. Guiraud, J. and Cadier, L. Vol. I. EcfrAR. Paris. 1892.
Les Registres de Nicolas III (1277–80). Ed. Gay, J. Vol. I, pts. 1 and 2. EcfrAR. Paris. 1898–1904.
Les Registres de Martin IV. Ed. École française de Rome. Vol. I, pts. 1, 2. EcfrAR. Paris. 1901.
Les Registres d'Honorius IV. Ed. Prou, M. EcfrAR. Paris. 1888.
Les Registres de Nicolas IV. Ed. Langlois, E. 2 vols. EcfrAR. Paris. 1886–93.
Les Registres de Boniface VIII. Ed. Digard, G., Faucon, M., and Thomas, A. Vols. I–III. EcfrAR. Paris. 1884–1911.
Les Registres de Benoit XI. Ed. Grandjean, C. EcfrAR. Paris. 1905.
Regestum Clementis Papae V. Benedictine edition. 9 vols. Rome. 1885–92.
Jean XXII (1316–34). Lettres secrètes et curiales. Ed. Coulon, A. Vols. I and II, pt. 1. EcfrAR. Paris. 1906.
—— Lettres communes. Ed. Mollat, G. Vols. I–VIII, pt. 1. EcfrAR. Paris. 1904–20.
—— Lettres de. Vols. I and II, pt. 1. (1316–30.) Ed. Fayen, A. Rome. 1908–9.
Benoit XII (1334–42). Lettres closes, patentes, et curiales. Ed. Daumet, G. Vol. I, pts. 1 and 2. EcfrAR. Paris. 1899–1902.
—— Lettres communes. Ed. Vidal, J. M. 3 vols. EcfrAR. Paris. 1902–11.
Clément VI (1342–52). Lettres closes, patentes, et curiales. Ed. Déprez, E. Vol. I, pt. 1. EcfrAR. Paris. 1901.
Innocent VI (1352–62). Lettres closes, patentes, et curiales. Ed. Déprez, E. Vol. I, pt. 1. EcfrAR. Paris. 1909.
Lettres secrètes et curiales du Pape Urbain V (1362–70). Ed. Lecacheux, P. Vol. I, pts. 1 and 2. EcfrAR. Paris. 1902–6.

(*d*) VARIOUS DOCUMENTS.

Archives de l'Orient latin. 2 vols. Paris. 1881–4.
Atti della Società ligure di storia patria. Genoa. 1859 ff., in progress.
Canciani, P. Barbarorum Leges Antiquae. Vol. III. Venice. 1785.
Charrière, E. Négociations de la France dans le Levant. Vols. I–III. Paris. 1848–53.
Delaville le Roulx, J. Cartulaire général de l'ordre des Hospitaliers de S. Jean de Jérusalem. 4 vols. Paris. 1894–1906.
Documenti riguardanti alcuni dinasti dell' Arcipelago. *In* Giornale Ligustico di Archeologia, Storia, e Belle Arti, I, 84–90, 217–21; II, 86–93, 292–7; III, 313–16; V, 345–72. Genoa. 1874–8. [Deal with the Gattilusj.]
Guardione, F. Sul dominio dei Ducati di Atene e Neopatras. Palermo. 1895.
Lámpros (Lambros), Sp. P. *Ἔγγραφα ἀναφερόμενα εἰς τὴν μεσαιωνικὴν ἱστορίαν τῶν Ἀθηνῶν*. (Forming vol. III of his Greek tr. of Gregorovius, F. Geschichte der Stadt Athen im Mittelalter.) Athens. 1906.
—— Κατάλογος τῶν ἐν ταῖς βιβλιοθήκαις τοῦ Ἁγίου Ὄρους Ἑλληνικῶν κωδίκων. Vol. II. p. 305. Cambridge. 1900.
Liber Jurium Reipublicae Genuensis. 2 vols. MHP. VII and IX. 1854–7.
Makuscev (Makushev), V. Monumenta historica Slavorum meridionalium vicinorumque populorum. 2 vols. Warsaw and Belgrade. 1874–82.
Mas Latrie, Comte L. de. Documents et mémoires servant de preuves à l'histoire de l'île de Chypre sous les Lusignans. (Form vols. II and III of his Histoire de l'île de Chypre.) Paris. 1852–5.
—— Nouvelles preuves de l'histoire de Chypre sous le règne des princes de la maison de Lusignan. BEC. Vols. XXXIII–IV, and separately. Paris. 1873–4.
—— Documents nouveaux servant de preuves à l'histoire de l'île de Chypre sous le règne des princes de la maison de Lusignan. *In* Mélanges historiques. Vol. IV. pp. 337–619. Paris. 82.

Mas Latrie, Comte L. de. Commerce et expéditions militaires de la France et de Venise au moyen âge. *In* Mélanges historiques. Choix de Documents. Vol. III. pp. 1–240. Paris. 1880.
Miklosich, F. and Müller, J. Acta et diplomata graeca medii aevi. *See Gen. Bibl.* IV.
Müller, G. Documenti sulle relazioni delle città toscane coll' Oriente. Florence. 1879.
Pauli, S. Codice diplomatico del sacro militare Ordine Gerosolimitano. 2 vols. Lucca. 1733–7.
Riant, P. Exuviae sacrae Constantinopolitanae. 2 vols. Geneva. 1877–8.
Ross, L. and Schmeller, J. A. Urkunden zur Geschichte Griechenlands im Mittelalter. *In* Abhandlungen der philos.-philol. Classe der K. bayer. Akademie. Vol. II. Munich. 1837.
Rubió y Lluch, A. Documentos inéditos relativos á la expedición navarra y el Ducado catalán de Atenas. *In* Memorias de la R. Acad. de Buenas Letras de Barcelona. Vol. IV. pp. 425–92. Barcelona. 1887.
—— Documents per l'Historia de la cultura catalana mig-eval. Vol. I. Barcelona. 1908.
Sáthas, K. N. *Κυπριακοὶ Νόμοι. In Μεσαιωνικὴ βιβλιοθήκη.* Vol. VI. *See Gen. Bibl.* IV.

(e) Greek Historians.

Acominatus Choniates, Michael. *Τὰ σωζόμενα.* Ed. Lámpros (Lambros), Sp. P. 2 vols. Athens. 1879–80.
Acropolites, Georgius. Ed. Heisenberg, A. 2 vols. Leipsic. 1903.
Bessaríon. MPG. Vol. CLXI. Paris. 1866.
Canabutzes, J. Ad principem Aeni et Samothraces in Dionysium Halicarnassensem Commentarius. Leipsic. 1890.
Cantacuzene, John. 3 vols. CSHB. 1828–32.
Chalcocondyles, Laonicus. CSHB. 1843.
Chomatianus, Demetrius. *Πονήματα διάφορα. In* Pitra, J. B. Analecta sacra et classica. Vol. VII. Paris and Rome. 1891.
Chronicle of Morea, The. Ed. Schmitt, J. (Byzantine Texts.) London. 1904.
Χρονογράφοι βασιλείου Κύπρου. In Sáthas, K. N. *In Μεσαιωνικὴ βιβλιοθήκη.* Vol. II. *See Gen. Bibl.* IV.
Critobulus. *In* Müller, C. Fragmenta historicorum graecorum. Vol. V. *See Gen. Bibl.* IV.
Cydones, Demetrius. *Ἐπιστολαί. In* Boissonade, J. F. Anecdota Nova. Paris. 1844.
Doróthеos of Monemvasia. *Βιβλίον Ἱστορικόν.* Venice. 1814.
Ducas and Chronicon breve. CSHB. 1834.
Ecthesis chronica and Chronicon Athenarum. Ed. Lámpros (Lambros), Sp. P. London. 1902.
Ephraim. CSHB. 1840.
Epirotica. CSHB. 1849.
Gemistós (Pléthon). MPG. Vol. CLX. Paris. 1866. Also *in* Ellissen, A. Analekten der mittel- und neugriechischen Literatur. Vol. IV. Leipsic. 1860.
Gregoras, Nicephorus. CSHB. 3 vols. 1829–55.
Historia politica et patriarchica Constantinopoleos. CSHB. 1849.
Mázaris. *Ἐπιδημία ἐν ᾍδου. In* Boissonade, J. F. Anecdota Graeca. Vol. III. Paris. 1831. Also *in* Ellissen, A. Analekten der mittel- und neugriechischen Literatur. Vol. IV. Leipsic. 1860.
Nicetas Choniates. CSHB. 1835.
Noúkios, Andronicus. *Ἀποδημιῶν βιβλία. In* Mustoxidi, M. A. *Ἱστορικὰ καὶ φιλολογικὰ Ἀνέκδοτα.* Corfù. 1872.
Pachymeres, Georgius. 2 vols. CSHB. 1835.
Palaeologus, Manuel. MPG. Vol. CLVI. Paris. 1866.
Palaeologus, Michael. De Vitâ suâ. Ed. Troitski, J. G. St Petersburg. 1885.
Phrantzes, Georgius. CSHB. 1838.

Theódoulos Rhétor. Πρεσβευτικὸς πρὸς τὸν Βασιλέα Ἀνδρόνικον τὸν Παλαιολόγον. And Περὶ τῶν ἐν τῇ Ἰταλῶν καὶ Περσῶν ἐφόδῳ γεγενημένων. *In* Boissonade, J. F. Anecdota Graeca. Vol. II. Paris. 1830.
Θρῆνος τῆς Κωνσταντινουπόλεως. *In* Wagner. Mediaeval Greek Texts. London. 1870.

(*f*) MISCELLANEOUS.

Adam, G. De modo Sarracenos extirpandi. Rec. hist. Cr. Documents arméniens. II. 519–55. *See Gen. Bibl.* IV.
Aeneas Sylvius (Pius II). Europa. *In* Opera. Ed. Gobellinus, J. Basle. *n.d.*
—— Commentarii rerum memorabilium, quae temporibus suis contigerunt. Frankfort. 1614.
Albricus Monachus Trium Fontium. Chronicon. MGH. Script. Vol. XXIII. 1874.
Amadi et Stambaldi. Chroniques (615–1458). Ed. Mas Latrie, R. de. *In* Collection de documents inédits sur l'histoire de la France. 2 vols. Paris. 1891–3.
Bartolomeo dalli Sonnetti. Periplus. *n.d.*
Bembo, P. Rerum Venetarum historia. Paris. 1551.
Benedict of Peterborough. Gesta Regis Ricardi. (Forms vol. II of Gesta Regis Henrici II.) Ed. Stubbs, W. (Rolls.) 1867.
Benjamin of Tudela, The Itinerary of. Ed. Adler, M. Oxford. 1907.
Boucicaut, Messire Jean le Maingre dit. Le livre des faicts du bon. Paris. 1825.
Breuning von und zu Buochenbach, H. J. Orientalische Reyss. Strasbourg. 1612.
Brocquière, B. de la. Voyage d'Outremer. *In* vol. XII of Recueil de voyages et de documents. Ed. Schefer, Ch. Paris. 1892.
Buondelmonti, Ch. Liber insularum Archipelagi. Ed. Sinner. Leipsic and Berlin. 1824. *Also* Version grecque par un anonyme. Ed. Legrand, É. Paris. 1897.
Bustron, Florio. Chronique de l'île de Chypre. Ed. Mas Latrie, R. de. *In* Mélanges historiques. Vol. V. 1–532. Paris. 1886.
Campofulgosus, B. Exemplorum, hoc est, dictorum factorumque memorabilium.... lib. IX. Basle. *n.d.*
Canal, Martin da. La Chronique des Veniciens. ASI. Vol. VIII. Florence. 1845.
Casola, P. Viaggio a Gerusalemme. Ed. Porro, G. Milan. 1855.
Cippico (Cepio), C. Petri Mocenici imperatoris gesta. Appended to P. Justiniani, Rerum Venetarum historia. Strasbourg. 1611.
Clavijo, Ruy Gonzalez de. Itinéraire de l'ambassade espagnole à Samarkande en 1402–6. English transl. Markham, C. R. (Hakluyt Society.) London. 1859.
Colucci, G. Delle antichità picene. Vol. XV. Fermo. 1792–6.
Contarini, G. P. Historia delle cose successe dal principio della guerra mossa da Selim Ottomano á Venetiani. Venice. 1572.
Conti, N. Delle historie de' suoi tempi. 2 vols. Venice. 1589.
Cronaca di Morea [Italian version]. *In* Hopf, K. Chroniques gréco-romanes, pp. 414–68. *See Gen. Bibl.* IV.
Crusius (Kraus), M. Turcograecia. Basle. 1584.
Cyriacus Anconitanus. Epigrammata reperta per Illyricum. *n.d.*
—— Itinerarium. Ed. Mehus, L. Florence. 1742.
Édrisi, Géographie de. Transl. Jaubert, A. Vol. II. Paris. 1840.
Faber (Fabri), F. Evagatorium. 3 vols. Stuttgart. 1843–9.
Fabricius, J. A. Bibliotheca latina mediae et infimae aetatis. Vol. VI. Padua. 1754.
Feyerabend. Reyssbuch des Heyligen Lands. Frankfort. 1584.
Foglietta (Folieta), U. Clarorum Ligurum Elogia. Rome. 1573.
—— Historiae Genuensium libri XII. Genoa. 1585.
Froissart, Chroniques de. Ed. Kervyn de Lettenhove. Vols. XV and XVI. Brussels. 1870–7.
Gerlach. Türkisches Tagebuch. Frankfort. 1674.
Guazzo, M. Historie [1524–49]. Venice. 1549.
Jordanus, Friar. Mirabilia descripta. Transl. Yule, H. London. 1863.
Joseph Ben Joshua, Rabbi. The Chronicles of. Transl. Bialloblotzky, C. H. F. London. 1835.
Jovius, P. Historiae sui temporis. Venice. 1553.
Les Gestes des Chyprois. Ed. Raynaud, G. Geneva. 1887.

Libro de los Fechos et Conquistas del Principado de la Morea. [Aragonese version of the Chronicle of the Morea.] Ed. and transl. Morel-Fatio, A. Geneva. 1885.
Livre de la Conqueste de la Princée de l'Amorée. Chronique de Morée (1204–1305). Ed. Longnon, J. Paris. 1911.
Luccari, G. Copioso ristretto degli annali di Rausa. Venice. 1605.
Ludolph von Suchem. De Itinere Terrae Sanctae. Ed. Deycks, F. Stuttgart. 1851.
Machaut, Guillaume de. La Prise d'Alexandrie, ou chronique du Roi Pierre de Lusignan. Ed. Mas Latrie, L. de. Geneva. 1877.
Marthono, Nicolaus de, notarius. Liber Peregrinationis ad Loca Sancta. *In* Revue de l'Orient latin. Vol. III. pp. 566–669. Paris. 1895.
Maurocenus (Morosini), Andreas. Historia Veneta ab anno MDXXI usque ad annum MDCXV. Venice. 1623.
Monacis, Laurentius de. Chronicon de rebus Venetis ab u. c. ad annum MCCCLIV. Venice. 1758.
Morosini, Antonio. Chronique. Ed. Dorez, L. 4 vols. Paris. 1848–52.
Mouskés, Philippe. Chronique rimée. Vol. II. *In* Collection de chroniques belges inédites. Brussels. 1838.
Muntaner, Ramón. Chronica. Ed. Lanz, K. Stuttgart. 1844. Also *in* Cronache catalane del secolo XIII e XIV. Vol. I. Transl. Moisé, F. Florence. 1844. Engl. transl. Goodenough, Lady. (Hakluyt Soc.) 2 vols. London. 1920–1.
Nigropontis, De Captione. *In* Basle edn. of Chalcocondyles. Basle. 1556.
Pagnini. Della Decima e di varie altre gravezze imposte dal comune di Firenze. 4 vols. Lisbon and Lucca. 1765–6.
Paris, Matthew. Chronica Majora. Ed. Luard, H. R. 7 vols. (Rolls.) 1872–83.
—— Historia Minor. Ed. Madden, F. 3 vols. *Ibid.* 1866–9.
Paruta, P. Historia Venetiana. Venice. 1703.
Rizzardo, G. La Presa di Negroponte. Ed. Cicogna, E. A. Venice. 1844.
Sabellico, M. A. Historia Rerum Venetarum. Basle. 1556.
Sa'd-ad-Dīn. Chronica dell' origine e progressi di casa ottomana. Transl. Bratutti, V. 2 vols. Vienna and Madrid. 1649–52.
Sansovino, F. Cronologia del Mondo. Venice. 1582.
—— Historia universale dell' origine et imperio de' Turchi. Venice. 1573.
Sanudo, M. Diarii. 58 vols. Venice. 1879–1903.
Sanudo Torsello, Marino. Istoria del Regno di Romania. *In* Hopf, K. Chroniques gréco-romanes. pp. 90–170. *See Gen. Bibl.* IV.
—— Secreta Fidelium Crucis. Forms vol. II of Gesta Dei per Francos. Ed. Bongars, J. Hanover. 1611.
Spandugino, Th. I Commentari di Theodoro Spandugino dell' origine de' Principi Turchi. Florence. 1551.
Symon Simeonis. Itinerarium. Ed. Nasmith, J. Cambridge. 1778.
Tozzetti, G. T. Relazioni di alcuni viaggi fatti in diverse parti della Toscana. 2nd edn. 6 vols. Florence. 1777.
Villehardouin, Geoffroy de. La conquête de Constantinople. Avec la continuation de Henri de Valenciennes. Ed. Wailly, N. de. Paris. 1872. Also ed. Bouchet, É. 2 vols. Paris. 1891.

IV. SECONDARY AUTHORITIES.

Albánas, Ph. Περὶ τῶν ἐν Κερκύρᾳ τίτλων εὐγενείας καὶ περὶ τῶν τιμαρίων. Corfù. 1894.
Andreádes, A. M. Περὶ τῆς οἰκονομικῆς διοικήσεως τῆς Ἑπτανήσου ἐπὶ Βενετοκρατίας. 2 vols. Athens. 1914.
Anonymous. Historia del Regno di Negroponte e sue isole adjacenti. Venice. 1695.
—— [Delês, J.] Οἱ Γατελοῦζοι ἐν Λέσβῳ. 1355–1462. Athens. 1901.
Aravantinós, P. A. Χρονογραφία τῆς Ἠπείρου. 2 vols. Athens. 1856–7.
Belabre, Baron de. Rhodes of the Knights. Oxford. 1908.
Beving, Ch. A. La Principauté d'Achaïe et de Morée. 1204–1430. Brussels. 1879.
Blantês, Sp. A. Ἡ Λευκὰς ὑπὸ τοὺς Φράγκους, τοὺς Τούρκους, καὶ τοὺς Ἑνετοὺς (1204–1797). Levkás. 1902.

Blastós, A. M. *Χιακά.* 2 vols. Hermoupolis. 1840. Engl. transl. Ralli, A. P. London. 1913.
Borchgrave, E. de. Croquis d'Orient. Brussels. 1908.
Boschini, M. L'Arcipelago. Venice. 1658.
Bosio, G. Dell' Istoria della sacra Religione et ill[ma] Militia di S. Gio. Gierosol[mo]. 2 vols. Rome. 1594.
Botta, C. Storia naturale e medica dell' isola di Corfù. Milan. 1823.
Bozzo, S. V. Notizie storiche siciliane del secolo xiv. Palermo. 1882.
Brokínes, L. S. *Περὶ τῶν ἐτησίως τελουμένων ἐν Κερκύρᾳ λιτανειῶν τοῦ θ. λειψάνου τοῦ Ἁγίου Σπυρίδωνος.* 2nd edn. Corfù. 1894. Engl. transl. by Mrs Dawes. Bonn. *n.d.*
—— *Ἡ περὶ τὰ μέσα τοῦ ΙΣ′ αἰῶνος ἐν Κερκύρᾳ ἀποίκησις τῶν Ναυπλιέων καὶ τῶν Μονεμβασιέων.* Corfù. 1905.
Buchon, J. A. Recherches et matériaux pour servir à une histoire de la domination française, etc. 2 vols. Paris. 1840.
—— Recherches historiques sur la Principauté française de Morée. 2 vols. Paris. 1845.
—— Nouvelles recherches historiques sur la Principauté française de Morée. 2 vols. Paris. 1843.
—— Histoire des conquêtes et de l'établissement des français dans les états de l'ancienne Grèce. Paris. 1846.
—— Atlas des nouvelles recherches historiques. Paris. *n.d.*
—— La Grèce continentale et la Morée. Paris. 1843.
—— La Grèce, les Cyclades, et les Iles Ioniennes. *In* Revue de Paris. Vols. xiii, 37–56; xvi, 330–51; xvii, 268–80. [Euboea and the Cyclades.] Paris. 1843.
—— Excursions historiques dans les Cyclades. *In* Revue Indépendante. Vol. xiii, 554–72. Paris. 1844.
—— Voyage dans l'Eubée, les Iles Ioniennes, et les Cyclades en 1841. Publié... par J. Longnon. Préface de M. Barrès. Paris. 1911.
Carmoly, E. Don Joseph Nassy, Duc de Naxos. 2nd ed. Frankfort. 1868.
Chiótes, P. *Ἱστορικὰ Ἀπομνημονεύματα Ἑπτανήσου.* Vols. ii, iii. Corfù. 1858–63.
C[icogna], E. A. Cenni storici intorno Paolo de Campo da Catania. Venice. 1836.
Conze, A. Reise auf den Inseln des Thrakischen Meeres. Hanover. 1860.
—— Reise auf der Insel Lesbos. Hanover. 1865.
Conze, A., Hauser, A., and Niemann, G. [Benndorf, O. in Vol. ii.] Archaeologische Untersuchungen auf Samothrake. 2 vols. Vienna. 1875–80.
Cornelius (Corner.), F. Ecclesiae Venetae. Vol. viii. Venice. 1749.
—— Creta Sacra. Venice. 1755.
Coronelli, V. M. and Parisotti. Isola di Rodi geografica-storica, antica, e moderna, coll' altre adjacenti. Venice. 1688.
Coronelli, V. M. Memorie Istoriografiche de' Regni della Morea, Negroponte, e Littorali fin' a Salonichi. 2nd edn. Venice. *n.d.*
Çurita (Zurita), G. Anales de la Corona de Aragon. 7 vols. Saragossa. 1610–21.
Curtius, E. Naxos. Berlin. 1846.
Daru, P. Histoire de la République de Venise. 3rd edn. 8 vols. Paris. 1826.
Datta, P. L. Spedizione in Oriente di Amadeo VI. Turin. 1826.
—— Storia dei Principi di Savoia del ramo d' Acaja. 2 vols. Turin. 1832.
Delaville le Roulx, J. La France en Orient au xive siècle. 2 vols. Paris. 1886.
—— Les Hospitaliers en Terre Sainte et en Chypre. Paris. 1904.
—— Mélanges sur l'Ordre de S. Jean de Jérusalem. Paris. 1910.
Diehl, Ch. L'église et les mosaïques du couvent de Saint Luc en Phocide. Paris. 1889.
Du Cange, C. du Fresne. Histoire de l'Empire de Constantinople. Ed. Buchon, J. A. *See Gen. Bibl.* v.
Dugit, M. E. Naxos et les établissements latins de l'Archipel. *In* Bulletin de l'Académie Delphinale. Ser. iii. Vol. x. Grenoble. 1875.
Emerson, J. The History of Modern Greece. 2 vols. London. 1830.
Eubel, C. Hierarchia Catholica Medii Aevi [1198–1600]. 3 vols. Münster. 1898–1910.

Fallmerayer, J. P. Geschichte der Halbinsel Morea während des Mittelalters. 2 vols. Stuttgart and Tübingen. 1830–6.
Fanelli, F. Atene Attica. Venice. 1707.
Finlay, G. A History of Greece. Ed. Tozer, H. F. Vols. III, IV. *See Gen. Bibl.* v.
Foscolo, Ugo. Narrazione delle fortune e della cessione di Parga. *In* Opere edite e postume. Prose politiche. Florence. 1850.
Gaddi, G. Corollarium poeticum. Florence. 1636.
—— Elogiographus. Florence. 1638.
Gerakáres, N. S. Κερκυραϊκαὶ σελίδες. 1204–1386. Corfù. 1906.
Gerland, E. Neue Quellen zur Geschichte des lateinischen Erzbisthums Patras. Leipsic. 1903.
—— Geschichte des lateinischen Kaiserreiches von Konstantinopel. Pt. I. *See Gen. Bibl.* v.
—— Histoire de la Noblesse crétoise au moyen âge. (Extrait de la Revue de l'Orient latin. Vols. x and XI.) Paris. 1907.
Gerola, G. Monumenti Veneti nell' Isola di Creta. 3 vols. Venice. 1905–17. [Incomplete.]
—— La Dominazione genovese in Creta. (Estratto dagli Atti dell' I. R. Accademia di Scienze....in Rovereto. Ser. III. Vol. VIII.) Rovereto. 1902.
—— Topografia delle chiese della città di Candia. (Estratto dal Bessarione.) Rome. 1918.
—— Per la cronotassi dei vescovi cretesi all' epoca Veneta. (Estratto da Miscellanea di Storia Veneta. Series III. Vol. VII.) Venice. 1914.
—— L'arte Veneta a Creta. Rome. 1905.
—— I Monumenti Medioevali delle Tredici Sporadi. 2 vols. Bergamo. 1914, 15.
—— Un piccolo feudo napoletano nell' Egeo. (L' isoletta di Castelrosso, ora Kastellòrizo.) (Estratto da Ausonia.) Rome. 1913.
—— Sèrfino (Sèriphos). Bergamo. 1921.
Giannópoulos, N. I. Οἱ δύο μεσαιωνικοὶ Ἀλμυροὶ καὶ ὁ νῦν. Athens. 1904.
Gittio, A. G. Lo Scettro del Despota. Naples. 1697.
Gkión, K. I. Ἱστορία τῆς νήσου Σίφνου. Syra. 1876.
Grandi, Jacopo. Risposta di...sopra alcune richieste intorno S. Maura, e la Prevesa. Venice. 1686.
Gregorovius, F. Geschichte der Stadt Athen im Mittelalter. *See Gen. Bibl.* v.
Guglielmotti, A. Storia della Marina pontificia nel medio evo, dal 728 al 1499. 2nd edn. Vol. II. Rome. 1886–93.
Guichenon, S. Histoire généalogique de la royale maison de Savoye. 2 vols. Lyons. 1660.
Guillaume, Abbé. Histoire généalogique des Sires de Salins. 2 vols. Besançon. *n.d.*
Guldencrone, Baronne Diane de. L'Achaïe feódale. Paris. 1886.
Ḥājjī Khalīfah. Cronologia historica. Transl. Carli, G. R. Venice. 1697.
—— The history of the Maritime Wars of the Turks. Transl. Mitchell, J. London. 1831.
Hammer-Purgstall, J. von. Geschichte des osmanischen Reiches. Vols. I and II. *See Gen. Bibl.* v.
Hertzberg, G. F. Geschichte Griechenlands seit dem Absterben des antiken Lebens bis zur Gegenwart. Vols. II and III. *See Gen. Bibl.* v.
Heyd, W. von. Le Colonie commerciali degli Italiani in Oriente. Transl. Müller, J. Venice and Turin. 1866–8.
—— Geschichte des Levantehandels im Mittelalter. *See Gen. Bibl.* v.
Hidroménos, A. M. Συνοπτικὴ ἱστορία τῆς Κερκύρας. Corfù. 1895.
Hopf, K. Geschichte Griechenlands vom Beginn des Mittelalters bis auf unsere Zeit. *See Gen. Bibl.* v.
—— Ghisi. *In* Ersch-Gruber. Vol. LXVI. (*See Gen. Bibl.* I.) Leipsic. 1857.
—— Giorgi. *Ibid.* Vol. LXVII. Leipsic. 1858.
—— Giustiniani. *Ibid.* Vol. LXVIII. Leipsic. 1859. French transl. by Vlasto, E. A. Les Giustiniani, dynastes de Chios. Paris. 1888. Italian transl. by Sardagna, G. B. Di alcune dinastie latine nella Grecia. *In* Archivio Veneto. Vol. XXXI. Venice. 1886. And by Wolf, A. Storia dei Giustiniani di Genova. *In*

Giornale Ligustico. Anni VII–IX. Genoa. 1881–2. Greek transl. *in* Χρυσαλλίς. Vol. II. Athens. 1864.
Hopf, K. Gozzadini. *In* Ersch-Gruber. Vol. LXXVI. (*See Gen. Bibl.* I.) Leipsic. 1863.
—— Geschichtlicher Ueberblick über die Schicksale von Karystos. *In* SKAW. Vol. XI. Vienna. 1853. Italian transl. by Sardagna, G. B., with author's additions. Dissertazione documentata sulla storia di Karystos. Venice. 1856. Greek transl. by Galánes, E. Athens. 1867.
—— Geschichte der Insel Andros und ihrer Beherrscher. SKAW. Vol. XVI. Vienna. 1855.
—— Urkunden und Zusätze zur Geschichte der Insel Andros. *Ibid.* Vol. XXI. Vienna. 1856. Italian transl. of both by Sardagna, G. B. Dissertazione documentata sulla storia dell' Isola di Andros. Venice. 1859. Greek transl. by Delagrammátika, Z. Andros. 1886.
—— Veneto-byzantinische Analekten. SKAW. Vol. XXXII. Vienna. 1859.
—— [*Re* Lesbos.] *In* Monatsberichte d. PAW. (1862.) pp. 79–91. Berlin. 1863.
—— De Historiae Ducatus Atheniensis fontibus. Bonn. 1852.
—— Walther VI von Brienne, Herzog von Athen und Graf von Lecce. *In* Raumer, F. v. Historisches Taschenbuch. Vol. III. Pt. 5. Leipsic. 1854.
—— Chroniques gréco-romanes inédites ou peu connues. *See Gen. Bibl.* IV.
Jervis, Henry Jervis-White. History of the Island of Corfù and of the Republic of the Ionian Islands. London. 1852.
Jubainville, H. d'Arbois de. Voyage paléographique dans le département de l'Aube. Troyes. 1855.
Kampoúroglos, D. G. *Ἱστορία τῶν Ἀθηναίων.* 3 vols. Athens. 1889–96.
—— *Μνημεῖα τῆς Ἱστορίας τῶν Ἀθηναίων.* 3 vols. Athens. 2nd edn. 1891–2.
Karavías, Grívas N. *Ἱστορία τῆς νήσου Ἰθάκης.* Athens. 1849.
Konstantinídes, G. *Ἱστορία τῶν Ἀθηνῶν ἀπὸ Χριστοῦ γεννήσεως μέχρι τοῦ ἔτους* 1821. 2nd edn. Athens. 1894.
Laborde, Cte de. Athènes aux XVe, XVIe, et XVIIe siècles. 2 vols. Paris. 1854.
Lami, G. Deliciae eruditorum. Vols. V, IX. Florence. 1738–40.
Lampákes, G. *Χριστιανικὴ ἀρχαιολογία τῆς μονῆς Δαφνίου.* Athens. 1889.
Lámpros (Lambros), P. Monete inedite dei Gran maestri dell' Ordine di S. Giovanni di Gerusalemme in Rodi. Transl. by C. Kunz. Venice. 1865. Primo supplemento. Venice. 1866. Originals in Πανδώρα. Vols. IX and XVI. Athens. 1859–65.
—— Monnaies inédites des Grands Maîtres de Rhodes de l'Ordre de Saint-Jean de Jérusalem. Paris. 1877.
—— Illustrazione di due monete inedite battute dai Conti di Salona. Transl. Athens. 1866.
—— Unedirte Münzen und Bleibullen der Despoten von Epirus. Vienna. 1873.
—— *Ἀνέκδοτα νομίσματα τοῦ μεσαιωνικοῦ Βασιλείου τῆς Κύπρου* (with French transl.). Athens. 1876.
—— *Ἀνέκδοτα νομίσματα κοπέντα ἐν Γλαρέντσᾳ κατὰ μίμησιν τῶν Ἑνετικῶν ὑπὸ Ῥοβέρτου τοῦ ἐξ Ἀνδηγαυῶν, ἡγεμόνος τῆς Πελοποννήσου* (1346–64). Athens. 1876.
—— Monnaies inédites de Chio. Paris. 1877.
—— Monnaies inédites de Pierre-Raymond Zacosta. Athens. 1877.
—— *Ἀνέκδοτα νομίσματα καὶ μολυβδόβουλλα τῶν κατὰ τοὺς μέσους αἰῶνας Δυναστῶν τῆς Ἑλλάδος.* Athens. 1880.
—— Νομίσματα τῶν ἀδελφῶν Μαρτίνου καὶ Βενεδίκτου Β′ Ζαχαριῶν Δυναστῶν τῆς Χίου. Athens. 1884.
—— *Μεσαιωνικὰ νομίσματα τῶν Δυναστῶν τῆς Χίου.* Athens. 1886.
Lámpros (Lambros), Sp. P. *Αἱ Ἀθῆναι περὶ τὰ τέλη τοῦ δωδεκάτου αἰῶνος.* Athens. 1878.
—— *Ἱστορία τῆς Ἑλλάδος.* Vols. V, VI. *See Gen. Bibl.* V.
—— Μικταὶ Σελίδες. Athens. 1905. (*See also* Νέος Ἑλληνομνήμων. *See below,* V.)
—— Παλαιολόγεια καὶ Πελοποννησιακά. 2 vols. Athens. 1912. [Incomplete.]
Lamprynídes, M. G. *Ἡ Ναυπλία.* Athens. 1898.
Le Quien, M. Oriens Christianus. Vol. II. *See Gen. Bibl.* IV.
Levy, M. A. Don Joseph Nasi, Herzog von Naxos. Breslau. 1859.
Litta, P. Le famiglie celebri italiane. *See Gen. Bibl.* III.

[Loredano, Gio. Fr.] Historie de' Rè Lusignani publicate da Henrico Giblet. Venice. 1667.
Loúntzes [Lunzi], E. *Περὶ τῆς πολιτικῆς καταστάσεως τῆς Ἑπτανήσου ἐπὶ Ἐνετῶν.* Athens. 1856. Enlarged Italian version: Della condizione politica delle Isole Ionie sotto il dominio veneto. Venice. 1858.
Lovérdos, J. P. K. *Ἱστορία τῆς νήσου Κεφαλληνίας.* Greek transl. from the Italian MS by Gratsiátos, P. K. Cephalonia. 1888.
Magni, Cornelio. Relazione della città di Atene. Parma. 1688.
—— Quanto di più curioso e vago ha potuto raccorre Cornelio Magni in viaggi e dimore per la Turchia. Parma. 1692.
Mai, A. Spicilegium Romanum. 10 vols. Rome. 1839–44.
Marmora, A. Historia di Corfù. Venice. 1672.
Martène, E. and Durand, U. Thesaurus novus Anecdotorum. *See Gen. Bibl.* IV.
Mas Latrie, L. de. Histoire de l'île de Chypre sous le Règne des Princes de la Maison de Lusignan. 3 vols. Paris. 1852–61.
—— Généalogie des Rois de Chypre de la famille de Lusignan. *In* Archivio Veneto. Vol. XXI. 309–59. Venice. 1881.
—— Histoire des Archevêques latins de l'île de Chypre. Genoa. 1882.
—— Les Princes de Morée. *In* R. Deputazione Veneta. Miscell. (Ser. I.) Vol. II. Venice. 1883.
—— Les ducs de l'Archipel. *Ibid.* Vol. IV. Venice. 1887.
—— Les seigneurs terciers de Négrepont. *In* Revue de l'Orient latin. Vol. I. 413–32. Paris. 1893.
Mazella, Sc. Descrittione del Regno di Napoli. Naples. 1601.
Meliarákes, A. *Ἄνδρος, Κέως.* Athens. 1880.
—— *Ἀμοργός. In Δελτίον τῆς Ἱστ. καὶ Ἐθν. Ἑτ.* Vol. I. 569–656. Athens. 1884.
—— *Κίμωλος. Ibid.* Vol. VI. 3–48. Athens. 1902.
—— *Γεωγραφία πολιτικὴ νέα καὶ ἀρχαία τοῦ νομοῦ Ἀργολίδος καὶ Κορινθίας.* Athens. 1886.
—— *Γεωγραφία πολιτικὴ νέα καὶ ἀρχαία τοῦ νομοῦ Κεφαλληνίας.* Athens. 1890.
—— *Ἱστορία τοῦ Βασιλείου τῆς Νικαίας καὶ τοῦ Δεσποτάτου τῆς Ἠπείρου. See Gen. Bibl.* V.
—— *Οἰκογένεια Μαμωνᾶ.* Athens. 1902.
Mercati, P. Saggio storico statistico di Zante. 1811.
Miller, W. The Latins in the Levant. *See Gen. Bibl.* V. Greek transl. by Lámpros, Sp. P. *See above,* I.
—— Essays on the Latin Orient. *See Gen. Bibl.* V.
—— The Latin Orient. *See Gen. Bibl.* V.
Millet, G. Le monastère de Daphni. Paris. 1899.
—— Monuments byzantins de Mistrâ. Album. Paris. 1910.
Missioni. Lettere edificanti scritte dalle missioni straniere. Vol. VII. Milan. 1827.
Mommsen, A. Athenae Christianae. Leipsic. 1868.
Moncada, F. de. Expedicion de los Catalanes y Aragones contre Turcos y Griegos. *In* Biblioteca de Autores Españoles. Vol. XXI. Madrid. 1868.
Moresini, A. Corsi di penna e catena di materie sopra l' Isola della Ceffalonia. Venice. 1628.
Moschídes, A. *Ἡ Λῆμνος.* Vol. I. [To 1770.] Alexandria. 1907.
Muratori, L. A. Antiquitates italicae medii aevi. *See Gen. Bibl.* IV.
Mustoxidi, A. Illustrazioni Corciresi. 2 vols. Milan. 1811–14.
—— Delle Cose Corciresi. Vol. I. Corfù. 1848. [Incomplete.]
Mustoxidi [Μουστοξύδης], M. A. *Ἱστορικὰ καὶ φιλολογικὰ Ἀνάλεκτα.* Corfù. 1872.
Orlándos, A. K. *Ἡ Παρηγορήτισσα τῆς Ἄρτης.* Athens. 1921.
Pagano, C. Delle Imprese e del Dominio dei Genovesi nella Grecia. Genoa. 1846.
Panvinius, O. Antiquitatum Veronensium libri VIII. Verona. 1648.
Paparrhegópoulos, K. *Ἱστορία τοῦ Ἑλληνικοῦ ἔθνους.* Vol. V. *See Gen. Bibl.* V.
Paschàles, D. P. *Νομισματικὴ τῆς νήσου Ἄνδρου.* Athens. 1892.
Pasch di Krienen, Conte. Breve descrizione dell' Arcipelago. Leghorn. 1773.
Pègues, Abbé. Histoire et phénomènes du volcan et des îles volcaniques de Santorin. Paris. 1842.
Perrhaibós, Ch. *Ἱστορία σύντομος τοῦ Σουλίου καὶ Πάργας.* Athens. 1857.

Petritzopoulos, D. Saggio storico sull' età di Leucadia. Venice. 1824.
Philadelpheús, Th. N. Ἱστορία τῶν Ἀθηνῶν ἐπὶ Τουρκοκρατίας. 2 vols. Athens. 1902.
Piacenza, F. L'Egeo redivivo. Modena. 1688.
Pinder and Friedländer. Beiträge zur älteren Münzkunde. [*Re* Lesbos, pp. 29–50.] Berlin. 1851.
Polýkarpos. Τὰ Μετέωρα. Athens. 1882.
Porcacchi, T. L'Isole più famose al mondo. Venice. 1572.
Pouqueville, F. C. H. L. Voyage dans la Grèce. 5 vols. Paris. 1820–1.
Promis, D. La Zecca di Scio durante il dominio dei Genovesi. Turin. 1865.
Psilákes, B. Ἱστορία τῆς Κρήτης, ἀπὸ τῆς ἀπωτάτης ἀρχαιότητος μέχρι τῶν καθ' ἡμᾶς χρόνων. 3 vols. Canea. 1901–10.
Raynaldus, O. Annales ecclesiasticae. [1198–1565.] *See Gen. Bibl.* v *under* Baronius, C.
Reinhard, J. P. Vollständige Geschichte des Königreichs Cypern. 2 vols. Erlangen. 1766–8.
Remondini, B. M. De Zacynthi antiquitatibus et fortuna. Venice. 1756.
Rodd, Sir Rennell. The Princes of Achaia and the Chronicles of Morea. 2 vols. London. 1907.
Rodokanákes, Prince D. Ἰουστινιᾶναι—Χίος. Syra. 1900.
Romanin, S. Storia documentata di Venezia. Vols. II–VI. Venice. 1854–7.
Romanós, J. A. Γρατιανὸς Ζῶρζης αὐθέντης Λευκάδος. Corfù. 1870.
—— Δημοσία Κερκυραϊκὴ πρᾶξις. Corfù. 1882.
—— Ἡ Ἑβραϊκὴ Κοινότης τῆς Κερκύρας. [Reprint from the Ἑστία.] Athens. 1891.
—— Περὶ τοῦ Δεσποτάτου τῆς Ἠπείρου. Corfù. 1895.
Rosario, Gregorio. Considerazioni sopra la storia di Sicilia. Vol. II. Palermo. 1833.
Rubió y Lluch, A. La Expedición y Dominación de los Catalanes en Oriente. Los Navarros en Grecia. Both *in* Memorias de la R. Academia de Buenas Letras de Barcelona. Vol. IV. Barcelona. 1887. The latter also separately published.
—— Catalunya a Grecia. Barcelona. 1906.
—— La Acrópolis de Atenas en la época catalana. Barcelona. 1908.
—— Tradicions sobre la caiguda del comtat català de Salona. Barcelona. 1910.
—— La llengua catalana a Grecia. *In* Primer Congrés Internacional de la llengua catalana. pp. 235–48. Barcelona. 1908.
—— Atenes en temps dels Catalans. *In* Anuari de l'Institut d' Estudis Catalans. Barcelona. 1907. Also separately published.
—— Els Castells catalans de la Grecia continental. *Ibid.* 1910. Also separately published. Greek transl. Mavrákes, G. N. Athens. 1912.
—— Els governs de Matheu de Moncada y Roger de Lluria en la Grecia catalana (1359–70). *Ibid.* 1912. Also separately published.
—— La Grècia catalana des de 1370 a 1377. *Ibid.* 1914. Also separately published.
—— La Grècia catalana des de 1377 a 1379. *Ibid.* 1920. Also separately published.
—— Contribució a la biografia de l'infant Ferràn de Mallorca. (Extract from Revista Estudis Universitaris Catalans. Vol. VIII.) Barcelona. 1915.
St Genois, Comte J. de. Droits primitifs des anciennes terres et seigneuries du pays et comté de Haynaut. Vol. I. Paris. 1782.
Saint-Sauveur, A. G. Voyage historique, littéraire, et pittoresque dans les îles et possessions çi-devant vénitiennes du Levant. 4 vols. Paris. An VIII. (1799–1800.)
S[alapántas], P. A. Ἡ Πάργα. Athens. 1861.
[Salvator, Archduke Ludwig.] Paxos und Antipaxos. 2nd edn. Würzburg and Vienna. 1889.
—— Zante. Allgemeiner Teil. Prague. 1904.
—— Zante. Specieller Teil. Prague. 1904.
—— Anmerkungen über Leukas. Prague. 1908.
—— Parga. Prague. 1907.
—— Versuch einer Geschichte von Parga. Prague. 1908.
Sassenay, Cte F. de. Les Brienne de Lecce et d'Athènes. Paris. 1869.
Sáthas, K. N. Χρονικὸν ἀνέκδοτον Γαλαξειδίου. Athens. 1865.
—— Τουρκοκρατουμένη Ἑλλάς. Athens. 1869.
Sauger. Histoire nouvelle des anciens ducs et autres souverains de l'Archipel. Paris. 1699. Greek transl. by Karáles, A. Hermoupolis. 1878.

Sauli, L. Della colonia dei Genovesi in Galata. 2 vols. Turin. 1831.
Schlumberger, G. Les Principautés franques du Levant. Paris. 1877.
—— Numismatique de l'Orient latin. *See Gen. Bibl.* III.
—— Expédition des "Almugavares" ou routiers catalans en Orient de l'an 1302 à l'an 1311. Paris. 1902.
Schultz, R. W. and Barnsley, S. H. The Monastery of St Luke of Stiris, in Phocis. London. 1901.
Schultz-Gora, O. Le epistole del trovatore Rambaldo di Vaqueiras. Florence. 1898.
Servion, J. Gestez et chroniques de la Mayson de Savoye. Ed. Bollati, F. E. 2 vols. Turin. 1879.
Sourmelês, D. Κατάστασις συνοπτικὴ τῆς πόλεως Ἀθηνῶν. 3rd edn. Athens. 1846.
Spon, J. and Wheler, G. Voyage d'Italie, de Dalmatie, de Grèce, et du Levant. 3 vols. Lyons. 1678.
Stai, N. Raccolta di antiche autorità...riguardanti l' Isola di Citera oggidì Cerigo. Pisa. 1847.
Stamatélos, I. Φιλολογικαὶ διατριβαὶ περὶ Λευκάδος. Athens. 1851.
Stamatiádes, E. Οἱ Καταλάνοι ἐν τῇ Ἀνατολῇ. Athens. 1869.
—— Ἰκαριακά, ἤτοι ἱστορία καὶ περιγραφὴ τῆς νήσου Ἰκαρίας. Samos. 1893.
Struck, A. Mistra. Eine mittelalterliche Ruinenstadt. Vienna and Leipsic. 1910.
Stubbs, W. The mediaeval kingdoms of Cyprus and Armenia. *In* Seventeen lectures on the study of mediaeval and modern history. 3rd edn. Oxford. 1900. pp. 179–239.
Torr, C. Rhodes in modern times. Cambridge. 1887.
Tournefort, P. de. Relation d'un voyage du Levant. 2 vols. Amsterdam. 1718.
Ubaldini, G. B. Origine della famiglia delli Acciaioli. Florence. 1638.
Volonakes, M. D. The Island of Roses and her eleven sisters, or the Dodecanese. London. 1922.
Wadding, L. Annales Minorum. *See Gen. Bibl.* IV.
Zabarella, G. Tito Livio Padovano. Padua. 1669.
—— Il Galba. Padua. 1671.

V. PERIODICAL LITERATURE.

Académie des Sciences, Belles-Lettres, et Arts de Besançon. Année 1880. Besançon. 1881.
Gauthier, J. Othon de la Roche, conquérant d'Athènes et sa famille (1217–1335). pp. 139–55.
Terrier de Loray, Marquis. Un parlement de dames au XIIIe siècle. pp. 205–21.
Annual of the British School at Athens, The. London. 1895 ff., in progress.
Hasluck, F. W. Albanian Settlements in the Aegean Islands. Vol. XV. 223–8.
—— Monuments of the Gattelusi. *Ibid.* 248–69.
—— Frankish Remains at Adalia. *Ibid.* 270–3.
—— The Latin Monuments of Chios. Vol. XVI. 137–84.
—— A French Inscription at Adalia. *Ibid.* 185–6.
—— Heraldry of the Rhodian Knights, formerly in Smyrna Castle. Vol. XVII. 145–50.
—— Depopulation in the Aegean Islands and the Turkish Conquest. *Ibid.* 151–81.
—— Note on a Greek Inscription of the Knights at Budrum. Vol. XVIII. 215.
—— On imitations of the Venetian Sequin struck for the Levant. *Ibid.* 261–4.
—— Contributions to the history of Levant Currencies. Vol. XIX. 174–81.
Put, A. van de. Note on the Armorial Insignia in the Church of St George, Geraki. Vol. XIII. 281–4.
Traquair, R. Laconia: The Mediaeval Fortresses. Vol. XII. 258–76.
—— Mediaeval Fortresses of the North-Western Peloponnesus. Vol. XIII. 268–81.

Annual of the British School at Athens, The.

Traquair, R. The Churches of Western Mani. Vol. xv. 177–213.

Wace, A. J. B. Frankish Sculptures at Parori and Geraki. Vol. xi. 139–45.

Archivio storico Siciliano. Vols. vii, xi. Palermo. 1879–83.

Ἁρμονία. Vol. iii. Athens. 1902.

Papadópoulos-Kerameús, A. Ἀθηναϊκὰ ἐκ τοῦ ΙΒ′ καὶ ΙΓ′ αἰῶνος. pp. 209–24, 273–93.

Bulletin de correspondance hellénique. 40 vols. Athens and Paris. 1877–1916.

Caron. Trouvailles de monnaies du moyen-âge à Delphes. Vol. xxi (1897). 26–39.

Giannópoulos, N. I. Χριστιανικαὶ ἐπιγραφαὶ Θεσσαλίας. Vol. xxiii (1899). 396–416.

Millet, G. Rapport sur une mission à Mistra. Vol. xix (1895). 268–72.

—— Inscriptions byzantines de Mistra. Vol. xxiii (1899). 97–156.

—— Inscriptions inédites de Mistra. Vol. xxx (1906). 453–66.

Byzantinisch-Neugriechische Jahrbücher. 2 vols. Berlin. 1920–1.

Jireček, C. Die Wittwe und die Söhne des Despoten Esau von Epirus. Vol. i. (1920.) 1–16.

BZ. Leipsic. 1892 ff., in progress.

Bées, N. A. Μνεῖαι τοῦ Ἄστρους κατὰ τοὺς μέσους αἰῶνας καὶ τὰ παρ᾽ αὐτὸ κάστρα. Τὸ τοπωνυμικὸν "Ἄρια." Vol. xvii (1908). 92–107.

Bogiatzídes, I. K. Ὁ Λακεδαιμόνιος βιβλιογράφος Στρατηγόπουλος. [*In* Andros, 1538–9.] Vol. xix (1910). 122–6.

Dräseke, J. Aus dem Athen der Acciaiuoli. Vol. xiv (1905). 239–53.

Foerster, R. Eine Monodie auf Theodoros Palaiologos. Vol. ix (1900). 641–8.

Gerland, E. Bericht über Carl Hopfs litterarischen Nachlass und die darin vorhandenen fränkisch-griechische Regestensammlung. Vol. viii (1899). 347–86.

—— Noch einmal der litterarische Nachlass Carl Hopfs. Vol. xi (1902). 321–32.

Gheyn, J. van den. Le siège épiscopal de Diaulia en Phocide. Vol. vi (1897). 92–5.

Giannópoulos, N. J. Μολυβδόβουλλα προερχόμενα ἐκ τοῦ Νοτίου Μεσαιωνικοῦ Ἁλμυροῦ. Vol. xvii (1908). 131–40.

—— Χριστιανικαὶ ἐπιγραφαὶ Θεσσαλίας. Vol. xxi (1912). 150–68.

Hatzidákis, G. N. Ὁ Μορέας oder τὸ Μόρεον. Vol. v (1896). 341–6.

Jegerlehner, J. Der Aufstand der kandiotischen Ritterschaft gegen das Mutterland Venedig. 1363–5. Vol. xii (1903). 78–125.

—— Beiträge zur Verwaltungsgeschichte Kandias im xiv Jahrhundert. Vol. xiii (1904). 435–79.

Jireček, K. Eine Urkunde von 1238–40 zur Geschichte von Korfù. Vol. i (1892). 336–7.

Kugéas, S. Notizbuch eines Beamten der Metropolis in Thessalonike aus dem Anfang des xv Jahrhunderts. Vol. xxiii (1914). 144–63.

Kurtz, E. Georgios Bardanes, Metropolit von Kerkyra. Vol. xv (1906). 603–13.

—— Christophoros von Ankyra als Exarch des Patriarchen Germanos II. Vol. xvi (1907). 120–42.

Lambros (Lámpros), Sp. P. Die erste Erwähnung von Astros, Leonidion, und Areia. Vol. ii (1893). 73–5.

—— Mazaris und seine Werke. Vol. v (1896). 63–73.

—— Tavia, eine verkannte mittelgriechische Stadt. Vol. vii (1898). 309–15.

Miller, W. Der älteste Stammbaum der Herzöge von Naxos. Vol. xvi (1907). 258–61.

—— Two Letters of Giovanni IV, Duke of the Archipelago. Vol. xvii (1908). 463–70.

—— The Gattilusj of Lesbos (1355–1462). Vol. xxii (1913). 406–47. Republished *in* Essays on the Latin Orient. *See Gen. Bibl.* v.

BZ. Leipsic. 1892 ff., in progress.

Papadópoulos-Kerameús, A. *Περὶ τῆς ἐπισκοπῆς Διαυλείας*. Vol. VII (1898). 50–6.

—— *Δυρραχηνά*. Vol. XIV (1905). 568–74.

Treu, M. Demetrios Kydones. Vol. I (1892). 60.

—— Mazaris und Holobolos. *Ibid.* 86–97.

Zerléntes, P. G. *Ναξία νῆσος καὶ πόλις*. Vol. XI (1902). 491–9.

—— *Γράμματα Φράγκων δουκῶν τοῦ Αἰγαίου πελάγους* (,αυλγ'—,αφξδ'). Vol. XIII (1904). 136–57.

Βυζαντίς. 2 vols. Athens. 1909–12.

Rubió y Lluch, A. Collection de documents relatifs à l'histoire de la ville d'Athènes pendant la domination catalane. Vol. II. 297–328.

Δελτίον τῆς Ἱστορικῆς καὶ Ἐθνολογικῆς Ἑταιρίας τῆς Ἑλλάδος. 7 vols. Athens. 1883–1918.

Δελτίον τῆς Χριστιανικῆς ἀρχαιολογικῆς Ἑταιρείας. 10 parts. Athens. 1892–1911.

Ἑλληνομνήμων. Athens. 1843–7.

EHR.

Fotheringham, J. K. Genoa and the Fourth Crusade. Vol. XXV (1910). 26–57.

Miller, W. The Name of Santa Maura. Vol. XVIII (1903). 513–14.

—— The Name of Navarino. Vols. XX (1905). 307–9. XXI (1906). 106.

—— Ithake under the Franks. Vol. XXI (1906). 513–17.

—— The Mad Duke of Naxos. *Ibid.* 737–9.

—— The Last Venetian Islands in the Aegean. Vol. XXII (1907). 304–8.

—— Notes on Athens under the Franks. *Ibid.* 518–22.

—— The Turkish Capture of Athens. Vol. XXIII (1908). 529–30.

—— The Genoese in Chios, 1346–1566. Vol. XXX (1915). 418–32.

—— Salonika. Vol. XXXII (1917). 161–74.

The above are republished *in* Essays on the Latin Orient. *See Gen. Bibl.* V.

Ἐπετηρὶς τοῦ Φιλολογικοῦ Συλλόγου Παρνασσοῦ. Athens. 1897–1906.

Journal of Hellenic Studies. 1880 ff., in progress.

Bury, J. B. The Lombards and Venetians in Euboia (1205–1470). Vols. VII (1886). 309–52. VIII (1887). 194–213. IX (1888). 91–117.

Miller, W. Monemvasia. Vol. XXVII (1907). 229–41, 300–1.

—— The Marquisate of Boudonitza. Vol. XXVIII (1908). 234–49.

—— The Frankish Inscription at Karditza. Vol. XXIX (1909). 197–201.

—— The Zaccaria of Phocaea and Chios. Vol. XXXI (1911). 42–55.

The above are republished *in* Essays on the Latin Orient. *See Gen. Bibl.* V.

Miller, W. The last Athenian historian : Laonikos Chalkokondyles. Vol. XLII (1922). 36–49.

Ramsay, W. M. A Romaic Ballad. Vol. I (1880). 293–300.

Tozer, H. F. Byzantine Satire. Vol. II (1881). 233–70.

—— The Franks in the Peloponnese. Vol. IV (1883). 165–236.

—— A Byzantine Reformer (Gemistus Plethon). Vol. VII (1886). 353–80.

Mélanges de l'École française de Rome. Paris. 1881 ff., in progress.

Faure, M. C. Le Dauphin Humbert II à Venise et en Orient (1345–7). Vol. XXVII (1907). 509–62.

Mitteilungen des k. deutschen Archäologischen Instituts. (Athenische Abtheilung.) 39 vols. Athens. 1876–1914.

Fredrich, E. Aus Samothrake. Vol. XXXIV (1909). 23–8.

Herzog, R. Ein türkisches Werk über das ägäische Meer aus dem Jahre 1520. Vol. XXVII (1902). 417–30.

Jacobs, E. Die Thasiaca des Cyriacus von Ancona im Codex Vaticanus 5250. Vol. XXII (1897). 113–38.

Judeich, W. Athen im Jahre 1395 nach der Beschreibung des Niccolò da Martoni. *Ibid.* 423–38.

Michel, K. and Struck, A. Die mittelbyzantinischen Kirchen Athens. Vol. XXXI (1906). 279–324.

Struck, A. Vier byzantinische Kirchen der Argolis. Vol. XXXIV (1909). 189–236.

Mitteilungen des k. deutschen Archäologischen Instituts.

Ziebarth, E. Ein griechischer Reisebericht des fünfzehnten Jahrhunderts. Vol. XXIV (1899). 72–88.

Νέα Πανδώρα. Vols. VI–X. Athens. 1856–60.

Νέος Ἑλληνομνήμων. Athens. 1904 ff., in progress.

Παρνασσός. Athens. 1877–95.

Revue de l'Orient latin. 11 vols. Paris. 1893–1908.

Desimoni, C. Actes passés à Famagouste, de 1299 à 1301, par devant le notaire Lamberto di Sambuceto. Vol. I (1893). 58–139, 275–312, 321–53.

—— Notes et observations sur les actes du notaire génois Lamberto di Sambuceto. Vol. II (1894). 1–34, 216–34.

—— Observations sur les monnaies, les poids, et les mesures cités dans les actes du notaire génois Lamberto di Sambuceto. Vol. III (1895). 1–26.

Kohler, Ch. Documents chypriotes du début du XIVe siècle. Vol. XI (1908). 440–52.

Omont, H. Un nouvel évêque latin de Milo, Étienne Gatalusio (1563). Vol. I (1893). 537–9.

VV. 15 vols. St Petersburg. 1894–1910.

Bées, N. A. *Βυζαντιναὶ ἐπιγραφαὶ Γορτυνίας.* And *Προσθῆκαι.* Vol. XI. 63–72, 384–5. 1904.

Hatzidákis, G. N. *Μυζήθρα, Μυζηθρᾶς, Μυστρᾶς.* Vol. II. 58–77. 1895.

Haviarâs, D. *Μελέται περὶ τῆς νήσου Σύμης.* Vol. XII. 172–90. Vol. XIV. 237–45. 1906–9.

Papadópoulos-Kerameús, A. *Παρατηρήσεις εἰς τὰ* Epirotica saeculi XIII. Vol. XI. 849–66.

—— *Κερκυραϊκά. Ἰωάννης Ἀπόκαυκος καὶ Γεώργιος Βαρδάνης.* Vol. XIII. 334–51. 1906.

Vasil'evski, V. *Ἠπειρωτικὰ κατὰ τὴν ιγ' ἑκατονταετηρίδα.* Vol. III. 233–99. 1896.

Χριστιανικὴ Κρήτη. Creta Christiana. 2 vols. Candia. 1912–15.

CHAPTER XVI.

THE EMPIRE OF NICAEA AND THE RECOVERY OF CONSTANTINOPLE.

I. SPECIAL BIBLIOGRAPHY.

Of Theodore II Lascaris and his works. *In* Pappadópoulos, J. B. Théodore II Lascaris, Empereur de Nicée. *See below,* IV (*b*).

II. ORIGINAL DOCUMENTS.

Boeckh, A. Corpus Inscriptionum Graecarum. Vol. IV. Nos. 8744–8. Berlin. 1877.

Carini, I. Gli archivi e le biblioteche di Spagna. Vol. II. Palermo. 1884.

Henry, Latin Emperor, Letter of. *In* Buchon, J. A. Recherches et matériaux pour servir à une histoire de la domination française, etc. II. 211–13. Paris. 1840.

Miklosich, F. and Müller, J. Acta et diplomata graeca medii aevi. *See Gen. Bibl.* IV.

Nicole, J. Bref inédit de Germain II, Patriarche de Constantinople (année 1230). *In* Revue des études grecques. VII. (1894.) 68–80.

Papal Letters.

Epistolarum Innocentii III libri XVI. Ed. Baluze, S. Paris. 1682. Also MPL. CCXV, CCXVI.

Regesta Honorii Papae III. Ed. Pressutti, P. 2 vols. Rome. 1888–95.

Les Registres de Grégoire IX. Ed. Auvray, L. Vols. I, II and III, pts. 1 and 2. EcfrAR. Paris. 1896–1910.

Les Registres d'Innocent IV. Ed. Berger, É. Vols. I–III. EcfrAR. Paris. 1884–97.

Les Registres d'Alexandre IV. Ed. Bourel de la Roncière, C., etc. Vol. I. EcfrAR. Paris. 1895–1902.

Pavlov. *Συνοδικὸν Γράμμα τοῦ 1213ου ἔτους περὶ γάμου τινὸς μεταξὺ Ἕλληνος αὐτοκράτορος καὶ τῆς θυγατρὸς Ἀρμενίου ἡγεμόνος.* *In* VV. IV (1897). 160–6.

Sakellíon, I. *Ἀνέκδοτος ἐπιστολὴ τοῦ αὐτοκράτορος Ἰωάννου Δούκα Βατάτση πρὸς τὸν πάπαν Γρηγόριον.* *In* Ἀθηναῖον. I. 369–78. Athens. 1873.

Tafel, G. L. F. and Thomas, G. M. Urkunden zur älteren Handels- und Staatsgeschichte der Republik Venedig. (Fontes Rerum Austriac. II. Vols. XII, XIII.) Vienna. 1856.

Vasil'evski, V. Epirotica saeculi XIII. (Letters of Joánnes Apokaukos, Metropolitan of Naupactus.) *In* VV. III (1896). 233–99.

III. CONTEMPORARY AUTHORITIES.

Abū'l-Fidā' Ismā'īl. Résumé de l'histoire des Croisades tiré des Annales. Rec. hist. Cr., Hist. Orient. Vol. I. 1872.

Abulpharagius (Barhebraeus). Historia Orientalis. Ed. Pocock, E. Oxford. 1672.

Acropolites, Georgius. Ed. Heisenberg, A. 2 vols. Leipsic. 1903.

Albricus Monachus Trium Fontium. Chronicon. MGH. Script. XXIII. 1874.

῾Η ῞Αλωσις τῆς Κωνσταντινουπόλεως. *In* Buchon, J. A. Recherches historiques sur la principauté française de Morée. Vol. II. 335–67. Paris. 1845.
Anonymous (c. 1361). Βίος τοῦ ῾Αγίου ᾿Ιωάννου Βασιλέως τοῦ ᾿Ελεήμονος. Ed. Heisenberg, A. BZ. XIV (1905). 193–233.
Anonymous (? Th. Scutariota). Σύνοψις Χρονική. *In* Sáthas, K. N. Μεσαιωνικὴ βιβλιοθήκη. Vol. VII. *See Gen. Bibl.* IV.
Arsenius (Patriarch). Διαθήκη. MPG. CXL.
Chomatianus, Demetrius. Πονήματα διάφορα. *In* Pitra, J. B. Analecta sacra et classica. Vol. VII. Paris. 1891.
Continuator Caffari. Annales Genuenses. Ed. Muratori. RR.II.SS. 1st edn. Vol. VI. Also ed. Belgrano, L. T. etc. *in* Fonti.
Dandolo, A. Chronicon. Ed. Muratori. RR.II.SS. 1st edn. Vol. XII.
Ephraim. Imperatorum et Patriarcharum Recensus. CSHB. 1840.
Eugenicus. Τῇ Τραπεζουντίων πόλει ἐγκωμιαστικὴ ἔκφρασις. *In* Tafel, G. L. F., Eustathii opuscula. pp. 370–3. Frankfort. 1832.
Georgius Cyprius. Διηγήσεως Μερικῆς Λόγος. MPG. CXLII.
Germanus II (Patriarch). ᾿Επιστολαί. MPG. CXL. Also in Sáthas, K. N. Μεσαιωνικὴ βιβλιοθήκη. Vol. II. 5–49. *See Gen. Bibl.* IV.
Gregoras, Nicephorus. ῾Ρωμαϊκὴ ῾Ιστορία. Vol. I. CSHB. 1829.
Hethum, Count of Gorigos. Chronological Table. Rec. hist. Cr., Doc. Arméniens. Vol. I. 1869.
Ibn al-Athīr. Extracts from the Chronicle. Rec. hist. Cr., Hist. Orient. Vol. II, 1. 1887.
Joinville, Jean Sire de. Histoire de Saint Louis. Ed. Wailly, N. de. Paris. 1874.
Martin da Canal. La Cronique des Veniciens. ASI. Ser. I. Vol. VIII. 1845.
Michael Palaeologus. De Vitâ Suâ. Ed. Troitski, J. G. St Petersburg. 1885.
Monachus Patavinus. Chronicon. Ed. Muratori. RR.II.SS. 1st edn. Vol. VIII. Re-ed. Jaffé, P. as Annales S. Justinae *in* MGH. Script. XIX. And re-ed. Botteghi, L. A. as Chronicon Marchiae Tarvisinae et Lombardiae in the new edn. of Muratori (*see Gen. Bibl.* IV). 1916.
Navagiero, A. Storia della Repubblica Veneziana. Ed. Muratori. RR.II.SS. 1st edn. Vol. XXIII.
Nicephorus Blemmydes. Opera. MPG. CXLII. 1865.
—— Διήγησις Μερική. Ed. Heisenberg, A. Leipsic. 1896.
—— Epistulae. *In* Festa's edn. of Theodorus Ducas Lascaris. *See below.*
—— Inedita. *Ibid.* And ed. Bury, J. B. *in* BZ. VI (1897). 526–37.
Nicetas Choniates. ῾Ιστορία. CSHB. 1835.
—— Σελέντιον and two addresses to Theodore I Lascaris. *In* Sáthas, K. N. Μεσαιωνικὴ βιβλιοθήκη. Vol. I. 97–136. *See Gen. Bibl.* IV.
Nicodemus Agioreites. ᾿Ασματικὴ ᾿Ακολουθία τοῦ ῾Αγίου Βασιλέως ᾿Ιωάννου τοῦ Βατάτση τοῦ ᾿Ελεήμονος. Ed. Agathángelos, K. Constantinople. 1872.
Nicolaus de Jamsilla. Historia de rebus gestis Frederici II Imperatoris ejusque filiorum. Ed. Muratori. RR.II.SS. 1st edn. Vol. VIII.
Pachymeres, Georgius. Μιχαὴλ Παλαιολόγος. Vol. I. CSHB. 1835.
Panarétos. Περὶ τῶν τῆς Τραπεζοῦντος βασιλέων, τῶν μεγάλων Κομνηνῶν. Ed. Lámpros, Sp. P. *in* Νέος ῾Ελληνομνήμων. Vol. IV. 257–95. Athens. 1907. Also *in* Tafel, G. L. F. Eustathii opuscula. pp. 362–70. Frankfort. 1832. Also *in* Fallmerayer, J. P. Original-fragmente. Abhand. d. hist. Cl. d. k. bayer. Akad. Vol. IV. Abt. 1. Munich. 1844.
Papadópoulos-Kerameús, A. Fontes Historiae Imperii Trapezuntini. St Petersburg. 1897. *Cf.* BZ. VI (1897). 630–2. XI (1902). 79–104. A portion of these sources is also to be found in Fallmerayer, J. P. Original-fragmente. Abhand. d. hist. Cl. d. k. bayer. Akad. Vol. III. Abt. 3. Munich. 1843.
Paris, Matthew. Chronica Majora. Ed. Luard, H. R. Vols. III–V. (Rolls.) 1876–80.
—— Historia Minor. Ed. Madden, F. Vols. II, III. *Ibid.* 1866–9.
Phrantzes, Georgius. Χρονικόν. CSHB. 1838.
Rubruquis, Guillaume de (William of Rubruck). Itinerarium. *In* Bergeron, P. Voyages faits principalement en Asie. Vol. I. Hague. 1735.
Sanudo, M. Vite de' Duchi di Venezia. Ed. Muratori. RR.II.SS. 1st edn. Vol. XXII. Re-ed. Monticolo, G. in the new edn. *See Gen. Bibl.* IV.

Sanudo Torsello, Marino. Fragmentum. *In* Hopf, K. Chroniques gréco-romanes. pp. 171–4. *See Gen. Bibl.* IV.
Sĕmpad (Smbat). Chronique du Royaume de la Petite Arménie. *In* Rec. hist. Cr., Doc. Arméniens. Vol. I. 1869.
Spandugino. De la origine de li Imperatori Ottomani. *In* Sáthas, K. N. Μνημεῖα Ἑλληνικῆς Ἱστορίας. IX. 140–2. Paris. 1890.
Theodorus Ducas Lascaris. Epistulae CCXVII. Ed. Festa, N. Florence. 1898. *Cf.* Festa, N. Noterelle alle epistole di Teodoro Duca Lascaris. *In* Studi italiani di filologia classica. VI. 228, 458. VII. 204. Florence and Rome. 1898–9. *Cf. also* BZ. IX (1900). 211–23. XI (1902). 16–32.
—— Éloge de Nicée. Ed. Bachmann, L. Rostock. 1847.
—— Éloge de l'empereur Vatatzes. Partially publ. by Uspenski, F. *in* ZMNP. (1877). 194.
Theodorus Metochites. Νικαεύς. *In* Sáthas, K. N. Μεσαιωνικὴ βιβλιοθήκη. Vol. I. 139–53. *See Gen. Bibl.* IV.
Villehardouin, Geoffroy de. La conquête de Constantinople. Avec la continuation de Henri de Valenciennes. Ed. Wailly, N. de. Paris. 1872. Also ed. Bouchet, É. 2 vols. Paris. 1891.
Vincent of Beauvais. Speculum historiale. Lib. XXX. Cap. 144. Douai. 1624.
William of Tyre, Continuation of. Rec. hist. Cr., Hist. Occident. Vol. II. 1859.
Xanthopulus, Nicephorus Callistus. Διήγησις περὶ τῶν ἐπισκόπων Βυζαντίου. MPG. CXLVII.

IV. MODERN WORKS.

(a) General.

Fallmerayer, J. P. Geschichte des Kaiserthums von Trapezunt. *See Gen. Bibl.* V.
Finlay, G. History of Greece. Ed. Tozer, H. F. Vols. III, IV. *See Gen. Bibl.* V.
Gardner, A. The Lascarids of Nicaea. *See Gen. Bibl.* V.
Joannides, S. Ἱστορία καὶ στατιστικὴ Τραπεζοῦντος. Constantinople. 1870.
Meliarákes, A. Ἱστορία τοῦ Βασιλείου τῆς Νικαίας καὶ τοῦ Δεσποτάτου τῆς Ἠπείρου (1204–61). *See Gen. Bibl.* V.
Sabatier, J. Description générale des monnaies byzantines. Vol. II. *See Gen. Bibl.* III.
Wroth, W. Catalogue of the coins of the Vandals, etc., and of the Empires of Thessalonica, etc. *See Gen. Bibl.* III.

(b) Monographs.

Diehl, C. Constance de Hohenstaufen, Impératrice de Nicée. *In* Figures byzantines. 2de série. 207–25. *See Gen. Bibl.* V.
—— Mosaïques byzantines de Nicée. BZ. I (1892). 74–85, 340–1, 525–6. Republd *in* Études byzantines. *See Gen. Bibl.* V.
Dräseke, J. Theodoros (II) Laskaris. BZ. III (1894). 498–515.
Freshfield, E. The Palace of the Greek Emperors of Nicaea at Nymphio. *In* Archaeologia. XLIX. London. 1886. 382–90.
Heisenberg, A. Analecta. Munich. 1901.
—— Kaiser Johannes Batatzes der Barmherzige. BZ. XIV (1905). 160–233. *Cf.* XVI (1907). 143–8.
Kurtz, E. Christophóros von Ankyra als Exarch des Patriarchen Germanós II. BZ. XVI. 120–42.
Lámpros (Lambros), P. Unedirte Münze Michaels Paläologus, des Kaisers von Nicäa. Zeit. f. Numismatik. IX (1882). 44–6.
Manfroni, C. Le relazioni fra Genova, l' Impero bizantino, e i Turchi. *In* Atti della Soc. Ligure di Storia Patria. XXVIII. 577 ff. Genoa. 1898.
Millet, G. Les monastères et les églises de Trébizonde. *In* Bull. de Correspondance hellénique. XIX. 419–59. Paris. 1895.
—— Inscriptions byzantines de Trébizonde. *Ibid.* XX (1896). 496–501.

Papadópoulos-Kerameús, A. Θεόδωρος Εἰρηνικὸς πατριάρχης οἰκουμενικὸς ἐν Νικαίᾳ. BZ. x (1901). 182–92.
Pappadópoulos, J. B. Théodore II Lascaris, Empereur de Nicée. Paris. 1908.
Pfaffenhofen, F. de. Essai sur les aspres comnénats. Paris. 1847.
Schlumberger, G. Sceaux byzantins inédits. *In* Revue des études grecques. iv (1891). 130–1. xiii (1900). 480–1. [Seals of Theodore Lascaris and Theodore III Vatatzes Ducas Lascaris.]
—— Le tombeau d'une Impératrice byzantine à Valence. *In* Revue des deux mondes. 15 March, 1902.
Strzygowski, J. Les chapiteaux de Sainte Sophie à Trébizonde. *In* Bull. de Correspondance hellénique. xix (1895). 517–72.
Texier, C. Tombeaux du moyen âge à Kutayah et à Nymphi. RA. i (1844). 320-5.
Wulff. Ἡ ἀρχιτεκτονικὴ καὶ τὰ ψηφιδωτὰ τοῦ ἐν Νικαίᾳ ναοῦ τῆς Κοιμήσεως τῆς Θεοτόκου. *In* VV. vi (1900). 315–425. *Cf.* BZ. x (1901). 707–10.
—— Die Koimesiskirche in Nicäa und ihre Mosaiken. Strasbourg. 1903. *Cf.* BZ. xii (1903). 634–6.

CHAPTERS XVII AND XVIII.

THE BALKAN STATES (1186–1483).

I. SPECIAL BIBLIOGRAPHIES.

Bianu, J. and Hodoş, N. Bibliografia Românescă veche 1508–1830. Vol. I and 3 parts. [To 1784.] Bucharest. 1903–7.
Bulletin de l'Institut pour l'étude de l'Europe sud-orientale. 9 vols. Bucharest. 1914–22. [Contains bibliography and reviews of practically every new work about the Balkan peninsula.]
Hammer-Purgstall, J. von. Geschichte des osmanischen Reiches. Vol. I. *See Gen. Bibl.* v. pp. xxix–xlii. [Contains a bibliography of the Oriental sources down to 1453.]
Legrand, É. Bibliographie albanaise. Description rais. des ouvrages publ. en Albanais ou relat. à l'Albanie du xve siècle jusqu'à 1900. Complétée par H. Gûys. Paris. 1912.
Nopcsa, F. Az Albániárol szóló legujabb irodalom. ("The most recent literature on Albania.") Buda-Pest. 1918.
Srpska Kraljevska Akademija. Essai de bibliographie française sur les Serbes et les Croates (1554–1900). Belgrade. 1900.
Tenneroni, A. Per la bibliografia del Montenegro. 2nd edn. Rome. 1896.

II. PRIMARY AUTHORITIES.

(a) Original Documents.

Fejér, G. Codex diplomaticus Hungariae ecclesiasticus et civilis. Vols. III–XI. *See Gen. Bibl.* IV.
Fermendžin, E. Acta Bosnae, potissimum ecclesiastica. MHSM. Vol. XXIII. Agram. 1892.
Gelcich, J. and Thallóczy, L. von. Diplomatarium Relationum Reipublicae Ragusanae cum Regno Hungariae. Buda-Pest. 1887.
Hasdeu, B. P. Arhiva istorică a Românieĭ. Vol. I. Bucharest. 1865.
Hurmuzaki, E. de. Documente privitóre la Istoria Românilor. Vols. I, II, pts. i and ii, XIV. Bucharest. 1887–1915.
Innocent III. Opera Omnia. Vols. I, II. MPL. Vols. CCXIV–XV.
Kukuljević, I. von. Codex diplomaticus Regni Croatiae, Dalmatiae, et Slavoniae. Vol. II. Agram. 1875.
—— Jura Regni Croatiae, Dalmatiae, et Slavoniae. Vol. I. Agram. 1862.
Ljubić, S. Commissiones et Relationes Venetae. Vol. I (1433–1527). MHSM. Vol. VI. Agram. 1876.
—— Listine. 11 vols. *Ibid.* Vols. I–V, IX, XII, XVII, XXI, XXII, XXIV. Agram. 1868–93. [Venetian documents regarding the Southern Slavs, 960–1469.]
Makuscev (Makushev), V. Monumenta historica Slavorum Meridionalium vicinorumque populorum. 2 vols. Warsaw and Belgrade. 1874–82.
Miklosich, F. Monumenta Serbica spectantia historiam Serbiae, Bosnae, Ragusii. Vienna. 1858.
—— and Müller, J. Acta et diplomata graeca medii aevi. Vols. I, II. *See Gen. Bibl.* IV.
Monumenta Hungariae historica. Acta extera. Vols. I–V. 1875–7.
—— Vol. XXXIII. Codex diplomaticus partium Regno Hungariae adnexarum (1198–1526). 1907. *See Gen. Bibl.* IV.

Monumenta Vaticana Hungariae. Series I, Vols. II–IV, VI. Buda-Pest. 1885–91.
Pucić, Count Medo. Spomenici srpski od. g. 1395–1423. Belgrade. 1858.
—— Spomenici srpski iz dubrovačke Arhive. Belgrade. 1862.
Rački, F. and Gelcich, J. Monumenta Ragusina. Libri Reformationum. 5 vols. [1301–96.] MSHM. Vols. X, XIII, XXVII–XXIX. Agram. 1879–97.
Šafařík, P. J. Památky dřevního pismenictví Jihoslovanův. Prague. 1851.
Smičiklas, T. Codex diplomaticus Regni Croatiae, Dalmatiae, et Slavoniae. Vols. III–XIII (1201–90). Agram. 1905–15.
Thallóczy, L. de, Jireček, C., and Sufflay, E. de. Acta et diplomata res Albaniae mediae aetatis illustrantia. Vols. I, II (344–1406). *See Gen. Bibl.* IV. [Contains a bibliography.]
Theiner, A. Vetera Monumenta historica Hungariam sacram illustrantia. 2 vols. Rome. 1859–60.
—— Vetera Monumenta Slavorum Meridionalium historiam illustrantia. Vol. I. Rome. 1863.
Zakonik Stefana Dušana, cara Srpskog, 1349 e 1354. Ed. Novaković, S. Belgrade. 1898. [New edition of Dušan's Code. Other editions are those of Šafařík, P. J. Prague. 1851; of Jireček, H. *in* Svod zákonův slovanských (Codex legum Slavonicarum). Prague. 1880; and of Zigel, M. Zakonnik Stefana Dushana. St Petersburg. 1872. Boué, A. La Turquie d'Europe. IV. 426 ff. Paris. 1840. Contains a French transl. of articles 1–105. *Cf.* Journal des Savants (1886), pp. 82–86, for a review of Jireček's edition and a summary of the Code by Dareste, R.]

(*b*) Contemporary Authorities.

Acropolites, Georgius. Ed. Heisenberg, A. 2 vols. Leipsic. 1903.
Adam, G. Directorium ad passagium faciendum. Rec. hist. Cr., Doc. arméniens. II. 365–517. [The part about Bulgaria and Serbia is pp. 422–85.]
Albricus Monachus Trium Fontium. Chronicon. MGH. Script. Vol. XXIII. 1874.
Annales Senenses. MGH. Script. Vol. XIX. 1866.
Bonfinius, A. Rerum Hungaricarum decades quatuor cum dimidia. 3rd edn. Hanover. 1606.
Brocquière, B. de la. Voyage d'Outremer. *In* vol. XII of Recueil de voyages et de documents. Ed. Schefer, Ch. Paris. 1892. [Pp. 582–692 refer to the Near East.]
Callimachus, P. De Rebus gestis a Vladislao Polonorum atque Hungarorum Rege ad Casimirum Regem. *In* Schwandtner, J. G. Scriptores Rerum Hungaricarum. Vol. I. pp. 433–518. Vienna. 1746; or vol. II. pp. 40–142. Vienna. 1768.
Cantacuzene, John. 3 vols. CSHB. 1828–32.
Chalcocondyles, Laonicus. CSHB. 1843.
Chomatianus, Demetrius. Πονήματα διάφορα. *In* Pitra, J. B. Analecta sacra et classica. Vol. VII. Paris and Rome. 1891.
Chronique du Religieux de Saint-Denis. Ed. Bellaguet, M.L. Vol. II. pp. 386–91. Paris. 1840. [Contains accounts of the battles of Kossovo and Nicopolis.]
Critobulus. *In* Müller, C. Fragmenta historicorum graecorum. Vol. V. *See Gen. Bibl.* IV.
Cydones, Demetrius. Ῥωμαίοις Συμβουλευτικός and Συμβουλευτικὸς ἕτερος περὶ Καλλιπόλεως αἰτήσαντος τοῦ Μουράτου. MPG. Vol. CLIV. pp. 961–1035. Paris. 1866.
Danilo [Serbian Archbishop]. Živote kraljeva i arhiepiskopa srpskih. Ed. Daničić, G. Agram. 1866.
Długosz, J. Historia Polonica. Vols. II–V (=Opera Omnia. Vols. XI–XIV). Cracow. 1873–8.
Domentijan. Život Svetoga Simeuna i Svetoga Save. Ed. Daničić, G. Belgrade. 1865. [French transl. of C. Živković's abridgment (made in 1794) of this biography by Chodźko, A. Légendes slaves du moyen âge, 1169–1237. Les Nemania, vie de St Syméon et de St Sabba. Paris. 1858.]
Ducas. CSHB. 1834.

Froissart, Chroniques de. Ed. Kervyn de Lettenhove. Vols. xv and xvi. Brussels. 1870–7.
Gregoras, Nicephorus. CSHB. 3 vols. 1829–55.
Histoire de Charles VI, Roy de France, par un autheur contemporain, Religieux de l'Abbaye de St Denis. Vol. i. Paris. 1663.
Mazzerius (=Maizières, P. de). Vita S. Petri Thomasii. *In* ASBoll. 29 Jan. Vol. ii. Antwerp. 1643. [Pp. 997–9 give a description of Dušan and his court in 1355.]
Metochites, Th. Πρεσβευτικός. *In* Sáthas, K. N. Μεσαιωνικὴ βιβλιοθήκη. Vol. i. pp. 154–93. *See Gen. Bibl.* iv.
Nicetas Choniates. CSHB. 1835.
—— Ἐπαναγνωστικὸν εἰς τὸν πατριάρχην καὶ τὴν σύνοδον. *In* Sáthas, K. N. Μεσαιωνικὴ βιβλιοθήκη. Vol. i. pp. 78–90. *See Gen. Bibl.* iv.
Pachymeres, Georgius. 2 vols. CSHB. 1835.
Phrantzes, Georgius. CSHB. 1838.
Reisen des Johannes Schiltberger aus München. Ed. Neumann, K. F. Munich. 1859. Engl. transl. The bondage and travels of Johann Schiltberger. London. 1879.
Sa'd-ad-Dīn. Chronica dell' origine e progressi di casa ottomana. Transl. Bratutti, V. 2 vols. Vienna and Madrid. 1649–52.
Servion, J. Gestez et chroniques de la Mayson de Savoye. Vol. ii. Ed. Bollati, F. E. Turin. 1879.
Srpske narodne pjesme. Belgrade. 1895. [The national edition of Vuk Karadžić's collection of Serbian ballads.] French selection and transl. by Dozon, A. Poésies populaires serbes. Paris. 1877. English by Bowring, Sir J. Servian popular poetry. London. 1827; and by Meredith, Owen. Serbski Pesme; or, National Songs of Servia. London. 1861; and by Low, D. H. The ballads of Marko Kraljević. Cambridge, 1922. Italian by Kasandrić, P. Canti popolari serbi e croati. Milan. 1914.
Thomas Archidiaconus Spalatensis. Historia Salonitanorum Pontificum atque Spalatensium. MHSM. Vol. xxvi. Agram. 1894.
Thurócz, J. de. Chronica Hungarorum. *In* Schwandtner, J. G. Scriptores Rerum Hungaricarum. Vol. i. 39–291. Vienna. 1746; or vol. i. 47–366. Vienna. 1766.
Vechele cronice moldovenesti pana la Ureche. Ed. Bogdan, J. Bucharest, 1891.
Yanich, V. and Hankey, C. P. Lives of the Serbian Saints. London. 1921.

III. SECONDARY AUTHORITIES.

Angyal, David. Le traité de paix de Szeged avec les Turcs (1444). (Extract from Revue de Hongrie, 15 March, 15 April, 1911.) Buda-Pest. 1911.
Borchgrave, É. de. L'empereur Étienne Douchan et la péninsule balcanique au xive siècle. Brussels. 1884.
Coquelle, P. Histoire du Monténégro et de la Bosnie. Paris. 1895.
Ducange, C. du Fresne. Illyricum vetus et novum. Pressburg. 1749.
Erber, T. La Contea di Poglizza: studio storico. Zara. 1886.
Farlati, D. Illyricum Sacrum. Vols. i–viii. Venice. 1751–1819.
Galanti, A. L'Albania. Rome. 1901.
Gelcich, G. La Zedda e la Dinastia dei Balšidi. Spalato. 1899.
Hammer-Purgstall, J. von. Geschichte des osmanischen Reiches. Vols. i and ii. *See Gen. Bibl.* v.
Hecquard, H. Histoire et description de la Haute Albanie ou Guégarie. Paris. *n.d.* [1858–64.]
Jireček, C. Geschichte der Bulgaren. *See Gen. Bibl.* v.
—— Geschichte der Serben. *See Gen. Bibl.* v.
—— Staat und Gesellschaft im mittelalterlichen Serbien. Studien zur Kulturgeschichte des 13–15 Jahrhunderts. 1–3. Teil. *In* Denkschriften d. KAW. Vols. lvi and lviii. Vienna. 1912–14.
Jorga, N. Geschichte des rumänischen Volkes. Vol. i. *See Gen. Bibl.* v.
—— Geschichte des osmanischen Reiches. Vols. i and ii. *See Gen. Bibl.* v.

Jorga, N. Brève histoire de l'Albanie et du peuple Albanais. Bucharest. 1919.
—— Istoria Romînilor din Peninsula Balcanica. Bucharest. 1919.
Klaić, V. Geschichte Bosniens. German transl. Bojničić, I. von. Leipsic. 1885.
Marković, G. Gli Slavi ed i Papi. Vol. II. Agram. 1897.
Mijatović, C. Despot Gjuragj Branković. 2 vols. Belgrade. 1880–2. 2nd edn. of vol. I. Belgrade. 1907.
Miklosich, F. Die serbischen Dynasten Crnojević. Ein Beitrag zur Geschichte von Montenegro. Vienna. 1886.
Orbini, M. Il regno degli Slavi hoggi corrottamente detti Schiavoni. Pesaro. 1601.
Petrović, V. Istoriya o Chernoy Gorê. Moscow. 1754. Italian transl. by Ciàmpoli, D. Lanciano. 1901.
Šafařík, P. J. Slavische Alterthümer. Vol. II. German transl. Leipsic. 1844.
—— Geschichte der südslavischen Literatur. Vol. III. Ed. Jireček, J. Prague. 1865.
Stevenson, F. S. A history of Montenegro. London. *n.d.* [1913.]
Temperley, H. W. V. History of Serbia. *See Gen. Bibl.* v.
Thallóczy, L. von. Illyrisch-Albanische Forschungen. 2 vols. Munich and Leipsic. 1916.
—— Studien zur Geschichte Bosniens und Serbiens im Mittelalter. German transl. Eckhart, F. Munich and Leipsic. 1914.
Villari, L. The Republic of Ragusa. London. 1904.
Xénopol, A. D. Histoire des Roumains de la Dacie Trajane. *See Gen. Bibl.* v.
Zinkeisen, J. W. Geschichte des osmanischen Reiches in Europa. Vols. I and II. Gotha. 1840–54.

IV. PERIODICAL LITERATURE.

Archives de l'Orient latin. Vol. II. Paris. 1884.
Archiv für slavische Philologie. Vols. VIII–XXXIV. Berlin. 1886–1912.
Bées, N. A. Über einen Kodex der serbischen Königin Milica oder Helena, als Nonne Eugenia genannt, in den Meteoren. Vol. XXXIV. 298–304.
Bogdan, J. Ein Beitrag zur bulgarischen und serbischen Geschichtschreibung. Vol. XIII. 481–543.
—— Eine bulgarische Urkunde des Caren Joan Sracimir. Vol. XVII. 544–7.
Ćorović, V. Serbische Volkslieder über den Abgang des heil. Sava zu den Mönchen. Vol. XXVIII. 629–33.
Ivić, A. Wann wurden die Reliquien des serbischen heil. Sava verbrannt? *Ibid.* 90–3.
Jireček, C. Eine altserbische Glockeneinschrift. Vol. VIII. 133.
—— Zur Würdigung der neuentdeckten bulgarischen Chronik. Vol. XIV. 255–77.
—— Reiterspiele im mittelalterlichen Serbien. [At Priština.] *And* Nachtrag zu den Reiterspielen. [At Sinj.] Vols. XIV, 73–5; XV, 457–9.
—— Stanjanin. [A phrase in Dušan's Code.] Vol. XIV. 75–7.
—— Das Gesetzbuch des serbischen Caren Stephan Dušan. Vol. XXII. 144–214.
Novaković, Stojan. Les problèmes serbes. Vols. XXXIII, 438–66; XXXIV, 203–33.
Radonić, J. Der Grossvojvode von Bosnien Sandalj Hranić-Kosača. Vol. XIX. 380–465.
Stanojević, S. Die Biographie Stefan Lazarević's von Konstantin dem Philosophen als Geschichtsquelle. Vol. XVIII. 409–72.
Atti del R. Istituto Veneto. Venice. 1873–4.
Cecchetti, B. Intorno agli stabilimenti politici della Repubblica Veneta nell' Albania. Vol. III. Ser. 4. pp. 977–98.
BZ.
Čajkanović, V. Über die Echtheit eines serbisch-byzantinischen Verlobungsringes. Vol. XIX (1910), 111–14. [Supporting K. Krumbacher's article in Sitzungsberichte der kgl. bayerischen Akad. der Wissensch., 1906 pp. 421–51, which ascribed the ring to Stephen Radoslav.]
Papadópoulos-Kerameús, A. Δυρραχηνά. Vol. XIV (1905). 568–74.

EHR.
Bain, R. Nisbet. The Siege of Belgrade by Muhammad II, July 1–23, 1456. Vol. VII (1892). 235–52.
Miller, W. The Founder of Montenegro. Vol. XXV (1910). 308. Republished in Essays on the Latin Orient. *See Gen. Bibl.* v.
—— Bosnia before the Turkish Conquest. Vol. XIII (1898). 643–6. Republished in Essays on the Latin Orient. *See Gen. Bibl.* v.
Journal of the British and American Archaeological Society of Rome.
Miller, W. Balkan Exiles in Rome. Vol. IV. No. 5 (1912). pp. 479–97. Republished in Essays on the Latin Orient. *See Gen. Bibl.* v.
JHS.
Miller, W. Valona. Vol. XXXVII (1917). pp. 184–94. Republished in Essays on the Latin Orient. *See Gen. Bibl.* v.
Quarterly Review.
Miller, W. The Mediaeval Serbian Empire. Vol. 226. No. 449 (1916). pp. 488–507. Republished in Essays on the Latin Orient. *See Gen. Bibl.* v.
Sitzungsberichte der k. böhmischen Gesellschaft der Wissenschaften. 1885. Prague. 1885.
Jireček, C. Die Beziehungen der Ragusaner zu Serbien unter Car Uroš und König Vlkašin (1355–71). pp. 114–41.
SKAW. Vienna. 1852.
Müller, J. Byzantinische Analekten. Vol. IX. 392–3; 403–10.
Wissenschaftliche Mittheilungen aus Bosnien und der Hercegovina. 12 vols. Vienna. 1893–1912.
Barišić, Fra. R. Kloster und Kirche der Franziskaner in Sućeska. Vol. I (1893). 268–80.
Bašagić, I. Das Todesurtheil des Stjepan Tomašević, letzten bosnischen Königs. Vol. I (1893). 496.
Čatić, A. Volkssage über die Ruine von Prozor. Vol. VI (1898). 654–5. [That it was the last Bosnian castle to fall, in 1469.]
Fraknói, Bishop W. Cardinal Carvajal in Bosnien, 1457. Vol. I (1893). 330–2.
Franić, D. Die Lage auf der Balkanhalbinsel zu Beginn des 13 Jahrhunderts. Vol. V (1897). 304–36.
Ippen, Th. Alte Kirchen und Kirchenruinen in Albanien. Vols. VII (1889). 231–42; and VIII (1900). 131–44.
—— Verschiedene Altersstufen in Albanien. Vol. X (1907). 3 ff. [Pp. 23–70 deal with the mediaeval remains.]
Jagić, V. Die goldene Bulle des Despoten Stefan [Lazarević]. Vol. I. 314–16.
Jireček, C. Glasinac im Mittelalter. *Ibid.* 320–2.
Lilek, E. Die Schatzkammer der Familie Hranići (Košaca). Vol. II (1894). 125–51.
Pavich von Pfauenthal, A. Beiträge zur Geschichte der Republik Poljica bei Spalato. Vol. X. 156–344.
Pavich von Pfauenthal, A., Matić, T., and Rešetar, M. Statut der Poljica. Vol. XII (1912). 324–40.
Peez, C. Achmed Pascha Hercegović. Vol. IV (1896). 395–6.
Pogatschnig, L. Alter Bergbau in Bosnien. Vol. II. 152–7.
Ruvarac, H. Katharina, die Tochter Tvrtko's I. Vol. I. 173–8.
—— Draga, Danica, und Resa. Vol. II. 163–72.
—— Zwei bosnische Königinnen. Vols. III (1895). 372–87; and IV. 395. [Catherine and Maria.]
—— Die Regierung des Banus Tvrtko (1353–77). Vol. IV. 324–42.
Šišić, F. v. Die Schlacht bei Nikopolis (25 September, 1396). Vol. VI. 291–327.
Stratimirović, G. v. Bosnische Königsschlösser. Vol. I. 323–7.
Thallóczy, L. v. Herzog Hervoja und sein Wappen. Vol. II. 108–24. *Cf.* his Studien, pp. 303–6. *See above,* III.
—— Bruchstücke aus der Geschichte der nordwestlichen Balkanländer. Vol. III. 298–371.

Thallóczy, L. v. Wie und wann wurde Hervoja Grossvojvode von Bosnien? Vol. vi. 284–90.
—— Untersuchungen über den Ursprung des bosnischen Banates mit besonderer Berücksichtigung der Urkunden im Körmender Archive. Vol. xi (1909). 237–85. Reprinted in his Studien, pp. 1–75. *See above*, iii.
Truhelka, C. Auszug aus der Chronik des Fra Nikolaus von Lašva. Vol. i. 281–2. [A deed of Stephen Tomašević of 1461.]
—— Der Maler des Wappenbuches von Fojnica. *Ibid.* 337–41.
—— Die Katakomben von Jajce. Vol. ii. 94–107.
—— Verzeichniss der bosnischen, serbischen, und bulgarischen Münzen des Landesmuseums in Sarajevo. Vol. iv. 303–23.
—— Eine handschriftliche Chronik aus Sarandapon. *Ibid.* 363–80.
—— Eine Inschrift des Banus Kulin. Vol. vii. 215–20.
—— Das mittelalterliche Staats- und Gerichtswesen in Bosnien. Vol. x. 71–155.
—— Der bosnische Münzenfund von Ribiči. Vol. xi. 184–236.
—— Chronikalische Notizen im "Liber Reformationum" des Archivs in Ragusa (1395–9). *Ibid.* 369–74.
—— Die Klosterchronik von Fojnica. Vol. xii. 301–23. [Important document of 1461.]
Vjekoslav, C. Eine Münze Georgs II Stracimir geprägt in der Stadt Scutari. Vol. vi. 538–40.
—— Beschreibung einiger bosnischen Münzen des städtischen Museums in Essegg. Vol. vii. 221–30.
Vuletić-Vukasović, V. Bündnissvertrag Herzog Hervojes und der Republik Ragusa gegen König Ostoja von Bosnien. Vol. iv. 390–3.

Articles too numerous for citation may be found in:
Académie Roumaine. Bulletin de la section historique. 5 vols. Bucharest. 1913–21.
Glas srpske kraljevske akademije, drugi razred. Belgrade. 1887 ff.
Glasnik srpskoga učenog društva. Belgrade. 1841–91.
Rad jugoslavenske akademije znanosti i umjetnosti. Agram. 1867 ff.
Sbornik za narodni umotvoreniya, nauka i knizhnina. Sofia. 1889 ff.
Spomenik srbske kraljevske akademije. Belgrade. 1888 ff.

CHAPTER XIX.

ATTEMPTS AT REUNION OF THE GREEK AND LATIN CHURCHES.

I. SOURCES.

(i) Collections of Documents.

Jorga, N. Notes et extraits pour servir à l'hist. des croisades au xve siècle. 5 vols. Paris and Bucharest. 1899–1915.
Mansi. Concilia. New edn. Vols. xix–xxxii. *See Gen. Bibl.* iv.
Theiner, A. Monumenta spectantia ad unionem Ecclesiarum graecae et romanae. Vienna. 1872.

(ii) Acts of Councils. Constitutions of Popes and Patriarchs.

Council of Lyons, 1274. Mansi. xxv. 38–136. *See also* Delisle, L. Recueils épist. de Bérard de Naples (Notices et extr. des MSS de la Bibl. Nationale). Paris. xxvii, 2. 1879. pp. 87–167. *Ibid.* pp. 150–63. [Latin transl. of documents laid before the Council of Lyons by the Greek ambassadors.]
Council of Basle, 1431–9. Mansi. xxx–xxxi a. 1–247.
Councils of Ferrara and Florence, 1438–9. Mansi. xxxi a–xxxi b.
Greek Council of St Sophia, 1450. Mansi. New edn. xxxii. Paris. 1912. pp. 99–114.
Diplomas of patriarchs of Constantinople. Miklosich, F. and Müller, J. Acta et diplomata graeca. Vols. i and ii. *See Gen. Bibl.* iv.

(iii) Correspondence of Emperors, Popes and Patriarchs.

Jaffé. Regesta Pontif. Romanorum (to 1198). *See Gen. Bibl.* iv. Potthast, A. Regesta Pontif. Romanorum (1198–1304). *See Gen. Bibl.* iv. For papal letters see bibliography in Giry, A. Manuel de diplomatique. pp. 662 ff. *See Gen. Bibl.* i. Most of these letters may be found in Mansi and MPL. The papal registers are printed in Bibl. EcfrAR. from Gregory IX (1227–41) to Benedict XI (1303–4). For letters of Innocent III see MPL. ccxiv.
See also:
Theodore Irenicus, Patriarch of Constantinople. Encyclical to the orthodox still under Latin rule (1214). Ed. Papadopoulos-Kerameus, A. BZ. x. 1901. pp. 187–92.
Lampros (Lambros), Sp. P. Chrysobulles des empereurs byzantins rel. à l'union des Églises (from the Vatican Archives). Neos Hellenomnemon. xi. 1914. pp. 94–128 and 241–54 (with facsimiles).
Schlumberger, G. Bulles d'or byzantines cons. aux arch. vaticanes. RN. 1894. p. 194.

(iv) Graeco-Latin Dogmatic and Polemical Treatises.

Many of these are still unprinted.
Bibliography in Krumbacher, K. Gesch. der byzant. Litteratur. *See Gen. Bibl.* v. pp. 50, 85, 93–5, 113–15.

Among the most important are:

(*a*) *Greek.*

Allatius, L. De Ecclesiae occidentalis atque orientalis perpetua consensione libri III. Cologne. 1648. [Though beyond the scope of this chapter, Allatius is important as representing the Uniate tradition of the Council of Florence. *See* Dict. d'hist. et de géogr. ecclésiastiques. Paris. 1912. *s.v.* Allatius.]

Basil, Archbp. of Ochrida (Achrida). Dialogues with Anselm of Havelberg, 1155. Ed. Schmidt. Des Basilius aus Achrida bisher unedierte Dialoge. Munich. 1901. Letter to Pope Hadrian IV. Mansi. XXXI. 799.

Bessarion, Cardinal, Archbp. of Nicaea. 1395–1472. Oration to the Council of Florence. Works. MPG. CLXI. 137–745.

Camaterus. Ἱερὰ ὁπλοθήκη. Dialogues of the Emperor Manuel Comnenus and the cardinals. 1166–7. MPL. CXLI. 396–613. [Incomplete.] *See* Hergenröther, J. A. G. Photios. III. Ratisbon. 1869. pp. 811–14.

Eustratius, Archbp. of Nicaea. Speech on the Holy Ghost (*c.* 1115). Ed. Demetrakopoulos, A. Ἐκκλησιαστικὴ βιβλιοθήκη. I. Leipsic. 1866. pp. 84–198.

Gennadius, Patriarch of Constantinople. 1453–68. Oration on the Union and treatises against the Latins. MPG. CLX. 320–73.

George of Cyprus, Patriarch of Constantinople. 1241–89. Treatises against Beccus and the Latins. MPG. CXLII. 233–45.

Germanus II, Patriarch (at Nicaea). 1222–40. Against the Latins. MPG. CXL. 621–757.

John Beccus, Patriarch of Constantinople (*ob.* 1293). Oration on the Union and polemical treatises. MPG. CXLI. 16 ff.

Joseph, Bp. of Methona. Apology for the Council of Florence. MPG. CLIX. 960.

Manuel Comnenus and the Patriarch Michael of Anchialus. Dialogue (1169). Ed. Loparev. *In* VV. XIV. 344.

Marcus Eugenicus, Archbp. of Ephesus (*ob.* 1447). Treatises against the Latins and encyclicals against the Council of Florence. MPG. CLX. 1071–1100.

Nicephorus Blemmydes, Patriarch (at Nicaea). 1260. On the Procession of the Holy Ghost. MPG. CXLII. 533–84.

Nicetas, Chartophylax (under Manuel Comnenus). Dialogues on the Holy Ghost (favouring the Latins). MPG. CXXXIX. 169.

Theophylact, Archbp. of Ochrida (Achrida) (end of eleventh century). On the errors of the Latins (*c.* 1091). MPG. CXXVI. 224.

(*b*) *Latin.*

Anselm, Bp. of Havelberg. Controversy with Nicetas, Archbp. of Nicomedia (1136) and Basil, Archbp. of Ochrida (1135). Achery, L. d'. Spicilegium. I. 161. *See Gen. Bibl.* IV. Dräseke, J. Bischof Anselm von Havelberg. ZK. XXXI. 79.

Anselm, St (1033–1109). On the Procession of the Holy Ghost against the Greeks. MPL. CLVIII.

Nicholas of Otranto, Abbot of Casole. Treatises on the Procession of the Holy Ghost and the Azymites. Gk. edn. after Cod. Mosquensis Arsenii. Novgorod. 1896. (Interpreting Benedict, Cardinal of Santa Susanna, at Constantinople, 1205.) *See* Norden, W. Das Papsttum und Byzanz. p. 184. *See Gen. Bibl.* V.

Peter Chrysolanus, Archbp. of Milan, Papal legate to Constantinople, 1113. Oration on the Holy Ghost. MPL. CXXVII. 912–20.

Thomas Aquinas, St. Treatise against the errors of the Greeks addressed to Urban IV. Ed. Fretté, S. E. *in* Opera. XXIX. 344–73. Paris. 1876.

Ugo Eteriano of Pisa. De haeresibus quas Graeci in Latinos devolvunt. MPL. CCII. 232–3.

(v) HISTORY.

Various documents in the different Western or Byzantine historical collections. The principal are referred to in the notes.

II. MODERN WORKS.

(i) GENERAL WORKS.

(*a*) *Bibliography.*

In Krumbacher, K. Gesch. d. byzant. Litteratur. *See Gen. Bibl.* v.

(*b*) *Histories.*

Bréhier, L. L'Église et l'Orient au moyen âge: les Croisades. *See Gen. Bibl.* v.
—— Origin of the Misunderstanding between the Roman Church and the East. The Constructive Quarterly. New York. 1917.
Hefele. Conciliengeschichte. Vols. IV, VIII. *See Gen. Bibl.* v.
Kremos. Ἱστορία τοῦ σχίσματος.... Athens. 1905.
Norden, W. Das Papsttum und Byzanz. *See Gen. Bibl.* v.

(ii) MONOGRAPHS.

(*a*) *From* 1054 *to* 1204.

Chalandon, F. Essai sur le règne d'Alexis Comnène. *See Gen. Bibl.* v.
—— Jean II et Manuel I Comnène. *See Gen. Bibl.* v.
—— Histoire de la domination normande en Italie et en Sicile. 2 vols. Paris. 1907.
Dräseke, J. Bischof Anselm von Havelberg. ZK. XXXI.
—— Nikolaos von Methone. BZ. I. 1892. p. 438.
—— Zu Eustratios von Nikaea. BZ. v. 1896. p. 318.

(*b*) *From* 1204 *to* 1274.

Gerland, E. Geschichte des lateinischen Kaiserreiches. I. 1204–16. *See Gen. Bibl.* v.
Loparev. Ob uniatovê imperatora Manuela Komnena. *In* VV. XIV. p. 344.
Luchaire, A. Innocent III: la question d'Orient. Paris. 1907.
Papadopoulos-Kerameus, A. Documents p. servir à l'hist. de la quatrième croisade. Rev. de l'Orient Latin. I. Paris. 1893. pp. 540–55. [Greek transl. of the Latin mass.]

(*c*) *From* 1274 *to* 1453.

Dräseke, J. Kircheneinigung Kaisers Michael VIII Palaeologos. ZWT. XXXIV. 325.
—— Analecta byzantina. Wandsbeck. 1909. [Monograph on John Beccus.]
—— Johannes Bekkos und seine theologische Zeitgenossen. Neue kirchliche Zeitschrift. XVIII. 1907. p. 877.
—— Zur Friedenschrift des Patriarchen Johannes Bekkos. ZWT. L. 1907. p. 231.
Gay, J. Le pape Clément VI et les affaires d'Orient. 1342–92. Paris. 1904.
Gottlob, A. Aus den Rechnungsbüchern Eugens IV zur Geschichte des Florentinums. HJ. XIV. 1893.
Jorga, N. Gesch. des osmanischen Reiches. Vols. I, II. *See Gen. Bibl.* v.
Kalogeras, N. Markos Eugenikos und Cardinal Bessarion. Revue Internat. de Théologie. 1893. [German transl. from the Greek.]
Omont, H. Projet de réunion des églises grecque et latine sous Charles le Bel en 1327. BEC. 1892. pp. 254–7.
Pears, E. The destruction of the Greek Empire. London. 1903.
Pierling, P. Les Russes au concile de Florence. RQH. LII. 1892.
Schlumberger, G. Un empereur de Byzance à Paris et à Londres. Paris. 1916.
Vasil'ev. Puteshestvie vizantiyskago imperatora Manuila II Paleologa po zapadnoy Evropê. St Petersburg. 1912. *See also* the Bibliographie relative au voyage de Manuel II, by Lampros (Lambros), Sp. P. Neos Hellenomnemon. XIII. 1916. pp. 132–3.
Vast, H. Le Cardinal Bessarion. Paris. 1878. *See also* articles in the periodical *Bessarione*, Rome.

CHAPTER XX.

THE MONGOLS.

[*An asterisk is prefixed to the more important works.*]

I. SPECIAL BIBLIOGRAPHIES.

*Browne, E. G. Literary History of Persia. Vol. II. *See below,* III (*a*).
*—— History of Persian Literature under Tartar Dominion. *See below,* III (*a*).
*EncBr. Vol. XVIII. pp. 719–21, at end of article "Mongols." [For history and linguistics.]
—— Vol. XVIII. p. 712, at end of article "Mongolia." [For geography and ethnology.]
Horn, P. *See below,* III (*b*).
*Howorth, H. H. History of the Mongols. Vol. I. *See below,* III (*a*). [In great detail.]
*Rockhill, W. W. William of Rubruck. *See below,* II (*b*), Rubruquis. [Large number of entries.]

II. SOURCES.

(*a*) HISTORIES.

Abū-l-Fidā' Ismā'īl. Annales Muslemici, Arabice et Latine. Ed. Reiske, J. J. and Adler, J. G. C. 5 vols. Copenhagen. 1789–94.
Aḥmad ibn Arabshāh. Biography of Tīmūr. Arabic text and Latin transl. Manger, S. H. 2 vols. Lieuwarden. 1767–72. French transl. Vattier, P. L'histoire du Grand Tamerlan. Paris. 1658.
'Alā-ad-Dīn 'Aṭā Malik-i-Juwainī. Ta'rikh-i-Jahān-Gushā. (History of Jenghiz Khan.) Ed. Mīrzā Muḥammad of Qazwīn. (Gibb Memorial Series.) 2 vols. London. 1912–16. [Juwainī's Ta'rīkh was completed by the Ta'rīkh-i-Waṣṣaf, which deals with the earlier period omitted by Juwainī. Ed. with German transl. Hammer-Purgstall, J. von. Geschichte Wassafs. Vienna. 1856.]
Bābur, Emperor of Hindustān. Memoirs of Zehīr-ed-Dīn Muhammed Bābur. English transl. Leyden, J. and Erskine, W. Ed. King, Sir Lucas. 2 vols. Oxford. 1921.
Barhebraeus (Abulpharagius, Gregorius). Chronicon Arabicum. Ed. with Latin transl. Pocock, E. Oxford. 1663.
—— Chronicon Syriacum. Ed. with Latin transl. Bruns, P. J. and Kirsch, G. W. 2 vols. Leipsic. 1789.
Ibn aṭ-Ṭiqṭaqà, Al-Fakhrī. Histoire du Khilafat et du Vizirat. Ed. Derenbourg, H. Paris. 1895. French transl. Amar, E. *in* Archives Marocaines. Vol. XVI. Paris. 1910.
Muḥammad Ḥaidar, Dughlāt. Tarīkh-i-Rashīdī. (History of the Moghuls of Central Asia.) English transl. Ross, E. D. Ed. Elias, N. London. 1898.
Muṣṭafà Effendi al-Jannābī. History of Tīmūr. Latin transl. Podesta, J. B. De gestis Timurlenkii seu Tamerlani opusculum turcicum, arabicum, persicum. Vienna. 1680.

Rashīd-ad-Dīn, Ṭabīb. Jami at-Tawārīkh. (History of the Mongols of Persia.) Ed. with French transl. Quatremère, E. Paris. 1836 ff. [For an introduction by Blochet, E., *see below*, III (*a*).]
Sharaf-ad-Dīn 'Alī Yazdī. Ẓafar-Nāmah. Ed. Maulavi Muḥammad Ilahdad. (Bibliotheca Indica. No. 533.) Calcutta. 1885. French transl. Pétis de la Croix, F. Histoire de Timur-Bec. 4 vols. Paris 1722 and Delf 1723. English transl. [Darby, J.] 2 vols. London. 1723.
Ssanang Ssetsen, Chungtaidschi. History of the East Mongols and their dynasty. Ed. with German transl. Schmidt, I. J. St Petersburg. 1829.

(*b*) Travellers' Accounts.

Benjamin ben Jonah of Tudela. Itinerary. Ed. with transl. Adler, M. N. London. 1907. [Description of Tartars, pp. 60 ff.]
Bernier, François. Travels in the Mogul Empire, 1656–68. Transl. Brock, I. 2 vols. London. 1826. Rev. edn., Constable, A. London. 1891.
Gonzalez de Clavijo, Ruy. Narrative of his Embassy...to the Court of Timour, at Samarcand, 1403–6. Transl. Markham, C. R. (Hakluyt Society. Vol. 26.) London. 1859.
Hayton, King of Lesser Armenia. Visit to Mangu and Batu in 1254. (Written by Kirakos Gandsaketsi.) French transl. Brosset, M. *in* Mém. AcadIP. 1870.
Ibn Baṭūṭah. Travels. Ed. with French transl. Defrémery, C. and Sanguinetti, B. R. Voyage d'Ibn Batoutah. 3rd edn. 4 vols. Paris. 1893. English transl. Lee, S. London. 1829. [*See also* Yule, H. Cathay and the way thither. Vol. II. p. 397. *See below*, III (*b*).]
Naṣīr ibn Khusrau. Safar Nāmah. Ed. with French transl. Schefer, C. Sefer Nameh. Relation du voyage...en Syrie, Palestine, Égypte, Arabie, et en Perse (1035–42). (Publ. de l'École des Langues Orientales vivantes. Ser. II. Vol. I.) Paris. 1891.
Pian del Carpine (John de Plano Carpini). *See below*, Rubruquis.
*Polo, Marco. The Book of Marco Polo...concerning the kingdoms and marvels of the East. Transl. and ed. by Yule, H. 3rd edn. revised by Cordier, H. 2 vols. London. 1903. Notes and addenda, by Cordier, H. London. 1920.
Roe, Sir Thomas. Embassy to the Great Mogul, 1615–19. Ed. Foster, W. 2 vols. (Hakluyt Society. Series II. Vols. 1, 2.) London. 1899.
Rubruquis, Guillaume de (William of Rubruck). Itinerarium. Transl. and ed. *Rockhill, W. W. The journey of William of Rubruck to the eastern parts of the world, 1253–5. With two accounts of the earlier journey of John of Pian de Carpine. (Hakluyt Society. Series II. Vol. 4.) London. 1900. [Very important bibliography.] *Also* ed. Beazley, C. R. The texts and versions of John de Plano Carpini and William de Rubruquis as printed by Hakluyt in 1598. (Hakluyt Society. Extra series.) London. 1903.

III. MODERN WORKS.

(*a*) General Histories.

Blochet, E. Introduction à l'histoire des Mongols de Fadl Allah Rashid ed-Din. (Gibb Memorial Series. Vol. XII.) London. 1910.
*Browne, E. G. Literary History of Persia. Vol. II, ch. VII ff. London. 1906. [Excellent account of the Mongols.]
*—— History of Persian Literature under Tartar Dominion. Cambridge. 1920. [Invaluable.]
Cahun, L. Introduction à l'histoire de l'Asie, Turcs et Mongols, des origines à 1405. Paris. 1896.
Curtin, J. The Mongols; a history. Boston. 1908. [Popular.]
**Douglas, R. K. Article "Mongols" in EncBr. [Indispensable.]
Guignes, J. de. Histoire générale des Huns, des Turcs, des Mogols, et des autres Tartares. 4 vols. in 5. Paris. 1756–8.
**Howorth, H. H. History of the Mongols. 3 vols. in 4. London. 1876–88. [A monumental work; for the student.]

*Lane-Poole, S. The Mohammadan Dynasties. *See Gen. Bibl.* III.
Mouradja d'Ohsson, A. C. Histoire des Mongols depuis Tchinguiz-Khan jusqu'à Timour Bey. 4 vols. Hague 1834–5 and Amsterdam 1852.

(*b*) Special Subjects.

Curtin, J. The Mongols in Russia. London. 1908.
EncBr. Articles: Carpini, Golden Horde, Hayton, Jenghiz Khan, Kublai Khan, Mongolia, Rubruquis, Timūr, Turkestan. Also, in part, Assassin, Caliphate, China, Poland, etc.
Encyclopaedia of Islam. Articles. *See Gen. Bibl.* I.
Hammer-Purgstall, J. von. Geschichte der Assassinen. Stuttgart and Tübingen. 1818. English transl. Wood, O. C. London. 1835.
—— Geschichte der Chane der Krim. Vienna. 1856.
—— Geschichte der Goldenen Horde in Kiptschak...Mongolen in Russland. Buda-Pest. 1840.
—— Geschichte der Ilchane...Mongolen in Persien. Darmstadt. 1842.
Herbelot, B. d'. Bibliothèque Orientale. Articles. Paris. 1697. Hague. 4 vols. 1777–9.
Horn, P. Sections on the Mongols in Persia (pp. 573–6), and Tīmūr (pp. 576–9) *in* Geiger, W. and Kuhn, E. Grundriss der iranischen Philologie. Strasbourg. 1896–1904. [Full bibliographies.]
*Kennedy, P. History of the Great Moghuls; or, a history of the Badshahate of Delhi, 1398–1739, with introd. concerning the Mongols and Moghuls of Central Asia. 2 vols. Calcutta. 1905–11.
Lane-Poole, S. Mediaeval India under Mohammedan rule, A.D. 712–1764. (Story of the Nations.) London. 1903.
*Nicholson, R. A. A literary history of the Arabs. London. 1907.
Rémusat, A. Mémoires sur les relations politiques des princes chrétiens...avec les empereurs Mongols. Paris. 1822.
Yule, H. Cathay and the way thither. (Hakluyt Society, No. 37.) Vol. II. London. 1866–7. [Contains extracts from Goës, Ibn Baṭūṭah, and others.]

Maps.

For maps see Howorth, *op. cit. See above,* III (*a*). *Also* Spruner-Menke. Hand-Atlas. No. 87. *See Gen. Bibl.* II. *Also* Poole, R. L. Historical Atlas. No. 80. *See Gen. Bibl.* II.

CHAPTER XXI.

THE OTTOMAN TURKS TO THE FALL OF CONSTANTINOPLE.

I. SPECIAL BIBLIOGRAPHIES.

No complete special bibliography has yet been published. That of Auboyneau, G. and Fevret, A. (Essai de bibliographie pour servir à l'histoire de l'Empire Ottoman; livres turcs, livres imprimés à Constantinople, et livres étrangers à la Turquie, mais pouvant servir à son histoire. Fasc. I. Religion, moeurs, coutumes. Paris. 1911) has remained unfinished. Jacob, G. Hilfsbuch für...d. Osmanisch-türkische. IV. Bibliographischer Wegweiser. 2nd edn. Berlin. 1917 is scanty. Gibbons, H. A. *in* The Foundation of the Ottoman Empire (*see below*, III B (i)) gives a bibliography not without inaccuracies.

The Western Sources are mostly to be found in

Chevalier, C. U. J. Répertoire des sources historiques du moyen âge (*see Gen. Bibl.* I) and in Potthast, A. Bibliotheca historica medii aevi. (*See Gen. Bibl.* I.)

The Oriental Sources are best described in

Hammer-Purgstall, J. von. Geschichte des osmanischen Reiches. Vol. IX, pp. 177 ff., X, pp. 699 ff. (*see Gen. Bibl.* V) and in the standard work of Oriental bibliography by Ḥājjī Khalīfah (Kātib Chelebi). Kashf aẓ-ẓunūn. Ed. in Arabic and Latin by Flügel, G. Lexicon bibliographicum et encyclopaedicum a Mustapha b. Abdallah Katib Jelebi dicto et nomine Haji Khalfa (*ob.* 1658) celebrato compositum. 7 vols. London and Leipsic. 1835–58.

There are also the recent but inadequate works:

Jamāl-ad-Dīn. Āyīne-i ẓurefā. Ed. and continued by Aḥmad Jevdet. 'Oṣmānli tarīkh muverrikhleri. Constantinople. A.H. 1314, and Brusali Muḥammad Ṭāhir. 'Oṣmānli mu'ellifleri. Constantinople. A.H. 1333 ff.

Certain catalogues of collections of Oriental MSS are also indispensable for bibliography, especially

Flügel, G. Die arab., pers., und türk. Handschriften der k. k. Hofbibliothek zu Wien. 3 vols. Vienna. 1865–7.

Rieu, C. Catalogue of Turkish MSS in the British Museum. London. 1888.

See also

Browne, E. G. Catalogue of the Persian MSS in the Library of the University of Cambridge. Cambridge. 1896.

—— Hand-list of the Muḥammadan MSS, including all those in the Arabic character, in the Library of the University of Cambridge. Cambridge. 1900.

—— Supplementary hand-list of the Muḥammadan MSS, etc., in the Libraries of the University and Colleges of Cambridge. Cambridge. 1922.

—— Hand-list of the Gibb Collection of Turkish and other books in the Library of the University of Cambridge. Cambridge. 1906.

Dozy, R. P. A. and others. Catalogus Codicum Orientalium Bibliothecae Academiae Lugduno-Batavae. 6 vols. Leiden. 1851–77.

Pertsch, L. C. W. Verzeichniss der persischen Handschriften der königlichen Bibliothek zu Berlin. Berlin. 1888.

—— Verzeichniss der türkischen Handschriften der königlichen Bibliothek zu Berlin. Berlin. 1889.

Slane, G. de. Catalogue des MSS arabes de la Bibliothèque Nationale, Paris. In MS. 2 vols. 1883–95.

—— Catalogue des Bibliothèques de Constantinople. In MS. Bibliothèque Nationale, Paris. Fonds arabes. No. 4474. [Forty of these Libraries have catalogues registering 57000 MSS.]

There are bibliographies of the Arabic and Persian sources by Brockelmann, C. *in* Geschichte der arabischen Litteratur (*see Gen. Bibl.* v) and by Ethé, H. *in* Grundriss der iranischen Philologie. Ed. Geiger, W. and Kuhn, E. Vol. II. pp. 212–363. Strasbourg. 1895–1904.

For printed works only the following are useful:

Fitzclarence, G. and Sprenger, A. Kitab Fihrist al-Koutoub. 1840.

Orientalische Bibliographie. Ed. Müller, A., Kuhn, E., Scherman, L. Berlin. 1888 ff.

Zenker, J. T. Bibliotheca orientalis. 2 vols. Leipsic. 1848–61.

II. SOURCES.

A. Oriental.

(*a*) *Archives.*

There exists an immense mass of documents, including many of great historical importance, in the archives of the Ottoman Government. General rumour has prevailed for years that such documents existed, but visitors, even with permits from the Government, were not able to see more than a few hundred bound volumes, mostly of well-known foreign authors and a disorderly heap of MSS. The great mass was re-discovered some years ago in the Palace of Tōp-Qāpū of Constantinople.

Many thousands of registers exist in the Imperial Divan, including Imperial Decrees and the decisions of the Great Council of the Empire presided over by the Grand Vizier. This Council dates back to an early period of Ottoman History and was continued until the reign of Mahomet the Conqueror. In the same place are a great number of registers containing the secret Orders of the Court and of the State.

(*b*) *Historical Works.*

(*In chronological order.*)

Aḥmadī (*ob.* 1408). Iskandar Nāmah. Publ. in Ta'rīkh-i ʻoṣmānī enjumeni mejmūʻasi. Vol. I. 1910. pp. 41 ff. Almost entirely publ. in "Anonymous Giese." *See below.*

Niẓām Shāmī. Ẓafar Nāmah. (Written in the lifetime of Tīmūr.) Brit. Mus. Addit. MSS. No. 23,980. [Unpublished; matter contained in the following.]

Sharaf-ad-Dīn (*ob.* 1454). Ẓafar Nāmah. Publ. in Bibliotheca Indica. Calcutta. 1887–8. French transl. Pétis de la Croix, F. Histoire de Timour-Bec. 4 vols. Paris. 1722; and Delf. 1723. English transl. [Darby, J.] 2 vols. London. 1723.

Ibn Arabshāh (*ob.* 1450). ʻAjāib al-maqdūr fī nawāib Tīmūr. Arabic text. Cairo. A.H. 1285–1305. Ed. Golius, J. Ahmedis Arabsiadis vitae et rerum gestarum Timuris historia. Leiden. 1676. Latin transl. Manger, S. H. Lieuwarden. 1767–72. Turkish transl. by Naẓmī Zādah. Ta'rīkh-i Tīmūr-i Gūrkān. Constantinople. 1729.

Ṭursun Beg. Ta'rīkh-i Abī'l-fatḥ. (Written in the lifetime of Mahomet II.) Vienna MSS. Flügel's Catalogue. No. 984.

Shukru'llāh. Bahjatu't-tavārīkh. (General history written at Constantinople in Persian.) Brit. Mus. Oriental MSS. 1627. Vienna MSS. Flügel's Catalogue. No. 828. Turkish transl. by Fārasī. MS in Constantinople University Library. No. 881.

ʻĀshiq Pasha Zādah. Tavārīkh-i āl-i ʻoṣmān. (Written shortly after 1481.) The best MS is at Dresden. Codices turcicae. No. 60. A bad edn., with continuation, ed. ʻĀlī Beg. Constantinople. A.H. 1332.

Ḥasan ibn Maḥmūd Beyātī. Jām Jam Āyīn. Silsilah-Nāmah-i Salāṭīn-i āl-i ʿoṣmān. (Written in 1482.) Ed. ʿĀlī Emīrī. Constantinople. A.H. 1331.

Neshrī. Jihān numā. (Written after 1512.) Vienna MSS. Flügel's Catalogue. No. 986. Parts publ., with German transl., *in* Behrnauer, W. Aus türkischen Urkunden. Vol. I. Vienna. 1857. Also Nöldeke, T. *in* ZDMG. XIII (1859). pp. 176 ff.; XV (1861). pp. 333 ff. Parts also publ. Wittek, P. *in* Mitteilungen zur osmanischen Geschichte. Vol. I. Vienna. 1921–2. pp. 77 ff. Nearly identical with the so-called Hanivaldanus *in* Leunclavius, J. Historiae musulmanae turcorum. Frankfort. 1591.

Tavārīkh-i āl-i ʿoṣmān. Anonymous chronicles written between 1490 and 1512. The so-called "Anonymous Giese." *See below.*

Bihishtī. Ta'rīkh. (Written between 1501 and 1512.) Brit. Mus. Addit. MSS. No. 7869. A later redaction, Brit. Mus. Addit. MSS. No. 24,955.

Idrīs Bitlisī (*ob.* 1520). Hasht Bihisht. In Persian. Brit. Mus. Addit. MSS. Nos. 7646, 47. Vienna MSS. Flügel's Catalogue. No. 994. (Partly in Turkish translation.)

Ḥadīdī (*ob.* shortly after 1523). Shāh Nāmah-i āl-i ʿoṣmān. Berlin MSS. Pertsch's Catalogue. No. 206.

Tavārīkh-i āl-i ʿoṣmān. A continuation up to 1550 of the "Anonymous Giese." (*See above.*) Perhaps written by Muḥyī-ad-Dīn (*ob.* 1550). Ed. Giese, F. Die altosmanischen anonymen Chroniken. Vol. I (text). Breslau. 1922. Vol. II (German transl.) in preparation. Nearly identical with the so-called Verantianus in Leunclavius, J. Historiae musulmanae turcorum. Frankfort. 1591; and with Leunclavius, J. Annales Sultanorum Othmanidarum. Frankfort. 1588. (The latter follows a shorter redaction.)

Luṭfī Pasha (*ob.* 1550[?]). Ta'rīkh-i āl-i ʿoṣmān. Vienna MSS. Flügel's Catalogue. No. 1001.

Rustam Pasha (*ob.* 1561). Ta'rīkh. Camb. MSS. Browne's Catalogue. Nos. 167, 8. Vienna MSS. Flügel's Catalogue. No. 1012.

ʿĀlī (*ob.* 1599). Kunhu'l-Akhbār. 5 vols. Constantinople. A.H. 1277. In 4 vols. Constantinople. A.H. 1284. [Both editions are incomplete.] Vienna MSS. Flügel's Catalogue. No. 1022.

Saʿd-ad-Dīn (*ob.* 1599). Tāj-at-tavārīkh. 2 vols. Constantinople. A.H. 1279–80. Italian transl. Bratutti, V. Cronica dell' origine e progressi della casa ottomana composta da Saidino Turco. Vol. I. Vienna. 1649; Vol. II. Madrid. 1652. Latin transl. Kollar, A. F. Saad ed-dini scriptoris Turcici annales Turcici. Vienna. 1758. [Incomplete.] English transl. Seaman, W. The reign of Sultan Orkhan. Translated from Hodja effendi. London. 1652. The part containing the fall of Constantinople was transl. into French by De Sacy, G. *in* Michaud, J. F. Bibliothèque des Croisades. Vol. III. Paris. 1829; into English by Gibb, E. J. W. Glasgow. 1879; and into German by Krause, J. H. Die Eroberungen von Konstantinopel. *See below,* III B (ii).

ʿAbdu'r-Raḥmān ibn Ḥasan, called Parvarī. Anīsu'l-musāfirīn (History of Hadrianople, written 1636). Vienna MSS. Flügel's Catalogue. No. 1052.

Ḥājjī Khalīfah (*ob.* 1657). Tuḥfatu'l-Kibār fī Asfāri'l-Bihār. Constantinople. 1728. English transl. (first part only) Mitchell, J. London. 1831.

—— Taqvīmu't-tavārīkh. Constantinople. A.H. 1146. Ital. transl. Carli, R. Chronologia historica da Hagi Halife Mustafa. Venice. 1697.

(*c*) *Geographical Works.*

Ibn Baṭūṭah (*ob.* 1377). Ed. with French transl. Defrémery, C. and Sanguinetti, B. R. Voyages d'Ibn Batoutah. 4 vols. Paris. 1853–9. 3rd edn. 1893. [Vol. II, pp. 255–353, gives travels in Asia Minor.] Arabic text only. Cairo. A.H. 1287–8. English transl. by Muhammed Hussein. The travels of Ibn Batuta. Lahore. 1898.

Shahāb-ad-Dīn (*ob.* 1348). Masāliku'l-abṣār fī mamāliki'l amṣār. Bibl. Nat., Paris, Arabic MSS. Slane's Catalogue. Nos. 2325–9. The part on Asia Minor transl. in French, Quatremère, E. M. *in* Notices et extraits des MSS. XIII, i, pp. 151–353.

ʻĀshiq (*ob.* 1600 [?]). Manāẓiru'l-ʻavālim. Vienna MSS. Flügel's Catalogue. No. 1279.

Ḥājji Khalīfah (Kātib Chelebi) (*ob.* 1658). Jihān numā. Constantinople. 1732. French transl. of the part on Asia Minor by Reinaud *in* Vivien de St Martin, L. Histoire des découvertes géographiques. Vol. III. p. 637. Paris. 1846. German transl. of the part on Rumeli and Bosna by Hammer-Purgstall, J. von. Vienna. 1812.

Evliyā Efendi (*ob.* shortly after 1679). Siyāḥat Nāmah (Ta'rīkh-i sayyāḥ). In ten books. MSS in the Beshīr Agha and ʻUmmumīye Library at Constantinople. Published Constantinople. A.H. 1316–18. [Incomplete. Vols. I–VI only.] English transl. Hammer-Purgstall, J. von. Narrative of travels in Europe, Asia, and Africa by Evliya Efendi. 2 vols. London. 1846–50. [Incomplete.]

(*d*) *Biographical Works.*

Sehī (*ob.* 1548). Hasht Bihisht. Ed. Muḥammad Shukrī. Constantinople. A.H. 1325.

Laṭīfī (ʻAbdu'l-laṭīf) (*ob.* 1582). Taẕkiratu'sh-shuʻarā. Constantinople. A.H. 1314. German partial transl. Chabert, T. Latifi oder biographische Nachrichten von türkischen Dichtern. Vienna and Zurich. 1800.

Ṭashkupri Zādah (*ob.* 1560). Shaqāiq an-nuʻmānīya. Turkish transl., with additions, by Mejdī (*ob. circa* 1590). Constantinople. A.H. 1269.

Ḥasan Chelebi (Qinālī Zādah) (*ob.* 1603). Taẕkiratu'sh-shuʻarā. Brit. Mus. Addit. MSS. No. 24,957. Vienna MSS. Flügel's Catalogue. No. 1228. Bibl. Nat., Paris. No. 246. Munich MSS. Aumer's Catalogue. No. 147.

ʻĀshiq Chelebi (*ob.* 1571). Vienna MSS. Flügel's Catalogue. No. 1218. Munich MSS. Aumer's Catalogue. No. 149. German partial transl. in Chabert, T. Latifi, etc. *See above.*

ʻOṣmān Zādah Tāib Aḥmad (*ob.* 1723). Hadīqatu'l-vuzarā. (With continuations.) Constantinople. A.H. 1271 and A.H. 1283.

(*e*) *Documents.*

On the oldest Ottoman documents see Kraelitz, F. Osman. Urkunden in türkischer Sprache. Vienna. 1922. No original document is known of this period; but some copies of old decrees are published by Kraelitz, F. *in* Ta'rīkh-i ʻoṣmānī enj. mejm. Vol. V. No. 28. 1915.

There are also the various "Qānūn-Nāmah" (Codes of Law) which consist of parts of such decrees. The earliest, composed between 1453 and 1457, contains many decrees of older date; it is published by Kraelitz, F. *in* Mitteilungen zur osman. Geschichte. Vol. I (1921–2). pp. 13 ff. For the other "Qānūn-Nāmah" *see* Kraelitz, F. *ibid.*

Official documents and letters are also to be found in the two following collections, which, however, for this period, must be used with caution:

Ibrāhīm Beg el-Defterdār. Munsha'āt. (Written under Sulaimān I.) Vienna MSS. Flügel's Catalogue. No. 310.

Aḥmad Nishānji, called Ferīdūn Bey (*ob.* 1583). Munsha'āt-i salāṭīn. Constantinople. A.H. 1264–5. [The most important collection of Turkish state-papers.]

B. Western.

(*a*) *General Histories.*

Professor Bury, in his edition of Gibbon, at the end of the volumes gives very valuable bibliographies on the subject-matter.

Acropolites, Georgius. Chronicon Constantinopolitanum. (1203–61.) Ed. Bekker, I. CSHB. 1836. [Not of great value for Ottoman history.]

Blemmydes, Nicephorus. Autobiography. Ed. Heisenberg, A. Leipsic. 1896.

Cantacuzene, John, Emperor. Historia. (1314–54.) Ed. Schopen, L. 3 vols. CSHB. 1828–32.

Chalcondyles, Laonicus. Historiae. (1298–1463.) Gr. and Lat. texts. Ed. Bekker, I. CSHB. 1843; and MPG. CLIX. 1866. French transl. Vigenère, B. de. Paris. 1577 and later edns. [Athenian in Turkish service. Fullest account of Turks.]
Ducas. Historia Byzantina. (1341–1462.) Ed. Bekker, I. CSHB. 1834. [Detailed, but inaccurate.]
Gregoras, Nicephorus. Historia Romana (Byzantina). (1203–1359.) Ed. Schopen, L. and Bekker, I. 3 vols. CSHB. 1829–55.
Pachymeres, Georgius. Historia. (1255–1308.) Ed. Bekker, I. CSHB. 1835. [Valuable.]
Phrantzes, Georgius. Chronicon. (1258–1476.) Ed. Bekker, I. CSHB. 1838. [Grand Logothete, eye-witness, valuable, Turcophobe.]

(*b*) *Sources for capture of Constantinople.*

(i) Known to Gibbon.

Cantemir, D. *See below,* III B (i).
Chalcondyles. *See above,* II B (*a*).
Ducas. *See above,* II B (*a*).
Isidore, Cardinal. De capta Constantinopoli. MPG. CLIX.
Leonard, Archbishop of Chios. Historia Constantinopolitanae urbis...captae. MPG. CLIX. Also ed. Sreznevski, I. I. *in* Povêst' o Tsaregradê. St Petersburg. 1855. Ital. transl. in Sansovino. *See below,* III B (i).
Phrantzes. *See above,* II B (*a*).
[These authors, contemporaries of the siege except Cantemir and Chalcondyles, were eye-witnesses of much which they relate, but were either Latins, or favoured the Union of the two Churches.]

(ii) Unknown to Gibbon.

Barbaro, Nicolò. Giornale dell' Assedio di Constantinopoli. Ed. Cornet, E. Vienna. 1856. Ed. Dethier, P. A. *In* Mon. Hungariae hist. Vol. XXII. Pt. I. *See Gen. Bibl.* IV. [This diary of an eye-witness, revised later, carries conviction of its truthfulness.]
Critobulus of Imbros. Life of Mahomet II. Ed. Müller, C. *In* Fragmenta historicorum graecorum. Vol. V. p. 40. *See Gen. Bibl.* IV. Ed. Dethier, P. A. *In* Mon. Hungariae hist. Vol. XXI. Pt. I. *See Gen. Bibl.* IV. [Critobulus was Archon of the Island of Imbros under Mahomet II. His history covers the first seventeen years of Mahomet's reign. As he belonged to the Greek as opposed to the Romanising party he is free from the bias of the authors known to Gibbon.]
Pusculus, Ubertinus, of Brescia. Constantinopoleos Libri IV. Ed. Ellissen, A. *In* Analekten der mittel- und neugriechischen Literatur. Vol. III. Leipsic. 1857. Ed. Dethier, P. A. *In* Mon. Hungariae hist. Vol. XXII. Pt. I. *See Gen. Bibl.* IV. [Poem by eye-witness.]
Tedaldi, J. Account of the Siege in two versions. (1) Ed. Vallet de Viriville. *In* Chronique de Charles VII by Jean Chartier. Vol. III. Paris. 1858. (2) Ed. Martène, E. and Durand, U. Thesaurus novus anecdotorum. Vol. I. *See Gen. Bibl.* IV. [Florentine eye-witness.]
The following are of secondary importance.
Cambini, A. Della Origine de' Turchi et Imperio delli Ottomanni. Florence. 1529 and later years. Also printed by Sansovini. *See below,* III B (i). [Book II, which treats of the siege, suggests information from eye-witnesses. Useful.]
Dolphin, Zorzi (Zorsi Dolfin). Assedio e presa di Constantinopoli nell' anno 1453. Ed. Thomas, G. M. *In* Sitzungsberichte k. bayer. Akad. Wissensch. Munich. 1868. Ed. Dethier, P. A. *In* Mon. Hungariae hist. Vol. XXII. Pt. I. *See Gen. Bibl.* IV. [Mainly from Leonard, but also from other eye-witnesses.]
Hierax, Grand Logothete. Θρῆνος, or History of the Turkish Empire. Ed. Dethier, P. A. *In* Mon. Hungariae hist. Vol. XXII. Pt. I. *See Gen. Bibl.* IV. [*c.* 1590; useful for topography.]

Michael Constantinovich of Ostrovića. Pamiętniki Janczara Polaka napisane. (Memoirs of the Polish Janissary.) Ed. Galezowski. *In* Zbiór Pisarzów Polskich. Vol. v. Warsaw. 1828. [Claims to be eye-witness.]
Montaldo, A. de. De Constantinopolitano excidio. Ed. Desimoni, C. *In* Atti d. Soc. Ligure di stor. pat. x (1874). Ed. Hopf, K. and Dethier, P. A. *In* Mon. Hungariae hist. Vol. xxii. Pt. i. *See Gen. Bibl.* iv. [Eye-witness.]
Rapporto del Superiore dei Franciscani presente all' assedio e alla presa di Constantinopoli. Ed. Muratori. RR.II.SS. xviii. Ed. Dethier, P. A. *In* Mon. Hungariae hist. Vol. xxii. Pt. i. [Eye-witness.]
Riccherio, Christoforo. La Presa di Constantinopoli. Ed. Sansovino, F. *See below* iii b (i). Ed. Dethier, P. A. *In* Mon. Hungariae hist. Vol. xxii. Pt. i. *See Gen. Bibl.* iv. [Valuable.]
Slavic account of the Siege (Skazaniya o vzyatii Tsargrada bezbozhnym turetskym sultanom). Ed. Sreznevski, I. I. under the title: Povêst' o Tsaregradê *in* Uchen'iya Zapiski of the 2nd Division, AcadIP. Reprinted with addns. St Petersburg. 1855. Transl. from another text, Dethier, P. A. *In* Mon. Hungariae hist. Vol. xxii. Pt. i (*see Gen. Bibl.* iv) as "Muscovite Chronicle." [Balkan Slav dialect. Eye-witness's account, but interpolated.]
Zacharia, Angelus Johannes, Podestà of Pera. Epistola de excidio Constantinopolitano. Ed. de Sacy, S. *In* Notices et extraits des MSS. de la Bibl. du Roi, xi. Paris. 1827. Ed. Dethier, P. A. and Hopf, K. *In* Mon. Hungariae hist. Vol. xxii. Pt. i. *See Gen. Bibl.* iv. [Eye-witness; written within a month of the capture of the city.]

III. MODERN WORKS.

A. Turkish Histories.

Muḥammad Saʿīd Effendi, called Ferāʾizī Zādah. Gulshen-i maʿārif. Constantinople. a.h. 1252.
Ṭayyār Zādah Aṭā. Ta'rīkh-i Aṭā. 4 vols. Constantinople. a.h. 1293.
Khairullāh Effendi. Ta'rīkh. Constantinople. 1851.
ʿAbdu'r-Raḥmān Sharaf Bey. Ta'rīkh-i devlet-i ʿoṣmānīye. 2 vols. Constantinople. a.h. 1315. [The best.]
Najīb ʿĀṣim. Turk ta'rīkhi. Constantinople. a.h. 1330.
Muḥammad Ghālib. Nataiju'l-vuqūʿāt. 2nd edn. 4 vols. Constantinople. a.h. 1329.
ʿOṣmānli Ta'rīkhi. Ed. by the Institute of Ottoman History. Vol. i. Constantinople. a.h. 1335.
Aḥmad Jevād Pasha. Ta'rīkh-i ʿasker-i ʿoṣmānī. (With maps.) 2 vols. Constantinople. a.h. 1297–9. French transl. Macrides, G. État militaire ottoman. Vol. i. Le corps des Janissaires. Paris. 1882. [All publ.]

B. Western Works.

(i) *General Histories.*

Cantemir, Demetrius, Prince of Moldavia. Histoire de l'empire Othoman. French transl. 1743. Engl. transl. Tindal, N. 1734–5. [Many curious statements, *e.g.*, that the Turks recognised that Constantinople capitulated on terms. Valuable as often giving the Turkish view. Originally written in Latin.]
Creasy, E. History of the Ottoman Empire. New edn. London. 1877. [Popular abridgment of Hammer-Purgstall.]
Finlay, G. History of Greece. Ed. Tozer, H. F. Vols. iii, iv, v. *See Gen. Bibl.* v. [Valuable.]
Gibbon, E. History of the Decline and Fall of the Roman Empire. Ed. Bury, J. B. *See Gen. Bibl.* v. [Gibbon depended on the Byzantine sources. Valuable notes by Bury.]
Gibbons, H. A. The Foundation of the Ottoman Empire. *See Gen. Bibl.* v.
Hammer-Purgstall, J. v. Geschichte des osmanischen Reiches. *See Gen. Bibl.* v.
Jorga, N. Geschichte des osmanischen Reiches. *See Gen Bibl.* v.

Knolles, R. The Generall Historie of the Turkes. London. 1603, and later edns.
Lane-Poole, S. Turkey. (Story of the Nations.) London. 1888. [Good summary.]
(Newman, J. H.) Lectures on the history of the Turks. Dublin. 1854. [Suggestive.]
Sansovino, F. Historia Universale dell' Origine et Imperio de' Turchi. Venice. 1600, and later edns. [Useful compilation, especially as to Greece and eastern shores of Adriatic. Contains Italian transl. of Archbishop Leonard's Capture of Constantinople, with important modifications; and Cardinal Isidore's Report on the same subject; with other notices otherwise difficult to find.]

(ii) *Fall of Constantinople.*

Krause, J. H. Die Eroberungen von Konstantinopel im dreizehnten und fünfzehnten Jahrhundert. Halle. 1870.
Mijatović (Mijatovich), C. Constantine, the last Emperor of the Greeks. London. 1892. [Slav standpoint. Bibliography.]
Mordtmann, A. D. Belagerung und Eroberung Constantinopels...im Jahre 1453. Stuttgart. 1858. [Uses some authorities unknown to Gibbon, but not the chief, Critobulus.]
Paspates, A. G. Πολιορκία καὶ ἅλωσις τῆς Κωνσταντινουπόλεως. Athens. 1890. [Careful; local knowledge.]
Pears, E. Destruction of the Greek Empire. London. 1903. [Uses authorities unknown to Gibbon.]
Vlasto, E. A. Les derniers jours de Constantinople. Paris. 1883. [Picturesque.]

CHAPTER XXII.

BYZANTINE LEGISLATION FROM THE DEATH OF JUSTINIAN (565 A.D.) TO 1453 A.D.

I. SPECIAL BIBLIOGRAPHY.

Krumbacher, K. Geschichte d. byzant. Litteratur. (*See Gen. Bibl.* v.) pp. 608–13. [To be supplemented by Siciliano Villanueva, L. Diritto bizantino. *See below,* III (*a*) (i).]

II. ORIGINAL AUTHORITIES.

(*a*) Collections of Sources.

Ferrari, G. I documenti greci medioevali di diritto privato dell' Italia meridionale e loro attinenze con quelli bizantini d'Oriente e coi papiri greco-egizii. Leipsic. 1910. [Forms Heft IV of the Byzantinisches Archiv.]
—— Formulari notarili inediti dell' età bizantina. *In* BISI. 33. 1912.
Heimbach, G. E. Ἀνέκδοτα. 2 vols. Leipsic. 1838–40.
Rhalles, G. A. and Potles, M. *Σύνταγμα ... κανόνων*. *See Gen. Bibl.* IV. [Contains sources of Byzantine Canon Law.]
Zachariae von Lingenthal, K. E. Ἀνέκδοτα. Leipsic. 1843.
—— Jus graeco-romanum. In 7 pts. *See Gen. Bibl.* IV. [The contents of each part appear separately below, II (*b*).]

(*b*) Separate Sources.

(*Arranged in chronological order according to the certain or probable date of their composition.*)

Institutionum graeca Paraphrasis Theophilo Antecessori vulgo tributa, etc. Ed. Ferrini, E. C. 2 vols. Berlin. 1884–97.
Αἱ Ῥοπαί oder der Schrift über die Zeitabschnitte. Ed. Zachariae von Lingenthal, K. E. Heidelberg. 1843. (Re-edited Sgoutas, L. *in* Θέμις. Vol. III. Athens. 1847. pp. 256–95.)
De Actionibus. This treatise has been published by Heimbach, G. E. *in* Observat. iuris graeco-romani. Vol. I. Leipsic. 1830. Re-edited Sgoutas, L. *in* Θέμις. Vol. I. 1846. pp. 117–26. And by Zachariae von Lingenthal. *In* ZSR. Romanistische Abt. Vol. XIII. 1892. pp. 88 ff.
The Novels of the Emperors from 566 to 1453 form Part III (Novellae Constitutiones) of Zachariae von Lingenthal. Jus graeco-romanum. (*See Gen. Bibl.* IV.) They are sub-divided as follows:
Collatio prima. Novellae Constitutiones annorum 566–866.
Collatio secunda. Imp. Leonis Novellae Constitutiones inter 886–910 editae.
Collatio tertia. Novellae Constitutiones annorum 911–1057.
Collatio quarta. Novellae Constitutiones annorum 1057–1204.
Collatio quinta. Novellae Constitutiones annorum 1204–1453.
Ecloga. Epanagoge. Ed. Zachariae von Lingenthal, K. E. Collectio librorum juris graeco-romani ineditorum. *See Gen. Bibl.* IV. (The Ecloga has been re-edited by Monferratos, A. G. Athens. 1889.)
Νόμος στρατιωτικός. Ed. Zachariae von Lingenthal, K. E. Die sogenannte Leges militares. BZ. III. 1894. pp. 450–5.

The Νόμος Ῥόδιος is published by Pardessus, J. M. Collection de Loix maritimes. Vol. I. Paris. 1828. Re-edited by Ferrini, E. C. and Mercati, J. *In* Editionis Basilicorum Heimbachianae supplementum alterum. Leipsic. 1897. Also by Dareste, R. *In* Revue de Philologie. 1905. pp. 1–29. And NRDF. XXIX. (1905.) pp. 428–49. Also by Ashburner, W. The Rhodian Sea-Law. Oxford. 1909.

Νόμος γεωργικός. Ed. Ferrini, E. C. Edizione critica del Νόμος γεωργικός. BZ. VII. (1898.) pp. 558–71. Also ed. Ashburner, W. *in* JHS. Vol. XXX. (1910.) pp. 97 ff.

Prochiron. Ed. Zachariae von Lingenthal, K. E. Ὁ Πρόχειρος Νόμος. Imperatorum Basilii, Constantini, et Leonis Prochiron, etc. *See Gen. Bibl.* IV. Re-edited Brandileone, F. *In* Fonti. 1895.

Epanagoge. *See above under* Ecloga.

Basilicorum libri LX. Vols. I–VI. Ed. Heimbach, W. E. *See Gen. Bibl.* IV. [Vol. VI contains Heimbach's Prolegomena et manuale Basilicorum.]

The work has been completed by two supplements:

1. Supplementum editionis Basilicorum Heimbachianae lib. XV–XVIII Basilicorum...nec non lib. XIX Basilicorum...continens. Ed. Zachariae von Lingenthal. Leipsic. 1846.
2. Editionis Basilicorum Heimbachianae supplementum alterum. Ed. Ferrini, E. C. and Mercati, J. Leipsic. 1897.

Tipucitus (Τιπούκειτος). Still unpublished. Extracts in Mai, A. Scriptorum veterum nova collectio. Vol. VII. Rome. 1833.

Prefect, Book of the. Ed. Nicole, J. Λέοντος τοῦ Σοφοῦ τὸ ἐπαρχικὸν βιβλίον. Le Livre du Préfet. *See Gen. Bibl.* IV.

Epitome Legum (920). Ed. Zachariae von Lingenthal. Jus graeco-romanum. Pts. II and VII. *See Gen. Bibl.* IV.

Ecloga privata aucta. *Ibid.* Pt. IV.

Ecloga ad Prochiron mutata. *Ibid.* Pt. IV.

Synopsis Basilicorum (major). *Ibid.* Pt. V.

Epanagoge aucta. *Ibid.* Pt. IV.

Πεῖρα *or* Practica ex actis Eustathii Romani. *Ibid.* Pt. I.

The opusculum of Eustathius and George Phobenos on the *Hypobolon* has been published by Zachariae von Lingenthal *in* Gesch. d. griechisch-römischen Rechts. § 14. *See Gen. Bibl.* V.

The treatises De peculiis and De privilegiis creditorum are in Heimbach, G. E. Ἀνέκδοτα. Vol. II. pp. 247–69. *See above*, II (*a*).

Novel of Constantine Monomachus (1045). Ed. Lagarde, P. de. Abhand. d. Göttinger Gesell. d. Wissen. Hist.-phil. Kl. XXVIII (1881), pp. 195–202; also ed. Cozza-Luzi, I. Studi e documenti di storia e diritto. Vol. V. (1884.) pp. 289–316. Also ed. Ferrini, E. C. Archivio giuridico. Vol. XXXIII. 1884.

Meditatio de nudis pactis. Ed. Monnier, H. and Platon, G. NRDF. Vols. XXXVII (1913), XXXVIII (1914).

Synopsis Legum. MPG. CXXII. 925–74. Also ed. Sathas, K. N. Μεσαιωνικὴ βιβλιοθήκη. Vol. IV. *See Gen. Bibl.* IV.

Ποίημα νομικόν. Ed. Leunclavius, J. and Freherius, M. Juris graeco-romani. Vol. II. Frankfort. 1596. Also ed. Sgoutas, L. *in* Θέμις. Vol. VIII. Athens. 1861.

Synopsis minor. Ed. Zachariae von Lingenthal, K. E. Jus graeco-romanum. Pt. II. *See Gen. Bibl.* IV.

Prochiron auctum. *Ibid.* Pt. VI.

Constantine Harmenopulus. Manuale legum sive Hexabiblos. Ed. Heimbach, G. E. Leipsic. 1851. [The extracts from Julianus Ascalonita, source of the Hexabiblos, have been published by Ferrini, E. C. *in* Rendiconti dell' Istit. lomb. Vol. XXXV. (1902.) pp. 613 ff.]

Brandileone, F. Frammenti di legislazione normanna e di giurisprudenza bizantina nell' Italia meridionale. *In* Rendiconti della R. Accad. dei Lincei. 1885–6. [Contains the fragments of Cod. Vatic. 845 on the Theoretron and the Hypobolon.]

Tamassia, N. Una collezione italiana di leggi bizantine. *In* Archivio giuridico. Vol. LV. (1895.) pp. 488 ff.

III. MODERN WORKS.

(a) Works of a General Character.

(i) *On Byzantine Legislation.*

Heimbach, W. E. Griechisch-römisches Recht. *In* Ersch-Gruber. Sect. i. Teil 86. 1868. pp. 191 ff. [Unfinished.]
Krueger, P. Geschichte der Quellen und Litteratur des römischen Rechts. 2nd edn. Munich. 1912. § 49. pp. 405–17. French transl. of 1st edn. Brissaud, J. Paris. 1894. [Summary.]
Krumbacher, K. Gesch. d. byzant. Litteratur. 2nd edn. *See Gen. Bibl.* v. [Summary.]
Mortreuil, J. A. B. Histoire du droit byzantin. 3 vols. Paris. 1843–6. [Still useful.]
Siciliano Villanueva, L. Diritto bizantino. (Extract from the Enciclopedia giuridica italiana.) Milan. 1906. [The most recent work.]
Zachariae von Lingenthal, K. E. Geschichte des griechisch-römischen Rechts. 3rd edn. *See Gen. Bibl.* v. [Indispensable and complete.]
—— Historiae juris graeco-romani delineatio cum appendice ineditorum. Heidelberg. 1839. French transl. Lauth, E. Histoire du droit privé gréco-romain. Paris. 1870. [Work replaced by the preceding.]

(ii) *Diffusion of Byzantine Law.*

Brandileone, F. Il diritto greco-romano nell' Italia meridionale dall' viii al xii secolo. *In* Archivio giuridico. Vol. xxxvi. (1886.) pp. 239 ff.
—— Nuovi studi sul diritto bizantino nell' Italia meridionale. *In* Studi e documenti di storia e diritto. Vol. viii. (1887.) pp. 65 ff.
Hubé, R. de. Roman and Graeco-Byzantine Law among the Slav peoples. With an appendix containing a Serbian extract of Romano-Byzantine Laws. Warsaw. 1868. (In Russian.) French transl. Stekert, A. Paris. 1880. (*Cf.* Review by Pertile *in* Archivio giuridico. Vol. xxvi. (1881.) pp. 391 ff.)
Pič, J. L. Les lois roumaines et leur connexité avec le droit byzantin et slave. Bucharest. 1887.
Siciliano Villanueva, L. Sul diritto greco-romano (privato) in Sicilia. *In* Riv. di storia e filosofia del diritto. Vol. ii. 1901.

(b) Monographs and Articles in Periodicals.

Andreadès, A. La vénalité des offices est-elle d'origine byzantine? NRDF. xlv. 1921.
Ashburner, W. The Farmers' Law. *In* JHS. Vol. xxx. (1910.) pp. 85 ff. [On the Νόμος γεωργικός, with critical text.]
Bonfante, P. and Brandileone, F. Nuovi studii e ricerche sulla storia del diritto romano in Oriente. *In* Atti del V congresso naz. giuridico-forense. Palermo. Vol. iii. 1903.
Brandileone, F. Sulla storia e la natura della donatio propter nuptias. Bologna. 1892.
—— Studio sul Prochiron legum. BISI. xvi. 1894.
—— La Traditio per cartam (παράδοσις δι' ἐγγράφου) nel diritto bizantino. *In* Studii...in onore di V. Scialoia. Vol. i. Milan. 1905.
Desminis, D. D. Die Eheschenkung nach römischen und insbesondere nach byzantinischen Recht. Athens. 1897.
Dyobuniates, G. Τὸ Φαλκίδιον τρίτον ἐν τῷ Βυζαντιακῷ δικαίῳ. *In* Ἐπετηρὶς τοῦ Φιλολ. Συλλόγου Παρνασσοῦ. Athens. 1902. pp. 219–56.
Ferrari, G. Il diritto penale nelle "Novelle" di Leone il Filosofo. *In* Riv. Penale. Vol. lxvii. 4. 1908.

Fischer, W. Studien zur byzant. Geschichte des 11 Jahrh. Plauen. 1883. [III. Die Entstehungszeit des "Tractatus de peculiis," des "Tractatus de privilegiis creditorum," der "Synopsis legum," des M. Psellus und der Peira und deren Verfasser.]

Jobbé-Duval, E. La Nature de la Querela inofficiosi testamenti selon les jurisconsultes byzantins. *In* Mélanges Fitting. I. Paris. 1908. pp. 437-64.

Laborde, L. Les Écoles de droit dans l'Empire d'Orient. Bordeaux. 1912. [diss.]

Maridakis, G. S. Τὸ ἀστικὸν δίκαιον ἐν ταῖς Νεαραῖς τῶν Βυζαντινῶν αὐτοκρατόρων. Athens. 1922.

Monferratos, A. G. Πραγματεία περὶ προγαμιαίας δωρεᾶς. Athens. 1884.

Monnier, H. Études de droit byzantin. I. L' Ἐπιβολή. NRDF. XVI (1892), XVIII (1894), XIX (1895).

—— La Protimesis dans les coutumes et les lois siciliennes. *Ibid.* XX. (1896.)

—— Études de droit byzantin. Méditation sur la constitution Ἑκατέρῳ et le *jus poenitendi*. *Ibid.* XXIV. (1900.)

—— Du Casus non existentium liberorum dans les Novelles de Justinien. *In* Mélanges Gérardin. Paris. 1907.

—— La Novelle XX de Léon le Sage. *In* Mélanges Fitting. II. Paris. 1908.

—— La Novelle L de Léon le Sage. *In* Mélanges P. F. Girard. II. Paris. 1912.

—— Les Novelles de Léon le Sage. [A French transl. which will be published shortly at Bordeaux.]

Paturini, G. [or Platon, G.] Pactes et contrats. Simples remarques. Paris. 1917. (Extract from Rev. générale du Droit.)

Platon, G. Observations sur le droit de προτίμησις en droit byzantin. *In* Rev. générale du Droit. Vols. XXVII-XXIX. 1903-5.

Schupfer, F. La comunità dei beni tra coniugi e l'Ecloga Isaurica. *In* Riv. ital. per le scienze giuridiche. Vol. XXXVI. (1904.) pp. 319 ff.

Tamassia, N. L'Affratellamento. Turin. 1886.

Testaud, G. Des rapports des puissants et des petits propriétaires ruraux dans l'Empire byzantin au Xe siècle. Bordeaux. 1898. [diss.]

CHAPTER XXIII.

THE GOVERNMENT AND ADMINISTRATION OF THE BYZANTINE EMPIRE.

I. SOURCES.

Basilicorum libri LX. *See Gen. Bibl.* IV.
Codex Justinianus. *See Gen. Bibl.* IV, Justinian.
Codinus, G. De officiis. Ed. Bekker, I. CSHB. 1839.
Constantine Porphyrogenitus. De cerimoniis. De thematibus. De administrando imperio. *See Gen. Bibl.* IV.
Ibn Khurdādhbih. Liber viarum et provinciarum. (Arabic.) Ed. with French transl. De Goeje, M. J. (Bibliotheca Geographorum Arabicorum. VI.) Leiden. 1889.
Jus graeco-romanum. Ed. Zachariae v. Lingenthal. Pt. III. Novellae constitutiones. *See Gen. Bibl.* IV.
Justiniani Novellae. *See Gen. Bibl.* IV.
Leo VI. Tactica. MPG. CVII.
Liber de re militari. (Incerti scriptoris byzantini saeculi x.) Ed. Vári, R. Leipsic. 1901.
Mauricius. Strategicon. Ed. Scheffer, J. Upsala. 1664.
Nicephorus Phocas. Περὶ παραδρομῆς πολέμου. Ed. Hase, C. B. (*with* Leo Diaconus). CSHB. 1828. Also ed. Kulakovski, Y. A. (Στρατηγικὴ ἔκθεσις καὶ σύνταξις.) Mém. AcadIP. 8th series. Vol. VIII. 1908.
Philotheus. Kletorologion. Ed. Bury, J. B. *in* The imperial administrative system. *See Gen. Bibl.* v.
Prefect, Book of the (τὸ ἐπαρχικὸν βιβλίον). Ed. Nicole, J. *See Gen. Bibl.* IV.
Qudāma. Liber tributi. (Arabic.) Ed. De Goeje, M. J. (Bibl. Geog. Arab. VI.) Leiden. 1889.
Schlumberger, G. Sigillographie de l'empire byzantin. *See Gen. Bibl.* III.
Taktikon. Ed. Uspenski, F. *in* Izvêstiya russk. arkheol. Inst. v Konstantinopolê. III. 1898.

II. MODERN WORKS.

Andreadès, A. Ἱστορία τῆς ἑλληνικῆς δημοσίας οἰκονομίας. Vol. I. Athens. 1918.
—— Les finances byzantines. Revue des sciences politiques. II. 1911.
—— Le montant du budget de l'empire byzantin. Revue des études grecques. XXXIV. 1921.
Aussaresses, F. L'armée byzantine à la fin du VIe siècle. Paris. 1909.
Bêlyáev, D. F. Byzantina. Vols. I–III. St Petersburg. 1891–1908. (In Russian.)
Bréhier, L. and Batiffol, P. Les survivances du culte impérial romain. Paris. 1920.
Brentano, L. Die byzant. Volkswirthschaft. *In* Schmoller, G. Jahrbuch f. Gesetzgebung, 41. Munich. 1917.
Brightman, F. E. Byzantine imperial coronations. JTS. II. 1901.
Brooks, E. W. Arabic lists of the byzantine themes. JHS. XXI. 1901.
Bury, J. B. The Ceremonial Book of Constantine Porphyrogennetos. EHR. XXII. 1907.
—— The constitution of the Later Roman Empire. (Creighton memorial lecture.) *See Gen. Bibl.* v.
—— The imperial administrative system in the ninth century. British Academy. Supplemental papers. I. *See Gen. Bibl.* v.

Bury, J. B. The naval policy of the Roman Empire in relation to the Western provinces from the seventh to the ninth century. (Centenario d. nascita di M. Amari. Vol. II.) Palermo. 1900.

Diehl, C. Études sur l'administration byzantine dans l'exarchat de Ravenne. Paris. 1888.

—— L'Afrique byzantine. Paris. 1896.

—— Justinien et la civilisation byzantine au VIe siècle. Paris. 1901.

—— La civilisation byzantine: les institutions. *In* Études byzantines. *See Gen. Bibl.* v.

—— L'origine du régime des thèmes dans l'empire byzantin. *Ibid. See Gen. Bibl.* v.

—— Sur la date de quelques passages du livre des Cérémonies. *Ibid. See Gen. Bibl.* v.

—— Byzance: grandeur et décadence. *See Gen. Bibl.* v.

Dieterich, K. Hofleben in Byzanz. Leipsic. 1914?

Gelzer, H. Die Genesis der byzant. Themenverfassung. *In* Abhandl. d. k. sächs. Gesell. d. Wissen. Phil.-hist. Kl. XVIII. 1899.

—— Das Verhältnis von Staat und Kirche in Byzanz. HZ. 1901.

—— Byzantinische Kulturgeschichte. *See Gen. Bibl.* v.

Gelzer, M. Studien zur byzantinischen Verwaltung Aegyptens. Leipsic. 1909.

Gfrörer, A. F. Das byzant. Seewesen. *In* Byzantinische Geschichten *See Gen. Bibl.* v.

Hartmann, L. M. Untersuchungen zur Geschichte der byzantinischen Verwaltung in Italien. Leipsic. 1889.

Kalligas, P. Μελέται καὶ λόγοι. Athens. 1882.

Koch, P. Die byzantinischen Beamtentitel von 400 bis 700. Jena. 1903. [diss.]

Kulakovski, Y. A. Istoriya Vizantii. 3 vols. Kiev. 1910–15.

—— Drung i drungarii. *In* VV. IX. 1902.

—— Vizantiyski lager kontsa x vêka. *In* VV. x. 1903.

—— K voprosu ob imeni i istorii themy "Opsikii." *In* VV. XI. 1904.

Lécrivain, C. Le sénat romain depuis Dioclétien à Rome et à Constantinople. EcfrAR. Paris. 1884.

Maspero, J. Organisation militaire de l'Égypte byzantine. Paris. 1912.

Mitard, M. Note sur la fonction d' ἐκ προσώπου τῶν θεμάτων. BZ. XII. 1903.

Mommsen, T. Ostgotische Studien. Neu. Arch. XIV. 1888.

Monnier, H. Études de droit byzantin: l' ἐπιβολή. NRDF. XVI. 1892. XVIII. 1894. XIX. 1895.

—— Méditation sur la constitution ἑκατέρῳ. *Ibid.* XXIV. 1900.

Neumann, C. Die byzantinische Marine. HZ. 1898.

Rambaud, A. N. Études sur l'histoire byzantine. Paris. 1912.

—— L'empire grec au dixième siècle. Paris. 1870.

Ramsay, W. M. The Orthodox Church in the Byzantine Empire. *In* The Expositor. Oct. 1908.

Reiske, J. J. Commentarii ad Constantinum Porph. de Cerimoniis. *In* Constant. Porph. opera. Vol. II. CSHB. *See Gen. Bibl.* IV.

Schlumberger, G. Un empereur byzantin au Xe siècle: Nicéphore Phocas. *See Gen. Bibl.* v.

Sickel, W. Das byzant. Krönungsrecht bis zum x Jahrhundert. BZ. VI. 1897.

Stein, E. Studien zur Geschichte des byzant. Reiches. Stuttgart. 1919.

Uspenski, F. Partii tsirka i dimy v Konstantinopolê. *In* VV. I. 1894.

—— Vizantiyskaya tabel o rangakh. *In* Izvêstiya russk. arkheol. Inst. v Konstantinopolê. III. 1898.

—— Konstantinopol'ski Eparkh. *Ibid.* IV. 1899.

—— Voennoe ustroystvo vizantiyskoi imperii. *Ibid.* VI. 1900.

Vogt, A. Basile Ier. Paris. 1908.

Zachariae von Lingenthal, K. E. Geschichte des griech.-römischen Rechts. *See Gen. Bibl.* v.

—— Zur Kenntniss der röm. Steuerwesens in der Kaiserzeit. Mém. AcadIP. 7th series. VI. 1863.

—— Wissenschaft und Recht für das Heer vom VI bis zum Anfang des x Jahrhunderts. BZ. III. 1894.

CHAPTER XXIV.

BYZANTINE CIVILISATION.

I. SOURCES.

[The data for the history of Byzantine Civilisation are derived from the whole of Byzantine literature. It would therefore be impossible as well as useless to give a complete list of sources. Only the sources concerning the monuments and life of Constantinople are enumerated below.]

Anonymous. De antiquitatibus Constantinopolitanis. Ed. Banduri, A. *in* Imperium orientale. Vol. I. *See Gen. Bibl.* II.

Anonymous. *Περὶ τῶν τάφων τῶν βασιλέων τῶν ὄντων ἐν τῷ ναῷ τῶν ἁγίων ἀποστόλων.* Ed. Banduri, A. *Ibid.* Vol. I.

Cecaumenus. Strategikon. Ed. Vasil'evski, V. and Jernstedt, V. *in* Zapiski Ist.-Filol. Fakult. AcadIP. 1896. [For life in the provinces.]

Constantine Porphyrogenitus. De cerimoniis aulae Byzantinae. *See Gen. Bibl.* IV.

Constantine the Rhodian. Description of the works of art and of the church of the Holy Apostles at Constantinople. Ed. Legrand, E. and Reinach, T. *In* Revue des études grecques. 1896.

Itinéraires russes en Orient. French transl. Khitrovo, Mme. B. de. Geneva. 1889.

Mesarites, Nicholas. Description of the church of the Holy Apostles. Ed. Heisenberg, A. *in* Die Apostelkirche in Konstantinopel. Leipsic. 1908.

Nicetas Acominatus (Choniates). De signis Constantinopolitanis. Ed. Bekker, I. CSHB. 1835.

Notitia urbis Constantinopolitanae. Ed. Seeck, O. *in* Notitia dignitatum. Berlin. 1876.

Pachymeres, George. *Ἔκφρασις τοῦ Αὐγουστεῶνος.* Ed. Banduri, A. *in* Imperium orientale. Vol. I. *See Gen. Bibl.* II.

Paul the Silentiary. *Ἔκφρασις τοῦ ναοῦ τῆς ἁγίας Σοφίας.* Ed. Bekker, I. CSHB. 1837.

—— *Ἔκφρασις τοῦ ἄμβωνος. Ibid.*

Photius. *Ἔκφρασις τῆς ἐν τοῖς βασιλείοις νέας ἐκκλησίας.* Ed. Banduri, A. *in* Imperium orientale. Vol. I. *See Gen. Bibl.* II.

Prefect, Book of the. *See Gen. Bibl.* IV.

Procopius. De aedificiis. Ed. Haury, J. *in* Opera omnia. Vol. III 2. Leipsic. 1913.

Scriptores originum Constantinopolitanarum. Ed. Preger, T. 2 vols. Leipsic. 1901–7.

II. MODERN WORKS.

(a) ON BYZANTINE CIVILISATION IN GENERAL.

Diehl, C. Byzance: grandeur et décadence. *See Gen. Bibl.* V.

—— Figures byzantines. *See Gen. Bibl.* V.

—— La sagesse de Cecaumenos. *In* Dans l'Orient byzantin. Paris. 1917.

—— La société byzantine. *In* Études byzantines. *See Gen. Bibl.* V.

Dieterich, K. Byzantinische Charakterköpfe. Leipsic. 1908.

Gelzer, H. Byzantinische Kulturgeschichte. *See Gen. Bibl.* V.

Hesseling, D. C. Essai sur la civilisation byzantine. French transl. Paris. 1907.

Krause, J. H. Die Byzantiner des Mittelalters. Halle. 1869. [Unreliable.]

Paparrhegopoulos, K. Histoire de la civilisation hellénique. *See Gen. Bibl.* V.

Roth, K. Sozial und Kulturgeschichte des byzantinischen Reichs. Leipsic. 1917.

Turchi, N. La civiltà bizantina. Florence. 1915.

Uspenski, F. Ocherki po istorii vizantiyskoi obrazovannosti. St Petersburg. 1892.

(*b*) On the topography of Constantinople.

[Bibliography in Destunis, G. The topography of Constantinople in the Middle Ages. ZMNP. 1882, 83. (Russian.) *See also* Pauly-Wissowa, article Constantinopolis.]

Andreadès, A. De la population de Constantinople sous les empereurs byzantins. *In* Metroon. i. 1920.
Aristarches, S. Ἀρχαιολογικὸς χάρτης τῶν χερσαίων τειχῶν Κωνσταντινουπόλεως. Παράρτημα of the Ἑλληνικὸς Φιλολογικὸς Σύλλογος of Constantinople. Vol. xiv. 1884.
Banduri, A. Imperium orientale. *See Gen. Bibl.* ii.
Bêlyáev, D. F. Byzantina. Vols. i–iii. St Petersburg. 1891–1908. (In Russian.)
Beylié, L. M. E. de. L'habitation byzantine. Paris. 1912.
Constantius Patriarcha. Κωνσταντινιὰς παλαιά τε καὶ νεωτέρα. Venice. 1824.
Djelal Essad. Constantinople. Paris. 1909.
Du Cange, C. du Fresne. Constantinopolis Christiana. *In* Historia Byzantina. Pts. ii and iii. *See Gen. Bibl.* v.
Ebersolt, J. Constantinople byzantine et les voyageurs du Levant. Paris. 1919.
Glück, H. Das Hebdomon von Konstantinopel. Vienna. 1920.
Gyllius, P. De topographia Constantinopoleos. Lyons. 1561.
Hammer-Purgstall, J. von. Constantinopolis und der Bosporos. 2 vols. Pest. 1822.
Mordtmann, A. Esquisse topographique de Constantinople. *See Gen. Bibl.* ii.
Oberhummer, E. Constantinopolis. Stuttgart. 1899.
Paspates, A. G. Βυζαντιναὶ μελέται τοπογραφικαὶ καὶ ἱστορικαί. Constantinople. 1877.
Richter, J. P. Quellen der byzant. Kunstgeschichte. Vienna. 1897.
Skarlatos Byzantios, C. D. Ἡ Κωνσταντινούπολις. 3 vols. Athens. 1851–69.
Strzygowski, J. and Forchheimer, P. Die byzant. Wasserbehälter von Konstantinopel. Vienna. 1897.
Unger, F. W. Quellen der byzant. Kunstgeschichte. Vienna. 1878.
Van Millingen, A. Byzantine Constantinople: the walls of the city and adjoining historical sites. *See Gen. Bibl.* ii.

(*c*) On St Sophia and the churches of Constantinople.

Antoniades. Ἔκφρασις τῆς ἁγίας Σοφίας. Paris. 1917.
Diehl, C. Justinien et la civilisation byzantine au vi[e] siècle. Paris. 1901.
Ebersolt, J. Sainte Sophie de Constantinople. Paris. 1910.
—— Sanctuaires du Constantinople. Paris. 1921.
—— and Thiers, A. Les églises de Constantinople. Paris. 1913.
Gurlitt, C. Die Baukunst Konstantinopels. Berlin. 1908 ff.
Heisenberg, A. Die Apostelkirche in Konstantinopel. Leipsic. 1908.
Kondakov (Kondakoff), N. P. Vizantiyskiya tserkvi i pamyatniki Konstantinopolya. Odessa. 1887.
Lethaby, W. R. and Swainson, H. The church of Sancta Sophia. London. 1894.
Pulgher, D. Les anciennes églises byzantines de Constantinople. (With atlas.) Vienna. 1878–80.
Salzenberg, W. Alt-christliche Baudenkmäler von Constantinopel. Berlin. 1854.
Van Millingen, A. Byzantine churches in Constantinople. London. 1912.

(*d*) On monastic life.

Ferradou, A. Les biens des monastères à Byzance. Paris. 1896.
Marin, E. Les moines de Constantinople. Paris. 1897.
Nissen, W. Die Regelung des Klosterwesens im Rhomäerreiche. Hamburg. 1897.
Oeconomos, L. La vie religieuse dans l'empire byzantin au temps des Comnènes et des Anges. Paris. 1918.

(*e*) On the Imperial Palaces.

Bury, J. B. The Great Palace. BZ. xx. 1911.
Dieterich, K. Hofleben in Byzanz. Leipsic. 1912.

Ebersolt, J. Le Grand Palais de Constantinople et le livre des Cérémonies. Paris. 1910.
—— Recherches dans les ruines du Grand Palais. *In* Mission archéologique à Constantinople. Paris. 1921.
—— Études sur la vie publique et privée à la cour byzantine. *In* Mélanges d'histoire et d'archéologie byzantine. Paris. 1917.
Labarte, J. Le Palais impérial à Constantinople. Paris. 1861.
Papadopoulos, J. Αἱ Βλαχερναί. Constantinople. 1921.
Paspates, A. G. Τὰ βυζαντινὰ ἀνακτορά. Athens. 1885.

(*f*) On the Hippodrome.

Grosvenor, E. A. The hippodrome of Constantinople. London. 1889.
Rambaud, A. Le sport et l'hippodrome à Constantinople. *In* Études sur l'histoire byzantine. Paris. 1912.
Uspenski, F. Partii tsirka i dimy v Konstantinopolê. *In* VV. i. 1894.

(*g*) On commerce and industry.

Brentano, L. Die byzant. Volkswirthschaft. Munich. 1917.
Heyd, W. Histoire du commerce du Levant. *See Gen. Bibl.* v.

(*h*) On literature.

Krumbacher, K. Geschichte der byzant. Litteratur. *See Gen. Bibl.* v. [Indispensable.]

(*i*) On the history of art.

Bayet, C. L'art byzantin. 2nd edn. Paris. 1904.
Dalton, O. M. Byzantine art and archaeology. *See Gen. Bibl.* v.
Diehl, C. Manuel d'art byzantin. *See Gen. Bibl.* v.
Kondakoff (Kondakov), N. P. Histoire de l'art byzantin. *See Gen. Bibl.* v.
Millet, G. L'art byzantin. *In* Michel, A. Histoire de l'art. Vols. i and iii. Paris. 1905, 8.
Wulff, O. Altchristliche und byzantinische Kunst. Berlin. 1914.

(*j*) On the agrarian question and the Byzantine feudal lords.

Neumann, C. Die Weltstellung des byzant. Reiches vor den Kreuzzügen. *See Gen. Bibl.* v.
Rambaud, A. N. L'empire grec au xe siècle. Paris. 1870.
Testaud, G. Des rapports des puissants et des petits propriétaires ruraux dans l'empire byzantin au xe siècle. Bordeaux. 1898.

CHRONOLOGICAL TABLE
OF
LEADING EVENTS MENTIONED IN THIS VOLUME

330 (11 May) Inauguration of Constantinople, 'New Rome,' by Constantine the Great.
428–633 Persian rule in Armenia.
476 Deposition of Romulus Augustus.
529 Justinian's Code.
533 Justinian's *Digest* and *Institutes*.
535 Justinian's *Novels*.
537 Inauguration of St Sophia.
558 The Avars appear in Europe.
565 Death of Justinian.
568 The Lombards invade Italy.
The Avars enter Pannonia.
c. 582 Creation of the exarchates of Africa and Ravenna.
626 The Avars besiege Constantinople.
627 Defeat of the Persians by Heraclius at Nineveh.
631 The Avars defeat the Bulgarians.
633-693 Byzantine rule in Armenia.
635 The Bulgarians free themselves from the power of the Chazars.
c. 650 Creation of the Asiatic themes.
679 Establishment of the Bulgarians south of the Danube.
693–862 Arab rule in Armenia.
713 First Venetian Doge elected.
717 (25 March) Accession of Leo III the Isaurian.
717–718 The Arabs besiege Constantinople.
726 Edict against images.
727 Insurrections in Greece and Italy.
732 Victory of Charles Martel at Poitiers (Tours).
739 Battle of Acroïnon.
740 Publication of the *Ecloga*.
Death of Leo III the Isaurian, and accession of Constantine V Copronymus.
741 Insurrection of Artavasdus.
742 (2 Nov.) Recovery of Constantinople by Constantine V.
744 Murder of Walīd II. The Caliphate falls into anarchy.
747 Annihilation of the Egyptian fleet.
750 Foundation of the Abbasid Caliphate.
751 Taking of Ravenna by the Lombards.
753 Iconoclastic Council of Hieria.
754 Donation of Pepin to the Papacy.
755 The war with the Bulgarians begins.
756 'Abd-ar-Raḥmān establishes an independent dynasty in Spain.
757 Election of Pope Paul IV. Ratification of Papal elections ceases to be asked of the Emperor of the East.
758 Risings of the Slavs of Thrace and Macedonia.
759 Defeat of the Bulgarians at Marcellae.
762 Baghdad founded by the Caliph Manṣūr.
Defeat of the Bulgarians at Anchialus.
764–771 Persecution of the image-worshippers.
772 Defeat of the Bulgarians at Lithosoria.

774 Annexation of the Lombard kingdom by Charlemagne.
775 (14 Sept.) Death of the Emperor Constantine V and accession of Leo IV the Chazar.
780 (8 Sept.) Death of Leo IV and Regency of Irene.
781 Pope Hadrian I ceases to date official acts by the regnal years of the Emperor.
787 Ecumenical Council of Nicaea. Condemnation of Iconoclasm.
788 Establishment of the Idrīsid dynasty in Morocco.
790 (Dec.) Abdication of Irene. Constantine VI assumes power.
797 (17 July) Deposition of Constantine VI. Irene becomes Emperor.
800 Establishment of the Aghlabid dynasty in Tunis.
(25 Dec.) Charlemagne crowned Emperor of the West.
802 (31 Oct.) Deposition of Irene and accession of Nicephorus I.
803 Destruction of the Barmecides.
809 Death of Hārūn ar-Rashīd and civil war in the Caliphate.
The Bulgarian Khan Krum invades the Empire.
Pepin of Italy's attack upon Venice.
810 Nicephorus I's scheme of financial reorganisation.
Concentration of the lagoon-townships at Rialto.
811 The Emperor Nicephorus I is defeated and slain by the Bulgarians: accession of Michael I Rangabé.
812 Treaty of Aix-la-Chapelle recognises Charlemagne's imperial title.
813 Michael I defeated at Versinicia: Krum appears before Constantinople.
Deposition of Michael I and accession of Leo V the Armenian.
Battle of Mesembria.
Ma'mūn becomes sole Caliph.
814 (14 April) Death of Krum: peace between the Empire and the Bulgarians.
815 Iconoclastic synod of Constantinople.
Banishment of Theodore of Studion.
820 (25 Dec.) Murder of Leo V, and accession of Michael II the Amorian.
822 Insurrection of Thomas the Slavonian.
826 Death of Theodore of Studion.
Conquest of Crete by the Arabs.
827 Arab invasion of Sicily.
829–842 Reign of Theophilus.
832 Edict of Theophilus against images.
833 Death of the Caliph Ma'mūn.
836 The Abbasid capital removed from Baghdad to Sāmarrā.
839 Treaty between the Russians and the Greeks.
840 Treaty of Pavia between the Emperor Lothar I and Venice.
842 The Arabs take Messina.
Disintegration of the Caliphate begins.
842–867 Reign of Michael III.
843 Council of Constantinople, and final restoration of image-worship by the Empress Theodora.
846 Ignatius becomes Patriarch.
852–893 Reign of Boris in Bulgaria.
856–866 Rule of Bardas.
858 Deposition of Ignatius and election of Photius as Patriarch.
860 The Russians appear before Constantinople.
860–861 (?) Cyril's mission to the Chazars.
863 (?) Mission of Cyril and Methodius to the Moravians.
864 Conversion of Bulgaria to orthodoxy.
867 The Schism of Photius.
The Synod of Constantinople completes the rupture with Rome.
(23 Sept.) Murder of Michael III and accession of Basil I the Macedonian.
Deposition of Photius. Restoration of Ignatius.
867 (13 Nov.) Death of Pope Nicholas I.
(14 Dec.) Election of Pope Hadrian II.
868 Independence of Egypt under the Ṭūlūnid dynasty.

869 (14 Feb.) Death of Cyril.
Ecumenical Council of Constantinople. End of the Schism.
870 Methodius becomes the first Moravo-Pannonian archbishop.
871 War with the Paulicians.
876 Capture of Bari from the Saracens by the Greeks.
877 Death of Ignatius and reinstatement of Photius as Patriarch.
(22 July) Council of Ravenna.
878 (21 May) Capture of Syracuse by the Arabs.
878 (?) Promulgation of the *Prochiron.*
882 Fresh rupture between the Eastern and Western Churches; excommunication of Photius.
885 (6 April) Death of Methodius.
886–912 Reign of Leo VI the Wise.
886 Deposition and exile of Photius.
887–892 Reign of Ashot I in Armenia.
c. 888 Publication of the *Basilics.*
891 Death of Photius.
892 The Abbasid capital restored to Baghdad.
892–914 Reign of Smbat I in Armenia.
893–927 Reign of Simeon in Bulgaria.
895–896 The Magyars migrate into Hungary.
898 Reconciliation between the Eastern and Western Churches.
899 The Magyars invade Lombardy.
900 Victory of Nicephorus Phocas at Adana.
The Magyars occupy Pannonia.
902 (1 Aug.) Fall of Taormina, the last Greek stronghold in Sicily.
904 Thessalonica sacked by the Saracens.
906 Leo VI's fourth marriage: contest with the Patriarch.
The Magyars overthrow the Great Moravian State.
907 Russian expedition against Constantinople.
909–1171 The Fāṭimid Caliphate in Africa.
912 (11 May) Death of Leo VI and accession of Constantine VII Porphyrogenitus under the regency of Alexander.
913 Simeon of Bulgaria appears before Constantinople.
915–928 Reign of Ashot II in Armenia.
917 (20 Aug.) Bulgarian victory at Anchialus.
919 (25 Mar.) Usurpation of Romanus Lecapenus.
920 (June) A Council at Constantinople pronounces upon fourth marriages.
923 Simeon besieges Constantinople.
927 (8 Sept.) Peace with Bulgaria.
932 Foundation of the Buwaihid dynasty.
933 Venice establishes her supremacy in Istria.
941 Russian expedition against Constantinople.
944 (16 Dec.) Deposition of Romanus Lecapenus. Personal rule of Constantine VII begins.
945 The Buwaihids enter Baghdad and control the Caliphate.
954 Princess Olga of Russia embraces Christianity.
955 Battle of the Lechfeld.
959 (9 Nov.) Death of Constantine VII and accession of Romanus II.
959–976 Reign of the Doge Peter IV Candianus.
961 Recovery of Crete by Nicephorus Phocas.
(Mar.) Advance in Asia by the Greeks.
Athanasius founds the convent of St Laura on Mt Athos.
963 (15 Mar.) Death of Romanus II: accession of Basil II: regency of Theophano.
(16 Aug.) Usurpation of Nicephorus II Phocas.
964 *Novel* against the monks.
965 Conquest of Cilicia.
967 Renewal of the Bulgarian war.
968 The Russians in Bulgaria.

969 (28 Oct.) Capture of Antioch.
The Fāṭimid Caliphs annex Egypt.
(10 Dec.) Murder of Nicephorus Phocas and accession of John Tzimisces.
970 Capture of Aleppo.
Accession of Géza as Prince of the Magyars.
971 Revolt of Bardas Phocas.
The Emperor John Tzimisces annexes Eastern Bulgaria.
972 Death of Svyatoslav of Kiev.
976 (10 Jan.) Death of John Tzimisces: personal rule of Basil II Bulgaroctonus begins.
Peter Orseolo I elected Doge.
976–979 Revolt of Bardas Sclerus.
980 Accession of Vladímir in Russia.
985 Fall of the eunuch Basil.
986–1018 Great Bulgarian War.
987–989 Conspiracy of Phocas and Sclerus.
988 The Fāṭimid Caliphs occupy Syria.
989 Baptism of Vladímir of Russia.
Vladímir captures Cherson.
991 The Fāṭimids re-occupy Syria.
991–1009 Reign of Peter Orseolo II as Doge.
992 (19 July) First Venetian treaty with the Eastern Empire.
994 Saif-ad-Daulah takes Aleppo and establishes himself in Northern Syria.
994–1001 War with the Fāṭimids.
995 Basil II's campaign in Syria.
996 (Jan.) *Novel* against the Powerful.
Defeat of the Bulgarians on the Spercheus.
997 Accession of St Stephen in Hungary, and conversion of the Magyars.
998–1030 Reign of Maḥmūd of Ghaznah.
1006 Vladímir of Russia makes a treaty with the Bulgarians.
1009 The Patriarch Sergius erases the Pope's name from the diptychs.
1014 Battle of Cimbalongu; death of the Tsar Samuel.
1015 Death of Vladímir of Russia.
1018–1186 Bulgaria a Byzantine province.
1021–1022 Annexation of Vaspurakan to the Empire.
1024 The Patriarch Eustathius attempts to obtain from the Pope the autonomy of the Greek Church.
1025 (15 Dec.) Death of Basil II and accession of Constantine VIII.
1026 Fall of the Orseoli at Venice.
1028 (11 Nov.) Death of Constantine VIII and succession of Zoë and Romanus III Argyrus.
1030 Defeat of the Greeks near Aleppo.
1031 Capture of Edessa by George Maniaces.
1034 (12 April) Murder of Romanus III and accession of Michael IV the Paphlagonian.
Government of John the Orphanotrophos.
1038 Death of St Stephen of Hungary.
Success of George Maniaces in Sicily.
The Seljūq Ṭughril Beg proclaimed.
1041 (10 Dec.) Death of Michael IV and succession of Michael V Calaphates.
Banishment of John the Orphanotrophos.
1042 (21 April) Revolution in Constantinople; fall of Michael V.
Zoë and Theodora joint Empresses.
(11–12 June) Zoë's marriage; accession of her husband, Constantine IX Monomachus.
1043 Michael Cerularius becomes Patriarch.
Rising of George Maniaces; his defeat and death at Ostrovo.
1045 Foundation of the Law School of Constantinople.
1046 Annexation of Armenia (Ani) to the Empire.
1047 Revolt of Tornicius.

1048 Appearance of the Seljūqs on the eastern frontier of the Empire.
1050 Death of the Empress Zoë.
1054 (20 July) The Patriarch Michael Cerularius breaks with Rome; schism between the Eastern and Western Churches.
1055 (11 Jan.) Death of Constantine IX; Theodora sole Empress.
The Seljūq Ṭughril Beg enters Baghdad.
1056 (31 Aug.) Death of Theodora and proclamation of Michael VI Stratioticus.
1057 Revolt of Isaac Comnenus. Deposition of Michael VI.
(1 Sept. ?) Isaac I Comnenus crowned Emperor at Constantinople.
1058 Deposition and death of Michael Cerularius.
1059 Treaty of Melfi.
Abdication of Isaac Comnenus.
1059–1067 Reign of Constantine X Ducas.
1063 Death of Ṭughril Beg.
1063–1072 Reign of the Seljūq Alp Arslān.
1064 Capture of Ani by the Seljūqs, and conquest of Greater Armenia.
1066 Foundation of the Nīẓamīyah University at Baghdad.
1067–1071 Reign of Romanus III Diogenes.
1071 Capture of Bari by the Normans and loss of Italy.
Battle of Manzikert.
The Seljūqs occupy Jerusalem.
1071–1078 Reign of Michael VII Parapinaces Ducas.
1072–1092 Reign of the Seljūq Malik Shāh.
1077 Accession of Sulaimān I, Sultan of Rūm.
1078 The Turks at Nicaea.
1078–1081 Reign of Nicephorus III Botaniates.
1080 Alliance between Robert Guiscard and Pope Gregory VII.
Foundation of the Armeno-Cilician kingdom.
1081–1118 Reign of Alexius I Comnenus.
1081–1084 Robert Guiscard's invasion of Epirus.
1082 Treaty with Venice.
1086 Incursions of the Patzinaks begin.
1091 (29 April) Defeat of the Patzinaks at the river Leburnium.
1094–1095 Invasion of the Cumans.
1094 Council of Piacenza.
1095 (18–28 Nov.) Council of Clermont proclaims the First Crusade.
1096 The Crusaders at Constantinople.
1097 The Crusaders capture Nicaea.
1098 Council of Bari. St Anselm refutes the Greeks.
1099 Establishment of the Kingdom of Jerusalem.
1100 (18 July) Death of Godfrey of Bouillon.
1104 Defeat of the Crusaders at Ḥarrān.
1107 Bohemond's expedition against Constantinople.
1108 Battle of Durazzo.
Treaty with Bohemond.
1116 Battle of Philomelium.
1118–1143 Reign of John II Comnenus.
1119 First expedition of John Comnenus to Asia Minor.
1122 Defeat of the Patzinaks near Eski-Sagra.
1122–1126 War with Venice.
1128 The Emperor John Comnenus defeats the Hungarians near Haram.
1137 (May) Roger II of Sicily's fleet defeated off Trani.
1137–1138 Campaign of John Comnenus in Cilicia and Syria.
1143–1180 Reign of Manuel I Comnenus.
1147–1149 The Second Crusade.
1147–1149 War with Roger II of Sicily.
1151 The Byzantines at Ancona.
1152–1154 Hungarian War.
1154 Death of Roger II of Sicily.

1158 Campaign of Manuel Comnenus in Syria.
1159 His solemn entry into Antioch; zenith of his power.
1163 Expulsion of the Greeks from Cilicia.
1164 Battle of Ḥārim.
1168 Annexation of Dalmatia.
1170 The Emperor Manuel attempts to re-unite the Greek and Armenian Churches.
1171 Rupture of Manuel with Venice.
1173 Frederick Barbarossa besieges Ancona.
1176 Battle of Myriocephalum.
Battle of Legnano.
1177 Peace of Venice.
1180–1183 Reign of Alexius II Comnenus.
1180 Foundation of the Serbian monarchy by Stephen Nemanja.
1182 Massacre of Latins in Constantinople.
1183 (Sept.) Andronicus I Comnenus becomes joint Emperor.
(Nov.) Murder of Alexius II.
1185 The Normans take Thessalonica.
Deposition and death of Andronicus; accession of Isaac II Angelus.
1185–1219 Reign of Leo II the Great of Cilicia.
1186 Second Bulgarian Empire founded.
1187 Saladin captures Jerusalem.
1189 Sack of Thessalonica.
1189–1192 Third Crusade.
1190 Death of Frederick Barbarossa in the East.
Isaac Angelus defeated by the Bulgarians.
1191 Occupation of Cyprus by Richard Coeur-de-Lion.
1192 Guy de Lusignan purchases Cyprus from Richard I.
1193–1205 Reign of the Doge Enrico Dandolo.
1195 Deposition of Isaac II; accession of Alexius III Angelus.
1197–1207 The Bulgarian Tsar Johannitsa (Kalojan).
1201 (April) Fourth Crusade. The Crusaders' treaty with Venice.
(May) Boniface of Montferrat elected leader of the Crusade.
1203 (17 July) The Crusaders enter Constantinople.
Deposition of Alexius III; restoration of Isaac II with Alexius IV Angelus.
1203–1227 Empire of Jenghiz Khan.
1204 (8 Feb.) Deposition of Isaac II and Alexius IV; accession of Alexius V Ducas (Mourtzouphlos).
(13 April) Sack of Constantinople.
(16 May) Coronation of Baldwin, Count of Flanders, and foundation of the Latin Empire of Constantinople.
The compulsory union of the Eastern and Western Churches.
The Venetians purchase the island of Crete.
Alexius Comnenus founds the state of Trebizond.
1205 (14 April) The Bulgarians defeat the Emperor Baldwin I at Hadrianople.
1206 (21 Aug.) Henry of Flanders crowned Latin Emperor of Constantinople.
Theodore I Lascaris crowned Emperor of Nicaea.
1208 Peace with the Bulgarians.
1210 The Turks of Rūm defeated on the Maeander by Theodore Lascaris.
1212 Peace with Nicaea.
1215 The Fourth Lateran Council.
1216 Death of the Emperor Henry, and succession of Peter of Courtenay.
1217 Stephen crowned King of Serbia.
1218 Death of Geoffrey of Villehardouin, Prince of Achaia.
1219 Creation of a separate Serbian Church.
1221–1228 Reign of Robert of Courtenay, Latin Emperor of Constantinople.
1222 Recovery of Thessalonica by the Greeks of Epirus.
Death of Theodore Lascaris, Emperor of Nicaea. Accession of John III Vatatzes.

1222 First appearance of the Mongols in Europe.
1224 The Emperor of Nicaea occupies Hadrianople.
1228 Death of Stephen, the first King of Serbia.
1228–1237 Reign of John of Brienne, Latin Emperor of Constantinople.
1230 Destruction of the Greek Empire of Thessalonica by the Bulgarians.
1234 Fall of the Kin Dynasty in China.
1235 Revival of the Bulgarian Patriarchate.
1236 Constantinople attacked by the Greeks and Bulgarians.
1236 (?) Alliance between the Armenians and the Mongols.
1237 Invasion of Europe by the Mongols.
1237–1261 Reign of Baldwin II, last Latin Emperor of Constantinople.
1241 Battles of Liegnitz and Mohi.
Death of John Asên II; the decline of Bulgaria begins.
1244 The Despotat of Thessalonica becomes a vassal of Nicaea.
1245 Council of Lyons.
1246 Reconquest of Macedonia from the Bulgarians.
1254 (30 Oct.) Death of John Vatatzes; Theodore II Lascaris succeeds as Emperor of Nicaea.
Submission of the Despot of Epirus to Nicaea.
Mamlūk Sultans in Egypt.
1255–1256 Theodore II's Bulgarian campaigns.
1256 Overthrow of the Assassins by the Mongols.
1258 Death of Theodore II Lascaris. Accession of John IV Lascaris.
Destruction of Baghdad by the Mongols and overthrow of the Caliphate.
1259 (1 Jan.) Michael VIII Palaeologus proclaimed Emperor of Nicaea.
1259–1294 Reign of Kublai Khan.
1260 The Egyptians defeat the Mongols at ʿAin Jālūt.
1261 (25 July) Capture of Constantinople by the Greeks; end of the Latin Empire.
1261–1530 Abbasid Caliphate in Cairo.
1266 (Feb.) Charles of Anjou's victory over Manfred at Benevento.
1267 (27 May) Treaty of Viterbo.
1267–1272 Progress of Charles of Anjou in Epirus.
1270 (25 Aug.) Death of St Louis.
1274 Ecumenical Council at Lyons; union of the Churches again achieved.
1276 Leo III of Cilicia defeats the Mamlūks.
1278 Leo III of Cilicia defeats the Seljūqs of Iconium.
1281 Joint Mongol and Armenian forces defeated by the Mamlūks on the Orontes.
(18 Nov.) Excommunication of Michael Palaeologus; breach of the Union.
Victory of the Berat over the Angevins.
1282 (30 May) The Sicilian Vespers.
(11 Dec.) Death of Michael Palaeologus. Accession of Andronicus II.
c. 1290 Foundation of Wallachia.
1291 Fall of Acre.
1299 Osmān, Emir of the Ottoman Turks.
1302 Osmān's victory at Baphaeum.
End of the alliance between the Armenians and the Mongols.
1302–1311 The Catalan Grand Company in the East.
1308 Turks enter Europe.
Capture of Ephesus by the Turks.
1309 Capture of Rhodes from the Turks by the Knights of St John.
1311 Battle of the Cephisus.
1326 Brūsa surrenders to the Ottoman Turks.
(Nov.) Death of Osmān.
1326–1359 Reign of Orkhān.
1328–1341 Reign of Andronicus III Palaeologus.
1329 The Ottomans capture Nicaea.
1330 (28 June) Defeat of the Bulgarians by the Serbians at the battle of Velbužd.

1331 (8 Sept.) Coronation of Stephen Dušan as King of Serbia.
1336 Birth of Tīmūr.
1337 The Ottomans capture Nicomedia.
Conquest of Cilicia by the Mamlūks.
1341 Succession of John V Palaeologus. Rebellion of John Cantacuzene.
1342–1344 Guy of Lusignan King of Cilicia.
1342–1349 Revolution of the Zealots at Thessalonica.
1344–1363 Reign of Constantine IV in Cilicia.
1345 Stephen Dušan conquers Macedonia.
1346 Stephen Dušan crowned Emperor of the Serbs and Greeks.
1347 John VI Cantacuzene takes Constantinople.
1348 Foundation of the Despotat of Mistra.
1349 Independence of Moldavia.
1350 Serbo-Greek treaty.
1354 The Turks take Gallipoli.
1355 Abdication of John VI Cantacuzene. Restoration of John V.
(20 Dec.) Death of Stephen Dušan.
1356 The Turks begin to settle in Europe.
1357 The Turks capture Hadrianople.
1359–1389 Reign of Murād I.
1360 Formation of the Janissaries from tribute-children.
1363–1373 Reign of Constantine V in Cilicia.
1365 The Turks establish their capital at Hadrianople.
1368 Foundation of the Ming dynasty in China.
1369 (21 Oct.) John V abjures the schism.
1371 (26 Sept.) Battle of the Maritza.
Death of Stephen Uroš V.
1373 The Emperor John V becomes the vassal of the Sultan Murād.
1373–1393 Leo VI of Lusignan, the last King of Armenia.
1375 Capture and exile of Leo VI of Armenia.
1376–1379 Rebellion of Andronicus IV.
Coronation of Tvrtko as King of the Serbs and Bosnia.
1379 Restoration of John V.
1382 Death of Louis the Great of Hungary.
1387 Turkish defeat on the Toplica.
Surrender of Thessalonica to the Turks.
1389 (15 June) Battle of Kossovo; fall of the Serbian Empire.
1389–1403 Reign of Bāyazīd.
1390 Usurpation of John VII Palaeologus.
1391 Death of John V. Accession of Manuel II Palaeologus.
(23 Mar.) Death of Tvrtko I.
Capture of Philadelphia by the Turks.
1393 Turkish conquest of Thessaly.
(17 July) Capture of Trnovo; end of the Bulgarian Empire.
1394 (10 Oct.) Turkish victory at Rovine in Wallachia.
1396 (25 Sept.) Battle of Nicopolis.
1397 Bāyazīd attacks Constantinople.
1398 The Turks invade Bosnia.
Tīmūr invades India and sacks Delhi.
1401 Tīmūr sacks Baghdad.
1402 (28 July) Tīmūr defeats the Ottoman Sultan Bāyazīd at Angora.
1402–1413 Civil war among the Ottoman Turks.
1403 (21 Nov.) Second battle of Kossovo.
1405 Death of Tīmūr.
1409 Council of Pisa.
1413–1421 Reign of Mahomet I.
1413 (10 July) Turkish victory at Chamorlū.
1416 The Turks declare war on Venice.
(29 May) Turkish fleet defeated off Gallipoli.
1418 Death of Mirčea the Great of Wallachia.

1421–1451 Reign of Murād II.
1422 Siege of Constantinople by the Turks.
1423 Turkish expedition into the Morea.
Thessalonica purchased by Venice.
1423–1448 Reign of John VIII Palaeologus.
1426 Battle of Choirokoitia.
1430 Capture of Thessalonica by the Turks.
1431 Council of Basle opens.
1432 Death of the last Frankish Prince of Achaia.
1438 (9 April) Opening of the Council of Ferrara.
1439 (10 Jan.) The Council of Ferrara removed to Florence.
(6 July) The Union of Florence.
Completion of the Turkish conquest of Serbia.
1440 The Turks besiege Belgrade.
1441 John Hunyadi appointed *voïvode* of Transylvania.
1443–1468 Skanderbeg's war of independence against the Turks.
1444 (July) Peace of Szegedin.
(10 Nov.) Battle of Varna.
1446 Turkish invasion of the Morea.
1448 (17 Oct.) Third battle of Kossovo. Accession of Constantine XI Palaeologus.
1451 Accession of Mahomet II.
1453 (29 May) Capture of Constantinople by the Turks.
1456 The Turks again besiege Belgrade.
1457 Stephen the Great succeeds in Moldavia.
1458 The Turks capture Athens.
1459 Final end of medieval Serbia.
1461 Turkish conquest of Trebizond.
1462–1479 War between Venice and the Turks.
1463 Turkish conquest of Bosnia.
1468 Turkish conquest of Albania.
1475 Stephen the Great of Moldavia defeats the Turks at Racova.
1479 Venice cedes Scutari to the Turks.
1484 The Montenegrin capital transferred to Cetinje.
1489 Venice acquires Cyprus.
1499 Renewal of Turco-Venetian War.
1517 Conquest of Egypt by the Turks.
1523 Conquest of Rhodes by the Turks.
1537–1540 Third Turco-Venetian War.
1571 Conquest of Cyprus from Venice by the Turks.

INDEX

Aaron, son of Shishman, Bulgarian chief, 239; executed, 240, 242
Aaron the Bulgarian, general of Michael VI, 321
Abāghā, Īl-Khān of Persia, 175; and Leo III of Armenia, 176
Abas Bagratuni, Armenian prince, 159
Abas, King of Armenia, 161
Abasgia, Abasgians (Abkhaz), King of, and Basil II, 95, *see* Bagarat, Ber
'Abbās, Abbasid prince, defeats Byzantines, 122 sq.
'Abbās, son of the Caliph Ma'mūn, 128 sq.; conspires against Mu'taṣim, 130
'Abbās ibn al-Faḍl ibn Ya'qūb, commander in Sicily, 137; death of, 138
'Abbās ibn al-Walīd, Umayyad prince, general in Paphlagonia, 120
Abbasid dynasty of Caliphs at Baghdad, 36, 38, 122; decline of, 151 sq., 157, 277 sqq., 302; civilization during, Chap. x (A) *passim*; religious orthodoxy of, 288, 292, 301; literature under, 289 sqq.; churches built under, 289; dynasty at Cairo, 279; *see* Caliphs
'Abd-al-'Azīz, Saracen emir, captured by Nicephorus Phocas, 69
'Abd-al-Kabīr, Saracen general, 124
'Abdallāh, Abbasid prince, emir of Syria, 122
'Abdallāh ibn Ṭāhir, Saracen general, 127
'Abdallāh ibn Tūmait, founder of the Almohad dynasty, 306
'Abd-al-Malik, emir of Mesopotamia, captures Camacha, 125 sq.
'Abd-al-Wahhāb, Abbasid prince, emir of Mesopotamia, 122
'Abd-ar-Rahīm, invades Armenia, 156
'Abd-ar-Raḥmān, Saracen general, 125 sq.
'Abd-ar-Raḥmān, Umayyad prince, conquers Spain, 275, 300
'Abd-ar-Raḥmān, farms Mongol taxes, 640
Abgar, King of Edessa, supposed relics of Our Lord possessed by him, 63, 150
Abharī, author of textbook of logic, 297
Abkhaz, *see* Abasgians
Aboba, *see* Pliska
Abubacer (Ibn Tufail), Spanish Arab philosopher, 296
Abū-Dīnār, Saracen admiral, 131
Abū-Firās, Arab poet, captured by Nicephorus II, 144 sq.
Abū-Isḥāq ash-Shīrāzī, author of legal treatises, 306
Abū'l-'Abbās, Saracen chief, captures Reggio, 141
Abū'l-Aghlab, Saracen governor of Sicily, 136 sq.
Abū'l-'Alà al-Ma'arrī, blind Arab poet, 290
Abū'l-Aswār, governor of Dwin, 164 sq.
Abū'l-'Atāhiyah, Arab poet, 290
Abu'l-Faraj Iṣfahānī, Arab writer, 290; his *Book of Songs*, 293
Abū'l-Fidā, on death of Kai-Khusrū I, 484 *note*
Abū'l-Futūḥ, Arab mystical author, 306
Abū'l Maḥāsin, 133 *note*
Abu'l-Qāsim, Turkish emir of Nicaea, and Alexius I, 331
Abū-Muslim, governor of Rai, and Sultan Barkiyāruq, 309
Abū-Naṣr al-Kundurī, vizier of Ṭughril Beg, 305
Abū-Nuwās, Arab poet, 290
Abū-Sa'īd, emir of Syria and Mesopotamia, 130, 132
Abū-Sa'īd, Īl-Khān of Persia, 644, 652
Abū Ṭālib al-Makki, author of Sufi treatise *Sustenance of the Souls*, 293
Abydos, Bardas Phocas defeated at, 88 sqq.; 119; captured by Saracens, 141; 344; captured by Latins, 424; 481
Acarnania, assigned to Venetians, 421; held by Carlo Tocco, 461; by Serbia, 543, 552
Acciajuoli, Florentine family, and duchy of Athens, 431, 454; *see* Antonio, Francesco, Franco, Nerio, Niccolò
Achaia, principality of, founded, 422, 433 sq.; 423; 431; organization of, 437; 443; Charles of Naples becomes Prince, 446; given to Philip of Taranto, 448 sq.; claimants for, 452; held by John of Gravina, 453; 454; conquered by Navarrese, 456; rule of Zaccaria in, 459; becomes Byzantine, 460; 511; Latin Church in, 606; 609; Turks in, 675, 689; Table of rulers, 474; *see also* Geoffrey, Isabelle, William
Achelous, town of, 552
Achilleus, St, bishop of Larissa, 240; church of, at Prespa, 245
Acominatus, *see* Michael, Nicetas
Acre (St Jean d'Acre), 376; captured by Turks, 469; Venetians at, 510; 643
Acrocorinth, fortress of, 433, 436; surrenders to Turks, 463
Acroïnon, in Phrygia, victory of Leo III at, 3, 121
Acroïnon (Prymnessus), 120
Acropolis, the, at Athens, 443; 454; 456 sq.; 463; holds out against Turks, 458, 464;

fortifications on, 462; church of Our Lady on, 433
Acropolita, George, Byzantine historian, 765; on death of Kai-Khusrū, 484 *note*; 422 *note*; sent as envoy to Michael of Epirus, 494 sq.; on death of Empress Irene, 495; 499; funeral oration on John III, 500; and Theodore II, 502, 506; taken prisoner by Epirotes, 504, 508; 505; 509 *note*; sent to Bulgaria, 510, 525; 513
Acyndinus, Gregory, Byzantine scholastic philosopher, 766
Adalbert, *see* Vojtěch, St
Adalia, *see* Attalia
Adam, archbishop (Pseudo-Brochart), on condition of Serbia, 537; 539 *note*
Adam, Armenian commander against Seljūqs, 173 sq.
Adam, Muslim belief concerning, 286
Adana, in Cilicia, in Saracen wars, 120, 122, 124, 127 sqq., 145; victory of Nicephorus Phocas at, 141; held by Armenian Kingdom, 168 sq., 358; 340 sq.; restored to Byzantium, 343, 359; taken by Mamlūks, 669; council of, 179
Adata, pass of, 122 sqq., 127, 129 sq.; Saracen military colony at, 132
Adelaide, Empress, wife of Otto I, 402
Adelaide, wife of Géza, Prince of the Magyars, 213
Adelchis, Lombard prince, son of Desiderius, 19, 22
Ademar of Puy, Papal legate at the First Crusade, 337
Adernesih, curopalates of Iberia, and Romanus I, 62
Ádharbayjàn, *see* Azarbā'ījān
'Adīb Ṣābir, poet, and envoy of Sanjar, 313
Adramyttium, 344; taken by Henry of Flanders, 422, 424; Genoese at, 431, 511; Hospitallers at, 480; 481; 485
Adrasus, in Isauria, 125 *note*
Adria, territory of, 402
Adriatic Sea, Byzantine fleet in, 10, 36, 394; Saracens in, 39, 139; Bulgaria on, 241; crossed by Normans, 329; Venice and, Chap. XIII *passim*; 436; 504; 523; Serbia on, 535; 537; 541; Bosnia on, 544, 559; 553; 565; 568; 570; "an Italian lake," 583; 584; 637; themes on, 733; 742
Adscriptitii, 5
Aḍud-ud-Daulah, Buwaihid prince, 289, 297
Aegean Sea, Saracen piracy in, 45, 127 sq., 141, 144; 131; under Latin domination, Chap. XV; 489; 541; Turkish tribes on, 654 sq.; 662; Venetian fleet in, 666; 668; 672; 675; Hospitallers in, 677; 683; 699; 700; coast, 238, 657; theme of (Dodecanese), 3, 35, 733, 742; *see also* Archipelago
Aegina, attacked by Saracen pirates, 141; under Lombard rule, 435; Catalan, 457; Venetian, 465; Turkish, 467; 476
Aeneas, bishop of Paris, 250 *note*
Aeneas Sylvius, *see* Pius II, Pope
Aenus, given to Demetrius Palaeologus, 464; 465; Genoese possession, 477
Aeolian Islands, raided by Saracens, 136
Aëtius, favourite of the Empress Irene, 24
Aëtius, strategus of the Anatolics, defeated and killed by the Saracens, 130
Aetolia, assigned to Venice, 421; Serbian, 543, 552
Afḍal, vizier of the Caliph of Egypt, captures Jerusalem, 316
Afghanistan, conquered by 'Alā-ud-Dīn Muḥammad of Khwārazm, 278; 633; 651
Afrāsiyāb, King of Turkestan, supposed ancestor of Seljūq, 300
Africa, Saracens in, and Byzantium, 37, 74, 119; conquer Sicily, 134 sqq.; 274; becomes independent of Caliphate, 275; rise of Fāṭimids in, 277, 302; African slaves in Caliph's army, 285 sq.; African trade with Constantinople, 762; exarchate of, 732; emirs of, *see* Aghlab, Aḥmad, Ibrāhīm, Mahomet, Ziyādatallāh
Afshīn, ostikan of Azarbā'ījān, wars of with Ashot I of Armenia, 160; 166
Afshīn, Saracen general, 129 sq.
Afyon-Qara-Hisār (Maurocastrum), Phrygian fortress, 655
Agallianus, turmarch of the Helladics, rebels against Leo III, 9
Agapius, bishop of Aleppo, made Patriarch of Antioch, 89
Agatha, daughter of Constantine VII, 68
Agatha, daughter of Romanus I, 98 *note*
Agathias, Byzantine historian, 765
Aghlab, emir of Africa, 136
Aghlabid emirs of Africa, dynasty founded, 275, 300; overthrown, 302; policy in Sicily, 138; conflict with eastern Saracens, 141; *see* Aghlab, Aḥmad, Ibrāhīm, Mahomet, Ziyādatallāh
Aghthamar, in Armenia, church at, 163 *note*
Agnellus Particiacus, *see* Particiacus
Agnes, duchess of Mačva and Bosnia, 591
Agnes of France, married to Alexius II, 379; to Andronicus I, 382
Agnes of Montferrat, betrothed to Henry of Flanders, 425
Agylaeus, translator into Latin of the Novels of Leo VI, 714
Ahil, island in Lake Prespa, 240
Aḥmad, Ottoman, brother of Mahomet II, put to death by him, 693
Aḥmad, Aghlabid emir of Africa, 138
Aḥmad, emir of Tarsus, 131
Aḥmad, Īl-Khān of Persia, becomes a Muslim, 644
Aḥmad, ostikan of Mesopotamia, defeats Smbat I, 160
Aḥmad, son of the Caliph Mu'taṣim, 295
Aḥmad Khān, governor of Samarqand, and Sanjar, 311 sq.
Aḥmad Malik, Turkish emir, and Armeno-Cilicia, 169
Aḥmad Pasha Hercegović, *see* Stephen

Aḥmad ibn Ṭūlūn, founds independent dynasty in Egypt, 276
Ahwāz, sacked by marauders, 276
Aibak, son of, driven from Egyptian throne, 643
Aidīn (Tralles), Turks at, 655 sq.; troops from at battle of Angora, 682; emir of, 662
'Ain-ad-Daulah, Dānishmandite ruler of Melitene, 365, 374
'Ain Jālūt, Mamlūks defeat Mongols at, 279, 643
'Ain Tāb, taken by Tīmūr, 680
Aistulf, King of the Lombards, captures Ravenna, 17, 391
Aix-la-Chapelle, treaty of, 36, 395 sq., 398, 402; Bulgarian mission at, 234
Akhtum, *see* Aytony
Akhurian, Armenian river, 163, 166
Akova, "the Lady of," daughter of William of Achaia, 452
Akritas, Digenes, hero of Byzantine popular poem, 733, 740, 767, 772
'Alā-ad-Dīn, brother and vizier of Sultan Orkhān, 661; and Janissaries, 663; and army, 664
'Alā-ad-Dīn, Sultan of Rūm; *see* Qai-Qubād I
Alagöz, *see* Aragatz, Mount
Alans, the, in Byzantine army, 347, 656; revolt against Andronicus II, 657; Roger de Flor and, 658; tribes in Southern Russia, 184, 207; "Gate of the Alans" (Dariel), 187; princess of, (1) mistress of Constantine IX, 109, 115, 265; (2) wife of Isaac Comnenus, 326
'Alā-ud-Dīn, Shāh of Khwārazm, *see* Muhammad
Al-Baidā = the White City, Arab name of Itil, 191
Albania (Arran, Shirvan), Albanians (Aluans), King of, invades Armenia, 165; occupied by Persia, 187; Russian raid on, 206
Albania (in Balkans), 231; separated from Old Bulgaria, 238; included in Samuel's kingdom, 240 sqq.; bishoprics in, 243; 428 sqq.; given to Philip of Taranto, 448; 452; 494; 517; 522; 541; 542; 572; Turks overrun, 583 sqq.; 689; Skanderbeg in, 572, 692; 587; Venetian colonies in, 583, 592; Carlo Thopia in, 553
Albanians, autochthonous, 230; settle in Attica, 456, 459, 463; in Joánnina, 461; 504; Stephen Uroš II and, 535, 537; defeat Epirotes, 552; Turks and, 557, 674, 678
Alberic, Prince of the Romans, son of Marozia, 259, 263
Albert, ambassador of Conrad III to John II, 360
Albert of Aix, on First Crusade, 337; 334 *note*
Albiola, taken by Pepin, 394; Magyars at, 400
Alboin, King of the Lombards, invades Italy, 386
Albricus Trium Fontium, 478 *note*, 491 *note*
Aldobrandini, the, Pisan family, at Attalia, 480
Alemdar, Mongol chief, 645
Aleppo, taken by Nicephorus Phocas, 73, 144; 76; 124; taken by Peter Phocas, 146; attacked by Egyptians, 149; Romanus III defeated near, 150; Ḥamdānids establish themselves in, 277; 295 sq.; Fāṭimids in, 302; Seljūqs in, 314, 317; 359; taken by Mongols, 279, 643; by Tīmūr, 651, 680; bishop of, *see* Agapius; Sultan of, 172; *see* Bakjūr, Nāṣir, Nūr-ad-Dīn, Qarghūyah, Saif-ad-Daulah, Shibl-ad-Daulah
Alessio, in Albania, becomes Venetian, 564, 583; 584; death of Skanderbeg at, 585; 591
Alexander (the Great), 49; legendary connexion of with the Mongols, 630, 639; 705
Alexander, Emperor, son of Basil I, 51; 53; joint ruler with Leo VI, 56; Regent, 59; death, 60; 83 sq.; 96; 142; and Simeon of Bulgaria, 237; and Nicholas Mysticus, 257; 712
Alexander II, Pope, disputed election of, 597
Alexander III, Pope, and Emperor Manuel, 370, 596, 601 sq.; and Venetians, 412, 414
Alexander IV, Pope, and Theodore II, 505, 609; 496 *note*
Alexander I, the Good, Prince of Moldavia, 568; 593
Alexander II, Prince of Moldavia, 593
Alexandretta, battle of, 170; captured by Constantine IV of Armeno-Cilicia, 181
Alexandria, occupied by Spanish Arabs, 127; 128; besieged by Latins, 177; 396 sq.; captured by Peter I of Cyprus, 470; trade of, 770; Patriarch of, 250
Alexiad, the, of Anna Comnena, 346
Alexius I, Comnenus, Emperor, early life, 326; accession, 327; character, 328; and Crusaders, 315 sq., 333 sqq.; and Normans, 329 sq.; and Patzinaks, 330; and Turks, 331, 344; plots against, 332, 342; war with Bohemond of Antioch, 341 sq.; persecutes Bogomiles, 243; Papacy and, 345, 596, 598 sqq., 626; and Byzantine Church, 349; theological interests, 350, 362; organizes army and navy, 347; and finances, 348; last illness and death, 346; 351 sqq.; 355; 366; and Venetians, 408 sq., 412; Novels of, 720
Alexius II, Comnenus, Emperor, minority of, 379; murdered by Andronicus, 382; 720
Alexius III, Angelus, Emperor, reign of, 384; deposes Isaac II, 417; flees from Constantinople, 418 sq.; 423; 478 sq.; Theodore I and, 484; 486; 503; sends crown to Leo of Armeno-Cilicia, 172; Bulgarians and, 519; Papacy and, 603 sq.
Alexius IV, Angelus, Emperor, son of Isaac II, appeals to Philip of Swabia, 417, 604;

crowned, 418; deposition and death, 419; promises Crete to Boniface of Montferrat, 432
Alexius V, Ducas, Mourtzouphlos, Emperor, overthrows the Angeli, 419; flees from Constantinople, 419; 478
Alexius I, Grand Comnenus, makes himself Emperor of Trebizond, 479 sq.; and Theodore I, 482; and Seljūqs, 485; death, 487; 514 sq.; coins of, 516
Alexius, the Caesar, son-in-law of Theophilus, defeats Saracens in Sicily, 136
Alexius of the Studion, Patriarch of Constantinople, 92, 264; marries Zoë to Michael IV, 101; 103; 106; crowns Theodora, 107; death, 112
Alexius Juraševič, ruler in the Zeta, 592
Alexius Apocaucus, Byzantine grand-duke, 615
Alexius Muselé, *see* Muselé
Alexius Strategopulus, *see* Strategopulus
Alexius, nephew of Alexius Strategopulus, 511
Alfonso Fadrique, chief of the Catalans in Greece, 453
Alfonso V, King of Aragon and Sicily, claims duchy of Athens, 461
'Alī, Caliph, son-in-law of Mahomet, 275; venerated by the Shī'ites, 301 sq.; Mongols and tomb of, 643
'Alī, emir of Tarsus, 132 sq.; killed, 134
'Alī, murderer of Prince Aḥmad, 693
'Alī ibn al-'Abbās (Haly Abbas), Arab medical writer, 297 sq.
'Alī ibn Rabban, Arab medical writer, 297
'Alids, *see* Shī'ites
Aliza, niece of Leo the Great of Armeno-Cilicia, married to Raymond of Antioch, 172
Allelengyon, the, tax, 92 sq.; abolished by Romanus III, 99
Almissa, in Dalmatia, 564
Almohad dynasty of Spain, founded, 306
Almos, Hungarian prince, and Emperor John II, 355 sq.
Alp Arslān, Great Seljūq Sultan, conquers Armenia, 166 sq.; empire of, 277; reign of, 305 sq.; meaning of his name, 306; murdered, 307; 309; 311; 314; 316
Alp Arslān Akhras, Seljūq ruler of Syria, 314
Alpheus, valley of the, 438
Alptigīn, founder of the Ghaznawids, 300
Altino, on Venetian mainland, 386
Aluans, the, *see* Albania
Alusian, Bulgarian prince, and Emperor Michael IV, 244
Alypius, father-in-law of Emperor Constantine VIII, 84
Amadeus VI, Count of Savoy, helps Emperor John V against Turks, 554 sq., 617, 669
Amalfi, 134; rivalry with Venice, 405, 408 sq.; bishop of, *see* Peter; *see* Pantaleone of; Amalfitans at Constantinople, 750, 762; *see* St Mary of *under* Constantinople
Amanus, mountain passes of, 343
Amasia, 79; 340; 378; Mahomet I at, 686; 688
Amastris, annexed by Emperor Theodore I, 483; *see* Gregory, St
Amaury I, King of Jerusalem, marries Byzantine princess, 376; 377
Amaury of Lusignan, King of Cyprus, feudal code of, 437, 469; 172; 476
Amaury of Lusignan, Prince of Tyre, becomes Regent of Cyprus, 469; 477; marriage of Armenian princess to, 178, 180
Amaury, Latin Patriarch of Antioch, 376
Amaury de Narbonne, French admiral in service of the Pope, 614
Amida (Dīyārbakr), 46; 86; 132; 145; Byzantine defeat at, 147; Emir of, received by Emperor Constantine VII, 66; taken by Mongols, 636
'Amīd-al-Mulk, the, *see* Abū-Naṣr al-Kundurī
Amīn, Abbasid Caliph, 275 sq.
'*Amīr-al-Mu'minīn* (Commander of the Faithful), title of the Caliphs, given to Seljūq Sultans, 307, 310 sq.
Amisus, taken by Omar of Melitene, 46, 133
Ammiana, Venetian island, 386
ἀμνημόνευτοι, Emperor Constantine V's epithet for the monks, 15
Amorgos, Venetian colony, 476
Amorian dynasty, its interest in learning and culture, 44; *see* Michael II, Theophilus, Michael III
Amorium, besieged by Saracens, 2; birthplace of Michael II, 32, 130; sacked by Saracens, 38, 130; Bardas Phocas defeated at, 86; 121; 125; 344
Amphissa, barony of Sálona founded at, 433
Ampûn, Seljūq defeat at, 344
'Amr ibn al-'Āṣ, in Egypt, 302
Amur, Asiatic river, 631
Anacatharsis (Repurgatio veterum legum), code of Basil I, 52, 712
Anagay, prince of the Utigurs, attacks Byzantines in Crimea, 188
Anagay, *see* A-na-Kuei
Anagni, Greek archbishops at, 608; bishop of, *see* Zacharias
Anaia, Genoese at, 511
A-na-Kuei (Anagay), Khagan of the Yuan-Yuan, 186
Anapa, *see* Gorgippia
Anastasius II, ex-Emperor, and Bulgarians, 3, 231; and Venice, 387 sq.
Anastasius III, Pope, and Emperor Alexander, 257
Anastasius, syncellus, made Patriarch of Constantinople by Emperor Leo III, 10; declares against Constantine V, 12; death of, 14
Anastasius, archbishop of Gran (Esztergom), and conversion of Hungary, 214
Anastasius, librarian of the Vatican, ambassador of Western Emperor at Constan-

tinople, 252 sq.; on Cyril and Methodius, 216, 219 sq.
Anastasius, advocate, commentator on the *Digest*, 707
Anastaso, *see* Theophano, Empress
Anatolia, "the East" (Asia Minor), 732; Domestic of the Scholae (generalissimo) of, *see* John I Tzimisces, Nicephorus II, Bardas Sclerus, Peter Phocas; 278; 335; 428; governed by Aḥmad Hercegović, 582; 587; Turkish tribes in, 653; Catalans in, 657; Osmān's successes in, 660; 663; 689; 694; 737; Anatolian troops at Angora, 682; at siege of Constantinople, 696, 702; themes in, 733, 744, 773; *see also* Asia Minor
Anatolia-Hisār, fort of, built by Bāyazīd, 676 sq.; Sulaimān at, 683; 694
Anatolic theme, creation of, 732; subdivided, 3; 2; 29; 127; strategus of, 731; *see also* Leo III, Leo V, Turcus Bardanes, Photinus; troops, 119, 121, 123; district, 125, 130
Anatolius, professor of law at Berytus (Beyrout), 705
Anavarzetsi, *see* Grigor VII
Anazarbus in Cilicia, ravaged by Saracens, 126; gipsies at, 132; taken by Emperor Nicephorus II, 144 sq.; 168; Emperor John II at, 169; held by Byzantines, 171, 343, 359; 178
Anbār, on the Euphrates, 289
Ancelin de Toucy ('Ασέλ), and Emperor Michael VIII, 509
Anchialus, victory of Emperor Constantine V at, 12, 231; Bulgarian victories at, 231, 238; sacked by Turks, 695; *see* Michael
Ancona, held by Emperor Manuel I, 369 sqq., 412; bishop of, *see* Paul
Ancyra, *see* Angora
Andravida, capital of princes of Achaia, 437; church of St James at, 444
Andrea, Venetian tribune, 389
Andreas, Prince of Hum, 591
Andrew, King of Hungary, 427
Andrew, St, patron of Patras, 6, 37
Andrew, the strategus, degrades Photius, 254
Andronicus I Comnenus, Emperor, and Thoros II of Armeno-Cilicia, 170 sq.; 373; 375; governor of Cilicia, 380; character and amours, 381; seizes the throne, 382; administration, 383, 364; attacks Latins at Constantinople, 362, 414; 479 sq.; 603; Géza of Hungary and, 368; murdered, 384; 775
Andronicus II Palaeologus, Emperor, 593; 444; 512; takes Catalans into his service, 449; Andronicus and Bulgaria, 530 sq.; and Serbia, 532 sq., 535, 537; and his grandson, 536, 659; Orthodox reaction under, 613 sq.; 658; Novels of, 720; and Hethum II of Armeno-Cilicia, 178
Andronicus III Palaeologus, Emperor, 593; quarrels with his grandfather, 535 sqq.; 659; alliance with Serbia, 538, 540; death of, 541; and Benedict XII, 614 sq.; and Orkhān, 661 sq.; Novel of, 720
Andronicus IV Palaeologus, Emperor, 593; revolts against his father, 671
Andronicus I Gídos, Emperor of Trebizond, defeats Latins, 483; defeats Seljūqs, 514 sq.; his death, 515; 516
Andronicus Euphorbenus, murders Stephanê, Armenian prince, 171, and *note*
Andros, ravaged by Venetians, 354; becomes Venetian, 421, 435, 467, 473, 476
Androûsa, Navarrese capital in the Morea, 456
Anemas, brothers, Turkish conspirators against Alexius I, 342
Anemas, tower of, 671
Angeli, dynasty of, decadence under, 384; *see* Alexius III, IV, Isaac II; Michael VIII's descent from, 507; dynasty in Epirus, 604, *see also* Demetrius, John, Manuel, Michael, Theodore, dukes of Neopatras
Angelo, Duke of the Archipelago, 475
Angelus, Andronicus, declares for Andronicus I, 382
Anglo-Saxons in Varangian Guard, 264, 738; in Byzantine army, 598
Angora (Ancyra), 123; taken by Saracens, 125 sq., 130; 128 sq.; 344; 357; 377; 656; 681; Tīmūr's victory at, 459, 562, 619, 651, 682 sqq., 688
Anholin, David, Albanian prince, and Armenia, 165
Ani, in Armenia, capital of Ashot III, 161; commercial prosperity of, 162; importance and culture of, 163, 167; willed by John Smbat to Byzantines, 164; betrayed to them, 112, 165 sq.; taken by Turks, 166, 325
Anjou, *see* Charles, Fulk, Joan; Angevins of Naples, and Greece, 442, 444, 446, 448
Anna Angelus, wife of Emperor Theodore I, 478
Anna, Empress, *see* Constance of Hohenstaufen
Anna Comnena, daughter of Emperor Alexius I, 328; plots against her brother, 346, 351; *Alexiad* of, 346, 363; 344; 347; 350; 598 *note*; 655; learning of, 763, 765
Anna Dalassena, mother of Emperor Alexius I, 326, 328; regent, 332; retirement, 346
Anna of Epirus, married to William of Achaia, 442
Annam (Tongking), conquered by Mongols, 645
Anne, daughter of Emperor Constantine VII, 68
Anne, daughter of Emperor Leo III, married to Artavasdus, 3
Anne, daughter of Emperor Romanus II, married to Vladímir of Russia, 68, 90, 209
Anne of Lusignan, last heiress of Armeno-Cilicia, 181

Anne of Savoy, mother of Emperor John V, and Stephen Dušan, 541, 543; and Pope Clement VI, 615
Anne of Vidin, Tsaritsa of Bulgaria, her patronage of learning, 561
Anonymus, the, commentator on the *Digest*, 707, 711, 714, 716
Anonymus regis Belae notarius, ancient Hungarian chronicler, 211
Anseau de Cayeux, governor of Chorlu, 493; 509 *note*
Anselm, St, and Byzantine Church, 595; speech at Council of Bari, 600
Anselm of Havelberg, ambassador to Constantinople, 358, 600
Antae, Eastern Slav race, 186; identified with Ukrainians, 200
Anthemius of Tralles, architect of St Sophia, 752
Anthony, bishop of Syllaeum, made Patriarch of Constantinople, 33
Anthony Cauleas, Patriarch of Constantinople, concludes the Photian schism, 56, 256; opposition to Emperor Leo VI, 57
Anthony of the Studion, appointed Patriarch of Constantinople, 80; resignation of, 89; 260
Anthony, general of Empress Irene, made prisoner by the Saracens, 124
Anthony, igumen of the Studion, exiled under Photius, 255
Anthypatus, title, 730
Antigus, surrenders to Saracens, 128
Antinomies, the Book of (τὸ τῶν ἐναντιοφάνων μονοβιβλίον), 707
Antioch, taken by Saracens, 76; 84; 89; siege of and capture by Emperor Nicephorus II, 145 sq.; besieged by Egyptians, 147 sqq.; 168; captured by Seljūqs, 307, 325, 330; Crusaders at, 335 sq., 338; siege and relief of, 339, 316; Latin principality of, 168 sqq.; succession dispute, 173; "assises of," adopted as Armenian law, 173; taken by Mamlūks, 175; 344; Emperor John II and, 352, 355, 357 sqq.; 365; Emperor Manuel I in, 374 sq.; 377; taken by Mongols, 643; princess of, 446; 711; Byzantine duchy of, 733 sq.; *see also* Bohemond, Constance, Mary, Philip, Raymond, Roger, Tancred; Patriarch of, crowns Thomas the Slavonian, 35; crowns imperial pretender, 129; Latin Patriarchate of, 599; Patriarchs of, *see* Agapius, Amaury, Athanasius, Peter, Theodore Balsamon, Theodore of Colonea; dukes of, *see* Cecaumenus, Nicetas
Antioch on the Maeander, victory of Theodore I at, 484
Anti-Taurus range, in Asia Minor, 274, 278
Antivari, included in Serbian state, 517; 537; 542; 553; Venetian, 564, 570, 583; taken by Turks, 585; 592
Antonio I Acciajuoli, and duchy of Athens, 458; becomes Duke, 459; and Turks, 460; reign in Athens, 461; death of, 462; 475
Antonio II Acciajuoli, secures duchy of Athens, 462; 463; 475
Antonio Tocco, recaptures Cephalonia from Turks, 466; 475
Antsevatsi, the Armenian principality of, 157
Anūshtigīn, ancestor of the Khwārazm Shāhs, 312, 633
Anzetene, Emperor Theophilus in, 129
Apamea, death of Emperor Basil I at, 54
Apamea in Syria, Byzantine defeat at, 149
Apennines, trade route across, 396
Aphameia, fort of, near Constantinople, 509
Apirat, Armenian prince, and John-Smbat, 163 sq.; *see also* Grigor VII
Apocaucus, *see* Alexius, John
Apollonia, on Black Sea, taken by Alexius I, 331; 344; occupied by Murād I, 672
Apulia, Greek sees in, 259 sq., 266 sq.; Latin ritual in, 266, 268; 341; annexed by Roger of Sicily, 358, 597; 601; Greek monks in, 737; dukes of, *see* Robert Guiscard, Roger Borsa
A̲q-Gyul, *see* Philomelium
A̲q-Hisār, *see* Asprocastrum, Kroja
A̲qinji, Turkish light horsemen, 665
A̲q-Shehr, death of Bāyazīd at, 684
Aquileia, see of, 224; 397; rivalry with Grado, 407 sq., 414; Patriarch of, 386, 412; *see* Lupus, Paulinus, Poppo, Serenus, Walpert
Aquitaine, 403; *see* William IX
'Arab, brother of Mas'ūd of Rūm, 357
Arabia, 124; merchandise from, 162
Arabian Nights, 647; 755
Arabic language, 2; spread of, 286, 290; grammar, 290 sq.; language and literature under Abbasids, 289 sqq.; numerals introduced in Europe, 298
Arabissus, 124; 134
Arabs, *see* Saracens; and the Caliphate, 276; compared with Turks, in treatises of Jāḥiẓ, 294; culture, and Mongols, 647; Byzantine influence on, 152, 775 sq.; Arabs in Byzantine army, 738; in Byzantine administration, 736; influence on Byzantium, 152, 735, 773; merchants in Constantinople, 762; coins in Russia, 201, 206; in Jerusalem, and Christian pilgrims, 316; effects of conquest of Spain, 629
Ara Coeli, church of, at Rome, 581
Aragatz, Mount (Alagöz), Armenians defeat Saracens at, 160
Aragon, *see* Constance; kings of, dukes of Athens, 442, 453; King of, assists Emperor John VI, 666; Murād II and, 691; 574 *note*; *see* Frederick, John, Pedro; Queen of, *see* Sibylla; Admiral of, *see* Loria; and Sicily, 448 sq.
Aral, Sea of, 198, 631, 633
Arangio, Count, rules in Icaria, 468
Ararat, province of, in Armenia, 158
Araxes, river, 187
Arbe, Dalmatian island, taken by Venetians, 406, 582

Arca, in Syria, attacked by Emperor John I, 146
Arcadia, Doxapatrês in, 434
Arcadiopolis, Thomas the Slavonian at, 35; 111
Arcadius, Forum of, at Constantinople, 749
Archipelago, the, fleet of Alexius I in, 347; subdivision of by Latins, 421, 431; 432; duchy of, 439, 465, 467 sq.; dukes of, *see* Table, 475, sq.; Latin clergy in, 606; "Crusade of," 616; Turks in, 654, 672; 733; Saracen ravages in, 742
Architecture, Byzantine: under Basil I, 52 sq.; churches built by Leo VI, 59; under Constantine VII, 67; repairs of St Sophia by Basil II, 96; buildings of Romanus III, 100; under Constantine IX, 114; buildings of Manuel I, 364; of Andronicus I, 383; of Theodore I, 487; churches at Nicaea, 479; buildings at Constantinople, 748 sqq.; 752 sqq.; building of St Sophia, 752; churches at Constantinople, 753; 754; apogee of, 768; influence of, 776 sq.; churches built under Islām, 289; Turkish architecture, 688; Armenian architecture, 162 sq.; in Serbia, 550; early Venetian, 396, 407
Archon, Greek, and Western *Baron*, 772; office of, held by Methodius, 217, 221; archon of the Pantheon, title of Michael the Paphlagonian, 101
Arcruni, the, Armenian princely family, 157 sq., 161
Ardashes, last Arsacid king of Armenia, 155
Ardskê in Armenia, 166
Ardzen, town in Armenia, 162; sacked by Seljūqs, 166 sq.
Argaus, Paulicians settled in, 132
Arghūn, Īl-Khān of Persia, 177
Argolid, the, 438
Argos, fortresses in, 434; 438; 441; purchased by Venetians, 457 sq., 461, 465; lost, 466; captured by Turks, 675; 476
Argyropulus, Romanus, ancestor of Emperor Romanus III, 98 *note*
Argyrus of Bari, 356
Argyrus the Lombard, catapan in Italy, efforts of for reunion of Churches, 113, 266 sqq.; 269 sqq.; 273, 597
Argyrus, Romanus, *see* Romanus III
Arianism, among the Lombards, 387
Arianites Comnenus, Albanian chief, 584
Arichis, duke of Benevento, and Emperor Leo IV, 19
Ariebes, Armenian general, plots against Emperor Alexius I, 332
Arikbuka, Mongol chief, 645; rebels against Kublai, 646
Arindz, Cilician fortress, 170
Aristinus, Alexius, nomophylax of the School at Constantinople, 720; work on canon law, 723
Aristophanes, study of, 763; 744
Aristotle, study of, 236, 763 sq.; 237; among the Arabs, 292, 295 sq.; "Theology of," 295; "Study of" at Athens, 459; Latin translations of, 447, 474; 506
Arithmus (*Vigla*), regiment of the Byzantine Guard, 739
Armenia, Chap. VI *passim*; Paulicians in, 42; 78 sq.; 85; 97; 111; annexation of by Byzantium, 112, 165 sq., 259, 737; 138; 143; Emperor John I and, 148; 150; invaded by Chazars, 126, 187 sqq.; its civilization, 162, 166; 295; Seljūqs in, 278, 325; 310; conquered by Mongols, 636, 640, 653; conquered by Tīmūr, 181, 689; Cyprus and, 477; kings of, *see* Abas, Ashot, Gagik, John-Smbat, Smbat; *see also* Greater Armenia, Armeno-Cilicia; emirs of, *see* 'Alī, Yūsūf
Armenia, ancient Roman province of, 155, 159
Armenia Quarta, ancient province, 120; ravaged by Saracens, 122; 129
Armeniac theme, 3; 61; 120; its loyalty to the Empire, 36; 127; 344; creation of, 732; 733; troops of, 123, 125; strategus of, *see* Artavasdus, Leo, Paul
Armenian, Armenians, origin of Emperor Basil I, 47, 49, 159, 253 *note*; of John I, 240; troops, mutiny among, 22 sq.; in Byzantine army, 738; soldiers of Nicephorus II, 75; generals of Byzantine Empire, 736; in Empire, 735, 746; at Constantinople, 750, 762; driven from Constantinople by Constantine IX, 109; 103; 123; colony in the Troad, 479, 481; colonists in Thrace, 231; missionaries in Bulgaria, 236; trade with Bulgaria, 193; 343; notable for iconoclasm, 14; persecution of, 350, 737; wife of Theodore I, 486; influence on Byzantium, 773; Byzantine influence on, 776; Armenian Church, *see* Church, Armenian; Leo the, *see* Leo V, Emperor
Armeno-Cilicia (lesser Armenia), principality of, founded, 154, 168; character of, 167 sq.; influence of Crusades on, 168; becomes a kingdom, 172; conquered by Mamlūks, 180; and Cyprus, 181, 470, 479; 278; *see also* Constantine, Guy, Hethum, Leo, Mleh, Oshin, Philip, Ruben, Ruben-Raymond, Smbat, Thoros
Army, Byzantine, 732 sqq., 737 sqq.; *see* Themes; under Isaurian Emperors, 4, 13; hostility to image worship, 21 sq.; publication of the "Tactics," 58; and Nicephorus II, 72, 75 sq.; military revolts, 87 sqq., 111, 117, 325; and Isaac I, 322; and Constantine X, 324; reorganized by Alexius I, 328, 347 sq.; and John II, 352; and Manuel I, 364; and Theodore II, 505
Army, of the Caliphs, 284 sq.; Chazar army, 190; Magyar army, 212; Mongol army and Kublai Khan, 647; Ottoman army, 664 sq.; 673; 675
Arno, river, 461
Arnulf, Western Emperor, war with Moravians, 198; 211

Arnulf, archbishop of Milan, ambassador to Emperor Basil II, 94
Árpád, Magyar chief, enters Hungary, 199; 212
Arran, *see* Albania
Arras, *see* Lambert of
Arsaber, patrician and quaestor, plots against Nicephorus I, 35
Arsacids, the, of Parthia, 49; of Armenia, 154, 158
Arsafius, the spatharius, and Charlemagne, 394 sq.
Arsamosata, 122; taken by Emperor Theophilus, 129; 131 sq.; besieged by Michael III, 133
Arsanias, river, 122
Arsenal, the, at Venice, founded, 410
Arsenius, Patriarch at Nicaea, 506; resignation of, 509; crowns Michael VIII in St Sophia, 513
Arslān, Seljūq prince of Kirmān, 314
Arslān Arghūn, Seljūq prince, uncle of Barkiyāruq, 310
Arslān ibn Seljūq, ancestor of the dynasty of Rūm, 315
Art, Byzantine: periods of, 767 sqq.; influence of, 769, 777; ancient art at Constantinople, 748; works of art under Constantine V, 13; under the Iconoclasts, 26; under Theophilus, 39 sq.; under the Caesar Bardas, 43 sq.; under Basil I, 53 sq.; under Leo VI, 59; under Constantine VII, 67; artistic renaissance under Constantine IX, 114; works of art under Manuel, 363 sq.; under Andronicus I, 383; under Theodore II, 506; destruction of works of art by Michael III, 51; Armenian art, 162, 182; art in Baghdad, 152, 642; remains of Latin art in Greece, 473; early Slav art, 549; *see also* Architecture
Arta, court of Michael Angelus at, 436; church at, 452, 504; entered by Emperor Michael VIII, 508; annexed by Stephen Dušan, 543; gulf of, 465
Artavasdus, son-in-law of Emperor Leo III, 3; rebels against Constantine V, 12, 121; 17
Artopolia, baker's quarter at Constantinople, 748
Asad, Saracen leader in Sicily, 135
Aṣbagh, Spanish Arab, commands in Sicily, 135
Ascalon, 340; Venetian naval victory off, 411
Ascalonita, *see* Julianus
'Ασέλ, *see* Ancelin
Asên, ruling family of Bulgaria, *see* Constantine, John, Michael, Peter; extinct, 525
Ash'arī, Arab theologian, 292
Ashnās, Saracen general in Asia Minor, 128 sqq.
Ashod, *see* Ashot
Ashot Bagratuni, Armenian leader, resists Emperor Justinian II, 157
Ashot Bagratuni, governor of Armenia under Saracens, 156 sq.
Ashot I, King of Armenia, made King by the Caliph, 158; Emperor Basil I and, 140, 158; journey to Constantinople, and death, 159; 163
Ashot II, King of Armenia, reign of, 160 sq.; received by Emperor Romanus I, 62, 160
Ashot III, King of Armenia, reign of, 161 sq.; and Emperor John I, 148, 161; buildings at Ani, 163
Ashot IV, brother of John-Smbat, wars against him, 163 sq.
Ashraf, Mamlūk Sultan, 177 sq.
Asia, Muslim Asia, 295; Seljūq rule in, 300; Crusaders in, 338 sqq.; unification of under Mongols, 629 sq.
Asia, proconsular, 121
Asia Minor (Anatolia), Saracen wars in, Chapter v *passim*; preponderance in the Empire, 25, 733, 742, 773; themes and clisurae of, 39, 732 sqq., 740 sq.; support to Iconoclasts, 7 sq.; Leo III from, 7; Slavs deported into, 13; Paulicians in, 7, 42; Manichaeans in, 498; rebellion of Thomas the Slavonian in, 33 sqq., 127; Sclerus' rebellion in, 85 sqq.; famine in, 89; 115; themes of, support Isaac I, 117; 154; 168; Mongols in, 175, 182, 279; Chazars in, 187; Russian raids in, 203; 217 *note*; bishops of, 261; 274; Seljūqs in, 278, 302, 315, 325, 329; 318; 320 sq.; 327; 331; Crusaders in, 315 sqq., 338 sq.; 366 sqq.; 348; John II in, 353, 357; Manuel's villas in, 364; ravaged by Seljūqs, 365; 377; 382; 383; Latin Empire in, 421 sqq., 480; Henry of Flanders in, 424 sqq.; 481 sqq.; 485; Latins lose, 427 sq.; Catalans in, 449; 468; 479; Chap. XVI *passim*; 514; 532; 560; 597; Tīmūr in, 651, 680 sqq.; Turkish tribes in, 653 sqq.; 657; 662; power of Ottomans in, 668 sq., 678; 684; 687; great cities of, 770; influence on conception of Emperor, 726; great families in, 771 sq.
Asicritus, supposed companion of St Cyril to the Saracens, 218 sq.
Askania, lake of, at Nicaea, 478, 513
Askin, Askil, *see* Sse-Kin
Askol'd, Prince of Kiev, 203
Asparuch, *see* Isparich
Asprocastrum (Āq-Hisār), 655
Assassins, Shī'ite sect, 301, 305, 308 sqq.; overthrown by the Seljūq Muḥammad, 311; embassies to Europe, 638; conquered by Mongols, 628, 641 sq.; *see* Ismā'īlī
Assises "of Antioch," adopted as Armenian law, 173; "of Jerusalem," 437; "of Romania" (constitution of Latin Empire), 422
Assisi, 438; Byzantine envoys at, 608
Astrakhan, 191; 650
Astrik, archbishop of Kalocsa, and conversion of Hungary, 214
Astronomy, under the Abbasids, 298; under Seljūqs, 308; under Mongols, 299, 646

Asturia, in North Spain, holds out against Saracens, 274
Astypálaia (Stampalia), acquired by Quirini family, 435
Atābegs (Atābeys) = guardians, or Lesser Seljūqs, found dynasties, 278, 300, 317; office and position of, 313 sq.; 315; of Mosul, 293; of Damascus, 314
Atel, *see* Itil; *see also* Volga
Atel Kuzu (Atel Köz), Magyar territory, 198 sq.
Athanasius, St, orations of, translated into Bulgarian, 237
Athanasius, made Patriarch of Constantinople by Constantine XI, 624
Athanasius, Patriarch of Antioch, 376
Athanasius, St, abbot of the Great Laura, and Emperor Nicephorus II, 70, 72 sqq.; revolt against his rule, 80; 90; 260
Athanasius, the advocate, commentator on the Novels, 707, 718
Atharib, fortress of, captured by Zangī, 317
Athenian origin of Empress Irene, 19
Athenians, ancient, Byzantines compared with, 774; (modern), 243
Athens, 24; 56, 254; visit of Emperor Basil II to, 95, 242; Latin duchy of, 422, 424, 426, 431 sqq.; 435, 438; Othon de la Roche in, 439; under suzerainty of Naples, 446; 447 sq.; Catalans in, 450 sq.; 452 sqq.; conquered by Navarrese, 456; by Acciajuoli, 457 sqq.; Florentine, 461 sq.; taken by Turks, 463 sq.; 466; condition in early fifteenth century, 459; birthplace of Chalcocondyles, 474; Greek monasteries in, 498; Latin Church in, 606; 764; dukes of, *see* Table, 475; *see* Guy, John, William; church of Our Lady at, *see* Acropolis, Parthenon
Athos, Mount (The Holy Mountain), monasteries on, 66; 70; 74; 90; 92; 260; 518; 532; Stephen Uroš II's gifts to, 535; reunion party in, 620; anti-union, 623; 753; churches of, 768 sq.
Atsiz, Khwārazm Shāh, revolts against Sanjar, 312 sq.
Atsiz, Seljūq general, occupies Palestine and Syria, 277
Attalia (Adalia, Satalia), taken by Saracens, 133, 141; fortified by Byzantines, 142; 353 sq.; Emperor John II at, 361; Crusaders at, 367; 383; Templars at, 480; ruled by Turks, 654; taken by King of Cyprus, 669; Byzantine sailors drawn from, 742; bay of, 125; governor of, *see* Philocales
Attaliates, Michael, *see* Michael
Attica, 441; exports corn to Venice, 447; Latin rule in, 451, 473; 455; Navarrese in, 456; 462; Turks in, 692; 769
Attila, King of the Huns, 184; 385
Augusta, title of, bestowed on Zoë, third wife of Emperor Leo VI, 57; on mistresses of Constantine IX, 108, 115
Augustus, Roman Emperor, 24
Aurillac, *see* Gerald, St
Aurius, tribune of the Venetians, settles in Torcello, 386
Austria, duchy of, *see* Henry, Isabella
Autocephalous Church, eastern doctrine of, 595; 262 sq.; 273
Autokrator, title of Eastern Emperors, 726 sq.
Auxerre, count of; *see* Peter of Courtenay
Avaraïr, Armenian defeat at, 155
Avarino, Greek castle, 446
Avars, nomad tribe, appear in Europe, 185; and Bulgarians, 186; 199; and the Antae, 200; 747
Avenpace (Ibn Bājja), Spanish Arab philosopher, 296
Averroes (Ibn Rushd), Spanish Arab philosopher, 296
Avicenna (Ibn Sīnā), Arab philosopher, 296 sqq.; surviving writings of, 289
Avignon, Byzantine envoys at, 615; 617; 621
Avlona, 243; taken by Normans, 329; 338; 342
'Awāṣim, al-, Saracen province of North Syria, 126, 132
ἀχειροποίητοι, epithet of icons, 751
Axoûchos, *see* John I, Emperor of Trebizond
Axuch, Grand Domestic, minister of Emperor John II, 352; of Manuel, 362, 364, 368
Ayas, maritime town of Armeno-Cilicia, 168; 180 sq.
Ayāz, governor of Khuzistān, 310
Aytony (Akhtum), principality of, conquered by St Stephen of Hungary, 215
Ayuka Khan, Mongol leader, and Peter the Great, 650
Ayyūb (Job), father of Saladin, 317
Ayyūbid dynasty, established by Saladin, 278, 302; 317
'Azabs, Turkish infantry, 665
Azarbā'ījān (Adharbayján), 128; relations with Armenia, 158 sqq., 161; 206; 312; included in empire of Khwārazm Shāh, 633; conquered by Mongols, 636
Azov, Sea of, 185 sq., 188; trade on, 193; 200; 207; 230
Azymites, 267; 625

Baalbek, taken by Emperor John I, 148; by Tīmūr, 680
Baanes, the Patrician, at Council of Constantinople, 251 sq.
Bābak, rebel against the Caliphate, 38, 128 sq.
Bāb-al-Abwāb, *see* Darband
Bābī, modern Persian Shī'ite sect, 301
Babuna mountains, in Bulgaria, 238
Babuni, name of Bulgarian Bogomiles, 238
Bābur, conqueror of India, 651 sq.
Babylon, culture at, 629; 747
Babylonia, Saracen capital moved to, 119; 310
Bachu, Mongol general, and Armenians, 175

Badī'-uz-Zamān Hamadhānī, Persian author, 294
Bagaran, town of Armenia, 158 sq.
Bagarat, founder of the Bagratuni family of Armenia, 157
Bagarat, King of Georgia and Abasgia, 165
Bagatur, hero, title in old Bulgaria, 231
Baghdad, Chap. x *passim*; buildings of, 39, 152; 124; feeling against Turks in, 131, 276, 285; revolution in, 147; taken by Tīmūr, 181, 651, 680; by Hūlāgū, 279, 628, 642, 654; made capital by Abbasids, 274, 281; again by Mu'tamid, 276; siege of, by Ṭāhir, 276; Russian traders at, 201; 218; 277; Manichaeans at, 287; Nestorian Patriarchs of, 289; culture in, 294, 296 sq.; 298; 300; Buwaihids in, 277, 301; Ṭughril Beg in, 304; University at, 305 sq.; 309 sq.; 317; 653; 656; compared with Constantinople, 745; traders from, 750; *see also* Caliphate
Baghras, fortress of, 146; 343
Bagratid (Bagratuni), Kings of Armenia, 111; 140; 154 sq.; 157; wealth and power of, 158; 159; extinction of, 166 sq.; 182; *see* Abas, Ashot, Gagik, John-Smbat, Smbat
Bahā-ad-Dīn, biographer of Saladin, 306
Bahrām, Seljūq prince of Kirmān, 314
Bahrām Shāh, made ruler of Ghaznah by Sanjar, 311
Baiane, *see* Eudocia
Baibars, Mamlūk Sultan of Egypt, general of Sultan Quṭuz, 643; slays Quṭuz, 644; captures Antioch, 175; defeated and slain, 176; 642
Baiḍāwī, commentator on the Koran, 291
Baidu, Mongol rebel, 178
Bajnak, Arab name for Patzinaks, *q.v.*
Bakjūr, emir of Aleppo, and Emperor Nicephorus II, 146
Balādhurī, Arab historian and biographer, 293
Balanea (Bulunyās), taken by Emperor John I, 148; 339; 343
Balanjar, town of the Chazars, 191 sq.
Balat, near Antioch, taken by Emperor John II, 359
Balāṭa, Armenian general of the Byzantines in Sicily, 135
Balaton, Lake, *see* Blatno
Baldwin I, count of Flanders, Latin Emperor of the East, 421; weakness of, 422; defeat and death, 424, 520; 427; 478 *note*; 480 sq.
Baldwin II, Latin Emperor, minority of, 427 sq.; appeals to Europe, 429; driven from Constantinople, 431, 443, 512; 488; and Michael VIII, 509; 511; 527; surrenders his rights to Charles of Anjou, 610
Baldwin I of Edessa, King of Jerusalem, 317; 335; at Tarsus, 338; and Venetians, 411
Baldwin II, King of Jerusalem, and Venetians, 411
Baldwin III, King of Jerusalem, mediates between Emperor Manuel I and Armeno-Cilicia, 171; marries Byzantine princess, 374, 381
Baldwin IV, King of Jerusalem, and Emperor Manuel I, 377
Baldwin, count of Germanicea, and Leo I of Armeno-Cilicia, 169
Baldwin, marshal of Armeno-Cilicia, 181
Balitza, ceded to Bohemond of Antioch, 343
Balkan peninsula, Chap. VIII, Chap. XVII, Chap. XVIII; Slav tribes in, 4; 13; ecclesiastical provinces of, 58; Avars in, 186; Bulgars migrate to, 200; Russians and, 207 sq.; Magyars in, 212; 213; 330; 432; Ottomans in, Chap. XXI *passim*; passes, Emperor Nicephorus I killed in, 37, 233; 676; medievalism of, 550, 586; themes of, 733
Balkash, Lake, 631, 652
Balkh, conquered by Seljūqs, 304; 312; destroyed by Mongols, 633; Tīmūr at, 650
Balša family, in the Zeta (Montenegro), 553, 559, 564, 583, 585 sq.; 592; *see* George II Balša
Balša I, ruler of Montenegro, 592
Balša II, ruler of Montenegro, 592
Balša III, ruler of Montenegro, 592
Balša, last duke of Herzegovina, 582
Balsamon, *see* Theodore
Balta-oghlu, admiral of Mahomet II, at siege of Constantinople, 699
Baltic Sea, 202
Balukli, outside Constantinople, 512
Banda, subdivision of a Byzantine army corps or theme, 734, 739
Banjaluka, residence of Turkish viceroy in Bosnia, 582
Baphaeum (Qoyun-Hisār), Ottoman victory at, 657
Barbaro, Nicolò, Venetian surgeon at siege of Constantinople, 695 sqq., 700 *note*; 702 sq.
Barbarossa, *see* Frederick I, Khair-ad-Dīn
Barcelona, "Customs of," Athens governed by, 451; 456
Bardanes Turcus, *see* Turcus
Bardas, the Caesar, brother of the Regent Theodora, 40; plots of, 42; made Caesar, 43; administration, 43; patronage of learning, 44, 710 sq.; 763; 45; 66; Bardas and Photian schism, 46, 248; 47; murdered, 48, 50, 250; 53; and Saracens, 120, 133 sq., 137; 251
Bardas Sclerus, *see* Sclerus
Bardsrberd (the High Fortress), in Armeno-Cilicia, 168, 177
Bari, 94; taken by Emperor Louis II, 139; attacked by Saracens, 149, 406; captured by Normans, 325, 356, 408, 597; archbishop of, and Pope John XIX, 263, 267; council of, 599 sq.; 601; church of St Nicholas at, 537
Barkiyrāuq, Great Seljūq Sultan, 308; reign of, 309 sq.; 311; 314; 343

Barlaam, Abbot, Byzantine theologian, 595; at Avignon, 615
Barmecides (Barmakids), family, 274, *see* Yaḥyà
Barozzi family, at Santorin, 435
Barsuls, the, Bulgarian tribe, 192
Bartletus, 691 *note*
Barzūyah (Borzo), taken by Emperor John I, 148
Basaraba, *see* Ivanko, Laïote, Nicholas
Basāsīrī, the Isfahsālār, and the Caliph of Baghdad, 304
Bashi-bazuks, Turkish irregular troops, 665; 696; failure before Constantinople, 702
Bashkirs (Bashgurt), Caspian tribes, 195
Basil I, the Macedonian, Emperor, 43 sqq.; intrigues against Bardas, 47; gains the throne, 48, 50; early life, 49, 234; family, 50; financial reforms, 51; legislation, 52, 706, 710 sqq., 717, 722; encouragement of art, 52, 67; Photian schism and, 53, 250 sq.; death of, 54; 55 sq.; 58 sq.; 61; 63; life of, by Constantine VII, 67, 69; 100; foreign policy, 138 sq.; losses in Sicily, 140; relations with Armenia, 138, 140, 158; and St Methodius, 228; 753 sq.
Basil II Bulgaroctonus, Emperor, 67; crowned, 68; 79; 81 sq.; character, 83; early years, 84; seizes power, 86; war with Bulgarians, 87, 240 sqq.; organizes government of Bulgaria, 243, 735; and Bulgarian Church, 94, 243 sq.; defeats Phocas, 88; legislation of, 89, 92 sq., 715, 718; alliance with Russians, 90, 209; Papacy and, 91, 94, 259, 262 sqq.; and Western Empire, 94; and Venice, 94, 405 sq.; travels, 95; death of, 96, 150; 97; 144; Saracen campaigns, 148 sq.; and Armenia, 164; 239; 318; 425; 484; 492; and feudal nobility, 92, 771; discovery of body of, 509
Basil, the Scamandrian, Patriarch of Constantinople, disgrace and exile of, 80, 260
Basil, archbishop of Ochrida, correspondence of with Pope Hadrian IV, 601
Basil, archbishop of Thessalonica, on Photius, 255
Basil, metropolitan of Caesarea, 65
Basil "the Bird," favourite of Emperor Constantine VII, 64; conspires against Romanus II, 68
Basil, the Parakoimomenos, natural son of Emperor Romanus I, 64; supporter of Nicephorus II, 72; minister of John I, 79; 82; of Basil II, 84 sq.; downfall and death, 86 sq.; estates of, 93
Basilaces, heretical priest, condemned by Emperor Manuel, 363
Basilaces, rebel against Emperor Nicephorus III, 327
Basilacius, plotter against Emperor Alexius I, 342
Basileopator, title of Zaützes, 57; assumed by Romanus Lecapenus, 61
Basileus (Eastern Emperor), titles and attributes of, 726 sq.
Basilian monks in South Italy, 259
Basilics (τὰ βασιλικά), code of Leo VI, 52, 58, 66; 706 sqq.; 713 sqq.; 720 sqq.
Βασιλικοπλόϊμον, τὸ, division of Byzantine navy, 743
Basiliscianus, favourite of Emperor Michael III, 50
Basle, Council of, and Reunion of the Churches, 620 sq.
Baṣrah, sacked by marauders, 276; commercial importance of, 286; school of grammarians at, 291
Batbayan, Bulgarian chieftain, and Chazars, 188
Batnae (Sarūj), *see* Sarūj
Baṭṭāl, Saracen general, 120 sq.
Bātu, grandson of Jenghiz Khan, invades Europe, 637 sq.; 643; rule of, 652
Baux, house of, 553, *see* Jacques
Bavaria, colonists from, in Pannonia, 211; Magyars in, 212; duke of, *see* Welf
Bayan, Khan of Bulgaria, and Emperor Constantine V, 232
Bāyazīd I, Ottoman Sultan, descent of, 360 *note*; at Kossovo, 558; 559; and Bulgaria, 560; victory at Nicopolis, 561; defeated at Angora, 562, 619, 651, 682; 593; 671; 673; character of, 674; his attempt to capture Constantinople, 675 sqq.; Tīmūr and, 679 sqq.; captivity and death, 683 sq.; 685 sq.; 694; supposed son of, 567
Bāyazīd II, Ottoman Sultan, annexes Herzegovina, 582; 593
Bāyazīd, grand vizier of Mahomet I, 688
Bayber, Seljūq victory at, 166; 167
Bazaars, at Constantinople, 761
Beatus, doge-consort of Venice, and Byzantium, 393 sqq.
Beauvais, bishop of, *see* Odo; *see also* Vincent
Beccus, *see* John
Bedouins, 294
Beglerbey (Beglerbeg) among Ottomans, 664; of Rumelia, 555, 571
Béla I, King of Hungary, and Emperor Manuel I, 372 sq.
Béla II, the Blind, King of Hungary, 356
Béla III, King of Hungary, and Mary of Antioch, 380; invades Byzantium, 383
Béla IV, King of Hungary, and Emperor John III, 608; defeated by Mongols, 637
Béla, Duke of Mačva and Bosnia, 591
Béla, son of Uroš of Rascia, 356; and Emperor Manuel, 373
Bêla vêzha, Russian name of Sarkel, *q.v.*
Belgrade, 234, 238; governed by Stephen Dragutin, 532; lost to Serbia, 535; taken by Stephen Dušan, 545; 562 sq.; 569; besieged by Murād II, 570; 571; 573 sq.; besieged by Mahomet V, 576; held by Hungary, 577 sq.; 688; 705; bishopric of, 243

Belisarius, general of Justinian, and Venetia, 385; 739
Bella Paise, Latin monastery in Greece, 473
Bellini, Gentile, Venetian painter, and Sultan Mahomet II, 705
Belluno, bishop of, *see* John
Beluchistan, *see* Mukrān
Bender-Eregli, inscription of Emperor Theodore I at, 487
Benedict III, Pope, and the Patriarch Ignatius, 247
Benedict VIII, Pope, and Emperor Basil II, 92, 262
Benedict XI, Pope, and Roman Church in Serbia, 537
Benedict XII, Pope, and Emperor Andronicus III, 614 sq.
Benedict XIII, Pope, and Emperor Manuel II, 619
Benedict of Como, Dominican friar, sent to Emperor Andronicus II, 614
Benedict, cardinal of Santa Susanna, signs treaty with Henry of Flanders, 606
Benedict the Pole, missionary to the Mongols, 640
Benedictine monastery, founded in Hungary, 213; in Greece, 438
Benevento, ceded to Franks, 24; submits to the Pope, 266; council of, 341; duke of, 136, 390, *see* Arichis; battle of, 496, 610
Benjamin of Tudela, on Ghuzz Turkomans, 303, 313, 631 *note*; on Constantinople, 745, 763
Benzo, Piedmontese bishop (of Alba), and Papal election, 597
Ber, King of the Abasgians, defeated by Armenians, 161
Berat, in Albania (Balkans), 242
Berdaa, capital of Albania (Shirvan), captured by Russian raiders, 206
Bereke, Mongol chief, raids Poland and Silesia, 652
Berengar I, Western Emperor, King of Italy, and Magyars, 211; and Venice, 400
Berengar II, King of Italy, 66; 402; 405
Bernard, St, and Byzantine Church, 596, 601
Berrhoea, *see* Veria
Bertha, of Sulzbach, wife of Emperor Manuel I, 360, 365
Bertha, wife of Emperor Romanus II, 64
Berthold, margrave of Hohenburg, and Emperor John III, 496, 499
Bertrand, Prince of Tripolis, natural son of Raymond of Toulouse, 342 sq.
Bertrandon de la Brocquière, French traveller in Serbia, 569; on Bashi-bazuks, 696
Berūnī, Arab astronomer, and writer, 298
Berytus, *see* Beyrout
Bêshir, ostikan of Armenia, 161
Bessarabia, Magyars in, 198; Bulgars migrate to, 230
Bessarion, Cardinal, archbishop of Nicaea, and Constantine Palaeologus, 462; 480 *note*; and Roman Church, 595, 620; at Ferrara, 623; 624; birth-place of, 620
Bessi, *see* Patzinaks
Bestes, Theodore, Byzantine canonist, 718, 723
Béthune, *see* Conon
Beuthen, in Poland, captured by Mongols, 652
Beyrout (Berytus), taken by Emperor John I, 148; law professors in, 707
Bezant, gold coin of Byzantium, 39, *see* Coinage
Bhatnir, in India, captured by Tīmūr, 651
Biandrate, *see* Hubert
Bibiones, Venetian township, 386
Bilarghu, Mongol leader, 178 sq.
Bilijik, captured by Ertughril, 655; 656
Biliktu, Mongol ruler, and Chinese, 649
Bisseni, *see* Patzinaks
Bithynia, 21; 24; 33; 67; 119; 131 *note*; Russians in, 205; 216 sq.; 256; assigned to Latin Emperor, 421, 424; 426; Theodore I in, 479; Michael Palaeologus in, 503 sq., 509; 513; 656; Turks in, 657, 662 sq.; 667; 675; 753
Bitlis, commercial town of Armenia, 162, 167
Bizā'a, in Syria, 359
Bizou, in Cappadocia, 112; given to Gagik II, 166
Blachernae, quarter of Constantinople, 41, 749; palace of, *see* Constantinople
"Black George" (Karageorge), founder of modern Serbia, 578
"Black Prince," the (Edward, Prince of Wales), 454
Black Sea, the (Euxine), 38 sq.; Greek colonies on, 183 sqq., 201; 192; 194; 203; 230; 232; 238; 331; 344; 353; 381; 421; Genoese in, 431, 511, 549; 478 sqq.; 487; 527; 535; 554; 572; 631; 653; 655; 660; Venetian fleet in, 666; 668; 672; 680; 692; 695 sq.; 733; 763
Black Stone, the, at Mecca, 276
Blagaj, capital of the duchy of Herzegovina, 580
Blastares, Matthew, Byzantine writer on law, 715; *Syntagma* of, 724
Blatno (Mosaburch, urbs paludum), town of, 211; lake of (Balaton), 211
Blemmýdes, Nicephorus, abbot of St Gregory's, 486 *note*; 488 *note*; 494 *note*; and Emperor John III, 495 sq.; and Latin theologians, 497; 498 sq.; refuses Patriarchate, 500; 505; and Theodore II, 506; 513
Blois, *see* Louis, Stephen
"Blue Fortress," in Armenia, Smbat I besieged in, 160
Blues, circus faction of Constantinople, 758 sq.

Blum, *see* Roger de Flor
Bobovac, Bosnian castle, besieged by Stephen Dušan, 545; 556; 565 sq.; surrendered to Turks, 580
Boccaccio, and "Duke of Athens," 442
Bodin, *see* Constantine
Boeotia, Latin rule in, 440 sq.; 450 sq.; Albanians settle in, 456; Constantine Palaeologus in, 462; given to Franco Acciajuoli, 464; Turkish, 465, 692
Bogdan I, Prince of Moldavia, 593
Bogdan II, Prince of Moldavia, 593
Bogdan III, Prince of Moldavia, 593; tributary to Turks, 588
Bogdan, Bulgarian commander, and Emperor Basil II, 242
Bogdan, Serbian chief, 553
Bogislav, Serbian leader, 110
Bogomile, heresy in Bulgaria, 238, 243, 518, 520, 523, 548, 550; in Bosnia, 518, 526, 545, 559, 574 sq., 580; 245; and Emperor Alexius I, 350; 363; persecuted by Stephen Dragutin, 532; Stephen Uroš II and, 535; 551; Islām and, 582 sq.; 737; *see also* Babuni, Manichaeans
Bohemia, 209, 214; ruler of, *see* Bořivoi
Bohemians, and conversion of Hungary, 214; at battle of Kossovo, 693
Bohemond I, of Taranto, Prince of Antioch, leader in First Crusade, captured by Seljūqs, 315, 340; invades Empire, 329, 600; Emperor Alexius I and, 335 sqq.; takes possession of Antioch, 338; 339; war with Alexius I, 341 sqq.; death of, 343; 347; 352
Bohemond II, Prince of Antioch, captures Leo I of Armeno-Cilicia, 169; 359
Bohemond III, Prince of Antioch, and Ruben II of Armeno-Cilicia, 171; 172; and Emperor Manuel, 376
Bohemond IV, the One-Eyed, count of Tripolis, seizes government of Antioch, 173 sq.
Bohemond of Lusignan, brother of Guy, King of Armeno-Cilicia, 181
Boiannes, Basil, catapan, reorganizes Southern Italy, 263
Boiditzes, surrenders Amorium to the Saracens, 130
Bojana, river of Albania, 527; 534
Boleslav the Mighty, King of Poland, and Vladímir of Russia, 209 sq.
Boljarin, nobility of old Bulgaria, 231
Bolkan, Župan of Rascia, makes himself independent of Byzantium, 330; Serbia and, 356
Bologna, friars of, at Negropont, 438; *see* Gozzadini
Boniface VI, Pope, and Photian schism, 256
Boniface VII, anti-Pope, in exile at Constantinople, 80
Boniface IX, Pope, and the Turks, 618 sq., 675
Boniface, marquess of Montferrat, King of Thessalonica, chosen to lead Fourth Crusade, 416, 604; and diversion of the Crusade, 417; 418 sq.; passed over for the Empire, 421; King of Thessalonica, 422 sqq.; 432 sq.; 435; death, 425, 520; 426 sq.; 436
Boniface of Verona, Euboean nobleman, and Guy II of Athens, 447; and Catalans, 451
Bordi (Gordi), in Armenia, 56
Borić, ban of Bosnia, 591
Boril, Tsar of Bulgaria, and Latin Empire, 425; deposed 521; 550; 591
Borilus, minister of Emperor Nicephorus III, 327
Boris, Khan of Bulgaria, becomes a Christian, 45, 235 sqq.; and Pope Nicholas I, 252
Boris II, Tsar of Bulgaria, 239 sq.
Boris of Hungary, son of Koloman, at Constantinople, 356
Bořivoi, Bohemian prince, baptized, 227
Borsa, *see* Roger
Borzo, *see* Barzūyah
Bosna, river of Bosnia, 518, 545, 560, 566, 573
Bosnia, 238; "banat" of, 432; rule of Kulin in, 517 sq.; Hungary and, 519 sq., 523, 526 sq.; Dragutin in, 532; lost to Serbia, 535; 541, 543; Stephen Dušan and, 544 sq.; and Ragusa, 549; hegemony of, 555 sqq., 559; Bosniaks at Kossovo, 558; and Turks, 557, 562, 566; and Cattaro, 564; 565; 567; 573 sq.; last years of kingdom, 578 sqq.; Upper Bosnia conquered by Turks, 580 sq.; 582; 687; Mahomet II and, 694; Manichaeans in, 498; Bogomiles in, 518; Chronicles, 546 *note*; Table of rulers, 591
Bosphorus (Panticapaeum, Kerch), 86, 183 submits to Utigurs, 185; 189
Bosphorus, the, 14, 86, 165, 316; Russians in, 46, 205; 320, 331, 336 sq.; Manuel's monastery on, 364; 367 sq., 382, 427, 486, 513, 546, 572, 660; Genoese and Venetians in, 666; 670, 677 sq.; Mahomet II in, 694, 696; 699, 701, 705, 755
Botaniates, *see* Nicephorus III, Emperor
Boua, Albanian clan, 552
Boua Spata, *see* Paul
Boucicaut, Marshal, at Constantinople, 618, 676 sq.; 678
Boudonitza, in Greece, marquesses of, 422; 433; castle of, 437; Zorzi family at, 458; conquered by Turks, 459
Bouillon, *see* Godfrey
Boyana, near Sofia, church of, 514; frescoes at, 550
Brabant, duke of, and Mongols, 639
Bracheuil, *see* Pierre de
Bragadino, defends Famagosta against Turks, 472
Branas, Theodore, adheres to Latin Empire, 423; 425
Branichevo, taken by Hungarians, 355
Branković, estates in Hungary, 573; ancestral territory, 576; *see* George, Vuk
Braslav, Croatian prince, 211

Brenta, Italian river, 211, 397
Breslau, 637
Breviarium, law treatise of Theodore, 714
Brevis Historia, work of St Cyril, 220
Břevnov, abbot of, becomes archbishop of Gran; *see* Anastasius
Brienne family, 449; *see* John, Walter
Bringas, Joseph, favourite of Theophano, 68 sqq.; defeated and imprisoned by Emperor Nicephorus II, 72; 116; 145
Brondolo, Venetian fortress, 391; captured by Pepin, 394
Browne, Professor E. G., on Avicenna's *Qānūn*, 297
Brumalia, Byzantine court fête, 26, 755
Brunelleschi, 622
Brunswick, *see* Otto of
Brūsa (Prusa), 542; Turkish capital, 543; 560; 562; 656; threatened by Osmān, 657 sq.; captured by Orkhān, 660; 661 sqq.; death of Orkhān at, 667; 674; 676; 678; captured by Tīmūr, 683; Bāyazīd I buried at, 684; 685; buildings of Mahomet I at, 688; 690; bishop of, *see* Joakim; *see also* Prusa
Bryennii, family, 771
Bryennius, Nicephorus, general, dismissed by Empress Theodora, 116; conspires against Michael VI, 117; executed, 320
Bryennius, Nicephorus, the Caesar, husband of Anna Comnena, plots against John II, 346, 351; work on Alexius I, 363, 765
Bryennius, Theoctistus, general of the regent Theodora, 42
Bryennius, revolts against Nicephorus III, 327
Bucellarian theme, 3, 733; (troops), 123 sq.; *see* Tadjat
Buda-Pesth, 546; 566; captured by Mongols, 638; 690
Buddhism among Mongols, 640, 646 sq., 649, 651
Budrun (Halicarnassus), taken by Hospitallers, 677
Budua, Adriatic town, Statutes of, 547; 553; occupied by Venice, 564, 570
Bug, river, 198, 200
Bugha, Saracen leader, 133
Bukaia, the, battle of, 375
Bukhārā, conquered by 'Alā-ud-Dīn of Khwārazm, 278; destroyed by Mongols, 279, 633; 303; 304; captured by Uzbeg Mongols, 651
Bukhārī, compiler of Arab traditions, 291
Bukhtyishū', Nestorian Christian, 297
Bulgar, Bulgary, capital of the White Bulgars, 193; destroyed by Mongols, 637
Bulgaria, Bulgarians, Chaps. VIII, XVII, XVIII; 3; 11; and Emperor Constantine V, 12, 231 sq.; 15; defeat Irene, 22; and Michael I, 29; besiege Constantinople, 30, 233 sq.; defeat Byzantines, 35, 37; 39; 42; conversion of, 45, 235 sq.; 47; 49; Romanus I and, 62; 70; Nicephorus II and, 76; Basil II and, 85, 148 sq., 241 sq., 263; 85 sq.; cost of war with, 93; and Michael IV, 104, 244; defeat Saracens, 119; 122 sq.; 126 sq.; and Basil I, 138; and Leo VI, 140; and Constantine VII, 142 sq.; 145; Armenian contingent sent to, 159; Slavonic liturgy in, 229; and Roman Church, 249, 252; *see also* Church, Bulgarian; Bulgaro-Roumanian frontier, 235; Byzantine government of, 243 sqq., 734 sqq.; risings in, 244 sq., 325; 257; Bulgarians in Byzantine army, 347; and Latin Empire, 423 sqq., 427 sqq., 481, 483; and John III, 430, 489 sq., 492; 432; victory of Klokonitsa, 428, 440; 478; 491; Manichaeans in, 498; and Theodore II, 501 sq.; and Michael VIII, 510; 511; defeat at Velbužd, 538; overrun by Turks, 555, 557; 571; finally conquered, 560 sq.; 617; 624; 659; and John V, 666; 669 sq.; 672 sq.; and Bāyazīd I, 674; 678; and Mūsà, 685; 687; 689; and Murād II, 691; 733 sq.; Bulgarian officials of Byzantium, 736; 746; Bulgarians at Constantinople, 750; trade with Constantinople, 762; influence of Byzantium on, 776; Table of rulers, 590; khans of, *see* Bayan, Boris, Isparich, Kardam, Kormisosh, Kovrat, Krum, Omurtag, Presiam, Sabin, Telerig, Telets, Tervel, Toktu; tsars of, *see* Boril, Boris, Constantine, Gabriel, George, John, Kaliman, Kalojan, Michael, Peter, Samuel, Shishman, Simeon, Theodore; archbishop of, *see* John Camaterus, Theophylact; *see also* Bulgars
Bulgarian Chronicle, 544 *note*
"Bulgaroctonus," epithet of Basil II, *q.v.*
Bulgaróphygos, Bulgarian victory at, 237
Bulgars, Chap. VII A; original home of, 184; and Justinian II, 185; trade and coinage, 193; political organization, 194; and Magyars, 198 sq.; migrate to Balkans, 200; and Svyatoslav of Kiev, 208, 213; and Vladímir, 202 sqq.; and St Cyril, 221, 223; Black Bulgars, 185; White (Silver) Bulgars, 192 sq.; 637
Bulotes, Manuel, ambassador of Emperor John VIII to the Pope, 621
Bulunyās, *see* Balanea
Bundārī, on date of Sultan Sanjar's birth, 311
Buondelmonti, *see* Esau
Burdas (Burtas), Chazar tribe, 192 sqq.
Burdas river, *see* Samara
Burgas, town of Thrace, 212; 667 *note*
Burgundy, *see* La Roche family; duke of, at La Crémonie, 441; at battle of Nicopolis, 675 sq.; fleet of, 571; *see* Louis
Būrī, Atābeg of Duqāq, 315
Būrid dynasty of Syria, 314 sq.
Burkan Khaldun, burial-place of Mangu Khan, 645
Burma, Mongols in, 646
Burtas, *see* Burdas

Burtasians (foxhides), export of, by the Burdas, 192
Burtzes, Constantine, disgraced by Emperor Constantine VIII, 97
Burtzes, Michael, 84; takes Antioch, 146; 147; defeated by Egyptians, 149
Burtzes, Michael, conspires against Emperor Michael VI, 320
Bury, Professor, on Emperor Michael IV, 105
Busta Gallorum, Byzantine victory of, 386
Butera, in Sicily, surrenders to Saracens, 137
Butrinto, Venetian naval victory at, 409; castle of, 448; Bulgarian bishopric of, 243
Butumites, general of Emperor Alexius I, 341, 343
Buwaih, founder of Persian dynasty, 301
Buwaihids, Persian dynasty, 276 sq.; 300; 302; 304; founded, 301
Buyur, lake, Chinese defeat Mongols at, 649
Būzhān, general of Malik Shāh, and Emperor Alexius I, 331
Byblus, *see* Jiblah
Byzantium, *see* Constantinople
Byzantius, Nicetas, teaches in University under Emperor Constantine IX, 114

Cabasilas, the, Byzantine mystical writers, 766
Cadalus, bishop of Parma, chosen anti-Pope (Honorius II), 597
Cadi (Muslim judge), 284; among Chazars, 191; at Constantinople, 675
Cadmea, castle of, at Thebes, 443; 446
Caesar, title, 730; *see* Alexius, Andronicus I, Bardas, Bryennius, Ducas, John-Roger; uncles of Emperor Constantine VI, 19, 23 sq.; title bestowed on Bulgarian prince, 213; in Serbia, 542 sq.; assumed by Gabalas of Rhodes, 488; 13; 61; 104; 118; 321; Caesars of Rome, 261, 626, 726; *see also* Tsar
Caesarea in Cappadocia (Qaisarīyah), Nicephorus II proclaimed at, 71, 145; Bardas Phocas proclaimed at, 81; 85 sq.; in Saracen wars, 120, 122; 167; 177; ruled by Dānishmandites, 315, 365; Crusaders at, 338; metropolitan of, *see* Basil, Mark
Caesarea in Palestine, taken by Emperor John I, 148
Caesaropapism, doctrines of, in Byzantine Church, 246
Cairo, 181; founded by Fāṭimids, 302; culture at, 629, 642; Abbasid Caliphate of, 279; 644
Calabria, province of, 4; remains Eastern, 36; 135; 141; diocese of, placed under Patriarch of Constantinople, 10; 259; hellenization of, 266; Norman, 597; theme of, 733; Byzantine monks in, 737
Calabrian admiral of Theodore I, 482; origin of Barlaam, 615
Calamus, Turks at, 657
Calaphates, *see* Michael V, Emperor
Calicadnus, river, Frederick Barbarossa drowned in, 172
Caliphate, of Baghdad, Chap. x (A); *see* Caliphs; and Armenia, 156, 158, 160 sq.; disintegration and decay of, 131, 139, 151, 300 sq.; 642; decline in revenue of, 151 *note*; frontier system of, 132; war with rulers of Aleppo, 143; 188; theory of the Caliphate, 275, 281 sq., 641; destroyed by Mongols, 642, 654; Ottoman Sultans heirs of, 642; Egyptian Caliphate, decay of, 376; *see* Khalīfah
Caliphs, *see* 'Alī, Omar I, Othman
Caliphs, Abbasids of Baghdad, *see* Amīn, Hārūn-ar-Rashīd, Mahdī, Ma'mūn, Manṣūr, Muhtadī, Muqtadī, Muqtadir, Mustakfī, Musta'ṣim, Mustaẓhir, Mu'taḍid, Mu'tamid, Mu'taṣim, Mutawakkil, Mutī', Qādir, Qā'im, Rāḍī, Saffāḥ, Wāthiq; 10; 86
Caliphs, Fāṭimids, *see* Ḥākim, Mahdī, Mu'izz, 'Ubaid-Allāh, Ẓāhir
Caliphs, Umayyads of Damascus, *see* Hishām, Marwān II, Omar II, Sulaimān, Walīd II, Yazīd II
Calixtus II, Pope, and Emperor John II, 354 sq., 596, 600
Calixtus III, Pope, and Hunyadi, 576
Callimachus, 691 *note*
Callinicus, inventor of Greek fire, 743
Callistus, Patriarch of Constantinople, and Pope Innocent VI, 617
Calocyrus, the patrician, and Russians, 208
Caloprini, Stefano, and Emperor Otto II, 404
Caloprini, Venetian faction, 403 sq.
Caltabellotta, in Sicily, tributary to Saracens, 136; revolts, 137
Caltagirone, in Sicily, sacked by Saracens, 136
Caltavuturo, in Sicily, and Saracens, 137
Camacha, fortress of, in Saracen wars, 120, 122 sq., 125, 127, 131 sq.
Camaterus, Gregory, logothete under Emperor John II, 352
Camaterus, John, Patriarch, *see* John
Camaterus, John, prefect of Constantinople, conspires against Mary of Antioch, 380
Cambalu (Pekin, Daitu, Taitu, Tatu, Khan Balig), founded by Kublai Khan, 647; captured by Chinese, 649; university of, 629
Cambini, on siege of Constantinople, 702
Cameniates, John, on siege of Salonica, 142
Camerino, battle of, 379
Campagna, the, revolts against Emperor Leo III, 9; Roman barons of, 258
Campofregoso, Pietro di, Genoese admiral, in Cyprus, 470
Campulung, Wallachian colony at, 540
Canale, Venetian admiral, 466
Candia (Chandax), Saracen stronghold in Crete, 36; captured by Nicephorus II, 69 sq.; seat of Venetian governor, 433; captured by Turks, 472

Candiani, Venetian noble family, 399; absolutism of, 407; *see* Peter
Canicleum, convent of, 68
Canina, occupied by Normans, 329; 342; bishopric of, 243
Canon Law (Nomocanones), Byzantine collections of, 229; 711; 715; 718; 723 sq.; in Serbia, 547
Cantacuzene family, 711
Cantacuzene, admiral of Emperor Alexius I, 341
Cantacuzene, John, *see* John VI, Emperor
Cantacuzene, Manuel, *see* Manuel
Cantacuzene, Matthew, and Turks, 553; 666 sq.
Cantacuzene, Theodore, sent by Manuel II to Paris, 618
Cantemir, 667 *note*; on exploits of Mahomet II, 704
Caopena, Catalan family in Aegina, 465
Caorle, settlement of, 386; bishopric of, 387; 412
Capella Palatina, at Palermo, mosaics at, 777
Capello Zen, at Venice, 397
Capistrano, Franciscan friar, at siege of Belgrade, 576
Capitol, the, at Constantinople, 748
Capo d'Istria, and Venice, 412
Cappadocia, clisura of, 39; 69; 85; 95; in Saracen wars, 121 sq., 125 sq., 128, 145; 153; 166; ruled by Seljūqs, 315; 320; 374; overrun by Mongols, 175, 177, 689; 670; 740; monks in, 753; emir of, *see* Ḥasan, Pulchas, *also* Dānishmand
Cappello, Victor, Venetian admiral, in Turkish war, 466
Captains, Serbian title, 542
Capua, Prince of, *see* Robert
Carabisiani, the, theme of, 732, 742
Carantenus, Theodore, admiral of Basil II, 85
Carbeas, Paulician chief, 42, 133
Carbonupsina, *see* Zoë
Carceri, dalle, *see* Giberto, Niccolò, Ravanò
Cardicon, Greek stronghold, taken by Turks, 690
Caria, emir of, allied with Byzantines, 662; 670; independent of Ottomans, 684; 753
Carlo I, Tocco, Count of Cephalonia, disputes for Corinth, 458; conquers Epirus and Joánnina, 461; 475
Carlo II, Tocco, ruler of Epirus, dethroned by Turks, 461; 475
Carlo Thopia, Albanian chief, 553, 583
Carmathians, attack Egyptians at Antioch, 147; revolt against Caliphate, 276
Carniola, 578
Carolingian Empire, 213; renaissance, 777
Carosus, Venetian tribune, conspires against doge, 397
Carpathian mountains, 200, 210; Turkish defeats on, 571; 637
Carpathos, held by Turkish pirates, 657
Casis, captured by Saracens, 123
Caspax, admiral of Alexius I, 339
Caspian Gate, 187
Caspian Sea, boundary of Armenia, 153; 186; 188; trade on, 193; 198; 201; Russian raids on, 206; 274; 277; 295; 490; 630 sq.; 633; 636; 651 sq.; 762
Cassandria, Genoese privileges at, 511
Cassiodorus, letter of, concerning Venetia, 385
Cassiopo, victory of Venetian fleet at, 409
Cassiteras, *see* Theodotus
Castamon (Castamona), Comnenian lands near, 318; captured by John II, 357
Castamunites, plots against Emperor Alexius I, 342
Castel dell' Uovo, at Naples, 452, 567
Castello, Venetian island (Olivolo), 392, 400
Castelnuovo (Novi), founded by Tvrtko I of Bosnia, 557; 564; 582
Castel Tornese, *see* Chloumoûtsi
Castoria, occupied by Normans, 329; ceded to Emperor John III, 494
Castriota, George, *see* Skanderbeg
Castrogiovanni, *see* Enna
Catacalon Cecaumenus, *see* Cecaumenus
Catalan, Grand Company, in Asia, 449, 657 sqq.; win battle of Cephisus, and seize duchy of Athens, 431, 450 sqq.; 453; degeneration of, 455; 456; in Monemvasia, 464; in Greece, 474, 614; Catalan trade with Constantinople, 762; *see* Muntaner, Roger de Flor
Catania, Byzantines defeated at, 135; raided by Saracens, 137
Catapan, office of, 733 sq.; in Attalia, 742; *see* Argyrus, Boiannes
Cataphracts, Byzantine heavy cavalry, 740
Caterina Cornaro, Queen of Cyprus, cedes it to Venice, 466, 471, 477
Catherine of Bulgaria, wife of Isaac I, 322; 324
Catherine of Valois, titular Latin Empress, marries Philip of Taranto, 452 sq.; Acciajuolo and, 454; 534 sq.; 474, 476
Catherine Vukčić, marries Stephen Thomas of Bosnia, 575; escapes to Rome, 581; death of, 581
Cattaro, 535; 537; 542; 545; 547; Serbian mint at, 550; captured by Tvrtko I, 557; 559; Venetian, 564 sq., 567; 574; cathedral at, 527; Bocche di, the, 517, 556 sq.
Cauca, ceded to Bohemond of Antioch, 343
Caucasian languages, 195; Caucasians in Byzantine Empire, 773
Caucasus, boundary of Empire under Basil II, 96; Goths in, 184; 187 sq.; 190; 638
Cauleas, *see* Anthony
Cavalry, Byzantine, 739 sq.
Cavarzere, revolts against Venice, 404 sq.
Cavazuccherina (Equilio Jesolo), settlement of, 386
Cayeux, *see* Anseau de
Cayster, river, 684
Cecaumenus, Catacalon, dismissed by Michael VI, 117; at battle of Petroë, 118; crown offered to, 320; plots against Alexius I, 333

Cecaumenus, treatise of, 773; on Byzantine fleet, 742; 774
Cedrenus, the chronicler, on Constantine VII, 66; on foundation of Sarkel, 192; 233 *note*; 239 *note*; on waterfall of Vodena, 241; 765
Cefalù in Sicily, 136; captured by Saracens, 137; 138; mosaics at, 777
Celestine III, Pope, sends crown to Leo the Great of Armeno-Cilicia, 172
"Celts from beyond the Alps," trade of, with Constantinople, 762; with Salonica, 770
Ceneda, bishop of, opposes Venice, 404
Centarch of the Spatharii, assistant of the strategus, 734
Centurione, Zaccaria, becomes Prince of Achaia, 459; defeated by Thomas Palaeologus, 460; 474
Ceos, 484
Cephalonia, and Normans, 330; occupied by Venetians, 354, 467; Orsini family in, 432, 473; Franciscans in, 438; 446; held by John of Gravina, 453; 455; 457; taken by Turks, 466; counts of, *see* Table, 475 sq.; theme of, 39, 733, 742; praetor of, *see* Paul
Cephisus, the, battle of, 431; 450 sqq., 455
Cerasus, Turkish defeat at, 656; trade with Constantinople, 762
Cerdagne, count of, *see* William-Jordan
Ceremonies, Book of, by Constantine VII, 58; 67; 142; 144; 746; 754
Cerigo, ravaged by Sicilian fleet, 368; becomes Venetian seigniory, 421, 436; recovered for Michael VIII, 445; Venetian colony, 457, 465 sq.; Byzantine fleet destroyed off, 488; 475
Cerigotto, island of, becomes Venetian seigniory, 436; becomes Byzantine, 445
Cerines, Cypriote fortress, 471
Certosa, the, at Florence, 454
Cerularius, *see* Michael
Cesarini, Cardinal Julian, killed at Varna, 572; at Council of Ferrara, 622; and Treaty of Szegedin, 571, 624, 691
Cetina, the, ceded to Bosnia, 556; 587
Cetinje, made capital of Montenegro, 587
Ceylon, trade with Constantinople, 762
Chagrī Beg, ruler of the Seljūqs, 304 sq.; 314
Chalandritza in Greece, 460
Chalcedon, 78; 667; Council of, 155; metropolitan of; *see* Leo
Chalcidice, peninsula of, 141
Chalcis (Negropont), *see* Negropont
Chalcocondyles, kinsman of Duchess of Athens, 462
Chalcocondyles (Chalcondyles), Demetrius, Athenian scholar, 462
Chalcocondyles (Chalcondyles), Laónikos, Athenian historian, 461 sq., 474; 558 *note*; 579 *note*; 659; 671 *note*; 677 *note*; 685 *note*; 688 *note*; 692 *note*; 695 *note*; 700 *note*, 765
Chalcondyles, *see* Chalcocondyles
Chalcutzes, Nicetas, conquers Cyprus, 145
Chaldaïsm, Michael Cerularius accused of, 323
Chaldeans, the, and Pope Eugenius IV, 623; *see* Nestorian
Chaldia, theme of, 39, 733; trade with Constantinople, 762
Chamáretos, John, in Laconia, 434
Chamber of Loans (*Camera degli imprestidi*) at Venice, 413
Chamorlu, battle of, 563
Champagne, *see* Theobald; marshal of, *see* Villehardouin
Champlitte, *see* Robert, William
Chandax, *see* Candia
Chapar Khan, Mongol ruler, 641
Charices, rebels against Alexius I, 331
Charisius, gate of, *see* Hadrianople Gate
Charistikarioi, beneficiaries of monastic revenues, 349
Charlemagne, Emperor of the West, and the Lombards 18 sq.; and Empress Irene, 20, 22, 24; crowned Emperor, 24; and Nicephorus I, 36; 226; 385; and Venice, 392 sqq.; embassy to Constantinople, 393; signs treaty of Aix, 395; 396
Charles Martel, victory of, at Poitiers, 2; and Pope Gregory III, 10; 391 sq.
Charles III the Fat, Emperor of the West, and Venice, 399 sq.
Charles I (of Anjou), King of Naples, and Achaia, 444; becomes Prince of Achaia, 446, 448; 496; and Emperor John IV, 513 *note*; plans to recover the Latin Empire, 527, 596; and Emperor Michael VIII, 610 sqq.; 474; 476
Charles II, King of Naples, 446; and suzerainty of Greece, 448, 474, 476
Charles III, King of Naples, Lord of Corfù, 476
Charles IV the Fair, King of France, and Andronicus II, 614
Charles V, King of France, and John V, 618
Charles VI, King of France, and Theodore Cantacuzene, 618, 678
Charles of Valois, and the Latin Empire, 534, 614
Charlotte, titular Queen of Cyprus, 466, 471; 477
Charsianum, theme of, 39, 733 sq.; troops of, 137; victory of Sclerus at, 86; fortress of, taken by Saracens, 120; Saracens defeated at, 129; 134
Chartularii, office of, 730
Chartulary of the Sakellion, office of, 731
Chartulary of the Theme, assistant of the strategus, 734
Chatalar, inscription at, 235
Chatalja, near Constantinople, 234
Chateaumorant, defends Constantinople, 677 sq.
Chatillon, *see* Reginald
Chaucer, and dukes of Athens, 442
Chazars, Turkish tribe, 38; 42; Cyril's mis-

sion to, 44, 219 sq.; 122; invade Armenia, 126; 187; Chazar Empire, 187 sqq.; religious tolerance of, 191; 192 sqq.; 199; and Russian trade, 201; 203; decline of, 207; 210; in Byzantine army, 738, 750; Leo the Chazar, *see* Leo IV, Emperor
Cheimarra, Bulgarian bishopric, 243
Χελάνδια, Chelandia (Zalandria) (Byzantine bireme), 398 *note*, 743
Chelebi, "gentleman," epithet applied to Mahomet I, 688
Chelidonia in Lycia, Saracen fleet destroyed off, 131
Chemishgadzak (Hierapolis), birthplace of John I, 78
Chemshkik, Chemishgig, real name of Tzimisces, 78
Chena, Turkish defeat at, 656
Chêpina, Bulgarian fortress, ceded to Theodore II, 502, 525
Cheremises, Ugrian tribe, 194
Cherkesses, *see* Kasogs
Chernigov, destroyed by Mongols, 637; *see* Rostislav
Cherson (Korsun), 19; and Justinian II, 189; 192; 208; ceded to Vladimir the Great, 209; St Cyril at, 220; 264; held by Turks, 659; theme of, 39, 733; bishop of, 32; ancient Greek colony (Chersonesus), 183
Chidmas (Chingylus), river, in Magyar territory, 195
Chiftliks, Turkish military lands, 674
Chiliandarion, death of Stephen Nemanja at, 518
China, Chinese Empire, 185; 198; and Mongols, 279, 628 sq., 632 sqq., 636, 644 sqq.; Kublai Khan's government of, 647 sq.; Mongols expelled from, 649; and Tīmūr, 651, 686; Mongol massacres in, 634; Chinese derivation of "Mongol," 630; Chinese annals, 187, 632; Keraits in, 650; Muslim trade with, 286; 631; trade with Constantinople, 762; *see* Kin, Ming, Sung
Chinardo, lord of Corfù, 476
Chingylus, *see* Chidmas
Chioggia (Clugies major), settlement of, 386; captured by Pepin, 394
Chios (Scio), 81, 110; and Venetians, 354, 371, 411; Venetian disaster at, 413; in Latin Empire, 421; taken by Emperor John III, 428, 487; Genoese in, 431, 465, 467, 511, 616, 672, 684; Zaccaria family in, 455; Turks in, 468, 654, 657; 672; 675; archbishop of, *see* Leonard
Chirmen, near Hadrianople, 555; *see* Maritza
Chliara, 344; fortified by Emperor Manuel, 378; conferred on Hospitallers, 480
Chloumoûtsi (Clermont, Castel Tornese), castle of, built by Geoffrey II, 439, 441, 473; Constantine Palaeologus at, 460; bishop of, *see* Stephen
Choirokoitia, victory of, 470
Choisy, on Byzantine art, 768
Choki, Tartar chief, and Bulgaria, 530 sq.
Chonae, given to Mavrozómes, 482; ceded by Seljūqs to Theodore II, 504
Chonarium, defeat of Michael III by Saracens at, 46, 133
Choniates, *see* Nicetas
Chora, abbot of, 32; *see* Constantinople, churches of
Chorene, *see* Moses of
Chorlu (Tzurulum), 327; 421; 429 sq.; captured by Latins, 490; by John III, 493; by Turks, 667
Chosroes I Nūshirwān, Sasanid King of Persia, builds the Caspian Gate against the Chazars, 187
Chosroes II, Sasanid King of Persia, 280
Chozan, theme of, 733
Chrabr, monk, on Slav script, 222
Chresianus, Bardas Phocas proclaimed Emperor at, 87
Christian of Mayence, arch-chancellor of Frederick I, 379
Christianity and image worship, 6; the Eastern Empire its champion against Islām, 25; Leo III on Christianity and paganism, 30; brought to the Slavs, 44; 215 sqq.; Bulgarians, 235 sqq., 45; Vladímir of Russia converted, 90, 207 sqq.; conversion of the Magyars, 213 sqq.; the Chazars and, 190 sq., 219 sqq.; character of Byzantine Christianity, 774; under Islām, 287 sqq.; 316; *see* Crusades; Mongols and, 493, 640; under Mahomet II, 625; under early Sultans, 661, 663
Christodulus of Patmos, St, monastic reformer, and Alexius I, 349; 754
Christopher, son of Romanus I, crowned by his father, 61; death, 63
Christopher, son-in-law of Basil I, 51
Christopher, Patriarch of Antioch, 80
Christopher, bishop of Olivolo, 393
Christópolis (Kavala), Lombards in, 426 sq.; pass of, 541; *see also* Kavala
Christos Philanthropos, monastery of, Alexius I buried at, 347
"Chronicle of the Morea," found at Thebes, 454; quoted on prosperity of Achaia, 445; 473 sq.; 509 *note*
Chrysoberges, *see* Nicholas
Chrysochir, Paulician leader, 139
Chrysopolis, 20; 55; 72; victory of Basil II at, 88; 124; 322; abbot of, 32
Chrysostom, St John, speeches of, 237; and Byzantine learning, 758
Chrysotriclinium, Imperial throne-room, *see under* Constantinople
Chudes, Slavonic tribe, 209
Chumnus, Michael, nomophylax of the School at Constantinople, 720, 724
Church, Armenian, its solidarity, 153, 155 sq., 182; 163; 167; *see* Messalians; attempts to unite it with Roman Church, 172; 178; 180; and Byzantine Church, 259; 737; Alexius I and, 350; Manuel and, 363, 376; Patriarch accepts Union of Florence, 623; *see* Councils, Katholikos

Church, Bulgarian; foundation of, 235 sq.; 45; and the Papacy, 47, 236, 252 sq., 520, 612; obtains Patriarchate, 238, 523; and Romanus I, 62, 238; and John I, 240; and Basil II, 94, 243, 259; under Tsar John Alexander, 548; subordinate to Patriarch of Constantinople, 53, 560; autocephalia of, 595; 736; *see* Councils
Church, Byzantine (Orthodox), 26; church property and taxation, 27; Church and State, 25, 31; Photian schism, 248 sqq., 47, 53 sq., 56; and Leo V's marriages, 57, 62, 256 sq.; and Nicephorus II, 73 sqq., 91; Schism with Rome, 112 sqq., Chaps. IX, XIX; and Armenian Church, 156, 363; and Russian Church, 207; and Isaac I, 323; and Alexius I, 332, 349; and Manuel I, 363 sq.; and Roman Church, 333, 345, 497; Latin oppression of, 423, 437, 446, 451; Theodore I and, 486 sqq.; schism with Epirus, 496; John II and, 498; Theodore II and, 505; and Bulgarian Church, 236, 523, 560; in Cyprus, 471; in Crete, 472; Serbian Patriarchate and, 548, 551, 554; and Moldavia, 568; and unification of Empire, 737; power of, 751 sqq.; preachers and theologians of, 766; relations with Papacy, Chaps. IX, XIX; *see also* Canon Law, Christianity, Councils, Iconoclasm, Moechian, Monasticism, Patriarchate, Studion
Church, Serbian, sees of, 90; use of Slavonic liturgy, 229; autocephalous, 487, 498, 521 sq., 528, 537, 595; its Patriarch at Ipek, 542; 554; 578; and Council of Lyons, 612
Church, Latin, *see* Latin, Roman
Cibyrrhaeots, theme of, 3, 35, 733, 742, 744; 123, 125; strategus of, *see* Craterus
Cilicia, campaigns of Nicephorus II in, 70, 74, 78, 145 sqq.; fighting in, 120, 123, 126; 128 sqq.; 140, 142; Saracen province of, 132; 153; 187; John II's campaign in, 348, 353, 359 sq.; Crusaders in, 338, 341, 343; 360; 365; 367; 374; 376; Andronicus Comnenus in, 373, 375, 381; Cyprus and, 470; Turkish tribes in, 653; finally annexed by Turks, 182; Mamlūks invade, 669; *see* Armeno-Cilicia
Cilician Gates, frontier fighting at, 120, 124 sqq., 131; 140; 653
Cimmerian Bosphorus, 185; Jews of, 190; 205; *see* Bosphorus
Cinnamus, Byzantine chronicler, 351; 362; 602; 765
Circassian Mamlūks at Damascus, 680
Cistercians, in Greece, 438
Civitate, Leo IX made prisoner at, 268
Civita Vecchia, bishop of, *see* Orbevieto
Civitot (Gemlik), fortress of, built by Alexius I, 331; 336; disaster of Crusaders at, 337; and Theodore I, 483; taken by Orkhān, 665; sacked by Tīmūr, 683
Clans, in ancient Bulgaria and modern Albania, 231
Clari, *see* Robert of
Claudiâs, taken by Constantine V from the Saracens, 122
Claudiopolis, bishop of, *see* Thomas
Clavijo, Ruy Gonzalez de, ambassador to Tīmūr, 640; 650
Clazomenae, 488
Clement IV, Pope, and Michael VIII, 610, 612
Clement V, Pope, and Stephen Uroš II, 534; 638
Clement VI, Pope, and Armenia, 180; and union with Byzantine Church, 615 sq.
Clement, St, relics of discovered by St Cyril, 220, 224, 250
Clement the Slav, supposed author of "Pannonian" Legends of SS. Methodius and Cyril, 217 *note*
Clermont, Council of, 410, 599
Clermont, *see* Chloumoûtsi
Clisurae (military governments), 39, 734
Clisurarchs, 734
Clugies major, *see* Chioggia
Clugies minor, *see* Sottomarina
Cluny, abbey of and Pope John XIX, 262 sq.; *see* Bernard, Peter
Cobidas, commentator on the *Digest*, 707
Coco, James, attempts to destroy Turkish fleet in Golden Horn, 700
Code of Justinian, Chap. XXII *passim*; 5, 52, 58 sq., 369
Coela, port of, 376
Coinage of Byzantium, 39; of Isaac I, 322; debasement of, 348; Theodore I and, 487; of Nicene Emperors, 514; of Trebizond, 516; of Bulgars, 193; Arab coins in Russia, 201, 206; Persian coins in Russia, 193; coinage expedients of Latin Emperors, 420, 429; of Neopatras, 449; of Latin princes of Greece, 439, 441, 451 sq.; of Lesbos, 465; counterfeit coinage of Stephen Uroš II, 535; Serbian mint, 550; Bosnian coinage, 550, 556; of Duke of Spalato, 566; coins of Semendria, 569; currency of Kublai Khan, 630, 640, 647; of Orkhān, 663; copper currency in India, 651; Venetian right to coin, 400, 514; in Cyprus, 469; *see* Bezant, Keration, Nomisma, Solidus
Colbigni, foreign mercenaries in Byzantine army, 347
Collectio Canonum, part of *Syntagma*, 723
Collectio Constitutionum Ecclesiasticarum Tripertita, 711
Collectio XXV Capitulorum, 711
Collectio LXXXVII Capitulorum, 711
Cologne, archbishop of, and Photius, 249; *see* Gero; 336; marks of, 414
Colonea, military government of, 39; 733; 381; *see* Theodore
Colonies, Byzantine, 736
Comacchio, defeat of Byzantine fleet at, 394; salt trade at, 396, 399; coveted by Venice, 399; sacked and taken, 400
Comana, conquered by Ghāzī, 357
Comania (Kūmistān), in Persia, 631

Comitatus, *comites*, in Hungary, 215
Comitopouloi, "Young Counts," the sons of Shishman of Bulgaria, 240
Commagene, 2
Comne, original home of the Comneni, 318
Comnena, *see* Anna
Comneni, dynasty, Chaps. XI, XII; 82 sq.; 118; 318, 378; end of, 384; 421; found Empire of Trebizond and despotat of Epirus, 423; 424; 428; 479 sq.; and Bulgaria, 245; and the Church, 603; 724; 726, 728, 733, 737 sqq.; court of, 756; churches built by, 753, 770; renaissance under, 769; *see* Alexius, Andronicus, Epirus, Isaac, John, Manuel, Michael Angelus, Trebizond
Comnenus, Alexius, eldest son of John II, death of, 361
Comnenus, Alexius, natural son of Manuel, 380
Comnenus, Alexius, Protosebastos, nephew of Manuel, and favourite of Mary of Antioch, 380
Comnenus, Andronicus, son of Alexius I, 346
Comnenus, Andronicus, son of John II, 361, 363, 376, 380
Comnenus, Arianites, *see* Arianites
Comnenus, David, brother of Alexius I of Trebizond, successes of, 425, 480; defeated by Theodore I, 482; Latin Empire and, 483; death of, 485
Comnenus, Isaac, *see* Isaac I Comnenus, Emperor
Comnenus, Isaac, brother of Alexius I, 326 sq.; 332
Comnenus, Isaac, the Sebastocrator, son of Alexius I, father of Andronicus I, 346, 352; plots against John II, 357; 360; 365; 381
Comnenus, Isaac, Sebastocrator, son of Emperor John II, at siege of Anazarbus, 169; 364 sq., 374
Comnenus, Isaac, rebel Emperor in Cyprus, 384
Comnenus, John, brother of Isaac I, 318; declines the crown, 324; family of, 326
Comnenus, John, nephew of Alexius I, plots against him, 332
Comnenus, John, nephew of John II, deserts to the Turks, 360
Comnenus, John, nephew of Manuel I, 376
Comnenus, John, son of Emperor Andronicus, 380
Comnenus, Manuel (Eroticus), defends Nicaea against Sclerus, 85; father of Emperor Isaac I, 318
Comnenus, Manuel, brother of Alexius I, 326
Comnenus, Manuel, son of Emperor Andronicus, 380
Comnenus, Nicephorus, disgraced by Constantine VIII, 97; 318
Como, 405; *see* Benedict of
Concordia, on Venetian mainland, 386
Conon of Béthune, governs Latin Empire, 427
Conrad II, the Salic, Emperor of the West, embassy of to Constantine VIII, 97; and Venice, 407 sq.
Conrad III, King of the Romans, and John II, 360 sq., 365; at Second Crusade, 366 sqq.; 369
Conrad, Moravian prince, 356
Conrad of Montferrat, 379
Conrad of Wittelsbach, archbishop of Mayence, at coronation of Leo the Great of Armeno-Cilicia, 172
Conradin, last of the Hohenstaufen, 444
Constance, Council of, Byzantine embassy at, 619; canon of, *see* John of Ragusa
Constance of Aragon, wife of Leo V of Armeno-Cilicia, 179
Constance of Hohenstaufen (Anna), wife of Emperor John III, 429, 495; her varied career, 496
Constance, Princess of Antioch, daughter of Bohemond, 359; and Manuel, 373; 381
Constans II, Emperor, 230 *note*
Constantine the Great, Emperor, 24; supposed ancestor of Basil I, 49; 318; 489; 542; 679; 729; 754
Constantine III, Emperor, visits Armenia, 156
Constantine IV (Pogonatus), Emperor, defeated by the Bulgarians, 230
Constantine V Copronymus, Emperor, birth and coronation, 3; succeeds his father, 11; character, 12; internal administration, 13, 4; organizes army, 4; military exploits, 12, 121 sq.; war against Bulgars, 13, 231 sq.; struggle with image worship, 13 sqq.; Novels, 708, 710; loses Italy, 18; death of, 19; 20; 29; 73; his leniency to Arab prisoners, 122; marriage to Chazar princess, 189
Constantine VI, Emperor, 19; proposal for his marriage, 20; struggle with his mother, 22 sq.; marriage with Maria, 22; marries Theodote, 23, 28; his character, 22; conquered and blinded by Irene, 24; impersonated, 35; campaigns against Arabs, 125, and Bulgarians, 232, 256; Novels, 710
Constantine VII Porphyrogenitus, Emperor, birth and baptism, 57, 256; crowned, 257; character, 59, 66; marriage to Helena, 61; personal government, 63; family circle, 64; poisoned, 65; and religious affairs, 65; and Papacy, 260; administration, 66; literary works, 67; death, 67; Saracen campaigns, 142 sq.; on Romanus I, 61 *note*; 51; 53; 58; 68; 70 sq.; relationship to Romanus III, 98 *note*; on foundation of Sarkel, 192; on Magyars, 195 sq.; on the Patzinaks, 197 sq.; on Russians, 204, 206; 237; on Torcello, 391; on Pepin's repulse from Venice, 394; 714; Novels of, 715 sq., 721, 725; on

ceremonial, 727 sq., 746, 754; on nationality, 735; 765
Constantine VIII, Emperor, birth of and coronation, 68, 83; 79; his character, 83, 97; 88; personal government, 96 sq., 318; and Arabs, 97; death, 98; 107; 148; and Armenia, 164
Constantine IX Monomachus, Emperor, marriage and coronation, 108; character, 109; revolts against, 110 sq., 271; and the Schism, 112 sq., 269 sqq.; literary renaissance under, 114; death, 115; 117; and Seljūq Turks, 150; and Armenia, 111, 165; 259; 265; 319; 364; and Papacy, 595; and School of Law, 706, 716, 718 sqq., 734; 715; 721
Constantine X Ducas, Emperor, plots against Michael VI, 320, 325; nominated by Isaac I to succeed him, 324; and Papal election, 597; Novel of, 720
Constantine XI Palaeologus (Dragases), Emperor, conquests in Morea, 460 sq.; crowned at Mistra, 462; and Union of the Churches, 624 sq.; and Mūrād II, 692; 694; defends Constantinople, 695 sqq.; 698, 700, 703; death, 463, 704; 593
Constantine I, Prince of Armeno-Cilicia, consolidates his kingdom, 168; 169
Constantine, regent of Armeno-Cilicia, 173 sqq.
Constantine III, King of Armeno-Cilicia, 177
Constantine IV, King of Armeno-Cilicia, 181
Constantine V, King of Armeno-Cilicia, 181
Constantine, King of Serbia, natural son of Stephen Uroš II, 536, 590
Constantine Bodin of Dioclea, Serbian prince, proclaimed Tsar of Bulgaria, 244; 245; deserts Alexius I, 330; 356
Constantine Asên, Tsar of Bulgaria, 510; 525 sqq.; death, 528; 531; 590
Constantine, son of Emperor Basil I, 50; death, 51, 253; 54 sq.; 708; 712; 717
Constantine, son of Emperor Romanus I, crowned by his father, 61; death of, 64
Constantine, the Paphlagonian, brother of Michael IV, made Domestic of the Oriental Scholae, 102; favourite of Michael V, 105; intrigues against Zoë and the Patriarch, 106; fall and punishment, 107; 110
Constantine Ducas, *see* Ducas
Constantine Lascaris, brother of Theodore I, defeated by Latins, 481
Constantine, the patrician, commander in Sicily, 134; defeated and slain, 135
Constantine, King of the Ethiopians, accepts the Council of Florence, 623
Constantine, Duke of Neopatras, 475
Constantine, the Serbian, friend of Marko, 555; rules at Köstendil, 557; killed, 561
Constantine, Patriarch of Constantinople, 15; executed by Constantine V, 16
Constantine Lichudes, made Patriarch of Constantinople, 324; 106; 110; learning of, 114
Constantine II, Katholikos of Armenia, 179
Constantine, Patriarch of the Armenians, accepts the Union of Florence, 623
Constantine, bishop of Nacolea, Iconoclast, 8
Constantine, bishop of Nicomedia, Iconoclast, 8
Constantine the Philosopher, Bulgarian scholar, at Serbian court, 561; biographer of Stephen Lazarević, 565; 465 *note*
Constantine the Rhodian, poem of, on Constantinople, 746, 749
Constantine, *see* Cyril, St
Constantine, pupil of St Methodius, 237
Constantine Nicaeus, Byzantine jurisconsult, 714, 722
Constantinople, *passim*; besieged by Saracens, 2, 119, 151; earthquake at, 4, 95; anti-iconoclast riots at, 9; stormed by Constantine V, 12; Charlemagne's embassy in, 393; besieged by Krum Khan, 29, 37, 233; by Thomas the Slavonian, 35, 235; Russian ambassadors at, 38, 90; attacked by Russians, 46, 140, 203, 205, 743; Russian merchants at, 205 sq.; Olga at, 207; walls, 40, 269, 696 sqq.; foreign embassies at, under Constantine VII, 66; risings in, against Bringas, 72; against Nicephorus II, 76; embassy of Gero at, 81; threatened by Sclerus, 85 sq.; Venetians at, 94, 391, 396, 407, 411, 413, 606; embassy of Conrad II at, 97; Saracen embassy at, 100; insurrection against Michael V, 106; threatened by Tornicius, 111; rising in favour of Cerularius, 113, 271; revolt against Michael VI, 118, 321; threatened by Saracen fleet, 141; Armenian kings at, 62, 159 sq., 165; Armenian colony at, 182; besieged by Avars, 186; Turkish embassies at, 187; threatened by Magyars, 212; SS. Cyril and Methodius at, 217 sq., 228; Moravian embassy at, 221 sq.; besieged by Simeon of Bulgaria, 238; captured by Alexius I, 327; Crusaders at, 316, 336 sq.; threatened by Normans, 325, 408; massacre of Latins at, 382, 414; Qilij Arslān at, 377; Fourth Crusade at, Chap. XIV; sack of, 420, 605, 777; partition of, 421; influence of, 777; attacked by Theodore I, 484; by John III, 429, 489, 493, 523; by Michael VIII, 509; taken, 429, 431, 443, 511 sqq., 526; threatened by Bulgarians, 537; attacked by Mahomet I, 619; Boucicaut at, 618, 676 sq.; attacked by Bāyazīd, 675 sqq.; by Mūsà, 686; by Murād II, 689; siege of, and capture, by Mahomet II, 693 sqq., 463, 575; Western pilgrims at, 258, 264, 266; Papal legates at, 256, 261, 269 sqq.; intellectual activity of, 66 sq., 114, 763 sqq.; Pisan quarter at, 344; Italians at, 362; Manuel's buildings at, 364; Andronicus I's buildings at, 383; description of, 744 sqq.; fortifications of, 40, 697; population, 750, 758 sqq.; included in theme of Thrace, 733

churches of, 769: *see* St Sophia; St George of Mangana, 114 sq., 346, 719; St Irene, 753; St Mary, 511; St Mary of the Amalfitans, 264; St Mary Peribleptos, 100; St Mocius, 256; SS. Sergius and Bacchus (Little St Sophia), 753, 768; St Stephen, 264; St Theodosius (Gul-jāmi‘), 704; Chora (Qahrīye-jāmi‘), 749, 753, 769, 770; Forty Martyrs, 383; Holy Apostles, 21, 30, 47, 55, 69, 77, 248, 746, 748, 753, 764, 768, 776; New Church (νέα), 53, 100, 753, 769; Pammakaristos (Fetḥīye-jāmi‘), 749, 753; Pantokrator (Kilīsa-jāmi‘), 352, 365, 625, 749, 753; of the Theotokos (Vefa-jāmi‘), 753; Latin churches at, *see* Latin Church; convent of Nine Orders, 323; icon of Path-finding Virgin, 513; Pantepoptes monastery (Eski-Imaret-jāmi‘), 346, 749; Petrion, convent of, 100, 107; St John monastery, 509; St Paul hospital, 349; Soter monastery, 615

palaces at: Blachernae, 756; Bucoleon, 76, 754; Caenurgium, 53, 754; Chalce, 52 (vestibule), 754; Chrysotriclinium, 754; Dolma Bagcha (modern), 696, 699; Eleutherian, 25; Hieria, 14; Magnaura (and School of Law), 21, 39, 42, 52, 711, 764; Petrion, 73; Porphyrogenitus, 698, 700; Sacred Palace, 9, 41, 68, 79, 107, 118, 321, 346, 727, 748, 750, 753 sqq.; St Mamas, 48, 50 sq., 234; of the Springs, 269 sqq.; Sigma terrace, 39, 107; Triconchus, 39, 754; 748

Amastrianon Square, 749, 761; Ātmeydān, *see* Hippodrome; Augusteum, 748, 754, 761; Bous (Taurus) Square, 748 sq., 761; Capitol, 748; Cyclobium fortress, 666; Forum, 51, 748, 761; ancient, 759; of Arcadius, 749; Golden Milestone, 748; Hebdomon quarter at, 509; Hippodrome (Circus, Ātmeydān), 758 sqq.; 12, 16, 52, 65, 68 sq., 87, 384, 699, 750 sq., 754, 757; Lausiacus Arcade, 754; Law Courts, 719; Long Portico, 761; Maḥmūdīye mosque, 698; Mese, street, 748 sq., 761; district, 749; Philadelphion cross-roads, 748; Praetorium, 748; Senate House, 748; Strategion, 761; Gates, *see* Golden, Hadrianople, Holy Angels, Pege, St Romanus

Constantinople, Patriarchs of, *see* Alexius, Anastasius, Anthony Cauleas, Anthony of the Studion, Arsenius, Athanasius, Basil, Callistus, Constantine, Constantine Lichudes, Cosmas, Eustathius, Euthymius, Gennadius, Germanus, Gregory, Ignatius, John Beccus, John Hylilas, Joseph, Methodius, Metrophanes, Michael Anchialus, Michael Cerularius, Nicephorus, Nicholas Chrysoberges, Nicholas Mysticus, Paul, Philotheus, Photius, Polyeuctes, Sergius, Sisinnius, Stephen, Tarasius, Theodotus Cassiteras, Theophylact, Tryphon; (Latin) Thomas Morosini.

Constitutional History, Muslim political theory, 280 sq.; constitution of Venice, 397, 407, 409, 413; Serbian, 547; Byzantine political theory, 727 sqq.

Contarini, Bartolomeo, and Duchess of Athens, 463 sq.

Contarini, Domenico, doge of Venice, 408

Contomytes, Constantine, strategus of the Thracesians, defeats Arabs, 131; defeated in Sicily, 137

Contostephanus, Alexius, commander under Emperor Manuel I, 368, 376

Copronymus, nickname of Emperor Constantine V, 11

Coquerel, Mahiot de, Navarrese leader, conquers Attica, 456, 474

Cordova, emirs of, and Theophilus, 38

Corfù, *see* Table, 476; reduced by Guiscard, 329; 330; 354; taken by Normans, 368; 371; Venetians at, 409, 411; 412, 414; Crusaders at, 414; becomes Venetian seigniory, 421; 428; 432; 434 sqq.; 440; 453; 456; Venetian, 457, 464 sqq., 583; besieged by Turks, 467; Latin culture in, 472; 493; sect of "Naked" at, 760

Coriatović, *see* Juga

Corinth, taken by Normans, 368; 424; 434; taken by Geoffrey Villehardouin, 438; 441; 447; 456; 458; Hospitallers at, 459, 677; becomes Turkish, 463; tournament at, 473; silk manufacture at, 770; Gulf of, 436, 439, 459, 465; Isthmus of, 690; made archbishopric, 438; archbishop of, and Aristotle, 474; *see* Acrocorinth, Hexamilion

Corleone, tributary to Arabs, 136

Coron, in Messenia, held by Venice, 421, 431, 434, 438, 453; 457; 461, 465; captured by Turks, 467; 476

Coronation of Emperors in St Sophia, 728; 752; at Nicaea, 488; coronation oath of Venetian doge, 413

Coronea, Turks at, 675

Coronello, Francesco, Spanish Jew, governs Naxos, 468

Corpus Iuris civilis, 714, *see* Code of Justinian

Corpus Legum, 722

Corum, besieged by Arabs, 126; destroyed, 128, 130

Corvinus, *see* Matthias

Cos, 128; plundered by Venetians, 411; assigned to Latin Empire, 491; taken by Emperor John III, 428

Cosmas, Byzantine illustrated MS. of, at Vatican, 768

Cosmas, Patriarch of Constantinople, crowns Alexius I and Irene, 328

Cosmas, Patriarch of Constantinople, deposed by Manuel, 362

Cosmas, the presbyter, opponent of the Bogomile heresy, 238

Cossacks, and Mongols, 650

Cotyaeum, 85

Council of Regency, in minority of Emperor Constantine VII, 59 sq.
Council of Ten, Venetian, created, 409
Councils (and Synods), *see especially* Chaps. IX, XIX; Ecumenical Councils and Justinian's Code, 711; Fourth Ecumenical Council, at Chalcedon (451), 155
Armenian Church: at Sis (1307), conforms to Latin uses, 178
Bulgarian Church: two Councils against Bogomiles, 548
Byzantine Church: at Constantinople, in the palace of Hieria (753), against image worship, 14; at Nicaea (787, Seventh Ecumenical Council), restores images, 1, 21, 246; at Constantinople (807), starts Moechian controversy, 28; (809), against Studites, 28; (815), in St Sophia, renews decrees against image worship, 31, 246; (843), finally restores images, 41, 246 sq.; (861), in church of Holy Apostles, declares for Photius, 47, 248; (867), condemns Latin uses and declares independence of Byzantine Church, 249 sqq.; (869–870, Eighth Ecumenical Council), in St Sophia, deposes Photius, 53, 251 sq.; (879), re-instates Photius, 253 sq.; (920), condemns fourth marriages, 62; (1009), re-asserts independence of Byzantine Church, 91, 261; (1054), in St Sophia, schism with Rome, 113 sq., 595; (1450), in St Sophia, refuses union with Rome, 624
Roman Church: in the Lateran (732), 389; (769), condemns iconoclasts, 18; at Mantua (827), 407; in the Lateran (863), condemns Photius, 47, 249; in St Peter's (868), condemns Council of Constantinople (867), 251; at Ravenna (877), 399; at Clermont (1095), proclamation of First Crusade, 410, 599; at Bari (1098), 599 sq.; in St Peter's (1099), 599; at Benevento (1102), 341; in the Lateran (1215, Fourth Lateran Council), 607; at Lyons (1245), 495, 608; at Lyons (1274), union with Byzantine Church, 527, 611 sqq., 615, 623; at Pisa (1409), 619; at Constance (1414–18), 619; at Basle (1431), 620 sq.; at Ferrara (1438), 621 sq.; at Florence (1439), union with Byzantine Church, 182, 595 sq., 622 sq., 690
Count of the Hetairia, assistant of the strategus, 734
Count of the Tent (κόρτη), assistant of the strategus, 734
Counts, Byzantine officials, 734, 739; Serbian title, 542
Court, Byzantine, splendour of, 13; 24; 40, 727, 754 sqq.
Courtenay, *see* Peter, Philip, Robert
Cracow, captured by Mongols, 652
Craina, the, on Dalmatian coast, metropolitan see of the Zeta, transferred from, 587
Craiova, "little Wallachia," held by Hungary, 540
Crasus in Phrygia, 121; Emperor Nicephorus I defeated at, 126
Craterus, father of the Empress Theophano, 67
Craterus, strategus of the Cibyrrhaeots, defeated by Arabs, 128
Cremona, subsidized by Manuel I, 370; bishop of, *see* Liudprand
Crescentius II, patrician of Rome, and the Papacy, 91; 259; 263
Crete, province of, 4; seized by Spanish Arabs, 36, 119, 128 sq.; raids by pirates of, 45, 131 sq., 134, 141 sq.; captured by Nicephorus II, 69, 144, 239; 70; diocese of, placed under Patriarch of Constantinople, 10; revolt in, against Alexius I, 331; becomes Venetian, 421, 431; Venetian government of, 434 sqq., 457; 465 sqq.; native aristocracy in, 473; rebellion against Venetians in, 488, 494, 616; Genoese in, 511; Latin Church in, 606, 616, 621; 737; Muslim conquest of, 472; 476
Crimea, the, 39; attacked by the Russians, 90, 209; Goths in, 184; Turks and Chazars in, 188 sq.; 190; Patzinaks and, 199; 207 sq., 220; Justinian II in, 189, 231; tributary to empire of Trebizond, 487, 514
Crispo, dynasty in Archipelago, 467, 473 sq.; *see* Francesco, Giovanni; dukes of, *see* Table, 475 sq.
Critobulus, Imbrian historian, 474; description of Serbia, 576; on siege of Constantinople, 695 *note*, 696 *note*, 698, 700 *note*, 702; 703 sq.; 765
Crnagora (Montenegro), derivation of, 586
Crnojević, family in Montenegro, 586
Croatia, Slavonic liturgy in, 229; 234; and Bulgarians, 235, 238; independent of Byzantium, 325; 545; "King of Croatia," 559, 575, 579; 580 sq.; influence of Byzantium on, 776; Croats, 399; 406; 545; 559; 565; Bogomiles among, 583; prince of, *see* Braslav
Crusades, the, First Crusade, 333 sqq., 410, 599; Second Crusade, 366 sqq., 600 sq.; Third Crusade, 384, 414, 519, 603; Fourth Crusade, 414, Chap. XIV; and Armenia, 153 sq., 167 sq., 172, 180; and Seljūqs, 278, 299, 302, 314 sqq.; Alexius I and, 315 sq., 333 sqq., 352, 599; Manuel and, 366 sqq., 600 sq.; Pisan Crusades, 344, 407; Venice and, 409 sq., 414, Chap. XIV; Popes and, Chap. XIX *passim*, *see* Eugenius, Innocent, Urban; John I's plans for, 148; Peter of Cyprus and, 470; Crusade of the Archipelago, 616; Eighth Crusade, 610; and Mongols, 628; 638 sq.; 643; 656; 697; 747; 777
"Crutched Friars," of Bologna, in Negropont, 438
Csanád, bishopric of, 214; bishop of, *see* Gerard, St
Ctesiphon, ancient capital of Persia, 274
Cubicularii, office of, 730

Cumans (Kipchaks, Polovtzi), Turkish tribe in the Ural, 197; raid Bulgaria, 245; and Alexius I, 330, 334, 344; 368; 490; in service of John III, 491; in Byzantine army, 507, 511; and Bulgarians, 502, 519, 525; in Roumania, 540; Cuman wife of Kalojan, 520 sq.; origin of George Terteri, 529; 631
Curcuas, family, 69, 78
Curcuas, general of Nicephorus II, 71
Curcuas, John, Domestic of the Hicanati, rebels against Emperor Basil I, 55
Curcuas, John, acquires the "Image of Edessa," 63, 143; campaigns against Arabs, 143; 739
Curiales, Roman law as to, 94
Curopalates, of Armenia, 155, 157; of Iberia, 62, 86; title given to Bardas Sclerus, 88; 135 *note*; *see* Adernesih, Artavasdus, Phocas (Leo); title reserved for royalty, 730
Curticius, admiral of the pretender Bardas Sclerus, 85
Curticius, plots against Alexius I, 342
Cusa, in Aquitaine, monastery of, 403
Cybistra, *see* Heraclea
Cyclades, revolts against Leo III, 9; becomes Venetian, 432, 434; 435; 437: annexed by Turks, 468; Latin influence in, 473; "Lord of the Cyclades," 436, 488
Cydones, Demetrius, Byzantine theologian, *see* Kydónis
Cyprian, Nestorian bishop under the Abbasids, 289
Cyprus, reconquered by Emperor Constantine V, 12; 74; revolts against Constantine IX, 110; in Saracen wars, 121, 123, 125, 127; 140; 142; conquered by Nicephorus II, 145; attacked by Reginald of Antioch, 170, 374; 174; 177; 178; revolts against Alexius I, 331; 340; 341; rising in, 383, 384; governed by Lusignan dynasty, 180 sq., 437, 468 sq.; 441; 454; 465; Venetian, 466 sq.; 471; history of, 468 sqq.; captured by Turks, 472; Latin life in, 473; 511; seized by Richard I, 384, 603; 617; 669; and Armenia, 180 sq.; 470; kings of, *see* Table, 476 sq.; Patriarch of, independence of, 593; *see* George of; duke of, *see* Philocales
Cyriacus of Ancona, medieval archaeologist, at Athens, 462, 465
Cyril, St (Constantine), Apostle of the Slavs, Chap. VII (B); his work in Moravia, 44; and the Chazars, 190 sq., 219 sq.; literary work, 220, 225; at Rome, 224, 250; 776
Cyril, St, Patriarch of Alexandria, 250
Cyril, the Younger, commentary on the *Digest*, 707, 714
Cyrus (Kūr), river, 187, 206; battles at, 161
Cyzicus, Seljūqs in, 327; Byzantines in, 331; Latins in, 425, 482 sq.; 657 sq.; 660; Metropolitan of, 513, 608; bishop of, *see* Metrophanes, Theodore
Cyzistra, *see* Sideropalus

Dābiq, 123
Dabiša, *see* Stephen
Dagno, Venetian colony on the Drin, 583 592; taken by Turks, 585
Dailam, country of Buwaih, founder of Buwaihids, 301
Daimbert, archbishop of Pisa, brings Pisan fleet to Palestine, 340
Daimonoyánnes, archon of Monemvasía, 440
Daitu, *see* Cambalu
Dalassena, *see* Anna
Dalasseni family, 771
Dalassenus, Constantine, 98; imprisoned by Michael IV, 103; released, 105
Dalassenus, Constantine, defeats Tzachas, 331
Dalassenus, Damianus, defeated by Saracens, 149
Dalmatia, and Charlemagne, 394 sq.; Slavonic liturgy in, 229; and Samuel of Bulgaria, 240; and Robert Guiscard, 325; 338; recovered by Manuel, 371 sqq.; pirates of, 397, 400 sq.; doge of Venice "Dux Dalmatiae," 406; 409 sq.; Venetian counts in, 412; Vukan, King of, 521 sqq., 556; 557; held by Bosnia, 559: 560; Venice in, 564, 566, 583; 565; 575; "King of Dalmatia," 559, 575; 579; Turks and, 578, 670; 674; 678; 689; theme of, 733
Damascus, Saracen capital removed from, 119, 274; 128; 133; surrender to Emperor John I, 148; 156 sq.; 172; 176; occupied by Seljūqs, 277, 314, 316; taken by Mongols, 279, 643; by Tīmūr, 651, 680; 374, 641, *see* Nūr-ad-Dīn, Susamish
Damietta, attacked by Byzantines, 121, 127; captured by Michael III, 45, 132; besieged by Manuel, 376
Dan I, Prince of Wallachia, 593
Dan II, Prince of Wallachia, 593
Dan III, Prince of Wallachia, 593
Dandolo, Enrico, doge of Venice, and Fourth Crusade, 414 sq., 417 sqq.; defeat by Bulgarians, 424; death of, 424; nephews of, 435; armour of, presented to Bellini, 705
Dandolo, Stephen, sent to Avignon by Andronicus III, 615
Daniel, Serbian archbishop and historian, 534; 537; and Stephen Dušan, 539, 550
Danielis, patroness of Basil the Macedonian, 50
Dānishmand, Seljūq dynasty, 315; 340; 357, 365; 374; *see* 'Ain-ad-Daulah, Dhū'l-Nūn, Dhū'l-Qarnain, Ghāzī, Malik, Mahomet, Ya'qūb-Arslān
Dante, and dukes of Athens, 442; 469; and Stephen Uroš II, 535
Danube, river, 184; 186; 197 sqq.; 210 sq.; 213; 215; Chap. VIII *passim*; 324 sq.; 330; 355; 368; 373; 383; 490; Chaps. XVII, XVIII *passim*; 601; 631; 656; 670; 675 sq.; 687; 689 sqq.; Danubian frontier, 322; "Bulgaria beyond the Danube," *see* Wallachia

Daphní in Attica, Cistercian monastery at, 438, 449; mosaics at, 769
Daphnusia, attacked by Venetians, 431, 511; 512
Dara, taken by Curcuas, 143; 145
Darband, on the Caspian, 187
Dardanelles, 481, 487, 502; 544, 572; 658 sq.; 668; 670; controlled by Bāyazīd, 678; 761
Dardel, John, Armenian chronicler, 181
Dariel, fortress of, built by Kawad of Persia, 187
Dauphiné, *see* Humbert
D'Avesnes, *see* Florent, Jacques
David, Bulgarian chief, son of Shishman, 239 sq.
David, King of Sebastea, 166
David Mamikonian, Armenian leader, 157
David, Patriarch of Bulgaria, 242
Dazimon, Lachanodraco defeated at, 20; Emperor Theophilus defeated at, 38, 130; 46; 133
Deabolis, interview of Alexius I and Bohemond at, 342
De Actionibus, legal treatise, 708; *Liber*, of Garidas, 721
De Administratione Imperii, by Constantine VII, 67, 198
De Caerimoniis, *see* Ceremonies, Book of
Dečani, monastery of, 536
Dečanski, Stephen, *see* Stephen Uroš III
De Creditis, legal treatise, 722
De Homicidiis, legal treatise by Garidas, 721
Delhi, 633, 636; Mogul dynasty at, 650; Tīmūr enters, 651
Deligun Buldagha (Onan Kerule), birthplace of Jenghiz Khan, 632
Delyan, Peter, leads Serbo-Bulgarian rising against Michael IV, 244
Demarchs, presidents of Byzantine circus factions, 759
Demes, circus factions at Constantinople, 729, 731
Demetrias, destroyed by Arab fleet, 141; Byzantine victory over Latins, 445
Demetrius Angelus, despot of Salonica, expelled by John III, 430, 440, 476, 492 sq.
Demetrius Palaeologus, brother of John VIII, sent to Basle, 620; at Council of Ferrara, 621; opposes Union, 623; becomes despot of the Morea, 462 sq.; surrenders to Turks, 464
Demetrius of Montferrat, King of Thessalonica, 426; dethroned by Theodore Angelus, 427
Demetrius Chomatianós, archbishop of Ochrida, crowns Theodore Angelus, 497
Demetrius, St, patron of Salonica, 6, 104, 244; and Kalojan of Bulgaria, 425, 521; 518 sq.; feast of, 556; fair of, 770
Democrats, chiefs of Byzantine circus factions, 759
Demona, in Sicily, 141
Demosthenes, study of, 236, 763
Demotika (Didymotichus), 88; lordship of, founded, 422; given to Branas, 425; 502; taken by Turks, 555; 666; taken by Murād I, 669, 671
De peculiis, legal monograph, 718
De privilegiis creditorum, legal monograph, 718
Derbessak, fortress of Armeno-Cilicia, 175
Derevlyans, Slavonic tribe, 206, 208
Derkos on Black Sea, surrendered to Turks, 690
Desiderius, King of the Lombards, and Constantine V, 18; and Leo IV, 19; and Franks, 391
Desiderius (Pope Victor III), abbot-designate of Monte Cassino, chosen legate to Constantinople, 597
Desna, Russian river, 193
"Despot," title of, assumed by doge of Venice, 421; of Morea, *see* Constantine XI, Demetrius Palaeologus, Theodore Palaeologus, Thomas; *see* Epirus, Serbia, Thessalonica (*see* Tables 475 sq.)
Despotes, title of the Emperor, 726
Dessa, *see* Stephen Nemanja
De Thematibus, by Constantine VII, 67
Deuil, *see* Odo of
Deusdedit, doge of Venice, 391
Develtus, on frontier of Thrace, 37; 212; 233 sq.
Dhakīra-i Khwārazmshāhī, Persian medical encyclopaedia, 298
Dhimmī (non-Muslim under Arab rule), 287
Dhū'l Kilā', 126 *note*
Dhū'l-Nūn, son of Mahomet, Dānishmandite ruler, 365; and Emperor Manuel, 377 sq.
Dhū'l-Qarnain, Dānishmandite ruler, 374, 377
Diavoli, death of Stephen Dušan at, 546
Didymotichus, *see* Demotika
Dieterici, editor of Arabic treatises, 292
Dieu d'Amour, Latin castle in Greece, 473
Digest of Justinian, the, commentators on, 707 sq.; 713 sq.; 716; 721
Digor, in Armenia, church at, 163
Dijon, 262
Dikeraton, tax of Leo III, 4
Dīnawarī, Arab historian, 293
Dioclea, Serbian state, 517, 521, 534, 542; rulers of, *see* Constantine Bodin, George, Gradicna, Grubessa, John Vladimir, Michael
Diocletian, Roman Emperor, 662; 729
Diogenes, *see* Romanus IV, Emperor
Diogenes, Constantine, conspires against Romanus III, 100
Diogenes, Constantine, son of Romanus IV, 326
Diogenes, Nicephorus, son of Romanus IV, plots against Alexius I, 333
Dios, abbot of, 32
Dioscorides, Greek medical writer, translated into Arabic, 297; Byzantine illustrated MS of, at Vienna, 768
Diplokionion, Turkish fleet lands at, 696

Dir, Prince of Kiev, 203
Dirhem, coin used by Bulgars, 193
Dishypatus, title of, 730
Dīwān, instituted by Caliph Omar, 282; *Dīwān-al-Barīd* (State post), 283
Dīyārbakr, *see* Amida
Dizabul (Silzibul), Khagan of the Turks, *see* Sinjibu
Dizkūh, Persian castle, 310
Djakovo, in Slavonia, treaty of, 559, 565
Djed, the, chief of the Bogomiles, 535; 545
Dnieper, river, 186; 195; 197; identified by Westberg with Kotsho and Kuzu, 198; 201 sqq.; 206; 230; 636; 637
Dniester, river, 198
Dobor, Bosnian fortress, 560; Hungarian victory at, 566
Dobrotich, independent Bulgarian prince, 554; 572
Dobrudzha, the, 554; 560; 659
Doda, house of, Mirdites governed by, 585
Dodecahemeron, festival of, 755
Dodecanese, the, *see* Aegean, theme of
Doge of Venice, creation of first, 387; early doges, 387 sqq.; development of power of, 395; becomes constitutional monarchy, 407. *See* Chap. XIII, Contarini, Dandolo, Deusdedit, Fabiani, Falier, Fortunatus, John, Marcellus, Mastropiero, Mauritius, Michiel, Monegarius, Morosini, Obelerius, Orseolo, Peter Candianus, Particiacus, Paulutio, Silvio, Tradonicus, Tribunus
Dolgoruki, George, candidate for princedom of Kiev, 368
Doliche (Dulūk), taken by Constantine, 121; taken by Nicephorus II, 144
Domenico Gattilusio, of Lesbos, 465
Domestic, title of governor of the Optimatian theme, 734
Domestic of the Hicanati, office of, 739; *see* Curcuas
Domestic, of the Scholae, office of, 731, 739; held by Nicephorus II, 70; held by Tzimisces, 78; by Bardas Phocas, 87; Bohemond of Taranto and, 335, 338; *of the Oriental Scholae*, Constantine the Paphlagonian appointed, 102; 739
Domestic of the theme, chief of staff to the strategus, 734
Dominic, Patriarch of Grado, sent to Michael VII, 598
Dominicans, in Bosnia, 545; Dominican helps to defend Scutari, 586; at Nicaea, 608; and Andronicus II, 614; at Pera, 615; sent to John VI, 616; *see* John of Ragusa
Dominicus, bishop of Torcello, dispute about, 399
Dominicus, bishop sent to Moravia to establish Latin liturgy, 229
Dominicus, relative of the doge Tradonicus, 399
Don, river, 38, 185, 192 sq., 195 sqq., 202, 680
Donatus, cardinal-bishop of Ostia, legate of Hadrian II at Constantinople, 251 sq.
Donatus, Patriarch of Grado, attacked by Serenus, Patriarch of Aquileia, 389
Doras, Gothic town in the Crimea, 189
Dorino Gattilusio of Lesbos, his love of archaeology, 465
Dorotheus, professor of law at Beyrout, 707
Dorylaeum (Eski-Shehr), occupied by Saracens, 123; 130; 353; fortified by Manuel, 378; 602; 655 sq.; Ertughril established at, 656; 657; Osmān transfers his capital from, 659; 660
Douglas, on Mongol massacre at Herat, 634
Doxapatrês, holds out against Latins in Greece, 434
Doxopater, Gregory, Byzantine jurisconsult, 714; 722; nomophylax at Constantinople, 720; *Nomocanon of*, 723
Dracon, river of Asia Minor, 337
Dragases, *see* Constantine XI, Emperor
Dragoche, founds principality of Moldavia, 540
Dragovitchi, Bogomile heresy among, 238
Dragutin, *see* Stephen
Drama, district in Serbia, 553
Drave, river, 211
Dravidian language, 195
Dregoviches, Slav tribe, 206
Drin, Albanian river, 240; 583
Dristra, *see* Silistria
Drivasto, castle of, on the Adriatic, becomes Venetian, 564, 570; 583; taken by Turks, 585, 592
Dromon, Byzantine ship of the line, 743
Drungarius, of the Fleet (*Grand Drungarius*), office of, 731, 743; held by Romanus Lecapenus, 61; 331; *of the Watch*, 721; *Drungarii*, subordinates of the strategus, 734, 739
"Drunkard," the, epithet applied to Emperor Michael III, 43
Druses, sect, 301
Druzhina, detachment, of the Varangians in Asia Minor, 88; in Sicily, 150; 204
Drvenglave, tomb of Stephen Lazarević at, 565
Ducas family, 771; and Alexius I, 327 sq., 332
Ducas, Andronicus, conspiracy of, against Leo VI, 257
Ducas, Constantine, pretender to the throne, 60
Ducas, Constantine, *see* Constantine X
Ducas, Constantine, son of Michael VII, 327; temporary heir presumptive, 328 sq.; 346; deposed by Alexius, 332
Ducas, John, Caesar, plots against Michael VI, 320, 326; 327
Ducas, John, Grand Drungarius of Alexius I, 331, 339
Ducas, the historian, 765; and Gattilusi family, 465, 474, 553 *note*; 558 *note*; 568 *note*; 570 *note*; 623; on numbers of Turks, 670, 689; 671 *note*; 676; 677 *note*; 678; 685 *note*; 686; 688 *note*; 691 *note*; 692

note; 695 *note*; 696 *note*; estimate of defenders of Constantinople, 697 *note*; 700 *note*; on fall of Constantinople, 704
Duke, title of governor of Antioch, 734
Dulcigno, Latin bishopric of, 537; becomes Venetian, 564, 583; taken by Turks, 585, 592
Dulo, Bulgarian dynasty of, 231
Dulūk, *see* Doliche
Δυνατοί, οἱ (the Powerful), 51; legislation against them, 62, 93, 708, 715; 771
Duqāq, Seljūq ruler of Damascus, 314 sq.
Durazzo (Dyrrhachium), 110; and Bulgarians, 240 sqq.; 244; besieged by Guiscard, 329, 408 sq.; 332; 337; 423; 426 sqq.; 452; 456; 497; obtained by Theodore II, 503 sq.; 522; vicissitudes of, 535 *note*; 536; 541; 553; 564; 583; taken by Turks, 585; 592; 600; 675; theme of, 39, 733
Durostolus (Dristra), *see* Silistria
Dušan, *see* Stephen
Dvina, Western, Russian river, 193; 202
Dwin, in Saracen Armenia, 156; taken by Smbat I, 160 sq.; governor of, *see* Abū'l-Aswār
Dyrrhachium, *see* Durazzo
Dzmndav, castle of Armeno-Cilicia, 167

Eagle, double-headed, first used by Nicene Empire, 514; assumed by Stephen Dušan, 542
Echmiadzin, in Armenia, Katholikos at, 182
Ecloga, code of Leo III, 5, 11, 708 sqq.; Basil I and, 712; treatises founded on it, 717, 721, 723, 725
Ecloga ad Prochiron Mutata, 717, 725
Ecloga cum appendice, 718
Ecloga Legis Mosaicae, 717
Ecloga legum in epitome expositarum, see *Epitome legum*
Ecloga Novellarum, abridgment of Leo VI's Novels, 715; 717; 723
Ecloga privata, 717
Ecloga privata aucta, 717, 725
Ecri-sur-Aisne, Fourth Crusade planned at, 415
Edessa, 147; captured by Maniaces, 150, 175; 316; taken by Zangī, 317; Crusaders at, 335, 343; "Image" of, taken by Curcuas, 63, 143; "Discourse on the Image" by Constantine VII, 67; second relic taken, 150; and Manuel I, 373, 375; count of, *see* Joscelin; *see also* Matthew of
Edifices, Book of, by Procopius, 746
Edward I, King of England, Mongol letter to, 176
Edward III, King of England, Gregory XI's letter to, 618
Eger (Erlau), bishopric of, founded, 214
Egidius, Duke of Mačva and Bosnia, 591
Egilius Gaulus, of Jesolo, attacks the doge Deusdedit, 391
Egypt, 38; 45; 125 sqq.; independent of Abbasid Caliphate, 139, 276, 300; annexed by Fāṭimids, 277: Ayyūbid dynasty in, 278, 302; 304; rule of the Mamlūks, 279; relations with Alexius I, 339, 341; and Manuel I, 376 sq.; and Crusaders, 415 sq., 418; and Cyprus, 470 sqq.; and Maria of Bulgaria, 528; 604; effect of Mongols on, 629; and Caliphate, 642; and Īl-Khāns of Persia, 651 sq.; Turkish tribes in, 653; monks in, 753; 770; Egyptian army at Antioch, 147; attacks Aleppo, 149; captures Antioch, 275; defeats Mongols, 279; defeated by Tīmūr, 680; Egyptian officials of Caliphate, 280; Egyptian Christians in Arab fleet, 2; Egyptian fleet, 119 sqq., 132, 145, 286; defeated by Venetians, 411; *see also* Ayyūbids, Fāṭimids, Ikhshīdids, Mamlūks, Ṭūlūnids
Eidikos, office of, 731
Einhard, biographer of Charlemagne, 36; on Pepin's invasion of Venice, 394
Eladas, John, rival of the Patriarch Nicholas Mysticus, 60
Elbassan, monument of Carlo Thopia near, 553
Elcimon, monastery of, 107
Eleusis, 438
Elias Pasha, rebels against Murād II, 690
Elias, Prince of Moldavia, 593
Elis, Templars in, 437; 473
Elizabeth, Queen of Hungary, Duchess of Mačva and Bosnia, 591
Elpidius, rebel in Sicily, 124; acknowledged Emperor by the Saracens, 125; 134
Emeric, King of Hungary, occupies part of Serbia, 519
Emeric, son of St Stephen of Hungary, 214
Emesa (Hims), 146; 148; captured by Basil II, 149; 359; 643; defeat of Mongols and Armenians by Mamlūks at, 176
Emperors of the East, *see* Alexander, Alexius I, II, III, IV, V, Andronicus I, II, III, IV, Basil I, II, Constantine V, VI, VII, VIII, IX, X, XI, Isaac I, II, John I, II, III, IV, V, VI, VII, VIII, Leo III, IV, V, VI, Manuel I, II, Michael I, II, III, IV, V, VI, VII, VIII, IX, Nicephorus I, II, III, Romanus I, II, III, IV, Stauracius, Theodore I, II, Theophilus. Empresses: Irene, Theodora, Zoë
Emperors of the West, *also* Kings of the Romans, *see* Arnulf, Berengar, Charlemagne, Charles the Fat, Conrad II, III, Frederick I, II, III, Guy, Henry II, III, IV, V, VI, Lothar I, III, Louis the Pious, Louis II, Otto I, II, III, Sigismund
"Enantiophanes," anonymous author of the *Book of Antinomies*, 707
Encheiridion, 717
Enghien family, claims of on Athens, 454; *see* Marie
England, Manuel II in, 618, 678; envoy of "Assassins" sent to, 638; 669; kings of, *see* Edward, Henry, John, Richard
English captains at the court of Leo of Ar-

menia, 172; in Byzantine bodyguard, 209; English work on Cyril and Methodius, 216; garrison of Civitot, 331; in Byzantine army, 347; at court of Manuel I, 362; at battle of Nicopolis, 675
Enna (Castro Giovanni), in Sicily, besieged by Saracens, 35, 136; finally captured, 461; 137 sq.
Enneads of Plotinus, translated into Arabic, 295
Epanagoge, law book of Basil I, 52, 59, 712, 717 sq., 721 sqq.
Epanagoge aucta, 717
Eparch (prefect of Constantinople), office of, 731
Eparchics (edicts of praetorian prefects), 714, 723
Eparchies (civil provinces), become *themes*, 732
Ephesus, 16; 126; 131; recaptured by Alexius I, 339; 367 sq.; 495; 624; held by Osmān, 657 sq.; Tīmūr at, 684; 770; archbishops of, *see* Mark, Nicholas, Theodosius
Epibatus in Thrace, taken by Turks, 667, 695
ἐπιβολή (adiectio), suspended by Tiberius II, 708
Epirus, becomes Venetian, 421; Greek kingdom in, 423, 427, 478 sq.; Michael Angelus, lordship in, 429 sq., 436 sqq., 493; 432; 440; Neapolitan claims on, 446; 447 sq.; Orsini in, 453; Serbs in, 455, 543, 545; Turks in, 461; 472; 489; 505; 507; 524; Florentines in, 553; 586; 604 sq.; sees in, 95, 243, (Latin) 607; Franciscans in, 609; schism with Nicaea, 486, 497 sq., 612; rulers, *see* Table, 475 sq.
Epitome (*Synagoge*) *canonum*, 718, 723
Epitome canonum of Harmenopulus, 724
Epitome canonum antiqua, 723
Epitome legum (*Ecloga legum in epitome expositarum*), 716 sq.
Epitome novellarum of Athanasius, 718
Epitropi (ἐπιτρόποι), executors, in S. Italy, 725
Equilio Jesolo, *see* Cavazuccherina
Erbil, conquered by Mongols, 636; 642
Erghin, emir of Ostan, 182
Eric the Good, King of Denmark, crusading expedition of, 341
Erivan, 163
Erizzo, Venetian defender of Negropont against Turks, 466, 472
Erkesiya, *see* "Great Fence"
Erlau, *see* Eger
Ernjak, Mongol massacre at, 181
Eroticus, *see* Comnenus (Manuel)
Eroticus, Theophilus, revolts against Constantine IX, 110
Ertughril, father of Osmān, founder of the Ottoman Turks, 655 sq., 660
Erzerūm, *see* Theodosiopolis
Erzinjān, taken by Tīmūr, 679 sq.
Esau Buondelmonti, becomes ruler of Epirus, 457; 461; 475
Esegels, Bulgar tribe, 192, 195
Eski-Imaret-jāmi', *see* Pantepoptes *under* Constantinople, churches of
Eski-Sagra (Stara-Zagora), Alexius I meets Robert of Flanders at, 334; John I defeats Patzinaks at, 354; captured by Theodore II, 502; 519
Eski-Shehr, *see* Dorylaeum
Esztergom, *see* Gran
Étampes, assembly of, 366
Ethiopians, the, adhere to the Council of Florence, 623
Etna, Mt, 138
Euboea (Negropont), island of, ravaged by Normans, 368; 371; 413; becomes Venetian, 421, 431 sq., 457; Latin nobles in, 422; Venetian government of, 435; under Achaian suzerainty, 439; 441; captured by Licario, 445; 447; 451; 457 sqq.; 486; Latin life in, 473; Genoese at, 511; 675; 476; *see* Negropont; *see also* Boniface, Theophylact
Euchaita, victory of the Saracens at, 127; see of, 56, 254
Eudocia Baiane, the Phrygian, third wife of Leo VI, 57, 256
Eudocia Ingerina, mother of Leo VI, and empress of Basil I, 43; 47; 50 sq.; 53; 55; 256
Eudocia Lascaris, daughter of Theodore I, 486
Eudocia Macrembolitissa, wife of Constantine X and of Romanus IV, 325 sq.; 757
Eudocia, cousin and mistress of Andronicus I, 381
Eudocia, daughter of Alexius I, 346
Eudocia, daughter of Constantine VIII, 84, 96
Eudocia, daughter of Leo VI, 55
Eugenicus, Marcus, *see* Mark of Ephesus
Eugenius III, Pope, and Emperor Manuel I, 366, 369, 601
Eugenius IV, Pope, and Hunyadi, 571; and John VIII, 620 sqq.; holds Council of Florence, 623 sq.
Eugenius, St, patron of Trebizond, 487, 515
Eulogia, sister of Michael VIII, opposed to union with Rome, 612
Euphemia, mother of Boris of Hungary, 356
Euphemius, rebel in Sicily, 37, 134; killed, 135
Euphorbenus, *see* Andronicus
Euphrates, river, Theophilus' campaign on, 38; 120; 132; 143 sqq.; 178; 289; 291; 358; 736 sq.
Euprepia, sister of Constantine IX, 111
Euripus, strait, 435
Europe, Armenia and, 159, 167; Mongols in, 628, 637 sqq., 642 sq.; Ottomans established in, 705; European provinces of Eastern Empire anti-iconoclast, 35; nobility of, 326, 771
Eustathius, Patriarch of Constantinople, and the Papacy, 92, 262; 264

Eustathius, archbishop of Thessalonica, orations of, 363; 754; classical commentaries of, 764; sermons of, 766
Eustathius, patrician, and the Magyars, 199
Eustathius, admiral of Alexius I, 340
Eustathius, author of work on the *Hypobolon*, 718
Eustathius Romanus, Byzantine jurisconsult, 718
Eustratius Garidas, Patriarch of Constantinople, 328
Eustratius, bishop of Nicaea, and archbishop Peter of Milan, 345, 600
Euthymius, Patriarch of Constantinople, 57, 60, 65, 257
Euthymius, Patriarch of Jerusalem, 329
Euthymius the Younger, St, of Thessalonica, life of, 255
Eutychian heresy, in Armenia, 155
Eutychius, exarch of Ravenna under Leo III, 9; and Venetians, 390
Euxine, *see* Black Sea
'Εξάβιβλος, see *Basilics*, *Promptuarium*
Exarchate of Africa, created, 732
Exarchate of Italy (Ravenna), created, 732; 387; attacked by Lombards, 17, 390; Manuel I and, 412
Exarchs, *see* Eutychius, John, Paul
Excubitors, regiment of the Byzantine Guard, 739; count of, *see* Michael II, Emperor
Exegesis Canonum, of Theodore Balsamon, 724
'Εξηκοντάβιβλος, see *Basilics*
Eyyūb, *see* Kosmidion
Ezerites, Slav tribe, 42

Fabiani, Domenico, doge of Venice, 407
Fabriacus, last magister militum of Venice, 390
Faḍl, Arab admiral, 133
Faḍl, Arab general, 125
Faḍl ibn Ja'far, takes Messina, 136; 137
Faḍl ibn Ya'qūb, commander in Sicily, 136
Fadriques, the, of Sálona, fate of the last heiress of, 458; *see* Alfonso
Fakhr-al-Mulk, vizier of Barkiyāruq, 310
Fakhr-ud-Dīn Rāzī, commentator on the Koran, 296
Falak-ad-Dīn 'Alī Chatrī, rebellious chamberlain of Sanjar, 313
Falier, Ordelafo, doge of Venice, founds the Arsenal, 410
Falier, Vitale, doge of Venice, and the Normans, 409
"Falling Asleep of the Virgin," church of, at Nicaea, 479
Famagosta in Cyprus, obtained by Genoa, 455, 465; 470; regained by Cyprus, 466, 471; captured by Turks, 472; 477; coronation city of Cypriote kings of Jerusalem, 469
Fano, and Venice, 412
Fārābī, Arab author, 290, 296
Faraj, Arab leader, rebuilds Adana, 127
Fārs, province, included in empire of Khwārazm Shāh, 633; 642
Fāṭimah, daughter of Mahomet, 302
Fāṭimid (Fāṭimite) Caliphs, *see* Ḥākim, Mu'izz, 'Ubaid-Allāh (Mahdī), Ẓāhir; 132; in Syria, 148 sq., 302; 277; and Shī'ites, 301; 304; in Palestine, 316
Fëdor Ivanovich, Tsar of Russia, 200
Felix, bishop of Malamocco, 399
Felix, the tribune, Francophil conspirator at Venice, 393
Fenestrelle pass into Italy, 391
Ferdinand I, King of Naples, 466
Ferdinand of Majorca, and principality of Achaia, 452
Fermo, on the Adriatic, 398
Ferrara, 410; and Venice, 412; Council of, 621; transferred to Florence, 622
Fetḥīye-jāmi', *see* Pammakaristos, *under* Constantinople, churches of
Feu, Chinese river, 645
Feudalism: in Byzantine Empire, military fiefs in Asia Minor, 75, 771 sqq.; Basil II's legislation against, 92 sqq.; strength of, 117, 771 sq.; Alexius I and small fiefholders, 347; Andronicus I and, 382; effects on army and navy, 738, 742; in Armeno-Cilicia, 167; compared with Russian system, 206; under the Caliphate, 278, 285; in Latin Empire, 422, 480; in Latin Greece, 433, 437, Chap. xv *passim*; in Crete, 434; in Cyprus, 469, 472; in Serbia, 547; in Bosnia, 585; of Turkish military system, 664
Filelfo, Francesco, interpreter to Byzantine embassy, 619; 693 *note*; 695 *note*; on Bashi-bazuks, 696
Filioque clause, in Creed, *see* Holy Ghost, Doctrine of Procession of
Finances, under Leo III, 4; under Constantine V, 13; under Irene, 27; under Nicephorus I, 27; under Theophilus, 39; Basil I's reforms of, 51; reforms of Romanus I, 62; fiscal measures and taxation of Nicephorus II, 76; abolition of the poll tax by John I, 82; under Basil II, 93; under Constantine VIII, 97; under Romanus III, 99; under Michael IV, 103; financial measures of Isaac I, 322; of Alexius I, 332, 348 sq.; of Manuel I, 364, 370; of John III, 498; of Theodore II, 505; financial administration of Byzantine Empire, 731, 735, 771; 763; strained by Saracen wars, 151; finances of Caliphate, 151 *note*; fiscal system of Caliphate, 280; taxation of non-Muslims, 287; Mahomet II and Turkish revenue, 705; finances of Venice, 413
Finns, 184; Finnish origin of Bulgars, 184, 230; trade with Bulgars, 193 sq.; Finnish foundation of Magyar language, 195; tribes in Russian Empire, 199 sq., 204
Fiorenza, Duchess of the Archipelago, 475
Fiqh (Muslim legal literature), 291 sq.
Firdausī, Persian poet, 303

Flanders, count of, *see* Baldwin, Henry, Philip, Robert
Flavigny, *see* Hugh of
Fleet, Byzantine, 741 sqq.; in the Adriatic, 101, 139; under Constantine V, 18; at Venice, 36, 386, 394; in Sicily, 46, 105, 134, 136, 147; attacks Damietta, 121, 127, 132, 376; in Sclerus' revolt, 85; pillages Seleucia, 130; defeat under Craterus, 128; attacks Pelusium, 133; captures Cyprus, 140; defeated at Mylae, 141; expeditions against the Cretans, 142 sqq.; and the Magyars, 199; in the Black Sea, 232; aids the Pope against the Saracens, 253; 260; reorganized by Alexius I, 328, 347; navy tax of Manuel, 364; captures Laodicea, 341; Normans and, 342; and John II, 411; and John III, 428, 488, 490; victories of Michael VIII, 445; and Theodore I, 482, of Andronicus III, 662; Grand Drungarius of, 731; merchant marine, 762; themes of, *see* Aegean, Carabisiani, Cibyrrhaeots, Dodecanese, Samos
Fleet, Ottoman, 582; of Mahomet I, 687; of Mahomet II at Belgrade, 576; at siege of Constantinople, 696, 699 sqq.; at Trebizond, 690; at Cyprus, 472; at Chios, 675
Fleet, Saracen, defeated before Constantinople, 2, 119; 38; piracy in Mediterranean, 36; under Thumāma, 123; victory in bay of Attalia, 125; ravages Cyprus, 127; defeats Craterus, 128; 131; captures Attalia, 133; successes off Sicily, 136 sq.; raids in the tenth century, 141; 150; under the Abbasids, 286; fleet of Smyrna, 331; helps Venice, 404; defeated by Venetians, 741; 406; *see also* Egypt
Flemings in Greece, 447, 474; *see* Florent, Jacques; Flemish duchy of Philippopolis, 520; *see* Renier
Florence, Walter de Brienne at, 454; Byzantine Bible at, 768; Council of, *see* Councils
Florent d'Avesnes, becomes Prince of Achaia, 446 sq., 474
Florentines, in Athens, 431; 461 sq.; successes in Greece, 457, 553; 513; and battle of Kossovo, 558
Foča, Turkish province of Bosnia, 579
Fogaras, Wallachia colonized from, 540
Foglia, *see* Phocaea
Formosus, cardinal-bishop of Porto (afterwards Pope), Roman missionary in Bulgaria, 45, 236; 252; and Photian schism, 256
Fortunatus, Patriarch of Grado, and Charlemagne, 393; failure of his policy, 395
Forty Martyrs, church of, *see* Constantinople; at Trnovo, 522; becomes mosque, 560
Foscarini, mission of, to Crete, 472
France: Pope Stephen II in, 17; Bohemond of Antioch in, 336, 341; trade route to, 396; 601; Manuel I's embassy to, 602; Michael VIII's embassy to, 610; John V and, 618, 670; Manuel II and, 618, 678; 677; Assassin envoy in, 638; 669; kings of, *see* Charles, Louis, Philip
Francesco I Crispo, becomes Duke of the Archipelago, 457, 475
Francesco II, Duke of the Archipelago, 476
Francesco III, Duke of the Archipelago, 476
Francesco Gattilusio, of Lesbos, 455; 465
Francesco, son of Nerio II, Duke of Athens, 463 sq.; 475
Franche-Comté, 440
Franciscans (Minorites), in Euboea, 438; at Nicaea, 497, 608; in Bosnia, 532, 545, 575, 581, 583; sent to Michael VIII, 609 sq.; Hethum II of Armenia joins the, 177; *see* John Parastron, John of Parma, John of Pian di Carpine, Rubruquis
Franco, son of Antonio II of Athens, and Turks, 463; made "Lord of Thebes," 464; executed, 465; 475
Francophil, party at Venice, 393; failure of, 395
Frankfort, Council of, 261 *note*
Franks, in Italy, 17, 22; and Irene, 24; and Nicephorus I, 36 sq.; invade Africa, 135; and Theophilus, 136; 211; Frankish Empire, 212; and Bulgars, 231, 234 sq.; 259; and Venetia, 385, 388, 391, 393; *see also* West, relations with
Fraunduni, tribune of Ammiana, 386
Frederick I Barbarossa, Western Emperor, and Leo II of Armeno-Cilicia, 172; and Manuel I, 369 sqq., 378 sq., 601; 385; 412; at Venice, 414; and Bulgarians, 519; Crusade of, 384, 519, 603
Frederick II, Western Emperor, and John III, 429, 495 sqq.; 608; and Cyprus, 469; Theodore II's funeral oration, on, 498, 501; and Mongol menace, 638 sq.
Frederick III, Western Emperor, and Stephen Vukčić, 574
Frederick II of Aragon, King of Sicily, and Catalans, 449; and duchy of Athens, 451; 453
Frederick III, King of Sicily, and Duke of Athens, 455, 475
Frederick of Lorraine, *see* Stephen IX, Pope
Frederick of Randazzo, ruler of Athens, 475
French, captains with Leo II of Armeno-Cilicia, 172; works on SS. Cyril and Methodius, 216; at court of Emperor Manuel, 362; at Second Crusade, 366 sqq.; at conquest of Constantinople, 419; in Genoa, 468; at battle of the Cephisus, 450; in Greece, 474; at battle of Nicopolis, 561, 675 sq.; 691; in Byzantine army, 738; traveller at Constantinople, 746, 750; fleet, 614; language at Theban court, 447
Friars, *see* "Crutched Friars," Dominicans, Franciscans
Friesland, fishermen of, and Mongols, 639
Friuli, and Venice, 398; 402; duke of, *see* Lupus
Froissart, on court of Epirus, 461
Fruyin (Prusianus), Bulgarian prince, and

Basil II, 242; conspires against Romanus III, 100, 244
Fucine lake, 448
Fulk of Anjou, King of Jerusalem, 359
Fulk of Neuilly, preaches Fourth Crusade in France, 415
Fundi, military fiefs in Armenia, 75
Fünfkirchen, *see* Pécs
Fusṭāt, in Egypt, 302

Gabala, taken by John I, 148; 343
Gabalâs, John, ruler of Rhodes, 493 sq.; and Emperor John III, 477
Gabalâs, Leo, founds seigniory at Rhodes, 423, 432, 436, 445, 477; and John III, 488, 494
Gabras, general of Manuel I, 378
Gabras, Constantine, general of Alexius I, 344; duke of Trebizond, 353, 357
Gabriel of Melitene, and the Seljūqs, 315
Gabriel, private physician of Caliph Hārūn, 289
Gabriel Radomir Roman, Tsar of Bulgaria, 241; murdered, 242; 244
Gaeta, 134
Gagik I, King of Armenia, reign of, 162 sq.
Gagik II, last King of Armenia, 112; reign of, 112, 164 sq.; death of, 166 sq., 169
Gagik, King of Vanand, 166
Gagliano, in Sicily, taken by Saracens, 137
Gaikhātū, Īl-Khān of Persia, and paper currency, 630
Gaiucome (Gīvē), captured by Ertughril, 655
Galata, 431; 509; Genoese at, 666, 680, 761; 677, 695 sq., 699; position of, at siege of Constantinople, 697, 700; tower of, stormed by Crusaders, 418
Galen, translation into Arabic, 297
Galicia, *see* Halicz, Red Russia
Galilee, prince of, *see* Hugh of Lusignan
Gallipoli, Frederick Barbarossa at, 384; becomes Venetian, 421; taken by John III, 428 sq., 489; occupied by Turks, recovered by Amadeus of Savoy, 544, 555, 617, 669; Alans revolt at, 657; 659 sq.; 677; Bāyazīd at, 678; Venetian naval victory at, 687; 693; 696; taken by Murād II, 689
Gangra, captured by Saracens, 120; 344; taken by John II, 357; 377
Ganos, on Sea of Marmora, attacked by Turks, 658
Garatoni, Christopher, legate of Eugenius IV, 620; at Constantinople, 621
Gardarik, Swedish name for Russia, 204
Garidas, Byzantine lawyer, 718, 720; works, 721; *see* Eustratius
Gastin, castle of, 361
Gattilusio, Genoese family, rulers in Lesbos, 455; 464 sqq.; 474
Gauderic, and Anastasius the Librarian, 220
Gaul, Byzantine trade with, 762
Gebseh, in Asia Minor, captured by John III, 490; 676
Gemistus, *see* Plethon
Gemlik, *see* Civitot; gulf of, 668
Genesis, Byzantine illustrated MS. of, at Vienna, 768
Genesius, cited, 133 *note*
Gennadius (George Scholarius), Byzantine theologian, afterwards Patriarch, opposition to Union, 624 sq., 698; and Mahomet II, 705; 766
Genoa, Genoese, and Alexius I, 341; and Manuel I, 371; and Baldwin II, 429, 431; and Michael VIII, 431, 510 sq., 609; and John VI, 666; at Constantinople, 362, 615, 678, 697, 700, 750; at siege of Constantinople, 695, 699; trade with Constantinople, 762; with Cilicia, 173; and First Crusade, 410; 411; in Crete, 434, 476; in Chios and Lesbos, 455, 616 sq., 672; in Rhodes, 441, 494, 658; in Thebes, 440; in Cyprus, 466, 469 sqq.; lose Chios and Phocaea, 468; 465; in Tenedos, 670; on Black Sea, 549; and Catalans, 657; and Murād I, 670; and Tīmūr, 680, 684 sq.; fleet of, 742; "castle" at Nymphaeum, 514; bishop of Kaffa, 614; Genoese colonies, *see* Table, 477; Manuel II at Genoa, 618; Genoa occupied by French, 468
Geoffrey I de Villehardouin, nephew of the historian, founds principality of Achaia, 422 sq., 426; 433 sq.; 437; regent, becomes Prince, 438; 452; 459; 474
Geoffrey II de Villehardouin, Prince of Achaia, helps Latin Emperor, 429; 439; prosperity of, 439; 474
George, King of Dioclea, and John II, 356
George Branković, Prince of Serbia, 562; and Turks, 563 sq.; becomes Despot of Serbia, 564; and Murād II, 568 sqq.; 690, 697; recovers his kingdom, 571; and battle of Varna, 572; and Bosnia, 573, 575; and walls of Constantinople, 575 *note*; and Mahomet II, 575 sq.; death of, 577; 590
George I, ruler of the Zeta, 592
George II Balša, ruler of the Zeta, and Venetians, 564; 592
George Juraśević, Montenegrin ruler, 592
George I Crnojević, Prince of Montenegro, driven from his throne, 587; 592
George II Crnojević, Montenegrin ruler, 592
George Terteri I, made Tsar of Bulgaria, 529 sq.; deposed by his son, 531; 533; 590
George Terteri II, Tsar of Bulgaria, 536; 590
George, the Paphlagonian, brother of Michael IV, made Protovestiary, 102
George Monachus, Byzantine chronicler, 765
George Scholarius, *see* Gennadius
George, supposed companion of St Cyril, 218 sq.
George Syncellus, 26
George of Cyprus, at Nicaea, 506
Georgia, *see* Iberia

Georgios, Christian physician under Abbasids, 297
Geráki, Greek fortress, 443; frescoes at, 446, 473
Gerald of Aurillac, St, life of, 396
Gerard, abbot of Monte Cassino, Alexius I's letter to, 345
Gerard de Stroem, duke of Philippopolis, 523; 590
Gerard of Cremona, translation of Avicenna, 297
Gerard, St, bishop of Csanád, and the conversion of Hungary, 214
Germanicea (Mar'ash), 2; in Saracen wars, 19, 51, 121, 123, 127, 130, 132, 143 sq.; 168; Crusaders at, 338, 341; ceded to Bohemond, 343; count of, *see* Baldwin
Germans, influence in Western Europe, 183; in Pannonia, 211, 213; methods, 212, 215; at court of Leo of Armeno-Cilicia, 172; 210; 216; in Byzantine army, 347, 738; at court of Manuel, 362; at Second Crusade, 366 sq.; in Athens, 474; at battle of Velbužd, 538; at Kossovo, 692 sq.; at Nicopolis, 676; mercenaries, 657; 691; guard of Stephen Dušan, 546, 549; opposition to Byzantine missions, 44, 227
Germanus, minister of Nicephorus III, 327
Germanus I, Patriarch of Constantinople, crowns Leo III, 2; deposition and death, 10 sq.
Germanus II, Patriarch at Nicaea, 499, 607
Germanus III, ex-Patriarch of Constantinople, 612
Germany, and Hungary, 213; trade route to, 396; Boniface and Montferrat in, 416; Alexius Angelus in, 417, 604; Mongols in, 628; Manuel II in, 678; and Byzantium, *see* West, relations with; *see* Emperors of the West, Germans
Germiyān, Turkish rule in, 654, *see also* Phrygia
Gero, archbishop of Cologne, ambassador to John I, 81
Getadartz, *see* Petros
Géza II, King of Hungary, and the Empire, 368, 372, 381
Géza, Prince of the Magyars, converted to Christianity, 213
Ghamr, Arab prince, 121, 123
Ghazālī, Arab theologian and mystic, 292; works of, 289, 293; 296; 306
Ghāzān Khān, Īl-Khān of Persia, 644; alliance with Armenia, 177 sq.; war with Egypt, 652
Ghāzī (Malik Ghāzī), Dānishmandite emir, opposes First Crusade, 340; wars with Empire, 353 sq., 357
Ghaznah, 299; 305; conquered by Seljūqs, 311; 312
Ghaznawids, Turkish dynasty, 277, 300, 303 sq.; *see* Maḥmūd, Ma'sūd
Ghibellines at Pisa, 371; and Fourth Crusade, 604; and Charles of Anjou, 610 sq.
Ghisi, the brothers, lordship of, in the Sporades, 435; 445; bequest to Venice, 457, 474
Ghīyāth-ad-Dīn Ghāzī, Sultan of Aleppo, defeated by Leo the Great, 173
Ghīyāth-ad-Dīn, Khwārazmian prince, 636
Ghīyāth-ad-Dunyà-w'ad-Dīn, title bestowed on Muḥammad the Seljūq, 310
Ghūr, Sultan of, *see* Ḥusain ibn Ḥasan Jahānsūz
Ghuzz (Guzes, Torki, Uzes), nomad tribe, 197 sq., 631; 303; 312; war against Sanjar, 303, 313; 325
Giacomo I, Duke of the Archipelago, 476
Giacomo II, Duke of the Archipelago, 476
Giacomo III, Duke of the Archipelago, 476
Giacomo IV, last Duke of the Archipelago, 468, 476
Gian Giacomo, Duke of the Archipelago, 476
Gibbon, on the captivity of Bāyazīd, 683
Giberto dalle Carceri, receives fief in Euboea, 435
Gídos, *see* Andronicus I Gídos
Gilds at Constantinople, 58, 716, 719, 731, 761
Giorgi, King of Iberia, attacks John-Smbat of Armenia, 163
Giovanna, divorced wife of Peter IV Candianus, 402
Giovanni I, Duke of the Archipelago, 475
Giovanni II, Duke of the Archipelago, 476
Giovanni III, Duke of the Archipelago, 476
Giovanni IV, Duke of the Archipelago, 467, 474, 476
Giovanni Asan, natural son of Centurione Zaccaria, 463
Gipsies, settled in Anazarbus, 132
Girgenti in Sicily, 135
Gisela, German princess, wife of St Stephen of Hungary, 214
Giurgevo, Roumanian town, occupied by Turks, 567, 687
Giustiniani, John, Genoese noble, defends Constantinople, 695, 697 sqq.; wound and death of, 703; 704
Giustiniani, maona of, Genoese company at Chios, 455; 468; 474; 672
Gīvē (Gaiucome), captured by Ertughril, 655
Glaber, Radulphus, on Patriarch Eustathius and John XIX, 262 *note*, 263
Glagolitic script (Slavonic alphabet), 44; 220; 225; 526; 776
Glaréntza, hill of, 439, 452; Constantine Palaeologus at, 460; Thomas Palaeologus at, 461; ruins of, 474
Gliavar, *see* Vusir
Glokhov, destroyed by Mongols, 637
Glossae Nomicae, Byzantine law book, 722
Glycas, Byzantine chronicler, 363
Gnostic influence on Muslim mysticism, 293; on Shī'ah doctrine, 301
Godefroy, biographer of Marshal Boucicaut, 677
Godfrey of Bouillon, and the Seljūqs, 315;

316; 335; at Constantinople, 337; death of, 340; 367; 655
Golden Gate of Constantinople, 232 sq., 243, 251; 509; 512; 666; 675; 749
"Golden-headed Virgin," monastery of, at Trebizond, 487, 515
Golden Horde (Western Kipchaks), 652; destroys Bulgary, 193; Cumans included in, 631
Golden Horn, 73; 418; 431; 512; 623; 626; 677; 695; walls of Constantinople on, 697 sqq., 747; Mahomet II's fleet in, 700 sq.; 702; 747 sq.; fish market on the, 761; 762
Golden Milestone, *see* Constantinople
Gongylas, Constantine, patrician, defeated in Crete, 144
Gorazd, successor of St Methodius in Moravia, 229
Gordi in Armenia, 56
Gorgippia, Jewish community at, 190
Gorigos in Cilicia, occupied by Byzantines, 340; held by Cyprus, 470; lost, 471; *see* Mary, Oshin
Goromozol in Cilicia, 168
Gospels, translated into Slav dialect, 44, 222, 226; Armenian MSS copies of, 162; Byzantine MS of, at Florence, 768
Gothic Art, 777
Gothland, fishermen from, and Mongols, 639
Goths, in Western Russia, 184; and Justinian I, 385; in Byzantine army, 738; King of, *see* Witigis
Gozzadini, Bolognese dynasty in Aegean, 467 sq.
Grabusa, Cretan fortress, 472
Gradenigo, Marco, Venetian podestà at Constantinople, 511; abandons Constantinople, 512
Gradicna, Prince of Dioclea, 356
Grado, settlement of, 386; raid of Lupus on, 387; see of, 224; Patriarchate of, founded, 387 sq.; and Istria, 389; Patriarch murdered at, 393; 395; struggle with Doge, 399; with Aquileia, 401, 407 sq.; Patriarchate transferred from, 397, 408, 414; Patriarch of, 266; *see* Dominic, Donatus, Fortunatus, John, Orso; church of Santa Eufemia at, 386, 400
Graïtzas Palaeologus, and the Turks, 464
Gran (Esztergom), archbishopric of, founded, 214; *see* Anastasius; captured by Mongols, 638
Grangerin, *see* Henri de
Grantmesnil, *see* William of
Graptoi, name given to image worshipping martyrs, 34
Graviá, pass of, 433
Great Bridge at Stamboul, 750
Great Bulgaria, 637; *see* Bulgars (White)
Great Council of Venice (Maggior Consiglio), 409, 413
Great Fence, Greco-Bulgarian boundary, 234
Great Laura, the, on Mount Athos, 70, 79, 81, 260; Basil II's gifts to, 90
Great Moravia, evangelised by Cyril and Methodius, 44, 210; prince of, *see* Rostislav, Svatopluk; conquered by the Magyars, 212; *see* Moravia
Great Prêslav, *see* Prêslav
Greece, risings in, 9, 11, 20; raids on coast of, 143; Varangians in, 209; Bulgarians in, 240 sq., 244; and Boniface of Montferrat, 421, 424; 423; Latin States in, Chap. xv; results of Latin rule in, 473 sq.; 512; Serbians in, 543, 552; Michael VIII attacks, 612; Turks in, 458 sqq.; 671 sqq., 689 sq.; 629; Byzantine law in, 723; churches in, 768 sq.; translations into Arabic, 290, 292, 296 sqq.; language, 447, 736, 763, 774, 777; scholarships at Paris, 616; colonies on Black Sea, 183 sqq.
Greek fire, 2, 19, 205, 743 sq.
"Greek Hollow," the, supposed scene of the defeat of Nicephorus I by the Bulgarians, 233
Greens and Blues, circus factions (*demes*) in Constantinople, 758 sq.
Gregoras, Nicephorus, Byzantine historian and theologian, 765 sq.; on Serbian court, 536 sq.; 539 *note*; 544 *note*; 616 *note*
Gregoras, patrician, killed in Sicily, 134
Gregory II, Pope, 9 sq., 41
Gregory III, Pope, and Leo III, 10; 17; and Exarchate, 390
Gregory V, Pope, election of, 91
Gregory VII (Hildebrand), Pope, and Croatia, 325; and Alexius I, 329, 333; 521; 595 sqq.; his letters appealing for Crusade, 598; struggle with Henry IV, 598; 626
Gregory IX, Pope, and John III, 489, 497, 608; and Manuel Angelus, 607; 638; and Mongol menace, 639
Gregory X (Tedaldo Visconti), Pope, and Michael VIII, 611; and Council of Lyons, 612; 626
Gregory XI, Pope, and the Turks, 618, 670; 671
Gregory, Patriarch of Constantinople, deposed as pro-unionist, 624; proclaims the Union, 625; 698
Gregory Asbestas, archbishop of Syracuse, and Pope Leo IV, 247
Gregory Nazianzen, St, St Cyril and, 217; MS of, 53, 769
Gregory of Amastris, St, biography of, on Russian raids in Asia Minor, 203
Gregory, son of George Branković, blinded by Turks, 570; 577 sq.
Gregory, Byzantine admiral, 134
Gregory of Klath, Armenian churchman, 182
Gregory of Tathew, Armenian churchman, 182
Grigor VII Apirat, Katholikos of Armenia, crowns Leo the Great, 172
Grigor VIII Anavarzetsi, Katholikos of Armenia, and Roman Church, 178
Grigor IX, Katholikos of Armenia, 182

Grigor Mamikonian, Armenian leader, 157
Grigori, Bulgarian translator, 237
Grotta Ferrata, St Nilus at, 258; abbot of, sent to Alexius I, 598
Grubessa, Prince of Dioclea, and John II, 356
Gualdrada of Tuscany, wife of Peter IV Candianus, 402 sq.
Gugarkh, in Armenia, 158; revolts against Ashot, 159
Guglielmo I, Duke of the Archipelago, 475
Guglielmo II, Duke of the Archipelago, 476
Guibert de Nogent, 599 *note*
Guillaume de Sains, at Hereke, 483
Guiragos, *see* Kirakos
Guiscard, *see* Robert
Gul-jāmi' (church of St Theodosius), *see under* Constantinople, churches of
Gumaljina, captured by Turks, 672
γυμνοί, *see* Naked
Gumushtagīn, Seljūq Atābeg, 309
Gunaria in Paphlagonia, 117, 320
Gunter (Wintker), Marquess of Istria, and Venice, 401
Gurdizi, on location of Magyars, 195
Guy, Western Emperor, King of Italy, and Venice, 400
Guy de Lusignan, ex-King of Jerusalem, King of Cyprus, 468 sq., 476
Guy of Lusignan, King of Armeno-Cilicia, 180 sq.
Guy I de la Roche, Lord of Athens, succeeds his uncle, 439 sq.; and William of Achaia, 441, 443; made Duke, 442, 475
Guy II, Duke of Athens, minority of, 446; brilliancy of his court, 447; death, 449 sqq.; 475
Guzes, *see* Ghuzz
Gyla, *Gyula*, Magyar title, 196
Gynaeceum, at Constantinople, 756
Györ (Raab), bishopric of, founded, 214
Gyulafehérvár (Karlsburg), bishopric of, founded, 214

Habsburg, House of, 559
Ḥadath, in Syria, 143
Ḣades, victory of Isaac Comnenus at, 321
Hadrian, Emperor, 629; "house of" at Athens, 459
Hadrian I, Pope, 18; and Empress Irene, 21; 246
Hadrian II, Pope, and Basil I, 54, 139, 253; and Moravian princes, 221, 226; and SS. Cyril and Methodius, 224, 250; and Bulgaria, 236; convokes council of Constantinople, 251 sq.
Hadrian III, Pope, and Photian schism, 254
Hadrian IV, Pope, and Union of the Churches, 369, 596, 601
Hadrianople, in Bulgarian wars, 29, 37, 233 sq., 237 sq.; 49; 110 sq.; 318; 327; 330; Crusaders at, 366, 384; Venetian, 421; defeat of Baldwin I at, 424, 520; given to Branas, 425; 427; taken by John III, 428; 491; 502; 522; Turkish, 555, 562, 576, 579, 617, 667 sqq.; 658; 670; 674; 678; 685; 687; death of Mahomet I at, 688; 689 sq.; 692; death of Murād II at, 693; 695 sq.; palace of Mahomet II at, 705; capital of Macedonian theme, 733
Hadrianople (Charisius) Gate, at Constantinople, 696 sqq., 702, 704, 748
Haemus, the, passes of, 354
Hagiopolites, John, superintendent of posts, and Photius, 254
Hagiotheodorita, *see* Theodorita
Haguenau, 604
Ḥaifa, taken by Crusaders, 410
Ḣainault, count of, 447; *see* Matilda of
Ḥājjī Bektāsh, dervish, and naming of the Janissaries, 663
Ḥākim, Fāṭimid Caliph of Egypt, concludes peace with Basil II, 149; persecutes Christians at Jerusalem, 316
Halicarnassus, *see* Budrun
Halicz, prince of, *see* Vladimirko, Yaroslav
Halil Ganem, on character of Mahomet I, 688; on Mahomet II, 704
Halmyrus in Greece, 433
Haly Abbas, *see* 'Alī ibn al-'Abbās
Halys, river, 46; 129; 134
Hamadān, taken by Seljūqs, 304; 309 sq.
Ḥamāh, taken by Zangī, 317; 359; by Tīmūr, 680
Ḥamdānids, rulers of Aleppo, 143 sq., 146, 148 sq.; rise of, 277; *see* Sa'd-ad-Daulah, Saif-ad-Daulah
Hammer, von, on Janissaries, 663, 673
Hangchow, *see* Lingan
Haram (Uj Palanka), Hungarians defeated at, 355
Hārim, Latin defeat at, 359; 375
Ḥarīrī, Arab author of *Maqāmāt*, 294
Ḣarmenopulus, Constantine, Byzantine legal writer, 715, 717; nomophylax at Constantinople, 720; *Promptuarium* of, 721 sqq., 724
Harnack, quoted on iconoclastic struggle, 41
Harold Fairhair, King of Norway, leader of the Varangians in Sicily, 150
Ḥarrān, Arabic language in, 290; Greek translators at, 297 sq.; Crusaders defeated at, 341; emir of, *see* Qāraja
Ḥarrānians, and Islām, 287
Ḣarthama, Arab commander in Cilicia, 127
Hārūn ar-Rashīd (Rashīd), Abbasid Caliph of Baghdad, victorious over Irene, 22, 24, 124 sqq.; 39; and Nicephorus I, 126; death, 127, 275; revenue, 151; and Armenians, 157; and Chazars, 189; and Barmecides, 274; and postal service, 283; and non-Muslims, 288 sq.; 291; 293 sq.; poets of his court, 290
Ḥasan, Turkish emir of Cappadocia, 344
Ḥasan ibn Ṣabbāh, founder of the Assassins, 305
Ḥasan, Persian commander under the Arabs, 122 sqq.
Ḥasan, Seljūq leader, 164

Hasan, the Janissary, first to enter Constantinople, 703
Havelberg, *see* Anselm
Hayton, *see* Hethum
Hebrew language, and St Cyril, 220, 225
Heimbach, G. E., modern editor of Harmenopulus, 723
Helen (Palaeologus), Queen of Cyprus, 471
Helena, Empress, mother of Constantine the Great, 25
Helena, daughter of Romanus I, marriage to Constantine VII, 61; 64; 67; death, 61; 98 *note*
Helena, daughter of Alypius, wife of Constantine VIII, 84, 96
Helena, Empress, wife of John V, 617
Helena, niece of Romanus III, married to King of Iberia, 100
Helena, Queen of Serbia, daughter of Emperor Baldwin II, 527, 530, 533
Helena Gruba, regent in Bosnia, 560; deposed, 565, 591
Helež, Bosnian family, 583
Helladics, turmarch of the, *see* Agallianus
Hellas, theme of, 733, 742
"Hellenes," connotation at Constantinople, 261
Hellenisation of the Empire, 731, 736
Hellespont, Saracen fleet in, 141, 148; 234; 431; Venetian colonies on, 480 sq.; 487
Helsingfors, Ugro-Finnish Society of, and site of Karakorum, 640
Henri de Grangerin, at Pegae, 485
Henry of Flanders, Latin Emperor, becomes lord of Adramyttium, 422 sq.; in Asia Minor, 424; 481 sqq., 485; becomes Emperor of the East, 425; successful reign of, 426; 427; and Marco Sanudo, 436; and Geoffrey de Villehardouin, 438; and Boril of Bulgaria, 521; and Pope Innocent III, 606
Henry II, Emperor of the West, 406
Henry III, Emperor of the West, and Venice, 408; embassy of Argyrus to, 597
Henry IV, Emperor of the West, and Alexius I, 329, 408; Gregory VII and, 598
Henry V, Emperor of the West, 345; 354; and the Papacy, 600
Henry VI, Emperor of the West, sends crown to Leo of Armeno-Cilicia, 172; Byzantium and, 416 sq., 603
Henry I of Lusignan, King of Cyprus, and Frederick II, 469; 476
Henry II of Lusignan, King of Cyprus, 179 sq.; deposed by his brother, 469; 477
Henry III, King of England, letter of Latin Emperor to, 490; and Mongols, 638
Henry IV, King of England, visited by Manuel II, 618, 678
Henry VI, King of England, 691
Henry, duke of Austria, and Manuel I, 371
Henry, duke of Silesia, defeated by Mongols, 637
Henry, Latin Patriarch, and Clement VI, 615
Heraclea (Cybistra), taken by Arabs, 126, 128; Crusaders defeated at, 341; 421; 480; 482; annexed by Nicaea, 483; ceded to Genoese, 666; bishop of, *see* Nicephorus
Heraclea, Venetian township, settlement of, 386 sqq.; 389; quarrels with Jesolo, 387, 390 sqq.; taken by Pepin, 394; devastated by Magyars, 400; diocese of, 387, 405
Heraclian dynasty, 729
Heraclius, Emperor, 625, 707; Novels of, 708, 711
Herāt, destroyed by Mongols, 279, 634; 313
Hercules, 484
Hereke, taken by Latins, 483
Hermanric, bishop of Passau, and Methodius, 227
Hermopolis, *see* Theodore of
Hermus valley, 354; 512; river, 378
Herodotus, 447
Hersek, on the Gulf of Izmid, 582
Hervé, the Francopol, ill-treated by Michael VI, 117
Herzegovina, the, 517; *see* Hum; derivation of name, 574
Hesiod, 763
Hetairia, regiment of the Imperial bodyguard, 738
Hethum I (Hayton), King of Armeno-Cilicia, crowned by his father, 174; his alliance with the Mongols, 175, 638 *note*
Hethum II (Hayton), the One-Eyed, King of Armeno-Cilicia, 176 sqq.; and Mongols, 178, 180; 181
Hethum (Hayton), of Lambron, son-in-law of Thoros II, 170; wars against Ruben II, 171, 174
Hethumian princes of Armeno-Cilicia, 154; extinct, 180
Hexabiblos, *see* Promptuarium
Hexameron (*Shestodnev*), work of John the exarch, 237
Hexamilion, Greek stronghold at Isthmus of Corinth taken by Turks, 690; *see* Isthmus
Hia (Tangut), Chinese province, invaded by Mongols, 633
Hicanati, regiment of the Byzantine Guards, 739; Domestic of the, *see* Curcuas, John
Hierapolis (Chemishgadzak in Armenia), birthplace of John I, 78
Hierapolis in North Syria, *see* Manbij
Hieria, palace of, *see* Constantinople, Councils
Hiericho, captured by Normans, 329, 342
Hieronymus, Byzantine canonist, 711
"High Fortress." *See* Bardsrberd
Hildebrand, Duke, takes Ravenna, 390
Hildebrand, *see* Gregory VII, Pope
Himalayas, 651
Himerius, Byzantine admiral, 141; defeated and disgraced, 142
Ḥimṣ, *see* Emesa
Hincmar, archbishop of Rheims, and Photius, 250
Hindu, *see* India
Hindu Kush, mountain range, 277

Hippocrates, translated into Arabic, 297
Hippodrome (Circus), *see* Constantinople
Hishām, Umayyad Caliph, 120 sq.
Hisn Manṣūr, *see* Perrhe
Ḥiṭṭīn, battle of, 278
Hochau, Chinese town, death of Mangu Khan at, 645
Hohenburg, *see* Berthold
Hohenstaufen, the, ambitions of, 596; 603; *see* Constance of
Holland, 449
Holy Angels, the, Gate of, at Constantinople, 323
Holy Apostles, church of, *see* Constantinople
Holy Argyri, monastery of the, founded by Michael IV, 104
Holy Ghost, Doctrine of the Procession of the, 91; in Armenia, 179; St Methodius and, 228; Photius and, 249 sq., 254; Emperor Leo VI on, 258, 261, 267, 271; John III and, 497; Theodore II and, 505; 594 sq.; John Beccus and, 613; Manuel II and, 618; Plethon and, 624; at Council of Bari, 600; at Ferrara, 621, 623
"Holy Mountain," *see* Athos
Holy Sepulchre, church of, *see* Jerusalem
Homa, *see* Sublaeum
Homer, taught at Constantinople, 114; 218; 703; Epirote paraphrase of, 453, 474; commentary on, 764
Honan, Chinese province, 635 sq., 645
Honorius II, Pope, and John II, 355, 596; 600
Honorius III, Pope, sends legate to crown Stephen of Serbia, 521
Honorius II, anti-Pope, *see* Cadalus
Hospitallers (Knights of St John, Knights of Rhodes), at Antioch, 173; and Hethum of Armenia, 177 sq.; in Greece, 437, 456, 459; in Rhodes, 455, 458, 465, 467, 665, 671; in Icaria, 468, 477; and Peter of Cyprus, 470; 474; share in Latin Empire, 480; in Roumania, 540; 511; 617; take Attalia, 669; and Theodore of Mistrâ, 677 sq.; defend Smyrna, 683 sq.; and Mahomet II, 687; Grand Master of, 672
Howorth, Sir H., on origin of name Tartar, 630; on Mongol massacre, 634; on Kublai Khan, 648
Hranić, *see* Sandalj
Hratchea, ancestor of the Bagratuni, 157
Hring, among Avars, 199
Hrushevsky, on early Russian history, 203 sqq.
Hrvoje Vukčić, Grand Duke, "Kingmaker," in Bosnia, 560; 565; death, 566, 578
Hubaira, *see* Omar
Hubert of Biandrate, *baile* of Thessalonica, 426
Hubert, marquess of Tuscany, 402
Hugh I of Lusignan, King of Cyprus, 476
Hugh II of Lusignan, King of Cyprus, 476
Hugh III, King of Cyprus, father-in-law of Oshin of Armeno-Cilicia, 179, 477
Hugh IV, King of Cyprus, 477; and Constantine IV of Armeno-Cilicia, 181
Hugh of Lusignan, Prince of Galilee, and the Morea, 454
Hugh of Provence, King of Italy, 64; and Constantine VII, 260; and Venice, 400; 402
Hugh of St Pol, made lord of Demotika, 422
Hugh of Vermandois reaches Constantinople, 337; 339
Hugh of Flavigny, 262 *note*
Hūlāgū, Mongol Īl-Khān of Persia, and Hethum I, 179; captures Baghdad, 279, 300, 642; conquers "Assassins," 641; 638; 643; founds Persian dynasty, 644; 645; 647; becomes a Muslim, 646, 651; 654; patronage of astronomy, 299, 629
Hum, land of (Herzegovina), 517; 523; Župan of, 524; seized by Hungary, 526, 556; 531; by Serbia, 534; 542; by Bosnia, 544; 566 sq.; 579; made Hungarian duchy, 520; 553; Hranič rules over, 573; 575; attacked by Turks, 580 sq., 673; finally annexed, 582; Table of rulers, 591
Ḥumaid, Saracen admiral, ravages Cyprus, 127
Humbert of Dauphiné, founds Greek scholarships at Paris, 616
Humbert, cardinal-bishop of Sylva Candida, legate of the Pope at Benevento, 266 sq.; at Constantinople, 269, 271
Humbertopulus, Norman leader, conspires against Alexius I, 332
Ḥunain ibn Isḥāq (Johannitius), Arab translator of medical works, 297
Hundred Years' War, 669
Hunfalvy, on origin of Magyars, 194 sq.
Hungaria, Great, 195
Hungarians, *see also* Magyars; 140, 170; and Isaac I, 322, 324; 325; and John II, 355 sqq.; and Manuel, 368 sqq., 372; 379; and Venice, 409 sqq., 416; and Serbia, 519, 531, 535, 545, 553 sq., 563 sq., 569, 571, 578; and Bulgaria, 526 sq., 554; and Bosnia, 526, 544, 556, 559, 566, 574, 579, 581; and Turks, 617 sq.; 669 sq.; at Nicopolis, 676; at Kossovo, 573, 693; 689; 692; and Mahomet II, 694
Hungary, Magyars in, 198 sq., 210 sqq.; Bulgars in, 234; and Turks, 617 sq.; 652; 675; 685; 687; Murād II in, 690; invaded by Mongols, 608, 628, 637, 639; kings of, *see* Andrew, Béla, Emeric, Géza, Koloman, Ladislas, Louis, Matthias, Sigismund, Stephen, Vladislav; *see also* Margaret of
Hung-Wu, Chinese Emperor, founder of Ming dynasty, 649
Huns, 184 sq.; (Utigurs) 188; in Justinian's army, 738; and Constantinople, 747
Hunyadi, John, voïvode of Transylvania, victories of, over Turks, 462, 571, 584, 624; at battle of Varna, 572, 691 sq.; at Kossovo, 573, 692 sq.; and Bosnia, 574 sq.; saves Belgrade, 576; and Mahomet II, 694; death, 577; 701

Ḥusain, Muslim martyr, 288
Ḥuṣain, brother-in-law of Tīmūr, 650
Ḥusain ibn Ḥasan Jahānsūz, Sultan of Ghūr, defeated by Sanjar, 313
Hyakinthos, monastery of, at Nicaea, 484, 486
Hylilas, John, *see* John
Hypatos (consul), title conferred on the Doge Marcellus, 390
Hyperperi, 514; *see* Coinage
Hypobolon (ὑπόβολον), bridal gift in Byzantine law, 716, 718

Ibelin, *see* John of
Iberia (Georgia), Basil II in, 95 sq., 149, 164; and Armenia, 155; devastated by Chazars, 189; and Trebizond, 472, 480, 515; and Seljūqs, 310; conquered by Mongols, 636, 639; influence of Byzantine law in, 724; 653; enamel work in, 162; kings of, *see* Bagarat, Giorgi, Liparid, Parakat; queen of, 639; *see also* Katholikos; curopalates of, 62, 86
Iberians, 97, 103; in Byzantine army, 738; convent of, on Mount Athos, 66; clergy at Council of Ferrara, 621
Ibn al-Athīr, Arab historian, 106, 133 *note*; works of, 293
Ibn al-Habbārīyah, Arab satirist, 305
Ibn Bājja, *see* Avenpace
Ibn Faḍlan, on Chazar judges, 191; on Bulgars, 194
Ibn Haukal, on town of Bulgary, 193
Ibn Hishām, Arab grammarian, 293
Ibn Isḥāq, biographer of Mahomet, 293
Ibn Khurdādhbih, Persian post-master, official handbook by, 295; on Russian trade, 201
Ibn Mangū, son-in-law of Ghāzī, 353
Ibn Rushd, *see* Averroes
Ibn Rusta, on town of Itil, 191; on Burdas, 192; on Magyars, 195 sqq.
Ibn Sa'd, Arab biographer, 293
Ibn Sīnā, *see* Avicenna
Ibn Tufail, *see* Abubacer
Ibrāhīm, Abbasid prince, rival to the Caliph Ma'mūn, 127
Ibrāhīm, Arab general, 126
Ibrāhīm, emir of Qaramān, and Mahomet II, 693 sq.
Ibrāhīm ibn al-Aghlab, emir of Africa, 134; 141; 275; 300
Ibrāhīm ibn Īnāl (Nīyāl), Seljūq prince, 304
Icaria, island taken by John III, 428; 488; Genoese and Hospitallers in, 468; 477
Iceland, Northmen from, 738
Iconium (Qonya), capital of Seljūqs of Rūm, 315; Crusaders at, 338; Manuel I fails at, 365; Manuel's last attack on, 378; 654
Iconium (Rūm), Sultans of, 168, 315; raids on Armeno-Cilicia, 171 sqq.; and Mongols, 174 sqq., 653; and Alexius I, 343 sq.; and John II, 307; 312; 317; 357; and Frederick I, 372; and Manuel I, 365 sqq., 373, 377 sq.; invade Empire, 383; John III and, 429, 492; 479; 642; *see* Kai-Kā'ūs, Kai-Khusrū, Kai-Qubād, Malik-Shāh, Mas'ūd, Qilij-Arslān, Shāhinshāh, Sulaimān
Iconoclasm, 5 sq., 13 sq., 20 sq., 26, 30 sq., 33 sq., 41, 390
Iconoclastic Emperors, *see* Chap. I *passim*; general estimate, 1, 6 sqq.; 41; legislation of, 708 sqq.
Ida, Mt, passes of, 481
Idrīs ibn 'Abdallāh, founder of dynasty in Morocco, 300
Idrīsid, dynasty in Morocco, 300
Ignatius, Patriarch of Constantinople, deposed by Bardas, 46, 248 sq.; appeals to Rome, 47; reinstated by Basil I, 53, 251; death, 54, 253; 218 sq.; and Pope Leo IV, 247; conflict with Photius, 248 sq., 255
Igor, Prince of Kiev, expedition against Greeks, 205; 207, 743
Igumen (abbot), of the Laura, authority of, 81
Ikhshīdids, Egyptian dynasty, 143, 300, 302
Ikhtiman, in Bulgaria, 240
Ilek, title of supreme Khagan of the Chazars, 189 sq.
Īl-Ghāzī, of the Urtuqid dynasty, 316 sq.
Īl-Khāns, Mongol dynasty of Persia, founded, 279; converted to Islām, 644; and Egypt, 651 sq.
Ilkilig, son of Atsiz Shāh, 312
"Illumination," Persian Islāmic philosophy of, 296
Illyria, 675
Illyricum, 329; dioceses of, placed under the jurisdiction of the Patriarch of Constantinople, 10, 58, 246
Ilmen', Lake, 202
Ilovayski, on early Russian princes, 205
Ilya, *see* St Elias
'Imād-ad-Dīn, biographer of Saladin, 306
'Imād-ad-Dīn Zangī, *see* Zangī
Image worship, *see* Iconoclasm
Imām-Caliph, the, ideal of, 279, 282; Shī'ites and the Imāmship of 'Alī, 301
Imāms, spared by Tīmūr, 680
Imbros, 323; given to Demetrius Palaeologus, 464; 465; birthplace of Critobulus, 474
Imperator, *see* Basileus
"Independents," Greek farmers of country round Constantinople, 509; and capture of, 511 sq.
"Index" to Arab literature by Nādīm, 290
India, Mas'ūdī's travels in, 295; Shī'ite doctrines in, 301 sq.; Maḥmūd's campaigns in, 303; Mas'ūd in, 304; Seljūq expedition to, 311; 551; Mogul dynasty in, 629, 650, 652; Tīmūr's conquest of, 650 sq.; Indian (Hindu) medicine, 297; astronomy, 298; Indian Ocean, 274
Indies, the, merchandise of, in Armenia, 162
Ἴνδικες, abridgments of Justinian's legal work, 707
Indo-Bactrian coins, used by Bulgars, 193

Indus, river, 274; 633; 636; 651
Ineboli, on Black Sea, 660, 668
Ingerina, *see* Eudocia
Inn, Bavarian river, 212
Innocent II, Pope, and John II, 355
Innocent III, Pope, and Fourth Crusade, 415 sq., 418, 603 sq.; on sack of Constantinople, 420; 423; and Bulgaria, 424, 520; and Henry of Flanders, 426; and Princes of Achaia, 434, 438; and Theodore I, 483 sq., 487 *note*; 480 *note*; 481 *note*; 595 sq.; and Antioch, 173; and Byzantine Church, 606, 611, 626
Innocent IV, Pope, and Mongol envoys, 493; and John III, 608; and Tartars, 630; and Mongol menace, 639
Innocent V, Pope, ultimatum of, to Michael VIII, 612
Innocent VI, Pope, and Stephen Dušan, 546; and John V, 617
Institutes of Justinian, commentaries on, 707 sq, 712 sq.
Investiture conflict, compared with Iconoclastic controversy, 31, 729
Ioannoúpolis, new name given to Prêslav, 240
Ionian Islands, become Venetian, 421, 432; ruled by Leonardo Tocco, 455; become Turkish, 466; Venetian again, 467; last relic of Venetian colonies, 472; results of Latin conquest of, 473; 733; 742
Ionian Sea, 238, 436
Ipek, residence of Serbian Metropolitan, 524; made seat of Patriarch, 542; 578
Iranian races in South Russia, 184; language, 195
'Irāq ('Irāk), 276; 286; 289; 291; Buwaihids in, 301; 307; Zangī governor of, 317
'Irāq 'Ajamī (Media), 304, 311, 633, 636; Seljūq dynasty in, 315 sq.
Irene, Chazar princess, wife of Constantine V, 189
Irene, Empress, reign of, 19 sqq.; origin and character, 19; summons Council at Nicaea, 21; deposes her son and assumes title of Emperor, 24; deposition, 25; 31; 34 sqq.; losses to the Saracens, 124 sqq.; 246; Novels of, 710; 757
Irene (Ducas), wife of Alexius I, 326; crowned, 328; intrigues against her son John, 346
Irene (Piriska), Hungarian princess, wife of John II, 355, 363
Irene, wife of Andronicus II, 533
Irene, first wife of John III, 495, 498 sq.
Irene, wife of Andronicus Comnenus, sister-in-law of Emperor Manuel I, patroness of scholars, 363
Irene (Angelus), wife of Philip of Swabia, 417
Irene, daughter of Theodore II, portrait of, 514
Irene, daughter of Michael VIII, married to John Asên III, 529
Irene, wife of George Branković, poisoned by her son, 577; 590
Irene, St, church of, *see under* Constantinople
Iris, river, 130
'Īsà, Abbasid prince, uncle of the Caliph Mahdī, 123 sq.
'Īsà, son of Bāyazīd I, at Angora, 682; killed by Sulaimān, 684
Isaac I Comnenus, Emperor, disgraced by Theodora, 116; defeated by Turks at Bayber, 166; revolts against Michael VI, 117, 319 sqq.; crowned Emperor, 118, 322; family, 318; character, 322; and Cerularius, 323 sq.; abdication, 324; 326; Novel of, 720
Isaac II Angelus, Emperor, arrested by Andronicus I, 383; proclaimed Emperor, 384, 414; reign of, 384; vicissitudes of, 417 sqq., 421, 604; 480; Bulgarians revolt against, 518 sq., 529; alliance with Saladin, 384, 603; Novels of, 720
Isaac, general of Mahomet I, in Bosnia, 566 sq.
Isabel of Lusignan, wife of Oshin of Armeno-Cilicia, 179
Isabella of Austria, wife of Leo the Great of Armeno-Cilicia, 172
Isabelle of Villehardouin, Princess of Achaia, "the lady of the Morea," marriage to Neapolitan prince, 444; 446; married to Florent, 447; marries Philip of Savoy, 448; death, 449; 452; 474
Isapostolos, title of the Emperor, 726
Isauria, 170; incorporated with Armeno-Cilicia, 172; 174 sq.; 125 *note*; Isaurian coast, 123, 340
Isaurian Emperors, Chap. I; 34; 49; 729; care for army, 737; and navy, 741 sq.; 739
Isha, deputy-khagan of the Chazars, 190
Ishmaelites, *see* Assassins, Ismā'īlī
Īsho'yath, Nestorian Patriarch in Baghdad, 289
Isidore, abbot of St Demetrius, in favour of Union, 620; made archbishop of Kiev, 621; Cardinal, 623; 625; 690; at siege of Constantinople, 695, 698
Isidore, commentator on Justinian, 707
Isidore of Miletus, architect of St Sophia, 752
Iskander (Alexander), *see* Skanderbeg
Islām, among Chazars, 190, 219; among Bulgars, 194; influence of Christian catechisms on, 280; political theory of, 280 sqq.; toleration under, 286 sqq.; sects in, 301; internal dissensions of, 642 sq.; consolidation under Seljūqs, 299 sqq.; position of Baghdad in, 641; Seljūqs converted to, 644; among Mongols, 640, 646 sq., 651; religion of Tīmūr, 650; Īl-Khān dynasty and, 644; Slav conversions to, 560, 581, 587; and Bosnian Bogomiles, 582; and Janissaries, 664; and Ottomans, 668; *see* Chap. x
Ismā'īl, uncle of Barkiyāruq, 309

Ismā'īlī, Shī'ah doctrine, 276, 292; sect of (Assassins), 301; Ishmaelites, *see* Assassins
Isova, Benedictine abbey of, in Greece, 438, 473
Ispahan, captured by Seljūqs, 304; 308 sqq.
Ispanok, Magyar official, 215
Isparich (Asparuch), Bulgarian khan migrates to Bessarabia, 230; and Justinian II, 231
Israelites, 303
Isrā'īl, former name of Alp Arslan, *q.v.*
Isrā'īl, son of Seljūq, 303 sq.
Isthmus of Corinth, wall built across, 460, 462, 690; *see* Hexamilion
Istria, ceded to the Franks, 24, 36; Slavonic liturgy in, 229; 386; separated from Venice, 387, 389; taken by Charlemagne, 393 sq.; returned to Byzantium, 395; 398; and Venice, 401, 403, 406, 578; 768; marquess of, *see* Gunter
Italian, Italians, captains at Armenian court, 172; in Byzantine army, 347, 738; in Empire, 736, 773; in Constantinople, 701 sqq., 746, 750; trade with Constantinople, 762; with Salonica, 770; with Bulgaria, 523; volunteers against Turks, 675 sq., 691; bankers in Greece, 473; Italians in Bosnia, 517, 566; Italian marriage of Stephen of Serbia, 521; wife of Andronicus II, 533; favourite of John III, 495 sq.; literature at court of Manuel I, 362; revision of *Prochiron*, 717, 725
Italus, John, "Consul of the Philosophers," teaching of condemned, 350; 764
Italy, taxation in, 4; anti-Iconoclast risings, 9 sq., 388, 390; lost to Eastern Empire, 5, 18, 22, 25, 36, 273, 328 sqq.; Leo IV and, 19; 16 sq.; 69; Nicephorus II and, 76 sq., 145; 80 sq.; 86; Basil II and, 91 sq., 94; Constantine VIII and, 97; 103; 108; 141; 147; 246; 250; John II and, 358, 360; Manuel I and, 368 sqq., 374, 412 sq.; 456; 463 sq.; 595 sq.; 598; 601; 608; John V in, 618; Manuel II in, 618; 619; John VIII in, 621, 690; 624; themes in, 733 sq., 736; exarchate of, created, 732; decay of Byzantine rule in, 387, 389, 597; influence of Byzantine law in, 724 sq.; of Byzantium on, 776 sq.; Byzantine Church in, 112 sq., 259, 263; monks in, 253, 258, 737; Saracens in, 37, 139, 142, 144, 149, 151, 260; Magyar raids in, 211 sq.; Lombards in, 9 sq.; 17 sq., 22, 386; Charlemagne in, 18, 392 sq.; kings of, and Venice, 400 sq.; Conrad II in, 407; 456; 463 sq.; 466; Normans in, 92, 112, 266, 268, 325, 328 sqq.; slaves from, 286; 333; 337; 341; 343 sq.; 352 sq.; 499, 504; 508; 624; Turkish designs on, 570, 578; Chaps. v, XIII *passim*
Itil (Atel), capital of the Chazars, 190 sqq.; river, *see* Volga
Ivailo, the Swineherd, Tsar of Bulgaria, 528; marries Tsaritsa Maria, 529; killed by Tartars, 530; 590
Ivan I Crnojević, the Black, Montenegrin ruler, 586 sq., 592
Ivan II Crnojević, Montenegrin ruler, 592
Ivanko, Basaraba, Prince of Wallachia, at battle of Velbužd, 538; 539 sq.; 593
Ivanko, Bulgarian rebel, 478; slays John Asên I, 520
Ivats, Bulgarian noble, resistance to Basil II, 242
Ivats, Bulgarian chamberlain of Michael IV, 244
Iviron, convent of, 90
Izmid, *see* Nicomedia
Iznīq, *see* Nicaea
Izyaslav, candidate for the princedom of Kiev, 368
'Izz-ad-Dīn, *see* Kai-Kā'ūs; title of Alp Arslān, 306

Jabal Hamrīn, Mongol defeat at, 636
Jacobites, Syrian Christians, 123, 290; Jacobite bishop, 289; and Union of Florence, 623
Jacques D'Avesnes, occupies Euboea, 435
Jacques de Baux, nephew of Philip II of Taranto, and Achaia, 456; 474; 476
Jaffa, Venetians at, 411
Jagatai, son of Jenghiz Khan, Mongol ruler of Transoxiana, 279; 633; share of his father's dominions, 635, 640; 641; 645; descendants of, 650
Jāhiẓ, Arab theologian and author, 294
Jajce, in Bosnia, 566; Stephen Tomašević crowned at, 578; taken by Turks, 580; Hungarian banat of, 581
Jalāl-ad-Dīn, Shāh of Khwārazm, overthrown by Mongols, 312, 515, 633; 636
Jalāl-ad-Dīn, title of Malik Shāh, 307
Jamāl-ad-Dīn, Persian astronomer, and Kublai Khan, 646
James I, King of Cyprus, hostage at Genoa, 470; 477
James II, King of Cyprus, regains Famagosta, 466, 471; 477
James III, King of Cyprus, death of, 467, 471; 477
James II, King of Aragon, 496
James II, King of Majorca, 452
Jamnia, schools of, 629
Jand on the Jaxartes, 313
Janissaries, formation of, by Orkhān, 663 sq.; at Nicopolis, 676; at Angora, 682; desert Sulaimān, 685; desert Mūsà, 686; 689; 692; at Kossovo, 693; at siege of Constantinople, 696, 702 sq.; and Mahomet II, 705
Janjići, chief seat of the Bosnian Bogomiles, 545
Jantra, river at Trnovo, 523
Janus, King of Cyprus, misfortunes of, 470; 477
Japan, Mongol expedition to, 646
Japhet, supposed ancestor of Mongols, 632

Jaquinta, widow of Constantine Bodin of Serbia, 356
Java, Mongol expedition to, 646
Jaxartes, river, 313; 650
Jele, see *Jila*
Jenghiz Khan, early history of, 632; 627; 631; conquests of, 279, 633; death and burial, 634 sq.; administration, 634; division of Empire, 635; 636; 638; 641; worshipped in China, 646; army of, 647; 648 sqq.; 653 sqq.
Jerusalem, 148; 175; taken by Crusaders, 335, 338 sqq.; Seljūqs in, 277; Egyptians in, 316; conquered by Saladin, 278, 361; 410; 416; kingdom of, 422; and Cyprus, 469, 477; "Assises of," 437; Serbian foundations at, 535; 599; 629; 643; saved from Tīmūr, 680; kings of, *see* Amaury, Baldwin, Fulk, Godfrey, Guy, John of Brienne; Patriarch of, 173, 264, *see* Euthymius; church of the Holy Sepulchre at, 98, 100, 598 sq.; church of the Theotokos at, 768
Jesolo, bishopric of, 387 sq.; jealousy of Heraclea, 390 sq.; 392; devastated by Magyars, 400; *see* Cavazuccherina
Jews, their hostility to images, 7; Leo III's edict against, 7; driven from Constantinople, 109; massacred at Zapetra, 129; 153; communities in Caucasus and Crimea, 190; disputation with St Cyril, 219 sq.; Islām and, 286 sqq.; Jewish Arabic works, 290; Jewish law, 292; trade in the East, 405; in Thebes, 440; Jewish rulers in the Cyclades, 468, 472; in Crete, 472; Jewish wife of John Alexander of Bulgaria, 548; 554; Jewish archbishop of Bulgaria, 243; *see* Judaism
Jiblah (Byblus), 146; captured by John I, 148
Jīhād, Muslim holy war, 282; demanded by Arabs against John I, 147; against Mongols, 636
Jila (*Jele*), Magyar title, 196
Jizyah, poll tax paid by non-Muslims, 287
Joakim, bishop of Brūsa, made Armenian Patriarch by Mahomet II, 182
Joan of Anjou, wife of Oshin of Armeno-Cilicia, 179
Joanna I, Queen of Naples, and Achaia, 456; 474; 476
Joannicius, son of John I of Trebizond, 515
Joánnina, bishopric of, 243; taken by Normans, 329; by Buondelmonti, 457; captured by Turks, 461, 690; 462; held by Serbians, 543, 552 sq.
Job, *see* Ayyūb
Johannicius the Saracen, betrays Basil the Bird, 68
Johannitius, *see* Ḥunain ibn Isḥāq
Johannitsa, *see* Kalojan
John I Tzimisces, Emperor, 68, 71, 75; early life, 78; murders Nicephorus II and becomes Emperor, 77; 79; crowned by Patriarch, 80; his reign, 81 sqq.; 84, 87 *note*; in the East, 72, 143 sq., 147 sq.; and Armenia, 161; and Bulgaria, 239 sq.; 259; Novels of, 715; relations with Rome, 260; 401; and Venice, 402; 403; 739
John II Comnenus, Emperor, birth, 328; 332; coronation and accession, 346; and coinage, 348; character, 351; foreign policy, 352; and Seljūqs, 353, 357; and Venetians, 354, 411; and Hungarians, 355; and Serbs, 356; and Armeno-Cilicia, 169, 358; Cilician campaign, 359 sq.; death, 361, 170; and Papacy, 596, 600; Novels of, 720; and Canon Law, 723
John III Ducas Vatatzes, Emperor at Nicaea, accession of, 427, 486; successes, 428 sq., 440; reign of, 487 sqq.; and Bulgaria, 489, 523; and Thessalonica, 490 sqq.; conquers Macedonia, 492; and Michael of Epirus, 494; second marriage, 495; ecclesiastical policy, 497 sq., 596, 607 sq.; administration, 498 sq.; and Michael Palaeologus, 503 sq.; and Genoese, 510; 515 sq.; 524; and Latin bishops, 607; Novel of, 720, 722; death and canonization, 430, 501
John IV Lascaris, minority of, 506 sq.; 508; 510; 512; blinded and imprisoned, 513 sq.; 516; 525
John V Palaeologus, Emperor, minority of, 541, 615; and John Cantacuzene, 543, 665 sq.; 546; and Bulgarians, 554; attempts to gain help from West, 617 sq., 670; Orkhān and, 667; and Murād I, 671; and Bāyāzid I, 675; and Lesbos, 455; 593
John VI Cantacuzene, Emperor, and the Morea, 454; and Stephen Dušan, 540 sqq.; 543; and Turks, 544; deposed, 546; 615; and Papacy, 616; 617; at siege of Nicaea, 661; Orkhān and, 665 sq.; on condition of Empire, 669; as historian, 765; 775; death, 462; 593
John VII Palaeologus, Emperor, nephew of Manuel II associated with him, 677; defends Constantinople, 678 sq.; 685; 593
John VIII Palaeologus, Emperor, and Council of Basle, 620; at Ferrara, 621 sq.; and Act of Union, 623, 690; death, 624; and Murād II, 689 sqq.; embassy to the West, 619; 593
John I Axoûchos, son of Alexius I of Trebizond, set aside from succession, 514; becomes Emperor, 515; 516
John of Brienne, King of Jerusalem, Latin Emperor (regent), 427; invades Asia Minor, 488 sq.; and John III, 608
John Angelus, crowned Emperor at Salonica, 429 sq., 440; made Despot by Emperor John III, 491; death, 492; 476
John Asên I, Tsar of Bulgaria, 517; revolts against Byzantium, 518 sq.; murdered, 519; 590
John Asên II, Tsar of Bulgaria, and Latins, 428; and John III, 429; 489 sqq.; re-

covers his throne, 521; prosperity of, 522 sq.; death, 524; 525; 590
John Asên III, Tsar of Bulgaria, son of Mytzês, short reign of, 529; with the Tartars, 530; 590
John Alexander Asên, Tsar of Bulgaria, 539; and the Pope, 540; and Turks, 544; and Church, 548; patron of learning, 549; 554; 590
John Shishman, last Tsar of Bulgaria, 554; defeated by Turks, 557; death, 560, 590
John Stephen, Tsar of Bulgaria, 538; exiled, 539; 590
John Vladislav, Tsar of Bulgaria, 242; 244; 322
John Sracimir, of Vidin in Bulgaria, carried off by Hungarians, 554; Turks and, 557, 561; 590
John I of Lusignan, King of Cyprus, 477
John II of Lusignan, King of Cyprus, 471, 477
John I Ducas Angelus (the Bastard), son of Michael II of Epirus, deserts William of Achaia, 442; Duke of Neopatras, 444; 445; 532; and reunion, 612; 475
John II, Duke of Neopatras, 449 sq., 475
John Vladimir, Prince of Dioclea, 240; and Samuel of Bulgaria, 241; murdered, 242
John of Gravina, Prince of Achaia, 452 sq.; 474
John, Duke of Athens, and John Ducas Angelus, 444 sq.; death, 446, 475
John of Randazzo, Duke of Athens, 475
John I, King of Aragon, Duke of Athens and Neopatras, 457; 475
John Lackland, King of England, 415; 480
John I Orsini, count of Cephalonia, 475
John II Orsini, rules Epirus and Cephalonia, 453; 475
John VIII, Pope, and Photius, 54, 253; 254; and St Methodius, 227 sqq.
John IX, Pope, and Anthony Cauleas, 56, 256
John X, Pope, and Nicholas Mysticus, 62; 257
John XI, Pope, recognises Theophylact as Patriarch, 63, 259
John XIII, Pope, legates of, at Constantinople, 261
John XIX, Pope, and the Patriarch Eustathius, 92, 262 sq.
John XXI, Pope, and Michael VIII, 612 sq.
John XXII, Pope, and Oshin of Armeno-Cilicia, 179; and Andronicus II, 614
John Gaetano Orsini, *see* Nicholas III, Pope
John Beccus (Veccus), and union, 595, 611; made Patriarch, 612; deposed, 613
John Camaterus, archbishop of Bulgaria, becomes Patriarch of Constantinople, 243
John Hylilas (the Grammarian), Patriarch of Constantinople, 34; iconoclastic zeal, 30; nickname, 40; deposed, 41; 43; sent as ambassador to Saracens, 128; and St Cyril, 218
John Apocaucus, metropolitan of Naupactus, and Union with Rome, 607
John, archbishop of Ochrida, 94
John, Katholikos of Armenia, 161
John Medzabaro, Katholikos of Armenia, 173
John, Patriarch of Grado, murdered by Doge, 393
John, Cardinal, papal legate (898 A.D.), 256
John, Cardinal, papal legate (1166 A.D.), 602
John, bishop of Belluno, and Venice, 404 sq.
John, bishop of Trani, letter of Cerularius to, 113, 266; at Constantinople, 268
John Damascene, St, treatises against Iconoclasm, 10; 26; 766
John of Rila, patron saint of Bulgaria, 238 sq.; 519; 524
John of Parma, General of the Franciscans, and John III, 608
John Parastron, Franciscan friar, emissary between Rome and Constantinople, 611
John of Pian di Carpine, friar, on Tartars, 630 sq.; mission to Mongols, 639 sq.
John of Ragusa, delegate of the Council of Basle, 620; at Constantinople, 621; at Council of Florence, 622
John Uroš, son of Simeon Uroš, becomes abbot of Metéoron, 552; 553
John of Khrna, Armenian churchman, 182
John of Orotn, Armenian churchman, 182
John Scholasticus, of Antioch, Byzantine canonist, 227, 711
John, priest sent by Pope Stephen V to Moravia, 229
John the Deacon, Venetian chronicler, on creation of first doge, 387 sq.; 398 *note*; 404; and Otto III, 405; on "New Venice," 406
John Asên, son of John Alexander of Bulgaria, 549
John Dishypatus, sent by Emperor John VIII to Council of Basle, 621
John Eladas, *see* Eladas
John the Exarch, and Simeon of Bulgaria, 237
John of Ibelin, Regent of Cyprus, 469
John of Lusignan, nephew of Hethum II, of Armeno-Cilicia, 180 sq.
John Mauropus, *see* Mauropus
John, nomophylax, *see* Xiphilin
John the Orphanotrophos, brother of Michael IV, 101; becomes chief minister, 102 sqq.; fall of, 105; 108, 265; executed by Constantine IX, 110; Bulgaria and, 244
John Uglješa, marshal of Serbia, 553 sq.; killed, 555
John, son of Simeon of Bulgaria, 238
John, treasurer of Irene, commander against Saracens, 124
John, general of Basil II, 90
John, son of Vitalian, general of Justinian I, 385
John, son of Mauritius, doge of Venice, 393
John-Roger, the Caesar, brother-in-law of Manuel I, 365; 373

John-Smbat (Sempad), King of Armenia, civil war with his brother, 163; 164; married to Byzantine princess, 100
Joinville, 515 *note*; on Greek fire, 743
Jolanda, *see* Yolande
Joscelin I, count of Edessa, 317; takes Germanicea, 341; 359; 361
Joscelin II, count of Edessa, 373
Joseph, Patriarch of Constantinople, opposition to Union, 611 sq.
Joseph, Patriarch of Constantinople, at Council of Ferrara, 621; death, 623
Joseph, archbishop of Salonica, exiled, 29
Joseph Bringas, *see* Bringas
Joseph Nasi, Jewish favourite of Selīm II, receives Naxos, 468; and Cyprus, 472; 476
Joseph the hymn-writer, St, life of, 255
Joseph, the Grand Oeconomus, and marriage of Constantine VI, 28 sq.
Joshua, Byzantine illustrated MS. of, at Vatican, 768
Jubilee, Papal (1300), 448
Judaea, 157; Roman conquest of, 629
Judaism among the Chazars, 190 sq., 219
Judge of the Theme, *see* Protonotary
Juga I Coriatović, Prince of Moldavia, 593
Juga II Mouchate, Prince of Moldavia, 593
Juji, son of Jenghiz Khan, 633; death, 635
Julian, professor of law in Constantinople, collector of the *Epitome Juliani*, 707; 711
Julianus Ascalonita, Byzantine legal writer, 723
Junaid, Turkish rebel against Mahomet I, 687 sq.
Jundī-Shāpūr, Persian medical school, 297
Juraševič brothers, Montenegro chieftains, 586, 592
Jurjān, conquered by Seljūqs, 304
Justin I, Emperor, 185
Justin II, Emperor, sends convoy to Central Asia, 187; 707; Novels of, 708, 714; builds throne-room, 754
Justinian I, Emperor, laws of, *see* Chap. XXII *passim*; 24, 53, 100; and Venetia, 385; 726; 730 sqq.; army of, 738; statue of, 748; and St Sophia, 752, 754; 758; 760; 764; Byzantine art under, 768; pre-Justinian law sources, 723
Justinian II, Emperor, exiled to Cherson, 189; Armenia and, 2; 13; 157; and Bulgarians, 231; pretended son of, *see* Tiberius; buildings of, 754
"Justiniana Prima," added to archbishopric of Bulgaria, 243
Justinianus, arcade of, in Imperial Palace, 754

Καβαλλάριοι, military tenants, 773
Καβάλλινος (Stable Boy), nickname of Constantine V, 11
Kabars, Chazar tribe, join Magyars, 196
Kabul Khan, grandfather of Jenghiz, 632
Kadykei, fortress of Bulgaria, 235
Kaffa, Genoese colony on Black Sea, 549; bishop of, 614
Kaidu Khan, grandson of Ogdai, 641; rebels against Kublai, 646
Kaifā, branch of Urtuqids, 317
Kai-Kā'ūs I, 'Izz-ad-Dīn, Sultan of Rūm, 173; captures Theodore I, 485
Kai-Kā'ūs II, 'Izz-ad-Dīn, Sultan of Rūm, and Hethum I, 175; and Theodore II, 504; and Michael Palaeologus, 503 sq., 510
Kai-Khusrū I, Sultan of Rūm, and Theodore I, 479; captured and slain, 482
Kai-Khusrū II, Sultan of Rūm, and John III, 492; defeated by Mongols, 515
Kai-Qubād I, 'Alā-ad-Dīn, Sultan of Rūm, 514; and Trebizond, 515; and Ertughril, 655 sq.
Kaisariané, abbot of, 464
Kaisum in Syria, 132
Kalabaka, *see* Stagi
Kalamáta, fief of the Villehardouins, 440; 444; 449
Kālanjar, castle in India, 304
Kalávryta, capital of Constantine Palaeologus in Morea, 461; ceded to Turks, 463
Kalīlah and Dimnah, Arab stories of, 294
Kaliman I, Tsar of Bulgaria, 492; 523 sq.; 590
Kaliman II, Tsar of Bulgaria, slays Michael Asên and is himself slain, 525; 590
Kalocsa, archbishopric of, founded, 214; archbishop of, and Bosnia, 526; *see* Astrik
Kalojan (Johannitsa), Tsar of Bulgaria, 423; 481; 483; defeats Emperor Baldwin, 424, 520; ravages and death of, 425, 428, 519 sqq., 590
Kama, river of Southern Russia, 184; 192 sq.; Kama Bulgars, 184
Kambalu, *see* Cambalu
Kāmil, Arab compilation, 294
Kang-hi, Chinese Emperor, and Mongols, 649
K'ang-li, Chinese name for Patzinaks and other tribes, 198
Kankali (K'ang-li), Turkish tribe, 631
Kapan, Armeno-Cilician fortress, 68; seized by Turks, 169, 174
Kapnikon (poll tax), abolished by John I, 82
Kara Khitai, Mongol tribe, 631, 633
Karakorum, Mongol capital, 631 sqq., 638; Ogdai's palace at, 640; 645; capital transferred from, 647 sq.
Karamania, *see* Qaramān
Karamzin, Russian historian, 199
Karbalā, pilgrimages to forbidden, 288; taken by Tīmūr, 651
Karchas, Magyar title, 196 sq.
Kardam, Khan of Bulgaria, and Constantine VI, 232
Karin, in Armenia, taken by Turks, 167
Karisiya (*al-arsīya*, *al-lārisīya*), Chazar bodyguard, 190
Karkh, Magyar trading centre, 197
Karlovic, Serbian Patriarch at, 578
Karlsburg, *see* Gyulafehérvár

Kars, in Armenia, 158; taken by Saracens, 160; intellectual centre of Armenia, 162; taken by Turks, 167; taken by Mongols, 181, 636; cathedral of, 161
Karýdi, Mount (the Walnut Mountain), battle of, between Latins of Athens and Sparta, 441
Karýkes, Demetrius, Byzantine philosopher, at Smyrna, 485
Kárystos, division of Euboea, 435; taken by Licario for Michael VIII, 445; 463
Kashgar, 312, 651
Kashmir, 651
Kashshāf, famous commentary on the Koran, 291
Kasogs (Cherkesses), subdued by Russians, 207
Kastoria, Macedonian bishopric, 243
Katákolo, 438
Kathīr, Arab general, 120
Katholikos (Patriarch), of Armenia, 112; 155 sq.; position of, 159; 160; visits of, 171; 177; 180; 182; *see also* Constantine, Grigor, Joakim, John, Kirakos, Nerses, Petros, Sahak; of Iberia, 97
Kātibī, author of text-book on logic, 297
Katunska, district in Montenegro, 587
Kavala, 541 sq.; taken by Turks, 672; *see* Christopolis
Kawad (Kobad), Sasanid King of Persia, and the Chazars, 187
Kazan, 650
Keghard, Armenian church at, 163
Kem, river, *see* Kien
Kende (*Knda*), Magyar title, 196
Keraits, Mongol tribes, 631 sq.; migrate to China, 650
Keration, Byzantine coin, 4
Kerbogha (Qawwām-ad-Daulah Karbuqā), prince of Mosul, at Antioch, 316, 339
Kerch, *see* Bosphorus
Kerulen, river, 631
Kesh, in Transoxiana, birthplace of Tīmūr, 650
Ketbogha, Mongol leader, slain at 'Ain Jālūt, 643
Khabur, river, 315
Khafāja, Saracen governor of Sicily, 138
Khagan, title first assumed by chief of the Yuan-Yuan, 185; and Chazars, 186 sq.; supreme Khagan, 190; applied to prince of Kiev, 203
Khair-ad-Dīn (Barbarossa), Turkish admiral, and Naxos, 467
Khālid, lieutenant of Mahomet, 302
Khalīfah (Caliph), title of the chief of Islām, 275, 281 sq.; *see* Caliphate, Caliphs
Khalīl, called Qāra (Black), and formation of Janissaries, 663 sq.
Khalīl, son of Sultan Orkhān and Theodora, 667
Khalīl, Turkish leader, and Andronicus II, 659
Khalīl Pasha, Grand Vizier of Murād II and Mahomet II, 693, 684; counsels the abandonment of siege of Constantinople, 701
Khalkhas, central Mongols, merged in Chinese Empire, 649
Khan, of Bulgaria, 231; of the Chazars, 38; of the Mongols, 175 sq.; Jenghiz Khan, title of Temujin, 632; of Turkestan, 300
Khan Balig, *see* Cambalu
Kharput, fortress of, captured by Bardas Sclerus, 85
Khatà, the, Sultan Sanjar's war against, 312 sq.
Khātūn, *see* Turkan Khātūn
Khawinjī, author of text-book on logic, 297
Khilat, battle of, 515; town of, 636
Khitans, in Chinese Empire, 633
Khiva, *see* Khwārazm
Khrna, *see* John of
Khubilai, *see* Kublai
Khurāsān, 123 sq.; Ṭāhir appointed governor of, 276; 285; 297; 303; Seljūqs in, 304; 307; 310; Sanjar, King of, 310 sqq.; invaded by Ghuzz, 313; 633; 636
Khurramites, Arab sect, 38; 128 sq.
Khushan, Armenian general of Constantine V, 121; successes of, 122 sq.
Khusrau, Fīrūz ar-Raḥīm, Buwaihid ruler of Persia, 304
Khuṭbah, Muslim bidding prayer, 301, 304 sq., 311 sq., 651
Khūzistān, 310, 633
Khwārazm (Khiva), 190; Khwārazm Shāhs, kingdom of the, 278, 312, 314 sqq.; 298; conquered by Seljūqs, 304, 306; 311; conquered by Mongols, 629, 631, 633, 635 sq.; trade with Bulgars, 193; nationality of Sultan Quṭuz, 643; *see* Anūshtigīn, Atsiz, Jalāl-ad-Dīn, Muḥammad, Qutb-ad-Dīn
Kialing, Chinese river, 645
Kien, river (Kem, Yenisey), 187; 631
Kiersy, *see* Quierzy
Kiev, early history of, 202 sqq.; heathenism at, 208; centre of Russian trade, 193, 199; 201; treaty of, 88, 209; 240; contest for throne of, 368; destroyed by Mongols, 637; princes of, *see* Igor, Oleg, Olga, Svyatoslav, Vladímir, Yaropolk
Kilīsa-jāmi', *see* Pantokrator, *under* Constantinople, churches of
Kilīsa-jāmi' (church-mosque), at Tarsus, 179
Kin (Golden), dynasty of China, destroyed by Mongols, 629, 632 sq., 635 sq.
Kindī, Arab translator and philosopher, 295
Kinsai, *see* Lingan
Kipchaks, *see* Cumans, Golden Horde
Kirakos (Guiragos), Armenian priest, and Constantine VIII, 164
Kirakos Virapensis, Katholikos of Armenia, removes his see to Echmiadzin, 182
Kirghiz Steppes, 303
Kirmān, province of, 307; Seljūq dynasty of, 314 sq.; 633; 642
Kisā'ī, Persian grammarian, 291

Kitubuka, Mongol general, overthrows the Assassins, 641
Klath, *see* Gregory of
Kleidion, Bulgarian defeat at, 241
Κλείσουρα (mountain pass), *see* Clisurae
Κλητορολόγιον (*Notitia*), book of ceremonial, by Philotheus, 58, 256, 730
Ključ, Bosnian fortress, surrenders to Turks, 580
Klokotinitza, victory of Bulgarians at, 428, 440, 489; 491; 522
Klyuchevski, Professor V., on early Russian history, 200, 203 sq., 206
Knda, see *Kende*
Knęzĭ (ἄρχων), appointment of St Methodius as, 217
Knights, of St John, of Rhodes, *see* Hospitallers; of the Temple, *see* Templars; *see also* Teutonic Knights
Knin, battle of, 560
Kobad, *see* Kawad
Kobilić (Obilić), *see* Miloš
Kocel, Slavonic prince in Pannonia, 211; and St Methodius, 224, 226 sq.
Koitonitai, office of the, 730
Kolb, Armenian town, 158
Kolberg, bishop of, *see* Reinberg
Koloman, King of Hungary, 355 sq.; occupies Bosnia and Hum, 526
Konjica, Bosnian assembly at, 574, 583
Konung, title of Varangian chiefs, 202, 204, 206
Kopány, cousin of St Stephen of Hungary, revolts against him, 214
Koran (*Qur'ān*), and Islāmic theory, 280 sq.; and toleration, 286 sq.; doctrine of the Mu'tazilites about, 288, 301; and the study of Arabic, 290 sq.; commentaries on, 290 sq., 293; rhyme in, 294; 684
Korea, 185; Mongol expedition against, 636 sq., 640, 646; revolts against Mongols, 649
Kormisosh, Bulgarian usurper, 231 sq.
Korsun, *see* Cherson
Κόρτη, *see* Count of the Tent
Kosača, Bosnian family, 567
Kosara, daughter of Samuel of Bulgaria, 241
Koselsk (Mobalig), Mongol barbarity at, 637
Kosmidion (Eyyūb), monastery of, 512
Kossovo, 1st battle of, 550, 557 sq., 672 sqq.; 2nd battle, 562; 3rd battle (1448), 573, 584, 692 sq., 696, 702; battlefield of, 245; plain of, 554
Köstendil, in Bulgaria, *see* Velbužd; derivation of, 555
Kotromanić, *see* Stephen; extinction of dynasty, 574
Kotsho, *see* Dnieper, river
Κουβουκλεῖον, the imperial household, 730
Koúndoura, Latin victory at, 434, 436
Koupharas, Theodore, Greek monk, and Boris of Bulgaria, 236
Koutritzákes, Alexius, and the capture of Constantinople, 519
Koutzo-Wallachs, 550; *see* Wallachs
Kovrat (Kurt), Bulgarian khan, defeats Avars, 186, 188; 230 sq.
Kriviches, East Slavonic tribe, 204, 206, 209 sq.
Kroja (Āq-Hisār), Albanian fortress, ceded to John III, 494; defence of, by Skanderbeg, 584 sq., 692 sq.
Krum, Khan of the Bulgarians, wars with Byzantines, 29 sq., 37, 49, 234 sqq.; siege of Constantinople, 233
Kruševac, Serbian capital, taken by Turks, 558; 569; 571
Kuban, Russian river, 230
Kublai (Khubilai) Khan, Great Khan, Chinese Emperor, at Pekin, 629; and paper currency, 630; 637; 640; in China, 644; elected Khan, 645; reign and government, 646 sqq.; death, 649
Kuchu, son of Ogdai Khan, 640
Kuchuk Chekmejeh, village near Constantinople, 511
Kūfah, school of grammar at, 291
Kugler, on the First Crusade, 334
Kūhistān, invaded by Mongols, 641
Kulenović, Bosnian family, 518
Kulin, ban of Bosnia, 517; and Bogomiles, 518; 520; 526; 591
Kuma, river, 631
Kūmistān, *see* Comania
Kunovica, Turks defeated at, 571
Kūr, river, *see* Cyrus
Kurdistān, 128; Seljūq dynasty in, 315; 633; conquered by Tīmūr, 652
Kurds, 130; *see* Naṣr
Kuriltai, general convocation of Mongols, 632, 634 sq., 640 sq., 643, 645
Kurt, *see* Kovrat
Kurya, prince of the Patzinaks, kills Svyatoslav of Russia, 208
Kushluk, Khan of the Naimans, 631
Kutrigurs (Kuturgurs), Bulgar tribe, 185
Kuyuk, son of Ogdai, succeeds his father as Great Khan, 640; death, 641
Kuza-Dāgh, Mongol victory at, 515
Kuzu, *see* Dnieper, river
Kydónis (Cydones), Demetrius, Byzantine rhetorician, and Bulgarians, 554; 555; as theologian, 766
Kyparissià, 460
Kyuchuk Āghā, Turkish general, defeated by Trapezuntines, 656
Kyūtāhiya, 683

Labarum, imperial standard, removed from the coinage by Isaac I, 322
Lacedaemon, *see* La Crémonie
Lachanâs, nickname of Ivailo, 528
Lachanodraco, Michael, strategus of the Thracesians, and image worshippers, 16; and Saracens, 20, 123 sq.
Laconia, 434; Laconian origin of the Empress Theophano, 68
La Crémonie (Lacedaemon), residence of princes of Achaia, 437; court of William

de Villehardouin at, 441; taken by Turks, 690
"Ladies' Parliament" of Níkli, 443
Ladislas I, the Saint, King of Hungary, decree of, 197
Ladislas II, King of Hungary, and Manuel I, 372
Ladislas, King of Naples, confers duchy of Athens on Nerio Acciajuolo, 458; Bosnia and, 565; 566
Ladoga, lake, 202
Laïote Basaraba, Prince of Wallachia, 593
Laïote Basaraba, "the Young," Prince of Wallachia, 593
Lama, name first given by Mongols to Buddhist priests, 646
Lambron, Cilician fortress, 168, 170; revolts from Armenia, 174 sq.; lords of, *see* Hethum, Oshin
Lambronatsi, *see* Nerses
Lamia, memorials of Catalan rule at, 457
Lampe, 344; 378
Lampedusa, Byzantine naval victory off, 134
Lampsacus, Venetian colony at, 480; 487 sq.; 509; 660; Genoese tower at, 687
Lamus, river, 120, 131 sq.
Lancia, Galvano, relation of the Empress Constance, 496
Landolf, admiral of Alexius I, 341
Langres, bishop of, and Louis VII, 601
Laodicea, in Phrygia, 367; 480; ceded by Seljūqs to Theodore II, 504
Laodicea, in Syria, 146; Malik Shāh at, 307; captured by Crusaders, 339; by Byzantines, 341; 343
Laodicea Combusta, taken by Saracens, 123
Larissa, in Argos, 434
Larissa, in Thessaly, Samuel of Bulgaria at, 240; 242; Normans at, 329; Henry of Flanders at, 426; becomes Lombard fief, 433; 494; bishop of, *see* Achilleus, St
La Roche, Burgundian family, become lords of Athens, 422, 431, 449; *see* Guy, Othon
Lascaris, *see* Theodore I, Emperor
Lateran, St John, *see* Councils; 623
Latin Church, controversies with, *see* Roman Church; liturgy in Apulia, 266; liturgy in Bulgaria, 45, 249, 252; in Moravia, 223 sq.; and Slavonic liturgy, 226, 228; ritual in Crete, 616; relations with Armenian Church, 172 sq., 177 sqq.; Church in Syria, 599; Church in Cyprus, 469; Church in Greece, 606 sq.; Latin Patriarchs of Constantinople, 615, 617, *see* Thomas Morosini; churches in Constantinople, 113, 264, 267, 271; *see also*, Church, Councils
Latin Empire of Constantinople, Chaps. XIV, XV, XVI *passim*; conquest of Constantinople, 243, 777, *see* Constantinople; Empire and Bulgaria, 520 sqq.; and Popes, 606 sqq.; fall of, 431, 511 sq., 609; principalities in Greece, Chap. XV *passim*, 612; and Turkish invasion, 654; Latin Emperors, *see* Baldwin, Henry, John, Peter, Robert; *see also* Assises of Romania; Geoffrey de Villehardouin, seneschal of, 438
Latin language and script, influence on Glagolitic script, 225; Latin titles, 731; translations from Arabic, 297 sq.
Latin states in Syria, and Alexius I, 341 sqq.; and John II, 352 sqq., 357 sqq.; and Manuel I, 365, 370, 373 sqq.; and Armeno-Cilicia, 154, 168 sqq.; Armeno-Cilicia under Latin kings, 180 sqq.; *see also* Antioch, Crusades, Cyprus, Jerusalem
Latins, hatred of, in Constantinople, 362, 380; massacre of, 382, 414, 603; anti-Latin feeling in East, 616, 690; Latins in Byzantine service, 245, 355, 484, 507, 738, 750; Latins and Byzantine feudal system, 772; Byzantine influence on, 775; intermarriage of Byzantines and Latins, 619
Λατρεία (adoration) of images, condemned by the Council of Nicaea, 21
Latros, in Caria, monastery on, 753
Latzcou, Prince of Moldavia, 593
Laura, the, *see* Great Laura, the
Law, Byzantine, Chap. XXII; Laws of Leo III, 5, 708 sqq.; of Basil I, 52, 711 sq.; of Leo VI, 58, 713 sqq.; of Constantine VII, 66, 715; of Basil II, 92 sqq.; external influence of, 724 sq.; school of, under Constantine IX, 114, 719 sq.; law-book, translated into Bulgarian, 550; *see* Novels
Albanian "code," 585; Bulgarian code, attributed to Krum, 233; Hungarian code of St Stephen, 215; laws of Latin Empire, *see* Assises of Romania; Mongol code of Jenghiz Khan, 634; Muslim theories of law, 280 sqq., 291 sq.; Serbian code (Zakonnik) of Stephen Dušan, 547 sqq.
See also Canon Law, Roman Law
Lazar I Hrebeljanović, rules at Mačva, 553; made Prince of Serbia, 555; and Tvrtko of Bosnia, 556; and Turks, 555, 557; death of, at Kossovo, 558, 672 sq., 590
Lazar II, *see* Stephen Lazarević
Lazar III, son of George Branković, accession and reign, 570; 577; 590
Lazarus, painter of icons, 34
Lebanon, Mt, 148; Druses in, 301; Mardaites in, 742
Lebedia, original territory of the Magyars, 195, 197
Leburnium, river, Patzinaks defeated on, 330 sq.
Lecapenides, sons of Romanus I, 63 sq.; *see also* Basil, Constantine, Michael, Romanus, Stephen
Lecapenus, *see* Romanus I, Emperor
Lecce, 450; counts of, 449
Lechfeld, battle of the, 212 sq.
Lefke (Leucae), in Asia Minor, captured by Ertughril, 655; Turks defeated at, 657
Legend, of St Cyril, see *Vita Cyrilli*; *of St Methodius*, see *Vita Methodii*
Legnano, battle of, 414
Lekanomantis, nickname of John Hylilas, 40

Lek Ducagin, Albanian "code," 585
Lembos, Mt, monastery on, 498
Lemnos, Byzantine naval victory off, 143; becomes a Venetian seigniory, 421, 435, 476 sq.; retaken by Michael VIII, 445, given to Demetrius Palaeologus, 464; 465; 624
Lentianá, near Prusa, 485
Leo III, the Isaurian, Emperor, Chap. I; work of reconstruction, 1; coronation and character, 2; and Saracens, 2, 151, 119 sqq.; and Armenia, 156, 167; and Chazars, 189; domestic and economic policy, 3 sqq.; and the army, 4; promulgates *Ecloga*, 5, 708 sqq.; iconoclastic zeal, 6 sqq.; and Italy, 10, 388, 390; death, 11; 14; 30; 49; 58; 231
Leo IV, the Chazar, Emperor, 19; successes against Saracens, 123; 124; 189; and Telerig of Bulgaria, 232; Novels, 710
Leo V, the Armenian, Emperor, strategus of the Anatolics, 29 sqq.; proclaimed Emperor, 29; defeats the Bulgarians, 30, 37, 233 sq.; his iconoclastic zeal, 30 sq.; his fall and death, 32; defeats Saracens, 127; 35; 38; 132; Novels of, 710
Leo VI, Emperor (the Wise, the Philosopher), 50; parentage, 50 sq., 54; reign of, 55 sqq.; portrait of, 53; general policy, 56; marriages of, 57, 60, 91, 256 sqq., 267, 272; legislative and administrative works, 58; literary and theological works of, 59, 258; death of, 59; weakness in Asia Minor, 134, 140; loses Sicily, 141 sq.; Armenia and, 159 sq.; and the Magyars, 198; and the Russian Church, 207; and the Bulgarians, 237; and Photius, 56, 254 sq.; 262; 708; legislation of, 711, 713 sq.; 712; 720; *Book of the Prefect*, 715 sqq., 761; Novels of, 722 sqq.; and army, 741
Leo I, Prince of Armeno-Cilicia, reign and misfortunes of, 169; 358 sq.; 361; 373
Leo II, the Great, King of Armeno-Cilicia, 171; his European connexions, 172; campaigns, 173; death, 174; crowns sent him by the Eastern and Western Emperors, 172
Leo III, King of Armeno-Cilicia, 175: defeated by Mamlūks, 176
Leo IV, King of Armeno-Cilicia, 177 sq.
Leo V, King of Armeno-Cilicia, 179 sq.
Leo VI, of Lusignan, last King of Armeno-Cilicia, exile and death in Paris, 181; 470
Leo IV, Pope, and Byzantine Church, 247
Leo IX, Pope, and Michael Cerularius, 112 sq., 264 sqq., 597; death, 270; and see of Grado, 408
Leo, metropolitan of Chalcedon, and Alexius I, 332
Leo, archbishop of Ochrida, letter of, against the Latin Church, 112; 267 sq.; 270
Leo the Deacon, chronicler, 80; 238 *note*; 239 *note*; 765
Leo the Drungarius, father of SS. Methodius and Cyril, 216
Leo Melissenus, *see* Melissenus
Leo Phocas, *see* Phocas
Leo the protovestiary, 85; defeated by Bardas Sclerus, 85
Leo of Salonica, famous mathematician, 43 sq., 218
Leo of Tripolis, leader of Saracen fleet, 141; defeated off Lemnos, 142
Leo, strategus of the Armeniacs, defeated by Saracens, 127
Leo, supposed son of Romanus IV, leader of the Cumans, 330
"Leo's hill" (battle of Mesembria), 234
Leonard, archbishop of Chios, at siege of Constantinople, 695 sqq.; 702 sq.
Leonardo I Tocco, count of Cephalonia, 455; 475
Leonardo III Tocco, count of Cephalonia, 465; loses his State, 466; 475
Leontini (Lentini), in Sicily, captured by Saracens, 46, 137
Leontius, Emperor, 6
Leontius of Neapolis, Byzantine theologian, 767
Leontokomes, theme of, 733
Lepanto, castle of, 448, 453, 476; bought by Venetians, 459; 465; becomes Turkish, 467; battle of, 468; metropolitan of, 494, 497
Lepara-Lycandus, battle of, 85
Lesbos, island of, Irene exiled to, 25; 64; 109; ravaged by Venetians, 354, 371; assigned to Latin Emperor, 421; taken by Vatatzes, 428, 487; Gattilusi at, 465; birthplace of historian Ducas, 474; Genoese at, 431, 455, 511, 655; 477
"Leucadia," Duke of, title of Tocco family in Cephalonia, 455
Leucae, *see* Lefke
Leucas, *see* Santa Mavra
Leunclavius, 677 *note*, 688 *note*, 691 *note*
Levant, the, 168; Venetians in, 395 sq., 410 sq., 416, 421, 431 sq.; Chap. XV *passim*; 677
Liau Tung, Mongols expelled from, 649
Libanius, 763
Libellus de conversione Bagoariorum et Carantanorum, polemic against Methodius, 222, 227
Libellus satisfactionis, against Photius, 252 sq.
Liburnia, restored to Byzantium, 395
Licario, lord high admiral of Michael VIII, triumphant career of, in Aegean, 445; 467
Lichudes, Constantine, *see* Constantine
Liegnitz, Mongol victory at, 637, 639
Limitanei (τὰ ἀκριτικὰ θέματα), frontier troops of the Empire, 740
Lingan (Hangchow, Kinsai), chief town of South China, 633
Liosa, Albanian clan, 552
Liparid, King of Iberia, captured by Seljūqs, 166
Lithosoria, battle of, 13, 232

Little Russians, *see* Ukrainians
Little St Sophia, *see* SS. Sergius and Bacchus *under* Constantinople, churches of
Liudprand, bishop of Cremona, envoy of Berengar II, 66; of Otto I, 76 sq., 260 sq.
Liutpold, duke of Bavaria, and the Magyars, 212
Liutprand, King of the Lombards, and Venice, 387 sqq., 396, 398
Livadia, captured by Navarrese, 456; Catalan memorials at, 457; 458
Logothete, Grand (*Logothete of the Dromos*), office of, 731
Logothete of the Public Treasury (τοῦ γενικοῦ, *logothete-general*), office of, 731
Logothete of the Military Chest (τοῦ στρατιωτικοῦ), office of, 731
Logothete of the Flocks (τῶν ἀγέλων), office of, 731
Λογοθέτης τῶν οἰκειακῶν, Venetians placed under jurisdiction of, 405
Lombards, and Emperor Leo III, 9 sq.; attack Rome, 17 sq.; 22; 112; 266; invade Venetia, 385; Venice and, 387 sqq.; defeated by Franks, 391 sq.; "Lombard" Crusade, 340 sq.; League of, against Frederick I, 412 sq., 602; 421; nobles in Salonica, 426; in Euboea, 435, 441, 445; imperialist party in Cyprus, known as, 469; in Byzantine service, 595, 738; influence on Byzantine law, 717; kings of, *see* Aistulf, Desiderius, Liutprand; *see also* Adelchis
Lombardy, Magyars in, 211; trade route to, 396
London, Armenian embassy sent to, 181; papal register at, 226 sq.; Peter of Cyprus at, 470; Manuel II at, 618
Longobardia, theme of, 733; threatened by Saracens, 403, 405 sq.; *see* Argyrus
Loos, *see* Thierri de
Lopadium, taken by Turks, 344; rising at, 383; taken by Latins, 424, 481, 485, 689
Loredan, Venetian admiral, defeats Turks, 687; and siege of Constantinople, 700 sq.
Loreo, revolts against Venice, 404 sq.
Loria, Roger, admiral of Aragon, raid of, on the Morea, 447
Loritello, *see* Robert of
Lorraine, duke of, *see* Godfrey; Frederick of, *see* Stephen IX, Pope
Lothar I, Emperor of the West, and Venetians, 398 sq., 401
Lothar II, King of Lorraine, 249
Lothar III, Emperor of the West, and John II, 358; 360; and Venetians, 412
Louis the Pious, Emperor of the West, correspondence with Michael II, 34; Theophilus and, 38, 203; and the Bulgarians, 234
Louis II, Emperor of the West, intervenes in South Italy, 139; and Photius, 249; and Council of Constantinople, 252
Louis II, the German, King of Germany, 197; and Moravia, 221, 227; 235
Louis VII, King of France, and Manuel I, 366 sqq.; 379, 600 sqq.
Louis IX (St Louis), King of France, buys relics from Latin Emperor, 429; William of Achaia and, 441; and Manuel of Trebizond, 515; and Michael VIII, 610; mission to Mongols, 640
Louis the Great, King of Hungary, and Bosnia, 545, 556; and Gregory XI, 618; 670 sq.
Louis I, Duke of Savoy, claimant to kingdom of Armenia, 181
Louis of Savoy, husband of Queen Charlotte of Cyprus, 471
Louis of Blois, and Chartres, made Duke of Nicaea, 422, 480; killed at Hadrianople, 481, 520; 516
Louis, Duke of Burgundy, marries Matilda of Hainault, and becomes Prince of Achaia, 452, 474
Lovat', Russian river, 202
Lucas Notaras, *see* Notaras
Luchaire, on Fourth Crusade, 415, 417
Lucian, 763
Lulum, Cilician fortress, annexed by Saracens, 120; 128; and Michael III, 133; ceded to Bohemond of Antioch, 343
Luparkos (Rhyndakos), river, defeat of Theodore I on, 426, 485; 689
Lupus, duke of Friuli, raids Grado, 387
Lupus, Patriarch of Aquileia, and Venice, 401
Lusignan family, rule of, in Cilicia, 154; 180 sqq.; in Cyprus, 468 sq., 172, 432; *see* Amaury, Guy, Henry, Hugh, Isabel, John, Leo, Peter
Lycandus, theme of, 733 sq.
Lycaonia, Mongols in, 689
Lycaonian desert, the, 125
Lycia, 131; 150; 670; independent of Ottomans, 684; Hospitallers in, 687
Lycus, valley, outside Constantinople, defences of, 696 sqq., 701 sq.; 749
Lydia, 126; 657
Lyons, Councils of, *see* Councils
Lyubech, Russian trading centre, 202, 204

Macaire of St Menehould, defeated in Asia Minor, 428; occupies Nicomedia, 481, 483
Macedo-Bulgarian dialect (Slovenian), basis of Glagolitic Script, 225
Macedonia, Slav risings in, 13, 20; Bulgarians and, 37, 39, 232, 235, 238, 240 sq.; 47; 49; 111; 217; Normans in, 245; Patzinaks invade, 354; assigned to Boniface of Montferrat, 422, 432; 427; 430; 442; Catalans in, 450; retaken by John III, 492, 494, 524; occupied by Michael of Epirus, 505; 519; 522; Serbians in, 532, 534, 538, 540; 541 sq.; 549; 553; Turks in, 555, 560, 568, 672, 674, 678; theme of, 133, 733, 737; sees in, 95, 243; churches in, and Byzantine Art, 769; manuscripts in, 499
Macedonian dynasty, Chaps. III, IV; founded,

50; 64; 69; 82; 96 sq.; 106; extinction of, 115, 118, 319; 259; 714 sq.; 728; renaissance under, 765, 769 sq., 777
Machiavelli family at Athens, 461
Macrembolitissa, *see* Eudocia
Mačva, banat of, governed by Rostislav, 526; by Stephen Dragutin, 532; taken by Stephen Uroš II, 534 sq.; 553; 591
"Mad Theodore," *see* Mankaphas
Madytus, 323; taken by John III, 428
Maeander, river, 134; valley of the, 353 sq.; 378; Seljūqs defeated on, 427; 428; 480
Magida, fortress of, taken by Saracens, 124, 128
Magister, title of, 730
Magister Militum, office in Venice, 390; in Oderzo, 387; in Istria, 389
Magnesia, 498 sq.; legend of John III at, 500; 508; 512; Turks at, 655; Michael IX at, 656; emir of, 662, 667; 692 sq.
Magyars, 194 sqq.; 198; migrate to Hungary, 199; 200; 202 sq.; 208; in Hungary, 210 sqq,; Italian raids of, 211, 400; Byzantines and, 140, 212; and Bulgarians, 234, 237 sq.; defeated at the Lechfeld, 212; kingdom organized by St Stephen, 215; manner of fighting, 212; language, 195, *see also* Hungarians
Mahbūb, Arab chronicler, 120 *note*
Mahdī, Abbasid Caliph, expedition against Leo IV, 123; 289
Mahdī, the, 'Ubaid-Allāh, the first Fātimid Caliph, claims to be, 302; 'Abdallah ibn Tūmart claims to be, 306
Maḥmūd, Ghaznawid Sultan, in India, 303; and Seljūqs, 304 sq.
Maḥmūd, son of Malik Shāh, 308; wars with his brother, 309; 310
Maḥmūd, Seljūq Sultan of 'Irāq, son of the Great Seljūq Muḥammad, dispossessed by Sanjar, 311; 315
Maḥmūdīye mosque, *see under* Constantinople
Mahomet, *see also* Muḥammad
Mahomet (Muḥammad), the Prophet, 275, 280 sq., 286; tribe of, 281; and religious tolerance, 287 sq.; biographies of, 293; 301 sq.; 641 sq.; 679
Mahomet I (the Gentleman), Ottoman Sultan, and Serbians, 563 sq.; and Bosnia, 566; and Wallachia, 567; conquers his brother and becomes Sultan, 686; reign and character of, 687 sq.; 593
Mahomet II, Ottoman Sultan, accession, 692 sq.; and Armenians, 182; in Greece, 463 sq.; and Chios, 468; and Serbia, 575 sq., 578; besieges Belgrade, 576; 577; Bosnia and, 579 sqq.; and Catholics in Bosnia, 583; and Albania, 584 sq.; and Moldavia, 587; 593; 624; and Byzantine Church, 625; 694; besieges and captures Constantinople, 696 sqq.; character of, 705
Mahomet, Aghlabid emir of Africa, 137
Mahomet, emir of Qaramān, 684
Mahomet ibn Gumishtigīn, Dānishmandite ruler in Cappadocia, 315
Mahomet, son of Malik Ghāzī, Dānishmandite ruler, 357, 360; 365
Mahomet, Dānishmandite prince, son of Dhū'l-Qarnain, 377
Mahomet, Saracen general in Sicily, cousin of the emir of Africa, 134, 136
Mahomet ibn Abī'l-Jawārī, Saracen general in Sicily, 135
Mahomet ibn Mu'āwiyah, Saracen general, 125
Mai, Cardinal Angelo, 719
Maimundiz, fort of the "Assassins," 641
Maina, district in Greece, 441; surrendered to Michael VIII, 443; and Manuel II, 460; Venetian colony, 476; 737
Majghariyah, Majghariyan, *see* Μεγέρη
Majorca, *see* Ferdinand, James
Majúsí, al-, Arab medical writer, 298
Makīn, Arab chronicler, 188
Makroliváda, Thracian frontier fortress, 37, 234
Makryplági, battle of, 444
Malacopea, taken by Saracens, 126
Malagina, attacked by Saracens, 126, 131
Malāḥidah, name of Assassins, *q.v.*
Malalas, John, Byzantine chronicler, 765; chronicle of, translated into Bulgarian, 237
Malamocco, foundation of, 386; 388; 390; made seat of Venetian government, 391 sq.; 393; taken by Pepin, 394; bishopric of, 387; bishop of, *see* Felix
Malatīyah, *see* Melitene
Maleinus family, 93
Maleinus, Eustathius, commander against Sclerus, 86; disgraced by Basil II, 93
Malik, Arab leader, killed in Phrygia, 121
Malik Ghāzī (Ghāzī), Dānishmandite emir, defeats Crusaders, 340 sq.; 342; 353 sq.; 357
Malik, Seljūq prince, failure before Trebizond, 514 sq.
Malik Shāh, Great Seljūq Sultan, conquers Transoxiana, 277; 278; 298 sq.; 306; succeeds his father, 307; empire of, 307 sq.; death, 309; 311 sq.; 314; 316 sq.; and Alexius I, 329, 331; 343; 633
Malik Shāh, Seljūq, son of Barkiyāruq, dispossessed by his uncle, 310
Malik Shāh, Seljūq Sultan of Rūm, son of Qilij Arslān, 343
Mallu Khān, Delhi general, defeated by Tīmūr, 651
Malomir, *see* Presiam
Malta, occupied by Saracens, 139
Māltepe, 700
Mamikonians, Armenian family, 157 sqq.
Mamistra, *see* Mopsuestia
Mamlūks of Egypt, and Armenia, 154, 175, 177 sq., 180 sqq., 669; and Mongols, 176, 279, 628, 643, 652; 314; massacre of, at Cyprus, 471; 642
Mamonâs, archon of Monemvasia, 440

Ma'mūn, Abbasid Caliph of Baghdad, campaigns against Byzantines, 127 sq.; Thomas the Slavonian and, 35, 127; death, 38, 129; and Manichaeans, 287; revenue of, 151 *note*; translation bureau of, 298; 275 sq.; 288; 300
Manalugh, Turkish emir, and Alexius I, 344
Manasses, Constantine, Byzantine scholar, 363; Slav translations of his *Chronicle*, 549; verses against the "Powerful," 708
Manassia, monastery in Serbia, 563
Manbij (Hierapolis), 144; Christian relic at, 145
Manchuria, 185
Manchus, become supreme in China, 649
Mandaeans, and Islām, 287
Μανδήλιον, Μανδίλιον, τὸ, see Edessa, image of,
Manegold, count, ambassador of Conrad II, 97
Manfred, King of Sicily, and Michael II of Epirus, 430, 442, 508; 446; 448; 495 sq.; 608; designs on Constantinople, 609; 475 sq.
Mangana, *see* St George of *under* Constantinople; John VI retires to, 666; arsenal at, 741
Mangu Khan, Mongol Great Khan, and Hethum I, 175, 638 *note*; 631; 640; reign of, 641; death, 643, 645; 644; 646
Mangū Tīmūr, Mongol general, defeated by Mamlūks, 176
Maniaces, George, Byzantine general, and Michael V, 105; made general in the West, 108; revolt and death, 110; 111; campaigns in East and in Sicily, 150
Manichaeans, 42; and Islām, 287 sq.; colony in Philippopolis, 330, 344; in Nicene Empire, 498; *see* Bogomile, Paulicians
Manicophagus, betrays Amorium to Saracens, 130
Mankaphas ("Mad Theodore"), founds lordship at Philadelphia, 423, 480; 481; conquered by Theodore I, 482
Manoláda, battle of, 452
Mansūr, Abbasid Caliph, 122 sq.; founds Baghdad, 274, 298, 641
Mantua, pact of, between Western Emperor and Venetians, 400; synod of, 407
Manuel I Comnenus, Emperor, 351; 356; 361; accession and character, 362 sq.; administration, 364; and Seljūqs, 365, 377 sq.; and Second Crusade, 366 sqq., 601; and Roger II of Sicily, 368; and Italy, 369 sqq.; and Hungarians, 372; and Serbs, 373; and Armeno-Cilicia, 373, 170; and Antioch, 374 sq.; marriages of, 360, 375; and Amaury of Jerusalem, 376; defeated at Myriocephalum, 378; and Venetians, 412 sq.; and Papacy, 345, 596, 602 sq.; death, 379; 380 sq.; and coinage, 348; ambitions of, 626; Novels of, 720, 723
Manuel II Palaeologus, Emperor, and the Morea, 460; 617; visit to the West, 618; 678; attitude to Union, 619; 670; 672; 675; and Bāyazīd, 677; and Sulaimān, 685; and Mūsà, 686; and Mahomet I, 687; 689; 593
Manuel I, Emperor of Trebizond, 515 sq.
Manuel III, Emperor of Trebizond, and Bāyazīd I, 674
Manuel Angelus, Emperor of Thessalonica, despot of Epirus, 428; deposed, 429; 440; and John III, 491; 497; 522; and Gregory IX, 607; 475 sq.
Manuel Cantacuzene, made despot of the Morea, 454
Manuel Mamikonian, Armenian general, 157
Manuel, strategus of the Anatolics, and Saracens, 127 sq., 130
Manuel, the magister, uncle of Empress Theodora, 40
Manuel, Byzantine admiral, 147
Manuel monastery, the, 91, 261
Manzikert, besieged by Turks, 166; battle of, 167, 306, 325, 348, 378
Maona, *see* Giustiniani
Maqāmah, *Maqāmāt*, Arabic rhymed prose, 294
Maqdīsī, Arab traveller, 295
Maqrīzī, Arab geographer, on treaty of Constantine VIII and Zāhir, 97
Maraclea (Maraqīyah), on the Syrian coast, 146; 339; restored to the Empire, 343
Mar'ash, *see* Germanicea
Marcellae, battle of, 12
Marcellus, magister militum, in Venice, 389
Marcellus Tegalianus, doge of Venice, 389; made *Hypatos* by the Emperor, 390
Marco Polo, on Mongols, 631; 640; on Cambalu, 647
Marco I Sanudo, founds duchy of the Archipelago, 435 sq., 439; and Theodore I, 485; 475
Marco II, Duke of the Archipelago, 475
Marcus Eugenicus, *see* Mark of Ephesus
Mardaites, of Mt Lebanon, 742
Mārdīn, Jacobite bishop of, and Caliph Hārūn, 289
Margaret of Hungary, widow of Isaac II, marries Boniface of Montferrat, 421; regent of Thessalonica, 426
Marghah, astronomical observatory at, 299
Maria, the Paphlagonian, first wife of Constantine VI, 22 sq.
Maria, first wife of Basil I, 50 sq.
Maria, first wife of John I, 78
Maria, wife of Michael VII, and Nicephorus III, 326; and Alexius I, 327 sq., 333
Maria de Courtenay, wife of Theodore I, 486
Maria, Tsaritsa of Bulgaria, widow of John Vladislav of Bulgaria, Basil II and, 242 sqq.
Maria, Tsaritsa of Bulgaria, niece of Michael VIII, 527 sq.; marries Ivailo, 529; 530 sq.
Maria Argyrus, sister of Romanus III, married to John Orseolo, 94, 406
Maria, daughter of Alexius I, 346
Maria, granddaughter of John III, 494

Maria Lazarević, married to Bāyazīd I, 559, 562, 674
Maria, daughter of George Branković, married to Murād II, 568 sq.; Mahomet II and, 575, 577
Maria, daughter of Lazar III, wife of Stephen Tomašević, 577 sq.; 581
Maria, heiress of Frederick III of Sicily, and Athens, 455 sq.
Maria Zaccaria of Achaia, 474
Maria Angelina, of Epirus, 475
Mariam of Iberia, visits Constantinople, 100
Mariam, sister of Hethum II of Armeno-Cilicia, 178
Marianus, prefect of Constantinople, proclaims Basil I, 51
Māridīn, Urtuqids of, 317
Marie de Bourbon, Princess of Achaia, 474, 476
Marie d'Enghien, sells Argos and Nauplia to Venetians, 457
Marino Dandolo, lord of Andros, 435
Marino Sanudo, 511 *note*
Marinus, Papal legate (later Pope), and Photian schism, 250, 254
Marinus, count of Comacchio, 399
Marinus, joint-compiler of the *Ecloga*, 709
Maritime Code (*νόμος ναυτικός*) of Leo III, 5; 708; 710
Maritime theme, divided by Leo III, 3, 742; *see* Carabisiani
Maritime-Venice, *see* Venice
Maritza, river, 241; 489; 492; 509; Turkish victory on, 555, 670, 672 sq.; 671
Marj-as-Suffar, Mongol defeat at, 651 sq.
Mark (Marcus Eugenicus), archbishop of Ephesus, theologian, opposition to Union, 595, 621 sqq.; banished to Lemnos, 624; death, 624; 766
Mark, metropolitan of Caesarea, murdered by Gagik II of Armenia, 166
Mark, St, body of, brought to Venice, 396 sq.
Marko, son of Vukašin, and Turks, 555; death at Rovine, 561
Marmora, Sea of, 323; 331; 382; 421; 462; 478; 480; 490; Turkish pirates in, 657; 658 sqq.; 665 sq.; Boucicaut on, 683; 685; Ottoman defeat in, 686; 677; 687; 695 sq.; walls of Constantinople on, 697 sq.; 701; 747; 754 sq.; 762; island of, 482
Maronites, the, and Eugenius IV, 623
Maros, Hungarian river, 215
Marozia, senatrix, 259
Marquart, on town of Itil, 191; on Burdas River, 192; 212
Marriage in Byzantine law, 708 sq., 712, 720, 723
Martin IV, Pope, and Michael VIII, 613
Martin V, Pope, and Manuel II, 619; 620
Martin, abbot of Pairis in Germany, preaches Fourth Crusade, 415
Martorana church, mosaics at, 777
Marturius, Patriarch of Grado, *see* Peter
Martyropolis (Mayyāfarīqīn), 134; taken by Curcuas, 143; 147
Marwān II, Umayyad Caliph, 120, 122; governor of Armenia, 156 sq.
Mary of Antioch, second wife of Manuel, 375; regency of, 379 sqq.; murdered by Andronicus, 382; 757
Mary, granddaughter of Romanus I, marriage to Peter of Bulgaria, 62, 238
Mary, mother of Michael V, 104
Mary, daughter of Manuel I, 370 sqq.; married to Renier of Montferrat, 379; intrigues against Empress Mary, 380
Mary, daughter of Emperor Andronicus I, 382
Mary, daughter of Uroš of Rascia, 356
Mary of Gorigos, regent of Armeno-Cilicia, 181
Mary, mother of SS. Methodius and Cyril, 216
Marzpans, Persian governors of Armenia, 155
Marzpetuni, Gêorg, Armenian leader, 161
Maslamah (Maslama), Arab general, defeated before Constantinople, 2, 119; 120 sq.
Mastalici, Venetian noble family, 397
Mastropiers, Orio, doge of Venice, invades Empire, 414
Mas'ūd I, Sultan of Rūm, and John II, 353; at Constantinople, 357; and Manuel, 365; 373 sq.; 377; and Armeno-Cilicia, 170 sq.
Mas'ūd ibn Maḥmūd, Sultān of Ghaznah, 299, 304
Mas'ūdī, Arab writer, journeys and universal history of, 295; on Chazar bodyguard 190; on town of Itil, 191; on Burdas tribe, 192; on Walinana, 200; on Magyars in Thrace, 212
Matilda, Countess of Tuscany, 410
Matilda, of Hainault, widow of Guy II and Princess of Achaia, her marriages and misfortunes, 452, 474
Matteo Orsini, the Apulian, Lord of Cephalonia and Zante, 432; and Venetians, 434; and Achaia, 439, 475
Matthew of Edessa, Armenian chronicler, John I's letter preserved by, 148; on numbers of Turks, 655
Matthew Ninoslav, ban of Bosnia, 526, 591
Matthew Paris, chronicler, 490 *note*, 493 *note*; on Tartars, 630 *note*, 638 *note*, 639
Matthias Corvinus, King of Hungary, 578; in Bosnia, 581
Maurice, Emperor, 707
Mauritius, doge of Venice, 392
Mauritius, the Younger, son of John, murders Patriarch of Grado, 393
Mauro family, 264
Maurocastrum (Afyon-Qara-Hisār), Phrygian fortress, 655
Mauropotamus, river, Byzantine defeat on, 131, 133 *note*
Mauropus, John, learning of, 114; drafts Novel founding school of law, 719
Maurus, bishop, settles in Torcello, 386

Mavrozómes, holds lordship in Asia Minor, 480; and Theodore I, 482
Mā-warā-an-Nahr, *see* Transoxiana
Mayence, archbishop of, *see* Christian, Conrad
Mayyāfarīqīn, *see* Martyropolis
Māzandarān, ruled by Ghīyāth-ad-Dīn, 636
Mázares, Byzantine satirist, on the Moreotes, 460
Mazzara, in Sicily, 135
Mecca, plundered by Carmathians, 276, 286; 312, 641
Media, 310, *see* 'Irāq Ajamī
Medici family, at Athens, 461; 620
Medicine, Arab, 297 sq.; at Constantinople, 764
Medina, 280 sq.; 641
Meditatio de nudis pactis, eleventh century Byzantine legal monograph, 721
Mediterranean Sea, Saracen activity in, 37, 144 sq., 274; 277; 302; Venice in, 409 sq.; 473; Norman plan of Mediterranean Empire, 596; Turkish pirates in, 662; 741; Byzantine fleet in, 742, 762; ports of, 286, 770; 776
Medzabaro, *see* John
Medzoph, *see* Thomas of
Meerut, taken by Tīmūr, 651
Megara, 441; 464
Megaskyr, the, of Athens, and Latin Emperor, 426; Othon de la Roche becomes, 433
Μεγέρη (Majghariyah, Majghariyan), eponymous Magyar tribe, 196
Melas, river, Byzantine defeat on, 122; 131 *note*
Melchi, *see* Mleh
Meleona, Balkan hills, 233
Melfi, treaty of, 273 *note*, 597
Melisseni, family of, 771
Melissenus, Leo, plots against Basil II, 86; 87 sq.
Melissenus, Nicephorus, rival of Alexius I, 327
Melitene (Malatīyah), captured by Constantine V, 12; 85; 87; in Saracen wars, 120 sqq., 127, 129 sq., 134, 139; captured by Curcuas, 143; 147; 218; attacked by Seljūqs, 322; ruled by Seljūqs, 315, 325, 357, 365; taken by Tīmūr, 680; emirs of, *see* Omar, Ṭughril Arslān
Melkê, Queen of Armenia, MSS. Gospel of, 162
Melnik, in Macedonia, taken by John III, 430, 492; 493; delivered by Theodore II, 502 sq.; 522
Memmo, *see* Tribunus Menius
Menander, Byzantine historian, 765
Menologium, of Basil II, 95, 769
Merkits, Mongol tribe, 631
Merseburg, Byzantine embassy at, 358
Merv, Mas'ūd defeated by Seljūqs at, 304; 312; plundered by Ghuzz, 313; destroyed by Mongols, 633
Mesarites, *see* Nicholas
Mese, *see under* Constantinople
Mesembria, battle of, 30; Leo V's victory at, 37, 234; 230; 233; 525; 527
Mesimerius, Basil, envoy of Alexius I to Pope Paschal II, 345
Mesopotamia, 74; 120 sq.; 123 sq.; 127; 132; Nicephorus II in, 134; 143; 147; 150; Seljūqs in, 164, 277 sq., 302, 317; 176; 201; ravaged by Carmathians, 276; Mongols in, 279, 636, 640, 643, 654; Turkish tribes in, 653, 655; Roman Law in, 292; theme of, 84, 733; emirs of, *see* 'Abd-al-Malik, 'Abd-al-Wahhāb, Abū-Sa'īd; ostikan of, *see* Aḥmad
Messalians, Armenian sect, 7
Messenia, 433 sq., 456, 609
Messina, captured by Saracens, 46, 136; recaptured by Maniaces, 150; 603
Metaphrastes, Simeon, Byzantine author, 95, 766
Meteorion, in the Hermus valley, 512
Metéoron, monastery of, 552; church at, 553
Methodius, Byzantine artist, and Boris of Bulgaria, 236
Methodius, messenger of Paschal I, imprisoned by Michael II, 33; made Patriarch, 41; relations with Roman Church, 246; 247; 255
Methodius, St, "Apostle of the Slavs," Chap. VII (B); and Chazars, 44; 197; made archbishop of Pannonia, 211; 236 sq.; at Rome, 224, 250; death, 229; 776
Methone, *see* Modon; *see also* Nicholas of
Methymna, 79
Metochites, Theodore, panegyric of, on Nicaea, 506, 479 *note*
Metrophanes, bishop of Cyzicus, elected Patriarch of Constantinople, 623
Michael I Rangabé, Emperor, reign of, 29; 35; defeated by the Bulgars, 37, 233; 46; Sicily and, 134; 247
Michael II (the Stammerer, the Amorian), Emperor, plots against Leo V and seizes the throne, 32; his religious policy, 33; 34; war against Thomas the Slavonian, 35 sq., 235; 41; and Saracens, 127; 128; Venice and, 396
Michael III (the Drunkard), Emperor, character of, 43; minority of, 40 sqq.; reign of, 43 sqq.; murder of, 48, 50, 251; 49; wasteful finance of, 51; 54; burial by Leo VI, 55; 66; 96; Saracens and, 131, 133 sq.; 203; and St Methodius, 217 sq., 220 sqq.; and Bulgaria, 235 sqq.; and Nicholas I, 249 sq.; 254
Michael IV, the Paphlagonian, marriage to Zoë and accession, 101; character of, 102; 103 sq.; abdication and death, 104; exiles Cerularius, 112; attempts to recapture Sicily, 150; 164; and Bulgarian rising, 244; 265; 319
Michael V Calaphates, 103; parentage and accession, 104; crowned, 105; disgraces John the Orphanotrophos, 105; exiles

Zoë, 106; fall and punishment, 107, 110; attacks Armenia, 165; 318
Michael VI Stratioticus, proclaimed Emperor, 116; army revolts against him, 117, 319 sq.; fall and death of, 118, 321; Novel of, 720
Michael VII Ducas, Emperor, 325 sqq.; and the Normans, 329; 346; 408; and the Papacy, 596, 598; Novels of, 720 sqq.; and canon law, 723
Michael VIII Palaeologus, Emperor, 493; 496; and Theodore II, 503 sqq.; crowned as despot, 507; as Emperor, 430, 508; first attempt on Constantinople, 509; captures it, 431, 443, 512 sqq.; crowned at Constantinople, 513; and William of Achaia, 442 sqq.; successes over Latins, 445; Genoese and, 431, 510; and Bulgaria, 525, 527 sq.; and Turks, 656 sq.; and Papacy, 596, 609 sqq., 626; death, 532, 613; coins of, 514; Novel of, 720; 94; 593
Michael IX Palaeologus, Emperor, at Magnesia, 656 sq.; death, 659; 593; marries sister of Hethum II, 178
Michael I Angelus Comnenus, founds "Despotat" in Epirus, 423, 427, 436; 475
Michael II Angelus, despot of Epirus, 429 sq.; and William of Achaia, 440; 442; death, 444; 493; and John III, 494 sq.; and Theodore II, 503 sqq.; and Michael VIII, 508; 524; 475
Michael, name taken at his baptism by Boris of Bulgaria, *q.v.*
Michael Asên, Tsar of Bulgaria, assassinated, 430, 502, 525; 492; and Theodore II, 501 sq., 524 sq.
Michael Shishmanich, of Vidin, becomes Tsar of Bulgaria, 536; killed at Velbužd, 538, 590
Michael, King of Dioclea, and Bulgarians, 244
Michael I, Prince of Wallachia, 593
Michael Cerularius, Patriarch of Constantinople, 91, 103; conspires against Michael IV, 104; minister of Constantine IX, 109; made Patriarch, 110, 112, 265; breach with the Western Church, 112 sqq., 265 sqq., 271 sq.; learning of, 114; 115 sq.; revolts against Michael VI, 117 sq., 319 sqq.; crowns Isaac I, 118, 322; imprisonment and death, 323; character, 265, 324; 594; 597; 753
Michael Anchialus, Patriarch of Constantinople, and Manuel I, 602; 724
Michael Acominatus, metropolitan of Athens, retires before Latins, 433; 482 *note*; Theodore I and, 484, 486; sermons of, 766
Michael, son of Romanus I, 64
Michael Burtzes, *see* Burtzes
Michael, son of Simeon of Bulgaria, 238
Michael Asên, son of Constantine Asên and Maria, 531, 590
Michael Konstantinović, and Turkish conquest of Bosnia, 579
Michael Attaliates, historian, 765; on Michael V, 106; teaches in the University, 114; on Isaac I and Cerularius, 323; law treatise of, 715, 722
Michael of Thessalonica, heretical priest, condemned by Manuel, 363
Michiel, Domenico, doge of Venice, and Emperor John II, 354, 410
Michiel, Vitale, doge of Venice, in the First Crusade, 410
Michieli, dynasty in the Aegean, 467
Mīkā'īl, son of Seljūq, 303
Milan, and Manuel I, 370; Manuel II at, 618; duke of, and Galata, 697; archbishop of, *see* Arnulf, Peter Chrysolanus
Milazzo, *see* Mylae
Milengi, Slav tribe in Greece, 42
Mileševo, monastery in Novibazar, 522, 556
Miletus, *see* Isidore of
Milica, widow of Lazar I of Serbia, 558
Military Code (*νόμος στρατιωτικός*), 4; 708; 710
Millicent of Tripolis, 375
Miloš Kobilić (Obilić), Serbian noble, stabs Murād II, 558, 672
Milutin, "child of grace," *see* Stephen Uroš II
Mineo, Byzantine defeat at, 37; 135
Ming, dynasty of China, replaces Mongols, 635, 649
Minorites, *see* Franciscans
Mīrān Shāh, son of Tīmūr, 182
Mirčea, the Great, Prince of Wallachia, 557; tributary to Turks, 560; 561 sq.; death, 567, 572; 593
Mirdāsid emirs, *see* Shibl-ad-daulah
Mirdites, in Albania, and memory of Skanderbeg, 585; autonomous, 587
Miroslav, prince of Hum, 517; 591
Mistrá, near Sparta, castle of, 441; surrendered to Michael VIII, 443; 444 sq.; called Sparta in the Middle Ages, 454; 458; 460 sqq.; surrenders to Turks, 464; palace of, 473; learning at, 474; frescoes in, 769; despots of, *see* Theodore Palaeologus
Mitrovica, 539
Mitylene, 108; 110; Genoese in, 684; metropolitan of, absolves Theodore II, 506
Mladen Šubić, ban of Bosnia, 591
Mleh (Melchi), the Armenian, Byzantine commander against Saracens, 147
Mleh, King of Armeno-Cilicia, 170 sq., 376
"Mobalig" (town of woe), name applied to Koselsk, 637
Modica, Sicilian fortress, taken by Saracens, 136; 137
Modon (Methone), ravaged by Venetians, 354; becomes Venetian, 421, 431, 434, 476; 433; Hospitallers at, 437; 438; 453; 457; 461; 465; becomes Turkish, 467, 675, 690
Modrina, victory of Constantine V at, 12
Moechian controversy, 28
Moesia, 230

Moglena, temporary capital of Samuel of Bulgaria, 240; captured by Normans, 329
Mogul dynasty in India, 629 sq.; 650; 652
Mohi, Hungarians defeated by Mongols at, 637
Moldavia, Magyars in, 198; foundation of principality of, 540; 567; and Turks, 587 sq.; Table of rulers, 593; Church in, 568
Moldo-Wallachia, Patriarch of, independence of, 595; delegates at Ferrara, 621
Momchilo, Bulgarian guerrilla leader, 542
Monasticism, Byzantine, danger from, to the Empire, 8; zeal for images, 8, 21; Constantine V and, 15; and Nicephorus I, 28; and Leo V, 30 sq.; Nicephorus II and, 74; Basil II and, 89; Michael IV's favour to, 102; Photius, and the Azymites, 267; Alexius I and monastic system, 349; Manuel I and the monasteries, 364; reformation under Theodore of Studion, 26; monastic property treated as fiefs, 349; influence of, in Byzantine life, 751, 753 sq.; monks and the Roman Church, 247, 259, 270; opposition to Union, 614; Byzantine monks in Italy, 258, 737
Monasteries in Armenia, 162 sq.; in Cilicia, 168, 182; monasticism in Bulgaria, 548; Benedictines in Hungary, 214; Western monks in Greece, 438; *see also* Athos (Mt), Studion
Monastir, Macedonian bishopric, 243; 493; 672
Monastras, general of Alexius I, 341, 344
Monegarius, Dominicus, doge of Venice, reign and deposition of, 392
Monemvasía, Greek fortress, 434; taken by Villehardouin, 440; given up to Michael VIII, 443; 445; resists Turks and becomes Venetian, 464 sq.; captured by Turks, 467; art at, 473; birthplace of Phrantzes, 474, 476
Mongolia, 185, 631, 634; Mongolian Turks, 303
Mongols, the, Chap. xx; alliance with Armeno-Cilicia, 175 sqq.; defeated by Mamlūks, 176, 279, 643; 177, 179; destroy Bulgary, 193; invade Armenia under Tīmūr, 181 sq.; conquests of Jenghiz Khān, 279, 300, 302, 312, 429, 632 sqq., 653; Cumans and, 490; and Seljūqs, 315, 491 sq., 504, 510, 515; and Innocent IV, 493, 499; and Theodore II, 505; 507; 514; invade Hungary, 608; early history of, 627 sq.; derivation of, 630; in Europe, 637 sqq.; conquer Baghdad, 279, 642; accept civilisation, 647 sq.; driven from China, 649; patronage of astronomy, 298 sq., 646; language, 195; Great Khans of, *see* Jenghiz Khan, Kublai, Kuyuk, Mangu, Ogdai
Monnier, on Tiberius II's economic measures, 708; on the *Synopsis Legum*, 721
Monobatae, monastery of, 105
Monomachus, *see* Constantine IX, Vladímir
Monoyánnes, Paul, made Lord of Cerigotto, 445
Monreale, mosaics at, 777
Monselice, and Venice, 398
Mons Lactarius, battle of, 386
Montaldo, on numbers of Turks at siege of Constantinople, 695 *note*
Monte Cassino, monastery of, 258; 599; 612; abbot of, 599, 612; *see* Desiderius, Gerard
Montenegro, history of, 585 sqq.; 244; 517; 547; and battle of Kossovo, 558; 564; 573; 578; 582; 584; resistance to Turks, 585; partially subdued, 587; Table of rulers, (the Zeta), 592
Montferrat, *see* Boniface, Conrad, William
Moors from Africa, in Justinian's army, 738
Mopsuestia (Mamistra), in Saracen wars, 122, 124, 126, 130, 145; under princes of Armeno-Cilicia, 168; 169 sq.; restored to the Empire, 171, 343; Ruben of Antioch defeated at, 174; 340 sq.; 358 sq.; 373 sq.
Morava, river, 517
Moravia, evangelised by Cyril and Methodius, 42, 44 sq., 221 sqq., 776; and Magyars, 198, 210, 236; *see* Great Moravia, Rostislav, Svatopluk
Moravian translation of the Gospels, 222
Moravo-Pannonian, archbishopric created, 211; princes, Pope Hadrian's letter to, 221; dialects, 225
Morea, the, *see also* Peloponnesus, Chap. xv *passim*; becomes French, 433; prosperity of, 447, 452, 456; conquered by Turks, 463 sq.; by Venetians, 466; Moreote influence in Cyprus, 471; results of Latin rule in, 473 sq.; 530; Latin Church in, 607; cavalry of, in Rhodes, 494; Charles of Anjou in, 611; 620; Turks in, 675, 677 sq., 692; 687; despots of, *see* Constantine XI, Demetrius, Manuel, Theodore, Thomas; "Lady of," *see* Isabelle of Villehardouin
Morocco, Idrīsid dynasty in, 300; 302
Morosini, Venetian commander, 467; reconquers Santa Mavra, 472
Morosini, Venetian faction in favour of Byzantines, 403 sq.
Morosini, Domenico, doge of Venice, and Emperor Manuel I, 412
Morosini, *see* Thomas
Μορτή (land rent), 5
Μορτῖται (peasants), 5
Mosaburch, *see* Blatno
Mosaic law, 267; 717
Mosaics, at Constantinople, 11; 39; in the New Church, 53; in St Sophia, 96, 752; in the Blachernae, 364; in church of the Forty Martyrs, 383; at the Chora, 753, 769 sq.; in the Forum, 748; in Ani cathedral, 163; at Nicaea, 479; at Ravenna, 758; 754; 767; 769 sq.; 772; in Western Europe, 777
Moschopulus, Byzantine professor, 764
Moscow, Armenian MSS of the Gospels at, 162; conquered by Mongols, 637; 652

Moses, Bulgarian chief, son of Shishman, 239 sq.
Moses of Chorene, Armenian historian, on origin of Bagratuni, 157; 198
Moses, *see* Mūsà
Mosque, at Constantinople, restored by Constantine VIII, 97; mosque at Bulgar, 194; built by Saracens at Tyana, 126; at Enna, 137; Christian dwellings turned into mosques by Mutawakkil, 288; 301; mosque at Trnovo, 560; mosques spared by Tīmūr, 651, 680; built by Mahomet I, 688; *see under* Constantinople, churches of
Mostar, 575
Mostenitsa, Teutonic Knights at, 437
Mosul, 277; 293; 315 sq.; 642; atābeg of, 357; *see* Kerbogha, Zangī
Mouchate, Moldavian dynasty, *see* Juga, Peter, Roman, Stephen
Mouchroutas, pavilion at imperial palace, 754
Mt St Auxentius, Stephen, abbot of, 16
Mourtzouphlos, *see* Alexius V
Mu'āwiyah I (Mu'āwiya), Umayyad Caliph, 641
Mu'āwiyah, Umayyad prince, 120 sq.
Mu'ayyid-al-Mulk, and Barkiyāruq, 310
Mubarrad, Arab compiler, 294
Muḥammad, *see also* Mahomet
Muḥammad, name adopted by Alp Arslān, 306
Muḥammad, 'Alā-ud-Dīn, Khwārazm Shāh, conquers Bukhārā, Samarqand, and Afghanistan, 278; driven out by Mongols, 312, 633, 636
Muḥammad II, last Seljūq ruler of Kirmān, 314
Muḥammad ibn Malik Shāh, Great Seljūq Sultan, brother of Barkiyāruq, reign of, 310 sq.; founds dynasty in 'Irāq, 315; 317; 343
Muḥammad ibn Mūsà al-Khwārazmī, Arab translator, and writer on algebra, 298
Muḥammad Shaibānī (Shāhī Beg), conquers Transoxiana, 651
Muḥammad, Sultan of Delhi, defeated by Tīmūr, 651
Muhtadī, Abbasid Caliph of Baghdad, and the court of appeal, 284
Muḥtasib, the, Muslim prefect of police, functions of, 283 sq.
Mu'izz, Fāṭimite Caliph, and Nicephorus II, 147
Mu'izz-ad-Dunyà-wa'd-Dīn, title of Malik Shāh, 307; of Sanjar, 311
Mukrān (Beluchistān), 312, 633
Mülhausen, treaty of, 398; 405
Multān, captured by Tīmūr, 651
Mumdzhilar, Balkan village, 235
Mumin, White Bulgarian ruler, 193
Muntaner, Ramón, Catalan chronicler, on the court of Guy II of Athens, 447; 451
Muqtadī, Abbasid Caliph of Baghdad, and Barkiyāruq, 309
Muqtadir, Abbasid Caliph of Baghdad, and the Bulgars, 194; his mother, 284; his slaves, 286
Murād I, Ottoman Sultan, accession of, 668 in Bulgaria, 555, 557; and John V, 617 sq., 671; and Janissaries, 664; in Thrace, 667; European policy of, 669; wins battle of the Maritza, 555, 670; assassination of, at Kossovo, 558, 672; character, 673; importance of reign, 674; 593
Murād II, Ottoman Sultan, accession, 569, 688; in Greece, 462; Serbia and, 568 sqq.; treaty of Szegedin, 571; victory at Varna, 572, 624, 691 sq.; Bosnia and, 575; 577; and Manuel II, 619; conquests of, 689 sq.; abdications of, 692; death of, 693; 694; 593
Murano, settlement of, 386
Murom, pagans in, 210
Mūsà, son of Bāyazīd I, at battle of Angora, 682; struggle for the throne and defeat, 562 sqq., 684 sqq.; 567; 593
Mūsà (Moses), son of Seljūq, 303
Muselé, Alexius, general of Constantine VI, 23
Mush, Armenian town, 158
Mushegh Mamikonian, Armenian leader, defeats Saracens, 156 sq.
Mushel Bagratuni, King of Vanand, brother of Ashot III, 161 sq.
Music, Serbian, 550; musicians at University of Constantinople, 764
Muslim, Chaps. v, x, xviii, xx, xxi; *see also* Islām, Musulmans
Mustaḍī, Abbasid Caliph of Baghdad, 289
Musṭafà, brother of Murād II, rebels against him, 690
Musṭafà, son of Bāyazīd, at Angora, 682; impersonator of, 688 sq.
Mustakfī, Abbasid Caliph of Baghdad, dethroned by the Buwaihids, 277, 301
Musta'sim, last Abbasid Caliph of Baghdad, put to death by Mongols, 279, 642
Mustaẓhir, Abbasid Caliph of Baghdad, and Muḥammad the Seljūq, 310
Musulmans, the, opposed to images, 7; driven from Constantinople, 109; Musulmans and Chazars, 190, 219 sq.; in Byzantine Empire, 737; *see* Islām
Mu'taḍid, Abbasid Caliph of Baghdad, 288
Mu'tamid, Abbasid Caliph of Baghdad; and Ashot of Armenia, 158; 276; 285
Mutanabbi, Arab poet, 290
Mu'taṣim, Abbasid Caliph of Baghdad, 38, 128 sq.; and Byzantines, 131 sq.; 151; moves his capital to Sāmorrā, 131, 276, 285; 295
Mutawakkil, Abbasid Caliph of Baghdad, intolerance of, 288, 292; 131; and Egyptian fleet, 132
Mutawakkil, last Abbasid Caliph of Cairo, 642
Mu'tazilites, Muslim sect, persecution of, 288; 291 sq.; 294; 301
Muṭī', Abbasid Caliph of Baghdad, 277
Muwaffaq, famous teacher at Nīshāpūr, 305

Muzalon, Byzantine general, defeated by Osmān, 657
Muzalon, George, made regent by Theodore II, 506; murdered, 430, 507
Myconus, island of, becomes Venetian, 457, 465; becomes Turkish, 466; 476
Mylae (Milazzo), Byzantine fleet defeated at, 141
Myra in Lycia, 127, 150; Venetians at, 410
Myriocephalum, defeat of Manuel I at, 362, 378
Mysia, assigned to Latin Emperor, 421, 426, 657
Mysticus, *see* Nicholas Mysticus
Mytzês, son-in-law of John Asên II of Bulgaria, 525, 528

Nacolea in Phrygia, besieged by Saracens, 124; bishop of, *see* Constantine
Nadīm, compiler of Arabic "Index," 290
Naimans, Mongol tribe, and Jenghiz Khan, 631; 632
"Naked" (γυμνοί), of Corfù, twelfth century communistic sect, 760
Nakhijevan, commercial town in Armenia, 162; church of, burnt by Arabs, 156
Nanchao, in Yunnan, 644
Naples, remains Byzantine, 36; and Saracens, 136; Angevins of, and Achaia, 442, 444, 446 sq.; Tocco family at, 455, 466; 539; and Herzegovina, 582; and Skanderbeg, 584 sq.; Castel dell' Uovo at, 452; King of, 559; *see* Charles, Ladislas, Robert
Narbonne, *see* Amaury
Narenta, on Dalmatian coast, 587
Narses, general of Justinian I, 385, 739
Nasi, *see* Joseph
Nāṣir, Abbasid Caliph of Baghdad, 278
Nāṣir, Mamlūk Sultan of Egypt, defeats Mongols, 651 sq.; conquers Armeno-Cilicia, 180
Nāṣir Ṣalāḥ-ad-Dīn Yūsuf, Sultan of Aleppo, defeated by Mongols, 175, 643
Naṣīr-ud-Dīn Ṭūsī, Persian philosopher and astronomer, 296, 299
Naṣr, emir of Tarsus, 131
Naṣr, Syrian rebel, and Emperor Leo V, 127
Naṣr the Kurd, rebel against the Caliph, 129; killed, 130
Naṣr the Shī'ite, Arab emissary, 132 sq.
Naupactus, 244, 423; metropolitan of, blinded by Constantine VIII, 97; *see* John Apocaucus
Nauplia, 424, 433 sq.; captured by Villehardouin, 438; 441; bought by Venetians, 457, 461, 465, 476; becomes Turkish, 467; archon of, *see* Sgourós
Navarino, bay of, 446; becomes Venetian, 461, 465; lost to Turks, 467
Navarre, King of, 455; Navarrese Company conquer Achaia, 456, 474; Nerio Acciajuoli and, 458
Navigajosi family at Lemnos, 436; driven out, 445
Navy, *see* Fleet, Byzantine; Fleet, Saracen; the "Tactics," 58; *see* Maritime Code
Naxos, attacked by Saracen pirates, 141; becomes Venetian seigniory, 421, 435, 439; 459; 465; dukes of, *see* Archipelago; annexed by Turks, 468; Latin rule in, 473
Nazareth, surrendered to John I, 148
Nazianzen, *see* Gregory
Nea, *see* New Church *under* Constantinople
Neapolis, *see* Leontius
Νεαραί, *see* Novels
Νέα Τακτικά, list of ecclesiastical dioceses drawn up by Leo VI, 58
Negropont (Chalcis), city of, under Venetians, 435; taken by Turks, 466, 472; hospice of friars in, 438; Latin Patriarch in, 615
Negropont, island of, *see* Euboea
Nemanja, Stephen, *see* Stephen: dynasty extinct, 555; 586
Neo-Caesarea, taken by Saracens, 120; 360; Byzantine defeat at, 378
"Neokastra, duchy of," 480; 488
Neopatras, principality of, founded by John Ducas Angelus, 444; duchy of, conquered by Catalans, 453; 455; 457; captured by Turks, 458; dukes of, *see* Table, 475; *see* John I, II
Neoplatonic, influence on Islām, 292 sq.
Nepi, bishop of, *see* Stephen
Nera, river, tributary of Danube, 355
Nerio I Acciajuoli, lord of Corinth, 456; seizes Athens, 457; death, 458; 475
Nerio II Acciajuoli, Duke of Athens, 462 sq., 475
Neropch, aboriginal Balkan tribe, 550
Nerses, Katholikos of Armenia, and Byzantine Church, 363
Nerses Lambronatsi, 170
Nesteutes, John, Byzantine canonist, 711
Nestóngos, cousin of John III, conspires against him, 488
Nestor, Russian chronicle, 204, 209, 264 *note*
Nestorian, Patriarchs of Baghdad, wealth of, 289; bishop, *see* Cyprian; Christians, and Arabic language, 290; Christians translate Greek medical works into Arabic, 297; Christians among Mongols, 631, 640; *see* Chaldeans
Neuilly, *see* Fulk
Neva, river, 202
Nevers, count of, *see* William
Nicaea (Iznīq), captured by Bardas Sclerus, 85; 117; 120; captured by Isaac I, 320; 321; 344; 365; capital of Seljūqs of Rūm, 315; Crusaders and, 337; captured by Crusaders, 338, 352, 655; 383; 421; Latin dukedom of, 422; Emperors at, Chap. XVI; 423 sqq., 426 sqq., 430, 439, 604 sq.; loses its importance, 513, 658; 607; 609; taken by Ottomans, 542, 661; 657; 660 sq.; 665; 667; sacked by Tīmūr, 683; 722; capital of Opsician theme, 733; description of, 479; churches at, 479, 498; hospitals at, 498, 513; Table of rulers, 516; Theo-

dore II's eulogies on, 501, 506; emir of, *see* Abu'l-Qāsim; Councils of, *see* Councils; bishop of, *see* Eustratius; archbishop of, *see* Bessarion
Patriarch of Constantinople at, Theodore I crowned by, 482; 486; 488; 497; jurisdiction of, 498; Theodore II and, 500 sq., 506; Michael VIII crowned by, 508; and Epirus, 490, 497, 607; and Serbian Church, 521; and Bulgarians, 523; *see* Arsenius, Germanus; *see also* Church
Niccolò Acciajuoli, invested with Corinth, 454
Niccolò Altomanović, Bosnian ruler, 591
Niccolò I, Duke of the Archipelago, 475
Niccolò II Sanudo, "Spezzabanda," Duke of the Archipelago, 475
Niccolò III dalle Carceri, Duke of the Archipelago, murder of, 457; 475
Nicene Creed, 228, 254, 478
Nicephoritza, supporter of the Comneni, 326
Nicephorus I, Emperor, Logothete-general, 24; proclaimed Emperor, 25; reign of, 27 sqq.; his death in battle, 29, 233; 34 sq.; his foreign policy, 36; war against Krum Khan, 37, 232 sq.; 38; wars against Hārūn ar-Rashīd, 126, 288; Italy and, 394 sq.; re-establishes the ἐπιβολή, 708; Novels of, 710
Nicephorus II Phocas, Emperor, 68 sqq.; proclaimed Emperor, 71; crowned, 72; reign of, 72 sqq.; Novels of, 74 sq., 79, 89, 260, 715, 753; murdered, 77; 78 sqq.; 83; 86; 100; 134; victories over Saracens, 144 sqq.; Sicily and, 147; 151; and Svyatoslav of Russia, 208; and Bulgarians, 239; 259; and Otto the Great, 76 sq., 261; and army, 741; and navy, 742; 754
Nicephorus III Botaniates, Emperor, 325 sq.; abdicates, 327; 329; 331 sq.; 408; excommunicated by Pope Gregory VII, 598; Novels of, 720
Nicephorus I Angelus, despot of Epirus, son of Michael II of Epirus, betrothed to grand-daughter of John III, 494; defeats Nicaeans, 508; 444; 448; 475; married, 503
Nicephorus II, despot of Epirus, 455; 552; 475
Nicephorus, Patriarch of Constantinople, 11; 13; 17; 26; quarrel with Studites, 28; Leo V and, 30, 38; 32 sq.; 35; account of Bulgarian settlement, 230; 248; 765
Nicephorus, bishop of Heraclea, 65
Nicephorus, nominated by Constantine IX as his successor, 115
Nicephorus, sacellarius of Michael Cerularius, 268, 270
Nicephorus Uranus, *see* Uranus
Nicetas, archbishop of Nicomedia, and Anselm of Havelberg, 600
Nicetas, count of Opsicium, defeated by Saracens, 124
Nicetas, the Paphlagonian, brother of Michael IV, made duke of Antioch, 102
Nicetas, the Patrician, Byzantine admiral, and Venice, 394
Nicetas Acominatus (Choniates), Byzantine historian and theologian, 765 sq.; on Prêslav, 237; on sack of Constantinople, 420, 605; 423; 480 *note*; 351; 353 *note*; 363; and Theodore I, 482; 484 *note*; 486; on death of Baldwin I, 520
Nicetas, joint compiler of the *Ecloga*, 709
Nicetas Stethatus, *see* Stethatus
Nicetas the quaestor, and the *Ecloga*, 709
Nicholas, St, Venetians and relics of, 410
Nicholas Chrysoberges, Patriarch of Constantinople, 89; death, 91
Nicholas Mysticus, Patriarch of Constantinople, and Leo VI, 57 sq., 60, 62, 65, 256; and Romanus I, 61; issues the *Tomus Unionis*, 60, 257; 753
Nicholas I, Pope, relations with Bulgaria, 45, 47; and Photius, 47, 53, 221; 248 sqq.; 251; and Boris of Bulgaria, 236, 252
Nicholas II, Pope, signs treaty of Melfi, 597
Nicholas III (John Gaetano Orsini), Pope, appealed to by Hethum II of Armenia, 177; and Michael VIII, 613
Nicholas IV, Pope, and the Tsar George Terteri, 530
Nicholas V, Pope, and Constantine XI, 624; and Turks, 692
Nicholas II de St Omer of Thebes, regent in the Morea, 446
Nicholas Alexander Basaraba, Prince of Wallachia, 593
Nicholas of Ilok, made King of Lower Bosnia by Matthias Corvinus, 581
Nicholas Orsini, count of Cephalonia, 453, 475; despot of Epirus, 475
Nicholas Mesarites, metropolitan of Ephesus, and Cardinal Pelagius, 606; 746
Nicholas, bishop, Papal legate, 256
Nicholas, abbot of the Studion, and Photius, 248, 255
Nicholas of Methone, Byzantine theologian, 766
Nicholson, Dr, on Arab poetry, 290
Nicole, discoverer of Leo VI's *Book of the Prefect*, 716
Nicomedia (Izmid), 118; 321; taken by Byzantines, 331; 367; taken by Latins, 424 sq.; 480 sqq.; Thierri de Loos at, 483; Latin bishopric at, 487; "duchy" of, 488; 490; 494; 657; 660 sq.; taken by Orkhān, 662 sq.; 668; 676 sq.; capital of Optimatian theme, 733; gulf of, 33, 483, 582; bishop of, *see* Constantine; archbishop of, *see* Nicetas
Nicopolis, theme of, 733; 244, 436
Nicopolis, Great, on the Danube, 557; Ottoman victory at, 561, 618, 675 sq.; 688
Nicopolis, Little, on the Danube, 675
Nicosia, coronation city of kings of Cyprus, 469; burnt by Egyptians, 470; captured by Turks, 472; archbishop of, 470 sq.
Nihāwand, 308
Nika riot at Constantinople, 754, 759

Níkli, High Court of Achaia at, 441; "Ladies' Parliament" at, 443
Nile, river, 295
Nīlufer, mother of Murād I, 673
Nilus, heresy of, 350
Nilus, St, in Italy, 258
Nīmrūz, *see* Tāj-ad-Dīn
Nine Orders, convent of, *see under* Constantinople, churches of
Ninoslav, ban of Bosnia, *see* Matthew
Niphon, Bogomile monk, 363
Niš, Bulgarian and Serbian town, 238; Crusaders at, 336; 519; taken by Turks, 557, 673; 571; Turkish defeat at, 584, 624; 688; bishopric of, 243
Nīshāpūr, Seljūqs at, 304; 305; university founded at, 306; ravaged by Ghuzz, 313; destroyed by Mongols, 633
Nisibis, in Mesopotamia, captured by Curcuas, 143; 147; church built at, 289
Niẓām-al-Mulk, vizier of the Great Seljūq Alp Arslān, 299; 305 sq.; treatise of, 305; and Antioch, 307; disgrace and death, 308; 309 sq.; 313
Nīzāmīyah University at Baghdad, founded, 305; at Nīshāpūr, 306
Njeguš, in Montenegro, 586
Nobilissimus, title, reserved for royalty, 730; bestowed on sons of Constantine V, 13; on Constantine the Paphlagonian, 105
"Noble War" of Constantine V against Bulgarians, 232
Nogai Khan, Tartar chief, marries daughter of Michael VIII, 527; kills Ivailo, 530
Nogent, *see* Guibert de
Nomisma, Byzantine gold coin, 4; under the Comneni, 348; *see also* Coinage
Nomocanon (digest of Canon Law), translation into Slavonic by Methodius, 229
Nomocanon titulorum, 711
Nomocanon XIV titulorum, 711; see *Syntagma*
Nomocanon of Doxopater, 723; of Aristinus, 723; ascribed to Photius, 724
Nomocanones, *see* Canon Law
Νόμοι πολιτικοί (civil laws), 720
Nomophylax, office of, instituted by Constantine IX, 114, 719 sq.
Νόμος γεωργικός, *see* Rural Code
Νόμος ναυτικός, *see* Maritime Code
Νόμος στρατιωτικός, *see* Military Code
Normans, in Italy, 92, 112, 266, 352, 354, 358; in Sicily, 103; in Macedonia, 245; defeat Argyrus, 268; 273; 322; 325; Michael VII and, 326; and Alexius I, 328 sq., 332 sq., 341 sqq.; at court of Manuel I, 362; war with Manuel I, 368 sq.; 383; and Venice, 407 sqq., 411 sq., 414; 595 sqq.; in Byzantine army, 347, 598, 738; influenced by Byzantine law, 725; by Byzantine art, 776 sq.
Norway, Northmen from, 738; 746
Nossiae, convent of, built by Leo VI, 59
Notaras, Lucas, Grand Duke, opposition to Union, 625; at siege of Constantinople, 698
Notarial profession at Constantinople, 716
Notitia, work of Philotheus, *see* Kleterologion
Notitia urbis Constantinopolitanae, 450, 746, 748
Noto in Sicily, raided by Saracens, 137 sq.
Novels, Chap. XXII *passim*; of Leo VI, 58, 723 sqq.; of Romanus I, against the "Powerful," 62, 92 sq.; of Constantine VII, 66; of Nicephorus II against monks, 74, 260, 753; abrogated, 79; of John I, 82; of Basil II, 89, 92, 94; of Constantine VIII, 98; of Romanus III, 99; of Constantine IX, founding school of law, 114, 706; of Alexius I, 332, 349; of Manuel I, 364, 720
Novgorod, Russian trading centre, 202; government united with Kiev, 204; Vladímir made prince of, 208 sq.; saved from Mongols, 637
Novi, *see* Castelnuovo, 557
Novibazar, destroyed by Serbians, 356, 517; Serbian capital, 523; Sanjak of, 522, 556; *see* Rascia
Novobrdo, silver mines of, 549; captured by Turks, 570, 576
Nur, destroyed by Mongols, 633
Nūr-ad-Dīn, son of Zangī, Sultan of Damascus, and Mleh of Armenia, 170 sq.; 299; 317, 374 sqq.
Nyitra, Hungarian river, 214; bishop of, *see* Wiching
Nymphaeum, 344; 430; residence of John III at, 488, 495, 513; 497; 500; ruins at, 514; treaty of, 431, 510 sq.
Nyssa in Cappadocia, 130; 134

Ob, river, 631
Obdormitio S. Cyrilli, 221
Obelerius, Francophil doge of Venice, 393; made spatharius, 394; deposed, 395
Obilić, *see* Miloš Kobilić
Obod, first Slavonic printing press at, 587
Ochrida, 242; taken by Normans, 329; by Theodore Angelus, 427; ceded to John III, 494; 524; 538; lake of, 240; see of, created, 243, 259; metropolitan of, crowns Theodore Angelus, 427; Bulgarian Patriarch resides at, 522; Moldavian and Wallachian Churches dependent on, 568; archbishops of, *see* Basil, Demetrius, John, Leo, Theophylact
Oderzo, sack of, 386 sq.
Odo, bishop of Beauvais, 250 *note*
Odo of Deuil, 601 *note*
Oeconomus, Grand, *see* Joseph
Oenaeum, on Black Sea, 381; declares for Emperors of Trebizond, 480; 487
Oeta, Mount, 444
Ogdai Khan, Mongol Great Khan, and Hethum I of Armeno-Cilicia, 175; 633; succeeds his father, 635; conquests of, 636 sq.; death, 638 sqq.; house of, ceases to rule, 645; worshipped in China, 646; 648
Ogelen Eke, *see* Yulun
Oghuz Khan, Turkish chief, 631

Oka, Russian river, 193
Olbia, Greek colony on Black Sea, 183
Old Testament, translated into Slavonic, 226, 229
Oleg, Prince of Kiev, 204; treaty with Byzantines, 205; 207
Oleg, son of Svyatoslav, killed by his brother, 208
Olga, Princess of Kiev, baptised, 66, 207; 208
Olivolo (Castello), bishopric of, 387, 398; foundation of, 392 sq.; 397; bishop of, *see* Christopher
Olona, *pactum* of, between Venice and Berengar, 400
Olovo, silver mines of, 556
Olympus, Mt, in Bithynia, 67; 80; 114; 216 sq.; 219; 256; 660; 753
Omar Beg, Emir of Aidīn, 662
Omar I, Caliph, the fiscal system of, 282; 288; 302
Omar II, Umayyad Caliph (ibn 'Abd-al-'Azīz), 119, 288
Omar, Caliph, Leo VI's letter to, 59
Omar, emir of Melitene, captures Amisus, 42, 46; 129, 131 sqq.; killed, 134
Omar ibn Hubaira, Saracen leader, 119 sq.
Omar Khayyām, poet and astronomer, 298 sq., 305, 308
Omar, Ottoman governor of Thessaly, 463; captures Athens, 464
Omurtag, Khan of Bulgaria, reign of, 234 sq.; and Leo V, 30, 37; defeats Thomas the Slavonian, 35
Onan Kerule, *see* Deligun Buldagha
Onon, river, 631 sq.
Ooryphas, Byzantine admiral, 128
Opsician theme, created, 732; 2 sq.; 12 sq.; loyalty of, 36; 479; conquered by Latins, 481; count of, 124, 126, 734
Optimatian theme, 3, 733; *Domestic* of, 734
Opus, Constantine, leader of unsuccessful expedition to Sicily, 150
Opus, general of Alexius I, 331
Oracles, work of Leo VI, 59
Orbevieto, bishop of Civitavecchia, sent to Nicaea, 609
Ordinatio, of Thionville, for government of Venice, 394 sq., 398
Ordu Balig, palace of Ogdai Khan, 640
Organas, chief of the Utigurs, becomes a Christian, 188
Orkhān, Ottoman Sultan, marries Byzantine princess, 543; 544; captures Brūsa, 660; succeeds his father, 661; successes of, 662; assumes title of Sultan, 663; military policy, 663 sq.; and John VI, 665 sqq.; death of, 668; 669; 673; 593
Orkhān, Ottoman prince, son of Sulaimān, blinded by Mūsà, 686
Orkhān, Ottoman prince, 693; claims supported by Constantine XI, 694; at siege of Constantinople, 701
Orkhon, river, 631
Orleans, duke of, 618; canon of, 620; *see* Payen
Orontes, river, Burtzes defeated on, 149; 176; 359 sq.; valley of, 343
Orotn, *see* John of
Orphanotrophos, *see* John
Orseoli, Venetian noble family, 403, 407
Orseolo, John, doge-consort of Venice, 404; marries Maria Argyra, 94, 406
Orseolo, Orso, *see* Orso
Orseolo I, Peter, doge of Venice, 403
Orseolo II, Peter, doge of Venice, 94; 395 sq.; foreign policy of, 404 sq.; and Otto II, 405; significance of his reign, 406
Orseolo III, Otto, doge of Venice, 404, 406 sq.
Orseolo, Vitalis, *see* Vitalis
Orsini dynasty in Cephalonia, 455, 461, 473 sq.; monument at Arta, 453; *see* John, Matteo
Orsini, John Gaetano, *see* Nicholas III, Pope
Orso, *see* Ursus
Orso Orseolo, bishop of Torcello, and Patriarch of Grado, 404, 407
Orthodoxy, festival of, 41
Oshin, King of Armeno-Cilicia, 179
Oshin of Gorigos, regent of Armeno-Cilicia, 179
Oshin, lord of Lambron, taken prisoner by Thoros II, 170
Osmān (Othmān, 'Uthmān), founder of the Ottoman dynasty, 653 sqq.; and Catalans, 657 sq.; and Andronicus II, 659; death, 660; 661; 668; 593
Ossetes, Alan tribe, subdued by Russians, 207
Ostan, 182
Ostia, bishop of, *see* Donatus, Ubaldo
Ostikans, Saracen governors of Armenia, 156; 161; of Azarbā'ījān, 158; *see* Afshīn, Yūsuf; of Mesopotamia, *see* Aḥmad
Ostoja, Stephen, King of Bosnia, 565 sqq., 573 sq.; 591
Ostrovo, battle of, 110; 494; lake of, 493
Othmān, Caliph, and the Chazars, 188
Othmān, *see* Osmān
Othon de la Roche, becomes *Megaskyr* (*Sire*) of Athens, 433; 438 sq.; 451; 475
Othrys, Mt, 444
Otranto, 18; 110; province created by Nicephorus II, 260; Church in, 737
Otrar, death of Tīmūr at, 651
Otto I, the Great, Emperor of the West, 66; 260 sq.; embassy to Nicephorus II, 76; plan of a Byzantine marriage for his son, 77; 145; and Géza of Hungary, 213; coronation of, 259; and Venetians, 402
Otto II, Emperor of the West, marriage to Theophano, daughter of Romanus II, 68, 81, 147; defeated by Saracens in South Italy, 149; 385; Venetians and, 403 sqq.
Otto III, Emperor of the West, 91; at Venice, 405 sq.; proposed marriage, 94; death, 94
Otto IV, of Brunswick, Emperor of the West, 415

Otto of Brunswick, husband of Joanna of Naples, Prince of Achaia, 456, 474
Ottoman Turks, Chap. XXI; Chap. XVIII *passim*; in Greece, 458 sq., 463 sqq., 543; wars with Venetians, 466 sq.; capture Naxos and Chios, 468; Cyprus, 472; 473; Magnesia, 499; 513; 517; 522; 530; 532; 534; 542; and John VI, 543, 616; first settlement in Europe, 544; threaten Byzantium, 614 sq., 617 sqq.; 620; 623 sq.; peril to Europe, 596, 675; and the Caliphate, 642; and Mongols, 650 sq.; weakened by battle of Angora, 684 sqq.; effects of conquest of Constantinople, 629; and Byzantine Church, 625; become European power, 705; Table of Sultans, 593; Armenians and, 182; heirs of the Seljūqs, 300, 315, 317
Ousiai, Byzantine warships, 743
Oxus, river, 303 sq., 306 sq., 311, 313
Oxylithus, battle of, 85

Pachymeres (Pachymer), George, Byzantine historian, 499 sq., 508 *note*; on Turks, 655, 765
Pacta, Venetian treaties with Western Empire, 395; *pactum* of Pavia, 398; Mantua, 400; Olona, 400; with Lothar, 401; of Rome, 402; of Mülhausen, 405; Conrad II refuses to ratify, 407
Padua, and Venice, 412; Manuel II at, 618
Pagasaean Gulf, 453, 465
Pahlavi, Arabic translations from, 298
Pahlavuni, Vahram, Armenian generalissimo, 164; crowns Gagik II, 165
Pahlavuni, Vasak, Armenian general, his mysterious death, 164
Pairis, in Germany, abbot of, *see* Martin
Palaeologi, family, 454, 771; origin of, 503; dynasty, 777; 764 sq.; *see* Andronicus, Constantine, Demetrius, John, Manuel, Michael, Theodore, Thomas
Palaeologus, Andrew, son of the despot Thomas of the Morea, 464
Palaeologus, Andronicus, father of Michael VIII, 492 sq.
Palaeologus, John, brother of Michael VIII, made governor of Rhodes, 504; and Epirotes, 508
Palaeologus, Michael, general of Manuel I, in Italy, 369 sq.
Παλαιὰ Τακτικά, list of ecclesiastical dioceses, 58
Palamas, Byzantine mystical writer, 766
Palermo, captured by Saracens, 37, 135 sqq.; by Normans, 408; Byzantine mosaics at, 777
Palestine (Holy Land), 10; monks of, 34, 753; 123; 125; John I's victories in, 148; Egyptians in, 175 sq., 178; Byzantine protectorate in, 259; occupied by Seljūqs, 277; Mongols in, 279; 280; Latin princes of, 333; 339; 354; 373; 375; 377; Venetians in, 410 sq.; 519; 521; 611; Byzantine law in, 723
Pallavicini, the, become lords of Boudonitza, 422
Pallavicini, Guido, Marquess, lord of Boudonitza, 433, 439
Palli, Cape, Venetian victory at, 329
Palmann, captain of the guard to Stephen Dušan, 546
Pamirs, the, included in empire of Khwārazm Shāh, 633
Pamphylia, 353 sq.
Pamphylians, Byzantine warships, 743
Pancalia, battle of, 86, 90
Panderma, occupied by Latins, 481
Pannonia, Roman province, 184; Avars and Turks in, 186; in ninth century, 211; overrun by Bulgars, 234; 386; Upper, conquered by Magyars, 212 sq.; *Pannonian Lives* of SS. Cyril and Methodius, 216 sqq., 224, 226
Pansebastos, title, granted to Thoros II of Armeno-Cilicia by Byzantines, 171
Pantaleone, of Amalfi, and Papal election, 597
Pantellaria, island, 136
Pantepoptes, church of, *see under* Constantinople, churches of
Panteugenus, Soterichus, heretical priest condemned by Manuel I, 363
Panticapaeum, *see* Bosphorus
Pantokrator, church and monastery of, *see under* Constantinople, churches of
Paoki, in China, 635
Paolo Veronese, picture of defence of Scutari, 586
Papacy, the, and Byzantine Church, Chaps. IX, XIX, 112 sqq.; and Photian schism, 47, 53 sq.; 56, 248 sqq.; and Leo VI's marriage, 57, 256; and Iconoclastic Emperors, 4, 8, 17 sq.; and Constantine VII, 139; and Alexius I, 329, 333, 345; and Manuel I, 366, 369 sq.; and Michael VIII, 444, 528; and John III, 496 sq.; and Theodore II, 505; and Franks, 17 sq., 391; and Lombards, 17 sq., 391; and SS. Cyril and Methodius, 121, 224 sqq.; and dispute between Grado and Aquileia, 389, 408; and Venice, Chap. XIII *passim*; and Normans, 595 sqq., 601; and Western Empire, 596, 600 sq., 603, 608; and Illyricum, 58; sends crown to Simeon of Bulgaria, 238; and Bulgarian Church, 45, 47, 62, 252; and Bosnians, 518, 526, 532; and Serbia, 534, 537, 548; and Lemnos, 477; and Samothrace, 477; and Latin clergy of Antioch, 361; and Armenian Church, 159, 172, 178, 189; and Ottomans, 669 sq., 690 sq.; and Mongols, 639 sq.; disputed Papal election, 91; *see also* Councils, Popes, Latin Church, Roman Church
Paphlagonia, theme of, 39, 733; 117; 120; 320; 382; subdued for Trebizond, 480; Turks in, 656; Paphlagonian wife of Constantine VI, 22; "the Paphlagonian," *see* Michael IV, Emperor
Paphlagonians, family of Michael IV, 102, 106 sqq.

Paracamus, Byzantine commander, takes possession of Armenia, 166
Παραγραφαί, explanatory notes on laws, 707
Parakat IV, King of Iberia, treaty with Romanus III, 100
Parakoimomenos (chief chamberlain), office of, 730; *see* Basil
Paraphrase of the Institutes, by Theophilus, 707, 721
Paraspondylus, Leo, minister of Theodora, and Michael VI, 116 sq.; 320
Parastron, *see* John
Παράτιτλα, method of explaining Justinian's laws, 707; in *Prochiron auctum*, 722
Parenzo, and Venice, 412; Byzantine art at, 768
Paris, Baldwin II at, 429; Manuel II at, 618, 678; Parlement at, 441; 558; Greek scholarships at, 616; 637; Armenian embassy to, 181; Armenian church at, 163; Byzantine MSS. at, 510, 713, 769; Constantinople compared with, 745; bishop of, *see* Aeneas
Paristrium, duchy of, created, 243
Parium, ravaged by Turks, 344
Parma, *see* John of; bishop of, *see* Cadalus
Paroikia, castle of, 437
Πάροικος, Byzantine peasant, compared with Western *villein*, 772
Paroïr, ancestor of the Bagratuni, 157
Paros, attacked by Saracen pirates, 141; Venetian, 467, 476
Parthenon, the, 242; as Latin cathedral, 433, 458 sq.; Latin archbishop leaves, 464
Parthia, 154, 157
Particiaci, Venetian ducal house, 396 sqq., 401, 407
Particiacus, Agnellus, doge of Venice, 395; builds first ducal palace, 396; appoints tribunes, 397
Particiacus, Badoero, brother of doge John, 399
Particiacus, John, doge of Venice, 399 sq.
Particiacus, Justinian, doge of Venice, builds first church of St Mark, 396 sq.
Particiacus, Peter Badoero, doge of Venice, 401
Particiacus, Ursus, doge of Venice, and Patriarch of Grado, 399
Particiacus, Ursus (Paureta), doge of Venice, 400
Particiacus, Ursus, *see* Ursus
Paschal I, Pope, appealed to by Theodore of Studion, 32; 33
Paschal II, Pope, and Alexius I, 345, 354, 596; and Bohemond of Antioch, 600
Pasha (Sanjakbey), Ottoman title, 664
Passau, bishopric of, 211, 221, 223; 227; bishop of, *see* Hermanric
Passavâ, Latin castle in Greece, 473
Paterikon, Slavonic translation of a, by St Methodius, 229
Pathfinding Virgin, famous image of, *see under* Constantinople
Patmos, attacked by Saracen pirates, 141; monastery at, 349; surrendered to Turks, 672; *see* Christodulus of
Patras, 6; attacked by the Slavs, 37; 50; frescoes at, 446; Acciajuoli at, 454; leased by Venetians, 459, 476; surrenders to Constantine Palaeologus, 460; ceded to Turks, 463; burned by Turks, 692; silk manufactures at, 770; Latin archbishop of, 437
Patria Potestas, in Byzantine law, 709
Patriarchate, Patriarchs, of Constantinople, *see under* Constantinople, Nicaea; and the Emperor, 729, 753; Patriarchate of Antioch, 343; Patriarchate of Aquileia, *see* Aquileia; Patriarchate of Baghdad, 289; Patriarchate of Grado, *see* Grado; Patriarchate of Bulgaria (Prêslav), 238, 240, 243, 490, 520, 522; recreated by John Asên II, 523; Patriarch executed by Theodore Svetslav; 531; 542; 560; Patriarchate of Jerusalem, 173; *see* Euthymius; Patriarchate of Moldavia, 568; and Serbia, 542, 554; Patriarchate of Serbia, created by Stephen Dušan, 542, 547 sq.; and Constantinople, 554, 578; Latin Patriarchate of Constantinople, 419, 421, 426, 431; of Antioch, and Jerusalem, 599; Eastern Patriarchs at Ferrara, 621; Patriarch of the Armenians, *see* Katholikos; *see* Church
Patrician, title of, 730, 733; 742
Patzinaks (Patzinakitai), Turkish tribe, 38 sq., 112, 192, 195, 197 sqq., 204, 207 sq.; and Vladímir the Great, 209 sq.; before Constantinople, 212; 238 sq.; raids in Bulgaria, 242, 245; 322; raids into the Empire, 324 sq.; and Alexius I, 330 sqq., 597; defeated by John II, 354; in Byzantine army, 347, 738; prince of, *see* Kurya
Patzus, Byzantine jurisconsult, 714, 722
Pau, Pedro de, defends Acropolis at Athens, 457
Paul, St, the Apostle, 42; *Epistles* of, translated into Slavonic, 225
Paul, Patriarch of Constantinople, zealous against images, 20; resigns, 20
Paul I, Pope, and confirmation of papal election, 246
Paul II, Pope, and Skanderbeg, 585
Paul Boua Spata, sells Lepanto to Venetians, 459
Paul, exarch, killed at Ravenna, 390
Paul the Silentiary, poem on Constantinople, 746, 762
Paul, strategus of the Armeniac theme, defeated and killed by Saracens, 122
Paul Subić, ban of Bosnia, 591
Paul, count of Opsicium, defeated by Saracens, 126
Paul, bishop of Ancona, Papal legate, and St Methodius, 227 sq.
Paul, the patrician, Byzantine admiral, 394
Paul, praetor of Cephalonia, Byzantine admiral, 395
Pauler, on Magyars, 195 sqq.
Paulicians, in Asia Minor, their iconoclastic

zeal, 7; at Constantinople, 29; persecuted by Theodora, 42, 46, 132; raids on the Empire, 134; war with Basil I, 139; 737
Paulinus, Patriarch of Aquileia, takes refuge at Grado, 386
Paulus, punished for circulating Papal Bull against Cerularius, 271
Paulutius Anafestus (Paulutio, Paulitio), first doge of Venice, 388; 389
Paun (the "peacock" castle), defeat of Bulgarians at, 245
Pavia, helped by Manuel, receives Byzantine subsidy, 370; taken by Franks, 391; trade at, 396; *pactum* of, 398; *see* William of
Paxo, island of, held by Venice, 466
Payen of Orleans, lands in Asia Minor, 480, 482
Pechenêgs, Slav name for Patzinaks, *q.v.*
Pécs (Fünfkirchen), bishopric of, founded, 214
Pécsvárad, abbot of, *see* Astrik
Pectoratus, *see* Stethatus
Pedro III, King of Aragon, 496
Pedro IV, King of Aragon, and Greek duchies, 455 sqq., 475
Pegae, Latin colony at, 480 sq., 483; given to Henri de Grangerin, 485; ceded to John III, 487; recaptured, 488
Pege (Selymbria, Silivri), gate of Constantinople, 512, 671, 697 sq.
Pegoraro dei Pegorari, receives fief in Euboea, 435
Πεῖρα (*Romaics of the Magister*), Byzantine legal manual, 718, 723
Pekin, 632; *see* Cambalu
Pelagonia, taken by Theodore Angelus, 427; defeat of Michael Angelus at, 430; defeat of William of Achaia at, 442 sq., 508 sq., 524
Pelagius, Cardinal, mission of, to the Byzantine Church, 606
Pelecanum, Crusaders and Alexius I at, 338
Pelestrina, taken by Pepin, 394
Peloponnesus (Morea), Slavs of, 37, 42; theme of, 39, 733, 737; and Byzantine navy, 742; Saracen raids on, 141; Bulgarian raids on, 240 sq.; becomes Venetian, 421, 432; Latin lordship in, 422 sq.; partly recovered by Nicaea, 430; Chap. xv *passim*; *see also* Morea; strategus of, *see* Theophylitzes
Pelusium, attacked by Byzantines, 133
Pempton Gate, *see* St Romanus
Πένητες (the "poor"), 51, 771
Pentapolis, the, revolt against Leo III, 9; abandoned to the Franks, 36, 392; 393
Pentapyrgion, imperial coffer, 40
Pepin, King of the Franks, and Pope Stephen II, 17 sq., 391 sq.
Pepin, King of Italy, son of Charlemagne, 393; attacks Venice, 36, 394; death, 395
Pera, Dominicans at, 615; 696; 699
Perche, *see* Stephen of
Peredeo, Lombard duke, takes Ravenna, 390
Pereslavl, in Russia, destroyed by Mongols, 637
Pereyaslavets, *see* Prêslav
Pergamus, captured by Saracens, 2, 117; 344; 378; given to Hospitallers, 480; Henry of Flanders at, 485; held by Turks, 657
Perge, bishop of, *see* Sisinnius
Peribleptos, St Mary, church of, *see under* Constantinople
Perinthus, sacked by Turks, 695
Perm, Russian government of, 193
Permyaks, Ugrian tribe, 194
Pernik, in Bulgaria, besieged by Basil II, 242
Perrhe (Hiṣn Manṣūr), 121
Persia, Sasanian dynasty of, 152, 274, 276; Sasanian administration, and the Caliphate, 280, 283; learning under the Sasanids, 297 sq.; Sasanian coins in Bulgar, 193; Sasanid kings, *see* Chosroes, Kawad, Piroz, Sapor, Yezdegerd; and Armenia, 153 sq., 159; 178; 287; 289; 631; 653; 689; Buwaihids in, 277; Seljūqs in, 164, 168, 278, 300, 302, 306, 317; war with Byzantines, 386; conquered by Mongols, 175, 279, 629, 640; Īl-Khān dynasty in, 644, 647; conquered by Tīmūr, 651, 679; Chazars and, 188; Magyars in, 195; vassal dynasties in, 300; Shī'ites in, 301; overrun by Ghuzz, 303; "History of," 293; Persians in Armenia, 158, 162 sq.; in Saracen army, 122 sq., 125, 127; in Byzantine army, 38, 130, 736, 738; influence on Abbasid dynasty, 274, 276, 285; writers in Saracen literature, 290 sq., 295, 298; language, 295; philosophy, 296; converts to Islām, 281; Persian favourite of Mahomet II, 580; spelling of Tartar, 630; trade with Constantinople, 762; influence on Byzantium, 773; Persian Gulf, 278, 314, 633
Perugia, 608
Pervoslav Uroš, Župan of Rascia, and Manuel I, 368, 373
Pescatore, Enrico, buccaneer in Crete, 434
Pesth, *see* Buda-Pesth
Peter, St, the Apostle, 32, 247; church of, *see* Saint Peter
Peter of Courtenay, count of Auxerre, Latin Emperor of Constantinople, defeat and death, 427; 438; 607
Peter, Tsar of Bulgaria, 62; and Constantine VII, 143; and Svyatoslav of Russia, 208; 243; 245; reign of, 238 sq.
Peter Asên, Tsar of Bulgaria, revolts against Empire, 517 sqq.; 590
Peter Bodin, Tsar of Bulgaria, *see* Constantine Bodin
Peter I of Lusignan, King of Cyprus, offered crown of Armenia, 181, 468; vigorous reign of, 469 sq.; 477
Peter II, King of Cyprus, and Genoese, 455, 470, 477
Peter, Prince of Hum, 591
Peter I Mouchate, Prince of Moldavia, 593

Peter II Mouchate, Prince of Moldavia, 593
Peter III Mouchate, Prince of Moldavia, 593
Peter the Great, of Russia, and Mongols, 650
Peter I Candianus, doge of Venice, and Slav pirates, 389, 400 sq.
Peter II Candianus, doge of Venice, and Istria, 401
Peter III Candianus, doge of Venice, and Patriarch of Aquileia, 401
Peter IV Candianus, doge of Venice, dynastic ambition of, 401; murdered, 402; 403 sq.; 407
Peter, Patriarch of Antioch, Michael Cerularius and, 113, 262, 268, 270; and Leo IX, 264, 267
Peter Marturius, Patriarch of Grado, 399
Peter Chrysolanus, archbishop of Milan, and Greek Church, 345, 600
Peter the Venerable, abbot of Cluny, and seizure of Constantinople, 601
Peter, bishop of Amalfi, legate of Leo IX, and Cerularius, 269
Peter Damian, St, quoted, 408 *note*
Peter, bishop of Jesolo, 399
Peter Boua, Albanian leader, 463
Peter the Hermit, and his lawless troops, 334; reaches Constantinople, 336; defeated, 337
Peter the Sicilian, sent to Paulicians by Basil I, 139
Peter the magister, general of Irene, captured by Saracens, 124
Petitions, Master of (ὁ ἐπὶ τῶν δεήσεων), office of, 731
Petrarch, on Greek feeling against Latins, 616
Petrion, *see under* Constantinople, churches of
Petroë, battle of, 117 sq.
Petronas, brother of Theodora, campaign against the Saracens, 46, 133; builds Sarkel, 192
Petros Getadartz, Katholikos of Armenia, mediates between John-Smbat and his brother, 112; 163; betrays Ani to Constantine IX, 165
Petrović, family in Montenegro, 587
Pettau, 211; 227
Pezineigi, *see* Patzinaks
Pezola, 64
Phanagoria (Tamatarcha, Tmutorakan), Justinian II at, 189; Jews at, 190, 208
Phanariote Greeks, 588
Philadelphia, 344, 377, 383; Greek lordship founded at, 423; French duke of, 480, 516; Turkish rule of, 654; 655; surrendered to Turks, 671; metropolitan of, and Michael VIII, 503
Philadelphion, *see under* Constantinople
Philagathus, John, anti-Pope, 91
Phileta, attacked by Seljūqs, 377
Philip of Swabia, King of the Romans, 415; and Fourth Crusade, 416 sq.; 421; 596, 603 sq.
Philip I of Anjou-Taranto (Philip II, titular Latin Emperor), 179; becomes suzerain of Greece, 448 sq.; 452 sq.; 614; 474; 476
Philip II of Taranto (Philip III, titular Latin Emperor), 454; death, 456; 535 sq.; 474; 476
Philip I, King of France, 337
Philip II Augustus, King of France, 415 sq.
Philip IV the Fair, King of France, 177
Philip VI of Valois, King of France, 179; and Leo V of Armenia, 180
Philip of Antioch, made King of Armeno-Cilicia, 174
Philip, count of Flanders and Vermandois, 377; arranges marriage of Alexius II, 379
Philip of Courtenay, declines Latin Empire, 427
Philip of Savoy, marries Isabelle of Achaia, 448, 474
Philip of Macedon, 49
Philippa of Antioch, and Andronicus Comnenus, 375, 381
Philippi, 492
Philippicus, Emperor, 6
Philippopolis, 37; 234; taken by Russians, 240; Manichaeans at, 243; 344; Latin dukedom of, 422, 520, 523, 590; Bulgarians defeated at, 425, 521; 427; 481; 502; ceded to Bulgaria, 541; 553; taken by Turks, 555; 571; 676; 691
Philocales, Eumathius, stratopedarch of Alexius I, 331; duke of Cyprus, 340 sq.; governor of Attalia, 344
Philomelium (Āq-Gyul), Alexius I at, 339, 344; captured by Ertughril, 655
Philosopher, the, *see* Leo VI; title applied to St Cyril, 217
Philotheus, author of *Kleterologion*, 58, 256, 730
Philotheus, Patriarch of Constantinople, friend of Harmenopulus, 617; 722
Philoxenus, commentator on the Novels, 707
Phobenus, George, Byzantine legal writer, 718
Phocaea (Foglia), in Asia Minor, 468, 662; 667; Genoese in, 684, 477; trade of, 775; 477
Phocas family, 64, 69, 78; its riches, 93; 95; 711; generals of, 739
Phocas, Emperor, 707
Phocas, Bardas, general, father of Nicephorus II, 70; defeated by Saracens, 72; 143
Phocas, Bardas, nephew of Nicephorus II, rebels against John I, 81, 147; defeats Bardas Sclerus, 85, 148; rebels again, 87, 208; defeat and death, 88, 149; captures Antioch, 89; 772
Phocas, Bardas, disgraced by Constantine VIII, 97
Phocas, Leo, general, uncle of Nicephorus II, 70; revolts under Constantine VII, 60 sq.

Phocas, Leo, brother of Nicephorus II, general of Theophano, 68; 69 sq.; made curopalates 72; enmity to John I, 78; banished, 79; revolts and failure, 81
Phocas, Nicephorus, patrician, general of Basil I, 69; victories in Italy, 140; victory at Adana, 141; 142; leader against the Bulgars, 199
Phocas, Nicephorus, *see* Nicephorus II, Emperor
Phocas, Nicephorus, son of Bardas Phocas, rebels against Basil II, 95
Phocas, Peter, son of Leo, patrician, 79; takes Antioch, 146; made commander in Anatolia, 84; killed at Rhegeas, 85
Phocis, mosaics in, 769
Phoenicia, freed from the Saracens, 148
Photian schism, *see* Photius
Photinus, strategus of the Anatolics, defeated in Crete, 132
Photius, Patriarch of Constantinople, made Patriarch, 46, 248 sqq.; and Roman Church, 47, 248 sqq.; deposed and exiled, 53, 250 sq.; again becomes Patriarch, 54 sq., 253; exiled by Leo VI, 56; death, 254; and Bulgaria, 45, 236; 255; 103; 261 sq.; 264; 267; 271 sq.; and St Cyril, 218 sq., 221; defends Constantinople, 46; 594; 625; 711; 718; 723 sq.; 753; learning of, 763; sermons of, 766
Phrantzes, Byzantine historian, and Constantine Palaeologus, 460; 474; 585 *note*; on Manuel II, 619; on resignation of John VI, 666, 671 *note*; 685 *note*; 695 *note*; 696 *note*; 697; 700; 765
Phrygia (Germiyān), 42; 121; 124; 170; Turks in, 654 sq., 657; Bāyazīd I and, 675; emir of, 690; Phrygian dynasty, 32, 36, 38, *see* Michael II, Theophilus; nationality of Empress Eudocia, 57
Piacenza, Council of, Byzantine ambassadors at, 599
Piale Pasha, Turkish admiral, occupies Naxos and Chios, 468
Pian di Carpine, John of, *see* John
Piave, river, and Magyar raid, 400; 405
Picardy, 415
Picenati, *see* Patzinaks
Piedmont, 181; Piedmontese in Greece, 448; 513; *see* Benzo
Pierre de Bracheuil, lands in Asia Minor, 480, 482 sq.; turns traitor, 484
"Pillars of Hercules," 742
Pindar, 763 sq.
Pindus, Mt, passes of, 241
Piraeus, the, 675
Piriska, *see* Irene
Piroz, Sasanid King of Persia, persecutes Armenians, 155
Pisa, fleet of, allied with Bohemond, 339 sq.; Alexius I and, 341, 344; and John II, 358; and Manuel I, 370 sq.; and First Crusade, 410 sq.; and Baldwin II, 429; 511; Byzantine fleet and, 742; Council of, 619; Pisans at Constantinople, 362, 750; trade with Constantinople, 762; archbishop of, *see* Daimbert
Pisani dynasty, in the Aegean, 467
Pithecas, in Asia Minor, 365
Pitti family at Athens, 461
Pius II (Aeneas Sylvius), Pope, sends crown to Stephen Tomašević of Bosnia, 578 sqq.; Skanderbeg and, 584; 692 *note*
Piyādē, Turkish infantry, 665
Plague, in Cilicia, 170, 176; Venetians attacked by, at Chios, 413; at Ferrara, 622
Planudes, Byzantine professor, 764
Plataea, in the Marmora, Turkish fleet defeated at, 686
Platani, in Sicily, tributary to Saracens, 136; revolts, 137
Plato, abbot of the Sakkudion, 21, 23, 28
Plato, Platonic doctrines in Arabic, 296; philosophy of, 350; 363; taught by Plethon at Mistrâ, 460, 766; 501; *Dialogues* of, 763 sq.; brought to Italy by Byzantines, 777
Platonion, 11
Plethon, George Gemistus, teaches Platonism at Mistrâ, 460, 766; 474; controversy with Roman Church, 595, 624
Pliska (Aboba), early capital of the Bulgarians, 231, 235, 237; taken by Nicephorus I, 232 sq.; 241
Plotinus, translated into Arabic, 295
Plutarch, 763
Po valley, importance as a trade route, 396; 399
Podandus, 127; death of Ma'mūn at, 129; river, 131; theme of, 343
Podgorica, in Montenegro, 534, 586
Pogodin, Russian historian, 199
Pogonatus, *see* Constantine IV
Ποίημα νομικόν, legal treatise of Michael Attaliates, 722
Poimanenon, Theodore I, defeated at, 424, 481; John III victorious at, 428, 487; 485; 488
Poitiers, Charles Martel's victory at, 2; Black Prince's, 454; *see* Raymond
Poland, 214; 556; Mongols in, 637, 652; kings of, *see* Boleslav, Vladislav; suzerain of Moldavia, 568; Poles, and Turks, 557; 692; *see* Benedict the Pole
Polani, John, Venetian admiral, 412
Political verse, Greek national metre, 721 *note*
Poljica, republic of, becomes vassal of Venice, 564; 587; 592
Polotsk, Russian trading centre, 202
Polovtzi, *see* Cumans
Polyans, Slav tribe at Kiev, 201, 203 sq.
Polybius, 763
Polychronium, Methodius made abbot of, 221
Polyeuctes, made Patriarch of Constantinople by Constantine VII, 65; his character, 65; 66; 68; supports Nicephorus II, 71 sq.; excommunicates Nicephorus,

74; 75; John I and, 79; death, 80; 260; and Liudprand, 261; 753
Pomposa, abbey of, 405
Pons, count of Tripolis, 343
Ponthion, convention of, 17
Pontus, 81, 121; trade with Constantinople, 762; *see also* Chaldia, Trebizond
Popes. *See* Alexander II, III, IV; Benedict III, VIII, XI, XII, XIII; Boniface VI, IX; Calixtus II, III; Celestine III; Clement IV, V, VI; Eugenius III, IV; Formosus; Gregory II, III, V, VII, IX, X, XI; Hadrian I, II, III, IV; Honorius II, III; Innocent II, III, IV, V, VI; John VIII, IX, X, XI, XIII, XIX, XXI, XXII; Leo IV, IX; Martin IV, V; Nicholas I, II, III, IV, V; Paschal I, II; Pius II; Romanus; Sergius III; Stephen II, V, VI, IX; Theodore II; Urban II, IV, V; Victor II; Zacharias. *See also* Papacy, Roman Church
Poppo, Patriarch of Aquileia, attacks Grado, 407
Porphyrogenitus, Constantine, *see* Constantine VII; palace of the, *see under* Constantinople; title of, 728
Porphyry Chamber, in the Palace at Constantinople, 24
Porto, bishop of, *see* Formosus, Radoald
Porus, in Thrace, 662
Posádniki, deputies of Oleg in Russian towns, 205
Poson, victory of Petronas at, 46, 134
Postal service, 731; under the Caliphate, 283; under Mongols, 629, 634, 647
Potenza, Louis VII at, 601
Poveglia, settlement of, 386
"Powerful," *see* Δυνατοί
Praecepta, of the Western Empire for Venice, 395; *praeceptum* of Thionville, 398; of Pavia, 400
Praepositus (Grand Master of Ceremonies), office of, 730
Praetorium, *see under* Constantinople
Prague, 214; bishop of, *see* Vojtěch, St
Prefect of the City (Constantinople), office of, 760 sq., *see* Eparch
"*Prefect, Book of the*," 58, 716, 719, 760 sq.
Prefect of Police (Muslim), *see* Muḥtasib
Pregadi, Venetian senate, beginnings of, 407
Preljub, Serbian governor of Joánnina, 543, 552
Preljubović, *see* Thomas
Presiam (Malomir), Khan of Bulgaria, 235
Prêslav, Great (Pereyaslavets), Bulgarian royal residence, 235; taken by Russians, 208; by Byzantines, 240 sq.; splendour under Simeon, 237; made capital by Peter Asên, 519; Patriarch of, 238, 522
Prêslav, Little, captured by Basil II, 241
Prespa, capital of Samuel of Bulgaria, 240 sqq.; ceded to John III, 494; lake of, 245
Prester John, 631, 639; identity of, 650
Pribina, Slavonic prince in Pannonia, 211
Prijesda I, "the great," ban of Bosnia, 591
Prijesda II, ban of Bosnia, 591
Prilep in Macedonia, 238; 241; 430; 502; taken by Epirotes, 504; 524; ceded to Serbia, 534; 555
Princes Islands, used as place of banishment, 16, 25, 29, 46, 95, 247, 265, 319, 657
Prinkipo, destroyed by Turks, 698; convent of, 106
Priština, temporary capital of Serbia, 523, 541; Vuk Branković at, 559; 562
Prizren, 244, 523, 554; bishopric of, 243
Prochiron, law book of Basil I, 52; 59; 710; 712 sq.; 716; revision of, 717; 718; 721 sqq.
Prochiron auctum, 717, 722
Prochiron legum, 717, 725
Proconnesus, 68; 134; 323
Procopius, Byzantine historian, 765; on Slav colonisation, 200; book of *Edifices*, 746; on dome of St Sophia, 752
Proedros (President of the Senate), title conferred on Basil Lecapenides, 72
Prokuy, revolts against St Stephen of Hungary, 214
Promptuarium (*Hexabiblos*), legal treatise of Harmenopulus, 721 sqq.
Pronishta, Albanian castle, 242
Pronoetes, of Bulgaria, office created, 243, 733 sq.
Propontis, the, *see* Marmora
Propylaea, the, at Athens, made ducal palace, 461, 464
Prosêk, Bulgarian fortress, 519, 522
Προσκύνησις (veneration), of images, 21; of the Emperor, 726
Proteuon, title of administrator of Cherson, 189; 192
Proti, island of, 63; 65; 79
Protimesis (law of redemption), in Novels of later Emperors, 715; commentary on, 718; 721; 725
Protoasecretis, office of the, 731; held by Photius, 248
Protochancellor of the theme, 734
Protomandator of the theme, 734
Protonotary of the theme, 734
Protosebastos, title of, conferred on doges, 412
Protospatharius, title of, 730
Protovestiary, office of, 730
Provence, 64; 260; *see* Hugh of
Prüm, *see* Regino of
Prusa (Brūsa), 344; 383; resists Latins, 481; 483; 485; Theodore I at, 479, 487; marriage of John III at, 495; 613; church at, 498; baths of, 23; *see also* Brūsa.
Prusianus, *see* Fruyin
Pruth, river, 198
Prymnessus, *see* Acroïnon
Psalms, translated into Slavonic by St Cyril, 226; Byzantine psalters, 769
Psará, Genoese at, 468, 477
Psellus, Michael, statesman and historian, 84 *note*; 96; 98; on Michael IV, 102; 103 sqq.; 110; teaches philosophy, 114, 764; 115; 118; and Cerularius, 265, 271; on

Isaac I, 321 sq.; 323 sq.; legal writings of, 715, 719, 721, 724; learning of, 763; history, 765; 764; 766; 774 sq.
Pseudo-Tipucitus, legal treatise, 720
Ptéleon, occupied by Venice, 453, 457, 465, 476; becomes Turkish, 466
Ptochotropheion, founded by Michael IV, 102
Pulchas, Turkish emir of Cappadocia, 331
Pulcheria, sister of Romanus III, 101: marriage to Constantine Monomachus, 108 sq.
Puy, *see* Ademar
Puzes, John, minister of John II and of Manuel I, 362
Pyramus, river, 122
Pyrgus, in Thrace, taken by Turks, 667

Qādir, Abbasid Caliph of Baghdad, 277
Qahrīye-jāmi', *see* Chora *under* Constantinople, churches of
Qā'im, Abbasid Caliph of Baghdad, and Seljūqs, 304, 306
Qairawān (Kairawān), Aghlabid capital, 300
Qaisarīyah, *see* Caesarea
Qalā'ūn (Saif-ad-Dīn Qalā'ūn al-Alfi), Mamlūk Sultan of Egypt, defeats Mongols and Armenians, 176; 177
Qānūn (Canon) of Avicenna, 297
Qāraja, emir of Ḥarrān, defeats Crusaders, 341
Qaramān (Karamania), city and emirate of, 654; and Ottoman Turks, 668, 672; Tīmūr in, 683; independent of Ottomans, 684 sq.; emir of, 690 sq., 694
Qaramān, Turkish chief in Asia Minor, 654
Qarghūyah, emir of Aleppo, treaty with Byzantines, 146
Qāsim, Abbasid prince, 126
Qāsim, a name of Barkiyāruq, *q.v.*
Qāsim, Saracen commander in Armenia, 156
Qāsim, youngest son of Bāyazīd I, 686
Qāsim Pasha, on Golden Horn, 700
Qāwurd, 'Imād-ad-Dīn, ruler of Kirmān, uncle of Malik Shāh, 307, 314
Qawwām-ad-Daulah Karbuqā, *see* Kerbogha
Qazwīn, *see* Zakarīyā
Qilij Arslān I ibn Sulaimān, Sultan of Rūm, 341; and Crusaders, 315 sqq., 340; and Alexius I, 331; 343; 353
Qilij Arslān II, son of Mas'ūd, Sultan of Rūm, 373; at Constantinople, 377; defeats Manuel, 378
Qonya (Iconium), *see* Iconium
Qoyun-Hisār, *see* Baphaeum
Quaestor, office of, 731
Quarnero, the, 559
Quierzy (Kiersy), assembly of, 17
Quirini, Venetian family, lordship of, at Astypálaia, 435; downfall of dynasty, 467; at Lampsacus, 480, 488
Quraish (Kuraish), the tribe of the Prophet, 281
Qur'ān, *see* Koran
Qutalmish, Seljūq prince, 304
Qutb-ad-Dīn Muḥammad, Khwārazm Shāh, 312
Quṭlughshāh, Mongol general, 178
Quṭuz, Mamlūk Sultan of Egypt, defeats Mongols, 643; killed by Baibars, 644

Raab, bishopric of, *see* Györ
Raab, Hungarian river, 211
Ra'bān, captured by Nicephorus II, 144
Rabbāh, Saracen leader in Sicily, 137
Rabī', Arab general, 124
Racova, Moldavian victory over Turks, 588
Radak, governor of Bobovac, surrenders to the Turks, 580
Radakovica, cliff of, 580
Rāḍī, Abbasid Caliph of Baghdad, 282
Radić Crnoje, "Lord of the Zeta," 586; 592
Radimiches, Slav tribe, subdued by Vladímir, 209
Radivoj, son of Stephen Ostoja of Bosnia, 573; slays his brother, 578; executed by Turks, 581
Radla, Bohemian priest, and the conversion of Hungary, 214
Radlov, and site of Karakorum, 640
Radoald, cardinal-bishop of Porto, legate of Pope Nicholas I, 248
Radoslav, ruler of Dioclea, 356
Radoslav, of Serbia, dispossessed by his brother, 522
Radoslav, Župan of Hum, 591
Radou I Negrou (Rudolf the Black), founds principality of Wallachia, 540, 593
Radou II, Prince of Wallachia, 593
Radou III, Prince of Wallachia, 593
Radou IV, "The Fair," Prince of Wallachia, 593
Radou V, "The Great," Prince of Wallachia, 593
Rāghib, Saracen admiral, victory off Asia Minor, 141
Ragusa, raided by Saracens, 137; 138 sq.; Robert Guiscard and, 325; surrenders to Venetians, 413; Bosnia and, 517, 565 sq., 583; and Bulgaria, 523 sq.; and Serbia, 535, 549, 553 sq., 570; 556 sq.; 559; 581; and Murād II, 690; *see* John of
Rai (Rayy), 303; taken by Seljūqs, 304, 309; 310; 314
"Rama, King of", title taken by kings of Hungary, 519, 527
Ramaḍān, Muslim fast, 284
Rambaud, A., on Byzantine Empire, 735, 737; on Constantinople, 750, 770; on Greek language, 774
Rametta, in Sicily, 144; captured by Saracens, 147
Randazzo, *see* Frederick, John
Rangabé, *see* Michael I, Emperor
Raphanea, taken by Basil II, 149
Rapsomates, rebels against Alexius I, 331
Rasa, bishopric of, 243
Rascia, *see* Novibazar; Chap. XVII *passim*; King of Hungary and, 519, 527; fertility

of, 537; Župan of, *see* Bolkan, Pervoslav, Stephen
Rashīd, *see* Hārūn ar-Rashīd
Rashīd, on Mongols, 631 sq.
Rationalis, title, superseded by that of *Logothete*, 731
Ravano dalle Carceri of Verona, becomes *terziere* of Euboea, 435
Ravenna, revolts against Leo III, 9; captured by Lombards, 17, 390 sq.; 18; 36; 385 sqq.; given to Pope, 392; 393; 398; *pactum* of, 399 sq.; 405 sq.; church of San Vitale at, 758, 768; monuments at, 776
Ravennika, Henry of Flanders at, 426
Rāwandī, Persian historian, on the Ghuzz, 303; 305
Raymond, of Saint-Gilles, count of Toulouse, 335; in First Crusade, 336, 338 sqq.; death, 342
Raymond of Poitiers, Prince of Antioch, 359; and John II, 361; and Manuel, 365
Raymond III of Antioch, count of Tripolis, 375; marries niece of Leo the Great, 172
Rayy, *see* Rai
Razboina, in the Balkans, 233
Rāzī, Arab medical writer, 297 sq.
Rector, impersonates Michael VII, 329
Red Russia (Eastern Galicia), and Vladímir, 209
Red Sea, 762
Regency, council of, during minority of Constantine VII, 59 sq.
Reggio, captured by Saracens, 141
Regina, duke of, last representative of Tocco family, 466
Reginald of Chatillon, regent of Antioch, and Armenia, 170; 374 sq.
Regino of Prüm, chronicler, on arrival of Magyars, 198
Register of Papal Letters, discovered in London, 226 sq.
Reinberg, bishop of Kolberg, imprisoned by Vladímir the Great, 210
Remigius Lellius, supposed ancestor of Palaeologi, 503
Renaissance, the, Byzantine influence on, 777; influence of Mongols on, 628
Renascence, in the tenth century: debt to Iconoclastic art, 26; 777
Renier, the Caesar, son of William of Montferrat, marries Mary, daughter of Manuel I, 379; 380; murdered by Andronicus, 382
Renier of Trit, duke of Philippopolis, 422, 425, 520, 590
Repurgatio veterum legum, see *Anacatharsis*, 714
Reshtuni, Armenian state, 157
Rhaedestus, *see* Rodosto
Rhegeas, battle of, 85
Rheims, archbishop of, *see* Hincmar
Rhodes, 64; Saracens land in, 127; pillaged by Venetians, 354, 411; 410; lordship of Gabalas at, 423, 432; and John III, 428, 488, 494; 441; and Michael VIII, 445; Hospitallers at, *see* Hospitallers; John Palaeologus, governor of, 504; 510; and Turks, 467, 654 sq., 657 sq., 665, 705; rulers of, *see* Table, 477
Rhodope, Mts., district of, 478; rebels against Theodore II, 501 sq., 525; 524
"Rhos," the, identified with Russians of Kiev, 203; *see* Rus
Rhosus, captured by Byzantines, 145
Rhyndakos, river, *see* Luparkos
Rialto, settlement of, 386; formed into city of Venice, 388 sqq., 394; defies Pepin, 394; 397
Ribnica, river, 517
Richard I, King of England, 362; 432; seizes Cyprus, 384, 603; sells Cyprus to Guy of Lusignan, 470
Richard II, King of England, made executor of last king of Armeno-Cilicia, 181
Richard, abbot of St Vannes, and Pope John XIX, 262; at Constantinople, 264
Richard, count of Cephalonia, 475
Ridwān, Seljūq ruler in Aleppo, 314, 340
Rila, mountains, 239, 502, 548, 577; *see* John of
Ripaticum, river toll, 400, 404
Ritha, sister of Hethum II of Armeno-Cilicia, 177
Riva degli Schiavoni, at Venice, 400
Rjeka, in Montenegro, 587
Robert of Courtenay, Latin Emperor, 427 sq.; 486
Robert of Taranto, Prince of Achaia (Robert II, titular Latin Emperor), 453 sq.; 474; 476
Robert, King of Naples, 179
Robert Guiscard, Duke of Apulia, and Alexius I, 325, 328 sq., 408 sq.; death, 330; 334; 337; 341 sq.; 352; 411 sq.; and Pope Nicholas II, 597; and Pope Gregory VII, 598
Robert, son of Robert Guiscard, 330
Robert, count of Flanders, and Alexius I, 333 sq.
Robert, Prince of Capua, on embassy of Conrad III, 360
Robert of Champlitte, dispossessed by Geoffrey Villehardouin, 438
Robert of Clari, on wealth of Constantinople, 745
Robert of Loritello, revolts against William of Sicily, 369
Roccafort, Catalan leader, 658
Rodolph, King of Italy, and Venice, 400
Rodoni, cape, Skanderbeg's castle on, 585
Rodosto (Rhaedestus), siege of, by Tornicius, 111; becomes Venetian, 421; taken by Catalans, 658; Turks defeated at, 662
Roe, Sir Thomas, ambassador to Mogul Empire, 652
Roger Borsa, Duke of Apulia, 345, 354
Roger II, King of Sicily, claims to Antioch, 358; and Manuel, 360, 365 sq., 368; death of, 369, 411; fleet defeated at Trani, 412; plans against Constantinople, 596, 600 sq.

Roger, Prince of Antioch, and Leo of Armeno-Cilicia, 169
Roger Bacon, on Tartars, 630; 764
Roger de Flor (Blum), leader of the Catalan Grand Company, 657; death, 658
Roger Deslaur, becomes ruler of Athens for the Catalans, 451; 475
Romaics of the Magister, see Πεῖρα
Romaioctonos, epithet applied to Kalojan of Bulgaria, 425
Ῥωμαῖοι, οἱ, in Byzantine administrative language, 738
Roman I Mouchate, Prince of Moldavia, 593
Roman II Mouchate, Prince of Moldavia, 593
Roman III, Prince of Moldavia, 593
Roman Armenia, *see* Armenia
Roman Church, *see* Councils, Papacy, Popes; relations with Byzantine Church, Chaps. IX, XIX; share in conversion of Hungary, 214; and Russians, 210; and Kalojan of Bulgaria, 520 sq.; in Serbia, 537; in Bosnia, 574 sq., 582; in Montenegro, 586
Roman Law, Byzantine legislation based on, Chap. XXII *passim*; and the *allelengyon*, 93; *Ecloga* contrasted with, 709; influence on Muslim legal system, 280, 292
Roman, conquest of Greece, 629; of Judea, 629; Roman division of Empire, 732; Roman protectorate of Black Sea towns, 184; Roman influence on Muslim postal system, 283; Roman and Byzantine Empires compared, 728 sq.; Alexius I's letter to the Romans, 600
Roman, son of Peter of Bulgaria, 240
Romania (Latin Empire), *see* Assises of; *see also* Latin Empire
Romanus I Lecapenus, Emperor, regent, 59 sq.; seizes throne, 61; plebeian origin of, 61 *note*; policy, 62 sq.; deposition and death, 63; legislation, 62, 93, 715 sq., 725; 64; 72; 79; 98 *note*; 142 sq.; and Magyars, 212; 238; 257; and Patriarchate, 63, 259 sq.
Romanus II, Emperor, worthless character of, 64; succeeds to throne, 67; family of, 68; death, 69; 70 sq.; 73; 77; 81 sq.; 84; 98; 144; 239
Romanus III Argyrus, Emperor, married forcibly to Zoë, 98; character and government of, 99; conspiracies against, 100; murder, 101; 102; 108; 150; 319; Novels of, 715; 718
Romanus IV Diogenes, Emperor, defeated and captured by Seljūqs at Manzikert, 167, 306 sqq., 325, 597; 326; 330; 333; 344; 378
Romanus, son of Romanus I, 64
Romanus, Pope, and Photian Schism, 256
Romanus, Byzantine hymnographer, 766
Rome, 5; revolts against Leo III, 9; attacked by Lombards, 17; Charlemagne crowned in, 24; 153; Cyril and Methodius at, 216, 224, 226 sq., 250; 249; 253; 261; 263; 271 sq.; 345; 399; 405; Baldwin II at, 429; 448; Greek pensioners at, 463 sq.; 578; Queen of Bosnia in, 581; 602; Boniface of Montferrat at, 604; ambassadors of John II at, 608; 617; John V at, 618, 670; 637; Eastern monks at, 258; Byzantine churches at, 264; trade route to, 396; Synods and Councils at, *see* Councils; *see* Lateran; *pactum* of, 402; monuments at, 776; compared with Constantinople, 745
Romkla in Armeno-Cilicia, 171; captured by Mamlūks, 177
Ῥοπαί, αἱ, collection of excerpts from Justinianean law, 707 sq., 723
Rosafa, fortress at Scutari, 564
Rossano, Byzantine MS. at, 768
Rostislav, Prince of Chernigov, and Theodore II, 502, 525; rules duchy of Mačva, 526
Rostislav, Prince of Great Moravia, asks for Christian teaching, 44, 235; 221 sq.; 225 sq.
Rotrude, daughter of Charlemagne, 20
"Rough Passes" of Nicomedia, battle of, 483
Roumania, Cumans in, 519; early history of, 540; Byzantine law in, 724; Church in, 568; Roumanians, at Kossovo, 573; Roumanian birth of Hunyadi, 571; *see also* Moldavia, Wallachia
Roussel de Bailleul, Norman leader against the Byzantines, 326
Roussillon, 451
Rovigno, and Venice, 412
Rovine, Turks defeat Wallachians at, 561
Ruben (Rupen) I, Armenian prince, founds principality of Armeno-Cilicia, 154, 167 sq.; 358
Ruben II, son of Thoros II, King of Armeno-Cilicia, 171
Ruben III, King of Armeno-Cilicia, 171, 376
Ruben, son of Leo I of Armeno-Cilicia, 358 sq.; put to death, 169
Ruben-Raymond, heir of Antioch, protected by Leo the Great, 173; defeat and death of, 174
Rubruquis (William of Rubruck), the friar, visits Mongols, 515; 630 sqq., 640 sq.
Rudolf the Black, *see* Radou Negrou
Rukn-ad-Daulah-w'ad Dīn, title of Barkiyāruq, 305, 309
Rukn-ad-Dīn, Sultan of Rūm, 173
Rukn-ad-Dīn, ruler of the Assassins, defeated by Mongols, 641
Rūm, *see* Iconium
Rumelia, 555, 571
Rumelia-Hisār, fortress, built by Mahomet II, 694
Rupel, pass of, Bulgarians defeated at, 430
Rupen, *see* Ruben
Rural Code of Leo III (νόμος γεωργικός), 4, 708; importance to historian, 710
Rurik, supposed founder of Russian dynasty, 200, 205
Rus, 200; means Swedes in Eastern writers, 204; *see* Rhos, Russians

Rusa, 338
Ruschuk, 687
Russia, early history of, 183 sqq., 199 sqq.; Turks in, 186; Mongols in, 279, 628, 631, 638; Andronicus Comnenus in, 381; John Asên II in, 521; 527; 659; Byzantine law in, 723 sq.; Byzantine influence on, 776; Slavonic ecclesiastical literature in, 229; churches in, 769
Russians, ambassadors in Constantinople, 38 sq.; attack Constantinople, 46, 140, 743, 747; princess of, *see* Olga; 96; 133; Basil I and, 138; war with John I, 81; Basil II and, 88, 149; conversion of, 89, 207, 210, 259; Constantine IX and, 111; 190; ravage Bulgary, 193; 194; 197; and Patzinaks, 199; early history of, 199 sqq.; and Bulgaria, 239 sq.; 263; and Manuel I, 368; and Mongols, 649 sq., 652; trade with Seljūqs, 516; with Constantinople, 762; in Byzantine army, 347, 738; in Constantinople, 746, 750; and Byzantine navy, 743; Russian Church, 261, 595, 712; *see also* Church, Byzantine; and Council of Ferrara, 621; Russian language, 220, 222; liturgies translated into, 92; "Russian Chronicle" (Nestor), 204, 209, 264 *note*; *see* Kiev, Svyatoslav, Vladímir, Yaroslav
Rustam, Sultan of Rūm, defeated by Leo the Great, 172
Ryazan, destroyed by Mongols, 637

Sabaeans, sect of, at Ḥarrān, 297 sq.
Sabaktagīn, father of Maḥmūd of Ghaznah, 303
Σαβάρτοι (Eastern Magyars), 195
Sábbas, lordship of, on Black Sea coast, 480; conquered by Theodore I, 482
Sabbioncello, peninsula of, ceded to Ragusans, 549
Sabin, Khan of Bulgaria, takes refuge at Constantinople, 232
Sabor, Serbian Parliament of nobles, 547
Sabutai, Mongol general, 637; 644
Sacellarius, office of, 731
Sacred Way, between Athens and Eleusis, 438
Sa'd-ad-Daulah, Ḥamdānid emir of Aleppo, 146
Sa'd-ad-Dīn, Turkish chronicler, on battle of Kossovo, 558 *note*; on capture of Constantinople, 704
Sa'd-al-Mulk, minister of the Great Seljūq Muḥammad, 311
Ṣadaqah, guardian of Seljūq prince Malik Shāh, 310
Sa'dī, Persian poet, 306
Ṣafavids, Persian dynasty, 301
Saffāḥ, Abbasid Caliph, death of, 122
Ṣaffārid dynasty, 300
Ṣafṣāf (the Willow), fort captured by Saracens, 125
Sahak IV, Katholikos of Armenia, taken prisoner by Saracens, 156
Sa'īd, Umayyad prince, 120
Saif-ad-Daulah, Ḥamdānid emir of Aleppo, wars with Constantine VII, 143 sq.; death, 146; master of North Syria, 277; patron of literature, 290, 296
Saif-ad-Dīn Qalā'ūn al-Alfi, *see* Qalā'ūn
Sains, *see* Guillaume de
St Andronicus, see of, in Pannonia, Methodius made bishop of, 226
St Anne, monastery of, 92
St Anthony the Great, church of, at Nicaea, 498
St Benignus at Dijon, abbot of, *see* William
St Bertin, Annals of the monastery of, on the "Rhos," 203
St Clement, church of, at Rome, 225
St Demetrius, *see* Demetrius; church of, at Salonica, 768, 770; chapel of, at Trnovo, 518; abbot of, *see* Isidore
St Denis, abbey of, 181; *see* Suger; Pantokrator church compared with, 753
St Elias (Ilya), cathedral of, at Kiev, 207
St Gall, the monk of, on Venetian trade at Pavia, 396
St George, Genoese bank of, and Famagosta, 471; *see* Mangana
St Germain, Philip de, of Savoy, sent to Pope Clement VI, 615
St Gilles, *see* Raymond; 602
St Gregory, abbey of, near Ephesus, 495
St John, Knights of, *see* Hospitallers; church of, at Valencia, 496; monastery of, *see under* Constantinople
St John Baptist, church of, at Prusa, 498; convent of, at Thessalonica, 66
St John Lateran, *see* Lateran
St Luke, church of, at Phocis, 769
St Mark, Venice, first church of, 396; 400; 402; new church of, 407; assembly in, 411; annual tribute to, 412; 415; modelled on church of the Holy Apostles at Constantinople, 753, 776; column of, erected, 413
St Martin's, Hungary, abbot of, becomes archbishop of Gran, *see* Anastasius
St Menehould, *see* Macaire
St Nicholas, church of, at Bari, 537
St Omer, brothers, fief of, in Greece, 433; *see* Nicholas; castle of, at Thebes, 446, 453
St Paul, hospital and orphanage of, *see under* Constantinople
St Peter, church of, at Rome, 18; Charlemagne crowned in, 24; 618; Councils at, *see* Councils; school at Constantinople, founded by Constantine IX, 114; cathedral of, at Olivolo, 397
St Pol, *see* Hugh of
St Romanus gate (Pempton, Tōp Qāpū), at Constantinople, 696, 698 sq., 701 sq., 704, 749
St Sabas, Laura of, 10
St Sava of Serbia, *see* Sava
St Servolo, abbot of, 397; island of, 406
St Simeon, port of Antioch, 341
St Sophia, church of, at Constantinople, 15,

30, 41, 46, 51, 53, 57, 71 sq., 79; repaired, 95 sq.; 99 sq., 107; decorated by Constantine IX, 114; 117 sq.; St Cyril made librarian of, 218; 220, 248, 257, 270 sqq., 320, 322 sq., 346, 380, 383, 418 sq.; desecrated by Latins, 420; Venetian, 421, 606; Dandolo buried in, 424; 431, 478; Michael VIII crowned in, 513; Union proclaimed at, 625, 695; last Christian service in, 701; Emperors anointed in, 728; 748 sqq.; building of, 751, 753 sq., 768; 770; dome of, 52; Councils in, *see* Councils; clergy of, 243, 343, 349, 623; church of, at Nicaea, 479; at Nicomedia, 483; at Salonica, 768; monastery of, at Trebizond, 515
St Tryphon, church of, at Nicaea, 513; schools at, 506
St Vannes, abbot of, *see* Richard
San Gregorio, at Venice, 400
San Marino, republic of, 564
San Michele del Quarto, Venetian market at, 405
San Niccolò di Lido, island of, Crusaders at, 416
San Stefano, sacked by Turks, 695
San Superan, Pedro de (Bordo), Navarrese leader in Achaia, 456, 459; 474
San Teodoro, column of, at Venice, 413
San Vitale, church of, at Ravenna, 758, 768
San Zaccaria, convent of, at Venice, 397, 399, 404, 406
Sant' Angelo, castle of, at Rome, 597
Sant' Angelo (in Pescheria), cardinal of, sent to Constantinople, 619
Sant' Apollinare Nuovo, church of, at Ravenna, 768
Sant' Ilario, on the Brenta, monastery of, founded, 397
Santa Maria Zobenigo, at Venice, 400, 402
Santa Mavra (Leucas), island, Venice obtains, 467, 472, 476; held by Michael Angelus, 436
Santa Susanna, *see* Benedict
Santo Spirito, hospital at Rome, 581
Sakkudion, the, monks of, oppose Constantine VI's divorce, 23; 24; abbot of, *see* Plato
Saksin, late name of Itil, *q.v.*
Saladin (Ṣalāḥ-ad-Dīn), 173; conquers Jerusalem, 278; 299; founds Ayyūbid dynasty, 302; biographers of, 306; 317; alliance of Isaac II with, 384, 603; and Assassins, 638; 643
Sale, Mongolian river, death of Jenghiz Khan by, 634
Salic Law, abrogated in Latin States of Greece, 437
Salīḥ, Abbasid prince, emir of Syria, 122
Sallustius Crispus (Sallust), quoted by Duke of the Archipelago, 467, 474
Salmenikón, last Greek fortress taken by Turks, 464
Sálona (Amphissa), barony of, founded, 433; castle of, 437; Roger Deslaur master of, 451; 456 sq.; captured by Turks, 458 sq.
Salonica (Thessalonica), 3, 6, 43 sq., 66, 104, 110, 115, 141; captured by Saracen fleet, 142, 151; attacked by Avars, 186; birthplace of SS. Cyril and Methodius, 215 sqq.; *Salonica legend of St Cyril*, 221; 237; 240 sqq.; Bulgarians defeated at, 244; taken by Normans, 383, 603; 408; Latin kingdom of, 422 sq., 432 sq., *see* Boniface, Demetrius; Greek Empire of, under despots of Epirus, 427 sqq., 439, 490 sq., 522 sqq., *see* Demetrius, John, Manuel, Theodore; conquered by Emperor John III, 430, 493; 497; 503; 505; 509; 511; 519; 521; 532 sq.; 541 sqq., 607; 609; 662; 665 sq.; 669; conquered by Murād I, 672; ceded to Manuel II, 685; captured by Mūsà, 686; purchased by Venice, 459; conquered by Murād II, 461, 690; 722; Genoese privileges at, 431; Serbian pious foundations at, 535; theme of, 39, 733; communist sect at, 760; churches at, 769 sq.; trade of, 770; archbishops of, *see* Basil, Eustathius, Joseph; *see also* Leo, Michael
Salzburg, archbishopric of, 211; and St Methodius, 221, 223; 226; archbishop of, *see* Theotmar
Samandar, town of the Chazars, 191
Sāmānids, princes of Khurāsān, 297, 300, 303
Samara, river, 192
Samaritan language, 220; signs in Glagolitic script, 225
Samarqand, conquered by 'Alā-ud-Dīn of Khwārazm, 278; 303; captured by Malik Shāh, 307; 311 sq.; destroyed by Mongols, 633: Tīmūr rules at, 650; 651; 684
Sāmarrā, 129 sq.; Abbasid Caliph removes to, 131, 276, 285; 133
Samkarsh, Jewish name of Phanagoria, 190
Samo, founds kingdom among West Slavs, defeats Avars, 186
Samokov, death of John Shishman at, 560; 563
Samos, 110; attacked by Saracen pirates, 141; Byzantine fleet defeated near, 142; ravaged by Venetians, 354, 411; assigned to Latin Emperor, 421; taken by John III, 428, 487; Genoese at, 468, 477; taken by Turks, 654, 657; theme of, 733, 742
Samosata, taken by Theophilus, 38; defeat of Michael III at, 46, 123; 133 *note*; captured by Basil I, 139; captured by John I, 143, 145; theme of, 733
Samothrace, island of, 421; 465, 477
Samsûn, held by Sábbas, 480
Samuel, Tsar of Bulgaria, 148; 239 sq.; defeat and death of, 241; 242 sqq.
Sanang Setzen, Mongol chronicler, on derivation of "Mongol," 630
Sandalj Hranić, Bosnian noble, 567; and Serbia, 573 sq., 591
Sangarius, river, 124, 133 *note*, 331, 360,

428, 480, 483; Ottomans established on, 656
Sanjakbey, *see* Pasha
Sanjar, Great Seljūq Sultan, 277, 298; defeated by Ghuzz, 303, 313; ruler of Khurāsān, 310; reign of, 311 sqq.; death, 313; 314; 317
Sanskrit, influence on Arab astronomy, 298 sq.
Santabarenus, Theodore, betrays Leo VI to Basil I, 55; exiled and punished by Leo VI, 56, 254
Santaméri, in the Morea, 446
Santorin, island of, 435
Sanudo, dynasty in the Aegean, 445; *see* Marco
Sanudo (the elder), 511 *note*, 514, 587 *note*
Sapor III, Sasanid King of Persia, partitions Armenia, 154
Saracens (Arabs), and the Empire, Chap. v; attack Constantinople under Leo III, 2 sq., 119; 20 sq.; Thomas the Slavonian and, 35; and Paulicians, 42; Nicephorus II's campaign against, 68; 74; 91; 103; in Crete, 36, 142, 144; in Sicily, 37, 134 sqq., 141, 147, 149; and Armenia, Chap. vi *passim*; and Chazars, 188 sq.; and Venice, 397 sq., 402, 404, 406, 410; in South Italy, 37, 39, 112, 139, 403; influence on Empire, 39, 152; Mongol invasions and, 628; *see* Chap. x; *see also* Africa, Asia Minor, Crete, Ottomans, Seljūqs, Sicily
Sarajevo, 566, 575
Sardica (Sofia), captured by Bulgars, 37, 232, 519; 239 sqq.; 324; 355; 502; 514; 525; 555; captured by Turks, 557; 571; 576; 624; 691; bishopric of, 243
Sardinia, tributary to Saracens, 134
Sardis, captured by Saracens, 119; victory of Constantine V at, 12; archbishop of, 608
Sarkel (White Town, Bêlavêzha, Ἄσπρον ὀσπίτιον), fortress of, 38, 191 sq.; captured by Russians, 207
Sarmatians, ancient inhabitants of Russia, 183 sq.
Saronic Gulf, islands of, 432
Sarūj (Batnae), 129, 143
Sarus, river, 120, 122
Sarygshar (Yellow City), part of the town of Itil, inhabited by the Khagan, 191
Sasanids, *see* Persia
Sassun, governed by Mamlūks, 182
Satalia, *see* Attalia
Satti, on the Drin, Venetian colony, 583; taken by Turks, 585; 592
Sauji, son of Murād I, conspires against him, 671; 673
Sava, St, son of Stephen Nemanja, made archbishop of Serbia, 518; and crowns his brother, 521; death of, 522; grave of, 556; "duke of St Sava," *see* Stephen Vukčić, Vlatko
Savastopoli, boundary of Empire of Trebizond, 487
Save, river, 211; 368; 545 sq.; 565; 569
Savoy, *see* Amadeus, Anne, Louis
Saxon, Emperors, 213, 401; *see* Otto I, II, III; Saxon Council, 261; Saxons in Serbia, 549
Saxony, 212
Scamander, monastery on the, 80
Scandinavian, crusading expedition, 341; Scandinavians at Constantinople, 750; trade with Constantinople, 762; *see also* Varangians
Schism, the, of Eastern and Western Churches, 182 sqq.; Chaps. IX, XIX; Great Schism in the West, 619
Schlözer, theory of Varangian origin of Russian Empire, 199
Schlumberger, on the murder of Nicephorus II, 77; on the death of John I, 82
Scholae, regiment of the Guard, 739; *see* Domestic of the
Scholarius, George, *see* Gennadius
Scholasticus, *see* John
Schools, church schools at Constantinople closed by Leo III, 10; foundations of Constantine IX, 114, 719 sq., 734; at Constantinople, 754, 764; of the Magnaura, 43, 711; encouraged by Alexius I, 328; founded by Theodore II at Nicaea, 506; in Armenia, 162; of Jamnia, 629; of Kublai Khan, 646; spared by Tīmūr, 680
Scicli, taken by Saracens, 138
Scio, *see* Chios
Sclerena, mistress of Constantine IX, 109 sq., 115
Sclerus family, 93, 771
Sclerus, Bardas, brother-in-law of John I, 78; 81; revolt of, 84 sqq., 148; defeated, 86; conspires again with Phocas, 87; his fate, 88 sq.; advice to Basil II, 92; 109; 149; 739; 772
Sclerus, Romanus, son of Bardas Sclerus, 84; betrays his father, 87
Sclerus, Romanus, grandson of Bardas Sclerus, favourite of Constantine IX, 110
Sclerus, plots against Alexius I, 342
Scopia, *see* Skoplje
Scutari, 517; 542; 553; Venetians in, 564, 584; defence of, 586; ceded to Turks, 584, 587; Orkhān at, 665; 666; 592; Sanjak of, 587; lake of, battle at, 110, 587; Latin Church at, 537
Scutariota, *see* Theodore
Scylitzes, Byzantine chronicler, judgment on Constantine VIII, 96; 101; 110; 765
Scyros, island of, 435
Scythians, ancient inhabitants of Russia, 183 sq.; 239; 748
Sdephanê, *see* Stephanê
Sea-Venice (Maritime-Venice), *see* Venice
Sebastea (Sīwās), 112, 129, 164, 166 sq.; Mongols at, 181, 679 sqq.; 315; 322; 325; 340; 365; theme of, 733 sq.
Sebastocrator, *see* Comnenus (Isaac)
Σεκρετικοί, Byzantine bureaucracy, importance of, 731 sq.

Seleucia, theme of, 39, 733 sq.; town of, pillaged by Byzantine fleet, 130; 169; occupied by Byzantines, 340
Selīm II, Ottoman Sultan, gains Naxos and Chios, 468; and Cyprus, 472
Seljūq ibn Yakāk, ancestor of Seljūq dynasties, 300, 304, 314
Seljūq Turks, Chap. x B, 111; 150 sq., 154; overrun Persia, 164; 165; conquer Greater Armenia, 166 sqq.; split-up of empire, 168; attack Armeno-Cilicia, 169 sqq., 178; 172; 182; rise of, 277; Empire of, 278; influence of, 299; save Islām, 302 sq.; Mongols and, 175, 279; 491, 504, 653 sq.; local dynasties, 314 sqq.; conquests in Asia, 325; Great Seljūq Sultans, *see* Alp Arslān, Barkiyāruq, Maḥmūd, Malik Shāh, Muḥammad, Sanjar, Ṭughril Beg; and Isaac I, 322, 324; and Alexius I, 326 sqq., 331 sq., 343 sq.; and First Crusade, 316 sq., 333 sqq., 337 sqq.; and John II, 353 sqq.; and Manuel I, 365 sq., 377; and Second Crusade, 367; and Andronicus I, 383; defeated by Nicenes, 425, 428 sq., 484; 479 sq.; capture Theodore I, 485; Michael Palaeologus and, 503 sq., 510; and Andronicus of Trebizond, 514 sq.; and Bulgarians, 527; 596 sqq.; 602; and Ottomans, 656; results of conquests of, 733, 742; trade with Nicaea, 498; trade with Russia, 516; architecture, 754; *see also* Iconium
Seltz, Charlemagne at, 393
Selymbria (Silivri), 271; taken by Michael VIII, 431, 509; Basil II buried at, 510; Selymbria gate of Constantinople, *see* Pege; 659; granted to Genoese, 666; 677; Turks in, 678, 695
Semaluos, taken by Saracens, 120, 128, 133; besieged by, 124
Semendria (Smederevo), built by George Branković, 569; 570; 573; 576; occupied by Turks, 578; 579
Semlin, sacked by Crusaders, 336; taken by Manuel I, 368 sq.
Sempad, *see* John-Smbat, Smbat
Senate, the, accepts Basil I, 50; and Michael IV, 102, 106; and Michael VI, 117 sq., 321; 342; 346; 728 sq.; of Venice, *see* Pregadi
Senekherim, King of Van, 163; resigns his kingdom to Basil II, 164; 166
Seraglio Point, at Constantinople, 698 sq.
Serbia, wasted by Tsar Simeon, 238; 240; 325; 338; 356; 368; independent under Stephen Nemanja, 373, 384, 517; Chaps. XVII, XVIII *passim*; 492; Turks in, 557, 559, 571 sq., 668, 672; annexation by Ottomans, 576 sqq., 670, 690; influence of Byzantine law, 724; influence of Byzantine civilisation, 776; Byzantine art in, 769; Table of rulers, 590. *See also* Church, Serbians
Serbians, Serbs, Chaps. XVII, XVIII *passim*; rising under Bogislav, 110; 230; first Serbo-Bulgarian war, 235; 238; 240 sqq.; rising under Delyan, 244; rising under Bodin, 244, 325; Alexius I and, 330, 332 sq.; and John II, 356; and Manuel I, 368 sqq., 373; 406; independence of, 373, 384, 517; and John Asên, 428; and Epirus, 430, 457, 504; and Greece, 455, 552; 465; and Theodore II, 504; and Papacy, 534; under Stephen Dušan, 539 sqq.; victory of Velbužd, 538; defeat on the Maritza, 555, 670, 672; defeat at Kossovo, 558; and Turks, 559, 568 sqq., 575 sq., 666, 669, 674 sq., 678, 685, 687 sq., 690 sqq.; and Bosnia, 562, 573 sq.; and Montenegro, 578, 585 sq., 617, 659; at battle of Angora, 562, 682; at siege of Constantinople, 696; Table of rulers, 590. *See also* Bosnia, Dioclea, Hum, Rascia, Serbia
Serenus, Patriarch of Aquileia, and Patriarch of Grado, 389
Seres, Balkan town, 240, 333; Lombard nobles at, 426; Latins defeated at, 428; 430; 492 sq.; 502 sq.; 532; 542 sq.; 553 sq.; 577; taken by Murād I, 669; 672
Seret, river, 198
Sergius and Bacchus, SS., 564; church of (Little St Sophia), 753, 768
Sergius III, Pope, and Leo VI, 256 sq.
Sergius, Patriarch of Constantinople, and Roman Church, 91, 258, 261 sqq.
Sergius, strategus of Sicily, proclaimed Emperor, 3
Serkevil, Mount, in Armenia, 164
Sermo Declamatorius, work of St Cyril, 220
Servia, Macedonian town, 241; captured by Normans, 329; obtained by Theodore II, 503
Sestieri, Crete divided into, 434
Sestos, 366; 376; 659; 667
Sevan, island of, victory of Ashot II over Saracens, 161; church of, 163
Severin, fortified by Mahomet I, 688
Sêveryans, Slav tribe, 204
Sextus, Calocyrus, Byzantine jurisconsult, 714, 722
Sgourós, Leo, founds lordship in Greece, 423, 433 sq.; death, 436
Shāfi'ite law, treatise on, 306
Shāhanshāh, title of Sasanid kings, 274
Shahap the Persian, defeated by Ashot I, 158
Shāhī Beg, *see* Muhammad Shaibānī
Shāhinshāh, Sultan of Rūm, 353
Shāhinshāh, Seljūq prince of Rūm, and Manuel I, 377 sq.
Shaizar, in Syria, 149; 359
Shakespeare, and "Duke of Athens," 442
Shamanism, original religion of Chazars, 190; among Mongols, 640, 646
Shamo, desert of, 187
Shangtu, Kublai elected Great Khan at, 645
Shangtung, Chinese province of, 648
Sharakans, Armenian sacred songs, 162
Shelun, Khagan of the Yuan-Yuan, 185
Shensi, province of China, 635; 644
Shestodnev, *see* Hexameron

Shī'ah (Shī'ites), sect, 301; factions in the Caliphate, 275; 277; Fāṭimids, 282, 302; persecuted by Mutawakkil, 288; legal system, 292, 304; feud with Sunnīs, 642 sq.; *see* Assassins, Mu'tazilites
Shibl-ad-daulah, Ḥamdānid emir of Aleppo, embassy to Romanus III, 100
Shihāb-ad-Dīn, Indian general, defeated by Tīmūr, 651
Shihāb-ud-Dīn Suhrawardī, Persian idealist philosopher, 296
Shiramun, grandson of Ogdai Khan, 640
Shirvan, *see* Albania
Shishman of Trnovo, founder of West Bulgarian Empire, 238; sons of, 239; 240; 244
Shtiponye, Bulgarians defeat Basil II at, 240
Shümeg, *see* Somogy
Shumla in Bulgaria, 231, 235
Siang-Hua, island of, off Korea, 637
Sībawaihi, Persian grammarian, 291
Sibylla, Queen of Aragon, at Athens, 459
Sibylla of Lusignan, second wife of Leo the Great of Armeno-Cilicia, 172
Sicily, insurrection in, 20; 36 sq.; 124; Saracens in, 37, 46, 69, 74, 96, 119, 135 sqq., 140; Byzantine successes in, 103; naval defeats off, 105; 128; finally lost, 141 sq., 147, 149; Maniaces in, 150; 151; Normans in, 352, 408, 416, 597; Catalans in, 449; 450; 513 *note*; 596; 608; 742; province of, 4; dioceses of, 10; influence of Byzantine law in, 725; Byzantine influence on art of, 776; kings of, *see* Alfonso, Charles, Frederick, Manfred, Roger, William; Sicilians in Byzantine army, 657, 738; "Sicilian Vespers," 448, 613; *see* Peter the Sicilian
Sideropalus (Cyzistra), taken by the Saracens, 126; Gagik II murdered at, 166, 169
Sidon, captured by John I, 148; Louis IX at, 515
Siena, John Stephen of Bulgaria at, 539
Sigismund, King of Hungary, later Western Emperor, and Stephen Dabiša, 569 sq.; defeated at Nicopolis, 561, 618, 675 sq.; and Serbia, 564; and Bosnia, 565 sq.; 620; and Mahomet I, 688; and Murād II, 690
Sile, river in Calabria, 405
Silesia, Mongols in, 628, 637, 639, 652; duke of, *see* Henry
Silistria (Dristra, Durostolus), 81; residence of Bulgarian Patriarch, 238; 239 sq.; Patzinak victory at, 330; ceded to Turks, 557; 560
Silivri, *see* Selymbria; Silivri gate at Constantinople, *see* Pege
Silver Bulgars, *see* Bulgars (White)
Silvio, Domenico, doge of Venice, marries Theodora Ducas, 408; defeats Normans, 409
Silzibul, *see* Sinjibu
Simanakla, Cilician fortress, 170
Simeon, name given to Stephen Nemanja as a monk and saint, 518, 535
Simeon, Tsar of Bulgaria, 62; war with Constantine VII, 142; 143; war with Magyars, 199, 236 sqq.; assumes the title of Tsar, 238; 243; 245
Simeon Uroš, brother of Stephen Dušan, rules Thessaly, 552; 475, 590
Simeon Magister, Byzantine chronicler, 765
Simocatta, Theophylact, on the Avars, 186
Simon the Logothete, Byzantine canonist, 718
Simonis, daughter of Andronicus II, married to Stephen Uroš II, 533
Sinai, monasteries in, 753
Sinān, taken by Saracens, 126, 128
"Sincerity, Brethren of," Muslim theological school, 292
Sind, 295
Sineus, Swedish chieftain in Russia, 200
Sinjibu (Silzibul, Dizabul), Khagan of the Turks, 187 sq.
Sinope, 133; declares for Empire of Trebizond, 480; captured by Theodore I, 485; Seljūqs at, 487, 514
Sipāhīs, division of Turkish army, 665
Sir Janni, ally of Stephen Dušan, 540
Sis, capital of Armeno-Cilicia, 168; 172; repulses Mamlūks, 176; 177; council at, 178 sq.; seat of Katholikos, 182
Sisia, Franciscan monastery in Cephalonia, 438
Sisinnius, Patriarch of Constantinople, 91, 261
Sisinnius, bishop of Perge, 8
Sīstān, 295, 311, 633
Siwni (Siunia), Armenian kingdom, 157; 158
Skanderbeg (George Castriota), Albanian chieftain, 572; career of, 584 sq., 691 sq.
Skanderbeg Crnojević, Turkish governor of Montenegro, 587; 592
Skepes, monastery of, 53
Skópelos, captured by Licario, 445
Skoplje (Scopia, Uskūb), in Macedonia, 241; captured by Normans, 329; 430; held by John III, 492; 519; 532; 536; Stephen Dušan crowned Emperor at, 542 sq.; 555; 690; bishopric of, 243
Slav, Bulgarian ruler of Melnik, 522
Slav, Slavs, tribes, Chap. VII, 4, 13, 20; of the Peloponnesus, 37, 42, 44; 119; 127; and Avars, 116; in Chazar bodyguard, 190; and Magyars, 194 sqq., 211, 215; 209; in Pannonia, 213 sq.; of the Balkans, 230; 244; 389; in Greece, 441; pirates, 253, 397, 399 sqq.; trade with Bulgars, 193; in Empire, 735 sq., 773; in Byzantine army, 738, 746, 770; language, 220, 222; culture in fourteenth century, 549; Byzantine influence on, 775 sq.; conversion of, 44 sq., 259, Chap. VII (B), 737; "Apostle of the," *see* Cyril, St; "Fort of the," captured by Saracens, 126; Eastern Slavs, *see* Russians

Slavery, under the Caliphate, 286; in Byzantine law, 720; Turkish slave girls of Mu'taṣim, 285; slave trade condemned at Venice, 399
Slavonia, 559, 581
Slavonian, the, *see* Thomas
Slavonic, alphabet, *see* Glagolitic; liturgy, 223 sqq., 228, 250, 568; abandoned in Moravia, 229; introduced into Bulgaria, 236 sq.; in Bosnia, 526; speech of Bulgaria, 235; literature in Russia, 229; first printed books, 587; law of succession, 559
Slovaks, in Hungary, 210
Slovenian, dialect, *see* Macedo-Bulgarian; "Slovenian lands," 227
Slovêns, East Slavonic tribe, 204
Smaragdus, punished for circulating Papal bull against Cerularius, 270
Smbat (Sempad), chronicle of, 172 *note*
Smbat Bagratuni, pro-Byzantine ruler in Armenia in early eighth century, 156 sq.
Smbat Bagratuni, the Confessor, father of Ashot I, 158
Smbat I, King of Armenia, 159; reign of, 160
Smbat II, King of Armenia, 162; buildings at Ani, 163
Smbat (Sempad), seizes throne of Armeno-Cilicia from Hethum II, 177; 178
Smbataberd, sacked by Seljūqs, 166
Smederevo, *see* Semendria
Smilec, Tsar of Bulgaria, 530 sq., 590
Smolensk, Russian trading centre, 202; 204
Smyrna, captured by Alexius I, 339; 344; Genoese at, 431, 511, 477; 485; logic taught at, 486; 498; miraculous image at, 500; recaptured from Seljūqs, 615; defended by Hospitallers, 683 sq.; 685; Junaid at, 687; trade of, 770; bishop of, 32; archbishop of, 617; emir of, *see* Tzachas; gulf of, 667
Soandus, surrenders to Saracens, 128
Sofia, *see* Sardica
Soissons, 416
Soldane of Georgia, mother of Leo VI of Armeno-Cilicia, 181
Solidus, coin, 4, 39; *see* Coinage
Solomon, senator, plots against Alexius I, 342
Solov'ëv, Russian historian, 199
Sommaripa, dynasty in Aegean, 467, 474
Somogy (Shümeg), chief of, *see* Kopány
Sophianós, archon of Monemvasía, 440
Sophon, lake, in Asia Minor, 331
Sorbonne, the, 619
Sósandra, monastery of, 498; tomb of John III at, 500; murder of Muzalon at, 507
Soter, monastery of the, *see under* Constantinople
Soterichus Panteugenus, *see* Panteugenus
Sotiriopolis, waters of, 67
Sottomarina (Clugies minor), settlement of, 386
Sozopetra, *see* Zapetra
Sozopolis, occupied by John II, 354; 361; taken by Seljūqs, 383
Spain, 36, 66; Saracen adventurers from, 127 sq., 135 sq.; Emperor Theophilus and emir of, 136; relations of Constantine VII with, 144; 295; lost to the Abbasid Caliphate, 300; Umayyad dynasty in, 139, 274 sq.; slaves from, 286; 629; Spanish Arab philosophers, 296; medical writers, 297; mercenaries, 657, *see* Catalan; trade with Constantinople, 762; travellers in Constantinople, 746, 750
Spalato, taken by Venetians, 406, 411; 557; 564; Hrvoje, "Duke of," 565 sq.
Sparta, capital of princes of Achaia, 441, 443, 454
Spatharius, title of, 730; bestowed on the doge Obelerius, 394; *see* Arsafius
Spatharocandidatus, title of, 730
Spercheus, river, Bulgarians defeated at, 241 sq.; valley of, 444
Spinalonga, Cretan fortress, 472
Spoleto, duke of, revolts against Byzantium, 390
Sporades, governed by Venetians, 434 sq.; captured by Byzantines, 445; Venice in, 465, 476; lost to Venice, 466
Sracimir, *see* John Sracimir
Srebrenica, silver mines of, 556, 566
Srebrenik, banat of, 581
Sse-Kin, Khagan of the Turks, sends embassy to Constantinople, 187
Staffolo, *placitum* of, 405
Stagi (Kalabaka), Thessalian bishopric, 243
Stamboul, derivation of, 696; size of, 747, 750, 761
Stampalia, *see* Astypálaia
Stara-Zagora, *see* Eski-Sagra
Stauracius, Emperor, son of Nicephorus I, defeated by Bulgarians, 29, 233
Stauracius, Logothete of the Dromos, favourite of Irene, 20; 22 sq.; captured by Saracens, 124; 125 sq.; death, 24
Stenimachus, 425
Stephanê (Sdephanê), brother of Thoros II of Armeno-Cilicia, 170; his fate, 171, 375; 376
Stephen II, Pope, 17 sq., 391
Stephen V, Pope, and Moravia, 229; and Photian schism, 254, 256
Stephen VI, Pope, and Photian schism, 256
Stephen IX (Frederick of Lorraine), Pope, and Cerularius, 269, 597
Stephen, brother of Leo VI, 51; made Patriarch of Constantinople, 56, 254; 58
Stephen, Patriarch of Constantinople under Romanus I, 63; 2
Stephen Nemanja (Dessa, St Simeon), Prince of Serbia, and Manuel I, 373; 517; reign and death, 518; 519; 550; 553; 590
Stephen, the First-Crowned, King of Serbia, "Great Župan," son of Stephen Nemanja, 518; crowned, 551; death, 522; Greek wife of, 532; 590

Stephen Dragutin, King of Serbia, drives his father from the throne, 531; rules Bosnia, 532; death, 534; 556; 590 sq.
Stephen Uroš I, King of Serbia, 524; and Michael VIII, 527; dethroned by his son, 531; 590
Stephen Uroš II Milutin, King of Serbia, 531; Byzantine marriage of, 532 sq.; and Papacy, 534; opportunist policy, 537; institutes trial by jury, 535; 547; 549; relic of, at Ragusa, 570
Stephen Uroš III Dečanski, King of Serbia, natural son of Stephen Uroš II, 534; seizes the crown, 535; marriage, 536; victory at Velbužd, 538; deposition and death, 539; 590
Stephen Uroš IV Dušan, Tsar of Serbia, 234; in N. Greece, 455; dispossesses his father, 539; reign of, 540 sqq.; and John VI, 541, 543; crowned Emperor, 542; and Bosnia, 544 sq.; death, 546; 552; legislation, 547; and the Church, 548; and foreigners, 549; his Empire, 550 sq.; break-up of his Empire, 554; 590; 553 and Turks, 666
Stephen Uroš V, Tsar of Serbia, crowned King by his father, 542; marriage, 549; accession as Tsar, 552; 553; dethroned, 554; death, 555; 590
Stephen Lazarević, "Despot" of Serbia, 559, 674; tributary to Turks at battle of Nicopolis, 561; at battle of Angora, 562, 682; reign of, 563; death, 564; 575; 585; 590
Stephen, ban of Bosnia, 591
Stephen Kotroman, founder of Bosnian dynasty, 532
Stephen Kotromanić, Bosnian ruler, 541; and Stephen Dušan, 544 sq.; death, 545; 550; 556; 591
Stephen Dabiša, King of Bosnia, 559 sq., 591
Stephen Ostoja, *see* Ostoja
Stephen Ostojić, King of Bosnia, 567, 591
Stephen Thomas Ostojić, King of Bosnia, *see* Thomas
Stephen Tomašević, King of Bosnia, 577; receives crown from Pope, 578 sq.; slain by Turks, 580; 591
Stephen Vukčić, Bosnian noble, made "Duke of St Sava," 574; King of Bosnia and, 575, 579; and Turks, 580; death, 581; 582; 591
Stephen Borić, Duke of Mačva and Bosnia, 591
Stephen I, St, King of Hungary, reign of, 213 sqq.
Stephen II, King of Hungary, and John II, 355 sq.
Stephen III, King of Hungary, and Manuel I, 372; 373
Stephen IV, King of Hungary and Manuel I, 372
Stephen I Mouchate, Prince of Moldavia, 593
Stephen II Mouchate, Prince of Moldavia, 593
Stephen III, Prince of Moldavia, 593
Stephen IV, the Great, Prince of Moldavia, 588, 593
Stephen I Crnojević, of Montenegro, and Venice, 586; 592
Stephen II Crnojević, becomes ruler of Montenegro, 587, 592
Stephen, son of Romanus I, crowned by his father, 61
Stephen, father of Michael V, 104; defeated in Sicily, 105
Stephen (Aḥmad Pasha Hercegović), son of Stephen Vukčić, 581; career in Turkish service, 582
Stephen, son of George Branković, blinded by Turks, 570, 577
Stephen of Blois, leader in First Crusade, 339
Stephen of Perche, made duke of Philadelphia, 480; 516
Stephen, bishop of Clermont, charge of, 599 *note*
Stephen, bishop of Nepi, legate of Hadrian II at Constantinople, 251 sq.
Stephen the Younger, St, murdered, 16
Stephen of Surozh (Sugdaea), St, biography of, on Russian raids in Asia Minor, 203
Stephen, priest sent by Pope Stephen V to Moravia, 229
Stephen, the deacon, on Constantine V, 11
Stephen of Ephesus, Byzantine canonist, 711
Stephen, eminent jurisconsult, 707, 714, 716
Stethatus (Pectoratus), Nicetas, and the Latin Church, 113, 267; treatise of, condemned, 269 sq.
Ştilo, Otto II defeated by Saracens at, 149
Ŝtip, Macedonian town, ceded to Stephen Uroš II, 534
Stracimir, Montenegrin ruler, 592
Strategion, *see under* Constantinople
Strategopulus, Alexius, general of Michael VIII, takes Constantinople, 431, 511 sqq.; at Chepina, 502; captured by Nicephorus Angelus, 508
Strategus, office of, 731, 733 sq.; in the navy, 742 sqq.
Stratioticus, *see* Michael VI, Emperor
Stratores (grooms), office of, 730
Strêz, Bulgarian prince, 519; 522
Struma, *see* Strymon
Strumitsa in Bulgaria (Macedonia), 242, 547
Strymon (Struma), river, 232; valley of the, 241, 502; 538; theme of, 733
Studenica, monastery of, 518; 535
Studion (the), monastery of, 24, 26, 28 sq.; zeal for images, 31; Ignatius and, 46; 80; 107; and Roman Church, 247 sqq.; and Stethatus, 269 sq., 255; 259 sq.; 266; 324; Michael VIII at, 513; 749; *see* Alexius, Anthony, Nicholas, Theodore
Stylianus Zaützes, *see* Zaützes
Stylianus, court chaplain, 73 sq.
Styria, 688

Šubić, Croatian family, and Serbia, 535; 541
Sublaeum (Homa), 378
"Sublima Porta," 697
"Sublime Khan," title of early rulers of Bulgaria, 231
Suchuan, Chinese province, 645
Suda, Cretan fortress, 472
Suetius, ceded to Bohemond of Antioch, 343
Sufiism, Sufis, 292
Suger, abbot of St Denis, 596, 601
Sugdaea, *see* Stephen of
Sughd, 303, 633
Συγκλητικοί, senatorial order, 729, 734, 757
Sugyut, made headquarters of Ottoman Turks, 656; 660
Suidas, on Bulgarian code of laws, 233
Sukmān, Urtuqid ruler, 316 sq.
Sulaimān, Umayyad Caliph, 119
Sulaimān, Umayyad prince, 120 sq.
Sulaimān, lieutenant of Maslamah, 2, 119
Sulaimān, Saracen general, 125
Sulaimān, Seljūq, nephew of Sanjar, 312
Sulaimān ibn Qutalmish, Sultan of Rūm, captures Antioch, 307 sq.; founds Sultanate of Rūm, 315; Alexius I and, 329; death, 331
Sulaimān, son of Orkhān, Ottoman prince, 666 sq.; death, 668; takes Hadrianople, 669; 673; 593
Sulaimān, son of Bāyazīd, at battle of Angora, 682; at Anatolia Hisār, 683; and Serbians, 562 sq.; and Manuel II, 685; death, 686
Sultān Shāh, Seljūq ruler in Syria, 314
Sulzbach, count of, father of the Empress Bertha, 360
Sung Dynasty, in South China, and Mongols, 633 sqq., 640, 644 sqq.
Sunnīs, Sunnah, orthodox Muslims, 277; six great traditions of, 281 sq., 301; schools of law, 292
Surozh (Sugdaea), *see* Stephen of
Susamish, Mamlūk viceroy of Damascus, invades Cilicia, 177
Sutera, in Sicily, tributary to Saracens, 136; revolts, 137
Sutjeska, seat of the Bosnian court, 556; Franciscan monastery at, 581
Suvar, Bulgarian town, 193
Svatopluk, Prince of Great Moravia, 198, 210, 226; and St Methodius, 227
Svętslav, James, Bulgarian chieftain, assassination of, 528; *see* Theodore
Svinimir of Croatia, crowned by the Papal legates, 325
Svyatopolk, son of Vladímir the Great, 209 sq.
Svyatoslav, Prince of Kiev, reign of, 207 sq.; and Byzantines, 145, 147; 213; and Bulgarians, 239 sq.
Swabia, 227; *see* Philip of
Swedes, commerce with Bulgars, 192 sq.; and foundation of Russia, 199 sq.; 202; Vladímir flees to, 208; *see also* Varangians
"Sweet waters of Asia," river, 676
Syce, besieged by Saracens, 123
Syllaeum, bishop of, *see* Anthony
Sylvester II, Pope, sends crown to St Stephen, 214
Symbatius, advocate and commentator on the Novels, 707
Symbatius, protospatharius, and promulgation of the Basilics, 713; 717
Synada, taken by Saracens, 121
Synadenós, general of David Comnenus, defeated by Theodore I, 482
Synagoge canonum, 711
Syncellus, creation of the office of, 58; *see* George
Synodal Edict, the, of Cerularius, 271
Synods, *see* Councils
Synopsis canonum, of Stephen of Ephesus, 711
Synopsis legum, legal treatise in verse, attributed to Psellus, 721
Synopsis Maior, 715, 717, 722 sq.
Synopsis Minor, 717, 722 sq.
Syntagma canonum et legum, of Blastares, 724
Syntagma, of Photius, (so-called) collection of Byzantine canon law, 718, 723 sq.
Syracuse, Saracen failure before, 37, 135; 103; 136 sqq.; captured, 140; recaptured and lost again, 150; archbishop of, *see* Gregory
Syria, 12, 19, 38, 70, 74, 76 sqq., 86, 99; Chap. v *passim*; Nicephorus II in, 134, 145 sqq.; Basil II in, 149 sq.; 178; 274; Seljūqs in, 168, 218, 277, 307, 310, 312, 314 sqq.; independent of Caliphate, 276; Mongols in, 279 sq., 643, 645, 654; Crusaders in, 339 sqq., 348, 353; Latin princes of, 357, 599; 358; 361; 376; 415; 418; kings of Cyprus and, 469; 564; Assassins in, 628; Turkish tribes in, 653; Tīmūr in, 680; Roman law in, 292; Byzantine law in, 723; monasteries in, 168; Syrian colonists in Thrace, 231; Syrian Christians, 298, 623; Syrians in Byzantine Empire, 735; in army, 738, 742; in Constantinople, 750; trade with Constantinople, 762, 776; ports, 770
Syriac literature, decline of, 290; translated into Arabic, 292, 297
Syrmia, held by Bulgarians, 234
"Sythines," fourteenth century name for Athens, 459
Szegedin, 576; Hungarian Parliament at, 578; treaty of, 571, 691
Szilágyi, governor of Belgrade, 577

Ṭabarī, Arab writer, 128 *note*; 133 *note*; 218; commentary on the Koran, 291; history of the world, 293
Ṭabaristān, conquered by Seljūqs, 304
Ṭabrīz, 182
Tactics, military work of Leo VI on, 58; *see* Army
Tadjat, Armenian general of Irene, deserts to Saracens, 124

Tagliacozzo, battle of, 444
Τάγματα, divisions of Byzantine army in Constantinople, 739
Ṭāhir, Persian general of the Caliph Ma'mūn, 276
Tā'i', Abbasid Caliph of Baghdad, 277
Tā'if, 312
Ṭaïkh, the, Armenian province, 157 sq., 160
Taine, on Byzantine courtiers, 755
Tai-Tsung, Chinese Emperor and Mongols, 632
Taitu, *see* Cambalu
Tāj-ad-Dīn, King of Nīmrūz, captured by the Khaṭa', 312
Tāj-al-Mulk Abu'l-Ghanā'im, vizier of Malik Shāh, 308
Tajki-Gar (Rock of Tajik), Cilician stronghold, 170
Takrīt, 278
Tali, Chinese city, taken by Kublai, 644
Talib, White Bulgarian ruler, 193
Tall-Baṭriq, Saracens defeat John I near, 143
Taman, peninsula of, 189
Tamatarcha, *see* Phanagoria
Tamburlaine (Tamerlane), *see* Tīmūr
Ṭamghāj Khān, father-in-law of Malik Shāh, 307
Tanais, Greek colony on Black Sea, 183; Jewish community at, 190
Tancred, nephew of Bohemond, leader in First Crusade, 335, 338, 340 sq.; becomes Prince of Antioch, 343
T'ang dynasty of China, 632
Tangut, *see* Hia
Taormina, harried by Saracens, 137; remains Byzantine, 138 sq.; captured, 141, 144
Taranta, 119
Taranto, Venetian fleet defeated by Saracens, 136, 398; 139; occupied by Otto II, 149; 369; *see* Philip, Robert
Tarasius, Patriarch of Constantinople, appointed by Irene, 21; opposes Constantine VI's divorce, 23; crowns Nicephorus I, 25; 26, 28; 248
Ṭaratūs (Tortosa), attacked by Byzantines, 146; regained by Alexius I, 343
Ta'rīkh Jalālī, Turkish era, named after title of Malik Shāh, 308
Tarim, river of Central Asia, 187
Taron, Armenian family, 62; 88
Taron, Armenian province, 131, 160; 161; ravaged by Mongols, 181
Taronites, governor of Salonica, killed by Bulgarians, 241
Taronites, Gregory, duke of Trebizond, and Alexius I, 342
Taronites, Gregory, minister of John I, 352
Taronites, Michael, brother-in-law of Alexius I, plots against him, 333
Tarsia, province of, 480
Tarsus, 89; in Saracen wars, 120, 124 sqq., 129, 132, 134; taken by Nicephorus II, 145; by John II, 169, 358 sq.; capital of Armeno-Cilicia, 168; 171 sq.; 174; captured by Mamlūks, 176, 669; Tancred at, 335, 338, 340 sq.; 343; church at, 179; commerce of, 770; emirs of, *see* 'Alī, Thābit
Tartars, and Bulgaria, 527 sqq.; in Serbia, 531 sq.; in Roumania, 540; mercenaries at Velbužd, 538; in Thrace, 659, 663, 665; languages, 628; derivation of name of, 630; finally absorbed by Mongols, 632; *see also* Mongols
Tartary, 175, 633
Tashkent, destroyed by Mongols, 633
Tataeum, 120
Tatar-Pazardzhik, 531
Taticius, Byzantine general with the Crusaders, 338
Tatu, *see* Cambalu
Taurus range, in Asia Minor, 120, 151, 167 sq., 274, 278, 358, 653, 740
Taurus, square at Constantinople, *see under* Constantinople
Tavia, Greek stronghold taken by Turks, 690
Taygetus, Mt, 42, 441; *see also* Maina
Tedaldi, Florentine soldier, at siege of Constantinople, 695, 697 *note*, 700 *note*
Tedaldo Visconti, *see* Gregory X, Pope
Tegea, 441
Teias, King of the Ostrogoths, 385
Tekfūr Serai (Palace of the Porphyrogenitus), *see under* Constantinople
Telerig, Khan of Bulgaria, and Constantine V, 232
Telets, Khan of Bulgaria, 231
Teloneum, land tolls, 400
Teluseh, ceded to Bohemond of Antioch, 343
Tempe, valley of, 241
Templars, the 171; and Leo the Great of Armeno-Cilicia, 173; help Hethum II, 177; 178; in Greece, 437; refuse Cyprus, 469; receive Attalia, 480
Temujin, *see* Jenghiz Khan; derivation of name, 632
Tenedos, island of, 500; taken by Turks, 654, 657; Venetians in 671; 677
Tenos, island of, 435; Venetian, 457, 465, 467 sq., 476; lost to the Ottomans, 472
Tephrice, occupied by Paulicians, 42; attacked by Petronas, 46; 132; captured by Basil I, 139
Terebinthus, island of, 248
Terter, river, 206
Terteri dynasty in Bulgaria, extinction of, 536; *see* George
Tervel, Bulgarian prince, and Justinian II, 189, 231
Terzieri, rulers in Euboea, 435
Teutonic Knights, in Greece, 437; in Roumania, 540
Thābit, emir of Tarsus, defeated by Byzantines, 127
Thābit ibn Qurrah, Arab translator of medical works, 297

Thalelaeus, author of commentary on the Code, 707, 714, 716
Thamar, aunt of Alexius Comnenus, Emperorof Trebizond, 479
Thamar of Bulgaria, married to Murād I, 555
Thasos, Byzantine fleet defeated off, 128; 465; Genoese in, 477
Thebasa, in Cappadocia, captured by Saracens, 125 sq.
Thebes, Bulgarian victory at, 244; Normans at, 368; 433; in dukedom of Athens, 439 sqq., 447, 472 sq.; Catalan vicar-general at, 451; 453; the Acciajuoli at, 458 sq., 464; 461 sq.; Turkish, 465; 508; silk manufacture at, 440, 447, 770
Thecla, sister of Basil I, 51
Theiss, river of Hungary, 210 sq., 214 sq., 637
Themes (θέματα), Byzantine provinces and army-corps, institution and arrangement of, 732 sqq.; command and government of, 734; names of army-corps, 739 sq.; maritime themes, 742 sqq., 364; development of system by Leo III, 3; reorganisation by Theophilus, 39; *Book of the*, by Constantine VII, 67; composition changed by Irene, 125; imitated by Saracens, 132; Bulgaria included in system, 243; Manuel I levies tax instead of ships from maritime themes, 364; *see* Army, Fleet
Theobald (Thibaut) III of Champagne, chosen leader of Fourth Crusade, 415; death, 416
Theocritus, 763
Theoctiste, mother of Theodora, 34
Theoctistus, the Logothete, uncle and counsellor of Theodora, 40, 42; murdered, 43; expedition against Saracen pirates, 45; defeated by Saracens, 131; patronage of St Cyril, 217 *note*, 218
Theoctistus Bryennius, *see* Bryennius
Theodates of Rhodes, helps Constantine IV of Armeno-Cilicia, 181
Theodonis Villa, *see* Thionville
Theodora, Empress, wife of Justinian I, 98, 757 sq.
Theodora, Empress, Chazar princess, wife of Justinian II, 189
Theodora, Empress, wife of Theophilus, left regent, 34, 40; restores image worship, 41, 246; Paulicians and, 42, 133, 139; Saracen campaigns, 139 sq.; and St Methodius, 217; end of her political career, 43; 46
Theodora, Empress, wife of Romanus I, 61
Theodora, Empress, daughter of Constantine VIII, 84; 94; 96; plots against Zoë and exiled, 100; crowned co-Empress, 107; joint government, 108; 109; becomes sole Empress, 115; disgraces Cerularius, 116, 597; death, 116; 319
Theodora, daughter of Constantine VII, 68; marries John I, 81
Theodora Comnena, marries Constantine Diogenes, 326
Theodora, daughter of Alexius I, 346
Theodora, niece of Manuel I, 363; married to Baldwin of Jerusalem, 374; carried off by Andronicus, 381
Theodora Ducas, marries Domenico Silvio, doge of Venice, 408
Theodora Cantacuzene, daughter of John VI, married to Sultan Orkhān, 665, 667
Theodora, the Senatrix, wife of Theophylact, 256, 259
Theodore I Lascaris, Emperor, crowned, 423; and Latins, 424, 426, 481, 485; defeats Seljūqs, 425, 484; death, 427; 478 sqq.; and Papacy, 596, 604, 607; 516
Theodore II Lascaris, Emperor, 489; 496; 499; accession and coronation, 500 sq.; Bulgarian campaigns, 502; 430; and Epirus, 503 sqq.; and Papacy, 505, 596, 609; illness and death, 506; 507; 513 sq.; 516; 525
Theodore Ducas Angelus, despot of Epirus, successes of, 427, 439; crowned Emperor, 497; and Theodore I, 479; and John III, 428 sq., 493 sq.; 436; 439 sq.; captured by Bulgarians, 523 sq.; ruler at Vodená, 493, 524; 475 sq.
Theodore I Palaeologus, despot of Mistrâ, 458 sq., 675: and Bāyazīd, 677 sq.
Theodore II Palaeologus, despot of Mistrâ, 460 sqq.; 471
Theodore Svętslav, Tsar of Bulgaria, son of George Terteri I, 530 sq.; seizes the throne, 536; 590
Theodore II, Pope, and Photian schism, 256
Theodore Balsamon, Patriarch of Antioch; nomophylax at Constantinople and legal author, 714 sq., 720; his *Exegesis Canonum*, 724
Theodore of Colonea, appointed Patriarch of Antioch, 80; death, 89
Theodore, bishop of Cyzicus, opposition to Polyeuctes, 65
Theodore of Studion, aims of, 21; 23; praise of Irene, 25; 28; appeals to Rome, 29, 32, 247; and Leo V, 30 sq.; 33; death, 34; final defeat of his policy, 41; 233; and Byzantine luxury, 758; 766
Theodore, Palestinian monk, champion of icons, 34
Theodore, son of John III, 489
Theodore, general of Michael VI, 117, 321
Theodore of Hermopolis, legal commentator, 707, 714, 716
Theodore Scutariota, 506 *note*
Theodore, tutor of Constantine VII, 61
Theodorita (Hagiotheodorita), Byzantine jurisconsult, 714, 720, 722
Theodosia, Greek colony on the Black Sea, 183
Theodosiopolis (Erzerum), captured by Constantine V, 12, 122; 129; 132; occupied by Mongols, 653

Theodosius I, Emperor, 154; column of, at Constantinople, 748
Theodosius II, Emperor, enlarges Constantinople, 747, 749; founds university of Constantinople, 764
Theodosius III, Emperor, 3
Theodosius, St, of Trnovo, adviser of John Alexander of Bulgaria, 550
Theodosius, father of Constantine IX, 108
Theodosius, cousin of Constantine IX, revolts against Michael VI, 117
Theodosius, bishop of Ephesus, 8
Theodosius, the patrician, sent by Theophilus to the doge, 397
Theodote, second wife of Constantine VI, 23 sq., 28
Theodotus Cassiteras, made Patriarch of Constantinople by Leo V, 31; dies, 33
Theodotus, Patriarch of Constantinople, 380; and Andronicus I, 381 sq.
Theodotus, the patrician, commander in Sicily, defeated and killed by Saracens, 135
Theognostus, the archimandrite, partisan of Ignatius, 249
Theophanes, Byzantine historian, 2, 11, 13, 16, 19, 24 sqq., 29; continuation of, by Constantine VII, 67; 120 *note*; 765
Theophanes, Palestinian monk, champion of icons, 34
Theophanes, the patrician, envoy of Romanus I to the Magyars, 212
Theophanes the Sicilian, author of *Life of St Joseph*, 255
Theophano (St Theophano), Empress, wife of Leo VI, 55; death, 56; 59, 256
Theophano, Empress, wife of Romanus II, character, 65, 67; governs, 68; 69; regency of, 70; and Nicephorus Phocas, 71 sqq., 145; 77 sq.; banished, 79; 81; 84; 757
Theophano, daughter of Romanus II, 68; 147; marries Otto II, 77; 81; 94
Theophano, daughter of Constantine VII, 68
Theophilus, Emperor, accession and iconoclastic zeal of, 34; Saracen war, 38, 128 sqq.; and Louis the Pious, 38, 203; internal administration, 39; buildings and love of the arts, 39 sq., 754; 41 sq.; 136; 152; 189; 192; and Venice, 396 sq.; Novels of, 710
Theophilus, Byzantine admiral, captured by Saracens, 125
Theophilus, professor of law, under Justinian, 707, 714, 721
Theophobus, the Persian, leads Saracen rebels to Theophilus, 38, 128; executed, 40
Theophylact, son of Romanus I, made Patriarch of Constantinople, 63, 259; 64; character and death of, 65, 260
Theophylact of Euboea, archbishop of Ochrida, 243; book *On the Errors of the Latins*, 333, 598
Theophylact, *see* Simocatta
Theophylact of Torcello, 397
Theophylact, Roman Senator, 256
Theophylitzes, patron of Basil the Macedonian, 50
Θεώρητρον (bridal gift of husband to wife), in Byzantine law, 716
Theorianus, and the Armenian Church, 363
Theotmar, archbishop of Salzburg, 227
Theotokos, title of the Virgin Mary, 2; 13 sq.; church of at Constantinople, *see under* Constantinople; at Jerusalem (Vefa jāmi‘), 768
Thera, eruption at, 9
Therapia, destroyed by Turks, 698
Therasia, eruption at, 9
Thermodon, river, 487
Thermopylae, pass of, 242, 433
Theseus, "Duke of Athens," 442
Thessalonica, *see* Salonica
Thessaly, 141, 217, 240; Normans in, 329; Latin lordships in, 422; 424, 426, 428, 432, 436, 439; given to Philip of Taranto, 448; 449 sq.; Turks conquer, 458, 463; 491; annexed by Stephen Dušan, 543, 545; ruled by Simeon Uroš, 552 sq.; 687; MSS. in, 499; sees in, 95, 243
Thierri de Loos, seneschal of Latin Empire, in Asia Minor, 482 sq.
Thietmar, German chronicler, on the Byzantine Χελάνδια, 398 *note*
Thionville (Theodonis Villa), 394 sq., 398
Thomas Angelus, last despot of Epirus, murdered by Orsini, 453, 475
Thomas Ostojić, Stephen, King of Bosnia, 574; and Bogomiles, 575; death, 578; 591
Thomas Palaeologus, despot of the Morea, 460 sq.; and Turks, 463 sq.; daughter of, 578
Thomas Preljubović, ruler of Epirus, 552; assassinated, 553; 457; 475
Thomas the Slavonian, rebels against Michael II, 33 sqq., 235; and Saracens, 127
Thomas de Stromoncourt, founds barony of Sálona, 433
Thomas Aquinas, St, and Byzantine Church, 595
Thomas Morosini, Latin Patriarch of Constantinople, 421, 426, 606
Thomas, bishop of Claudiopolis, 8
Thomas of Medzoph, Armenian churchman, 182
Thopia, clan of Albania, 584; *see* Carlo
Thoros I, ruler of Armeno-Cilicia, prosperous reign, 169; 357 sq.
Thoros II, ruler of Armeno-Cilicia, 169; reconquers his kingdom from Manuel I, 170 sq.; 359, 373 sqq., 381
Thoros III, King of Armeno-Cilicia, put to death, 177
Thrace, 13 sq., 35, 37, 119; Magyars invade, 212, 230, 234, 240, 323; anti-Latin rising in, 424, 481; 427, 432, 483, 486, 489 sq., 511, 520, 523 sqq.; Tartars in, 527, 663; 546; Ottoman Turks in, 555,

617, 658 sq., 662, 665, 668 sqq., 672, 675, 685, 695; 689; Asiatic colonists in, 231; Thracian origin of Emperor John III, 487; theme of, 733; Thracians in Byzantine Empire, 773
Thracesian theme, 5, 339, 732 sq.; strategus of, *see* Contomytes, Lachanodraco
Thucydides, 763
Thughūr-al-Jazīra, Saracen province, 132
Thughūr-ash-Shām, Saracen province, 132
Thumāma, Saracen general, 123; defeated, 124
Thuringia, landgrave of, and Mongols, 639
Ṭibb-i-Yúnání, and Greek medicine, 298
Tiberias, surrendered to John I, 148
Tiberius II, Emperor, 187; Novels of, 708, 714
Tiberius III Apsimar, Emperor, exiles Justinian II, 189
Tiberius, pretended son of Justinian II, 121
Tibet, raided by Mongols, 649
Tiflis, in Iberia, taken by Mongols, 636, 679
Tigris, river, 276, 306, 636
Tikhomir, Bulgarian leader, 244
Timariots, Ottoman military tenants, 664
Tīmūr (Tīmūrleng, Tamerlane, Tamburlane, Timurlane), Mongol leader, birth and career, 650 sqq.; and Bāyazīd I, 679 sqq.; at battle of Angora, 562, 619; besieges Smyrna, 683; death, 651, 684; 181 sq.; 193; 644; 674; 685 sq.; 688 sqq.; 695
Tīmūrid dynasties, displaced by Uzbegs, 651
Tinnis, 119
Tipucitus, 722; 713
Tiridates (Trdat), Armenian architect, restores St Sophia, 96; architect of the cathedral at Ani, 163
Tirmidh, fortress of, 312 sq.
Tirmidhī, compiler of Arab traditions, 291
Titles, of the Emperor, 726; of the hierarchy, 730 sq.
Tito Venier, marquess of Cerigo, rebels against Venice, 457
Tivertsy, Slav tribe, and Magyars, 198
Tivoli, 241, 601
Tmutorakan, *see* Phanagoria
Tmutorakanian Russia, 208
Tocco family, dominions annexed by Turks, 463, 466; at Naples, 455, 466; and archaeology, 474; *see* Antonio, Carlo, Leonardo
Toitzakia, Chazar garment introduced at Constantinople by Irene, 189
Tokat, modern name of Dazimon, 38
Toktu, Khan of Bulgaria, slain by Byzantines, 232
Tolen, Prince of Hum, 591
Tolonor, conference of, between Mongols and Chinese, 649
Tomor, Mt, in Albania, 242
Τόμος τῆς ἑνώσεως (Tomus Unionis), decree of Nicholas Mysticus, 62, 257
Tongking, *see* Annam
T'o-pa, empire of, in East Asia, 185 sq.
Tophana, 700
Toplica, river, Turkish defeat on the, 557
Topoteresiae (lieutenancies), subdivisions of theme, 734
Tōp Qāpu, gate at Constantinople, *see* St Romanus
Torcello, settlement of, 386; bishopric of, 387; trade of, 391; bishop of, *see* Dominicus, Orso, Vitalis, *see also* Theophylact
Torgods, Mongol tribe, 650
Torki, *see* Ghuzz
Tornesi, coins of Tours, 439
Tornicius (Tornig), general of Basil II, builds the convent of Iviron, 90
Tornicius, Leo, revolts against Constantine IX, 110 sq., 266
Tortosa, *see* Taraṭūs
Toucy, *see* Ancelin de
Toul, diocese of, 265
Toulouse, *see* Raymond
Tours, battle of, 637; coins of, 439
Trade and commerce, of Constantinople, 761 sq.; of provincial towns, 770; trade between Saracens and Byzantines, 152; commercial treaty with Russians, 205; trade with Bulgaria, 237; Alexius I and Pisans, 344; and Venetians, 354: Manuel I and Pisans, 371; clauses of treaty of Nymphaeum, 511; trade between Nicaea and Seljūqs, 498; of Armenia, 162, 173; of Chazars, 191; of White Bulgars, 193; slave trade of Magyars, 197; trade of Patzinaks, 199; Russian commerce, 201 sqq., 206, 209; Saracen commerce under Abbasids, 286, 289; under Faṭimids, 302; Venetian trade and commerce, Chap. XIII *passim*, 416; in Euboea, 435; in Cyprus, 469, 471; commercial prosperity of Lesbos, 465; trade of Bosnia, 517; of Ragusa and Bulgaria, 523; of Serbia, 535, 541, 549; Byzantine mercantile marine, 5, 762
Tradonicus, Peter, doge of Venice, 397 sq.; murdered, 398
Trajan's, column, 748; bridge, 688
Trajanopolis, Turks defeated at, 662
Tralles, *see* Aidīn; Anthemius of
Trani, defeat of Normans off, 412; 513 *note*; bishop of, *see* John
Transcaucasia, 154; tribes of, 207; *see also* Abasgia, Albania, Iberia
Translatio S. Clementis, Latin account of St Cyril, 216, 218 sqq.
Transoxiana (Mā-warā-an-Nahr), conquered by Seljūqs, 277; by Mongols, 279; Seljūq emigrates to, 300, 303; 311; invaded by the Khatá, 312; 317; 633; 650 sq.; *see also* Turkestan
Transylvania (Black Hungary), in the ninth century, 211; 214 sq.; 540; 571; Murād II in, 690
Trapezitae, Byzantine light cavalry, 740
Traù, submits to Venetians, 406; 411
Traulus, mutinies against Alexius I, 330
Travnik, Turkish residence in Bosnia, 582
Trdat, *see* Tiridates
Trebizond, 56, 88, 96; duke of, 344, 381; Empire of, founded by Comneni, 423 sq.,

479 sq.; 465; and Empire of Nicaea, 482, 486 sq.; and Nicene Patriarch, 486, 498; besieged by Seljūqs, 514 sq.; Turks and, 656, 665, 674; 690; Table of rulers, 516; trade of, 762, 770; country of Bessarion, 620; Armenian MS. Gospels of, 162; *see also* Chaldia
Trèves, archbishop of, and Photius, 249
Trevisan, Gabriel, Venetian commander, at siege of Constantinople, 695, 697 sq., 700
Treviso, 393; bishop of, 404 sq.; Trevisan march, 398, 402
Tribunes at Venice, 386, 389, 392, 397; tribunitian families, 387 sq.
Tribuni Maritimorum of Venetia, 385
Tribunus, Peter, doge of Venice, 400
Tribunus Menius (Memmo), doge of Venice, 403; deposed, 404
Triclinius, Byzantine professor, 764
Tricocca, near Nicaea, taken by Osmān, 657
Triconchus, *see under* Constantinople
Trikala, captured by Normans, 329; 552 sq.
Triphyllius, Constantine, negotiates with Saracens, 133
Tripolis, emir of, treaty with Romanus III, 100; 146; 148 sq.; 173; besieged by Crusaders, 341; princes of, *see* Bertrand, Pons, Raymond; *see also* Leo of
Trit, *see* Renier of
Trnovo, capital of Bulgarian Tsars, 234, 238, 428, 489, 518 sq., 522; Kalojan crowned at, 520; 521; splendour of, 525; 527 sq.; besieged by Byzantines, 529; 531; 544; 557; taken by Turks, 560; 577; Patriarch of, 542; church of the Forty Martyrs at, 560
Troad, the, held by Latins, 485; ceded to John III, 487; Armenian colony in, 479, 481
Troy, 525; Latin bishopric of, 485; Trojan War, 506; frescoes of, at Patras, 446; 705
Trstivnica, river, 581
Truvor, Swedish chieftain in Russia, 200
Tryphon, Patriarch of Constantinople, 63, 260
Tryphon, St, patron saint of Nicaea, 506; figure of, on coins, 514
Tsar (*Caesar*), of Bulgaria, title assumed by Simeon, 238; Table of Tsars, 590
Tsar (*Caesar*), of Serbia, title assumed by Stephen Dušan, 542; Table of Tsars, 590
Tsarigrad, Russian name for Constantinople, 746
Tudela, *see* Benjamin of
Tuduns, lieutenants of the Chazar khagan, 189
Ṭughril Arslān, emir of Melitene, 353
Ṭughril Beg, Great Seljūq Sultan, reign and conquests of, 304 sq.; and Armenia, 164, 166; enters Baghdad, 277, 304; death, 305
Ṭughril II, last Seljūq ruler in ʻIrāq, 315
Ṭughril Shāh, Seljūq ruler in Kirmān, 314
Ṭughtigīn, founder of the Būrid dynasty of Syria, 314 sq.
T'u-Küe, Turkish hordes of Central Asia, 185
Tulē, youngest son of Jenghiz Khan, 633, 635 sq., 641
Ṭūlūnid dynasty in Egypt, founded, 139; 300
T'u-mên, leader of Turkish tribes, 185 sqq.
Tunis, Aghlabids in, 300; Crusade against, 610
Tunja valley, near Hadrianople, 318
Tuqtāmish, Mongol Khan of the Golden Horde, sacks Moscow, 652
Tura-Khān, Ottoman captain, in the Morea, 460; 463
Turakina, widow of Ogdai Khan, 640
Tūrān, Seljūq prince of Kirmān, 314
Turbessel, John II before, 361
Turcopuli, Turks employed by Byzantines, 658
Turco-Tartar races, 194 sq.
Turcus, Bardanes, rebels against Nicephorus I, 34
Turkān Khātūn, wife of Malik Shāh, 307; intrigues and death, 308 sq.; 310
Turkestan, 185, 188, 303; Alp Arslān's campaigns in, 307; conquered by Mongols, 633; Manichaeans in, 288; king of, 300; *see also* Transoxiana
Turkomans, invade Cilicia, 169; 171; 180; 307; *see also* Ghuzz
Turks, Chaps. VII (A), X (B), XVIII, XXI *passim*; of Central Asia, 185 sqq.; and Chazars, 188; Turkish elements in Bulgar race, 184; in Magyars, 194, 196; Turkish soldiers of the Caliphs, 129, 131, 139, 276 sq., 285 sq.; Turkish princes in Cilicia, 470; Turkish tribes in Anatolia, 653 sqq.; among Mongols, 631; Turkish mercenaries in Greece, 443 sq.; 450; in Serbia, 553; in Byzantine army, 347, 738; as subjects of the Empire, 735 sqq.; modern Turks compared with Byzantines, 774; Turkish language, 195, 295; *see also* Mongols, Ottomans, Seljūqs
Turmae, subdivisions of army and theme, 734, 739
Turmarchs, 734
Turnu-Severin, Roumanian town, 567
Turov, 210
Turtukai, on the Danube, 235
Turuberan, in higher Armenia, 158; ravaged by Tīmūr, 181
Turxanth, Turkish khagan, receives Byzantine embassy, 188
Ṭūs, governor of, and Seljūqs, 304
Tuscany, marquess of, *see* Hubert
Tusla, fortress of, captured by John III, 490
Tutsa, Bulgarian river, 235
Tutush, Seljūq ruler in Syria, son of Alp Arslān, 309 sq., 314 sq.; captures Jerusalem, 316; 317
Tvrtko I, King of Bosnia, succeeds as ban of Bosnia, 545; victories of, 555 sq.; crowned king, 556; joins anti-Turkish

league, 557 sq.; death of, 559; 565; 575; 591
Tvrtko II, Tvrtković, King of Bosnia, 565 sqq., 573 sq., 591
Tyana, 121; mosque built at, 126; 127 sqq.
Tymphrestos, Greek mountain, 444
Typikon, monastic rule, of St Athanasius, 80
Tyras, Greek colony on Black Sea, 183
Tyre, 376; captured by Venetians, 411; *see* Amaury, William
Tyropaeum, castle of, 88
Tyrrhenian Sea, 742
Tzachas, emir of Smyrna, designs on Constantinople, 331
Tzetzes, Byzantine writer, 763; *Chiliads* of, 368
Tzimisces, family, 69, 93; *see* John I, Emperor
Tzurulum, *see* Chorlu
Tzympe, first Turkish settlement in Europe, 544; 667

'Ubaid-Allāh (Mahdī), first Fāṭimid Caliph, conquers North Africa, 302
'Ubaid-Allāh, governor of Antioch, 89
Ubaldo, cardinal-bishop of Ostia, sent to Constantinople, 602
Udine, proposed council at, 621
Ugain, nobility of old Bulgaria, 231; clan of, 231
Uglješa, *see* John
Ugrian tribes, 194; Ugro-Finnish Society, and site of Karakorum, 640
Ugrin, Duke of Mačva and Bosnia, 591
Uighurs, Mongol tribe, 631; ruled by Jagatai, 635; script of, among Mongols, 634, 646
'Ujaif, Saracen general, 128 sq.
Uj Palanka, *see* Haram
Ukil, Bulgarian clan, 231
Ukrainians (Little Russians), 200
'*Ulama*, the, Murād I and, 668
Uldza, river, 630
Uljāitū, Mongol Īl-khān of Persia, becomes Musulman, 178
Ulnia (Zeithun), in Armeno-Cilicia, 168
Ulubad, *see* Lopadium
Umago, and Venice, 412
Umar, claimant for the Bulgarian throne, 232
Ummán, 312
Umayyad Caliphs of Damascus, 139, 274 sq.; unorthodoxy of, 280 sqq., 288; churches built under, 289; 290 sq.; 293; 300; and the Shī'ites, 301; 641; naval power of, 741; emirs of Cordova, 38, 139, 274 sq.; *see* Caliphate, Caliphs
Uniates, in Armenia, 179, 182; Uniate Greeks and Papacy, 594
University, of Constantinople, 44, 217, 248, 764; reopened by Constantine IX, 114; at Latin Athens, 462; at Baghdad, 305; at Kars, 162, 167; at Nīshāpūr, 306; of Paris, Greek scholarships at, 616
Unrū Bulkà, the Isfahsālār, rebels against Barkiyāruq, 310
'Uqailids, dynasty of Mosul, 317
Ural-Altaic peoples, 192, 194
Ural, river, *see* Yaik
Uranus, Nicephorus, ambassador to Baghdad, 86; victorious over Bulgarians, 241
Urban II, Pope, and Alexius I, 333, 596, 598 sq.
Urban IV, Pope, and Michael VIII, 609
Urban V, Pope, and Petrarch, 616; and John V, 617 sq., 670
Urban, Hungarian engineer, casts monster-gun for siege of Constantinople, 696, 698
Urdu language, 295
Uriang Kadai, Mongol general, in China, 644
Uroš, Župan of Rascia, and his family, 356; *see also* Pervoslav, Stephen
Ursus (Orso), third doge of Venice, 388; independent election of, 390; 391
Ursus, son of John Particiacus, bishop of Olivolo, 397
Urtuq ibn Aksab, founder of the Urtuqid dynasty, 316 sq.
Urtūqid dynasty of Aleppo, 314 sq., 317
Uskūb, *see* Skoplje
Usora, Bosnian district, annexed by Serbia, 573
Uspenski, on foundation of Sarkel, 192
Ussakhal, Mongol ruler, defeated by Chinese, 649
'Uthmān, *see* Osmān
Utigurs, Utrigurs, Bulgar tribe, 185, 200; prince of, *see* A-na-kuei, Organas
Uzbeg Mongols, 651 sq.
Uzes, Byzantine name for Ghuzz, *q.v.*

Vácz (Waitzen), bishopric of, founded, 214
Vahan Kamsarakan, Armenian leader against the Persians, 157
Vahan Mamikonian, "the Wolf," Armenian leader against Persians, 157
Vahka, Armeno-Cilician fortress, 168 sqq.
Vajk, former name of St Stephen of Hungary, *q.v.*
Vakhtang, Code of (Iberian), Byzantine influence on, 724
Valarsaces, Arsacid King of Armenia, 157
Valencia, tomb of the Empress Constance at, 496
Valens, Emperor, 233; aqueduct of, 96
Valentinus, Byzantine ambassador to the supreme khagan, 187 sq.
"Valerian, wall of," at Athens, 462
Valley of Flowers, at Ani, 163
Valois, *see* Catherine, Charles, Philip
Vámbéry, on Magyars, 194 sqq.; on Patzinaks, 197
Van, kingdom of (Vaspurakan), in Armenia, 157, 161, 163; overrun by Seljūqs, 164; 166 sq.; by Mongols, 181 sq.; 318; fortress of, 157, 167; lake of, 157
Vanand, in Armenia, 129; kingdom of, founded by Mushel, 161; revolts against Ashot I, 159, 162; given to Byzantines,

166; taken by Seljūqs, 167; King of, *see* Gagik
Vandals, in Justinian's army, 738
Varangians, and Basil II, 88, 90, 209; detachment in Sicily, 150; in Russia, 202 sqq.; Byzantine bodyguard, 209, 327, 738, 750; in navy, 742; church of, at Constantinople, 264; theory of foundation of Russian Empire, 199 sq.; *see also* Russians, Scandinavians, Swedes
Varaztirots Bagratuni, Armenian curopalates, 157
Vardan, Armenian rebel against Saracens, 126
Vardan Mamikonian, Armenian leader, killed in the battle of Avaraïr, 155, 157
Vardar, river, 241, 508, 519, 533, 553, 737, 770
Varna, in Bulgaria, 230, 519, 549, 584; Ottoman victory at, 462, 572 sq., 624, 691 sq., 696
Varyag, *see* Varangian
Vasak Mamikonian, Armenian general, 157
Vaspurakan, *see* Van
Vassal, John and James, messengers from Mongols to Edward I of England, 176
Vatatzes, Andronicus, defeated by Seljūqs, 378
Vatatzes, John Ducas; *see* John III, Emperor
Vatatzes, lieutenant of Tornicius, executed by Constantine IX, 111
Vatican, librarian of, *see* Anastasius; Bulgarian MS. at, 549; Byzantine MSS. at, 768 sq.
Vatopedi, convent of, founded by Basil II, 90
Veccus, *see* John Beccus
Vefa-jāmi', *see* Theotokos, church of the
Veglia, submits to Venetians, 406
Velbužd (Köstendil), 492; battle of, 538 sq.; 555; Murād I at, 557
Velehrad, in Moravia, 229
Velestino, fief of, 433
Venetia, 385 sq., *see* Venice
Venetians, Chap. XIII; and Leo III, 9, 388; 18; and Charlemagne, 36, 395 sq.; and Basil II, 94, 138; fleet in Sicily, 135; defeat at Taranto, 136; at Bari, 149; and Armenia, 173, 181; and Alexius I, 329 sq., 341, 347; and John II, 354; 362; and Manuel, 368, 370 sq.; and Fourth Crusade, 414, 604, Chap. XIV *passim*; share in partition of Empire, 421, 427, 432, 434, 606; and Baldwin II, 429, 431; 433; and Geoffrey of Achaia, 438; 440; possessions in Greece, 453, 457 sqq., 461, 464; wars with Ottomans, 466 sq., 687 sq.; administration of foreign possessions, 434 sqq.; in Cyprus, 469 sqq.; and Rhodes, 494; in Chios and Icaria, 468, 477; rising in Crete against, 616; rivalry with Genoese, 469, 666; lose Gallipoli, 489; lose Salonica, 461, 690; colonies in Asia Minor, 480; in Albania, 583 sqq., 592; in Dalmatia, 564, 566, 575; Table of colonies, 486; colonies left after Ottoman conquest, 465; lost, 472; Serbia and, 535, 541 sq., 546; suzerainty over Montenegro, 586 sq.; Bosnia and, 544, 556, 559, 574 sq., 579; and Balkans, Chap. XVII *passim*; and Theodore I, 487; and Michael VIII, 609, 613; 617; 623; and Andronicus II, 657; aid Boucicaut, 677; help to defend Constantinople, 695; Byzantine navy and, 742; in Constantinople, 750, 762; Byzantine influence on Venetian art, 776
Venice, *see* Venetians, Chap. XIII; Maritime Venetia made into a separate *ducatus*, 387, 389, 392; SS. Cyril and Methodius at, 224; Otto II at, 406; John V at, 618, 670; John VIII at, 621; Manuel II at, 678; 447; Byzantine psalter at, 769; peace of, 370, 372, 414
Venier, Venetian family, lordship of, in Aegean, 436; *see* Tito
Veregava, Bulgarians defeat Constantine V at, 231
Veria (Berrhoea), in Macedonia, 241; captured by Normans, 329
Vermandois, *see* Hugh, Philip
Verona, and Venice, 412; treaty of, 404; Veronese lords in Euboea, 435, 451
Versinicia, battle of, 29, 35, 37, 233
Vestiarii, office of the, 730
Vest Sarkis Siwni, regent of Armenia, betrays country to Constantine IX, 164
Veszprém, bishopric of, founded, 214
Vetalonia, 503
Vetrano, Leo, Genoese pirate, threatens Corfù, 432; executed, 434
Via Egnatia, threatened by Normans, 408
Viaro, Venetian family, lordship of, in Aegean, 436
Vicenza, and Venice, 398
Victor II, Pope, and the Schism, 270
Vidin, Bulgarian fortress, 240 sq.; captured by Hungarians, 527, 554; 557; captured by Ottomans, 561, 572; bishopric of, 243; *see* Anne, John Sracimir, Michael
Vienna, Byzantine MSS. at, 768
Vigla, *see* Arithmus
Villehardouin, Geoffrey de, the historian, negotiates with Venetians, 415; impression of Constantinople, 418; on booty of, 420, 745; 422; 433
Villehardouins of Achaia, 431; *see* Geoffrey, Isabelle, William
Vincent of Beauvais, 515 *note*
Visdomino, of Venice, established at Ferrara, 410
Vita Basilii (Basil I), 711
Vita Clementis, 229
Vita Cyrilli (Pannonian legend), credibility of, 216; 217 sq.
Vita Ignatii, 253
Vita Methodii (Pannonian legend), credibility of, 216; 217 sq.
Vitalian, 386
Vitalis Candianus, doge of Venice, 403

Vitalis Orseolo, bishop of Torcello, 407
Viterbo, treaty of, 444, 610; Palaeologus legend at, 503
Vitichev, Russian fortress, 206
Vitoš, Mt, monastery at, 584
Vizier, *see* Wazīr
Vizye, taken by John III, 430; sacked by Ottomans, 695
Vlachia (Thessaly), 448, 543
Vlachs, *see* Wallachs
Vlad I, Prince of Wallachia, 593
Vlad II, "the Devil," Prince of Wallachia, and Ottomans, 571; and Hunyadi, 572; 593
Vlad III, "the Impaler," Prince of Wallachia, 588; 593
Vlad IV, "the Monk," Prince of Wallachia, 593
Vladika, prince-bishop of Montenegro, office of, 587
Vladímir the Great, Prince of Kiev, 208 sqq.; baptism and marriage of, 68, 89 sq., 264; 149; importance in Russian history, 210; ambassadors of, at St Sophia, 752
Vladimir, son of Boris of Bulgaria, 235, 237
Vladímir Monomachus, Prince of Kiev, 356, 368
Vladímir, town in Russia, conquered by Mongols, 637
Vladimirko, Prince of Halicz, and the princedom of Kiev, 368
Vladislav I (Władisław), King of Poland and Hungary, and Hunyadi, 571, 624; killed at Varna, 572, 690 sq.; Bosnia and, 574
Vladislav, King of Serbia, dispossesses his brother, 522; 524; 590
Vladislav, King of Serbia, son of Stephen Dragutin, imprisoned by his uncle, 534; 535; deposed, 536; 590
Vladislav I, Prince of Wallachia, 593
Vladislav II, Prince of Wallachia, 593
Vladislav, son of Stephen Vukčić, 580 sqq., 591
Vlastele, Vlasteličići, Serbian nobles, 547
Vlastimir, Serbian prince, and the Bulgarians, 235
Vlatko, son of Stephen Vukčić, 581; becomes "Duke of St Sava," 582; 591
Vlatko Hranić, Bosnian leader, at Kossovo, 558
Vodená, capital of Samuel of Bulgaria, 240; waterfall of, 241; 243; captured by Normans, 329; Theodore Angelus rules at, 493; 494
Voijihna, "Caesar" of Serbia, and Matthew Cantacuzene, 553
Vojeslav Vojnov, count of Hum, 591
Vojtěch, St (Adalbert), bishop of Prague, converts Magyars, 213 sq.
Voleros, on the Maritza, 241
Volga, river (Turkish Itil, Atel), 184, 188, 191 sq., 197 sq., 202, 631, 636, 651
Volga Bulgars, 184; Volga-Bulgarian kingdom, 192 sqq., 202; *see* Bulgars (White)
Volkhov, river, 202 sq.
Volo, gulf of, 445
Vólosti, Russian city-states, 202 sq.
Volpiano, *see* William of
Vónitza, castle of, held by Leonardo Tocco, 465; annexed by Ottomans, 466
Vostitza, Venetian colony, 476
Votyaks, Ugrian tribe, 194
Vračar, 522 *note*
Vranina, sacred island on Lake Scutari, 586
Vrbas, Bosnian river, 581
Vrbitsa pass, in Bulgaria, 231
Vrdnik, monastery of, 558
Vrhbosna, in Bosnia, Ottomans in, 566 sq., 574, 582
Vsévolod, Russian prince, marriage to Byzantine princess, 111
Vuk Branković, alleged treachery of, at Kossovo, 558; rules at Priština, 559; 590
Vuk Lazarević, Serbian prince, and his brother, 563
Vukan, son of Stephen Nemanja, 518; calls in Hungarians, 519; 521; 590
Vukašin, King of Serbia, guardian of Stephen Uroš V, 553; becomes king, 554; death in battle, 555, 670; 590
Vukčić, Bosnian family, *see* Catherine, Hrvoje, Stephen, Vladislav, Vlatko
Vusir (Wazir) Gliavar, khagan of the Chazars, and Justinian II, 189
Vyatiches, tributary to Russians, 207 sqq.

Waitzen, *see* Vácz
Walandar (probably Develtus), 212
Walīd II, Umayyad Caliph, murder of, 121
Walīd ibn Hishām, 121
Walinana, East Slav tribe, 200
Wallachia (Bulgaria beyond the Danube), included in kingdom of Krum, 232, 234; under Kalojan, 424; 518; foundation of principality, 540; tributary to Turks, 560; 561; 567; 575; 669; rises against Turks, 688; 694; primate of, 520; Church in, 568; Table of rulers, 593
Wallachs (Vlachs), 240; at battle of the Maritza, 555, 670; 685; at Kossovo, 692 sq.; of Macedonia, 674; Wallach wife of Stephen Uroš V, 549; of John Alexander, 548
"Walnut Mountain," battle of, *see* Karýdi
Walpert, Patriarch of Aquileia, 401
Walter of Brienne, becomes Duke of Athens, 449; defeat by the Catalans and death of, 450, 475
Walter of Brienne, the Younger, tries to regain duchy of Athens, 453; subsequent career, 454
Walter the Penniless, defeated by Seljūqs, 315
Wang Khan, defeated by Jenghiz Khan, 632; identified with "Prester John," 650
Wāqidī, Arab biographer and historian, 293
Wāsiṭ, sacked by marauders, 276
Wāthiq, Abbasid Caliph, 131
Wazīr (Vizier), office of, under the Abbasids, 282 sqq.; under Seljūqs, 313 sq.

Welf I, duke of Bavaria, defeated by Seljūqs, 341
Welf, count (duke of Tuscany), and Conrad III, 368
Werner, bishop of Strasbourg, 97
West, the relations of Byzantium with: Leo III and, 9 sq.; Constantine V and, 17 sq.; Irene and, 20, 22, 24; recognition of the Western Empire by Nicephorus I, 36, 394 sq.; Theophilus and, 38; Basil I and Louis II, 139; missions and embassies of Constantine VII, 66, 260; Nicephorus II and Otto the Great, 76 sq., 260; embassy of Gero, 80; Basil II and Crescentius, 91, 94; Constantine VIII and Conrad II, 97; Otto II and Greek Italy, 149; Alexius I and Henry IV, 329; John II and Lothar, 358; and Conrad III, 360; Manuel I and Conrad III, 365 sqq.; and Frederick I, 369 sqq., 379; Henry VI and Byzantine Empire, 416 sq.; John III and Frederick II, 495, 608; Theodore's eulogy on Frederick II, 496, 501; the Empire and Venice, 394, 398 sqq., 402, 405 sq., 408, 412; and Papacy, *see* Chaps. IX, XIX; *see also* Crusades, Papacy
Westberg, on Chazar bodyguard, 190; on Dnieper river, 198
White Bulgars, *see* Bulgars
White Town (Sarkel), *see* Sarkel
Wiching, bishop of Nyitra, opposition to St Methodius, 228 sq.
William I of Champlitte, Prince of Achaia, founds principality, 422, 433 sq.; death, 437; 474
William of Villehardouin, Prince of Achaia, and Michael II of Epirus, 430; wars of, 440, 442; taken prisoner by Michael VIII, 442 sq., 508; death, 444; and Rhodes, 494; 474
William, Duke of Athens, 446; 475
William I, King of Sicily, and Manuel I, 369 sq., 596, 601; treaty with Venice, 412
William II, King of Sicily, and Manuel I, 370; 371 sq.; 374; invades Byzantium, 383 sq., 596, 603
William IX, duke of Aquitaine, 341
William of Grantmesnil, leader in First Crusade, 339
William, marquess of Montferrat, supported by Manuel I, 379
William, count of Nevers, crusade of, 341
William of Pavia, papal legate in France, and Manuel I, 601
William of Volpiano, St, abbot of St Benignus at Dijon, and Pope John XIX, 262
William of Rubruck, *see* Rubruquis
William of Tyre, chronicler, on numbers of Turks, 655
William-Jordan, count of Cerdagne, and Alexius I, 342
Winkler, on Magyar language, 195
Wintker, *see* Gunter
Witigis, King of the Goths, and Venetia, 385
Wittelsbach, Bavarian dynasty, 212
Wuchang, Chinese city, besieged by Mongols, 646

Xerigordon, Crusaders defeated at, 337
Xerus, prefect of Constantinople, plots against Alexius I, 342
Xiphias, Nicephorus, general of Basil II, rebels, 95; victorious over Bulgarians, 241
Xiphilin, John, nomophylax, 110; teaches law under Constantine IX, 114, 714; 719; 721 sq.
Xylocastron, turret on Byzantine ship of the line, 743

Yadrintsev, N., expedition of, to Central Asia, 640
Yaḥyà, the Barmecide, Saracen general, defeats Byzantines, 124; minister of Hārūn, 283
Yaḥyà, Saracen general, takes Tyana, 128
Yaḥyà ibn ʻAlī-at-Tabrīzi, Arab lecturer, 306
Yaik (Ural), river, 197 sq., 631, 651
Yaman, the, 312
Yamboli, in Bulgaria, 231
Yamīnu-Amīri'l-Mu'minīn, title bestowed on Ṭughril Beg, 305
Yangtse Kiang, Chinese river, 645
Yaʻqūb, brother of Bāyazīd, put to death by him, 558, 673
Yaʻqūb, general of Bāyazīd, in the Morea, 675
Yaʻqūb Arslān, brother of Mahomet, Dānishmandite ruler, 365, 375; 377
Yaʻqūbī, Arab historian, 293
Yāqūt, Arab geographer, 194, 295
Yarmouth, herring trade of, 639
Yaropolk, son of Svyatoslav of Russia, 208
Yaroslav, prince of Russia, 111
Yaroslav, prince of Halicz, 381
Yazīd II, Umayyad Caliph, 119 sq.
Yellow River, in China, 633
Yenisey, river, *see* Kien
Yeni-Shehr, taken by Ertughril, 655; Osmān's capital transferred to, 659
Yenkin, ancient capital of North China, 632, 647
Yeshil-jāmiʻ (Green Mosque), at Brūsa, 688
Yesukai, Mongol chieftain, father of Jenghiz Khan, 632
Yezdegerd II, Sasanid King of Persia, persecutes Armenians, 155
Yilderim (Thunderbolt), epithet applied to Bāyazīd I, 562, 674
Yolande (Jolanda), Latin Empress, wife of Peter de Courtenay, Latin Emperor, regency of, 427; 486
Yuan-Yuan (Yü-Küe-lü), Asiatic nomads, 185; overthrown by Turks, 186
Yugers, Ugrian tribe, 194
Yulun (Ogelen Eke), mother of Jenghiz Khan, 632
Yunnan, Chinese province, 644
Yūnus, son of Seljūq, 303

Yūsuf, emir of Armenia, killed by Byzantines, 131
Yūsuf, Mamlūk Sultan of Egypt, 182
Yūsuf, ostikan of Azarbā'ījān, captures Smbat I of Armenia, 160 sq.
Yūsuf Barzamī, murders Alp Arslān, 307

Zabel, daughter and heiress of Leo the Great of Armeno-Cilicia, 174
Zabel, sister of Hethum II of Armeno-Cilicia, 178, 180 sq.
Žabljak, capital of Montenegro, 586; Turks at, 587
Zaccaria, Genoese family of, in Chios, 455; *see* Centurione, Maria
Zacharias, Pope, 17
Zacharias, bishop of Anagni, legate of Pope Nicholas I, 248
Zagan, Turkish governor in the Morea, 465
Zāhir, Fāṭimite Caliph, agreement with Constantine VIII, 97
Za'im, Ottoman military tenant, 664
Zain-ud-Dīn Ismā'īl, Persian medical writer, 298
Zakarīyā of Qazwīn, Arab encyclopaedist and geographer, 295
Zakonnik, Serbian code of law, 547
Zala, Pannonian river, 211
Zamakhsharī, famous commentator on the Koran, 291
Zangī, 'Imād-ad-Dīn, prince of Mosul, founder of Zangid dynasty, 299, 316 sq.; defeats King of Jerusalem, 359
Zangids, Atābeg dynasty, 315 sq.
Zante, ruled by Orsini, 432; under suzerainty of Naples, 446; Venetian, 466 sq., 473, 476
Zanzibar, 295
Zapetra (Sozopetra), in Saracen wars, 38, 121, 125, 128 sqq.; captured by Basil I, 139
Zara, submits to Venetians, 406; Venetian "counts" in, 412; Fourth Crusade captures, 416 sqq., 604; 559; Ladislas of Naples crowned at, 565
Zara Vecchia, captured by Venetians, 411
Zaützes, Stylianus, guardian and father-in-law of Leo VI, 54, 56, 58, 256
"Zealots" of Salonica, fourteenth century communists, 760
Zeithun, *see* Ulnia
Zemarchus, Byzantine ambassador to the Turks of Central Asia, 187
Zeta, the (Montenegro), original Serbian Kingdom (Dioclea), 517; left to Vukan, 518 sq.; 534; 542; Balša family in, 553, 559, 564, 586; see of, 587: Table of rulers, 592; *see also* Dioclea
Zeus, Olympian, temple of the, at Athens, 459
Žiča, coronation church of Serbian kings, 521
Zichna, frontier town of John III, 492
Zigabenus, Euthymius, compiler of Alexius I's theological treatise, 350; 766
Zīj-i-Malikshāhī, astronomical tables drawn up by Omar Khayyam, 308
Ziyādatallāh, Aghlabid emir of Africa, in Sicily, 37, 134; death, 136
Zlatica, near Philippopolis, 571
Zobor, Benedictine monastery, in Hungary, founded, 214
Zoë, Empress, daughter of Constantine VIII, 84, 94, 96 sq.; marriage and accession of, 98; 99 sq.; marriage to Michael IV, 101 sqq.; adopts Michael V, 104; 105; exiled, 106, 319; joint reign with Theodora, 107; marriage to Constantine IX, 108 sq.; death, 115; 265: 757; Novels of, 715
Zoë, Empress, daughter of Zaützes, mistress of Leo VI, 56; marriage and death of, 57; 59; 256
Zoë Carbonupsina, Empress, wife of Leo VI, 57, 60, 256; supports Phocas, 61; 142
Zoë, daughter of Constantine VII, 68
Zonaras, John, Grand Drungarius of the Watch, historian and legal writer, 363, 724; on Basil II, 87; 110; on coinage of Alexius I, 348; 765
Zoroastrianism, 155; and Islām, 287
Zorzi, Venetian family, become marquesses of Boudonitza, 458
Zuhair, Saracen leader in Sicily, 135
Župan, *župy*, 517; see *Ispanok*; of Rascia, *see* Bolkan, Pervoslav, Stephen, Uroš
Zvečan, castle of, 539

CAMBRIDGE: PRINTED BY W. LEWIS AT THE UNIVERSITY PRESS

[illegible]

Zambia, [illegible]

Zeila, [illegible]

Zeno, [illegible]

Zoe, [illegible]

[illegible]

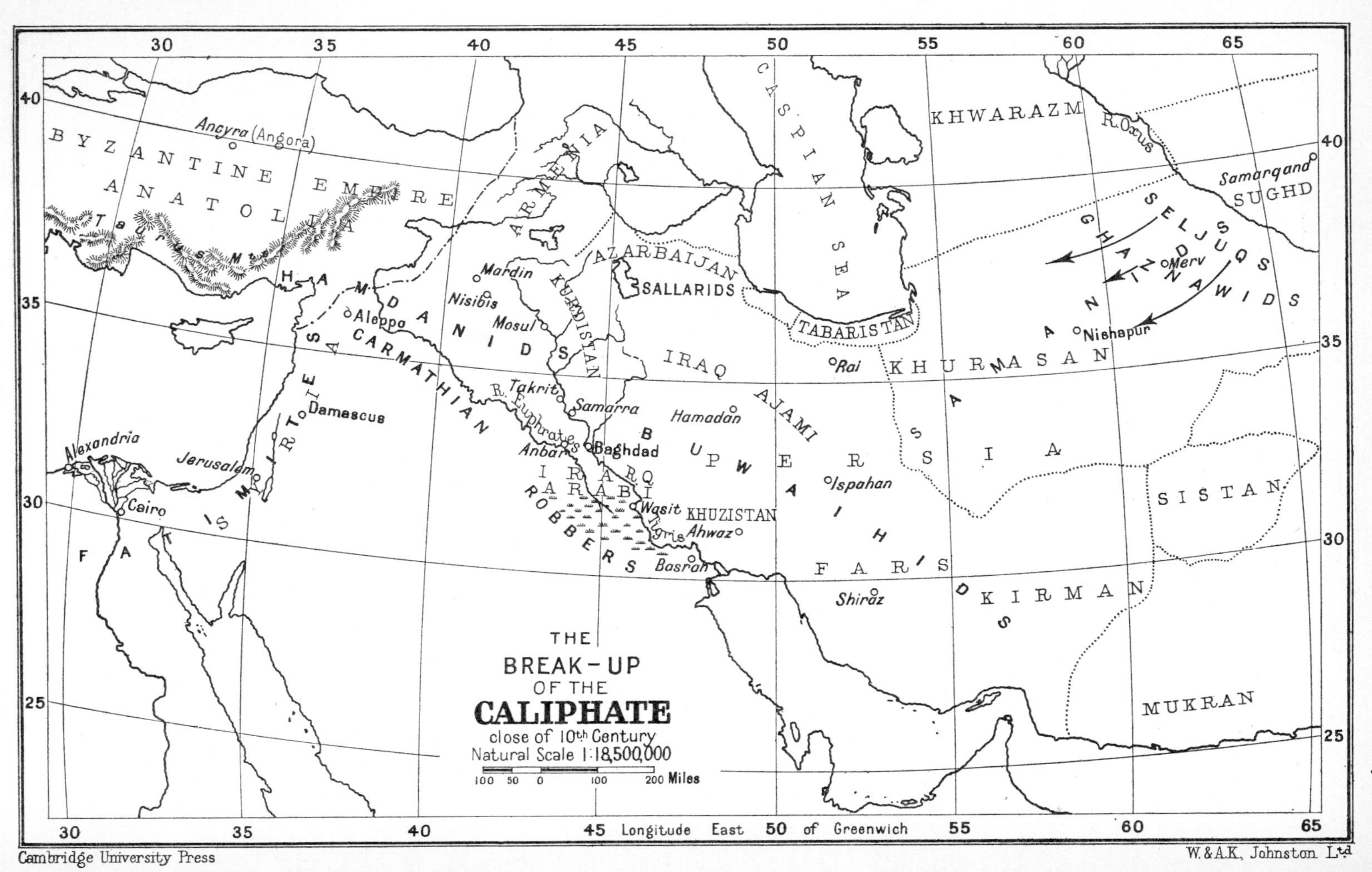

Cambridge University Press
W. & A.K. Johnston Ltd

Map 39

Asia Minor

showing themes of
10th century

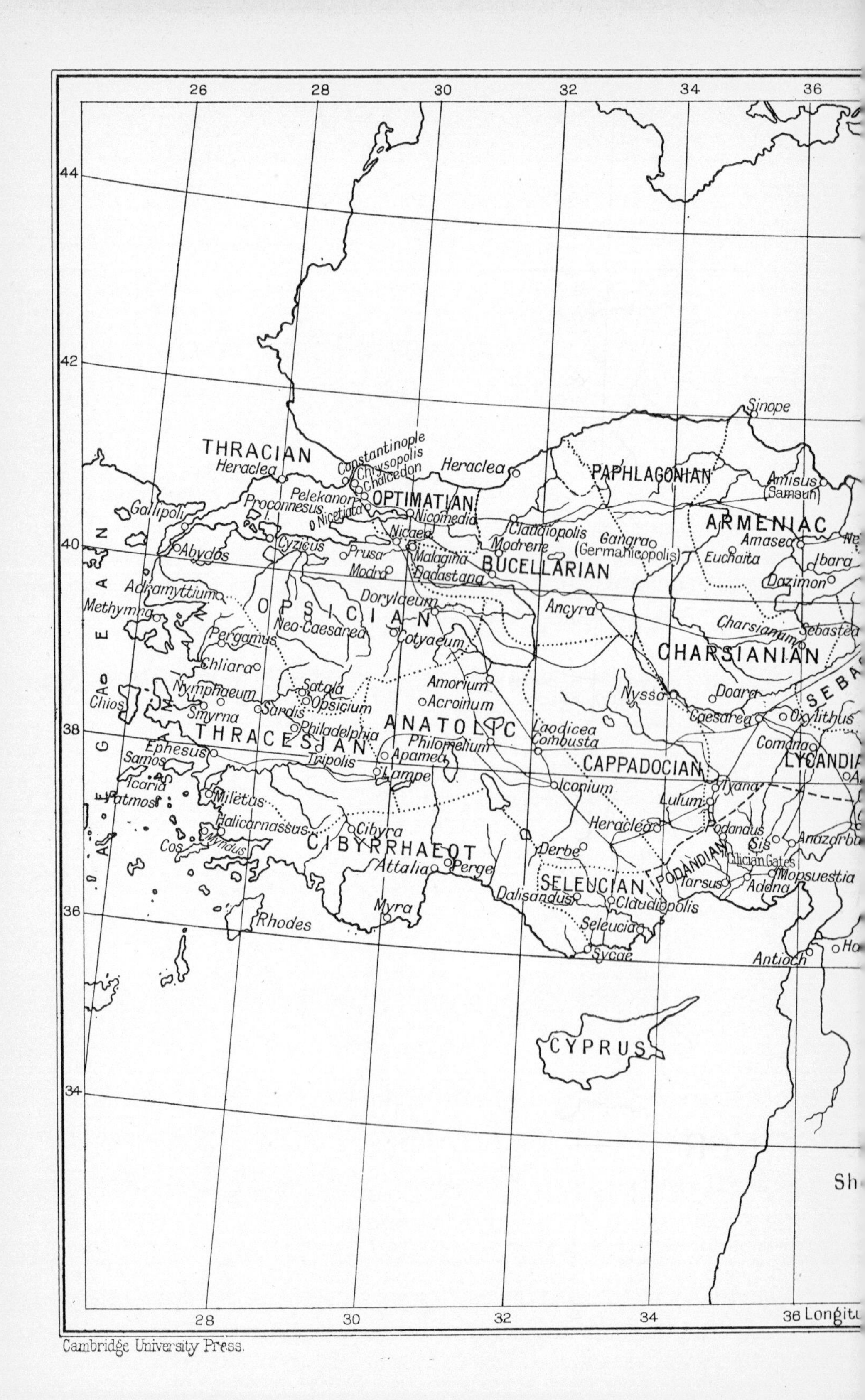

Cambridge University Press.

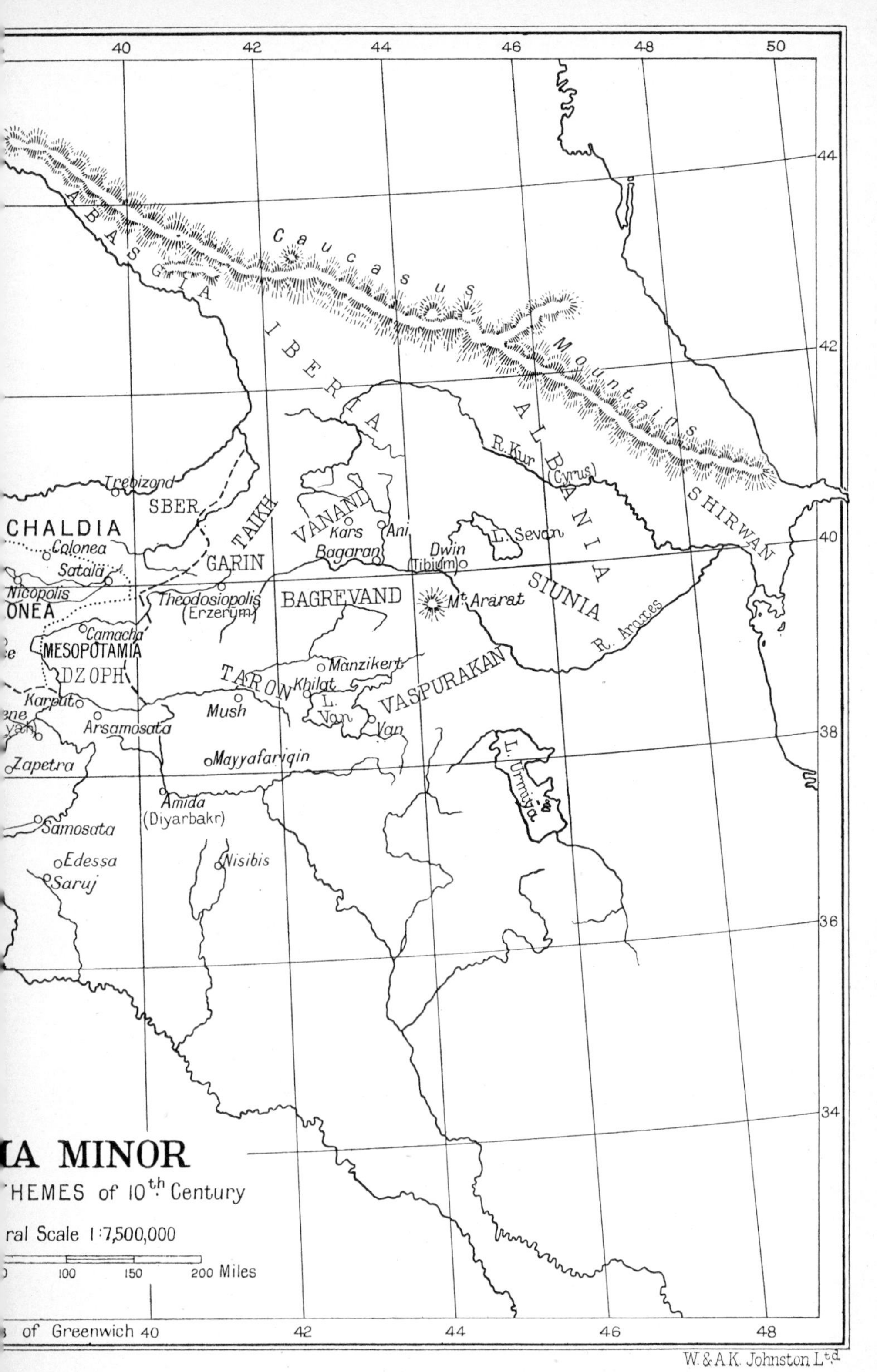

Caucasus Mountains
ABASGIA
IBERIA
ALBANIA
SHIRWAN
R. Kur (Cyrus)
L. Sevan
Trebizond
SBER
CHALDIA
Colonea
Satala
Nicopolis
TAIKH
VANAND
Kars
Ani
Bagaran
Dwin (Tibium)
GARIN
Theodosiopolis (Erzerum)
BAGREVAND
Mt Ararat
SIUNIA
R. Araxes
MESOPOTAMIA
Camacha
DZOPH
TARON
Manzikert
Khilat
L. Van
Van
VASPURAKAN
Karput
Arsamosata
Mush
Zapetra
Mayyafariqin
Amida (Diyarbakr)
L. Urmiya
Samosata
Edessa
Saruj
Nisibis
A MINOR
HEMES of 10th Century
ral Scale 1:7,500,000
100
150
200 Miles
of Greenwich 40
42
44
46
48
50
44
42
40
38
36
34
W. & A.K. Johnston Ltd.

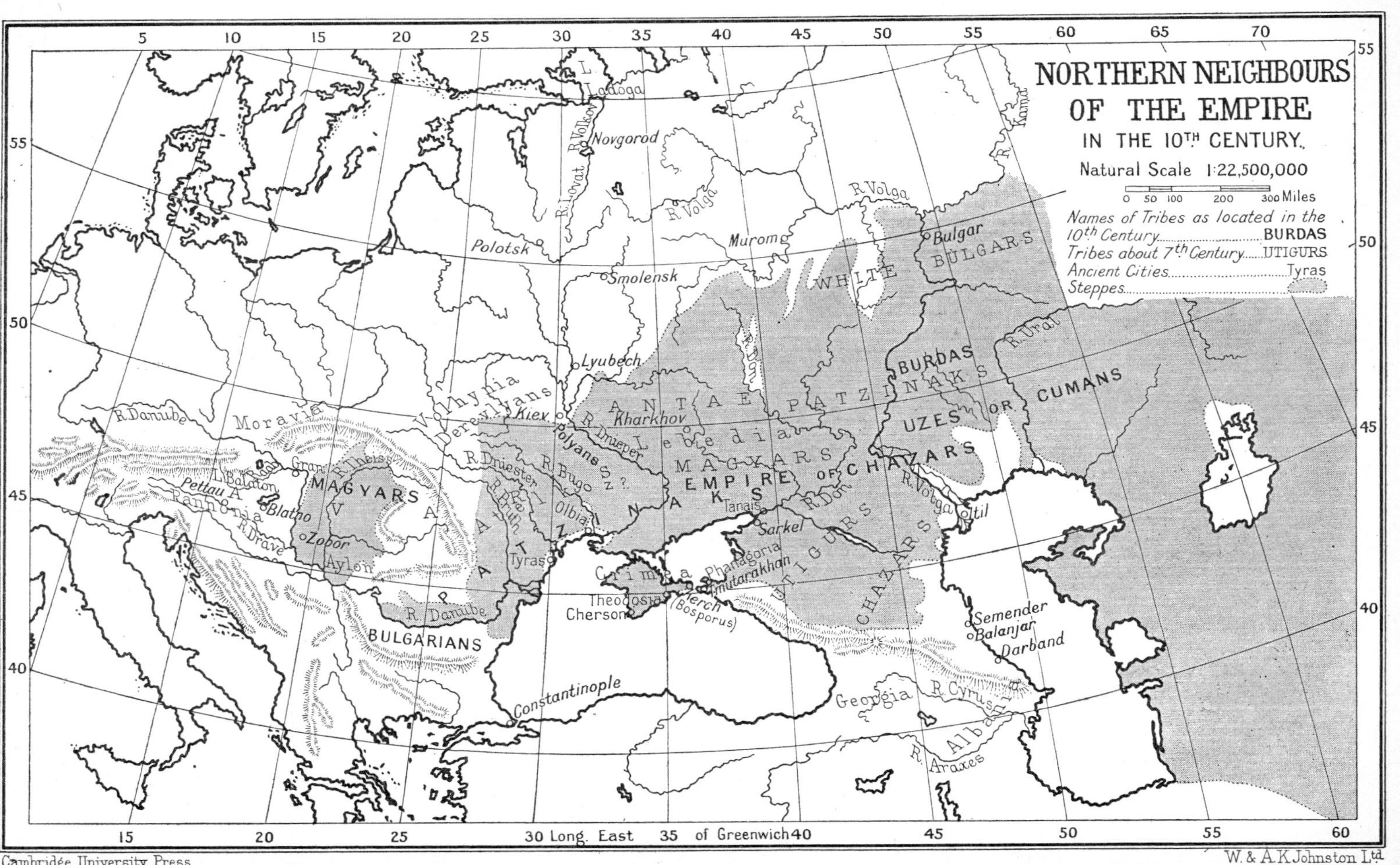
NORTHERN NEIGHBOURS OF THE EMPIRE
IN THE 10TH CENTURY.
Natural Scale 1:22,500,000
0 50 100 200 300 Miles
Names of Tribes as located in the 10th Century........BURDAS
Tribes about 7th Century......UTIGURS
Ancient Cities..........Tyras
Steppes..........
30 Long. East 35 of Greenwich 40
L. Ladoga
R. Volkov
Novgorod
R. Lovat
R. Volga
R. Kama
Murom
Bulgar
BULGARS
WHITE
Polotsk
Smolensk
Lyubech
R. Don
R. Ural
BURDAS
PATZINAKS
CUMANS
UZES OR
ANTAE
Kharkhov
Lebedia
MAGYARS
EMPIRE OF CHAZARS
Kiev
Volhynia
Derevlyans
Polyans
R. Dnieper
R. Bugo
R. Dniester
R. Pruth
Olbia
Tyras
Tanais
Sarkel
R. Volga
Itil
UTIGURS
CHAZARS
Crimea
Phanagoria
Tmutarakhan
Theodosia
Kerch (Bosporus)
Cherson
Semender
Balanjar
Darband
Constantinople
Georgia
R. Cyrus
Albania
R. Araxes
R. Danube
Moravia
Gran
R. Theiss
L. Balaton
Pettau
Pannonia
Blatno
MAGYARS
Zobor
Aylon
R. Drave
BULGARIANS
Cambridge University Press
W. & A. K. Johnston Ltd

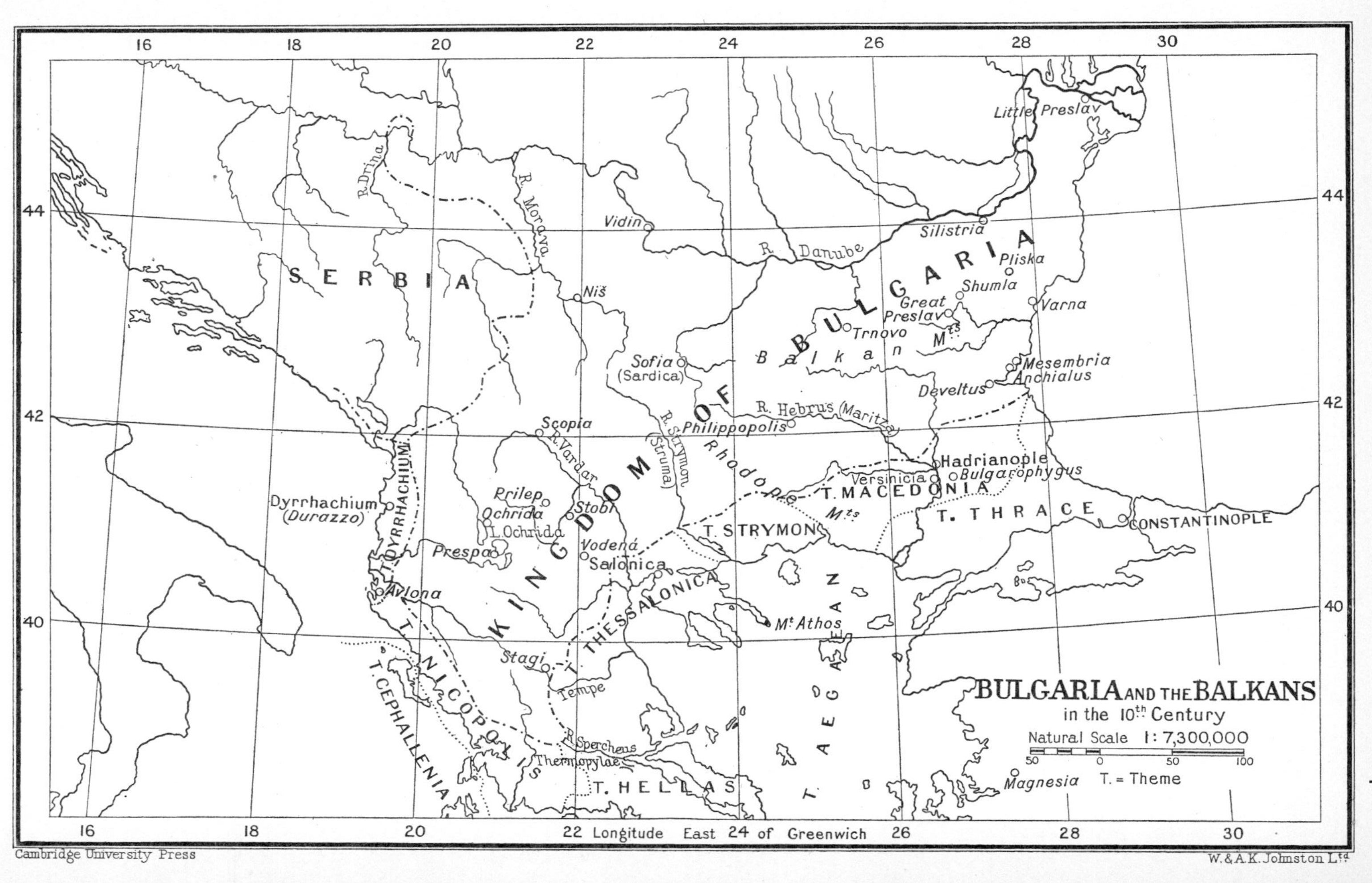

Cambridge University Press

W. & A. K. Johnston Ltd

Map 42
The Empire of
the Comneni

THE
EMPIRE OF THE COMNENI
(about 1130)
Natural Scale 1: 7,800,000
0 50 100 200 Miles
Eastern Frontier of Alexius (C.1118)
Names of THEMES in Europe THRACE
Nominal Limits of Empire of John Comnenus at furthest extent
PATZINAKS
PARISTRIUM
SERBIA
BULGARIA
DYRRHACHIUM
MACEDONIA
THRACE
THESSALONICA
NICOPOLIS
CEPHALLENIA
HELLAS AND PELOPONNESUS
NEGROPONT
PROCONNESSUS
CRETE
Semlin
Semendria
(Belgrade)
Haram
Branduizium
(Branichevo)
R. Morava
R. Danube
Durostolus
Trnovo
Sardica
(Sofia)
Eski-Zagra
Mesembria
Sozopolis
Philippopolis
R. Maritza
Hadrianople
Scopia
R. Vardar
R. Struma
Durazzo
Deabolis
Castoria
Seres
Thessalonica
Chorlu
Chalcedon
Chrysopolis
Avlona
Canina
Hiericho
CORFU
Mt. Athos
IMBROS
Cyzicus
Parium
Lopadium
Abydos
LEMNOS
Apollonia
Halmyrus
Adramyttium
Cotyaeum
LESBOS
Pergamus
Chliara
CEPHALONIA
CHIOS
R. Hermus
Sardis
Philadelphia
Smyrna
Nymphaeum
SAMOS
R. Meander
Antioch
Laodicea
Chonae
Modon
PATMOS
Miletus
COS
RHODES
Chandax (Candia)
Longitude East
18
20
22
24
26
28
44
42
40
38
36
34
32
Cambridge University Press

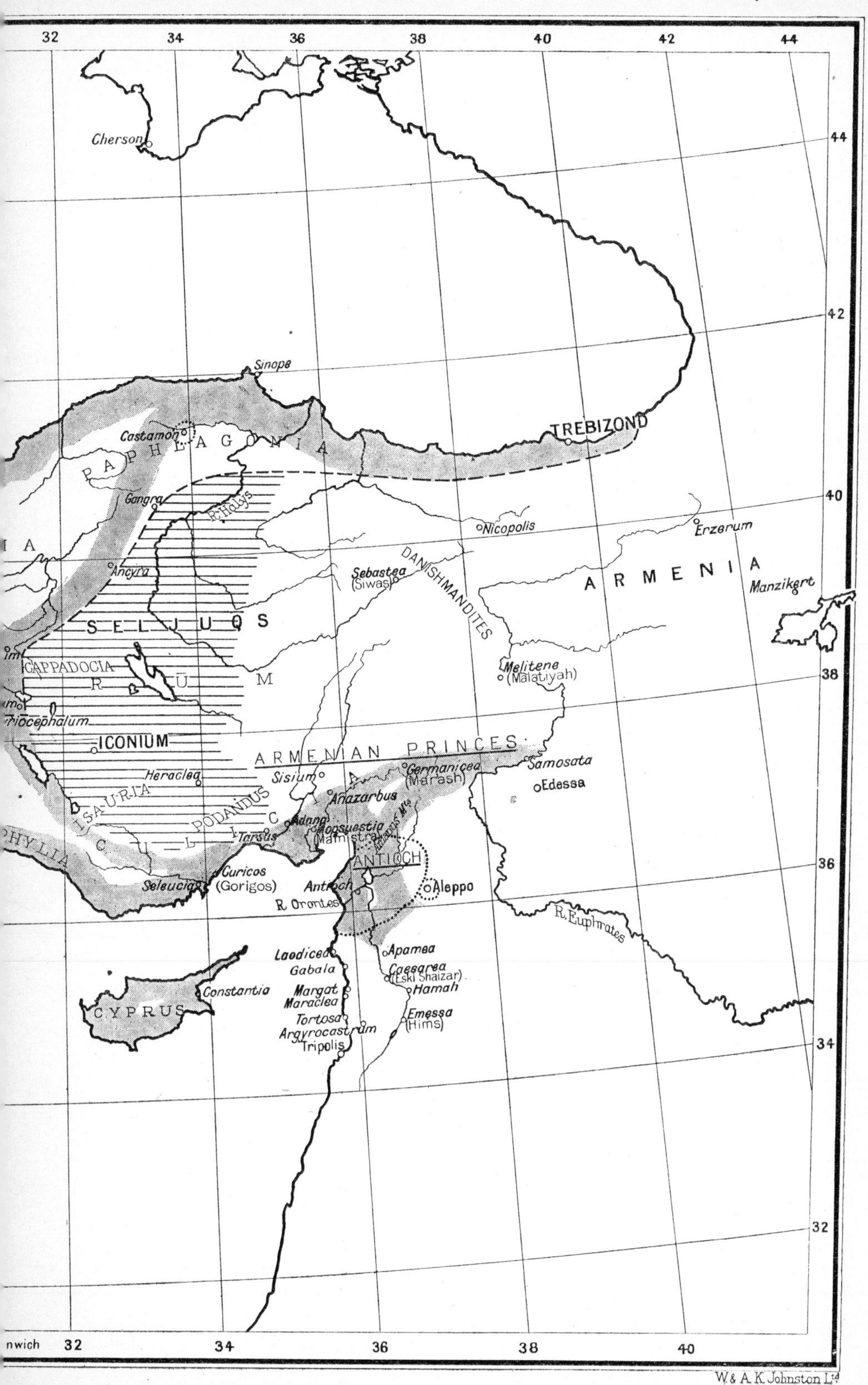
Cherson
Sinope
Castamon
PAPHLAGONIA
TREBIZOND
Gangra
R. Halys
Nicopolis
Erzerum
Ancyra
Sebastea
(Siwas)
DANISHMANDITES
ARMENIA
Manzikert
SELJUQS
CAPPADOCIA
RUM
Melitene
(Malatiyah)
Triocephalum
ICONIUM
ARMENIAN PRINCES
Samosata
Heraclea
Sisium
Germanicea
(Marash)
Edessa
ISAURIA
Anazarbus
PODANDUS
Adana
Mopsuestia
Mamistra
Tarsus
CILICIA
ANTIOCH
Curicos
(Gorigos)
Seleucia
Antioch
Aleppo
R. Orontes
R. Euphrates
Laodicea
Apamea
Gabala
Caesarea
(Eski Shaizar)
Hamah
Margat
Maraclea
Constantia
CYPRUS
Tortosa
Emessa
(Hims)
Argyrocastrum
Tripolis
W. & A. K. Johnston Ltd

Map 43
Latin States
in the East
in 1214

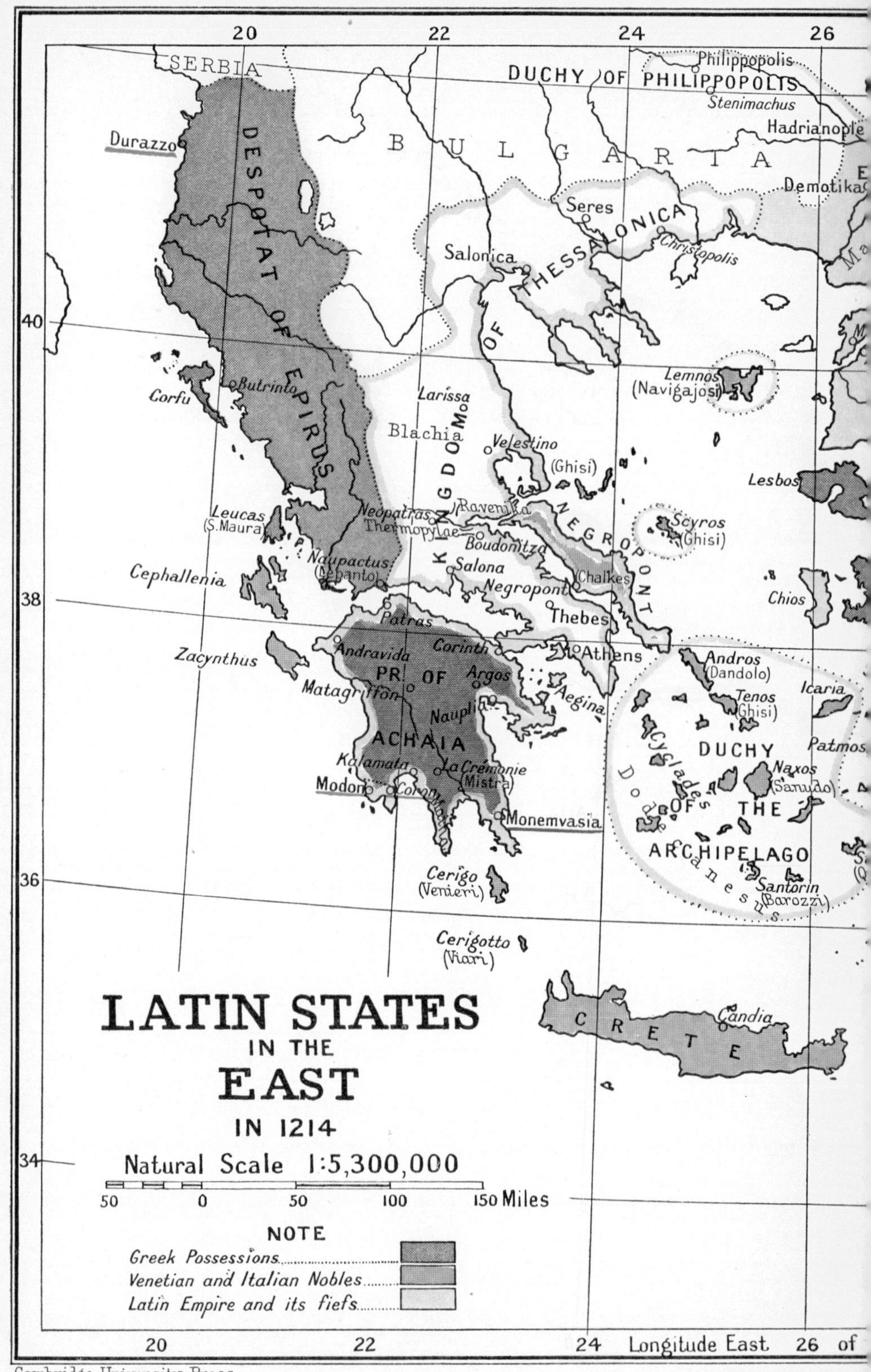
LATIN STATES
IN THE
EAST
IN 1214
Natural Scale 1:5,300,000
50 0 50 100 150 Miles
NOTE
Greek Possessions
Venetian and Italian Nobles
Latin Empire and its fiefs
Longitude East
SERBIA
DUCHY OF PHILIPPOPOLIS
Philippopolis
Stenimachus
Hadrianople
Demotika
BULGARIA
Durazzo
DESPOTAT OF EPIRUS
KINGDOM OF THESSALONICA
Seres
Christopolis
Salonica
Lemnos
(Navigajosi)
Corfu
Butrinto
Larissa
Blachia
Velestino
(Ghisi)
Lesbos
Leucas
(S. Maura)
Neopatras
Thermopylae
Ravenika
NEGROPONT
Scyros
(Ghisi)
Naupactus
(Lepanto)
Boudonitza
Salona
Cephallenia
Negropont
Chalkes
Chios
Thebes
Patras
Zacynthus
Andravida
Corinth
Athens
Andros
(Dandolo)
PR. OF ACHAIA
Argos
Matagriffon
Aegina
Tenos
(Ghisi)
Icaria
Nauplia
DUCHY OF THE ARCHIPELAGO
Cyclades
Dodecanesus
Patmos
Kalamata
La Crémonie
(Mistra)
Naxos
(Sanudo)
Modon
Coron
Monemvasia
Santorin
(Barozzi)
Cerigo
(Venieri)
Cerigotto
(Viari)
CRETE
Candia
20
22
24
26
40
38
36
34
Cambridge University Press

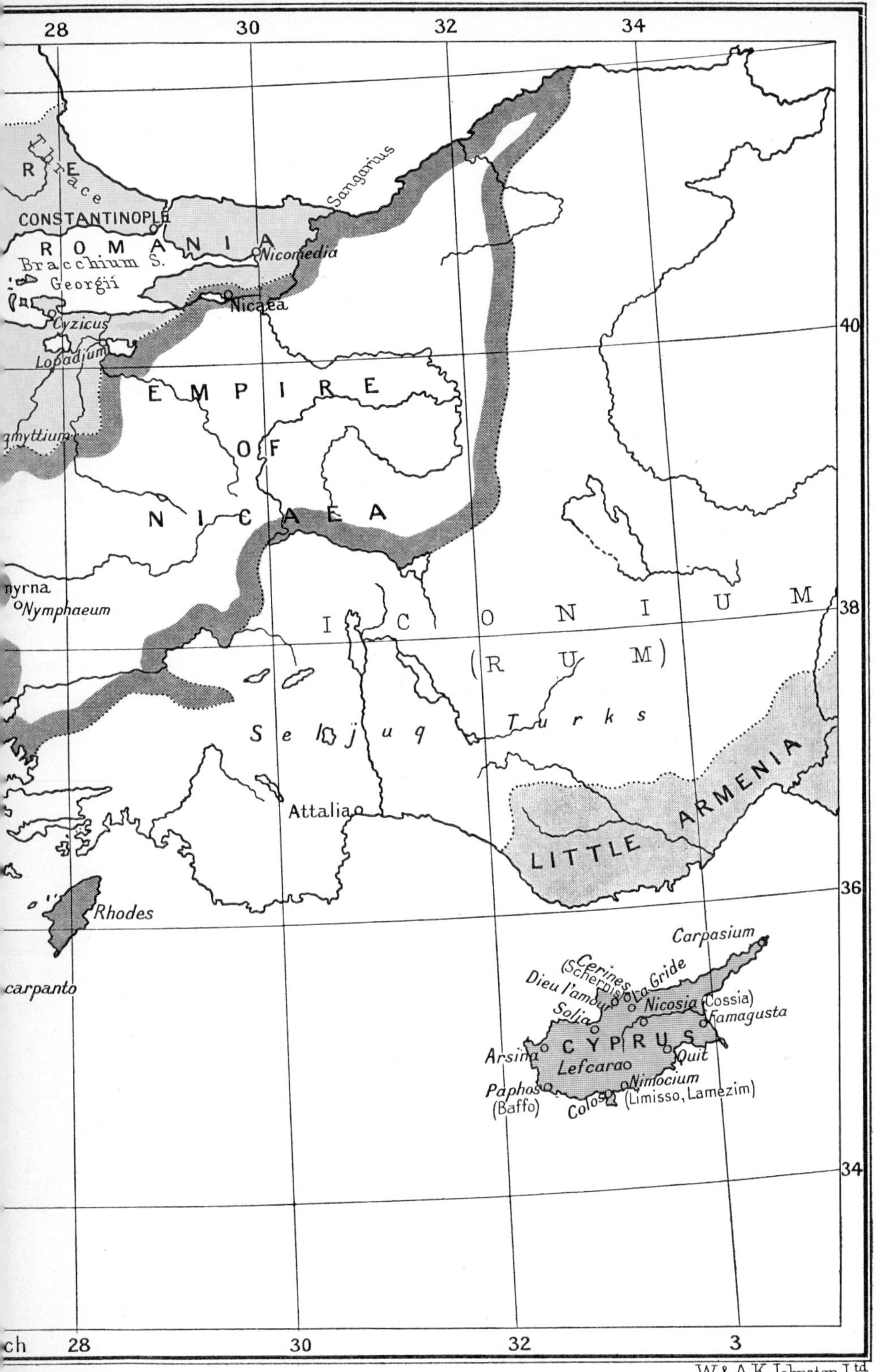
28
30
32
34
Thrace
CONSTANTINOPLE
ROMANIA
Bracchium S. Georgii
Sangarius
Nicomedia
Nicaea
Cyzicus
Lopadium
EMPIRE OF NICAEA
Nymphaeum
ICONIUM
(RUM)
Seljuq Turks
Attalia
LITTLE ARMENIA
Rhodes
Carpasium
Cerines (Scherpis)
Dieu l'amour
La Gride
Nicosia
(Cossia)
Famagusta
Solia
CYPRUS
Arsina
Lefcara
Quit
Paphos (Baffo)
Nimocium (Limisso, Lamezim)
Colos
40
38
36
34
W. & A. K. Johnston Ltd.

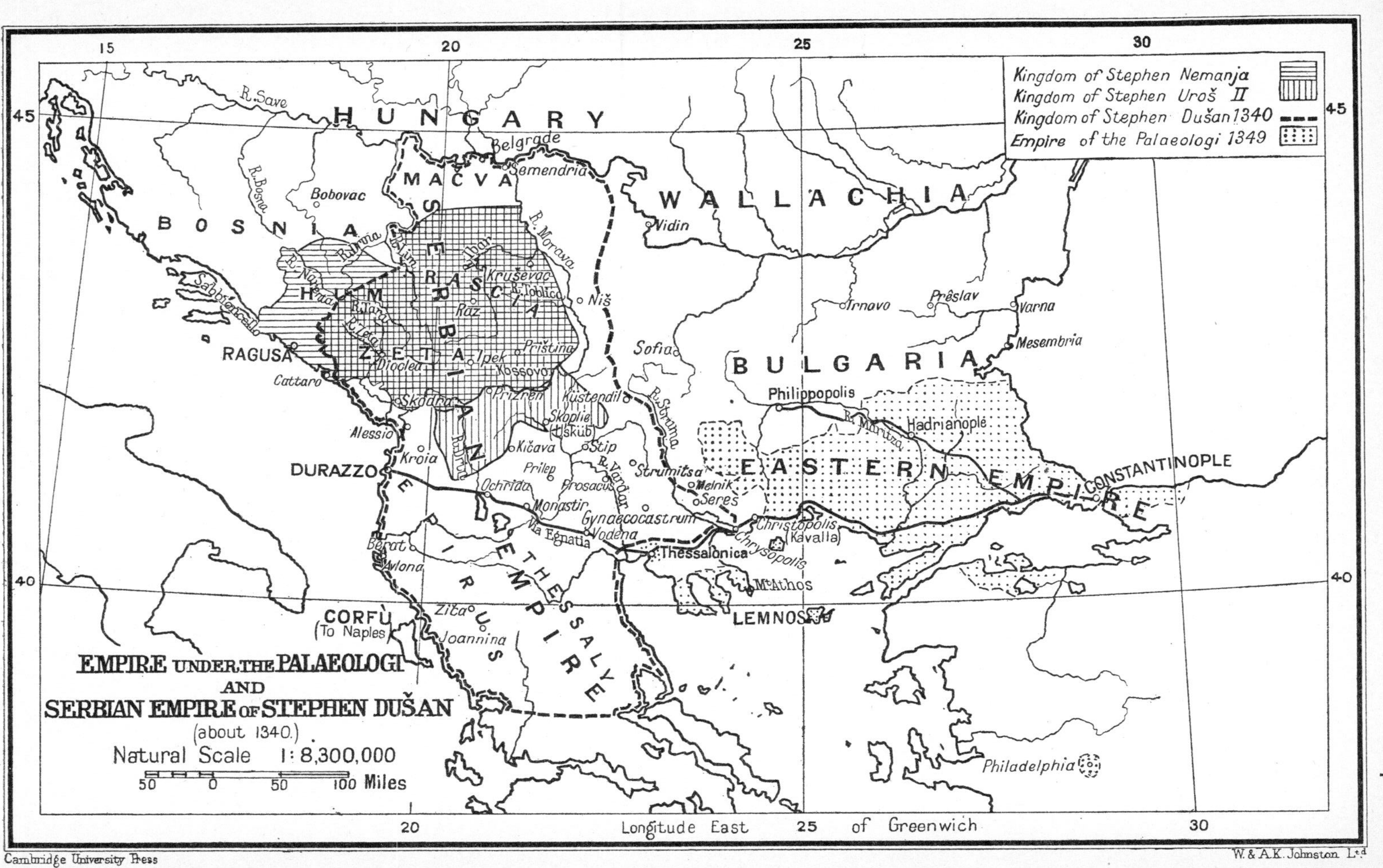

Cambridge University Press
W. & A.K. Johnston Ltd

Map 45
Turkish Sultanate
in 1481

Cambridge University Press

W. & A.K. Johnston Ltd.

Map 46

Mongol Empire

(about 1250)

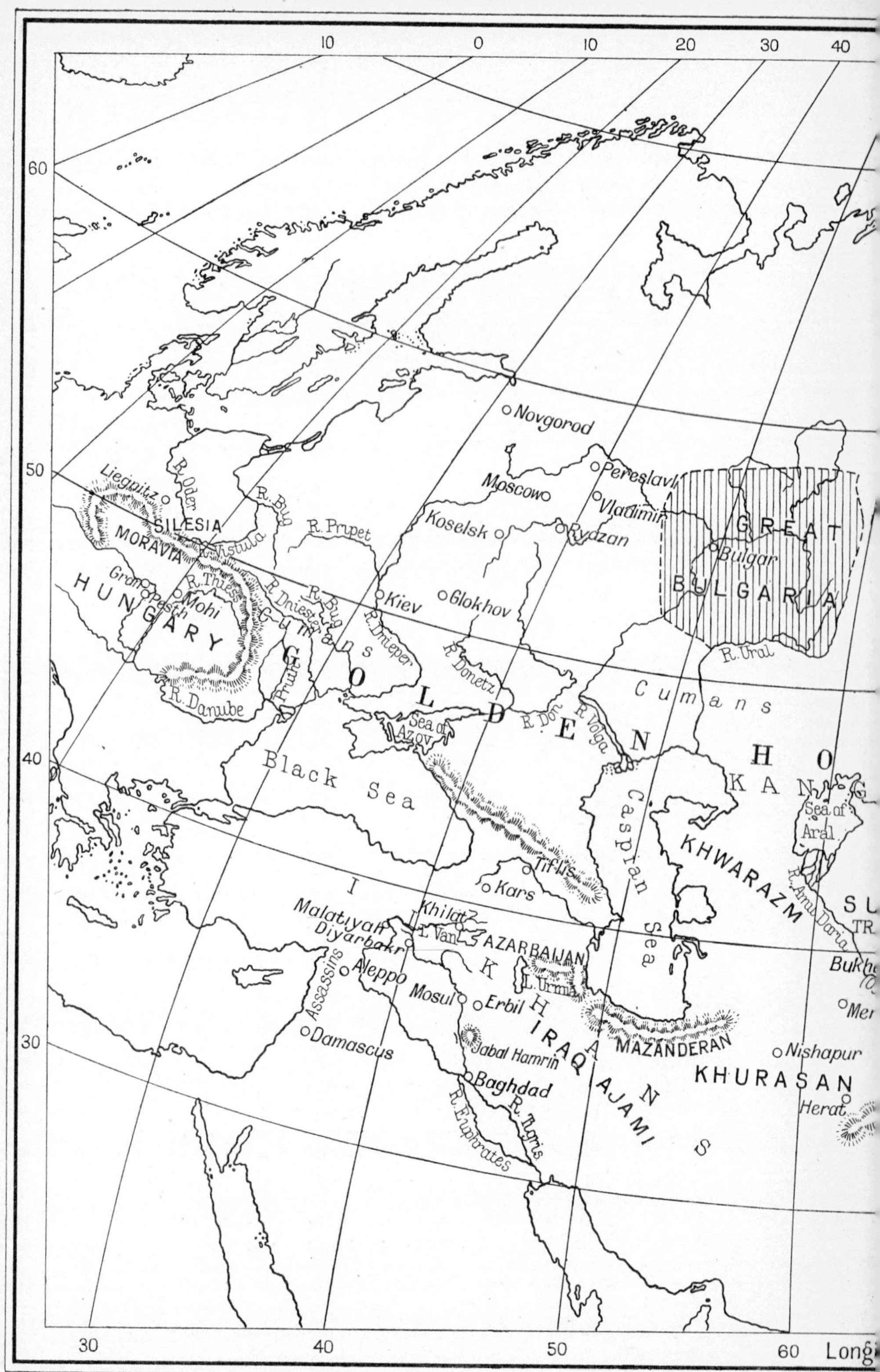

Cambridge University Press

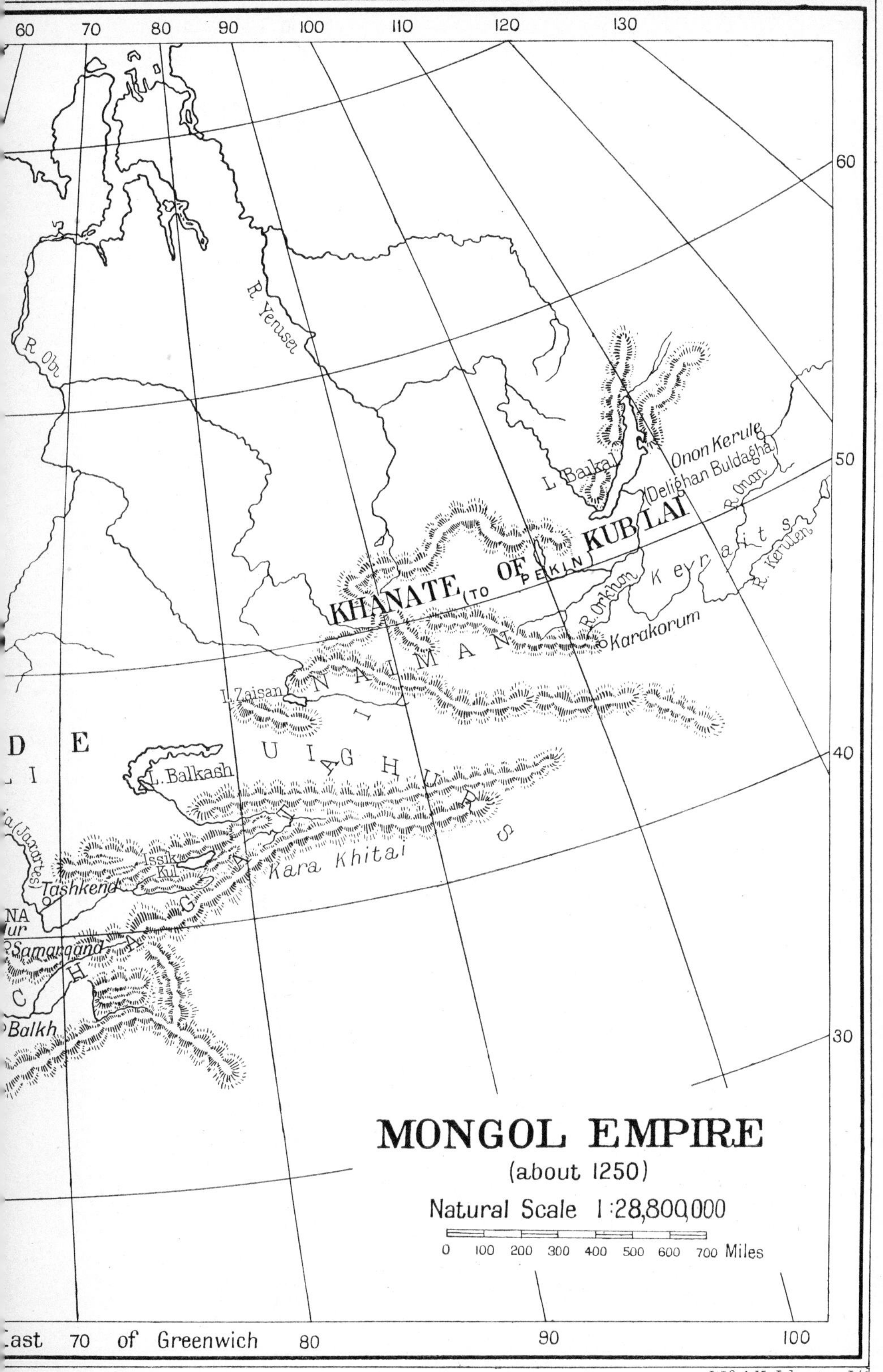

W. & A. K. Johnston Ltd.

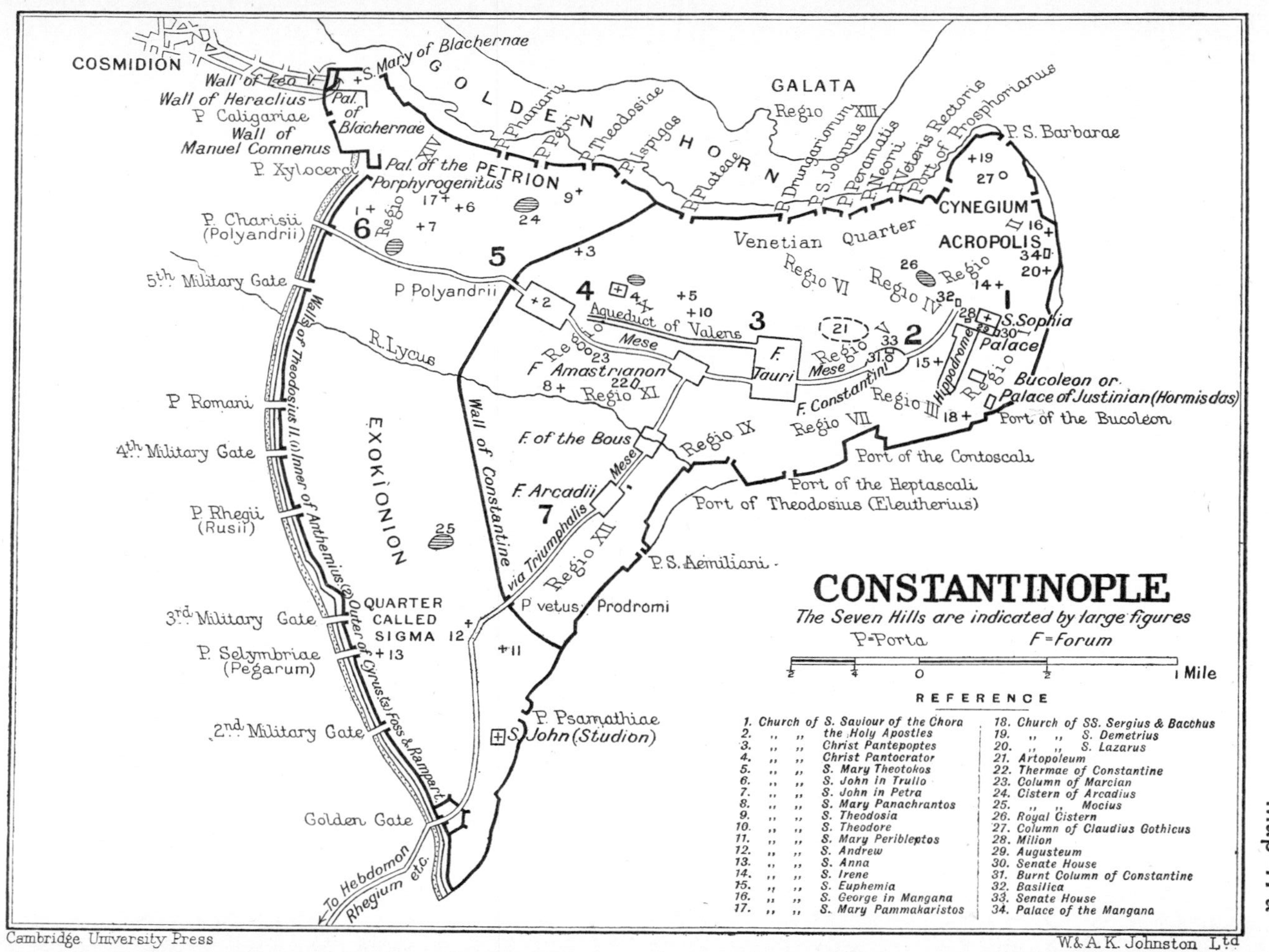

Cambridge University Press
W. & A. K. Johnston Ltd

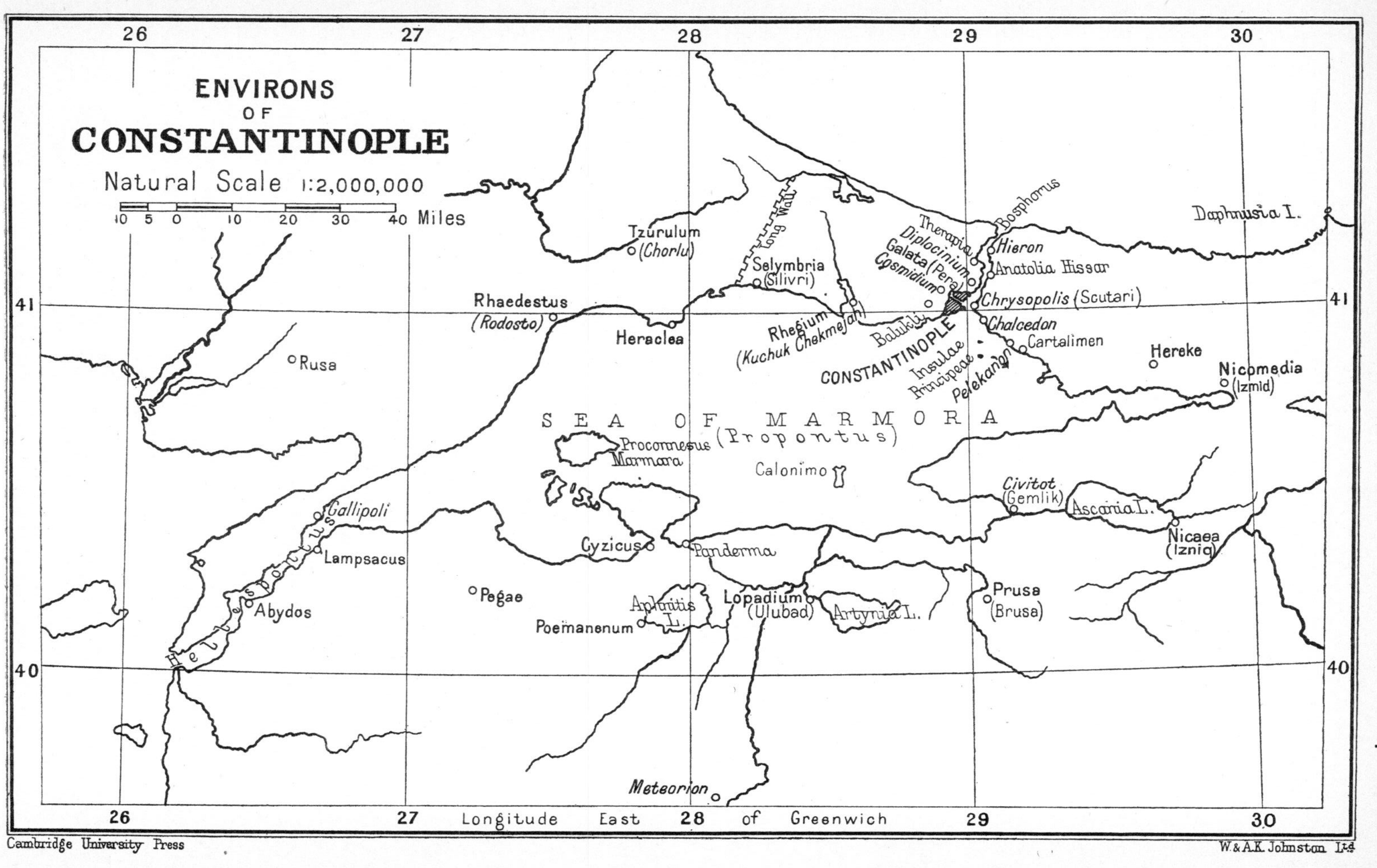

Cambridge University Press

W. & A.K. Johnston Ltd.